15TH EDITION

Doing Business 2018

Reforming to Create Jobs

COMPARING BUSINESS REGULATION FOR DOMESTIC FIRMS IN 190 ECONOMIES

A World Bank Group Flagship Report

Doing Business 2018

Resources
on the *Doing Business* website

Current features
News on the *Doing Business* project
http://www.doingbusiness.org

Rankings
How economies rank—from 1 to 190
http://www.doingbusiness.org/rankings

Data
All the data for 190 economies—topic
rankings, indicator values, lists of
regulatory procedures and details
underlying indicators
http://www.doingbusiness.org/data

Reports
Access to *Doing Business* reports as well
as subnational and regional reports, case
studies and customized economy and
regional profiles
http://www.doingbusiness.org/reports

Methodology
The methodologies and research papers
underlying *Doing Business*
http://www.doingbusiness.org/methodology

Research
Abstracts of papers on *Doing Business*
topics and related policy issues
http://www.doingbusiness.org/research

Doing Business reforms
Short summaries of DB2018 business
regulation reforms and lists of reforms
since DB2006
http://www.doingbusiness.org/reforms

Historical data
Customized data sets since DB2004
http://www.doingbusiness.org/custom-query

Law library
Online collection of business laws and
regulations relating to business
http://www.doingbusiness.org/law-library

Contributors
More than 13,000 specialists in 190
economies who participate in
Doing Business
*http://www.doingbusiness.org/contributors
/doing-business*

Entrepreneurship data
Data on new business density (number
of newly registered companies per 1,000
working-age people) for 143 economies
*http://www.doingbusiness.org/data
/exploretopics/entrepreneurship*

Distance to frontier
Data benchmarking 190 economies to
the frontier in regulatory practice and a
distance to frontier calculator
*http://www.doingbusiness.org
/data/distance-to-frontier*

Information on good practices
Showing where the many good
practices identified by *Doing Business*
have been adopted
*http://www.doingbusiness.org/data
/good-practice*

Doing Business 2018

Contents

- *Doing Business 2018* is the 15th in a series of annual reports investigating the regulations that enhance business activity and those that constrain it. *Doing Business* presents quantitative indicators on business regulation and the protection of property rights that can be compared across 190 economies—from Afghanistan to Zimbabwe—and over time.

- *Doing Business* measures aspects of regulation affecting 11 areas of the life of a business. Ten of these areas are included in this year's ranking on the ease of doing business: starting a business, dealing with construction permits, getting electricity, registering property, getting credit, protecting minority investors, paying taxes, trading across borders, enforcing contracts and resolving insolvency. *Doing Business* also measures features of labor market regulation, which is not included in this year's ranking.

- Data in *Doing Business 2018* are current as of June 1, 2017. The indicators are used to analyze economic outcomes and identify what reforms of business regulation have worked, where and why.

- This publication is the printed version of *Doing Business 2018*. The full report (which includes the Data Notes, Distance to Frontier and Ease of Doing Business chapter and the Reform Summaries) can be downloaded from the *Doing Business* website at http://www.doingbusiness.org.

Doing Business 2018

Foreword

In its 14 years of publication, *Doing Business* has come a long way. At a recent international forum, I heard the leaders of India and the Russian Federation talking about how important it is for their countries to improve their *Doing Business* rankings and create more jobs for young workers.

When the first edition was published in September 2003, little data was available on regulation affecting business activity. *Doing Business* created a new approach to policy reform—one informed by hard data and focused on domestic companies. The objectives of *Doing Business* are as clear as they are ambitious: to inform the design of reforms and motivate these reforms through country benchmarking. Behind each set of indicators lies rigorous academic analysis, done in cooperation with leading scholars. For example, the indicators on efficient insolvency systems were created with the help of Professor Oliver Hart from Harvard University, the 2016 Nobel Prize winner in economics.[1] In the years since the start of the project, over 3,000 peer-reviewed academic papers and another 7,000 working papers have been written using the *Doing Business* data. Their findings improve our knowledge of how economic policy works.

Since its inception—when *Doing Business* covered 145 economies—the scope of the report has expanded to 190 economies worldwide. The regulatory areas measured by the report have also been expanded to include more aspects that are relevant to the daily operations of domestic small and medium-size firms. For eight of the 11 *Doing Business* indicator sets, the report's traditional focus on efficiency—defined as the time, cost and number of interactions necessary to incorporate a new business or connect a warehouse to the electrical grid—has been complemented with a new focus on regulatory quality. *Doing Business* data shows that efficiency and quality go hand in hand, reinforcing each other.

Despite these additions and improvements, one aspect of *Doing Business* has remained unchanged: its focus on promoting regulatory reform that strengthens the ability of the private sector to create jobs, lift people out of poverty and create more opportunities for the economy to prosper. The notion that the private sector has substantial economic, social and development impact is now universally recognized. Responsible for an estimated 90% of employment in developing economies, the private sector

---

1. Djankov and others 2008.

is ideally placed to alleviate poverty by providing the opportunities to secure a good and sustainable standard of living.

Policy reforms catalyze private investment. Promoting a well-functioning private sector is a major undertaking for any government. It requires long-term policies of removing administrative barriers and strengthening laws that promote entrepreneurship.

Hard data helps do that. It gives a voice to the people to demand improved public services. It also increases government accountability. Over the past decade, more than 60 economies have established regulatory reform committees that use the *Doing Business* indicators. As a result, governments have reported more than 3,180 regulatory reforms, including about 920 reforms that have been inspired by *Doing Business*. This is true impact.

Kristalina Georgieva
Chief Executive Officer
The World Bank
Washington, DC

Overview

This year marks the 15th *Doing Business* report. Since the inception of the project in 2003, the global business regulatory environment has changed dramatically. Governments around the world have embraced and nurtured advances in information technology to reduce bureaucratic hurdles and increase transparency. Today, in 65 of the 190 economies covered by *Doing Business*, entrepreneurs can complete at least one business incorporation procedure online, compared with only nine of the 145 economies measured in *Doing Business 2004*. Furthermore, in 31 economies it is now possible to initiate a commercial dispute online. This kind of progress can also be observed in the other areas measured by *Doing Business*.

Doing Business measures aspects of business regulation and their implications for firm establishment and operations. It does not include all the issues that are relevant for businesses' decisions, but it does cover important areas that are under the control of policy makers. Governments worldwide recognize the economic and political benefits of improved business regulation. In fact, 119 of the 190 economies measured by *Doing Business 2018* enacted at least one business regulation reform in 2016/17. Of these, 79.8% implemented at least one reform for a second consecutive year and 64.7% for a third.

Business regulation can enable new ideas to come to life. When a software engineer realizes that she can develop a better and less-expensive product than is currently available, she may choose to start her own company to develop the idea. She will be more likely to become an entrepreneur in an economy where the rules governing start-ups are accessible, transparent

and predictable. Conversely, in an economy where business regulation is cumbersome or ambiguous, she may be less willing to start her own company. In this case, the economy forfeits a new entrepreneur —as well as the associated capital investment and job creation. In turn, consumers have fewer, lower quality and more expensive product choices. Such a scenario highlights the way in which cumbersome regulation can distort resource allocation by stifling entrepreneurial endeavors in favor of maintaining a less optimal status quo.

Consider the case of the potential software entrepreneur. If she were a national of Canada, it would take just two procedures, one and a half days and less than 1% of income per capita to start her business in Toronto. First, she would need to file for federal incorporation and provincial registration online via Industry Canada's Electronic Filing Centre; this costs 200 Canadian dollars ($159) and is completed within a day. Second, she would need to

- *Doing Business* uses 11 indicator sets to measure aspects of business regulation that matter for entrepreneurship.

- Although good regulatory practices can be found around the world, they are most common in OECD high-income economies and the economies of Europe and Central Asia.

- Sub-Saharan Africa has the widest variation in performance among the areas measured by *Doing Business*, with Mauritius standing at 25 in the ranking and Somalia at 190.

- South Asia is the only region not represented in the top 50 ranking for ease of doing business. However, India stands out this year as one of the 10 economies that improved the most in the areas measured by *Doing Business*.

- The regions with the highest share of reforming economies in *Doing Business 2018* are Europe and Central Asia, South Asia and Sub-Saharan Africa.

- Crises are opportunities for reform; economies are more likely to implement regulatory reforms in the areas measured by *Doing Business* when there is fiscal distress. Evidence shows that an economic crisis creates a stronger motivation for reform than a change of government.

- Better performance in *Doing Business* is associated with lower levels of unemployment and poverty.

register online for value added tax; this costs nothing and is completed within half a day. She can perform these steps online from the comfort of her home. As her business expands and becomes profitable, she would be expected to pay 20.9% of her commercial profits in taxes and contributions annually. However, if the same entrepreneur were a national of the Philippines, living in Quezon City, the business incorporation process would require 16 procedures, take 28 days and cost around 16% of income per capita. She would need to make 20 different tax and contribution payments and visit multiple agencies in person. Furthermore, her business would be expected to pay 42.9% of its commercial profits in taxes and contributions annually. Cumbersome business regulatory structures such as these constrain the ability of entrepreneurs to transform their ideas into viable businesses.

Doing Business measures the processes for starting a business, obtaining a building permit, getting an electricity connection, transferring property, paying taxes, taking a commercial dispute to court, and resolving an insolvency case, as well as credit and equity market regulations and logistics of importing and exporting goods (figure 1.1). There are many other factors that influence firm decisions—such as the availability of skilled labor or market size—that are not captured in *Doing Business*. But *Doing Business* focuses on key areas of interaction between the government and entrepreneurs, where policy makers and regulators can directly influence procedures to facilitate these interactions. For more information on what is measured and what is not, see the chapter About *Doing Business*.

WHAT ARE THE BENEFITS OF IMPROVED BUSINESS REGULATION?

The 11 *Doing Business* indicator sets capture the effectiveness and quality of business regulation. Research findings substantiate the economic relevance of the aspects of business regulation measured by *Doing Business*. Recent research, for example, examines the impact of improving business regulation. One study finds that high start-up costs can result in lower overall productivity.

Specifically, incumbent firms are more likely to continue operating despite poor productivity because there is little competition from new, more productive firms. In the absence of effective regulation, firms are also less inclined to leave the informal sector.[1]

In addition, *Doing Business* measures the coverage, scope and quality of credit information available from credit registries and bureaus. When functioning well, these institutions form an essential element of an economy's financial infrastructure by strengthening access to financial services, particularly credit. By collecting and sharing credit information, such agencies reduce information asymmetries, increase access to credit for small firms, lower interest rates, improve borrower discipline and strengthen bank supervision and credit risk monitoring. Indeed, a study of a credit bureau serving the equipment finance industry in the United States found that better exchange of information between lenders results in improved repayment behavior by firms, including lower incidences of delinquencies and defaults. This impact was stronger for firms that typically lack

FIGURE 1.1   What is measured in *Doing Business*?

Source: Doing Business database.
Note: Labor market regulation is not included in the ease of doing business ranking.

informational transparency, such as small and young firms.[2]

Doing Business places emphasis on the quality of legal infrastructure and the strength of legal institutions. The protecting minority investors indicator set, for example, measures the protection of minority shareholders. For businesses to secure equity finance, legal mechanisms are needed to prevent the use of corporate assets by company insiders for personal gain—especially during financial crises or times of market distress. Research has shown that during the 2008 global financial crisis, for example, companies in economies with better investor protections and stronger corporate governance experienced a smaller decrease in their market value. Conversely, firms in economies with weak legal structures saw a more significant decline in value.[3]

The *Doing Business* indicators on resolving insolvency provide evidence of a strong relationship between regulatory quality and efficient outcomes. The indicator set measures the quality of regulation as the recovery rate for secured creditors and the extent to which domestic law has incorporated certain internationally-accepted principles on liquidation and reorganization proceedings. Efficient outcomes occur when viable businesses are given a chance to survive, while loss-prone, inefficient firms exit the market, putting resources to better use elsewhere in the economy. In the absence of strong legal bankruptcy legislation, however, the balance between firm survival and efficient exit is distorted. This distortion was highlighted by research using data from Hungary, where the majority of firms in bankruptcy were preserved and allowed to continue operating as going concerns—despite generating substantial operating losses and resulting in low recovery rates for creditors. The main cause of this distortion was the inadequate allocation of control rights between secured and unsecured creditors, which decreased the recovery value

by not allowing creditors to take important decisions related to the company assets during insolvency procedures. Another cause was the establishment of a compensation scheme for agents managing bankruptcy proceedings based on assets sold and operating revenues of a firm, which created a significant increase in the cost of bankruptcy procedures and reduced creditors' recovery rate.[4]

In the area of cross-border trade, *Doing Business* measures the effectiveness of trade logistics. Several studies have underscored the importance of port automation and efficiency for both trade facilitation and regional economic development. These studies have found that ports that are more automated require less maintenance, are more cost-effective and ensure better worker safety. Furthermore, a study of the determinants of shipping costs from Latin America to the United States found that—for most exporting economies—high transportation costs pose even greater barriers to trade than import tariffs, and that port inefficiencies significantly add to these costs. One of the most striking findings is that by improving port efficiency from the 25th to the 75th percentile, shipping costs are lowered by 12%, substantially increasing the volume of bilateral trade.[5] One of the principal causes of port inefficiency is excessive regulation—precisely what *Doing Business* advocates to curb.

WHERE IS BUSINESS REGULATION BETTER?

The overall measure of the ease of doing business gives an indication of where it is easier for domestic small and medium-size firms to do business. Although the economies with the most business-friendly regulation in this year's ease of doing business ranking are relatively diverse, the economies within the top 20 share some common features. Fourteen of the top 20 are OECD high-income economies; three are from Europe and

Central Asia and three from East Asia and the Pacific. Eighteen of the top 20 are classified as high-income economies. The top 5 performers are New Zealand, Singapore, Denmark, the Republic of Korea and Hong Kong SAR, China. The former Yugoslav Republic of Macedonia is the only upper-middle-income economy on the list, while Georgia is the only lower-middle-income one (table 1.1). To date, no low-income economy has reached the top 20 group. However, being wealthy does not guarantee a front-runner position in the ease of doing business ranking; many high-income economies still have room for progress. Having few bureaucratic hurdles, robust legal institutions and laws and regulations that are based on international good practices is what matters most for a good performance in the ease of doing business ranking.

Among the top 20 economies, Georgia, with a ranking of 9, has implemented the highest number of business regulation reforms since the launch of *Doing Business* in 2003—a total of 47. With 41, FYR Macedonia has carried out the second highest number of reforms among the top 20. During the same period, Latvia and Lithuania have also actively reformed their business regulatory environments, with 28 and 31 reforms respectively. Among other reforms, Lithuania has made six reforms to its business incorporation processes, five reforms to bankruptcy proceedings and four reforms to its taxation system. Many other top-ranked economies have followed this pattern of continuous reform, demonstrating that comprehensive reform efforts can lead to considerable improvements in an economy's regulatory and business environment. Another feature that the top 20 economies have in common—albeit not measured by *Doing Business*—is that on average they have higher labor force participation rates and lower levels of income inequality. Indeed, the average Gini coefficient[6] of the top 20 economies is 0.3 (with 0 representing perfect equality and 1 representing perfect inequality), compared to 0.4 for the lowest 20.[7]

TABLE 1.1   Ease of doing business ranking

DB 2018 Rank	Economy	DTF score	DTF change	DB 2018 Rank	Economy	DTF score	DTF change	DB 2018 Rank	Economy	DTF score	DTF change
1	New Zealand	86.55	-0.18	65	Albania	68.70	+0.96	129	St. Vincent and the Grenadines	55.72	+0.01
2	Singapore	84.57	+0.04	66	Bahrain	68.13	+0.01	130	Palau	55.58	+0.46
3	Denmark	84.06	-0.01	67	Greece	68.02	+0.01	131	Nicaragua	55.39	+0.09
4	Korea, Rep.	83.92	0.00	68	Vietnam	67.93	+2.85	132	Barbados	55.20	-0.09
5	Hong Kong SAR, China	83.44	+0.29	69	Morocco	67.91	-0.03	133	Lebanon	54.67	-0.10
6	United States	82.54	-0.01	70	Jamaica	67.27	+0.57	134	St. Kitts and Nevis	54.52	+0.18
7	United Kingdom	82.22	-0.12	71	Oman	67.20	+0.08	135	Cambodia	54.47	+0.23
8	Norway	82.16	-0.25	72	Indonesia	66.47	+2.25	136	Maldives	54.42	+0.64
9	Georgia	82.04	+2.12	73	El Salvador	66.42	+3.54	137	Tanzania	54.04	+0.11
10	Sweden	81.27	+0.03	74	Uzbekistan	66.33	+4.46	138	Mozambique	54.00	+0.97
11	Macedonia, FYR	81.18	-0.21	75	Bhutan	66.27	+1.06	139	Côte d'Ivoire	53.71	+2.04
12	Estonia	80.80	+0.05	76	Ukraine	65.75	+1.90	140	Senegal	53.06	+3.75
13	Finland	80.37	-0.11	77	Kyrgyz Republic	65.70	+0.54	141	Lao PDR	53.01	+0.43
14	Australia	80.14	0.00	78	China	65.29	-0.40	142	Grenada	52.94	-0.11
15	Taiwan, China	80.07	+0.41	79	Panama	65.27	+1.25	143	Mali	52.92	+0.30
16	Lithuania	79.87	+1.05	80	Kenya	65.15	+2.59	144	Niger	52.34	+2.26
17	Ireland	79.51	-0.19	81	Botswana	64.94	+0.07	145	Nigeria	52.03	+3.85
18	Canada	79.29	-0.09	82	South Africa	64.89	-0.08	146	Gambia, The	51.92	-0.01
19	Latvia	79.26	-0.79	83	Qatar	64.86	+0.61	147	Pakistan	51.65	+0.71
20	Germany	79.00	-0.19	84	Malta	64.72	+0.43	148	Burkina Faso	51.54	+0.20
21	United Arab Emirates	78.73	+1.87	85	Zambia	64.50	+3.92	149	Marshall Islands	51.45	+0.03
22	Austria	78.54	-0.15	86	Bosnia and Herzegovina	64.20	+0.42	150	Mauritania	50.88	+1.56
23	Iceland	78.50	+0.01	87	Samoa	63.89	+2.06	151	Benin	50.47	+1.85
24	Malaysia	78.43	+0.96	88	Tunisia	63.58	-0.20	152	Bolivia	50.18	+0.32
25	Mauritius	77.54	+2.09	89	Tonga	63.43	+0.50	153	Guinea	49.80	+0.32
26	Thailand	77.44	+5.68	90	Vanuatu	63.08	+0.02	154	Djibouti	49.58	+3.99
27	Poland	77.30	+0.18	91	St. Lucia	62.88	+0.01	155	Micronesia, Fed. Sts.	48.99	+0.01
28	Spain	77.02	0.00	92	Saudi Arabia	62.50	+2.92	156	Togo	48.88	+0.64
29	Portugal	76.84	-0.14	93	San Marino	62.47	-0.03	157	Kiribati	48.74	-0.31
30	Czech Republic	76.27	+0.03	94	Uruguay	61.99	+0.35	158	Comoros	48.52	+0.47
31	France	76.13	-0.06	95	Seychelles	61.41	+1.01	159	Zimbabwe	48.47	+0.80
32	Netherlands	76.03	+0.51	96	Kuwait	61.23	+1.52	160	Sierra Leone	48.18	-0.06
33	Switzerland	75.92	+0.19	97	Guatemala	61.18	-0.43	161	Ethiopia	47.77	+2.08
34	Japan	75.68	+0.07	98	Dominica	60.96	+0.34	162	Madagascar	47.67	+3.05
35	Russian Federation	75.50	+0.81	99	Dominican Republic	60.93	+2.52	163	Cameroon	47.23	+2.18
36	Kazakhstan	75.44	+1.06	100	India	60.76	+4.71	164	Burundi	46.92	+0.06
37	Slovenia	75.42	+0.99	101	Fiji	60.74	+0.04	165	Suriname	46.87	+0.11
38	Belarus	75.06	+0.55	102	Trinidad and Tobago	60.68	-0.19	166	Algeria	46.71	-0.01
39	Slovak Republic	74.90	-0.25	103	Jordan	60.58	+2.38	167	Gabon	46.19	+1.33
40	Kosovo	73.49	+4.98	104	Lesotho	60.42	+0.54	168	Iraq	44.87	+0.48
41	Rwanda	73.40	+3.21	105	Nepal	59.95	+2.35	169	São Tomé and Príncipe	44.84	+0.39
42	Montenegro	73.18	+1.64	106	Namibia	59.94	+0.54	170	Sudan	44.46	+0.17
43	Serbia	73.13	+0.26	107	Antigua and Barbuda	59.63	+0.98	171	Myanmar	44.21	+0.30
44	Moldova	73.00	+0.20	108	Paraguay	59.18	+0.06	172	Liberia	43.55	+3.10
45	Romania	72.87	+0.17	109	Papua New Guinea	59.04	+0.17	173	Equatorial Guinea	41.66	+1.77
46	Italy	72.70	+1.15	110	Malawi	58.94	+6.33	174	Syrian Arab Republic	41.55	+0.08
47	Armenia	72.51	+0.59	111	Sri Lanka	58.86	+0.13	175	Angola	41.49	+1.38
48	Hungary	72.39	+0.26	112	Swaziland	58.82	+0.25	176	Guinea-Bissau	41.45	+0.23
49	Mexico	72.27	+0.18	113	Philippines	58.74	+0.42	177	Bangladesh	40.99	+0.15
50	Bulgaria	71.91	+0.10	114	West Bank and Gaza	58.68	+3.80	178	Timor-Leste	40.62	-0.07
51	Croatia	71.70	+0.05	115	Honduras	58.46	-0.07	179	Congo, Rep.	39.57	-0.52
52	Belgium	71.69	-0.23	116	Solomon Islands	58.13	-0.01	180	Chad	38.30	-0.28
53	Cyprus	71.63	-0.49	117	Argentina	58.11	+0.07	181	Haiti	38.24	+0.01
54	Israel	71.42	+0.05	118	Ecuador	57.83	-0.01	182	Congo, Dem. Rep.	37.65	+0.22
55	Chile	71.22	+0.37	119	Bahamas, The	57.47	+0.82	183	Afghanistan	36.19	-1.80
56	Brunei Darussalam	70.60	+5.83	120	Ghana	57.24	+0.34	184	Central African Republic	34.86	+0.78
57	Azerbaijan	70.19	+3.12	121	Belize	57.11	+0.01	185	Libya	33.21	+0.03
58	Peru	69.45	+0.01	122	Uganda	56.94	+0.42	186	Yemen, Rep.	33.00	+0.06
59	Colombia	69.41	-0.11	123	Tajikistan	56.86	+0.93	187	South Sudan	32.86	-0.33
60	Turkey	69.14	+1.16	124	Iran, Islamic Rep.	56.48	+0.26	188	Venezuela, RB	30.87	-0.79
61	Costa Rica	69.13	+1.23	125	Brazil	56.45	+0.38	189	Eritrea	22.87	+0.42
62	Mongolia	69.03	+1.27	126	Guyana	56.28	+0.39	190	Somalia	19.98	-0.31
63	Luxembourg	69.01	+0.35	127	Cabo Verde	56.24	+0.42				
64	Puerto Rico (U.S.)	68.85	+0.05	128	Egypt, Arab Rep.	56.22	+0.10				

Source: Doing Business database.

Note: The DB 2018 rankings are benchmarked to June 2017 and based on the average of each economy's distance to frontier (DTF) scores for the 10 topics included in the aggregate ranking. For the economies for which the data cover two cities, scores are a population-weighted average for the two cities. A positive change indicates an improvement in the score between 2016 and 2017 (and therefore an improvement in the overall business environment as measured by Doing Business), while a negative change indicates a deterioration and 0.00 indicates no change in the score.

What can the *Doing Business 2018* data tell us about global patterns? Good regulatory practices are present in almost all of the world's regions. Aside from 28 OECD high-income economies, the 50 highest-ranked economies include 13 from Europe and Central Asia, five from East Asia and the Pacific, two from Sub-Saharan Africa and one each from the regions of Latin America and the Caribbean and the Middle East and North Africa. Each region also has a relatively wide spectrum of strong and weak performers. Economies are ranked based on the distance to frontier score. This measure shows the distance of each economy to the "frontier," which represents the best performance observed on each of the indicators across all economies in the *Doing Business* sample (box 1.1). In OECD high-income economies, for example, New Zealand, Denmark and Korea have the highest overall distance to frontier scores at 86.55, 84.06 and 83.92, respectively. Conversely, Greece, Luxembourg and Chile have the lowest scores in this group, at 68.02, 69.01 and 71.22. However, the OECD high-income group has the smallest gap between the highest and the lowest scores, of only 18.53 percentage points (figure 1.2). Sub-Saharan Africa has the widest gap (57.56 percentage points), with a regional average score of only 50.43—the lowest

FIGURE 1.2 Where it is easier to do business and where it is more difficult

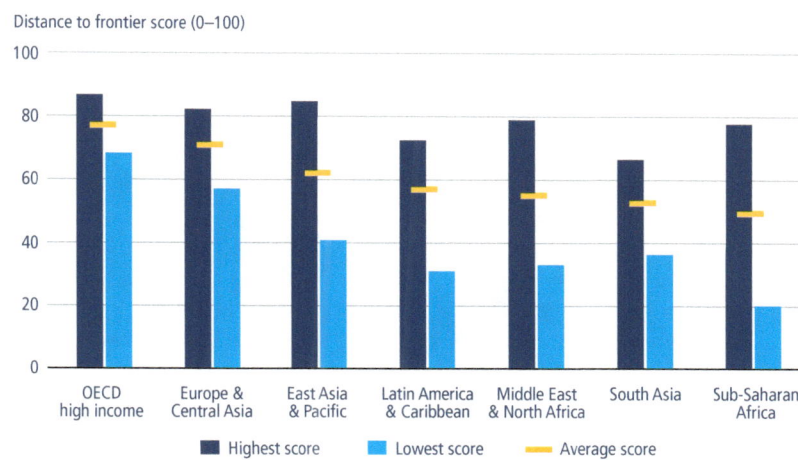

Distance to frontier score (0–100)

Source: Doing Business database.

across all regions. Among the economies of Sub-Saharan Africa, Mauritius has the highest distance to frontier score (77.54), while Somalia the lowest (19.98).

Regional rankings across different *Doing Business* indicator sets also show large variations. South Asia, for example—the only region not represented in the top 50 list—scores comparatively well for starting a business, with an average distance to frontier score of 83.27. In contrast, South Asia's regional average score for resolving

insolvency is only 33.04. Indeed, *Doing Business* data show considerable variation in performance between economies within the same region and within the same regulatory area. Within South Asia, India has the highest score (80) for protecting minority investors compared to Afghanistan's score of 10. Similarly, there is a substantial difference in scores between economies in the Middle East and North Africa region. Malta, for example, has a distance to frontier score for trading across borders of 91.01, while Algeria only scores 24.15. Interestingly, all regions have at least one economy in the top 20 ranking on the protecting minority investors indicators and all regions—except the OECD high-income group—have at least one economy in the bottom 20 ranking on the protecting minority investors indicators. These patterns indicate that there is further room for improvement across all regions and at all income levels.

WHICH ECONOMIES IMPROVED THE MOST IN *DOING BUSINESS 2018*?

Doing Business 2018 captures 264 business regulation reforms across the 10 measured indicator sets. As in previous years, Sub-Saharan Africa is the region

BOX 1.1 What is the distance to frontier score?

Doing Business measures many different dimensions of business regulation. To combine measures with different units such as the number of days to obtain a construction permit and the number of procedures to start a business into a single score, *Doing Business* computes the distance to frontier score. The distance to frontier score captures the gap between an economy's current performance and the best practice across the entire sample of 41 indicators across 10 *Doing Business* indicator sets. For example, according to the *Doing Business* database across all economies and over time, the least time to start a business is 0.5 days while in the worst 5% of cases it takes more than 100 days to incorporate a company. Half a day is, therefore, considered the frontier of best performance, while 100 days is the worst. Higher distance to frontier scores show absolute better ease of doing business (as the frontier is set at 100 percentage points), while lower scores show absolute poorer ease of doing business (the worst performance is set at 0 percentage points). The percentage point distance to frontier scores of an economy on different indicators are averaged to obtain an overall distance to frontier score. For more details, see the chapter on the distance to frontier and ease of doing business ranking available at www.doingbusiness.org.

with the highest number of reforms (83 in total), followed by East Asia and the Pacific (45) and Europe and Central Asia (44). The regions with the highest share of reforming economies are Europe and Central Asia (79%), South Asia (79%) and Sub-Saharan Africa (75%), while the OECD high-income group has the lowest share (46%). The indicator sets for starting a business and getting credit record the highest number of reforms (38 each) in 2016/17. They are closely followed by the trading across borders indicator set with 33 reforms. The least-reformed areas as captured by *Doing Business* continue to be the indicators with a legal focus—for example, resolving insolvency (13 reforms) and enforcing contracts (20). Legal reforms are typically slow to advance, mainly because they require long-term political commitments, substantial resources and close collaboration between multiple regulatory agencies and rulemaking institutions.

It is important to look at both the number of reforms and their impact on the distance to frontier score because they provide different information. The number of reforms indicates *how many* areas an

economy chose to target for improvement, while the change in the distance to frontier score indicates *the size* of the impact those changes had on the *Doing Business* data. Across all economies, the average distance to frontier score increase is 0.76 percentage points, with the highest regional increase in Sub-Saharan Africa (1.18), although this region does not have the highest percentage of economies implementing at least one business regulatory reform. Nevertheless, there is a strong correlation between the number of reforms and the actual improvement in the distance to frontier score.[8] *Doing Business* data show that it has become easier for small and medium-size enterprises to do business in 62.6% of economies worldwide (or 119 of the 190 economies measured by *Doing Business*).

While economies in the Sub-Saharan Africa region show the highest average increase in the distance to frontier score, economies in the OECD high-income group have the lowest average increase (0.11 percentage points). This is not surprising as most OECD high-income economies are already near to global good practices. The *Doing Business*

indicator sets capturing the most business regulation reforms across regions in 2016/17 are paying taxes and trading across borders. Indeed, the reform agendas of OECD high-income and East Asia and the Pacific economies appear to be dominated by regulatory changes captured by the paying taxes indicator set (figure 1.3). Lower-middle-income economies have the highest average reform count at 1.9 reforms each; low-income economies are second highest at 1.3 reforms. Unsurprisingly, high-income economies recorded the lowest average reform count (1).

Of the 10 economies showing the most improvement in performance on the *Doing Business* indicators, three are from Sub-Saharan Africa, two from East Asia and the Pacific, two from Europe and Central Asia, one from Latin America and the Caribbean, one from the Middle East and North Africa and one from South Asia. Brunei Darussalam, the only high-income economy on the list of top 10 improvers, showed the largest advance toward the global good practice frontier after implementing eight reforms in 2016/17; it joins this list for the second year in a

FIGURE 1.3 The average number of reforms per economy is highest in South Asia but the average impact is biggest in Sub-Saharan Africa

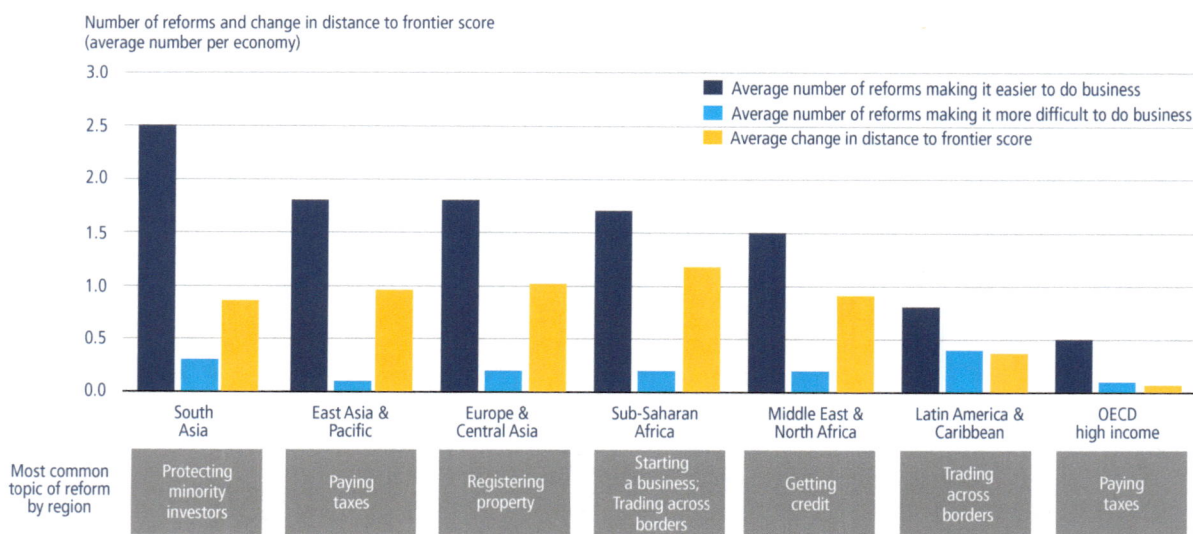

Source: Doing Business database.
Note: The average change in the distance to frontier score shows the change between Doing Business 2018 and Doing Business 2017.

row. E Salvador, India, Malawi, Nigeria and Thailand also made impressive strides and joined the 10 top improvers for the first time. Among top improvers, Brunei Darussalam, India and Thailand implemented the highest number of business regulation reforms in 2016/17, with eight reforms each. The remaining four economies in the list of top improvers are: Kosovo, Uzbekistan, Zambia and Djibouti. For details on the reforms these countries undertook, see the chapter on reforming the business environment in 2016/17.

The database of *Doing Business* reforms indicates differences in reform momentum, both within topics and across regions. Why are reforms more common in some years than others? When do economies tend to reform in the areas covered in *Doing Business*? Two main theories explain the timing of regulatory reform. The first suggests that economies reform when they must—that is, when there is no choice but to implement a regulatory change. In this case, an increase in reforms would be more likely during crises.[9] A second theory argues that economies reform when they can—that is, when governments are recently elected and are in the "honeymoon period."[10]

Doing Business data can be used to explore which theory is more likely to hold true in practice. Recent research shows that governments are more likely to reform business regulation when their economy is experiencing a fiscal crisis.[11] This is particularly true for regulation concerning resolving insolvency, which showed a spike in reform activity in 2010/11,[12] a couple of years after the 2008/09 financial crisis. The reason is that these kinds of reforms take time to be implemented and captured by *Doing Business* (figure 1.4). However, the effect of fiscal crises on reform intensity is less robust when public debt is lower. When a fiscal crisis can be solved—albeit temporarily—by increasing borrowing, the need for reform becomes less urgent. In contrast, the "honeymoon" theory of reforms has less evidence to support

FIGURE 1.4   Reform intensity tends to rise in response to crises

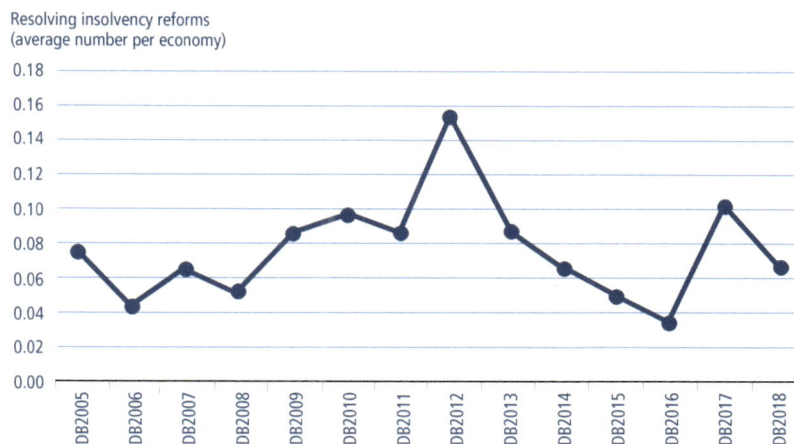

Source: Djankov, Georgieva and Ramalho 2017a.

it. In general, political change is not associated with more reform unless the political change takes place after the fiscal crisis. Indeed, economies tend to reform when they must, rather than when they can.

WHAT IMPACT DOES BUSINESS REGULATION HAVE ON EMPLOYMENT AND POVERTY?

Many factors explain poverty. These can include vulnerability to natural disasters, remoteness, quality of governance, property rights, availability of infrastructure and services, proximity to markets, social relationships, the gender of the head of household, employment status, hours worked, property owned and educational attainment.[13] Several of these factors have a direct link to the areas measured in *Doing Business* since the *Doing Business* indicators measure factors such as the quality of governance and property rights. Furthermore, *Doing Business* can have an indirect link to these factors as improvements to business regulation can drive additional job creation. And ultimately, as a reliable source of income, employment can lift people out of poverty.

Reforming in the areas measured by *Doing Business* can be particularly beneficial to employment creation when those reforms take place in the areas of starting a business and labor market regulation.[14] Such an assertion, however, is made with some caveats from other research exploring causal relationships between business entry regulation and job creation.[15] Nonetheless, one of the mechanisms through which business regulation can impact employment directly is the simplification of business start-up regulations. Across economies there is a significant positive association between employment growth and the distance to frontier score (figure 1.5). While this result shows an association, and cannot be interpreted in a causal fashion, it is reassuring to see that economies with better business regulation, as measured by *Doing Business*, also tend to be the economies that are creating more job opportunities.[16] When it comes to unemployment, the expected opposite result is evident. Economies with less streamlined business regulation are those with higher levels of unemployment on average. In fact, a one-point improvement in the distance to frontier score is associated with a 0.02 percentage point decline in unemployment growth rate.[17]

FIGURE 1.5 Better business regulation is associated with employment growth and poorer regulation with higher unemployment

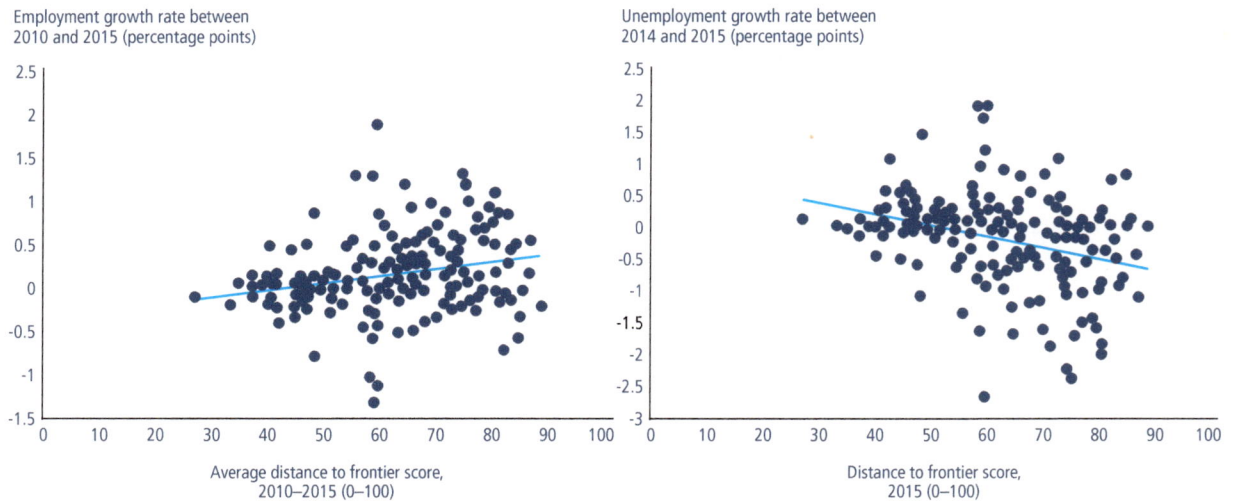

Employment growth rate between
2010 and 2015 (percentage points)

Average distance to frontier score,
2010–2015 (0–100)

Unemployment growth rate between
2014 and 2015 (percentage points)

Distance to frontier score,
2015 (0–100)

Sources: Doing Business database; International Labor Organization data (http://www.ilo.org/ilostat).

Note: The relationships are significant at the 1% level after controlling for income per capita. The left-hand side relationship also holds when using employment growth rate and distance to frontier average score between 2010 and 2015.

Doing Business 2017 reported that there is a negative association between the Gini index, which measures income inequality within an economy, and the distance to frontier score. Economies with poor quality business regulation have higher levels of income inequality on average. This relationship can be partially explained by the strong association between measures of poverty and the distance to frontier score. When business regulation is overly cumbersome, entrepreneurs and workers are pushed out of the formal sector and must resort to operating in the informal sector.[18, 19] The informal sector is characterized by a lack of regulation, minimal social protection and increased levels of poverty.[20] Individuals living in poverty are likely to gain the most from smarter and more streamlined business regulation. When bureaucratic hurdles are high, only the most privileged members of society can get things done, either through hiring third parties or paying bribes. In economies with complex company incorporation processes, for example, entrepreneurs tend to hire lawyers to

assist with the process of registering their businesses.

The data support this interpretation as there is a strong association between inequality, poverty and business regulation. In fact, economies with better business regulation have lower levels of poverty on average. Indeed, a 10 percentage point improvement in the distance to frontier is associated with a 2 percentage point reduction in the poverty rate, measured as the percentage of people earning less than $1.90 a day.[21] Fragility is also a factor linked to poverty. However, even fragile economies can improve in areas that ultimately reduce poverty levels. Despite their fragile status, several economies implemented reforms as captured by *Doing Business 2018* (box 1.2).

WHAT IS NEW IN THIS YEAR'S REPORT?

This year's report presents four case studies, two of which focus on transparency. The case study on starting a

business analyzes new data about the information available at business registries. It finds that economies with more transparent and accessible information have lower levels of corruption on average. The case study on registering property analyzes the transparency of information as captured by the quality of land administration index and shows that transparent land administration systems are associated with a lower incidence of bribery.

The case study on dealing with construction permits analyzes private sector participation in construction regulation. It demonstrates that economies which employ some form of private sector involvement in construction regulation tend to have more efficient processes and better quality controls. However, they also exhibit higher costs and a propensity for conflicts of interest. Finally, the case study on resolving insolvency discusses three successful insolvency reforms—in France, Slovenia and Thailand—and the lessons learned that are transferable to other economies.

BOX 1.2   Crises as opportunities?

Fragile states, often characterized by weak governance, residual violence, concentrated poverty and inequality, face myriad development and humanitarian challenges. Depleted human capital, minimal rule of law and violence all contribute to significant—and often extreme—rates of poverty in fragile states.[a] While fragile states are not home to the majority of the world's poor, the poor are disproportionately located in fragile states,[b] underscoring the need to address poverty in these economies. In poor and fragile states, the private sector is often constrained by a lack of infrastructure, political instability, high rates of informality and poor business skills. Private sector job creation is one of the factors that can diminish the incentives to engage in violence, thereby reducing both fragility and poverty.[c]

Doing Business data show that fragile economies are reforming and approaching crises as opportunities for better business regulations. As a result, the gap with non-fragile economies in some areas of business regulation has been narrowing over time (see figure). In 2016/17, of the 34 economies classified as most vulnerable by the World Bank Group's 2017 Harmonized List of Fragile Situations,[d] 14 implemented at least one business regulation reform and six economies implemented two reforms or more. Getting credit was the most reformed area of business regulation, accounting for eight of the 24 reforms implemented by this group. Djibouti recorded five reforms, the highest number among all fragile states. Djibouti reduced the fees associated with starting a business and construction inspections, implemented decennial liability for all professionals involved in construction projects, increased the transparency of its land administration system and established a new credit information system. As a result of these reforms, Djibouti's distance to frontier score improved by 3.79 percentage points.

Fragile states are converging with non-fragile states on the cost to register property and start a business

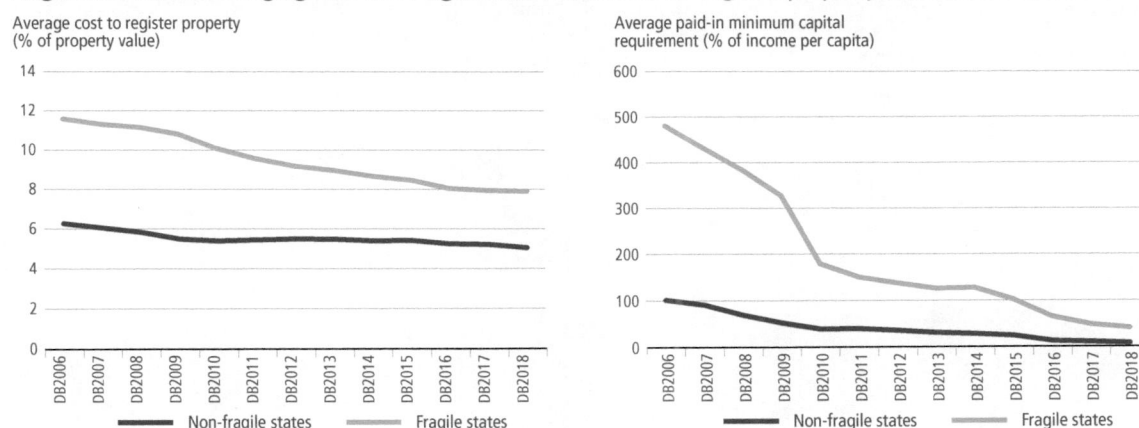

Average cost to register property
(% of property value)

Average paid-in minimum capital
requirement (% of income per capita)

Source: Doing Business database.
Note: Fragile states are classified based on the World Bank Group's Harmonized List of Fragile Situations for fiscal year 2017. The sample includes 174 economies where data is available back to *Doing Business 2006*.

Kosovo, the second most-reformed country in the fragile states group, implemented three business regulation reforms. Iraq, Madagascar, Myanmar, and Sierra Leone made two reforms each in 2016/17. Iraq simplified the process of starting a business by combining multiple registration procedures and reducing the time to register a company. It also launched a new credit registry, improving access to credit information. Similarly, Myanmar adopted a regulation that allows the creation of credit bureaus, while Madagascar increased the coverage of its credit registry. Kosovo and Liberia undertook reforms in the area of resolving insolvency in 2016/17. Both of these economies introduced a legal framework for corporate insolvency, making liquidation and reorganization procedures available to debtors and creditors.

a. World Bank 2011.
b. Burt, Hughes and Milante 2014.
c. Collier and Hoeffler 2004.
d. The harmonized list also includes Tuvalu, the only economy from the list that is not measured by *Doing Business*.

NOTES

1. Moscoso Boedo and Mukoyama 2012.
2. Doblas-Madrid and Minetti 2013.
3. Enikolopov, Petrova and Stepanov 2014.
4. Franks and Loranth 2014.
5. Clark, Dollar and Micco 2004.
6. The Gini coefficient, the most commonly-used measure of inequality, is a measure of statistical dispersion intended to represent the income or wealth distribution of an economy's residents.
7. The relationship is significant at the 1% level after controlling for income per capita.
8. The correlation between the number of reforms and the actual improvement in the distance to frontier score is 0.57.
9. Drazen and Grilli 1993; Ranciere and Tornell 2015.
10. Haggard and Williamson 1994.
11. Djankov, Georgieva and Ramalho 2017a.
12. The second peak is explained by substantial business regulation reforms undertaken by the 17 member states of the Organization for the Harmonization of Business Law in Africa, known by its French acronym OHADA. The organization adopted a revised Uniform Act Organizing Collective Proceedings for Wiping Off Debts in 2015, which introduced a simplified preventive settlement procedure for small companies and a new reconciliation procedure for companies facing financial difficulties, encouraging an agreement between a debtor and its main creditors. The OHADA Uniform Act also introduced provisions on cross-border insolvency that were implemented in all 17 OHADA member states.
13. Kraay and McKenzie 2014; Banerjee and Duflo 2011; Rodrick, Subramanian and Trebbi 2004; Buvinic and Gupta 1997.
14. Bruhn 2011; Bruhn 2013; Branstetter and others 2014.
15. Bruhn 2013; Fajnzylber, Maloney and Montes-Rojas 2011; Kaplan, Piedra and Seira 2011.
16. The relationship is significant at the 1% level after controlling for income per capita.
17. The relationship is significant at the 1% level after controlling for income per capita and population size; it is shown in figure 1.5.
18. De Soto 1989.
19. Dabla-Norris, Gradstein, and Inchauste 2008.
20. Loayza and Serven 2010.
21. Djankov, Georgieva and Ramalho 2017b. This association is significant when using the following indicator sets individually: starting a business, dealing with construction permits, getting credit and enforcing contracts. The relationship holds after controlling for income per capita and government expenditure.

About
Doing Business

The foundation of *Doing Business* is the notion that economic activity benefits from clear and coherent rules: rules that set out and clarify property rights and facilitate the resolution of disputes. And rules that enhance the predictability of economic interactions and provide contractual partners with essential protections against arbitrariness and abuse. Such rules are much more effective in shaping the incentives of economic agents in ways that promote growth and development where they are reasonably efficient in design, are transparent and accessible to those for whom they are intended and can be implemented at a reasonable cost. The quality of the rules also has a crucial bearing on how societies distribute the benefits and finance the costs of development strategies and policies.

Good rules create an environment where new entrants with drive and good ideas can get started in business and where good firms can invest, expand and create new jobs. The role of government policy in the daily operations of domestic small and medium-size firms is a central focus of the *Doing Business* data. The objective is to encourage regulation that is designed to be efficient, accessible to all and simple to implement. Onerous regulation diverts the energies of entrepreneurs away from developing their businesses. But regulation that is efficient, transparent and implemented in a simple way facilitates business expansion and innovation, and makes it easier for aspiring entrepreneurs to compete on an equal footing.

Doing Business measures aspects of business regulation for domestic firms through an objective lens. The focus of the project is on small and medium-size companies in the largest business city of an economy. Based on standardized case studies, *Doing Business* presents quantitative indicators on the regulations that apply to firms at different stages of their life cycle. The results for each economy can be compared with those for 189 other economies and over time.

FACTORS *DOING BUSINESS* MEASURES

Doing Business captures several important dimensions of the regulatory environment as it applies to local firms. It provides quantitative indicators on regulation for starting a business, dealing with construction permits, getting electricity, registering property, getting credit, protecting minority investors, paying taxes, trading across borders, enforcing contracts and resolving insolvency (table 2.1). *Doing Business* also measures features of labor market regulation. Although *Doing Business* does not present rankings of economies on the labor market regulation indicators or include the topic in the aggregate distance to frontier score or ranking on the ease of doing business, it does present the data for these indicators.

- *Doing Business* measures aspects of business regulation affecting domestic small and medium-size firms defined based on standardized case scenarios and located in the largest business city of each economy. In addition, for 11 economies a second city is covered.

- *Doing Business* covers 11 areas of business regulation across 190 economies. Ten of these areas—starting a business, dealing with construction permits, getting electricity, registering property, getting credit, protecting minority investors, paying taxes, trading across borders, enforcing contracts and resolving insolvency—are included in the distance to frontier score and ease of doing business ranking. *Doing Business* also measures features of labor market regulation, which is not included in these two measures.

- *Doing Business* relies on four main sources of information: the relevant laws and regulations, *Doing Business* respondents, the governments of the economies covered and the World Bank Group regional staff.

- More than 43,000 professionals in 190 economies have assisted in providing the data that inform the *Doing Business* indicators over the past 15 years.

- *Doing Business* data are widely used by governments, researchers, international organizations and think tanks to guide policies, conduct research and develop new indexes.

TABLE 2.1	What *Doing Business* measures—11 areas of business regulation
Indicator set	**What is measured**
Starting a business	Procedures, time, cost and paid-in minimum capital to start a limited liability company
Dealing with construction permits	Procedures, time and cost to complete all formalities to build a warehouse and the quality control and safety mechanisms in the construction permitting system
Getting electricity	Procedures, time and cost to get connected to the electrical grid, the reliability of the electricity supply and the transparency of tariffs
Registering property	Procedures, time and cost to transfer a property and the quality of the land administration system
Getting credit	Movable collateral laws and credit information systems
Protecting minority investors	Minority shareholders' rights in related-party transactions and in corporate governance
Paying taxes	Payments, time and total tax and contribution rate for a firm to comply with all tax regulations as well as post-filing processes
Trading across borders	Time and cost to export the product of comparative advantage and import auto parts
Enforcing contracts	Time and cost to resolve a commercial dispute and the quality of judicial processes
Resolving insolvency	Time, cost, outcome and recovery rate for a commercial insolvency and the strength of the legal framework for insolvency
Labor market regulation	Flexibility in employment regulation and aspects of job quality

How the indicators are selected

The design of the *Doing Business* indicators has been informed by theoretical insights gleaned from extensive research and the literature on the role of institutions in enabling economic development.[1] In addition, the background papers developing the methodology for each of the *Doing Business* indicator sets have established the importance of the rules and regulations that *Doing Business* focuses on for such economic outcomes as trade volumes, foreign direct investment, market capitalization in stock exchanges and private credit as a percentage of GDP.[2]

The choice of the 11 sets of *Doing Business* indicators has also been guided by economic research and firm-level data, specifically data from the World Bank Enterprise Surveys.[3] These surveys provide data highlighting the main obstacles to business activity as reported by entrepreneurs in more than 131,000 companies in 139 economies. Access to finance and access to electricity, for example, are among the factors identified by the surveys as important to businesses—inspiring the design of the *Doing*

Business indicators on getting credit and getting electricity.

Some *Doing Business* indicators give a higher score for more regulation and better-functioning institutions (such as courts or credit bureaus). Higher scores are given for stricter disclosure requirements for related-party transactions, for example, in the area of protecting minority investors. Higher scores are also given for a simplified way of applying regulation that keeps compliance costs for firms low—such as by easing the burden of business start-up formalities with a one-stop shop or through a single online portal. Finally, *Doing Business* scores reward economies that apply a risk-based approach to regulation as a way to address social and environmental concerns—such as by imposing a greater regulatory burden on activities that pose a high risk to the population and a lesser one on lower-risk activities. Thus, the economies that rank highest on the ease of doing business are not those where there is no regulation—but those where governments have managed to create rules that facilitate interactions in the

marketplace without needlessly hindering the development of the private sector.

The distance to frontier and ease of doing business ranking

To provide different perspectives on the data, *Doing Business* presents data both for individual indicators and for two aggregate measures: the distance to frontier score and the ease of doing business ranking. The distance to frontier score aids in assessing the absolute level of regulatory performance and how it improves over time. This measure shows the distance of each economy to the "frontier," which represents the best performance observed on each of the indicators across all economies in the *Doing Business* sample since 2005 or the third year in which data were collected for the indicator. The frontier is set at the highest possible value for indicators calculated as scores, such as the strength of legal rights index or the quality of land administration index. This underscores the gap between a particular economy's performance and the best performance at any point in time and is used to assess the absolute change in the economy's regulatory environment over time as measured by *Doing Business*. The distance to frontier is first computed for each topic and then averaged across all topics to compute the aggregate distance to frontier score. The ranking on the ease of doing business complements the distance to frontier score by providing information about an economy's performance in business regulation relative to the performance of other economies as measured by *Doing Business*.

Doing Business uses a simple averaging approach for weighting component indicators, calculating rankings and determining the distance to frontier score.[4] Each topic covered by *Doing Business* relates to a different aspect of the business regulatory environment. The distance to frontier scores and rankings of each economy vary, often considerably, across topics, indicating that a strong performance by an economy in one area of regulation can coexist with weak performance in another (figure 2.1). One way to assess the variability of

FIGURE 2.1   An economy's regulatory environment may be more business-friendly in some areas than in others

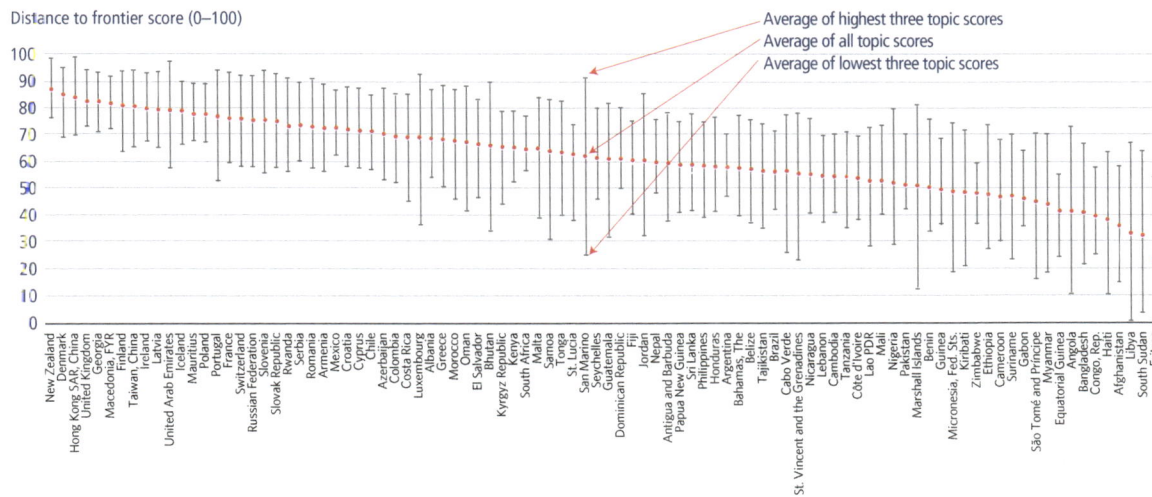

Source: Doing Business database.
Note: The distance to frontier scores reflected are those for the 10 *Doing Business* topics included in this year's aggregate distance to frontier score. The figure is illustrative only; it does not include all 190 economies covered by this year's report. See the country tables for the distance to frontier scores for each *Doing Business* topic for all economies.

an economy's regulatory performance is to look at its distance to frontier scores across topics (see the country tables). Morocco, for example, has an overall distance to frontier score of 67.91, meaning that it is about two-thirds of the way from the worst to the best performance. Its distance to frontier score is 92.46 for starting a business, 85.72 for paying taxes and 81.12 for trading across borders. At the same time, it has a distance to frontier score of 34.03 for resolving insolvency, 45 for getting credit and 58.33 for protecting minority investors.

FACTORS *DOING BUSINESS* DOES NOT MEASURE

Many important policy areas are not covered by *Doing Business*; even within the areas it covers its scope is narrow (table 2.2). *Doing Business* does not measure the full range of factors, policies and institutions that affect the quality of an economy's business environment or its national competitiveness. It does not, for example, capture aspects of macroeconomic stability, development of the financial system,

market size, the incidence of bribery and corruption or the quality of the labor force.

The focus is deliberately narrow even within the relatively small set of indicators included in *Doing Business*. The time and cost required for the logistical process of exporting and importing goods is captured in the trading across borders indicators, for example, but they do not measure the cost of tariffs or of international transport. *Doing Business* provides a narrow perspective on the infrastructure challenges that firms face, particularly in the developing world, through these indicators. It does not address the extent to which inadequate roads, rail, ports and communications may add to firms' costs and undermine competitiveness (except to the extent that the trading across borders indicators indirectly measure the quality of ports and border connections). Similar to the indicators on trading across borders, all aspects of commercial legislation are not covered by those on starting a business or protecting minority investors. And while *Doing Business* measures only a few aspects within each area that it covers, business regulation

reforms should not focus only on these aspects, because those that it does not measure are also important.

Doing Business does not attempt to quantify all costs and benefits of a particular law or regulation to society as a whole. The paying taxes indicators measure the tax and contribution rate, which, in isolation, is a cost to businesses. However, the indicators do not measure—nor are they intended to measure—the benefits of the social and economic programs funded with tax revenues. Measuring the quality and efficiency of business regulation provides only one input into the debate on the regulatory burden associated with achieving regulatory objectives, which can differ across economies. *Doing Business* provides

TABLE 2.2   Examples of areas not covered by *Doing Business*

Macroeconomic stability

Development of the financial system

Quality of the labor force

Incidence of bribery and corruption

Market size

Lack of security

a starting point for this discussion and should be used in conjunction with other data sources.

ADVANTAGES AND LIMITATIONS OF THE METHODOLOGY

The *Doing Business* methodology is designed to be an easily replicable way to benchmark specific aspects of business regulation. Its advantages and limitations should be understood when using the data (table 2.3).

Ensuring comparability of the data across a global set of economies is a central consideration for the *Doing Business* indicators, which are developed using standardized case scenarios with specific assumptions. One such assumption is the location of a standardized business—the subject of the *Doing Business* case study—in the largest business city of the economy. The reality is that business regulations and their enforcement may differ within a country, particularly in federal states and large economies. But gathering data for every relevant jurisdiction in each of the 190 economies covered by *Doing Business* is infeasible. Nevertheless, where policy makers are interested in generating data at the local level, beyond

the largest business city, and learning from local good practices, *Doing Business* has complemented its global indicators with subnational studies (box 2.1). Also, coverage was extended to the second largest business city in economies with a population of more than 100 million (as of 2013) in *Doing Business 2015*.

Doing Business recognizes the limitations of the standardized case scenarios and assumptions. But while such assumptions come at the expense of generality, they also help to ensure the comparability of data. Some *Doing Business* topics are complex, and so it is important that the standardized cases are defined carefully. For example, the standardized case scenario usually involves a limited liability company or its legal equivalent. There are two reasons for this assumption. First, private limited liability companies are the most prevalent business form (for firms with more than one owner) in many economies around the world. Second, this choice reflects the focus of *Doing Business* on expanding opportunities for entrepreneurship: investors are encouraged to venture into business when potential losses are limited to their capital participation.

Another assumption underlying the *Doing Business* indicators is that entrepreneurs have knowledge of and comply

with applicable regulations. In practice, entrepreneurs may not be aware of what needs to be done or how to comply with regulations and may lose considerable time trying to find out. Alternatively, they may intentionally avoid compliance—by not registering for social security, for example. Firms may opt for bribery and other informal arrangements intended to bypass the rules where regulation is particularly onerous—an aspect that helps explain differences between the de jure data provided by *Doing Business* and the de facto insights offered by the World Bank Enterprise Surveys.[5] Levels of informality tend to be higher in economies with particularly burdensome regulation. Compared with their formal sector counterparts, firms in the informal sector typically grow more slowly, have poorer access to credit and employ fewer workers—and these workers remain outside the protections of labor law and, more generally, other legal protections embedded in the law.[6] Firms in the informal sector are also less likely to pay taxes. *Doing Business* measures one set of factors that help explain the occurrence of informality and provides policy makers with insights into potential areas of regulatory reform.

DATA COLLECTION IN PRACTICE

The *Doing Business* data are based on a detailed reading of domestic laws and regulations as well as administrative requirements. The report covers 190 economies—including some of the smallest and poorest economies, for which little or no data are available from other sources. The data are collected through several rounds of communication with expert respondents (both private sector practitioners and government officials), through responses to questionnaires, conference calls, written correspondence and visits by the team. *Doing Business* relies on four main sources of information: the relevant laws and regulations, *Doing Business* respondents, the governments of the economies covered and the World Bank Group regional staff (figure 2.2).

TABLE 2.3	Advantages and limitations of the *Doing Business* methodology	
Feature	Advantages	Limitations
Use of standardized case scenarios	Makes data comparable across economies and methodology transparent	Reduces scope of data; only regulatory reforms in areas measured can be systematically tracked
Focus on largest business city[a]	Makes data collection manageable (cost-effective) and data comparable	Reduces representativeness of data for an economy if there are significant differences across locations
Focus on domestic and formal sector	Keeps attention on formal sector—where regulations are relevant and firms are most productive	Unable to reflect reality for informal sector—important where that is large—or for foreign firms facing a different set of constraints
Reliance on expert respondents	Ensures that data reflect knowledge of those with most experience in conducting types of transactions measured	Indicators less able to capture variation in experiences among entrepreneurs
Focus on the law	Makes indicators "actionable"—because the law is what policy makers can change	Where systematic compliance with the law is lacking, regulatory changes will not achieve full results desired

a. In economies with a population of more than 100 million as of 2013, *Doing Business* covers business regulation in both the largest and second largest business city.

BOX 2.1 Subnational *Doing Business* indicators: regional-level benchmarking in the European Union

Subnational *Doing Business* studies point to differences in business regulation and its implementation—as well as in the pace of regulatory reform—across locations in a single economy or region. For several economies, subnational studies are now periodically updated to measure change over time or to expand geographic coverage to additional cities. Six economies completed subnational studies this year: Afghanistan, Colombia, three EU member states (Bulgaria, Hungary and Romania) and Kazakhstan. In addition, an ongoing study updated data for Nigeria.

With funding from the European Commission's Directorate-General for Regional and Urban Policy (DG REGIO), the first of a series of new subnational reports was launched focusing on the European Union member states. *Doing Business in the European Union 2017: Bulgaria, Hungary and Romania* builds on subnational studies completed in Italy, Spain and Poland. The next study in the subnational series will cover Croatia, the Czech Republic, Portugal and the Slovak Republic.

These studies will provide valuable input to individual country reports produced for the European Semester, the European Union's economic and fiscal policy coordination framework, and will be closely linked with the Lagging Regions initiative launched by the European Commission in June 2015, which studies constraints to growth and investment in the European Union's low-income and low-growth regions.

Doing Business in the European Union 2017: Bulgaria, Hungary and Romania goes beyond the largest business cities of Sofia, Budapest and Bucharest to benchmark an additional 19 locations. In total, the study measures business regulation in 22 locations—six in Bulgaria, seven in Hungary and nine in Romania. The study benchmarks the locations using five *Doing Business* indicator sets: starting a business, dealing with construction permits, getting electricity, registering property and enforcing contracts.

The study finds that there are locations in each economy that outperform the EU average in at least one area. In Bulgaria, for example, Varna and Pleven outperform the EU average on the starting a business indicators. This is also the case in Pecs and Szeged (Hungary), which outperform the EU average on the dealing with construction permits indicators. All Hungarian cities and Oradea (Romania) perform above the EU average for registering property; most locations also do so for enforcing contracts. However, none of the subnational locations surveyed came close to the EU average on the indicators for getting electricity.

While no single location excels in all five areas covered by the study, most demonstrate a noteworthy performance in at least one area, providing reform-minded officials with examples of existing good practices that can be replicated. For example, Bulgarian cities could make starting a business easier by adopting the good practices observed in Varna. Cities in Hungary could make it easier to get electricity by emulating the good practices of Szeged and Szekesfehervar. And Romanian cities could strengthen their own contract enforcement regimes by studying the example of Timisoara. The study, which also includes comparisons with 187 other economies worldwide, provides practical recommendations and showcases good practices for improving the business environment.

FIGURE 2.2 How *Doing Business* collects and verifies the data

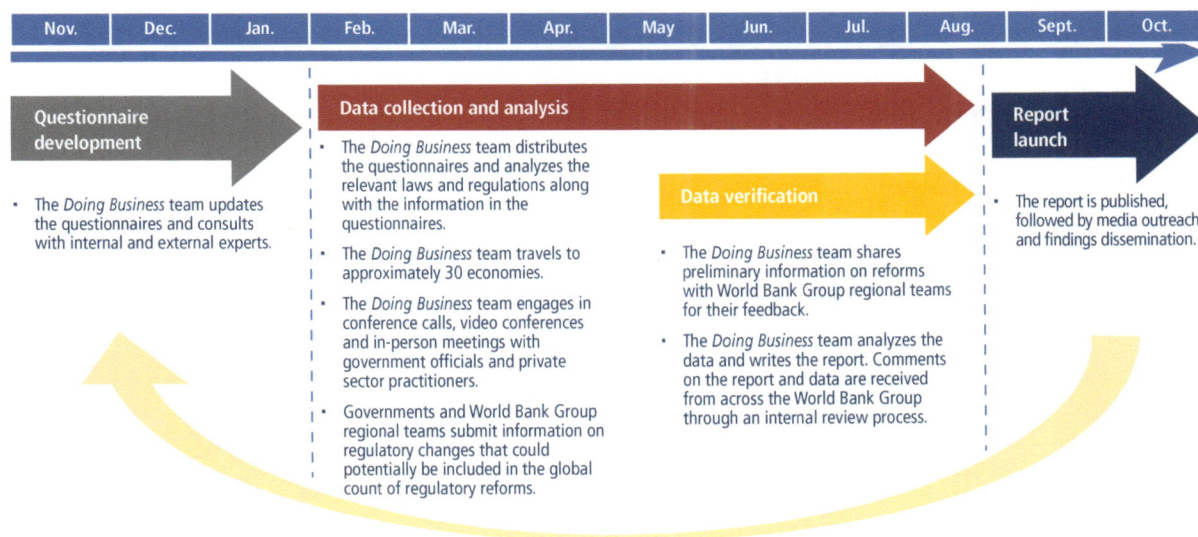

For a detailed explanation of the *Doing Business* methodology, see the data notes at www.doingbusiness.org.

Relevant laws and regulations

The *Doing Business* indicators are based mostly on laws and regulations: approximately two-thirds of the data embedded in the *Doing Business* indicators are based on a reading of the law. In addition to filling out questionnaires, *Doing Business* respondents submit references to the relevant laws, regulations and fee schedules. The *Doing Business* team collects the texts of the relevant laws and regulations and checks the questionnaire responses for accuracy. The team will examine the civil procedure code, for example, to check the maximum number of adjournments in a commercial court dispute, and read the insolvency code to identify if the debtor can initiate liquidation or reorganization proceedings. These and other types of laws are available on the *Doing Business* law library website.[7] Since the data collection process involves an annual update of an established database, having a very large sample of respondents is not strictly necessary. In principle, the role of the contributors is largely advisory—helping the *Doing Business* team to locate and understand the laws and regulations. There are quickly diminishing returns to an expanded pool of contributors. This notwithstanding, the number of contributors rose by 60% between 2010 and 2017.

Extensive consultations with multiple contributors are conducted by the team to minimize measurement error for the rest of the data. For some indicators—for example, those on dealing with construction permits, enforcing contracts and resolving insolvency—the time component and part of the cost component (where fee schedules are lacking) are based on actual practice rather than the law on the books. This introduces a degree of judgment by respondents on what actual practice looks like. When respondents disagree, the time indicators reported by *Doing Business* represent the median values of several responses given under the assumptions of the standardized case (box 2.2).

BOX 2.2 Where is the implementation of regulation more predictable and does it matter?

Doing Business measures the median duration of each procedure or process individually across the different indicator sets with time components. However, in practice, the time it takes to complete the same transaction can differ significantly from one entrepreneur to another. Because entrepreneurs place a premium on reliability and low risk, this variability in time can have important implications.

This year, *Doing Business* sets out to better understand these differences for the eight indicators with a time component, namely starting a business, dealing with construction permits, getting electricity, registering property, paying taxes, trading across borders, enforcing contracts and resolving insolvency. To do so, *Doing Business* collected data estimating the time to complete a procedure in both the best and worst case scenarios in an economy. The data show that in Spain, for example, a commercial dispute trial takes 280 days on average in a normal case, but can range from 180 days to 550 days depending on the individual circumstances.

The data show that—across the eight *Doing Business* indicators mentioned above—high-income economies have lower time variability and, therefore, more predictable regulatory environments than low- or middle-income economies (see figure below for an example). In addition, the data confirm that the median is very much at the center of the time distribution. In the United Kingdom, for example, the median time for dealing with construction permits is 90 days. The worst case scenario is 120 days and the best case scenario is 60 days, meaning that the distribution is centered around the median plus or minus 30 days.

High-income economies have the smallest difference between the best and worst case scenario time estimates

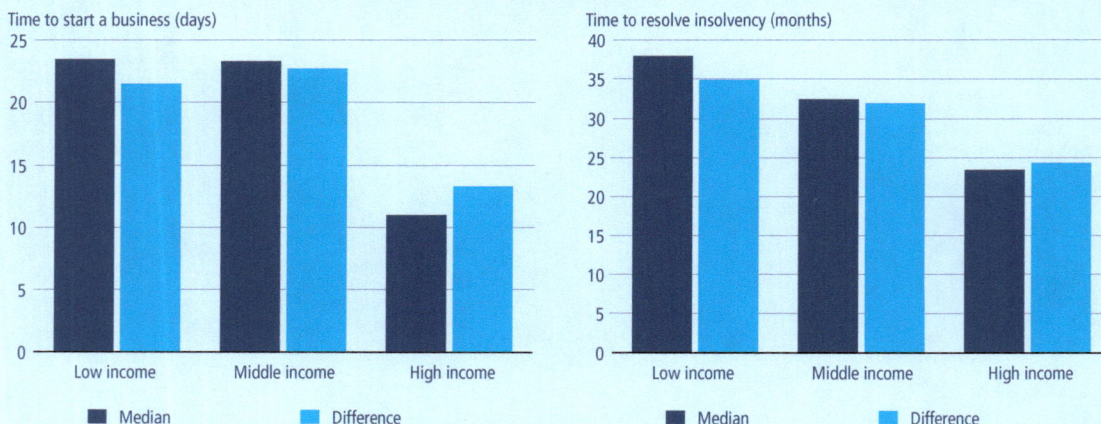

Source: *Doing Business* database.

(continued)

BOX 2.2 Where is the implementation of regulation more predictable and does it matter? *(continued)*

Doing Business data also show that the median is positively correlated with the difference between the best and worst case scenarios (see figure below). The longer the median time to comply with a regulation, the more difficult it becomes to predict the time needed to do so—the median becomes a measure for the unpredictability in time. In fact, economies with more variability in time do not experience higher levels of corruption on average other than what is already predicted by the median.

In economies where it takes longer to start or close a business, the time to do so is less predictable

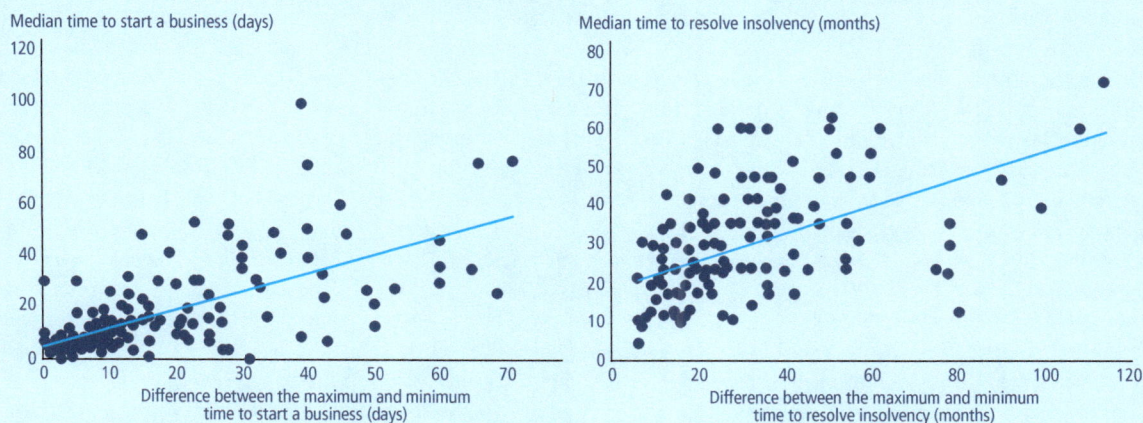

Median time to start a business (days) — Difference between the maximum and minimum time to start a business (days)

Median time to resolve insolvency (months) — Difference between the maximum and minimum time to resolve insolvency (months)

Source: Doing Business database.

Doing Business respondents

More than 43,000 professionals in 190 economies have assisted in providing the data that inform the *Doing Business* indicators over the past 15 years.[8] This year's report draws on the inputs of more than 13,000 professionals.[9] The *Doing Business* website shows the number of respondents for each economy and each indicator set.

Selected on the basis of their expertise in these areas, respondents are professionals who routinely administer or advise on the legal and regulatory requirements in the specific areas covered by *Doing Business*. Because of the focus on legal and regulatory arrangements, most of the respondents are legal professionals such as lawyers, judges or notaries. In addition, officials of the credit bureau or registry complete the credit information questionnaire. Accountants, architects, engineers, freight forwarders and other professionals answer the questionnaires related to paying taxes, dealing with construction permits, trading across borders

and getting electricity. Information that is incorporated into the indicators is also provided by certain public officials (such as registrars from the company or property registry).

The *Doing Business* approach is to work with legal practitioners or other professionals who regularly undertake the transactions involved. Following the standard methodological approach for time-and-motion studies, *Doing Business* breaks down each process or transaction, such as starting a business or registering a building, into separate steps to ensure a better estimate of time. The time estimate for each step is given by practitioners with significant and routine experience in the transaction.

There are two main reasons that *Doing Business* does not survey firms. The first relates to the frequency with which firms engage in the transactions captured by the indicators, which is generally low. For example, a firm goes through the start-up process once in its existence, while

an incorporation lawyer may carry out 10 such transactions each month. The incorporation lawyers and other experts providing information to *Doing Business* are therefore better able to assess the process of starting a business than are individual firms. They also have access to current regulations and practices, while a firm may have faced a different set of rules when incorporating years before. The second reason is that the *Doing Business* questionnaires mostly gather legal information, which firms are unlikely to be fully familiar with. For example, few firms will know about all the main legal procedures involved in resolving a commercial dispute through the courts, even if they have gone through the process themselves. But a litigation lawyer should have little difficulty in providing the requested information on all the procedures.

Governments and World Bank Group regional staff

After receiving the completed questionnaires from the *Doing Business* respondents, verifying the information against the law and conducting follow-up inquiries to ensure that all relevant information is captured, the *Doing Business* team shares the preliminary descriptions of regulatory reforms with governments (through the World Bank Group's Board of Executive Directors) and regional staff of the World Bank Group. Through this process, government authorities and World Bank Group staff working on the economies covered by *Doing Business* can alert the team about, for example, regulatory reforms not reported by the respondents or additional achievements of regulatory reforms. The *Doing Business* team can then turn to the local private sector experts for further consultation and, as needed, corroboration. In addition, the team responds formally to the comments of governments or regional staff and provides explanations of the scoring decisions.

Data adjustments

Information on data corrections is provided in the data notes available at the *Doing Business* website. A transparent complaint procedure allows anyone to challenge the data. From November 2016 to October 2017 the team received and responded to over 180 queries on the data.

USES OF THE *DOING BUSINESS* DATA

Doing Business was designed with two main types of users in mind: policy makers and researchers. It is a tool that governments can use to design sound business regulatory policies. Nevertheless, the *Doing Business* data are limited in scope and should be complemented with other sources of information. *Doing Business* focuses on a few specific rules relevant to the specific case studies analyzed. These rules and case studies are chosen to be illustrative of the business regulatory environment, but they are not a comprehensive description of that environment. By providing a unique data set that enables analysis aimed at better understanding the role of business regulation in economic development, *Doing Business* is also an important source of information for researchers.

Governments and policy makers

Doing Business offers policy makers a benchmarking tool useful in stimulating policy debate, both by exposing potential challenges and by identifying good practices and lessons learned. Despite the narrow focus of the indicators, the initial debate in an economy on the results they highlight typically turns into a deeper discussion on areas where business regulatory reform is needed, including areas well beyond those measured by *Doing Business*. In economies where subnational studies are conducted, the *Doing Business* indicators go one step further in offering policy makers a tool to identify good practices that can be adopted within their economies (box 2.1).

Many *Doing Business* indicators can be considered "actionable." For example, governments can set the minimum capital requirement for new firms, invest in company and property registries to increase their efficiency, or improve the efficiency of tax administration by adopting the latest technology to facilitate the preparation, filing and payment of taxes by the business community. And they can undertake court reforms to shorten delays in the enforcement of contracts. But some *Doing Business* indicators capture procedures, time and costs that involve private sector participants, such as lawyers, notaries, architects, electricians or freight forwarders. Governments may have little influence in the short run over the fees these professions charge, though much can be achieved by strengthening professional licensing regimes and preventing anticompetitive behavior. And governments have no control over the geographic location of their economy, a factor that can adversely affect businesses.

While many *Doing Business* indicators are actionable, this does not necessarily mean that they are all "action-worthy" in a particular context. Business regulatory reforms are only one element of a strategy aimed at improving competitiveness and establishing a solid foundation for sustainable economic growth. There are many other important goals to pursue—such as effective management of public finances, adequate attention to education and training, adoption of the latest technologies to boost economic productivity and the quality of public services, and appropriate regard for air and water quality to safeguard public health. Governments must decide what set of priorities best suits their needs. To say that governments should work toward a sensible set of rules for private sector activity (as embodied, for example, in the *Doing Business* indicators) does not suggest that doing so should come at the expense of other worthy policy goals.

Over the past decade governments have increasingly turned to *Doing Business* as a repository of actionable, objective data providing unique insights into good practices worldwide as they have come to understand the importance of business regulation as a driving force of competitiveness. To ensure the coordination of efforts across agencies, economies such as Colombia, Malaysia and the Russian Federation have formed regulatory reform committees. These committees use the *Doing Business* indicators as one input to inform their programs for improving the business environment. More than 60 other economies have also formed such committees. In East Asia and the Pacific, they include Brunei Darussalam; Indonesia; the Republic of Korea; the Philippines; Taiwan, China; and Thailand. In the Middle East and North Africa: the Arab Republic of Egypt, Kuwait, Morocco, Saudi Arabia and the United Arab Emirates. In South Asia: Bangladesh, India and Pakistan. In Europe and Central Asia: Albania, Croatia, Georgia, Kazakhstan, Kosovo, the Kyrgyz Republic, the former Yugoslav Republic of Macedonia, Moldova, Montenegro, Poland, Tajikistan, Turkey, Ukraine and Uzbekistan. In Sub-Saharan Africa: Benin,

Burundi, the Comoros, the Democratic Republic of Congo, the Republic of Congo, Côte d'Ivoire, Guinea, Guinea-Bissau, Kenya, Liberia, Malawi, Mali, Mauritius, Niger, Nigeria, Rwanda, Senegal, Sierra Leone, Sudan, Tanzania, Togo, Zambia and Zimbabwe. And in Latin America and the Caribbean: Argentina, Brazil, Chile, Costa Rica, the Dominican Republic, Guatemala, Jamaica, Mexico, Nicaragua, Panama, Peru and St. Lucia. Since 2003, governments have reported more than 3,180 regulatory reforms, about 920 of which have been informed by *Doing Business*.[10]

Many economies share knowledge on the regulatory reform process related to the areas measured by *Doing Business*. Among the most common venues for this knowledge sharing are peer-to-peer learning events—workshops where officials from different governments across a region or even across the globe meet to discuss the challenges of regulatory reform and to share their experiences.

Think tanks and other research organizations

Doing Business data are widely used by think tanks and other research organizations, both for the development of new indexes and to produce research papers.

Many research papers have shown the importance of business regulation and how it relates to different economic outcomes.[11] One of the most cited theoretical mechanisms on how excessive business regulation affects economic performance and development is that it makes it too costly for firms to engage in the formal economy, causing them not to invest or to move to the informal sector. Recent studies have conducted extensive empirical testing of this proposition using *Doing Business* and other related indicators. According to one study, for example, a reform that simplified business registration in Mexican municipalities increased registration by 5% and wage employment by 2.2%—and, as a result of increased competition, reduced the income of incumbent businesses by 3%.[12] Business

registration reforms in Mexico also resulted in 14.9% of informal business owners shifting to the formal economy.[13]

Efficient and non-distortionary business regulations are important drivers of productivity. A study on India, for example, shows that inefficient licensing and size restrictions cause a misallocation of resources, reducing total factor productivity by preventing efficient firms from achieving their optimal scale and allowing inefficient firms to remain in the market.[14] The study shows that removing these restrictions would boost total factor productivity by an estimated 40-60%. In the European Union and Japan, implicit taxes on capital use were shown to reduce the average size of firms by 20%, output by 8.1% and output per firm by 25.6%.[15] A recent study on Côte d'Ivoire, Ethiopia, Ghana and Kenya demonstrates large productivity gains following the removal of firm-level distortions caused by uneven regulations and a poor business environment.[16] Research also shows that raising the efficiency level of bankruptcy laws in select OECD high-income economies to that of the United States would increase the total factor productivity of the former by about 30% through a rise in bank loans to large firms.[17]

Considerable effort has been devoted to studying the link between government regulation of firm entry and employment growth. In Portugal, business reforms resulted in a reduction of the time and cost needed for company formalization, increasing the number of business startups by 17% and creating 7 new jobs per 100,000 inhabitants per month. New start-ups were more likely to be female-owned, were smaller and headed by less experienced, less-educated entrepreneurs than before the reform, suggesting that the reform created a more inclusive environment for aspiring entrepreneurs.[18]

In many economies, companies engaged in international trade struggle with high trade costs arising from transport, logistics and regulations that impede their

competitiveness and prevent them from taking full advantage of their productive capacity. With the availability of *Doing Business* indicators on trading across borders—which measure the time, procedural and monetary costs of exporting and importing—several empirical studies have assessed how trade costs affect the export and import performance of economies. A rich body of empirical research shows that efficient infrastructure and a healthy business environment are positively linked to export performance.[19]

Improving infrastructure efficiency and trade logistics bring documented benefits to an economy's balance of trade and individual traders. However, delays in transit time can reduce exports: a study analyzing the importance of trade logistics found that a 1-day increase in transit time reduces exports by an average of 7% in Sub-Saharan Africa.[20] Another study found that a 1-day delay in transport time for landlocked economies and for time-sensitive agricultural and manufacturing products has a particularly large negative impact, reducing trade by more than 1% for each day of delay.[21] Delays while clearing customs procedures also negatively impact a firm's ability to export, particularly when goods are destined for new clients.[22] And in economies with flexible entry regulations, a 1% increase in trade is associated with an increase of more than 0.5% in income per capita, but has no positive income effects in economies with more rigid regulation.[23] Research has also found that—although domestic buyers benefit from having goods of varying quality and price to choose from—import competition only results in minimal quality upgrading in OECD high-income economies with cumbersome regulation while it has no effect on quality upgrading in non-OECD economies with cumbersome regulation.[24] Therefore, the potential gains for consumers from import competition are reduced where regulation is cumbersome.

Doing Business measures aspects of business regulation affecting domestic firms.

However, research shows that better business regulation—as measured by *Doing Business*—is associated with higher levels of foreign direct investment.[25] Furthermore, foreign direct investment can either impede or promote domestic investment depending on how business friendly entry regulations are in the host economy. In fact, foreign direct investment has been shown to crowd out domestic investment in economies with costly processes for starting a business.[26] Another study showed that economies with higher international market integration have, on average, easier and simpler processes for starting a business.[27]

Recent empirical work shows the importance of well-designed credit market regulations and well-functioning court systems for debt recovery. For example, a reform making bankruptcy laws more efficient significantly improved the recovery rate of viable firms in Colombia.[28] In a multi-economy study, the introduction of collateral registries for movable assets was shown to increase firms' access to finance by approximately 8%.[29] In India the establishment of debt recovery tribunals reduced non-performing loans by 28% and lowered interest rates on larger loans, suggesting that faster processing of debt recovery cases cut the cost of credit.[30] An in-depth review of global bank flows revealed that firms in economies with better credit information sharing systems and higher branch penetration evade taxes to a lesser degree.[31] Strong shareholder rights have been found to lower financial frictions, especially for firms with large external finance relative to their capital stock (such as small firms or firms in distress).[32]

There is also a large body of theoretical and empirical work investigating the distortionary effects of high tax rates and cumbersome tax codes and procedures. According to one study, business licensing among retail firms rose 13% after a tax reform in Brazil.[33] Another showed that a 10% reduction in tax complexity is comparable to a 1% reduction in effective corporate tax rates.[34]

Labor market regulation—as measured by *Doing Business*—has been shown to have important implications for the labor market. According to one study, graduating from school during a time of adverse economic conditions has a persistent, harmful effect on workers' subsequent employment opportunities. The persistence of this negative effect is stronger in economies with stricter employment protection legislation.[35] Rigid employment protection legislation can also have negative distributional consequences. A study on Chile, for example, found that the tightening of job security rules was associated with lower employment rates for youth, unskilled workers and women.[36]

By expanding the time series dimension and the scope of the data, *Doing Business* hopes to continue being a key reference for the debate on the importance of business regulation for economic development both within and outside the World Bank Group (box 2.3).

Indexes

Doing Business identified 17 different data projects or indexes that use *Doing Business* as one of its sources of data.[37] Most of these projects or institutions use indicator level data and not the aggregate ease of doing business ranking. The indicator set most widely used is starting a business, followed by labor market regulation and paying taxes. These indexes typically combine *Doing Business* data with data from other sources to assess an economy along a particular aggregate dimension such as competitiveness or innovation.

BOX 2.3 Recent *Doing Business* research drawing on new data from *Doing Business* and World Bank Enterprise Surveys

The *Doing Business* team conducted several studies in 2016/17 analyzing how the current data on business regulations from *Doing Business* and the World Bank Enterprise Surveys are associated with various economic and institutional outcomes. These studies found that:

• Small and medium-size firms are more likely to be credit constrained. In addition, a more advanced credit information system is associated with lower levels of credit constraints, particularly for smaller firms, firms that are not externally audited or firms that lack a quality certification.[a]

• Fiscal pressures encourage regulatory reform. However, the effect of fiscal imbalances on reform weakens when governments can rely on low borrowing costs.[b]

• Service unreliability is a significant factor in low-income economies, where power outages fluctuate significantly from year to year. Furthermore, burdensome electricity connections are associated with utility corruption and higher electricity sector constraints reduce firm demand for energy inputs.[c]

• There is a significant negative relationship between corruption and firm productivity when business regulation is high, but there is no significant relationship when business regulation is low.[d]

a. Chávez 2017.
b. Djankov, Georgieva and Ramalho 2017a.
c. Arlet 2017.
d. Amin and Ulku 2017.

The Heritage Foundation's Index of Economic Freedom, for example, has used 22 *Doing Business* indicators to measure the degree of economic freedom in the world in four areas, including rule of law, government size, regulatory efficiency and market openness.[38] Economies that score better in these four areas also tend to have a high degree of economic freedom.

Similarly, the World Economic Forum uses *Doing Business* data in its Global Competitiveness Index to demonstrate how competitiveness is a global driver of economic growth. The organization also uses 13 *Doing Business* indicators in five indexes that measure institutions, product market efficiency, labor market efficiency, financial market development and business dynamism. These publicly accessible sources expand the general business environment data generated by *Doing Business* by incorporating it into the study of other important social and economic issues across economies and regions. They prove that, taken individually, *Doing Business* indicators remain a useful starting point for a rich body of analysis across different areas and dimensions in the research world.

NOTES

1. Djankov 2016.
2. These papers are available on the *Doing Business* website at http://www.doingbusiness.org/methodology.
3. For more on the World Bank Enterprise Surveys, see the website at http://www.enterprisesurveys.org.
4. For getting credit, indicators are weighted proportionally, according to their contribution to the total score, with a weight of 60% assigned to the strength of legal rights index and 40% to the depth of credit information index. In this way, each point included in these indexes has the same value independent of the component it belongs to. Indicators for all other topics are assigned equal weights. For more details, see the chapter on the distance to frontier and ease of doing business ranking available at www.doingbusiness.org.
5. Hallward-Driemeier and Pritchett 2015.
6. Schneider 2005; La Porta and Shleifer 2008.
7. For the law library, see the website at http://www.doingbusiness.org/law-library.
8. The annual data collection exercise is an update of the database. The *Doing Business* team and the contributors examine the extent to which the regulatory framework has changed in ways relevant for the features captured by the indicators. The data collection process should therefore be seen as adding each year to an existing stock of knowledge reflected in the previous year's report, not as creating an entirely new data set.
9. While about 13,000 contributors provided data for this year's report, many of them completed a questionnaire for more than one *Doing Business* indicator set. Indeed, the total number of contributions received for this year's report is more than 16,000, which represents a true measure of the inputs received. The average number of contributions per indicator set and economy is more than seven. For more details, see http://www.doingbusiness.org/contributors/doing-business.
10. These are reforms for which *Doing Business* is aware that information provided by *Doing Business* was used in shaping the reform agenda.
11. The papers cited here are just a few examples of research done in the areas measured by *Doing Business*. Since 2003, when the *Doing Business* report was first published, more than 10,000 working papers and research articles published in peer-reviewed academic journals have discussed how regulation in the areas measured by *Doing Business* influences economic outcomes.
12. Bruhn 2011.
13. Bruhn 2013.
14. Hsieh and Klenow 2009.
15. Guner, Ventura and Xu 2008.
16. Cirera, Fattal Jaef and Maemir 2017.
17. Neira 2017.
18. Branstetter and others 2014.
19. Portugal-Perez and Wilson 2011.
20. Freund and Rocha 2011.
21. Djankov, Freund and Pham 2010.
22. Martincus, Carballo and Graziano 2015.
23. Freund and Bolaky 2008.
24. Amiti and Khandelwal 2011.
25. Corcoran and Gillanders 2015.
26. Munemo 2014.
27. Norbäck, Persson and Douhan 2014.
28. Giné and Love 2006.
29. Love, Martinez-Peria and Singh 2013.
30. Visaria 2009.
31. Beck, Lin and Ma 2014.
32. Claessens, Ueda and Yafeh 2014.
33. Monteiro and Assunção 2012.
34. Lawless 2013.
35. Kawaguchi and Murao 2014.
36. Montenegro and Pagés 2003.
37. The projects or indexes using *Doing Business* as a source of data are the following: Fraser Institute's Economic Freedom of the World (EFW); The Heritage Foundation's Index of Economic Freedom (IEF); The World Economic Forum's Global Competitiveness Index (GCI); Networked Readiness Index (NRI, jointly with INSEAD); Human Capital Index (HCI); Enabling Trade Index (ETI); Travel and Tourism Competitiveness Index (TTCI); INSEAD's Global Talent Competitiveness Index (GTCI); Global Innovation Index (GII, jointly with Cornell University and the World Intellectual Property Organization); KPMG's Change Readiness Index (CRI); Citi and Imperial College London's Digital Money Index; International Institute for Management Development's World Competitiveness Yearbook; DHL's Global Connectedness Index (GCI); PricewaterhouseCoopers' Paying Taxes 2016: The Global Picture; Legatum Institute's Legatum Prosperity Index; The Millennium Challenge Corporation's Open Data Catalog; International Civil Service Effectiveness (InCiSE) Index of Oxford University, Blavatnik School of Government and The Institute for Government.
38. For more on the Heritage Foundation's Index of Economic Freedom, see the website at http://heritage.org/index.

Reforming
the Business Environment in 2016/17

- From June 2, 2016, to June 1, 2017, *Doing Business* recorded 264 regulatory reforms making it easier to do business—with 119 economies implementing at least one reform across the different areas measured by *Doing Business*.

- The economies that showed the most notable improvement in *Doing Business* 2018 are Brunei Darussalam, Thailand, Malawi, Kosovo, India, Uzbekistan, Zambia, Nigeria, Djibouti and El Salvador.

- Starting a business and getting credit were the areas with the highest incidence of reforms in 2016/17, with 38 reforms recorded in each area. Simplifying registration formalities was the most common feature of reforms making it easier to start a business. The most common feature of reforms making it easier to get credit was the introduction of new credit bureaus and registries.

- Europe and Central Asia continued to be the region with the highest share of economies (79%) implementing at least one business regulation reform, a trend that began over a decade ago. Sub-Saharan Africa, however, was the region with the highest total number of reforms in 2016/17, with 83 reforms recorded across all areas measured by *Doing Business*.

- East Asia and the Pacific had the highest number of economies recording the greatest overall number of reforms making it easier to do business in 2016/17. Brunei Darussalam and Thailand each implemented eight reforms while Indonesia implemented seven reforms.

Starting a business in Thailand used to take 27.5 days. Today, thanks to a series of business regulation reforms, the process takes only 4.5 days. First, Thailand eliminated the requirement that companies obtain a company seal. Previously, every certificate of shares had to be signed by at least one director and bear the company seal. And second, Thailand repealed the requirement to obtain approval of the company's work regulations from the Labor Department. Before the reform, companies with more than 10 employees were required to submit their work regulations to the Labor Department for approval. The company's work regulations are now checked during regular labor inspections. Thailand's case is not unique. In all, 38 economies reduced the complexity and cost of business incorporation processes in 2016/17, making it easier and faster for entrepreneurs to start a business.

Reform pays off. Reducing administrative burdens, simplifying regulation, strengthening competition and cutting red tape are reforms that are positively associated with higher manufacturing productivity growth in low-income economies and aggregate productivity growth in middle-income economies.[1] There is ample evidence of the positive impact of reforming in the *Doing Business* areas with a historically higher number of reforms—namely starting a business, paying taxes and trading across borders. Regulatory reforms that make it easier to start a formal business, for example, are associated with an increase in the number of registered firms and with a higher level of employment and productivity.[2] The composition and quality of taxation can have a significant impact on productivity and economic growth.[3] Tax policies can negatively impact productivity by creating disincentives for firms to engage in innovative activities or distorting the capital-labor allocation when considering labor taxes, including mandatory social contributions. Research shows that eliminating such fiscal barriers would lift real GDP growth rates by about 1 percentage point per year on average over the next two decades.[4] Improving infrastructure efficiency and trade logistics bring documented benefits to an economy's external trade balance and individual traders but transit delays can reduce exports. A study analyzing the importance of trade logistics found that a 1-day increase in transit time reduces exports by an average of 7% in Sub-Saharan Africa.[5]

WHO REFORMED THE MOST IN 2016/17?

From June 2, 2016, to June 1, 2017, *Doing Business* recorded 264 regulatory reforms making it easier to do business—with 119 economies implementing at least one reform across the different areas measured by *Doing Business* (see table 3A.1 at the end of this chapter). However, starting a business, getting credit and trading across borders are the topics with the highest incidence of reforms in 2016/17 (table 3.1).

TABLE 3.1   Economies in Europe and Central Asia recorded the highest share of reforms making it easier to do business in 2016/17

Area of reform	Number of reforms in 2016/17	Region with the highest share of reformers in 2016/17
Starting a business	38	South Asia
Dealing with construction permits	22	Sub-Saharan Africa
Getting electricity	20	Europe & Central Asia
Registering property	29	Europe & Central Asia
Getting credit	38	South Asia
Protecting minority investors	21	South Asia
Paying taxes	30	East Asia & Pacific
Trading across borders	33	South Asia
Enforcing contracts	20	South Asia
Resolving insolvency	13	South Asia

Source: *Doing Business* database.

Note: The labor market regulation indicators also recorded 17 regulatory changes in the *Doing Business 2018* report. These changes are not included in the total reform count.

The region with the highest share of economies reforming across all topics is Europe and Central Asia, continuing a trend that began over a decade ago. Indeed, 79% of economies in the region implemented at least one business regulation reform recorded by *Doing Business 2018*. With five reforms, Uzbekistan is the regional leader on the total count of reforms, followed by Lithuania and Azerbaijan with four reforms each. However, Sub-Saharan Africa is the region with the highest total number of reforms in 2016/17 with 83 reforms recorded across all areas measured by *Doing Business*. Three-quarters of economies in the region implemented at least one business regulation reform in 2016/17. Similarly, 75% of economies in South Asia have implemented at least one business regulation reform captured in *Doing Business 2018*.

East Asia and the Pacific has the greatest number of economies recording the greatest overall number of reforms making it easier to do business in 2016/17; Brunei Darussalam and Thailand each implemented eight reforms while Indonesia implemented seven reforms. Latin America and the Caribbean and the OECD high-income group had the smallest shares of economies implementing business regulation reforms. The Middle East and North Africa was also among the regions with a relatively small share of economies reforming (65%). Nonetheless, Saudi Arabia implemented six reforms.

The 10 economies showing the most notable improvement in performance on the *Doing Business* indicators in 2016/17 were Brunei Darussalam, Thailand, Malawi, Kosovo, India, Uzbekistan, Zambia, Nigeria, Djibouti and El Salvador (table 3.2). These economies together implemented 53 business regulation reforms across 10 of the areas measured by *Doing Business*. Overall, the 10 top improvers implemented the most regulatory reforms in the area of getting credit (eight reforms), starting a business, dealing with construction permits and paying taxes (seven reforms in each area).

TABLE 3.2   The 10 economies improving the most across three or more areas measured by *Doing Business* in 2016/17

Economy	Ease of doing business rank	Change in DTF score	Starting a business	Dealing with construction permits	Getting electricity	Registering property	Getting credit	Protecting minority investors	Paying taxes	Trading across borders	Enforcing contracts	Resolving insolvency
Brunei Darussalam	56	5.77	✔	✔		✔	✔	✔	✔	✔	✔	
Thailand	26	5.65	✔		✔	✔	✔	✔	✔		✔	✔
Malawi	110	5.42		✔			✔			✔		✔
Kosovo	40	4.94	✔				✔					✔
India	100	4.66	✔	✔			✔	✔	✔	✔	✔	✔
Uzbekistan	74	4.50	✔	✔	✔			✔	✔			
Zambia	85	3.94					✔		✔	✔		
Nigeria	145	3.82	✔	✔		✔	✔		✔			
Djibouti	154	3.79	✔	✔		✔	✔	✔				
El Salvador	73	3.56		✔	✔					✔	✔	

Source: *Doing Business* database.

Note: Economies are selected on the basis of the number of reforms and ranked on how much their distance to frontier (DTF) score improved. First, Doing Business selects the economies that implemented reforms making it easier to do business in three or more of the 10 areas included in this year's aggregate distance to frontier score. Regulatory changes making it more difficult to do business are subtracted from the number of those making it easier. Second, Doing Business ranks these economies on the increase in their distance to frontier score due to reforms from the previous year (the impact due to changes in income per capita and the lending rate is excluded). The improvement in their score is calculated not by using the data published in 2016 but by using comparable data that capture data revisions and methodology changes. The choice of the most improved economies is determined by the largest improvements in the distance to frontier score among those with at least three reforms.

Among the 10 top improvers, Brunei Darussalam made the biggest advance toward the regulatory frontier for the second consecutive year by implementing eight reforms making it easier to do business. Brunei Darussalam removed post-incorporation procedures and implemented new building guidelines for construction, eliminating the requirement to obtain a hoarding permit and to submit both the commencement and completion notice to the one-stop shop. Additionally, Brunei Darussalam adopted a new secured transactions law that strengthened the rights of borrowers and creditors and strengthened minority investor protections by increasing shareholders' rights and role in major corporate decisions, clarifying ownership and control structures and requiring greater corporate transparency. The economy also introduced an electronic case management system for use by judges and lawyers and introduced an online system for filing and payment of the contributions to the employee provident fund. Finally, in 2016/17 Brunei Darussalam enhanced its National Single Window for goods clearance.

Thailand, the other economy in East Asia and the Pacific that made it to the list of the 10 top improvers, implemented changes in eight areas measured by *Doing Business*. Thailand streamlined the post-registration process to start a new business. Thailand also adopted a new secured transactions law that strengthened the rights of borrowers and creditors, introduced an automated risk-based system for selecting companies for tax audit and increased the automation and efficiency of enforcement processes in Bangkok. In addition, Thailand strengthened its land administration system by implementing a geographic information system and scanning the majority of maps in Bangkok.

Three Sub-Saharan African economies—Nigeria, Malawi and Zambia—made it to the list of 10 top improvers in 2016/17. Nigeria made starting a business faster by introducing the electronic approval of registration documents. Nigeria also

increased the transparency of dealing with construction permits by publishing all relevant regulations, fee schedules and pre-application requirements online. In addition, Nigeria improved access to credit information by legally guaranteeing borrowers the right to inspect their own data and by starting to provide credit scores to banks, financial institutions and borrowers. Nigeria also introduced new centralized electronic payment channels for the payment of all federal taxes. Malawi halved the fees charged by the city council and reduced the time to process building plan approvals. It also improved access to credit information by establishing a new credit bureau. Zambia made exporting and importing easier by implementing the ASYCUDA World data management system and made tax compliance easier by introducing an online platform for filing and paying taxes. All three economies introduced or made amendments to their secured transactions laws.

Kosovo and Uzbekistan are the two economies in Europe and Central Asia that made the biggest advances toward the frontier in 2016/17. Kosovo recorded three reforms making it easier to do business, including adopting a new law that establishes clear priority rules inside bankruptcy for secured creditors and clear grounds for relief from a stay for secured creditors during reorganization procedures. Uzbekistan, which recorded five reforms, streamlined the process of obtaining an electricity connection by introducing a "turnkey" service at the utility that fulfills all connection-related services, including the design and construction completion of the external connection.

With eight reforms making it easier to do business in 2016/17, India was the only economy in South Asia to join the list of the 10 top improvers. India made obtaining a building permit faster by implementing an online Single Window System for the approval of building plans; the new system allows for the submission and approval of building plans prior to requesting the building permit. India also streamlined

the business incorporation process by introducing the SPICe form (INC-32), which combined the application for the Permanent Account Number (PAN) and the Tax Account Number (TAN) into a single submission. Furthermore, following improvements to the online system in 2016, the time needed to complete the applications for Employee's Provident Fund Organization (EPFO) and the Employee's State Insurance Corporation (ESIC) decreased. The joint application for the Mumbai Value Added Tax (VAT) and the Profession Tax (PT) also was fully implemented in January 2017. India also strengthened access to credit by amending the rules on priority of secured creditors outside reorganization proceedings and adopting a new insolvency and bankruptcy code that introduced a reorganization procedure for corporate debtors. In trading across borders, India reduced border compliance time by improving infrastructure at the Nhava Sheva Port in Mumbai. Export and import border compliance costs were also reduced in both Delhi and Mumbai after merchant overtime fees were abolished. Thanks to the increased use of electronic and mobile platforms, since July 2016 importers under the Authorized Economic Operator (AEO) program have been able to clear cargo faster through simplified customs procedures.

With four reforms—captured in the indicators for dealing with construction permits, getting electricity, paying taxes and trading across borders—El Salvador is the only economy in Latin America and the Caribbean on this year's list of 10 top improvers. Similarly, Djibouti (with five reforms) is the only economy in the Middle East and North Africa region on the list.

REMOVING OBSTACLES TO STARTING A BUSINESS

Entrepreneurs in many economies continue to face significant barriers to entry when starting a business. Burdensome and costly regulation can prevent entrepreneurs from entering the formal economy, negatively impacting both the public and private sectors. Formalization allows entrepreneurs and employees to access the legal and financial services available to registered companies (such as obtaining loans and social security benefits). There is clear evidence that streamlining regulatory procedures can encourage business entry, business growth, job creation and rising national incomes.

Thirty-eight economies made starting a business easier in 2016/17 by reducing the procedures, time or cost associated with the process. Two-thirds of these economies simplified registration formalities by, for example, abolishing requirements to obtain various approvals or consolidating several registration processes into one. Others streamlined postregistration procedures by eliminating the need to obtain a general business license or company seal. And still others set up or improved one-stop shops, reduced or eliminated minimum capital requirements and set up online platforms for entrepreneurs. Of the 38 economies that reformed in this area, 12 implemented complex improvements associated with two or more types of reforms.

Equatorial Guinea advanced the most toward the frontier in starting a business in 2016/17. It did this by abolishing the requirement to obtain an authorization of establishment from the Office of the Prime Minister to start a business. Previously, it took four months on average for each new business to obtain this authorization.

Niger, another economy that notably improved the ease of starting a business, reduced its minimum capital requirement, allocated more personnel to its one-stop shop—resulting in a reduction in the time required to register a company—and allowed for the publication of the notice of company incorporation online free of charge.

Since its inception, *Doing Business* has captured at least one reform making it easier to start a business in almost 95% of economies. These reforms have made it faster and easier for firms to launch and formally operate. Fifteen years ago, it took entrepreneurs worldwide 52 days on average to start and formally operate a firm. Today, it takes 20 days.

Simplifying registration requirements can range from merging registration procedures to eliminating redundant processes. Several economies in Sub-Saharan Africa took steps to streamline these formalities in 2016/17 (figure 3.1). By eliminating the requirement that a woman must obtain her husband's permission to operate a business, the Democratic Republic of Congo made it easier for women to register firms. And by combining multiple business registration procedures, the Democratic Republic of Congo also reduced the time required to start a business by nearly a business week.

STREAMLINING THE PROCESS OF OBTAINING A BUILDING PERMIT

The construction sector is a critical indicator of the health of an economy. An abundance of stalled construction projects is a visible sign of economic hardship, while a booming construction industry is indicative of economic growth. Although various obstacles remain—including the fragmented nature of the construction industry and its hesitancy to adapt to technological change—governments around the world are focused on implementing reforms that reduce the time and cost to obtain permission to build.[6] In 2016/17, five of the 22 economies that reformed their construction permitting processes focused their reforms on reducing the time to obtain the building permit itself (figure 3.2).

Côte d'Ivoire, which showed the most significant improvement in this area in

FIGURE 3.1   Economies in South Asia and Sub-Saharan Africa have the highest share of reforms making it easier to start a business in 2016/17

Share of economies that made it easier to start a business in 2016/17 (%)

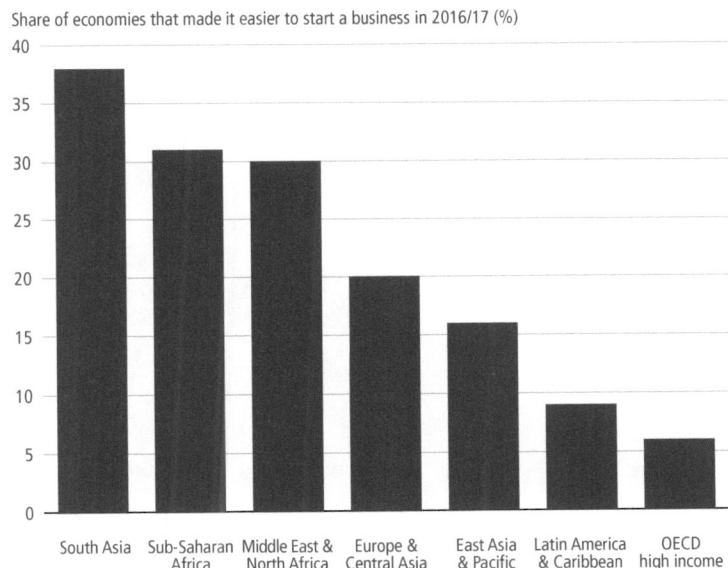

Source: Doing Business database.

FIGURE 3.2   Many economies made getting construction permits faster in 2016/17

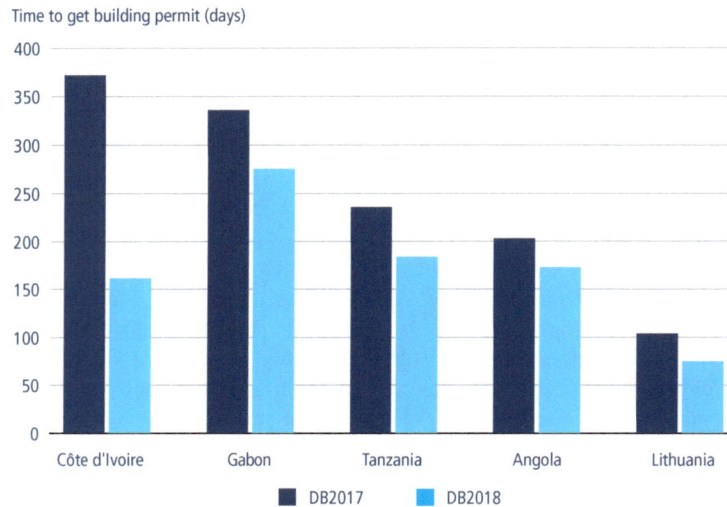

Time to get building permit (days)

Source: Doing Business database.

2016/17, established a one-stop shop for building permits and published deadlines, costs and procedures related to obtaining the urban planning certificate. As a result, Côte d'Ivoire reduced the number of required procedures by four and the time to process applications by 210 days.

Notable progress was also made elsewhere in Sub-Saharan Africa, where 15 economies reformed multiple aspects of their construction permitting processes. Gabon streamlined procedures and reduced the time to obtain a building permit by setting up an internal pre-approval meeting of relevant technical experts who examine the application prior to a formal committee meeting. Gabon also made its building regulations, fee schedules and requirements to obtain a building permit available online. Similarly, Benin and Ghana improved transparency by making regulations concerning construction openly accessible online while Rwanda increased quality control during construction by introducing risk-based inspections. Kenya reduced construction fees by eliminating clearance fees from the National Environment Management Authority and the National Construction Authority. Malawi halved building permit fees. Tanzania streamlined

its permitting process by improving the efficiency of its one-stop shop and increasing the frequency of building permit council meetings to once a month.

In Europe and Central Asia, Ukraine reduced the cost of construction by significantly lowering mandatory investor contributions to Kyiv's social and engineering-transport infrastructure. Lithuania reduced the time needed to obtain technical conditions and the building permit. Uzbekistan streamlined the process for obtaining approvals of land plot allocations from various agencies.

MAKING ACCESS TO ELECTRICITY MORE EFFICIENT AND RELIABLE

World Bank Enterprise Surveys data show that business owners in developing economies identify access to reliable electrical services as the fourth largest obstacle to doing business.[7] However, electricity sector constraints vary. A difficult connection process is associated with utility corruption and may hamper firms,[8] while an unreliable electricity supply is linked to low firm productivity.[9]

Both an efficient connection process and safeguards to mitigate outage risks are crucial to business owners. Effective customer protections and regulations also provide predictability for firms, enabling them to better forecast risks.

Given the importance of the electricity sector, many economies aim to improve access to electricity and the quality of supply to strengthen the operating environment for small and medium-size enterprises. *Doing Business* recorded reforms in 20 economies making it easier to get electricity in 2016/17. Of these, 12 economies focused on improving the connection process and eight on the reliability of electricity supply.

The most common feature of electricity reforms in the past year was improvement to the connection process. Regulatory changes that reduce the number of interactions required between the utility or other third parties and customers when they apply for an electricity connection are an effective way to improve the connection process. Armenia successfully reduced the number of interactions required in 2016/17 by installing a geographic information system, eliminating the need for a site inspection to issue the technical conditions. As a result, the total time to obtain a connection was reduced from 138 days in 2016 to 127 days in 2017.

In the Dominican Republic and Kenya changes were made to improve the reliability of power supply. Major upgrades were made to the network infrastructure in Santo Domingo and Nairobi, resulting in a notable reduction in the duration of outages (figure 3.3). In Kenya, the utility in Nairobi invested in its distribution lines and transformers and set up a squad specializing in restoring power when outages occur. In the Dominican Republic, the utility in Santo Domingo built new substations, redesigned the network zoning plan and established a response squad to quickly restore service after an outage. The initiatives implemented by

FIGURE 3.3   The duration of power outages has decreased in the Dominican Republic and Kenya

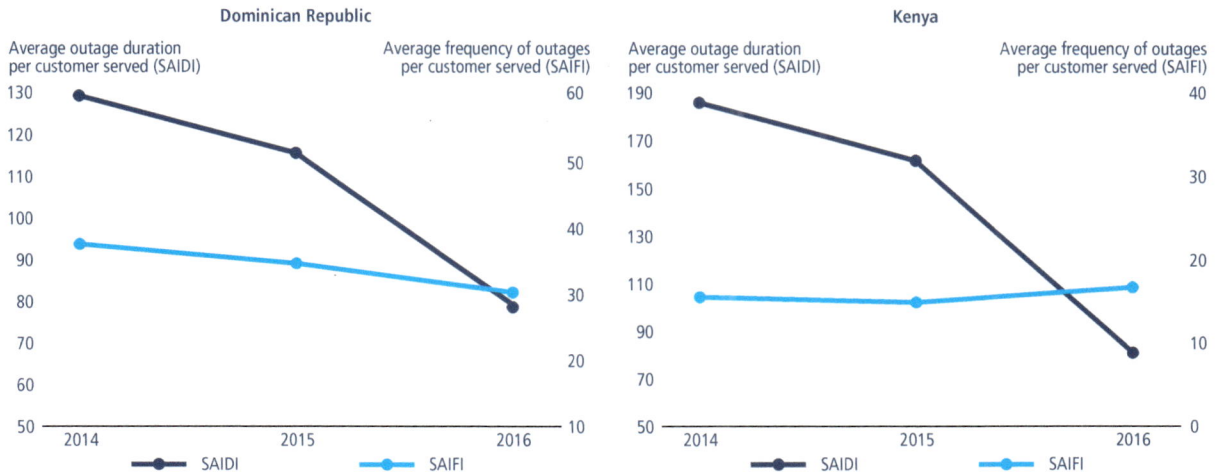

Source: *Doing Business* database.

Note: The figures show the average number of hours without electricity supply (as measured by SAIDI) and the average number of power outages (as measured by SAIFI) per customer served over the course of a year in the largest business city in each economy.

the utilities in both economies resulted in significant improvements in the reliability of electric supply. As a result, Kenya and the Dominican Republic became eligible to score on *Doing Business'* reliability of supply and transparency of tariff index as their System Average Interruption Duration Index (SAIDI) and System Average Interruption Frequency Index (SAIFI) scores are now below 100.

IMPROVING THE QUALITY OF LAND ADMINISTRATION

Valid property rights are necessary to support investment, productivity and economic growth. Evidence from economies around the world suggests that property owners with registered titles are more likely to invest. They also have a better chance of getting credit when using their property as collateral. Likewise, having reliable, up-to-date information in cadasters and land registries is essential for governments to correctly assess and collect property taxes.

Twenty-nine economies made registering a property easier by increasing the efficiency of property transfers and

improving the quality of land administration in 2016/17. The most common improvements included increasing transparency of information and increasing administrative efficiency by reducing the time to transfer property.

Mauritius made the biggest improvement in the ease of registering property in 2016/17. It did this by eliminating the

10% transfer tax and registration duty, implementing a complaint mechanism and publishing service standards. Rwanda also made improvements to its property registration process in 2016/17. Rwanda reduced the time for a property transfer by introducing new online services such as user searches of property information and online property transfer filing and registration (figure 3.4). It is

FIGURE 3.4   Rwanda has consistently reduced the time it takes to transfer property

Source: *Doing Business* database.

now possible to search online for owners of specific properties, locations and the encumbrances affecting the property. In addition, the parties, or their notary, can file the property transfer deed for registration online. Niger significantly reduced registration costs by reducing notary fees from 4% of the property value to a regressive fee scheme based on the property value. The government also made changes to the General Tax Code to lower property transfer registration fees.

Among regions, Europe and Central Asia and Sub-Saharan Africa tie as the regions with the most reforms relating to the transfer of property in 2016/17. In Europe and Central Asia, Croatia passed the Real Estate Transfer Act, which decreased the real estate transfer tax from 5% to 4%, while Kazakhstan made cadastral plans in Almaty available to the public via the government's website and began publishing statistics on land disputes. The Russian Federation made property registration services available at its one-stop shop and passed legislation requiring that property registrations be completed within nine working days. In Sub-Saharan Africa, the land registry in Mauritania launched a website that provides relevant information to the public on land registry services, including property transfer regulations, procedures and fees. Senegal decreased property registration times by streamlining the interactions between different departments at the property registry, introducing internal mechanisms to identify bottlenecks and enacting internal time limits to speed up the registration process.

STRENGTHENING ACCESS TO CREDIT

Twenty-four economies implemented reforms improving their credit information systems in 2016/17. The most common feature of reform was the introduction of new credit bureaus and registries to improve the sharing of credit information. Malawi made the most improvement in

credit reporting by operationalizing a new credit bureau, Credit Data CRB, in July 2016. The credit bureau distributes positive and negative credit information on both firms and individuals and borrowers have a legally-guaranteed right to inspect their own data. Cameroon, Indonesia, Iraq, Jordan and Slovenia all established a new credit bureau or registry in 2016/17. Azerbaijan, Djibouti and Myanmar improved their regulatory framework for credit reporting, enabling the creation of new credit bureaus in the near future.

Economies in West Africa also implemented reforms in 2016/17 to improve their credit reporting systems. All West African Economic and Monetary Union (WAEMU) member states have now formally adopted the Uniform Law on the Regulation of Credit Information Bureaus. WAEMU's regional credit bureau, Creditinfo VoLo, began operations in Burkina Faso, Guinea-Bissau and Togo in early 2017. These economies joined Côte d'Ivoire, Mali, Niger and Senegal, where Creditinfo VoLo was launched in 2016 (figure 3.5).

Elsewhere, economies adopted global good practices in credit reporting. The

credit bureaus in Nigeria, Qatar and the United Arab Emirates began offering credit scores to their data users as a value-added service. Improvements were also made in the distribution of data from sources other than financial institutions. In Bhutan, two utility companies began submitting positive and negative information on consumer accounts to the credit bureau. In Kenya, public utility companies and savings and credit cooperative organizations are now required to share credit information. In the Islamic Republic of Iran, a vehicle dealership began sharing information on credit-based transactions with the credit bureau.

In 2016/17, 18 economies made it easier for businesses to obtain credit by modifying legislation to encourage the use of moveable property as collateral. The most common feature of reform included improvements in the legislative framework for secured transactions encompassing functional equivalents to security interests and creating modern, searchable collateral registries which are accessible on-line for the registration, modification and cancelation of security interests. West Bank and Gaza

---

FIGURE 3.5   Timeline of West African Economic and Monetary Union regional credit bureau

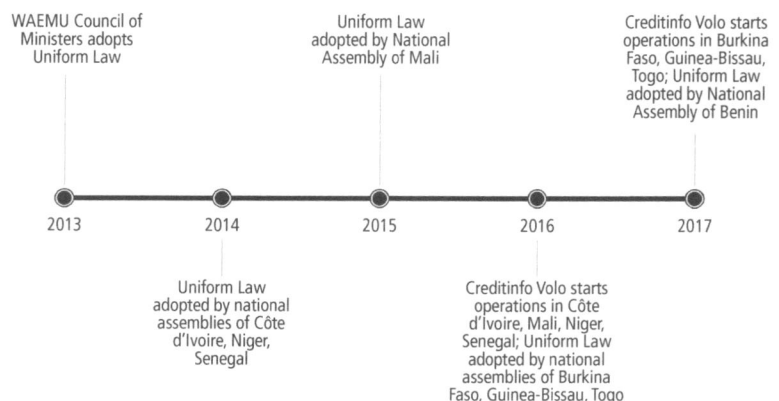

| 2013 | 2014 | 2015 | 2016 | 2017 |

Above timeline:
WAEMU Council of Ministers adopts Uniform Law — 2013

Uniform Law adopted by National Assembly of Mali — 2015

Creditinfo VoLo starts operations in Burkina Faso, Guinea-Bissau, Togo; Uniform Law adopted by National Assembly of Benin — 2017

Below timeline:
Uniform Law adopted by national assemblies of Côte d'Ivoire, Niger, Senegal — 2014

Creditinfo VoLo starts operations in Côte d'Ivoire, Mali, Niger, Senegal; Uniform Law adopted by national assemblies of Burkina Faso, Guinea-Bissau, Togo — 2016

Source: Doing Business database.

made the most noteworthy improvement in 2016/17 by adopting a secured transactions law in 2016 that establishes a modern collateral registry and allows a general description of present and future assets used as security interests. The new rules also establish priority for secured creditors outside insolvency and permit out-of-court enforcement.

Belarus created the Registry of Encumbrances on Movable Property in 2016 to record, store and provide information on security interests in movable assets. Mongolia's Law on Movable and Intangible Property Pledges, which entered into force in March 2017, regulates the assignment of receivables, financial leases and retention-of-title sales, requiring their registration with the collateral registry. Similarly, Brunei Darussalam, the Kyrgyz Republic, Mongolia, Malaysia, Nepal, Nigeria, Russia, Samoa, Turkey and Zambia introduced new laws establishing modern collateral registries.

PROTECTING THE RIGHTS OF MINORITY SHAREHOLDERS

Djibouti made the most noteworthy improvements to minority investor protections in 2016/17. A new law, Law No. 191/AN/17/7, which modified the Code of Commerce, takes significant steps to mitigate the risk of prejudicial conflicts of interest in companies. The law requires directors to inform their board in detail of any conflict of interest they may have on a proposed transaction. If they decide to proceed, they must also include the terms of the transaction and the extent of the conflict of interest in the annual report. Even after these precautions, shareholders can file in court to cancel the transaction and recover any profits made by the interested parties if the transaction was prejudicial to the company. Shareholders can also inspect transaction documents before filing a suit and seek reimbursement of their legal expenses. In addition, the law stipulates that transactions representing

51% of a company's assets must be authorized by its shareholders and that the notice of meeting should be sent 21 days in advance. As a result of these and other amendments, Djibouti improved its score on all six indices of the indicator set, resulting in a 21.67-percentage point increase in its distance to frontier score for minority investor protections (figure 3.6).

Twenty other economies also strengthened minority shareholder protections in 2016/17.[10] Costa Rica enacted Law No. 9392 in October 2016 which provides specific protections for minority investors and strengthens safeguards against conflicts of interest. The board of directors now must vote on transactions with interested parties and board members who have a personal interest must clearly disclose their interest and abstain from voting in this case. Should shareholders choose to file a claim against the transaction, the law also increases their access to evidence both before and during court proceedings. As a result, Costa Rica's score improved significantly on both the extent of disclosure index and the ease of shareholder suits index, resulting in a 10 percentage point increase in its distance to frontier score for minority investor protections.

Thirteen economies—Azerbaijan, Brunei Darussalam, Djibouti, Arab Republic of Egypt, France, Indonesia, Kazakhstan, Lithuania, Malaysia, Nepal, Rwanda, Saudi Arabia and Uzbekistan—passed legislation in 2016/17 that increased corporate transparency requirements. These laws give more agenda-setting power to shareholders and disclose board member activities in other companies, executive compensation and audit reports. As a result, all of these economies improved their scores on the extent of corporate transparency index.

Azerbaijan, Bhutan, Brunei Darussalam, Djibouti, Georgia, Kazakhstan, Rwanda, Saudi Arabia and Thailand took steps to clarify corporate governance, ownership and control structures by, for example, enacting legislation that requires companies to nominate independent board members and set up an audit committee. These changes resulted in improvements in the scores of these nine economies on the extent of ownership and control index.

Finally, 11 economies enacted regulation in 2016/17 enhancing approval and disclosure requirements for related-party transactions. Among them, Luxembourg

FIGURE 3.6 Djibouti strengthened minority investor protections the most in 2016/17

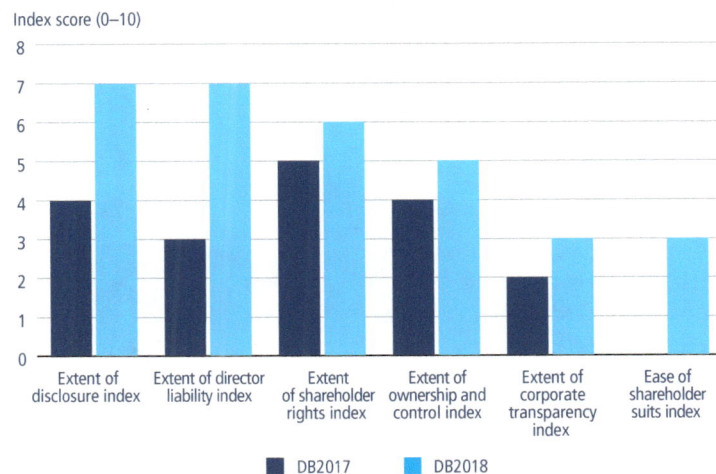

Source: Doing Business database.

made it easier for shareholders representing 10% of the share capital of their company to get access to corporate information and to sue directors in cases of prejudicial third-party transactions. These 11 economies—Costa Rica, Djibouti, Georgia, India, Kazakhstan, Luxembourg, Pakistan, Rwanda, Saudi Arabia, Thailand and Ukraine—improved on the extent of approval, extent of director liability and ease of shareholder suits indices.

ENHANCING TAX COMPLIANCE SYSTEMS

Properly developed, effective taxation systems are crucial for a well-functioning society. In most economies, taxes are the main source of revenue to fund public spending on education, health care, public transport, infrastructure and social programs, among others. Tax policy is one of the most contentious areas of public policy. A large body of theoretical and empirical work examines the effects of high tax rates and complex fiscal systems. Although determining the optimal tax system can be challenging because context matters when economies want to maximize their welfare, there is less uncertainty—from both theoretical and empirical perspectives—about the distortionary effects of high taxes and cumbersome tax systems. A good tax system should ensure that taxes are proportionate and certain (not arbitrary) and that the method of paying taxes is convenient to taxpayers. Lastly, taxes should be easy to administer and collect.

El Salvador made the greatest advances in tax payment systems in 2016/17. Following regulatory changes, all companies are now required to submit their tax returns electronically. Electronic payments are now used by a majority of companies in El Salvador for profit taxes, value added taxes and labor taxes, including mandatory contributions. The tax administration also moved to a

different assessment criteria for selecting companies for a tax audit, with its focus now primarily on larger companies. Low-risk companies and small businesses would not be selected for a tax audit in the case of an underpayment or self-reporting an error in the corporate income tax return.

The most common feature of reforms in the area of paying taxes over the past year was the implementation or enhancement of electronic filing and payment systems. Besides El Salvador, 16 other economies—Botswana, Brunei Darussalam, India, Indonesia, Kenya, Lithuania, Maldives, Morocco, New Zealand, the Philippines, Rwanda, Saudi Arabia, Uruguay, Uzbekistan, Vietnam and Zambia—introduced or enhanced systems for filing and paying taxes online. India eased tax compliance on businesses by implementing an online platform for the electronic payment of the Employee Provident Fund and introducing administrative measures to ease corporate income tax compliance (figure 3.7).

The use of electronic tax filing and payment systems has increased substantially since 2006, with the most notable

progress in the economies of Europe and Central Asia. Sub-Saharan Africa remains the region with the smallest share of economies using electronic filing or payments. However, in 2016 the use of online systems for filing and payment of taxes resulted in efficiency gains in several economies in the region, including Botswana, Kenya, Rwanda and Zambia. Angola, Mauritania, Senegal and Togo are improving their systems to enable taxpayers to shift from manual to online filing of tax returns in the near future.

Other economies directed efforts at reducing the financial burden of taxes on businesses and keeping tax rates at a reasonable level to encourage private sector development. With the objective of promoting more stable employment conditions, Italy exempted employers from social security contributions for a maximum of 36 months for hires with open-ended contracts from January 1, 2015 to December 31, 2015. Japan reduced the corporate income tax rate at the national level from 25.5% to 23.9% for tax years beginning on or after April 1, 2015. The Bahamas reduced the rate of stamp duty on land sales from 10% in 2015 to 2.5% in 2016.

FIGURE 3.7   India made paying taxes faster by requiring the electronic payment of some taxes

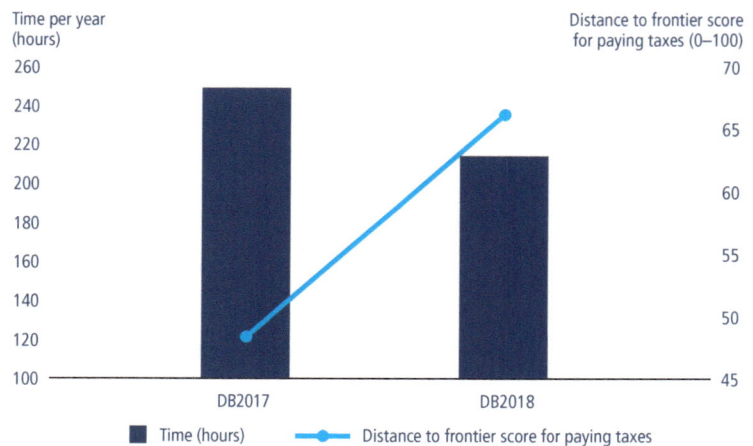

FACILITATING INTERNATIONAL TRADE

International trade is a cornerstone of economic development, as access to international markets is strongly correlated with economic growth.[11] Although tariffs on exports and imports have fallen on average in recent decades, non-tariff measures have gained increasing prominence.[12] Optimizing time and costs in the trade sector is strongly associated with trade growth, diversification and economic expansion.[13] Accordingly, global trade policies have shifted their focus from tariffs to trade facilitation, including the elimination of trade-related transactions costs. *Doing Business* tracks global trade policies and reforms that facilitate trade by implementing cost-effective, time-efficient and transparent regulatory practices (figure 3.8).

Of the 33 economies that undertook reforms making it easier to trade across borders in 2016/17, 22 improved their existing electronic systems for exports or imports, reducing the time of documentary and border compliance by more than 760 hours overall. More than half of this time savings is associated with the enhancement of existing electronic systems. Zambia reduced the time to complete documentary and border compliance by about 30%, underscoring the impact of roll out of the ASYCUDA World system, an automated customs data management system, to multiple customs offices nationwide. In 2017 Zambia increased the functionality of the platform, enabling the electronic submission of declarations, supporting documents and the online payment of customs fees. Following its upgrade from ASYCUDA to the *Sistema Único de Modernización Aduanera* (Single Customs Modernization System; SUMA), Bolivia has enabled traders to clear their goods electronically, submitting customs declarations and supporting documents online and eliminating the need for visits to multiple government agencies to obtain clearance. As a result, Bolivia reduced the time required to prepare and submit all required documentation by 72 hours overall.

Eleven economies significantly upgraded their trade logistics infrastructure in 2016/17. Inadequate infrastructure is one of the main burdens in international trade.[14] As part of its National Development Plan 2013-2017, Angola has significantly rehabilitated and upgraded the port of Luanda, expanding the terminals, adding new berths and acquiring equipment. This has resulted in improvements in handling processes and reduced border compliance time for both exports and imports.

The regions implementing the most reforms making it easier to trade across borders in 2016/17 were Sub-Saharan Africa (46% of reforms in this area) and East Asia and the Pacific (18%). Together, the economies in these two regions account for nearly 64% of reforms in this area as captured by *Doing Business 2018*. The remainder of reforms were made by economies in Latin America and the Caribbean (15%), the Middle East and North Africa (9%), South Asia (9%) and Europe and Central Asia (3%).

ENHANCING JUDICIAL EFFICIENCY

A judicial system that provides effective commercial dispute resolution is crucial to a healthy economy.[15] Case management systems supporting manual case flow through forms and files contribute to the overall timeliness and efficiency of the justice system, especially when combined with increased court automation and information communication technology solutions.[16] The introduction of new case management features, or the expansion of existing case management or court automation systems, was the most common reform feature recorded in 2016/17. Some economies—Guyana and Kazakhstan, for example—focused on strengthening regulatory case management principles by introducing tighter time standards for key court events. Others—such as Switzerland and Taiwan, China—focused on the

FIGURE 3.8 Reforms affecting customs, especially those regarding the implementation of electronic systems, produce the highest time savings across regions

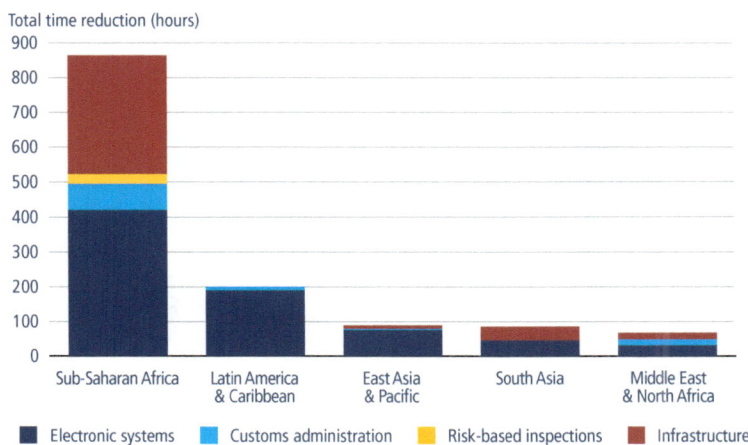

Source: *Doing Business* database.
Note: The time reduction captures reforms that were implemented and had a positive impact on time for the trading across borders indicator set from 2016 to 2017. The reforms recorded during this period are aggregated in four wide-ranging categories: electronic systems, customs administration, risk-based inspections and infrastructure. Regions with no reforms on time are excluded from the figure.

implementation of a platform for the electronic submission of the initial complaint. Hungary strengthened its existing electronic-filing system by integrating it with a platform that allows litigants to pay court fees electronically.

Namibia, the economy that improved most notably in the area of enforcing contracts in 2016/17, is witnessing the results of a seven-year reform process in case management and information communication technology systems that began with a peer learning exercise with some of the top-performing economies on the enforcing contracts indicators. The reform process led to the approval of new court rules in 2014 that incorporated many case management principles such as time limits for key court events, early case management through pre-trial conferences, earlier intervention by the judge, tools to dispose of cases that have been "abandoned" by the parties and court-connected mediation. The court also upgraded its information communication technology systems and court users are now able to submit their initial complaint online, while judges and lawyers have access to a dedicated

online case management system. Today the Windhoek High Court has a case clearance rate of above 110% (figure 3.9), higher than some of the most sophisticated economies in the world, including Finland and Sweden.[17]

Other economies have strengthened judicial efficiency through the introduction of a specialized commercial court. Bhutan introduced dedicated benches that only hear commercial cases. Guyana, Nicaragua, the Slovak Republic and Vietnam strengthened their regulatory environment by introducing a new Code of Civil Procedure.

PROMOTING EFFICIENT BANKRUPTCY REGIMES

Efficient regulation of corporate insolvency is associated with increased access to credit for firms and on better terms.[18] Creditors are more willing to lend because they are more likely to recover their loans. Additionally, economies that reform their insolvency law to provide a mechanism for business rescue may reduce the failure rate among firms, help maintain

a higher overall level of entrepreneurship in the economy and preserve jobs.[19] By facilitating the efficient business exit and liquidation of nonviable companies, an insolvency framework supports the efficient reallocation of resources across the economy.[20]

In 2016/17 *Doing Business* recorded 13 reforms making it easier to resolve insolvency. The most common feature of reform was the introduction of a reorganization procedure as an alternative to liquidation. Cabo Verde, the Dominican Republic, Grenada, India, Kosovo, Liberia, Malawi, Panama, Singapore and the United Arab Emirates adopted legal regulations enabling parties to make use of reorganization procedures for the purpose of saving viable businesses where there is a prospect of financial recovery.

The reform in Kosovo is particularly noteworthy. A comprehensive insolvency law, which was adopted in July 2016, introduced a number of modern features that are aligned with international good practices. In addition to establishing reorganization and liquidation procedures, the law provided the debtor with

FIGURE 3.9 Namibia has reduced its case backlog by implementing a case management system

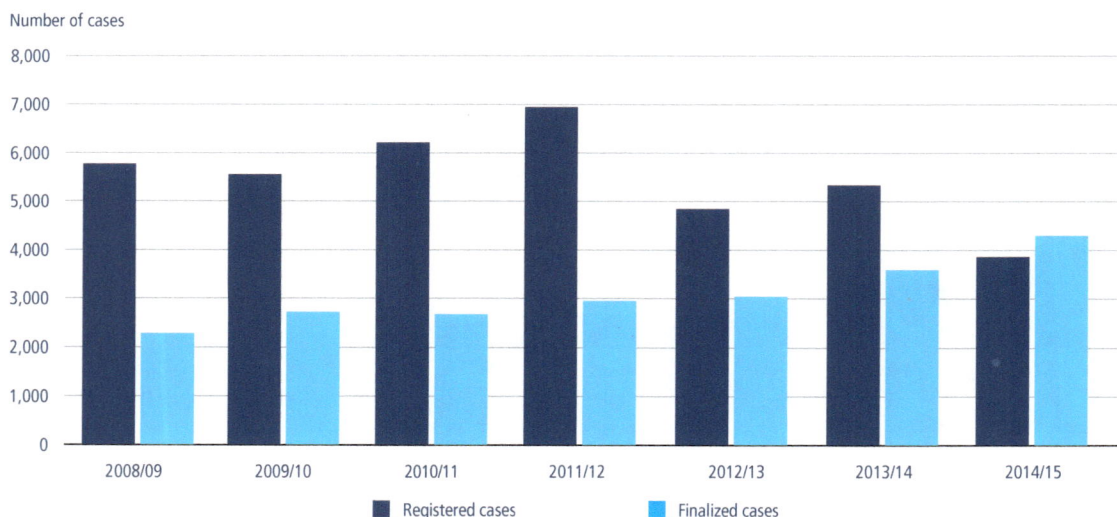

Source: Namibia Superior Courts data (http://www.ejustice.moj.na).

the option to submit a pre-packaged rehabilitation plan before the commencement of reorganization proceedings and established expedited insolvency proceedings for small and medium-size enterprises. These new elements not only streamline liquidation and reorganization proceedings in Kosovo in general, but are also likely to shorten the timeframe for resolving insolvency. The law also allows the debtor to obtain new financing after the commencement of insolvency proceedings to facilitate continued operations, regulates the treatment of contracts and establishes a cross-border insolvency regime (table 3.3).

Upper-middle-income and high-income economies mainly focused their efforts on strengthening the rights of creditors in insolvency proceedings in 2016/17. Azerbaijan, the Dominican Republic, Grenada, and Panama made important amendments to their legal frameworks to provide creditors with additional safeguards and enable their participation in important decisions that affect their interests. The Dominican Republic and Grenada granted creditors the right to approve the sale of substantial assets of the debtor. Azerbaijan and Grenada provided creditors with the right to request information on the financial affairs of the debtor at any time. Additionally, Azerbaijan and Georgia granted creditors the right to object to the decision accepting or rejecting creditors' claims.

CHANGING LABOR MARKET REGULATION

Regulation of labor markets is essential for the achievement of primary economic goals, such as the efficient allocation of resources—that is, the distribution of resources to their most productive uses.[21] Labor regulation is also indispensable in protecting vulnerable groups from market failures, such as forced labor and discrimination.[22] In addition to these fundamental functions, smart labor regulation can help advance a myriad of economic and social goals, ranging from better responses to economic shocks to the promotion of equal opportunities and social cohesion. The challenge in developing labor policies is to prevent both over- and under-regulation by balancing labor flexibility with worker protection.[23]

In 2016/17, *Doing Business* recorded 17 reforms in the areas covered by the indicators for labor market regulation,

TABLE 3.4 Puerto Rico (U.S.)'s Transformation and Labor Flexibility Act (TLFA)

Old framework	Labor reform
Length of the maximum probationary period for permanent employees	
3 months	9 months
Wage premium for daily overtime work and weekly holiday work	
100% premium rate	50% premium rate
Mandatory paid annual leave, workers with 1 year tenure	
15 days	9 days
Mandatory paid annual leave, workers with 5-10 years tenure	
15 days	12 days

Source: Doing Business database.

including the hiring of workers, working hours, redundancy rules and job quality. Some economies made their labor regulation more rigid while others made it more flexible; in some economies, the changes were in both directions. Puerto Rico (U.S.), for example, undertook a substantial regulatory reform effort by adopting the Transformation and Labor Flexibility Act (TLFA), which introduced comprehensive changes to regulation in all areas measured by the indicator for labor market regulation (table 3.4). The TLFA increased the length of the maximum probationary period for permanent employees, decreased the premium for daily overtime work and the wage premium for weekly holiday, decreased the mandatory paid annual leave and established severance payments for all employees wrongfully made redundant.

Kiribati also implemented significant changes to labor regulation by approving the Employment and Industrial Relation Code (EIRC) which regulates the number of work hours per day, establishes paid annual leave and paid sick-leave and clarifies rules governing redundancies.

Changes to the regulation of working hours was a common feature of reform in 2016/17. Albania reduced the number of work hours to 48 per week. Similarly, the Democratic Republic of Congo

TABLE 3.3 Kosovo's previous and new insolvency frameworks

Previous framework	New framework
Can a debtor initiate liquidation or reorganization procedures?	
No liquidation or reorganization available.	Yes. Debtors can initiate both procedures.
Do creditors vote on the reorganization plan?	
No reorganization available.	Yes. Creditors whose rights are affected by the proposed plan vote on it.
Can a court invalidate preferential and undervalued transactions concluded before insolvency proceedings?	
No provisions.	Yes.
Can a debtor obtain credit after commencement of insolvency proceedings?	
No provisions.	Yes. The debtor or the administrator may obtain new financing after the commencement of insolvency proceedings and the priorities of the new financing are clearly established.
Can creditors participate in important decisions?	
No provisions.	Yes. Every creditor has the right to request information on the debtor's financial situation from the insolvency representative and may object to the decision regarding its own claims as well as claims of other creditors.

Source: Doing Business database.

established a standard workday of eight hours per day and designated Sunday as a weekly rest day. Taiwan, China, increased the number of weekly rest days from one to two and also extended the length of mandatory paid annual leave. Bosnia and Herzegovina decreased wage premiums for overtime work, night work and weekly holiday work. Tajikistan abolished restrictions on night work by non-pregnant women and non-nursing mothers.

In addition, some economies made changes to legislation regulating redundancy rules and costs. Tajikistan increased the amount of severance pay that an employer must provide when making an employee redundant. The Bahamas amended its legislation to introduce priority rules that apply to reemployment and Singapore adopted legislation requiring employers to notify the Ministry of Manpower when terminating a group of nine redundant workers.

Economies also implemented legislation in the area of job quality in 2016/17. The United States (Los Angeles) established a maximum of six working days of paid sick leave a year. Colombia, the Dominican Republic, India and Paraguay increased the duration of paid maternity leave.

NOTES

1. Dabla-Norris and others 2013.
2. Klapper and Love 2011.
3. IMF 2015.
4. IMF 2017.
5. Freund and Rocha 2011.
6. World Economic Forum 2017.
7. Enterprise Surveys database (http://www.enterprisesurveys.org/), World Bank.
8. Geginat and Ramalho 2015.
9. Grimm, Hartwig and Lay 2012.
10. The economies that strengthened minority shareholder rights in 2016/17 are Azerbaijan, Bhutan, Brunei Darussalam, Costa Rica, Djibouti, Egypt, France, Georgia, India, Indonesia, Kazakhstan, Lithuania, Luxembourg, Malaysia, Nepal, Pakistan, Rwanda, Saudi Arabia, Thailand, Ukraine and Uzbekistan.
11. World Bank Group and WTO 2015.
12. Hoekman and Nicita 2011.
13. Arvis and others 2016.
14. Lanz, Roberts and Taal 2016.
15. Ramello and Voigt 2012.
16. Gramckow and others 2016.
17. CEPEJ 2016.
18. Cirmizi, Klapper and Uttamchandani 2010.
19. Klapper and Love 2011.
20. For more on how insolvency frameworks support the efficient reallocation of resources across the economy, see Djankov 2009, Funchal 2008, Klapper 2011 and Visaria 2009.
21. World Bank 2012.
22. Agell 1999.
23. Kuddo and others 2015.

TABLE 3A.1   Who reduced regulatory complexity and cost and/or strengthened legal institutions in 2016/17—and what did they do?

Feature	Economies	Some highlights
Making it easier to start a business		
Simplified preregistration and registration formalities (publication, notarization, inspection, and other requirements)	Bhutan; China; Democratic Republic of Congo; Republic of Congo; Czech Republic; Djibouti; Dominican Republic; Equatorial Guinea; Ethiopia; Gabon; Indonesia; Iraq; Jamaica; Kenya; Madagascar; Mauritius; Morocco; Nigeria; Pakistan; Saudi Arabia; Senegal; Serbia; Thailand; Uzbekistan	Djibouti made starting a business more affordable by reducing the fees to register and publish the notice of commencement of activity.
Cut or simplified postregistration procedures (tax registration, social security registration, licensing)	The Bahamas; Brunei Darussalam; Greece; India; Iraq; Kenya; Kosovo; Madagascar; Malta; Niger; Tajikistan; Thailand; Zimbabwe	The Bahamas made starting a business easier by merging the process of registering for the business license and value added tax. Greece made starting a business easier by creating a unified social security institution.
Introduced or improved online procedures	India; Kuwait; Saudi Arabia	Saudi Arabia made starting a business easier through the use of an online system, which merges the name reservation and submission of the articles of association into one procedure. Saudi Arabia also improved the online payment system, removing the need to pay fees in person.
Created or improved one-stop shop	Democratic Republic of Congo; Kuwait; Mauritania; Moldova; Niger; Sierra Leone	Mauritania made starting a business easier by combining multiple registration procedures.
Abolished or reduced minimum capital requirement	Cameroon; Republic of Congo; Ethiopia; Gabon; Niger	Cameroon made starting a business easier by reducing the minimum capital requirement. Gabon made starting a business easier by reducing the minimum capital requirement and by making the notarization of incorporation documents optional.
Making it easier to deal with construction permits		
Reduced time for processing permit applications	Angola; Brunei Darussalam; Côte d'Ivoire; El Salvador; Gabon; India; Kenya; Lithuania; Mauritius; Niger; Nigeria; Tanzania; United Arab Emirates; Uzbekistan	Lithuania reduced the time it takes to obtain technical conditions and the building permit. Niger introduced new rules to obtain a water connection as well as service delivery objectives, resulting in a reduction in the time to obtain a water connection. The Waste Water Management Authority (WMA) in Mauritius outsourced the design and construction of sewage connection works to five private companies, thereby reducing the time to provide sewage connection.
Improved transparency	Benin; Cabo Verde; Gabon; Ghana; Niger; Nigeria; Seychelles	Gabon improved the transparency of information by publishing legislation related to the construction industry online. Nigeria (Kano and Lagos) increased transparency by publishing all relevant regulations, fee schedules and pre-application requirements online.
Streamlined procedures	Brunei Darussalam; Gabon; Niger; Nigeria; Uzbekistan	Brunei Darussalam eliminated the requirement to obtain a hoarding permit and to submit both the commencement and completion notice to the one-stop shop. Niger streamlined its internal processes and set up a building permit commission which meets every Thursday to rule on permit applications.
Adopted new building regulations	Djibouti; El Salvador; Niger; Rwanda; United Arab Emirates; Uzbekistan	Djibouti implemented a decree clearly establishing decennial liability for all professionals engaged in construction projects. Uzbekistan introduced a new system of allocating land through a competitive selection process for land plots of up to a hectare.
Reduced fees	Djibouti; Kenya; Malawi; Niger; Ukraine; United Arab Emirates	Kenya eliminated fees to obtain clearance from the National Environment Management Authority and the National Construction Authority. Malawi halved the fees to obtain a building permit. The National Laboratory of Djibouti published new official fees for its services, reducing the cost of concrete inspections.
Improved or introduced electronic platforms or online services	Angola; El Salvador; India	El Salvador introduced a single window system, making preliminary construction fees payable online. The Municipality of Greater Mumbai introduced an online single window system that allows for the submission and approval of building plans prior to requesting the building permit along with various other services.
Introduced or improved one-stop shop	Côte d'Ivoire; Tanzania	Côte d'Ivoire created a one-stop shop for processing building permits. Tanzania increased the efficiency of its one-stop shop by improving coordination among agencies.
Making it easier to get electricity		
Facilitated more reliable power supply and transparency of tariff information	Dominican Republic; El Salvador; Jamaica; Kenya; Mexico; Montenegro; Senegal; Vietnam	Jamaica improved the reliability of supply in Kingston by investing in the distribution network through several initiatives, including the installation of smart meters and distribution automation switches.
Improved process efficiency	Angola; Armenia; Indonesia; Italy; Niger; Philippines	Armenia made getting electricity easier by imposing new deadlines for connection procedures and introducing a new geographic information system at the utility.
Streamlined approval process	Indonesia; Lithuania; Mozambique; Thailand; United Arab Emirates; Uzbekistan	Mozambique reduced the time to get an electricity connection by streamlining procedures through the utility instead of various agencies. Mozambique also reduced costs by eliminating the security deposit for large commercial clients.
Improved regulation of connection processes and costs	Georgia; Indonesia; Mozambique; United Arab Emirates	Georgia made getting electricity more affordable by reducing connection costs for new customers.

TABLE 3A.1	Who reduced regulatory complexity and cost and/or strengthened legal institutions in 2016/17—and what did they do?	
Feature	**Economies**	**Some highlights**
Making it easier to register property		
Increased transparency of information	Benin; Brunei Darussalam; Djibouti; Hong Kong SAR, China; Kazakhstan; Kuwait; Mauritania; Mauritius; Nigeria; Pakistan; Seychelles; Suriname	Mauritania created a new section on the government website containing information on the services provided by the land registry. Kazakhstan made cadastral plans in Almaty available to the public and began publishing statistics on the number of land disputes.
Increased administrative efficiency	Antigua and Barbuda; Costa Rica; Guyana; Kuwait; Nigeria; Russian Federation; Rwanda; Saudi Arabia; Senegal; Tajikistan	Saudi Arabia implemented an online system to check for property ownership and encumbrances. Rwanda reduced the time to complete a property transfer from 12 to seven days, by reducing the time needed to conduct a title search and registration.
Reduced taxes or fees	Benin; Croatia; Indonesia; Mauritius; Myanmar; Niger; Senegal; Turkey	Niger decreased registration fees, effectively lowering the cost to register a property by 15%. Turkey made registering property easier by reducing mortar dues (property transfer registration fees) from 4% to 3%.
Increased reliability of infrastructure	Hong Kong SAR, China; Romania; Serbia; Seychelles; Thailand	Serbia and Thailand improved the reliability of their land administration systems by implementing a geographic information system. Hong Kong SAR, China, linked information recorded by the Lands Department with that of the Land Registry. Romania digitized its land book system in Bucharest.
Improved the accessibility of the land dispute resolution mechanism	Armenia; Brunei Darussalam; Kazakhstan; Saudi Arabia	Armenia, Brunei Darussalam, Kazakhstan and Saudi Arabia made their land dispute mechanism more accessible by publishing statistics on land-related cases filed at the court of first instance.
Strengthening legal rights of borrowers and lenders		
Created a unified and/or modern collateral registry for movable property	Belarus; Brunei Darussalam; Kyrgyz Republic; Malaysia; Mongolia; Nepal; Nigeria; Russian Federation; Samoa; Turkey; West Bank and Gaza; Zambia	Zambia strengthened access to credit by adopting a new law on secured transactions that establishes a modern and centralized collateral registry.
Introduced a functional and secured transactions system	Brunei Darussalam; Mongolia; Nepal; Nigeria; Samoa; West Bank and Gaza; Zambia	West Bank and Gaza strengthened access to credit by adopting the Security Interests in Moveable Property Act. The new law on secured transactions implements a functional secured transactions system. The law regulates functional equivalents to loans secured with movable property, such as financial leases and retention-of-title sales.
Allowed for general description of assets that can be used as collateral	Albania; Thailand; West Bank and Gaza	Albania implemented new laws allowing for the general description of assets that can be used as collateral.
Expanded range of movable assets that can be used as collateral	Thailand; Vietnam	Thailand introduced a law that broadens the scope of assets which can be used as collateral to secure a loan.
Granted absolute priority to secured creditors or allowed out-of-court enforcement	Albania; Brunei Darussalam; India; Kosovo; Malawi; Thailand; Turkey; West Bank and Gaza	Turkey introduced a law that allows out-of-court enforcement.
Granted exemptions to secured creditors from automatic stay in insolvency proceedings	India; Kosovo; Thailand	Kosovo adopted a new bankruptcy law that includes protections for secured creditors during an automatic stay in reorganization proceedings.
Improving the sharing of credit information		
Established a new credit bureau or registry	Burkina Faso; Cameroon; Guinea-Bissau; Indonesia; Iraq; Jordan; Malawi; Slovenia; Togo	Indonesia improved access to credit information by launching a new credit bureau.
Improved regulatory framework for credit reporting	Azerbaijan; Benin; Djibouti; Guinea-Bissau; Kyrgyz Republic; Myanmar; Turkey	Djibouti improved access to credit information by adopting a law that creates a new credit information system.
Expanded scope of information collected and reported by credit bureau or registry	Bhutan; Islamic Republic of Iran; Kenya; Netherlands	In Bhutan, two utility companies began submitting positive and negative information on consumer accounts to the credit bureau.
Introduced bureau or registry credit scores as a value-added service	Nigeria; Qatar; United Arab Emirates	In the United Arab Emirates, the credit bureau began offering consumer credit scores to banks and financial institutions as a value-added service to help them assess the creditworthiness of borrowers.
Guaranteed by law borrowers' right to inspect data	Nigeria; Swaziland	Swaziland adopted the Consumer Credit Act 2016 guaranteeing borrowers' right to inspect their own data.
Expanded borrower coverage by credit bureau or registry	Madagascar	In Madagascar, the credit registry for microfinance institutions was consolidated with the registry for banks, expanding the number of borrowers listed in the registry's database with information on their borrowing history from the past five years to more than 5% of the adult population.

TABLE 3A.1   Who reduced regulatory complexity and cost and/or strengthened legal institutions in 2016/17—and what did they do?

Feature	Economies	Some highlights
Strengthening minority investor protections		
Expanded shareholders' role in company management	Azerbaijan; Bhutan; Brunei Darussalam; Djibouti; Arab Republic of Egypt; France; Georgia; Indonesia; Kazakhstan; Lithuania; Malaysia; Nepal; Rwanda; Saudi Arabia; Thailand; Uzbekistan	Lithuania enacted a law requiring the disclosure of information about board members' other directorships as well as basic information on their primary employment.
Enhanced access to information in shareholder actions	Costa Rica; Djibouti; Georgia; Kazakhstan; Luxembourg; Rwanda; Thailand	Luxembourg adopted legislation allowing shareholders that represent at least 10% of the share capital to inspect transactions documents before filing a suit.
Increased disclosure requirements for related-party transactions	Costa Rica; Djibouti; India; Saudi Arabia; Ukraine	Costa Rica adopted a law requiring board members who have a personal interest in a proposed transaction to clearly disclose it and not participate in the decision.
Increased director liability	Djibouti; India; Luxembourg; Pakistan	Djibouti adopted a law allowing shareholders to hold interested directors (as well as other board members) liable when a transaction with interested parties is unfair or prejudicial to the company and to have them repay profits made from the transaction upon a successful claim.
Making it easier to pay taxes		
Introduced or enhanced electronic systems	Botswana; Brunei Darussalam; El Salvador; India; Indonesia; Kenya; Lithuania; Maldives; Morocco; New Zealand; Philippines; Rwanda; Saudi Arabia; Uruguay; Uzbekistan; Vietnam; Zambia	El Salvador mandated all business taxpayers to file their annual income tax return through one of the available electronic methods (DET software or online processing). The general online tax processing and payment system was also consolidated.
Reduced profit tax rate	Japan; Norway	Japan adopted the 2016 Tax Reform Bill on February 5, 2016, which reduced the corporate income tax rate at the national level from 25.5% to 23.9% for tax years beginning on or after April 1, 2015.
Reduced labor taxes and mandatory contributions	Belgium; France; Italy; Japan; Ukraine	Ukraine introduced in 2016 a flat rate of 22% for the Unified Social Contribution tax paid by employers, which replaced the previous differentiated rates ranging from 36.76% to 49.7%.
Reduce taxes other than profit and labor	The Bahamas; Indonesia; Thailand; Zambia	Indonesia reduced the statutory rate for capital gains tax from 5% to 2.5% in 2016.
Simplified tax compliance processes or decreased number of tax filings or payments	China; India; Italy; Nigeria; Mauritania; Palau; Ukraine	India introduced the Income Computation and Disclosure Standards (ICDS) in 2016 to standardize the methods of computing taxable income and other tax accounting standards. Data gathering became more automated in India due to the use of modern enterprise resource planning (ERP) software.
Introduced a risk-based tax audit selection system	El Salvador; Thailand	Thailand implemented a new automatic risk-based system for selecting companies for a tax audit in 2016. The system does not flag for a tax audit in cases of self-reporting an error or an underpayment of tax liability due.
Introduced time limits for processing VAT cash refunds	Senegal	Senegal mandated by law that value added tax refunds be paid within 90 days from the moment the tax authority receives the documents from the taxpayer and the request for value added tax credit refund must be taken into account by the administration within 30 days from the time the request has been submitted. These changes were applied in practice.
Making it easier to trade across borders		
Introduced or improved electronic submission and processing of documents for exports	Bolivia; Botswana; Brazil; Brunei Darussalam; Cabo Verde; Comoros; Malawi; Mauritius; Oman; Pakistan; Sierra Leone; Sri Lanka; St. Kitts and Nevis; Swaziland; Taiwan, China; Uganda; Vietnam; Zambia	Bolivia upgraded its automated customs system (SUMA) and reduced documentary compliance time to export. Zambia expanded its customs management system nationwide, allowing electronic payments.
Introduced or improved electronic submission and processing of documents for imports	Bolivia; Brazil; Brunei Darussalam; Cabo Verde; Comoros; Indonesia; Jamaica; Kenya; Malawi; Mauritius; Oman; Pakistan; Sri Lanka; Swaziland; Vietnam; Zambia	Due to improvements made to their respective electronic customs platforms, Cabo Verde and Kenya both reduced import documentary compliance time by 24 hours. Brazil made trading across borders faster by enhancing its electronic system—integrating customs, tax and administrative agencies—reducing import documentary compliance time by 72 hours.
Strengthened transport or port infrastructure for exports	Angola; India; Malaysia; Mauritania; Mauritius; Mozambique; Pakistan; Qatar; Russian Federation; Singapore; Uganda	Angola rehabilitated the Port of Luanda, improving handling processes and reducing border compliance time. The Russian Federation opened a deep water port on the coast of the Gulf of Finland, increasing competition and reducing the cost of border compliance at the Port of St. Petersburg.
Strengthened transport or port infrastructure for imports	Angola; India; Malaysia; Mauritania; Mauritius; Pakistan; Qatar; Russian Federation; Singapore	Qatar made trading across borders easier by inaugurating the Hamad Port. Expansion of existing ports in Singapore and Malaysia improved the terminal handling process.
Facilitated customs administration for exports and imports	Botswana; Brunei Darussalam; El Salvador; Ethiopia; India; Mauritania; Mauritius; São Tomé e Príncipe; Saudi Arabia; Sierra Leone; Vietnam	El Salvador increased the number of customs officers for clearance and inspections, reducing border compliance time. Mauritius decreased the number of intrusive inspections, which reduced border compliance time for both exports and imports by 10 hours.

TABLE 3A.1   Who reduced regulatory complexity and cost and/or strengthened legal institutions in 2016/17—and what did they do?

Feature	Economies	Some highlights
Making it easier to enforce contracts		
Introduced significant changes to the applicable civil procedure or enforcement rules	Guyana; Kazakhstan; Nicaragua; Senegal; Serbia; Slovak Republic; Spain; Vietnam	Nicaragua and the Slovak Republic each introduced a new Code of Civil Procedure. Serbia adopted a new enforcement law that broadens and clarifies the responsibilities of enforcement agents. Spain reduced the fees to file new cases.
Expanded court automation by introducing electronic payment or by publishing judgments	Azerbaijan; Hungary; Mauritania; Rwanda; Thailand	Azerbaijan, Hungary and Thailand implemented platforms to pay fees electronically. Mauritania and Rwanda made decisions rendered at all levels in commercial cases publicly available.
Introduced or expanded the electronic case management system	Brunei Darussalam; India; Namibia; Saudi Arabia	India introduced the possibility of generating performance measurement reports. Brunei Darussalam, Namibia and Saudi Arabia introduced electronic case management systems.
Introduced electronic filing	Namibia; Switzerland; Taiwan, China	Namibia, Switzerland and Taiwan, China, introduced electronic filing systems for commercial cases, allowing attorneys to submit the initial summons online.
Introduced or expanded specialized commercial court	Bhutan	Bhutan introduced a dedicated bench to resolve commercial disputes.
Expanded the alternative dispute resolution framework	Vietnam	Vietnam introduced a new law regulating voluntary mediation.
Making it easier to resolve insolvency		
Improved the likelihood of successful reorganization	Azerbaijan; Cabo Verde; Dominican Republic; Georgia; Grenada; India; Kosovo; Liberia; Malawi; Panama; Thailand; United Arab Emirates	Cabo Verde established the possibility for the debtor to receive new financing after the commencement of insolvency proceedings and introduced corresponding priority rules.
Introduced a new restructuring procedure	Cabo Verde; Dominican Republic; Grenada; India; Kosovo; Liberia; Malawi; Panama; Singapore; United Arab Emirates	The United Arab Emirates introduced the option of reorganization for commercial entities as an alternative to liquidation.
Strengthened creditors' rights	Azerbaijan; Cabo Verde; Dominican Republic; Georgia; Grenada; Kosovo; Liberia; Panama	The Dominican Republic granted creditors the right to object to decisions of special importance made by the insolvency representative, such as the sale of substantial assets of the debtor in the course of insolvency proceedings.
Improved provisions on treatment of contracts during insolvency	Azerbaijan; Cabo Verde; Dominican Republic; Georgia; Kosovo; Liberia; Malawi; Panama; United Arab Emirates	Liberia allowed avoidance of preferential and undervalued transactions concluded prior to commencement of insolvency proceedings.
Regulated the profession of insolvency administrators	India; Liberia; Malawi; Panama	Malawi regulated the profession of insolvency administrator, including its duties, powers and liabilities.
Changing labor legislation		
Altered hiring rules and probationary period	Finland; Mongolia; Puerto Rico (U.S.)	Puerto Rico (U.S.) increased the length of the maximum probationary period for permanent employees, hired after the effective date of the Transformation and Labor Flexibility Act (TLFA).
Amended regulation of working hours	Albania; Bosnia and Herzegovina; Democratic Republic of Congo; Kiribati; Taiwan, China; Tajikistan	Kiribati established rules for the number of work hours per day and the maximum number of working days per week.
Changed redundancy rules and cost	The Bahamas; Kiribati; Puerto Rico (U.S.); Singapore; Tajikistan	Singapore adopted legislation requiring employers to notify the Ministry of Manpower when terminating a group of nine redundant workers.
Reformed legislation regulating worker protection and social benefits	Albania; Colombia; Dominican Republic; India; Kiribati; Latvia; Paraguay; Puerto Rico (U.S.); United States	The United States (Los Angeles) adopted the Paid Sick Leave Ordinance, allowing for a maximum of six working days of paid sick leave a year upon the oral or written request of an employee.

Source: Doing Business database.

Note: Reforms affecting the labor market regulation indicators are included here but do not affect the ranking on the ease of doing business.

Starting
a Business

Transparency of information at business registries

Governments and civil society have come together in recent years to increase the transparency of business information. New regulations have been adopted to improve transparency, particularly regarding the dissemination of company data. These changes have been made in the wake of a series of revelations—such as the Panama papers and the Bahamas leaks—that showed the extent to which individuals take advantage of obscure company ownership structures to illicitly move money around the globe. There is now strong momentum behind expanding access to corporate information, including company ownership.

- Transparent information provided to the public by business registries can reduce transactions costs and facilitate investment decisions.

- The most common types of information shared by business registries include the company's name, its legal address and the names of its directors.

- Information on beneficial ownership, corporate structure and annual financial returns is less commonly collected and made available to the public.

- Technological advances have greatly enhanced access to information.

- There is a strong association between a transparent business registry and higher efficiency, as well as a lower incidence of bribery.

One way to increase transparency in the business environment is to disclose beneficial ownership information publicly—that is, to reveal the identity of individuals who ultimately enjoy the benefits of property rights in equity, even if they are not legal owners. Disclosure of beneficial ownership is useful in identifying suspected money laundering and potential terrorist financing.

To make ownership more transparent, Singapore amended its Companies Act to require locally-incorporated companies and foreign companies registered in Singapore to maintain beneficial ownership information and to make the data public upon request. Ghana amended its Companies Act in 2016 to regulate disclosure of information on beneficial ownership. In May 2017 Germany's parliament passed a law requiring that the owners of all German enterprises (including offshore entities) be identified in an electronic beneficial ownership registry. Access to corporate information is vital for individuals and institutions looking to make sound investment decisions. It is crucial for investors to know who they are doing business with in the global economy.

Providing public access to company information through business registries strengthens confidence in businesses and institutions, but it also helps to manage financial exposure and increase market stability, thereby reducing the risks associated with doing business. Improving transparency necessitates the drafting of laws that expand public access to additional corporate data, such as the identities of the company directors, shareholders and beneficial owners.

This year, *Doing Business* has collected preliminary data on the information gathered and shared by business registries in 190 economies. *Doing Business* collects data on the public availability of both detailed corporate information (such as company name, directors, shareholders, beneficial owners and so on) and the information needed to start a business (for example, a documents list, fee schedule, services standards and official statistics on firm creation). Each type of information obtained without the need for any personal interaction is assigned points to reflect greater transparency. The features of transparency of information range from 0 (least transparent) to 18 (most transparent). The aim is to capture new and actionable aspects related to the business incorporation framework and to understand how transparency of information in business registration varies across regions and how it is associated with other institutional and economic outcomes.

HOW IMPORTANT IS TRANSPARENCY IN BUSINESS REGISTRIES?

As the principal agency responsible for registering firms, business registries allow companies to acquire a legal identity. This legal status enables a firm to enter into contracts with other firms, access formal financial systems and bid on public-sector contracts.[1] Business registries play a vital role by ensuring that the information they collect from these companies is not only captured within their systems but is also available to the public. Sharing information publicly makes it easier to ensure that the information is accurate.

Business registry transparency can increase the accountability of firms and public officials. By improving the

predictability of transactions, transparency can also benefit financial institutions and company services providers as it becomes easier for them to obtain the information they need to comply effectively with due diligence requirements.[2] Registries with clearly-stipulated requirements facilitate the process of registering and verifying information. There tends to be a culture of greater competition and economic growth in economies where it is easier for companies to enter the market.[3]

Transparency of information can broaden the pool of potential investors by reducing the need for personal connections. It can level the playing field for a budding entrepreneur who may lack the necessary connections to formally launch his or her company. By reducing the risk associated with an investment, transparency can help investors determine the viability of a transaction.[4] Revealing public information to curb information asymmetry can also reduce a firm's cost of capital by attracting increased demand from large investors (due to increased liquidity of its securities).[5] The financial cost of a lack of data transparency can be significant: in

2011 alone it is estimated that developing economies suffered nearly $1 trillion in illicit financial outflows.[6] Transparent data on company ownership are vital in combating money laundering, tax evasion, corruption and other illegal activities.

WHAT KIND OF BUSINESS INFORMATION IS AVAILABLE TO THE PUBLIC?

Most business registries share some data with the public about the companies registered with them. The types of information that are most commonly made public by the business registry are the company's name, legal address, year of incorporation, type of business activity and the names of its directors.[7]

Information regarding a firm's corporate structure, annual returns and beneficial ownership is less commonly made available to the public. It is possible to access information on a company's corporate structure—that is, whether it has subsidiaries or belongs to a holding company—and its beneficial ownership in only a few economies (figure 4.1).

FIGURE 4.1   Data on shareholders and directors are more accessible than data on beneficial owners

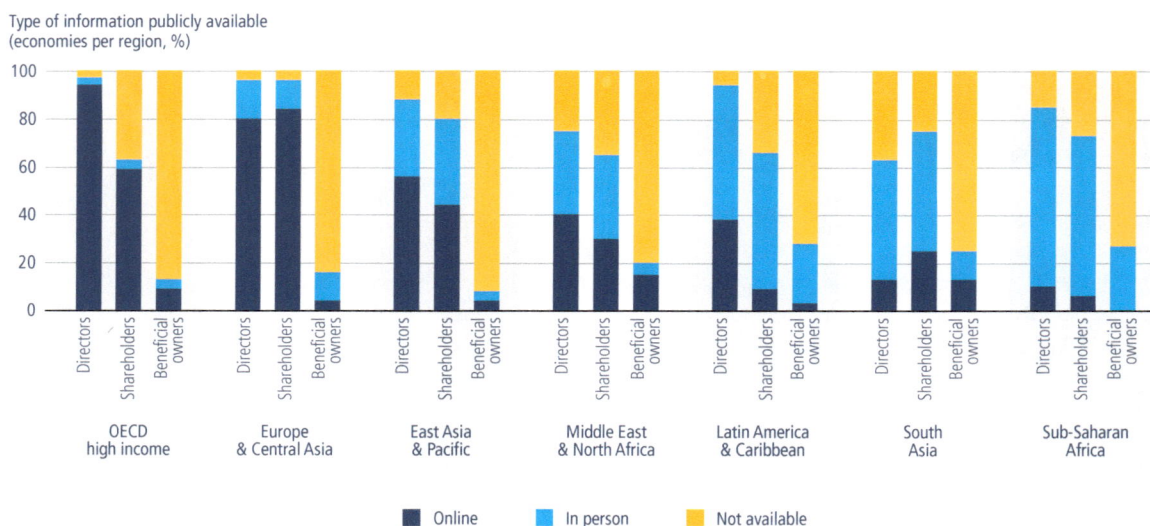

Source: Doing Business database.

Data on a firm's corporate structure, for example, is readily available in less than one-third of economies worldwide. Furthermore, the identity of a company's beneficial owners is made public in fewer than one-quarter of economies globally; only 8% of economies in East Asia and the Pacific and 15% of OECD high-income economies collect data on beneficial ownership and make it publicly available.

In general, the types of business registry information made available to the public vary little across economies. The names of a company's directors, for example, are publicly available in 92% of high-income economies covered by *Doing Business*; this figure is only slightly lower in low-income economies (84%). For other categories of information, however, public access is not equally provided across economies. In 75% of high-income economies, for example, one can verify the number and type of company shares. This information can be publicly accessed at business registries in fewer than half of low-income economies. Similarly, while businesses' annual accounts are available for public consultation in most high-income economies, these are available in only 10% of low-income economies. Registries in many developing economies either do not require companies to file annual accounts with the business registry or provide limited access to businesses' annual accounts. As a result, the economy may be negatively impacted as poor quality corporate governance regimes can restrict access to information and reduce investment returns.[8]

Some kinds of business data are more accessible than others. In general, public access is greater when the information available is considered less sensitive. Basic data such as a company's type of activity or year of incorporation can be found easily in most economies, but for business reasons some companies

may prefer not to disclose their annual returns or annual accounts.

HOW IS INFORMATION MADE AVAILABLE TO THE PUBLIC?

During the past decade government agencies around the world have explored ways to increase business registry transparency. The need for access to corporate information in the name of greater transparency pushed many economies to digitize their business registries and publish data online. By allowing around-the-clock, online access to registry information, the need for personal visits has been reduced, significantly enhancing the utility of these registries.

Where company details can be searched remotely, information and transaction costs are reduced. Basic information underlying potential trade or business dealings—for example, whether an entity has the legal authority to commit to an export contract or whether a particular company is in good financial standing—can be obtained quickly. The majority of the business registries in the economies covered by *Doing Business* share some company information online. Business registries in OECD high-income

economies publish most of the information collected on their websites.

The business registry information most widely available online includes the name of the company, its identification number, its legal address and the year the company was incorporated. The most basic information—the company name—is the information most commonly made available online. The names of existing companies are available online in 62% of economies covered by *Doing Business*, primarily because a company name must be verified before it can be registered as a new business. The business registries in all OECD high-income economies offer online company name search. In contrast, business registries in fewer than 10 economies in Sub-Saharan Africa—including Nigeria and Rwanda—offer this service (figure 4.2). More detailed information—such as information on a firm's shareholders, directors or beneficial ownership—is less commonly made available online.

Information on a company's directors, shareholders and beneficial owners is particularly important because it allows both business representatives and private individuals to identify the ownership of companies with which they may choose to do business or invest. In some

FIGURE 4.2 Company name search is mostly done in person in Sub-Saharan Africa

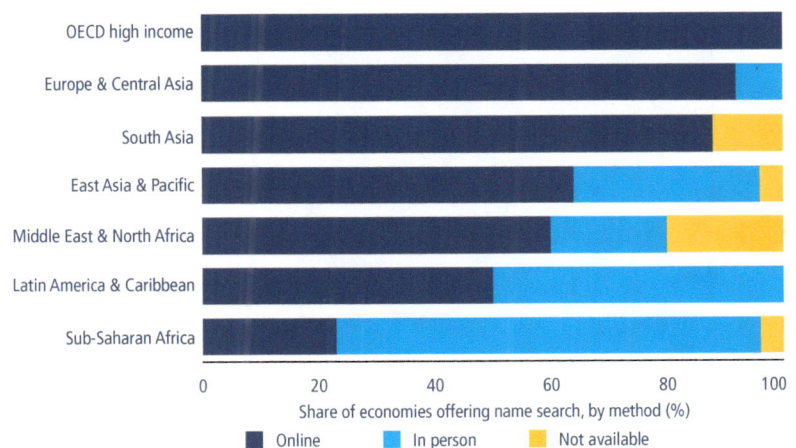

Source: *Doing Business* database.

regions, however, this information is either not available or can only be obtained in person. In South Asia, for example, business registries in 75% of economies only allow information about shareholders to be made available in person. In contrast, less than 20% of economies in Europe and Central Asia require that those seeking this information appear in person at the business registry; in the vast majority of economies in this region, shareholder information can be obtained online. In Sub-Saharan Africa, business registries in 77% of economies do not make the names of registered companies available online. In East Asia and the Pacific, one-third of economies do not publish the legal address or the names of company directors online. This type of information would allow a company, before doing business with an individual, to verify, for example, whether that person is a legitimate company representative.

Even when business registry information is published online, it is not always provided free of charge or made easily searchable. In many economies, online access to company information is only available after preregistration or the payment of a subscription fee, limiting the information to those people who can pay for it. In contrast, Denmark and the United Kingdom publish their entire business registry database free of charge.[9] The presentation of the information can also be a barrier. If data are available only through record-by-record searches, for example, a person must begin their search with the company name or identification number to access information about it.

FIGURE 4.3 Higher levels of transparency at the business registry are associated with higher overall levels of transparency in an economy

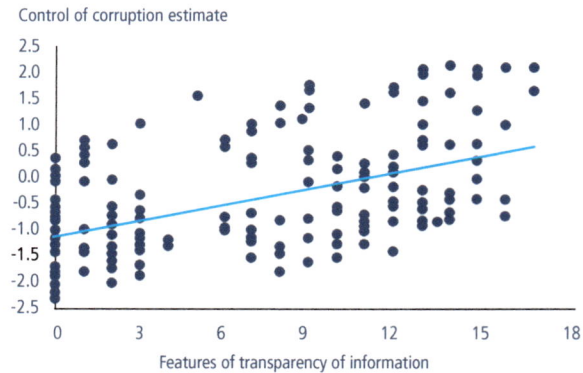

Sources: Doing Business database; Worldwide Governance Indicators (https://www.govindicators.org), World Bank.

Note: The Worldwide Governance Indicators control of corruption indicator captures perceptions of the extent to which public power is exercised for private gain, including both petty and grand forms of corruption, as well as "capture" of the state by elites and private interests. Estimate gives the economy's score on the aggregate indicator in units of a standard normal distribution, ranging from approximately -2.5 to 2.5, with higher values representing lower corruption perceptions. The features of transparency of information range from 0 (not transparent) to 18 (transparent). The sample includes 189 economies covered by both *Doing Business* and the control of corruption estimate (data on control of corruption estimate not available for San Marino). The relationship is significant at the 1% level after controlling for income per capita.

HOW IS TRANSPARENCY OF INFORMATION ASSOCIATED WITH EFFICIENCY AND CORRUPTION?

Business registries facilitate the operation of firms in the formal economy and they are often the first public institution

FIGURE 4.4 The time and cost to start a business tend to be lower in economies with higher transparency of information at the business registry

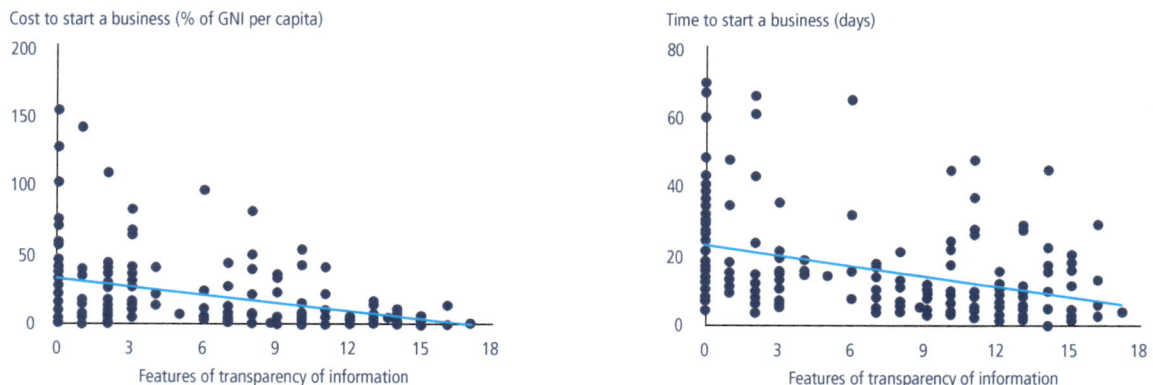

Source: Doing Business database.

Note: The cost of starting a business is recorded as percentage of GNI per capita. The time required to start a business is recorded in calendar days. The features of transparency of information range from 0 (not transparent) to 18 (transparent). Samples include 185 and 184 economies after the five highest cost estimates and the six highest time estimates are removed as outliers, respectively. The relationship between the cost of starting a business and the features of transparency of information is significant at the 1% level after controlling for income per capita. The same applies when the analysis is done using the time to start a business.

with which entrepreneurs interact. This first interaction can have a formative impact on the entrepreneur's perception of the efficacy of the public administration. Indeed, the level of transparency and trust in an economy has been shown to be highly correlated with the level of transparency of information at the business registry (figure 4.3). When business registry information is easily accessible and can be searched remotely, it can facilitate business transactions by removing unnecessary steps and reducing transactions costs.

The level of transparency of information at business registries is also associated with the time and cost to start a business. Data show that, on average, economies with greater transparency of information tend to have faster and less costly processes for starting a business (figure 4.4). In economies where official information on how to incorporate a business is not made readily available, entrepreneurs may have to seek legal advice from third parties or visit various government offices to find reliable information. In contrast, when the information is consolidated and easily obtained, entrepreneurs can spend less time and money finding it; they can dedicate more time to running their business.

Transparency can be approached from multiple aspects. Beyond providing readily available and reliable information about existing companies, it is important that entrepreneurs can openly access information about the requirements to establish a business (such as a list of required documents, fee schedules and services standards). When public access to information on company incorporation requirements is limited, it can represent a substantial obstacle to entrepreneurs who want to start a business. However, when transparency is a priority for business registries and all requirements are made public, more firms are able to enter the formal sector. If anyone can easily obtain transparent information before a business transaction, it can increase the ability of companies to conduct proper Know-Your-Client procedures, raising the level of trust in transactions and counterparts. Easy access to relevant information is also correlated with increased transparency of interactions with public officials. *Doing Business* data show that economies with transparent business registries tend to have lower incidences of bribery, both asked and given (figure 4.5). Transparent information provides citizens with the data they need to hold their counterparts accountable and improves trust in public agencies (including business

registries), particularly when transparency is conveyed on multiple levels (such as clearly stating business registration fees and the expected time to receive incorporation documents).

CONCLUSION

The transparency of the information provided by the business registry plays a vital role in an economy. Transparent business registries reduce information asymmetry among entrepreneurs and broaden the pool of potential investors by reducing the need for personal connections. Transparency can also raise the accountability of public officials and strengthen trust in public agencies. In the past decade, government agencies around the world have used technology to increase the transparency of public services. Technology can be utilized by governments to improve transparency of company ownership and the procedures to start a business. This case study has shown that the public availability of information on company ownership and starting a business is associated with an increase in an economy's overall level of transparency, an increase in the efficiency of business registration and a decrease in bribery.

FIGURE 4.5   Levels of bribery tend to be lower in economies with higher transparency of information at the business registry

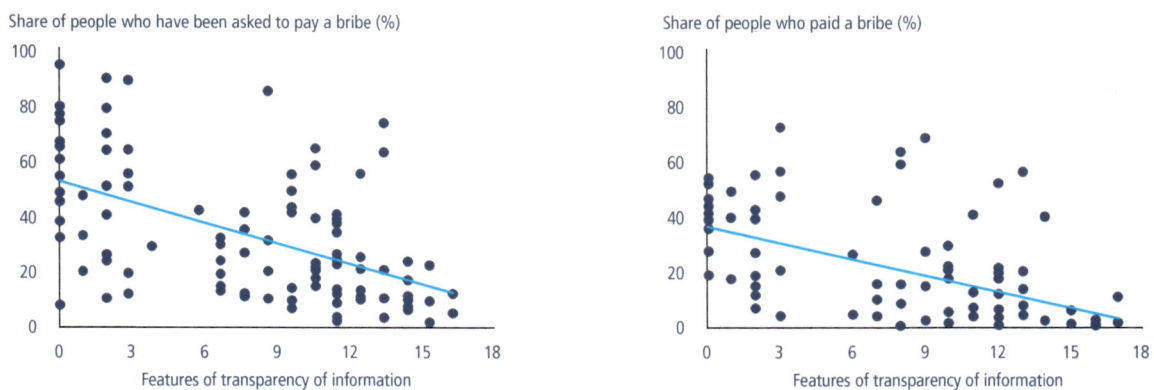

Sources: Doing Business database; Transparency International database (https://www.transparency.org).
Note: The features of the transparency of information range from 0 (not transparent) to 18 (transparent). The samples include 100 and 89 economies covered by both the *Doing Business* database and the Transparency International database. The relationships are significant at the 1% level after controlling for income per capita.

NOTES

This case study was written by Cyriane Coste, Frederic Meunier, Nadia Novik, Morgann Reeves and Erick Tjong.

1. ASORLAC, CRF, ECRF and IACA 2016.
2. De Simone and Fagan 2014.
3. Klapper, Laeven and Rajan 2006.
4. Malesky, McCulloch and Duc Nhat 2015.
5. Diamond and Verrecchia 1991.
6. Palstra 2014.
7. Accessibility to 14 types of business information is included in this case study. These are the following: name of company, name of directors, name of shareholders, name of beneficial owners, articles of association, year of incorporation, company identification number, legal address, physical address, type of activity, annual accounts, annual returns, capital structure and corporate structure. In addition, the documents to start a business, fees, service standards and statistics are also included.
8. Bradley 2003.
9. Quintanilla and Darbishire 2016.

Dealing
with Construction Permits

Private sector participation in construction regulation

The world has witnessed an unparalleled expansion of cities in recent decades. The urban population of developing economies is projected to double by 2030, while the area covered by cities could triple.[1] In tandem with this trend, the construction industry is forecast to grow by more than 70%,[2] reaching $15 trillion by 2025.[3] With the population of cities rising around the world, municipal authorities are struggling to keep up with increased demand for their services. In developing economies, in particular, building departments operating under tight budgets and resource constraints are finding it increasingly difficult to enforce building codes, ensure that quality standards are met and adhere to efficient service delivery processing times.

- Involving private sector engineers or firms in construction regulation is a trend that has been gaining traction in economies around the world.

- Some form of private sector participation in construction regulation is employed in 93 of the 190 economies covered by *Doing Business*.

- Private sector participation in building regulatory processes has shown positive results in achieving regulatory goals. However, the delegation of authority from the public to the private sector has generated significant challenges.

- Economies that employ some form of private sector involvement in construction regulation tend to have more efficient processes and better quality controls. Yet, they also exhibit higher costs and a propensity for conflicts of interest.

- The policy choice to integrate private sector entities in construction regulation should be accompanied by appropriate safeguards that favor the public interest over private profits.

In some economies, local municipalities have partnered with the private sector to supplement their strained capacity to oversee construction. However, faster and more efficient services provided by third-party inspectors inevitably cost more. *Doing Business* data show that the need to hire qualified third-party professionals on construction projects raises the cost of regulatory compliance by 1% on average in lower-middle-income economies and by 1.3% on average in upper-middle-income economies. The average cost of regulatory compliance in low-income economies without third-party involvement is 7.8% lower; the tradeoff is that it takes longer than in those with third-party involvement.

The use of independent, private-sector entities in construction regulation has provided a conduit for the increased participation of the private sector in the regulatory process and—when appropriate safeguards are in place—has offered an innovative way of addressing regulatory gaps. Low compensation for public sector regulators has resulted in a scarcity of qualified building professionals in

local governments. Hiring private sector experts has addressed this critical gap while improving the efficiency of the regulatory process. When it solicits the experts of private third-party engineering and architectural firms, the public sector taps into specialized skills that enable more robust compliance checks. These firms play a key role in monitoring the enforcement of building regulations and ensuring adherence to adequate standards of quality control at various stages of construction.

Initially pioneered in high-income economies—such as Australia, Japan and the United Kingdom—the trend toward involving private third-party engineers or specialized construction firms in public service delivery has been gradually gaining traction in lower-middle-income and upper-middle-income economies. Modern construction systems increasingly involve licensed or approved private engineers or firms, often enabled by the municipality and local enforcement agencies, to fulfill a building control function. Indeed, data show that 93 out of the 190 economies covered by *Doing Business* use some form of private third-party service in construction regulation. Of high-income and upper-middle-income economies, 66.1% and 56.9%, respectively, use third-party services in construction regulation, while 37.7% of lower-middle-income economies use third-party services. In contrast, only 25% of low-income economies make use of private third-party services in construction regulation (figure 5.1).

THE PRIVATE SECTOR'S ROLE IN CONSTRUCTION REGULATION

Over the past two decades, several models of private sector participation in building regulatory processes have emerged in economies around the world. Private participation in construction regimes can range from a very limited role for the private sector—such as in the Arab Republic of Egypt, where the Syndicate of Licensed Engineers merely certifies the qualifications of the supervising engineer—to a more comprehensive role where a private firm has complete authority over the entire process—such as in Australia, where private building surveyors directly oversee building design, control and inspection. In the United Kingdom, builders are given the option of either working with an approved private inspector or completing the required procedures with the public authorities. In other economies, such as France and the Republic of Congo, building controls are associated with an insurance-driven regulatory regime in which insurance and warranty firms engage private inspection firms in third-party reviews. While these two economies share the same insurance regime, there is a large disparity in terms of their performance on the quality control index, where France scores significantly higher than the Republic of Congo. At least two parties are held liable for any construction failure for a period of 10 years in 32% of high-income economies allowing third-party involvement, but this figure falls to just 9% for

FIGURE 5.1   Private third-party services are more commonly used in construction regulation in high-income and upper-middle-income economies

Share of economies using private third-party services in construction regulation (%)

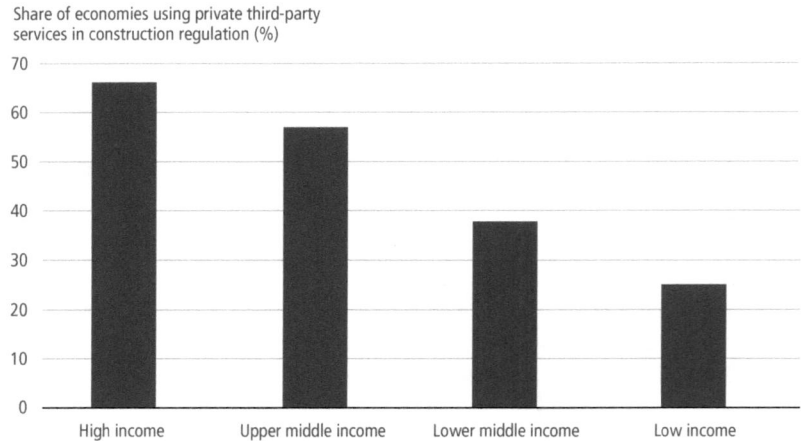

Source: *Doing Business* database.

low-income economies. Under this legal framework, only buildings deemed safe by independent third-party entities can be insured by an insurance company.

The degree to which the private sector is engaged in regulatory activities varies significantly across economies (figure 5.2). However, the primary function of private third-party entities involved in construction regulation tends to focus on

building inspections during project execution, as is the case in 92% of economies with private participation mechanisms. Of these economies, 61% engage private entities in reviewing building plans, 54% in conducting final inspections upon the completion of construction and 33% in conducting risk assessments of projects. Nonetheless, the issuance of building and occupancy permits remains largely under the purview of local authorities with only

FIGURE 5.2   Almost all economies employing private-sector regulatory support allow third-party inspections during construction

Share of economies allowing specified third-party service (%)

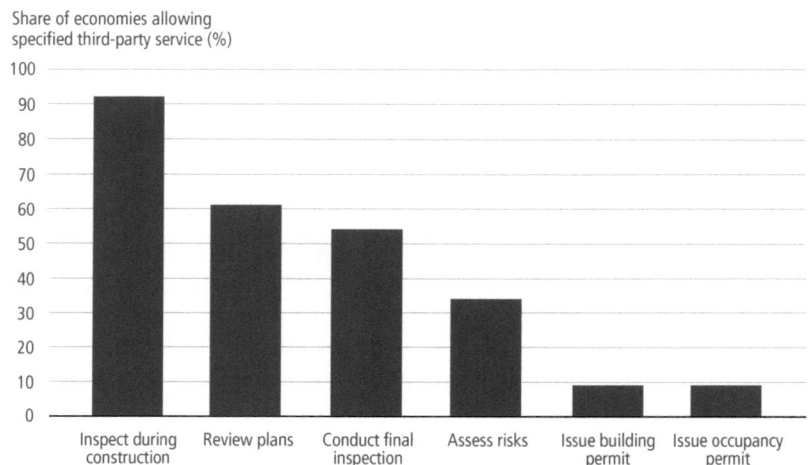

Source: *Doing Business* database.

9% of economies delegating these regulatory roles to the private sector.

BENEFITS OF THIRD-PARTY INVOLVEMENT IN CONSTRUCTION REGULATION

Economies can reap numerous benefits when private sector involvement is carefully implemented within a coherent regulatory framework. In most EU economies, there has been a complete shift from public to private governance mechanisms in building regulation, reflecting a desire to improve the quality of regulation, reduce the administrative burden for applicants and support a greater focus on risk mitigation.[4]

Public-private collaboration on construction regulation has shown positive results including improved compliance with building regulations, more rigorous quality control throughout the project lifecycle and better processing efficiency. *Doing Business* data show that private third-party involvement is associated with better building quality in construction as measured by the building quality control index.[5] Private sector involvement in construction regulation can support the enforcement of building codes and other applicable regulations. It effectively promotes compliance with the existing legal framework, particularly in economies where clear, transparent rules and specific technical instructions are prescribed.

Economies that integrated the private sector into regulatory functions decades ago have seen notable improvements in building quality control. Japan, for example, suffers from an extremely high exposure to natural hazards such as typhoons and earthquakes. The authorities reformed building regulations in 1998 by introducing private third-party services to significantly expand its capacity to carry out building inspections. By doing so, it managed to increase the rate of final inspections to more than 90% in 2016

compared with just 40% before June 2000. By establishing a successful regulatory system that relies on third-party checks, Japan increased its capacity to detect deficiencies in building design and construction, offering timely and appropriate remedies. Private third-party firms now play an instrumental and dominant role in inspection works (figure 5.3).

Similarly, to improve the energy efficiency of its large stock of new buildings, in 2005 the Chinese government introduced an innovative private third-party mechanism to carry out compliance checks of green building code provisions, effectively tapping a vast and readily-available pool of private sector expertise. Five years after the reform, compliance rates with regulatory requirements had effectively doubled.[6]

The former Yugoslav Republic of Macedonia initiated sweeping construction reforms in 2007/08 mandating the use of private engineers licensed by the Chamber of Engineers to undertake independent building plan reviews. Since then, FYR Macedonia has seen significant improvements in the efficiency of construction regulation as measured by *Doing Business*. The tradeoff has been an increase

in regulatory cost (figure 5.4). Even the Netherlands—one of the few EU economies that has maintained exclusive public enforcement of building regulation—is now preparing to shift toward a more hybrid system of enforcement involving private third-party mechanisms.

Introducing private third-party involvement in construction regimes can also expand regulatory capacity through efficiency gains. The use of private sector third-party services allows for the flexibility to hire specialized expertise that is usually scarce in local municipal governments, particularly in low- and middle-income economies. Local governments are often subject to hiring restrictions and operate with less competitive pay scales that limit their capacity to hire well-qualified staff or contain the high level of staff turnover. These limitations are usually compounded by a wide range of factors, including inadequate local tax bases to fund service delivery, limited transfers from national governments and institutional capacity constraints.

Doing Business data show that the process of dealing with construction permits tends to be faster in economies with private participation in construction

FIGURE 5.3 Private third-party inspection firms have become instrumental players in Japan

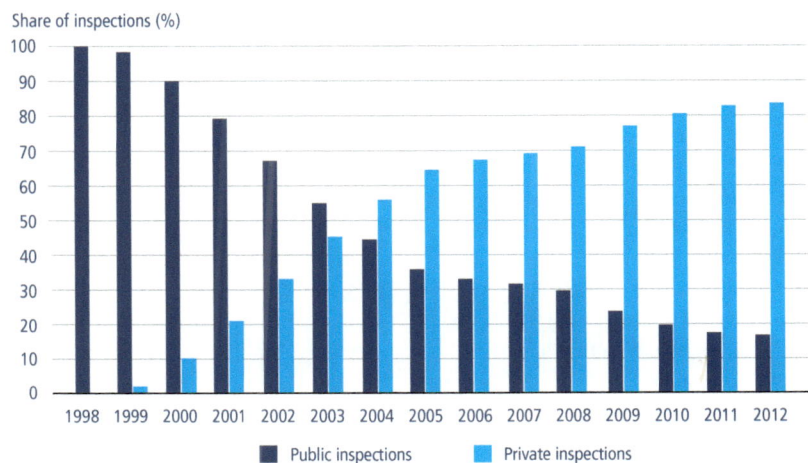

Source: Japan, Ministry of Land, Infrastructure, Transport and Tourism database (http://www.mlit.go.jp).

FIGURE 5.4   FYR Macedonia reduced the number of procedures and time it takes to build a warehouse following the introduction of private third-party building plan review

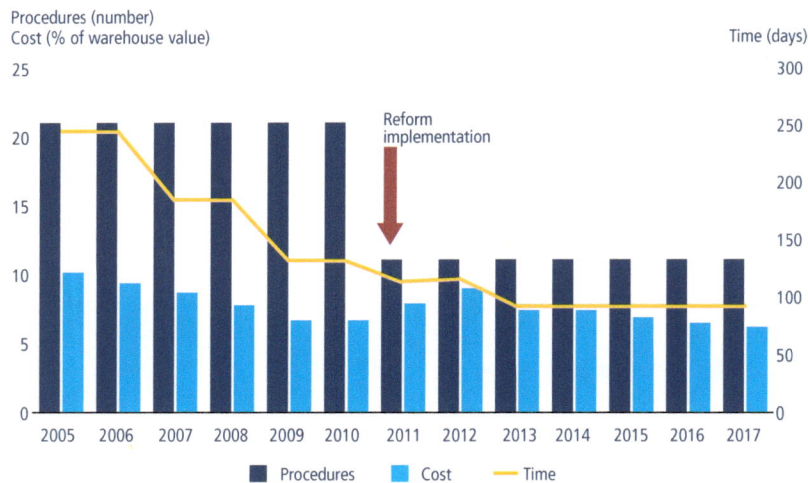

Source: *Doing Business* database.

regulation. High-income economies employing private sector regulatory support experience time savings of up to 60 days on average compared to economies that do not rely on third-party participation. Private sector involvement in building control activities has the potential to promote administrative efficiency, which in turn results in favorable economic outcomes. A study of the economic impact of expediting permit processing reveals that improving administrative efficiency results in a 16.5% increase in property tax collection, a 5.7% increase in construction spending and a 0.6% increase in the rate of financial return for the investor.[7] In contrast, regulatory delays could undermine the profitability of building projects,[8] adding a financial burden that amounts to 5% of total construction costs incurred by developers[9] and reducing the likelihood of further investment.

Economies with the least efficient construction permitting procedures have enforcement systems that rely exclusively on public authorities. Conversely, some economies that have transitioned from a public approach to a more open system involving partnerships with the private sector have experienced significant gains in efficiency. The planning office in Bogotá, Colombia, for example, reduced the average time needed to process a construction permit from three years in 1995 to 73 days in 2012 after it began using private professionals to carry out plan reviews and issue building permits. Given the successful integration of third-party professionals in building control activities, the authorities are now considering extending the use of specialized engineers to building inspections, which remain under the jurisdiction of local public officials.

CHALLENGES OF THIRD-PARTY INVOLVEMENT IN CONSTRUCTION REGULATION

Models of private sector participation in construction regimes vary. While third-party involvement in construction regulation can facilitate doing business in the construction industry by reducing the burden on local authorities, it comes with tradeoffs—including higher construction costs. Privatization of public services should be implemented carefully, with due regard to standards of transparency and accountability. The delegation of such a key regulatory mandate to the private sector should always be coupled with strict oversight safeguards designed to hold public interest above private profits.

For the private sector to successfully assume such an important regulatory role, a robust vetting system should be in place. Private third-party entities carrying out controls on construction are entrusted to promote compliance with building codes and regulations and enforce rigorous safeguards in favor of the public interest. For such an arrangement to work as intended, the public sector should regulate private third-party professionals and firms. Public sector agencies do so by enforcing professional certification criteria that render individuals and firms eligible to take on a regulatory mandate. Insufficient qualifications of private individuals or firms would undermine the objective of such a regulatory mechanism as the quality of service provided by these professionals would fail to meet the required standards of safety.

Economies with third-party involvement in regulatory functions often adopt specific standards of eligibility for private sector entities to be able to fulfill such a critical regulatory role. These standards typically include a minimum number of years of professional experience, certification by a recognized professional body and proof of performance on previous contracts. When private certification requirements were not properly implemented in New Zealand in the 1990s, the authorities quickly abandoned the shift to private sector building controls and reverted to the traditional public sector regulatory role. New Zealand's attempt to adopt third-party inspections failed due to the lack of strong regulatory safeguards. This resulted in the "leaky building syndrome." In 2008, the cost to repair 42,000 leaky buildings was estimated around 11.3 billion New Zealand dollars (approximately $8.3 billion).[10] Third-party involvement in construction regulation holds the promise of improving the regulatory framework, but it could also result in unintended adverse consequences if inadequately implemented. Although 22.2% of high-income economies with third-party involvement covered by *Doing Business* have standard eligibility requirements—including number of years of experience, a university degree and proof of performance on similar projects—only 3.3% of low-income economies require these standard qualifications.

Certifying agencies are mandated with monitoring the enforcement of professional standards. Government agencies represent the largest share of certifying bodies (68.5%) in those economies covered by *Doing Business*, followed by the national order of engineers (19.6%) and other independent bodies (13%) (table 5.1). In the United States, professional certification for third-party services is provided by the International Code Council (ICC), a non-governmental organization. Japan and China, by contrast, host this important function under central ministerial authorities.[11] The United Kingdom has mandated an independent organization—the Construction Industry Council—to administer the registration system for Approved Inspectors (AIs).

Having strict qualification standards in place is an essential and necessary element of a third-party regulatory regime, but this alone is insufficient to ensure that qualified professionals are delivering a satisfactory service. Special attention should be given to the effective enforcement of these professional certification

TABLE 5.1 Distribution of certifying bodies for third-party entities involved in construction regulation	
Certification agency for third-party entities in construction	Number of economies
Government	63
Order of architects or engineers	18
Other independent body	12

Source: Doing Business database.

requirements. This may entail the introduction of oversight mechanisms, a liability and insurance regime and a disciplinary framework that accompanies the transfer of regulatory authority from public officials to third-party entities as part of an essential quality assurance mechanism of third-party providers. China, for example, directed the Ministry of Housing and Urban-Rural Development to certify private third-party companies to carry out compliance checks of green building code provisions. The ministry maintains a comprehensive online public database that contains information on certified third-party firms. It requires the management of construction inspection companies to maintain accountability and quality of service, enforcing penalties when violations are discovered by regular inspections of third-party firms.

When the regulatory framework clearly defines the roles and responsibilities of private service providers, third-party entities are aware of their rights and obligations under the law and can exercise their authority within a legally transparent environment. Furthermore, accountability provisions governing conflicts of interest should be put in place to minimize their incidence and promote unbiased and independent regulatory control. Regulations in 76% of economies that make use of third-party inspectors explicitly require the independence of third-party inspectors; they should have no financial interests in the project and should not be related to the investor or builder.

Without strong liability and insurance regimes and rigorous professional certification mechanisms, third-party involvement in construction regulation can become inefficient or fail to ensure high quality building standards. Moreover, builders could incur the high costs that often accompany private-sector regulatory control without fully benefiting from the advantages that this control is intended to offer. Some economies regulate the cost of such services to

acceptable levels by enforcing fee schedules (within suggested industry guidelines) or by requiring fewer external professionals to be engaged by investors or local construction companies. In the Republic of Korea, for example, an independent third-party may not charge more than 1.29% of the estimated construction cost, in accordance with the Regulation for Scope of Architect Services and Fee Standard. In other economies, the local building authority either conducts all construction oversight or absorbs the cost of engaging external third-party professionals in the process through outsourcing. In South Africa, local authorities can temporarily appoint external building inspectors to conduct inspections on behalf of the local authority.

CONCLUSION

Sound construction regulation can save human lives, improve health and safety and support a prosperous and sustainable building sector and economy.[12] It can help facilitate doing business by safeguarding lucrative investments, strengthening property rights and protecting the public from faulty building practices. Private sector involvement in the enforcement of building regulations has shown positive results in achieving regulatory goals.[13] However, several challenges should be addressed before a policy of private sector involvement in construction regulation is pursued. The transfer of authority from the public to the private sphere could undermine the public interest. Public-private collaboration in building regulation has delivered successful results when authorities have enforced strict qualification requirements, effective oversight mechanisms and provisions on conflicts of interest, among other fundamental safeguards. A wealth of peer experience accumulated over the past 20 years is now available to economies considering integrating third-party entities in construction regulation.

NOTES

This case study was written by Baria Nabil Daye, Marie Lily Delion, Imane Fahli, Thomas Moullier, Keiko Sakoda, Jayashree Srinivasan and Yelizaveta Yanovich.

1.   UN-Habitat 2016.
2.   Moullier 2013.
3.   Global Construction Perspectives and Oxford Economics 2013.
4.   Meijer and Visscher 2005.
5.   For more on the building quality control index, see the data notes.
6.   As reported by the American Council for an Energy-Efficient Economy. http://aceee.org /research-report/i121.
7.   PricewaterhouseCoopers 2005.
8.   Wrenn and Irwin 2015.
9.   Hsueh 2010.
10. Lovegrove 2016.
11. The Ministry of Land, Infrastructure, Transport and Tourism (MLIT) in Japan and the Ministry of Housing and Urban-Rural Development (MoHURD) in China.
12. Van der Heijden 2009.
13. Moullier 2017.

Registering
Property

Using information to curb corruption

Transparency is a key element of the quality of land administration systems. Transparency eliminates asymmetrical information between users and officials with respect to services provided by the land administration, thereby increasing the efficiency of the real estate market. Transparent systems also strengthen public confidence in governments and facilitate substantial reductions in the cost of doing business.

In 2013 Transparency International reported that one in five users of land services globally claimed to have paid a bribe for services such as registering a land title or obtaining updated property ownership information. The prevalence of bribery in the land sector creates a substantial informal cost for those trying to register or transfer land. For those unable to afford illegal payments, it can also reduce access to land administration services, hindering property registration and increasing land tenure informality. In addition to bribes, corruption can take the form of land record fraud or alteration, land document forgery and multiple allocations of the same plot of land. Officials may also leverage their position to benefit from parties with an interest in acquiring, disposing of and developing land.[1]

Integral components of a transparent and efficient land administration system include easy access to clear and credible information on property ownership, open public access to information on procedures and fees for public services as well as active public dissemination of regulations affecting land rights. These measures can reduce corruption and increase accountability of land administration authorities.[2]

As a component of its registering property indicator set, *Doing Business* has measured the transparency of land administration systems for the past four years.[3] This research has focused on whether information concerning the ownership and physical location of a property is public, whether essential information on the property transfer process is made accessible, if there is an independent and specific complaint mechanism to respond to issues raised by land registry users and whether statistics on property transfers in the largest business city of an economy are published.[4]

Since 2013, 25 economies have improved transparency by launching websites, publishing fee schedules, setting time limits and implementing specific complaint mechanisms. Senegal introduced a comprehensive website for its land administration system, which includes a list of procedures, required documents, service standards and official fees to complete any property transaction.[5] Similarly, Qatar and Guyana have increased transparency in their land administration systems by expanding web-based land administration portals to include dedicated and comprehensive sections on the services provided.[6, 7]

- Transparency of information provided by land administration systems can reduce transaction costs and facilitate investment in immovable property.

- In economies where information on fee schedules and documentary requirements is easily available, the process of completing property transfers tends to be more efficient.

- Since 2013, 25 economies have become more transparent by launching websites, publishing fee schedules, setting time limits and implementing specific complaint mechanisms.

- In 51 economies, the only way to obtain information about documentary requirements for property registration is by having an in-person interaction with a public official.

- Property-specific and independent complaint mechanisms are not common around the globe, indicating an area for improvement to increase transparency.

- A transparent land administration system reduces opportunities for corruption.

ACCESS TO INFORMATION DURING DUE DILIGENCE

Information on the property, the parties and the transfer process is fundamental for a property transaction to occur. Buyers and sellers will only be able to make informed decisions when this information is widely available, either at a low cost or free of charge. The parties should know the costs, required documents and the expected duration of the transfer process before the transaction takes place. Although these conditions are necessary for a sound land administration, whether an agency can deliver its services with efficiency and accountability depends on other variables such as the capacity and reliability of its infrastructure.

Around the world, 158 economies publish fee schedules for services offered at the land registry. If a fee schedule is public, it is also likely to be available online. In 131 economies, this information can be accessed through a dedicated website. Although the use of online platforms is common in high-income economies—where 80% publish fees on websites—only a third of low-income economies have such portals. One example is Zimbabwe. In 2016, the economy launched an official website that includes a list of documents and fees required to complete a land transaction, as well as a specific time frame for delivering legally-binding documents proving property ownership.

The documentary requirements for land registration should also be made available to the public. Parties involved in a property transaction can streamline their interactions with the agency in charge of property registration if they know beforehand what documents they will be required to submit. This greatly reduces the risk of unforeseen delays or obstacles to submitting a property transfer—including the incidence of informal payments. When the list of required documents is public and complete, for example, the likelihood that the parties would be requested to come back with additional documents is reduced, expediting the registration process.

Transparency of documentary requirements may also simplify a transaction by potentially reducing the need to resort to third-party professionals to prepare a property transfer application (figure 6.1). In 51 economies, the only way to obtain information about documentary requirements for property registration is by having an in-person interaction with a public official. In Zambia, for example, where the list of required documents is not publicly available, a lawyer is hired to complete most of the property transfer steps for a commercial warehouse, costing an entrepreneur an additional 2.5% of the property value.

To promote full transparency, in addition to document and fee schedules, all services provided by land registries—such as title search, ownership certificate or

transfer of ownership—should be clearly specified, including the timeframes for their completion. This allows the public to know beforehand what level of service they can expect to receive, how much it will cost and how long it will take. Moreover, by providing clear public guidelines, governments set the standard for accountability of services offered by their land administration systems. Land registry services that lack established timeframes for completion can foster corruption in the form of bribes. An official might purposely delay registration, for example, to encourage clients to make facilitation payments to accelerate the process. Furthermore, in the absence of enforced time limits, land registry users are unable to monitor the status of their transactions.

Service standards at land registries are rare. Land registry users are not aware of any specific time limits promulgated by law in 122 economies covered by *Doing Business*. In addition, economies that do not establish service standards, such as specific time limits, tend to complete property transfers less efficiently (figure 6.2).

The Land Revenues Office charter, published in June 2013 by Nepal's Department of Land Reform and Management, provides a good example of how to set effective time limits. The charter contains a comprehensive list of services provided by the Land Revenue Office, the list of documents needed to

FIGURE 6.1   Transparency in land systems can bring efficiency gains

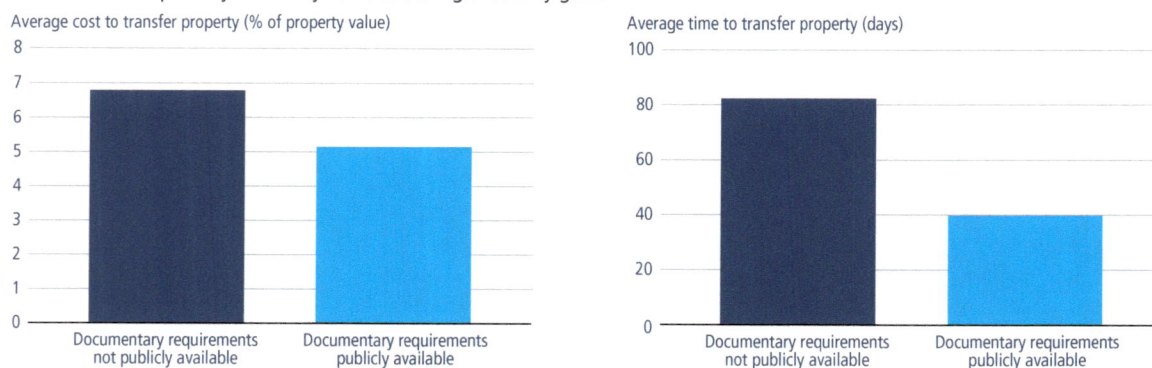

FIGURE 6.2 Economies that publish effective time limits tend to be more efficient in completing property transfers

Average time to complete property transfer (days)

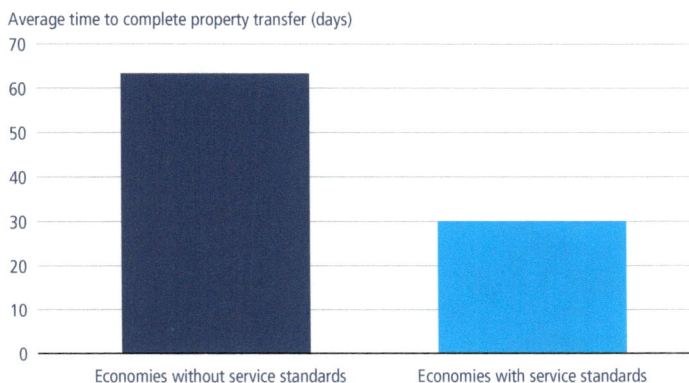

Source: Doing Business database.

complete each service, the applicable fees and the effective deadline within which the agency commits to deliver specific services. Similarly, the government of Thailand established a one-day service standard to register property transactions. To comply with this commitment, the number of staff is determined based on the average number of transactions, preventing delays.[8]

ACCESS TO INFORMATION DURING A PROPERTY TRANSACTION

Land administration is defined by the United Nations Economic Commission for Europe (UNECE) as "the processes of determining, recording and disseminating information about the ownership, value and use of land when implementing land management policies."[9] One of the major roles of a land registry is to make land transactions public. By doing so, it safeguards the interests of all parties involved in sales or leases.

When parties engage in a property transaction, it is essential that they obtain legally reliable information regarding the actual property involved in the transaction. The availability of information on the property—as well as

its owners or creditors—helps to eliminate uncertainty over property rights or obligations that may encumber the property. In the absence of any public records or any related rights to a property, the transaction costs can become overwhelming, risking that ownership becomes untraceable.

In 127 of the 190 economies covered by *Doing Business*, the information recorded by the land registry is openly available to the public. In the remaining economies, mainly because of privacy concerns, only owners or third parties who prove legitimate interest can access the information

kept in the land registry. In those economies, parties must hire an authorized professional to obtain ownership information, making the process more burdensome. In both cases, the agency in charge of registering immovable property can reject applications to access and retrieve ownership information on a discretionary basis. Public access should be embedded in land administration systems.

Among the economies covered by *Doing Business*, more than 70% of upper-middle-income and high-income economies make information on property ownership available to the public, whether for a nominal fee or free of charge. By contrast, only 50% of low-income economies open their records on land ownership to the public. Globally, information about land ownership is restricted to intermediaries and interested parties in 31% of economies. In 27 out of 190 economies—including Chile, Poland and the United States—this information is freely available (figure 6.3).

Because cadastral maps do not usually contain any personal information about the property owner, privacy concerns do not typically impact mapping agencies. However, the number of economies offering open access to maps is similar to the ones with open ownership information.[10] Overall, among the economies covered by *Doing Business*, 33% do not

FIGURE 6.3 Citizens in low-income economies have limited access to land ownership information

Share of economies by type of access to land records (%)

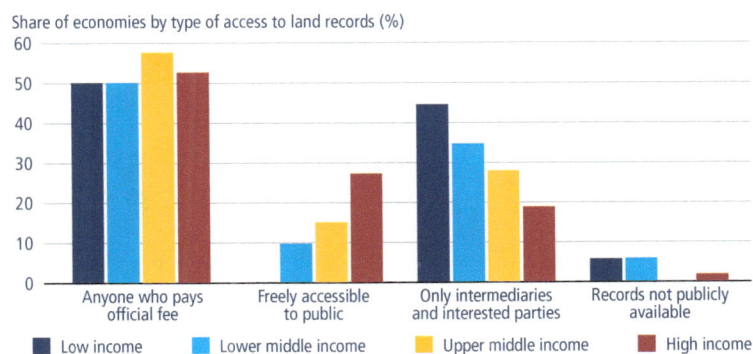

Source: Doing Business database.

make information on land boundaries publicly available. Sweden, on the other hand, has an online system allowing anyone to freely access property ownership information and maps dating back 400 years.[11]

ACCESS TO INFORMATION AFTER COMPLETION OF A PROPERTY TRANSACTION

After property transactions are completed, it is important to provide citizens with a safe environment where they can register complaints. Unlike courts, an informal structure allows users to be more forthcoming about possible abuses, relieving the courts of additional cases. In addition to allowing citizens to contribute to a better business environment, an independent and specific mechanism for filing complaints would also help governments to track issues and respond accordingly.[12]

Such complaint mechanisms promote three desired outcomes. First, the rights of citizens are safeguarded against any sub-standard service—whether by mistake or fault—provided by the land registry. Consequently, citizens can expect the land registry to provide services in accordance with the applicable rules and service guidelines. Second, citizens can have more confidence in a land tenure governance system where information is transparent and the officials providing land transfer services are held accountable for their actions. Third, candid feedback can help improve the administrative tasks performed by the land registry, resulting in a higher quality of service.

Only 24 economies measured by *Doing Business* have established complaint mechanisms that improve the overall quality of land registries; half of these (12) are OECD high-income economies or East Asia and the Pacific economies. Such complaint mechanisms are not in place in any of the economies of South Asia or the Middle East and North Africa

(figure 6.4). Globally, 22 economies offer complaint mechanisms in their cadastre or mapping agency. *Doing Business* data suggest that this is one of the areas with the most room for improvement worldwide.

An independent and specific complaint mechanism is important in the fight against corruption. A study by Transparency International conducted in Burundi, Kenya, Rwanda, Tanzania and Uganda found that about 90% of respondents that encountered a bribery incident did not report it or make a complaint to any authority or official; the reasons differed from economy to economy. In Kenya, most of the respondents indicated that they did not know where to report the incident, while in Tanzania most felt that no action would be taken to resolve their complaint.[13] As of June 2017 it was possible to file a complaint online in only 19 economies covered by *Doing Business*. The Singapore Land Authority recently introduced a web portal to file complaints about any issues related to their services. The Swedish Land and Cadastral Authority introduced a new mechanism for filing complaints regarding errors identified on maps of land plots.[14] Similarly, Guatemala and Vanuatu have successfully implemented alternative offline solutions. In Guatemala, an agency within the public ministry investigates claims related to the land registry. In 2014 Vanuatu appointed the first Land's

Ombudsman, an official responsible for following up on all complaints, whose duty is to report to the lands ministry as well as the client within 30 days.

Governments can keep their stakeholders engaged by collecting and publishing statistics on land transactions. Transaction statistics benefit regulators as well as the real estate sector, serving as a data analysis tool for policy makers to monitor the real estate market. Currently, 122 economies covered by *Doing Business* publish statistics on land transactions. In Japan, for example, data on land transactions are published monthly at the municipal level. In the United Arab Emirates, numbers on land transactions in Dubai are compiled daily and published on the land registry's web portal.

REDUCING OPPORTUNITIES FOR CORRUPTION THROUGH TRANSPARENCY

Transparency in a land administration system provides a defense against bribes intended to expedite the process of registering property, changing a title, acquiring information on land or processing cadastral surveys. Corruption in land administration can result in fraudulent land transfers, undermine public confidence in existing land rights while reducing investment and formal land

FIGURE 6.4 Most economies do not provide an independent and specific complaint mechanism for land registry issues

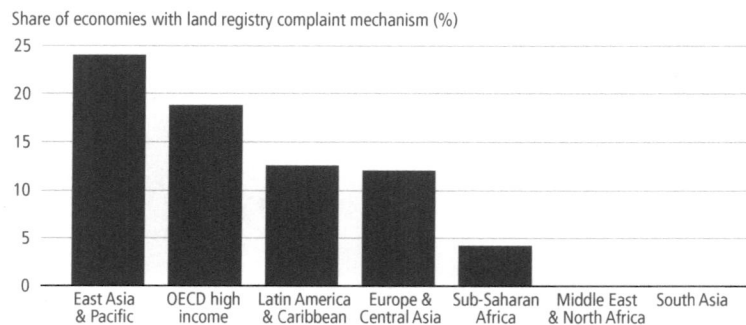

Source: Doing Business database.

registration.[15] Such corrupt behaviors spur inefficient land ownership, with land being owned by those most able to participate in corrupt activities.[16]

Furthermore, corruption and abuse of power can hinder the development of the real estate market. It can have adverse consequences on the business climate and economic activities by increasing the costs of doing business, thus undermining private sector confidence. High costs, together with inefficient procedures discourage people from registering land transactions, steering them instead into the informal land market. Corruption in land management can have a direct negative impact on business operations.

To be successfully deployed, full-fledged land reforms are time-consuming, costly, demanding an immense effort from governments and stakeholders. But a transparent land administration system—one in which all land-related information is publicly available, all procedures regarding property transactions are clearly documented and information on fees for public services is easy to access—minimizes the opportunities for informal payments and abuses of the system. Indeed, cross-country data show that the greater the quality and transparency of a land administration system, the lower the incidence of bribery at the land registry (figure 6.5).

CONCLUSION

Transparency is one of the most important tools for combating corruption—it is the basic pillar of enhancing the quality of land administration.[17] Moreover, rather than serving as a complementary tool, transparency should be considered as a key component when designing land policies. It is crucial that citizens have complete access to official land information, regulations and applicable fees. By establishing mechanisms that shield citizens from informal payments or other abuses, governments not only strengthen institutions but also increase the public's

FIGURE 6.5   A more transparent land administration system is associated with a lower incidence of bribery at the land registry

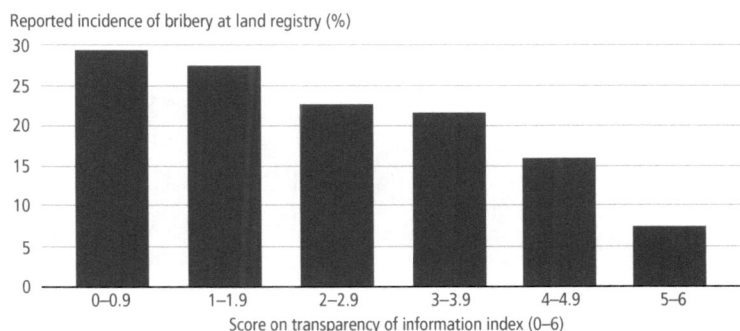

Sources: Doing Business database; Transparency International data (https://www.transparency.org/gcb2013).
Note: The analysis is based on data collected for the 95 economies covered in 2013/14 by both *Doing Business* and Transparency International's Global Corruption Barometer 2013. The relationship is significant at the 1% level after controlling for income per capita.

confidence in them. Having well-defined rules and standards—in addition to a safe environment to censure wrongdoing—is essential to ensure quality and efficiency in the administration of land tenure rights.

NOTES

This case study was written by Yuriy Valentinovich Avramov, Albert Nogués i Comas, Laura Diniz, Brendan Meighan, Esperanza Pastor Nunes and Geyi Zheng.

1. Kakai 2012; Obala and Mattingly 2014.
2. Zakout, Wehrmann and Törhönen 2006.
3. For more information on the transparency of information index, see the data notes.
4. In 11 economies with a population of more than 100 million as of 2013, *Doing Business* also collects data for the second largest business city.
5. For more on Senegal's land administration system, see http://www.impotsetdomaines.gouv.sn/fr/demarches-affaires-domaniales-cadastres.
6. For more on Qatar's web portal, see https://sak.gov.qa/.
7. For more on Guyana's efforts to increase transparency in land administration, see http://minbusiness.gov.gy/doing-business/3-how-to-get-property/.
8. Zakout, Wehrmann and Törhönen 2006.
9. UNECE 1996.
10. According to *Doing Business* data, 129 economies provide for open access to maps recorded at the agency in charge of surveying privately held land plots, while 127 economies provide for open access to ownership information recorded at the land registry.
11. For more information on Sweden's mapping, cadastral and land registration authority, see http://www.lantmateriet.se.
12. The registering property indicator set only considers dispute resolution mechanisms that (i) have been designed specifically to cover the services provided by the agency in charge of land registration and (ii) are managed by a body that is independent from the agency in charge. These requirements are essential in constituting an efficient, fair and legitimate governance system over land tenure rights.
13. Transparency International 2014.
14. For more on Sweden's mechanism for filing complaints regarding errors identified on maps of land plots, see http://www.sla.gov.sg/.
15. Transparency International 2013.
16. Søreide and Williams 2014.
17. Peisakhin 2012; Rose-Ackerman 2004.

Resolving
Insolvency

The challenges of successfully implementing insolvency reforms

- Since 2013/14, 19 economies have introduced reorganization procedures and another nine economies have improved their existing procedures. However, making them workable in practice can be challenging.

- France introduced a restructuring procedure—the *procédure de sauvegarde* (safeguard procedure)— in 2005 to enable debtors to prevent economic and financial difficulties. Today, the procedure facilitates business survival in three out of four initiated cases.

- Slovenia brought its legal framework closer to international good practices in 2013. Greater access to the reorganization procedures for creditors has been accompanied by an impressive survival rate of viable companies.

- Although it took some time for stakeholders in Thailand to get accustomed to reorganization procedures, filings at the Central Bankruptcy Court increased steadily from 1% of total insolvency cases in 2011 to almost 9% in 2016.

Access to finance is key to the development of the private sector. Lenders need tools to assess not only the risk of non-repayment but also what happens if a debtor cannot repay debts as they mature. A good insolvency framework—one with clear rules, that efficiently rehabilitates viable companies and liquidates non-viable ones—provides entrepreneurs and lenders with tools to evaluate the consequences of a worst-case scenario.

Existing literature shows that legal protection of creditors and efficient enforcement are conducive to larger and more developed capital markets and that there is a link between insolvency reforms and access to credit.[1] The specific features of an economy's insolvency regime and its enforcement are important aspects for the legal protection of creditors. Several studies show that reforms strengthening the insolvency framework may reduce the cost of credit, increase the level of credit and lower interest rates on large loans.[2] A study on the 2005 Brazilian bankruptcy reform found a reduction in the cost of debt together with a significant increase in the amount of total and long-term debt.[3] A more recent study found that the same reform led to an increase in secured loans, as well as an increase in investment and value of output in the years after the reform in Brazilian municipalities with less-congested courts.[4] Another study shows that, across a sample of Organisation for Economic Co-operation and Development (OECD) countries, efficient bankruptcy procedures are associated with a higher proportion of new bank loans to large firms.[5]

Other studies show that insolvency reforms that introduce or promote reorganization procedures through the adoption of several international good practices

may decrease the failure rate of insolvent firms. Research on the 1999 Colombian bankruptcy reform shows that by reducing reorganization costs through, for example, streamlining the reorganization process and establishing mandatory deadlines on the length of proceedings, the new law enabled viable companies to reorganize and inefficient ones to liquidate (this was not possible before the reform).[6]

Doing Business tracks insolvency reforms across 190 economies. Since *Doing Business 2005*, 110 economies have introduced 205 changes aimed at facilitating the efficient resolution of corporate insolvency. This case study uses the specific examples of France, Slovenia and Thailand to illustrate successful insolvency reforms that can inspire similar efforts elsewhere.

HOW HAVE ECONOMIES REFORMED THEIR INSOLVENCY SYSTEMS?

Insolvency laws have traditionally focused on enabling the swift liquidation of insolvent companies while organizing the repayment of creditors. The focus of modern insolvency regimes has been to offer restructuring tools to companies that are economically viable but face temporary financial distress in order to maintain the business activity. Recent reform efforts around the world have introduced this modern feature to insolvency frameworks while also allowing the speedy liquidation of nonviable businesses.

In 2013/14, the resolving insolvency indicators started measuring whether insolvency laws complied with certain international standards, including access to reorganization proceedings for debtors and creditors. Since then, the most common type of reform recorded by the indicators has been the introduction of or improvements to reorganization procedures. During this period, 19 economies introduced reorganization procedures and another nine economies improved their existing procedures.[7]

Providing creditors with greater access to and participation in insolvency proceedings has been another common area of reform. Economies including Cyprus, Jamaica, Kazakhstan, Mexico, Mozambique, St. Vincent and the Grenadines, Switzerland and Uganda have implemented reforms in this direction. Enabling creditors' meaningful participation in the process can make them more cooperative and less litigious, and it can result in shorter proceedings.

Many factors, however, can make it challenging to implement insolvency reforms. Doing so requires not only the adoption of an insolvency law or amendments to existing legislation but also changes to regulation to make the law workable in practice. An insolvency law often requires setting up new structures under the regulatory framework such as, for example, a professional body of insolvency administrators. Successful implementation also requires the buy-in and active participation of the judiciary.

WHAT DID SUCCESSFUL REFORMERS DO DIFFERENTLY?

Doing Business has recorded several notable insolvency reforms. However, France, Slovenia and Thailand were selected for this case study because they implemented insolvency reforms that brought them closer to internationally-recognized good practices—particularly through the introduction and improvement of restructuring procedures (table 7.1). There is also a significant amount of information available on the evolution of court procedures following these reforms. Business reorganization has become an increasingly utilized option for viable firms in financial distress in all three countries.

The case of France

Since the 1980s France has regularly assessed and updated its insolvency legal framework to encourage business rescue. In the mid-1980s—when the number of firms declaring bankruptcy doubled compared to the previous decade—liquidation was the only option available to companies in financial distress. The number of business liquidations rose from 11,000 in 1970 to 25,000 in 1984. Members of the legislature realized that some of these companies could have been saved had they been given the tools to restructure. The legislature subsequently adopted three laws in 1985 with the objective of saving viable businesses. A reorganization procedure, open to debtors in cessation of payments that had a prospect of survival, was introduced.

Many companies, however, still ended up stopping operations and being liquidated, mainly because they began the reorganization process when their financial situation was already severely compromised. In response, the government amended the insolvency law in 2005 to focus on preventing firms' economic and financial difficulties. A new restructuring tool—the *procédure de sauvegarde* (safeguard procedure)—was introduced. It allowed debtors that are facing difficulties (but which have not yet ceased payments) to apply for court protection while they negotiate a restructuring plan with creditors.

Contrary to initial expectations, the safeguard procedure was not widely used. When the procedure became available for the first time in 2006, only 509 safeguard applications were filed (compared to 16,046 judicial reorganizations and 31,045 judicial liquidations).[8] One reason was that the criteria required to initiate the safeguard procedure were too strict. Debtors had to demonstrate that they were facing difficulties that would result in insolvency, which was challenging. Another reason was that the law did not clearly stipulate which party—the company managers or the court-appointed administrator—was responsible for the preparation of the safeguard plan, an issue which could deter managers from starting the proceedings.

TABLE 7.1	France, Slovenia and Thailand successfully implemented insolvency reforms		
Country	**Motivation**	**Reform content**	**Outcome**
France	High number of bankruptcy cases; no possibility for companies to reorganize prior to the reform	Starting in 1985, introduced restructuring procedures with focus on preventing firms economic and financial difficulties	Increased number of initiated and successful reorganization cases
Slovenia	High number of insolvent companies as a result of the 2008 global financial crisis; features of restructuring procedures not suited; no preventive procedures available	Starting in 2008, introduced preventive restructuring procedure for medium and large-size companies and simplified reorganization procedure for micro and small-size companies; improved access to reorganization proceedings for creditors	Increased number of initiated and successful reorganization cases
Thailand	High number of non-performing loans in the context of the 1997 Asian financial crisis; no possibility for companies to reorganize prior to the reform	Starting in 1998, introduced reorganization procedure for corporate debtors; created specialized bankruptcy court	Increased number of initiated and successful reorganization cases

Source: Doing Business database.

The insolvency law was amended again in 2008 to make the safeguard procedure more accessible and attractive to debtors by simplifying the eligibility criteria. Debtors had only to demonstrate difficulties—economic, financial, or legal—that they could not overcome, without having to define or qualify the gravity or extent of those difficulties. The 2008 amendment also made the procedure more attractive by clarifying that the managers of the company were responsible for preparing the safeguard plan with the assistance of the court-appointed administrator. Furthermore, in 2011 France introduced a procedure—the *sauvegarde financière accélérée* (accelerated financial safeguard)—under which a debtor can reach an out-of-court arrangement with a majority of its financial creditors and then initiate summary court proceedings to validate the agreement without negatively impacting non-financial creditors.

These changes led to a significant increase in the number of new safeguard procedures filed, to 1,386 cases in 2009. Since then the number of filings has risen steadily, to 1,620 new cases in 2014. Not only did the use of safeguard procedures increase, but three out of four cases terminated with an agreement with creditors to enable the company to continue operating (figure 7.1). However, the increased use of the safeguard procedure was accompanied by a significant number of filings for liquidation, which in 2014 amounted to 69% of all insolvency cases filed.

By allowing viable companies to restructure and continue operating as going concerns, the amendments to the insolvency law aimed to support entrepreneurial risk-taking and encourage enterprise creation. Insolvency reforms may have contributed in part to the surge in new businesses in France—525,000 companies were created in 2015, twice as many as in 2000. This growth underscores the connection made in the literature between sound insolvency systems and the level of entrepreneurship development as

measured by the rate of new firm entry and entrepreneurship support.[9]

The case of Slovenia

The early 2000s were a period of significant reform in Slovenia as the country prepared to join the European Union in 2004. A new insolvency law was adopted in 2007, but it was insufficient to cope with the challenging economic and financial conditions brought on by the global financial crisis of 2008; many companies became insolvent. Firms suffered from over-indebtedness and had difficulties repaying their loans, leading to an increase in corporate non-performing loans to around 20% of total loans.[10] Firms in Slovenia needed effective corporate restructuring procedures to guide the restructuring of their debt.

To address these needs and to bring the legal framework closer to international good practices, the government modified the corporate restructuring framework in 2013. The changes included the creation of a new pre-insolvency restructuring procedure for distressed medium and large-size companies to restructure their

financial claims, as well as a new simplified compulsory settlement procedure to offer a reorganization option for micro and small companies. A change was also made to the existing compulsory settlement procedure to enable creditors to initiate the reorganization of companies for the first time.

The procedures quickly became a popular option for debtors and creditors. In the first two years following the reform, the proportion of companies using one of the three procedures more than doubled, rising from 6% of total insolvency proceedings in 2013 to 14% in 2015.[11] Microenterprises, however, underwent corporate liquidation proceedings in the vast majority of cases (96%) in 2016. Microenterprises have less capacity to face a reorganization and to secure resources to enable them to operate in a situation of financial distress. Despite these challenges, microenterprises have also benefited from the restructuring options. Indeed, the number of simplified compulsory settlement proceedings for the benefit of microenterprises increased from 59 cases in 2014 to 85 in 2016.

FIGURE 7.1 A significant number of companies undergoing restructuring proceedings in France continue operating at the end of proceedings

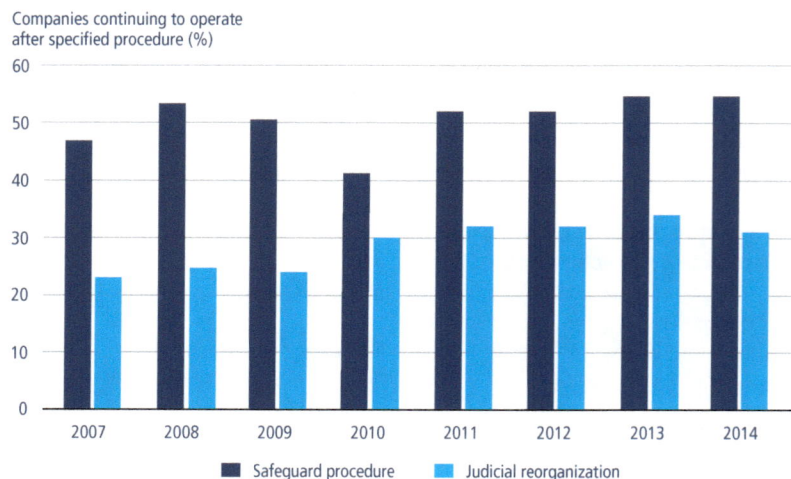

Source: Deloitte and Altares 2016.
Note: Companies that continue operating include companies that adopted a reorganization or safeguard plan, or that were sold as a whole.

Creditors have progressively taken advantage of the enabled access to compulsory settlement proceedings granted to them in 2013; by 2016 they initiated almost one-third of all cases. During the same period, the number of successfully terminated reorganization proceedings increased significantly. In 2016, most ended with an approved settlement (figure 7.2).

One of the companies that benefited from the restructuring procedures was Pivovarna Laško, Slovenia's largest brewer. By the end of 2014, the company's total financial liabilities stood at 226.8 million euros (about $268 million). It negotiated a restructuring plan with its creditors, which included a two-year debt rescheduling, the sale of shares in other companies and an intensive search for additional capital. Following the agreement, the company was bought by Heineken International BV, which committed to provide financial stability to the company. Following the sale of its assets in various corporations and entering into long-term loan agreements with Heineken, the company was able to repay its creditors in full in October 2015. Its value increased, the brewery was able to continue operating, saving hundreds of jobs.

Apart from increasing the likelihood of business survival—as shown by the rising number of successfully-terminated compulsory settlement and simplified settlement procedures—the insolvency reform may have contributed to broader positive economic effects. First, the level of entrepreneurship and company formation in Slovenia increased. One year after the reform was introduced, 6,243 new businesses were registered in Slovenia, the highest number in a decade (and similar to pre-crisis levels). Second, progress has been made in addressing Slovenia's high level of non-performing loans, which decreased from 15% of total loans in 2012 to 7.9% in 2016. While these results do not establish a causal relationship with the insolvency reform, they suggest that sound insolvency

FIGURE 7.2 Corporate reorganizations in Slovenia have become more successful over time

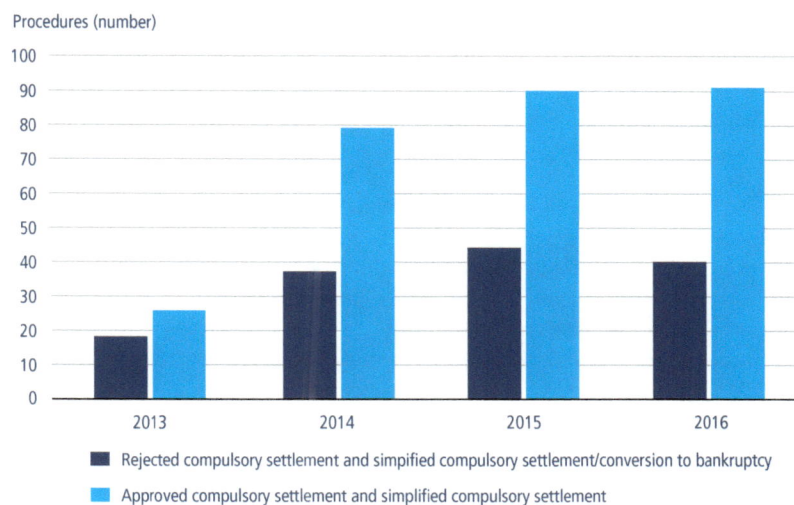

Source: Slovenia Ministry of Justice 2017.

regimes may encourage entrepreneurship and accelerate the speed of adjustment of non-performing loans.[12]

The case of Thailand

The 1997 Asian financial crisis prompted a major insolvency reform in Thailand. Non-performing loans had been increasing before the crisis, reaching a peak of 42.9% of total loans in 1998. Thailand's antiquated insolvency law needed to be revised and given the features necessary to perform. The 1940 Thai Bankruptcy Act established the procedure of judicial liquidation for debtors unable to meet their financial commitments. It relied on an agency within the Ministry of Justice— the Legal Execution Department—to direct the proceedings. The only aim of the law was to organize the repayment of creditors through liquidation procedures; it did not offer a channel for viable companies to survive.

Amendments brought by the Bankruptcy Act of 1998 built on the existing legal and institutional framework. They introduced a reorganization procedure for corporate entities, giving insolvent debtors the chance to negotiate a reorganization

plan with creditors. A specialized bankruptcy court was established in 1999 to adjudicate cases. Also, the Business Reorganization Office (within the Legal Execution Department) was set up to administer new reorganization cases.

Considerable time was needed in Thailand for stakeholders to become accustomed to reorganization procedures. Finding expertise within Thailand to prepare reorganization plans proved challenging; it required the capacity to negotiate a plan with multiple creditors in a short period of time to return the company to profitability. Managers of companies in financial difficulties found it challenging to formulate a reorganization plan effectively. Debtors turned to large companies with foreign human capital that had expertise in drafting such plans. However, this approach was expensive, making reorganization procedures accessible to only a small number of large debtors.

As a result, in the years following the reform, the number of annual applications for reorganization was modest, averaging 30 to 70 (compared to approximately 700 annual applications for liquidation).[13] Realizing that the benefits of the procedure had to be explained to stakeholders, the government undertook outreach efforts. As local firms gained the necessary expertise to advise debtors during the reorganization process, reorganization practices progressively became more widespread in Bangkok. Consequently, all parties were able to experience the advantages of the new mechanism, enabling them to make use of it to save viable businesses. Together with a greater understanding of the law, reorganization filings rose to 3.5% of total insolvency cases in 2014 (from 1.1% in 2011).[14] The share almost doubled in 2015 and continued to rise in 2016, when 8.5% of insolvency petitions received by the judiciary were reorganization cases (figure 7.3).

The rising use of reorganization proceedings in Thailand has driven an increase in the rate of successful reorganizations (that is, cases that end up with the approval of the reorganization plan, regardless of whether they continue operating in the longer term). The Central Bankruptcy Court's reorganization plan approval rate reached 25% in 2016, up from 20% in 2015.

The connection between the insolvency reform and the likelihood of business survival is reflected in *Doing Business* data. Resolving simple reorganization cases in Bangkok has become easier over time. Companies are now more likely to continue operating at the end of reorganization procedures. Also, today it takes 18 months on average, half the time it took in 2010, for a small company to go through reorganization, counted up to the moment the reorganization plan is approved by creditors.

Studies on the effect of insolvency reforms that accelerate the procedures find that they increase the aggregate level of credit. Other studies suggest that where insolvency regimes are most effective, creditors are more willing to lend because they are more likely to recoup a larger share of a troubled loan.[15] Following the reform in Thailand, domestic credit to the private sector rose from 93% of GDP in 2001 to 147% of GDP in 2016.[16] Banks are more willing to lend in Thailand than in other parts of East Asia and the Pacific. Data from the World Bank Enterprise Surveys show that only 2.4% of firms in Thailand identify access to finance as a major constraint to doing

business, compared to 12.2% of firms in the region and 26.5% in all economies. While no causal relationship can be established between these results and the bankruptcy reform in Thailand, they do show that access to credit improved in the years following the reform.

CONCLUSION

The successful implementation of insolvency reforms is not easy. Many factors must come into play for an insolvency reform to yield positive effects in both insolvency practice and the economy. Even in economies with strong legal frameworks and institutions, insolvency reforms take time. It is a complex area of law, which is why different agencies—including the judiciary as well as insolvency administrators—need to be trained and given the means to carry out the tasks envisioned in the law.

Lessons can be drawn from reforms implemented worldwide. The French and Slovenian examples show the importance of constantly assessing the insolvency system. Insolvency law is not a static field. Rather, it serves the economic system and needs to adapt as the structure of the economy evolves. Implementing and refining insolvency reform takes time; a quick fix will not bring positive long-term results. The example of Thailand illustrates the importance of utilizing the existing infrastructure to drive change—the focus should be on building on existing laws and institutions and creating new ones only when the existing system cannot be adapted. A new framework requires training along with patience. Amending the law should not be seen as a goal in itself, but rather as a first step to be followed by the thorough implementation of the amended law.

All in all, the three examples suggest that sound insolvency reforms can have a positive impact on an economy. Providing corporate debtors with the option to

FIGURE 7.3 Distressed businesses in Bangkok are more likely to pursue reorganization today than seven years ago

New reorganization cases as a share of total insolvency cases (%)

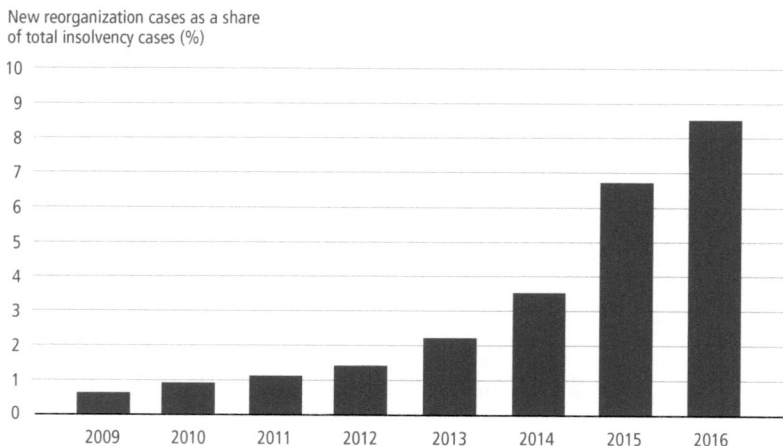

reorganize increases the chances of debt recovery by creditors, positively influencing their willingness to lend. The availability of reorganization procedures also increases the likelihood that viable firms will continue operating despite financial difficulties, thus decreasing the failure rate of firms, preserving jobs and encouraging entrepreneurship.

NOTES

This case study was written by Faiza El Fezzazi El Maziani, Raman Maroz and María A. Quesada.

1. La Porta and others 1997; La Porta and others 1998; Klapper 2011.
2. Visaria 2009; Funchal 2008; Rodano, Serrano-Velarde and Tarantino 2011.
3. Araujo, Ferreira and Funchal 2012.
4. Ponticelli and Alencar 2016.
5. Neira 2017.
6. Foley 1999; Dewaelheyns and Van Hulle 2006. For Colombia, Giné and Love 2008.
7. The 19 economies that have introduced reorganization procedures are Brunei Darussalam, Cabo Verde, Cyprus, the Dominican Republic, Grenada, India, Jamaica, Kenya, Kosovo, Liberia, Malawi, Mozambique, Panama, St. Kitts and Nevis, St. Vincent and the Grenadines, the Seychelles, Trinidad and Tobago, Uganda, and the United Arab Emirates. The nine economies that improved their existing reorganization procedures are Chile, Georgia, Kazakhstan, Kenya, Mexico, Romania, Slovenia, Thailand, and Switzerland.
8. Deloitte and Altares 2016.
9. Lee and others 2011; Peng, Yamakawa and Lee 2010.
10. IMF 2015.
11. Slovenia, Ministry of Justice 2017.
12. Carpus-Carcea and others 2015.
13. Wisitsora-at 2015.
14. Thailand, Office of the Judiciary 2016.
15. Visaria 2009; Funchal 2008.
16. These data are from the World Development Indicators database (http://data.worldbank.org/indicator), World Bank.

References

Agell, Jonas. 1999. "On the Benefits from Rigid Labour Markets: Norms, Market Failures, and Social Insurance." *The Economic Journal* 109 (453): 143–64.

Amin, Mohammad. 2007. "Are Labor Regulations Driving Computer Usage in India's Retail Stores?" Policy Research Working Paper 4274, World Bank, Washington, DC.

Amin, Mohammad, and Hulya Ulku. 2017. "Corruption, Regulatory Burden and Firm Productivity." World Bank, Washington, DC.

Amiti, Mary, and Amit K. Khandelwal. 2011. "Import Competition and Quality Upgrading." *Review of Statistics and Economics* 95 (2): 476–90.

Araujo, Aloisio P., Rafael V. X. Ferreira, and Bruno Funchal. 2012. "The Brazilian Bankruptcy Law Experience." *Journal of Corporate Finance* 18 (4): 994–1004.

Arlet, Jean. 2017. "Electricity Sector Constraints for Firms Across Economies: A Comparative Analysis." Doing Business Research Notes No.1, World Bank Group, Washington, DC.

Arvis, Jean-François, Daniel Saslavsky, Lauri Ojala, Ben Shepherd, Christina Busch, Anasuya Raj, and Tapio Naula. 2016. *Connecting to Compete 2016: Trade Logistics in the Global Economy— The Logistics Performance Index and Its Indicators*. World Bank, Washington, DC.

ASORLAC (Association of Registers of Latin America and the Caribbean), CRF (Corporate Registers Forum), ECRF (European Commerce Registers' Forum) and IACA (International Association of Commercial Administrators). 2016.
The International Business Registers Report. Available from http://www .corporateregistersforum.org/wp-content /uploads/IBRR_2016_webb.pdf.

Banerjee, Abhijit V., and Esther Duflo. 2011. *Poor Economics: A Radical Rethinking of the Way to Fight Global Poverty*. New York, NY: Public Affairs.

Beck, Thorsten, Chen Lin, and Yue Ma. 2014. "Why Do Firms Evade Taxes? The Role of Information Sharing and Financial Sector Outreach." *Journal of Finance* 69: 763–817.

Bradley, Nick. 2003. "Corporate Governance: A Risk Worth Measuring?" In *Selected Issues in Corporate Governance: Regional and Country Experiences*. New York and Geneva: UNCTAD (United Nations Conference on Trade and Development).

Branstetter, Lee G., Francisco Lima, Lowell J. Taylor, and Ana Venâncio. 2014. "Do Entry Regulations Deter Entrepreneurship and Job Creation? Evidence from Recent Reforms in Portugal." *Economic Journal* 124 (577): 805–32. doi:10.1111// ecoj.12044.

Bruhn, Miriam. 2011. "License to Sell: The Effect of Business Registration Reform on Entrepreneurial Activity in Mexico." *Review of Economics and Statistics* 93 (1): 382–86.

———. 2013. "A Tale of Two Species: Revisiting the Effect of Registration Reform on Informal Business Owners in Mexico." *Journal of Development Economics* 103: 275–83.

Burt, Alison, Barry Hughes, and Gary Milante. 2014. "Eradicating Poverty in Fragile States: Prospects of Reaching the 'High-Hanging' Fruit by 2030." Policy

Research Working Paper 7002, World Bank, Washington, DC.

Buvinic, M., and G. R. Gupta. 1997. "Female-Headed Households and Female-Maintained Families: Are They Worth Targeting to Reduce Poverty in Developing Countries?" *Economic Development and Cultural Change* 45 (2): 259–80.

Carpus-Carcea, Mihaela, Daria Ciriaci, Carlos Cuerpo, Dimitri Lorenzani, and Peter Pontuch. 2015. "The Economic Impact of Rescue and Recovery Frameworks in the EU." EU Discussion Paper 004, European Union, Luxembourg.

CEPEJ (European Commission for the Efficiency of Justice). 2016. *European Judicial Systems. Efficiency and Quality of Justice.* Strasbourg: European Commission for the Efficiency of Justice.

Chávez, Édgar. 2017. "Credit Information and Firms' Access to Finance: Evidence from an Alternative Measure of Credit Constraints." Doing Business Research Notes No. 2, World Bank Group, Washington, DC.

Cirera, Xavier, Roberto N. Fattal Jaef, and Hibret B. Maemir. 2017. "Taxing the Good? Distortions, Misallocation, and Productivity in Sub-Saharan Africa." Policy Research Working Paper 7949, World Bank, Washington, DC.

Cirmizi, Elena, Leora Klapper, and Mahesh Uttamchandani. 2010. "The Challenges of Bankruptcy Reform." Policy Research Working Paper 5448, World Bank, Washington, DC.

Claessens, Stijn, Kenichi Ueda, and Yishay Yafeh. 2014. "Institutions and Financial Frictions: Estimating with Structural Restrictions on Firm Value and Investment." *Journal of Development Economics* 110: 107-22.

Clark, Ximena, David Dollar, and Alejandro Micco. 2004. "Port Efficiency, Maritime Transport Costs and Bilateral Trade." *Journal of Development Economics* 75 (2): 417–50.

Collier, Paul, and Anke Hoeffler. 2004. "Greed and Grievance in Civil War." *Oxford Economic Papers* 56 (2004): 563–95.

Corcoran, Adrian, and Robert Gillanders. 2015. "Foreign Direct Investment and the Ease of Doing Business." *Review of World Economics* 151 (1): 103–26.

Dabla-Norris, Era, Mark Gradstein, and Gabriela Inchauste. 2008. "What Causes Firms to Hide Output? The Determinants of Informality." *Journal of Development Economics* 85 (1–2): 1–27.

Dabla-Norris, Era, Giang Ho, Kalpana Kochhar, Annette Kyobe, and Robert Tchaidze. 2013. "Anchoring Growth: The Importance of Productivity-Enhancing Reforms in Emerging Market and Developing Economies." IMF Staff Discussion Notes 13/08, International Monetary Fund, Washington, DC.

Deloitte and Altares. 2016. *L'entreprise en difficulté en France. Gagner plus de lisibilité pour aller de l'avant.* 11th edition, March.

De Simone, Matteo, and Craig Fagan. 2014. "Ending Secrecy to End Impunity: Tracing the Beneficial Owner." Transparency International Policy Brief 02/2014, Berlin: Transparency International.

De Soto, H. 1989. *The Other Path: The Invisible Revolution in the Third World.* New York: Harper and Row.

Dewaelheyns, Nico, and Cynthia Van Hulle. 2006. "Legal Reform and Aggregate Small and Micro Business Bankruptcy Rates: Evidence from the 1997 Belgian Bankruptcy Code." *Small Business Economics* 31 (4): 409–24.

Diamond, Douglas, and Robert E. Verrecchia. 1991. "Disclosure, Liquidity, and the Cost of Capital." *Journal of Finance* (46): 1325–59.

Djankov, Simeon. 2009. "Bankruptcy Regimes during Financial Distress." Working Paper 50332, World Bank, Washington, DC.

———. 2016. "The Doing Business Project: How It Started: Correspondence." *Journal of Economic Perspectives* 30 (1): 247–48.

Djankov, Simeon, Caroline Freund, and Cong S. Pham. 2010. "Trading on Time." *Review of Economics and Statistics* 92 (1): 166–73.

Djankov, Simeon, Dorina Georgieva, and Rita Ramalho. 2017a. "Determinants of Regulatory Reform." LSE Discussion Paper 765, Financial Management Group, London School of Economics, London. Available from http://www .lse.ac.uk/fmg/news/newsPDFs /DjankovDeterminantsOfRegulatoryReform .pdf.

———. 2017b. "Business Regulation and Poverty." LSE Discussion Paper 766, London School of Economics, London. Available from http://www.lse.ac.uk /fmg/dp/discussionPapers/fmgdps /DP766.pdf.

Djankov, Simeon, Oliver Hart, Caralee McLiesh, and Andrei Shleifer. 2008. "Debt Enforcement around the World." *Journal of Political Economy* 116 (6): 1105–49.

Djankov, Simeon, Darshini Manraj, Caralee McLiesh, and Rita Ramalho. 2005. "Doing Business Indicators: Why Aggregate, and How to Do It." World Bank, Washington, DC.

Doblas-Madrid, Antonio, and Raoul Minetti. 2013. "Sharing Information in the Credit Market: Contract-Level Evidence from US firms." *Journal of Financial Economics* 109 (1): 198–223.

Drazen, Allan, and Vittorio Grilli. 1993. "The Benefit of Crises for Economic Reforms." *American Economic Review* 83 (3): 598–607.

Enikolopov, Ruben, Maria Petrova, and Sergey Stepanov. 2014. "Firm Value in Crisis: Effects of Firm-Level Transparency and Country-Level Institutions." *Journal of Banking and Finance* 46 (C): 72–84.

Fajnzylber, P., W. Maloney, and G. Montes-Rojas. 2011. "Does Formality Improve Micro-Firm Performance? Evidence from the Brazilian SIMPLES Program." *Journal of Development Economics* 94 (2): 262–76.

Foley, C. Fritz. 1999. "Going Bust in Bangkok: Lessons from Bankruptcy Law Reform in Thailand." Harvard Business School, Cambridge, MA. Available from http://www.people.hbs.edu/ffoley /ThaiBankruptcy.pdf.

Franks, Julian, and Gyongyi Loranth. 2014. "A Study of Bankruptcy Costs and the Allocation of Control." *The Review of Finance* 18 (3): 961–97.

Freund, Caroline, and Bineswaree Bolaky.
2008. "Trade, Regulations, and Income."
Journal of Development Economics 87:
309–21.

Freund, Caroline, and Nadia Rocha. 2011.
"What Constrains Africa's Exports?"
The World Bank Economic Review 25 (3):
361–86.

Funchal, Bruno. 2008. "The Effects of the
2005 Bankruptcy Reform in Brazil."
Economics Letters 101 (2008): 84–86.

Geginat, Carolin, and Rita Ramalho. 2015.
"Electricity Connections and Firm
Performance in 183 Countries." Global
Indicators Group, World Bank Group,
Washington, DC. Available from
http://www.doingbusiness
.org/~/media/GIAWB/Doing%20
Business/Documents/Special-Reports
/DB15-Electricity-Connections-and-
Firm-Performance.pdf.

Giné, Xavier, and Inessa Love. 2006.
"Do Reorganization Costs Matter for
Efficiency? Evidence from a Bankruptcy
Reform in Colombia." Policy Research
Working Paper 3970, World Bank,
Washington, DC.

Global Construction Perspectives and
Oxford Economics. 2013. *Global
Construction 2025*. London: Global
Construction Perspectives.

Gramckow, Heike, Omniah Ebeid, Erica
Bosio, and Jorge Luis Silva Mendez.
2016. "Good Practices for Courts
Report: Helpful Elements for Good
Court Performance and the World
Bank's Quality of Judicial Process
Indicators—Key Elements, Lessons
Learned, and Good Practice Examples."
Working Paper 108234, World Bank,
Washington, DC.

Grimm, Michael, Renate Hartwig, and Jann
Lay. 2012. "How Much Does Utility
Access Matter for the Performance of
Micro and Small Enterprises?" Policy
Research Working Paper 77935, World
Bank, Washington, DC.

Guner, Nezih, Gustavo Ventura, and Yi Xu.
2008. "Macroeconomic Implications
of Size-Dependent Policies." *Review of
Economic Dynamics* 11: 721–44.

Haggard, Stephan, and John Williamson.
1994. "The Political Conditions for

Economic Reform." In *The Political
Economy of Policy Reform*, edited by J.
Williamson, 525–96. Washington, DC:
Institute for International Economics.

Hallward-Driemeier, Mary, and Lant
Pritchett. 2015. "How Business Is Done
in the Developing World: Deals versus
Rules." *Journal of Economic Perspectives*
29 (3): 121–40.

Hoekman, Bernard, and Alessandro Nicita.
2011. "Trade Policy, Trade Costs, and
Developing Country Trade." *World
Development* 39 (12): 2069–79.

Hsieh, Chang-Tai, and Peter J. Klenow. 2009.
"Misallocation and Manufacturing TFP
in China and India." *Quarterly Journal of
Economics* 124 (4): 1403–48.

Hsueh, Natalie. 2010. "Philadelphia's
Development Permit Review Process:
Recommendations for Reform."
Presented to the City of Philadelphia,
Pennsylvania, January 2010.

IMF (International Monetary Fund). 2015.
*Country Report No. 15/42, Republic of
Slovenia*. Washington, DC: International
Monetary Fund.

———. 2017. *Fiscal Monitor: Achieving More
with Less*. Washington, DC, April.

Kakai, Sèdagban Hygin F. 2012. "Government
and Land Corruption in Benin." Land Deal
Politics Initiative Working Paper 12, The
Land Deal Politics Initiative, International
Institute of Social Studies, The Hague.

Kawaguchi, Daiji, and Tetsushi Murao. 2014.
"Labor-Market Institutions and Long-
Term Effects of Youth Unemployment."
Journal of Money Credit and Banking
46 (S2): 95–116.

Kaplan, David, Eduardo Piedra, and Enrique
Seira. 2011. "Entry Regulation and
Business Start-ups: Evidence from
Mexico." *Journal of Public Economics*
95 (11–12): 1501–15.

Klapper, Leora. 2011. "Saving Viable
Businesses." Public Policy Journal Note
328, World Bank Group, Washington DC.

Klapper, Leora, Luc Laeven, and Raghuram
Rajan. 2006. "Entry Regulation as a
Barrier to Entrepreneurship." *Journal of
Financial Economics* (82): 591–629.

Klapper, Leora, and Inessa Love. 2011. "The
Impact of Business Environment Reforms
on New Firm Registration." Policy

Research Working Paper 5493, World
Bank, Washington, DC.

Kraay, Aart, and David McKenzie. 2014.
"Do Poverty Traps Exist? Assessing the
Evidence." *Journal of Economic Perspectives*
28 (3): 127–48.

Lanz, Rainer, Michael Roberts, and Sainabou
Taal. 2016. "Reducing Trade Costs
in LDCs: The Role of Aid for Trade."
WTO Working Paper, World Trade
Organization, Geneva.

La Porta, Rafael, Florencio Lopez-de-Silanes,
Andrei Shleifer, and Robert W. Vishny. 1997.
"Legal Determinants of External Finance."
The Journal of Finance (52): 1131–50.

———. 1998. "Law and Finance." *Journal of
Political Economy* (106): 1113–55.

La Porta, Rafael, and Andrei Shleifer. 2008.
"The Unofficial Economy and Economic
Development." Tuck School of Business
Working Paper 2009-57, Dartmouth
College, Hanover, NH. Available from
Social Science Research Network (SSRN).
http://ssrn.com/abstract=1304760.

Lawless, Martina. 2013. "Do Complicated
Tax Systems Prevent Foreign Direct
Investment?" *Economica* 80 (317): 1–22.

Lee, Seung-Hyun, Yasuhiro Yamakawa,
Mike W. Peng, and Jay B. Barney. 2011.
"How do Bankruptcy Laws Affect
Entrepreneurship Development Around
the World?" *Journal of Business Venturing*
26 (5): 505–20.

Loayza, Norman, and Luis Serven. 2010.
*Business Regulation and Economic
Performance*. Washington,
DC: World Bank.

Love, Inessa, María Soledad Martínez Pería,
and Sandeep Singh. 2013. "Collateral
Registries for Movable Assets: Does
Their Introduction Spur Firms' Access to
Bank Finance?" Policy Research Working
Paper 6477, World Bank, Washington,
DC.

Lovegrove, Kim. 2016. "Australasian Building
Control: A Journey from Monopoly to
Free Market to Benefits of Hindsight."
Background paper, World Bank,
Washington, DC.

Malesky, Edmund, Neil McCulloch, and
Nguyen Duc Nhat. 2015. "The Impact of
Governance and Transparency on Firm

Investment in Vietnam." *Economics of Transition* (23): 677–715.

Martin, John P. P., and Stefano Scarpetta. 2012. "Setting It Right: Employment Protection, Labour Reallocation and Productivity." *De Economist* 160 (2): 89–116.

Martincus, Christian Volpe, Jeronimo Carballo, and Alejandro Graziano. 2015. "Customs." *Journal of International Economics* 96 (2015): 119–37.

Meijer, Frits, and Henk Visscher. 2005. "Building Control: Private Versus Public Responsibilities." Delft University, Delft.

Monteiro, Joana, and Juliano J. Assunção. 2012. "Coming Out of the Shadows? Estimating the Impact of Bureaucracy Simplification and Tax Cut on Formality in Brazilian Microenterprises." *Journal of Development Economics* 99: 105–15.

Montenegro, Claudio, and Carmen Pagés. 2003. "Who Benefits from Labor Market Regulations?" Policy Research Working Paper 3143, World Bank, Washington DC.

Moscoso Boedo, Hernan J., and Toshihiko Mukoyama. 2012. "Evaluating the Effects of Entry Regulations and Firing Costs on International Income Differences." *Journal of Economic Growth* 17 (2): 143–70.

Moullier, Thomas. 2013. "Good Practices for Construction Regulation and Enforcement Reform: Guidelines for Reformers." World Bank Working Paper 77100, World Bank, Washington, DC.

———. 2017. "Building Regulatory Capacity Assessment: Level 1 – Initial Screening." Global Facility for Disaster Reduction and Recovery (GFDRR) Working Paper, World Bank, Washington, DC.

Munemo, Jonathan. 2014. "Business Start-Up Regulations and the Complementarity Between Foreign and Domestic Investment" *Review of World Economics* 150 (4): 745–61.

Neira, Julian. 2017. "Bankruptcy and Cross-Country Differences in Productivity." *Journal of Economic Behavior and Organization* (2017). Available from http://dx.doi.org/10.1016/j.jebo.2017.07.011.

Norbäck, Pehr-Johan, Lars Persson, and Robin Douhan. 2014. "Entrepreneurship Policy and Globalization." *Journal of Development Economics* 110: 22–38

Obala, Luke, and Michael Mattingly. 2014. "Ethnicity, Corruption and Violence in Urban Land Conflict in Kenya." *Urban Studies* 51: 2735–51.

Palstra, Nienke. 2014. "Fighting Money Laundering in the EU: From Secret Ownership to Public Registries." EU Policy Paper 01/2014, Brussels: Transparency International.

Peisakhin, Leonid. 2012. "Transparency and Corruption: Evidence from India." *The Journal of Law and Economics* 55 (1): 129–49.

Peng, Mike W., Yasuhiro Yamakawa, and Seung-Hyun Lee. 2010. "Bankruptcy Laws and Entrepreneur-Friendliness." *Entrepreneurship Theory and Practice* (34): 517–30.

Ponticelli, Jacopo, and Leonardo S. Alencar. 2016. "Court Enforcement, Bank Loans and Firm Investment: Evidence from a Bankruptcy Reform in Brazil." Working Paper 425, Research Department, Central Bank of Brazil.

Portugal-Perez, Alberto, and John S. Wilson. 2011. "Export Performance and Trade Facilitation Reform: Hard and Soft Infrastructure." *World Development* 40 (7): 1295–1307.

PricewaterhouseCoopers. 2005. "Economic Impact of Accelerating Permit Processes on Local Development and Government Revenues." Report prepared for the American Institute of Architects, Washington, DC.

Quintanilla, Pamela Bartlett and Helen Darbishire. 2016. "It's None of Your Business! 10 Obstacles to Accessing Company Register Data Using the Right to Information." Access Info Europe and Organized Crime and Corruption Reporting Project. Available from http://slideflix.net/doc/4075921/%E2%80%9Cit%E2%80%99s-none-of-your-business-%E2%80%9D-10-obstacles-to-accessing-c.

Ramello, Giovanni, and Stephen Voigt. 2012. "The Economics of Efficiency and the Judicial System." *International Review of Law and Economics* 32: 1–2.

Ranciere, Romain, and Aaron Tornell. 2015. "Why Do Reforms Occur in Crises Times?" Economics Department Working Paper, University of California at Los Angeles (UCLA), Los Angeles.

Rodano, Giacomo, Nicolas Andre Benigno Serrano-Velarde, and Emanuele Tarantino. 2011. "The Causal Effect of Bankruptcy Law on the Cost of Finance." Available from Social Science Research Network (SSRN): http://dx.doi.org/10.2139/ssrn.1967485.

Rodrik, D., A. Subramanian, and F. Trebbi. 2004. "Institutions Rule: The Primacy of Institutions over Geography and Integration in Economic Development." *Journal of Economic Growth* 9 (2): 131–65.

Rose-Ackerman, Susan. 2004. "Governance and Corruption." In *Global Crises, Global Solutions*, edited by Bjorn Lomborg, 301–38. Cambridge: Cambridge University Press.

Schneider, Friedrich. 2005. "The Informal Sector in 145 Countries." Department of Economics, University Linz, Austria.

Slovenia, Ministry of Justice. 2017. "Evaluation of the Implementation of ZFPPIPP after the enforcement of ZFPPIPP-E and ZFPPIPP-F Amending Acts, Including ZFPPIPP-G Amending act (January 2017) Preliminary Report." Ministry of Justice, Slovenia.

Søreide, Tina, and Aled Williams, ed. 2014. *Corruption, Grabbing and Development: Real World Problems*. Edward Elgar: Cheltenham.

Thailand, Office of the Judiciary. 2016. *Annual Judicial Statistics (2008–2016)*. Statistics Division, Planning and Budget Department, Bangkok.

Transparency International. 2013. *Global Corruption Barometer 2013*. Berlin: Transparency International. Available from http://www.wingia.com/web/files/news/61/file/61.pdf.

———. 2014. *East African Bribery Index 2014*. Nairobi: Transparency International Kenya.

UNECE (United Nations Economic Commission for Europe). 1996. *Land Administration Guidelines with Special Reference to Countries in Transition*. New York and Geneva: UNECE.

UN-Habitat (United Nations Human Settlements Programme). 2016. *World Cities Report 2016. Urbanization and Development: Emerging Futures.* Nairobi: UN-Habitat.

Van der Heijden, Jeroen. 2009. "Building Regulatory Enforcement Regimes: Comparative Analysis of Private Sector Involvement in the Enforcement of Public Building Regulations." PhD thesis, Delft University of Technology.

Visaria, Sujata. 2009. "Legal Reform and Loan Repayment: The Microeconomic Impact of Debt Recovery Tribunals in India." *American Economic Journal: Applied Economics* 1(3): 59–81.

Wisitsora-at, Wisit. 2015. "Bankruptcy Reform in Thailand and the Lessons to be Learned from this." *Assumption University* 50 (2550): 129-135.

World Bank. 2011. *World Development Report 2011.* Washington DC: World Bank.

———. 2012. *World Development Report 2013: Jobs.* Washington, DC: World Bank.

World Bank Group and World Trade Organization (WTO). 2015. *The Role of Trade in Ending Poverty.* Geneva: WTO.

World Economic Forum. 2017. *Shaping the Future of Construction: Inspiring Innovators Redefine the Industry.* Geneva: World Economic Forum.

WTO (World Trade Organization). 2015. *World Trade Report 2015.* Geneva: WTO.

Wrenn, Douglas H., and Elena G. Irwin. 2015. "Time is Money: An Empirical Examination of the Effects of Regulatory Delay on Residential Subdivision Development." *Regional Science and Urban Economics* (51): 25–36.

Zakout, Wael, Babette Wehrmann, and Mika-Petteri Törhönen. 2006. "Good Governance in Land Administration Principles and Good Practices." Food and Agriculture Organization of the United Nations (FAO), Rome, Italy.

Country
Tables

✔ Reform making it easier to do business   ✘ Change making it more difficult to do business

AFGHANISTAN

		South Asia		GNI per capita (US$)	580
Ease of doing business rank (1–190)	183	Overall distance to frontier (DTF) score (0–100)	36.19	Population	34,656,032

✘ **Starting a business** (rank)	107	**Getting credit** (rank)	105	**Trading across borders** (rank)	175
DTF score for starting a business (0–100)	84.28	DTF score for getting credit (0–100)	45.00	DTF score for trading across borders (0–100)	30.63
Procedures (number)	3.5	Strength of legal rights index (0–12)	9	Time to export	
Time (days)	7.5	Depth of credit information index (0–8)	0	Documentary compliance (hours)	228
Cost (% of income per capita)	82.3	Credit bureau coverage (% of adults)	0.0	Border compliance (hours)	48
Minimum capital (% of income per capita)	0.0	Credit registry coverage (% of adults)	1.0	Cost to export	
				Documentary compliance (US$)	344
Dealing with construction permits (rank)	185	**Protecting minority investors** (rank)	189	Border compliance (US$)	453
DTF score for dealing with construction permits (0–100)	22.54	DTF score for protecting minority investors (0–100)	10.00	Time to import	
Procedures (number)	13	Extent of disclosure index (0–10)	1	Documentary compliance (hours)	324
Time (days)	354	Extent of director liability index (0–10)	1	Border compliance (hours)	96
Cost (% of warehouse value)	89.8	Ease of shareholder suits index (0–10)	3	Cost to import	
Building quality control index (0–15)	2.5	Extent of shareholder rights index (0–10)	0	Documentary compliance (US$)	900
		Extent of ownership and control index (0–10)	0	Border compliance (US$)	750
		Extent of corporate transparency index (0–10)	1		
Getting electricity (rank)	163			**Enforcing contracts** (rank)	181
DTF score for getting electricity (0–100)	44.58			DTF score for enforcing contracts (0–100)	31.76
Procedures (number)	6	**Paying taxes** (rank)	176	Time (days)	1,642
Time (days)	114	DTF score for paying taxes (0–100)	41.97	Cost (% of claim)	29.0
Cost (% of income per capita)	2,426.7	Payments (number per year)	19	Quality of judicial processes index (0–18)	5.0
Reliability of supply and transparency of tariffs index (0–8)	0	Time (hours per year)	275		
		Total tax and contribution rate (% of profit)	71.4		
Registering property (rank)	186	Postfiling index (0–100)	0.00	**Resolving insolvency** (rank)	161
DTF score for registering property (0–100)	27.50			DTF score for resolving insolvency (0–100)	23.62
Procedures (number)	9			Time (years)	2.0
Time (days)	250			Cost (% of estate)	25.0
Cost (% of property value)	5.0			Recovery rate (cents on the dollar)	26.5
Quality of land administration index (0–30)	3.0			Strength of insolvency framework index (0–16)	3.0

ALBANIA

		Europe & Central Asia		GNI per capita (US$)	4,250
Ease of doing business rank (1–190)	65	Overall distance to frontier (DTF) score (0–100)	68.70	Population	2,876,101

Starting a business (rank)	45	✔ **Getting credit** (rank)	42	**Trading across borders** (rank)	24
DTF score for starting a business (0–100)	91.49	DTF score for getting credit (0–100)	70.00	DTF score for trading across borders (0–100)	96.29
Procedures (number)	5	Strength of legal rights index (0–12)	8	Time to export	
Time (days)	5	Depth of credit information index (0–8)	6	Documentary compliance (hours)	6
Cost (% of income per capita)	12.0	Credit bureau coverage (% of adults)	0.0	Border compliance (hours)	9
Minimum capital (% of income per capita)	0.0	Credit registry coverage (% of adults)	51.6	Cost to export	
				Documentary compliance (US$)	10
Dealing with construction permits (rank)	106	**Protecting minority investors** (rank)	20	Border compliance (US$)	55
DTF score for dealing with construction permits (0–100)	66.27	DTF score for protecting minority investors (0–100)	71.67	Time to import	
Procedures (number)	17	Extent of disclosure index (0–10)	9	Documentary compliance (hours)	8
Time (days)	220	Extent of director liability index (0–10)	7	Border compliance (hours)	10
Cost (% of warehouse value)	3.5	Ease of shareholder suits index (0–10)	7	Cost to import	
Building quality control index (0–15)	13.0	Extent of shareholder rights index (0–10)	6	Documentary compliance (US$)	10
		Extent of ownership and control index (0–10)	6	Border compliance (US$)	77
Getting electricity (rank)	157	Extent of corporate transparency index (0–10)	8		
DTF score for getting electricity (0–100)	48.31			**Enforcing contracts** (rank)	120
Procedures (number)	6	**Paying taxes** (rank)	125	DTF score for enforcing contracts (0–100)	53.66
Time (days)	134	DTF score for paying taxes (0–100)	63.94	Time (days)	525
Cost (% of income per capita)	513.0	Payments (number per year)	35	Cost (% of claim)	34.9
Reliability of supply and transparency of tariffs index (0–8)	0	Time (hours per year)	261	Quality of judicial processes index (0–18)	6.0
		Total tax and contribution rate (% of profit)	37.3		
Registering property (rank)	103	Postfiling index (0–100)	57.61	**Resolving insolvency** (rank)	41
DTF score for registering property (0–100)	59.28			DTF score for resolving insolvency (0–100)	66.13
Procedures (number)	6			Time (years)	2.0
Time (days)	19			Cost (% of estate)	10.0
Cost (% of property value)	9.6			Recovery rate (cents on the dollar)	41.6
Quality of land administration index (0–30)	15.5			Strength of insolvency framework index (0–16)	14.0

Note: Most indicator sets refer to a case scenario in the largest business city of an economy, though for 11 economies the data are a population-weighted average for the two largest business cities. For some indicators a result of "no practice" may be recorded for an economy; see the data notes for more details. In starting a business, procedures (number), time (days) and cost (% of income per capita) are calculated as the average of both men and women. For the postfiling index, a result of "not applicable" may be recorded for an economy.

✔ Reform making it easier to do business   ✘ Change making it more difficult to do business

ALGERIA

		Middle East & North Africa		GNI per capita (US$)	4,270
Ease of doing business rank (1–190)	166	Overall distance to frontier (DTF) score (0–100)	46.71	Population	40,606,052

Starting a business (rank)	145	**Getting credit** (rank)	177	**Trading across borders** (rank)	181
DTF score for starting a business (0–100)	77.54	DTF score for getting credit (0–100)	10.00	DTF score for trading across borders (0–100)	24.15
Procedures (number)	12	Strength of legal rights index (0–12)	2	*Time to export*	
Time (days)	20	Depth of credit information index (0–8)	0	Documentary compliance (hours)	149
Cost (% of income per capita)	11.1	Credit bureau coverage (% of adults)	0.0	Border compliance (hours)	118
Minimum capital (% of income per capita)	0.0	Credit registry coverage (% of adults)	2.9	*Cost to export*	
				Documentary compliance (US$)	374
Dealing with construction permits (rank)	146	**Protecting minority investors** (rank)	170	Border compliance (US$)	593
DTF score for dealing with construction permits (0–100)	58.89	DTF score for protecting minority investors (0–100)	33.33	*Time to import*	
Procedures (number)	19	Extent of disclosure index (0–10)	4	Documentary compliance (hours)	249
Time (days)	146	Extent of director liability index (0–10)	1	Border compliance (hours)	327
Cost (% of warehouse value)	8.1	Ease of shareholder suits index (0–10)	5	*Cost to import*	
Building quality control index (0–15)	10.0	Extent of shareholder rights index (0–10)	3	Documentary compliance (US$)	400
		Extent of ownership and control index (0–10)	4	Border compliance (US$)	466
		Extent of corporate transparency index (0–10)	3		
Getting electricity (rank)	120			**Enforcing contracts** (rank)	103
DTF score for getting electricity (0–100)	60.56			DTF score for enforcing contracts (0–100)	55.49
Procedures (number)	5	**Paying taxes** (rank)	157	Time (days)	630
Time (days)	180	DTF score for paying taxes (0–100)	54.11	Cost (% of claim)	19.9
Cost (% of income per capita)	1,335.3	Payments (number per year)	27	Quality of judicial processes index (0–18)	5.5
Reliability of supply and transparency of tariffs index (0–8)	5	Time (hours per year)	265		
		Total tax and contribution rate (% of profit)	65.6		
Registering property (rank)	163	Postfiling index (0–100)	49.77	**Resolving insolvency** (rank)	71
DTF score for registering property (0–100)	43.83			DTF score for resolving insolvency (0–100)	49.24
Procedures (number)	10			Time (years)	1.3
Time (days)	55			Cost (% of estate)	7.0
Cost (% of property value)	7.1			Recovery rate (cents on the dollar)	50.8
Quality of land administration index (0–30)	7.0			Strength of insolvency framework index (0–16)	7.0

ANGOLA

		Sub-Saharan Africa		GNI per capita (US$)	3,440
Ease of doing business rank (1–190)	175	Overall distance to frontier (DTF) score (0–100)	41.49	Population	28,813,463

Starting a business (rank)	134	**Getting credit** (rank)	183	✔ **Trading across borders** (rank)	180
DTF score for starting a business (0–100)	80.09	DTF score for getting credit (0–100)	5.00	DTF score for trading across borders (0–100)	25.28
Procedures (number)	7	Strength of legal rights index (0–12)	1	*Time to export*	
Time (days)	36	Depth of credit information index (0–8)	0	Documentary compliance (hours)	169
Cost (% of income per capita)	17.4	Credit bureau coverage (% of adults)	0.0	Border compliance (hours)	192
Minimum capital (% of income per capita)	0.0	Credit registry coverage (% of adults)	1.9	*Cost to export*	
				Documentary compliance (US$)	240
✔ **Dealing with construction permits** (rank)	80	**Protecting minority investors** (rank)	81	Border compliance (US$)	825
DTF score for dealing with construction permits (0–100)	68.80	DTF score for protecting minority investors (0–100)	55.00	*Time to import*	
Procedures (number)	10	Extent of disclosure index (0–10)	4	Documentary compliance (hours)	180
Time (days)	173	Extent of director liability index (0–10)	6	Border compliance (hours)	96
Cost (% of warehouse value)	0.5	Ease of shareholder suits index (0–10)	6	*Cost to import*	
Building quality control index (0–15)	6.0	Extent of shareholder rights index (0–10)	7	Documentary compliance (US$)	460
		Extent of ownership and control index (0–10)	6	Border compliance (US$)	1,030
		Extent of corporate transparency index (0–10)	4		
✔ **Getting electricity** (rank)	165			**Enforcing contracts** (rank)	186
DTF score for getting electricity (0–100)	44.08			DTF score for enforcing contracts (0–100)	26.26
Procedures (number)	7	**Paying taxes** (rank)	103	Time (days)	1,296
Time (days)	121	DTF score for paying taxes (0–100)	69.54	Cost (% of claim)	44.4
Cost (% of income per capita)	990.1	Payments (number per year)	31	Quality of judicial processes index (0–18)	4.5
Reliability of supply and transparency of tariffs index (0–8)	0	Time (hours per year)	287		
		Total tax and contribution rate (% of profit)	49.1		
Registering property (rank)	172	Postfiling index (0–100)	94.95	**Resolving insolvency** (rank)	168
DTF score for registering property (0–100)	40.86			DTF score for resolving insolvency (0–100)	0.00
Procedures (number)	7			Time (years)	no practice
Time (days)	190			Cost (% of estate)	no practice
Cost (% of property value)	2.9			Recovery rate (cents on the dollar)	0.0
Quality of land administration index (0–30)	7.0			Strength of insolvency framework index (0–16)	0.0

ANTIGUA AND BARBUDA

		Latin America & Caribbean		GNI per capita (US$)	13,400
Ease of doing business rank (1–190)	107	Overall distance to frontier (DTF) score (0–100)	59.63	Population	100,963

Starting a business (rank)	126	**Getting credit** (rank)	159	**Trading across borders** (rank)	101
DTF score for starting a business (0–100)	81.69	DTF score for getting credit (0–100)	25.00	DTF score for trading across borders (0–100)	68.73
Procedures (number)	9	Strength of legal rights index (0–12)	5	*Time to export*	
Time (days)	22	Depth of credit information index (0–8)	0	Documentary compliance (hours)	51
Cost (% of income per capita)	9.1	Credit bureau coverage (% of adults)	0.0	Border compliance (hours)	61
Minimum capital (% of income per capita)	0.0	Credit registry coverage (% of adults)	0.0	*Cost to export*	
				Documentary compliance (US$)	121
Dealing with construction permits (rank)	99	**Protecting minority investors** (rank)	96	Border compliance (US$)	546
DTF score for dealing with construction permits (0–100)	67.09	DTF score for protecting minority investors (0–100)	51.67	*Time to import*	
Procedures (number)	19	Extent of disclosure index (0–10)	4	Documentary compliance (hours)	48
Time (days)	135	Extent of director liability index (0–10)	8	Border compliance (hours)	61
Cost (% of warehouse value)	0.8	Ease of shareholder suits index (0–10)	8	*Cost to import*	
Building quality control index (0–15)	9.0	Extent of shareholder rights index (0–10)	4	Documentary compliance (US$)	100
		Extent of ownership and control index (0–10)	4	Border compliance (US$)	546
		Extent of corporate transparency index (0–10)	3		
Getting electricity (rank)	39			**Enforcing contracts** (rank)	33
DTF score for getting electricity (0–100)	83.50			DTF score for enforcing contracts (0–100)	68.11
Procedures (number)	4	**Paying taxes** (rank)	144	Time (days)	476
Time (days)	42	DTF score for paying taxes (0–100)	58.69	Cost (% of claim)	27.1
Cost (% of income per capita)	114.9	Payments (number per year)	57	Quality of judicial processes index (0–18)	11.5
Reliability of supply and transparency of tariffs index (0–8)	5	Time (hours per year)	192		
		Total tax and contribution rate (% of profit)	41.9		
✔ **Registering property** (rank)	118	Postfiling index (0–100)	69.40	**Resolving insolvency** (rank)	128
DTF score for registering property (0–100)	56.61			DTF score for resolving insolvency (0–100)	35.26
Procedures (number)	7			Time (years)	3.0
Time (days)	32			Cost (% of estate)	7.0
Cost (% of property value)	10.8			Recovery rate (cents on the dollar)	36.5
Quality of land administration index (0–30)	19.0			Strength of insolvency framework index (0–16)	5.0

Note: Most indicator sets refer to a case scenario in the largest business city of an economy, though for 11 economies the data are a population-weighted average for the two largest business cities. For some indicators a result of "no practice" may be recorded for an economy; see the data notes for more details. In starting a business, procedures (number), time (days) and cost (% of income per capita) are calculated as the average of both men and women. For the postfiling index, a result of "not applicable" may be recorded for an economy.

✔ Reform making it easier to do business   ✘ Change making it more difficult to do business

ARGENTINA

		Latin America & Caribbean		GNI per capita (US$)	11,960
Ease of doing business rank (1–190)	117	Overall distance to frontier (DTF) score (0–100)	58.11	Population	43,847,430

Starting a business (rank)	157	**Getting credit** (rank)	77	**Trading across borders** (rank)	116
DTF score for starting a business (0–100)	75.15	DTF score for getting credit (0–100)	55.00	DTF score for trading across borders (0–100)	65.36
Procedures (number)	13	Strength of legal rights index (0–12)	3	*Time to export*	
Time (days)	24	Depth of credit information index (0–8)	8	Documentary compliance (hours)	30
Cost (% of income per capita)	10.4	Credit bureau coverage (% of adults)	80.0	Border compliance (hours)	21
Minimum capital (% of income per capita)	0.0	Credit registry coverage (% of adults)	44.8	*Cost to export*	
				Documentary compliance (US$)	60
✘ **Dealing with construction permits** (rank)	171	**Protecting minority investors** (rank)	43	Border compliance (US$)	150
DTF score for dealing with construction permits (0–100)	49.27	DTF score for protecting minority investors (0–100)	63.33	*Time to import*	
Procedures (number)	22	Extent of disclosure index (0–10)	7	Documentary compliance (hours)	192
Time (days)	347	Extent of director liability index (0–10)	2	Border compliance (hours)	60
Cost (% of warehouse value)	3.1	Ease of shareholder suits index (0–10)	6	*Cost to import*	
Building quality control index (0–15)	11.0	Extent of shareholder rights index (0–10)	9	Documentary compliance (US$)	120
		Extent of ownership and control index (0–10)	7	Border compliance (US$)	1,200
Getting electricity (rank)	95	Extent of corporate transparency index (0–10)	7		
DTF score for getting electricity (0–100)	70.01			**Enforcing contracts** (rank)	102
Procedures (number)	6			DTF score for enforcing contracts (0–100)	55.66
Time (days)	92	**Paying taxes** (rank)	169	Time (days)	995
Cost (% of income per capita)	24.5	DTF score for paying taxes (0–100)	49.34	Cost (% of claim)	22.5
Reliability of supply and transparency of tariffs index (0–8)	5	Payments (number per year)	9	Quality of judicial processes index (0–18)	11.5
		Time (hours per year)	311.5		
		Total tax and contribution rate (% of profit)	106.0		
Registering property (rank)	117	Postfiling index (0–100)	47.94	**Resolving insolvency** (rank)	101
DTF score for registering property (0–100)	56.75			DTF score for resolving insolvency (0–100)	41.24
Procedures (number)	7			Time (years)	2.4
Time (days)	51.5			Cost (% of estate)	16.5
Cost (% of property value)	6.6			Recovery rate (cents on the dollar)	21.5
Quality of land administration index (0–30)	13.5			Strength of insolvency framework index (0–16)	9.5

ARMENIA

		Europe & Central Asia		GNI per capita (US$)	3,760
Ease of doing business rank (1–190)	47	Overall distance to frontier (DTF) score (0–100)	72.51	Population	2,924,816

Starting a business (rank)	15	**Getting credit** (rank)	42	**Trading across borders** (rank)	52
DTF score for starting a business (0–100)	94.47	DTF score for getting credit (0–100)	70.00	DTF score for trading across borders (0–100)	86.45
Procedures (number)	4	Strength of legal rights index (0–12)	6	*Time to export*	
Time (days)	4.5	Depth of credit information index (0–8)	8	Documentary compliance (hours)	2
Cost (% of income per capita)	0.9	Credit bureau coverage (% of adults)	77.2	Border compliance (hours)	39
Minimum capital (% of income per capita)	0.0	Credit registry coverage (% of adults)	0.0	*Cost to export*	
				Documentary compliance (US$)	150
Dealing with construction permits (rank)	89	**Protecting minority investors** (rank)	62	Border compliance (US$)	100
DTF score for dealing with construction permits (0–100)	67.99	DTF score for protecting minority investors (0–100)	58.33	*Time to import*	
Procedures (number)	19	Extent of disclosure index (0–10)	5	Documentary compliance (hours)	2
Time (days)	98	Extent of director liability index (0–10)	6	Border compliance (hours)	41
Cost (% of warehouse value)	0.9	Ease of shareholder suits index (0–10)	8	*Cost to import*	
Building quality control index (0–15)	8.0	Extent of shareholder rights index (0–10)	7	Documentary compliance (US$)	100
		Extent of ownership and control index (0–10)	2	Border compliance (US$)	100
✔ **Getting electricity** (rank)	66	Extent of corporate transparency index (0–10)	7		
DTF score for getting electricity (0–100)	78.53			**Enforcing contracts** (rank)	47
Procedures (number)	3			DTF score for enforcing contracts (0–100)	66.00
Time (days)	127	**Paying taxes** (rank)	87	Time (days)	570
Cost (% of income per capita)	78.9	DTF score for paying taxes (0–100)	72.49	Cost (% of claim)	16.0
Reliability of supply and transparency of tariffs index (0–8)	5	Payments (number per year)	14	Quality of judicial processes index (0–18)	9.5
		Time (hours per year)	313		
		Total tax and contribution rate (% of profit)	18.5		
✔ **Registering property** (rank)	13	Postfiling index (0–100)	49.08	**Resolving insolvency** (rank)	97
DTF score for registering property (0–100)	87.78			DTF score for resolving insolvency (0–100)	43.01
Procedures (number)	3			Time (years)	1.9
Time (days)	7			Cost (% of estate)	11.0
Cost (% of property value)	0.2			Recovery rate (cents on the dollar)	36.4
Quality of land administration index (0–30)	21.5			Strength of insolvency framework index (0–16)	7.5

AUSTRALIA

		OECD high income		GNI per capita (US$)	54,420
Ease of doing business rank (1–190)	14	Overall distance to frontier (DTF) score (0–100)	80.14	Population	24,127,159

Starting a business (rank)	7	**Getting credit** (rank)	6	**Trading across borders** (rank)	95
DTF score for starting a business (0–100)	96.47	DTF score for getting credit (0–100)	90.00	DTF score for trading across borders (0–100)	70.65
Procedures (number)	3	Strength of legal rights index (0–12)	11	*Time to export*	
Time (days)	2.5	Depth of credit information index (0–8)	7	Documentary compliance (hours)	7
Cost (% of income per capita)	0.7	Credit bureau coverage (% of adults)	100.0	Border compliance (hours)	36
Minimum capital (% of income per capita)	0.0	Credit registry coverage (% of adults)	0.0	*Cost to export*	
				Documentary compliance (US$)	264
Dealing with construction permits (rank)	6	**Protecting minority investors** (rank)	57	Border compliance (US$)	749
DTF score for dealing with construction permits (0–100)	84.39	DTF score for protecting minority investors (0–100)	60.00	*Time to import*	
Procedures (number)	11	Extent of disclosure index (0–10)	8	Documentary compliance (hours)	4
Time (days)	121	Extent of director liability index (0–10)	2	Border compliance (hours)	39
Cost (% of warehouse value)	0.9	Ease of shareholder suits index (0–10)	8	*Cost to import*	
Building quality control index (0–15)	14.0	Extent of shareholder rights index (0–10)	5	Documentary compliance (US$)	100
		Extent of ownership and control index (0–10)	4	Border compliance (US$)	525
Getting electricity (rank)	47	Extent of corporate transparency index (0–10)	9		
DTF score for getting electricity (0–100)	82.31			**Enforcing contracts** (rank)	3
Procedures (number)	5			DTF score for enforcing contracts (0–100)	79.00
Time (days)	75	**Paying taxes** (rank)	26	Time (days)	402
Cost (% of income per capita)	12.4	DTF score for paying taxes (0–100)	85.62	Cost (% of claim)	23.2
Reliability of supply and transparency of tariffs index (0–8)	7	Payments (number per year)	11	Quality of judicial processes index (0–18)	15.5
		Time (hours per year)	105		
		Total tax and contribution rate (% of profit)	47.5		
Registering property (rank)	51	Postfiling index (0–100)	95.34	**Resolving insolvency** (rank)	18
DTF score for registering property (0–100)	74.17			DTF score for resolving insolvency (0–100)	78.79
Procedures (number)	5			Time (years)	1.0
Time (days)	4.5			Cost (% of estate)	8.0
Cost (% of property value)	5.2			Recovery rate (cents on the dollar)	82.5
Quality of land administration index (0–30)	20.0			Strength of insolvency framework index (0–16)	11.0

Note: Most indicator sets refer to a case scenario in the largest business city of an economy, though for 11 economies the data are a population-weighted average for the two largest business cities. For some indicators a result of "no practice" may be recorded for an economy; see the data notes for more details. In starting a business, procedures (number), time (days) and cost (% of income per capita) are calculated as the average of both men and women. For the postfiling index, a result of "not applicable" may be recorded for an economy.

✔ Reform making it easier to do business   ✘ Change making it more difficult to do business

AUSTRIA

AUSTRIA		**OECD high income**		**GNI per capita (US$)**		45,230
Ease of doing business rank (1–190)	22	Overall distance to frontier (DTF) score (0–100)	78.54	Population		8,747,358

Indicator	Value	Indicator	Value	Indicator	Value
Starting a business (rank)	118	**Getting credit** (rank)	77	**Trading across borders** (rank)	1
DTF score for starting a business (0–100)	83.13	DTF score for getting credit (0–100)	55.00	DTF score for trading across borders (0–100)	100.00
Procedures (number)	8	Strength of legal rights index (0–12)	4	*Time to export*	
Time (days)	21	Depth of credit information index (0–8)	7	Documentary compliance (hours)	1
Cost (% of income per capita)	5.1	Credit bureau coverage (% of adults)	52.8	Border compliance (hours)	0
Minimum capital (% of income per capita)	12.5	Credit registry coverage (% of adults)	2.2	*Cost to export*	
				Documentary compliance (US$)	0
Dealing with construction permits (rank)	42	**Protecting minority investors** (rank)	29	Border compliance (US$)	0
DTF score for dealing with construction permits (0–100)	75.00	DTF score for protecting minority investors (0–100)	68.33	*Time to import*	
Procedures (number)	11	Extent of disclosure index (0–10)	5	Documentary compliance (hours)	1
Time (days)	222	Extent of director liability index (0–10)	5	Border compliance (hours)	0
Cost (% of warehouse value)	1.2	Ease of shareholder suits index (0–10)	7	*Cost to import*	
Building quality control index (0–15)	13.0	Extent of shareholder rights index (0–10)	7	Documentary compliance (US$)	0
		Extent of ownership and control index (0–10)	9	Border compliance (US$)	0
Getting electricity (rank)	22	Extent of corporate transparency index (0–10)	8		
DTF score for getting electricity (0–100)	87.71			**Enforcing contracts** (rank)	9
Procedures (number)	5	**Paying taxes** (rank)	39	DTF score for enforcing contracts (0–100)	75.49
Time (days)	23	DTF score for paying taxes (0–100)	83.34	Time (days)	397
Cost (% of income per capita)	93.5	Payments (number per year)	12	Cost (% of claim)	20.6
Reliability of supply and transparency of tariffs index (0–8)	7	Time (hours per year)	131	Quality of judicial processes index (0–18)	13.0
		Total tax and contribution rate (% of profit)	51.8		
Registering property (rank)	31	Postfiling index (0–100)	98.54	**Resolving insolvency** (rank)	23
DTF score for registering property (0–100)	79.97			DTF score for resolving insolvency (0–100)	77.43
Procedures (number)	3			Time (years)	1.1
Time (days)	20.5			Cost (% of estate)	10.0
Cost (% of property value)	4.6			Recovery rate (cents on the dollar)	80.0
Quality of land administration index (0–30)	23.0			Strength of insolvency framework index (0–16)	11.0

AZERBAIJAN

AZERBAIJAN		**Europe & Central Asia**		**GNI per capita (US$)**		4,760
Ease of doing business rank (1–190)	57	Overall distance to frontier (DTF) score (0–100)	70.19	Population		9,762,274

Indicator	Value	Indicator	Value	Indicator	Value
Starting a business (rank)	18	✔ **Getting credit** (rank)	122	**Trading across borders** (rank)	83
DTF score for starting a business (0–100)	94.36	DTF score for getting credit (0–100)	40.00	DTF score for trading across borders (0–100)	73.56
Procedures (number)	4	Strength of legal rights index (0–12)	2	*Time to export*	
Time (days)	4.5	Depth of credit information index (0–8)	6	Documentary compliance (hours)	33
Cost (% of income per capita)	1.8	Credit bureau coverage (% of adults)	0.0	Border compliance (hours)	29
Minimum capital (% of income per capita)	0.0	Credit registry coverage (% of adults)	37.5	*Cost to export*	
				Documentary compliance (US$)	300
Dealing with construction permits (rank)	161	✔ **Protecting minority investors** (rank)	10	Border compliance (US$)	214
DTF score for dealing with construction permits (0–100)	54.90	DTF score for protecting minority investors (0–100)	75.00	*Time to import*	
Procedures (number)	21	Extent of disclosure index (0–10)	10	Documentary compliance (hours)	38
Time (days)	242	Extent of director liability index (0–10)	5	Border compliance (hours)	30
Cost (% of warehouse value)	6.8	Ease of shareholder suits index (0–10)	8	*Cost to import*	
Building quality control index (0–15)	12.0	Extent of shareholder rights index (0–10)	8	Documentary compliance (US$)	200
		Extent of ownership and control index (0–10)	6	Border compliance (US$)	300
Getting electricity (rank)	102	Extent of corporate transparency index (0–10)	8		
DTF score for getting electricity (0–100)	67.98			✔ **Enforcing contracts** (rank)	38
Procedures (number)	7	**Paying taxes** (rank)	35	DTF score for enforcing contracts (0–100)	67.51
Time (days)	69	DTF score for paying taxes (0–100)	84.21	Time (days)	277
Cost (% of income per capita)	141.4	Payments (number per year)	6	Cost (% of claim)	18.5
Reliability of supply and transparency of tariffs index (0–8)	5	Time (hours per year)	195	Quality of judicial processes index (0–18)	6.5
		Total tax and contribution rate (% of profit)	39.8		
Registering property (rank)	21	Postfiling index (0–100)	83.79	✔ **Resolving insolvency** (rank)	47
DTF score for registering property (0–100)	82.07			DTF score for resolving insolvency (0–100)	62.27
Procedures (number)	3			Time (years)	1.5
Time (days)	5.5			Cost (% of estate)	12.0
Cost (% of property value)	0.2			Recovery rate (cents on the dollar)	40.2
Quality of land administration index (0–30)	14.5			Strength of insolvency framework index (0–16)	13.0

BAHAMAS, THE

BAHAMAS, THE		**Latin America & Caribbean**		**GNI per capita (US$)**		21,020
Ease of doing business rank (1–190)	119	Overall distance to frontier (DTF) score (0–100)	57.47	Population		391,232

Indicator	Value	Indicator	Value	Indicator	Value
✔ **Starting a business** (rank)	108	**Getting credit** (rank)	142	**Trading across borders** (rank)	157
DTF score for starting a business (0–100)	84.18	DTF score for getting credit (0–100)	30.00	DTF score for trading across borders (0–100)	53.07
Procedures (number)	7	Strength of legal rights index (0–12)	6	*Time to export*	
Time (days)	21.5	Depth of credit information index (0–8)	0	Documentary compliance (hours)	12
Cost (% of income per capita)	13.8	Credit bureau coverage (% of adults)	0.0	Border compliance (hours)	36
Minimum capital (% of income per capita)	0.0	Credit registry coverage (% of adults)	0.0	*Cost to export*	
				Documentary compliance (US$)	550
Dealing with construction permits (rank)	86	**Protecting minority investors** (rank)	129	Border compliance (US$)	512
DTF score for dealing with construction permits (0–100)	68.30	DTF score for protecting minority investors (0–100)	45.00	*Time to import*	
Procedures (number)	16	Extent of disclosure index (0–10)	2	Documentary compliance (hours)	6
Time (days)	180	Extent of director liability index (0–10)	5	Border compliance (hours)	51
Cost (% of warehouse value)	1.0	Ease of shareholder suits index (0–10)	8	*Cost to import*	
Building quality control index (0–15)	10.0	Extent of shareholder rights index (0–10)	8	Documentary compliance (US$)	550
		Extent of ownership and control index (0–10)	1	Border compliance (US$)	1,385
Getting electricity (rank)	117	Extent of corporate transparency index (0–10)	3		
DTF score for getting electricity (0–100)	60.96			**Enforcing contracts** (rank)	74
Procedures (number)	5	✔ **Paying taxes** (rank)	55	DTF score for enforcing contracts (0–100)	59.43
Time (days)	67	DTF score for paying taxes (0–100)	78.09	Time (days)	532
Cost (% of income per capita)	124.1	Payments (number per year)	31	Cost (% of claim)	28.9
Reliability of supply and transparency of tariffs index (0–8)	0	Time (hours per year)	233	Quality of judicial processes index (0–18)	8.0
		Total tax and contribution rate (% of profit)	31.5		
Registering property (rank)	167	Postfiling index (0–100)	95.00	**Resolving insolvency** (rank)	64
DTF score for registering property (0–100)	42.71			DTF score for resolving insolvency (0–100)	52.93
Procedures (number)	7			Time (years)	3.0
Time (days)	122			Cost (% of estate)	12.0
Cost (% of property value)	4.7			Recovery rate (cents on the dollar)	63.5
Quality of land administration index (0–30)	3.0			Strength of insolvency framework index (0–16)	6.0

Note: Most indicator sets refer to a case scenario in the largest business city of an economy, though for 11 economies the data are a population-weighted average for the two largest business cities. For some indicators a result of "no practice" may be recorded for an economy; see the data notes for more details. In starting a business, procedures (number), time (days) and cost (% of income per capita) are calculated as the average of both men and women. For the postfiling index, a result of "not applicable" may be recorded for an economy.

✔ Reform making it easier to do business   ✗ Change making it more difficult to do business

BAHRAIN

		Middle East & North Africa		GNI per capita (US$)	22,858
Ease of doing business rank (1–190)	66	Overall distance to frontier (DTF) score (0–100)	68.13	Population	1,425,171

Starting a business (rank)	75	**Getting credit** (rank)	105	**Trading across borders** (rank)	78
DTF score for starting a business (0–100)	87.87	DTF score for getting credit (0–100)	45.00	DTF score for trading across borders (0–100)	75.97
Procedures (number)	7.5	Strength of legal rights index (0–12)	1	*Time to export*	
Time (days)	9.5	Depth of credit information index (0–8)	8	Documentary compliance (hours)	24
Cost (% of income per capita)	1.0	Credit bureau coverage (% of adults)	27.8	Border compliance (hours)	71
Minimum capital (% of income per capita)	2.9	Credit registry coverage (% of adults)	0.0	*Cost to export*	
				Documentary compliance (US$)	100
Dealing with construction permits (rank)	47	**Protecting minority investors** (rank)	108	Border compliance (US$)	47
DTF score for dealing with construction permits (0–100)	73.73	DTF score for protecting minority investors (0–100)	50.00	*Time to import*	
Procedures (number)	11	Extent of disclosure index (0–10)	8	Documentary compliance (hours)	84
Time (days)	174	Extent of director liability index (0–10)	4	Border compliance (hours)	54
Cost (% of warehouse value)	3.7	Ease of shareholder suits index (0–10)	4	*Cost to import*	
Building quality control index (0–15)	12.0	Extent of shareholder rights index (0–10)	5	Documentary compliance (US$)	130
		Extent of ownership and control index (0–10)	4	Border compliance (US$)	397
		Extent of corporate transparency index (0–10)	5		
Getting electricity (rank)	79			**Enforcing contracts** (rank)	111
DTF score for getting electricity (0–100)	74.83	✗ **Paying taxes** (rank)	5	DTF score for enforcing contracts (0–100)	54.53
Procedures (number)	5	DTF score for paying taxes (0–100)	93.89	Time (days)	635
Time (days)	85	Payments (number per year)	14	Cost (% of claim)	14.7
Cost (% of income per capita)	57.0	Time (hours per year)	28.5	Quality of judicial processes index (0–18)	4.0
Reliability of supply and transparency of tariffs index (0–8)	5	Total tax and contribution rate (% of profit)	13.8		
		Postfiling index (0–100)	not applicable	**Resolving insolvency** (rank)	90
Registering property (rank)	25			DTF score for resolving insolvency (0–100)	44.42
DTF score for registering property (0–100)	81.07			Time (years)	2.5
Procedures (number)	2			Cost (% of estate)	9.5
Time (days)	31			Recovery rate (cents on the dollar)	41.9
Cost (% of property value)	1.7			Strength of insolvency framework index (0–16)	7.0
Quality of land administration index (0–30)	17.5				

BANGLADESH

		South Asia		GNI per capita (US$)	1,330
Ease of doing business rank (1–190)	177	Overall distance to frontier (DTF) score (0–100)	40.99	Population	162,951,560

✗ **Starting a business** (rank)	131	**Getting credit** (rank)	159	**Trading across borders** (rank)	173
DTF score for starting a business (0–100)	80.67	DTF score for getting credit (0–100)	25.00	DTF score for trading across borders (0–100)	34.86
Procedures (number)	9	Strength of legal rights index (0–12)	5	*Time to export*	
Time (days)	19.5	Depth of credit information index (0–8)	0	Documentary compliance (hours)	147
Cost (% of income per capita)	22.3	Credit bureau coverage (% of adults)	0.0	Border compliance (hours)	99.7
Minimum capital (% of income per capita)	0.0	Credit registry coverage (% of adults)	0.9	*Cost to export*	
				Documentary compliance (US$)	225
Dealing with construction permits (rank)	130	**Protecting minority investors** (rank)	76	Border compliance (US$)	408.2
DTF score for dealing with construction permits (0–100)	61.97	DTF score for protecting minority investors (0–100)	56.67	*Time to import*	
Procedures (number)	14.2	Extent of disclosure index (0–10)	6	Documentary compliance (hours)	144
Time (days)	269	Extent of director liability index (0–10)	7	Border compliance (hours)	183
Cost (% of warehouse value)	2.4	Ease of shareholder suits index (0–10)	6	*Cost to import*	
Building quality control index (0–15)	10.0	Extent of shareholder rights index (0–10)	5	Documentary compliance (US$)	370
		Extent of ownership and control index (0–10)	4	Border compliance (US$)	1,293.8
		Extent of corporate transparency index (0–10)	6		
Getting electricity (rank)	185			**Enforcing contracts** (rank)	189
DTF score for getting electricity (0–100)	16.97	**Paying taxes** (rank)	152	DTF score for enforcing contracts (0–100)	22.21
Procedures (number)	9	DTF score for paying taxes (0–100)	56.13	Time (days)	1,442
Time (days)	428.9	Payments (number per year)	33	Cost (% of claim)	66.8
Cost (% of income per capita)	2,602.9	Time (hours per year)	435	Quality of judicial processes index (0–18)	7.5
Reliability of supply and transparency of tariffs index (0–8)	0	Total tax and contribution rate (% of profit)	33.4		
		Postfiling index (0–100)	44.36	**Resolving insolvency** (rank)	152
Registering property (rank)	185			DTF score for resolving insolvency (0–100)	27.71
DTF score for registering property (0–100)	27.67			Time (years)	4.0
Procedures (number)	8			Cost (% of estate)	8.0
Time (days)	244			Recovery rate (cents on the dollar)	28.3
Cost (% of property value)	6.9			Strength of insolvency framework index (0–16)	4.0
Quality of land administration index (0–30)	4.5				

BARBADOS

		Latin America & Caribbean		GNI per capita (US$)	14,830
Ease of doing business rank (1–190)	132	Overall distance to frontier (DTF) score (0–100)	55.20	Population	284,996

Starting a business (rank)	99	**Getting credit** (rank)	133	**Trading across borders** (rank)	129
DTF score for starting a business (0–100)	85.11	DTF score for getting credit (0–100)	35.00	DTF score for trading across borders (0–100)	61.88
Procedures (number)	8	Strength of legal rights index (0–12)	7	*Time to export*	
Time (days)	15	Depth of credit information index (0–8)	0	Documentary compliance (hours)	54
Cost (% of income per capita)	7.6	Credit bureau coverage (% of adults)	0.0	Border compliance (hours)	41
Minimum capital (% of income per capita)	0.0	Credit registry coverage (% of adults)	0.0	*Cost to export*	
				Documentary compliance (US$)	109
Dealing with construction permits (rank)	155	**Protecting minority investors** (rank)	167	Border compliance (US$)	350
DTF score for dealing with construction permits (0–100)	56.63	DTF score for protecting minority investors (0–100)	35.00	*Time to import*	
Procedures (number)	9	Extent of disclosure index (0–10)	2	Documentary compliance (hours)	74
Time (days)	442	Extent of director liability index (0–10)	2	Border compliance (hours)	104
Cost (% of warehouse value)	0.2	Ease of shareholder suits index (0–10)	7	*Cost to import*	
Building quality control index (0–15)	6.5	Extent of shareholder rights index (0–10)	4	Documentary compliance (US$)	146
		Extent of ownership and control index (0–10)	1	Border compliance (US$)	1,585
		Extent of corporate transparency index (0–10)	5		
Getting electricity (rank)	160			**Enforcing contracts** (rank)	167
DTF score for getting electricity (0–100)	46.36	✗ **Paying taxes** (rank)	89	DTF score for enforcing contracts (0–100)	38.02
Procedures (number)	8	DTF score for paying taxes (0–100)	71.90	Time (days)	1,340
Time (days)	88	Payments (number per year)	29	Cost (% of claim)	19.7
Cost (% of income per capita)	64.0	Time (hours per year)	245	Quality of judicial processes index (0–18)	6.5
Reliability of supply and transparency of tariffs index (0–8)	0	Total tax and contribution rate (% of profit)	35.3		
		Postfiling index (0–100)	74.08	**Resolving insolvency** (rank)	34
Registering property (rank)	133			DTF score for resolving insolvency (0–100)	69.79
DTF score for registering property (0–100)	52.35			Time (years)	1.8
Procedures (number)	6			Cost (% of estate)	15.0
Time (days)	105			Recovery rate (cents on the dollar)	65.8
Cost (% of property value)	5.6			Strength of insolvency framework index (0–16)	11.0
Quality of land administration index (0–30)	11.5				

Note: Most indicator sets refer to a case scenario in the largest business city of an economy, though for 11 economies the data are a population-weighted average for the two largest business cities. For some indicators a result of "no practice" may be recorded for an economy; see the data notes for more details. In starting a business, procedures (number), time (days) and cost (% of income per capita) are calculated as the average of both men and women. For the postfiling index, a result of "not applicable" may be recorded for an economy.

✔ Reform making it easier to do business   ✘ Change making it more difficult to do business

BELARUS

BELARUS		Europe & Central Asia		GNI per capita (US$)		5,600
Ease of doing business rank (1–190)	38	Overall distance to frontier (DTF) score (0–100)	75.06	Population		9,507,120

Starting a business (rank)	30	✔ Getting credit (rank)	90	Trading across borders (rank)	30
DTF score for starting a business (0–100)	92.91	DTF score for getting credit (0–100)	50.00	DTF score for trading across borders (0–100)	93.71
Procedures (number)	5	Strength of legal rights index (0–12)	3	*Time to export*	
Time (days)	5	Depth of credit information index (0–8)	7	Documentary compliance (hours)	4
Cost (% of income per capita)	0.6	Credit bureau coverage (% of adults)	0.0	Border compliance (hours)	5
Minimum capital (% of income per capita)	0.0	Credit registry coverage (% of adults)	72.2	*Cost to export*	
				Documentary compliance (US$)	140
Dealing with construction permits (rank)	22	**Protecting minority investors** (rank)	40	Border compliance (US$)	108
DTF score for dealing with construction permits (0–100)	78.34	DTF score for protecting minority investors (0–100)	65.00	*Time to import*	
Procedures (number)	16	Extent of disclosure index (0–10)	7	Documentary compliance (hours)	4
Time (days)	115	Extent of director liability index (0–10)	2	Border compliance (hours)	1
Cost (% of warehouse value)	0.7	Ease of shareholder suits index (0–10)	8	*Cost to import*	
Building quality control index (0–15)	13.0	Extent of shareholder rights index (0–10)	6	Documentary compliance (US$)	0
		Extent of ownership and control index (0–10)	8	Border compliance (US$)	0
		Extent of corporate transparency index (0–10)	8		
Getting electricity (rank)	25				
DTF score for getting electricity (0–100)	86.04			**Enforcing contracts** (rank)	24
Procedures (number)	4	**Paying taxes** (rank)	96	DTF score for enforcing contracts (0–100)	70.36
Time (days)	105	DTF score for paying taxes (0–100)	70.81	Time (days)	275
Cost (% of income per capita)	110.0	Payments (number per year)	7	Cost (% of claim)	23.4
Reliability of supply and transparency of tariffs index (0–8)	8	Time (hours per year)	184	Quality of judicial processes index (0–18)	9.0
		Total tax and contribution rate (% of profit)	52.9		
		Postfiling index (0–100)	50.00	**Resolving insolvency** (rank)	68
Registering property (rank)	5			DTF score for resolving insolvency (0–100)	51.26
DTF score for registering property (0–100)	92.19			Time (years)	1.5
Procedures (number)	2			Cost (% of estate)	17.0
Time (days)	3			Recovery rate (cents on the dollar)	37.2
Cost (% of property value)	0.0			Strength of insolvency framework index (0–16)	10.0
Quality of land administration index (0–30)	23.5				

BELGIUM

BELGIUM		OECD high income		GNI per capita (US$)	41,860
Ease of doing business rank (1–190)	52	Overall distance to frontier (DTF) score (0–100)	71.69	Population	11,348,159

Starting a business (rank)	16	Getting credit (rank)	105	Trading across borders (rank)	1
DTF score for starting a business (0–100)	94.43	DTF score for getting credit (0–100)	45.00	DTF score for trading across borders (0–100)	100.00
Procedures (number)	3	Strength of legal rights index (0–12)	4	*Time to export*	
Time (days)	4	Depth of credit information index (0–8)	5	Documentary compliance (hours)	1
Cost (% of income per capita)	5.6	Credit bureau coverage (% of adults)	0.0	Border compliance (hours)	0
Minimum capital (% of income per capita)	16.8	Credit registry coverage (% of adults)	95.5	*Cost to export*	
				Documentary compliance (US$)	0
Dealing with construction permits (rank)	39	**Protecting minority investors** (rank)	57	Border compliance (US$)	0
DTF score for dealing with construction permits (0–100)	75.36	DTF score for protecting minority investors (0–100)	60.00	*Time to import*	
Procedures (number)	10	Extent of disclosure index (0–10)	8	Documentary compliance (hours)	1
Time (days)	212	Extent of director liability index (0–10)	6	Border compliance (hours)	0
Cost (% of warehouse value)	1.0	Ease of shareholder suits index (0–10)	7	*Cost to import*	
Building quality control index (0–15)	12.0	Extent of shareholder rights index (0–10)	4	Documentary compliance (US$)	0
		Extent of ownership and control index (0–10)	4	Border compliance (US$)	0
		Extent of corporate transparency index (0–10)	7		
Getting electricity (rank)	103				
DTF score for getting electricity (0–100)	67.30			**Enforcing contracts** (rank)	52
Procedures (number)	6	✔ **Paying taxes** (rank)	59	DTF score for enforcing contracts (0–100)	64.25
Time (days)	201	DTF score for paying taxes (0–100)	77.69	Time (days)	505
Cost (% of income per capita)	101.1	Payments (number per year)	11	Cost (% of claim)	18.0
Reliability of supply and transparency of tariffs index (0–8)	8	Time (hours per year)	136	Quality of judicial processes index (0–18)	8.0
		Total tax and contribution rate (% of profit)	57.1		
		Postfiling index (0–100)	83.45	**Resolving insolvency** (rank)	11
Registering property (rank)	138			DTF score for resolving insolvency (0–100)	81.46
DTF score for registering property (0–100)	51.40			Time (years)	0.9
Procedures (number)	8			Cost (% of estate)	3.5
Time (days)	56			Recovery rate (cents on the dollar)	84.6
Cost (% of property value)	12.7			Strength of insolvency framework index (0–16)	11.5
Quality of land administration index (0–30)	22.5				

BELIZE

BELIZE		Latin America & Caribbean		GNI per capita (US$)	4,410
Ease of doing business rank (1–190)	121	Overall distance to frontier (DTF) score (0–100)	57.11	Population	366,954

Starting a business (rank)	161	Getting credit (rank)	170	Trading across borders (rank)	104
DTF score for starting a business (0–100)	73.24	DTF score for getting credit (0–100)	20.00	DTF score for trading across borders (0–100)	68.13
Procedures (number)	9	Strength of legal rights index (0–12)	4	*Time to export*	
Time (days)	43	Depth of credit information index (0–8)	0	Documentary compliance (hours)	38
Cost (% of income per capita)	34.6	Credit bureau coverage (% of adults)	0.0	Border compliance (hours)	96
Minimum capital (% of income per capita)	0.0	Credit registry coverage (% of adults)	0.0	*Cost to export*	
				Documentary compliance (US$)	28
Dealing with construction permits (rank)	114	**Protecting minority investors** (rank)	132	Border compliance (US$)	710
DTF score for dealing with construction permits (0–100)	65.28	DTF score for protecting minority investors (0–100)	43.33	*Time to import*	
Procedures (number)	16	Extent of disclosure index (0–10)	3	Documentary compliance (hours)	36
Time (days)	127	Extent of director liability index (0–10)	4	Border compliance (hours)	48
Cost (% of warehouse value)	2.5	Ease of shareholder suits index (0–10)	7	*Cost to import*	
Building quality control index (0–15)	7.0	Extent of shareholder rights index (0–10)	6	Documentary compliance (US$)	75
		Extent of ownership and control index (0–10)	1	Border compliance (US$)	688
		Extent of corporate transparency index (0–10)	5		
Getting electricity (rank)	83				
DTF score for getting electricity (0–100)	72.97			**Enforcing contracts** (rank)	132
Procedures (number)	5	**Paying taxes** (rank)	48	DTF score for enforcing contracts (0–100)	50.11
Time (days)	66	DTF score for paying taxes (0–100)	79.90	Time (days)	892
Cost (% of income per capita)	317.7	Payments (number per year)	29	Cost (% of claim)	27.5
Reliability of supply and transparency of tariffs index (0–8)	4	Time (hours per year)	147	Quality of judicial processes index (0–18)	8.0
		Total tax and contribution rate (% of profit)	31.1		
		Postfiling index (0–100)	85.09	**Resolving insolvency** (rank)	83
Registering property (rank)	132			DTF score for resolving insolvency (0–100)	45.74
DTF score for registering property (0–100)	52.42			Time (years)	2.0
Procedures (number)	9			Cost (% of estate)	22.5
Time (days)	60			Recovery rate (cents on the dollar)	55.9
Cost (% of property value)	4.8			Strength of insolvency framework index (0–16)	5.0
Quality of land administration index (0–30)	11.0				

Note: Most indicator sets refer to a case scenario in the largest business city of an economy, though for 11 economies the data are a population-weighted average for the two largest business cities. For some indicators a result of "no practice" may be recorded for an economy; see the data notes for more details. In starting a business, procedures (number), time (days) and cost (% of income per capita) are calculated as the average of both men and women. For the postfiling index, a result of "not applicable" may be recorded for an economy.

✔ Reform making it easier to do business   ✘ Change making it more difficult to do business

BENIN

		Sub-Saharan Africa		GNI per capita (US$)	820
Ease of doing business rank (1–190)	151	Overall distance to frontier (DTF) score (0–100)	50.47	Population	10,872,298

Starting a business (rank)	56	✔ **Getting credit** (rank)	142	**Trading across borders** (rank)	136
DTF score for starting a business (0–100)	90.58	DTF score for getting credit (0–100)	30.00	DTF score for trading across borders (0–100)	60.78
Procedures (number)	5.5	Strength of legal rights index (0–12)	6	*Time to export*	
Time (days)	8.5	Depth of credit information index (0–8)	0	Documentary compliance (hours)	48
Cost (% of income per capita)	3.7	Credit bureau coverage (% of adults)	0.0	Border compliance (hours)	78
Minimum capital (% of income per capita)	5.4	Credit registry coverage (% of adults)	0.7	*Cost to export*	
				Documentary compliance (US$)	80
✔ **Dealing with construction permits** (rank)	46	**Protecting minority investors** (rank)	146	Border compliance (US$)	412
DTF score for dealing with construction permits (0–100)	73.85	DTF score for protecting minority investors (0–100)	40.00	*Time to import*	
Procedures (number)	13	Extent of disclosure index (0–10)	7	Documentary compliance (hours)	59
Time (days)	88	Extent of director liability index (0–10)	1	Border compliance (hours)	82
Cost (% of warehouse value)	2.9	Ease of shareholder suits index (0–10)	5	*Cost to import*	
Building quality control index (0–15)	9.0	Extent of shareholder rights index (0–10)	4	Documentary compliance (US$)	529
		Extent of ownership and control index (0–10)	3	Border compliance (US$)	599
		Extent of corporate transparency index (0–10)	4		
Getting electricity (rank)	174			**Enforcing contracts** (rank)	170
DTF score for getting electricity (0–100)	33.84	**Paying taxes** (rank)	174	DTF score for enforcing contracts (0–100)	36.34
Procedures (number)	5	DTF score for paying taxes (0–100)	44.73	Time (days)	750
Time (days)	90	Payments (number per year)	57	Cost (% of claim)	64.7
Cost (% of income per capita)	12,304.6	Time (hours per year)	270	Quality of judicial processes index (0–18)	6.0
Reliability of supply and transparency of tariffs index (0–8)	0	Total tax and contribution rate (% of profit)	57.4		
		Postfiling index (0–100)	49.31	**Resolving insolvency** (rank)	105
✔ **Registering property** (rank)	127			DTF score for resolving insolvency (0–100)	40.46
DTF score for registering property (0–100)	54.14			Time (years)	4.0
Procedures (number)	4			Cost (% of estate)	21.5
Time (days)	120			Recovery rate (cents on the dollar)	22.9
Cost (% of property value)	3.5			Strength of insolvency framework index (0–16)	9.0
Quality of land administration index (0–30)	6.5				

BHUTAN

		South Asia		GNI per capita (US$)	2,510
Ease of doing business rank (1–190)	75	Overall distance to frontier (DTF) score (0–100)	66.27	Population	797,765

✔ **Starting a business** (rank)	88	✔ **Getting credit** (rank)	77	**Trading across borders** (rank)	26
DTF score for starting a business (0–100)	86.33	DTF score for getting credit (0–100)	55.00	DTF score for trading across borders (0–100)	94.25
Procedures (number)	8	Strength of legal rights index (0–12)	4	*Time to export*	
Time (days)	12	Depth of credit information index (0–8)	7	Documentary compliance (hours)	9
Cost (% of income per capita)	3.9	Credit bureau coverage (% of adults)	25.9	Border compliance (hours)	5
Minimum capital (% of income per capita)	0.0	Credit registry coverage (% of adults)	0.0	*Cost to export*	
				Documentary compliance (US$)	50
Dealing with construction permits (rank)	82	✔ **Protecting minority investors** (rank)	124	Border compliance (US$)	59
DTF score for dealing with construction permits (0–100)	68.69	DTF score for protecting minority investors (0–100)	46.67	*Time to import*	
Procedures (number)	21	Extent of disclosure index (0–10)	4	Documentary compliance (hours)	8
Time (days)	150	Extent of director liability index (0–10)	4	Border compliance (hours)	5
Cost (% of warehouse value)	1.1	Ease of shareholder suits index (0–10)	6	*Cost to import*	
Building quality control index (0–15)	12.0	Extent of shareholder rights index (0–10)	4	Documentary compliance (US$)	50
		Extent of ownership and control index (0–10)	5	Border compliance (US$)	110
		Extent of corporate transparency index (0–10)	5		
Getting electricity (rank)	56			✔ **Enforcing contracts** (rank)	25
DTF score for getting electricity (0–100)	80.36	**Paying taxes** (rank)	17	DTF score for enforcing contracts (0–100)	69.99
Procedures (number)	4	DTF score for paying taxes (0–100)	88.00	Time (days)	225
Time (days)	61	Payments (number per year)	18	Cost (% of claim)	23.1
Cost (% of income per capita)	461.4	Time (hours per year)	85	Quality of judicial processes index (0–18)	8.0
Reliability of supply and transparency of tariffs index (0–8)	5	Total tax and contribution rate (% of profit)	35.3		
		Postfiling index (0–100)	95.50	**Resolving insolvency** (rank)	168
Registering property (rank)	56			DTF score for resolving insolvency (0–100)	0.00
DTF score for registering property (0–100)	73.41			Time (years)	no practice
Procedures (number)	3			Cost (% of estate)	no practice
Time (days)	77			Recovery rate (cents on the dollar)	0.0
Cost (% of property value)	5.0			Strength of insolvency framework index (0–16)	0.0
Quality of land administration index (0–30)	24.0				

BOLIVIA

		Latin America & Caribbean		GNI per capita (US$)	3,070
Ease of doing business rank (1–190)	152	Overall distance to frontier (DTF) score (0–100)	50.18	Population	10,887,882

Starting a business (rank)	179	**Getting credit** (rank)	133	✔ **Trading across borders** (rank)	89
DTF score for starting a business (0–100)	62.95	DTF score for getting credit (0–100)	35.00	DTF score for trading across borders (0–100)	71.59
Procedures (number)	14	Strength of legal rights index (0–12)	0	*Time to export*	
Time (days)	45	Depth of credit information index (0–8)	7	Documentary compliance (hours)	144
Cost (% of income per capita)	54.0	Credit bureau coverage (% of adults)	49.8	Border compliance (hours)	48
Minimum capital (% of income per capita)	0.0	Credit registry coverage (% of adults)	16.1	*Cost to export*	
				Documentary compliance (US$)	25
Dealing with construction permits (rank)	158	**Protecting minority investors** (rank)	146	Border compliance (US$)	65
DTF score for dealing with construction permits (0–100)	55.56	DTF score for protecting minority investors (0–100)	40.00	*Time to import*	
Procedures (number)	13	Extent of disclosure index (0–10)	1	Documentary compliance (hours)	72
Time (days)	322	Extent of director liability index (0–10)	5	Border compliance (hours)	114
Cost (% of warehouse value)	1.4	Ease of shareholder suits index (0–10)	6	*Cost to import*	
Building quality control index (0–15)	7.0	Extent of shareholder rights index (0–10)	6	Documentary compliance (US$)	30
		Extent of ownership and control index (0–10)	2	Border compliance (US$)	315
		Extent of corporate transparency index (0–10)	4		
Getting electricity (rank)	101			**Enforcing contracts** (rank)	109
DTF score for getting electricity (0–100)	68.18	**Paying taxes** (rank)	186	DTF score for enforcing contracts (0–100)	54.65
Procedures (number)	8	DTF score for paying taxes (0–100)	21.62	Time (days)	591
Time (days)	42	Payments (number per year)	42	Cost (% of claim)	25.0
Cost (% of income per capita)	689.0	Time (hours per year)	1,025	Quality of judicial processes index (0–18)	5.5
Reliability of supply and transparency of tariffs index (0–8)	6	Total tax and contribution rate (% of profit)	83.7		
		Postfiling index (0–100)	50.00	**Resolving insolvency** (rank)	99
Registering property (rank)	144			DTF score for resolving insolvency (0–100)	42.32
DTF score for registering property (0–100)	49.89			Time (years)	1.8
Procedures (number)	7			Cost (% of estate)	14.5
Time (days)	90			Recovery rate (cents on the dollar)	40.9
Cost (% of property value)	4.7			Strength of insolvency framework index (0–16)	6.5
Quality of land administration index (0–30)	7.0				

Note: Most indicator sets refer to a case scenario in the largest business city of an economy, though for 11 economies the data are a population-weighted average for the two largest business cities. For some indicators a result of "no practice" may be recorded for an economy; see the data notes for more details. In starting a business, procedures (number), time (days) and cost (% of income per capita) are calculated as the average of both men and women. For the postfiling index, a result of "not applicable" may be recorded for an economy.

✔ Reform making it easier to do business   ✘ Change making it more difficult to do business

BOSNIA AND HERZEGOVINA

Europe & Central Asia		GNI per capita (US$)	4,880			
Ease of doing business rank (1–190)	86	Overall distance to frontier (DTF) score (0–100)	64.20	Population	3,516,816	

Starting a business (rank) — 175
DTF score for starting a business (0–100) — 65.91
Procedures (number) — 12
Time (days) — 65
Cost (% of income per capita) — 7.7
Minimum capital (% of income per capita) — 12.0

Dealing with construction permits (rank) — 166
DTF score for dealing with construction permits (0–100) — 51.77
Procedures (number) — 16
Time (days) — 193
Cost (% of warehouse value) — 17.5
Building quality control index (0–15) — 13.0

Getting electricity (rank) — 122
DTF score for getting electricity (0–100) — 60.18
Procedures (number) — 8
Time (days) — 125
Cost (% of income per capita) — 357.7
Reliability of supply and transparency of tariffs index (0–8) — 6

Registering property (rank) — 97
DTF score for registering property (0–100) — 61.56
Procedures (number) — 7
Time (days) — 24
Cost (% of property value) — 5.2
Quality of land administration index (0–30) — 12.5

Getting credit (rank) — 55
DTF score for getting credit (0–100) — 65.00
Strength of legal rights index (0–12) — 7
Depth of credit information index (0–8) — 6
Credit bureau coverage (% of adults) — 12.1
Credit registry coverage (% of adults) — 41.5

Protecting minority investors (rank) — 62
DTF score for protecting minority investors (0–100) — 58.33
Extent of disclosure index (0–10) — 3
Extent of director liability index (0–10) — 6
Ease of shareholder suits index (0–10) — 5
Extent of shareholder rights index (0–10) — 8
Extent of ownership and control index (0–10) — 6
Extent of corporate transparency index (0–10) — 7

Paying taxes (rank) — 137
DTF score for paying taxes (0–100) — 60.43
Payments (number per year) — 33
Time (hours per year) — 411
Total tax and contribution rate (% of profit) — 23.7
Postfiling index (0–100) — 47.68

Trading across borders (rank) — 37
DTF score for trading across borders (0–100) — 91.87
Time to export
Documentary compliance (hours) — 4
Border compliance (hours) — 5
Cost to export
Documentary compliance (US$) — 92
Border compliance (US$) — 106
Time to import
Documentary compliance (hours) — 8
Border compliance (hours) — 6
Cost to import
Documentary compliance (US$) — 97
Border compliance (US$) — 109

Enforcing contracts (rank) — 71
DTF score for enforcing contracts (0–100) — 59.67
Time (days) — 595
Cost (% of claim) — 36.0
Quality of judicial processes index (0–18) — 10.5

Resolving insolvency (rank) — 40
DTF score for resolving insolvency (0–100) — 67.28
Time (years) — 3.3
Cost (% of estate) — 9.0
Recovery rate (cents on the dollar) — 37.9
Strength of insolvency framework index (0–16) — 15.0

BOTSWANA

Sub-Saharan Africa		GNI per capita (US$)	6,610			
Ease of doing business rank (1–190)	81	Overall distance to frontier (DTF) score (0–100)	64.94	Population	2,250,260	

Starting a business (rank) — 153
DTF score for starting a business (0–100) — 76.22
Procedures (number) — 9
Time (days) — 48
Cost (% of income per capita) — 0.7
Minimum capital (% of income per capita) — 0.0

Dealing with construction permits (rank) — 59
DTF score for dealing with construction permits (0–100) — 72.27
Procedures (number) — 19
Time (days) — 106
Cost (% of warehouse value) — 0.4
Building quality control index (0–15) — 10.5

Getting electricity (rank) — 124
DTF score for getting electricity (0–100) — 59.38
Procedures (number) — 5
Time (days) — 77
Cost (% of income per capita) — 283.8
Reliability of supply and transparency of tariffs index (0–8) — 0

✘ **Registering property** (rank) — 81
DTF score for registering property (0–100) — 65.45
Procedures (number) — 4
Time (days) — 27
Cost (% of property value) — 5.1
Quality of land administration index (0–30) — 10.0

Getting credit (rank) — 77
DTF score for getting credit (0–100) — 55.00
Strength of legal rights index (0–12) — 5
Depth of credit information index (0–8) — 6
Credit bureau coverage (% of adults) — 54.0
Credit registry coverage (% of adults) — 0.0

Protecting minority investors (rank) — 76
DTF score for protecting minority investors (0–100) — 56.67
Extent of disclosure index (0–10) — 7
Extent of director liability index (0–10) — 8
Ease of shareholder suits index (0–10) — 3
Extent of shareholder rights index (0–10) — 6
Extent of ownership and control index (0–10) — 3
Extent of corporate transparency index (0–10) — 7

✔ **Paying taxes** (rank) — 47
DTF score for paying taxes (0–100) — 80.01
Payments (number per year) — 34
Time (hours per year) — 120
Total tax and contribution rate (% of profit) — 25.1
Postfiling index (0–100) — 82.70

✔ **Trading across borders** (rank) — 50
DTF score for trading across borders (0–100) — 86.65
Time to export
Documentary compliance (hours) — 18
Border compliance (hours) — 5
Cost to export
Documentary compliance (US$) — 179
Border compliance (US$) — 317
Time to import
Documentary compliance (hours) — 3
Border compliance (hours) — 4
Cost to import
Documentary compliance (US$) — 67
Border compliance (US$) — 98

Enforcing contracts (rank) — 133
DTF score for enforcing contracts (0–100) — 49.99
Time (days) — 660
Cost (% of claim) — 39.8
Quality of judicial processes index (0–18) — 7.0

Resolving insolvency (rank) — 79
DTF score for resolving insolvency (0–100) — 47.76
Time (years) — 1.7
Cost (% of estate) — 18.0
Recovery rate (cents on the dollar) — 65.5
Strength of insolvency framework index (0–16) — 4.0

BRAZIL

Latin America & Caribbean		GNI per capita (US$)	8,840			
Ease of doing business rank (1–190)	125	Overall distance to frontier (DTF) score (0–100)	56.45	Population	207,652,865	

Starting a business (rank) — 176
DTF score for starting a business (0–100) — 65.05
Procedures (number) — 11
Time (days) — 79.5
Cost (% of income per capita) — 5.0
Minimum capital (% of income per capita) — 0.0

Dealing with construction permits (rank) — 170
DTF score for dealing with construction permits (0–100) — 49.83
Procedures (number) — 19.2
Time (days) — 434
Cost (% of warehouse value) — 0.8
Building quality control index (0–15) — 9.0

Getting electricity (rank) — 45
DTF score for getting electricity (0–100) — 82.46
Procedures (number) — 4
Time (days) — 64.4
Cost (% of income per capita) — 54.5
Reliability of supply and transparency of tariffs index (0–8) — 5.4

Registering property (rank) — 131
DTF score for registering property (0–100) — 52.60
Procedures (number) — 13.6
Time (days) — 31.4
Cost (% of property value) — 3.2
Quality of land administration index (0–30) — 13.8

Getting credit (rank) — 105
DTF score for getting credit (0–100) — 45.00
Strength of legal rights index (0–12) — 2
Depth of credit information index (0–8) — 7
Credit bureau coverage (% of adults) — 79.3
Credit registry coverage (% of adults) — 75.6

Protecting minority investors (rank) — 43
DTF score for protecting minority investors (0–100) — 63.33
Extent of disclosure index (0–10) — 5
Extent of director liability index (0–10) — 8
Ease of shareholder suits index (0–10) — 4
Extent of shareholder rights index (0–10) — 7
Extent of ownership and control index (0–10) — 6
Extent of corporate transparency index (0–10) — 8

Paying taxes (rank) — 184
DTF score for paying taxes (0–100) — 32.97
Payments (number per year) — 9.6
Time (hours per year) — 1,958
Total tax and contribution rate (% of profit) — 68.4
Postfiling index (0–100) — 7.80

✔ **Trading across borders** (rank) — 139
DTF score for trading across borders (0–100) — 59.78
Time to export
Documentary compliance (hours) — 12
Border compliance (hours) — 49
Cost to export
Documentary compliance (US$) — 226.4
Border compliance (US$) — 958.7
Time to import
Documentary compliance (hours) — 48
Border compliance (hours) — 63.1
Cost to import
Documentary compliance (US$) — 106.9
Border compliance (US$) — 969.6

Enforcing contracts (rank) — 47
DTF score for enforcing contracts (0–100) — 66.00
Time (days) — 731
Cost (% of claim) — 22.0
Quality of judicial processes index (0–18) — 13.1

Resolving insolvency (rank) — 80
DTF score for resolving insolvency (0–100) — 47.46
Time (years) — 4.0
Cost (% of estate) — 12.0
Recovery rate (cents on the dollar) — 12.7
Strength of insolvency framework index (0–16) — 13.0

Note: Most indicator sets refer to a case scenario in the largest business city of an economy, though for 11 economies the data are a population-weighted average for the two largest business cities. For some indicators a result of "no practice" may be recorded for an economy; see the data notes for more details. In starting a business, procedures (number), time (days) and cost (% of income per capita) are calculated as the average of both men and women. For the postfiling index, a result of "not applicable" may be recorded for an economy.

✔ Reform making it easier to do business   ✘ Change making it more difficult to do business

BRUNEI DARUSSALAM

		East Asia & Pacific		GNI per capita (US$)	32,840
Ease of doing business rank (1–190)	56	Overall distance to frontier (DTF) score (0–100)	70.60	Population	423,196

✔ Starting a business (rank)	58	Getting credit (rank)	2	✔ Trading across borders (rank)	144
DTF score for starting a business (0–100)	90.23	DTF score for getting credit (0–100)	95.00	DTF score for trading across borders (0–100)	58.70
Procedures (number)	5.5	Strength of legal rights index (0–12)	12	Time to export	
Time (days)	12.5	Depth of credit information index (0–8)	7	Documentary compliance (hours)	155
Cost (% of income per capita)	1.1	Credit bureau coverage (% of adults)	0.0	Border compliance (hours)	117
Minimum capital (% of income per capita)	0.0	Credit registry coverage (% of adults)	71.9	Cost to export	
				Documentary compliance (US$)	90
✔ Dealing with construction permits (rank)	48	✔ Protecting minority investors (rank)	40	Border compliance (US$)	340
DTF score for dealing with construction permits (0–100)	73.62	DTF score for protecting minority investors (0–100)	65.00	Time to import	
Procedures (number)	20	Extent of disclosure index (0–10)	4	Documentary compliance (hours)	132
Time (days)	83	Extent of director liability index (0–10)	8	Border compliance (hours)	48
Cost (% of warehouse value)	1.8	Ease of shareholder suits index (0–10)	8	Cost to import	
Building quality control index (0–15)	12.0	Extent of shareholder rights index (0–10)	7	Documentary compliance (US$)	50
		Extent of ownership and control index (0–10)	4	Border compliance (US$)	395
✘ Getting electricity (rank)	24	Extent of corporate transparency index (0–10)	8		
DTF score for getting electricity (0–100)	86.46			✔ Enforcing contracts (rank)	61
Procedures (number)	5	Paying taxes (rank)	104	DTF score for enforcing contracts (0–100)	60.95
Time (days)	36	DTF score for paying taxes (0–100)	69.41	Time (days)	540
Cost (% of income per capita)	41.5	Payments (number per year)	15	Cost (% of claim)	36.6
Reliability of supply and transparency of tariffs index (0–8)	7	Time (hours per year)	64.2	Quality of judicial processes index (0–18)	10.5
		Total tax and contribution rate (% of profit)	8.0		
✔ Registering property (rank)	136	Postfiling index (0–100)	0.00	Resolving insolvency (rank)	60
DTF score for registering property (0–100)	51.48			DTF score for resolving insolvency (0–100)	55.11
Procedures (number)	7			Time (years)	2.5
Time (days)	298.5			Cost (% of estate)	3.5
Cost (% of property value)	0.6			Recovery rate (cents on the dollar)	47.2
Quality of land administration index (0–30)	18.0			Strength of insolvency framework index (0–16)	9.5

BULGARIA

		Europe & Central Asia		GNI per capita (US$)	7,470
Ease of doing business rank (1–190)	50	Overall distance to frontier (DTF) score (0–100)	71.91	Population	7,127,822

Starting a business (rank)	95	Getting credit (rank)	42	Trading across borders (rank)	21
DTF score for starting a business (0–100)	85.37	DTF score for getting credit (0–100)	70.00	DTF score for trading across borders (0–100)	97.41
Procedures (number)	7	Strength of legal rights index (0–12)	9	Time to export	
Time (days)	23	Depth of credit information index (0–8)	5	Documentary compliance (hours)	2
Cost (% of income per capita)	1.2	Credit bureau coverage (% of adults)	0.0	Border compliance (hours)	4
Minimum capital (% of income per capita)	0.0	Credit registry coverage (% of adults)	74.3	Cost to export	
				Documentary compliance (US$)	52
Dealing with construction permits (rank)	51	Protecting minority investors (rank)	24	Border compliance (US$)	55
DTF score for dealing with construction permits (0–100)	73.35	DTF score for protecting minority investors (0–100)	70.00	Time to import	
Procedures (number)	18	Extent of disclosure index (0–10)	10	Documentary compliance (hours)	1
Time (days)	97	Extent of director liability index (0–10)	2	Border compliance (hours)	1
Cost (% of warehouse value)	4.2	Ease of shareholder suits index (0–10)	8	Cost to import	
Building quality control index (0–15)	13.0	Extent of shareholder rights index (0–10)	8	Documentary compliance (US$)	0
		Extent of ownership and control index (0–10)	5	Border compliance (US$)	0
Getting electricity (rank)	141	Extent of corporate transparency index (0–10)	9		
DTF score for getting electricity (0–100)	54.80			Enforcing contracts (rank)	40
Procedures (number)	6	Paying taxes (rank)	90	DTF score for enforcing contracts (0–100)	67.04
Time (days)	262	DTF score for paying taxes (0–100)	71.78	Time (days)	564
Cost (% of income per capita)	468.4	Payments (number per year)	14	Cost (% of claim)	18.6
Reliability of supply and transparency of tariffs index (0–8)	6	Time (hours per year)	453	Quality of judicial processes index (0–18)	10.5
		Total tax and contribution rate (% of profit)	27.1		
Registering property (rank)	67	Postfiling index (0–100)	69.30	Resolving insolvency (rank)	50
DTF score for registering property (0–100)	69.30			DTF score for resolving insolvency (0–100)	60.02
Procedures (number)	8			Time (years)	3.3
Time (days)	19			Cost (% of estate)	9.0
Cost (% of property value)	2.9			Recovery rate (cents on the dollar)	36.0
Quality of land administration index (0–30)	19.0			Strength of insolvency framework index (0–16)	13.0

BURKINA FASO

		Sub-Saharan Africa		GNI per capita (US$)	640
Ease of doing business rank (1–190)	148	Overall distance to frontier (DTF) score (0–100)	51.54	Population	18,646,433

Starting a business (rank)	74	✔ Getting credit (rank)	142	Trading across borders (rank)	113
DTF score for starting a business (0–100)	88.17	DTF score for getting credit (0–100)	30.00	DTF score for trading across borders (0–100)	66.58
Procedures (number)	3	Strength of legal rights index (0–12)	6	Time to export	
Time (days)	13	Depth of credit information index (0–8)	0	Documentary compliance (hours)	84
Cost (% of income per capita)	42.6	Credit bureau coverage (% of adults)	0.3	Border compliance (hours)	75
Minimum capital (% of income per capita)	6.7	Credit registry coverage (% of adults)	0.4	Cost to export	
				Documentary compliance (US$)	86
Dealing with construction permits (rank)	53	Protecting minority investors (rank)	146	Border compliance (US$)	261
DTF score for dealing with construction permits (0–100)	73.20	DTF score for protecting minority investors (0–100)	40.00	Time to import	
Procedures (number)	14	Extent of disclosure index (0–10)	7	Documentary compliance (hours)	96
Time (days)	121	Extent of director liability index (0–10)	1	Border compliance (hours)	102
Cost (% of warehouse value)	4.8	Ease of shareholder suits index (0–10)	5	Cost to import	
Building quality control index (0–15)	12.0	Extent of shareholder rights index (0–10)	4	Documentary compliance (US$)	197
		Extent of ownership and control index (0–10)	3	Border compliance (US$)	265
Getting electricity (rank)	179	Extent of corporate transparency index (0–10)	4		
DTF score for getting electricity (0–100)	29.42			Enforcing contracts (rank)	163
Procedures (number)	4	Paying taxes (rank)	153	DTF score for enforcing contracts (0–100)	41.05
Time (days)	169	DTF score for paying taxes (0–100)	55.89	Time (days)	446
Cost (% of income per capita)	9,438.4	Payments (number per year)	45	Cost (% of claim)	81.7
Reliability of supply and transparency of tariffs index (0–8)	0	Time (hours per year)	270	Quality of judicial processes index (0–18)	7.5
		Total tax and contribution rate (% of profit)	41.3		
Registering property (rank)	140	Postfiling index (0–100)	49.31	Resolving insolvency (rank)	104
DTF score for registering property (0–100)	50.44			DTF score for resolving insolvency (0–100)	40.68
Procedures (number)	4			Time (years)	4.0
Time (days)	67			Cost (% of estate)	21.0
Cost (% of property value)	12.0			Recovery rate (cents on the dollar)	23.3
Quality of land administration index (0–30)	11.5			Strength of insolvency framework index (0–16)	9.0

Note: Most indicator sets refer to a case scenario in the largest business city of an economy, though for 11 economies the data are a population-weighted average for the two largest business cities. For some indicators a result of "no practice" may be recorded for an economy; see the data notes for more details. In starting a business, procedures (number), time (days) and cost (% of income per capita) are calculated as the average of both men and women. For the postfiling index, a result of "not applicable" may be recorded for an economy.

✔ Reform making it easier to do business   ✘ Change making it more difficult to do business

BURUNDI

Sub-Saharan Africa		GNI per capita (US$)	280
Ease of doing business rank (1–190)	164	Population	10,524,117

✘ **Starting a business** (rank)	42	**Getting credit** (rank)	177	**Trading across borders** (rank)	164
DTF score for starting a business (0–100)	91.94	DTF score for getting credit (0–100)	10.00	DTF score for trading across borders (0–100)	47.02
Procedures (number)	3	Strength of legal rights index (0–12)	2	*Time to export*	
Time (days)	4	Depth of credit information index (0–8)	0	Documentary compliance (hours)	120
Cost (% of income per capita)	33.9	Credit bureau coverage (% of adults)	0.0	Border compliance (hours)	59
Minimum capital (% of income per capita)	0.0	Credit registry coverage (% of adults)	4.6	*Cost to export*	
				Documentary compliance (US$)	150
Dealing with construction permits (rank)	168	**Protecting minority investors** (rank)	132	Border compliance (US$)	136
DTF score for dealing with construction permits (0–100)	51.16	DTF score for protecting minority investors (0–100)	43.33	*Time to import*	
Procedures (number)	15	Extent of disclosure index (0–10)	8	Documentary compliance (hours)	180
Time (days)	70	Extent of director liability index (0–10)	7	Border compliance (hours)	154
Cost (% of warehouse value)	12.5	Ease of shareholder suits index (0–10)	2	*Cost to import*	
Building quality control index (0–15)	3.0	Extent of shareholder rights index (0–10)	6	Documentary compliance (US$)	1,025
		Extent of ownership and control index (0–10)	1	Border compliance (US$)	444
		Extent of corporate transparency index (0–10)	2		
Getting electricity (rank)	182			**Enforcing contracts** (rank)	150
DTF score for getting electricity (0–100)	26.45			DTF score for enforcing contracts (0–100)	45.74
Procedures (number)	5	**Paying taxes** (rank)	138	Time (days)	832
Time (days)	158	DTF score for paying taxes (0–100)	60.34	Cost (% of claim)	38.6
Cost (% of income per capita)	15,517.3	Payments (number per year)	25	Quality of judicial processes index (0–18)	7.0
Reliability of supply and transparency of tariffs index (0–8)	0	Time (hours per year)	232		
		Total tax and contribution rate (% of profit)	41.5		
Registering property (rank)	95	Postfiling index (0–100)	28.21	**Resolving insolvency** (rank)	144
DTF score for registering property (0–100)	62.54			DTF score for resolving insolvency (0–100)	30.71
Procedures (number)	5			Time (years)	5.0
Time (days)	23			Cost (% of estate)	30.0
Cost (% of property value)	3.1			Recovery rate (cents on the dollar)	7.7
Quality of land administration index (0–30)	4.5			Strength of insolvency framework index (0–16)	8.5

CABO VERDE

Sub-Saharan Africa		GNI per capita (US$)	2,970
Ease of doing business rank (1–190)	127	Population	539,560

Starting a business (rank)	98	**Getting credit** (rank)	122	✔ **Trading across borders** (rank)	107
DTF score for starting a business (0–100)	85.14	DTF score for getting credit (0–100)	40.00	DTF score for trading across borders (0–100)	67.41
Procedures (number)	8	Strength of legal rights index (0–12)	2	*Time to export*	
Time (days)	11	Depth of credit information index (0–8)	6	Documentary compliance (hours)	24
Cost (% of income per capita)	15.4	Credit bureau coverage (% of adults)	0.0	Border compliance (hours)	72
Minimum capital (% of income per capita)	0.0	Credit registry coverage (% of adults)	19.6	*Cost to export*	
				Documentary compliance (US$)	125
✔ **Dealing with construction permits** (rank)	67	**Protecting minority investors** (rank)	164	Border compliance (US$)	780
DTF score for dealing with construction permits (0–100)	71.25	DTF score for protecting minority investors (0–100)	36.67	*Time to import*	
Procedures (number)	16	Extent of disclosure index (0–10)	1	Documentary compliance (hours)	24
Time (days)	107	Extent of director liability index (0–10)	5	Border compliance (hours)	60
Cost (% of warehouse value)	4.2	Ease of shareholder suits index (0–10)	6	*Cost to import*	
Building quality control index (0–15)	11.0	Extent of shareholder rights index (0–10)	3	Documentary compliance (US$)	125
		Extent of ownership and control index (0–10)	5	Border compliance (US$)	588
		Extent of corporate transparency index (0–10)	2		
Getting electricity (rank)	145			**Enforcing contracts** (rank)	43
DTF score for getting electricity (0–100)	53.47			DTF score for enforcing contracts (0–100)	66.69
Procedures (number)	7	**Paying taxes** (rank)	75	Time (days)	425
Time (days)	88	DTF score for paying taxes (0–100)	75.15	Cost (% of claim)	19.8
Cost (% of income per capita)	1,136.3	Payments (number per year)	30	Quality of judicial processes index (0–18)	8.5
Reliability of supply and transparency of tariffs index (0–8)	2	Time (hours per year)	180		
		Total tax and contribution rate (% of profit)	36.6		
Registering property (rank)	71	Postfiling index (0–100)	80.65	✔ **Resolving insolvency** (rank)	168
DTF score for registering property (0–100)	66.57			DTF score for resolving insolvency (0–100)	0.00
Procedures (number)	6			Time (years)	no practice
Time (days)	22			Cost (% of estate)	no practice
Cost (% of property value)	2.3			Recovery rate (cents on the dollar)	0.0
Quality of land administration index (0–30)	10.0			Strength of insolvency framework index (0–16)	0.0

CAMBODIA

East Asia & Pacific		GNI per capita (US$)	1,140
Ease of doing business rank (1–190)	135	Population	15,762,370

Starting a business (rank)	183	**Getting credit** (rank)	20	**Trading across borders** (rank)	108
DTF score for starting a business (0–100)	51.91	DTF score for getting credit (0–100)	80.00	DTF score for trading across borders (0–100)	67.28
Procedures (number)	9	Strength of legal rights index (0–12)	10	*Time to export*	
Time (days)	99	Depth of credit information index (0–8)	6	Documentary compliance (hours)	132
Cost (% of income per capita)	51.3	Credit bureau coverage (% of adults)	49.9	Border compliance (hours)	48
Minimum capital (% of income per capita)	82.5	Credit registry coverage (% of adults)	0.0	*Cost to export*	
				Documentary compliance (US$)	100
Dealing with construction permits (rank)	179	**Protecting minority investors** (rank)	108	Border compliance (US$)	375
DTF score for dealing with construction permits (0–100)	41.73	DTF score for protecting minority investors (0–100)	50.00	*Time to import*	
Procedures (number)	20	Extent of disclosure index (0–10)	6	Documentary compliance (hours)	132
Time (days)	652	Extent of director liability index (0–10)	10	Border compliance (hours)	8
Cost (% of warehouse value)	5.3	Ease of shareholder suits index (0–10)	4	*Cost to import*	
Building quality control index (0–15)	8.0	Extent of shareholder rights index (0–10)	1	Documentary compliance (US$)	120
		Extent of ownership and control index (0–10)	3	Border compliance (US$)	240
		Extent of corporate transparency index (0–10)	6		
Getting electricity (rank)	137			**Enforcing contracts** (rank)	179
DTF score for getting electricity (0–100)	56.56			DTF score for enforcing contracts (0–100)	32.67
Procedures (number)	4	**Paying taxes** (rank)	136	Time (days)	483
Time (days)	179	DTF score for paying taxes (0–100)	61.28	Cost (% of claim)	103.4
Cost (% of income per capita)	1,993.2	Payments (number per year)	40	Quality of judicial processes index (0–18)	5.0
Reliability of supply and transparency of tariffs index (0–8)	3	Time (hours per year)	173		
		Total tax and contribution rate (% of profit)	21.7		
Registering property (rank)	123	Postfiling index (0–100)	25.97	**Resolving insolvency** (rank)	74
DTF score for registering property (0–100)	55.00			DTF score for resolving insolvency (0–100)	48.25
Procedures (number)	7			Time (years)	6.0
Time (days)	56			Cost (% of estate)	18.0
Cost (% of property value)	4.3			Recovery rate (cents on the dollar)	14.2
Quality of land administration index (0–30)	7.5			Strength of insolvency framework index (0–16)	13.0

Note: Most indicator sets refer to a case scenario in the largest business city of an economy, though for 11 economies the data are a population-weighted average for the two largest business cities. For some indicators a result of "no practice" may be recorded for an economy; see the data notes for more details. In starting a business, procedures (number), time (days) and cost (% of income per capita) are calculated as the average of both men and women. For the postfiling index, a result of "not applicable" may be recorded for an economy.

✔ Reform making it easier to do business ✘ Change making it more difficult to do business

CAMEROON

CAMEROON		Sub-Saharan Africa		GNI per capita (US$)	1,200
Ease of doing business rank (1–190)	163	Overall distance to frontier (DTF) score (0–100)	47.23	Population	23,439,189

✔ **Starting a business** (rank)	122	**Getting credit** (rank)	68	**Trading across borders** (rank)	186
DTF score for starting a business (0–100)	82.39	DTF score for getting credit (0–100)	60.00	DTF score for trading across borders (0–100)	15.99
Procedures (number)	6.5	Strength of legal rights index (0–12)	6	*Time to export*	
Time (days)	16.5	Depth of credit information index (0–8)	6	Documentary compliance (hours)	66
Cost (% of income per capita)	35.7	Credit bureau coverage (% of adults)	0.0	Border compliance (hours)	202
Minimum capital (% of income per capita)	16.6	Credit registry coverage (% of adults)	8.0	*Cost to export*	
				Documentary compliance (US$)	306
Dealing with construction permits (rank)	140	**Protecting minority investors** (rank)	138	Border compliance (US$)	983
DTF score for dealing with construction permits (0–100)	59.74	DTF score for protecting minority investors (0–100)	41.67	*Time to import*	
Procedures (number)	15	Extent of disclosure index (0–10)	7	Documentary compliance (hours)	163
Time (days)	135	Extent of director liability index (0–10)	1	Border compliance (hours)	271
Cost (% of warehouse value)	15.3	Ease of shareholder suits index (0–10)	6	*Cost to import*	
Building quality control index (0–15)	13.0	Extent of shareholder rights index (0–10)	4	Documentary compliance (US$)	849
		Extent of ownership and control index (0–10)	3	Border compliance (US$)	1,407
		Extent of corporate transparency index (0–10)	4		
Getting electricity (rank)	121			**Enforcing contracts** (rank)	162
DTF score for getting electricity (0–100)	60.35			DTF score for enforcing contracts (0–100)	41.76
Procedures (number)	4	**Paying taxes** (rank)	183	Time (days)	800
Time (days)	64	DTF score for paying taxes (0–100)	36.34	Cost (% of claim)	46.6
Cost (% of income per capita)	1,776.9	Payments (number per year)	44	Quality of judicial processes index (0–18)	6.0
Reliability of supply and transparency of tariffs index (0–8)	0	Time (hours per year)	624		
		Total tax and contribution rate (% of profit)	57.7		
Registering property (rank)	176	Postfiling index (0–100)	49.31	**Resolving insolvency** (rank)	125
DTF score for registering property (0–100)	37.33			DTF score for resolving insolvency (0–100)	36.73
Procedures (number)	5			Time (years)	2.8
Time (days)	86			Cost (% of estate)	33.5
Cost (% of property value)	19.0			Recovery rate (cents on the dollar)	16.0
Quality of land administration index (0–30)	7.0			Strength of insolvency framework index (0–16)	7.0

CANADA

CANADA		OECD high income		GNI per capita (US$)	43,660
Ease of doing business rank (1–190)	18	Overall distance to frontier (DTF) score (0–100)	79.29	Population	36,286,425

Starting a business (rank)	2	**Getting credit** (rank)	12	**Trading across borders** (rank)	46
DTF score for starting a business (0–100)	98.23	DTF score for getting credit (0–100)	85.00	DTF score for trading across borders (0–100)	88.36
Procedures (number)	2	Strength of legal rights index (0–12)	9	*Time to export*	
Time (days)	1.5	Depth of credit information index (0–8)	8	Documentary compliance (hours)	1
Cost (% of income per capita)	0.4	Credit bureau coverage (% of adults)	100.0	Border compliance (hours)	2
Minimum capital (% of income per capita)	0.0	Credit registry coverage (% of adults)	0.0	*Cost to export*	
				Documentary compliance (US$)	156
✘ **Dealing with construction permits** (rank)	54	**Protecting minority investors** (rank)	8	Border compliance (US$)	167
DTF score for dealing with construction permits (0–100)	72.87	DTF score for protecting minority investors (0–100)	78.33	*Time to import*	
Procedures (number)	12	Extent of disclosure index (0–10)	8	Documentary compliance (hours)	1
Time (days)	249	Extent of director liability index (0–10)	9	Border compliance (hours)	2
Cost (% of warehouse value)	1.9	Ease of shareholder suits index (0–10)	9	*Cost to import*	
Building quality control index (0–15)	14.0	Extent of shareholder rights index (0–10)	6	Documentary compliance (US$)	163
		Extent of ownership and control index (0–10)	7	Border compliance (US$)	172
		Extent of corporate transparency index (0–10)	8		
Getting electricity (rank)	105			**Enforcing contracts** (rank)	114
DTF score for getting electricity (0–100)	66.89			DTF score for enforcing contracts (0–100)	54.35
Procedures (number)	7	**Paying taxes** (rank)	16	Time (days)	910
Time (days)	137	DTF score for paying taxes (0–100)	88.05	Cost (% of claim)	22.3
Cost (% of income per capita)	125.3	Payments (number per year)	8	Quality of judicial processes index (0–18)	9.5
Reliability of supply and transparency of tariffs index (0–8)	7	Time (hours per year)	131		
		Total tax and contribution rate (% of profit)	20.9		
Registering property (rank)	33	Postfiling index (0–100)	73.23	**Resolving insolvency** (rank)	11
DTF score for registering property (0–100)	79.31			DTF score for resolving insolvency (0–100)	81.46
Procedures (number)	5			Time (years)	0.8
Time (days)	4			Cost (% of estate)	7.0
Cost (% of property value)	2.9			Recovery rate (cents on the dollar)	87.5
Quality of land administration index (0–30)	21.5			Strength of insolvency framework index (0–16)	11.0

CENTRAL AFRICAN REPUBLIC

CENTRAL AFRICAN REPUBLIC		Sub-Saharan Africa		GNI per capita (US$)	370
Ease of doing business rank (1–190)	184	Overall distance to frontier (DTF) score (0–100)	34.86	Population	4,594,621

Starting a business (rank)	188	**Getting credit** (rank)	142	**Trading across borders** (rank)	145
DTF score for starting a business (0–100)	37.02	DTF score for getting credit (0–100)	30.00	DTF score for trading across borders (0–100)	58.64
Procedures (number)	10	Strength of legal rights index (0–12)	6	*Time to export*	
Time (days)	22	Depth of credit information index (0–8)	0	Documentary compliance (hours)	48
Cost (% of income per capita)	154.7	Credit bureau coverage (% of adults)	0.0	Border compliance (hours)	141
Minimum capital (% of income per capita)	446.7	Credit registry coverage (% of adults)	3.3	*Cost to export*	
				Documentary compliance (US$)	60
Dealing with construction permits (rank)	180	**Protecting minority investors** (rank)	146	Border compliance (US$)	280
DTF score for dealing with construction permits (0–100)	38.86	DTF score for protecting minority investors (0–100)	40.00	*Time to import*	
Procedures (number)	16	Extent of disclosure index (0–10)	7	Documentary compliance (hours)	120
Time (days)	219	Extent of director liability index (0–10)	1	Border compliance (hours)	98
Cost (% of warehouse value)	17.0	Ease of shareholder suits index (0–10)	5	*Cost to import*	
Building quality control index (0–15)	6.0	Extent of shareholder rights index (0–10)	4	Documentary compliance (US$)	500
		Extent of ownership and control index (0–10)	3	Border compliance (US$)	209
		Extent of corporate transparency index (0–10)	4		
Getting electricity (rank)	183			**Enforcing contracts** (rank)	182
DTF score for getting electricity (0–100)	24.64			DTF score for enforcing contracts (0–100)	30.46
Procedures (number)	7	**Paying taxes** (rank)	187	Time (days)	660
Time (days)	98	DTF score for paying taxes (0–100)	18.89	Cost (% of claim)	82.0
Cost (% of income per capita)	12,688.1	Payments (number per year)	56	Quality of judicial processes index (0–18)	5.0
Reliability of supply and transparency of tariffs index (0–8)	0	Time (hours per year)	483		
		Total tax and contribution rate (% of profit)	73.3		
Registering property (rank)	169	Postfiling index (0–100)	5.13	**Resolving insolvency** (rank)	150
DTF score for registering property (0–100)	41.92			DTF score for resolving insolvency (0–100)	28.13
Procedures (number)	5			Time (years)	4.8
Time (days)	75			Cost (% of estate)	76.0
Cost (% of property value)	11.0			Recovery rate (cents on the dollar)	0.0
Quality of land administration index (0–30)	3.0			Strength of insolvency framework index (0–16)	9.0

Note: Most indicator sets refer to a case scenario in the largest business city of an economy, though for 11 economies the data are a population-weighted average for the two largest business cities. For some indicators a result of "no practice" may be recorded for an economy; see the data notes for more details. In starting a business, procedures (number), time (days) and cost (% of income per capita) are calculated as the average of both men and women. For the postfiling index, a result of "not applicable" may be recorded for an economy.

✔ Reform making it easier to do business ✘ Change making it more difficult to do business

CHAD — Sub-Saharan Africa

Ease of doing business rank (1–190)	180	**Overall distance to frontier (DTF) score (0–100)**	38.30	**GNI per capita (US$)**	720
				Population	14,452,543

Starting a business (rank)	185	**Getting credit** (rank)	142	**Trading across borders** (rank)	172
DTF score for starting a business (0–100)	50.26	DTF score for getting credit (0–100)	30.00	DTF score for trading across borders (0–100)	40.12
Procedures (number)	9	Strength of legal rights index (0–12)	6	*Time to export*	
Time (days)	60	Depth of credit information index (0–8)	0	Documentary compliance (hours)	87
Cost (% of income per capita)	171.3	Credit bureau coverage (% of adults)	0.0	Border compliance (hours)	106
Minimum capital (% of income per capita)	25.8	Credit registry coverage (% of adults)	2.4	*Cost to export*	
				Documentary compliance (US$)	188
Dealing with construction permits (rank)	153	**Protecting minority investors** (rank)	160	Border compliance (US$)	319
DTF score for dealing with construction permits (0–100)	56.79	DTF score for protecting minority investors (0–100)	38.33	*Time to import*	
Procedures (number)	13	Extent of disclosure index (0–10)	7	Documentary compliance (hours)	172
Time (days)	226	Extent of director liability index (0–10)	1	Border compliance (hours)	242
Cost (% of warehouse value)	12.0	Ease of shareholder suits index (0–10)	4	*Cost to import*	
Building quality control index (0–15)	11.5	Extent of shareholder rights index (0–10)	4	Documentary compliance (US$)	500
		Extent of ownership and control index (0–10)	3	Border compliance (US$)	669
Getting electricity (rank)	177	Extent of corporate transparency index (0–10)	4		
DTF score for getting electricity (0–100)	32.17			**Enforcing contracts** (rank)	154
Procedures (number)	6	**Paying taxes** (rank)	188	DTF score for enforcing contracts (0–100)	44.58
Time (days)	67	DTF score for paying taxes (0–100)	17.92	Time (days)	743
Cost (% of income per capita)	9,821.1	Payments (number per year)	54	Cost (% of claim)	45.7
Reliability of supply and transparency of tariffs index (0–8)	0	Time (hours per year)	766	Quality of judicial processes index (0–18)	6.5
		Total tax and contribution rate (% of profit)	63.5		
		Postfiling index (0–100)	13.07	**Resolving insolvency** (rank)	150
Registering property (rank)	159			DTF score for resolving insolvency (0–100)	28.13
DTF score for registering property (0–100)	44.67			Time (years)	4.0
Procedures (number)	6			Cost (% of estate)	60.0
Time (days)	44			Recovery rate (cents on the dollar)	0.0
Cost (% of property value)	12.9			Strength of insolvency framework index (0–16)	9.0
Quality of land administration index (0–30)	8.0				

CHILE — OECD high income

Ease of doing business rank (1–190)	55	**Overall distance to frontier (DTF) score (0–100)**	71.22	**GNI per capita (US$)**	13,530
				Population	17,909,754

Starting a business (rank)	65	**Getting credit** (rank)	90	**Trading across borders** (rank)	68
DTF score for starting a business (0–100)	89.55	DTF score for getting credit (0–100)	50.00	DTF score for trading across borders (0–100)	80.56
Procedures (number)	7	Strength of legal rights index (0–12)	4	*Time to export*	
Time (days)	5.5	Depth of credit information index (0–8)	6	Documentary compliance (hours)	24
Cost (% of income per capita)	3.0	Credit bureau coverage (% of adults)	14.3	Border compliance (hours)	60
Minimum capital (% of income per capita)	0.0	Credit registry coverage (% of adults)	49.5	*Cost to export*	
				Documentary compliance (US$)	50
Dealing with construction permits (rank)	15	**Protecting minority investors** (rank)	57	Border compliance (US$)	290
DTF score for dealing with construction permits (0–100)	80.28	DTF score for protecting minority investors (0–100)	60.00	*Time to import*	
Procedures (number)	12	Extent of disclosure index (0–10)	8	Documentary compliance (hours)	36
Time (days)	133	Extent of director liability index (0–10)	6	Border compliance (hours)	54
Cost (% of warehouse value)	1.3	Ease of shareholder suits index (0–10)	7	*Cost to import*	
Building quality control index (0–15)	13.0	Extent of shareholder rights index (0–10)	9	Documentary compliance (US$)	50
		Extent of ownership and control index (0–10)	4	Border compliance (US$)	290
Getting electricity (rank)	44	Extent of corporate transparency index (0–10)	2		
DTF score for getting electricity (0–100)	82.49			**Enforcing contracts** (rank)	56
Procedures (number)	5	**Paying taxes** (rank)	72	DTF score for enforcing contracts (0–100)	62.81
Time (days)	43	DTF score for paying taxes (0–100)	76.17	Time (days)	480
Cost (% of income per capita)	68.1	Payments (number per year)	7	Cost (% of claim)	28.6
Reliability of supply and transparency of tariffs index (0–8)	6	Time (hours per year)	291	Quality of judicial processes index (0–18)	9.0
		Total tax and contribution rate (% of profit)	33.0		
		Postfiling index (0–100)	58.36	**Resolving insolvency** (rank)	52
Registering property (rank)	61			DTF score for resolving insolvency (0–100)	59.47
DTF score for registering property (0–100)	70.90			Time (years)	2.0
Procedures (number)	6			Cost (% of estate)	14.5
Time (days)	28.5			Recovery rate (cents on the dollar)	40.8
Cost (% of property value)	1.2			Strength of insolvency framework index (0–16)	12.0
Quality of land administration index (0–30)	14.0				

CHINA — East Asia & Pacific

Ease of doing business rank (1–190)	78	**Overall distance to frontier (DTF) score (0–100)**	65.29	**GNI per capita (US$)**	8,260
				Population	1,378,665,000

✔ **Starting a business** (rank)	93	**Getting credit** (rank)	68	**Trading across borders** (rank)	97
DTF score for starting a business (0–100)	85.47	DTF score for getting credit (0–100)	60.00	DTF score for trading across borders (0–100)	69.91
Procedures (number)	7	Strength of legal rights index (0–12)	4	*Time to export*	
Time (days)	22.9	Depth of credit information index (0–8)	8	Documentary compliance (hours)	21.2
Cost (% of income per capita)	0.6	Credit bureau coverage (% of adults)	21.4	Border compliance (hours)	25.9
Minimum capital (% of income per capita)	0.0	Credit registry coverage (% of adults)	95.3	*Cost to export*	
				Documentary compliance (US$)	84.6
Dealing with construction permits (rank)	172	**Protecting minority investors** (rank)	119	Border compliance (US$)	484.1
DTF score for dealing with construction permits (0–100)	47.28	DTF score for protecting minority investors (0–100)	48.33	*Time to import*	
Procedures (number)	23	Extent of disclosure index (0–10)	10	Documentary compliance (hours)	65.7
Time (days)	247.1	Extent of director liability index (0–10)	1	Border compliance (hours)	92.3
Cost (% of warehouse value)	7.8	Ease of shareholder suits index (0–10)	4	*Cost to import*	
Building quality control index (0–15)	9.6	Extent of shareholder rights index (0–10)	3	Documentary compliance (US$)	170.9
		Extent of ownership and control index (0–10)	2	Border compliance (US$)	745
Getting electricity (rank)	98	Extent of corporate transparency index (0–10)	9		
DTF score for getting electricity (0–100)	68.83			**Enforcing contracts** (rank)	5
Procedures (number)	5.5	✔ **Paying taxes** (rank)	130	DTF score for enforcing contracts (0–100)	78.23
Time (days)	143.2	DTF score for paying taxes (0–100)	62.90	Time (days)	496
Cost (% of income per capita)	356.0	Payments (number per year)	9	Cost (% of claim)	16.2
Reliability of supply and transparency of tariffs index (0–8)	6	Time (hours per year)	207	Quality of judicial processes index (0–18)	15.1
		Total tax and contribution rate (% of profit)	67.3		
		Postfiling index (0–100)	49.08	**Resolving insolvency** (rank)	56
Registering property (rank)	41			DTF score for resolving insolvency (0–100)	55.82
DTF score for registering property (0–100)	76.15			Time (years)	1.7
Procedures (number)	4			Cost (% of estate)	22.0
Time (days)	19.5			Recovery rate (cents on the dollar)	36.9
Cost (% of property value)	3.4			Strength of insolvency framework index (0–16)	11.5
Quality of land administration index (0–30)	18.3				

Note: Most indicator sets refer to a case scenario in the largest business city of an economy, though for 11 economies the data are a population-weighted average for the two largest business cities. For some indicators a result of "no practice" may be recorded for an economy; see the data notes for more details. In starting a business, procedures (number), time (days) and cost (% of income per capita) are calculated as the average of both men and women. For the postfiling index, a result of "not applicable" may be recorded for an economy.

✔ Reform making it easier to do business ✘ Change making it more difficult to do business

COLOMBIA

		Latin America & Caribbean		GNI per capita (US$)	6,320
Ease of doing business rank (1–190)	59	Overall distance to frontier (DTF) score (0–100)	69.41	Population	48,653,419

Starting a business (rank)	96	Getting credit (rank)	2	Trading across borders (rank)	125
DTF score for starting a business (0–100)	85.32	DTF score for getting credit (0–100)	95.00	DTF score for trading across borders (0–100)	62.83
Procedures (number)	8	Strength of legal rights index (0–12)	12	Time to export	
Time (days)	11	Depth of credit information index (0–8)	7	Documentary compliance (hours)	60
Cost (% of income per capita)	14.0	Credit bureau coverage (% of adults)	94.5	Border compliance (hours)	112
Minimum capital (% of income per capita)	0.0	Credit registry coverage (% of adults)	0.0	Cost to export	
				Documentary compliance (US$)	90
Dealing with construction permits (rank)	81	Protecting minority investors (rank)	16	Border compliance (US$)	545
DTF score for dealing with construction permits (0–100)	68.71	DTF score for protecting minority investors (0–100)	73.33	Time to import	
Procedures (number)	13	Extent of disclosure index (0–10)	9	Documentary compliance (hours)	64
Time (days)	132	Extent of director liability index (0–10)	7	Border compliance (hours)	112
Cost (% of warehouse value)	7.2	Ease of shareholder suits index (0–10)	8	Cost to import	
Building quality control index (0–15)	11.0	Extent of shareholder rights index (0–10)	6	Documentary compliance (US$)	50
		Extent of ownership and control index (0–10)	8	Border compliance (US$)	545
Getting electricity (rank)	81	Extent of corporate transparency index (0–10)	6		
DTF score for getting electricity (0–100)	74.18			Enforcing contracts (rank)	177
Procedures (number)	5			DTF score for enforcing contracts (0–100)	34.29
Time (days)	106	Paying taxes (rank)	142	Time (days)	1,288
Cost (% of income per capita)	542.3	DTF score for paying taxes (0–100)	59.08	Cost (% of claim)	45.8
Reliability of supply and transparency of tariffs index (0–8)	6	Payments (number per year)	12	Quality of judicial processes index (0–18)	9.0
		Time (hours per year)	239		
		Total tax and contribution rate (% of profit)	69.8		
Registering property (rank)	60	Postfiling index (0–100)	48.17	Resolving insolvency (rank)	33
DTF score for registering property (0–100)	71.34			DTF score for resolving insolvency (0–100)	70.02
Procedures (number)	7			Time (years)	1.7
Time (days)	15			Cost (% of estate)	8.5
Cost (% of property value)	1.9			Recovery rate (cents on the dollar)	66.2
Quality of land administration index (0–30)	16.5			Strength of insolvency framework index (0–16)	11.0

COMOROS

		Sub-Saharan Africa		GNI per capita (US$)	760
Ease of doing business rank (1–190)	158	Overall distance to frontier (DTF) score (0–100)	48.52	Population	795,601

Starting a business (rank)	166	Getting credit (rank)	122	✔ Trading across borders (rank)	111
DTF score for starting a business (0–100)	72.01	DTF score for getting credit (0–100)	40.00	DTF score for trading across borders (0–100)	66.87
Procedures (number)	9	Strength of legal rights index (0–12)	6	Time to export	
Time (days)	16	Depth of credit information index (0–8)	2	Documentary compliance (hours)	50
Cost (% of income per capita)	84.1	Credit bureau coverage (% of adults)	0.0	Border compliance (hours)	51
Minimum capital (% of income per capita)	29.1	Credit registry coverage (% of adults)	9.8	Cost to export	
				Documentary compliance (US$)	124
Dealing with construction permits (rank)	79	Protecting minority investors (rank)	146	Border compliance (US$)	651
DTF score for dealing with construction permits (0–100)	69.19	DTF score for protecting minority investors (0–100)	40.00	Time to import	
Procedures (number)	10	Extent of disclosure index (0–10)	7	Documentary compliance (hours)	26
Time (days)	108	Extent of director liability index (0–10)	1	Border compliance (hours)	70
Cost (% of warehouse value)	1.3	Ease of shareholder suits index (0–10)	5	Cost to import	
Building quality control index (0–15)	4.0	Extent of shareholder rights index (0–10)	4	Documentary compliance (US$)	93
		Extent of ownership and control index (0–10)	3	Border compliance (US$)	765
Getting electricity (rank)	135	Extent of corporate transparency index (0–10)	4		
DTF score for getting electricity (0–100)	57.58			Enforcing contracts (rank)	180
Procedures (number)	3			DTF score for enforcing contracts (0–100)	32.05
Time (days)	120	Paying taxes (rank)	168	Time (days)	506
Cost (% of income per capita)	2,050.5	DTF score for paying taxes (0–100)	49.86	Cost (% of claim)	89.4
Reliability of supply and transparency of tariffs index (0–8)	0	Payments (number per year)	33	Quality of judicial processes index (0–18)	5.0
		Time (hours per year)	100		
		Total tax and contribution rate (% of profit)	216.5		
Registering property (rank)	111	Postfiling index (0–100)	57.33	Resolving insolvency (rank)	168
DTF score for registering property (0–100)	57.66			DTF score for resolving insolvency (0–100)	0.00
Procedures (number)	4			Time (years)	no practice
Time (days)	30			Cost (% of estate)	no practice
Cost (% of property value)	8.1			Recovery rate (cents on the dollar)	0.0
Quality of land administration index (0–30)	7.0			Strength of insolvency framework index (0–16)	0.0

CONGO, DEM. REP.

		Sub-Saharan Africa		GNI per capita (US$)	420
Ease of doing business rank (1–190)	182	Overall distance to frontier (DTF) score (0–100)	37.65	Population	78,736,153

✔ Starting a business (rank)	62	Getting credit (rank)	142	Trading across borders (rank)	188
DTF score for starting a business (0–100)	89.78	DTF score for getting credit (0–100)	30.00	DTF score for trading across borders (0–100)	1.26
Procedures (number)	4	Strength of legal rights index (0–12)	6	Time to export	
Time (days)	7	Depth of credit information index (0–8)	0	Documentary compliance (hours)	698
Cost (% of income per capita)	28.6	Credit bureau coverage (% of adults)	0.0	Border compliance (hours)	515
Minimum capital (% of income per capita)	9.7	Credit registry coverage (% of adults)	0.7	Cost to export	
				Documentary compliance (US$)	2,500
✘ Dealing with construction permits (rank)	121	Protecting minority investors (rank)	164	Border compliance (US$)	2,223
DTF score for dealing with construction permits (0–100)	63.91	DTF score for protecting minority investors (0–100)	36.67	Time to import	
Procedures (number)	12	Extent of disclosure index (0–10)	7	Documentary compliance (hours)	216
Time (days)	122	Extent of director liability index (0–10)	1	Border compliance (hours)	588
Cost (% of warehouse value)	8.4	Ease of shareholder suits index (0–10)	3	Cost to import	
Building quality control index (0–15)	8.0	Extent of shareholder rights index (0–10)	4	Documentary compliance (US$)	875
		Extent of ownership and control index (0–10)	3	Border compliance (US$)	3,039
Getting electricity (rank)	175	Extent of corporate transparency index (0–10)	4		
DTF score for getting electricity (0–100)	33.59			Enforcing contracts (rank)	172
Procedures (number)	6			DTF score for enforcing contracts (0–100)	36.06
Time (days)	54	Paying taxes (rank)	181	Time (days)	610
Cost (% of income per capita)	14,885.8	DTF score for paying taxes (0–100)	39.40	Cost (% of claim)	80.6
Reliability of supply and transparency of tariffs index (0–8)	0	Payments (number per year)	52	Quality of judicial processes index (0–18)	7.0
		Time (hours per year)	346		
		Total tax and contribution rate (% of profit)	54.6		
Registering property (rank)	158	Postfiling index (0–100)	27.08	Resolving insolvency (rank)	168
DTF score for registering property (0–100)	45.85			DTF score for resolving insolvency (0–100)	0.00
Procedures (number)	8			Time (years)	no practice
Time (days)	38			Cost (% of estate)	no practice
Cost (% of property value)	11.1			Recovery rate (cents on the dollar)	0.0
Quality of land administration index (0–30)	10.0			Strength of insolvency framework index (0–16)	0.0

Note: Most indicator sets refer to a case scenario in the largest business city of an economy, though for 11 economies the data are a population-weighted average for the two largest business cities. For some indicators a result of "no practice" may be recorded for an economy; see the data notes for more details. In starting a business, procedures (number), time (days) and cost (% of income per capita) are calculated as the average of both men and women. For the postfiling index, a result of "not applicable" may be recorded for an economy.

✔ Reform making it easier to do business   ✘ Change making it more difficult to do business

CONGO, REP. — Sub-Saharan Africa — GNI per capita (US$) 1,710

Ease of doing business rank (1–190)	179	Overall distance to frontier (DTF) score (0–100)	39.57	Population	5,125,821

✔ **Starting a business** (rank) — 177
- DTF score for starting a business (0–100) — 64.69
- Procedures (number) — 10
- Time (days) — 49
- Cost (% of income per capita) — 77.7
- Minimum capital (% of income per capita) — 2.9

Dealing with construction permits (rank) — 125
- DTF score for dealing with construction permits (0–100) — 63.07
- Procedures (number) — 12
- Time (days) — 164
- Cost (% of warehouse value) — 8.0
- Building quality control index (0–15) — 9.0

Getting electricity (rank) — 181
- DTF score for getting electricity (0–100) — 28.42
- Procedures (number) — 6
- Time (days) — 134
- Cost (% of income per capita) — 6,957.7
- Reliability of supply and transparency of tariffs index (0–8) — 0

Registering property (rank) — 177
- DTF score for registering property (0–100) — 36.04
- Procedures (number) — 6
- Time (days) — 55
- Cost (% of property value) — 16.1
- Quality of land administration index (0–30) — 3.5

Getting credit (rank) — 133
- DTF score for getting credit (0–100) — 35.00
- Strength of legal rights index (0–12) — 6
- Depth of credit information index (0–8) — 1
- Credit bureau coverage (% of adults) — 0.0
- Credit registry coverage (% of adults) — 11.9

Protecting minority investors (rank) — 146
- DTF score for protecting minority investors (0–100) — 40.00
- Extent of disclosure index (0–10) — 7
- Extent of director liability index (0–10) — 1
- Ease of shareholder suits index (0–10) — 5
- Extent of shareholder rights index (0–10) — 4
- Extent of ownership and control index (0–10) — 3
- Extent of corporate transparency index (0–10) — 4

Paying taxes (rank) — 185
- DTF score for paying taxes (0–100) — 26.79
- Payments (number per year) — 50
- Time (hours per year) — 602
- Total tax and contribution rate (% of profit) — 54.3
- Postfiling index (0–100) — 12.29

Trading across borders (rank) — 184
- DTF score for trading across borders (0–100) — 19.68
- *Time to export*
- Documentary compliance (hours) — 120
- Border compliance (hours) — 276
- *Cost to export*
- Documentary compliance (US$) — 165
- Border compliance (US$) — 1,975
- *Time to import*
- Documentary compliance (hours) — 208
- Border compliance (hours) — 397
- *Cost to import*
- Documentary compliance (US$) — 310
- Border compliance (US$) — 1,581

Enforcing contracts (rank) — 155
- DTF score for enforcing contracts (0–100) — 43.99
- Time (days) — 560
- Cost (% of claim) — 53.2
- Quality of judicial processes index (0–18) — 5.0

Resolving insolvency (rank) — 118
- DTF score for resolving insolvency (0–100) — 37.98
- Time (years) — 3.3
- Cost (% of estate) — 25.0
- Recovery rate (cents on the dollar) — 18.3
- Strength of insolvency framework index (0–16) — 9.0

COSTA RICA — Latin America & Caribbean — GNI per capita (US$) 10,840

Ease of doing business rank (1–190)	61	Overall distance to frontier (DTF) score (0–100)	69.13	Population	4,857,274

Starting a business (rank) — 127
- DTF score for starting a business (0–100) — 81.65
- Procedures (number) — 9
- Time (days) — 22.5
- Cost (% of income per capita) — 8.5
- Minimum capital (% of income per capita) — 0.0

Dealing with construction permits (rank) — 70
- DTF score for dealing with construction permits (0–100) — 71.02
- Procedures (number) — 17
- Time (days) — 135
- Cost (% of warehouse value) — 2.0
- Building quality control index (0–15) — 11.0

Getting electricity (rank) — 21
- DTF score for getting electricity (0–100) — 88.21
- Procedures (number) — 5
- Time (days) — 45
- Cost (% of income per capita) — 168.1
- Reliability of supply and transparency of tariffs index (0–8) — 8

✔ **Registering property** (rank) — 49
- DTF score for registering property (0–100) — 74.36
- Procedures (number) — 5
- Time (days) — 11
- Cost (% of property value) — 3.4
- Quality of land administration index (0–30) — 17.5

Getting credit (rank) — 12
- DTF score for getting credit (0–100) — 85.00
- Strength of legal rights index (0–12) — 10
- Depth of credit information index (0–8) — 7
- Credit bureau coverage (% of adults) — 100.0
- Credit registry coverage (% of adults) — 32.2

✔ **Protecting minority investors** (rank) — 119
- DTF score for protecting minority investors (0–100) — 48.33
- Extent of disclosure index (0–10) — 5
- Extent of director liability index (0–10) — 5
- Ease of shareholder suits index (0–10) — 8
- Extent of shareholder rights index (0–10) — 4
- Extent of ownership and control index (0–10) — 4
- Extent of corporate transparency index (0–10) — 3

Paying taxes (rank) — 60
- DTF score for paying taxes (0–100) — 77.46
- Payments (number per year) — 10
- Time (hours per year) — 151
- Total tax and contribution rate (% of profit) — 58.3
- Postfiling index (0–100) — 85.06

Trading across borders (rank) — 73
- DTF score for trading across borders (0–100) — 79.32
- *Time to export*
- Documentary compliance (hours) — 24
- Border compliance (hours) — 20
- *Cost to export*
- Documentary compliance (US$) — 80
- Border compliance (US$) — 375
- *Time to import*
- Documentary compliance (hours) — 26
- Border compliance (hours) — 80
- *Cost to import*
- Documentary compliance (US$) — 75
- Border compliance (US$) — 420

Enforcing contracts (rank) — 129
- DTF score for enforcing contracts (0–100) — 51.48
- Time (days) — 852
- Cost (% of claim) — 24.3
- Quality of judicial processes index (0–18) — 7.5

Resolving insolvency (rank) — 131
- DTF score for resolving insolvency (0–100) — 34.42
- Time (years) — 3.0
- Cost (% of estate) — 14.5
- Recovery rate (cents on the dollar) — 29.1
- Strength of insolvency framework index (0–16) — 6.0

CÔTE D'IVOIRE — Sub-Saharan Africa — GNI per capita (US$) 1,520

Ease of doing business rank (1–190)	139	Overall distance to frontier (DTF) score (0–100)	53.71	Population	23,695,919

Starting a business (rank) — 44
- DTF score for starting a business (0–100) — 91.72
- Procedures (number) — 4
- Time (days) — 7
- Cost (% of income per capita) — 16.5
- Minimum capital (% of income per capita) — 2.8

✔ **Dealing with construction permits** (rank) — 152
- DTF score for dealing with construction permits (0–100) — 57.50
- Procedures (number) — 21
- Time (days) — 162
- Cost (% of warehouse value) — 5.4
- Building quality control index (0–15) — 9.0

Getting electricity (rank) — 129
- DTF score for getting electricity (0–100) — 58.73
- Procedures (number) — 8
- Time (days) — 55
- Cost (% of income per capita) — 2,280.8
- Reliability of supply and transparency of tariffs index (0–8) — 5

Registering property (rank) — 113
- DTF score for registering property (0–100) — 57.56
- Procedures (number) — 6
- Time (days) — 30
- Cost (% of property value) — 7.4
- Quality of land administration index (0–30) — 10.5

Getting credit (rank) — 142
- DTF score for getting credit (0–100) — 30.00
- Strength of legal rights index (0–12) — 6
- Depth of credit information index (0–8) — 0
- Credit bureau coverage (% of adults) — 4.0
- Credit registry coverage (% of adults) — 0.3

Protecting minority investors (rank) — 146
- DTF score for protecting minority investors (0–100) — 40.00
- Extent of disclosure index (0–10) — 7
- Extent of director liability index (0–10) — 1
- Ease of shareholder suits index (0–10) — 5
- Extent of shareholder rights index (0–10) — 4
- Extent of ownership and control index (0–10) — 3
- Extent of corporate transparency index (0–10) — 4

Paying taxes (rank) — 175
- DTF score for paying taxes (0–100) — 43.88
- Payments (number per year) — 63
- Time (hours per year) — 270
- Total tax and contribution rate (% of profit) — 50.1
- Postfiling index (0–100) — 44.50

Trading across borders (rank) — 155
- DTF score for trading across borders (0–100) — 54.15
- *Time to export*
- Documentary compliance (hours) — 120
- Border compliance (hours) — 110
- *Cost to export*
- Documentary compliance (US$) — 136
- Border compliance (US$) — 387
- *Time to import*
- Documentary compliance (hours) — 89
- Border compliance (hours) — 125
- *Cost to import*
- Documentary compliance (US$) — 267
- Border compliance (US$) — 456

Enforcing contracts (rank) — 101
- DTF score for enforcing contracts (0–100) — 55.74
- Time (days) — 525
- Cost (% of claim) — 41.7
- Quality of judicial processes index (0–18) — 8.5

Resolving insolvency (rank) — 77
- DTF score for resolving insolvency (0–100) — 47.81
- Time (years) — 2.2
- Cost (% of estate) — 18.0
- Recovery rate (cents on the dollar) — 36.6
- Strength of insolvency framework index (0–16) — 9.0

Note: Most indicator sets refer to a case scenario in the largest business city of an economy, though for 11 economies the data are a population-weighted average for the two largest business cities. For some indicators a result of "no practice" may be recorded for an economy; see the data notes for more details. In starting a business, procedures (number), time (days) and cost (% of income per capita) are calculated as the average of both men and women. For the postfiling index, a result of "not applicable" may be recorded for an economy.

CROATIA

CROATIA		Europe & Central Asia		GNI per capita (US$)	12,110
Ease of doing business rank (1–190)	51	Overall distance to frontier (DTF) score (0–100)	71.70	Population	4,170,600

Starting a business (rank)	87	**Getting credit** (rank)	77	**Trading across borders** (rank)	1
DTF score for starting a business (0–100)	86.39	DTF score for getting credit (0–100)	55.00	DTF score for trading across borders (0–100)	100.00
Procedures (number)	8	Strength of legal rights index (0–12)	5	*Time to export*	
Time (days)	7	Depth of credit information index (0–8)	6	Documentary compliance (hours)	1
Cost (% of income per capita)	7.2	Credit bureau coverage (% of adults)	100.0	Border compliance (hours)	0
Minimum capital (% of income per capita)	12.5	Credit registry coverage (% of adults)	0.0	*Cost to export*	
				Documentary compliance (US$)	0
✘ **Dealing with construction permits** (rank)	126	**Protecting minority investors** (rank)	29	Border compliance (US$)	0
DTF score for dealing with construction permits (0–100)	63.00	DTF score for protecting minority investors (0–100)	68.33	*Time to import*	
Procedures (number)	18	Extent of disclosure index (0–10)	5	Documentary compliance (hours)	1
Time (days)	126	Extent of director liability index (0–10)	6	Border compliance (hours)	0
Cost (% of warehouse value)	9.4	Ease of shareholder suits index (0–10)	6	*Cost to import*	
Building quality control index (0–15)	12.0	Extent of shareholder rights index (0–10)	8	Documentary compliance (US$)	0
		Extent of ownership and control index (0–10)	9	Border compliance (US$)	0
Getting electricity (rank)	75	Extent of corporate transparency index (0–10)	7		
DTF score for getting electricity (0–100)	76.26			**Enforcing contracts** (rank)	23
Procedures (number)	5			DTF score for enforcing contracts (0–100)	70.60
Time (days)	65	**Paying taxes** (rank)	95	Time (days)	650
Cost (% of income per capita)	298.5	DTF score for paying taxes (0–100)	70.90	Cost (% of claim)	15.2
Reliability of supply and transparency of tariffs index (0–8)	5	Payments (number per year)	35	Quality of judicial processes index (0–18)	13.0
		Time (hours per year)	206		
		Total tax and contribution rate (% of profit)	20.6		
✔ **Registering property** (rank)	59	Postfiling index (0–100)	61.20	**Resolving insolvency** (rank)	60
DTF score for registering property (0–100)	71.44			DTF score for resolving insolvency (0–100)	55.11
Procedures (number)	5			Time (years)	3.1
Time (days)	62			Cost (% of estate)	14.5
Cost (% of property value)	4.0			Recovery rate (cents on the dollar)	32.7
Quality of land administration index (0–30)	22.5			Strength of insolvency framework index (0–16)	12.0

CYPRUS

CYPRUS		Europe & Central Asia		GNI per capita (US$)	23,680
Ease of doing business rank (1–190)	53	Overall distance to frontier (DTF) score (0–100)	71.63	Population	1,170,125

Starting a business (rank)	50	**Getting credit** (rank)	68	**Trading across borders** (rank)	45
DTF score for starting a business (0–100)	91.19	DTF score for getting credit (0–100)	60.00	DTF score for trading across borders (0–100)	88.44
Procedures (number)	5	Strength of legal rights index (0–12)	7	*Time to export*	
Time (days)	6	Depth of credit information index (0–8)	5	Documentary compliance (hours)	2
Cost (% of income per capita)	12.4	Credit bureau coverage (% of adults)	72.9	Border compliance (hours)	18
Minimum capital (% of income per capita)	0.0	Credit registry coverage (% of adults)	0.0	*Cost to export*	
				Documentary compliance (US$)	50
Dealing with construction permits (rank)	120	**Protecting minority investors** (rank)	43	Border compliance (US$)	300
DTF score for dealing with construction permits (0–100)	63.99	DTF score for protecting minority investors (0–100)	63.33	*Time to import*	
Procedures (number)	8	Extent of disclosure index (0–10)	8	Documentary compliance (hours)	2
Time (days)	507	Extent of director liability index (0–10)	4	Border compliance (hours)	15
Cost (% of warehouse value)	1.1	Ease of shareholder suits index (0–10)	7	*Cost to import*	
Building quality control index (0–15)	11.0	Extent of shareholder rights index (0–10)	6	Documentary compliance (US$)	50
		Extent of ownership and control index (0–10)	6	Border compliance (US$)	335
Getting electricity (rank)	67	Extent of corporate transparency index (0–10)	7		
DTF score for getting electricity (0–100)	78.32			**Enforcing contracts** (rank)	138
Procedures (number)	5			DTF score for enforcing contracts (0–100)	48.59
Time (days)	137	✘ **Paying taxes** (rank)	44	Time (days)	1,100
Cost (% of income per capita)	133.2	DTF score for paying taxes (0–100)	80.59	Cost (% of claim)	16.4
Reliability of supply and transparency of tariffs index (0–8)	8	Payments (number per year)	28	Quality of judicial processes index (0–18)	8.0
		Time (hours per year)	127		
		Total tax and contribution rate (% of profit)	22.7		
Registering property (rank)	92	Postfiling index (0–100)	76.07	**Resolving insolvency** (rank)	21
DTF score for registering property (0–100)	63.41			DTF score for resolving insolvency (0–100)	78.46
Procedures (number)	7			Time (years)	1.5
Time (days)	9			Cost (% of estate)	14.5
Cost (% of property value)	10.4			Recovery rate (cents on the dollar)	73.2
Quality of land administration index (0–30)	23.0			Strength of insolvency framework index (0–16)	12.5

CZECH REPUBLIC

CZECH REPUBLIC		OECD high income		GNI per capita (US$)	17,570
Ease of doing business rank (1–190)	30	Overall distance to frontier (DTF) score (0–100)	76.27	Population	10,561,633

✔ **Starting a business** (rank)	81	**Getting credit** (rank)	42	**Trading across borders** (rank)	1
DTF score for starting a business (0–100)	87.44	DTF score for getting credit (0–100)	70.00	DTF score for trading across borders (0–100)	100.00
Procedures (number)	8	Strength of legal rights index (0–12)	7	*Time to export*	
Time (days)	9	Depth of credit information index (0–8)	7	Documentary compliance (hours)	1
Cost (% of income per capita)	1.0	Credit bureau coverage (% of adults)	79.5	Border compliance (hours)	0
Minimum capital (% of income per capita)	0.0	Credit registry coverage (% of adults)	7.0	*Cost to export*	
				Documentary compliance (US$)	0
Dealing with construction permits (rank)	127	**Protecting minority investors** (rank)	62	Border compliance (US$)	0
DTF score for dealing with construction permits (0–100)	62.77	DTF score for protecting minority investors (0–100)	58.33	*Time to import*	
Procedures (number)	21	Extent of disclosure index (0–10)	2	Documentary compliance (hours)	1
Time (days)	247	Extent of director liability index (0–10)	6	Border compliance (hours)	0
Cost (% of warehouse value)	0.2	Ease of shareholder suits index (0–10)	9	*Cost to import*	
Building quality control index (0–15)	12.0	Extent of shareholder rights index (0–10)	6	Documentary compliance (US$)	0
		Extent of ownership and control index (0–10)	7	Border compliance (US$)	0
Getting electricity (rank)	15	Extent of corporate transparency index (0–10)	5		
DTF score for getting electricity (0–100)	90.33			**Enforcing contracts** (rank)	91
Procedures (number)	4			DTF score for enforcing contracts (0–100)	58.21
Time (days)	68	✘ **Paying taxes** (rank)	53	Time (days)	611
Cost (% of income per capita)	23.8	DTF score for paying taxes (0–100)	79.26	Cost (% of claim)	33.8
Reliability of supply and transparency of tariffs index (0–8)	8	Payments (number per year)	8	Quality of judicial processes index (0–18)	9.5
		Time (hours per year)	248		
		Total tax and contribution rate (% of profit)	50.0		
Registering property (rank)	32	Postfiling index (0–100)	90.75	**Resolving insolvency** (rank)	25
DTF score for registering property (0–100)	79.68			DTF score for resolving insolvency (0–100)	76.69
Procedures (number)	4			Time (years)	2.1
Time (days)	28			Cost (% of estate)	17.0
Cost (% of property value)	4.0			Recovery rate (cents on the dollar)	67.0
Quality of land administration index (0–30)	25.0			Strength of insolvency framework index (0–16)	13.0

Note: Most indicator sets refer to a case scenario in the largest business city of an economy, though for 11 economies the data are a population-weighted average for the two largest business cities. For some indicators a result of "no practice" may be recorded for an economy; see the data notes for more details. In starting a business, procedures (number), time (days) and cost (% of income per capita) are calculated as the average of both men and women. For the postfiling index, a result of "not applicable" may be recorded for an economy.

✔ Reform making it easier to do business ✗ Change making it more difficult to do business

DENMARK

OECD high income	
GNI per capita (US$)	56,730
Ease of doing business rank (1–190)	3
Overall distance to frontier (DTF) score (0–100)	84.06
Population	5,731,118

Starting a business (rank)	34
DTF score for starting a business (0–100)	92.50
Procedures (number)	5
Time (days)	3.5
Cost (% of income per capita)	0.2
Minimum capital (% of income per capita)	13.5

✗ Dealing with construction permits (rank)	1
DTF score for dealing with construction permits (0–100)	86.79
Procedures (number)	7
Time (days)	64
Cost (% of warehouse value)	1.4
Building quality control index (0–15)	11.0

Getting electricity (rank)	16
DTF score for getting electricity (0–100)	90.21
Procedures (number)	4
Time (days)	38
Cost (% of income per capita)	106.2
Reliability of supply and transparency of tariffs index (0–8)	7

Registering property (rank)	11
DTF score for registering property (0–100)	89.88
Procedures (number)	3
Time (days)	4
Cost (% of property value)	0.6
Quality of land administration index (0–30)	24.5

Getting credit (rank)	42
DTF score for getting credit (0–100)	70.00
Strength of legal rights index (0–12)	8
Depth of credit information index (0–8)	6
Credit bureau coverage (% of adults)	7.4
Credit registry coverage (% of adults)	0.0

Protecting minority investors (rank)	33
DTF score for protecting minority investors (0–100)	66.67
Extent of disclosure index (0–10)	7
Extent of director liability index (0–10)	5
Ease of shareholder suits index (0–10)	8
Extent of shareholder rights index (0–10)	6
Extent of ownership and control index (0–10)	5
Extent of corporate transparency index (0–10)	9

Paying taxes (rank)	8
DTF score for paying taxes (0–100)	91.22
Payments (number per year)	10
Time (hours per year)	130
Total tax and contribution rate (% of profit)	24.2
Postfiling index (0–100)	89.06

Trading across borders (rank)	1
DTF score for trading across borders (0–100)	100.00
Time to export	
Documentary compliance (hours)	1
Border compliance (hours)	0
Cost to export	
Documentary compliance (US$)	0
Border compliance (US$)	0
Time to import	
Documentary compliance (hours)	1
Border compliance (hours)	0
Cost to import	
Documentary compliance (US$)	0
Border compliance (US$)	0

Enforcing contracts (rank)	32
DTF score for enforcing contracts (0–100)	68.37
Time (days)	485
Cost (% of claim)	23.3
Quality of judicial processes index (0–18)	11.0

Resolving insolvency (rank)	7
DTF score for resolving insolvency (0–100)	84.93
Time (years)	1.0
Cost (% of estate)	4.0
Recovery rate (cents on the dollar)	88.1
Strength of insolvency framework index (0–16)	12.0

DJIBOUTI

Middle East & North Africa	
GNI per capita (US$)	1,908
Ease of doing business rank (1–190)	154
Overall distance to frontier (DTF) score (0–100)	49.58
Population	942,333

✔ Starting a business (rank)	115
DTF score for starting a business (0–100)	83.38
Procedures (number)	7
Time (days)	14
Cost (% of income per capita)	35.2
Minimum capital (% of income per capita)	0.0

✔ Dealing with construction permits (rank)	84
DTF score for dealing with construction permits (0–100)	68.48
Procedures (number)	17
Time (days)	111
Cost (% of warehouse value)	5.4
Building quality control index (0–15)	11.0

Getting electricity (rank)	169
DTF score for getting electricity (0–100)	40.75
Procedures (number)	4
Time (days)	125
Cost (% of income per capita)	5,979.9
Reliability of supply and transparency of tariffs index (0–8)	0

✔ Registering property (rank)	168
DTF score for registering property (0–100)	42.65
Procedures (number)	6
Time (days)	39
Cost (% of property value)	12.7
Quality of land administration index (0–30)	4.5

✔ Getting credit (rank)	183
DTF score for getting credit (0–100)	5.00
Strength of legal rights index (0–12)	1
Depth of credit information index (0–8)	0
Credit bureau coverage (% of adults)	0.0
Credit registry coverage (% of adults)	0.4

✔ Protecting minority investors (rank)	96
DTF score for protecting minority investors (0–100)	51.67
Extent of disclosure index (0–10)	7
Extent of director liability index (0–10)	7
Ease of shareholder suits index (0–10)	3
Extent of shareholder rights index (0–10)	6
Extent of ownership and control index (0–10)	5
Extent of corporate transparency index (0–10)	3

Paying taxes (rank)	108
DTF score for paying taxes (0–100)	68.91
Payments (number per year)	35
Time (hours per year)	76
Total tax and contribution rate (% of profit)	37.7
Postfiling index (0–100)	49.57

Trading across borders (rank)	159
DTF score for trading across borders (0–100)	51.87
Time to export	
Documentary compliance (hours)	72
Border compliance (hours)	109
Cost to export	
Documentary compliance (US$)	95
Border compliance (US$)	944
Time to import	
Documentary compliance (hours)	50
Border compliance (hours)	78
Cost to import	
Documentary compliance (US$)	100
Border compliance (US$)	1,209

Enforcing contracts (rank)	175
DTF score for enforcing contracts (0–100)	34.78
Time (days)	1,025
Cost (% of claim)	34.0
Quality of judicial processes index (0–18)	3.0

Resolving insolvency (rank)	73
DTF score for resolving insolvency (0–100)	48.32
Time (years)	2.3
Cost (% of estate)	11.0
Recovery rate (cents on the dollar)	37.5
Strength of insolvency framework index (0–16)	9.0

DOMINICA

Latin America & Caribbean	
GNI per capita (US$)	6,750
Ease of doing business rank (1–190)	98
Overall distance to frontier (DTF) score (0–100)	60.96
Population	73,543

Starting a business (rank)	67
DTF score for starting a business (0–100)	89.29
Procedures (number)	5
Time (days)	12
Cost (% of income per capita)	15.5
Minimum capital (% of income per capita)	0.0

Dealing with construction permits (rank)	74
DTF score for dealing with construction permits (0–100)	70.07
Procedures (number)	11
Time (days)	191
Cost (% of warehouse value)	0.3
Building quality control index (0–15)	8.0

Getting electricity (rank)	46
DTF score for getting electricity (0–100)	82.43
Procedures (number)	5
Time (days)	61
Cost (% of income per capita)	466.1
Reliability of supply and transparency of tariffs index (0–8)	7

Registering property (rank)	164
DTF score for registering property (0–100)	43.40
Procedures (number)	5
Time (days)	42
Cost (% of property value)	13.3
Quality of land administration index (0–30)	4.5

Getting credit (rank)	142
DTF score for getting credit (0–100)	30.00
Strength of legal rights index (0–12)	6
Depth of credit information index (0–8)	0
Credit bureau coverage (% of adults)	0.0
Credit registry coverage (% of adults)	0.0

Protecting minority investors (rank)	96
DTF score for protecting minority investors (0–100)	51.67
Extent of disclosure index (0–10)	4
Extent of director liability index (0–10)	8
Ease of shareholder suits index (0–10)	8
Extent of shareholder rights index (0–10)	4
Extent of ownership and control index (0–10)	4
Extent of corporate transparency index (0–10)	3

Paying taxes (rank)	77
DTF score for paying taxes (0–100)	74.91
Payments (number per year)	37
Time (hours per year)	117
Total tax and contribution rate (% of profit)	35.2
Postfiling index (0–100)	79.66

Trading across borders (rank)	81
DTF score for trading across borders (0–100)	74.26
Time to export	
Documentary compliance (hours)	12
Border compliance (hours)	36
Cost to export	
Documentary compliance (US$)	50
Border compliance (US$)	625
Time to import	
Documentary compliance (hours)	24
Border compliance (hours)	39
Cost to import	
Documentary compliance (US$)	50
Border compliance (US$)	906

Enforcing contracts (rank)	79
DTF score for enforcing contracts (0–100)	59.17
Time (days)	681
Cost (% of claim)	36.0
Quality of judicial processes index (0–18)	11.5

Resolving insolvency (rank)	132
DTF score for resolving insolvency (0–100)	34.41
Time (years)	4.0
Cost (% of estate)	10.0
Recovery rate (cents on the dollar)	29.1
Strength of insolvency framework index (0–16)	6.0

Note: Most indicator sets refer to a case scenario in the largest business city of an economy, though for 11 economies the data are a population-weighted average for the two largest business cities. For some indicators a result of "no practice" may be recorded for an economy; see the data notes for more details. In starting a business, procedures (number), time (days) and cost (% of income per capita) are calculated as the average of both men and women. For the postfiling index, a result of "not applicable" may be recorded for an economy.

✔ Reform making it easier to do business ✘ Change making it more difficult to do business

DOMINICAN REPUBLIC | Latin America & Caribbean | GNI per capita (US$) 6,390

Ease of doing business rank (1–190)	99	Overall distance to frontier (DTF) score (0–100)	60.93	Population	10,648,791

✔ Starting a business (rank)	116	Getting credit (rank)	105	Trading across borders (rank)	59
DTF score for starting a business (0–100)	83.23	DTF score for getting credit (0–100)	45.00	DTF score for trading across borders (0–100)	83.51
Procedures (number)	7	Strength of legal rights index (0–12)	1	Time to export	
Time (days)	16.5	Depth of credit information index (0–8)	8	Documentary compliance (hours)	10
Cost (% of income per capita)	14.5	Credit bureau coverage (% of adults)	68.3	Border compliance (hours)	16
Minimum capital (% of income per capita)	33.9	Credit registry coverage (% of adults)	26.4	Cost to export	
				Documentary compliance (US$)	15
Dealing with construction permits (rank)	62	Protecting minority investors (rank)	96	Border compliance (US$)	488
DTF score for dealing with construction permits (0–100)	71.73	DTF score for protecting minority investors (0–100)	51.67	Time to import	
Procedures (number)	15	Extent of disclosure index (0–10)	5	Documentary compliance (hours)	14
Time (days)	184	Extent of director liability index (0–10)	4	Border compliance (hours)	24
Cost (% of warehouse value)	2.8	Ease of shareholder suits index (0–10)	8	Cost to import	
Building quality control index (0–15)	13.0	Extent of shareholder rights index (0–10)	7	Documentary compliance (US$)	40
		Extent of ownership and control index (0–10)	2	Border compliance (US$)	579
✔ Getting electricity (rank)	108	Extent of corporate transparency index (0–10)	5		
DTF score for getting electricity (0–100)	64.74			Enforcing contracts (rank)	136
Procedures (number)	7	✘ Paying taxes (rank)	149	DTF score for enforcing contracts (0–100)	48.71
Time (days)	67	DTF score for paying taxes (0–100)	57.45	Time (days)	590
Cost (% of income per capita)	248.6	Payments (number per year)	7	Cost (% of claim)	40.9
Reliability of supply and transparency of tariffs index (0–8)	4	Time (hours per year)	317	Quality of judicial processes index (0–18)	5.5
		Total tax and contribution rate (% of profit)	48.8		
		Postfiling index (0–100)	10.71	✔ Resolving insolvency (rank)	121
Registering property (rank)	79			DTF score for resolving insolvency (0–100)	37.59
DTF score for registering property (0–100)	65.67			Time (years)	3.5
Procedures (number)	6			Cost (% of estate)	38.0
Time (days)	45			Recovery rate (cents on the dollar)	8.9
Cost (% of property value)	3.4			Strength of insolvency framework index (0–16)	10.5
Quality of land administration index (0–30)	14.5				

ECUADOR | Latin America & Caribbean | GNI per capita (US$) 5,820

Ease of doing business rank (1–190)	118	Overall distance to frontier (DTF) score (0–100)	57.83	Population	16,385,068

Starting a business (rank)	168	Getting credit (rank)	105	Trading across borders (rank)	102
DTF score for starting a business (0–100)	70.50	DTF score for getting credit (0–100)	45.00	DTF score for trading across borders (0–100)	68.65
Procedures (number)	11	Strength of legal rights index (0–12)	1	Time to export	
Time (days)	48.5	Depth of credit information index (0–8)	8	Documentary compliance (hours)	24
Cost (% of income per capita)	21.9	Credit bureau coverage (% of adults)	71.0	Border compliance (hours)	96
Minimum capital (% of income per capita)	0.0	Credit registry coverage (% of adults)	0.0	Cost to export	
				Documentary compliance (US$)	140
Dealing with construction permits (rank)	105	Protecting minority investors (rank)	124	Border compliance (US$)	560
DTF score for dealing with construction permits (0–100)	66.32	DTF score for protecting minority investors (0–100)	46.67	Time to import	
Procedures (number)	17	Extent of disclosure index (0–10)	2	Documentary compliance (hours)	120
Time (days)	132	Extent of director liability index (0–10)	5	Border compliance (hours)	24
Cost (% of warehouse value)	1.9	Ease of shareholder suits index (0–10)	6	Cost to import	
Building quality control index (0–15)	8.0	Extent of shareholder rights index (0–10)	9	Documentary compliance (US$)	75
		Extent of ownership and control index (0–10)	3	Border compliance (US$)	250
Getting electricity (rank)	85	Extent of corporate transparency index (0–10)	3		
DTF score for getting electricity (0–100)	72.16			Enforcing contracts (rank)	75
Procedures (number)	7	✘ Paying taxes (rank)	145	DTF score for enforcing contracts (0–100)	59.38
Time (days)	74	DTF score for paying taxes (0–100)	58.39	Time (days)	523
Cost (% of income per capita)	636.1	Payments (number per year)	10	Cost (% of claim)	27.2
Reliability of supply and transparency of tariffs index (0–8)	7	Time (hours per year)	666	Quality of judicial processes index (0–18)	7.5
		Total tax and contribution rate (% of profit)	32.5		
		Postfiling index (0–100)	49.54	Resolving insolvency (rank)	157
✘ Registering property (rank)	74			DTF score for resolving insolvency (0–100)	25.01
DTF score for registering property (0–100)	66.18			Time (years)	5.3
Procedures (number)	8			Cost (% of estate)	18.0
Time (days)	38			Recovery rate (cents on the dollar)	17.4
Cost (% of property value)	2.1			Strength of insolvency framework index (0–16)	5.0
Quality of land administration index (0–30)	16.5				

EGYPT, ARAB REP. | Middle East & North Africa | GNI per capita (US$) 3,460

Ease of doing business rank (1–190)	128	Overall distance to frontier (DTF) score (0–100)	56.22	Population	95,688,681

Starting a business (rank)	103	Getting credit (rank)	90	Trading across borders (rank)	170
DTF score for starting a business (0–100)	84.53	DTF score for getting credit (0–100)	50.00	DTF score for trading across borders (0–100)	42.23
Procedures (number)	8.5	Strength of legal rights index (0–12)	2	Time to export	
Time (days)	14.5	Depth of credit information index (0–8)	8	Documentary compliance (hours)	88
Cost (% of income per capita)	7.4	Credit bureau coverage (% of adults)	25.3	Border compliance (hours)	48
Minimum capital (% of income per capita)	0.0	Credit registry coverage (% of adults)	7.8	Cost to export	
				Documentary compliance (US$)	100
Dealing with construction permits (rank)	66	✔ Protecting minority investors (rank)	81	Border compliance (US$)	258
DTF score for dealing with construction permits (0–100)	71.43	DTF score for protecting minority investors (0–100)	55.00	Time to import	
Procedures (number)	19	Extent of disclosure index (0–10)	8	Documentary compliance (hours)	265
Time (days)	172	Extent of director liability index (0–10)	3	Border compliance (hours)	240
Cost (% of warehouse value)	1.9	Ease of shareholder suits index (0–10)	3	Cost to import	
Building quality control index (0–15)	14.0	Extent of shareholder rights index (0–10)	5	Documentary compliance (US$)	1,000
		Extent of ownership and control index (0–10)	7	Border compliance (US$)	554
Getting electricity (rank)	89	Extent of corporate transparency index (0–10)	7		
DTF score for getting electricity (0–100)	71.24			Enforcing contracts (rank)	160
Procedures (number)	5	Paying taxes (rank)	167	DTF score for enforcing contracts (0–100)	42.75
Time (days)	53	DTF score for paying taxes (0–100)	50.67	Time (days)	1,010
Cost (% of income per capita)	324.7	Payments (number per year)	29	Cost (% of claim)	26.2
Reliability of supply and transparency of tariffs index (0–8)	3	Time (hours per year)	392	Quality of judicial processes index (0–18)	5.5
		Total tax and contribution rate (% of profit)	45.3		
		Postfiling index (0–100)	26.62	Resolving insolvency (rank)	115
✘ Registering property (rank)	119			DTF score for resolving insolvency (0–100)	38.89
DTF score for registering property (0–100)	55.50			Time (years)	2.5
Procedures (number)	8			Cost (% of estate)	22.0
Time (days)	75			Recovery rate (cents on the dollar)	25.8
Cost (% of property value)	1.1			Strength of insolvency framework index (0–16)	8.0
Quality of land administration index (0–30)	1.5				

Note: Most indicator sets refer to a case scenario in the largest business city of an economy, though for 11 economies the data are a population-weighted average for the two largest business cities. For some indicators a result of "no practice" may be recorded for an economy; see the data notes for more details. In starting a business, procedures (number), time (days) and cost (% of income per capita) are calculated as the average of both men and women. For the postfiling index, a result of "not applicable" may be recorded for an economy.

✔ Reform making it easier to do business   ✗ Change making it more difficult to do business

EL SALVADOR

EL SALVADOR		**Latin America & Caribbean**		**GNI per capita (US$)**		**3,920**
Ease of doing business rank (1–190)	73	Overall distance to frontier (DTF) score (0–100)	66.42	Population		6,344,722

Starting a business (rank)	140	**Getting credit** (rank)	20	✔ **Trading across borders** (rank)	43
DTF score for starting a business (0–100)	78.88	DTF score for getting credit (0–100)	80.00	DTF score for trading across borders (0–100)	89.29
Procedures (number)	9	Strength of legal rights index (0–12)	9	*Time to export*	
Time (days)	16.5	Depth of credit information index (0–8)	7	Documentary compliance (hours)	9
Cost (% of income per capita)	41.4	Credit bureau coverage (% of adults)	35.4	Border compliance (hours)	30
Minimum capital (% of income per capita)	2.5	Credit registry coverage (% of adults)	28.6	*Cost to export*	
				Documentary compliance (US$)	50
✔ **Dealing with construction permits** (rank)	139	**Protecting minority investors** (rank)	160	Border compliance (US$)	128
DTF score for dealing with construction permits (0–100)	60.16	DTF score for protecting minority investors (0–100)	38.33	*Time to import*	
Procedures (number)	23	Extent of disclosure index (0–10)	3	Documentary compliance (hours)	13
Time (days)	122.5	Extent of director liability index (0–10)	0	Border compliance (hours)	36
Cost (% of warehouse value)	5.2	Ease of shareholder suits index (0–10)	7	*Cost to import*	
Building quality control index (0–15)	10.0	Extent of shareholder rights index (0–10)	6	Documentary compliance (US$)	67
		Extent of ownership and control index (0–10)	1	Border compliance (US$)	128
		Extent of corporate transparency index (0–10)	6		
✔ **Getting electricity** (rank)	88			**Enforcing contracts** (rank)	105
DTF score for getting electricity (0–100)	71.40	✔ **Paying taxes** (rank)	61	DTF score for enforcing contracts (0–100)	55.20
Procedures (number)	7	DTF score for paying taxes (0–100)	77.35	Time (days)	786
Time (days)	56	Payments (number per year)	7	Cost (% of claim)	19.2
Cost (% of income per capita)	502.0	Time (hours per year)	180	Quality of judicial processes index (0–18)	7.5
Reliability of supply and transparency of tariffs index (0–8)	6	Total tax and contribution rate (% of profit)	35.5		
		Postfiling index (0–100)	49.54	**Resolving insolvency** (rank)	84
Registering property (rank)	69			DTF score for resolving insolvency (0–100)	45.69
DTF score for registering property (0–100)	67.92			Time (years)	3.5
Procedures (number)	5			Cost (% of estate)	12.0
Time (days)	31			Recovery rate (cents on the dollar)	32.6
Cost (% of property value)	3.8			Strength of insolvency framework index (0–16)	9.0
Quality of land administration index (0–30)	13.5				

EQUATORIAL GUINEA		**Sub-Saharan Africa**		**GNI per capita (US$)**	**6,550**
Ease of doing business rank (1–190)	173	Overall distance to frontier (DTF) score (0–100)	41.66	Population	1,221,490

✔ **Starting a business** (rank)	182	**Getting credit** (rank)	122	**Trading across borders** (rank)	174
DTF score for starting a business (0–100)	54.96	DTF score for getting credit (0–100)	40.00	DTF score for trading across borders (0–100)	32.05
Procedures (number)	16	Strength of legal rights index (0–12)	6	*Time to export*	
Time (days)	33	Depth of credit information index (0–8)	2	Documentary compliance (hours)	154
Cost (% of income per capita)	103.4	Credit bureau coverage (% of adults)	0.0	Border compliance (hours)	132
Minimum capital (% of income per capita)	30.3	Credit registry coverage (% of adults)	6.3	*Cost to export*	
				Documentary compliance (US$)	85
Dealing with construction permits (rank)	160	**Protecting minority investors** (rank)	146	Border compliance (US$)	760
DTF score for dealing with construction permits (0–100)	54.95	DTF score for protecting minority investors (0–100)	40.00	*Time to import*	
Procedures (number)	13	Extent of disclosure index (0–10)	7	Documentary compliance (hours)	240
Time (days)	144	Extent of director liability index (0–10)	1	Border compliance (hours)	240
Cost (% of warehouse value)	4.2	Ease of shareholder suits index (0–10)	5	*Cost to import*	
Building quality control index (0–15)	1.0	Extent of shareholder rights index (0–10)	4	Documentary compliance (US$)	70
		Extent of ownership and control index (0–10)	3	Border compliance (US$)	985
		Extent of corporate transparency index (0–10)	4		
Getting electricity (rank)	146			**Enforcing contracts** (rank)	104
DTF score for getting electricity (0–100)	53.44	**Paying taxes** (rank)	177	DTF score for enforcing contracts (0–100)	55.25
Procedures (number)	5	DTF score for paying taxes (0–100)	41.54	Time (days)	475
Time (days)	106	Payments (number per year)	46	Cost (% of claim)	19.5
Cost (% of income per capita)	1,185.2	Time (hours per year)	492	Quality of judicial processes index (0–18)	3.0
Reliability of supply and transparency of tariffs index (0–8)	0	Total tax and contribution rate (% of profit)	79.4		
		Postfiling index (0–100)	93.12	**Resolving insolvency** (rank)	168
Registering property (rank)	162			DTF score for resolving insolvency (0–100)	0.00
DTF score for registering property (0–100)	44.45			Time (years)	no practice
Procedures (number)	6			Cost (% of estate)	no practice
Time (days)	23			Recovery rate (cents on the dollar)	0.0
Cost (% of property value)	12.5			Strength of insolvency framework index (0–16)	0.0
Quality of land administration index (0–30)	4.0				

ERITREA		**Sub-Saharan Africa**		**GNI per capita (US$)**	**823**
Ease of doing business rank (1–190)	189	Overall distance to frontier (DTF) score (0–100)	22.87	Population	5,869,869

Starting a business (rank)	184	**Getting credit** (rank)	186	**Trading across borders** (rank)	189
DTF score for starting a business (0–100)	50.60	DTF score for getting credit (0–100)	0.00	DTF score for trading across borders (0–100)	0.00
Procedures (number)	13	Strength of legal rights index (0–12)	0	*Time to export*	
Time (days)	84	Depth of credit information index (0–8)	0	Documentary compliance (hours)	no practice
Cost (% of income per capita)	27.0	Credit bureau coverage (% of adults)	0.0	Border compliance (hours)	no practice
Minimum capital (% of income per capita)	118.5	Credit registry coverage (% of adults)	0.0	*Cost to export*	
				Documentary compliance (US$)	no practice
Dealing with construction permits (rank)	186	**Protecting minority investors** (rank)	172	Border compliance (US$)	no practice
DTF score for dealing with construction permits (0–100)	0.00	DTF score for protecting minority investors (0–100)	31.67	*Time to import*	
Procedures (number)	no practice	Extent of disclosure index (0–10)	3	Documentary compliance (hours)	no practice
Time (days)	no practice	Extent of director liability index (0–10)	0	Border compliance (hours)	no practice
Cost (% of warehouse value)	no practice	Ease of shareholder suits index (0–10)	5	*Cost to import*	
Building quality control index (0–15)	0.0	Extent of shareholder rights index (0–10)	5	Documentary compliance (US$)	no practice
		Extent of ownership and control index (0–10)	3	Border compliance (US$)	no practice
		Extent of corporate transparency index (0–10)	3		
Getting electricity (rank)	187			**Enforcing contracts** (rank)	119
DTF score for getting electricity (0–100)	0.00	**Paying taxes** (rank)	148	DTF score for enforcing contracts (0–100)	53.68
Procedures (number)	no practice	DTF score for paying taxes (0–100)	57.50	Time (days)	490
Time (days)	no practice	Payments (number per year)	30	Cost (% of claim)	22.6
Cost (% of income per capita)	no practice	Time (hours per year)	216	Quality of judicial processes index (0–18)	3.0
Reliability of supply and transparency of tariffs index (0–8)	0	Total tax and contribution rate (% of profit)	83.7		
		Postfiling index (0–100)	99.54	**Resolving insolvency** (rank)	168
Registering property (rank)	178			DTF score for resolving insolvency (0–100)	0.00
DTF score for registering property (0–100)	35.29			Time (years)	no practice
Procedures (number)	11			Cost (% of estate)	no practice
Time (days)	78			Recovery rate (cents on the dollar)	0.0
Cost (% of property value)	9.0			Strength of insolvency framework index (0–16)	0.0
Quality of land administration index (0–30)	6.5				

Note: Most indicator sets refer to a case scenario in the largest business city of an economy, though for 11 economies the data are a population-weighted average for the two largest business cities. For some indicators a result of "no practice" may be recorded for an economy; see the data notes for more details. In starting a business, procedures (number), time (days) and cost (% of income per capita) are calculated as the average of both men and women. For the postfiling index, a result of "not applicable" may be recorded for an economy.

✔ Reform making it easier to do business   ✘ Change making it more difficult to do business

ESTONIA

ESTONIA		OECD high income		GNI per capita (US$)	17,750
Ease of doing business rank (1–190)	12	Overall distance to frontier (DTF) score (0–100)	80.80	Population	1,316,481

Starting a business (rank)	12	**Getting credit** (rank)	42	**Trading across borders** (rank)	17
DTF score for starting a business (0–100)	95.15	DTF score for getting credit (0–100)	70.00	DTF score for trading across borders (0–100)	99.92
Procedures (number)	3	Strength of legal rights index (0–12)	7	*Time to export*	
Time (days)	3.5	Depth of credit information index (0–8)	7	Documentary compliance (hours)	1
Cost (% of income per capita)	1.2	Credit bureau coverage (% of adults)	35.2	Border compliance (hours)	2
Minimum capital (% of income per capita)	16.0	Credit registry coverage (% of adults)	0.0	*Cost to export*	
				Documentary compliance (US$)	0
Dealing with construction permits (rank)	8	**Protecting minority investors** (rank)	76	Border compliance (US$)	0
DTF score for dealing with construction permits (0–100)	82.50	DTF score for protecting minority investors (0–100)	56.67	*Time to import*	
Procedures (number)	10	Extent of disclosure index (0–10)	8	Documentary compliance (hours)	1
Time (days)	103	Extent of director liability index (0–10)	3	Border compliance (hours)	0
Cost (% of warehouse value)	0.2	Ease of shareholder suits index (0–10)	6	*Cost to import*	
Building quality control index (0–15)	11.0	Extent of shareholder rights index (0–10)	8	Documentary compliance (US$)	0
		Extent of ownership and control index (0–10)	3	Border compliance (US$)	0
		Extent of corporate transparency index (0–10)	6		
Getting electricity (rank)	41			**Enforcing contracts** (rank)	11
DTF score for getting electricity (0–100)	83.21			DTF score for enforcing contracts (0–100)	74.34
Procedures (number)	5	**Paying taxes** (rank)	14	Time (days)	455
Time (days)	91	DTF score for paying taxes (0–100)	89.56	Cost (% of claim)	21.9
Cost (% of income per capita)	168.8	Payments (number per year)	8	Quality of judicial processes index (0–18)	13.5
Reliability of supply and transparency of tariffs index (0–8)	8	Time (hours per year)	50		
		Total tax and contribution rate (% of profit)	48.7		
		Postfiling index (0–100)	99.38	**Resolving insolvency** (rank)	44
Registering property (rank)	6			DTF score for resolving insolvency (0–100)	65.62
DTF score for registering property (0–100)	91.02			Time (years)	3.0
Procedures (number)	3			Cost (% of estate)	9.0
Time (days)	17.5			Recovery rate (cents on the dollar)	40.6
Cost (% of property value)	0.5			Strength of insolvency framework index (0–16)	14.0
Quality of land administration index (0–30)	27.5				

ETHIOPIA

ETHIOPIA		Sub-Saharan Africa		GNI per capita (US$)	660
Ease of doing business rank (1–190)	161	Overall distance to frontier (DTF) score (0–100)	47.77	Population	102,403,196

✔ **Starting a business** (rank)	174	**Getting credit** (rank)	173	✔ **Trading across borders** (rank)	167
DTF score for starting a business (0–100)	68.43	DTF score for getting credit (0–100)	15.00	DTF score for trading across borders (0–100)	45.34
Procedures (number)	12	Strength of legal rights index (0–12)	3	*Time to export*	
Time (days)	33	Depth of credit information index (0–8)	0	Documentary compliance (hours)	76
Cost (% of income per capita)	57.8	Credit bureau coverage (% of adults)	0.0	Border compliance (hours)	51
Minimum capital (% of income per capita)	0.0	Credit registry coverage (% of adults)	0.3	*Cost to export*	
				Documentary compliance (US$)	175
Dealing with construction permits (rank)	169	**Protecting minority investors** (rank)	176	Border compliance (US$)	172
DTF score for dealing with construction permits (0–100)	50.55	DTF score for protecting minority investors (0–100)	28.33	*Time to import*	
Procedures (number)	13	Extent of disclosure index (0–10)	3	Documentary compliance (hours)	194
Time (days)	130	Extent of director liability index (0–10)	0	Border compliance (hours)	166
Cost (% of warehouse value)	16.5	Ease of shareholder suits index (0–10)	2	*Cost to import*	
Building quality control index (0–15)	7.0	Extent of shareholder rights index (0–10)	5	Documentary compliance (US$)	750
		Extent of ownership and control index (0–10)	3	Border compliance (US$)	738
		Extent of corporate transparency index (0–10)	4		
Getting electricity (rank)	125			**Enforcing contracts** (rank)	68
DTF score for getting electricity (0–100)	59.29			DTF score for enforcing contracts (0–100)	59.99
Procedures (number)	4	**Paying taxes** (rank)	133	Time (days)	530
Time (days)	95	DTF score for paying taxes (0–100)	62.14	Cost (% of claim)	15.2
Cost (% of income per capita)	1,027.9	Payments (number per year)	30	Quality of judicial processes index (0–18)	5.5
Reliability of supply and transparency of tariffs index (0–8)	0	Time (hours per year)	306		
		Total tax and contribution rate (% of profit)	38.6		
		Postfiling index (0–100)	50.89	**Resolving insolvency** (rank)	122
Registering property (rank)	139			DTF score for resolving insolvency (0–100)	37.31
DTF score for registering property (0–100)	51.32			Time (years)	3.0
Procedures (number)	7			Cost (% of estate)	14.5
Time (days)	52			Recovery rate (cents on the dollar)	28.7
Cost (% of property value)	6.0			Strength of insolvency framework index (0–16)	7.0
Quality of land administration index (0–30)	6.0				

FIJI

FIJI		East Asia & Pacific		GNI per capita (US$)	4,840
Ease of doing business rank (1–190)	101	Overall distance to frontier (DTF) score (0–100)	60.74	Population	898,760

Starting a business (rank)	160	**Getting credit** (rank)	159	**Trading across borders** (rank)	75
DTF score for starting a business (0–100)	73.26	DTF score for getting credit (0–100)	25.00	DTF score for trading across borders (0–100)	77.57
Procedures (number)	11	Strength of legal rights index (0–12)	5	*Time to export*	
Time (days)	40	Depth of credit information index (0–8)	0	Documentary compliance (hours)	56
Cost (% of income per capita)	16.9	Credit bureau coverage (% of adults)	0.0	Border compliance (hours)	56
Minimum capital (% of income per capita)	0.0	Credit registry coverage (% of adults)	0.0	*Cost to export*	
				Documentary compliance (US$)	76
Dealing with construction permits (rank)	92	**Protecting minority investors** (rank)	96	Border compliance (US$)	317
DTF score for dealing with construction permits (0–100)	67.69	DTF score for protecting minority investors (0–100)	51.67	*Time to import*	
Procedures (number)	15	Extent of disclosure index (0–10)	2	Documentary compliance (hours)	34
Time (days)	141	Extent of director liability index (0–10)	8	Border compliance (hours)	42
Cost (% of warehouse value)	0.6	Ease of shareholder suits index (0–10)	7	*Cost to import*	
Building quality control index (0–15)	7.0	Extent of shareholder rights index (0–10)	5	Documentary compliance (US$)	58
		Extent of ownership and control index (0–10)	4	Border compliance (US$)	320
		Extent of corporate transparency index (0–10)	5		
Getting electricity (rank)	84			**Enforcing contracts** (rank)	89
DTF score for getting electricity (0–100)	72.19			DTF score for enforcing contracts (0–100)	58.44
Procedures (number)	4	**Paying taxes** (rank)	120	Time (days)	397
Time (days)	81	DTF score for paying taxes (0–100)	66.00	Cost (% of claim)	38.9
Cost (% of income per capita)	1,391.9	Payments (number per year)	38	Quality of judicial processes index (0–18)	7.5
Reliability of supply and transparency of tariffs index (0–8)	4	Time (hours per year)	247		
		Total tax and contribution rate (% of profit)	33.0		
		Postfiling index (0–100)	62.62	**Resolving insolvency** (rank)	92
Registering property (rank)	58			DTF score for resolving insolvency (0–100)	43.72
DTF score for registering property (0–100)	71.86			Time (years)	1.8
Procedures (number)	4			Cost (% of estate)	10.0
Time (days)	69			Recovery rate (cents on the dollar)	46.4
Cost (% of property value)	3.0			Strength of insolvency framework index (0–16)	6.0
Quality of land administration index (0–30)	19.5				

Note: Most indicator sets refer to a case scenario in the largest business city of an economy, though for 11 economies the data are a population-weighted average for the two largest business cities. For some indicators a result of "no practice" may be recorded for an economy; see the data notes for more details. In starting a business, procedures (number), time (days) and cost (% of income per capita) are calculated as the average of both men and women. For the postfiling index, a result of "not applicable" may be recorded for an economy.

✔ Reform making it easier to do business   ✘ Change making it more difficult to do business

FINLAND — OECD high income — GNI per capita (US$) 44,730

Ease of doing business rank (1–190)	**13**	**Overall distance to frontier (DTF) score (0–100)**	**80.37**	**Population**		**5,495,096**

Starting a business (rank)	26	**Getting credit** (rank)	55	**Trading across borders** (rank)	34
DTF score for starting a business (0–100)	93.15	DTF score for getting credit (0–100)	65.00	DTF score for trading across borders (0–100)	92.44
Procedures (number)	3	Strength of legal rights index (0–12)	7	*Time to export*	
Time (days)	14	Depth of credit information index (0–8)	6	Documentary compliance (hours)	2
Cost (% of income per capita)	1.0	Credit bureau coverage (% of adults)	20.9	Border compliance (hours)	36
Minimum capital (% of income per capita)	6.4	Credit registry coverage (% of adults)	0.0	*Cost to export*	
				Documentary compliance (US$)	70
Dealing with construction permits (rank)	37	**Protecting minority investors** (rank)	62	Border compliance (US$)	213
DTF score for dealing with construction permits (0–100)	75.74	DTF score for protecting minority investors (0–100)	58.33	*Time to import*	
Procedures (number)	17	Extent of disclosure index (0–10)	6	Documentary compliance (hours)	1
Time (days)	65	Extent of director liability index (0–10)	4	Border compliance (hours)	2
Cost (% of warehouse value)	0.9	Ease of shareholder suits index (0–10)	8	*Cost to import*	
Building quality control index (0–15)	10.0	Extent of shareholder rights index (0–10)	6	Documentary compliance (US$)	0
		Extent of ownership and control index (0–10)	2	Border compliance (US$)	0
Getting electricity (rank)	20	Extent of corporate transparency index (0–10)	9		
DTF score for getting electricity (0–100)	88.97			**Enforcing contracts** (rank)	46
Procedures (number)	5	**Paying taxes** (rank)	12	DTF score for enforcing contracts (0–100)	66.40
Time (days)	42	DTF score for paying taxes (0–100)	90.14	Time (days)	485
Cost (% of income per capita)	27.1	Payments (number per year)	8	Cost (% of claim)	16.2
Reliability of supply and transparency of tariffs index (0–8)	8	Time (hours per year)	93	Quality of judicial processes index (0–18)	8.5
		Total tax and contribution rate (% of profit)	38.4		
		Postfiling index (0–100)	93.09	**Resolving insolvency** (rank)	2
Registering property (rank)	27			DTF score for resolving insolvency (0–100)	92.82
DTF score for registering property (0–100)	80.73			Time (years)	0.9
Procedures (number)	3			Cost (% of estate)	3.5
Time (days)	47			Recovery rate (cents on the dollar)	88.3
Cost (% of property value)	4.0			Strength of insolvency framework index (0–16)	14.5
Quality of land administration index (0–30)	26.5				

FRANCE — OECD high income — GNI per capita (US$) 38,950

Ease of doing business rank (1–190)	**31**	**Overall distance to frontier (DTF) score (0–100)**	**76.13**	**Population**		**66,896,109**

Starting a business (rank)	25	**Getting credit** (rank)	90	**Trading across borders** (rank)	1
DTF score for starting a business (0–100)	93.28	DTF score for getting credit (0–100)	50.00	DTF score for trading across borders (0–100)	100.00
Procedures (number)	5	Strength of legal rights index (0–12)	4	*Time to export*	
Time (days)	3.5	Depth of credit information index (0–8)	6	Documentary compliance (hours)	1
Cost (% of income per capita)	0.7	Credit bureau coverage (% of adults)	0.0	Border compliance (hours)	0
Minimum capital (% of income per capita)	0.0	Credit registry coverage (% of adults)	47.2	*Cost to export*	
				Documentary compliance (US$)	0
Dealing with construction permits (rank)	18	✔ **Protecting minority investors** (rank)	33	Border compliance (US$)	0
DTF score for dealing with construction permits (0–100)	79.29	DTF score for protecting minority investors (0–100)	66.67	*Time to import*	
Procedures (number)	9	Extent of disclosure index (0–10)	8	Documentary compliance (hours)	1
Time (days)	183	Extent of director liability index (0–10)	3	Border compliance (hours)	0
Cost (% of warehouse value)	3.0	Ease of shareholder suits index (0–10)	6	*Cost to import*	
Building quality control index (0–15)	14.0	Extent of shareholder rights index (0–10)	5	Documentary compliance (US$)	0
		Extent of ownership and control index (0–10)	8	Border compliance (US$)	0
Getting electricity (rank)	26	Extent of corporate transparency index (0–10)	10		
DTF score for getting electricity (0–100)	85.89			**Enforcing contracts** (rank)	15
Procedures (number)	5	✔ **Paying taxes** (rank)	54	DTF score for enforcing contracts (0–100)	73.04
Time (days)	71	DTF score for paying taxes (0–100)	78.55	Time (days)	395
Cost (% of income per capita)	6.0	Payments (number per year)	9	Cost (% of claim)	17.4
Reliability of supply and transparency of tariffs index (0–8)	8	Time (hours per year)	139	Quality of judicial processes index (0–18)	11.0
		Total tax and contribution rate (% of profit)	62.2		
		Postfiling index (0–100)	92.40	**Resolving insolvency** (rank)	28
Registering property (rank)	100			DTF score for resolving insolvency (0–100)	73.91
DTF score for registering property (0–100)	60.69			Time (years)	1.9
Procedures (number)	8			Cost (% of estate)	9.0
Time (days)	64			Recovery rate (cents on the dollar)	73.5
Cost (% of property value)	7.3			Strength of insolvency framework index (0–16)	11.0
Quality of land administration index (0–30)	24.0				

GABON — Sub-Saharan Africa — GNI per capita (US$) 7,210

Ease of doing business rank (1–190)	**167**	**Overall distance to frontier (DTF) score (0–100)**	**46.19**	**Population**		**1,979,786**

✔ **Starting a business** (rank)	132	**Getting credit** (rank)	122	**Trading across borders** (rank)	169
DTF score for starting a business (0–100)	80.48	DTF score for getting credit (0–100)	40.00	DTF score for trading across borders (0–100)	43.94
Procedures (number)	8	Strength of legal rights index (0–12)	6	*Time to export*	
Time (days)	33	Depth of credit information index (0–8)	2	Documentary compliance (hours)	60
Cost (% of income per capita)	7.2	Credit bureau coverage (% of adults)	0.0	Border compliance (hours)	96
Minimum capital (% of income per capita)	2.5	Credit registry coverage (% of adults)	28.9	*Cost to export*	
				Documentary compliance (US$)	200
✔ **Dealing with construction permits** (rank)	149	**Protecting minority investors** (rank)	160	Border compliance (US$)	1,633
DTF score for dealing with construction permits (0–100)	58.33	DTF score for protecting minority investors (0–100)	38.33	*Time to import*	
Procedures (number)	14	Extent of disclosure index (0–10)	7	Documentary compliance (hours)	120
Time (days)	276	Extent of director liability index (0–10)	1	Border compliance (hours)	84
Cost (% of warehouse value)	1.1	Ease of shareholder suits index (0–10)	4	*Cost to import*	
Building quality control index (0–15)	7.0	Extent of shareholder rights index (0–10)	4	Documentary compliance (US$)	170
		Extent of ownership and control index (0–10)	3	Border compliance (US$)	1,320
Getting electricity (rank)	170	Extent of corporate transparency index (0–10)	4		
DTF score for getting electricity (0–100)	40.21			**Enforcing contracts** (rank)	178
Procedures (number)	7	**Paying taxes** (rank)	165	DTF score for enforcing contracts (0–100)	32.84
Time (days)	148	DTF score for paying taxes (0–100)	51.64	Time (days)	1,160
Cost (% of income per capita)	1,294.5	Payments (number per year)	26	Cost (% of claim)	34.3
Reliability of supply and transparency of tariffs index (0–8)	0	Time (hours per year)	488	Quality of judicial processes index (0–18)	4.0
		Total tax and contribution rate (% of profit)	46.8		
		Postfiling index (0–100)	42.47	**Resolving insolvency** (rank)	126
Registering property (rank)	173			DTF score for resolving insolvency (0–100)	36.11
DTF score for registering property (0–100)	40.00			Time (years)	5.0
Procedures (number)	5			Cost (% of estate)	14.5
Time (days)	102			Recovery rate (cents on the dollar)	14.8
Cost (% of property value)	10.5			Strength of insolvency framework index (0–16)	9.0
Quality of land administration index (0–30)	3.5				

Note: Most indicator sets refer to a case scenario in the largest business city of an economy, though for 11 economies the data are a population-weighted average for the two largest business cities. For some indicators a result of "no practice" may be recorded for an economy; see the data notes for more details. In starting a business, procedures (number), time (days) and cost (% of income per capita) are calculated as the average of both men and women. For the postfiling index, a result of "not applicable" may be recorded for an economy.

✔ Reform making it easier to do business   ✘ Change making it more difficult to do business

GAMBIA, THE

Sub-Saharan Africa		GNI per capita (US$)	440
Ease of doing business rank (1–190)	146	Overall distance to frontier (DTF) score (0–100)	51.92	Population	2,038,501

Starting a business (rank)	171
DTF score for starting a business (0–100)	69.00
Procedures (number)	7
Time (days)	25
Cost (% of income per capita)	128.2
Minimum capital (% of income per capita)	0.0

Dealing with construction permits (rank)	118
DTF score for dealing with construction permits (0–100)	64.31
Procedures (number)	12
Time (days)	144
Cost (% of warehouse value)	2.2
Building quality control index (0–15)	4.5

Getting electricity (rank)	156
DTF score for getting electricity (0–100)	49.29
Procedures (number)	5
Time (days)	78
Cost (% of income per capita)	3,517.9
Reliability of supply and transparency of tariffs index (0–8)	0

Registering property (rank)	129
DTF score for registering property (0–100)	53.28
Procedures (number)	5
Time (days)	66
Cost (% of property value)	7.6
Quality of land administration index (0–30)	8.5

Getting credit (rank)	122
DTF score for getting credit (0–100)	40.00
Strength of legal rights index (0–12)	8
Depth of credit information index (0–8)	0
Credit bureau coverage (% of adults)	0.0
Credit registry coverage (% of adults)	0.0

Protecting minority investors (rank)	164
DTF score for protecting minority investors (0–100)	36.67
Extent of disclosure index (0–10)	2
Extent of director liability index (0–10)	5
Ease of shareholder suits index (0–10)	5
Extent of shareholder rights index (0–10)	4
Extent of ownership and control index (0–10)	1
Extent of corporate transparency index (0–10)	5

Paying taxes (rank)	169
DTF score for paying taxes (0–100)	49.34
Payments (number per year)	49
Time (hours per year)	326
Total tax and contribution rate (% of profit)	51.3
Postfiling index (0–100)	53.46

Trading across borders (rank)	105
DTF score for trading across borders (0–100)	67.81
Time to export	
Documentary compliance (hours)	48
Border compliance (hours)	109
Cost to export	
Documentary compliance (US$)	133
Border compliance (US$)	381
Time to import	
Documentary compliance (hours)	32
Border compliance (hours)	87
Cost to import	
Documentary compliance (US$)	152
Border compliance (US$)	326

Enforcing contracts (rank)	107
DTF score for enforcing contracts (0–100)	54.84
Time (days)	407
Cost (% of claim)	37.9
Quality of judicial processes index (0–18)	5.5

Resolving insolvency (rank)	130
DTF score for resolving insolvency (0–100)	34.71
Time (years)	2.0
Cost (% of estate)	14.5
Recovery rate (cents on the dollar)	26.8
Strength of insolvency framework index (0–16)	6.5

GEORGIA

Europe & Central Asia		GNI per capita (US$)	3,810
Ease of doing business rank (1–190)	9	Overall distance to frontier (DTF) score (0–100)	82.04	Population	3,719,300

Starting a business (rank)	4
DTF score for starting a business (0–100)	97.84
Procedures (number)	2
Time (days)	2
Cost (% of income per capita)	2.5
Minimum capital (% of income per capita)	0.0

Dealing with construction permits (rank)	29
DTF score for dealing with construction permits (0–100)	77.57
Procedures (number)	11
Time (days)	63
Cost (% of warehouse value)	0.3
Building quality control index (0–15)	7.0

✔ Getting electricity (rank)	30
DTF score for getting electricity (0–100)	84.32
Procedures (number)	3
Time (days)	71
Cost (% of income per capita)	176.8
Reliability of supply and transparency of tariffs index (0–8)	5

Registering property (rank)	4
DTF score for registering property (0–100)	92.85
Procedures (number)	1
Time (days)	1
Cost (% of property value)	0.0
Quality of land administration index (0–30)	21.5

Getting credit (rank)	12
DTF score for getting credit (0–100)	85.00
Strength of legal rights index (0–12)	9
Depth of credit information index (0–8)	8
Credit bureau coverage (% of adults)	95.7
Credit registry coverage (% of adults)	0.0

✔ Protecting minority investors (rank)	2
DTF score for protecting minority investors (0–100)	81.67
Extent of disclosure index (0–10)	9
Extent of director liability index (0–10)	6
Ease of shareholder suits index (0–10)	9
Extent of shareholder rights index (0–10)	7
Extent of ownership and control index (0–10)	9
Extent of corporate transparency index (0–10)	9

Paying taxes (rank)	22
DTF score for paying taxes (0–100)	87.14
Payments (number per year)	5
Time (hours per year)	269
Total tax and contribution rate (% of profit)	16.4
Postfiling index (0–100)	85.89

Trading across borders (rank)	62
DTF score for trading across borders (0–100)	82.43
Time to export	
Documentary compliance (hours)	2
Border compliance (hours)	48
Cost to export	
Documentary compliance (US$)	35
Border compliance (US$)	383
Time to import	
Documentary compliance (hours)	2
Border compliance (hours)	15
Cost to import	
Documentary compliance (US$)	189
Border compliance (US$)	396

Enforcing contracts (rank)	7
DTF score for enforcing contracts (0–100)	75.97
Time (days)	285
Cost (% of claim)	25.0
Quality of judicial processes index (0–18)	12.5

✔ Resolving insolvency (rank)	57
DTF score for resolving insolvency (0–100)	55.59
Time (years)	2.0
Cost (% of estate)	10.0
Recovery rate (cents on the dollar)	39.4
Strength of insolvency framework index (0–16)	11.0

GERMANY

OECD high income		GNI per capita (US$)	43,660
Ease of doing business rank (1–190)	20	Overall distance to frontier (DTF) score (0–100)	79.00	Population	82,667,685

Starting a business (rank)	113
DTF score for starting a business (0–100)	83.46
Procedures (number)	9
Time (days)	10.5
Cost (% of income per capita)	1.9
Minimum capital (% of income per capita)	32.4

Dealing with construction permits (rank)	24
DTF score for dealing with construction permits (0–100)	78.16
Procedures (number)	9
Time (days)	126
Cost (% of warehouse value)	1.2
Building quality control index (0–15)	9.5

Getting electricity (rank)	5
DTF score for getting electricity (0–100)	98.79
Procedures (number)	3
Time (days)	28
Cost (% of income per capita)	40.2
Reliability of supply and transparency of tariffs index (0–8)	8

Registering property (rank)	77
DTF score for registering property (0–100)	65.71
Procedures (number)	6
Time (days)	52
Cost (% of property value)	6.7
Quality of land administration index (0–30)	22.0

Getting credit (rank)	42
DTF score for getting credit (0–100)	70.00
Strength of legal rights index (0–12)	6
Depth of credit information index (0–8)	8
Credit bureau coverage (% of adults)	100.0
Credit registry coverage (% of adults)	1.9

Protecting minority investors (rank)	62
DTF score for protecting minority investors (0–100)	58.33
Extent of disclosure index (0–10)	5
Extent of director liability index (0–10)	5
Ease of shareholder suits index (0–10)	5
Extent of shareholder rights index (0–10)	7
Extent of ownership and control index (0–10)	6
Extent of corporate transparency index (0–10)	7

Paying taxes (rank)	41
DTF score for paying taxes (0–100)	82.14
Payments (number per year)	9
Time (hours per year)	218
Total tax and contribution rate (% of profit)	48.9
Postfiling index (0–100)	97.67

Trading across borders (rank)	39
DTF score for trading across borders (0–100)	91.77
Time to export	
Documentary compliance (hours)	1
Border compliance (hours)	36
Cost to export	
Documentary compliance (US$)	45
Border compliance (US$)	345
Time to import	
Documentary compliance (hours)	1
Border compliance (hours)	0
Cost to import	
Documentary compliance (US$)	0
Border compliance (US$)	0

Enforcing contracts (rank)	22
DTF score for enforcing contracts (0–100)	71.32
Time (days)	499
Cost (% of claim)	14.4
Quality of judicial processes index (0–18)	11.0

Resolving insolvency (rank)	4
DTF score for resolving insolvency (0–100)	90.27
Time (years)	1.2
Cost (% of estate)	8.0
Recovery rate (cents on the dollar)	80.6
Strength of insolvency framework index (0–16)	15.0

Note: Most indicator sets refer to a case scenario in the largest business city of an economy, though for 11 economies the data are a population-weighted average for the two largest business cities. For some indicators a result of "no practice" may be recorded for an economy; see the data notes for more details. In starting a business, procedures (number), time (days) and cost (% of income per capita) are calculated as the average of both men and women. For the postfiling index, a result of "not applicable" may be recorded for an economy.

✔ Reform making it easier to do business   ✘ Change making it more difficult to do business

GHANA

		Sub-Saharan Africa		GNI per capita (US$)	1,380
Ease of doing business rank (1–190)	120	Overall distance to frontier (DTF) score (0–100)	57.24	Population	28,206,728

Starting a business (rank)	110	**Getting credit** (rank)	55	**Trading across borders** (rank)	158
DTF score for starting a business (0–100)	84.02	DTF score for getting credit (0–100)	65.00	DTF score for trading across borders (0–100)	52.32
Procedures (number)	8	Strength of legal rights index (0–12)	7	*Time to export*	
Time (days)	14	Depth of credit information index (0–8)	6	Documentary compliance (hours)	89
Cost (% of income per capita)	17.5	Credit bureau coverage (% of adults)	16.5	Border compliance (hours)	108
Minimum capital (% of income per capita)	1.7	Credit registry coverage (% of adults)	0.0	*Cost to export*	
				Documentary compliance (US$)	155
✔ **Dealing with construction permits** (rank)	131	**Protecting minority investors** (rank)	96	Border compliance (US$)	490
DTF score for dealing with construction permits (0–100)	61.90	DTF score for protecting minority investors (0–100)	51.67	*Time to import*	
Procedures (number)	16	Extent of disclosure index (0–10)	7	Documentary compliance (hours)	76
Time (days)	170	Extent of director liability index (0–10)	5	Border compliance (hours)	89
Cost (% of warehouse value)	5.4	Ease of shareholder suits index (0–10)	7	*Cost to import*	
Building quality control index (0–15)	9.0	Extent of shareholder rights index (0–10)	6	Documentary compliance (US$)	474
		Extent of ownership and control index (0–10)	3	Border compliance (US$)	553
		Extent of corporate transparency index (0–10)	3		
Getting electricity (rank)	136			**Enforcing contracts** (rank)	116
DTF score for getting electricity (0–100)	56.81	**Paying taxes** (rank)	116	DTF score for enforcing contracts (0–100)	54.00
Procedures (number)	5	DTF score for paying taxes (0–100)	66.47	Time (days)	710
Time (days)	78	Payments (number per year)	31	Cost (% of claim)	23.0
Cost (% of income per capita)	1,080.5	Time (hours per year)	224	Quality of judicial processes index (0–18)	6.5
Reliability of supply and transparency of tariffs index (0–8)	0	Total tax and contribution rate (% of profit)	33.2		
		Postfiling index (0–100)	49.54	**Resolving insolvency** (rank)	158
Registering property (rank)	119			DTF score for resolving insolvency (0–100)	24.77
DTF score for registering property (0–100)	55.50			Time (years)	1.9
Procedures (number)	6			Cost (% of estate)	22.0
Time (days)	47			Recovery rate (cents on the dollar)	22.8
Cost (% of property value)	6.2			Strength of insolvency framework index (0–16)	4.0
Quality of land administration index (0–30)	8.0				

GREECE

		OECD high income		GNI per capita (US$)	18,960
Ease of doing business rank (1–190)	67	Overall distance to frontier (DTF) score (0–100)	68.02	Population	10,746,740

✔ **Starting a business** (rank)	37	**Getting credit** (rank)	90	**Trading across borders** (rank)	29
DTF score for starting a business (0–100)	92.30	DTF score for getting credit (0–100)	50.00	DTF score for trading across borders (0–100)	93.72
Procedures (number)	4	Strength of legal rights index (0–12)	3	*Time to export*	
Time (days)	12.5	Depth of credit information index (0–8)	7	Documentary compliance (hours)	1
Cost (% of income per capita)	2.2	Credit bureau coverage (% of adults)	78.3	Border compliance (hours)	24
Minimum capital (% of income per capita)	0.0	Credit registry coverage (% of adults)	0.0	*Cost to export*	
				Documentary compliance (US$)	30
Dealing with construction permits (rank)	58	**Protecting minority investors** (rank)	43	Border compliance (US$)	300
DTF score for dealing with construction permits (0–100)	72.48	DTF score for protecting minority investors (0–100)	63.33	*Time to import*	
Procedures (number)	18	Extent of disclosure index (0–10)	7	Documentary compliance (hours)	1
Time (days)	124	Extent of director liability index (0–10)	4	Border compliance (hours)	1
Cost (% of warehouse value)	2.0	Ease of shareholder suits index (0–10)	5	*Cost to import*	
Building quality control index (0–15)	12.0	Extent of shareholder rights index (0–10)	7	Documentary compliance (US$)	0
		Extent of ownership and control index (0–10)	7	Border compliance (US$)	0
		Extent of corporate transparency index (0–10)	8		
Getting electricity (rank)	76			**Enforcing contracts** (rank)	131
DTF score for getting electricity (0–100)	75.97	**Paying taxes** (rank)	65	DTF score for enforcing contracts (0–100)	50.19
Procedures (number)	7	DTF score for paying taxes (0–100)	76.97	Time (days)	1,580
Time (days)	55	Payments (number per year)	8	Cost (% of claim)	14.4
Cost (% of income per capita)	70.1	Time (hours per year)	193	Quality of judicial processes index (0–18)	12.0
Reliability of supply and transparency of tariffs index (0–8)	7	Total tax and contribution rate (% of profit)	51.7		
		Postfiling index (0–100)	75.70	**Resolving insolvency** (rank)	57
Registering property (rank)	145			DTF score for resolving insolvency (0–100)	55.59
DTF score for registering property (0–100)	49.67			Time (years)	3.5
Procedures (number)	10			Cost (% of estate)	9.0
Time (days)	20			Recovery rate (cents on the dollar)	33.6
Cost (% of property value)	4.8			Strength of insolvency framework index (0–16)	12.0
Quality of land administration index (0–30)	4.5				

GRENADA

		Latin America & Caribbean		GNI per capita (US$)	8,830
Ease of doing business rank (1–190)	142	Overall distance to frontier (DTF) score (0–100)	52.94	Population	107,317

Starting a business (rank)	82	**Getting credit** (rank)	142	**Trading across borders** (rank)	131
DTF score for starting a business (0–100)	87.09	DTF score for getting credit (0–100)	30.00	DTF score for trading across borders (0–100)	61.52
Procedures (number)	6	Strength of legal rights index (0–12)	6	*Time to export*	
Time (days)	15	Depth of credit information index (0–8)	0	Documentary compliance (hours)	13
Cost (% of income per capita)	15.3	Credit bureau coverage (% of adults)	0.0	Border compliance (hours)	101
Minimum capital (% of income per capita)	0.0	Credit registry coverage (% of adults)	0.0	*Cost to export*	
				Documentary compliance (US$)	40
Dealing with construction permits (rank)	128	**Protecting minority investors** (rank)	132	Border compliance (US$)	1,034
DTF score for dealing with construction permits (0–100)	62.22	DTF score for protecting minority investors (0–100)	43.33	*Time to import*	
Procedures (number)	15	Extent of disclosure index (0–10)	4	Documentary compliance (hours)	24
Time (days)	146	Extent of director liability index (0–10)	8	Border compliance (hours)	37
Cost (% of warehouse value)	2.0	Ease of shareholder suits index (0–10)	8	*Cost to import*	
Building quality control index (0–15)	5.0	Extent of shareholder rights index (0–10)	3	Documentary compliance (US$)	50
		Extent of ownership and control index (0–10)	2	Border compliance (US$)	1,745
		Extent of corporate transparency index (0–10)	1		
Getting electricity (rank)	73			**Enforcing contracts** (rank)	76
DTF score for getting electricity (0–100)	76.41	✘ **Paying taxes** (rank)	141	DTF score for enforcing contracts (0–100)	59.33
Procedures (number)	5	DTF score for paying taxes (0–100)	59.39	Time (days)	688
Time (days)	38	Payments (number per year)	42	Cost (% of claim)	32.6
Cost (% of income per capita)	187.8	Time (hours per year)	140	Quality of judicial processes index (0–18)	11.0
Reliability of supply and transparency of tariffs index (0–8)	4	Total tax and contribution rate (% of profit)	48.4		
		Postfiling index (0–100)	48.85	✔ **Resolving insolvency** (rank)	168
Registering property (rank)	141			DTF score for resolving insolvency (0–100)	0.00
DTF score for registering property (0–100)	50.15			Time (years)	no practice
Procedures (number)	8			Cost (% of estate)	no practice
Time (days)	32			Recovery rate (cents on the dollar)	0.0
Cost (% of property value)	7.4			Strength of insolvency framework index (0–16)	0.0
Quality of land administration index (0–30)	7.0				

Note: Most indicator sets refer to a case scenario in the largest business city of an economy, though for 11 economies the data are a population-weighted average for the two largest business cities. For some indicators a result of "no practice" may be recorded for an economy; see the data notes for more details. In starting a business, procedures (number), time (days) and cost (% of income per capita) are calculated as the average of both men and women. For the postfiling index, a result of "not applicable" may be recorded for an economy.

✔ Reform making it easier to do business ✘ Change making it more difficult to do business

GUATEMALA

		Latin America & Caribbean		GNI per capita (US$)	3,790
Ease of doing business rank (1–190)	97	Overall distance to frontier (DTF) score (0–100)	61.18	Population	16,582,469

Starting a business (rank)	139	**Getting credit** (rank)	20	**Trading across borders** (rank)	79
DTF score for starting a business (0–100)	79.30	DTF score for getting credit (0–100)	80.00	DTF score for trading across borders (0–100)	75.31
Procedures (number)	8	Strength of legal rights index (0–12)	9	Time to export	
Time (days)	26.5	Depth of credit information index (0–8)	7	Documentary compliance (hours)	48
Cost (% of income per capita)	22.9	Credit bureau coverage (% of adults)	7.4	Border compliance (hours)	36
Minimum capital (% of income per capita)	16.3	Credit registry coverage (% of adults)	17.5	Cost to export	
				Documentary compliance (US$)	105
✘ **Dealing with construction permits** (rank)	116	**Protecting minority investors** (rank)	172	Border compliance (US$)	310
DTF score for dealing with construction permits (0–100)	64.63	DTF score for protecting minority investors (0–100)	31.67	Time to import	
Procedures (number)	12	Extent of disclosure index (0–10)	3	Documentary compliance (hours)	32
Time (days)	205	Extent of director liability index (0–10)	2	Border compliance (hours)	72
Cost (% of warehouse value)	7.0	Ease of shareholder suits index (0–10)	5	Cost to import	
Building quality control index (0–15)	11.0	Extent of shareholder rights index (0–10)	5	Documentary compliance (US$)	140
		Extent of ownership and control index (0–10)	1	Border compliance (US$)	405
		Extent of corporate transparency index (0–10)	3		
Getting electricity (rank)	36			**Enforcing contracts** (rank)	176
DTF score for getting electricity (0–100)	84.02			DTF score for enforcing contracts (0–100)	34.55
Procedures (number)	5	**Paying taxes** (rank)	100	Time (days)	1,402
Time (days)	44	DTF score for paying taxes (0–100)	70.30	Cost (% of claim)	26.5
Cost (% of income per capita)	550.6	Payments (number per year)	8	Quality of judicial processes index (0–18)	6.0
Reliability of supply and transparency of tariffs index (0–8)	7	Time (hours per year)	248		
		Total tax and contribution rate (% of profit)	35.2	**Resolving insolvency** (rank)	153
Registering property (rank)	85	Postfiling index (0–100)	33.04	DTF score for resolving insolvency (0–100)	27.57
DTF score for registering property (0–100)	64.44			Time (years)	3.0
Procedures (number)	7			Cost (% of estate)	14.5
Time (days)	24			Recovery rate (cents on the dollar)	28.0
Cost (% of property value)	3.7			Strength of insolvency framework index (0–16)	4.0
Quality of land administration index (0–30)	13.0				

GUINEA

		Sub-Saharan Africa		GNI per capita (US$)	490
Ease of doing business rank (1–190)	153	Overall distance to frontier (DTF) score (0–100)	49.80	Population	12,395,924

Starting a business (rank)	125	**Getting credit** (rank)	142	**Trading across borders** (rank)	165
DTF score for starting a business (0–100)	81.77	DTF score for getting credit (0–100)	30.00	DTF score for trading across borders (0–100)	46.24
Procedures (number)	6	Strength of legal rights index (0–12)	6	Time to export	
Time (days)	8	Depth of credit information index (0–8)	0	Documentary compliance (hours)	139
Cost (% of income per capita)	67.5	Credit bureau coverage (% of adults)	0.0	Border compliance (hours)	72
Minimum capital (% of income per capita)	8.9	Credit registry coverage (% of adults)	0.0	Cost to export	
				Documentary compliance (US$)	128
✘ **Dealing with construction permits** (rank)	75	**Protecting minority investors** (rank)	146	Border compliance (US$)	778
DTF score for dealing with construction permits (0–100)	69.92	DTF score for protecting minority investors (0–100)	40.00	Time to import	
Procedures (number)	15	Extent of disclosure index (0–10)	7	Documentary compliance (hours)	156
Time (days)	161	Extent of director liability index (0–10)	1	Border compliance (hours)	91
Cost (% of warehouse value)	4.3	Ease of shareholder suits index (0–10)	5	Cost to import	
Building quality control index (0–15)	12.0	Extent of shareholder rights index (0–10)	4	Documentary compliance (US$)	180
		Extent of ownership and control index (0–10)	3	Border compliance (US$)	909
		Extent of corporate transparency index (0–10)	4		
Getting electricity (rank)	158			**Enforcing contracts** (rank)	117
DTF score for getting electricity (0–100)	47.88			DTF score for enforcing contracts (0–100)	53.87
Procedures (number)	4	**Paying taxes** (rank)	182	Time (days)	311
Time (days)	69	DTF score for paying taxes (0–100)	38.93	Cost (% of claim)	45.0
Cost (% of income per capita)	5,639.8	Payments (number per year)	33	Quality of judicial processes index (0–18)	5.0
Reliability of supply and transparency of tariffs index (0–8)	0	Time (hours per year)	400		
		Total tax and contribution rate (% of profit)	61.4	**Resolving insolvency** (rank)	111
Registering property (rank)	143	Postfiling index (0–100)	12.77	DTF score for resolving insolvency (0–100)	39.27
DTF score for registering property (0–100)	50.07			Time (years)	3.8
Procedures (number)	6			Cost (% of estate)	8.0
Time (days)	44			Recovery rate (cents on the dollar)	20.7
Cost (% of property value)	8.9			Strength of insolvency framework index (0–16)	9.0
Quality of land administration index (0–30)	6.5				

GUINEA–BISSAU

		Sub-Saharan Africa		GNI per capita (US$)	620
Ease of doing business rank (1–190)	176	Overall distance to frontier (DTF) score (0–100)	41.45	Population	1,815,698

Starting a business (rank)	178	✔ **Getting credit** (rank)	142	**Trading across borders** (rank)	141
DTF score for starting a business (0–100)	63.76	DTF score for getting credit (0–100)	30.00	DTF score for trading across borders (0–100)	59.60
Procedures (number)	8.5	Strength of legal rights index (0–12)	6	Time to export	
Time (days)	8.5	Depth of credit information index (0–8)	0	Documentary compliance (hours)	60
Cost (% of income per capita)	48.9	Credit bureau coverage (% of adults)	0.3	Border compliance (hours)	118
Minimum capital (% of income per capita)	273.4	Credit registry coverage (% of adults)	0.1	Cost to export	
				Documentary compliance (US$)	160
Dealing with construction permits (rank)	176	**Protecting minority investors** (rank)	138	Border compliance (US$)	585
DTF score for dealing with construction permits (0–100)	44.40	DTF score for protecting minority investors (0–100)	41.67	Time to import	
Procedures (number)	13	Extent of disclosure index (0–10)	7	Documentary compliance (hours)	36
Time (days)	143	Extent of director liability index (0–10)	1	Border compliance (hours)	84
Cost (% of warehouse value)	28.2	Ease of shareholder suits index (0–10)	6	Cost to import	
Building quality control index (0–15)	6.5	Extent of shareholder rights index (0–10)	4	Documentary compliance (US$)	205
		Extent of ownership and control index (0–10)	3	Border compliance (US$)	550
		Extent of corporate transparency index (0–10)	4		
Getting electricity (rank)	180			**Enforcing contracts** (rank)	168
DTF score for getting electricity (0–100)	29.01			DTF score for enforcing contracts (0–100)	36.76
Procedures (number)	7	**Paying taxes** (rank)	155	Time (days)	1,785
Time (days)	257	DTF score for paying taxes (0–100)	54.93	Cost (% of claim)	28.0
Cost (% of income per capita)	1,399.8	Payments (number per year)	46	Quality of judicial processes index (0–18)	7.5
Reliability of supply and transparency of tariffs index (0–8)	0	Time (hours per year)	218		
		Total tax and contribution rate (% of profit)	45.5	**Resolving insolvency** (rank)	168
Registering property (rank)	126	Postfiling index (0–100)	45.34	DTF score for resolving insolvency (0–100)	0.00
DTF score for registering property (0–100)	54.41			Time (years)	no practice
Procedures (number)	5			Cost (% of estate)	no practice
Time (days)	48			Recovery rate (cents on the dollar)	0.0
Cost (% of property value)	5.5			Strength of insolvency framework index (0–16)	0.0
Quality of land administration index (0–30)	3.0				

Note: Most indicator sets refer to a case scenario in the largest business city of an economy, though for 11 economies the data are a population-weighted average for the two largest business cities. For some indicators a result of "no practice" may be recorded for an economy; see the data notes for more details. In starting a business, procedures (number), time (days) and cost (% of income per capita) are calculated as the average of both men and women. For the postfiling index, a result of "not applicable" may be recorded for an economy.

✔ Reform making it easier to do business   ✘ Change making it more difficult to do business

GUYANA

		Latin America & Caribbean		GNI per capita (US$)	4,250
Ease of doing business rank (1–190)	126	Overall distance to frontier (DTF) score (0–100)	56.28	Population	773,303

Starting a business (rank)	92	**Getting credit** (rank)	90	**Trading across borders** (rank)	142
DTF score for starting a business (0–100)	85.55	DTF score for getting credit (0–100)	50.00	DTF score for trading across borders (0–100)	59.33
Procedures (number)	7	Strength of legal rights index (0–12)	3	*Time to export*	
Time (days)	18	Depth of credit information index (0–8)	7	Documentary compliance (hours)	200
Cost (% of income per capita)	9.8	Credit bureau coverage (% of adults)	52.8	Border compliance (hours)	72
Minimum capital (% of income per capita)	0.0	Credit registry coverage (% of adults)	0.0	*Cost to export*	
				Documentary compliance (US$)	78
Dealing with construction permits (rank)	163	**Protecting minority investors** (rank)	96	Border compliance (US$)	378
DTF score for dealing with construction permits (0–100)	54.66	DTF score for protecting minority investors (0–100)	51.67	*Time to import*	
Procedures (number)	17	Extent of disclosure index (0–10)	5	Documentary compliance (hours)	156
Time (days)	208	Extent of director liability index (0–10)	5	Border compliance (hours)	84
Cost (% of warehouse value)	1.5	Ease of shareholder suits index (0–10)	8	*Cost to import*	
Building quality control index (0–15)	4.0	Extent of shareholder rights index (0–10)	6	Documentary compliance (US$)	63
		Extent of ownership and control index (0–10)	2	Border compliance (US$)	265
Getting electricity (rank)	132	Extent of corporate transparency index (0–10)	5		
DTF score for getting electricity (0–100)	58.35			✔ **Enforcing contracts** (rank)	93
Procedures (number)	8			DTF score for enforcing contracts (0–100)	57.87
Time (days)	82	**Paying taxes** (rank)	123	Time (days)	581
Cost (% of income per capita)	441.7	DTF score for paying taxes (0–100)	65.08	Cost (% of claim)	27.0
Reliability of supply and transparency of tariffs index (0–8)	4	Payments (number per year)	35	Quality of judicial processes index (0–18)	7.5
		Time (hours per year)	256		
		Total tax and contribution rate (% of profit)	32.3		
✔ **Registering property** (rank)	110	Postfiling index (0–100)	54.24	**Resolving insolvency** (rank)	162
DTF score for registering property (0–100)	57.90			DTF score for resolving insolvency (0–100)	22.38
Procedures (number)	6			Time (years)	3.0
Time (days)	45			Cost (% of estate)	28.5
Cost (% of property value)	4.6			Recovery rate (cents on the dollar)	18.4
Quality of land administration index (0–30)	7.5			Strength of insolvency framework index (0–16)	4.0

HAITI

		Latin America & Caribbean		GNI per capita (US$)	780
Ease of doing business rank (1–190)	181	Overall distance to frontier (DTF) score (0–100)	38.24	Population	10,847,334

Starting a business (rank)	189	**Getting credit** (rank)	177	**Trading across borders** (rank)	77
DTF score for starting a business (0–100)	33.70	DTF score for getting credit (0–100)	10.00	DTF score for trading across borders (0–100)	76.90
Procedures (number)	12	Strength of legal rights index (0–12)	2	*Time to export*	
Time (days)	97	Depth of credit information index (0–8)	0	Documentary compliance (hours)	22
Cost (% of income per capita)	200.2	Credit bureau coverage (% of adults)	0.0	Border compliance (hours)	28
Minimum capital (% of income per capita)	14.0	Credit registry coverage (% of adults)	1.5	*Cost to export*	
				Documentary compliance (US$)	48
Dealing with construction permits (rank)	177	**Protecting minority investors** (rank)	188	Border compliance (US$)	368
DTF score for dealing with construction permits (0–100)	44.15	DTF score for protecting minority investors (0–100)	20.00	*Time to import*	
Procedures (number)	14	Extent of disclosure index (0–10)	2	Documentary compliance (hours)	28
Time (days)	98	Extent of director liability index (0–10)	3	Border compliance (hours)	83
Cost (% of warehouse value)	21.6	Ease of shareholder suits index (0–10)	4	*Cost to import*	
Building quality control index (0–15)	5.0	Extent of shareholder rights index (0–10)	2	Documentary compliance (US$)	150
		Extent of ownership and control index (0–10)	1	Border compliance (US$)	563
Getting electricity (rank)	138	Extent of corporate transparency index (0–10)	0		
DTF score for getting electricity (0–100)	55.40			**Enforcing contracts** (rank)	125
Procedures (number)	4			DTF score for enforcing contracts (0–100)	52.49
Time (days)	60	✘ **Paying taxes** (rank)	147	Time (days)	530
Cost (% of income per capita)	3,522.0	DTF score for paying taxes (0–100)	57.55	Cost (% of claim)	42.6
Reliability of supply and transparency of tariffs index (0–8)	0	Payments (number per year)	47	Quality of judicial processes index (0–18)	7.0
		Time (hours per year)	184		
		Total tax and contribution rate (% of profit)	42.8		
Registering property (rank)	180	Postfiling index (0–100)	48.17	**Resolving insolvency** (rank)	168
DTF score for registering property (0–100)	32.22			DTF score for resolving insolvency (0–100)	0.00
Procedures (number)	5			Time (years)	no practice
Time (days)	312			Cost (% of estate)	no practice
Cost (% of property value)	6.9			Recovery rate (cents on the dollar)	0.0
Quality of land administration index (0–30)	2.5			Strength of insolvency framework index (0–16)	0.0

HONDURAS

		Latin America & Caribbean		GNI per capita (US$)	2,150
Ease of doing business rank (1–190)	115	Overall distance to frontier (DTF) score (0–100)	58.46	Population	9,112,867

Starting a business (rank)	150	**Getting credit** (rank)	12	**Trading across borders** (rank)	115
DTF score for starting a business (0–100)	76.98	DTF score for getting credit (0–100)	85.00	DTF score for trading across borders (0–100)	65.85
Procedures (number)	11	Strength of legal rights index (0–12)	9	*Time to export*	
Time (days)	13	Depth of credit information index (0–8)	8	Documentary compliance (hours)	48
Cost (% of income per capita)	41.3	Credit bureau coverage (% of adults)	44.9	Border compliance (hours)	88
Minimum capital (% of income per capita)	0.0	Credit registry coverage (% of adults)	20.9	*Cost to export*	
				Documentary compliance (US$)	80
Dealing with construction permits (rank)	113	**Protecting minority investors** (rank)	129	Border compliance (US$)	601
DTF score for dealing with construction permits (0–100)	65.44	DTF score for protecting minority investors (0–100)	45.00	*Time to import*	
Procedures (number)	17	Extent of disclosure index (0–10)	3	Documentary compliance (hours)	72
Time (days)	94	Extent of director liability index (0–10)	8	Border compliance (hours)	96
Cost (% of warehouse value)	7.5	Ease of shareholder suits index (0–10)	6	*Cost to import*	
Building quality control index (0–15)	10.0	Extent of shareholder rights index (0–10)	5	Documentary compliance (US$)	70
		Extent of ownership and control index (0–10)	2	Border compliance (US$)	483
Getting electricity (rank)	144	Extent of corporate transparency index (0–10)	3		
DTF score for getting electricity (0–100)	53.61			**Enforcing contracts** (rank)	152
Procedures (number)	7			DTF score for enforcing contracts (0–100)	45.54
Time (days)	39	**Paying taxes** (rank)	164	Time (days)	920
Cost (% of income per capita)	790.8	DTF score for paying taxes (0–100)	51.74	Cost (% of claim)	35.2
Reliability of supply and transparency of tariffs index (0–8)	0	Payments (number per year)	48	Quality of judicial processes index (0–18)	7.5
		Time (hours per year)	224		
		Total tax and contribution rate (% of profit)	44.4		
✘ **Registering property** (rank)	91	Postfiling index (0–100)	35.14	**Resolving insolvency** (rank)	142
DTF score for registering property (0–100)	63.42			DTF score for resolving insolvency (0–100)	32.07
Procedures (number)	6			Time (years)	3.8
Time (days)	29			Cost (% of estate)	14.5
Cost (% of property value)	5.7			Recovery rate (cents on the dollar)	18.9
Quality of land administration index (0–30)	14.0			Strength of insolvency framework index (0–16)	7.0

Note: Most indicator sets refer to a case scenario in the largest business city of an economy, though for 11 economies the data are a population-weighted average for the two largest business cities. For some indicators a result of "no practice" may be recorded for an economy; see the data notes for more details. In starting a business, procedures (number), time (days) and cost (% of income per capita) are calculated as the average of both men and women. For the postfiling index, a result of "not applicable" may be recorded for an economy.

✔ Reform making it easier to do business ✘ Change making it more difficult to do business

HONG KONG SAR, CHINA

		East Asia & Pacific		GNI per capita (US$)	43,240
Ease of doing business rank (1–190)	5	Overall distance to frontier (DTF) score (0–100)	83.44	Population	7,346,700

✘ **Starting a business** (rank)	3	**Getting credit** (rank)	29	**Trading across borders** (rank)	31
DTF score for starting a business (0–100)	98.14	DTF score for getting credit (0–100)	75.00	DTF score for trading across borders (0–100)	93.56
Procedures (number)	2	Strength of legal rights index (0–12)	8	*Time to export*	
Time (days)	1.5	Depth of credit information index (0–8)	7	Documentary compliance (hours)	1
Cost (% of income per capita)	1.1	Credit bureau coverage (% of adults)	100.0	Border compliance (hours)	2
Minimum capital (% of income per capita)	0.0	Credit registry coverage (% of adults)	0.0	*Cost to export*	
				Documentary compliance (US$)	57
Dealing with construction permits (rank)	5	**Protecting minority investors** (rank)	9	Border compliance (US$)	0
DTF score for dealing with construction permits (0–100)	84.86	DTF score for protecting minority investors (0–100)	76.67	*Time to import*	
Procedures (number)	11	Extent of disclosure index (0–10)	10	Documentary compliance (hours)	1
Time (days)	72	Extent of director liability index (0–10)	8	Border compliance (hours)	19
Cost (% of warehouse value)	0.7	Ease of shareholder suits index (0–10)	9	*Cost to import*	
Building quality control index (0–15)	12.0	Extent of shareholder rights index (0–10)	7	Documentary compliance (US$)	57
		Extent of ownership and control index (0–10)	4	Border compliance (US$)	266
Getting electricity (rank)	4	Extent of corporate transparency index (0–10)	8		
DTF score for getting electricity (0–100)	99.02			**Enforcing contracts** (rank)	28
Procedures (number)	3	**Paying taxes** (rank)	3	DTF score for enforcing contracts (0–100)	69.13
Time (days)	27	DTF score for paying taxes (0–100)	98.82	Time (days)	385
Cost (% of income per capita)	1.4	Payments (number per year)	3	Cost (% of claim)	23.6
Reliability of supply and transparency of tariffs index (0–8)	8	Time (hours per year)	72	Quality of judicial processes index (0–18)	10.0
		Total tax and contribution rate (% of profit)	22.9		
✔ **Registering property** (rank)	55	Postfiling index (0–100)	98.85	**Resolving insolvency** (rank)	43
DTF score for registering property (0–100)	73.54			DTF score for resolving insolvency (0–100)	65.69
Procedures (number)	5			Time (years)	0.8
Time (days)	27.5			Cost (% of estate)	5.0
Cost (% of property value)	7.7			Recovery rate (cents on the dollar)	87.2
Quality of land administration index (0–30)	27.5			Strength of insolvency framework index (0–16)	6.0

HUNGARY

		OECD high income		GNI per capita (US$)	12,570
Ease of doing business rank (1–190)	48	Overall distance to frontier (DTF) score (0–100)	72.39	Population	9,817,958

Starting a business (rank)	79	**Getting credit** (rank)	29	**Trading across borders** (rank)	1
DTF score for starting a business (0–100)	87.60	DTF score for getting credit (0–100)	75.00	DTF score for trading across borders (0–100)	100.00
Procedures (number)	6	Strength of legal rights index (0–12)	10	*Time to export*	
Time (days)	7	Depth of credit information index (0–8)	5	Documentary compliance (hours)	1
Cost (% of income per capita)	5.4	Credit bureau coverage (% of adults)	89.8	Border compliance (hours)	0
Minimum capital (% of income per capita)	43.8	Credit registry coverage (% of adults)	0.0	*Cost to export*	
				Documentary compliance (US$)	0
Dealing with construction permits (rank)	90	**Protecting minority investors** (rank)	108	Border compliance (US$)	0
DTF score for dealing with construction permits (0–100)	67.93	DTF score for protecting minority investors (0–100)	50.00	*Time to import*	
Procedures (number)	20	Extent of disclosure index (0–10)	2	Documentary compliance (hours)	1
Time (days)	205.5	Extent of director liability index (0–10)	4	Border compliance (hours)	0
Cost (% of warehouse value)	0.6	Ease of shareholder suits index (0–10)	6	*Cost to import*	
Building quality control index (0–15)	13.0	Extent of shareholder rights index (0–10)	6	Documentary compliance (US$)	0
		Extent of ownership and control index (0–10)	5	Border compliance (US$)	0
Getting electricity (rank)	110	Extent of corporate transparency index (0–10)	7		
DTF score for getting electricity (0–100)	63.26			✔ **Enforcing contracts** (rank)	13
Procedures (number)	5	**Paying taxes** (rank)	93	DTF score for enforcing contracts (0–100)	73.75
Time (days)	257	DTF score for paying taxes (0–100)	71.49	Time (days)	605
Cost (% of income per capita)	90.3	Payments (number per year)	11	Cost (% of claim)	15.0
Reliability of supply and transparency of tariffs index (0–8)	7	Time (hours per year)	277	Quality of judicial processes index (0–18)	14.0
		Total tax and contribution rate (% of profit)	46.5		
Registering property (rank)	29	Postfiling index (0–100)	63.94	**Resolving insolvency** (rank)	62
DTF score for registering property (0–100)	80.09			DTF score for resolving insolvency (0–100)	54.75
Procedures (number)	4			Time (years)	2.0
Time (days)	17.5			Cost (% of estate)	14.5
Cost (% of property value)	5.0			Recovery rate (cents on the dollar)	43.7
Quality of land administration index (0–30)	26.0			Strength of insolvency framework index (0–16)	10.0

ICELAND

		OECD high income		GNI per capita (US$)	56,990
Ease of doing business rank (1–190)	23	Overall distance to frontier (DTF) score (0–100)	78.50	Population	334,252

Starting a business (rank)	55	**Getting credit** (rank)	68	**Trading across borders** (rank)	69
DTF score for starting a business (0–100)	90.71	DTF score for getting credit (0–100)	60.00	DTF score for trading across borders (0–100)	80.27
Procedures (number)	5	Strength of legal rights index (0–12)	5	*Time to export*	
Time (days)	11.5	Depth of credit information index (0–8)	7	Documentary compliance (hours)	2
Cost (% of income per capita)	1.8	Credit bureau coverage (% of adults)	100.0	Border compliance (hours)	36
Minimum capital (% of income per capita)	6.8	Credit registry coverage (% of adults)	0.0	*Cost to export*	
				Documentary compliance (US$)	40
Dealing with construction permits (rank)	64	**Protecting minority investors** (rank)	29	Border compliance (US$)	655
DTF score for dealing with construction permits (0–100)	71.72	DTF score for protecting minority investors (0–100)	68.33	*Time to import*	
Procedures (number)	17	Extent of disclosure index (0–10)	7	Documentary compliance (hours)	3
Time (days)	84	Extent of director liability index (0–10)	5	Border compliance (hours)	24
Cost (% of warehouse value)	0.3	Ease of shareholder suits index (0–10)	8	*Cost to import*	
Building quality control index (0–15)	8.0	Extent of shareholder rights index (0–10)	6	Documentary compliance (US$)	0
		Extent of ownership and control index (0–10)	7	Border compliance (US$)	655
Getting electricity (rank)	11	Extent of corporate transparency index (0–10)	8		
DTF score for getting electricity (0–100)	92.24			**Enforcing contracts** (rank)	29
Procedures (number)	4	**Paying taxes** (rank)	33	DTF score for enforcing contracts (0–100)	69.10
Time (days)	22	DTF score for paying taxes (0–100)	84.54	Time (days)	417
Cost (% of income per capita)	9.4	Payments (number per year)	21	Cost (% of claim)	9.0
Reliability of supply and transparency of tariffs index (0–8)	7	Time (hours per year)	140	Quality of judicial processes index (0–18)	7.5
		Total tax and contribution rate (% of profit)	29.7		
Registering property (rank)	15	Postfiling index (0–100)	87.20	**Resolving insolvency** (rank)	13
DTF score for registering property (0–100)	86.61			DTF score for resolving insolvency (0–100)	81.44
Procedures (number)	3			Time (years)	1.0
Time (days)	3.5			Cost (% of estate)	3.5
Cost (% of property value)	3.6			Recovery rate (cents on the dollar)	84.5
Quality of land administration index (0–30)	26.5			Strength of insolvency framework index (0–16)	11.5

Note: Most indicator sets refer to a case scenario in the largest business city of an economy, though for 11 economies the data are a population-weighted average for the two largest business cities. For some indicators a result of "no practice" may be recorded for an economy; see the data notes for more details. In starting a business, procedures (number), time (days) and cost (% of income per capita) are calculated as the average of both men and women. For the postfiling index, a result of "not applicable" may be recorded for an economy.

✔ Reform making it easier to do business   ✘ Change making it more difficult to do business

INDIA

Ease of doing business rank (1–190)	**100**	**Overall distance to frontier (DTF) score (0–100)**	**60.76**	**Population**	**1,324,171,354**

South Asia — GNI per capita (US$) 1,680

✔ **Starting a business** (rank) — 156
DTF score for starting a business (0–100) — 75.40
Procedures (number) — 11.5
Time (days) — 29.8
Cost (% of income per capita) — 14.8
Minimum capital (% of income per capita) — 0.0

✔ **Dealing with construction permits** (rank) — 181
DTF score for dealing with construction permits (0–100) — 38.80
Procedures (number) — 30.1
Time (days) — 143.9
Cost (% of warehouse value) — 23.2
Building quality control index (0–15) — 11.5

Getting electricity (rank) — 29
DTF score for getting electricity (0–100) — 85.21
Procedures (number) — 5
Time (days) — 45.9
Cost (% of income per capita) — 96.7
Reliability of supply and transparency of tariffs index (0–8) — 7

Registering property (rank) — 154
DTF score for registering property (0–100) — 47.08
Procedures (number) — 8
Time (days) — 53
Cost (% of property value) — 8.4
Quality of land administration index (0–30) — 8.2

✔ **Getting credit** (rank) — 29
DTF score for getting credit (0–100) — 75.00
Strength of legal rights index (0–12) — 8
Depth of credit information index (0–8) — 7
Credit bureau coverage (% of adults) — 43.5
Credit registry coverage (% of adults) — 0.0

✔ **Protecting minority investors** (rank) — 4
DTF score for protecting minority investors (0–100) — 80.00
Extent of disclosure index (0–10) — 8
Extent of director liability index (0–10) — 7
Ease of shareholder suits index (0–10) — 7
Extent of shareholder rights index (0–10) — 10
Extent of ownership and control index (0–10) — 8
Extent of corporate transparency index (0–10) — 8

✔ **Paying taxes** (rank) — 119
DTF score for paying taxes (0–100) — 66.06
Payments (number per year) — 13
Time (hours per year) — 214
Total tax and contribution rate (% of profit) — 55.3
Postfiling index (0–100) — 49.31

✔ **Trading across borders** (rank) — 146
DTF score for trading across borders (0–100) — 58.56
Time to export
Documentary compliance (hours) — 38.4
Border compliance (hours) — 106.1
Cost to export
Documentary compliance (US$) — 91.9
Border compliance (US$) — 382.4
Time to import
Documentary compliance (hours) — 61.3
Border compliance (hours) — 264.5
Cost to import
Documentary compliance (US$) — 134.8
Border compliance (US$) — 543.2

✔ **Enforcing contracts** (rank) — 164
DTF score for enforcing contracts (0–100) — 40.76
Time (days) — 1,445
Cost (% of claim) — 31.0
Quality of judicial processes index (0–18) — 10.3

✔ **Resolving insolvency** (rank) — 103
DTF score for resolving insolvency (0–100) — 40.75
Time (years) — 4.3
Cost (% of estate) — 9.0
Recovery rate (cents on the dollar) — 26.4
Strength of insolvency framework index (0–16) — 8.5

INDONESIA

Ease of doing business rank (1–190)	**72**	**Overall distance to frontier (DTF) score (0–100)**	**66.47**	**Population**	**261,115,456**

East Asia & Pacific — GNI per capita (US$) 3,400

✔ **Starting a business** (rank) — 144
DTF score for starting a business (0–100) — 77.93
Procedures (number) — 11.2
Time (days) — 23.1
Cost (% of income per capita) — 10.9
Minimum capital (% of income per capita) — 0.0

Dealing with construction permits (rank) — 108
DTF score for dealing with construction permits (0–100) — 66.08
Procedures (number) — 17
Time (days) — 200.2
Cost (% of warehouse value) — 4.8
Building quality control index (0–15) — 13.0

✔ **Getting electricity** (rank) — 38
DTF score for getting electricity (0–100) — 83.87
Procedures (number) — 4
Time (days) — 34
Cost (% of income per capita) — 276.1
Reliability of supply and transparency of tariffs index (0–8) — 5

✔ **Registering property** (rank) — 106
DTF score for registering property (0–100) — 59.01
Procedures (number) — 5
Time (days) — 27.6
Cost (% of property value) — 8.3
Quality of land administration index (0–30) — 11.3

✔ **Getting credit** (rank) — 55
DTF score for getting credit (0–100) — 65.00
Strength of legal rights index (0–12) — 6
Depth of credit information index (0–8) — 7
Credit bureau coverage (% of adults) — 18.3
Credit registry coverage (% of adults) — 55.3

Protecting minority investors (rank) — 43
DTF score for protecting minority investors (0–100) — 63.33
Extent of disclosure index (0–10) — 10
Extent of director liability index (0–10) — 5
Ease of shareholder suits index (0–10) — 2
Extent of shareholder rights index (0–10) — 7
Extent of ownership and control index (0–10) — 7
Extent of corporate transparency index (0–10) — 7

✔ **Paying taxes** (rank) — 114
DTF score for paying taxes (0–100) — 68.04
Payments (number per year) — 43
Time (hours per year) — 207.5
Total tax and contribution rate (% of profit) — 30.0
Postfiling index (0–100) — 68.82

✔ **Trading across borders** (rank) — 112
DTF score for trading across borders (0–100) — 66.59
Time to export
Documentary compliance (hours) — 61.3
Border compliance (hours) — 53.3
Cost to export
Documentary compliance (US$) — 138.8
Border compliance (US$) — 253.7
Time to import
Documentary compliance (hours) — 119.2
Border compliance (hours) — 99.4
Cost to import
Documentary compliance (US$) — 164.4
Border compliance (US$) — 382.6

Enforcing contracts (rank) — 145
DTF score for enforcing contracts (0–100) — 47.23
Time (days) — 403
Cost (% of claim) — 70.3
Quality of judicial processes index (0–18) — 7.9

Resolving insolvency (rank) — 38
DTF score for resolving insolvency (0–100) — 67.61
Time (years) — 1.1
Cost (% of estate) — 21.6
Recovery rate (cents on the dollar) — 64.7
Strength of insolvency framework index (0–16) — 10.5

IRAN, ISLAMIC REP.

Ease of doing business rank (1–190)	**124**	**Overall distance to frontier (DTF) score (0–100)**	**56.48**	**Population**	**80,277,428**

Middle East & North Africa — GNI per capita (US$) 4,683

Starting a business (rank) — 97
DTF score for starting a business (0–100) — 85.16
Procedures (number) — 8.5
Time (days) — 15
Cost (% of income per capita) — 1.4
Minimum capital (% of income per capita) — 0.0

Dealing with construction permits (rank) — 25
DTF score for dealing with construction permits (0–100) — 78.07
Procedures (number) — 15
Time (days) — 99
Cost (% of warehouse value) — 2.0
Building quality control index (0–15) — 12.5

Getting electricity (rank) — 99
DTF score for getting electricity (0–100) — 68.43
Procedures (number) — 6
Time (days) — 77
Cost (% of income per capita) — 1,064.9
Reliability of supply and transparency of tariffs index (0–8) — 5

Registering property (rank) — 87
DTF score for registering property (0–100) — 64.16
Procedures (number) — 7
Time (days) — 12
Cost (% of property value) — 5.7
Quality of land administration index (0–30) — 15.0

✔ **Getting credit** (rank) — 90
DTF score for getting credit (0–100) — 50.00
Strength of legal rights index (0–12) — 2
Depth of credit information index (0–8) — 8
Credit bureau coverage (% of adults) — 55.8
Credit registry coverage (% of adults) — 54.7

Protecting minority investors (rank) — 170
DTF score for protecting minority investors (0–100) — 33.33
Extent of disclosure index (0–10) — 7
Extent of director liability index (0–10) — 4
Ease of shareholder suits index (0–10) — 1
Extent of shareholder rights index (0–10) — 3
Extent of ownership and control index (0–10) — 3
Extent of corporate transparency index (0–10) — 2

Paying taxes (rank) — 150
DTF score for paying taxes (0–100) — 56.57
Payments (number per year) — 20
Time (hours per year) — 344
Total tax and contribution rate (% of profit) — 44.7
Postfiling index (0–100) — 26.88

Trading across borders (rank) — 166
DTF score for trading across borders (0–100) — 46.11
Time to export
Documentary compliance (hours) — 120
Border compliance (hours) — 101
Cost to export
Documentary compliance (US$) — 125
Border compliance (US$) — 565
Time to import
Documentary compliance (hours) — 192
Border compliance (hours) — 141
Cost to import
Documentary compliance (US$) — 197
Border compliance (US$) — 660

Enforcing contracts (rank) — 80
DTF score for enforcing contracts (0–100) — 59.07
Time (days) — 505
Cost (% of claim) — 17.0
Quality of judicial processes index (0–18) — 5.0

Resolving insolvency (rank) — 160
DTF score for resolving insolvency (0–100) — 23.93
Time (years) — 4.5
Cost (% of estate) — 15.0
Recovery rate (cents on the dollar) — 15.4
Strength of insolvency framework index (0–16) — 5.0

Note: Most indicator sets refer to a case scenario in the largest business city of an economy, though for 11 economies the data are a population-weighted average for the two largest business cities. For some indicators a result of "no practice" may be recorded for an economy; see the data notes for more details. In starting a business, procedures (number), time (days) and cost (% of income per capita) are calculated as the average of both men and women. For the postfiling index, a result of "not applicable" may be recorded for an economy.

✔ Reform making it easier to do business   ✘ Change making it more difficult to do business

IRAQ

IRAQ		Middle East & North Africa		GNI per capita (US$)	5,430
Ease of doing business rank (1–190)	168	Overall distance to frontier (DTF) score (0–100)	44.87	Population	37,202,572

✔ **Starting a business** (rank)	154	✔ **Getting credit** (rank)	186	**Trading across borders** (rank)	179
DTF score for starting a business (0–100)	75.87	DTF score for getting credit (0–100)	0.00	DTF score for trading across borders (0–100)	25.33
Procedures (number)	8.5	Strength of legal rights index (0–12)	0	*Time to export*	
Time (days)	26.5	Depth of credit information index (0–8)	0	Documentary compliance (hours)	504
Cost (% of income per capita)	43.3	Credit bureau coverage (% of adults)	0.0	Border compliance (hours)	85
Minimum capital (% of income per capita)	18.5	Credit registry coverage (% of adults)	1.2	*Cost to export*	
				Documentary compliance (US$)	1,800
Dealing with construction permits (rank)	93	**Protecting minority investors** (rank)	124	Border compliance (US$)	1,118
DTF score for dealing with construction permits (0–100)	67.66	DTF score for protecting minority investors (0–100)	46.67	*Time to import*	
Procedures (number)	11	Extent of disclosure index (0–10)	4	Documentary compliance (hours)	176
Time (days)	167	Extent of director liability index (0–10)	5	Border compliance (hours)	131
Cost (% of warehouse value)	0.3	Ease of shareholder suits index (0–10)	5	*Cost to import*	
Building quality control index (0–15)	5.5	Extent of shareholder rights index (0–10)	8	Documentary compliance (US$)	500
		Extent of ownership and control index (0–10)	3	Border compliance (US$)	644
		Extent of corporate transparency index (0–10)	3		
Getting electricity (rank)	116			**Enforcing contracts** (rank)	144
DTF score for getting electricity (0–100)	61.64	**Paying taxes** (rank)	129	DTF score for enforcing contracts (0–100)	48.02
Procedures (number)	5	DTF score for paying taxes (0–100)	63.55	Time (days)	520
Time (days)	51	Payments (number per year)	15	Cost (% of claim)	28.1
Cost (% of income per capita)	466.6	Time (hours per year)	312	Quality of judicial processes index (0–18)	1.5
Reliability of supply and transparency of tariffs index (0–8)	0	Total tax and contribution rate (% of profit)	30.8		
		Postfiling index (0–100)	21.43	**Resolving insolvency** (rank)	168
Registering property (rank)	101			DTF score for resolving insolvency (0–100)	0.00
DTF score for registering property (0–100)	59.97			Time (years)	no practice
Procedures (number)	5			Cost (% of estate)	no practice
Time (days)	51			Recovery rate (cents on the dollar)	0.0
Cost (% of property value)	5.7			Strength of insolvency framework index (0–16)	0.0
Quality of land administration index (0–30)	10.5				

IRELAND

IRELAND		OECD high income		GNI per capita (US$)	52,560
Ease of doing business rank (1–190)	17	Overall distance to frontier (DTF) score (0–100)	79.51	Population	4,773,095

Starting a business (rank)	8	**Getting credit** (rank)	42	**Trading across borders** (rank)	47
DTF score for starting a business (0–100)	95.91	DTF score for getting credit (0–100)	70.00	DTF score for trading across borders (0–100)	87.25
Procedures (number)	3	Strength of legal rights index (0–12)	7	*Time to export*	
Time (days)	5	Depth of credit information index (0–8)	7	Documentary compliance (hours)	1
Cost (% of income per capita)	0.2	Credit bureau coverage (% of adults)	100.0	Border compliance (hours)	24
Minimum capital (% of income per capita)	0.0	Credit registry coverage (% of adults)	0.0	*Cost to export*	
				Documentary compliance (US$)	75
Dealing with construction permits (rank)	30	**Protecting minority investors** (rank)	10	Border compliance (US$)	305
DTF score for dealing with construction permits (0–100)	76.99	DTF score for protecting minority investors (0–100)	75.00	*Time to import*	
Procedures (number)	10	Extent of disclosure index (0–10)	9	Documentary compliance (hours)	1
Time (days)	149.5	Extent of director liability index (0–10)	8	Border compliance (hours)	24
Cost (% of warehouse value)	4.6	Ease of shareholder suits index (0–10)	9	*Cost to import*	
Building quality control index (0–15)	13.0	Extent of shareholder rights index (0–10)	7	Documentary compliance (US$)	75
		Extent of ownership and control index (0–10)	4	Border compliance (US$)	253
		Extent of corporate transparency index (0–10)	8		
Getting electricity (rank)	35			**Enforcing contracts** (rank)	98
DTF score for getting electricity (0–100)	84.22			DTF score for enforcing contracts (0–100)	56.03
Procedures (number)	5	**Paying taxes** (rank)	4	Time (days)	650
Time (days)	85	DTF score for paying taxes (0–100)	94.46	Cost (% of claim)	26.9
Cost (% of income per capita)	52.8	Payments (number per year)	9	Quality of judicial processes index (0–18)	7.5
Reliability of supply and transparency of tariffs index (0–8)	8	Time (hours per year)	82		
		Total tax and contribution rate (% of profit)	26.0	**Resolving insolvency** (rank)	17
Registering property (rank)	40	Postfiling index (0–100)	92.93	DTF score for resolving insolvency (0–100)	79.00
DTF score for registering property (0–100)	76.29			Time (years)	0.4
Procedures (number)	5			Cost (% of estate)	9.0
Time (days)	31.5			Recovery rate (cents on the dollar)	85.8
Cost (% of property value)	2.5			Strength of insolvency framework index (0–16)	10.5
Quality of land administration index (0–30)	21.0				

ISRAEL

ISRAEL		OECD high income		GNI per capita (US$)	36,190
Ease of doing business rank (1–190)	54	Overall distance to frontier (DTF) score (0–100)	71.42	Population	8,547,100

Starting a business (rank)	37	**Getting credit** (rank)	55	**Trading across borders** (rank)	60
DTF score for starting a business (0–100)	92.30	DTF score for getting credit (0–100)	65.00	DTF score for trading across borders (0–100)	82.85
Procedures (number)	4	Strength of legal rights index (0–12)	6	*Time to export*	
Time (days)	12	Depth of credit information index (0–8)	7	Documentary compliance (hours)	13
Cost (% of income per capita)	3.2	Credit bureau coverage (% of adults)	71.4	Border compliance (hours)	36
Minimum capital (% of income per capita)	0.0	Credit registry coverage (% of adults)	0.0	*Cost to export*	
				Documentary compliance (US$)	73
Dealing with construction permits (rank)	65	**Protecting minority investors** (rank)	16	Border compliance (US$)	150
DTF score for dealing with construction permits (0–100)	71.69	DTF score for protecting minority investors (0–100)	73.33	*Time to import*	
Procedures (number)	15	Extent of disclosure index (0–10)	7	Documentary compliance (hours)	44
Time (days)	209	Extent of director liability index (0–10)	9	Border compliance (hours)	64
Cost (% of warehouse value)	1.4	Ease of shareholder suits index (0–10)	9	*Cost to import*	
Building quality control index (0–15)	13.0	Extent of shareholder rights index (0–10)	7	Documentary compliance (US$)	70
		Extent of ownership and control index (0–10)	3	Border compliance (US$)	307
		Extent of corporate transparency index (0–10)	9		
Getting electricity (rank)	77			**Enforcing contracts** (rank)	92
DTF score for getting electricity (0–100)	75.20			DTF score for enforcing contracts (0–100)	57.93
Procedures (number)	6	**Paying taxes** (rank)	99	Time (days)	975
Time (days)	102	DTF score for paying taxes (0–100)	70.35	Cost (% of claim)	25.3
Cost (% of income per capita)	14.1	Payments (number per year)	33	Quality of judicial processes index (0–18)	13.0
Reliability of supply and transparency of tariffs index (0–8)	7	Time (hours per year)	235		
		Total tax and contribution rate (% of profit)	27.0	**Resolving insolvency** (rank)	29
Registering property (rank)	130	Postfiling index (0–100)	61.36	DTF score for resolving insolvency (0–100)	72.74
DTF score for registering property (0–100)	52.84			Time (years)	2.0
Procedures (number)	6			Cost (% of estate)	23.0
Time (days)	81			Recovery rate (cents on the dollar)	62.6
Cost (% of property value)	8.3			Strength of insolvency framework index (0–16)	12.5
Quality of land administration index (0–30)	14.0				

Note: Most indicator sets refer to a case scenario in the largest business city of an economy, though for 11 economies the data are a population-weighted average for the two largest business cities. For some indicators a result of "no practice" may be recorded for an economy; see the data notes for more details. In starting a business, procedures (number), time (days) and cost (% of income per capita) are calculated as the average of both men and women. For the postfiling index, a result of "not applicable" may be recorded for an economy.

✔ Reform making it easier to do business   ✘ Change making it more difficult to do business

ITALY

		OECD high income		GNI per capita (US$)	31,590
Ease of doing business rank (1–190)	46	Overall distance to frontier (DTF) score (0–100)	72.70	Population	60,600,590

Starting a business (rank)	66	**Getting credit** (rank)	105	**Trading across borders** (rank)	1
DTF score for starting a business (0–100)	89.42	DTF score for getting credit (0–100)	45.00	DTF score for trading across borders (0–100)	100.00
Procedures (number)	6	Strength of legal rights index (0–12)	2	*Time to export*	
Time (days)	6.5	Depth of credit information index (0–8)	7	Documentary compliance (hours)	1
Cost (% of income per capita)	13.7	Credit bureau coverage (% of adults)	100.0	Border compliance (hours)	0
Minimum capital (% of income per capita)	0.0	Credit registry coverage (% of adults)	30.1	*Cost to export*	
				Documentary compliance (US$)	0
				Border compliance (US$)	0
Dealing with construction permits (rank)	96	**Protecting minority investors** (rank)	62	*Time to import*	
DTF score for dealing with construction permits (0–100)	67.26	DTF score for protecting minority investors (0–100)	58.33	Documentary compliance (hours)	1
Procedures (number)	12	Extent of disclosure index (0–10)	7	Border compliance (hours)	0
Time (days)	227.5	Extent of director liability index (0–10)	4	*Cost to import*	
Cost (% of warehouse value)	3.6	Ease of shareholder suits index (0–10)	6	Documentary compliance (US$)	0
Building quality control index (0–15)	11.0	Extent of shareholder rights index (0–10)	6	Border compliance (US$)	0
		Extent of ownership and control index (0–10)	4		
✔ **Getting electricity** (rank)	28	Extent of corporate transparency index (0–10)	8		
DTF score for getting electricity (0–100)	85.27			**Enforcing contracts** (rank)	108
Procedures (number)	4	✔ **Paying taxes** (rank)	112	DTF score for enforcing contracts (0–100)	54.79
Time (days)	82	DTF score for paying taxes (0–100)	68.29	Time (days)	1,120
Cost (% of income per capita)	156.5	Payments (number per year)	14	Cost (% of claim)	23.1
Reliability of supply and transparency of tariffs index (0–8)	7	Time (hours per year)	238	Quality of judicial processes index (0–18)	13.0
		Total tax and contribution rate (% of profit)	48.0		
Registering property (rank)	23	Postfiling index (0–100)	52.39	**Resolving insolvency** (rank)	24
DTF score for registering property (0–100)	81.70			DTF score for resolving insolvency (0–100)	76.97
Procedures (number)	4			Time (years)	1.8
Time (days)	16			Cost (% of estate)	22.0
Cost (% of property value)	4.4			Recovery rate (cents on the dollar)	64.6
Quality of land administration index (0–30)	26.5			Strength of insolvency framework index (0–16)	13.5

JAMAICA

		Latin America & Caribbean		GNI per capita (US$)	4,660
Ease of doing business rank (1–190)	70	Overall distance to frontier (DTF) score (0–100)	67.27	Population	2,881,355

✔ **Starting a business** (rank)	5	**Getting credit** (rank)	20	✔ **Trading across borders** (rank)	130
DTF score for starting a business (0–100)	97.30	DTF score for getting credit (0–100)	80.00	DTF score for trading across borders (0–100)	61.54
Procedures (number)	2	Strength of legal rights index (0–12)	9	*Time to export*	
Time (days)	3	Depth of credit information index (0–8)	7	Documentary compliance (hours)	47
Cost (% of income per capita)	4.8	Credit bureau coverage (% of adults)	24.1	Border compliance (hours)	58
Minimum capital (% of income per capita)	0.0	Credit registry coverage (% of adults)	0.0	*Cost to export*	
				Documentary compliance (US$)	90
				Border compliance (US$)	876
Dealing with construction permits (rank)	98	**Protecting minority investors** (rank)	81	*Time to import*	
DTF score for dealing with construction permits (0–100)	67.22	DTF score for protecting minority investors (0–100)	55.00	Documentary compliance (hours)	56
Procedures (number)	19	Extent of disclosure index (0–10)	4	Border compliance (hours)	80
Time (days)	141.5	Extent of director liability index (0–10)	8	*Cost to import*	
Cost (% of warehouse value)	1.7	Ease of shareholder suits index (0–10)	5	Documentary compliance (US$)	90
Building quality control index (0–15)	10.0	Extent of shareholder rights index (0–10)	6	Border compliance (US$)	906
		Extent of ownership and control index (0–10)	4		
✔ **Getting electricity** (rank)	91	Extent of corporate transparency index (0–10)	6		
DTF score for getting electricity (0–100)	71.11			**Enforcing contracts** (rank)	127
Procedures (number)	7			DTF score for enforcing contracts (0–100)	51.87
Time (days)	95	**Paying taxes** (rank)	122	Time (days)	550
Cost (% of income per capita)	237.3	DTF score for paying taxes (0–100)	65.67	Cost (% of claim)	50.2
Reliability of supply and transparency of tariffs index (0–8)	7	Payments (number per year)	11	Quality of judicial processes index (0–18)	8.5
		Time (hours per year)	268		
Registering property (rank)	128	Total tax and contribution rate (% of profit)	33.1	**Resolving insolvency** (rank)	35
DTF score for registering property (0–100)	53.70	Postfiling index (0–100)	19.68	DTF score for resolving insolvency (0–100)	69.31
Procedures (number)	8			Time (years)	1.1
Time (days)	18			Cost (% of estate)	18.0
Cost (% of property value)	9.8			Recovery rate (cents on the dollar)	64.9
Quality of land administration index (0–30)	14.0			Strength of insolvency framework index (0–16)	11.0

JAPAN

		OECD high income		GNI per capita (US$)	38,000
Ease of doing business rank (1–190)	34	Overall distance to frontier (DTF) score (0–100)	75.68	Population	126,994,511

Starting a business (rank)	106	**Getting credit** (rank)	77	**Trading across borders** (rank)	51
DTF score for starting a business (0–100)	84.37	DTF score for getting credit (0–100)	55.00	DTF score for trading across borders (0–100)	86.51
Procedures (number)	9	Strength of legal rights index (0–12)	5	*Time to export*	
Time (days)	12.2	Depth of credit information index (0–8)	6	Documentary compliance (hours)	2.4
Cost (% of income per capita)	7.5	Credit bureau coverage (% of adults)	100.0	Border compliance (hours)	22.6
Minimum capital (% of income per capita)	0.0	Credit registry coverage (% of adults)	0.0	*Cost to export*	
				Documentary compliance (US$)	54
				Border compliance (US$)	264.9
Dealing with construction permits (rank)	50	**Protecting minority investors** (rank)	62	*Time to import*	
DTF score for dealing with construction permits (0–100)	73.36	DTF score for protecting minority investors (0–100)	58.33	Documentary compliance (hours)	3.4
Procedures (number)	12	Extent of disclosure index (0–10)	7	Border compliance (hours)	39.6
Time (days)	197	Extent of director liability index (0–10)	6	*Cost to import*	
Cost (% of warehouse value)	0.5	Ease of shareholder suits index (0–10)	8	Documentary compliance (US$)	107
Building quality control index (0–15)	11.0	Extent of shareholder rights index (0–10)	6	Border compliance (US$)	299.2
		Extent of ownership and control index (0–10)	3		
Getting electricity (rank)	17	Extent of corporate transparency index (0–10)	5		
DTF score for getting electricity (0–100)	89.88			**Enforcing contracts** (rank)	51
Procedures (number)	3.4	✔ **Paying taxes** (rank)	68	DTF score for enforcing contracts (0–100)	65.26
Time (days)	97.7	DTF score for paying taxes (0–100)	76.71	Time (days)	360
Cost (% of income per capita)	0.0	Payments (number per year)	14	Cost (% of claim)	23.4
Reliability of supply and transparency of tariffs index (0–8)	8	Time (hours per year)	151	Quality of judicial processes index (0–18)	7.5
		Total tax and contribution rate (% of profit)	47.4		
Registering property (rank)	52	Postfiling index (0–100)	71.69	**Resolving insolvency** (rank)	1
DTF score for registering property (0–100)	73.92			DTF score for resolving insolvency (0–100)	93.44
Procedures (number)	6			Time (years)	0.6
Time (days)	13			Cost (% of estate)	4.2
Cost (% of property value)	5.8			Recovery rate (cents on the dollar)	92.4
Quality of land administration index (0–30)	24.5			Strength of insolvency framework index (0–16)	14.0

Note: Most indicator sets refer to a case scenario in the largest business city of an economy, though for 11 economies the data are a population-weighted average for the two largest business cities. For some indicators a result of "no practice" may be recorded for an economy; see the data notes for more details. In starting a business, procedures (number), time (days) and cost (% of income per capita) are calculated as the average of both men and women. For the postfiling index, a result of "not applicable" may be recorded for an economy.

✔ Reform making it easier to do business   ✘ Change making it more difficult to do business

JORDAN

		Middle East & North Africa		GNI per capita (US$)	3,920
Ease of doing business rank (1–190)	103	Overall distance to frontier (DTF) score (0–100)	60.58	Population	9,455,802

Starting a business (rank)	105	✔ Getting credit (rank)	159	Trading across borders (rank)	53
DTF score for starting a business (0–100)	84.40	DTF score for getting credit (0–100)	25.00	DTF score for trading across borders (0–100)	85.93
Procedures (number)	7.5	Strength of legal rights index (0–12)	0	Time to export	
Time (days)	12.5	Depth of credit information index (0–8)	5	Documentary compliance (hours)	6
Cost (% of income per capita)	24.2	Credit bureau coverage (% of adults)	15.3	Border compliance (hours)	38
Minimum capital (% of income per capita)	0.1	Credit registry coverage (% of adults)	2.2	Cost to export	
				Documentary compliance (US$)	16
Dealing with construction permits (rank)	110	Protecting minority investors (rank)	146	Border compliance (US$)	131
DTF score for dealing with construction permits (0–100)	65.74	DTF score for protecting minority investors (0–100)	40.00	Time to import	
Procedures (number)	15	Extent of disclosure index (0–10)	4	Documentary compliance (hours)	55
Time (days)	62	Extent of director liability index (0–10)	4	Border compliance (hours)	79
Cost (% of warehouse value)	12.0	Ease of shareholder suits index (0–10)	2	Cost to import	
Building quality control index (0–15)	11.0	Extent of shareholder rights index (0–10)	2	Documentary compliance (US$)	30
		Extent of ownership and control index (0–10)	5	Border compliance (US$)	181
		Extent of corporate transparency index (0–10)	7		
Getting electricity (rank)	40			Enforcing contracts (rank)	118
DTF score for getting electricity (0–100)	83.33	Paying taxes (rank)	97	DTF score for enforcing contracts (0–100)	53.71
Procedures (number)	5	DTF score for paying taxes (0–100)	70.75	Time (days)	642
Time (days)	55	Payments (number per year)	25	Cost (% of claim)	31.2
Cost (% of income per capita)	384.1	Time (hours per year)	128.5	Quality of judicial processes index (0–18)	7.0
Reliability of supply and transparency of tariffs index (0–8)	7	Total tax and contribution rate (% of profit)	28.1		
		Postfiling index (0–100)	34.69	Resolving insolvency (rank)	146
Registering property (rank)	72			DTF score for resolving insolvency (0–100)	30.53
DTF score for registering property (0–100)	66.40			Time (years)	3.0
Procedures (number)	6			Cost (% of estate)	20.0
Time (days)	17			Recovery rate (cents on the dollar)	27.7
Cost (% of property value)	9.0			Strength of insolvency framework index (0–16)	5.0
Quality of land administration index (0–30)	22.5				

KAZAKHSTAN

		Europe & Central Asia		GNI per capita (US$)	8,710
Ease of doing business rank (1–190)	36	Overall distance to frontier (DTF) score (0–100)	75.44	Population	17,797,032

Starting a business (rank)	41	Getting credit (rank)	77	Trading across borders (rank)	123
DTF score for starting a business (0–100)	91.95	DTF score for getting credit (0–100)	55.00	DTF score for trading across borders (0–100)	63.19
Procedures (number)	5	Strength of legal rights index (0–12)	4	Time to export	
Time (days)	9	Depth of credit information index (0–8)	7	Documentary compliance (hours)	128
Cost (% of income per capita)	0.3	Credit bureau coverage (% of adults)	54.4	Border compliance (hours)	133
Minimum capital (% of income per capita)	0.0	Credit registry coverage (% of adults)	0.0	Cost to export	
				Documentary compliance (US$)	320
Dealing with construction permits (rank)	52	✔ Protecting minority investors (rank)	1	Border compliance (US$)	574
DTF score for dealing with construction permits (0–100)	73.30	DTF score for protecting minority investors (0–100)	85.00	Time to import	
Procedures (number)	19	Extent of disclosure index (0–10)	9	Documentary compliance (hours)	6
Time (days)	123	Extent of director liability index (0–10)	6	Border compliance (hours)	2
Cost (% of warehouse value)	1.9	Ease of shareholder suits index (0–10)	9	Cost to import	
Building quality control index (0–15)	13.0	Extent of shareholder rights index (0–10)	10	Documentary compliance (US$)	0
		Extent of ownership and control index (0–10)	8	Border compliance (US$)	0
		Extent of corporate transparency index (0–10)	9		
Getting electricity (rank)	70			✔ Enforcing contracts (rank)	6
DTF score for getting electricity (0–100)	76.77	Paying taxes (rank)	50	DTF score for enforcing contracts (0–100)	77.55
Procedures (number)	7	DTF score for paying taxes (0–100)	79.47	Time (days)	370
Time (days)	77	Payments (number per year)	7	Cost (% of claim)	22.0
Cost (% of income per capita)	47.4	Time (hours per year)	178	Quality of judicial processes index (0–18)	14.0
Reliability of supply and transparency of tariffs index (0–8)	8	Total tax and contribution rate (% of profit)	29.2		
		Postfiling index (0–100)	48.85	Resolving insolvency (rank)	39
✔ Registering property (rank)	17			DTF score for resolving insolvency (0–100)	67.52
DTF score for registering property (0–100)	84.61			Time (years)	1.5
Procedures (number)	3			Cost (% of estate)	15.0
Time (days)	3.5			Recovery rate (cents on the dollar)	38.3
Cost (% of property value)	0.1			Strength of insolvency framework index (0–16)	15.0
Quality of land administration index (0–30)	17.0				

KENYA

		Sub-Saharan Africa		GNI per capita (US$)	1,380
Ease of doing business rank (1–190)	80	Overall distance to frontier (DTF) score (0–100)	65.15	Population	48,461,567

✔ Starting a business (rank)	117	✔ Getting credit (rank)	29	✔ Trading across borders (rank)	106
DTF score for starting a business (0–100)	83.20	DTF score for getting credit (0–100)	75.00	DTF score for trading across borders (0–100)	67.63
Procedures (number)	6	Strength of legal rights index (0–12)	7	Time to export	
Time (days)	25	Depth of credit information index (0–8)	8	Documentary compliance (hours)	19
Cost (% of income per capita)	26.3	Credit bureau coverage (% of adults)	30.4	Border compliance (hours)	21
Minimum capital (% of income per capita)	0.0	Credit registry coverage (% of adults)	0.0	Cost to export	
				Documentary compliance (US$)	191
✔ Dealing with construction permits (rank)	124	Protecting minority investors (rank)	62	Border compliance (US$)	143
DTF score for dealing with construction permits (0–100)	63.16	DTF score for protecting minority investors (0–100)	58.33	Time to import	
Procedures (number)	16	Extent of disclosure index (0–10)	6	Documentary compliance (hours)	60
Time (days)	159	Extent of director liability index (0–10)	5	Border compliance (hours)	180
Cost (% of warehouse value)	5.0	Ease of shareholder suits index (0–10)	9	Cost to import	
Building quality control index (0–15)	9.0	Extent of shareholder rights index (0–10)	5	Documentary compliance (US$)	115
		Extent of ownership and control index (0–10)	6	Border compliance (US$)	833
		Extent of corporate transparency index (0–10)	4		
✔ Getting electricity (rank)	71			Enforcing contracts (rank)	90
DTF score for getting electricity (0–100)	76.68	✔ Paying taxes (rank)	92	DTF score for enforcing contracts (0–100)	58.27
Procedures (number)	3	DTF score for paying taxes (0–100)	71.67	Time (days)	465
Time (days)	97	Payments (number per year)	26	Cost (% of claim)	41.8
Cost (% of income per capita)	724.7	Time (hours per year)	185.5	Quality of judicial processes index (0–18)	9.0
Reliability of supply and transparency of tariffs index (0–8)	4	Total tax and contribution rate (% of profit)	37.4		
		Postfiling index (0–100)	62.03	Resolving insolvency (rank)	95
Registering property (rank)	125			DTF score for resolving insolvency (0–100)	43.11
DTF score for registering property (0–100)	54.49			Time (years)	4.5
Procedures (number)	9			Cost (% of estate)	22.0
Time (days)	61			Recovery rate (cents on the dollar)	27.9
Cost (% of property value)	6.0			Strength of insolvency framework index (0–16)	9.0
Quality of land administration index (0–30)	16.0				

Note: Most indicator sets refer to a case scenario in the largest business city of an economy, though for 11 economies the data are a population-weighted average for the two largest business cities. For some indicators a result of "no practice" may be recorded for an economy; see the data notes for more details. In starting a business, procedures (number), time (days) and cost (% of income per capita) are calculated as the average of both men and women. For the postfiling index, a result of "not applicable" may be recorded for an economy.

✔ Reform making it easier to do business   ✘ Change making it more difficult to do business

KIRIBATI

		East Asia & Pacific		GNI per capita (US$)	2,380
Ease of doing business rank (1–190)	157	Overall distance to frontier (DTF) score (0–100)	48.74	Population	114,395

Starting a business (rank)	147
DTF score for starting a business (0–100)	77.47
Procedures (number)	7
Time (days)	31
Cost (% of income per capita)	40.2
Minimum capital (% of income per capita)	16.2
Dealing with construction permits (rank)	111
DTF score for dealing with construction permits (0–100)	65.72
Procedures (number)	15
Time (days)	150
Cost (% of warehouse value)	0.3
Building quality control index (0–15)	6.0
Getting electricity (rank)	168
DTF score for getting electricity (0–100)	41.50
Procedures (number)	6
Time (days)	97
Cost (% of income per capita)	4,022.3
Reliability of supply and transparency of tariffs index (0–8)	0
Registering property (rank)	146
DTF score for registering property (0–100)	49.12
Procedures (number)	5
Time (days)	513
Cost (% of property value)	0.0
Quality of land administration index (0–30)	9.0

Getting credit (rank)	170
DTF score for getting credit (0–100)	20.00
Strength of legal rights index (0–12)	4
Depth of credit information index (0–8)	0
Credit bureau coverage (% of adults)	0.0
Credit registry coverage (% of adults)	0.0
Protecting minority investors (rank)	124
DTF score for protecting minority investors (0–100)	46.67
Extent of disclosure index (0–10)	6
Extent of director liability index (0–10)	5
Ease of shareholder suits index (0–10)	8
Extent of shareholder rights index (0–10)	5
Extent of ownership and control index (0–10)	2
Extent of corporate transparency index (0–10)	2
Paying taxes (rank)	94
DTF score for paying taxes (0–100)	71.42
Payments (number per year)	11
Time (hours per year)	168
Total tax and contribution rate (% of profit)	32.7
Postfiling index (0–100)	26.68

Trading across borders (rank)	127
DTF score for trading across borders (0–100)	62.08
Time to export	
Documentary compliance (hours)	24
Border compliance (hours)	72
Cost to export	
Documentary compliance (US$)	310
Border compliance (US$)	420
Time to import	
Documentary compliance (hours)	48
Border compliance (hours)	96
Cost to import	
Documentary compliance (US$)	120
Border compliance (US$)	685
Enforcing contracts (rank)	121
DTF score for enforcing contracts (0–100)	53.39
Time (days)	660
Cost (% of claim)	25.8
Quality of judicial processes index (0–18)	6.0
Resolving insolvency (rank)	168
DTF score for resolving insolvency (0–100)	0.00
Time (years)	no practice
Cost (% of estate)	no practice
Recovery rate (cents on the dollar)	0.0
Strength of insolvency framework index (0–16)	0.0

KOREA, REP.

		OECD high income		GNI per capita (US$)	27,600
Ease of doing business rank (1–190)	4	Overall distance to frontier (DTF) score (0–100)	83.92	Population	51,245,707

Starting a business (rank)	9
DTF score for starting a business (0–100)	95.83
Procedures (number)	2
Time (days)	4
Cost (% of income per capita)	14.6
Minimum capital (% of income per capita)	0.0
Dealing with construction permits (rank)	28
DTF score for dealing with construction permits (0–100)	77.74
Procedures (number)	10
Time (days)	27.5
Cost (% of warehouse value)	4.4
Building quality control index (0–15)	8.0
Getting electricity (rank)	2
DTF score for getting electricity (0–100)	99.89
Procedures (number)	3
Time (days)	13
Cost (% of income per capita)	37.0
Reliability of supply and transparency of tariffs index (0–8)	8
Registering property (rank)	39
DTF score for registering property (0–100)	76.34
Procedures (number)	7
Time (days)	5.5
Cost (% of property value)	5.1
Quality of land administration index (0–30)	27.5

Getting credit (rank)	55
DTF score for getting credit (0–100)	65.00
Strength of legal rights index (0–12)	5
Depth of credit information index (0–8)	8
Credit bureau coverage (% of adults)	100.0
Credit registry coverage (% of adults)	0.0
Protecting minority investors (rank)	20
DTF score for protecting minority investors (0–100)	71.67
Extent of disclosure index (0–10)	7
Extent of director liability index (0–10)	6
Ease of shareholder suits index (0–10)	8
Extent of shareholder rights index (0–10)	7
Extent of ownership and control index (0–10)	6
Extent of corporate transparency index (0–10)	9
Paying taxes (rank)	24
DTF score for paying taxes (0–100)	86.69
Payments (number per year)	12
Time (hours per year)	188
Total tax and contribution rate (% of profit)	33.1
Postfiling index (0–100)	93.04

Trading across borders (rank)	33
DTF score for trading across borders (0–100)	92.52
Time to export	
Documentary compliance (hours)	1
Border compliance (hours)	13
Cost to export	
Documentary compliance (US$)	11
Border compliance (US$)	185
Time to import	
Documentary compliance (hours)	1
Border compliance (hours)	6
Cost to import	
Documentary compliance (US$)	27
Border compliance (US$)	315
Enforcing contracts (rank)	1
DTF score for enforcing contracts (0–100)	84.15
Time (days)	290
Cost (% of claim)	12.7
Quality of judicial processes index (0–18)	14.5
Resolving insolvency (rank)	5
DTF score for resolving insolvency (0–100)	89.33
Time (years)	1.5
Cost (% of estate)	3.5
Recovery rate (cents on the dollar)	84.7
Strength of insolvency framework index (0–16)	14.0

KOSOVO

		Europe & Central Asia		GNI per capita (US$)	3,850
Ease of doing business rank (1–190)	40	Overall distance to frontier (DTF) score (0–100)	73.49	Population	1,816,200

✔ **Starting a business** (rank)	10
DTF score for starting a business (0–100)	95.67
Procedures (number)	3
Time (days)	5.5
Cost (% of income per capita)	1.0
Minimum capital (% of income per capita)	0.0
Dealing with construction permits (rank)	122
DTF score for dealing with construction permits (0–100)	63.72
Procedures (number)	15
Time (days)	152
Cost (% of warehouse value)	5.8
Building quality control index (0–15)	9.0
Getting electricity (rank)	106
DTF score for getting electricity (0–100)	66.12
Procedures (number)	6
Time (days)	36
Cost (% of income per capita)	219.1
Reliability of supply and transparency of tariffs index (0–8)	2
Registering property (rank)	34
DTF score for registering property (0–100)	78.12
Procedures (number)	6
Time (days)	27
Cost (% of property value)	0.3
Quality of land administration index (0–30)	20.5

✔ **Getting credit** (rank)	12
DTF score for getting credit (0–100)	85.00
Strength of legal rights index (0–12)	11
Depth of credit information index (0–8)	6
Credit bureau coverage (% of adults)	0.0
Credit registry coverage (% of adults)	40.5
Protecting minority investors (rank)	89
DTF score for protecting minority investors (0–100)	53.33
Extent of disclosure index (0–10)	6
Extent of director liability index (0–10)	6
Ease of shareholder suits index (0–10)	4
Extent of shareholder rights index (0–10)	9
Extent of ownership and control index (0–10)	2
Extent of corporate transparency index (0–10)	5
Paying taxes (rank)	45
DTF score for paying taxes (0–100)	80.28
Payments (number per year)	10
Time (hours per year)	155
Total tax and contribution rate (% of profit)	15.2
Postfiling index (0–100)	49.16

Trading across borders (rank)	48
DTF score for trading across borders (0–100)	86.87
Time to export	
Documentary compliance (hours)	38
Border compliance (hours)	28
Cost to export	
Documentary compliance (US$)	127
Border compliance (US$)	105
Time to import	
Documentary compliance (hours)	6
Border compliance (hours)	16
Cost to import	
Documentary compliance (US$)	42
Border compliance (US$)	128
Enforcing contracts (rank)	49
DTF score for enforcing contracts (0–100)	65.66
Time (days)	330
Cost (% of claim)	34.4
Quality of judicial processes index (0–18)	9.5
✔ **Resolving insolvency** (rank)	49
DTF score for resolving insolvency (0–100)	60.13
Time (years)	2.0
Cost (% of estate)	15.0
Recovery rate (cents on the dollar)	39.1
Strength of insolvency framework index (0–16)	12.5

Note: Most indicator sets refer to a case scenario in the largest business city of an economy, though for 11 economies the data are a population-weighted average for the two largest business cities. For some indicators a result of "no practice" may be recorded for an economy; see the data notes for more details. In starting a business, procedures (number), time (days) and cost (% of income per capita) are calculated as the average of both men and women. For the postfiling index, a result of "not applicable" may be recorded for an economy.

✔ Reform making it easier to do business   ✘ Change making it more difficult to do business

KUWAIT

		Middle East & North Africa		GNI per capita (US$)	39,050
Ease of doing business rank (1–190)	96	Overall distance to frontier (DTF) score (0–100)	61.23	Population	4,052,584

✔ **Starting a business** (rank)	149	**Getting credit** (rank)	133	**Trading across borders** (rank)	154
DTF score for starting a business (0–100)	77.21	DTF score for getting credit (0–100)	35.00	DTF score for trading across borders (0–100)	54.24
Procedures (number)	9.5	Strength of legal rights index (0–12)	1	*Time to export*	
Time (days)	38.5	Depth of credit information index (0–8)	6	Documentary compliance (hours)	72
Cost (% of income per capita)	1.7	Credit bureau coverage (% of adults)	31.0	Border compliance (hours)	96
Minimum capital (% of income per capita)	8.5	Credit registry coverage (% of adults)	15.0	*Cost to export*	
				Documentary compliance (US$)	191
Dealing with construction permits (rank)	129	**Protecting minority investors** (rank)	81	Border compliance (US$)	602
DTF score for dealing with construction permits (0–100)	62.20	DTF score for protecting minority investors (0–100)	55.00	*Time to import*	
Procedures (number)	23	Extent of disclosure index (0–10)	4	Documentary compliance (hours)	96
Time (days)	236	Extent of director liability index (0–10)	9	Border compliance (hours)	89
Cost (% of warehouse value)	1.1	Ease of shareholder suits index (0–10)	4	*Cost to import*	
Building quality control index (0–15)	13.0	Extent of shareholder rights index (0–10)	3	Documentary compliance (US$)	332
		Extent of ownership and control index (0–10)	5	Border compliance (US$)	491
		Extent of corporate transparency index (0–10)	8		
Getting electricity (rank)	97			**Enforcing contracts** (rank)	73
DTF score for getting electricity (0–100)	69.60			DTF score for enforcing contracts (0–100)	59.58
Procedures (number)	7	**Paying taxes** (rank)	6	Time (days)	566
Time (days)	85	DTF score for paying taxes (0–100)	92.48	Cost (% of claim)	18.6
Cost (% of income per capita)	64.2	Payments (number per year)	12	Quality of judicial processes index (0–18)	6.5
Reliability of supply and transparency of tariffs index (0–8)	6	Time (hours per year)	98		
		Total tax and contribution rate (% of profit)	13.0		
✔ **Registering property** (rank)	70	Postfiling index (0–100)	not applicable	**Resolving insolvency** (rank)	110
DTF score for registering property (0–100)	67.55			DTF score for resolving insolvency (0–100)	39.44
Procedures (number)	9			Time (years)	4.2
Time (days)	35			Cost (% of estate)	10.0
Cost (% of property value)	0.5			Recovery rate (cents on the dollar)	32.6
Quality of land administration index (0–30)	17.0			Strength of insolvency framework index (0–16)	7.0

KYRGYZ REPUBLIC

		Europe & Central Asia		GNI per capita (US$)	1,100
Ease of doing business rank (1–190)	77	Overall distance to frontier (DTF) score (0–100)	65.70	Population	6,082,700

Starting a business (rank)	29	✔ **Getting credit** (rank)	29	**Trading across borders** (rank)	84
DTF score for starting a business (0–100)	92.94	DTF score for getting credit (0–100)	75.00	DTF score for trading across borders (0–100)	73.34
Procedures (number)	4	Strength of legal rights index (0–12)	9	*Time to export*	
Time (days)	10	Depth of credit information index (0–8)	6	Documentary compliance (hours)	21
Cost (% of income per capita)	2.1	Credit bureau coverage (% of adults)	37.0	Border compliance (hours)	20
Minimum capital (% of income per capita)	0.0	Credit registry coverage (% of adults)	0.0	*Cost to export*	
				Documentary compliance (US$)	145
Dealing with construction permits (rank)	31	**Protecting minority investors** (rank)	51	Border compliance (US$)	445
DTF score for dealing with construction permits (0–100)	76.85	DTF score for protecting minority investors (0–100)	61.67	*Time to import*	
Procedures (number)	11	Extent of disclosure index (0–10)	7	Documentary compliance (hours)	36
Time (days)	142	Extent of director liability index (0–10)	5	Border compliance (hours)	72
Cost (% of warehouse value)	1.7	Ease of shareholder suits index (0–10)	8	*Cost to import*	
Building quality control index (0–15)	11.0	Extent of shareholder rights index (0–10)	4	Documentary compliance (US$)	200
		Extent of ownership and control index (0–10)	6	Border compliance (US$)	512
		Extent of corporate transparency index (0–10)	7		
Getting electricity (rank)	164			**Enforcing contracts** (rank)	139
DTF score for getting electricity (0–100)	44.19			DTF score for enforcing contracts (0–100)	48.57
Procedures (number)	7	**Paying taxes** (rank)	151	Time (days)	410
Time (days)	125	DTF score for paying taxes (0–100)	56.55	Cost (% of claim)	47.0
Cost (% of income per capita)	814.4	Payments (number per year)	51	Quality of judicial processes index (0–18)	4.0
Reliability of supply and transparency of tariffs index (0–8)	0	Time (hours per year)	225		
		Total tax and contribution rate (% of profit)	29.0		
✘ **Registering property** (rank)	8	Postfiling index (0–100)	37.38	**Resolving insolvency** (rank)	119
DTF score for registering property (0–100)	90.21			DTF score for resolving insolvency (0–100)	37.67
Procedures (number)	3			Time (years)	1.5
Time (days)	3.5			Cost (% of estate)	15.0
Cost (% of property value)	0.2			Recovery rate (cents on the dollar)	35.2
Quality of land administration index (0–30)	24.0			Strength of insolvency framework index (0–16)	6.0

LAO PDR

		East Asia & Pacific		GNI per capita (US$)	2,150
Ease of doing business rank (1–190)	141	Overall distance to frontier (DTF) score (0–100)	53.01	Population	6,758,353

Starting a business (rank)	164	**Getting credit** (rank)	77	**Trading across borders** (rank)	124
DTF score for starting a business (0–100)	72.56	DTF score for getting credit (0–100)	55.00	DTF score for trading across borders (0–100)	62.98
Procedures (number)	8	Strength of legal rights index (0–12)	6	*Time to export*	
Time (days)	67	Depth of credit information index (0–8)	5	Documentary compliance (hours)	216
Cost (% of income per capita)	3.5	Credit bureau coverage (% of adults)	0.0	Border compliance (hours)	12
Minimum capital (% of income per capita)	0.0	Credit registry coverage (% of adults)	11.2	*Cost to export*	
				Documentary compliance (US$)	235
Dealing with construction permits (rank)	40	**Protecting minority investors** (rank)	172	Border compliance (US$)	73
DTF score for dealing with construction permits (0–100)	75.25	DTF score for protecting minority investors (0–100)	31.67	*Time to import*	
Procedures (number)	11	Extent of disclosure index (0–10)	6	Documentary compliance (hours)	216
Time (days)	83	Extent of director liability index (0–10)	1	Border compliance (hours)	14
Cost (% of warehouse value)	0.4	Ease of shareholder suits index (0–10)	3	*Cost to import*	
Building quality control index (0–15)	6.5	Extent of shareholder rights index (0–10)	4	Documentary compliance (US$)	115
		Extent of ownership and control index (0–10)	4	Border compliance (US$)	153
		Extent of corporate transparency index (0–10)	1		
Getting electricity (rank)	149			**Enforcing contracts** (rank)	97
DTF score for getting electricity (0–100)	52.65			DTF score for enforcing contracts (0–100)	56.22
Procedures (number)	6	**Paying taxes** (rank)	156	Time (days)	443
Time (days)	134	DTF score for paying taxes (0–100)	54.18	Cost (% of claim)	31.6
Cost (% of income per capita)	1,132.5	Payments (number per year)	35	Quality of judicial processes index (0–18)	5.5
Reliability of supply and transparency of tariffs index (0–8)	2	Time (hours per year)	362		
		Total tax and contribution rate (% of profit)	26.2		
Registering property (rank)	65	Postfiling index (0–100)	18.57	**Resolving insolvency** (rank)	168
DTF score for registering property (0–100)	69.55			DTF score for resolving insolvency (0–100)	0.00
Procedures (number)	4			Time (years)	no practice
Time (days)	53			Cost (% of estate)	no practice
Cost (% of property value)	1.0			Recovery rate (cents on the dollar)	0.0
Quality of land administration index (0–30)	10.5			Strength of insolvency framework index (0–16)	0.0

Note: Most indicator sets refer to a case scenario in the largest business city of an economy, though for 11 economies the data are a population-weighted average for the two largest business cities. For some indicators a result of "no practice" may be recorded for an economy; see the data notes for more details. In starting a business, procedures (number), time (days) and cost (% of income per capita) are calculated as the average of both men and women. For the postfiling index, a result of "not applicable" may be recorded for an economy.

✔ Reform making it easier to do business   ✘ Change making it more difficult to do business

LATVIA

		OECD high income		GNI per capita (US$)	14,630
Ease of doing business rank (1–190)	19	Overall distance to frontier (DTF) score (0–100)	79.26	Population	1,960,424

Starting a business (rank)	21
DTF score for starting a business (0–100)	94.11
Procedures (number)	4
Time (days)	5.5
Cost (% of income per capita)	1.8
Minimum capital (% of income per capita)	0.0

Dealing with construction permits (rank)	49
DTF score for dealing with construction permits (0–100)	73.41
Procedures (number)	14
Time (days)	192
Cost (% of warehouse value)	0.5
Building quality control index (0–15)	12.0

Getting electricity (rank)	62
DTF score for getting electricity (0–100)	79.05
Procedures (number)	4
Time (days)	107
Cost (% of income per capita)	278.1
Reliability of supply and transparency of tariffs index (0–8)	6

Registering property (rank)	22
DTF score for registering property (0–100)	81.87
Procedures (number)	4
Time (days)	16.5
Cost (% of property value)	2.0
Quality of land administration index (0–30)	22.0

Getting credit (rank)	12
DTF score for getting credit (0–100)	85.00
Strength of legal rights index (0–12)	9
Depth of credit information index (0–8)	8
Credit bureau coverage (% of adults)	43.1
Credit registry coverage (% of adults)	88.8

Protecting minority investors (rank)	43
DTF score for protecting minority investors (0–100)	63.33
Extent of disclosure index (0–10)	5
Extent of director liability index (0–10)	4
Ease of shareholder suits index (0–10)	9
Extent of shareholder rights index (0–10)	7
Extent of ownership and control index (0–10)	5
Extent of corporate transparency index (0–10)	8

Paying taxes (rank)	13
DTF score for paying taxes (0–100)	89.79
Payments (number per year)	7
Time (hours per year)	168.5
Total tax and contribution rate (% of profit)	35.9
Postfiling index (0–100)	98.11

Trading across borders (rank)	25
DTF score for trading across borders (0–100)	95.26
Time to export	
Documentary compliance (hours)	2
Border compliance (hours)	24
Cost to export	
Documentary compliance (US$)	35
Border compliance (US$)	150
Time to import	
Documentary compliance (hours)	1
Border compliance (hours)	0
Cost to import	
Documentary compliance (US$)	0
Border compliance (US$)	0

Enforcing contracts (rank)	20
DTF score for enforcing contracts (0–100)	71.66
Time (days)	469
Cost (% of claim)	23.1
Quality of judicial processes index (0–18)	12.5

Resolving insolvency (rank)	53
DTF score for resolving insolvency (0–100)	59.10
Time (years)	1.5
Cost (% of estate)	10.0
Recovery rate (cents on the dollar)	40.1
Strength of insolvency framework index (0–16)	12.0

LEBANON

		Middle East & North Africa		GNI per capita (US$)	7,680
Ease of doing business rank (1–190)	133	Overall distance to frontier (DTF) score (0–100)	54.67	Population	6,006,668

Starting a business (rank)	143
DTF score for starting a business (0–100)	78.17
Procedures (number)	8
Time (days)	15
Cost (% of income per capita)	42.0
Minimum capital (% of income per capita)	42.3

Dealing with construction permits (rank)	142
DTF score for dealing with construction permits (0–100)	59.66
Procedures (number)	19
Time (days)	249
Cost (% of warehouse value)	5.6
Building quality control index (0–15)	13.0

Getting electricity (rank)	123
DTF score for getting electricity (0–100)	60.07
Procedures (number)	5
Time (days)	75
Cost (% of income per capita)	130.2
Reliability of supply and transparency of tariffs index (0–8)	0

Registering property (rank)	102
DTF score for registering property (0–100)	59.93
Procedures (number)	8
Time (days)	34
Cost (% of property value)	5.9
Quality of land administration index (0–30)	16.0

Getting credit (rank)	122
DTF score for getting credit (0–100)	40.00
Strength of legal rights index (0–12)	2
Depth of credit information index (0–8)	6
Credit bureau coverage (% of adults)	0.0
Credit registry coverage (% of adults)	22.9

Protecting minority investors (rank)	138
DTF score for protecting minority investors (0–100)	41.67
Extent of disclosure index (0–10)	9
Extent of director liability index (0–10)	1
Ease of shareholder suits index (0–10)	5
Extent of shareholder rights index (0–10)	4
Extent of ownership and control index (0–10)	1
Extent of corporate transparency index (0–10)	5

Paying taxes (rank)	113
DTF score for paying taxes (0–100)	68.21
Payments (number per year)	20
Time (hours per year)	181
Total tax and contribution rate (% of profit)	30.3
Postfiling index (0–100)	27.48

Trading across borders (rank)	140
DTF score for trading across borders (0–100)	59.71
Time to export	
Documentary compliance (hours)	48
Border compliance (hours)	96
Cost to export	
Documentary compliance (US$)	100
Border compliance (US$)	410
Time to import	
Documentary compliance (hours)	72
Border compliance (hours)	180
Cost to import	
Documentary compliance (US$)	135
Border compliance (US$)	695

Enforcing contracts (rank)	134
DTF score for enforcing contracts (0–100)	49.85
Time (days)	721
Cost (% of claim)	30.8
Quality of judicial processes index (0–18)	6.0

Resolving insolvency (rank)	147
DTF score for resolving insolvency (0–100)	29.42
Time (years)	3.0
Cost (% of estate)	15.0
Recovery rate (cents on the dollar)	31.4
Strength of insolvency framework index (0–16)	4.0

LESOTHO

		Sub-Saharan Africa		GNI per capita (US$)	1,210
Ease of doing business rank (1–190)	104	Overall distance to frontier (DTF) score (0–100)	60.42	Population	2,203,821

Starting a business (rank)	119
DTF score for starting a business (0–100)	83.06
Procedures (number)	7
Time (days)	29
Cost (% of income per capita)	7.7
Minimum capital (% of income per capita)	0.0

Dealing with construction permits (rank)	167
DTF score for dealing with construction permits (0–100)	51.57
Procedures (number)	10
Time (days)	183
Cost (% of warehouse value)	12.4
Building quality control index (0–15)	5.0

Getting electricity (rank)	152
DTF score for getting electricity (0–100)	52.09
Procedures (number)	5
Time (days)	114
Cost (% of income per capita)	1,341.8
Reliability of supply and transparency of tariffs index (0–8)	0

Registering property (rank)	109
DTF score for registering property (0–100)	58.12
Procedures (number)	4
Time (days)	43
Cost (% of property value)	8.1
Quality of land administration index (0–30)	9.5

Getting credit (rank)	77
DTF score for getting credit (0–100)	55.00
Strength of legal rights index (0–12)	5
Depth of credit information index (0–8)	6
Credit bureau coverage (% of adults)	7.5
Credit registry coverage (% of adults)	0.0

Protecting minority investors (rank)	108
DTF score for protecting minority investors (0–100)	50.00
Extent of disclosure index (0–10)	3
Extent of director liability index (0–10)	4
Ease of shareholder suits index (0–10)	9
Extent of shareholder rights index (0–10)	6
Extent of ownership and control index (0–10)	3
Extent of corporate transparency index (0–10)	5

Paying taxes (rank)	111
DTF score for paying taxes (0–100)	68.68
Payments (number per year)	32
Time (hours per year)	333
Total tax and contribution rate (% of profit)	13.6
Postfiling index (0–100)	66.94

Trading across borders (rank)	40
DTF score for trading across borders (0–100)	91.60
Time to export	
Documentary compliance (hours)	3
Border compliance (hours)	4
Cost to export	
Documentary compliance (US$)	90
Border compliance (US$)	150
Time to import	
Documentary compliance (hours)	3
Border compliance (hours)	5
Cost to import	
Documentary compliance (US$)	90
Border compliance (US$)	150

Enforcing contracts (rank)	95
DTF score for enforcing contracts (0–100)	57.18
Time (days)	615
Cost (% of claim)	31.3
Quality of judicial processes index (0–18)	8.5

Resolving insolvency (rank)	124
DTF score for resolving insolvency (0–100)	36.91
Time (years)	2.6
Cost (% of estate)	20.0
Recovery rate (cents on the dollar)	27.9
Strength of insolvency framework index (0–16)	7.0

Note: Most indicator sets refer to a case scenario in the largest business city of an economy, though for 11 economies the data are a population-weighted average for the two largest business cities. For some indicators a result of "no practice" may be recorded for an economy; see the data notes for more details. In starting a business, procedures (number), time (days) and cost (% of income per capita) are calculated as the average of both men and women. For the postfiling index, a result of "not applicable" may be recorded for an economy.

✔ Reform making it easier to do business   ✘ Change making it more difficult to do business

LIBERIA

		Sub-Saharan Africa		GNI per capita (US$)	370
Ease of doing business rank (1–190)	172	Overall distance to frontier (DTF) score (0–100)	43.55	Population	4,613,823

Starting a business (rank)	54	**Getting credit** (rank)	105	**Trading across borders** (rank)	177
DTF score for starting a business (0–100)	90.77	DTF score for getting credit (0–100)	45.00	DTF score for trading across borders (0–100)	27.77
Procedures (number)	5	Strength of legal rights index (0–12)	9	*Time to export*	
Time (days)	6	Depth of credit information index (0–8)	0	Documentary compliance (hours)	144
Cost (% of income per capita)	15.7	Credit bureau coverage (% of adults)	0.0	Border compliance (hours)	193
Minimum capital (% of income per capita)	0.0	Credit registry coverage (% of adults)	1.9	*Cost to export*	
				Documentary compliance (US$)	155
Dealing with construction permits (rank)	184	**Protecting minority investors** (rank)	177	Border compliance (US$)	1113
DTF score for dealing with construction permits (0–100)	28.94	DTF score for protecting minority investors (0–100)	26.67	*Time to import*	
Procedures (number)	25	Extent of disclosure index (0–10)	4	Documentary compliance (hours)	144
Time (days)	87	Extent of director liability index (0–10)	1	Border compliance (hours)	217
Cost (% of warehouse value)	39.1	Ease of shareholder suits index (0–10)	6	*Cost to import*	
Building quality control index (0–15)	2.0	Extent of shareholder rights index (0–10)	3	Documentary compliance (US$)	230
		Extent of ownership and control index (0–10)	1	Border compliance (US$)	1,013
Getting electricity (rank)	176	Extent of corporate transparency index (0–10)	1		
DTF score for getting electricity (0–100)	32.95			**Enforcing contracts** (rank)	174
Procedures (number)	4			DTF score for enforcing contracts (0–100)	35.23
Time (days)	482	**Paying taxes** (rank)	69	Time (days)	1,300
Cost (% of income per capita)	4,174.9	DTF score for paying taxes (0–100)	76.70	Cost (% of claim)	35.0
Reliability of supply and transparency of tariffs index (0–8)	0	Payments (number per year)	33	Quality of judicial processes index (0–18)	7.5
		Time (hours per year)	139.5		
		Total tax and contribution rate (% of profit)	45.5		
Registering property (rank)	183	Postfiling index (0–100)	98.62	✔ **Resolving insolvency** (rank)	106
DTF score for registering property (0–100)	31.04			DTF score for resolving insolvency (0–100)	40.43
Procedures (number)	10			Time (years)	3.0
Time (days)	44			Cost (% of estate)	30.0
Cost (% of property value)	13.8			Recovery rate (cents on the dollar)	17.1
Quality of land administration index (0–30)	3.5			Strength of insolvency framework index (0–16)	10.0

LIBYA

		Middle East & North Africa		GNI per capita (US$)	5,193
Ease of doing business rank (1–190)	185	Overall distance to frontier (DTF) score (0–100)	33.21	Population	6,293,253

Starting a business (rank)	167	**Getting credit** (rank)	186	**Trading across borders** (rank)	118
DTF score for starting a business (0–100)	71.72	DTF score for getting credit (0–100)	0.00	DTF score for trading across borders (0–100)	64.66
Procedures (number)	10	Strength of legal rights index (0–12)	0	*Time to export*	
Time (days)	35	Depth of credit information index (0–8)	0	Documentary compliance (hours)	72
Cost (% of income per capita)	30.3	Credit bureau coverage (% of adults)	0.0	Border compliance (hours)	72
Minimum capital (% of income per capita)	41.5	Credit registry coverage (% of adults)	0.6	*Cost to export*	
				Documentary compliance (US$)	50
Dealing with construction permits (rank)	186	**Protecting minority investors** (rank)	183	Border compliance (US$)	575
DTF score for dealing with construction permits (0–100)	0.00	DTF score for protecting minority investors (0–100)	25.00	*Time to import*	
Procedures (number)	no practice	Extent of disclosure index (0–10)	4	Documentary compliance (hours)	96
Time (days)	no practice	Extent of director liability index (0–10)	1	Border compliance (hours)	79
Cost (% of warehouse value)	no practice	Ease of shareholder suits index (0–10)	4	*Cost to import*	
Building quality control index (0–15)	0.0	Extent of shareholder rights index (0–10)	4	Documentary compliance (US$)	60
		Extent of ownership and control index (0–10)	1	Border compliance (US$)	637
Getting electricity (rank)	130	Extent of corporate transparency index (0–10)	1		
DTF score for getting electricity (0–100)	58.66			**Enforcing contracts** (rank)	141
Procedures (number)	4			DTF score for enforcing contracts (0–100)	48.41
Time (days)	118	**Paying taxes** (rank)	128	Time (days)	690
Cost (% of income per capita)	422.4	DTF score for paying taxes (0–100)	63.61	Cost (% of claim)	27.0
Reliability of supply and transparency of tariffs index (0–8)	0	Payments (number per year)	19	Quality of judicial processes index (0–18)	4.0
		Time (hours per year)	889		
		Total tax and contribution rate (% of profit)	32.6		
Registering property (rank)	187	Postfiling index (0–100)	90.16	**Resolving insolvency** (rank)	168
DTF score for registering property (0–100)	0.00			DTF score for resolving insolvency (0–100)	0.00
Procedures (number)	no practice			Time (years)	no practice
Time (days)	no practice			Cost (% of estate)	no practice
Cost (% of property value)	no practice			Recovery rate (cents on the dollar)	0.0
Quality of land administration index (0–30)	0.0			Strength of insolvency framework index (0–16)	0.0

LITHUANIA

		Europe & Central Asia		GNI per capita (US$)	14,770
Ease of doing business rank (1–190)	16	Overall distance to frontier (DTF) score (0–100)	79.87	Population	2,872,298

Starting a business (rank)	27	**Getting credit** (rank)	42	**Trading across borders** (rank)	19
DTF score for starting a business (0–100)	93.05	DTF score for getting credit (0–100)	70.00	DTF score for trading across borders (0–100)	97.70
Procedures (number)	4	Strength of legal rights index (0–12)	6	*Time to export*	
Time (days)	5.5	Depth of credit information index (0–8)	8	Documentary compliance (hours)	3
Cost (% of income per capita)	0.6	Credit bureau coverage (% of adults)	100.0	Border compliance (hours)	9
Minimum capital (% of income per capita)	19.3	Credit registry coverage (% of adults)	45.3	*Cost to export*	
				Documentary compliance (US$)	28
✔ **Dealing with construction permits** (rank)	12	✔ **Protecting minority investors** (rank)	43	Border compliance (US$)	58
DTF score for dealing with construction permits (0–100)	81.43	DTF score for protecting minority investors (0–100)	63.33	*Time to import*	
Procedures (number)	13	Extent of disclosure index (0–10)	7	Documentary compliance (hours)	1
Time (days)	75	Extent of director liability index (0–10)	4	Border compliance (hours)	0
Cost (% of warehouse value)	0.3	Ease of shareholder suits index (0–10)	7	*Cost to import*	
Building quality control index (0–15)	11.0	Extent of shareholder rights index (0–10)	6	Documentary compliance (US$)	0
		Extent of ownership and control index (0–10)	6	Border compliance (US$)	0
✔ **Getting electricity** (rank)	33	Extent of corporate transparency index (0–10)	8		
DTF score for getting electricity (0–100)	84.25			**Enforcing contracts** (rank)	4
Procedures (number)	5			DTF score for enforcing contracts (0–100)	78.80
Time (days)	85	✔ **Paying taxes** (rank)	18	Time (days)	370
Cost (% of income per capita)	42.0	DTF score for paying taxes (0–100)	87.81	Cost (% of claim)	23.6
Reliability of supply and transparency of tariffs index (0–8)	8	Payments (number per year)	11	Quality of judicial processes index (0–18)	15.0
		Time (hours per year)	109.3		
		Total tax and contribution rate (% of profit)	42.7		
✔ **Registering property** (rank)	3	Postfiling index (0–100)	97.52	**Resolving insolvency** (rank)	70
DTF score for registering property (0–100)	92.94			DTF score for resolving insolvency (0–100)	49.37
Procedures (number)	3			Time (years)	2.3
Time (days)	3.5			Cost (% of estate)	10.0
Cost (% of property value)	0.8			Recovery rate (cents on the dollar)	45.3
Quality of land administration index (0–30)	28.5			Strength of insolvency framework index (0–16)	8.0

Note: Most indicator sets refer to a case scenario in the largest business city of an economy, though for 11 economies the data are a population-weighted average for the two largest business cities. For some indicators a result of "no practice" may be recorded for an economy; see the data notes for more details. In starting a business, procedures (number), time (days) and cost (% of income per capita) are calculated as the average of both men and women. For the postfiling index, a result of "not applicable" may be recorded for an economy.

✔ Reform making it easier to do business   ✘ Change making it more difficult to do business

LUXEMBOURG

Ease of doing business rank (1–190)	63	**Overall distance to frontier (DTF) score (0–100)**	69.01	**Population**	582,972

OECD high income — GNI per capita (US$): 76,660

Starting a business (rank): 70
DTF score for starting a business (0–100): 88.76
Procedures (number): 5
Time (days): 16.5
Cost (% of income per capita): 1.7
Minimum capital (% of income per capita): 18.0

Dealing with construction permits (rank): 7
DTF score for dealing with construction permits (0–100): 83.71
Procedures (number): 11
Time (days): 157
Cost (% of warehouse value): 0.7
Building quality control index (0–15): 15.0

Getting electricity (rank): 31
DTF score for getting electricity (0–100): 84.31
Procedures (number): 5
Time (days): 56
Cost (% of income per capita): 34.4
Reliability of supply and transparency of tariffs index (0–8): 7

Registering property (rank): 88
DTF score for registering property (0–100): 63.85
Procedures (number): 7
Time (days): 26.5
Cost (% of property value): 10.1
Quality of land administration index (0–30): 25.5

Getting credit (rank): 173
DTF score for getting credit (0–100): 15.00
Strength of legal rights index (0–12): 3
Depth of credit information index (0–8): 0
Credit bureau coverage (% of adults): 0.0
Credit registry coverage (% of adults): 0.0

✔ **Protecting minority investors** (rank): 119
DTF score for protecting minority investors (0–100): 48.33
Extent of disclosure index (0–10): 6
Extent of director liability index (0–10): 5
Ease of shareholder suits index (0–10): 4
Extent of shareholder rights index (0–10): 5
Extent of ownership and control index (0–10): 2
Extent of corporate transparency index (0–10): 7

Paying taxes (rank): 21
DTF score for paying taxes (0–100): 87.37
Payments (number per year): 23
Time (hours per year): 55
Total tax and contribution rate (% of profit): 20.5
Postfiling index (0–100): 83.75

Trading across borders (rank): 1
DTF score for trading across borders (0–100): 100.00
Time to export
Documentary compliance (hours): 1
Border compliance (hours): 0
Cost to export
Documentary compliance (US$): 0
Border compliance (US$): 0
Time to import
Documentary compliance (hours): 1
Border compliance (hours): 0
Cost to import
Documentary compliance (US$): 0
Border compliance (US$): 0

Enforcing contracts (rank): 14
DTF score for enforcing contracts (0–100): 73.32
Time (days): 321
Cost (% of claim): 9.7
Quality of judicial processes index (0–18): 8.5

Resolving insolvency (rank): 86
DTF score for resolving insolvency (0–100): 45.42
Time (years): 2.0
Cost (% of estate): 14.5
Recovery rate (cents on the dollar): 43.8
Strength of insolvency framework index (0–16): 7.0

MACEDONIA, FYR

Ease of doing business rank (1–190)	11	**Overall distance to frontier (DTF) score (0–100)**	81.18	**Population**	2,081,206

Europe & Central Asia — GNI per capita (US$): 4,980

Starting a business (rank): 22
DTF score for starting a business (0–100): 93.94
Procedures (number): 4
Time (days): 7
Cost (% of income per capita): 0.1
Minimum capital (% of income per capita): 0.0

Dealing with construction permits (rank): 26
DTF score for dealing with construction permits (0–100): 78.01
Procedures (number): 11
Time (days): 96
Cost (% of warehouse value): 6.1
Building quality control index (0–15): 13.0

Getting electricity (rank): 53
DTF score for getting electricity (0–100): 81.42
Procedures (number): 3
Time (days): 97
Cost (% of income per capita): 200.1
Reliability of supply and transparency of tariffs index (0–8): 5

Registering property (rank): 48
DTF score for registering property (0–100): 74.49
Procedures (number): 7
Time (days): 30
Cost (% of property value): 3.2
Quality of land administration index (0–30): 25.0

Getting credit (rank): 12
DTF score for getting credit (0–100): 85.00
Strength of legal rights index (0–12): 10
Depth of credit information index (0–8): 7
Credit bureau coverage (% of adults): 100.0
Credit registry coverage (% of adults): 39.7

Protecting minority investors (rank): 4
DTF score for protecting minority investors (0–100): 80.00
Extent of disclosure index (0–10): 10
Extent of director liability index (0–10): 9
Ease of shareholder suits index (0–10): 5
Extent of shareholder rights index (0–10): 8
Extent of ownership and control index (0–10): 7
Extent of corporate transparency index (0–10): 9

Paying taxes (rank): 29
DTF score for paying taxes (0–100): 84.72
Payments (number per year): 7
Time (hours per year): 119
Total tax and contribution rate (% of profit): 13.0
Postfiling index (0–100): 56.36

Trading across borders (rank): 27
DTF score for trading across borders (0–100): 93.87
Time to export
Documentary compliance (hours): 2
Border compliance (hours): 9
Cost to export
Documentary compliance (US$): 45
Border compliance (US$): 103
Time to import
Documentary compliance (hours): 3
Border compliance (hours): 8
Cost to import
Documentary compliance (US$): 50
Border compliance (US$): 150

Enforcing contracts (rank): 35
DTF score for enforcing contracts (0–100): 67.79
Time (days): 634
Cost (% of claim): 28.8
Quality of judicial processes index (0–18): 14.0

Resolving insolvency (rank): 30
DTF score for resolving insolvency (0–100): 72.54
Time (years): 1.5
Cost (% of estate): 10.0
Recovery rate (cents on the dollar): 47.7
Strength of insolvency framework index (0–16): 15.0

MADAGASCAR

Ease of doing business rank (1–190)	162	**Overall distance to frontier (DTF) score (0–100)**	47.67	**Population**	24,894,551

Sub-Saharan Africa — GNI per capita (US$): 400

✔ **Starting a business** (rank): 76
DTF score for starting a business (0–100): 87.76
Procedures (number): 5
Time (days): 8
Cost (% of income per capita): 35.8
Minimum capital (% of income per capita): 0.0

Dealing with construction permits (rank): 183
DTF score for dealing with construction permits (0–100): 35.88
Procedures (number): 16
Time (days): 185
Cost (% of warehouse value): 54.5
Building quality control index (0–15): 5.0

Getting electricity (rank): 184
DTF score for getting electricity (0–100): 21.07
Procedures (number): 6
Time (days): 450
Cost (% of income per capita): 5,322.0
Reliability of supply and transparency of tariffs index (0–8): 0

Registering property (rank): 161
DTF score for registering property (0–100): 44.63
Procedures (number): 6
Time (days): 100
Cost (% of property value): 9.1
Quality of land administration index (0–30): 8.5

✔ **Getting credit** (rank): 133
DTF score for getting credit (0–100): 35.00
Strength of legal rights index (0–12): 2
Depth of credit information index (0–8): 5
Credit bureau coverage (% of adults): 0.0
Credit registry coverage (% of adults): 5.1

Protecting minority investors (rank): 96
DTF score for protecting minority investors (0–100): 51.67
Extent of disclosure index (0–10): 7
Extent of director liability index (0–10): 6
Ease of shareholder suits index (0–10): 5
Extent of shareholder rights index (0–10): 4
Extent of ownership and control index (0–10): 5
Extent of corporate transparency index (0–10): 4

Paying taxes (rank): 131
DTF score for paying taxes (0–100): 62.70
Payments (number per year): 23
Time (hours per year): 183
Total tax and contribution rate (% of profit): 38.1
Postfiling index (0–100): 21.84

Trading across borders (rank): 134
DTF score for trading across borders (0–100): 60.95
Time to export
Documentary compliance (hours): 49
Border compliance (hours): 70
Cost to export
Documentary compliance (US$): 117
Border compliance (US$): 868
Time to import
Documentary compliance (hours): 58
Border compliance (hours): 99
Cost to import
Documentary compliance (US$): 150
Border compliance (US$): 595

Enforcing contracts (rank): 158
DTF score for enforcing contracts (0–100): 42.85
Time (days): 871
Cost (% of claim): 33.6
Quality of judicial processes index (0–18): 5.0

Resolving insolvency (rank): 133
DTF score for resolving insolvency (0–100): 34.24
Time (years): 3.0
Cost (% of estate): 8.5
Recovery rate (cents on the dollar): 11.4
Strength of insolvency framework index (0–16): 9.0

Note: Most indicator sets refer to a case scenario in the largest business city of an economy, though for 11 economies the data are a population-weighted average for the two largest business cities. For some indicators a result of "no practice" may be recorded for an economy; see the data notes for more details. In starting a business, procedures (number), time (days) and cost (% of income per capita) are calculated as the average of both men and women. For the postfiling index, a result of "not applicable" may be recorded for an economy.

✔ Reform making it easier to do business   ✘ Change making it more difficult to do business

MALAWI

MALAWI		Sub-Saharan Africa		GNI per capita (US$)	320
Ease of doing business rank (1–190)	110	Overall distance to frontier (DTF) score (0–100)	58.94	Population	18,091,575

✘ **Starting a business** (rank)	152	✔ **Getting credit** (rank)	6	✔ **Trading across borders** (rank)	117
DTF score for starting a business (0–100)	76.43	DTF score for getting credit (0–100)	90.00	DTF score for trading across borders (0–100)	65.29
Procedures (number)	7	Strength of legal rights index (0–12)	11	Time to export	
Time (days)	37	Depth of credit information index (0–8)	7	Documentary compliance (hours)	75
Cost (% of income per capita)	44.6	Credit bureau coverage (% of adults)	23.5	Border compliance (hours)	78
Minimum capital (% of income per capita)	0.0	Credit registry coverage (% of adults)	0.0	Cost to export	
				Documentary compliance (US$)	342
✔ **Dealing with construction permits** (rank)	144	**Protecting minority investors** (rank)	96	Border compliance (US$)	243
DTF score for dealing with construction permits (0–100)	59.22	DTF score for protecting minority investors (0–100)	51.67	Time to import	
Procedures (number)	13	Extent of disclosure index (0–10)	4	Documentary compliance (hours)	55
Time (days)	153	Extent of director liability index (0–10)	7	Border compliance (hours)	55
Cost (% of warehouse value)	11.6	Ease of shareholder suits index (0–10)	7	Cost to import	
Building quality control index (0–15)	9.5	Extent of shareholder rights index (0–10)	7	Documentary compliance (US$)	162
		Extent of ownership and control index (0–10)	2	Border compliance (US$)	143
		Extent of corporate transparency index (0–10)	4		
Getting electricity (rank)	166			**Enforcing contracts** (rank)	151
DTF score for getting electricity (0–100)	43.43			DTF score for enforcing contracts (0–100)	45.55
Procedures (number)	6	**Paying taxes** (rank)	134	Time (days)	522
Time (days)	127	DTF score for paying taxes (0–100)	62.10	Cost (% of claim)	69.1
Cost (% of income per capita)	2,341.6	Payments (number per year)	35	Quality of judicial processes index (0–18)	8.5
Reliability of supply and transparency of tariffs index (0–8)	0	Time (hours per year)	177.5		
		Total tax and contribution rate (% of profit)	34.5	✔ **Resolving insolvency** (rank)	138
Registering property (rank)	96	Postfiling index (0–100)	33.41	DTF score for resolving insolvency (0–100)	33.28
DTF score for registering property (0–100)	62.45			Time (years)	2.6
Procedures (number)	6			Cost (% of estate)	25.0
Time (days)	69			Recovery rate (cents on the dollar)	12.5
Cost (% of property value)	1.6			Strength of insolvency framework index (0–16)	8.5
Quality of land administration index (0–30)	10.5				

MALAYSIA

MALAYSIA		East Asia & Pacific		GNI per capita (US$)	9,850
Ease of doing business rank (1–190)	24	Overall distance to frontier (DTF) score (0–100)	78.43	Population	31,187,265

Starting a business (rank)	111	✔ **Getting credit** (rank)	20	✔ **Trading across borders** (rank)	61
DTF score for starting a business (0–100)	83.78	DTF score for getting credit (0–100)	80.00	DTF score for trading across borders (0–100)	82.75
Procedures (number)	8.5	Strength of legal rights index (0–12)	8	Time to export	
Time (days)	18.5	Depth of credit information index (0–8)	8	Documentary compliance (hours)	10
Cost (% of income per capita)	5.4	Credit bureau coverage (% of adults)	82.6	Border compliance (hours)	45
Minimum capital (% of income per capita)	0.0	Credit registry coverage (% of adults)	63.6	Cost to export	
				Documentary compliance (US$)	45
Dealing with construction permits (rank)	11	✔ **Protecting minority investors** (rank)	4	Border compliance (US$)	321
DTF score for dealing with construction permits (0–100)	82.19	DTF score for protecting minority investors (0–100)	80.00	Time to import	
Procedures (number)	14	Extent of disclosure index (0–10)	10	Documentary compliance (hours)	10
Time (days)	78	Extent of director liability index (0–10)	9	Border compliance (hours)	69
Cost (% of warehouse value)	1.4	Ease of shareholder suits index (0–10)	7	Cost to import	
Building quality control index (0–15)	13.0	Extent of shareholder rights index (0–10)	8	Documentary compliance (US$)	60
		Extent of ownership and control index (0–10)	6	Border compliance (US$)	321
		Extent of corporate transparency index (0–10)	8		
Getting electricity (rank)	8			**Enforcing contracts** (rank)	44
DTF score for getting electricity (0–100)	94.33			DTF score for enforcing contracts (0–100)	66.61
Procedures (number)	4	**Paying taxes** (rank)	73	Time (days)	425
Time (days)	31	DTF score for paying taxes (0–100)	76.07	Cost (% of claim)	37.3
Cost (% of income per capita)	28.0	Payments (number per year)	8	Quality of judicial processes index (0–18)	12.0
Reliability of supply and transparency of tariffs index (0–8)	8	Time (hours per year)	188		
		Total tax and contribution rate (% of profit)	39.2	**Resolving insolvency** (rank)	46
Registering property (rank)	42	Postfiling index (0–100)	52.65	DTF score for resolving insolvency (0–100)	62.51
DTF score for registering property (0–100)	76.06			Time (years)	1.0
Procedures (number)	8			Cost (% of estate)	10.0
Time (days)	13			Recovery rate (cents on the dollar)	81.3
Cost (% of property value)	3.5			Strength of insolvency framework index (0–16)	6.0
Quality of land administration index (0–30)	27.5				

MALDIVES

MALDIVES		South Asia		GNI per capita (US$)	7,430
Ease of doing business rank (1–190)	136	Overall distance to frontier (DTF) score (0–100)	54.42	Population	417,492

Starting a business (rank)	68	**Getting credit** (rank)	133	**Trading across borders** (rank)	152
DTF score for starting a business (0–100)	89.06	DTF score for getting credit (0–100)	35.00	DTF score for trading across borders (0–100)	55.87
Procedures (number)	6	Strength of legal rights index (0–12)	2	Time to export	
Time (days)	12	Depth of credit information index (0–8)	5	Documentary compliance (hours)	48
Cost (% of income per capita)	4.7	Credit bureau coverage (% of adults)	0.0	Border compliance (hours)	42
Minimum capital (% of income per capita)	1.7	Credit registry coverage (% of adults)	18.8	Cost to export	
				Documentary compliance (US$)	300
Dealing with construction permits (rank)	54	**Protecting minority investors** (rank)	132	Border compliance (US$)	596
DTF score for dealing with construction permits (0–100)	72.87	DTF score for protecting minority investors (0–100)	43.33	Time to import	
Procedures (number)	10	Extent of disclosure index (0–10)	0	Documentary compliance (hours)	61
Time (days)	140	Extent of director liability index (0–10)	8	Border compliance (hours)	100
Cost (% of warehouse value)	0.5	Ease of shareholder suits index (0–10)	8	Cost to import	
Building quality control index (0–15)	7.0	Extent of shareholder rights index (0–10)	5	Documentary compliance (US$)	180
		Extent of ownership and control index (0–10)	1	Border compliance (US$)	981
		Extent of corporate transparency index (0–10)	4		
Getting electricity (rank)	143			**Enforcing contracts** (rank)	106
DTF score for getting electricity (0–100)	53.69			DTF score for enforcing contracts (0–100)	55.07
Procedures (number)	6	✔ **Paying taxes** (rank)	118	Time (days)	760
Time (days)	91	DTF score for paying taxes (0–100)	66.08	Cost (% of claim)	16.5
Cost (% of income per capita)	283.5	Payments (number per year)	17	Quality of judicial processes index (0–18)	6.5
Reliability of supply and transparency of tariffs index (0–8)	0	Time (hours per year)	390.5		
		Total tax and contribution rate (% of profit)	30.2	**Resolving insolvency** (rank)	139
Registering property (rank)	174	Postfiling index (0–100)	46.10	DTF score for resolving insolvency (0–100)	33.26
DTF score for registering property (0–100)	39.97			Time (years)	1.5
Procedures (number)	6			Cost (% of estate)	4.0
Time (days)	57			Recovery rate (cents on the dollar)	50.2
Cost (% of property value)	15.8			Strength of insolvency framework index (0–16)	2.0
Quality of land administration index (0–30)	8.5				

Note: Most indicator sets refer to a case scenario in the largest business city of an economy, though for 11 economies the data are a population-weighted average for the two largest business cities. For some indicators a result of "no practice" may be recorded for an economy; see the data notes for more details. In starting a business, procedures (number), time (days) and cost (% of income per capita) are calculated as the average of both men and women. For the postfiling index, a result of "not applicable" may be recorded for an economy.

✔ Reform making it easier to do business   ✘ Change making it more difficult to do business

MALI

		Sub-Saharan Africa		GNI per capita (US$)	750
Ease of doing business rank (1–190)	143	Overall distance to frontier (DTF) score (0–100)	52.92	Population	17,994,837

Starting a business (rank)	104	**Getting credit** (rank)	142	**Trading across borders** (rank)	85
DTF score for starting a business (0–100)	84.46	DTF score for getting credit (0–100)	30.00	DTF score for trading across borders (0–100)	73.30
Procedures (number)	5	Strength of legal rights index (0–12)	6	*Time to export*	
Time (days)	8.5	Depth of credit information index (0–8)	0	Documentary compliance (hours)	48
Cost (% of income per capita)	58.4	Credit bureau coverage (% of adults)	0.8	Border compliance (hours)	48
Minimum capital (% of income per capita)	5.6	Credit registry coverage (% of adults)	0.1	*Cost to export*	
				Documentary compliance (US$)	33
Dealing with construction permits (rank)	134	**Protecting minority investors** (rank)	146	Border compliance (US$)	242
DTF score for dealing with construction permits (0–100)	61.36	DTF score for protecting minority investors (0–100)	40.00	*Time to import*	
Procedures (number)	13	Extent of disclosure index (0–10)	7	Documentary compliance (hours)	77
Time (days)	124	Extent of director liability index (0–10)	1	Border compliance (hours)	98
Cost (% of warehouse value)	6.2	Ease of shareholder suits index (0–10)	5	*Cost to import*	
Building quality control index (0–15)	5.5	Extent of shareholder rights index (0–10)	4	Documentary compliance (US$)	90
		Extent of ownership and control index (0–10)	3	Border compliance (US$)	545
Getting electricity (rank)	154	Extent of corporate transparency index (0–10)	4		
DTF score for getting electricity (0–100)	51.12			**Enforcing contracts** (rank)	159
Procedures (number)	4	**Paying taxes** (rank)	166	DTF score for enforcing contracts (0–100)	42.80
Time (days)	120	DTF score for paying taxes (0–100)	51.55	Time (days)	620
Cost (% of income per capita)	2,794.6	Payments (number per year)	35	Cost (% of claim)	52.0
Reliability of supply and transparency of tariffs index (0–8)	0	Time (hours per year)	270	Quality of judicial processes index (0–18)	5.0
		Total tax and contribution rate (% of profit)	48.3		
Registering property (rank)	137	Postfiling index (0–100)	25.71	**Resolving insolvency** (rank)	94
DTF score for registering property (0–100)	51.43			DTF score for resolving insolvency (0–100)	43.22
Procedures (number)	5			Time (years)	3.6
Time (days)	29			Cost (% of estate)	18.0
Cost (% of property value)	11.1			Recovery rate (cents on the dollar)	28.0
Quality of land administration index (0–30)	8.0			Strength of insolvency framework index (0–16)	9.0

MALTA

		Middle East & North Africa		GNI per capita (US$)	24,140
Ease of doing business rank (1–190)	84	Overall distance to frontier (DTF) score (0–100)	64.72	Population	436,947

✔ **Starting a business** (rank)	102	**Getting credit** (rank)	142	**Trading across borders** (rank)	41
DTF score for starting a business (0–100)	84.83	DTF score for getting credit (0–100)	30.00	DTF score for trading across borders (0–100)	91.01
Procedures (number)	8	Strength of legal rights index (0–12)	2	*Time to export*	
Time (days)	16	Depth of credit information index (0–8)	4	Documentary compliance (hours)	3
Cost (% of income per capita)	7.3	Credit bureau coverage (% of adults)	0.0	Border compliance (hours)	24
Minimum capital (% of income per capita)	1.1	Credit registry coverage (% of adults)	53.6	*Cost to export*	
				Documentary compliance (US$)	25
Dealing with construction permits (rank)	45	**Protecting minority investors** (rank)	51	Border compliance (US$)	325
DTF score for dealing with construction permits (0–100)	73.86	DTF score for protecting minority investors (0–100)	61.67	*Time to import*	
Procedures (number)	15	Extent of disclosure index (0–10)	3	Documentary compliance (hours)	1
Time (days)	167	Extent of director liability index (0–10)	6	Border compliance (hours)	2
Cost (% of warehouse value)	2.1	Ease of shareholder suits index (0–10)	8	*Cost to import*	
Building quality control index (0–15)	13.0	Extent of shareholder rights index (0–10)	7	Documentary compliance (US$)	0
		Extent of ownership and control index (0–10)	4	Border compliance (US$)	230
Getting electricity (rank)	78	Extent of corporate transparency index (0–10)	9		
DTF score for getting electricity (0–100)	75.16			**Enforcing contracts** (rank)	37
Procedures (number)	5	**Paying taxes** (rank)	71	DTF score for enforcing contracts (0–100)	67.57
Time (days)	106	DTF score for paying taxes (0–100)	76.19	Time (days)	505
Cost (% of income per capita)	222.5	Payments (number per year)	8	Cost (% of claim)	21.5
Reliability of supply and transparency of tariffs index (0–8)	6	Time (hours per year)	139	Quality of judicial processes index (0–18)	10.5
		Total tax and contribution rate (% of profit)	43.9		
Registering property (rank)	147	Postfiling index (0–100)	52.51	**Resolving insolvency** (rank)	117
DTF score for registering property (0–100)	48.86			DTF score for resolving insolvency (0–100)	38.07
Procedures (number)	7			Time (years)	3.0
Time (days)	15			Cost (% of estate)	10.0
Cost (% of property value)	13.4			Recovery rate (cents on the dollar)	38.8
Quality of land administration index (0–30)	12.5			Strength of insolvency framework index (0–16)	5.5

MARSHALL ISLANDS

		East Asia & Pacific		GNI per capita (US$)	4,450
Ease of doing business rank (1–190)	149	Overall distance to frontier (DTF) score (0–100)	51.45	Population	53,066

Starting a business (rank)	72	**Getting credit** (rank)	90	**Trading across borders** (rank)	67
DTF score for starting a business (0–100)	88.49	DTF score for getting credit (0–100)	50.00	DTF score for trading across borders (0–100)	80.59
Procedures (number)	5	Strength of legal rights index (0–12)	10	*Time to export*	
Time (days)	17	Depth of credit information index (0–8)	0	Documentary compliance (hours)	24
Cost (% of income per capita)	11.9	Credit bureau coverage (% of adults)	0.0	Border compliance (hours)	60
Minimum capital (% of income per capita)	0.0	Credit registry coverage (% of adults)	0.0	*Cost to export*	
				Documentary compliance (US$)	20
Dealing with construction permits (rank)	71	**Protecting minority investors** (rank)	177	Border compliance (US$)	220
DTF score for dealing with construction permits (0–100)	70.93	DTF score for protecting minority investors (0–100)	26.67	*Time to import*	
Procedures (number)	7	Extent of disclosure index (0–10)	2	Documentary compliance (hours)	60
Time (days)	38	Extent of director liability index (0–10)	0	Border compliance (hours)	84
Cost (% of warehouse value)	2.3	Ease of shareholder suits index (0–10)	8	*Cost to import*	
Building quality control index (0–15)	1.0	Extent of shareholder rights index (0–10)	3	Documentary compliance (US$)	43
		Extent of ownership and control index (0–10)	1	Border compliance (US$)	220
Getting electricity (rank)	126	Extent of corporate transparency index (0–10)	2		
DTF score for getting electricity (0–100)	59.26			**Enforcing contracts** (rank)	99
Procedures (number)	5	**Paying taxes** (rank)	83	DTF score for enforcing contracts (0–100)	55.93
Time (days)	67	DTF score for paying taxes (0–100)	73.45	Time (days)	616
Cost (% of income per capita)	675.4	Payments (number per year)	9	Cost (% of claim)	32.1
Reliability of supply and transparency of tariffs index (0–8)	0	Time (hours per year)	120	Quality of judicial processes index (0–18)	8.0
		Total tax and contribution rate (% of profit)	64.8		
Registering property (rank)	187	Postfiling index (0–100)	not applicable	**Resolving insolvency** (rank)	167
DTF score for registering property (0–100)	0.00			DTF score for resolving insolvency (0–100)	9.19
Procedures (number)	no practice			Time (years)	2.0
Time (days)	no practice			Cost (% of estate)	38.0
Cost (% of property value)	no practice			Recovery rate (cents on the dollar)	17.1
Quality of land administration index (0–30)	0.0			Strength of insolvency framework index (0–16)	0.0

Note: Most indicator sets refer to a case scenario in the largest business city of an economy, though for 11 economies the data are a population-weighted average for the two largest business cities. For some indicators a result of "no practice" may be recorded for an economy; see the data notes for more details. In starting a business, procedures (number), time (days) and cost (% of income per capita) are calculated as the average of both men and women. For the postfiling index, a result of "not applicable" may be recorded for an economy.

✔ Reform making it easier to do business   ✘ Change making it more difficult to do business

MAURITANIA

		Sub-Saharan Africa		GNI per capita (US$)	1,120
Ease of doing business rank (1–190)	150	Overall distance to frontier (DTF) score (0–100)	50.88	Population	4,301,018

✔ Starting a business (rank)	43	Getting credit (rank)	159	✔ Trading across borders (rank)	138
DTF score for starting a business (0–100)	91.80	DTF score for getting credit (0–100)	25.00	DTF score for trading across borders (0–100)	60.30
Procedures (number)	4	Strength of legal rights index (0–12)	2	Time to export	
Time (days)	6	Depth of credit information index (0–8)	3	Documentary compliance (hours)	51
Cost (% of income per capita)	19.3	Credit bureau coverage (% of adults)	0.0	Border compliance (hours)	62
Minimum capital (% of income per capita)	0.0	Credit registry coverage (% of adults)	7.1	Cost to export	
				Documentary compliance (US$)	92
Dealing with construction permits (rank)	109	Protecting minority investors (rank)	108	Border compliance (US$)	749
DTF score for dealing with construction permits (0–100)	66.03	DTF score for protecting minority investors (0–100)	50.00	Time to import	
Procedures (number)	13	Extent of disclosure index (0–10)	6	Documentary compliance (hours)	64
Time (days)	104	Extent of director liability index (0–10)	3	Border compliance (hours)	69
Cost (% of warehouse value)	4.3	Ease of shareholder suits index (0–10)	7	Cost to import	
Building quality control index (0–15)	6.0	Extent of shareholder rights index (0–10)	5	Documentary compliance (US$)	400
		Extent of ownership and control index (0–10)	5	Border compliance (US$)	580
		Extent of corporate transparency index (0–10)	4		
Getting electricity (rank)	148			✔ Enforcing contracts (rank)	65
DTF score for getting electricity (0–100)	53.31	✔ Paying taxes (rank)	179	DTF score for enforcing contracts (0–100)	60.43
Procedures (number)	5	DTF score for paying taxes (0–100)	40.71	Time (days)	370
Time (days)	67	Payments (number per year)	33	Cost (% of claim)	23.2
Cost (% of income per capita)	4,628.4	Time (hours per year)	270	Quality of judicial processes index (0–18)	5.0
Reliability of supply and transparency of tariffs index (0–8)	2	Total tax and contribution rate (% of profit)	71.3		
		Postfiling index (0–100)	17.20	Resolving insolvency (rank)	168
✔ Registering property (rank)	98			DTF score for resolving insolvency (0–100)	0.00
DTF score for registering property (0–100)	61.25			Time (years)	no practice
Procedures (number)	4			Cost (% of estate)	no practice
Time (days)	49			Recovery rate (cents on the dollar)	0.0
Cost (% of property value)	4.6			Strength of insolvency framework index (0–16)	0.0
Quality of land administration index (0–30)	7.0				

MAURITIUS

		Sub-Saharan Africa		GNI per capita (US$)	9,760
Ease of doing business rank (1–190)	25	Overall distance to frontier (DTF) score (0–100)	77.54	Population	1,263,473

✔ Starting a business (rank)	40	Getting credit (rank)	55	✔ Trading across borders (rank)	70
DTF score for starting a business (0–100)	92.00	DTF score for getting credit (0–100)	65.00	DTF score for trading across borders (0–100)	79.90
Procedures (number)	5.5	Strength of legal rights index (0–12)	6	Time to export	
Time (days)	5.5	Depth of credit information index (0–8)	7	Documentary compliance (hours)	9
Cost (% of income per capita)	1.0	Credit bureau coverage (% of adults)	0.0	Border compliance (hours)	38
Minimum capital (% of income per capita)	0.0	Credit registry coverage (% of adults)	86.1	Cost to export	
				Documentary compliance (US$)	128
✔ Dealing with construction permits (rank)	9	Protecting minority investors (rank)	33	Border compliance (US$)	303
DTF score for dealing with construction permits (0–100)	82.45	DTF score for protecting minority investors (0–100)	66.67	Time to import	
Procedures (number)	15	Extent of disclosure index (0–10)	6	Documentary compliance (hours)	9
Time (days)	98	Extent of director liability index (0–10)	8	Border compliance (hours)	41
Cost (% of warehouse value)	0.6	Ease of shareholder suits index (0–10)	9	Cost to import	
Building quality control index (0–15)	14.0	Extent of shareholder rights index (0–10)	7	Documentary compliance (US$)	166
		Extent of ownership and control index (0–10)	3	Border compliance (US$)	372
		Extent of corporate transparency index (0–10)	7		
Getting electricity (rank)	51			Enforcing contracts (rank)	27
DTF score for getting electricity (0–100)	82.03	Paying taxes (rank)	10	DTF score for enforcing contracts (0–100)	69.58
Procedures (number)	4	DTF score for paying taxes (0–100)	90.85	Time (days)	519
Time (days)	81	Payments (number per year)	8	Cost (% of claim)	25.0
Cost (% of income per capita)	229.4	Time (hours per year)	152	Quality of judicial processes index (0–18)	12.5
Reliability of supply and transparency of tariffs index (0–8)	6	Total tax and contribution rate (% of profit)	21.9		
		Postfiling index (0–100)	87.65	Resolving insolvency (rank)	36
✔ Registering property (rank)	35			DTF score for resolving insolvency (0–100)	69.06
DTF score for registering property (0–100)	77.89			Time (years)	1.7
Procedures (number)	5			Cost (% of estate)	14.5
Time (days)	17			Recovery rate (cents on the dollar)	67.4
Cost (% of property value)	0.6			Strength of insolvency framework index (0–16)	10.5
Quality of land administration index (0–30)	17.0				

MEXICO

		Latin America & Caribbean		GNI per capita (US$)	9,040
Ease of doing business rank (1–190)	49	Overall distance to frontier (DTF) score (0–100)	72.27	Population	127,540,423

Starting a business (rank)	90	Getting credit (rank)	6	Trading across borders (rank)	63
DTF score for starting a business (0–100)	85.84	DTF score for getting credit (0–100)	90.00	DTF score for trading across borders (0–100)	82.09
Procedures (number)	7.8	Strength of legal rights index (0–12)	10	Time to export	
Time (days)	8.4	Depth of credit information index (0–8)	8	Documentary compliance (hours)	8
Cost (% of income per capita)	17.0	Credit bureau coverage (% of adults)	100.0	Border compliance (hours)	20.4
Minimum capital (% of income per capita)	0.0	Credit registry coverage (% of adults)	0.0	Cost to export	
				Documentary compliance (US$)	60
✘ Dealing with construction permits (rank)	87	Protecting minority investors (rank)	62	Border compliance (US$)	400
DTF score for dealing with construction permits (0–100)	68.28	DTF score for protecting minority investors (0–100)	58.33	Time to import	
Procedures (number)	14.7	Extent of disclosure index (0–10)	8	Documentary compliance (hours)	17.6
Time (days)	82.3	Extent of director liability index (0–10)	5	Border compliance (hours)	44.2
Cost (% of warehouse value)	9.9	Ease of shareholder suits index (0–10)	5	Cost to import	
Building quality control index (0–15)	11.7	Extent of shareholder rights index (0–10)	7	Documentary compliance (US$)	100
		Extent of ownership and control index (0–10)	6	Border compliance (US$)	450
		Extent of corporate transparency index (0–10)	4		
✔ Getting electricity (rank)	92			Enforcing contracts (rank)	41
DTF score for getting electricity (0–100)	70.99	Paying taxes (rank)	115	DTF score for enforcing contracts (0–100)	67.01
Procedures (number)	6.8	DTF score for paying taxes (0–100)	67.01	Time (days)	341
Time (days)	100.4	Payments (number per year)	6	Cost (% of claim)	33.0
Cost (% of income per capita)	314.3	Time (hours per year)	240.5	Quality of judicial processes index (0–18)	10.1
Reliability of supply and transparency of tariffs index (0–8)	7	Total tax and contribution rate (% of profit)	52.1		
		Postfiling index (0–100)	40.51	Resolving insolvency (rank)	31
✘ Registering property (rank)	99			DTF score for resolving insolvency (0–100)	72.31
DTF score for registering property (0–100)	60.81			Time (years)	1.8
Procedures (number)	7.7			Cost (% of estate)	18.0
Time (days)	38.8			Recovery rate (cents on the dollar)	67.6
Cost (% of property value)	5.6			Strength of insolvency framework index (0–16)	11.5
Quality of land administration index (0–30)	5.6				

Note: Most indicator sets refer to a case scenario in the largest business city of an economy, though for 11 economies the data are a population-weighted average for the two largest business cities. For some indicators a result of "no practice" may be recorded for an economy; see the data notes for more details. In starting a business, procedures (number), time (days) and cost (% of income per capita) are calculated as the average of both men and women. For the postfiling index, a result of "not applicable" may be recorded for an economy.

✔ Reform making it easier to do business   ✘ Change making it more difficult to do business

MICRONESIA, FED. STS.

MICRONESIA, FED. STS.		**East Asia & Pacific**		**GNI per capita (US$)**		**3,680**
Ease of doing business rank (1–190)	155	Overall distance to frontier (DTF) score (0–100)	48.99	Population		104,937

Starting a business (rank)	170	Getting credit (rank)	90	Trading across borders (rank)	58
DTF score for starting a business (0–100)	69.56	DTF score for getting credit (0–100)	50.00	DTF score for trading across borders (0–100)	84.00
Procedures (number)	7	Strength of legal rights index (0–12)	10	*Time to export*	
Time (days)	16	Depth of credit information index (0–8)	0	Documentary compliance (hours)	26
Cost (% of income per capita)	141.7	Credit bureau coverage (% of adults)	0.0	Border compliance (hours)	36
Minimum capital (% of income per capita)	0.0	Credit registry coverage (% of adults)	0.0	*Cost to export*	
				Documentary compliance (US$)	60
Dealing with construction permits (rank)	137	**Protecting minority investors** (rank)	183	Border compliance (US$)	168
DTF score for dealing with construction permits (0–100)	61.05	DTF score for protecting minority investors (0–100)	25.00	*Time to import*	
Procedures (number)	14	Extent of disclosure index (0–10)	0	Documentary compliance (hours)	35
Time (days)	86	Extent of director liability index (0–10)	0	Border compliance (hours)	56
Cost (% of warehouse value)	0.5	Ease of shareholder suits index (0–10)	8	*Cost to import*	
Building quality control index (0–15)	0.0	Extent of shareholder rights index (0–10)	5	Documentary compliance (US$)	80
		Extent of ownership and control index (0–10)	2	Border compliance (US$)	180
		Extent of corporate transparency index (0–10)	0		
Getting electricity (rank)	109			**Enforcing contracts** (rank)	183
DTF score for getting electricity (0–100)	64.48	**Paying taxes** (rank)	110	DTF score for enforcing contracts (0–100)	29.39
Procedures (number)	3	DTF score for paying taxes (0–100)	68.78	Time (days)	885
Time (days)	105	Payments (number per year)	21	Cost (% of claim)	66.0
Cost (% of income per capita)	343.2	Time (hours per year)	128	Quality of judicial processes index (0–18)	4.5
Reliability of supply and transparency of tariffs index (0–8)	0	Total tax and contribution rate (% of profit)	60.5		
		Postfiling index (0–100)	not applicable		
Registering property (rank)	187			**Resolving insolvency** (rank)	119
DTF score for registering property (0–100)	0.00			DTF score for resolving insolvency (0–100)	37.67
Procedures (number)	no practice			Time (years)	5.3
Time (days)	no practice			Cost (% of estate)	38.0
Cost (% of property value)	no practice			Recovery rate (cents on the dollar)	3.2
Quality of land administration index (0–30)	0.0			Strength of insolvency framework index (0–16)	11.5

MOLDOVA

MOLDOVA		**Europe & Central Asia**		**GNI per capita (US$)**	**2,120**
Ease of doing business rank (1–190)	44	Overall distance to frontier (DTF) score (0–100)	73.00	Population	3,552,000

✔ Starting a business (rank)	23	Getting credit (rank)	42	Trading across borders (rank)	35
DTF score for starting a business (0–100)	93.76	DTF score for getting credit (0–100)	70.00	DTF score for trading across borders (0–100)	92.32
Procedures (number)	4	Strength of legal rights index (0–12)	8	*Time to export*	
Time (days)	5	Depth of credit information index (0–8)	6	Documentary compliance (hours)	48
Cost (% of income per capita)	5.6	Credit bureau coverage (% of adults)	13.6	Border compliance (hours)	3
Minimum capital (% of income per capita)	0.0	Credit registry coverage (% of adults)	0.0	*Cost to export*	
				Documentary compliance (US$)	44
Dealing with construction permits (rank)	165	**Protecting minority investors** (rank)	33	Border compliance (US$)	76
DTF score for dealing with construction permits (0–100)	51.98	DTF score for protecting minority investors (0–100)	66.67	*Time to import*	
Procedures (number)	28	Extent of disclosure index (0–10)	7	Documentary compliance (hours)	2
Time (days)	276	Extent of director liability index (0–10)	4	Border compliance (hours)	4
Cost (% of warehouse value)	1.6	Ease of shareholder suits index (0–10)	8	*Cost to import*	
Building quality control index (0–15)	12.0	Extent of shareholder rights index (0–10)	8	Documentary compliance (US$)	41
		Extent of ownership and control index (0–10)	5	Border compliance (US$)	83
		Extent of corporate transparency index (0–10)	8		
Getting electricity (rank)	80			**Enforcing contracts** (rank)	62
DTF score for getting electricity (0–100)	74.65	**Paying taxes** (rank)	32	DTF score for enforcing contracts (0–100)	60.87
Procedures (number)	6	DTF score for paying taxes (0–100)	84.55	Time (days)	585
Time (days)	87	Payments (number per year)	10	Cost (% of claim)	28.6
Cost (% of income per capita)	721.4	Time (hours per year)	181	Quality of judicial processes index (0–18)	9.5
Reliability of supply and transparency of tariffs index (0–8)	7	Total tax and contribution rate (% of profit)	40.5		
		Postfiling index (0–100)	90.79		
Registering property (rank)	20			**Resolving insolvency** (rank)	65
DTF score for registering property (0–100)	82.60			DTF score for resolving insolvency (0–100)	52.56
Procedures (number)	5			Time (years)	2.8
Time (days)	5.5			Cost (% of estate)	15.0
Cost (% of property value)	1.1			Recovery rate (cents on the dollar)	28.0
Quality of land administration index (0–30)	22.0			Strength of insolvency framework index (0–16)	12.0

MONGOLIA

MONGOLIA		**East Asia & Pacific**		**GNI per capita (US$)**	**3,550**
Ease of doing business rank (1–190)	62	Overall distance to frontier (DTF) score (0–100)	69.03	Population	3,027,398

Starting a business (rank)	59	✔ Getting credit (rank)	20	Trading across borders (rank)	110
DTF score for starting a business (0–100)	90.08	DTF score for getting credit (0–100)	80.00	DTF score for trading across borders (0–100)	66.89
Procedures (number)	6	Strength of legal rights index (0–12)	9	*Time to export*	
Time (days)	10	Depth of credit information index (0–8)	7	Documentary compliance (hours)	168
Cost (% of income per capita)	1.4	Credit bureau coverage (% of adults)	0.0	Border compliance (hours)	62
Minimum capital (% of income per capita)	0.0	Credit registry coverage (% of adults)	45.0	*Cost to export*	
				Documentary compliance (US$)	64
Dealing with construction permits (rank)	23	**Protecting minority investors** (rank)	33	Border compliance (US$)	191
DTF score for dealing with construction permits (0–100)	78.19	DTF score for protecting minority investors (0–100)	66.67	*Time to import*	
Procedures (number)	17	Extent of disclosure index (0–10)	6	Documentary compliance (hours)	115
Time (days)	137	Extent of director liability index (0–10)	8	Border compliance (hours)	48
Cost (% of warehouse value)	0.1	Ease of shareholder suits index (0–10)	8	*Cost to import*	
Building quality control index (0–15)	14.0	Extent of shareholder rights index (0–10)	3	Documentary compliance (US$)	83
		Extent of ownership and control index (0–10)	7	Border compliance (US$)	210
		Extent of corporate transparency index (0–10)	8		
Getting electricity (rank)	139			**Enforcing contracts** (rank)	88
DTF score for getting electricity (0–100)	55.00	✘ **Paying taxes** (rank)	62	DTF score for enforcing contracts (0–100)	58.48
Procedures (number)	8	DTF score for paying taxes (0–100)	77.32	Time (days)	374
Time (days)	79	Payments (number per year)	19	Cost (% of claim)	30.6
Cost (% of income per capita)	618.9	Time (hours per year)	134	Quality of judicial processes index (0–18)	5.5
Reliability of supply and transparency of tariffs index (0–8)	3	Total tax and contribution rate (% of profit)	24.7		
		Postfiling index (0–100)	49.08		
Registering property (rank)	50			**Resolving insolvency** (rank)	93
DTF score for registering property (0–100)	74.18			DTF score for resolving insolvency (0–100)	43.54
Procedures (number)	5			Time (years)	4.0
Time (days)	10.5			Cost (% of estate)	15.0
Cost (% of property value)	2.1			Recovery rate (cents on the dollar)	17.0
Quality of land administration index (0–30)	14.5			Strength of insolvency framework index (0–16)	11.0

Note: Most indicator sets refer to a case scenario in the largest business city of an economy, though for 11 economies the data are a population-weighted average for the two largest business cities. For some indicators a result of "no practice" may be recorded for an economy; see the data notes for more details. In starting a business, procedures (number), time (days) and cost (% of income per capita) are calculated as the average of both men and women. For the postfiling index, a result of "not applicable" may be recorded for an economy.

✔ Reform making it easier to do business ✘ Change making it more difficult to do business

MONTENEGRO

MONTENEGRO		**Europe & Central Asia**		**GNI per capita (US$)**	6,970		
Ease of doing business rank (1–190)	42	Overall distance to frontier (DTF) score (0–100)	73.18	Population	622,781		

Starting a business (rank)	60	**Getting credit** (rank)	12	**Trading across borders** (rank)	44
DTF score for starting a business (0–100)	90.07	DTF score for getting credit (0–100)	85.00	DTF score for trading across borders (0–100)	88.75
Procedures (number)	6	Strength of legal rights index (0–12)	12	*Time to export*	
Time (days)	10	Depth of credit information index (0–8)	5	Documentary compliance (hours)	5
Cost (% of income per capita)	1.5	Credit bureau coverage (% of adults)	0.0	Border compliance (hours)	8
Minimum capital (% of income per capita)	0.0	Credit registry coverage (% of adults)	31.6	*Cost to export*	
				Documentary compliance (US$)	67
Dealing with construction permits (rank)	78	**Protecting minority investors** (rank)	51	Border compliance (US$)	158
DTF score for dealing with construction permits (0–100)	69.30	DTF score for protecting minority investors (0–100)	61.67	*Time to import*	
Procedures (number)	8	Extent of disclosure index (0–10)	5	Documentary compliance (hours)	10
Time (days)	152	Extent of director liability index (0–10)	8	Border compliance (hours)	23
Cost (% of warehouse value)	10.9	Ease of shareholder suits index (0–10)	6	*Cost to import*	
Building quality control index (0–15)	12.0	Extent of shareholder rights index (0–10)	6	Documentary compliance (US$)	100
		Extent of ownership and control index (0–10)	3	Border compliance (US$)	306
		Extent of corporate transparency index (0–10)	9		
✔ **Getting electricity** (rank)	127			**Enforcing contracts** (rank)	42
DTF score for getting electricity (0–100)	59.17			DTF score for enforcing contracts (0–100)	66.75
Procedures (number)	7	**Paying taxes** (rank)	70	Time (days)	545
Time (days)	142	DTF score for paying taxes (0–100)	76.67	Cost (% of claim)	25.7
Cost (% of income per capita)	425.6	Payments (number per year)	18	Quality of judicial processes index (0–18)	11.5
Reliability of supply and transparency of tariffs index (0–8)	5	Time (hours per year)	300		
		Total tax and contribution rate (% of profit)	22.1		
Registering property (rank)	76	Postfiling index (0–100)	70.49	**Resolving insolvency** (rank)	37
DTF score for registering property (0–100)	65.76			DTF score for resolving insolvency (0–100)	68.70
Procedures (number)	6			Time (years)	1.4
Time (days)	69			Cost (% of estate)	8.0
Cost (% of property value)	3.2			Recovery rate (cents on the dollar)	49.3
Quality of land administration index (0–30)	17.5			Strength of insolvency framework index (0–16)	13.5

MOROCCO

MOROCCO		**Middle East & North Africa**		**GNI per capita (US$)**	2,850		
Ease of doing business rank (1–190)	69	Overall distance to frontier (DTF) score (0–100)	67.91	Population	35,276,786		

✔ **Starting a business** (rank)	35	**Getting credit** (rank)	105	**Trading across borders** (rank)	65
DTF score for starting a business (0–100)	92.46	DTF score for getting credit (0–100)	45.00	DTF score for trading across borders (0–100)	81.12
Procedures (number)	4	Strength of legal rights index (0–12)	2	*Time to export*	
Time (days)	9	Depth of credit information index (0–8)	7	Documentary compliance (hours)	26
Cost (% of income per capita)	8.0	Credit bureau coverage (% of adults)	25.0	Border compliance (hours)	19
Minimum capital (% of income per capita)	0.0	Credit registry coverage (% of adults)	0.0	*Cost to export*	
				Documentary compliance (US$)	107
Dealing with construction permits (rank)	17	**Protecting minority investors** (rank)	62	Border compliance (US$)	156
DTF score for dealing with construction permits (0–100)	79.73	DTF score for protecting minority investors (0–100)	58.33	*Time to import*	
Procedures (number)	13	Extent of disclosure index (0–10)	9	Documentary compliance (hours)	26
Time (days)	88.5	Extent of director liability index (0–10)	2	Border compliance (hours)	106
Cost (% of warehouse value)	3.5	Ease of shareholder suits index (0–10)	6	*Cost to import*	
Building quality control index (0–15)	13.0	Extent of shareholder rights index (0–10)	6	Documentary compliance (US$)	116
		Extent of ownership and control index (0–10)	5	Border compliance (US$)	228
		Extent of corporate transparency index (0–10)	7		
Getting electricity (rank)	72			**Enforcing contracts** (rank)	57
DTF score for getting electricity (0–100)	75.52			DTF score for enforcing contracts (0–100)	61.85
Procedures (number)	5	✔ **Paying taxes** (rank)	25	Time (days)	510
Time (days)	49	DTF score for paying taxes (0–100)	85.72	Cost (% of claim)	26.5
Cost (% of income per capita)	1,791.6	Payments (number per year)	6	Quality of judicial processes index (0–18)	8.5
Reliability of supply and transparency of tariffs index (0–8)	6	Time (hours per year)	155		
		Total tax and contribution rate (% of profit)	49.8		
✘ **Registering property** (rank)	86	Postfiling index (0–100)	98.62	**Resolving insolvency** (rank)	134
DTF score for registering property (0–100)	64.35			DTF score for resolving insolvency (0–100)	34.03
Procedures (number)	6			Time (years)	3.5
Time (days)	22			Cost (% of estate)	18.0
Cost (% of property value)	6.4			Recovery rate (cents on the dollar)	28.4
Quality of land administration index (0–30)	15.5			Strength of insolvency framework index (0–16)	6.0

MOZAMBIQUE

MOZAMBIQUE		**Sub-Saharan Africa**		**GNI per capita (US$)**	480		
Ease of doing business rank (1–190)	138	Overall distance to frontier (DTF) score (0–100)	54.00	Population	28,829,476		

Starting a business (rank)	137	**Getting credit** (rank)	159	✔ **Trading across borders** (rank)	109
DTF score for starting a business (0–100)	79.86	DTF score for getting credit (0–100)	25.00	DTF score for trading across borders (0–100)	67.25
Procedures (number)	10	Strength of legal rights index (0–12)	1	*Time to export*	
Time (days)	19	Depth of credit information index (0–8)	4	Documentary compliance (hours)	70
Cost (% of income per capita)	18.1	Credit bureau coverage (% of adults)	0.0	Border compliance (hours)	66
Minimum capital (% of income per capita)	0.0	Credit registry coverage (% of adults)	7.4	*Cost to export*	
				Documentary compliance (US$)	220
Dealing with construction permits (rank)	56	**Protecting minority investors** (rank)	138	Border compliance (US$)	602
DTF score for dealing with construction permits (0–100)	72.80	DTF score for protecting minority investors (0–100)	41.67	*Time to import*	
Procedures (number)	11	Extent of disclosure index (0–10)	5	Documentary compliance (hours)	24
Time (days)	118	Extent of director liability index (0–10)	4	Border compliance (hours)	14
Cost (% of warehouse value)	6.3	Ease of shareholder suits index (0–10)	7	*Cost to import*	
Building quality control index (0–15)	11.0	Extent of shareholder rights index (0–10)	6	Documentary compliance (US$)	171
		Extent of ownership and control index (0–10)	2	Border compliance (US$)	354
		Extent of corporate transparency index (0–10)	1		
✔ **Getting electricity** (rank)	150			**Enforcing contracts** (rank)	184
DTF score for getting electricity (0–100)	52.54			DTF score for enforcing contracts (0–100)	27.32
Procedures (number)	5	**Paying taxes** (rank)	117	Time (days)	950
Time (days)	68	DTF score for paying taxes (0–100)	66.13	Cost (% of claim)	119.0
Cost (% of income per capita)	2,817.3	Payments (number per year)	37	Quality of judicial processes index (0–18)	9.0
Reliability of supply and transparency of tariffs index (0–8)	0	Time (hours per year)	200		
		Total tax and contribution rate (% of profit)	36.1		
Registering property (rank)	104	Postfiling index (0–100)	58.56	**Resolving insolvency** (rank)	75
DTF score for registering property (0–100)	59.27			DTF score for resolving insolvency (0–100)	48.20
Procedures (number)	6			Time (years)	1.5
Time (days)	40			Cost (% of estate)	20.5
Cost (% of property value)	5.1			Recovery rate (cents on the dollar)	31.5
Quality of land administration index (0–30)	9.5			Strength of insolvency framework index (0–16)	10.0

Note: Most indicator sets refer to a case scenario in the largest business city of an economy, though for 11 economies the data are a population-weighted average for the two largest business cities. For some indicators a result of "no practice" may be recorded for an economy; see the data notes for more details. In starting a business, procedures (number), time (days) and cost (% of income per capita) are calculated as the average of both men and women. For the postfiling index, a result of "not applicable" may be recorded for an economy.

✔ Reform making it easier to do business   ✘ Change making it more difficult to do business

MYANMAR

		East Asia & Pacific		GNI per capita (US$)	1,315
Ease of doing business rank (1–190)	171	Overall distance to frontier (DTF) score (0–100)	44.21	Population	52,885,223

Starting a business (rank)	155	✔ Getting credit (rank)	177	Trading across borders (rank)	163
DTF score for starting a business (0–100)	75.42	DTF score for getting credit (0–100)	10.00	DTF score for trading across borders (0–100)	47.67
Procedures (number)	12	Strength of legal rights index (0–12)	2	*Time to export*	
Time (days)	14	Depth of credit information index (0–8)	0	Documentary compliance (hours)	144
Cost (% of income per capita)	40.1	Credit bureau coverage (% of adults)	0.0	Border compliance (hours)	142
Minimum capital (% of income per capita)	0.0	Credit registry coverage (% of adults)	0.0	*Cost to export*	
				Documentary compliance (US$)	140
Dealing with construction permits (rank)	73	Protecting minority investors (rank)	183	Border compliance (US$)	432
DTF score for dealing with construction permits (0–100)	70.33	DTF score for protecting minority investors (0–100)	25.00	*Time to import*	
Procedures (number)	15	Extent of disclosure index (0–10)	3	Documentary compliance (hours)	48
Time (days)	95	Extent of director liability index (0–10)	0	Border compliance (hours)	230
Cost (% of warehouse value)	3.8	Ease of shareholder suits index (0–10)	3	*Cost to import*	
Building quality control index (0–15)	9.0	Extent of shareholder rights index (0–10)	5	Documentary compliance (US$)	210
		Extent of ownership and control index (0–10)	1	Border compliance (US$)	457
		Extent of corporate transparency index (0–10)	3		
Getting electricity (rank)	151			Enforcing contracts (rank)	188
DTF score for getting electricity (0–100)	52.52	Paying taxes (rank)	125	DTF score for enforcing contracts (0–100)	24.53
Procedures (number)	6	DTF score for paying taxes (0–100)	63.94	Time (days)	1,160
Time (days)	77	Payments (number per year)	31	Cost (% of claim)	51.5
Cost (% of income per capita)	1,155.3	Time (hours per year)	282	Quality of judicial processes index (0–18)	3.0
Reliability of supply and transparency of tariffs index (0–8)	0	Total tax and contribution rate (% of profit)	31.2		
		Postfiling index (0–100)	45.54		
✔ Registering property (rank)	134			Resolving insolvency (rank)	164
DTF score for registering property (0–100)	52.30			DTF score for resolving insolvency (0–100)	20.39
Procedures (number)	6			Time (years)	5.0
Time (days)	85			Cost (% of estate)	18.0
Cost (% of property value)	4.1			Recovery rate (cents on the dollar)	14.7
Quality of land administration index (0–30)	5.5			Strength of insolvency framework index (0–16)	4.0

NAMIBIA

		Sub-Saharan Africa		GNI per capita (US$)	4,620
Ease of doing business rank (1–190)	106	Overall distance to frontier (DTF) score (0–100)	59.94	Population	2,479,713

Starting a business (rank)	172	Getting credit (rank)	68	Trading across borders (rank)	132
DTF score for starting a business (0–100)	68.90	DTF score for getting credit (0–100)	60.00	DTF score for trading across borders (0–100)	61.47
Procedures (number)	10	Strength of legal rights index (0–12)	5	*Time to export*	
Time (days)	66	Depth of credit information index (0–8)	7	Documentary compliance (hours)	90
Cost (% of income per capita)	11.3	Credit bureau coverage (% of adults)	61.0	Border compliance (hours)	120
Minimum capital (% of income per capita)	0.0	Credit registry coverage (% of adults)	0.0	*Cost to export*	
				Documentary compliance (US$)	348
Dealing with construction permits (rank)	107	Protecting minority investors (rank)	89	Border compliance (US$)	745
DTF score for dealing with construction permits (0–100)	66.10	DTF score for protecting minority investors (0–100)	53.33	*Time to import*	
Procedures (number)	12	Extent of disclosure index (0–10)	5	Documentary compliance (hours)	3
Time (days)	160	Extent of director liability index (0–10)	5	Border compliance (hours)	6
Cost (% of warehouse value)	2.5	Ease of shareholder suits index (0–10)	7	*Cost to import*	
Building quality control index (0–15)	6.5	Extent of shareholder rights index (0–10)	4	Documentary compliance (US$)	63
		Extent of ownership and control index (0–10)	3	Border compliance (US$)	145
		Extent of corporate transparency index (0–10)	8		
Getting electricity (rank)	68			✔ Enforcing contracts (rank)	59
DTF score for getting electricity (0–100)	78.12	Paying taxes (rank)	79	DTF score for enforcing contracts (0–100)	61.58
Procedures (number)	6	DTF score for paying taxes (0–100)	74.52	Time (days)	460
Time (days)	37	Payments (number per year)	27	Cost (% of claim)	35.8
Cost (% of income per capita)	343.7	Time (hours per year)	302	Quality of judicial processes index (0–18)	9.5
Reliability of supply and transparency of tariffs index (0–8)	6	Total tax and contribution rate (% of profit)	20.7		
		Postfiling index (0–100)	77.17		
Registering property (rank)	175			Resolving insolvency (rank)	123
DTF score for registering property (0–100)	38.35			DTF score for resolving insolvency (0–100)	37.04
Procedures (number)	8			Time (years)	2.5
Time (days)	52			Cost (% of estate)	14.5
Cost (% of property value)	13.8			Recovery rate (cents on the dollar)	34.0
Quality of land administration index (0–30)	8.5			Strength of insolvency framework index (0–16)	6.0

NEPAL

		South Asia		GNI per capita (US$)	730
Ease of doing business rank (1–190)	105	Overall distance to frontier (DTF) score (0–100)	59.95	Population	28,982,771

Starting a business (rank)	109	✔ Getting credit (rank)	90	Trading across borders (rank)	76
DTF score for starting a business (0–100)	84.04	DTF score for getting credit (0–100)	50.00	DTF score for trading across borders (0–100)	77.17
Procedures (number)	7	Strength of legal rights index (0–12)	10	*Time to export*	
Time (days)	16.5	Depth of credit information index (0–8)	0	Documentary compliance (hours)	43
Cost (% of income per capita)	24.9	Credit bureau coverage (% of adults)	1.7	Border compliance (hours)	56
Minimum capital (% of income per capita)	0.0	Credit registry coverage (% of adults)	0.0	*Cost to export*	
				Documentary compliance (US$)	110
Dealing with construction permits (rank)	157	✔ Protecting minority investors (rank)	62	Border compliance (US$)	288
DTF score for dealing with construction permits (0–100)	55.74	DTF score for protecting minority investors (0–100)	58.33	*Time to import*	
Procedures (number)	12	Extent of disclosure index (0–10)	6	Documentary compliance (hours)	48
Time (days)	117	Extent of director liability index (0–10)	1	Border compliance (hours)	61
Cost (% of warehouse value)	16.6	Ease of shareholder suits index (0–10)	9	*Cost to import*	
Building quality control index (0–15)	9.0	Extent of shareholder rights index (0–10)	7	Documentary compliance (US$)	80
		Extent of ownership and control index (0–10)	6	Border compliance (US$)	190
		Extent of corporate transparency index (0–10)	6		
Getting electricity (rank)	133			Enforcing contracts (rank)	153
DTF score for getting electricity (0–100)	57.95	Paying taxes (rank)	146	DTF score for enforcing contracts (0–100)	45.26
Procedures (number)	5	DTF score for paying taxes (0–100)	58.01	Time (days)	910
Time (days)	70	Payments (number per year)	34	Cost (% of claim)	26.8
Cost (% of income per capita)	993.7	Time (hours per year)	339	Quality of judicial processes index (0–18)	5.5
Reliability of supply and transparency of tariffs index (0–8)	0	Total tax and contribution rate (% of profit)	29.6		
		Postfiling index (0–100)	33.35		
Registering property (rank)	84			Resolving insolvency (rank)	76
DTF score for registering property (0–100)	64.82			DTF score for resolving insolvency (0–100)	48.15
Procedures (number)	4			Time (years)	2.0
Time (days)	6			Cost (% of estate)	9.0
Cost (% of property value)	4.8			Recovery rate (cents on the dollar)	43.0
Quality of land administration index (0–30)	5.5			Strength of insolvency framework index (0–16)	8.0

Note: Most indicator sets refer to a case scenario in the largest business city of an economy, though for 11 economies the data are a population-weighted average for the two largest business cities. For some indicators a result of "no practice" may be recorded for an economy; see the data notes for more details. In starting a business, procedures (number), time (days) and cost (% of income per capita) are calculated as the average of both men and women. For the postfiling index, a result of "not applicable" may be recorded for an economy.

✔ Reform making it easier to do business   ✘ Change making it more difficult to do business

NETHERLANDS

NETHERLANDS		OECD high income		GNI per capita (US$)	46,310
Ease of doing business rank (1–190)	32	Overall distance to frontier (DTF) score (0–100)	76.03	Population	17,018,408

Starting a business (rank)	20	✔ **Getting credit** (rank)	105	**Trading across borders** (rank)	1
DTF score for starting a business (0–100)	94.28	DTF score for getting credit (0–100)	45.00	DTF score for trading across borders (0–100)	100.00
Procedures (number)	4	Strength of legal rights index (0–12)	2	*Time to export*	
Time (days)	3.5	Depth of credit information index (0–8)	7	Documentary compliance (hours)	1
Cost (% of income per capita)	4.4	Credit bureau coverage (% of adults)	95.2	Border compliance (hours)	0
Minimum capital (% of income per capita)	0.0	Credit registry coverage (% of adults)	0.0	*Cost to export*	
				Documentary compliance (US$)	0
Dealing with construction permits (rank)	76	**Protecting minority investors** (rank)	62	Border compliance (US$)	0
DTF score for dealing with construction permits (0–100)	69.33	DTF score for protecting minority investors (0–100)	58.33	*Time to import*	
Procedures (number)	13	Extent of disclosure index (0–10)	4	Documentary compliance (hours)	1
Time (days)	161	Extent of director liability index (0–10)	4	Border compliance (hours)	0
Cost (% of warehouse value)	3.7	Ease of shareholder suits index (0–10)	6	*Cost to import*	
Building quality control index (0–15)	10.0	Extent of shareholder rights index (0–10)	6	Documentary compliance (US$)	0
		Extent of ownership and control index (0–10)	7	Border compliance (US$)	0
Getting electricity (rank)	52	Extent of corporate transparency index (0–10)	8		
DTF score for getting electricity (0–100)	81.58			**Enforcing contracts** (rank)	69
Procedures (number)	5	**Paying taxes** (rank)	20	DTF score for enforcing contracts (0–100)	59.94
Time (days)	110	DTF score for paying taxes (0–100)	87.59	Time (days)	514
Cost (% of income per capita)	29.5	Payments (number per year)	9	Cost (% of claim)	23.9
Reliability of supply and transparency of tariffs index (0–8)	8	Time (hours per year)	119	Quality of judicial processes index (0–18)	7.0
		Total tax and contribution rate (% of profit)	40.7		
Registering property (rank)	30	Postfiling index (0–100)	91.95	**Resolving insolvency** (rank)	8
DTF score for registering property (0–100)	80.04			DTF score for resolving insolvency (0–100)	84.22
Procedures (number)	5			Time (years)	1.1
Time (days)	2.5			Cost (% of estate)	3.5
Cost (% of property value)	6.1			Recovery rate (cents on the dollar)	89.7
Quality of land administration index (0–30)	28.5			Strength of insolvency framework index (0–16)	11.5

NEW ZEALAND

NEW ZEALAND		OECD high income		GNI per capita (US$)	39,070
Ease of doing business rank (1–190)	1	Overall distance to frontier (DTF) score (0–100)	86.55	Population	4,692,700

Starting a business (rank)	1	**Getting credit** (rank)	1	**Trading across borders** (rank)	56
DTF score for starting a business (0–100)	99.96	DTF score for getting credit (0–100)	100.00	DTF score for trading across borders (0–100)	84.63
Procedures (number)	1	Strength of legal rights index (0–12)	12	*Time to export*	
Time (days)	0.5	Depth of credit information index (0–8)	8	Documentary compliance (hours)	3
Cost (% of income per capita)	0.3	Credit bureau coverage (% of adults)	100.0	Border compliance (hours)	37
Minimum capital (% of income per capita)	0.0	Credit registry coverage (% of adults)	0.0	*Cost to export*	
				Documentary compliance (US$)	67
Dealing with construction permits (rank)	3	**Protecting minority investors** (rank)	2	Border compliance (US$)	337
DTF score for dealing with construction permits (0–100)	86.36	DTF score for protecting minority investors (0–100)	81.67	*Time to import*	
Procedures (number)	11	Extent of disclosure index (0–10)	10	Documentary compliance (hours)	1
Time (days)	93	Extent of director liability index (0–10)	9	Border compliance (hours)	25
Cost (% of warehouse value)	2.3	Ease of shareholder suits index (0–10)	9	*Cost to import*	
Building quality control index (0–15)	15.0	Extent of shareholder rights index (0–10)	7	Documentary compliance (US$)	80
		Extent of ownership and control index (0–10)	7	Border compliance (US$)	367
Getting electricity (rank)	37	Extent of corporate transparency index (0–10)	7		
DTF score for getting electricity (0–100)	83.97			✘ **Enforcing contracts** (rank)	21
Procedures (number)	5	✔ **Paying taxes** (rank)	9	DTF score for enforcing contracts (0–100)	71.48
Time (days)	58	DTF score for paying taxes (0–100)	91.08	Time (days)	216
Cost (% of income per capita)	72.4	Payments (number per year)	7	Cost (% of claim)	27.2
Reliability of supply and transparency of tariffs index (0–8)	7	Time (hours per year)	140	Quality of judicial processes index (0–18)	9.5
		Total tax and contribution rate (% of profit)	34.5		
Registering property (rank)	1	Postfiling index (0–100)	96.90	**Resolving insolvency** (rank)	32
DTF score for registering property (0–100)	94.47			DTF score for resolving insolvency (0–100)	71.85
Procedures (number)	2			Time (years)	1.3
Time (days)	1			Cost (% of estate)	3.5
Cost (% of property value)	0.1			Recovery rate (cents on the dollar)	84.2
Quality of land administration index (0–30)	26.0			Strength of insolvency framework index (0–16)	8.5

NICARAGUA

NICARAGUA		Latin America & Caribbean		GNI per capita (US$)	2,050
Ease of doing business rank (1–190)	131	Overall distance to frontier (DTF) score (0–100)	55.39	Population	6,149,928

Starting a business (rank)	138	**Getting credit** (rank)	105	**Trading across borders** (rank)	74
DTF score for starting a business (0–100)	79.61	DTF score for getting credit (0–100)	45.00	DTF score for trading across borders (0–100)	78.99
Procedures (number)	7	Strength of legal rights index (0–12)	1	*Time to export*	
Time (days)	14	Depth of credit information index (0–8)	8	Documentary compliance (hours)	48
Cost (% of income per capita)	65.4	Credit bureau coverage (% of adults)	55.9	Border compliance (hours)	60
Minimum capital (% of income per capita)	0.0	Credit registry coverage (% of adults)	20.4	*Cost to export*	
				Documentary compliance (US$)	47
Dealing with construction permits (rank)	174	**Protecting minority investors** (rank)	167	Border compliance (US$)	150
DTF score for dealing with construction permits (0–100)	45.82	DTF score for protecting minority investors (0–100)	35.00	*Time to import*	
Procedures (number)	18	Extent of disclosure index (0–10)	1	Documentary compliance (hours)	16
Time (days)	225	Extent of director liability index (0–10)	5	Border compliance (hours)	72
Cost (% of warehouse value)	6.1	Ease of shareholder suits index (0–10)	6	*Cost to import*	
Building quality control index (0–15)	3.5	Extent of shareholder rights index (0–10)	4	Documentary compliance (US$)	86
		Extent of ownership and control index (0–10)	1	Border compliance (US$)	400
Getting electricity (rank)	100	Extent of corporate transparency index (0–10)	4		
DTF score for getting electricity (0–100)	68.33			✔ **Enforcing contracts** (rank)	87
Procedures (number)	6	**Paying taxes** (rank)	159	DTF score for enforcing contracts (0–100)	58.58
Time (days)	55	DTF score for paying taxes (0–100)	52.86	Time (days)	490
Cost (% of income per capita)	856.5	Payments (number per year)	43	Cost (% of claim)	26.8
Reliability of supply and transparency of tariffs index (0–8)	4	Time (hours per year)	201	Quality of judicial processes index (0–18)	6.5
		Total tax and contribution rate (% of profit)	60.2		
Registering property (rank)	148	Postfiling index (0–100)	52.55	**Resolving insolvency** (rank)	102
DTF score for registering property (0–100)	48.85			DTF score for resolving insolvency (0–100)	40.89
Procedures (number)	9			Time (years)	2.2
Time (days)	56			Cost (% of estate)	14.5
Cost (% of property value)	5.0			Recovery rate (cents on the dollar)	35.3
Quality of land administration index (0–30)	6.5			Strength of insolvency framework index (0–16)	7.0

Note: Most indicator sets refer to a case scenario in the largest business city of an economy, though for 11 economies the data are a population-weighted average for the two largest business cities. For some indicators a result of "no practice" may be recorded for an economy; see the data notes for more details. In starting a business, procedures (number), time (days) and cost (% of income per capita) are calculated as the average of both men and women. For the postfiling index, a result of "not applicable" may be recorded for an economy.

✔ Reform making it easier to do business   ✘ Change making it more difficult to do business

NIGER

NIGER		Sub-Saharan Africa		GNI per capita (US$)		370
Ease of doing business rank (1–190)	144	Overall distance to frontier (DTF) score (0–100)	52.34	Population		20,672,987

✔ **Starting a business** (rank)	24	**Getting credit** (rank)	142	**Trading across borders** (rank)	122
DTF score for starting a business (0–100)	93.65	DTF score for getting credit (0–100)	30.00	DTF score for trading across borders (0–100)	63.61
Procedures (number)	3	Strength of legal rights index (0–12)	6	*Time to export*	
Time (days)	7	Depth of credit information index (0–8)	0	Documentary compliance (hours)	51
Cost (% of income per capita)	8.3	Credit bureau coverage (% of adults)	0.2	Border compliance (hours)	48
Minimum capital (% of income per capita)	11.8	Credit registry coverage (% of adults)	0.3	*Cost to export*	
				Documentary compliance (US$)	39
✔ **Dealing with construction permits** (rank)	164	**Protecting minority investors** (rank)	146	Border compliance (US$)	543
DTF score for dealing with construction permits (0–100)	53.70	DTF score for protecting minority investors (0–100)	40.00	*Time to import*	
Procedures (number)	15	Extent of disclosure index (0–10)	7	Documentary compliance (hours)	156
Time (days)	91	Extent of director liability index (0–10)	1	Border compliance (hours)	78
Cost (% of warehouse value)	13.3	Ease of shareholder suits index (0–10)	5	*Cost to import*	
Building quality control index (0–15)	6.0	Extent of shareholder rights index (0–10)	4	Documentary compliance (US$)	282
		Extent of ownership and control index (0–10)	3	Border compliance (US$)	462
		Extent of corporate transparency index (0–10)	4		
✔ **Getting electricity** (rank)	162			**Enforcing contracts** (rank)	137
DTF score for getting electricity (0–100)	44.86	**Paying taxes** (rank)	160	DTF score for enforcing contracts (0–100)	48.70
Procedures (number)	4	DTF score for paying taxes (0–100)	52.49	Time (days)	430
Time (days)	97	Payments (number per year)	41	Cost (% of claim)	52.6
Cost (% of income per capita)	5,632.6	Time (hours per year)	270	Quality of judicial processes index (0–18)	5.5
Reliability of supply and transparency of tariffs index (0–8)	0	Total tax and contribution rate (% of profit)	47.3		
		Postfiling index (0–100)	38.02	**Resolving insolvency** (rank)	112
✔ **Registering property** (rank)	116			DTF score for resolving insolvency (0–100)	39.19
DTF score for registering property (0–100)	57.15			Time (years)	5.0
Procedures (number)	4			Cost (% of estate)	18.0
Time (days)	35			Recovery rate (cents on the dollar)	20.6
Cost (% of property value)	6.5			Strength of insolvency framework index (0–16)	9.0
Quality of land administration index (0–30)	4.0				

NIGERIA

NIGERIA		Sub-Saharan Africa		GNI per capita (US$)		2,450
Ease of doing business rank (1–190)	145	Overall distance to frontier (DTF) score (0–100)	52.03	Population		185,989,640

✔ **Starting a business** (rank)	130	✔ **Getting credit** (rank)	6	**Trading across borders** (rank)	183
DTF score for starting a business (0–100)	80.80	DTF score for getting credit (0–100)	90.00	DTF score for trading across borders (0–100)	19.93
Procedures (number)	8.5	Strength of legal rights index (0–12)	10	*Time to export*	
Time (days)	18.9	Depth of credit information index (0–8)	8	Documentary compliance (hours)	131.4
Cost (% of income per capita)	28.8	Credit bureau coverage (% of adults)	7.8	Border compliance (hours)	135.4
Minimum capital (% of income per capita)	0.0	Credit registry coverage (% of adults)	0.1	*Cost to export*	
				Documentary compliance (US$)	250
✔ **Dealing with construction permits** (rank)	147	**Protecting minority investors** (rank)	33	Border compliance (US$)	785.7
DTF score for dealing with construction permits (0–100)	58.81	DTF score for protecting minority investors (0–100)	66.67	*Time to import*	
Procedures (number)	15.1	Extent of disclosure index (0–10)	7	Documentary compliance (hours)	172.7
Time (days)	110.3	Extent of director liability index (0–10)	7	Border compliance (hours)	283.7
Cost (% of warehouse value)	18.5	Ease of shareholder suits index (0–10)	7	*Cost to import*	
Building quality control index (0–15)	11.8	Extent of shareholder rights index (0–10)	5	Documentary compliance (US$)	564.3
		Extent of ownership and control index (0–10)	5	Border compliance (US$)	1,076.8
		Extent of corporate transparency index (0–10)	9		
Getting electricity (rank)	172			**Enforcing contracts** (rank)	96
DTF score for getting electricity (0–100)	34.68	✔ **Paying taxes** (rank)	171	DTF score for enforcing contracts (0–100)	56.32
Procedures (number)	9.8	DTF score for paying taxes (0–100)	48.44	Time (days)	454
Time (days)	149.4	Payments (number per year)	59	Cost (% of claim)	42.3
Cost (% of income per capita)	334.8	Time (hours per year)	360.4	Quality of judicial processes index (0–18)	7.9
Reliability of supply and transparency of tariffs index (0–8)	0	Total tax and contribution rate (% of profit)	34.8		
		Postfiling index (0–100)	47.48	**Resolving insolvency** (rank)	145
✔ **Registering property** (rank)	179			DTF score for resolving insolvency (0–100)	30.60
DTF score for registering property (0–100)	34.08			Time (years)	2.0
Procedures (number)	11.3			Cost (% of estate)	22.0
Time (days)	68.9			Recovery rate (cents on the dollar)	27.8
Cost (% of property value)	10.5			Strength of insolvency framework index (0–16)	5.0
Quality of land administration index (0–30)	7.4				

NORWAY

NORWAY		OECD high income		GNI per capita (US$)		82,330
Ease of doing business rank (1–190)	8	Overall distance to frontier (DTF) score (0–100)	82.16	Population		5,232,929

Starting a business (rank)	19	**Getting credit** (rank)	77	**Trading across borders** (rank)	22
DTF score for starting a business (0–100)	94.30	DTF score for getting credit (0–100)	55.00	DTF score for trading across borders (0–100)	96.97
Procedures (number)	4	Strength of legal rights index (0–12)	5	*Time to export*	
Time (days)	4	Depth of credit information index (0–8)	6	Documentary compliance (hours)	2
Cost (% of income per capita)	0.9	Credit bureau coverage (% of adults)	100.0	Border compliance (hours)	2
Minimum capital (% of income per capita)	4.8	Credit registry coverage (% of adults)	0.0	*Cost to export*	
				Documentary compliance (US$)	0
Dealing with construction permits (rank)	21	**Protecting minority investors** (rank)	10	Border compliance (US$)	125
DTF score for dealing with construction permits (0–100)	78.83	DTF score for protecting minority investors (0–100)	75.00	*Time to import*	
Procedures (number)	11	Extent of disclosure index (0–10)	7	Documentary compliance (hours)	2
Time (days)	110.5	Extent of director liability index (0–10)	5	Border compliance (hours)	2
Cost (% of warehouse value)	0.6	Ease of shareholder suits index (0–10)	8	*Cost to import*	
Building quality control index (0–15)	10.0	Extent of shareholder rights index (0–10)	7	Documentary compliance (US$)	0
		Extent of ownership and control index (0–10)	8	Border compliance (US$)	125
		Extent of corporate transparency index (0–10)	10		
Getting electricity (rank)	23			**Enforcing contracts** (rank)	8
DTF score for getting electricity (0–100)	87.46	✔ **Paying taxes** (rank)	28	DTF score for enforcing contracts (0–100)	75.71
Procedures (number)	4	DTF score for paying taxes (0–100)	85.18	Time (days)	400
Time (days)	66	Payments (number per year)	4	Cost (% of claim)	9.9
Cost (% of income per capita)	11.4	Time (hours per year)	83	Quality of judicial processes index (0–18)	11.0
Reliability of supply and transparency of tariffs index (0–8)	7	Total tax and contribution rate (% of profit)	37.5		
		Postfiling index (0–100)	63.69	**Resolving insolvency** (rank)	6
Registering property (rank)	14			DTF score for resolving insolvency (0–100)	85.94
DTF score for registering property (0–100)	87.26			Time (years)	0.9
Procedures (number)	1			Cost (% of estate)	1.0
Time (days)	3			Recovery rate (cents on the dollar)	93.1
Cost (% of property value)	2.5			Strength of insolvency framework index (0–16)	11.5
Quality of land administration index (0–30)	20.0				

Note: Most indicator sets refer to a case scenario in the largest business city of an economy, though for 11 economies the data are a population-weighted average for the two largest business cities. For some indicators a result of "no practice" may be recorded for an economy; see the data notes for more details. In starting a business, procedures (number), time (days) and cost (% of income per capita) are calculated as the average of both men and women. For the postfiling index, a result of "not applicable" may be recorded for an economy.

✔ Reform making it easier to do business   ✘ Change making it more difficult to do business

OMAN

Middle East & North Africa		GNI per capita (US$)	15,871
Ease of doing business rank (1–190)	71	Population	4,424,762

Overall distance to frontier (DTF) score (0–100): 67.20

Starting a business (rank)	31
DTF score for starting a business (0–100)	92.85
Procedures (number)	4.5
Time (days)	6.5
Cost (% of income per capita)	4.0
Minimum capital (% of income per capita)	0.0

Dealing with construction permits (rank)	60
DTF score for dealing with construction permits (0–100)	72.15
Procedures (number)	14
Time (days)	172
Cost (% of warehouse value)	1.3
Building quality control index (0–15)	11.0

Getting electricity (rank)	61
DTF score for getting electricity (0–100)	79.35
Procedures (number)	6
Time (days)	62
Cost (% of income per capita)	77.7
Reliability of supply and transparency of tariffs index (0–8)	7

Registering property (rank)	54
DTF score for registering property (0–100)	73.62
Procedures (number)	2
Time (days)	16
Cost (% of property value)	5.0
Quality of land administration index (0–30)	13.0

Getting credit (rank)	133
DTF score for getting credit (0–100)	35.00
Strength of legal rights index (0–12)	1
Depth of credit information index (0–8)	6
Credit bureau coverage (% of adults)	0.0
Credit registry coverage (% of adults)	26.7

Protecting minority investors (rank)	124
DTF score for protecting minority investors (0–100)	46.67
Extent of disclosure index (0–10)	8
Extent of director liability index (0–10)	5
Ease of shareholder suits index (0–10)	3
Extent of shareholder rights index (0–10)	4
Extent of ownership and control index (0–10)	4
Extent of corporate transparency index (0–10)	4

Paying taxes (rank)	11
DTF score for paying taxes (0–100)	90.60
Payments (number per year)	15
Time (hours per year)	68
Total tax and contribution rate (% of profit)	23.9
Postfiling index (0–100)	85.32

✔ Trading across borders (rank)	72
DTF score for trading across borders (0–100)	79.39
Time to export	
Documentary compliance (hours)	7
Border compliance (hours)	52
Cost to export	
Documentary compliance (US$)	107
Border compliance (US$)	261
Time to import	
Documentary compliance (hours)	7
Border compliance (hours)	70
Cost to import	
Documentary compliance (US$)	124
Border compliance (US$)	394

Enforcing contracts (rank)	67
DTF score for enforcing contracts (0–100)	60.02
Time (days)	598
Cost (% of claim)	15.1
Quality of judicial processes index (0–18)	6.5

Resolving insolvency (rank)	98
DTF score for resolving insolvency (0–100)	42.40
Time (years)	4.0
Cost (% of estate)	3.5
Recovery rate (cents on the dollar)	38.1
Strength of insolvency framework index (0–16)	7.0

PAKISTAN

South Asia		GNI per capita (US$)	1,510
Ease of doing business rank (1–190)	147	Population	193,203,476

Overall distance to frontier (DTF) score (0–100): 51.65

✔ Starting a business (rank)	142
DTF score for starting a business (0–100)	78.61
Procedures (number)	12
Time (days)	17.5
Cost (% of income per capita)	7.6
Minimum capital (% of income per capita)	0.0

Dealing with construction permits (rank)	141
DTF score for dealing with construction permits (0–100)	59.72
Procedures (number)	15
Time (days)	262.1
Cost (% of warehouse value)	6.6
Building quality control index (0–15)	12.0

Getting electricity (rank)	167
DTF score for getting electricity (0–100)	42.39
Procedures (number)	5.4
Time (days)	180.7
Cost (% of income per capita)	1,663.7
Reliability of supply and transparency of tariffs index (0–8)	0

✔ Registering property (rank)	170
DTF score for registering property (0–100)	41.41
Procedures (number)	7.7
Time (days)	154.8
Cost (% of property value)	4.6
Quality of land administration index (0–30)	7.6

Getting credit (rank)	105
DTF score for getting credit (0–100)	45.00
Strength of legal rights index (0–12)	2
Depth of credit information index (0–8)	7
Credit bureau coverage (% of adults)	6.7
Credit registry coverage (% of adults)	9.9

✔ Protecting minority investors (rank)	20
DTF score for protecting minority investors (0–100)	71.67
Extent of disclosure index (0–10)	6
Extent of director liability index (0–10)	7
Ease of shareholder suits index (0–10)	6
Extent of shareholder rights index (0–10)	8
Extent of ownership and control index (0–10)	9
Extent of corporate transparency index (0–10)	7

Paying taxes (rank)	172
DTF score for paying taxes (0–100)	46.43
Payments (number per year)	47
Time (hours per year)	311.5
Total tax and contribution rate (% of profit)	33.8
Postfiling index (0–100)	10.49

✔ Trading across borders (rank)	171
DTF score for trading across borders (0–100)	41.94
Time to export	
Documentary compliance (hours)	55
Border compliance (hours)	75
Cost to export	
Documentary compliance (US$)	257
Border compliance (US$)	406
Time to import	
Documentary compliance (hours)	143
Border compliance (hours)	129.3
Cost to import	
Documentary compliance (US$)	735
Border compliance (US$)	936.6

Enforcing contracts (rank)	156
DTF score for enforcing contracts (0–100)	43.49
Time (days)	1,071
Cost (% of claim)	20.5
Quality of judicial processes index (0–18)	5.7

Resolving insolvency (rank)	82
DTF score for resolving insolvency (0–100)	45.83
Time (years)	2.6
Cost (% of estate)	4.0
Recovery rate (cents on the dollar)	44.5
Strength of insolvency framework index (0–16)	7.0

PALAU

East Asia & Pacific		GNI per capita (US$)	12,450
Ease of doing business rank (1–190)	130	Population	21,503

Overall distance to frontier (DTF) score (0–100): 55.58

Starting a business (rank)	124
DTF score for starting a business (0–100)	81.96
Procedures (number)	8
Time (days)	28
Cost (% of income per capita)	2.9
Minimum capital (% of income per capita)	7.7

Dealing with construction permits (rank)	85
DTF score for dealing with construction permits (0–100)	68.38
Procedures (number)	19
Time (days)	72
Cost (% of warehouse value)	0.8
Building quality control index (0–15)	7.0

Getting electricity (rank)	140
DTF score for getting electricity (0–100)	54.84
Procedures (number)	5
Time (days)	125
Cost (% of income per capita)	64.7
Reliability of supply and transparency of tariffs index (0–8)	0

Registering property (rank)	43
DTF score for registering property (0–100)	75.16
Procedures (number)	5
Time (days)	14
Cost (% of property value)	0.2
Quality of land administration index (0–30)	12.5

Getting credit (rank)	90
DTF score for getting credit (0–100)	50.00
Strength of legal rights index (0–12)	10
Depth of credit information index (0–8)	0
Credit bureau coverage (% of adults)	0.0
Credit registry coverage (% of adults)	0.0

Protecting minority investors (rank)	177
DTF score for protecting minority investors (0–100)	26.67
Extent of disclosure index (0–10)	0
Extent of director liability index (0–10)	0
Ease of shareholder suits index (0–10)	7
Extent of shareholder rights index (0–10)	5
Extent of ownership and control index (0–10)	2
Extent of corporate transparency index (0–10)	2

✔ Paying taxes (rank)	107
DTF score for paying taxes (0–100)	69.22
Payments (number per year)	11
Time (hours per year)	52
Total tax and contribution rate (% of profit)	75.5
Postfiling index (0–100)	not applicable

Trading across borders (rank)	133
DTF score for trading across borders (0–100)	60.98
Time to export	
Documentary compliance (hours)	72
Border compliance (hours)	102
Cost to export	
Documentary compliance (US$)	100
Border compliance (US$)	505
Time to import	
Documentary compliance (hours)	96
Border compliance (hours)	84
Cost to import	
Documentary compliance (US$)	100
Border compliance (US$)	605

Enforcing contracts (rank)	126
DTF score for enforcing contracts (0–100)	52.21
Time (days)	810
Cost (% of claim)	35.3
Quality of judicial processes index (0–18)	9.5

Resolving insolvency (rank)	166
DTF score for resolving insolvency (0–100)	16.38
Time (years)	2.0
Cost (% of estate)	22.5
Recovery rate (cents on the dollar)	30.4
Strength of insolvency framework index (0–16)	0.0

Note: Most indicator sets refer to a case scenario in the largest business city of an economy, though for 11 economies the data are a population-weighted average for the two largest business cities. For some indicators a result of "no practice" may be recorded for an economy; see the data notes for more details. In starting a business, procedures (number), time (days) and cost (% of income per capita) are calculated as the average of both men and women. For the postfiling index, a result of "not applicable" may be recorded for an economy.

✔ Reform making it easier to do business   ✘ Change making it more difficult to do business

PANAMA

		Latin America & Caribbean		GNI per capita (US$)	12,140
Ease of doing business rank (1–190)	79	Overall distance to frontier (DTF) score (0–100)	65.27	Population	4,034,119

Starting a business (rank)	39	Getting credit (rank)	29	Trading across borders (rank)	54
DTF score for starting a business (0–100)	92.02	DTF score for getting credit (0–100)	75.00	DTF score for trading across borders (0–100)	85.47
Procedures (number)	5	Strength of legal rights index (0–12)	7	*Time to export*	
Time (days)	6	Depth of credit information index (0–8)	8	Documentary compliance (hours)	6
Cost (% of income per capita)	5.7	Credit bureau coverage (% of adults)	66.8	Border compliance (hours)	24
Minimum capital (% of income per capita)	0.0	Credit registry coverage (% of adults)	0.0	*Cost to export*	
				Documentary compliance (US$)	60
Dealing with construction permits (rank)	88	Protecting minority investors (rank)	96	Border compliance (US$)	270
DTF score for dealing with construction permits (0–100)	68.16	DTF score for protecting minority investors (0–100)	51.67	*Time to import*	
Procedures (number)	18	Extent of disclosure index (0–10)	4	Documentary compliance (hours)	6
Time (days)	105	Extent of director liability index (0–10)	4	Border compliance (hours)	24
Cost (% of warehouse value)	2.5	Ease of shareholder suits index (0–10)	8	*Cost to import*	
Building quality control index (0–15)	9.0	Extent of shareholder rights index (0–10)	8	Documentary compliance (US$)	50
		Extent of ownership and control index (0–10)	1	Border compliance (US$)	490
Getting electricity (rank)	18	Extent of corporate transparency index (0–10)	6		
DTF score for getting electricity (0–100)	89.77			Enforcing contracts (rank)	148
Procedures (number)	5	Paying taxes (rank)	180	DTF score for enforcing contracts (0–100)	46.19
Time (days)	35	DTF score for paying taxes (0–100)	39.66	Time (days)	790
Cost (% of income per capita)	17.2	Payments (number per year)	52	Cost (% of claim)	38.0
Reliability of supply and transparency of tariffs index (0–8)	8	Time (hours per year)	417	Quality of judicial processes index (0–18)	6.5
		Total tax and contribution rate (% of profit)	37.2		
		Postfiling index (0–100)	12.84	✔ Resolving insolvency (rank)	107
Registering property (rank)	83			DTF score for resolving insolvency (0–100)	39.59
DTF score for registering property (0–100)	65.17			Time (years)	2.5
Procedures (number)	7			Cost (% of estate)	25.0
Time (days)	22.5			Recovery rate (cents on the dollar)	27.1
Cost (% of property value)	2.4			Strength of insolvency framework index (0–16)	8.0
Quality of land administration index (0–30)	11.0				

PAPUA NEW GUINEA

		East Asia & Pacific		GNI per capita (US$)	2,528
Ease of doing business rank (1–190)	109	Overall distance to frontier (DTF) score (0–100)	59.04	Population	8,084,991

Starting a business (rank)	129	Getting credit (rank)	42	Trading across borders (rank)	137
DTF score for starting a business (0–100)	81.04	DTF score for getting credit (0–100)	70.00	DTF score for trading across borders (0–100)	60.47
Procedures (number)	6	Strength of legal rights index (0–12)	9	*Time to export*	
Time (days)	41	Depth of credit information index (0–8)	5	Documentary compliance (hours)	96
Cost (% of income per capita)	11.5	Credit bureau coverage (% of adults)	7.0	Border compliance (hours)	42
Minimum capital (% of income per capita)	0.0	Credit registry coverage (% of adults)	0.0	*Cost to export*	
				Documentary compliance (US$)	75
Dealing with construction permits (rank)	117	Protecting minority investors (rank)	89	Border compliance (US$)	660
DTF score for dealing with construction permits (0–100)	64.42	DTF score for protecting minority investors (0–100)	53.33	*Time to import*	
Procedures (number)	17	Extent of disclosure index (0–10)	5	Documentary compliance (hours)	120
Time (days)	217	Extent of director liability index (0–10)	5	Border compliance (hours)	72
Cost (% of warehouse value)	1.2	Ease of shareholder suits index (0–10)	9	*Cost to import*	
Building quality control index (0–15)	10.0	Extent of shareholder rights index (0–10)	8	Documentary compliance (US$)	85
		Extent of ownership and control index (0–10)	2	Border compliance (US$)	790
Getting electricity (rank)	107	Extent of corporate transparency index (0–10)	3		
DTF score for getting electricity (0–100)	65.53			Enforcing contracts (rank)	171
Procedures (number)	4	Paying taxes (rank)	91	DTF score for enforcing contracts (0–100)	36.21
Time (days)	66	DTF score for paying taxes (0–100)	71.71	Time (days)	591
Cost (% of income per capita)	27.2	Payments (number per year)	32	Cost (% of claim)	110.3
Reliability of supply and transparency of tariffs index (0–8)	0	Time (hours per year)	199	Quality of judicial processes index (0–18)	8.5
		Total tax and contribution rate (% of profit)	39.3		
		Postfiling index (0–100)	77.12	Resolving insolvency (rank)	141
Registering property (rank)	122			DTF score for resolving insolvency (0–100)	32.31
DTF score for registering property (0–100)	55.38			Time (years)	3.0
Procedures (number)	4			Cost (% of estate)	23.0
Time (days)	72			Recovery rate (cents on the dollar)	25.2
Cost (% of property value)	5.2			Strength of insolvency framework index (0–16)	6.0
Quality of land administration index (0–30)	4.5				

PARAGUAY

		Latin America & Caribbean		GNI per capita (US$)	4,070
Ease of doing business rank (1–190)	108	Overall distance to frontier (DTF) score (0–100)	59.18	Population	6,725,308

Starting a business (rank)	146	Getting credit (rank)	122	Trading across borders (rank)	120
DTF score for starting a business (0–100)	77.52	DTF score for getting credit (0–100)	40.00	DTF score for trading across borders (0–100)	64.03
Procedures (number)	7	Strength of legal rights index (0–12)	1	*Time to export*	
Time (days)	35	Depth of credit information index (0–8)	7	Documentary compliance (hours)	24
Cost (% of income per capita)	39.9	Credit bureau coverage (% of adults)	44.6	Border compliance (hours)	120
Minimum capital (% of income per capita)	0.0	Credit registry coverage (% of adults)	25.4	*Cost to export*	
				Documentary compliance (US$)	120
Dealing with construction permits (rank)	72	Protecting minority investors (rank)	138	Border compliance (US$)	815
DTF score for dealing with construction permits (0–100)	70.52	DTF score for protecting minority investors (0–100)	41.67	*Time to import*	
Procedures (number)	14	Extent of disclosure index (0–10)	6	Documentary compliance (hours)	36
Time (days)	121	Extent of director liability index (0–10)	5	Border compliance (hours)	48
Cost (% of warehouse value)	1.6	Ease of shareholder suits index (0–10)	6	*Cost to import*	
Building quality control index (0–15)	8.0	Extent of shareholder rights index (0–10)	3	Documentary compliance (US$)	135
		Extent of ownership and control index (0–10)	3	Border compliance (US$)	500
Getting electricity (rank)	104	Extent of corporate transparency index (0–10)	2		
DTF score for getting electricity (0–100)	67.09			Enforcing contracts (rank)	70
Procedures (number)	5	Paying taxes (rank)	127	DTF score for enforcing contracts (0–100)	59.77
Time (days)	67	DTF score for paying taxes (0–100)	63.73	Time (days)	606
Cost (% of income per capita)	161.6	Payments (number per year)	20	Cost (% of claim)	30.0
Reliability of supply and transparency of tariffs index (0–8)	2	Time (hours per year)	378	Quality of judicial processes index (0–18)	9.5
		Total tax and contribution rate (% of profit)	35.0		
		Postfiling index (0–100)	46.56	Resolving insolvency (rank)	100
Registering property (rank)	75			DTF score for resolving insolvency (0–100)	41.32
DTF score for registering property (0–100)	66.12			Time (years)	3.9
Procedures (number)	6			Cost (% of estate)	9.0
Time (days)	46			Recovery rate (cents on the dollar)	21.6
Cost (% of property value)	1.8			Strength of insolvency framework index (0–16)	9.5
Quality of land administration index (0–30)	12.0				

Note: Most indicator sets refer to a case scenario in the largest business city of an economy, though for 11 economies the data are a population-weighted average for the two largest business cities. For some indicators a result of "no practice" may be recorded for an economy; see the data notes for more details. In starting a business, procedures (number), time (days) and cost (% of income per capita) are calculated as the average of both men and women. For the postfiling index, a result of "not applicable" may be recorded for an economy.

✔ Reform making it easier to do business   ✘ Change making it more difficult to do business

PERU

PERU		Latin America & Caribbean		GNI per capita (US$)	5,950		
Ease of doing business rank (1–190)	58	Overall distance to frontier (DTF) score (0–100)	69.45	Population	31,773,839		

Starting a business (rank)	114	**Getting credit** (rank)	20	**Trading across borders** (rank)	92
DTF score for starting a business (0–100)	83.39	DTF score for getting credit (0–100)	80.00	DTF score for trading across borders (0–100)	71.45
Procedures (number)	7	Strength of legal rights index (0–12)	8	*Time to export*	
Time (days)	26.5	Depth of credit information index (0–8)	8	Documentary compliance (hours)	48
Cost (% of income per capita)	10.0	Credit bureau coverage (% of adults)	100.0	Border compliance (hours)	48
Minimum capital (% of income per capita)	0.0	Credit registry coverage (% of adults)	37.4	*Cost to export*	
				Documentary compliance (US$)	50
Dealing with construction permits (rank)	61	**Protecting minority investors** (rank)	51	Border compliance (US$)	460
DTF score for dealing with construction permits (0–100)	71.90	DTF score for protecting minority investors (0–100)	61.67	*Time to import*	
Procedures (number)	15	Extent of disclosure index (0–10)	9	Documentary compliance (hours)	72
Time (days)	188	Extent of director liability index (0–10)	6	Border compliance (hours)	72
Cost (% of warehouse value)	1.1	Ease of shareholder suits index (0–10)	6	*Cost to import*	
Building quality control index (0–15)	12.0	Extent of shareholder rights index (0–10)	8	Documentary compliance (US$)	80
		Extent of ownership and control index (0–10)	3	Border compliance (US$)	583
Getting electricity (rank)	63	Extent of corporate transparency index (0–10)	5		
DTF score for getting electricity (0–100)	79.01			**Enforcing contracts** (rank)	63
Procedures (number)	5	**Paying taxes** (rank)	121	DTF score for enforcing contracts (0–100)	60.70
Time (days)	67	DTF score for paying taxes (0–100)	65.81	Time (days)	426
Cost (% of income per capita)	349.6	Payments (number per year)	9	Cost (% of claim)	35.7
Reliability of supply and transparency of tariffs index (0–8)	6	Time (hours per year)	260	Quality of judicial processes index (0–18)	8.5
		Total tax and contribution rate (% of profit)	35.6		
Registering property (rank)	44	Postfiling index (0–100)	19.24	**Resolving insolvency** (rank)	84
DTF score for registering property (0–100)	74.90			DTF score for resolving insolvency (0–100)	45.69
Procedures (number)	5			Time (years)	3.1
Time (days)	7.5			Cost (% of estate)	7.0
Cost (% of property value)	3.3			Recovery rate (cents on the dollar)	29.7
Quality of land administration index (0–30)	17.5			Strength of insolvency framework index (0–16)	9.5

PHILIPPINES		East Asia & Pacific		GNI per capita (US$)	3,580		
Ease of doing business rank (1–190)	113	Overall distance to frontier (DTF) score (0–100)	58.74	Population	103,320,222		

Starting a business (rank)	173	**Getting credit** (rank)	142	**Trading across borders** (rank)	99
DTF score for starting a business (0–100)	68.88	DTF score for getting credit (0–100)	30.00	DTF score for trading across borders (0–100)	69.39
Procedures (number)	16	Strength of legal rights index (0–12)	1	*Time to export*	
Time (days)	28	Depth of credit information index (0–8)	5	Documentary compliance (hours)	72
Cost (% of income per capita)	15.8	Credit bureau coverage (% of adults)	8.0	Border compliance (hours)	42
Minimum capital (% of income per capita)	3.0	Credit registry coverage (% of adults)	0.0	*Cost to export*	
				Documentary compliance (US$)	53
Dealing with construction permits (rank)	101	**Protecting minority investors** (rank)	146	Border compliance (US$)	456
DTF score for dealing with construction permits (0–100)	66.84	DTF score for protecting minority investors (0–100)	40.00	*Time to import*	
Procedures (number)	23	Extent of disclosure index (0–10)	2	Documentary compliance (hours)	96
Time (days)	122	Extent of director liability index (0–10)	3	Border compliance (hours)	72
Cost (% of warehouse value)	2.6	Ease of shareholder suits index (0–10)	7	*Cost to import*	
Building quality control index (0–15)	12.0	Extent of shareholder rights index (0–10)	0	Documentary compliance (US$)	50
		Extent of ownership and control index (0–10)	5	Border compliance (US$)	580
✔ **Getting electricity** (rank)	31	Extent of corporate transparency index (0–10)	7		
DTF score for getting electricity (0–100)	84.31			**Enforcing contracts** (rank)	149
Procedures (number)	4	✔ **Paying taxes** (rank)	105	DTF score for enforcing contracts (0–100)	45.96
Time (days)	37	DTF score for paying taxes (0–100)	69.27	Time (days)	962
Cost (% of income per capita)	25.3	Payments (number per year)	20	Cost (% of claim)	31.0
Reliability of supply and transparency of tariffs index (0–8)	5	Time (hours per year)	182	Quality of judicial processes index (0–18)	7.5
		Total tax and contribution rate (% of profit)	42.9		
Registering property (rank)	114	Postfiling index (0–100)	50.00	**Resolving insolvency** (rank)	59
DTF score for registering property (0–100)	57.55			DTF score for resolving insolvency (0–100)	55.22
Procedures (number)	9			Time (years)	2.7
Time (days)	35			Cost (% of estate)	32.0
Cost (% of property value)	4.3			Recovery rate (cents on the dollar)	21.3
Quality of land administration index (0–30)	12.5			Strength of insolvency framework index (0–16)	14.0

POLAND		OECD high income		GNI per capita (US$)	12,680		
Ease of doing business rank (1–190)	27	Overall distance to frontier (DTF) score (0–100)	77.30	Population	37,948,016		

Starting a business (rank)	120	**Getting credit** (rank)	29	**Trading across borders** (rank)	1
DTF score for starting a business (0–100)	82.78	DTF score for getting credit (0–100)	75.00	DTF score for trading across borders (0–100)	100.00
Procedures (number)	5	Strength of legal rights index (0–12)	7	*Time to export*	
Time (days)	37	Depth of credit information index (0–8)	8	Documentary compliance (hours)	1
Cost (% of income per capita)	12.0	Credit bureau coverage (% of adults)	85.7	Border compliance (hours)	0
Minimum capital (% of income per capita)	10.7	Credit registry coverage (% of adults)	0.0	*Cost to export*	
				Documentary compliance (US$)	0
Dealing with construction permits (rank)	41	**Protecting minority investors** (rank)	51	Border compliance (US$)	0
DTF score for dealing with construction permits (0–100)	75.16	DTF score for protecting minority investors (0–100)	61.67	*Time to import*	
Procedures (number)	12	Extent of disclosure index (0–10)	7	Documentary compliance (hours)	1
Time (days)	153	Extent of director liability index (0–10)	2	Border compliance (hours)	0
Cost (% of warehouse value)	0.3	Ease of shareholder suits index (0–10)	9	*Cost to import*	
Building quality control index (0–15)	10.0	Extent of shareholder rights index (0–10)	6	Documentary compliance (US$)	0
		Extent of ownership and control index (0–10)	5	Border compliance (US$)	0
Getting electricity (rank)	54	Extent of corporate transparency index (0–10)	8		
DTF score for getting electricity (0–100)	81.35			**Enforcing contracts** (rank)	55
Procedures (number)	4	**Paying taxes** (rank)	51	DTF score for enforcing contracts (0–100)	63.44
Time (days)	122	DTF score for paying taxes (0–100)	79.42	Time (days)	685
Cost (% of income per capita)	18.6	Payments (number per year)	7	Cost (% of claim)	19.4
Reliability of supply and transparency of tariffs index (0–8)	7	Time (hours per year)	260	Quality of judicial processes index (0–18)	10.5
		Total tax and contribution rate (% of profit)	40.5		
Registering property (rank)	38	Postfiling index (0–100)	77.36	**Resolving insolvency** (rank)	22
DTF score for registering property (0–100)	76.49			DTF score for resolving insolvency (0–100)	77.71
Procedures (number)	6			Time (years)	3.0
Time (days)	33			Cost (% of estate)	15.0
Cost (% of property value)	0.3			Recovery rate (cents on the dollar)	63.1
Quality of land administration index (0–30)	19.5			Strength of insolvency framework index (0–16)	14.0

Note: Most indicator sets refer to a case scenario in the largest business city of an economy, though for 11 economies the data are a population-weighted average for the two largest business cities. For some indicators a result of "no practice" may be recorded for an economy; see the data notes for more details. In starting a business, procedures (number), time (days) and cost (% of income per capita) are calculated as the average of both men and women. For the postfiling index, a result of "not applicable" may be recorded for an economy.

✔ Reform making it easier to do business   ✘ Change making it more difficult to do business

PORTUGAL

PORTUGAL		OECD high income		**GNI per capita (US$)**		**19,850**
Ease of doing business rank (1–190)	29	Overall distance to frontier (DTF) score (0–100)	76.84	Population		10,324,611

Starting a business (rank)	48	**Getting credit** (rank)	105	**Trading across borders** (rank)	1
DTF score for starting a business (0–100)	91.26	DTF score for getting credit (0–100)	45.00	DTF score for trading across borders (0–100)	100.00
Procedures (number)	6	Strength of legal rights index (0–12)	2	Time to export	
Time (days)	5	Depth of credit information index (0–8)	7	Documentary compliance (hours)	1
Cost (% of income per capita)	2.1	Credit bureau coverage (% of adults)	7.8	Border compliance (hours)	0
Minimum capital (% of income per capita)	0.0	Credit registry coverage (% of adults)	100.0	Cost to export	
				Documentary compliance (US$)	0
Dealing with construction permits (rank)	32	**Protecting minority investors** (rank)	57	Border compliance (US$)	0
DTF score for dealing with construction permits (0–100)	76.52	DTF score for protecting minority investors (0–100)	60.00	Time to import	
Procedures (number)	14	Extent of disclosure index (0–10)	6	Documentary compliance (hours)	1
Time (days)	113	Extent of director liability index (0–10)	5	Border compliance (hours)	0
Cost (% of warehouse value)	1.2	Ease of shareholder suits index (0–10)	7	Cost to import	
Building quality control index (0–15)	11.0	Extent of shareholder rights index (0–10)	4	Documentary compliance (US$)	0
		Extent of ownership and control index (0–10)	6	Border compliance (US$)	0
Getting electricity (rank)	58	Extent of corporate transparency index (0–10)	8		
DTF score for getting electricity (0–100)	80.18			**Enforcing contracts** (rank)	19
Procedures (number)	7			DTF score for enforcing contracts (0–100)	71.74
Time (days)	46	**Paying taxes** (rank)	38	Time (days)	547
Cost (% of income per capita)	36.0	DTF score for paying taxes (0–100)	83.75	Cost (% of claim)	17.2
Reliability of supply and transparency of tariffs index (0–8)	8	Payments (number per year)	8	Quality of judicial processes index (0–18)	12.5
		Time (hours per year)	243		
		Total tax and contribution rate (% of profit)	39.8		
Registering property (rank)	28	Postfiling index (0–100)	92.71	**Resolving insolvency** (rank)	15
DTF score for registering property (0–100)	80.26			DTF score for resolving insolvency (0–100)	79.67
Procedures (number)	1			Time (years)	3.0
Time (days)	1			Cost (% of estate)	9.0
Cost (% of property value)	7.3			Recovery rate (cents on the dollar)	63.8
Quality of land administration index (0–30)	21.0			Strength of insolvency framework index (0–16)	14.5

PUERTO RICO (U.S.)

PUERTO RICO (U.S.)		Latin America & Caribbean		**GNI per capita (US$)**		**29,697**
Ease of doing business rank (1–190)	64	Overall distance to frontier (DTF) score (0–100)	68.85	Population		3,411,307

Starting a business (rank)	47	**Getting credit** (rank)	6	**Trading across borders** (rank)	64
DTF score for starting a business (0–100)	91.29	DTF score for getting credit (0–100)	90.00	DTF score for trading across borders (0–100)	81.86
Procedures (number)	6	Strength of legal rights index (0–12)	11	Time to export	
Time (days)	5.5	Depth of credit information index (0–8)	7	Documentary compliance (hours)	2
Cost (% of income per capita)	0.8	Credit bureau coverage (% of adults)	100.0	Border compliance (hours)	48
Minimum capital (% of income per capita)	0.0	Credit registry coverage (% of adults)	0.0	Cost to export	
				Documentary compliance (US$)	75
Dealing with construction permits (rank)	138	**Protecting minority investors** (rank)	108	Border compliance (US$)	386
DTF score for dealing with construction permits (0–100)	60.17	DTF score for protecting minority investors (0–100)	50.00	Time to import	
Procedures (number)	22	Extent of disclosure index (0–10)	7	Documentary compliance (hours)	2
Time (days)	165	Extent of director liability index (0–10)	6	Border compliance (hours)	48
Cost (% of warehouse value)	6.3	Ease of shareholder suits index (0–10)	8	Cost to import	
Building quality control index (0–15)	12.0	Extent of shareholder rights index (0–10)	1	Documentary compliance (US$)	75
		Extent of ownership and control index (0–10)	2	Border compliance (US$)	386
Getting electricity (rank)	69	Extent of corporate transparency index (0–10)	6		
DTF score for getting electricity (0–100)	76.94			**Enforcing contracts** (rank)	113
Procedures (number)	5			DTF score for enforcing contracts (0–100)	54.41
Time (days)	32	**Paying taxes** (rank)	161	Time (days)	630
Cost (% of income per capita)	228.3	DTF score for paying taxes (0–100)	52.42	Cost (% of claim)	30.2
Reliability of supply and transparency of tariffs index (0–8)	4	Payments (number per year)	16	Quality of judicial processes index (0–18)	7.0
		Time (hours per year)	218		
		Total tax and contribution rate (% of profit)	63.4		
Registering property (rank)	153	Postfiling index (0–100)	13.76	**Resolving insolvency** (rank)	9
DTF score for registering property (0–100)	47.19			DTF score for resolving insolvency (0–100)	84.20
Procedures (number)	8			Time (years)	2.5
Time (days)	191			Cost (% of estate)	11.0
Cost (% of property value)	1.0			Recovery rate (cents on the dollar)	69.4
Quality of land administration index (0–30)	13.5			Strength of insolvency framework index (0–16)	15.0

QATAR

QATAR		Middle East & North Africa		**GNI per capita (US$)**		**67,630**
Ease of doing business rank (1–190)	83	Overall distance to frontier (DTF) score (0–100)	64.86	Population		2,569,804

Starting a business (rank)	89	✔ **Getting credit** (rank)	133	✔ **Trading across borders** (rank)	90
DTF score for starting a business (0–100)	86.00	DTF score for getting credit (0–100)	35.00	DTF score for trading across borders (0–100)	71.51
Procedures (number)	8.5	Strength of legal rights index (0–12)	1	Time to export	
Time (days)	9	Depth of credit information index (0–8)	6	Documentary compliance (hours)	10
Cost (% of income per capita)	6.7	Credit bureau coverage (% of adults)	0.0	Border compliance (hours)	25
Minimum capital (% of income per capita)	0.0	Credit registry coverage (% of adults)	28.1	Cost to export	
				Documentary compliance (US$)	150
Dealing with construction permits (rank)	19	**Protecting minority investors** (rank)	177	Border compliance (US$)	382
DTF score for dealing with construction permits (0–100)	79.16	DTF score for protecting minority investors (0–100)	26.67	Time to import	
Procedures (number)	16	Extent of disclosure index (0–10)	2	Documentary compliance (hours)	72
Time (days)	58	Extent of director liability index (0–10)	2	Border compliance (hours)	48
Cost (% of warehouse value)	2.0	Ease of shareholder suits index (0–10)	2	Cost to import	
Building quality control index (0–15)	12.0	Extent of shareholder rights index (0–10)	4	Documentary compliance (US$)	290
		Extent of ownership and control index (0–10)	2	Border compliance (US$)	558
Getting electricity (rank)	65	Extent of corporate transparency index (0–10)	4		
DTF score for getting electricity (0–100)	78.60			**Enforcing contracts** (rank)	123
Procedures (number)	4			DTF score for enforcing contracts (0–100)	52.79
Time (days)	90	**Paying taxes** (rank)	1	Time (days)	570
Cost (% of income per capita)	11.7	DTF score for paying taxes (0–100)	99.44	Cost (% of claim)	21.6
Reliability of supply and transparency of tariffs index (0–8)	5	Payments (number per year)	4	Quality of judicial processes index (0–18)	3.5
		Time (hours per year)	41		
		Total tax and contribution rate (% of profit)	11.3		
Registering property (rank)	26	Postfiling index (0–100)	not applicable	**Resolving insolvency** (rank)	116
DTF score for registering property (0–100)	81.06			DTF score for resolving insolvency (0–100)	38.41
Procedures (number)	7			Time (years)	2.8
Time (days)	13			Cost (% of estate)	22.0
Cost (% of property value)	0.3			Recovery rate (cents on the dollar)	30.7
Quality of land administration index (0–30)	24.5			Strength of insolvency framework index (0–16)	7.0

Note: Most indicator sets refer to a case scenario in the largest business city of an economy, though for 11 economies the data are a population-weighted average for the two largest business cities. For some indicators a result of "no practice" may be recorded for an economy; see the data notes for more details. In starting a business, procedures (number), time (days) and cost (% of income per capita) are calculated as the average of both men and women. For the postfiling index, a result of "not applicable" may be recorded for an economy.

✔ Reform making it easier to do business   ✘ Change making it more difficult to do business

ROMANIA

ROMANIA		Europe & Central Asia		GNI per capita (US$)	9,470
Ease of doing business rank (1–190)	45	Overall distance to frontier (DTF) score (0–100)	72.87	Population	19,705,301

Starting a business (rank)	64	**Getting credit** (rank)	20	**Trading across borders** (rank)	1
DTF score for starting a business (0–100)	89.67	DTF score for getting credit (0–100)	80.00	DTF score for trading across borders (0–100)	100.00
Procedures (number)	6	Strength of legal rights index (0–12)	9	*Time to export*	
Time (days)	12	Depth of credit information index (0–8)	7	Documentary compliance (hours)	1
Cost (% of income per capita)	0.4	Credit bureau coverage (% of adults)	54.8	Border compliance (hours)	0
Minimum capital (% of income per capita)	0.5	Credit registry coverage (% of adults)	17.3	*Cost to export*	
				Documentary compliance (US$)	0
Dealing with construction permits (rank)	150	**Protecting minority investors** (rank)	57	Border compliance (US$)	0
DTF score for dealing with construction permits (0–100)	58.13	DTF score for protecting minority investors (0–100)	60.00	*Time to import*	
Procedures (number)	24	Extent of disclosure index (0–10)	9	Documentary compliance (hours)	1
Time (days)	260	Extent of director liability index (0–10)	4	Border compliance (hours)	0
Cost (% of warehouse value)	2.1	Ease of shareholder suits index (0–10)	5	*Cost to import*	
Building quality control index (0–15)	13.0	Extent of shareholder rights index (0–10)	6	Documentary compliance (US$)	0
		Extent of ownership and control index (0–10)	5	Border compliance (US$)	0
Getting electricity (rank)	147	Extent of corporate transparency index (0–10)	7		
DTF score for getting electricity (0–100)	53.34			**Enforcing contracts** (rank)	17
Procedures (number)	9			DTF score for enforcing contracts (0–100)	72.25
Time (days)	174	**Paying taxes** (rank)	42	Time (days)	512
Cost (% of income per capita)	510.9	DTF score for paying taxes (0–100)	80.86	Cost (% of claim)	25.8
Reliability of supply and transparency of tariffs index (0–8)	7	Payments (number per year)	14	Quality of judicial processes index (0–18)	14.0
		Time (hours per year)	163		
		Total tax and contribution rate (% of profit)	38.4		
✔ **Registering property** (rank)	45	Postfiling index (0–100)	76.82	**Resolving insolvency** (rank)	51
DTF score for registering property (0–100)	74.70			DTF score for resolving insolvency (0–100)	59.78
Procedures (number)	6			Time (years)	3.3
Time (days)	16			Cost (% of estate)	10.5
Cost (% of property value)	1.4			Recovery rate (cents on the dollar)	35.6
Quality of land administration index (0–30)	17.0			Strength of insolvency framework index (0–16)	13.0

RUSSIAN FEDERATION

RUSSIAN FEDERATION		Europe & Central Asia		GNI per capita (US$)	9,720
Ease of doing business rank (1–190)	35	Overall distance to frontier (DTF) score (0–100)	75.50	Population	144,342,396

Starting a business (rank)	28	✔ **Getting credit** (rank)	29	✔ **Trading across borders** (rank)	100
DTF score for starting a business (0–100)	93.03	DTF score for getting credit (0–100)	75.00	DTF score for trading across borders (0–100)	69.20
Procedures (number)	4	Strength of legal rights index (0–12)	8	*Time to export*	
Time (days)	10.1	Depth of credit information index (0–8)	7	Documentary compliance (hours)	25.4
Cost (% of income per capita)	1.1	Credit bureau coverage (% of adults)	81.8	Border compliance (hours)	72
Minimum capital (% of income per capita)	0.0	Credit registry coverage (% of adults)	0.0	*Cost to export*	
				Documentary compliance (US$)	92
Dealing with construction permits (rank)	115	**Protecting minority investors** (rank)	51	Border compliance (US$)	665
DTF score for dealing with construction permits (0–100)	65.25	DTF score for protecting minority investors (0–100)	61.67	*Time to import*	
Procedures (number)	14.4	Extent of disclosure index (0–10)	6	Documentary compliance (hours)	42.5
Time (days)	239.4	Extent of director liability index (0–10)	2	Border compliance (hours)	38.6
Cost (% of warehouse value)	1.3	Ease of shareholder suits index (0–10)	7	*Cost to import*	
Building quality control index (0–15)	10.0	Extent of shareholder rights index (0–10)	9	Documentary compliance (US$)	152.5
		Extent of ownership and control index (0–10)	5	Border compliance (US$)	587.5
Getting electricity (rank)	10	Extent of corporate transparency index (0–10)	8		
DTF score for getting electricity (0–100)	92.81			**Enforcing contracts** (rank)	18
Procedures (number)	3			DTF score for enforcing contracts (0–100)	72.18
Time (days)	83	**Paying taxes** (rank)	52	Time (days)	337
Cost (% of income per capita)	41.5	DTF score for paying taxes (0–100)	79.29	Cost (% of claim)	16.5
Reliability of supply and transparency of tariffs index (0–8)	8	Payments (number per year)	7	Quality of judicial processes index (0–18)	9.5
		Time (hours per year)	168		
		Total tax and contribution rate (% of profit)	47.5		
✔ **Registering property** (rank)	12	Postfiling index (0–100)	73.14	**Resolving insolvency** (rank)	54
DTF score for registering property (0–100)	88.72			DTF score for resolving insolvency (0–100)	57.83
Procedures (number)	4			Time (years)	2.0
Time (days)	13			Cost (% of estate)	9.0
Cost (% of property value)	0.2			Recovery rate (cents on the dollar)	40.7
Quality of land administration index (0–30)	26.0			Strength of insolvency framework index (0–16)	11.5

RWANDA

RWANDA		Sub-Saharan Africa		GNI per capita (US$)	700
Ease of doing business rank (1–190)	41	Overall distance to frontier (DTF) score (0–100)	73.40	Population	11,917,508

Starting a business (rank)	78	**Getting credit** (rank)	6	**Trading across borders** (rank)	87
DTF score for starting a business (0–100)	87.66	DTF score for getting credit (0–100)	90.00	DTF score for trading across borders (0–100)	72.44
Procedures (number)	5	Strength of legal rights index (0–12)	10	*Time to export*	
Time (days)	4	Depth of credit information index (0–8)	7	Documentary compliance (hours)	42
Cost (% of income per capita)	44.6	Credit bureau coverage (% of adults)	19.5	Border compliance (hours)	97
Minimum capital (% of income per capita)	0.0	Credit registry coverage (% of adults)	8.2	*Cost to export*	
				Documentary compliance (US$)	110
✔ **Dealing with construction permits** (rank)	112	✔ **Protecting minority investors** (rank)	16	Border compliance (US$)	183
DTF score for dealing with construction permits (0–100)	65.56	DTF score for protecting minority investors (0–100)	73.33	*Time to import*	
Procedures (number)	15	Extent of disclosure index (0–10)	7	Documentary compliance (hours)	48
Time (days)	113	Extent of director liability index (0–10)	9	Border compliance (hours)	86
Cost (% of warehouse value)	13.2	Ease of shareholder suits index (0–10)	5	*Cost to import*	
Building quality control index (0–15)	14.0	Extent of shareholder rights index (0–10)	8	Documentary compliance (US$)	121
		Extent of ownership and control index (0–10)	8	Border compliance (US$)	282
Getting electricity (rank)	119	Extent of corporate transparency index (0–10)	7		
DTF score for getting electricity (0–100)	60.69			✔ **Enforcing contracts** (rank)	85
Procedures (number)	4			DTF score for enforcing contracts (0–100)	58.62
Time (days)	34	✔ **Paying taxes** (rank)	31	Time (days)	230
Cost (% of income per capita)	2,722.6	DTF score for paying taxes (0–100)	84.60	Cost (% of claim)	82.7
Reliability of supply and transparency of tariffs index (0–8)	0	Payments (number per year)	8	Quality of judicial processes index (0–18)	14.0
		Time (hours per year)	94.5		
		Total tax and contribution rate (% of profit)	33.2		
✔ **Registering property** (rank)	2	Postfiling index (0–100)	63.68	**Resolving insolvency** (rank)	78
DTF score for registering property (0–100)	93.26			DTF score for resolving insolvency (0–100)	47.79
Procedures (number)	3			Time (years)	2.5
Time (days)	7			Cost (% of estate)	29.0
Cost (% of property value)	0.1			Recovery rate (cents on the dollar)	19.1
Quality of land administration index (0–30)	28.0			Strength of insolvency framework index (0–16)	12.0

Note: Most indicator sets refer to a case scenario in the largest business city of an economy, though for 11 economies the data are a population-weighted average for the two largest business cities. For some indicators a result of "no practice" may be recorded for an economy; see the data notes for more details. In starting a business, procedures (number), time (days) and cost (% of income per capita) are calculated as the average of both men and women. For the postfiling index, a result of "not applicable" may be recorded for an economy.

✔ Reform making it easier to do business   ✘ Change making it more difficult to do business

SAMOA

		East Asia & Pacific		GNI per capita (US$)	4,100
Ease of doing business rank (1–190)	87	Overall distance to frontier (DTF) score (0–100)	63.89	Population	195,125

Starting a business (rank)	33	✔ **Getting credit** (rank)	105	**Trading across borders** (rank)	148
DTF score for starting a business (0–100)	92.54	DTF score for getting credit (0–100)	45.00	DTF score for trading across borders (0–100)	57.81
Procedures (number)	4	Strength of legal rights index (0–12)	9	*Time to export*	
Time (days)	9	Depth of credit information index (0–8)	0	Documentary compliance (hours)	24
Cost (% of income per capita)	7.3	Credit bureau coverage (% of adults)	0.0	Border compliance (hours)	51
Minimum capital (% of income per capita)	0.0	Credit registry coverage (% of adults)	0.0	*Cost to export*	
				Documentary compliance (US$)	180
Dealing with construction permits (rank)	83	**Protecting minority investors** (rank)	76	Border compliance (US$)	1,400
DTF score for dealing with construction permits (0–100)	68.68	DTF score for protecting minority investors (0–100)	56.67	*Time to import*	
Procedures (number)	18	Extent of disclosure index (0–10)	5	Documentary compliance (hours)	25
Time (days)	58	Extent of director liability index (0–10)	6	Border compliance (hours)	84
Cost (% of warehouse value)	0.8	Ease of shareholder suits index (0–10)	9	*Cost to import*	
Building quality control index (0–15)	6.0	Extent of shareholder rights index (0–10)	8	Documentary compliance (US$)	230
		Extent of ownership and control index (0–10)	3	Border compliance (US$)	900
		Extent of corporate transparency index (0–10)	3		
Getting electricity (rank)	60			**Enforcing contracts** (rank)	86
DTF score for getting electricity (0–100)	79.70	**Paying taxes** (rank)	64	DTF score for enforcing contracts (0–100)	58.59
Procedures (number)	4	DTF score for paying taxes (0–100)	77.04	Time (days)	455
Time (days)	34	Payments (number per year)	37	Cost (% of claim)	24.4
Cost (% of income per capita)	615.2	Time (hours per year)	224	Quality of judicial processes index (0–18)	5.5
Reliability of supply and transparency of tariffs index (0–8)	4	Total tax and contribution rate (% of profit)	19.3		
		Postfiling index (0–100)	91.88	**Resolving insolvency** (rank)	137
Registering property (rank)	66			DTF score for resolving insolvency (0–100)	33.38
DTF score for registering property (0–100)	69.51			Time (years)	2.0
Procedures (number)	5			Cost (% of estate)	38.0
Time (days)	15			Recovery rate (cents on the dollar)	18.5
Cost (% of property value)	3.8			Strength of insolvency framework index (0–16)	7.5
Quality of land administration index (0–30)	13.0				

SAN MARINO

		Europe & Central Asia		GNI per capita (US$)	46,447
Ease of doing business rank (1–190)	93	Overall distance to frontier (DTF) score (0–100)	62.47	Population	33,203

Starting a business (rank)	112	**Getting credit** (rank)	183	**Trading across borders** (rank)	20
DTF score for starting a business (0–100)	83.65	DTF score for getting credit (0–100)	5.00	DTF score for trading across borders (0–100)	97.48
Procedures (number)	8	Strength of legal rights index (0–12)	1	*Time to export*	
Time (days)	12.5	Depth of credit information index (0–8)	0	Documentary compliance (hours)	1
Cost (% of income per capita)	9.1	Credit bureau coverage (% of adults)	0.0	Border compliance (hours)	0
Minimum capital (% of income per capita)	30.4	Credit registry coverage (% of adults)	0.0	*Cost to export*	
				Documentary compliance (US$)	0
Dealing with construction permits (rank)	68	**Protecting minority investors** (rank)	175	Border compliance (US$)	0
DTF score for dealing with construction permits (0–100)	71.20	DTF score for protecting minority investors (0–100)	30.00	*Time to import*	
Procedures (number)	15	Extent of disclosure index (0–10)	3	Documentary compliance (hours)	3
Time (days)	145.5	Extent of director liability index (0–10)	2	Border compliance (hours)	4
Cost (% of warehouse value)	5.5	Ease of shareholder suits index (0–10)	8	*Cost to import*	
Building quality control index (0–15)	13.0	Extent of shareholder rights index (0–10)	4	Documentary compliance (US$)	100
		Extent of ownership and control index (0–10)	1	Border compliance (US$)	50
		Extent of corporate transparency index (0–10)	0		
Getting electricity (rank)	14			**Enforcing contracts** (rank)	78
DTF score for getting electricity (0–100)	90.63	**Paying taxes** (rank)	40	DTF score for enforcing contracts (0–100)	59.25
Procedures (number)	3	DTF score for paying taxes (0–100)	82.32	Time (days)	575
Time (days)	45	Payments (number per year)	18	Cost (% of claim)	13.9
Cost (% of income per capita)	60.8	Time (hours per year)	52	Quality of judicial processes index (0–18)	5.5
Reliability of supply and transparency of tariffs index (0–8)	6	Total tax and contribution rate (% of profit)	35.4		
		Postfiling index (0–100)	67.80	**Resolving insolvency** (rank)	109
Registering property (rank)	78			DTF score for resolving insolvency (0–100)	39.48
DTF score for registering property (0–100)	65.68			Time (years)	2.3
Procedures (number)	9			Cost (% of estate)	5.0
Time (days)	42.5			Recovery rate (cents on the dollar)	47.2
Cost (% of property value)	4.1			Strength of insolvency framework index (0–16)	4.5
Quality of land administration index (0–30)	23.0				

SÃO TOMÉ AND PRÍNCIPE

		Sub-Saharan Africa		GNI per capita (US$)	1,730
Ease of doing business rank (1–190)	169	Overall distance to frontier (DTF) score (0–100)	44.84	Population	199,910

Starting a business (rank)	148	**Getting credit** (rank)	159	✔ **Trading across borders** (rank)	114
DTF score for starting a business (0–100)	77.33	DTF score for getting credit (0–100)	25.00	DTF score for trading across borders (0–100)	66.03
Procedures (number)	6	Strength of legal rights index (0–12)	0	*Time to export*	
Time (days)	7	Depth of credit information index (0–8)	5	Documentary compliance (hours)	46
Cost (% of income per capita)	13.2	Credit bureau coverage (% of adults)	0.0	Border compliance (hours)	83
Minimum capital (% of income per capita)	192.4	Credit registry coverage (% of adults)	11.9	*Cost to export*	
				Documentary compliance (US$)	194
Dealing with construction permits (rank)	103	**Protecting minority investors** (rank)	187	Border compliance (US$)	426
DTF score for dealing with construction permits (0–100)	66.49	DTF score for protecting minority investors (0–100)	21.67	*Time to import*	
Procedures (number)	16	Extent of disclosure index (0–10)	3	Documentary compliance (hours)	17
Time (days)	67	Extent of director liability index (0–10)	1	Border compliance (hours)	150
Cost (% of warehouse value)	2.3	Ease of shareholder suits index (0–10)	6	*Cost to import*	
Building quality control index (0–15)	5.0	Extent of shareholder rights index (0–10)	2	Documentary compliance (US$)	75
		Extent of ownership and control index (0–10)	0	Border compliance (US$)	406
		Extent of corporate transparency index (0–10)	1		
Getting electricity (rank)	115			**Enforcing contracts** (rank)	185
DTF score for getting electricity (0–100)	61.97	**Paying taxes** (rank)	135	DTF score for enforcing contracts (0–100)	27.00
Procedures (number)	4	DTF score for paying taxes (0–100)	61.81	Time (days)	1,185
Time (days)	89	Payments (number per year)	46	Cost (% of claim)	50.5
Cost (% of income per capita)	370.8	Time (hours per year)	424	Quality of judicial processes index (0–18)	4.5
Reliability of supply and transparency of tariffs index (0–8)	0	Total tax and contribution rate (% of profit)	37.0		
		Postfiling index (0–100)	92.20	**Resolving insolvency** (rank)	168
Registering property (rank)	171			DTF score for resolving insolvency (0–100)	0.00
DTF score for registering property (0–100)	41.06			Time (years)	no practice
Procedures (number)	8			Cost (% of estate)	no practice
Time (days)	52			Recovery rate (cents on the dollar)	0.0
Cost (% of property value)	10.2			Strength of insolvency framework index (0–16)	0.0
Quality of land administration index (0–30)	4.5				

Note: Most indicator sets refer to a case scenario in the largest business city of an economy, though for 11 economies the data are a population-weighted average for the two largest business cities. For some indicators a result of "no practice" may be recorded for an economy; see the data notes for more details. In starting a business, procedures (number), time (days) and cost (% of income per capita) are calculated as the average of both men and women. For the postfiling index, a result of "not applicable" may be recorded for an economy.

✔ Reform making it easier to do business   ✘ Change making it more difficult to do business

SAUDI ARABIA

		Middle East & North Africa		GNI per capita (US$)	21,750
Ease of doing business rank (1–190)	92	Overall distance to frontier (DTF) score (0–100)	62.50	Population	32,275,687

✔ Starting a business (rank)	135	Getting credit (rank)	90	✔ Trading across borders (rank)	161
DTF score for starting a business (0–100)	80.04	DTF score for getting credit (0–100)	50.00	DTF score for trading across borders (0–100)	49.59
Procedures (number)	11	Strength of legal rights index (0–12)	2	Time to export	
Time (days)	18	Depth of credit information index (0–8)	8	Documentary compliance (hours)	81
Cost (% of income per capita)	6.8	Credit bureau coverage (% of adults)	50.2	Border compliance (hours)	69
Minimum capital (% of income per capita)	0.0	Credit registry coverage (% of adults)	0.0	Cost to export	
				Documentary compliance (US$)	105
Dealing with construction permits (rank)	38	✔ Protecting minority investors (rank)	10	Border compliance (US$)	363
DTF score for dealing with construction permits (0–100)	75.52	DTF score for protecting minority investors (0–100)	75.00	Time to import	
Procedures (number)	17	Extent of disclosure index (0–10)	9	Documentary compliance (hours)	122
Time (days)	89.5	Extent of director liability index (0–10)	8	Border compliance (hours)	228
Cost (% of warehouse value)	2.3	Ease of shareholder suits index (0–10)	4	Cost to import	
Building quality control index (0–15)	12.0	Extent of shareholder rights index (0–10)	7	Documentary compliance (US$)	390
		Extent of ownership and control index (0–10)	8	Border compliance (US$)	779
Getting electricity (rank)	59	Extent of corporate transparency index (0–10)	9		
DTF score for getting electricity (0–100)	79.88			✔ Enforcing contracts (rank)	83
Procedures (number)	5			DTF score for enforcing contracts (0–100)	58.78
Time (days)	68	✔ Paying taxes (rank)	76	Time (days)	575
Cost (% of income per capita)	32.1	DTF score for paying taxes (0–100)	75.00	Cost (% of claim)	27.5
Reliability of supply and transparency of tariffs index (0–8)	6	Payments (number per year)	3	Quality of judicial processes index (0–18)	8.0
		Time (hours per year)	47		
		Total tax and contribution rate (% of profit)	15.7	Resolving insolvency (rank)	168
✔ Registering property (rank)	24	Postfiling index (0–100)	0.00	DTF score for resolving insolvency (0–100)	0.00
DTF score for registering property (0–100)	81.19			Time (years)	no practice
Procedures (number)	2			Cost (% of estate)	no practice
Time (days)	1.5			Recovery rate (cents on the dollar)	0.0
Cost (% of property value)	0.0			Strength of insolvency framework index (0–16)	0.0
Quality of land administration index (0–30)	10.0				

SENEGAL

		Sub-Saharan Africa		GNI per capita (US$)	950
Ease of doing business rank (1–190)	140	Overall distance to frontier (DTF) score (0–100)	53.06	Population	15,411,614

✔ Starting a business (rank)	63	Getting credit (rank)	142	Trading across borders (rank)	135
DTF score for starting a business (0–100)	89.70	DTF score for getting credit (0–100)	30.00	DTF score for trading across borders (0–100)	60.85
Procedures (number)	4	Strength of legal rights index (0–12)	6	Time to export	
Time (days)	6	Depth of credit information index (0–8)	0	Documentary compliance (hours)	26
Cost (% of income per capita)	33.8	Credit bureau coverage (% of adults)	2.4	Border compliance (hours)	61
Minimum capital (% of income per capita)	4.6	Credit registry coverage (% of adults)	0.6	Cost to export	
				Documentary compliance (US$)	96
Dealing with construction permits (rank)	145	Protecting minority investors (rank)	138	Border compliance (US$)	547
DTF score for dealing with construction permits (0–100)	59.11	DTF score for protecting minority investors (0–100)	41.67	Time to import	
Procedures (number)	14	Extent of disclosure index (0–10)	7	Documentary compliance (hours)	72
Time (days)	177	Extent of director liability index (0–10)	1	Border compliance (hours)	53
Cost (% of warehouse value)	10.1	Ease of shareholder suits index (0–10)	6	Cost to import	
Building quality control index (0–15)	10.0	Extent of shareholder rights index (0–10)	4	Documentary compliance (US$)	545
		Extent of ownership and control index (0–10)	3	Border compliance (US$)	702
✔ Getting electricity (rank)	118	Extent of corporate transparency index (0–10)	4		
DTF score for getting electricity (0–100)	60.76			✔ Enforcing contracts (rank)	142
Procedures (number)	6			DTF score for enforcing contracts (0–100)	48.15
Time (days)	75	✔ Paying taxes (rank)	178	Time (days)	740
Cost (% of income per capita)	3,619.6	DTF score for paying taxes (0–100)	40.79	Cost (% of claim)	36.4
Reliability of supply and transparency of tariffs index (0–8)	5	Payments (number per year)	58	Quality of judicial processes index (0–18)	6.5
		Time (hours per year)	441		
		Total tax and contribution rate (% of profit)	45.1	Resolving insolvency (rank)	91
✔ Registering property (rank)	121	Postfiling index (0–100)	42.67	DTF score for resolving insolvency (0–100)	44.12
DTF score for registering property (0–100)	55.41			Time (years)	3.0
Procedures (number)	5			Cost (% of estate)	20.0
Time (days)	56			Recovery rate (cents on the dollar)	29.7
Cost (% of property value)	7.8			Strength of insolvency framework index (0–16)	9.0
Quality of land administration index (0–30)	10.0				

SERBIA

		Europe & Central Asia		GNI per capita (US$)	5,280
Ease of doing business rank (1–190)	43	Overall distance to frontier (DTF) score (0–100)	73.13	Population	7,057,412

✔ Starting a business (rank)	32	Getting credit (rank)	55	Trading across borders (rank)	23
DTF score for starting a business (0–100)	92.57	DTF score for getting credit (0–100)	65.00	DTF score for trading across borders (0–100)	96.64
Procedures (number)	5	Strength of legal rights index (0–12)	6	Time to export	
Time (days)	5.5	Depth of credit information index (0–8)	7	Documentary compliance (hours)	2
Cost (% of income per capita)	2.3	Credit bureau coverage (% of adults)	100.0	Border compliance (hours)	4
Minimum capital (% of income per capita)	0.0	Credit registry coverage (% of adults)	0.0	Cost to export	
				Documentary compliance (US$)	35
Dealing with construction permits (rank)	10	Protecting minority investors (rank)	76	Border compliance (US$)	47
DTF score for dealing with construction permits (0–100)	82.38	DTF score for protecting minority investors (0–100)	56.67	Time to import	
Procedures (number)	11	Extent of disclosure index (0–10)	4	Documentary compliance (hours)	3
Time (days)	110	Extent of director liability index (0–10)	6	Border compliance (hours)	4
Cost (% of warehouse value)	1.8	Ease of shareholder suits index (0–10)	5	Cost to import	
Building quality control index (0–15)	13.0	Extent of shareholder rights index (0–10)	6	Documentary compliance (US$)	35
		Extent of ownership and control index (0–10)	7	Border compliance (US$)	52
Getting electricity (rank)	96	Extent of corporate transparency index (0–10)	6		
DTF score for getting electricity (0–100)	69.97			✔ Enforcing contracts (rank)	60
Procedures (number)	5			DTF score for enforcing contracts (0–100)	61.41
Time (days)	125	Paying taxes (rank)	82	Time (days)	635
Cost (% of income per capita)	223.5	DTF score for paying taxes (0–100)	73.63	Cost (% of claim)	40.8
Reliability of supply and transparency of tariffs index (0–8)	5	Payments (number per year)	33	Quality of judicial processes index (0–18)	13.0
		Time (hours per year)	225.5		
		Total tax and contribution rate (% of profit)	39.7	Resolving insolvency (rank)	48
✔ Registering property (rank)	57	Postfiling index (0–100)	91.09	DTF score for resolving insolvency (0–100)	60.49
DTF score for registering property (0–100)	72.59			Time (years)	2.0
Procedures (number)	6			Cost (% of estate)	20.0
Time (days)	21			Recovery rate (cents on the dollar)	34.0
Cost (% of property value)	2.8			Strength of insolvency framework index (0–16)	13.5
Quality of land administration index (0–30)	18.0				

Note: Most indicator sets refer to a case scenario in the largest business city of an economy, though for 11 economies the data are a population-weighted average for the two largest business cities. For some indicators a result of "no practice" may be recorded for an economy; see the data notes for more details. In starting a business, procedures (number), time (days) and cost (% of income per capita) are calculated as the average of both men and women. For the postfiling index, a result of "not applicable" may be recorded for an economy.

✔ Reform making it easier to do business   ✘ Change making it more difficult to do business

SEYCHELLES

		Sub-Saharan Africa		GNI per capita (US$)	15,410
Ease of doing business rank (1–190)	95	Overall distance to frontier (DTF) score (0–100)	61.41	Population	94,677

Starting a business (rank)	141	**Getting credit** (rank)	133	**Trading across borders** (rank)	88
DTF score for starting a business (0–100)	78.68	DTF score for getting credit (0–100)	35.00	DTF score for trading across borders (0–100)	71.79
Procedures (number)	9	Strength of legal rights index (0–12)	2	*Time to export*	
Time (days)	32	Depth of credit information index (0–8)	5	Documentary compliance (hours)	44
Cost (% of income per capita)	13.2	Credit bureau coverage (% of adults)	0.0	Border compliance (hours)	82
Minimum capital (% of income per capita)	0.0	Credit registry coverage (% of adults)	66.9	*Cost to export*	
				Documentary compliance (US$)	115
✔ **Dealing with construction permits** (rank)	131	**Protecting minority investors** (rank)	108	Border compliance (US$)	332
DTF score for dealing with construction permits (0–100)	61.90	DTF score for protecting minority investors (0–100)	50.00	*Time to import*	
Procedures (number)	17	Extent of disclosure index (0–10)	4	Documentary compliance (hours)	33
Time (days)	151	Extent of director liability index (0–10)	8	Border compliance (hours)	97
Cost (% of warehouse value)	0.3	Ease of shareholder suits index (0–10)	5	*Cost to import*	
Building quality control index (0–15)	5.0	Extent of shareholder rights index (0–10)	4	Documentary compliance (US$)	93
		Extent of ownership and control index (0–10)	5	Border compliance (US$)	341
		Extent of corporate transparency index (0–10)	4		
Getting electricity (rank)	134			**Enforcing contracts** (rank)	130
DTF score for getting electricity (0–100)	57.86			DTF score for enforcing contracts (0–100)	51.25
Procedures (number)	6	**Paying taxes** (rank)	29	Time (days)	915
Time (days)	137	DTF score for paying taxes (0–100)	84.72	Cost (% of claim)	15.4
Cost (% of income per capita)	349.6	Payments (number per year)	29	Quality of judicial processes index (0–18)	6.5
Reliability of supply and transparency of tariffs index (0–8)	3	Time (hours per year)	85		
		Total tax and contribution rate (% of profit)	30.1		
✔ **Registering property** (rank)	62	Postfiling index (0–100)	93.42	**Resolving insolvency** (rank)	67
DTF score for registering property (0–100)	70.75			DTF score for resolving insolvency (0–100)	52.14
Procedures (number)	4			Time (years)	2.0
Time (days)	33			Cost (% of estate)	11.0
Cost (% of property value)	7.0			Recovery rate (cents on the dollar)	38.8
Quality of land administration index (0–30)	21.0			Strength of insolvency framework index (0–16)	10.0

SIERRA LEONE

		Sub-Saharan Africa		GNI per capita (US$)	490
Ease of doing business rank (1–190)	160	Overall distance to frontier (DTF) score (0–100)	48.18	Population	7,396,190

✔ **Starting a business** (rank)	83	**Getting credit** (rank)	159	✔ **Trading across borders** (rank)	162
DTF score for starting a business (0–100)	86.95	DTF score for getting credit (0–100)	25.00	DTF score for trading across borders (0–100)	48.99
Procedures (number)	5	Strength of legal rights index (0–12)	5	*Time to export*	
Time (days)	11	Depth of credit information index (0–8)	0	Documentary compliance (hours)	72
Cost (% of income per capita)	36.2	Credit bureau coverage (% of adults)	0.0	Border compliance (hours)	55
Minimum capital (% of income per capita)	0.0	Credit registry coverage (% of adults)	1.5	*Cost to export*	
				Documentary compliance (US$)	227
Dealing with construction permits (rank)	182	**Protecting minority investors** (rank)	81	Border compliance (US$)	552
DTF score for dealing with construction permits (0–100)	38.43	DTF score for protecting minority investors (0–100)	55.00	*Time to import*	
Procedures (number)	17	Extent of disclosure index (0–10)	6	Documentary compliance (hours)	137
Time (days)	182	Extent of director liability index (0–10)	8	Border compliance (hours)	120
Cost (% of warehouse value)	22.8	Ease of shareholder suits index (0–10)	6	*Cost to import*	
Building quality control index (0–15)	7.0	Extent of shareholder rights index (0–10)	5	Documentary compliance (US$)	387
		Extent of ownership and control index (0–10)	2	Border compliance (US$)	821
		Extent of corporate transparency index (0–10)	6		
Getting electricity (rank)	178			**Enforcing contracts** (rank)	100
DTF score for getting electricity (0–100)	30.65			DTF score for enforcing contracts (0–100)	55.92
Procedures (number)	8	**Paying taxes** (rank)	85	Time (days)	515
Time (days)	82	DTF score for paying taxes (0–100)	72.86	Cost (% of claim)	39.5
Cost (% of income per capita)	5,365.7	Payments (number per year)	34	Quality of judicial processes index (0–18)	8.0
Reliability of supply and transparency of tariffs index (0–8)	0	Time (hours per year)	343		
		Total tax and contribution rate (% of profit)	31.0		
Registering property (rank)	165	Postfiling index (0–100)	95.41	**Resolving insolvency** (rank)	159
DTF score for registering property (0–100)	43.27			DTF score for resolving insolvency (0–100)	24.72
Procedures (number)	7			Time (years)	2.3
Time (days)	56			Cost (% of estate)	42.0
Cost (% of property value)	10.8			Recovery rate (cents on the dollar)	11.1
Quality of land administration index (0–30)	6.5			Strength of insolvency framework index (0–16)	6.0

SINGAPORE

		East Asia & Pacific		GNI per capita (US$)	51,880
Ease of doing business rank (1–190)	2	Overall distance to frontier (DTF) score (0–100)	84.57	Population	5,607,283

Starting a business (rank)	6	**Getting credit** (rank)	29	✔ **Trading across borders** (rank)	42
DTF score for starting a business (0–100)	96.49	DTF score for getting credit (0–100)	75.00	DTF score for trading across borders (0–100)	89.57
Procedures (number)	3	Strength of legal rights index (0–12)	8	*Time to export*	
Time (days)	2.5	Depth of credit information index (0–8)	7	Documentary compliance (hours)	2
Cost (% of income per capita)	0.5	Credit bureau coverage (% of adults)	67.8	Border compliance (hours)	10
Minimum capital (% of income per capita)	0.0	Credit registry coverage (% of adults)	0.0	*Cost to export*	
				Documentary compliance (US$)	37
Dealing with construction permits (rank)	16	**Protecting minority investors** (rank)	4	Border compliance (US$)	335
DTF score for dealing with construction permits (0–100)	80.26	DTF score for protecting minority investors (0–100)	80.00	*Time to import*	
Procedures (number)	10	Extent of disclosure index (0–10)	10	Documentary compliance (hours)	3
Time (days)	54	Extent of director liability index (0–10)	9	Border compliance (hours)	33
Cost (% of warehouse value)	6.2	Ease of shareholder suits index (0–10)	9	*Cost to import*	
Building quality control index (0–15)	12.0	Extent of shareholder rights index (0–10)	7	Documentary compliance (US$)	40
		Extent of ownership and control index (0–10)	5	Border compliance (US$)	220
		Extent of corporate transparency index (0–10)	8		
Getting electricity (rank)	12			**Enforcing contracts** (rank)	2
DTF score for getting electricity (0–100)	91.33			DTF score for enforcing contracts (0–100)	83.61
Procedures (number)	4	**Paying taxes** (rank)	7	Time (days)	164
Time (days)	30	DTF score for paying taxes (0–100)	91.58	Cost (% of claim)	25.8
Cost (% of income per capita)	25.3	Payments (number per year)	5	Quality of judicial processes index (0–18)	15.0
Reliability of supply and transparency of tariffs index (0–8)	7	Time (hours per year)	64		
		Total tax and contribution rate (% of profit)	20.3		
Registering property (rank)	19	Postfiling index (0–100)	71.97	✔ **Resolving insolvency** (rank)	27
DTF score for registering property (0–100)	83.57			DTF score for resolving insolvency (0–100)	74.31
Procedures (number)	6			Time (years)	0.8
Time (days)	4.5			Cost (% of estate)	4.0
Cost (% of property value)	2.9			Recovery rate (cents on the dollar)	88.7
Quality of land administration index (0–30)	29.0			Strength of insolvency framework index (0–16)	8.5

Note: Most indicator sets refer to a case scenario in the largest business city of an economy, though for 11 economies the data are a population-weighted average for the two largest business cities. For some indicators a result of "no practice" may be recorded for an economy; see the data notes for more details. In starting a business, procedures (number), time (days) and cost (% of income per capita) are calculated as the average of both men and women. For the postfiling index, a result of "not applicable" may be recorded for an economy.

✔ Reform making it easier to do business   ✘ Change making it more difficult to do business

SLOVAK REPUBLIC

Ease of doing business rank (1–190)	**39**	**OECD high income**		**GNI per capita (US$)**	**16,810**	
		Overall distance to frontier (DTF) score (0–100)	**74.90**	**Population**	**5,428,704**	

Starting a business (rank)	83	**Getting credit** (rank)	55	**Trading across borders** (rank)	1
DTF score for starting a business (0–100)	86.95	DTF score for getting credit (0–100)	65.00	DTF score for trading across borders (0–100)	100.00
Procedures (number)	7	Strength of legal rights index (0–12)	7	*Time to export*	
Time (days)	12.5	Depth of credit information index (0–8)	6	Documentary compliance (hours)	1
Cost (% of income per capita)	1.1	Credit bureau coverage (% of adults)	79.4	Border compliance (hours)	0
Minimum capital (% of income per capita)	17.2	Credit registry coverage (% of adults)	3.2	*Cost to export*	
				Documentary compliance (US$)	0
Dealing with construction permits (rank)	91	**Protecting minority investors** (rank)	89	Border compliance (US$)	0
DTF score for dealing with construction permits (0–100)	67.82	DTF score for protecting minority investors (0–100)	53.33	*Time to import*	
Procedures (number)	10	Extent of disclosure index (0–10)	3	Documentary compliance (hours)	1
Time (days)	286	Extent of director liability index (0–10)	4	Border compliance (hours)	0
Cost (% of warehouse value)	0.1	Ease of shareholder suits index (0–10)	7	*Cost to import*	
Building quality control index (0–15)	10.0	Extent of shareholder rights index (0–10)	6	Documentary compliance (US$)	0
		Extent of ownership and control index (0–10)	6	Border compliance (US$)	0
Getting electricity (rank)	57	Extent of corporate transparency index (0–10)	6		
DTF score for getting electricity (0–100)	80.31			✔ **Enforcing contracts** (rank)	84
Procedures (number)	5			DTF score for enforcing contracts (0–100)	58.63
Time (days)	121	**Paying taxes** (rank)	49	Time (days)	775
Cost (% of income per capita)	50.8	DTF score for paying taxes (0–100)	79.88	Cost (% of claim)	30.6
Reliability of supply and transparency of tariffs index (0–8)	8	Payments (number per year)	8	Quality of judicial processes index (0–18)	11.5
		Time (hours per year)	192		
		Total tax and contribution rate (% of profit)	51.6		
Registering property (rank)	7	Postfiling index (0–100)	87.17	**Resolving insolvency** (rank)	42
DTF score for registering property (0–100)	91.00			DTF score for resolving insolvency (0–100)	66.08
Procedures (number)	3			Time (years)	4.0
Time (days)	16.5			Cost (% of estate)	18.0
Cost (% of property value)	0.0			Recovery rate (cents on the dollar)	47.3
Quality of land administration index (0–30)	26.5			Strength of insolvency framework index (0–16)	13.0

SLOVENIA

Ease of doing business rank (1–190)	**37**	**OECD high income**		**GNI per capita (US$)**	**21,660**
		Overall distance to frontier (DTF) score (0–100)	**75.42**	**Population**	**2,064,845**

Starting a business (rank)	46	✔ **Getting credit** (rank)	105	**Trading across borders** (rank)	1
DTF score for starting a business (0–100)	91.48	DTF score for getting credit (0–100)	45.00	DTF score for trading across borders (0–100)	100.00
Procedures (number)	4	Strength of legal rights index (0–12)	3	*Time to export*	
Time (days)	7	Depth of credit information index (0–8)	6	Documentary compliance (hours)	1
Cost (% of income per capita)	0.0	Credit bureau coverage (% of adults)	0.0	Border compliance (hours)	0
Minimum capital (% of income per capita)	39.6	Credit registry coverage (% of adults)	100.0	*Cost to export*	
				Documentary compliance (US$)	0
Dealing with construction permits (rank)	100	**Protecting minority investors** (rank)	24	Border compliance (US$)	0
DTF score for dealing with construction permits (0–100)	67.01	DTF score for protecting minority investors (0–100)	70.00	*Time to import*	
Procedures (number)	14	Extent of disclosure index (0–10)	5	Documentary compliance (hours)	1
Time (days)	239.5	Extent of director liability index (0–10)	9	Border compliance (hours)	0
Cost (% of warehouse value)	2.9	Ease of shareholder suits index (0–10)	8	*Cost to import*	
Building quality control index (0–15)	12.0	Extent of shareholder rights index (0–10)	8	Documentary compliance (US$)	0
		Extent of ownership and control index (0–10)	6	Border compliance (US$)	0
Getting electricity (rank)	19	Extent of corporate transparency index (0–10)	6		
DTF score for getting electricity (0–100)	89.16			**Enforcing contracts** (rank)	122
Procedures (number)	5			DTF score for enforcing contracts (0–100)	52.97
Time (days)	38	**Paying taxes** (rank)	58	Time (days)	1,160
Cost (% of income per capita)	107.1	DTF score for paying taxes (0–100)	77.78	Cost (% of claim)	12.7
Reliability of supply and transparency of tariffs index (0–8)	8	Payments (number per year)	10	Quality of judicial processes index (0–18)	10.5
		Time (hours per year)	245		
		Total tax and contribution rate (% of profit)	31.0		
Registering property (rank)	36	Postfiling index (0–100)	59.94	**Resolving insolvency** (rank)	10
DTF score for registering property (0–100)	77.05			DTF score for resolving insolvency (0–100)	83.69
Procedures (number)	5			Time (years)	0.8
Time (days)	49.5			Cost (% of estate)	4.0
Cost (% of property value)	2.0			Recovery rate (cents on the dollar)	88.7
Quality of land administration index (0–30)	23.5			Strength of insolvency framework index (0–16)	11.5

SOLOMON ISLANDS

Ease of doing business rank (1–190)	**116**	**East Asia & Pacific**		**GNI per capita (US$)**	**1,880**
		Overall distance to frontier (DTF) score (0–100)	**58.13**	**Population**	**599,419**

Starting a business (rank)	94	**Getting credit** (rank)	90	**Trading across borders** (rank)	156
DTF score for starting a business (0–100)	85.42	DTF score for getting credit (0–100)	50.00	DTF score for trading across borders (0–100)	53.45
Procedures (number)	7	Strength of legal rights index (0–12)	10	*Time to export*	
Time (days)	9	Depth of credit information index (0–8)	0	Documentary compliance (hours)	60
Cost (% of income per capita)	28.9	Credit bureau coverage (% of adults)	1.1	Border compliance (hours)	110
Minimum capital (% of income per capita)	0.0	Credit registry coverage (% of adults)	0.0	*Cost to export*	
				Documentary compliance (US$)	257
Dealing with construction permits (rank)	57	**Protecting minority investors** (rank)	108	Border compliance (US$)	630
DTF score for dealing with construction permits (0–100)	72.74	DTF score for protecting minority investors (0–100)	50.00	*Time to import*	
Procedures (number)	13	Extent of disclosure index (0–10)	3	Documentary compliance (hours)	37
Time (days)	98	Extent of director liability index (0–10)	7	Border compliance (hours)	108
Cost (% of warehouse value)	1.3	Ease of shareholder suits index (0–10)	9	*Cost to import*	
Building quality control index (0–15)	7.5	Extent of shareholder rights index (0–10)	7	Documentary compliance (US$)	215
		Extent of ownership and control index (0–10)	3	Border compliance (US$)	740
Getting electricity (rank)	113	Extent of corporate transparency index (0–10)	1		
DTF score for getting electricity (0–100)	63.10			**Enforcing contracts** (rank)	156
Procedures (number)	4			DTF score for enforcing contracts (0–100)	43.49
Time (days)	53	**Paying taxes** (rank)	37	Time (days)	497
Cost (% of income per capita)	1,273.7	DTF score for paying taxes (0–100)	83.81	Cost (% of claim)	78.9
Reliability of supply and transparency of tariffs index (0–8)	0	Payments (number per year)	34	Quality of judicial processes index (0–18)	9.0
		Time (hours per year)	80		
		Total tax and contribution rate (% of profit)	32.0		
Registering property (rank)	152	Postfiling index (0–100)	100.00	**Resolving insolvency** (rank)	143
DTF score for registering property (0–100)	47.37			DTF score for resolving insolvency (0–100)	31.95
Procedures (number)	10			Time (years)	1.0
Time (days)	86.5			Cost (% of estate)	38.0
Cost (% of property value)	4.7			Recovery rate (cents on the dollar)	24.5
Quality of land administration index (0–30)	11.0			Strength of insolvency framework index (0–16)	6.0

Note: Most indicator sets refer to a case scenario in the largest business city of an economy, though for 11 economies the data are a population-weighted average for the two largest business cities. For some indicators a result of "no practice" may be recorded for an economy; see the data notes for more details. In starting a business, procedures (number), time (days) and cost (% of income per capita) are calculated as the average of both men and women. For the postfiling index, a result of "not applicable" may be recorded for an economy.

✔ Reform making it easier to do business ✘ Change making it more difficult to do business

SOMALIA

Ease of doing business rank (1–190)	190

Sub-Saharan Africa	
Overall distance to frontier (DTF) score (0–100)	19.98

GNI per capita (US$)	442
Population	14,317,996

Starting a business (rank)	187
DTF score for starting a business (0–100)	45.77
Procedures (number)	9
Time (days)	70
Cost (% of income per capita)	203.6
Minimum capital (% of income per capita)	0.0

Getting credit (rank)	186
DTF score for getting credit (0–100)	0.00
Strength of legal rights index (0–12)	0
Depth of credit information index (0–8)	0
Credit bureau coverage (% of adults)	0.0
Credit registry coverage (% of adults)	0.0

Trading across borders (rank)	160
DTF score for trading across borders (0–100)	51.60
Time to export	
Documentary compliance (hours)	73
Border compliance (hours)	44
Cost to export	
Documentary compliance (US$)	350
Border compliance (US$)	495
Time to import	
Documentary compliance (hours)	76
Border compliance (hours)	85
Cost to import	
Documentary compliance (US$)	300
Border compliance (US$)	952

Dealing with construction permits (rank)	186
DTF score for dealing with construction permits (0–100)	0.00
Procedures (number)	no practice
Time (days)	no practice
Cost (% of warehouse value)	no practice
Building quality control index (0–15)	0.0

Protecting minority investors (rank)	190
DTF score for protecting minority investors (0–100)	0.00
Extent of disclosure index (0–10)	0
Extent of director liability index (0–10)	0
Ease of shareholder suits index (0–10)	0
Extent of shareholder rights index (0–10)	0
Extent of ownership and control index (0–10)	0
Extent of corporate transparency index (0–10)	0

Getting electricity (rank)	187
DTF score for getting electricity (0–100)	0.00
Procedures (number)	no practice
Time (days)	no practice
Cost (% of income per capita)	no practice
Reliability of supply and transparency of tariffs index (0–8)	0

Paying taxes (rank)	190
DTF score for paying taxes (0–100)	0.00
Payments (number per year)	no practice
Time (hours per year)	no practice
Total tax and contribution rate (% of profit)	no practice
Postfiling index (0–100)	no practice

Enforcing contracts (rank)	110
DTF score for enforcing contracts (0–100)	54.58
Time (days)	575
Cost (% of claim)	21.4
Quality of judicial processes index (0–18)	4.5

Registering property (rank)	150
DTF score for registering property (0–100)	47.83
Procedures (number)	5
Time (days)	188
Cost (% of property value)	1.6
Quality of land administration index (0–30)	7.5

Resolving insolvency (rank)	168
DTF score for resolving insolvency (0–100)	0.00
Time (years)	no practice
Cost (% of estate)	no practice
Recovery rate (cents on the dollar)	0.0
Strength of insolvency framework index (0–16)	0.0

SOUTH AFRICA

Ease of doing business rank (1–190)	82

Sub-Saharan Africa	
Overall distance to frontier (DTF) score (0–100)	64.89

GNI per capita (US$)	5,480
Population	55,908,865

Starting a business (rank)	136
DTF score for starting a business (0–100)	79.97
Procedures (number)	7
Time (days)	45
Cost (% of income per capita)	0.2
Minimum capital (% of income per capita)	0.0

Getting credit (rank)	68
DTF score for getting credit (0–100)	60.00
Strength of legal rights index (0–12)	5
Depth of credit information index (0–8)	7
Credit bureau coverage (% of adults)	64.4
Credit registry coverage (% of adults)	0.0

Trading across borders (rank)	147
DTF score for trading across borders (0–100)	58.01
Time to export	
Documentary compliance (hours)	68
Border compliance (hours)	100
Cost to export	
Documentary compliance (US$)	170
Border compliance (US$)	428
Time to import	
Documentary compliance (hours)	36
Border compliance (hours)	144
Cost to import	
Documentary compliance (US$)	213
Border compliance (US$)	657

Dealing with construction permits (rank)	94
DTF score for dealing with construction permits (0–100)	67.53
Procedures (number)	20
Time (days)	149
Cost (% of warehouse value)	1.6
Building quality control index (0–15)	11.0

Protecting minority investors (rank)	24
DTF score for protecting minority investors (0–100)	70.00
Extent of disclosure index (0–10)	8
Extent of director liability index (0–10)	8
Ease of shareholder suits index (0–10)	8
Extent of shareholder rights index (0–10)	8
Extent of ownership and control index (0–10)	6
Extent of corporate transparency index (0–10)	4

Getting electricity (rank)	112
DTF score for getting electricity (0–100)	63.21
Procedures (number)	4
Time (days)	84
Cost (% of income per capita)	146.6
Reliability of supply and transparency of tariffs index (0–8)	0

Paying taxes (rank)	46
DTF score for paying taxes (0–100)	80.02
Payments (number per year)	7
Time (hours per year)	210
Total tax and contribution rate (% of profit)	28.9
Postfiling index (0–100)	55.45

Enforcing contracts (rank)	115
DTF score for enforcing contracts (0–100)	54.10
Time (days)	600
Cost (% of claim)	33.2
Quality of judicial processes index (0–18)	7.0

Registering property (rank)	107
DTF score for registering property (0–100)	58.43
Procedures (number)	7
Time (days)	23
Cost (% of property value)	7.6
Quality of land administration index (0–30)	13.5

Resolving insolvency (rank)	55
DTF score for resolving insolvency (0–100)	57.59
Time (years)	2.0
Cost (% of estate)	18.0
Recovery rate (cents on the dollar)	34.4
Strength of insolvency framework index (0–16)	12.5

SOUTH SUDAN

Ease of doing business rank (1–190)	187

Sub-Saharan Africa	
Overall distance to frontier (DTF) score (0–100)	32.86

GNI per capita (US$)	182
Population	12,230,730

✘ **Starting a business** (rank)	181
DTF score for starting a business (0–100)	55.68
Procedures (number)	12
Time (days)	13
Cost (% of income per capita)	305.0
Minimum capital (% of income per capita)	0.0

Getting credit (rank)	177
DTF score for getting credit (0–100)	10.00
Strength of legal rights index (0–12)	2
Depth of credit information index (0–8)	0
Credit bureau coverage (% of adults)	0.0
Credit registry coverage (% of adults)	0.0

Trading across borders (rank)	178
DTF score for trading across borders (0–100)	26.19
Time to export	
Documentary compliance (hours)	192
Border compliance (hours)	146
Cost to export	
Documentary compliance (US$)	194
Border compliance (US$)	763
Time to import	
Documentary compliance (hours)	360
Border compliance (hours)	179
Cost to import	
Documentary compliance (US$)	350
Border compliance (US$)	781

Dealing with construction permits (rank)	178
DTF score for dealing with construction permits (0–100)	42.54
Procedures (number)	23
Time (days)	124
Cost (% of warehouse value)	15.3
Building quality control index (0–15)	7.0

Protecting minority investors (rank)	177
DTF score for protecting minority investors (0–100)	26.67
Extent of disclosure index (0–10)	2
Extent of director liability index (0–10)	1
Ease of shareholder suits index (0–10)	5
Extent of shareholder rights index (0–10)	2
Extent of ownership and control index (0–10)	3
Extent of corporate transparency index (0–10)	3

Getting electricity (rank)	187
DTF score for getting electricity (0–100)	0.00
Procedures (number)	no practice
Time (days)	no practice
Cost (% of income per capita)	no practice
Reliability of supply and transparency of tariffs index (0–8)	0

Paying taxes (rank)	66
DTF score for paying taxes (0–100)	76.75
Payments (number per year)	37
Time (hours per year)	210
Total tax and contribution rate (% of profit)	31.4
Postfiling index (0–100)	95.87

Enforcing contracts (rank)	81
DTF score for enforcing contracts (0–100)	58.99
Time (days)	228
Cost (% of claim)	30.0
Quality of judicial processes index (0–18)	3.5

Registering property (rank)	181
DTF score for registering property (0–100)	31.79
Procedures (number)	9
Time (days)	50
Cost (% of property value)	14.9
Quality of land administration index (0–30)	0.0

Resolving insolvency (rank)	168
DTF score for resolving insolvency (0–100)	0.00
Time (years)	no practice
Cost (% of estate)	no practice
Recovery rate (cents on the dollar)	0.0
Strength of insolvency framework index (0–16)	0.0

Note: Most indicator sets refer to a case scenario in the largest business city of an economy, though for 11 economies the data are a population-weighted average for the two largest business cities. For some indicators a result of "no practice" may be recorded for an economy; see the data notes for more details. In starting a business, procedures (number), time (days) and cost (% of income per capita) are calculated as the average of both men and women. For the postfiling index, a result of "not applicable" may be recorded for an economy.

✔ Reform making it easier to do business   ✘ Change making it more difficult to do business

SPAIN

SPAIN		OECD high income		GNI per capita (US$)	27,520
Ease of doing business rank (1–190)	28	Overall distance to frontier (DTF) score (0–100)	77.02	Population	46,443,959

Starting a business (rank)	86	**Getting credit** (rank)	68	**Trading across borders** (rank)	1
DTF score for starting a business (0–100)	86.65	DTF score for getting credit (0–100)	60.00	DTF score for trading across borders (0–100)	100.00
Procedures (number)	7	Strength of legal rights index (0–12)	5	Time to export	
Time (days)	13	Depth of credit information index (0–8)	7	Documentary compliance (hours)	1
Cost (% of income per capita)	4.8	Credit bureau coverage (% of adults)	15.9	Border compliance (hours)	0
Minimum capital (% of income per capita)	12.5	Credit registry coverage (% of adults)	79.3	Cost to export	
				Documentary compliance (US$)	0
Dealing with construction permits (rank)	123	**Protecting minority investors** (rank)	24	Border compliance (US$)	0
DTF score for dealing with construction permits (0–100)	63.50	DTF score for protecting minority investors (0–100)	70.00	Time to import	
Procedures (number)	15	Extent of disclosure index (0–10)	7	Documentary compliance (hours)	1
Time (days)	208	Extent of director liability index (0–10)	6	Border compliance (hours)	0
Cost (% of warehouse value)	5.4	Ease of shareholder suits index (0–10)	6	Cost to import	
Building quality control index (0–15)	11.0	Extent of shareholder rights index (0–10)	9	Documentary compliance (US$)	0
		Extent of ownership and control index (0–10)	5	Border compliance (US$)	0
Getting electricity (rank)	42	Extent of corporate transparency index (0–10)	9		
DTF score for getting electricity (0–100)	82.99			✔ **Enforcing contracts** (rank)	26
Procedures (number)	5			DTF score for enforcing contracts (0–100)	69.97
Time (days)	95	**Paying taxes** (rank)	34	Time (days)	510
Cost (% of income per capita)	100.1	DTF score for paying taxes (0–100)	84.44	Cost (% of claim)	17.2
Reliability of supply and transparency of tariffs index (0–8)	8	Payments (number per year)	9	Quality of judicial processes index (0–18)	11.0
		Time (hours per year)	152		
		Total tax and contribution rate (% of profit)	46.9	**Resolving insolvency** (rank)	19
Registering property (rank)	53	Postfiling index (0–100)	93.60	DTF score for resolving insolvency (0–100)	78.74
DTF score for registering property (0–100)	73.88			Time (years)	1.5
Procedures (number)	5			Cost (% of estate)	11.0
Time (days)	12.5			Recovery rate (cents on the dollar)	76.6
Cost (% of property value)	6.1			Strength of insolvency framework index (0–16)	12.0
Quality of land administration index (0–30)	22.5				

SRI LANKA

SRI LANKA		South Asia		GNI per capita (US$)	3,780
Ease of doing business rank (1–190)	111	Overall distance to frontier (DTF) score (0–100)	58.86	Population	21,203,000

Starting a business (rank)	77	**Getting credit** (rank)	122	✔ **Trading across borders** (rank)	86
DTF score for starting a business (0–100)	87.74	DTF score for getting credit (0–100)	40.00	DTF score for trading across borders (0–100)	73.29
Procedures (number)	7	Strength of legal rights index (0–12)	2	Time to export	
Time (days)	9	Depth of credit information index (0–8)	6	Documentary compliance (hours)	48
Cost (% of income per capita)	10.4	Credit bureau coverage (% of adults)	35.0	Border compliance (hours)	43
Minimum capital (% of income per capita)	0.0	Credit registry coverage (% of adults)	0.0	Cost to export	
				Documentary compliance (US$)	58
Dealing with construction permits (rank)	76	**Protecting minority investors** (rank)	43	Border compliance (US$)	366
DTF score for dealing with construction permits (0–100)	69.33	DTF score for protecting minority investors (0–100)	63.33	Time to import	
Procedures (number)	13	Extent of disclosure index (0–10)	8	Documentary compliance (hours)	48
Time (days)	115	Extent of director liability index (0–10)	5	Border compliance (hours)	72
Cost (% of warehouse value)	0.3	Ease of shareholder suits index (0–10)	7	Cost to import	
Building quality control index (0–15)	5.5	Extent of shareholder rights index (0–10)	6	Documentary compliance (US$)	283
		Extent of ownership and control index (0–10)	6	Border compliance (US$)	300
Getting electricity (rank)	93	Extent of corporate transparency index (0–10)	6		
DTF score for getting electricity (0–100)	70.98			**Enforcing contracts** (rank)	165
Procedures (number)	5			DTF score for enforcing contracts (0–100)	39.31
Time (days)	100	**Paying taxes** (rank)	158	Time (days)	1,318
Cost (% of income per capita)	777.0	DTF score for paying taxes (0–100)	53.70	Cost (% of claim)	22.8
Reliability of supply and transparency of tariffs index (0–8)	5	Payments (number per year)	47	Quality of judicial processes index (0–18)	7.5
		Time (hours per year)	168		
		Total tax and contribution rate (% of profit)	55.2	**Resolving insolvency** (rank)	88
Registering property (rank)	157	Postfiling index (0–100)	49.31	DTF score for resolving insolvency (0–100)	44.99
DTF score for registering property (0–100)	45.92			Time (years)	1.7
Procedures (number)	9			Cost (% of estate)	10.0
Time (days)	51			Recovery rate (cents on the dollar)	42.9
Cost (% of property value)	5.1			Strength of insolvency framework index (0–16)	7.0
Quality of land administration index (0–30)	2.5				

ST. KITTS AND NEVIS

ST. KITTS AND NEVIS		Latin America & Caribbean		GNI per capita (US$)	15,850
Ease of doing business rank (1–190)	134	Overall distance to frontier (DTF) score (0–100)	54.52	Population	54,821

Starting a business (rank)	91	**Getting credit** (rank)	159	✔ **Trading across borders** (rank)	66
DTF score for starting a business (0–100)	85.76	DTF score for getting credit (0–100)	25.00	DTF score for trading across borders (0–100)	81.04
Procedures (number)	7	Strength of legal rights index (0–12)	5	Time to export	
Time (days)	18.5	Depth of credit information index (0–8)	0	Documentary compliance (hours)	24
Cost (% of income per capita)	7.2	Credit bureau coverage (% of adults)	0.0	Border compliance (hours)	27
Minimum capital (% of income per capita)	0.0	Credit registry coverage (% of adults)	0.0	Cost to export	
				Documentary compliance (US$)	100
Dealing with construction permits (rank)	33	**Protecting minority investors** (rank)	119	Border compliance (US$)	335
DTF score for dealing with construction permits (0–100)	76.27	DTF score for protecting minority investors (0–100)	48.33	Time to import	
Procedures (number)	11	Extent of disclosure index (0–10)	4	Documentary compliance (hours)	33
Time (days)	105	Extent of director liability index (0–10)	8	Border compliance (hours)	37
Cost (% of warehouse value)	0.3	Ease of shareholder suits index (0–10)	8	Cost to import	
Building quality control index (0–15)	8.0	Extent of shareholder rights index (0–10)	4	Documentary compliance (US$)	90
		Extent of ownership and control index (0–10)	1	Border compliance (US$)	311
Getting electricity (rank)	94	Extent of corporate transparency index (0–10)	4		
DTF score for getting electricity (0–100)	70.10			**Enforcing contracts** (rank)	50
Procedures (number)	4			DTF score for enforcing contracts (0–100)	65.51
Time (days)	18	**Paying taxes** (rank)	124	Time (days)	578
Cost (% of income per capita)	239.2	DTF score for paying taxes (0–100)	64.41	Cost (% of claim)	26.6
Reliability of supply and transparency of tariffs index (0–8)	0	Payments (number per year)	39	Quality of judicial processes index (0–18)	11.5
		Time (hours per year)	203		
		Total tax and contribution rate (% of profit)	49.7	**Resolving insolvency** (rank)	168
Registering property (rank)	184	Postfiling index (0–100)	75.73	DTF score for resolving insolvency (0–100)	0.00
DTF score for registering property (0–100)	28.80			Time (years)	no practice
Procedures (number)	6			Cost (% of estate)	no practice
Time (days)	224			Recovery rate (cents on the dollar)	0.0
Cost (% of property value)	11.0			Strength of insolvency framework index (0–16)	0.0
Quality of land administration index (0–30)	11.0				

Note: Most indicator sets refer to a case scenario in the largest business city of an economy, though for 11 economies the data are a population-weighted average for the two largest business cities. For some indicators a result of "no practice" may be recorded for an economy; see the data notes for more details. In starting a business, procedures (number), time (days) and cost (% of income per capita) are calculated as the average of both men and women. For the postfiling index, a result of "not applicable" may be recorded for an economy.

✔ Reform making it easier to do business   ✗ Change making it more difficult to do business

ST. LUCIA

		Latin America & Caribbean		GNI per capita (US$)	7,670
Ease of doing business rank (1–190)	91	Overall distance to frontier (DTF) score (0–100)	62.88	Population	178,015

Starting a business (rank)	69
DTF score for starting a business (0–100)	88.79
Procedures (number)	5
Time (days)	11
Cost (% of income per capita)	21.5
Minimum capital (% of income per capita)	0.0

Dealing with construction permits (rank)	34
DTF score for dealing with construction permits (0–100)	76.21
Procedures (number)	14
Time (days)	116
Cost (% of warehouse value)	0.6
Building quality control index (0–15)	10.5

Getting electricity (rank)	43
DTF score for getting electricity (0–100)	82.88
Procedures (number)	6
Time (days)	26
Cost (% of income per capita)	203.7
Reliability of supply and transparency of tariffs index (0–8)	7

Registering property (rank)	105
DTF score for registering property (0–100)	59.16
Procedures (number)	9
Time (days)	17
Cost (% of property value)	7.6
Quality of land administration index (0–30)	18.5

Getting credit (rank)	159
DTF score for getting credit (0–100)	25.00
Strength of legal rights index (0–12)	5
Depth of credit information index (0–8)	0
Credit bureau coverage (% of adults)	0.0
Credit registry coverage (% of adults)	0.0

Protecting minority investors (rank)	96
DTF score for protecting minority investors (0–100)	51.67
Extent of disclosure index (0–10)	4
Extent of director liability index (0–10)	8
Ease of shareholder suits index (0–10)	8
Extent of shareholder rights index (0–10)	4
Extent of ownership and control index (0–10)	4
Extent of corporate transparency index (0–10)	3

Paying taxes (rank)	74
DTF score for paying taxes (0–100)	75.73
Payments (number per year)	35
Time (hours per year)	110
Total tax and contribution rate (% of profit)	34.7
Postfiling index (0–100)	77.80

Trading across borders (rank)	82
DTF score for trading across borders (0–100)	73.87
Time to export	
Documentary compliance (hours)	19
Border compliance (hours)	27
Cost to export	
Documentary compliance (US$)	63
Border compliance (US$)	718
Time to import	
Documentary compliance (hours)	14
Border compliance (hours)	27
Cost to import	
Documentary compliance (US$)	98
Border compliance (US$)	842

Enforcing contracts (rank)	71
DTF score for enforcing contracts (0–100)	59.67
Time (days)	645
Cost (% of claim)	37.3
Quality of judicial processes index (0–18)	11.5

Resolving insolvency (rank)	127
DTF score for resolving insolvency (0–100)	35.83
Time (years)	2.0
Cost (% of estate)	9.0
Recovery rate (cents on the dollar)	43.3
Strength of insolvency framework index (0–16)	4.0

ST. VINCENT AND THE GRENADINES

		Latin America & Caribbean		GNI per capita (US$)	6,790
Ease of doing business rank (1–190)	129	Overall distance to frontier (DTF) score (0–100)	55.72	Population	109,643

Starting a business (rank)	85
DTF score for starting a business (0–100)	86.82
Procedures (number)	7
Time (days)	10
Cost (% of income per capita)	15.8
Minimum capital (% of income per capita)	0.0

Dealing with construction permits (rank)	44
DTF score for dealing with construction permits (0–100)	74.42
Procedures (number)	14
Time (days)	92
Cost (% of warehouse value)	0.1
Building quality control index (0–15)	8.0

Getting electricity (rank)	90
DTF score for getting electricity (0–100)	71.14
Procedures (number)	3
Time (days)	52
Cost (% of income per capita)	52.5
Reliability of supply and transparency of tariffs index (0–8)	0

Registering property (rank)	166
DTF score for registering property (0–100)	43.10
Procedures (number)	7
Time (days)	47
Cost (% of property value)	11.8
Quality of land administration index (0–30)	7.0

Getting credit (rank)	159
DTF score for getting credit (0–100)	25.00
Strength of legal rights index (0–12)	5
Depth of credit information index (0–8)	0
Credit bureau coverage (% of adults)	0.0
Credit registry coverage (% of adults)	0.0

Protecting minority investors (rank)	96
DTF score for protecting minority investors (0–100)	51.67
Extent of disclosure index (0–10)	4
Extent of director liability index (0–10)	8
Ease of shareholder suits index (0–10)	8
Extent of shareholder rights index (0–10)	4
Extent of ownership and control index (0–10)	4
Extent of corporate transparency index (0–10)	3

Paying taxes (rank)	101
DTF score for paying taxes (0–100)	70.26
Payments (number per year)	36
Time (hours per year)	108
Total tax and contribution rate (% of profit)	39.3
Postfiling index (0–100)	63.89

Trading across borders (rank)	93
DTF score for trading across borders (0–100)	71.08
Time to export	
Documentary compliance (hours)	72
Border compliance (hours)	28
Cost to export	
Documentary compliance (US$)	80
Border compliance (US$)	425
Time to import	
Documentary compliance (hours)	24
Border compliance (hours)	48
Cost to import	
Documentary compliance (US$)	90
Border compliance (US$)	875

Enforcing contracts (rank)	53
DTF score for enforcing contracts (0–100)	63.66
Time (days)	595
Cost (% of claim)	30.3
Quality of judicial processes index (0–18)	11.5

Resolving insolvency (rank)	168
DTF score for resolving insolvency (0–100)	0.00
Time (years)	no practice
Cost (% of estate)	no practice
Recovery rate (cents on the dollar)	0.0
Strength of insolvency framework index (0–16)	0.0

SUDAN

		Sub-Saharan Africa		GNI per capita (US$)	2,140
Ease of doing business rank (1–190)	170	Overall distance to frontier (DTF) score (0–100)	44.46	Population	39,578,828

Starting a business (rank)	159
DTF score for starting a business (0–100)	73.51
Procedures (number)	10.5
Time (days)	36.5
Cost (% of income per capita)	27.8
Minimum capital (% of income per capita)	0.0

Dealing with construction permits (rank)	133
DTF score for dealing with construction permits (0–100)	61.63
Procedures (number)	15
Time (days)	270
Cost (% of warehouse value)	2.0
Building quality control index (0–15)	10.0

Getting electricity (rank)	110
DTF score for getting electricity (0–100)	63.26
Procedures (number)	5
Time (days)	70
Cost (% of income per capita)	2,311.2
Reliability of supply and transparency of tariffs index (0–8)	3

Registering property (rank)	89
DTF score for registering property (0–100)	63.62
Procedures (number)	6
Time (days)	11
Cost (% of property value)	2.6
Quality of land administration index (0–30)	5.5

Getting credit (rank)	173
DTF score for getting credit (0–100)	15.00
Strength of legal rights index (0–12)	3
Depth of credit information index (0–8)	0
Credit bureau coverage (% of adults)	2.4
Credit registry coverage (% of adults)	0.0

Protecting minority investors (rank)	186
DTF score for protecting minority investors (0–100)	23.33
Extent of disclosure index (0–10)	3
Extent of director liability index (0–10)	1
Ease of shareholder suits index (0–10)	4
Extent of shareholder rights index (0–10)	3
Extent of ownership and control index (0–10)	2
Extent of corporate transparency index (0–10)	1

Paying taxes (rank)	163
DTF score for paying taxes (0–100)	51.80
Payments (number per year)	42
Time (hours per year)	180
Total tax and contribution rate (% of profit)	45.4
Postfiling index (0–100)	20.20

Trading across borders (rank)	185
DTF score for trading across borders (0–100)	19.16
Time to export	
Documentary compliance (hours)	190
Border compliance (hours)	162
Cost to export	
Documentary compliance (US$)	428
Border compliance (US$)	950
Time to import	
Documentary compliance (hours)	132
Border compliance (hours)	144
Cost to import	
Documentary compliance (US$)	420
Border compliance (US$)	1,093

Enforcing contracts (rank)	146
DTF score for enforcing contracts (0–100)	46.91
Time (days)	810
Cost (% of claim)	19.8
Quality of judicial processes index (0–18)	3.5

Resolving insolvency (rank)	154
DTF score for resolving insolvency (0–100)	26.39
Time (years)	2.0
Cost (% of estate)	20.0
Recovery rate (cents on the dollar)	31.6
Strength of insolvency framework index (0–16)	3.0

Note: Most indicator sets refer to a case scenario in the largest business city of an economy, though for 11 economies the data are a population-weighted average for the two largest business cities. For some indicators a result of "no practice" may be recorded for an economy; see the data notes for more details. In starting a business, procedures (number), time (days) and cost (% of income per capita) are calculated as the average of both men and women. For the postfiling index, a result of "not applicable" may be recorded for an economy.

✔ Reform making it easier to do business   ✘ Change making it more difficult to do business

SURINAME

		Latin America & Caribbean		GNI per capita (US$)	7,070
Ease of doing business rank (1–190)	165	Overall distance to frontier (DTF) score (0–100)	46.87	Population	558,368

Starting a business (rank)	186	**Getting credit** (rank)	177	**Trading across borders** (rank)	80
DTF score for starting a business (0–100)	48.27	DTF score for getting credit (0–100)	10.00	DTF score for trading across borders (0–100)	75.02
Procedures (number)	13.5	Strength of legal rights index (0–12)	2	*Time to export*	
Time (days)	84.5	Depth of credit information index (0–8)	0	Documentary compliance (hours)	12
Cost (% of income per capita)	97.8	Credit bureau coverage (% of adults)	0.0	Border compliance (hours)	84
Minimum capital (% of income per capita)	0.3	Credit registry coverage (% of adults)	0.0	*Cost to export*	
				Documentary compliance (US$)	40
Dealing with construction permits (rank)	104	**Protecting minority investors** (rank)	167	Border compliance (US$)	468
DTF score for dealing with construction permits (0–100)	66.40	DTF score for protecting minority investors (0–100)	35.00	*Time to import*	
Procedures (number)	10	Extent of disclosure index (0–10)	1	Documentary compliance (hours)	24
Time (days)	223	Extent of director liability index (0–10)	0	Border compliance (hours)	48
Cost (% of warehouse value)	0.2	Ease of shareholder suits index (0–10)	6	*Cost to import*	
Building quality control index (0–15)	6.5	Extent of shareholder rights index (0–10)	8	Documentary compliance (US$)	40
		Extent of ownership and control index (0–10)	4	Border compliance (US$)	658
		Extent of corporate transparency index (0–10)	2		
Getting electricity (rank)	131			**Enforcing contracts** (rank)	187
DTF score for getting electricity (0–100)	58.55	**Paying taxes** (rank)	102	DTF score for enforcing contracts (0–100)	25.94
Procedures (number)	4	DTF score for paying taxes (0–100)	69.55	Time (days)	1,715
Time (days)	113	Payments (number per year)	30	Cost (% of claim)	37.1
Cost (% of income per capita)	633.7	Time (hours per year)	199	Quality of judicial processes index (0–18)	3.5
Reliability of supply and transparency of tariffs index (0–8)	0	Total tax and contribution rate (% of profit)	27.9		
		Postfiling index (0–100)	48.85	**Resolving insolvency** (rank)	135
✔ **Registering property** (rank)	156			DTF score for resolving insolvency (0–100)	33.98
DTF score for registering property (0–100)	45.95			Time (years)	5.0
Procedures (number)	6			Cost (% of estate)	30.0
Time (days)	46			Recovery rate (cents on the dollar)	8.0
Cost (% of property value)	13.7			Strength of insolvency framework index (0–16)	9.5
Quality of land administration index (0–30)	11.5				

SWAZILAND

		Sub-Saharan Africa		GNI per capita (US$)	2,830
Ease of doing business rank (1–190)	112	Overall distance to frontier (DTF) score (0–100)	58.82	Population	1,343,098

Starting a business (rank)	158	✔ **Getting credit** (rank)	77	✔ **Trading across borders** (rank)	32
DTF score for starting a business (0–100)	74.35	DTF score for getting credit (0–100)	55.00	DTF score for trading across borders (0–100)	92.92
Procedures (number)	12	Strength of legal rights index (0–12)	4	*Time to export*	
Time (days)	30	Depth of credit information index (0–8)	7	Documentary compliance (hours)	2
Cost (% of income per capita)	16.4	Credit bureau coverage (% of adults)	44.2	Border compliance (hours)	2
Minimum capital (% of income per capita)	0.3	Credit registry coverage (% of adults)	0.0	*Cost to export*	
				Documentary compliance (US$)	76
✘ **Dealing with construction permits** (rank)	102	**Protecting minority investors** (rank)	138	Border compliance (US$)	134
DTF score for dealing with construction permits (0–100)	66.72	DTF score for protecting minority investors (0–100)	41.67	*Time to import*	
Procedures (number)	14	Extent of disclosure index (0–10)	2	Documentary compliance (hours)	4
Time (days)	116	Extent of director liability index (0–10)	5	Border compliance (hours)	3
Cost (% of warehouse value)	3.6	Ease of shareholder suits index (0–10)	6	*Cost to import*	
Building quality control index (0–15)	7.0	Extent of shareholder rights index (0–10)	6	Documentary compliance (US$)	76
		Extent of ownership and control index (0–10)	3	Border compliance (US$)	134
		Extent of corporate transparency index (0–10)	3		
Getting electricity (rank)	159			**Enforcing contracts** (rank)	169
DTF score for getting electricity (0–100)	47.24	**Paying taxes** (rank)	63	DTF score for enforcing contracts (0–100)	36.72
Procedures (number)	6	DTF score for paying taxes (0–100)	77.27	Time (days)	956
Time (days)	137	Payments (number per year)	33	Cost (% of claim)	56.1
Cost (% of income per capita)	753.7	Time (hours per year)	122	Quality of judicial processes index (0–18)	7.5
Reliability of supply and transparency of tariffs index (0–8)	0	Total tax and contribution rate (% of profit)	35.2		
		Postfiling index (0–100)	83.15	**Resolving insolvency** (rank)	114
Registering property (rank)	115			DTF score for resolving insolvency (0–100)	38.90
DTF score for registering property (0–100)	57.40			Time (years)	2.0
Procedures (number)	9			Cost (% of estate)	14.5
Time (days)	21			Recovery rate (cents on the dollar)	37.4
Cost (% of property value)	7.1			Strength of insolvency framework index (0–16)	6.0
Quality of land administration index (0–30)	16.0				

SWEDEN

		OECD high income		GNI per capita (US$)	54,630
Ease of doing business rank (1–190)	10	Overall distance to frontier (DTF) score (0–100)	81.27	Population	9,903,122

Starting a business (rank)	13	**Getting credit** (rank)	77	**Trading across borders** (rank)	18
DTF score for starting a business (0–100)	94.67	DTF score for getting credit (0–100)	55.00	DTF score for trading across borders (0–100)	98.04
Procedures (number)	3	Strength of legal rights index (0–12)	6	*Time to export*	
Time (days)	7	Depth of credit information index (0–8)	5	Documentary compliance (hours)	1
Cost (% of income per capita)	0.5	Credit bureau coverage (% of adults)	100.0	Border compliance (hours)	2
Minimum capital (% of income per capita)	11.1	Credit registry coverage (% of adults)	0.0	*Cost to export*	
				Documentary compliance (US$)	40
Dealing with construction permits (rank)	27	**Protecting minority investors** (rank)	29	Border compliance (US$)	55
DTF score for dealing with construction permits (0–100)	77.89	DTF score for protecting minority investors (0–100)	68.33	*Time to import*	
Procedures (number)	8	Extent of disclosure index (0–10)	8	Documentary compliance (hours)	1
Time (days)	117	Extent of director liability index (0–10)	4	Border compliance (hours)	0
Cost (% of warehouse value)	2.0	Ease of shareholder suits index (0–10)	7	*Cost to import*	
Building quality control index (0–15)	9.0	Extent of shareholder rights index (0–10)	7	Documentary compliance (US$)	0
		Extent of ownership and control index (0–10)	7	Border compliance (US$)	0
		Extent of corporate transparency index (0–10)	8		
Getting electricity (rank)	6			**Enforcing contracts** (rank)	36
DTF score for getting electricity (0–100)	96.21	**Paying taxes** (rank)	27	DTF score for enforcing contracts (0–100)	67.61
Procedures (number)	3	DTF score for paying taxes (0–100)	85.28	Time (days)	483
Time (days)	52	Payments (number per year)	6	Cost (% of claim)	30.4
Cost (% of income per capita)	31.2	Time (hours per year)	122	Quality of judicial processes index (0–18)	12.0
Reliability of supply and transparency of tariffs index (0–8)	8	Total tax and contribution rate (% of profit)	49.1		
		Postfiling index (0–100)	90.75	**Resolving insolvency** (rank)	16
Registering property (rank)	9			DTF score for resolving insolvency (0–100)	79.53
DTF score for registering property (0–100)	90.11			Time (years)	2.0
Procedures (number)	1			Cost (% of estate)	9.0
Time (days)	7			Recovery rate (cents on the dollar)	78.1
Cost (% of property value)	4.3			Strength of insolvency framework index (0–16)	12.0
Quality of land administration index (0–30)	27.5				

Note: Most indicator sets refer to a case scenario in the largest business city of an economy, though for 11 economies the data are a population-weighted average for the two largest business cities. For some indicators a result of "no practice" may be recorded for an economy; see the data notes for more details. In starting a business, procedures (number), time (days) and cost (% of income per capita) are calculated as the average of both men and women. For the postfiling index, a result of "not applicable" may be recorded for an economy.

✔ Reform making it easier to do business   ✘ Change making it more difficult to do business

SWITZERLAND

		OECD high income		GNI per capita (US$)	81,240
Ease of doing business rank (1–190)	**33**	**Overall distance to frontier (DTF) score (0–100)**	**75.92**	**Population**	**8,372,098**

Starting a business (rank)	73	Getting credit (rank)	68	Trading across borders (rank)	38
DTF score for starting a business (0–100)	88.38	DTF score for getting credit (0–100)	60.00	DTF score for trading across borders (0–100)	91.79
Procedures (number)	6	Strength of legal rights index (0–12)	6	*Time to export*	
Time (days)	10	Depth of credit information index (0–8)	6	Documentary compliance (hours)	2
Cost (% of income per capita)	2.3	Credit bureau coverage (% of adults)	25.6	Border compliance (hours)	1
Minimum capital (% of income per capita)	25.4	Credit registry coverage (% of adults)	0.0	*Cost to export*	
				Documentary compliance (US$)	75
Dealing with construction permits (rank)	62	**Protecting minority investors** (rank)	108	Border compliance (US$)	201
DTF score for dealing with construction permits (0–100)	71.73	DTF score for protecting minority investors (0–100)	50.00	*Time to import*	
Procedures (number)	13	Extent of disclosure index (0–10)	0	Documentary compliance (hours)	2
Time (days)	156	Extent of director liability index (0–10)	5	Border compliance (hours)	1
Cost (% of warehouse value)	0.7	Ease of shareholder suits index (0–10)	5	*Cost to import*	
Building quality control index (0–15)	9.0	Extent of shareholder rights index (0–10)	8	Documentary compliance (US$)	75
		Extent of ownership and control index (0–10)	5	Border compliance (US$)	201
Getting electricity (rank)	7	Extent of corporate transparency index (0–10)	7		
DTF score for getting electricity (0–100)	94.41			✔ **Enforcing contracts** (rank)	45
Procedures (number)	3	**Paying taxes** (rank)	19	DTF score for enforcing contracts (0–100)	66.49
Time (days)	39	DTF score for paying taxes (0–100)	87.66	Time (days)	510
Cost (% of income per capita)	59.2	Payments (number per year)	19	Cost (% of claim)	24.0
Reliability of supply and transparency of tariffs index (0–8)	7	Time (hours per year)	63	Quality of judicial processes index (0–18)	10.5
		Total tax and contribution rate (% of profit)	28.8		
Registering property (rank)	16	Postfiling index (0–100)	83.21	**Resolving insolvency** (rank)	45
DTF score for registering property (0–100)	86.12			DTF score for resolving insolvency (0–100)	62.63
Procedures (number)	4			Time (years)	3.0
Time (days)	16			Cost (% of estate)	4.5
Cost (% of property value)	0.3			Recovery rate (cents on the dollar)	46.7
Quality of land administration index (0–30)	23.5			Strength of insolvency framework index (0–16)	12.0

SYRIAN ARAB REPUBLIC

		Middle East & North Africa		GNI per capita (US$)	1,037
Ease of doing business rank (1–190)	**174**	**Overall distance to frontier (DTF) score (0–100)**	**41.55**	**Population**	**18,430,453**

Starting a business (rank)	133	Getting credit (rank)	173	Trading across borders (rank)	176
DTF score for starting a business (0–100)	80.43	DTF score for getting credit (0–100)	15.00	DTF score for trading across borders (0–100)	29.83
Procedures (number)	7.5	Strength of legal rights index (0–12)	1	*Time to export*	
Time (days)	15.5	Depth of credit information index (0–8)	2	Documentary compliance (hours)	48
Cost (% of income per capita)	7.9	Credit bureau coverage (% of adults)	0.0	Border compliance (hours)	84
Minimum capital (% of income per capita)	84.0	Credit registry coverage (% of adults)	7.1	*Cost to export*	
				Documentary compliance (US$)	725
Dealing with construction permits (rank)	186	**Protecting minority investors** (rank)	89	Border compliance (US$)	1,113
DTF score for dealing with construction permits (0–100)	0.00	DTF score for protecting minority investors (0–100)	53.33	*Time to import*	
Procedures (number)	no practice	Extent of disclosure index (0–10)	7	Documentary compliance (hours)	149
Time (days)	no practice	Extent of director liability index (0–10)	5	Border compliance (hours)	141
Cost (% of warehouse value)	no practice	Ease of shareholder suits index (0–10)	3	*Cost to import*	
Building quality control index (0–15)	0.0	Extent of shareholder rights index (0–10)	6	Documentary compliance (US$)	742
		Extent of ownership and control index (0–10)	5	Border compliance (US$)	828
Getting electricity (rank)	153	Extent of corporate transparency index (0–10)	6		
DTF score for getting electricity (0–100)	51.99			**Enforcing contracts** (rank)	161
Procedures (number)	5	**Paying taxes** (rank)	81	DTF score for enforcing contracts (0–100)	42.58
Time (days)	146	DTF score for paying taxes (0–100)	73.97	Time (days)	872
Cost (% of income per capita)	247.3	Payments (number per year)	20	Cost (% of claim)	29.3
Reliability of supply and transparency of tariffs index (0–8)	0	Time (hours per year)	336	Quality of judicial processes index (0–18)	4.0
		Total tax and contribution rate (% of profit)	42.7		
Registering property (rank)	155	Postfiling index (0–100)	92.20	**Resolving insolvency** (rank)	163
DTF score for registering property (0–100)	46.88			DTF score for resolving insolvency (0–100)	21.44
Procedures (number)	4			Time (years)	4.1
Time (days)	48			Cost (% of estate)	16.0
Cost (% of property value)	28.0			Recovery rate (cents on the dollar)	10.8
Quality of land administration index (0–30)	10.5			Strength of insolvency framework index (0–16)	5.0

TAIWAN, CHINA

		East Asia & Pacific		GNI per capita (US$)	23,284
Ease of doing business rank (1–190)	**15**	**Overall distance to frontier (DTF) score (0–100)**	**80.07**	**Population**	**23,539,816**

Starting a business (rank)	16	Getting credit (rank)	90	✔ Trading across borders (rank)	55
DTF score for starting a business (0–100)	94.43	DTF score for getting credit (0–100)	50.00	DTF score for trading across borders (0–100)	84.94
Procedures (number)	3	Strength of legal rights index (0–12)	2	*Time to export*	
Time (days)	10	Depth of credit information index (0–8)	8	Documentary compliance (hours)	5
Cost (% of income per capita)	2.0	Credit bureau coverage (% of adults)	98.4	Border compliance (hours)	17
Minimum capital (% of income per capita)	0.0	Credit registry coverage (% of adults)	0.0	*Cost to export*	
				Documentary compliance (US$)	84
Dealing with construction permits (rank)	4	**Protecting minority investors** (rank)	24	Border compliance (US$)	335
DTF score for dealing with construction permits (0–100)	86.32	DTF score for protecting minority investors (0–100)	70.00	*Time to import*	
Procedures (number)	10	Extent of disclosure index (0–10)	9	Documentary compliance (hours)	4
Time (days)	93	Extent of director liability index (0–10)	5	Border compliance (hours)	47
Cost (% of warehouse value)	0.4	Ease of shareholder suits index (0–10)	6	*Cost to import*	
Building quality control index (0–15)	13.0	Extent of shareholder rights index (0–10)	7	Documentary compliance (US$)	65
		Extent of ownership and control index (0–10)	5	Border compliance (US$)	340
Getting electricity (rank)	3	Extent of corporate transparency index (0–10)	10		
DTF score for getting electricity (0–100)	99.45			✔ **Enforcing contracts** (rank)	10
Procedures (number)	3	**Paying taxes** (rank)	56	DTF score for enforcing contracts (0–100)	75.11
Time (days)	22	DTF score for paying taxes (0–100)	77.96	Time (days)	510
Cost (% of income per capita)	38.9	Payments (number per year)	11	Cost (% of claim)	18.3
Reliability of supply and transparency of tariffs index (0–8)	8	Time (hours per year)	221	Quality of judicial processes index (0–18)	14.0
		Total tax and contribution rate (% of profit)	34.3		
Registering property (rank)	18	Postfiling index (0–100)	63.17	**Resolving insolvency** (rank)	20
DTF score for registering property (0–100)	83.89			DTF score for resolving insolvency (0–100)	78.63
Procedures (number)	3			Time (years)	1.9
Time (days)	4			Cost (% of estate)	4.0
Cost (% of property value)	6.2			Recovery rate (cents on the dollar)	82.2
Quality of land administration index (0–30)	28.5			Strength of insolvency framework index (0–16)	11.0

Note: Most indicator sets refer to a case scenario in the largest business city of an economy, though for 11 economies the data are a population-weighted average for the two largest business cities. For some indicators a result of "no practice" may be recorded for an economy; see the data notes for more details. In starting a business, procedures (number), time (days) and cost (% of income per capita) are calculated as the average of both men and women. For the postfiling index, a result of "not applicable" may be recorded for an economy.

✔ Reform making it easier to do business   ✘ Change making it more difficult to do business

TAJIKISTAN

TAJIKISTAN		Europe & Central Asia		GNI per capita (US$)	1,110
Ease of doing business rank (1–190)	123	Overall distance to frontier (DTF) score (0–100)	56.86	Population	8,734,951

✔ Starting a business (rank)	57	Getting credit (rank)	122	Trading across borders (rank)	149
DTF score for starting a business (0–100)	90.54	DTF score for getting credit (0–100)	40.00	DTF score for trading across borders (0–100)	57.17
Procedures (number)	4	Strength of legal rights index (0–12)	1	Time to export	
Time (days)	11	Depth of credit information index (0–8)	7	Documentary compliance (hours)	66
Cost (% of income per capita)	19.3	Credit bureau coverage (% of adults)	39.4	Border compliance (hours)	75
Minimum capital (% of income per capita)	0.0	Credit registry coverage (% of adults)	0.0	Cost to export	
				Documentary compliance (US$)	330
Dealing with construction permits (rank)	136	Protecting minority investors (rank)	33	Border compliance (US$)	313
DTF score for dealing with construction permits (0–100)	61.21	DTF score for protecting minority investors (0–100)	66.67	Time to import	
Procedures (number)	25	Extent of disclosure index (0–10)	8	Documentary compliance (hours)	126
Time (days)	182	Extent of director liability index (0–10)	6	Border compliance (hours)	107
Cost (% of warehouse value)	2.0	Ease of shareholder suits index (0–10)	6	Cost to import	
Building quality control index (0–15)	12.0	Extent of shareholder rights index (0–10)	9	Documentary compliance (US$)	260
		Extent of ownership and control index (0–10)	4	Border compliance (US$)	223
		Extent of corporate transparency index (0–10)	7		
Getting electricity (rank)	171			Enforcing contracts (rank)	54
DTF score for getting electricity (0–100)	35.00	Paying taxes (rank)	132	DTF score for enforcing contracts (0–100)	63.49
Procedures (number)	9	DTF score for paying taxes (0–100)	62.27	Time (days)	430
Time (days)	133	Payments (number per year)	6	Cost (% of claim)	25.5
Cost (% of income per capita)	811.5	Time (hours per year)	224	Quality of judicial processes index (0–18)	8.0
Reliability of supply and transparency of tariffs index (0–8)	0	Total tax and contribution rate (% of profit)	65.2		
		Postfiling index (0–100)	40.40	Resolving insolvency (rank)	148
✔ Registering property (rank)	90			DTF score for resolving insolvency (0–100)	28.76
DTF score for registering property (0–100)	63.50			Time (years)	1.7
Procedures (number)	5			Cost (% of estate)	9.0
Time (days)	36			Recovery rate (cents on the dollar)	36.0
Cost (% of property value)	3.1			Strength of insolvency framework index (0–16)	3.0
Quality of land administration index (0–30)	7.5				

TANZANIA

TANZANIA		Sub-Saharan Africa		GNI per capita (US$)	900
Ease of doing business rank (1–190)	137	Overall distance to frontier (DTF) score (0–100)	54.04	Population	55,572,201

Starting a business (rank)	162	Getting credit (rank)	55	Trading across borders (rank)	182
DTF score for starting a business (0–100)	73.03	DTF score for getting credit (0–100)	65.00	DTF score for trading across borders (0–100)	20.21
Procedures (number)	11	Strength of legal rights index (0–12)	5	Time to export	
Time (days)	28	Depth of credit information index (0–8)	8	Documentary compliance (hours)	96
Cost (% of income per capita)	42.9	Credit bureau coverage (% of adults)	6.2	Border compliance (hours)	96
Minimum capital (% of income per capita)	0.0	Credit registry coverage (% of adults)	0.0	Cost to export	
				Documentary compliance (US$)	275
✔ Dealing with construction permits (rank)	156	Protecting minority investors (rank)	129	Border compliance (US$)	1,160
DTF score for dealing with construction permits (0–100)	56.43	DTF score for protecting minority investors (0–100)	45.00	Time to import	
Procedures (number)	24	Extent of disclosure index (0–10)	2	Documentary compliance (hours)	240
Time (days)	134	Extent of director liability index (0–10)	6	Border compliance (hours)	402
Cost (% of warehouse value)	6.6	Ease of shareholder suits index (0–10)	8	Cost to import	
Building quality control index (0–15)	12.0	Extent of shareholder rights index (0–10)	4	Documentary compliance (US$)	375
		Extent of ownership and control index (0–10)	2	Border compliance (US$)	1,350
		Extent of corporate transparency index (0–10)	5		
Getting electricity (rank)	82			Enforcing contracts (rank)	58
DTF score for getting electricity (0–100)	73.96			DTF score for enforcing contracts (0–100)	61.66
Procedures (number)	4	Paying taxes (rank)	154	Time (days)	515
Time (days)	109	DTF score for paying taxes (0–100)	55.49	Cost (% of claim)	14.3
Cost (% of income per capita)	843.8	Payments (number per year)	60	Quality of judicial processes index (0–18)	6.0
Reliability of supply and transparency of tariffs index (0–8)	5	Time (hours per year)	207		
		Total tax and contribution rate (% of profit)	44.1	Resolving insolvency (rank)	108
✘ Registering property (rank)	142	Postfiling index (0–100)	67.17	DTF score for resolving insolvency (0–100)	39.52
DTF score for registering property (0–100)	50.13			Time (years)	3.0
Procedures (number)	8			Cost (% of estate)	22.0
Time (days)	67			Recovery rate (cents on the dollar)	21.2
Cost (% of property value)	5.2			Strength of insolvency framework index (0–16)	9.0
Quality of land administration index (0–30)	7.5				

THAILAND

THAILAND		East Asia & Pacific		GNI per capita (US$)	5,640
Ease of doing business rank (1–190)	26	Overall distance to frontier (DTF) score (0–100)	77.44	Population	68,863,514

✔ Starting a business (rank)	36	✔ Getting credit (rank)	42	Trading across borders (rank)	57
DTF score for starting a business (0–100)	92.34	DTF score for getting credit (0–100)	70.00	DTF score for trading across borders (0–100)	84.10
Procedures (number)	5	Strength of legal rights index (0–12)	7	Time to export	
Time (days)	4.5	Depth of credit information index (0–8)	7	Documentary compliance (hours)	11
Cost (% of income per capita)	6.2	Credit bureau coverage (% of adults)	56.6	Border compliance (hours)	51
Minimum capital (% of income per capita)	0.0	Credit registry coverage (% of adults)	0.0	Cost to export	
				Documentary compliance (US$)	97
Dealing with construction permits (rank)	43	✔ Protecting minority investors (rank)	16	Border compliance (US$)	223
DTF score for dealing with construction permits (0–100)	74.58	DTF score for protecting minority investors (0–100)	73.33	Time to import	
Procedures (number)	18	Extent of disclosure index (0–10)	10	Documentary compliance (hours)	4
Time (days)	104	Extent of director liability index (0–10)	7	Border compliance (hours)	50
Cost (% of warehouse value)	0.1	Ease of shareholder suits index (0–10)	8	Cost to import	
Building quality control index (0–15)	11.0	Extent of shareholder rights index (0–10)	5	Documentary compliance (US$)	43
		Extent of ownership and control index (0–10)	7	Border compliance (US$)	233
		Extent of corporate transparency index (0–10)	7		
✔ Getting electricity (rank)	13			✔ Enforcing contracts (rank)	34
DTF score for getting electricity (0–100)	90.99			DTF score for enforcing contracts (0–100)	67.91
Procedures (number)	4	✔ Paying taxes (rank)	67	Time (days)	420
Time (days)	32	DTF score for paying taxes (0–100)	76.73	Cost (% of claim)	16.9
Cost (% of income per capita)	63.1	Payments (number per year)	21	Quality of judicial processes index (0–18)	8.5
Reliability of supply and transparency of tariffs index (0–8)	7	Time (hours per year)	262		
		Total tax and contribution rate (% of profit)	28.7	✔ Resolving insolvency (rank)	26
✔ Registering property (rank)	68	Postfiling index (0–100)	73.41	DTF score for resolving insolvency (0–100)	75.64
DTF score for registering property (0–100)	68.75			Time (years)	1.5
Procedures (number)	5			Cost (% of estate)	18.0
Time (days)	7			Recovery rate (cents on the dollar)	68.0
Cost (% of property value)	7.3			Strength of insolvency framework index (0–16)	12.5
Quality of land administration index (0–30)	18.0				

Note: Most indicator sets refer to a case scenario in the largest business city of an economy, though for 11 economies the data are a population-weighted average for the two largest business cities. For some indicators a result of "no practice" may be recorded for an economy; see the data notes for more details. In starting a business, procedures (number), time (days) and cost (% of income per capita) are calculated as the average of both men and women. For the postfiling index, a result of "not applicable" may be recorded for an economy.

✔ Reform making it easier to do business   ✘ Change making it more difficult to do business

TIMOR–LESTE

		East Asia & Pacific		GNI per capita (US$)	1,861
Ease of doing business rank (1–190)	178	Overall distance to frontier (DTF) score (0–100)	40.62	Population	1,268,671

Starting a business (rank)	151	**Getting credit** (rank)	170	**Trading across borders** (rank)	98
DTF score for starting a business (0–100)	76.60	DTF score for getting credit (0–100)	20.00	DTF score for trading across borders (0–100)	69.90
Procedures (number)	4	Strength of legal rights index (0–12)	0	*Time to export*	
Time (days)	9	Depth of credit information index (0–8)	4	Documentary compliance (hours)	33
Cost (% of income per capita)	0.5	Credit bureau coverage (% of adults)	0.0	Border compliance (hours)	96
Minimum capital (% of income per capita)	268.6	Credit registry coverage (% of adults)	5.6	*Cost to export*	
				Documentary compliance (US$)	100
Dealing with construction permits (rank)	159	**Protecting minority investors** (rank)	81	Border compliance (US$)	350
DTF score for dealing with construction permits (0–100)	55.29	DTF score for protecting minority investors (0–100)	55.00	*Time to import*	
Procedures (number)	16	Extent of disclosure index (0–10)	5	Documentary compliance (hours)	44
Time (days)	207	Extent of director liability index (0–10)	4	Border compliance (hours)	100
Cost (% of warehouse value)	0.5	Ease of shareholder suits index (0–10)	5	*Cost to import*	
Building quality control index (0–15)	3.0	Extent of shareholder rights index (0–10)	8	Documentary compliance (US$)	115
		Extent of ownership and control index (0–10)	6	Border compliance (US$)	410
		Extent of corporate transparency index (0–10)	5		
Getting electricity (rank)	114			**Enforcing contracts** (rank)	190
DTF score for getting electricity (0–100)	62.96	**Paying taxes** (rank)	139	DTF score for enforcing contracts (0–100)	6.13
Procedures (number)	3	DTF score for paying taxes (0–100)	60.32	Time (days)	1,285
Time (days)	93	Payments (number per year)	18	Cost (% of claim)	163.2
Cost (% of income per capita)	1,258.0	Time (hours per year)	276	Quality of judicial processes index (0–18)	2.5
Reliability of supply and transparency of tariffs index (0–8)	0	Total tax and contribution rate (% of profit)	11.2		
		Postfiling index (0–100)	1.38	**Resolving insolvency** (rank)	168
Registering property (rank)	187			DTF score for resolving insolvency (0–100)	0.00
DTF score for registering property (0–100)	0.00			Time (years)	no practice
Procedures (number)	no practice			Cost (% of estate)	no practice
Time (days)	no practice			Recovery rate (cents on the dollar)	0.0
Cost (% of property value)	no practice			Strength of insolvency framework index (0–16)	0.0
Quality of land administration index (0–30)	0.0				

TOGO

		Sub-Saharan Africa		GNI per capita (US$)	540
Ease of doing business rank (1–190)	156	Overall distance to frontier (DTF) score (0–100)	48.88	Population	7,606,374

Starting a business (rank)	121	✔ **Getting credit** (rank)	142	**Trading across borders** (rank)	121
DTF score for starting a business (0–100)	82.51	DTF score for getting credit (0–100)	30.00	DTF score for trading across borders (0–100)	63.66
Procedures (number)	5	Strength of legal rights index (0–12)	6	*Time to export*	
Time (days)	6	Depth of credit information index (0–8)	0	Documentary compliance (hours)	11
Cost (% of income per capita)	66.0	Credit bureau coverage (% of adults)	0.0	Border compliance (hours)	67
Minimum capital (% of income per capita)	31.5	Credit registry coverage (% of adults)	0.6	*Cost to export*	
				Documentary compliance (US$)	25
Dealing with construction permits (rank)	173	**Protecting minority investors** (rank)	146	Border compliance (US$)	163
DTF score for dealing with construction permits (0–100)	47.24	DTF score for protecting minority investors (0–100)	40.00	*Time to import*	
Procedures (number)	11	Extent of disclosure index (0–10)	7	Documentary compliance (hours)	180
Time (days)	163	Extent of director liability index (0–10)	1	Border compliance (hours)	168
Cost (% of warehouse value)	13.5	Ease of shareholder suits index (0–10)	5	*Cost to import*	
Building quality control index (0–15)	3.0	Extent of shareholder rights index (0–10)	4	Documentary compliance (US$)	252
		Extent of ownership and control index (0–10)	3	Border compliance (US$)	612
		Extent of corporate transparency index (0–10)	4		
Getting electricity (rank)	142			**Enforcing contracts** (rank)	143
DTF score for getting electricity (0–100)	54.30	**Paying taxes** (rank)	173	DTF score for enforcing contracts (0–100)	48.10
Procedures (number)	3	DTF score for paying taxes (0–100)	44.99	Time (days)	488
Time (days)	66	Payments (number per year)	49	Cost (% of claim)	47.5
Cost (% of income per capita)	5,017.6	Time (hours per year)	216	Quality of judicial processes index (0–18)	5.0
Reliability of supply and transparency of tariffs index (0–8)	0	Total tax and contribution rate (% of profit)	48.5		
		Postfiling index (0–100)	14.85	**Resolving insolvency** (rank)	81
Registering property (rank)	182			DTF score for resolving insolvency (0–100)	46.41
DTF score for registering property (0–100)	31.57			Time (years)	3.0
Procedures (number)	5			Cost (% of estate)	15.0
Time (days)	283			Recovery rate (cents on the dollar)	34.0
Cost (% of property value)	9.1			Strength of insolvency framework index (0–16)	9.0
Quality of land administration index (0–30)	6.0				

TONGA

		East Asia & Pacific		GNI per capita (US$)	4,020
Ease of doing business rank (1–190)	89	Overall distance to frontier (DTF) score (0–100)	63.43	Population	107,122

Starting a business (rank)	53	**Getting credit** (rank)	42	**Trading across borders** (rank)	103
DTF score for starting a business (0–100)	90.81	DTF score for getting credit (0–100)	70.00	DTF score for trading across borders (0–100)	68.20
Procedures (number)	4	Strength of legal rights index (0–12)	10	*Time to export*	
Time (days)	16	Depth of credit information index (0–8)	4	Documentary compliance (hours)	168
Cost (% of income per capita)	7.1	Credit bureau coverage (% of adults)	17.0	Border compliance (hours)	52
Minimum capital (% of income per capita)	0.0	Credit registry coverage (% of adults)	0.0	*Cost to export*	
				Documentary compliance (US$)	70
Dealing with construction permits (rank)	13	**Protecting minority investors** (rank)	138	Border compliance (US$)	201
DTF score for dealing with construction permits (0–100)	80.86	DTF score for protecting minority investors (0–100)	41.67	*Time to import*	
Procedures (number)	13	Extent of disclosure index (0–10)	3	Documentary compliance (hours)	72
Time (days)	77	Extent of director liability index (0–10)	3	Border compliance (hours)	26
Cost (% of warehouse value)	2.0	Ease of shareholder suits index (0–10)	9	*Cost to import*	
Building quality control index (0–15)	12.0	Extent of shareholder rights index (0–10)	2	Documentary compliance (US$)	148
		Extent of ownership and control index (0–10)	2	Border compliance (US$)	330
		Extent of corporate transparency index (0–10)	6		
Getting electricity (rank)	74			**Enforcing contracts** (rank)	94
DTF score for getting electricity (0–100)	76.28	**Paying taxes** (rank)	98	DTF score for enforcing contracts (0–100)	57.32
Procedures (number)	5	DTF score for paying taxes (0–100)	70.56	Time (days)	350
Time (days)	42	Payments (number per year)	30	Cost (% of claim)	30.5
Cost (% of income per capita)	89.9	Time (hours per year)	200	Quality of judicial processes index (0–18)	4.5
Reliability of supply and transparency of tariffs index (0–8)	4	Total tax and contribution rate (% of profit)	27.5		
		Postfiling index (0–100)	52.53	**Resolving insolvency** (rank)	136
Registering property (rank)	160			DTF score for resolving insolvency (0–100)	33.97
DTF score for registering property (0–100)	44.64			Time (years)	2.7
Procedures (number)	4			Cost (% of estate)	22.0
Time (days)	112			Recovery rate (cents on the dollar)	28.3
Cost (% of property value)	15.1			Strength of insolvency framework index (0–16)	6.0
Quality of land administration index (0–30)	17.0				

Note: Most indicator sets refer to a case scenario in the largest business city of an economy, though for 11 economies the data are a population-weighted average for the two largest business cities. For some indicators a result of "no practice" may be recorded for an economy; see the data notes for more details. In starting a business, procedures (number), time (days) and cost (% of income per capita) are calculated as the average of both men and women. For the postfiling index, a result of "not applicable" may be recorded for an economy.

✔ Reform making it easier to do business   ✘ Change making it more difficult to do business

TRINIDAD AND TOBAGO

		Latin America & Caribbean		GNI per capita (US$)	15,680
Ease of doing business rank (1–190)	102	Overall distance to frontier (DTF) score (0–100)	60.68	Population	1,364,962

Starting a business (rank)	71
DTF score for starting a business (0–100)	88.57
Procedures (number)	7
Time (days)	10.5
Cost (% of income per capita)	0.8
Minimum capital (% of income per capita)	0.0

Dealing with construction permits (rank)	119
DTF score for dealing with construction permits (0–100)	64.19
Procedures (number)	16
Time (days)	253
Cost (% of warehouse value)	0.1
Building quality control index (0–15)	10.0

Getting electricity (rank)	33
DTF score for getting electricity (0–100)	84.25
Procedures (number)	4
Time (days)	61
Cost (% of income per capita)	212.4
Reliability of supply and transparency of tariffs index (0–8)	6

Registering property (rank)	151
DTF score for registering property (0–100)	47.50
Procedures (number)	9
Time (days)	77
Cost (% of property value)	7.0
Quality of land administration index (0–30)	12.0

Getting credit (rank)	55
DTF score for getting credit (0–100)	65.00
Strength of legal rights index (0–12)	7
Depth of credit information index (0–8)	6
Credit bureau coverage (% of adults)	75.5
Credit registry coverage (% of adults)	0.0

Protecting minority investors (rank)	62
DTF score for protecting minority investors (0–100)	58.33
Extent of disclosure index (0–10)	4
Extent of director liability index (0–10)	9
Ease of shareholder suits index (0–10)	8
Extent of shareholder rights index (0–10)	7
Extent of ownership and control index (0–10)	5
Extent of corporate transparency index (0–10)	2

✘ Paying taxes (rank)	162
DTF score for paying taxes (0–100)	52.22
Payments (number per year)	39
Time (hours per year)	210
Total tax and contribution rate (% of profit)	36.2
Postfiling index (0–100)	8.00

Trading across borders (rank)	126
DTF score for trading across borders (0–100)	62.60
Time to export	
Documentary compliance (hours)	32
Border compliance (hours)	60
Cost to export	
Documentary compliance (US$)	250
Border compliance (US$)	499
Time to import	
Documentary compliance (hours)	44
Border compliance (hours)	78
Cost to import	
Documentary compliance (US$)	250
Border compliance (US$)	635

Enforcing contracts (rank)	173
DTF score for enforcing contracts (0–100)	35.62
Time (days)	1,340
Cost (% of claim)	33.5
Quality of judicial processes index (0–18)	8.0

Resolving insolvency (rank)	72
DTF score for resolving insolvency (0–100)	48.48
Time (years)	2.5
Cost (% of estate)	25.0
Recovery rate (cents on the dollar)	26.2
Strength of insolvency framework index (0–16)	11.0

TUNISIA

		Middle East & North Africa		GNI per capita (US$)	3,690
Ease of doing business rank (1–190)	88	Overall distance to frontier (DTF) score (0–100)	63.58	Population	11,403,248

Starting a business (rank)	100
DTF score for starting a business (0–100)	85.02
Procedures (number)	9
Time (days)	11
Cost (% of income per capita)	4.6
Minimum capital (% of income per capita)	0.0

Dealing with construction permits (rank)	95
DTF score for dealing with construction permits (0–100)	67.49
Procedures (number)	18
Time (days)	96
Cost (% of warehouse value)	6.2
Building quality control index (0–15)	11.0

Getting electricity (rank)	48
DTF score for getting electricity (0–100)	82.28
Procedures (number)	4
Time (days)	65
Cost (% of income per capita)	712.1
Reliability of supply and transparency of tariffs index (0–8)	6

Registering property (rank)	93
DTF score for registering property (0–100)	63.21
Procedures (number)	4
Time (days)	39
Cost (% of property value)	6.1
Quality of land administration index (0–30)	11.0

Getting credit (rank)	105
DTF score for getting credit (0–100)	45.00
Strength of legal rights index (0–12)	3
Depth of credit information index (0–8)	6
Credit bureau coverage (% of adults)	0.0
Credit registry coverage (% of adults)	26.9

Protecting minority investors (rank)	119
DTF score for protecting minority investors (0–100)	48.33
Extent of disclosure index (0–10)	4
Extent of director liability index (0–10)	7
Ease of shareholder suits index (0–10)	5
Extent of shareholder rights index (0–10)	4
Extent of ownership and control index (0–10)	3
Extent of corporate transparency index (0–10)	6

✘ Paying taxes (rank)	140
DTF score for paying taxes (0–100)	60.14
Payments (number per year)	9
Time (hours per year)	145
Total tax and contribution rate (% of profit)	64.1
Postfiling index (0–100)	22.91

Trading across borders (rank)	96
DTF score for trading across borders (0–100)	70.50
Time to export	
Documentary compliance (hours)	3
Border compliance (hours)	50
Cost to export	
Documentary compliance (US$)	200
Border compliance (US$)	469
Time to import	
Documentary compliance (hours)	27
Border compliance (hours)	80
Cost to import	
Documentary compliance (US$)	144
Border compliance (US$)	596

Enforcing contracts (rank)	76
DTF score for enforcing contracts (0–100)	59.33
Time (days)	565
Cost (% of claim)	21.8
Quality of judicial processes index (0–18)	7.0

Resolving insolvency (rank)	63
DTF score for resolving insolvency (0–100)	54.53
Time (years)	1.3
Cost (% of estate)	7.0
Recovery rate (cents on the dollar)	52.0
Strength of insolvency framework index (0–16)	8.5

TURKEY

		Europe & Central Asia		GNI per capita (US$)	11,180
Ease of doing business rank (1–190)	60	Overall distance to frontier (DTF) score (0–100)	69.14	Population	79,512,426

Starting a business (rank)	80
DTF score for starting a business (0–100)	87.59
Procedures (number)	7
Time (days)	6.5
Cost (% of income per capita)	12.8
Minimum capital (% of income per capita)	7.8

Dealing with construction permits (rank)	96
DTF score for dealing with construction permits (0–100)	67.26
Procedures (number)	18
Time (days)	103
Cost (% of warehouse value)	4.0
Building quality control index (0–15)	9.5

Getting electricity (rank)	55
DTF score for getting electricity (0–100)	81.02
Procedures (number)	4
Time (days)	55
Cost (% of income per capita)	457.7
Reliability of supply and transparency of tariffs index (0–8)	5

✔ Registering property (rank)	46
DTF score for registering property (0–100)	74.67
Procedures (number)	7
Time (days)	7
Cost (% of property value)	3.0
Quality of land administration index (0–30)	21.5

✔ Getting credit (rank)	77
DTF score for getting credit (0–100)	55.00
Strength of legal rights index (0–12)	4
Depth of credit information index (0–8)	7
Credit bureau coverage (% of adults)	0.0
Credit registry coverage (% of adults)	80.2

Protecting minority investors (rank)	20
DTF score for protecting minority investors (0–100)	71.67
Extent of disclosure index (0–10)	9
Extent of director liability index (0–10)	5
Ease of shareholder suits index (0–10)	6
Extent of shareholder rights index (0–10)	8
Extent of ownership and control index (0–10)	7
Extent of corporate transparency index (0–10)	8

Paying taxes (rank)	88
DTF score for paying taxes (0–100)	72.40
Payments (number per year)	11
Time (hours per year)	215.5
Total tax and contribution rate (% of profit)	41.1
Postfiling index (0–100)	50.00

Trading across borders (rank)	71
DTF score for trading across borders (0–100)	79.71
Time to export	
Documentary compliance (hours)	5
Border compliance (hours)	16
Cost to export	
Documentary compliance (US$)	87
Border compliance (US$)	376
Time to import	
Documentary compliance (hours)	11
Border compliance (hours)	41
Cost to import	
Documentary compliance (US$)	142
Border compliance (US$)	655

Enforcing contracts (rank)	30
DTF score for enforcing contracts (0–100)	68.87
Time (days)	580
Cost (% of claim)	24.9
Quality of judicial processes index (0–18)	13.0

✘ Resolving insolvency (rank)	139
DTF score for resolving insolvency (0–100)	33.26
Time (years)	5.0
Cost (% of estate)	14.5
Recovery rate (cents on the dollar)	15.3
Strength of insolvency framework index (0–16)	8.0

Note: Most indicator sets refer to a case scenario in the largest business city of an economy, though for 11 economies the data are a population-weighted average for the two largest business cities. For some indicators a result of "no practice" may be recorded for an economy; see the data notes for more details. In starting a business, procedures (number), time (days) and cost (% of income per capita) are calculated as the average of both men and women. For the postfiling index, a result of "not applicable" may be recorded for an economy.

✔ Reform making it easier to do business   ✘ Change making it more difficult to do business

UGANDA

UGANDA		Sub-Saharan Africa		GNI per capita (US$) 660
Ease of doing business rank (1–190)	122	Overall distance to frontier (DTF) score (0–100)	56.94	Population 41,487,965

Starting a business (rank)	165	**Getting credit** (rank)	55	✔ **Trading across borders** (rank)	127
DTF score for starting a business (0–100)	72.25	DTF score for getting credit (0–100)	65.00	DTF score for trading across borders (0–100)	62.08
Procedures (number)	13	Strength of legal rights index (0–12)	6	*Time to export*	
Time (days)	24	Depth of credit information index (0–8)	7	Documentary compliance (hours)	51
Cost (% of income per capita)	33.6	Credit bureau coverage (% of adults)	6.4	Border compliance (hours)	64
Minimum capital (% of income per capita)	0.0	Credit registry coverage (% of adults)	0.0	*Cost to export*	
				Documentary compliance (US$)	102
Dealing with construction permits (rank)	148	**Protecting minority investors** (rank)	108	Border compliance (US$)	209
DTF score for dealing with construction permits (0–100)	58.37	DTF score for protecting minority investors (0–100)	50.00	*Time to import*	
Procedures (number)	18	Extent of disclosure index (0–10)	3	Documentary compliance (hours)	138
Time (days)	122	Extent of director liability index (0–10)	5	Border compliance (hours)	154
Cost (% of warehouse value)	8.0	Ease of shareholder suits index (0–10)	7	*Cost to import*	
Building quality control index (0–15)	8.0	Extent of shareholder rights index (0–10)	4	Documentary compliance (US$)	296
		Extent of ownership and control index (0–10)	5	Border compliance (US$)	412
Getting electricity (rank)	173	Extent of corporate transparency index (0–10)	6		
DTF score for getting electricity (0–100)	34.11			**Enforcing contracts** (rank)	64
Procedures (number)	6			DTF score for enforcing contracts (0–100)	60.60
Time (days)	66	**Paying taxes** (rank)	84	Time (days)	490
Cost (% of income per capita)	7,508.4	DTF score for paying taxes (0–100)	73.10	Cost (% of claim)	31.3
Reliability of supply and transparency of tariffs index (0–8)	0	Payments (number per year)	31	Quality of judicial processes index (0–18)	8.5
		Time (hours per year)	195		
		Total tax and contribution rate (% of profit)	33.7		
Registering property (rank)	124	Postfiling index (0–100)	72.28	**Resolving insolvency** (rank)	113
DTF score for registering property (0–100)	54.99			DTF score for resolving insolvency (0–100)	38.94
Procedures (number)	10			Time (years)	2.2
Time (days)	42			Cost (% of estate)	29.5
Cost (% of property value)	3.1			Recovery rate (cents on the dollar)	37.5
Quality of land administration index (0–30)	10.5			Strength of insolvency framework index (0–16)	6.0

UKRAINE

UKRAINE		Europe & Central Asia		GNI per capita (US$) 2,310
Ease of doing business rank (1–190)	76	Overall distance to frontier (DTF) score (0–100)	65.75	Population 45,004,645

Starting a business (rank)	52	**Getting credit** (rank)	29	**Trading across borders** (rank)	119
DTF score for starting a business (0–100)	91.05	DTF score for getting credit (0–100)	75.00	DTF score for trading across borders (0–100)	64.26
Procedures (number)	6	Strength of legal rights index (0–12)	8	*Time to export*	
Time (days)	6.5	Depth of credit information index (0–8)	7	Documentary compliance (hours)	96
Cost (% of income per capita)	0.8	Credit bureau coverage (% of adults)	47.3	Border compliance (hours)	26
Minimum capital (% of income per capita)	0.0	Credit registry coverage (% of adults)	0.0	*Cost to export*	
				Documentary compliance (US$)	292
✔ **Dealing with construction permits** (rank)	35	✔ **Protecting minority investors** (rank)	81	Border compliance (US$)	75
DTF score for dealing with construction permits (0–100)	75.81	DTF score for protecting minority investors (0–100)	55.00	*Time to import*	
Procedures (number)	10	Extent of disclosure index (0–10)	7	Documentary compliance (hours)	168
Time (days)	76	Extent of director liability index (0–10)	2	Border compliance (hours)	72
Cost (% of warehouse value)	3.1	Ease of shareholder suits index (0–10)	6	*Cost to import*	
Building quality control index (0–15)	8.0	Extent of shareholder rights index (0–10)	5	Documentary compliance (US$)	212
		Extent of ownership and control index (0–10)	5	Border compliance (US$)	100
Getting electricity (rank)	128	Extent of corporate transparency index (0–10)	8		
DTF score for getting electricity (0–100)	58.80			**Enforcing contracts** (rank)	82
Procedures (number)	5			DTF score for enforcing contracts (0–100)	58.96
Time (days)	281	✔ **Paying taxes** (rank)	43	Time (days)	378
Cost (% of income per capita)	525.2	DTF score for paying taxes (0–100)	80.77	Cost (% of claim)	46.3
Reliability of supply and transparency of tariffs index (0–8)	6	Payments (number per year)	5	Quality of judicial processes index (0–18)	9.0
		Time (hours per year)	327.5		
		Total tax and contribution rate (% of profit)	37.8		
Registering property (rank)	64	Postfiling index (0–100)	85.95	**Resolving insolvency** (rank)	149
DTF score for registering property (0–100)	69.61			DTF score for resolving insolvency (0–100)	28.24
Procedures (number)	7			Time (years)	2.9
Time (days)	17			Cost (% of estate)	40.5
Cost (% of property value)	1.8			Recovery rate (cents on the dollar)	8.9
Quality of land administration index (0–30)	14.5			Strength of insolvency framework index (0–16)	7.5

UNITED ARAB EMIRATES

UNITED ARAB EMIRATES		Middle East & North Africa		GNI per capita (US$) 40,480
Ease of doing business rank (1–190)	21	Overall distance to frontier (DTF) score (0–100)	78.73	Population 9,269,612

Starting a business (rank)	51	✔ **Getting credit** (rank)	90	**Trading across borders** (rank)	91
DTF score for starting a business (0–100)	91.16	DTF score for getting credit (0–100)	50.00	DTF score for trading across borders (0–100)	71.50
Procedures (number)	4.5	Strength of legal rights index (0–12)	2	*Time to export*	
Time (days)	8.5	Depth of credit information index (0–8)	8	Documentary compliance (hours)	6
Cost (% of income per capita)	13.4	Credit bureau coverage (% of adults)	54.5	Border compliance (hours)	27
Minimum capital (% of income per capita)	0.0	Credit registry coverage (% of adults)	8.8	*Cost to export*	
				Documentary compliance (US$)	178
✔ **Dealing with construction permits** (rank)	2	**Protecting minority investors** (rank)	10	Border compliance (US$)	462
DTF score for dealing with construction permits (0–100)	86.38	DTF score for protecting minority investors (0–100)	75.00	*Time to import*	
Procedures (number)	14	Extent of disclosure index (0–10)	10	Documentary compliance (hours)	12
Time (days)	50.5	Extent of director liability index (0–10)	9	Border compliance (hours)	54
Cost (% of warehouse value)	2.3	Ease of shareholder suits index (0–10)	4	*Cost to import*	
Building quality control index (0–15)	15.0	Extent of shareholder rights index (0–10)	6	Documentary compliance (US$)	283
		Extent of ownership and control index (0–10)	9	Border compliance (US$)	678
✔ **Getting electricity** (rank)	1	Extent of corporate transparency index (0–10)	7		
DTF score for getting electricity (0–100)	99.92			**Enforcing contracts** (rank)	12
Procedures (number)	2			DTF score for enforcing contracts (0–100)	74.02
Time (days)	10	**Paying taxes** (rank)	1	Time (days)	445
Cost (% of income per capita)	25.2	DTF score for paying taxes (0–100)	99.44	Cost (% of claim)	21.0
Reliability of supply and transparency of tariffs index (0–8)	8	Payments (number per year)	4	Quality of judicial processes index (0–18)	13.0
		Time (hours per year)	12		
		Total tax and contribution rate (% of profit)	15.9		
Registering property (rank)	10	Postfiling index (0–100)	not applicable	✔ **Resolving insolvency** (rank)	69
DTF score for registering property (0–100)	90.02			DTF score for resolving insolvency (0–100)	49.80
Procedures (number)	2			Time (years)	3.2
Time (days)	1.5			Cost (% of estate)	20.0
Cost (% of property value)	0.2			Recovery rate (cents on the dollar)	28.7
Quality of land administration index (0–30)	21.0			Strength of insolvency framework index (0–16)	11.0

Note: Most indicator sets refer to a case scenario in the largest business city of an economy, though for 11 economies the data are a population-weighted average for the two largest business cities. For some indicators a result of "no practice" may be recorded for an economy; see the data notes for more details. In starting a business, procedures (number), time (days) and cost (% of income per capita) are calculated as the average of both men and women. For the postfiling index, a result of "not applicable" may be recorded for an economy.

✔ Reform making it easier to do business   ✘ Change making it more difficult to do business

UNITED KINGDOM

UNITED KINGDOM		OECD high income		GNI per capita (US$)	42,390
Ease of doing business rank (1–190)	7	Overall distance to frontier (DTF) score (0–100)	82.22	Population	65,637,239

Starting a business (rank)	14	**Getting credit** (rank)	29	**Trading across borders** (rank)	28
DTF score for starting a business (0–100)	94.58	DTF score for getting credit (0–100)	75.00	DTF score for trading across borders (0–100)	93.76
Procedures (number)	4	Strength of legal rights index (0–12)	7	*Time to export*	
Time (days)	4.5	Depth of credit information index (0–8)	8	Documentary compliance (hours)	4
Cost (% of income per capita)	0.0	Credit bureau coverage (% of adults)	100.0	Border compliance (hours)	24
Minimum capital (% of income per capita)	0.0	Credit registry coverage (% of adults)	0.0	*Cost to export*	
				Documentary compliance (US$)	25
Dealing with construction permits (rank)	14	**Protecting minority investors** (rank)	10	Border compliance (US$)	280
DTF score for dealing with construction permits (0–100)	80.39	DTF score for protecting minority investors (0–100)	75.00	*Time to import*	
Procedures (number)	9	Extent of disclosure index (0–10)	10	Documentary compliance (hours)	2
Time (days)	86	Extent of director liability index (0–10)	7	Border compliance (hours)	3
Cost (% of warehouse value)	1.0	Ease of shareholder suits index (0–10)	8	*Cost to import*	
Building quality control index (0–15)	9.0	Extent of shareholder rights index (0–10)	7	Documentary compliance (US$)	0
		Extent of ownership and control index (0–10)	5	Border compliance (US$)	0
		Extent of corporate transparency index (0–10)	8		
Getting electricity (rank)	9			**Enforcing contracts** (rank)	31
DTF score for getting electricity (0–100)	93.29			DTF score for enforcing contracts (0–100)	68.69
Procedures (number)	3	**Paying taxes** (rank)	23	Time (days)	437
Time (days)	79	DTF score for paying taxes (0–100)	86.70	Cost (% of claim)	45.7
Cost (% of income per capita)	24.9	Payments (number per year)	8	Quality of judicial processes index (0–18)	15.0
Reliability of supply and transparency of tariffs index (0–8)	8	Time (hours per year)	110		
		Total tax and contribution rate (% of profit)	30.7		
Registering property (rank)	47	Postfiling index (0–100)	71.00	**Resolving insolvency** (rank)	14
DTF score for registering property (0–100)	74.51			DTF score for resolving insolvency (0–100)	80.24
Procedures (number)	6			Time (years)	1.0
Time (days)	21.5			Cost (% of estate)	6.0
Cost (% of property value)	4.8			Recovery rate (cents on the dollar)	85.2
Quality of land administration index (0–30)	24.5			Strength of insolvency framework index (0–16)	11.0

UNITED STATES

UNITED STATES		OECD high income		GNI per capita (US$)	56,180
Ease of doing business rank (1–190)	6	Overall distance to frontier (DTF) score (0–100)	82.54	Population	323,127,513

Starting a business (rank)	49	**Getting credit** (rank)	2	**Trading across borders** (rank)	36
DTF score for starting a business (0–100)	91.23	DTF score for getting credit (0–100)	95.00	DTF score for trading across borders (0–100)	92.01
Procedures (number)	6	Strength of legal rights index (0–12)	11	*Time to export*	
Time (days)	5.5	Depth of credit information index (0–8)	8	Documentary compliance (hours)	1.5
Cost (% of income per capita)	1.1	Credit bureau coverage (% of adults)	100.0	Border compliance (hours)	1.5
Minimum capital (% of income per capita)	0.0	Credit registry coverage (% of adults)	0.0	*Cost to export*	
				Documentary compliance (US$)	60
Dealing with construction permits (rank)	36	**Protecting minority investors** (rank)	42	Border compliance (US$)	175
DTF score for dealing with construction permits (0–100)	75.77	DTF score for protecting minority investors (0–100)	64.67	*Time to import*	
Procedures (number)	15.8	Extent of disclosure index (0–10)	7.4	Documentary compliance (hours)	7.5
Time (days)	80.6	Extent of director liability index (0–10)	8.6	Border compliance (hours)	1.5
Cost (% of warehouse value)	0.9	Ease of shareholder suits index (0–10)	9	*Cost to import*	
Building quality control index (0–15)	10.0	Extent of shareholder rights index (0–10)	4	Documentary compliance (US$)	100
		Extent of ownership and control index (0–10)	4.4	Border compliance (US$)	175
		Extent of corporate transparency index (0–10)	5.4		
Getting electricity (rank)	49			**Enforcing contracts** (rank)	16
DTF score for getting electricity (0–100)	82.14			DTF score for enforcing contracts (0–100)	72.61
Procedures (number)	4.8	**Paying taxes** (rank)	36	Time (days)	420
Time (days)	89.6	DTF score for paying taxes (0–100)	84.13	Cost (% of claim)	30.5
Cost (% of income per capita)	23.7	Payments (number per year)	10.6	Quality of judicial processes index (0–18)	13.8
Reliability of supply and transparency of tariffs index (0–8)	7.2	Time (hours per year)	175		
		Total tax and contribution rate (% of profit)	43.8		
Registering property (rank)	37	Postfiling index (0–100)	94.04	**Resolving insolvency** (rank)	3
DTF score for registering property (0–100)	76.80			DTF score for resolving insolvency (0–100)	91.07
Procedures (number)	4.4			Time (years)	1.0
Time (days)	15.2			Cost (% of estate)	10.0
Cost (% of property value)	2.5			Recovery rate (cents on the dollar)	82.1
Quality of land administration index (0–30)	17.6			Strength of insolvency framework index (0–16)	15.0

URUGUAY

URUGUAY		Latin America & Caribbean		GNI per capita (US$)	15,230
Ease of doing business rank (1–190)	94	Overall distance to frontier (DTF) score (0–100)	61.99	Population	3,444,006

✘ **Starting a business** (rank)	61	**Getting credit** (rank)	68	**Trading across borders** (rank)	151
DTF score for starting a business (0–100)	89.80	DTF score for getting credit (0–100)	60.00	DTF score for trading across borders (0–100)	56.29
Procedures (number)	5	Strength of legal rights index (0–12)	4	*Time to export*	
Time (days)	6.5	Depth of credit information index (0–8)	8	Documentary compliance (hours)	24
Cost (% of income per capita)	22.5	Credit bureau coverage (% of adults)	100.0	Border compliance (hours)	120
Minimum capital (% of income per capita)	0.0	Credit registry coverage (% of adults)	100.0	*Cost to export*	
				Documentary compliance (US$)	231
Dealing with construction permits (rank)	161	**Protecting minority investors** (rank)	132	Border compliance (US$)	1,095
DTF score for dealing with construction permits (0–100)	54.90	DTF score for protecting minority investors (0–100)	43.33	*Time to import*	
Procedures (number)	21	Extent of disclosure index (0–10)	3	Documentary compliance (hours)	72
Time (days)	251	Extent of director liability index (0–10)	4	Border compliance (hours)	6
Cost (% of warehouse value)	1.0	Ease of shareholder suits index (0–10)	8	*Cost to import*	
Building quality control index (0–15)	8.0	Extent of shareholder rights index (0–10)	5	Documentary compliance (US$)	285
		Extent of ownership and control index (0–10)	5	Border compliance (US$)	375
		Extent of corporate transparency index (0–10)	1		
Getting electricity (rank)	50			**Enforcing contracts** (rank)	112
DTF score for getting electricity (0–100)	82.12			DTF score for enforcing contracts (0–100)	54.44
Procedures (number)	5	✔ **Paying taxes** (rank)	106	Time (days)	725
Time (days)	48	DTF score for paying taxes (0–100)	69.26	Cost (% of claim)	23.2
Cost (% of income per capita)	11.4	Payments (number per year)	20	Quality of judicial processes index (0–18)	7.0
Reliability of supply and transparency of tariffs index (0–8)	6	Time (hours per year)	190		
		Total tax and contribution rate (% of profit)	41.8		
Registering property (rank)	112	Postfiling index (0–100)	49.54	**Resolving insolvency** (rank)	66
DTF score for registering property (0–100)	57.59			DTF score for resolving insolvency (0–100)	52.15
Procedures (number)	9			Time (years)	1.8
Time (days)	66			Cost (% of estate)	7.0
Cost (% of property value)	7.0			Recovery rate (cents on the dollar)	41.7
Quality of land administration index (0–30)	22.5			Strength of insolvency framework index (0–16)	9.5

Note: Most indicator sets refer to a case scenario in the largest business city of an economy, though for 11 economies the data are a population-weighted average for the two largest business cities. For some indicators a result of "no practice" may be recorded for an economy; see the data notes for more details. In starting a business, procedures (number), time (days) and cost (% of income per capita) are calculated as the average of both men and women. For the postfiling index, a result of "not applicable" may be recorded for an economy.

✔ Reform making it easier to do business   ✘ Change making it more difficult to do business

UZBEKISTAN

Ease of doing business rank (1–190)	**74**	Europe & Central Asia		Overall distance to frontier (DTF) score (0–100)	66.33	

GNI per capita (US$) 2,220
Population 31,848,200

✔ **Starting a business** (rank) — 11
DTF score for starting a business (0–100) — 95.54
Procedures (number) — 3
Time (days) — 5
Cost (% of income per capita) — 3.1
Minimum capital (% of income per capita) — 0.0

✔ **Dealing with construction permits** (rank) — 135
DTF score for dealing with construction permits (0–100) — 61.26
Procedures (number) — 17
Time (days) — 246
Cost (% of warehouse value) — 3.4
Building quality control index (0–15) — 11.0

✔ **Getting electricity** (rank) — 27
DTF score for getting electricity (0–100) — 85.50
Procedures (number) — 4
Time (days) — 88
Cost (% of income per capita) — 883.1
Reliability of supply and transparency of tariffs index (0–8) — 8

Registering property (rank) — 73
DTF score for registering property (0–100) — 66.34
Procedures (number) — 9
Time (days) — 46
Cost (% of property value) — 1.2
Quality of land administration index (0–30) — 18.5

Getting credit (rank) — 55
DTF score for getting credit (0–100) — 65.00
Strength of legal rights index (0–12) — 6
Depth of credit information index (0–8) — 7
Credit bureau coverage (% of adults) — 40.1
Credit registry coverage (% of adults) — 0.0

✔ **Protecting minority investors** (rank) — 62
DTF score for protecting minority investors (0–100) — 58.33
Extent of disclosure index (0–10) — 8
Extent of director liability index (0–10) — 3
Ease of shareholder suits index (0–10) — 7
Extent of shareholder rights index (0–10) — 6
Extent of ownership and control index (0–10) — 4
Extent of corporate transparency index (0–10) — 7

✔ **Paying taxes** (rank) — 78
DTF score for paying taxes (0–100) — 74.78
Payments (number per year) — 10
Time (hours per year) — 181
Total tax and contribution rate (% of profit) — 38.3
Postfiling index (0–100) — 48.39

Trading across borders (rank) — 168
DTF score for trading across borders (0–100) — 44.31
Time to export
Documentary compliance (hours) — 174
Border compliance (hours) — 112
Cost to export
Documentary compliance (US$) — 292
Border compliance (US$) — 278
Time to import
Documentary compliance (hours) — 174
Border compliance (hours) — 111
Cost to import
Documentary compliance (US$) — 292
Border compliance (US$) — 278

Enforcing contracts (rank) — 39
DTF score for enforcing contracts (0–100) — 67.26
Time (days) — 225
Cost (% of claim) — 20.5
Quality of judicial processes index (0–18) — 6.0

Resolving insolvency (rank) — 87
DTF score for resolving insolvency (0–100) — 45.00
Time (years) — 2.0
Cost (% of estate) — 10.0
Recovery rate (cents on the dollar) — 37.2
Strength of insolvency framework index (0–16) — 8.0

VANUATU

Ease of doing business rank (1–190)	**90**	East Asia & Pacific		Overall distance to frontier (DTF) score (0–100)	63.08	

GNI per capita (US$) 2,815
Population 270,402

Starting a business (rank) — 128
DTF score for starting a business (0–100) — 81.23
Procedures (number) — 7
Time (days) — 18
Cost (% of income per capita) — 44.4
Minimum capital (% of income per capita) — 0.0

Dealing with construction permits (rank) — 151
DTF score for dealing with construction permits (0–100) — 57.58
Procedures (number) — 14
Time (days) — 124
Cost (% of warehouse value) — 7.8
Building quality control index (0–15) — 5.0

Getting electricity (rank) — 86
DTF score for getting electricity (0–100) — 72.01
Procedures (number) — 4
Time (days) — 120
Cost (% of income per capita) — 1,090.4
Reliability of supply and transparency of tariffs index (0–8) — 5

Registering property (rank) — 80
DTF score for registering property (0–100) — 65.63
Procedures (number) — 4
Time (days) — 58
Cost (% of property value) — 7.0
Quality of land administration index (0–30) — 18.5

Getting credit (rank) — 29
DTF score for getting credit (0–100) — 75.00
Strength of legal rights index (0–12) — 11
Depth of credit information index (0–8) — 4
Credit bureau coverage (% of adults) — 9.4
Credit registry coverage (% of adults) — 0.0

Protecting minority investors (rank) — 108
DTF score for protecting minority investors (0–100) — 50.00
Extent of disclosure index (0–10) — 5
Extent of director liability index (0–10) — 6
Ease of shareholder suits index (0–10) — 5
Extent of shareholder rights index (0–10) — 8
Extent of ownership and control index (0–10) — 2
Extent of corporate transparency index (0–10) — 4

Paying taxes (rank) — 57
DTF score for paying taxes (0–100) — 77.85
Payments (number per year) — 31
Time (hours per year) — 120
Total tax and contribution rate (% of profit) — 8.5
Postfiling index (0–100) — 69.04

Trading across borders (rank) — 143
DTF score for trading across borders (0–100) — 59.13
Time to export
Documentary compliance (hours) — 72
Border compliance (hours) — 38
Cost to export
Documentary compliance (US$) — 190
Border compliance (US$) — 709
Time to import
Documentary compliance (hours) — 48
Border compliance (hours) — 126
Cost to import
Documentary compliance (US$) — 183
Border compliance (US$) — 681

Enforcing contracts (rank) — 135
DTF score for enforcing contracts (0–100) — 49.27
Time (days) — 430
Cost (% of claim) — 56.0
Quality of judicial processes index (0–18) — 6.5

Resolving insolvency (rank) — 96
DTF score for resolving insolvency (0–100) — 43.04
Time (years) — 2.6
Cost (% of estate) — 38.0
Recovery rate (cents on the dollar) — 45.1
Strength of insolvency framework index (0–16) — 6.0

VENEZUELA, RB

Ease of doing business rank (1–190)	**188**	Latin America & Caribbean		Overall distance to frontier (DTF) score (0–100)	30.87	

GNI per capita (US$) 9,258
Population 31,568,179

✘ **Starting a business** (rank) — 190
DTF score for starting a business (0–100) — 25.00
Procedures (number) — 20
Time (days) — 230
Cost (% of income per capita) — 351.6
Minimum capital (% of income per capita) — 0.0

Dealing with construction permits (rank) — 143
DTF score for dealing with construction permits (0–100) — 59.27
Procedures (number) — 11
Time (days) — 434
Cost (% of warehouse value) — 1.8
Building quality control index (0–15) — 10.5

Getting electricity (rank) — 186
DTF score for getting electricity (0–100) — 16.85
Procedures (number) — 6
Time (days) — 208
Cost (% of income per capita) — 16,713.5
Reliability of supply and transparency of tariffs index (0–8) — 0

Registering property (rank) — 135
DTF score for registering property (0–100) — 52.29
Procedures (number) — 9
Time (days) — 52
Cost (% of property value) — 2.7
Quality of land administration index (0–30) — 5.5

Getting credit (rank) — 122
DTF score for getting credit (0–100) — 40.00
Strength of legal rights index (0–12) — 1
Depth of credit information index (0–8) — 7
Credit bureau coverage (% of adults) — 27.4
Credit registry coverage (% of adults) — 0.0

Protecting minority investors (rank) — 177
DTF score for protecting minority investors (0–100) — 26.67
Extent of disclosure index (0–10) — 3
Extent of director liability index (0–10) — 2
Ease of shareholder suits index (0–10) — 3
Extent of shareholder rights index (0–10) — 2
Extent of ownership and control index (0–10) — 3
Extent of corporate transparency index (0–10) — 3

Paying taxes (rank) — 189
DTF score for paying taxes (0–100) — 15.18
Payments (number per year) — 70
Time (hours per year) — 792
Total tax and contribution rate (% of profit) — 65.0
Postfiling index (0–100) — 19.72

Trading across borders (rank) — 187
DTF score for trading across borders (0–100) — 7.93
Time to export
Documentary compliance (hours) — 528
Border compliance (hours) — 288
Cost to export
Documentary compliance (US$) — 375
Border compliance (US$) — 1,250
Time to import
Documentary compliance (hours) — 1,090
Border compliance (hours) — 240
Cost to import
Documentary compliance (US$) — 400
Border compliance (US$) — 1,500

Enforcing contracts (rank) — 147
DTF score for enforcing contracts (0–100) — 46.89
Time (days) — 720
Cost (% of claim) — 43.7
Quality of judicial processes index (0–18) — 7.0

Resolving insolvency (rank) — 165
DTF score for resolving insolvency (0–100) — 18.66
Time (years) — 4.0
Cost (% of estate) — 38.0
Recovery rate (cents on the dollar) — 5.6
Strength of insolvency framework index (0–16) — 5.0

Note: Most indicator sets refer to a case scenario in the largest business city of an economy, though for 11 economies the data are a population-weighted average for the two largest business cities. For some indicators a result of "no practice" may be recorded for an economy; see the data notes for more details. In starting a business, procedures (number), time (days) and cost (% of income per capita) are calculated as the average of both men and women. For the postfiling index, a result of "not applicable" may be recorded for an economy.

✔ Reform making it easier to do business   ✗ Change making it more difficult to do business

VIETNAM

Ease of doing business rank (1–190)	**68**	East Asia & Pacific		Overall distance to frontier (DTF) score (0–100)	**67.93**	GNI per capita (US$)	**2,050**
						Population	**92,701,100**

Starting a business (rank)	123	✔ **Getting credit** (rank)	29	✔ **Trading across borders** (rank)		94
DTF score for starting a business (0–100)	82.02	DTF score for getting credit (0–100)	75.00	DTF score for trading across borders (0–100)		70.83
Procedures (number)	9	Strength of legal rights index (0–12)	8	Time to export		
Time (days)	22	Depth of credit information index (0–8)	7	Documentary compliance (hours)		50
Cost (% of income per capita)	6.5	Credit bureau coverage (% of adults)	19.7	Border compliance (hours)		55
Minimum capital (% of income per capita)	0.0	Credit registry coverage (% of adults)	51.0	Cost to export		
				Documentary compliance (US$)		139
Dealing with construction permits (rank)	20	**Protecting minority investors** (rank)	81	Border compliance (US$)		290
DTF score for dealing with construction permits (0–100)	79.03	DTF score for protecting minority investors (0–100)	55.00	Time to import		
Procedures (number)	10	Extent of disclosure index (0–10)	7	Documentary compliance (hours)		76
Time (days)	166	Extent of director liability index (0–10)	4	Border compliance (hours)		56
Cost (% of warehouse value)	0.7	Ease of shareholder suits index (0–10)	2	Cost to import		
Building quality control index (0–15)	12.0	Extent of shareholder rights index (0–10)	7	Documentary compliance (US$)		183
		Extent of ownership and control index (0–10)	6	Border compliance (US$)		373
		Extent of corporate transparency index (0–10)	7			
✔ **Getting electricity** (rank)	64			✔ **Enforcing contracts** (rank)		66
DTF score for getting electricity (0–100)	78.69			DTF score for enforcing contracts (0–100)		60.22
Procedures (number)	5	✔ **Paying taxes** (rank)	86	Time (days)		400
Time (days)	46	DTF score for paying taxes (0–100)	72.77	Cost (% of claim)		29.0
Cost (% of income per capita)	1,191.8	Payments (number per year)	14	Quality of judicial processes index (0–18)		6.5
Reliability of supply and transparency of tariffs index (0–8)	6	Time (hours per year)	498			
		Total tax and contribution rate (% of profit)	38.1			
Registering property (rank)	63	Postfiling index (0–100)	95.71	**Resolving insolvency** (rank)		129
DTF score for registering property (0–100)	70.61			DTF score for resolving insolvency (0–100)		35.16
Procedures (number)	5			Time (years)		5.0
Time (days)	57.5			Cost (% of estate)		14.5
Cost (% of property value)	0.6			Recovery rate (cents on the dollar)		21.8
Quality of land administration index (0–30)	14.0			Strength of insolvency framework index (0–16)		7.5

WEST BANK AND GAZA

Ease of doing business rank (1–190)	**114**	Middle East & North Africa		Overall distance to frontier (DTF) score (0–100)	**58.68**	GNI per capita (US$)	**3,230**
						Population	**4,551,566**

Starting a business (rank)	169	✔ **Getting credit** (rank)	20	**Trading across borders** (rank)	49
DTF score for starting a business (0–100)	69.59	DTF score for getting credit (0–100)	80.00	DTF score for trading across borders (0–100)	86.67
Procedures (number)	10.5	Strength of legal rights index (0–12)	8	Time to export	
Time (days)	43.5	Depth of credit information index (0–8)	8	Documentary compliance (hours)	72
Cost (% of income per capita)	45.1	Credit bureau coverage (% of adults)	0.0	Border compliance (hours)	6
Minimum capital (% of income per capita)	0.0	Credit registry coverage (% of adults)	19.0	Cost to export	
				Documentary compliance (US$)	80
Dealing with construction permits (rank)	154	**Protecting minority investors** (rank)	160	Border compliance (US$)	51
DTF score for dealing with construction permits (0–100)	56.70	DTF score for protecting minority investors (0–100)	38.33	Time to import	
Procedures (number)	20	Extent of disclosure index (0–10)	6	Documentary compliance (hours)	45
Time (days)	108	Extent of director liability index (0–10)	5	Border compliance (hours)	6
Cost (% of warehouse value)	13.9	Ease of shareholder suits index (0–10)	6	Cost to import	
Building quality control index (0–15)	12.0	Extent of shareholder rights index (0–10)	2	Documentary compliance (US$)	85
		Extent of ownership and control index (0–10)	1	Border compliance (US$)	50
		Extent of corporate transparency index (0–10)	3		
Getting electricity (rank)	87			**Enforcing contracts** (rank)	124
DTF score for getting electricity (0–100)	71.46			DTF score for enforcing contracts (0–100)	52.51
Procedures (number)	5	**Paying taxes** (rank)	109	Time (days)	540
Time (days)	47	DTF score for paying taxes (0–100)	68.84	Cost (% of claim)	27.0
Cost (% of income per capita)	1,475.3	Payments (number per year)	28	Quality of judicial processes index (0–18)	4.0
Reliability of supply and transparency of tariffs index (0–8)	4	Time (hours per year)	162		
		Total tax and contribution rate (% of profit)	15.3		
Registering property (rank)	94	Postfiling index (0–100)	34.47	**Resolving insolvency** (rank)	168
DTF score for registering property (0–100)	62.71			DTF score for resolving insolvency (0–100)	0.00
Procedures (number)	7			Time (years)	no practice
Time (days)	51			Cost (% of estate)	no practice
Cost (% of property value)	3.0			Recovery rate (cents on the dollar)	0.0
Quality of land administration index (0–30)	13.5			Strength of insolvency framework index (0–16)	0.0

YEMEN, REP.

Ease of doing business rank (1–190)	**186**	Middle East & North Africa		Overall distance to frontier (DTF) score (0–100)	**33.00**	GNI per capita (US$)	**1,040**
						Population	**27,584,213**

Starting a business (rank)	163	**Getting credit** (rank)	186	**Trading across borders** (rank)	189
DTF score for starting a business (0–100)	72.68	DTF score for getting credit (0–100)	0.00	DTF score for trading across borders (0–100)	0.00
Procedures (number)	6.5	Strength of legal rights index (0–12)	0	Time to export	
Time (days)	40.5	Depth of credit information index (0–8)	0	Documentary compliance (hours)	no practice
Cost (% of income per capita)	73.5	Credit bureau coverage (% of adults)	0.0	Border compliance (hours)	no practice
Minimum capital (% of income per capita)	0.0	Credit registry coverage (% of adults)	1.3	Cost to export	
				Documentary compliance (US$)	no practice
Dealing with construction permits (rank)	186	**Protecting minority investors** (rank)	132	Border compliance (US$)	no practice
DTF score for dealing with construction permits (0–100)	0.00	DTF score for protecting minority investors (0–100)	43.33	Time to import	
Procedures (number)	no practice	Extent of disclosure index (0–10)	6	Documentary compliance (hours)	no practice
Time (days)	no practice	Extent of director liability index (0–10)	4	Border compliance (hours)	no practice
Cost (% of warehouse value)	no practice	Ease of shareholder suits index (0–10)	3	Cost to import	
Building quality control index (0–15)	0.0	Extent of shareholder rights index (0–10)	5	Documentary compliance (US$)	no practice
		Extent of ownership and control index (0–10)	4	Border compliance (US$)	no practice
		Extent of corporate transparency index (0–10)	4		
Getting electricity (rank)	187			**Enforcing contracts** (rank)	140
DTF score for getting electricity (0–100)	0.00			DTF score for enforcing contracts (0–100)	48.52
Procedures (number)	no practice	**Paying taxes** (rank)	80	Time (days)	645
Time (days)	no practice	DTF score for paying taxes (0–100)	74.13	Cost (% of claim)	30.0
Cost (% of income per capita)	no practice	Payments (number per year)	44	Quality of judicial processes index (0–18)	4.0
Reliability of supply and transparency of tariffs index (0–8)	0	Time (hours per year)	248		
		Total tax and contribution rate (% of profit)	26.6		
Registering property (rank)	82	Postfiling index (0–100)	96.34	**Resolving insolvency** (rank)	156
DTF score for registering property (0–100)	65.21			DTF score for resolving insolvency (0–100)	26.14
Procedures (number)	6			Time (years)	3.0
Time (days)	19			Cost (% of estate)	15.0
Cost (% of property value)	1.8			Recovery rate (cents on the dollar)	19.5
Quality of land administration index (0–30)	7.0			Strength of insolvency framework index (0–16)	5.0

Note: Most indicator sets refer to a case scenario in the largest business city of an economy, though for 11 economies the data are a population-weighted average for the two largest business cities. For some indicators a result of "no practice" may be recorded for an economy; see the data notes for more details. In starting a business, procedures (number), time (days) and cost (% of income per capita) are calculated as the average of both men and women. For the postfiling index, a result of "not applicable" may be recorded for an economy.

✔ Reform making it easier to do business   ✘ Change making it more difficult to do business

ZAMBIA

ZAMBIA		**Sub-Saharan Africa**		**GNI per capita (US$)**		1,300
Ease of doing business rank (1–190)	85	Overall distance to frontier (DTF) score (0–100)	64.50	Population		16,591,390

Starting a business (rank)	101	✔ **Getting credit** (rank)	2	✔ **Trading across borders** (rank)		150
DTF score for starting a business (0–100)	84.89	DTF score for getting credit (0–100)	95.00	DTF score for trading across borders (0–100)		56.88
Procedures (number)	7	Strength of legal rights index (0–12)	11	*Time to export*		
Time (days)	8.5	Depth of credit information index (0–8)	8	Documentary compliance (hours)		96
Cost (% of income per capita)	34.2	Credit bureau coverage (% of adults)	8.7	Border compliance (hours)		120
Minimum capital (% of income per capita)	0.0	Credit registry coverage (% of adults)	0.0	*Cost to export*		
				Documentary compliance (US$)		200
Dealing with construction permits (rank)	69	**Protecting minority investors** (rank)	89	Border compliance (US$)		370
DTF score for dealing with construction permits (0–100)	71.04	DTF score for protecting minority investors (0–100)	53.33	*Time to import*		
Procedures (number)	10	Extent of disclosure index (0–10)	4	Documentary compliance (hours)		72
Time (days)	189	Extent of director liability index (0–10)	6	Border compliance (hours)		120
Cost (% of warehouse value)	3.1	Ease of shareholder suits index (0–10)	7	*Cost to import*		
Building quality control index (0–15)	10.0	Extent of shareholder rights index (0–10)	6	Documentary compliance (US$)		175
		Extent of ownership and control index (0–10)	5	Border compliance (US$)		380
Getting electricity (rank)	155	Extent of corporate transparency index (0–10)	4			
DTF score for getting electricity (0–100)	49.92			**Enforcing contracts** (rank)		128
Procedures (number)	6	✔ **Paying taxes** (rank)	15	DTF score for enforcing contracts (0–100)		51.74
Time (days)	117	DTF score for paying taxes (0–100)	88.71	Time (days)		611
Cost (% of income per capita)	588.5	Payments (number per year)	11	Cost (% of claim)		38.7
Reliability of supply and transparency of tariffs index (0–8)	0	Time (hours per year)	164	Quality of judicial processes index (0–18)		7.0
		Total tax and contribution rate (% of profit)	15.6			
Registering property (rank)	149	Postfiling index (0–100)	85.94	**Resolving insolvency** (rank)		89
DTF score for registering property (0–100)	48.69			DTF score for resolving insolvency (0–100)		44.85
Procedures (number)	6			Time (years)		1.0
Time (days)	45			Cost (% of estate)		9.0
Cost (% of property value)	9.9			Recovery rate (cents on the dollar)		48.5
Quality of land administration index (0–30)	7.0			Strength of insolvency framework index (0–16)		6.0

ZIMBABWE

ZIMBABWE		**Sub-Saharan Africa**		**GNI per capita (US$)**		940
Ease of doing business rank (1–190)	159	Overall distance to frontier (DTF) score (0–100)	48.47	Population		16,150,362

✔ **Starting a business** (rank)	180	✘ **Getting credit** (rank)	105	**Trading across borders** (rank)		153
DTF score for starting a business (0–100)	59.28	DTF score for getting credit (0–100)	45.00	DTF score for trading across borders (0–100)		55.47
Procedures (number)	9	Strength of legal rights index (0–12)	5	*Time to export*		
Time (days)	61	Depth of credit information index (0–8)	4	Documentary compliance (hours)		99
Cost (% of income per capita)	110.0	Credit bureau coverage (% of adults)	32.0	Border compliance (hours)		74
Minimum capital (% of income per capita)	0.0	Credit registry coverage (% of adults)	3.2	*Cost to export*		
				Documentary compliance (US$)		170
Dealing with construction permits (rank)	175	**Protecting minority investors** (rank)	89	Border compliance (US$)		285
DTF score for dealing with construction permits (0–100)	44.73	DTF score for protecting minority investors (0–100)	53.33	*Time to import*		
Procedures (number)	10	Extent of disclosure index (0–10)	8	Documentary compliance (hours)		81
Time (days)	238	Extent of director liability index (0–10)	2	Border compliance (hours)		228
Cost (% of warehouse value)	22.5	Ease of shareholder suits index (0–10)	5	*Cost to import*		
Building quality control index (0–15)	9.0	Extent of shareholder rights index (0–10)	7	Documentary compliance (US$)		150
		Extent of ownership and control index (0–10)	5	Border compliance (US$)		562
Getting electricity (rank)	161	Extent of corporate transparency index (0–10)	5			
DTF score for getting electricity (0–100)	44.90			**Enforcing contracts** (rank)		166
Procedures (number)	6			DTF score for enforcing contracts (0–100)		38.73
Time (days)	106	**Paying taxes** (rank)	143	Time (days)		410
Cost (% of income per capita)	2,602.6	DTF score for paying taxes (0–100)	58.83	Cost (% of claim)		83.1
Reliability of supply and transparency of tariffs index (0–8)	0	Payments (number per year)	51	Quality of judicial processes index (0–18)		6.0
		Time (hours per year)	242			
Registering property (rank)	108	Total tax and contribution rate (% of profit)	31.6	**Resolving insolvency** (rank)		155
DTF score for registering property (0–100)	58.21	Postfiling index (0–100)	52.84	DTF score for resolving insolvency (0–100)		26.21
Procedures (number)	5			Time (years)		3.3
Time (days)	36			Cost (% of estate)		22.0
Cost (% of property value)	7.6			Recovery rate (cents on the dollar)		19.7
Quality of land administration index (0–30)	10.0			Strength of insolvency framework index (0–16)		5.0

Note: Most indicator sets refer to a case scenario in the largest business city of an economy, though for 11 economies the data are a population-weighted average for the two largest business cities. For some indicators a result of "no practice" may be recorded for an economy; see the data notes for more details. In starting a business, procedures (number), time (days) and cost (% of income per capita) are calculated as the average of both men and women. For the postfiling index, a result of "not applicable" may be recorded for an economy.

Labor
Market Regulation

Regulation of the labor market is an important aspect of the business environment that can influence employment dynamics and productivity.[1] Labor market imperfections can negatively affect job quality and job creation.[2] Regulation can mitigate market failures and contribute to a more productive allocation of labor resources within an economy. While reforms toward more flexible labor regulation could increase employment,[3] labor under-regulation can also have negative impacts by, for example, creating an unsafe workplace or undermining worker quality of life. By setting the right incentives and deterrents for both employers and employees, labor regulation could contribute to labor mobility and productivity growth.[4]

The challenge in developing labor policies is to avoid the extremes of both over- and under-regulation by balancing labor flexibility with worker protection. More flexible regulation may allow an economy to better adjust to economic shocks, variations in the business cycle and long-term structural shifts, such as technological and demographic changes. Data collected for *Doing Business 2018* show that 64.7% of economies allow the use of fixed-term contracts for permanent tasks and 78.9% do not have restrictions on night work. In 21.4% of economies the law requires the employer to reassign or retrain a worker before making that worker redundant.

On the other hand, a lack of worker protection can lead to lower standards of living and—with unhealthy and unmotivated employees—poor firm productivity. *Doing Business 2018* data show that 68.9% of economies provide at least five fully-paid days of sick leave annually. The under-regulation of the labor market may disproportionally affect specific groups. For female employees, discrimination in access to employment and persistent gaps in income may discourage them from entering the labor market or participating in it to their full potential. *Doing Business 2018* data show that 48% of economies prohibit gender-based discrimination in hiring and 40.5% mandate equal remuneration for work of equal value.

In recent years *Doing Business* has developed a more nuanced approach to its labor market indicators by expanding its methodological scope, going beyond the areas traditionally measured by the report. Historically, *Doing Business* measured flexibility in the regulation of employment as it relates to the hiring and redundancy of employees and the scheduling of working hours. However, several new components were added since *Doing Business 2016*, including the availability of at least five fully-paid days of sick leave a year, length of paid maternity leave, unemployment protection, gender nondiscrimination in hiring and equal remuneration for work of equal value. This methodological expansion stemmed from a collaborative dialogue with interested stakeholders and the International Labor Organization. The changes implemented were aimed at providing a more comprehensive measure by setting the right balance in labor market regulation. The *Doing Business* labor market indicators serve as an essential resource for academics, journalists, private sector researchers and others interested in labor market regulation.

NOTES

1. Martin and Scarpetta 2012.
2. World Bank 2012.
3. Amin 2007.
4. Martin and Scarpetta 2012.

LABOR MARKET REGULATION DATA

Economy	Fixed-term contracts prohibited for permanent tasks?[a]	Maximum length of fixed-term contracts (months)[a]	Minimum wage for a cashier, age 19, with one year of work experience (US$/month)[b]	Ratio of minimum wage to value added per worker	Maximum length of probationary period (months)[c]	Maximum number of working days per week	Premium for night work (% of hourly pay)	Premium for work on weekly rest day (% of hourly pay)	Premium for overtime work (% of hourly pay)	Restrictions on night work?	Whether non-pregnant and non-nursing women can work the same night hours as men	Restrictions on weekly holiday work?	Restrictions on overtime work?	Paid annual leave (working days)[d]
	Hiring					Working hours								
Afghanistan	No	No limit	0.0	0.0	3.0	6.0	15.0	50.0	25.0	Yes	No	No	Yes	20.0
Albania	Yes	No limit	182.3	0.4	3.0	5.5	50.0	25.0	25.0	Yes	Yes	No	No	20.0
Algeria	Yes	No limit	187.1	0.3	6.0	6.0	0.0	0.0	50.0	Yes	No	No	No	22.0
Angola	No	120.0	148.4	0.3	3.0	6.0	10.0	75.0	20.0	Yes	Yes	Yes	No	22.0
Antigua and Barbuda	No	No limit	604.9	0.4	3.0	6.0	0.0	0.0	50.0	No	Yes	No	No	12.0
Argentina	Yes	60.0	936.7	0.6	3.0	5.5	13.0	100.0	50.0	No	Yes	No	No	18.0
Armenia	Yes	No limit	117.0	0.3	3.0	6.0	30.0	100.0	50.0	No	Yes	No	No	20.0
Australia	No	No limit	2,068.3	0.3	6.0	6.0	25.0	100.0	50.0	No	Yes	No	No	20.0
Austria	No	No limit	1,590.5	0.3	1.0	5.5	67.0	100.0	50.0	Yes	Yes	No	No	25.0
Azerbaijan	No	60.0	95.5	0.2	3.0	6.0	40.0	100.0	100.0	Yes	No	No	Yes	17.0
Bahamas, The	No	No limit	867.5	0.3	0.0	5.0	0.0	0.0	50.0	No	Yes	No	No	11.7
Bahrain	No	60.0	0.0	0.0	3.0	6.0	0.0	0.0	37.5	No	Yes	No	No	30.0
Bangladesh (Chittagong)	No	No limit	0.0	0.0	3.0	5.5	0.0	0.0	100.0	No	Yes	No	No	17.0
Bangladesh (Dhaka)	No	No limit	0.0	0.0	3.0	5.5	0.0	0.0	100.0	No	Yes	No	No	17.0
Barbados	No	No limit	518.2	0.3	n.a.	5.0	0.0	0.0	50.0	No	Yes	No	No	20.3
Belarus	No	No limit	156.9	0.2	3.0	6.0	20.0	100.0	100.0	No	Yes	No	No	18.0
Belgium	No	No limit	2,280.1	0.4	0.0	6.0	0.0	0.0	50.0	Yes	Yes	Yes	No	20.0
Belize	No	No limit	332.0	0.6	6.0	6.0	0.0	50.0	50.0	No	Yes	No	Yes	12.0
Benin	No	48.0	70.2	0.6	2.0	6.0	0.0	0.0	12.0	No	Yes	No	No	24.0
Bhutan	No	No limit	54.1	0.2	6.0	6.0	0.0	0.0	0.0	No	Yes	No	No	15.0
Bolivia[h]	Yes	24.0	291.7	0.7	3.0	6.0	25.0	100.0	100.0	No	No	No	No	21.7
Bosnia and Herzegovina	No	36.0	232.5	0.4	6.0	6.0	25.0	15.0	25.0	No	Yes	No	No	20.0
Botswana	No	No limit	84.5	0.1	3.0	6.0	0.0	100.0	50.0	No	Yes	No	No	15.0
Brazil (Rio de Janeiro)	Yes	24.0	382.0	0.4	3.0	6.0	20.0	0.0	50.0	Yes	Yes	No	No	26.0
Brazil (São Paulo)	Yes	24.0	348.9	0.3	3.0	6.0	20.0	0.0	60.0	Yes	Yes	No	No	26.0
Brunei Darussalam	No	No limit	0.0	0.0	n.a.	6.0	0.0	50.0	50.0	No	Yes	No	No	11.7
Bulgaria	No	36.0	266.8	0.3	6.0	6.0	7.6	0.0	50.0	Yes	Yes	No	Yes	20.0
Burkina Faso	No	No limit	90.8	0.9	2.0	6.0	0.0	0.0	15.0	No	Yes	Yes	No	22.0
Burundi	No	No limit	2.4	0.1	6.0	6.0	35.0	0.0	35.0	No	Yes	No	No	21.0
Cabo Verde	Yes	60.0	115.3	0.3	2.0	6.0	25.0	100.0	35.0	No	Yes	No	No	22.0
Cambodia	No	24.0	0.0	0.0	1.0	6.0	30.0	0.0	50.0	No	Yes	No	No	19.3
Cameroon	No	48.0	72.2	0.4	2.0	6.0	0.0	0.0	20.0	No	Yes	No	No	25.0

	Redundancy rules							Redundancy cost		Job quality							
Dismissal due to redundancy allowed by law?	Third-party notification if 1 worker is dismissed?	Third-party approval if 1 worker is dismissed?	Third-party notification if 9 workers are dismissed?	Third-party approval if 9 workers are dismissed?	Retraining or reassignment?[e]	Priority rules for redundancies?	Priority rules for reemployment?	Notice period for redundancy dismissal (weeks of salary)[d]	Severance pay for redundancy dismissal (weeks of salary)[d]	Equal remuneration for work of equal value?	Gender non-discrimination in hiring?	Paid/unpaid maternity leave mandated by law?[f]	Minimum length of maternity leave (calendar days)[g]	Receive 100% of wages on maternity leave?	Availability of five fully paid days of sick leave?	Whether an unemployment protection scheme exists after one year of employment[h]	Minimum duration of contribution period (in months) for unemployment protection
Yes	Yes	No	Yes	Yes	No	No	Yes	4.3	17.3	No	No	Yes	90	Yes	Yes	No	n.a.
Yes	No	No	No	No	No	No	Yes	10.1	10.7	Yes	Yes	Yes	365	No	No	Yes	12.0
Yes	Yes	No	Yes	No	Yes	Yes	No	4.3	13.0	Yes	No	Yes	98	Yes	No	No	36.0
Yes	Yes	Yes	Yes	Yes	No	No	Yes	4.3	13.6	Yes	No	Yes	90	Yes	No	No	n.a.
Yes	No	No	No	No	Yes	Yes	No	3.4	12.8	No	Yes	Yes	91	No	Yes	No	n.a.
Yes	No	No	No	No	No	No	No	7.2	23.1	Yes	Yes	Yes	90	Yes	Yes	Yes	6.0
Yes	No	No	No	No	Yes	No	No	8.7	4.3	No	No	Yes	140	Yes	No	No	n.a.
Yes	No	No	No	No	Yes	No	No	3.3	8.7	Yes	Yes	Yes	126	No	Yes	Yes	0.0
Yes	Yes	No	Yes	No	No	Yes	Yes	2.0	0.0	Yes	No	Yes	112	Yes	Yes	Yes	12.0
Yes	Yes	No	Yes	No	No	Yes	No	8.7	13.0	No	Yes	Yes	126	Yes	Yes	Yes	6.5
Yes	Yes	No	Yes	No	No	No	Yes	2.0	10.7	No	Yes	Yes	91	Yes	Yes	Yes	12.0
Yes	Yes	No	Yes	No	No	Yes	No	4.3	60.7	No	No	Yes	60	Yes	Yes	Yes	0.0
Yes	Yes	No	Yes	No	No	Yes	Yes	4.3	26.7	No	No	Yes	112	Yes	Yes	No	n.a.
Yes	Yes	No	Yes	No	No	Yes	Yes	4.3	26.7	No	No	Yes	112	Yes	Yes	No	n.a.
Yes	No	No	Yes	No	No	No	Yes	3.7	12.5	No	No	Yes	84	Yes	No	Yes	12.0
Yes	No	No	No	No	Yes	Yes	No	8.7	13.0	Yes	No	Yes	126	Yes	Yes	Yes	0.0
Yes	No	No	No	No	No	No	No	19.7	0.0	Yes	Yes	Yes	105	No	Yes	No	14.4
Yes	Yes	No	Yes	No	No	No	No	4.7	8.3	No	No	Yes	98	No	Yes	No	n.a.
Yes	Yes	No	Yes	No	No	Yes	Yes	4.3	7.3	Yes	Yes	Yes	98	Yes	Yes	No	n.a.
Yes	Yes	No	Yes	No	No	No	No	8.3	0.0	Yes	Yes	Yes	56	Yes	Yes	No	n.a.
No	n.a.	n.a.	n.a.	n.a.	n.a.	n.a.	n.a.	n.a.	n.a.	Yes	No	Yes	90	Yes	Yes	No	n.a.
Yes	No	No	Yes	No	Yes	No	Yes	2.0	7.2	Yes	Yes	Yes	365	No	Yes	Yes	8.0
Yes	Yes	No	Yes	No	No	Yes	Yes	3.8	16.8	No	No	Yes	84	No	Yes	No	n.a.
Yes	No	No	No	No	No	No	No	6.6	8.9	No	Yes	Yes	120	Yes	Yes	Yes	12.0
Yes	No	No	No	No	No	No	No	6.6	8.9	No	Yes	Yes	120	Yes	Yes	Yes	12.0
Yes	No	No	No	No	No	No	No	3.0	0.0	No	No	Yes	91	Yes	Yes	No	n.a.
Yes	No	No	No	No	No	No	No	4.3	4.3	Yes	Yes	Yes	410	No	Yes	Yes	9.0
Yes	No	No	Yes	No	No	Yes	Yes	4.3	6.1	Yes	No	Yes	98	Yes	Yes	No	n.a.
Yes	No	No	Yes	No	No	Yes	Yes	8.7	7.2	No	Yes	Yes	84	Yes	No	No	n.a.
Yes	Yes	No	Yes	No	No	Yes	No	2.1	15.2	No	No	Yes	60	Yes	Yes	Yes	6.0
Yes	No	No	Yes	No	No	Yes	Yes	7.9	11.4	No	Yes	Yes	90	No	No	No	n.a.
Yes	Yes	Yes	Yes	Yes	No	Yes	Yes	11.6	8.3	No	No	Yes	98	Yes	Yes	No	n.a.

LABOR MARKET REGULATION DATA

Economy	Fixed-term contracts prohibited for permanent tasks?	Maximum length of fixed-term contracts (months)[a]	Minimum wage for a cashier, age 19, with one year of work experience (US$/month)[b]	Ratio of minimum wage to value added per worker	Maximum length of probationary period (months)[c]	Maximum number of working days per week	Premium for night work (% of hourly pay)	Premium for work on weekly rest day (% of hourly pay)	Premium for overtime work (% of hourly pay)	Restrictions on night work?	Whether non-pregnant and non-nursing women can work the same night hours as men	Restrictions on weekly holiday work?	Restrictions on overtime work?	Paid annual leave (working days)[d]
		Hiring							Working hours					
Canada	No	No limit	1,565.7	0.3	3.0	6.0	0.0	0.0	50.0	No	Yes	No	Yes	10.0
Central African Republic	Yes	24.0	77.1	1.4	2.0	6.0	0.0	50.0	..	No	Yes	Yes	No	25.3
Chad	No	48.0	111.4	0.9	3.0	6.0	0.0	0.0	10.0	Yes	No	No	No	24.7
Chile	No	12.0	393.9	0.2	n.a.	6.0	0.0	30.0	50.0	No	Yes	No	No	15.0
China (Beijing)	No	No limit	290.1	0.3	6.0	6.0	0.0	100.0	50.0	No	Yes	No	No	6.7
China (Shanghai)	No	No limit	353.0	0.4	6.0	6.0	34.0	100.0	50.0	No	Yes	No	No	6.7
Colombia	No	No limit	267.5	0.3	2.0	6.0	35.0	75.0	25.0	No	Yes	No	No	15.0
Comoros	No	36.0	0.0	0.0	6.0	6.0	28.3	0.0	25.0	No	Yes	Yes	No	22.0
Congo, Dem. Rep.	Yes	48.0	65.0	1.0	1.0	6.0	25.0	0.0	37.5	Yes	Yes	No	No	13.0
Congo, Rep.	Yes	24.0	198.6	0.7	4.0	6.0	0.0	0.0	13.7	No	Yes	Yes	Yes	29.7
Costa Rica	Yes	12.0	588.3	0.4	3.0	6.0	0.0	100.0	50.0	Yes	No	No	No	12.0
Côte d'Ivoire	No	24.0	103.7	0.4	2.0	6.0	37.5	0.0	23.8	No	Yes	No	No	27.4
Croatia	Yes	No limit	497.1	0.3	6.0	6.0	0.0	0.0	0.0	Yes	Yes	Yes	No	20.0
Cyprus	No	30.0	1,076.2	0.4	24.0	5.5	0.0	100.0	100.0	No	Yes	No	No	20.0
Czech Republic	No	108.0	559.6	0.3	3.0	6.0	10.0	10.0	25.0	No	Yes	No	No	20.0
Denmark	No	No limit	0.0	0.0	3.0	6.0	0.0	0.0	0.0	No	Yes	No	No	25.0
Djibouti	Yes	24.0	0.0	0.0	2.0	6.0	0.0	0.0	0.0	No	Yes	No	Yes	30.0
Dominica	No	No limit	344.9	0.4	6.0	6.0	0.0	100.0	50.0	No	Yes	No	No	13.3
Dominican Republic	Yes	No limit	334.7	0.4	3.0	5.5	0.0	100.0	35.0	No	Yes	Yes	No	16.7
Ecuador	Yes	No limit	434.8	0.6	3.0	5.0	25.0	100.0	50.0	No	Yes	No	Yes	12.0
Egypt, Arab Rep.	No	No limit	0.0	0.0	3.0	6.0	0.0	0.0	35.0	No	Yes	No	No	24.0
El Salvador	Yes	No limit	252.7	0.5	1.0	6.0	25.0	100.0	125.0	Yes	Yes	Yes	No	11.0
Equatorial Guinea	Yes	24.0	745.9	0.8	1.0	6.0	25.0	50.0	25.0	No	Yes	Yes	No	22.0
Eritrea	Yes	No limit	0.0	0.0	3.0	6.0	0.0	0.0	25.0	No	Yes	No	No	19.0
Estonia	Yes	120.0	533.2	0.2	4.0	5.0	25.0	0.0	50.0	Yes	Yes	No	No	24.0
Ethiopia	Yes	No limit	0.0	0.0	1.5	6.0	0.0	0.0	25.0	No	Yes	No	No	18.3
Fiji	No	No limit	296.3	0.5	3.0	6.0	4.3	0.0	50.0	No	Yes	No	No	10.0
Finland	Yes	60.0	2,026.1	0.3	6.0	6.0	15.7	100.0	50.0	No	Yes	No	No	30.0
France	Yes	18.0	1,765.1	0.3	2.0	6.0	7.5	20.0	25.0	Yes	Yes	Yes	No	30.3
Gabon	No	48.0	275.0	0.3	6.0	6.0	0.0	0.0	10.0	No	Yes	No	No	24.0
Gambia, The	No	No limit	0.0	0.0	12.0	7.0	0.0	0.0	0.0	No	Yes	No	No	0.0
Georgia	No	30.0	17.7	0.0	6.0	7.0	0.0	0.0	0.0	No	Yes	No	No	24.0

Dismissal due to redundancy allowed by law?	Redundancy rules							Redundancy cost		Job quality							
	Third-party notification if 1 worker is dismissed?	Third-party approval if 1 worker is dismissed?	Third-party notification if 9 workers are dismissed?	Third-party approval if 9 workers are dismissed?	Retraining or reassignment?[e]	Priority rules for redundancies?	Priority rules for reemployment?	Notice period for redundancy dismissal (weeks of salary)[d]	Severance pay for redundancy dismissal (weeks of salary)[d]	Equal remuneration for work of equal value?	Gender non-discrimination in hiring?	Paid/unpaid maternity leave mandated by law?[f]	Minimum length of maternity leave (calendar days)[g]	Receive 100% of wages on maternity leave?	Availability of five fully paid days of sick leave?	Whether an unemployment protection scheme exists after one year of employment[i]	Minimum duration of contribution period (in months) for unemployment protection
Yes	No	No	No	No	No	No	No	5.0	5.0	Yes	No	Yes	105	No	No	Yes	3.2
Yes	Yes	No	Yes	Yes	No	Yes	Yes	4.3	17.3	No	No	Yes	98	No	Yes	No	n.a.
Yes	Yes	No	Yes	No	No	Yes	Yes	7.2	5.8	Yes	Yes	Yes	98	No	Yes	No	n.a.
Yes	Yes	No	Yes	No	No	No	No	4.3	23.1	No	No	Yes	126	Yes	No	Yes	12.0
Yes	Yes	No	Yes	No	Yes	Yes	Yes	4.3	23.1	No	Yes	Yes	98	Yes	Yes	Yes	12.0
Yes	Yes	No	Yes	No	Yes	Yes	Yes	4.3	23.1	No	Yes	Yes	128	Yes	Yes	Yes	12.0
Yes	No	No	No	No	No	No	No	0.0	16.7	No	No	Yes	126	Yes	Yes	Yes	12.0
Yes	Yes	No	Yes	No	No	Yes	Yes	8.7	5.0	Yes	Yes	Yes	98	Yes	..	No	n.a.
Yes	Yes	Yes	Yes	Yes	No	Yes	Yes	10.3	0.0	No	Yes	Yes	98	No	No	No	n.a.
Yes	Yes	Yes	Yes	Yes	No	Yes	Yes	8.7	6.9	No	No	Yes	105	Yes	Yes	No	n.a.
Yes	No	No	No	No	No	No	No	4.3	14.4	No	No	Yes	120	Yes	Yes	No	n.a.
Yes	No	No	Yes	No	No	No	Yes	5.8	7.3	Yes	Yes	Yes	98	Yes	Yes	No	n.a.
Yes	Yes	No	Yes	No	No	Yes	Yes	7.9	7.2	Yes	Yes	Yes	208	Yes	Yes	Yes	9.0
Yes	Yes	No	Yes	No	Yes	No	Yes	5.7	0.0	Yes	Yes	Yes	126	No	No	Yes	6.0
Yes	No	No	No	No	No	No	No	8.7	11.6	Yes	Yes	Yes	196	No	No	Yes	12.0
Yes	No	No	No	No	No	No	No	0.0	0.0	Yes	Yes	Yes	126	No	Yes	Yes	12.0
Yes	Yes	No	Yes	No	No	No	Yes	4.3	0.0	Yes	Yes	Yes	98	Yes	Yes	No	n.a.
Yes	No	No	No	No	No	No	Yes	10.1	9.3	No	No	Yes	84	No	No	No	n.a.
Yes	No	No	No	No	No	No	No	4.0	22.2	No	No	Yes	98	Yes	No	No	n.a.
Yes	Yes	No	Yes	No	No	No	No	0.0	31.8	Yes	No	Yes	84	Yes	No	No	n.a.
Yes	Yes	Yes	Yes	Yes	No	Yes	No	10.1	26.7	No	No	Yes	90	Yes	No	Yes	6.0
Yes	No	No	No	No	No	No	No	0.0	22.9	No	No	Yes	112	Yes	No	No	n.a.
Yes	Yes	Yes	Yes	Yes	No	Yes	Yes	4.3	34.3	Yes	No	Yes	84	No	Yes	No	n.a.
Yes	No	No	No	No	No	No	No	3.1	12.3	No	No	Yes	60	Yes	Yes	No	n.a.
Yes	No	No	No	No	Yes	Yes	No	8.6	4.3	Yes	Yes	Yes	140	Yes	No	Yes	12.0
Yes	No	No	Yes	No	Yes	Yes	No	8.7	10.5	No	No	Yes	90	Yes	Yes	No	n.a.
Yes	Yes	No	Yes	No	No	No	No	4.3	5.3	No	Yes	Yes	84	Yes	Yes	No	n.a.
Yes	Yes	No	Yes	No	Yes	No	Yes	10.1	0.0	Yes	Yes	Yes	105	No	Yes	Yes	6.0
Yes	No	No	Yes	No	Yes	Yes	Yes	7.2	4.6	Yes	Yes	Yes	112	Yes	No	Yes	4.0
Yes	Yes	Yes	Yes	Yes	No	Yes	Yes	14.4	4.3	No	No	Yes	98	Yes	Yes	No	n.a.
Yes	No	No	No	No	No	Yes	Yes	26.0	26.0	No	No	Yes	180	Yes	Yes	No	n.a.
Yes	No	No	No	No	No	No	No	4.3	4.3	No	No	Yes	183	Yes	Yes	No	n.a.

LABOR MARKET REGULATION DATA

Economy	Fixed-term contracts prohibited for permanent tasks?	Maximum length of fixed-term contracts (months)[a]	Minimum wage for a cashier, age 19, with one year of work experience (US$/month)[b]	Ratio of minimum wage to value added per worker	Maximum length of probationary period (months)[c]	Maximum number of working days per week	Premium for night work (% of hourly pay)	Premium for work on weekly rest day (% of hourly pay)	Premium for overtime work (% of hourly pay)	Restrictions on night work?	Whether non-pregnant and non-nursing women can work the same night hours as men	Restrictions on weekly holiday work?	Restrictions on overtime work?	Paid annual leave (working days)[d]
		Hiring				Working hours								
Germany	No	No limit	1,736.1	0.3	6.0	6.0	0.0	0.0	0.0	No	Yes	No	No	24.0
Ghana	No	No limit	45.4	0.2	n.a.	5.0	0.0	0.0	0.0	No	Yes	No	No	15.0
Greece	Yes	No limit	687.5	0.3	12.0	6.0	25.0	75.0	27.5	No	Yes	Yes	No	22.3
Grenada	Yes	No limit	250.4	0.2	1.0	6.0	0.0	0.0	50.0	No	Yes	No	No	13.3
Guatemala	Yes	No limit	411.2	0.7	2.0	6.0	0.0	50.0	50.0	Yes	Yes	Yes	Yes	15.0
Guinea	No	24.0	50.0	0.7	1.0	6.0	20.0	0.0	30.0	No	Yes	Yes	No	30.0
Guinea-Bissau	Yes	12.0	0.0	0.0	1.0	6.0	25.0	50.0	0.0	No	No	No	No	21.0
Guyana	No	No limit	202.9	0.4	n.a.	5.5	0.0	0.0	50.0	Yes	Yes	Yes	Yes	12.0
Haiti	No	No limit	154.1	1.5	0.0	6.0	50.0	50.0	50.0	No	Yes	No	No	13.0
Honduras	Yes	24.0	460.4	1.6	2.0	6.0	25.0	100.0	37.5	Yes	Yes	No	No	16.7
Hong Kong SAR, China	No	No limit	885.3	0.2	1.0	6.0	0.0	0.0	0.0	No	Yes	No	No	10.3
Hungary	No	60.0	465.9	0.3	3.0	5.0	15.0	50.0	50.0	No	Yes	No	Yes	21.3
Iceland	No	24.0	2,079.3	0.3	3.0	6.0	0.9	0.8	1.4	No	Yes	No	No	24.0
India (Delhi)	No	No limit	217.6	1.0	3.0	6.0	0.0	0.0	100.0	Yes	No	Yes	Yes	15.0
India (Mumbai)	No	No limit	134.1	0.6	3.0	6.0	0.0	0.0	100.0	Yes	No	Yes	Yes	21.0
Indonesia (Jakarta)	Yes	36.0	248.9	0.6	3.0	6.0	0.0	0.0	75.0	No	Yes	No	No	12.0
Indonesia (Surabaya)	Yes	36.0	244.5	0.6	3.0	6.0	0.0	0.0	75.0	No	Yes	No	No	12.0
Iran, Islamic Rep.	No	No limit	300.8	0.5	1.0	6.0	35.0	40.0	40.0	No	Yes	No	No	24.0
Iraq	Yes	12.0	120.4	0.1	3.0	6.0	0.0	50.0	50.0	Yes	No	No	No	23.0
Ireland	No	No limit	1,832.8	0.3	12.0	6.0	0.0	0.0	0.0	No	Yes	No	No	20.0
Israel	No	No limit	1,280.4	0.3	n.a.	5.5	0.0	50.0	25.0	No	Yes	Yes	No	18.0
Italy	No	36.0	1,973.7	0.5	2.0	6.0	15.0	30.0	15.0	No	Yes	No	No	26.0
Jamaica	No	No limit	213.7	0.4	3.0	6.0	0.0	100.0	0.0	No	Yes	No	No	11.7
Japan (Osaka)	No	No limit	1,329.5	0.3	n.a.	6.0	25.0	35.0	25.0	No	Yes	No	Yes	15.3
Japan (Tokyo)	No	No limit	1,403.3	0.3	n.a.	6.0	25.0	35.0	25.0	No	Yes	No	Yes	15.3
Jordan	No	No limit	299.4	0.6	3.0	6.0	0.0	50.0	25.0	Yes	No	No	Yes	18.7
Kazakhstan	No	No limit	91.4	0.1	3.0	6.0	50.0	50.0	50.0	No	Yes	No	No	18.0
Kenya	No	No limit	233.2	1.1	12.0	6.0	0.0	0.0	50.0	No	Yes	No	No	21.0
Kiribati	No	No limit	173.7	0.5	n.a.	5.0	0.0	0.0	0.0	Yes	Yes	No	Yes	30.0
Korea, Rep.	No	24.0	967.7	0.3	3.0	6.0	50.0	50.0	50.0	No	Yes	No	No	17.0
Kosovo	No	No limit	150.0	0.3	6.0	6.0	30.0	50.0	30.0	No	Yes	No	No	21.0
Kuwait	No	No limit	198.6	0.0	3.0	6.0	0.0	50.0	25.0	No	No	Yes	Yes	30.0

	Redundancy rules							Redundancy cost		Job quality							
Dismissal due to redundancy allowed by law?	Third-party notification if 1 worker is dismissed?	Third-party approval if 1 worker is dismissed?	Third-party notification if 9 workers are dismissed?	Third-party approval if 9 workers are dismissed?	Retraining or reassignment?[e]	Priority rules for redundancies?	Priority rules for reemployment?	Notice period for redundancy dismissal (weeks of salary)[d]	Severance pay for redundancy dismissal (weeks of salary)[d]	Equal remuneration for work of equal value?	Gender non-discrimination in hiring?	Paid/unpaid maternity leave mandated by law?[f]	Minimum length of maternity leave (calendar days)[g]	Receive 100% of wages on maternity leave?	Availability of five fully paid days of sick leave?	Whether an unemployment protection scheme exists after one year of employment[i]	Minimum duration of contribution period (in months) for unemployment protection
Yes	Yes	No	Yes	No	Yes	Yes	No	10.0	11.6	No	Yes	Yes	98	Yes	Yes	Yes	12.0
Yes	Yes	Yes	Yes	Yes	No	No	No	3.6	46.2	No	No	Yes	84	Yes	No	No	n.a.
Yes	No	No	Yes	Yes	No	Yes	No	0.0	15.9	Yes	Yes	Yes	119	Yes	No	Yes	4.0
Yes	No	No	No	No	No	No	No	7.2	5.3	Yes	Yes	Yes	84	No	Yes	No	n.a.
Yes	No	No	No	No	No	No	No	0.0	27.0	No	No	Yes	84	Yes	Yes	No	n.a.
Yes	Yes	No	Yes	No	No	No	No	4.3	5.8	Yes	Yes	Yes	98	Yes	No	No	n.a.
Yes	Yes	Yes	Yes	Yes	No	Yes	Yes	0.0	26.0	No	No	Yes	60	Yes	Yes	No	n.a.
Yes	Yes	No	Yes	No	No	No	No	4.3	7.0	Yes	Yes	Yes	91	No	No	No	n.a.
Yes	No	No	No	No	No	No	No	10.1	0.0	No	No	Yes	42	Yes	Yes	No	n.a.
Yes	Yes	Yes	Yes	Yes	No	Yes	No	7.2	23.1	No	Yes	Yes	84	Yes	Yes	No	n.a.
Yes	No	No	No	No	No	No	No	4.3	1.4	No	Yes	Yes	70	No	No	Yes	0.0
Yes	No	No	No	No	No	No	No	6.2	7.2	No	Yes	Yes	168	No	Yes	Yes	12.0
Yes	No	No	No	No	No	No	No	13.0	0.0	Yes	Yes	Yes	90	No	Yes	Yes	3.0
Yes	Yes	No	Yes	No	No	Yes	Yes	4.3	11.4	No	Yes	Yes	182	Yes	No	No	n.a.
Yes	Yes	No	Yes	No	No	Yes	Yes	4.3	11.4	No	Yes	Yes	182	Yes	No	No	n.a.
Yes	Yes	Yes	Yes	Yes	Yes	No	No	0.0	57.8	No	No	Yes	90	Yes	Yes	No	n.a.
Yes	Yes	Yes	Yes	Yes	Yes	No	No	0.0	57.8	No	No	Yes	90	Yes	Yes	No	n.a.
Yes	Yes	Yes	Yes	Yes	No	No	No	0.0	23.1	No	No	Yes	270	No	No	Yes	6.0
Yes	Yes	Yes	Yes	Yes	No	No	No	0.0	10.7	No	Yes	Yes	98	Yes	Yes	No	n.a.
Yes	No	No	Yes	No	No	No	No	3.7	10.7	Yes	Yes	Yes	182	No	No	No	24.0
Yes	No	No	No	No	No	No	No	4.3	23.1	Yes	Yes	Yes	98	Yes	No	Yes	12.0
Yes	Yes	No	Yes	No	Yes	Yes	Yes	4.5	0.0	Yes	No	Yes	150	No	No	Yes	3.0
Yes	No	No	No	No	No	No	No	4.0	10.0	No	No	Yes	56	Yes	Yes	No	n.a.
Yes	No	No	No	No	No	No	No	4.3	0.0	No	Yes	Yes	98	No	No	Yes	12.0
Yes	No	No	No	No	No	No	No	4.3	0.0	No	Yes	Yes	98	No	No	Yes	12.0
Yes	Yes	Yes	Yes	Yes	No	No	Yes	4.3	0.0	No	No	Yes	70	Yes	Yes	No	36.0
Yes	Yes	No	Yes	No	No	No	No	4.3	4.3	No	Yes	Yes	126	Yes	Yes	Yes	0.0
Yes	Yes	No	Yes	No	No	Yes	No	4.3	2.1	Yes	Yes	Yes	90	Yes	Yes	No	n.a.
Yes	Yes	No	Yes	No	Yes	No	No	3.7	0.0	Yes	Yes	Yes	84	No	Yes	No	n.a.
Yes	Yes	No	Yes	No	No	No	Yes	4.3	23.1	No	Yes	Yes	90	Yes	No	Yes	6.0
Yes	No	No	No	No	Yes	Yes	Yes	4.3	7.2	Yes	Yes	Yes	270	No	Yes	No	n.a.
Yes	No	No	No	No	No	No	No	13.0	15.1	No	No	Yes	70	Yes	Yes	Yes	6.0

LABOR MARKET REGULATION DATA

Economy	Hiring					Working hours								
	Fixed-term contracts prohibited for permanent tasks?	Maximum length of fixed-term contracts (months)[a]	Minimum wage for a cashier, age 19, with one year of work experience (US$/month)[b]	Ratio of minimum wage to value added per worker	Maximum length of probationary period (months)[c]	Maximum number of working days per week	Premium for night work (% of hourly pay)	Premium for work on weekly rest day (% of hourly pay)	Premium for overtime work (% of hourly pay)	Restrictions on night work?	Whether non-pregnant and non-nursing women can work the same night hours as men	Restrictions on weekly holiday work?	Restrictions on overtime work?	Paid annual leave (working days)[d]
Kyrgyz Republic	Yes	60.0	17.4	0.1	3.0	6.0	50.0	100.0	50.0	No	Yes	No	No	20.0
Lao PDR	No	36.0	105.8	0.4	2.0	6.0	15.0	150.0	50.0	No	Yes	No	No	15.0
Latvia	Yes	60.0	434.6	0.2	3.0	5.5	50.0	0.0	100.0	No	Yes	No	No	20.0
Lebanon	No	24.0	438.9	0.5	3.0	5.5	0.0	50.0	50.0	No	Yes	No	Yes	15.0
Lesotho	No	No limit	140.7	0.8	4.0	6.0	0.0	100.0	25.0	Yes	Yes	No	No	12.0
Liberia	No	No limit	141.4	2.5	3.0	5.5	0.0	0.0	50.0	No	Yes	No	Yes	16.5
Libya	No	48.0	323.7	0.5	1.0	6.0	0.0	0.0	50.0	No	Yes	No	No	30.0
Lithuania	No	60.0	433.5	0.2	3.0	5.5	50.0	100.0	50.0	No	Yes	No	No	20.7
Luxembourg	Yes	24.0	2,764.4	0.3	6.0	5.5	0.0	70.0	40.0	No	Yes	Yes	No	25.0
Macedonia, FYR	No	60.0	262.5	0.4	6.0	6.0	35.0	50.0	35.0	Yes	Yes	No	No	20.0
Madagascar	Yes	24.0	55.7	0.9	3.0	6.0	30.0	40.0	30.0	No	Yes	No	No	24.0
Malawi	Yes	No limit	27.5	0.5	12.0	6.0	0.0	0.0	50.0	No	Yes	No	No	18.0
Malaysia	No	No limit	257.2	0.2	n.a.	6.0	0.0	100.0	50.0	No	Yes	No	No	13.3
Maldives	No	24.0	0.0	0.0	3.0	6.0	0.0	50.0	25.0	No	Yes	No	No	30.0
Mali	Yes	72.0	67.4	0.5	6.0	6.0	0.0	0.0	10.0	No	Yes	No	No	22.0
Malta	No	48.0	837.4	0.3	6.0	6.0	0.0	100.0	50.0	No	Yes	No	No	24.0
Marshall Islands	No	No limit	517.5	0.8	n.a.	7.0	0.0	0.0	0.0	No	Yes	No	No	0.0
Mauritania	No	24.0	90.8	0.6	1.0	6.0	0.0	0.0	15.0	No	Yes	Yes	No	18.0
Mauritius	No	24.0	236.8	0.2	n.a.	6.0	0.0	100.0	50.0	No	Yes	No	No	17.0
Mexico (Mexico City)	Yes	No limit	151.7	0.1	1.0	6.0	0.0	25.0	100.0	No	Yes	No	Yes	12.0
Mexico (Monterrey)	Yes	No limit	151.7	0.1	1.0	6.0	0.0	25.0	100.0	No	Yes	No	Yes	12.0
Micronesia, Fed. Sts.	No	No limit	361.7	0.7	n.a.	7.0	0.0	0.0	50.0	No	Yes	No	No	0.0
Moldova	Yes	No limit	110.4	0.5	0.5	6.0	50.0	100.0	50.0	Yes	Yes	Yes	No	20.0
Mongolia	No	No limit	116.9	0.3	3.0	5.0	0.0	50.0	50.0	No	Yes	No	Yes	16.0
Montenegro	No	24.0	218.9	0.3	6.0	6.0	40.0	0.0	40.0	No	No	No	No	20.7
Morocco	Yes	12.0	268.3	0.8	1.5	6.0	0.0	0.0	25.0	No	Yes	Yes	No	19.5
Mozambique	Yes	72.0	103.4	1.3	3.0	6.0	25.0	100.0	50.0	No	Yes	Yes	No	24.0
Myanmar	No	No limit	68.3	0.4	n.a.	6.0	0.0	100.0	100.0	Yes	Yes	No	No	10.0
Namibia	No	No limit	0.0	0.0	n.a.	5.5	6.0	100.0	50.0	No	Yes	No	No	20.0
Nepal	Yes	No limit	89.1	0.9	12.0	6.0	0.0	50.0	50.0	No	No	No	No	18.0
Netherlands	No	24.0	931.8	0.2	2.0	5.5	0.0	0.0	0.0	No	Yes	No	No	20.0
New Zealand	No	No limit	1,942.8	0.4	3.0	7.0	0.0	0.0	0.0	No	Yes	No	No	20.0

	Redundancy rules							Redundancy cost		Job quality							
Dismissal due to redundancy allowed by law?	Third-party notification if 1 worker is dismissed?	Third-party approval if 1 worker is dismissed?	Third-party notification if 9 workers are dismissed?	Third-party approval if 9 workers are dismissed?	Retraining or reassignment?[e]	Priority rules for redundancies?	Priority rules for reemployment?	Notice period for redundancy dismissal (weeks of salary)[d]	Severance pay for redundancy dismissal (weeks of salary)[d]	Equal remuneration for work of equal value?	Gender non-discrimination in hiring?	Paid/unpaid maternity leave mandated by law?[f]	Minimum length of maternity leave (calendar days)[g]	Receive 100% of wages on maternity leave?	Availability of five fully paid days of sick leave?	Whether an unemployment protection scheme exists after one year of employment[i]	Minimum duration of contribution period (in months) for unemployment protection
Yes	No	No	No	No	No	No	No	4.3	13.0	No	No	Yes	126	No	No	Yes	12.0
Yes	Yes	No	Yes	No	No	No	No	6.4	27.7	No	No	Yes	105	Yes	Yes	No	n.a.
Yes	No	No	No	No	Yes	Yes	No	4.3	8.7	Yes	Yes	Yes	112	No	No	Yes	12.0
Yes	Yes	No	Yes	No	No	Yes	Yes	8.7	0.0	No	No	Yes	70	Yes	Yes	No	n.a.
Yes	No	No	No	No	No	No	No	4.3	10.7	Yes	No	Yes	84	Yes	Yes	No	n.a.
Yes	Yes	No	Yes	No	No	Yes	Yes	4.3	21.3	Yes	Yes	Yes	98	Yes	Yes	No	n.a.
Yes	Yes	No	Yes	No	No	No	No	4.3	15.2	Yes	No	Yes	98	Yes	Yes	No	n.a.
Yes	No	No	No	No	Yes	Yes	No	8.7	15.9	Yes	Yes	Yes	126	Yes	Yes	No	18.0
Yes	Yes	No	Yes	No	No	No	Yes	17.3	4.3	Yes	Yes	Yes	112	Yes	Yes	Yes	6.0
Yes	No	No	No	No	No	No	No	4.3	8.7	No	Yes	Yes	270	Yes	Yes	Yes	12.0
Yes	No	No	Yes	Yes	No	Yes	Yes	5.8	8.9	No	No	Yes	98	Yes	Yes	No	n.a.
Yes	No	No	No	No	No	No	No	4.3	12.3	Yes	Yes	Yes	56	Yes	Yes	No	n.a.
Yes	No	No	Yes	No	No	No	No	6.7	17.2	No	No	Yes	60	Yes	Yes	No	n.a.
Yes	No	No	No	No	No	No	No	7.2	0.0	No	Yes	Yes	60	Yes	Yes	No	n.a.
Yes	Yes	No	Yes	No	No	Yes	Yes	4.3	9.3	No	No	Yes	98	Yes	Yes	No	n.a.
Yes	No	No	No	No	No	Yes	Yes	7.3	0.0	Yes	Yes	Yes	126	No	Yes	Yes	6.0
Yes	No	No	No	No	No	No	No	0.0	0.0	No	No	No	n.a.	n.a.	No	No	n.a.
Yes	Yes	No	Yes	No	No	Yes	Yes	4.3	6.1	No	Yes	Yes	98	Yes	Yes	No	n.a.
Yes	Yes	No	Yes	No	No	Yes	No	4.3	69.3	Yes	Yes	Yes	98	Yes	Yes	Yes	6.0
Yes	Yes	Yes	Yes	Yes	No	Yes	Yes	0.0	22.0	No	Yes	Yes	84	Yes	No	No	n.a.
Yes	Yes	Yes	Yes	Yes	No	Yes	Yes	0.0	22.0	No	Yes	Yes	84	Yes	No	No	n.a.
Yes	No	No	No	No	No	No	No	0.0	0.0	No	No	No	n.a.	n.a.	No	No	n.a.
Yes	Yes	No	Yes	No	Yes	Yes	No	8.7	15.0	No	Yes	Yes	126	Yes	Yes	Yes	9.0
Yes	No	No	No	No	No	No	No	4.3	4.3	No	No	Yes	120	Yes	Yes	Yes	9.0
Yes	No	No	No	No	Yes	No	No	4.3	6.9	Yes	Yes	Yes	45	Yes	Yes	Yes	12.0
Yes	Yes	Yes	Yes	Yes	Yes	Yes	Yes	7.2	13.5	Yes	Yes	Yes	98	Yes	No	No	36.0
Yes	Yes	No	Yes	No	No	No	No	4.3	33.2	No	No	Yes	60	Yes	No	No	n.a.
Yes	No	No	No	No	No	No	No	4.3	18.8	No	No	Yes	98	No	Yes	No	36.0
Yes	No	No	Yes	No	No	No	No	4.3	5.3	Yes	Yes	Yes	84	Yes	Yes	No	n.a.
Yes	Yes	Yes	Yes	Yes	No	Yes	Yes	4.3	22.9	No	No	Yes	52	Yes	No	No	n.a.
Yes	Yes	Yes	Yes	Yes	Yes	Yes	No	8.7	7.2	Yes	Yes	Yes	112	Yes	No	Yes	6.0
Yes	No	No	No	No	Yes	No	No	0.0	0.0	No	Yes	No	n.a.	No	Yes	No	n.a.

LABOR MARKET REGULATION DATA

Economy	Fixed-term contracts prohibited for permanent tasks?	Maximum length of fixed-term contracts (months)[a]	Minimum wage for a cashier, age 19, with one year of work experience (US$/month)[b]	Ratio of minimum wage to value added per worker	Maximum length of probationary period (months)[c]	Maximum number of working days per week	Premium for night work (% of hourly pay)	Premium for work on weekly rest day (% of hourly pay)	Premium for overtime work (% of hourly pay)	Restrictions on night work?	Whether non-pregnant and non-nursing women can work the same night hours as men	Restrictions on weekly holiday work?	Restrictions on overtime work?	Paid annual leave (working days)[d]
		Hiring									**Working hours**			
Nicaragua	No	No limit	227.3	0.9	1.0	6.0	0.0	100.0	100.0	Yes	Yes	Yes	Yes	30.0
Niger	Yes	48.0	52.6	0.8	6.0	6.0	37.5	0.0	10.0	No	Yes	No	No	22.0
Nigeria (Kano)	No	No limit	81.8	0.2	n.a.	6.0	0.0	0.0	0.0	No	Yes	No	No	6.0
Nigeria (Lagos)	No	No limit	81.8	0.2	n.a.	6.0	0.0	0.0	0.0	No	Yes	No	No	6.0
Norway	No	48.0	3,286.3	0.3	6.0	6.0	0.0	0.0	40.0	Yes	Yes	Yes	No	21.0
Oman[h]	No	No limit	845.3	0.5	3.0	5.0	50.0	100.0	25.0	Yes	No	No	Yes	22.0
Pakistan (Karachi)	Yes	9.0	129.8	0.6	3.0	6.0	0.0	100.0	100.0	Yes	No	Yes	No	14.0
Pakistan (Lahore)	Yes	9.0	129.8	0.6	3.0	6.0	0.0	100.0	100.0	Yes	No	Yes	No	14.0
Palau	No	No limit	693.5	0.5	n.a.	7.0	0.0	0.0	0.0	No	Yes	No	No	0.0
Panama	Yes	12.0	558.8	0.4	3.0	6.0	13.0	50.0	50.0	No	Yes	Yes	Yes	22.0
Papua New Guinea	No	No limit	213.0	0.6	n.a.	6.0	0.0	0.0	50.0	No	Yes	No	No	11.0
Paraguay	Yes	No limit	365.0	0.7	1.0	6.0	30.0	100.0	50.0	Yes	Yes	No	Yes	20.0
Peru	Yes	60.0	258.3	0.3	3.0	6.0	35.0	100.0	25.0	No	Yes	No	No	13.0
Philippines	No	No limit	293.5	0.6	6.0	6.0	10.0	30.0	25.0	No	Yes	No	No	5.0
Poland	No	33.0	540.2	0.4	3.0	5.5	20.0	100.0	50.0	No	Yes	No	No	22.0
Portugal	Yes	36.0	735.2	0.3	3.0	6.0	25.0	50.0	31.3	No	Yes	Yes	No	22.0
Puerto Rico (U.S.)	No	No limit	1,256.7	0.3	9.0	7.0	0.0	100.0	50.0	No	Yes	No	No	11.0
Qatar	No	No limit	0.0	0.0	6.0	6.0	0.0	0.0	25.0	Yes	Yes	No	Yes	22.0
Romania	Yes	60.0	365.7	0.3	3.0	5.0	25.0	100.0	75.0	No	Yes	No	No	20.0
Russian Federation (Moscow)	Yes	60.0	299.0	0.3	3.0	6.0	20.0	100.0	50.0	No	Yes	Yes	No	22.0
Russian Federation (St. Petersburg)	Yes	60.0	272.5	0.2	3.0	6.0	20.0	100.0	50.0	No	Yes	Yes	No	22.0
Rwanda	No	No limit	0.0	0.0	6.0	6.0	0.0	0.0	0.0	No	Yes	No	No	19.3
Samoa	No	No limit	207.6	0.4	3.0	6.0	0.0	0.0	50.0	No	Yes	No	No	10.0
San Marino	Yes	18.0	2,147.1	0.4	1.6	6.0	35.0	0.0	26.3	No	Yes	No	No	26.0
São Tomé and Príncipe	Yes	36.0	71.0	0.3	1.0	6.0	25.0	100.0	37.5	No	No	Yes	No	26.0
Saudi Arabia	No	48.0	0.0	0.0	3.0	6.0	0.0	50.0	50.0	No	No	Yes	No	23.3
Senegal	Yes	24.0	160.9	1.1	2.0	6.0	38.0	0.0	10.0	No	Yes	Yes	Yes	24.3
Serbia	Yes	24.0	212.0	0.3	6.0	6.0	26.0	110.0	26.0	No	Yes	No	No	20.0
Seychelles	No	No limit	575.5	0.3	6.0	6.0	0.0	100.0	50.0	No	Yes	No	No	21.0
Sierra Leone	Yes	No limit	84.5	1.1	6.0	5.5	15.0	100.0	50.0	No	Yes	No	No	23.0
Singapore	No	No limit	0.0	0.0	6.0	6.0	0.0	100.0	50.0	No	Yes	No	No	10.7

	Redundancy rules							Redundancy cost		Job quality							
Dismissal due to redundancy allowed by law?	Third-party notification if 1 worker is dismissed?	Third-party approval if 1 worker is dismissed?	Third-party notification if 9 workers are dismissed?	Third-party approval if 9 workers are dismissed?	Retraining or reassignment?[e]	Priority rules for redundancies?	Priority rules for reemployment?	Notice period for redundancy dismissal (weeks of salary)[d]	Severance pay for redundancy dismissal (weeks of salary)[d]	Equal remuneration for work of equal value?	Gender non-discrimination in hiring?	Paid/unpaid maternity leave mandated by law?[f]	Minimum length of maternity leave (calendar days)[g]	Receive 100% of wages on maternity leave?	Availability of five fully paid days of sick leave?	Whether an unemployment protection scheme exists after one year of employment[i]	Minimum duration of contribution period (in months) for unemployment protection
Yes	No	No	No	No	No	No	No	0.0	14.9	No	Yes	Yes	84	Yes	No	No	n.a.
Yes	Yes	No	Yes	No	Yes	Yes	Yes	4.3	9.7	Yes	Yes	Yes	98	Yes	Yes	No	n.a.
Yes	No	No	Yes	No	No	Yes	No	3.2	0.0	No	No	Yes	84	No	Yes	No	n.a.
Yes	No	No	Yes	No	No	Yes	No	3.2	0.0	No	No	Yes	84	No	Yes	No	n.a.
Yes	No	No	No	No	Yes	Yes	Yes	8.7	0.0	Yes	Yes	Yes	343	No	Yes	Yes	0.0
No	n.a.	n.a.	n.a.	n.a.	n.a.	n.a.	n.a.	n.a.	n.a.	No	No	Yes	50	Yes	Yes	No	n.a.
Yes	No	No	No	No	No	Yes	Yes	4.3	22.9	No	No	Yes	84	Yes	Yes	No	n.a.
Yes	No	No	No	No	No	Yes	Yes	4.3	22.9	No	No	Yes	84	Yes	Yes	No	n.a.
Yes	No	No	No	No	No	No	No	0.0	0.0	No	No	No	n.a.	n.a.	No	No	n.a.
Yes	Yes	Yes	Yes	Yes	No	Yes	No	0.0	18.1	No	No	Yes	98	Yes	Yes	No	n.a.
Yes	No	No	No	No	No	No	No	3.3	9.2	No	No	Yes	0	n.a.	Yes	No	n.a.
Yes	Yes	Yes	Yes	Yes	No	No	Yes	10.8	18.6	Yes	No	Yes	126	No	Yes	No	n.a.
Yes	Yes	Yes	Yes	Yes	No	No	Yes	0.0	11.4	Yes	No	Yes	98	Yes	Yes	No	n.a.
Yes	Yes	No	Yes	No	No	Yes	No	4.3	23.1	Yes	No	Yes	60	Yes	No	No	n.a.
Yes	No	No	No	No	No	Yes	Yes	10.1	8.7	No	Yes	Yes	140	Yes	No	Yes	12.0
Yes	Yes	No	Yes	No	Yes	No	No	7.9	9.1	Yes	Yes	Yes	120	Yes	No	Yes	12.0
Yes	No	No	No	No	No	Yes	Yes	0.0	0.0	No	Yes	Yes	56	Yes	Yes	Yes	6.0
Yes	No	No	No	No	No	No	No	7.2	16.0	No	No	Yes	50	Yes	Yes	No	n.a.
Yes	No	No	No	No	No	Yes	Yes	4.0	0.0	Yes	Yes	Yes	126	No	Yes	Yes	12.0
Yes	Yes	No	Yes	No	Yes	Yes	No	8.7	8.7	No	Yes	Yes	140	Yes	Yes	Yes	0.0
Yes	Yes	No	Yes	No	Yes	Yes	No	8.7	8.7	No	Yes	Yes	140	Yes	Yes	Yes	0.0
Yes	Yes	No	Yes	No	No	Yes	No	4.3	8.7	No	No	Yes	84	Yes	Yes	No	n.a.
Yes	No	No	No	No	No	No	No	3.3	0.0	Yes	No	Yes	28	Yes	Yes	No	n.a.
Yes	Yes	Yes	Yes	Yes	No	Yes	Yes	0.0	0.0	No	No	Yes	630	No	Yes	Yes	9.0
Yes	Yes	Yes	Yes	Yes	No	No	Yes	4.3	26.0	No	No	Yes	98	Yes	No	No	n.a.
Yes	No	No	No	No	No	No	No	8.6	15.2	No	No	Yes	70	Yes	Yes	Yes	12.0
Yes	Yes	No	Yes	No	No	Yes	Yes	4.3	10.5	No	No	Yes	98	Yes	Yes	No	n.a.
Yes	No	No	No	No	Yes	No	Yes	0.0	7.7	Yes	Yes	Yes	135	Yes	No	Yes	12.0
Yes	Yes	Yes	Yes	Yes	No	No	No	4.3	7.6	No	No	Yes	98	No	Yes	No	n.a.
Yes	Yes	No	Yes	No	Yes	Yes	Yes	13.0	62.5	No	No	Yes	84	Yes	Yes	No	n.a.
Yes	No	No	Yes	No	No	No	No	3.0	0.0	No	No	Yes	105	Yes	Yes	No	n.a.

LABOR MARKET REGULATION DATA

Economy	Fixed-term contracts prohibited for permanent tasks?	Maximum length of fixed-term contracts (months)[a]	Minimum wage for a cashier, age 19, with one year of work experience (US$/month)[b]	Ratio of minimum wage to value added per worker	Maximum length of probationary period (months)[c]	Maximum number of working days per week	Premium for night work (% of hourly pay)	Premium for work on weekly rest day (% of hourly pay)	Premium for overtime work (% of hourly pay)	Restrictions on night work?	Whether non-pregnant and non-nursing women can work the same night hours as men	Restrictions on weekly holiday work?	Restrictions on overtime work?	Paid annual leave (working days)[d]
		Hiring					Working hours							
Slovak Republic	No	24.0	502.1	0.3	3.0	6.0	20.0	0.0	25.0	No	Yes	No	No	25.0
Slovenia	Yes	24.0	919.8	0.3	6.0	6.0	75.0	100.0	30.0	No	Yes	No	No	22.0
Solomon Islands	No	No limit	114.5	0.4	n.a.	6.0	0.0	0.0	50.0	No	No	No	No	15.0
Somalia	No	No limit	0.0	0.0	n.a.	6.0	0.0	0.0	25.0	No	No	No	No	80.0
South Africa	Yes	No limit	285.5	0.4	n.a.	6.0	0.0	100.0	50.0	Yes	Yes	No	No	18.3
South Sudan	No	48.0	0.0	0.0	3.0	0.0	0.0	0.0	50.0	No	No	No	No	23.3
Spain	Yes	48.0	1,005.9	0.3	6.0	5.5	6.6	0.0	0.0	No	Yes	No	No	22.0
Sri Lanka	No	No limit	75.1	0.2	n.a.	5.5	0.0	0.0	50.0	Yes	No	No	No	14.0
St. Kitts and Nevis	No	No limit	563.3	0.3	3.0	0.0	0.0	0.0	50.0	No	Yes	No	No	14.0
St. Lucia	No	24.0	0.0	0.0	3.0	6.0	0.0	100.0	50.0	No	Yes	No	No	21.0
St. Vincent and the Grenadines	No	No limit	311.9	0.4	6.0	6.0	0.0	0.0	50.0	No	Yes	No	No	18.7
Sudan	No	48.0	67.1	0.2	3.0	6.0	0.0	0.0	50.0	No	No	No	No	23.3
Suriname	No	No limit	215.4	0.2	2.0	6.0	0.0	100.0	50.0	No	Yes	No	No	16.0
Swaziland	No	No limit	130.5	0.3	3.0	5.5	0.0	0.0	50.0	No	Yes	No	No	15.0
Sweden	No	24.0	0.0	0.0	6.0	5.5	0.0	0.0	0.0	No	Yes	Yes	No	25.0
Switzerland	No	120.0	0.0	0.0	3.0	6.0	25.0	50.0	25.0	Yes	Yes	Yes	No	20.0
Syrian Arab Republic	No	60.0	35.2	0.2	3.0	6.0	0.0	100.0	37.5	No	No	Yes	No	21.7
Taiwan, China	Yes	No limit	649.8	0.2	n.a.	6.0	0.0	100.0	33.0	No	Yes	No	No	12.7
Tajikistan	Yes	No limit	60.4	0.4	3.0	6.0	50.0	100.0	100.0	Yes	Yes	No	No	18.0
Tanzania	Yes	No limit	54.5	0.4	6.0	6.0	5.0	100.0	50.0	No	Yes	No	No	20.0
Thailand	Yes	No limit	229.4	0.3	0.0	6.0	0.0	0.0	50.0	No	Yes	No	No	6.0
Timor-Leste	Yes	36.0	115.0	0.4	1.0	6.0	25.0	100.0	50.0	No	Yes	Yes	No	12.0
Togo	Yes	48.0	92.0	1.1	2.0	6.0	0.0	0.0	20.0	No	Yes	No	No	30.0
Tonga[h]	No	No limit	0.0	0.0	n.a.	0.0	0.0	0.0	0.0	No	Yes	Yes	No	0.0
Trinidad and Tobago	No	No limit	411.9	0.2	n.a.	6.0	0.0	100.0	50.0	No	Yes	No	No	10.0
Tunisia	No	48.0	243.4	0.5	6.0	6.0	0.0	100.0	25.0	No	No	No	No	19.0
Turkey	Yes	No limit	616.3	0.4	2.0	6.0	0.0	100.0	50.0	Yes	No	No	No	18.0
Uganda	No	No limit	1.9	0.0	12.0	6.0	0.0	0.0	50.0	No	Yes	No	No	21.0
Ukraine	Yes	No limit	133.8	0.5	3.0	5.5	20.0	100.0	100.0	No	No	Yes	Yes	18.0
United Arab Emirates	No	No limit	0.0	0.0	6.0	6.0	0.0	50.0	25.0	No	No	Yes	No	26.0
United Kingdom	No	No limit	1,409.2	0.3	6.0	6.0	0.0	0.0	0.0	No	Yes	No	No	28.0

	Redundancy rules							Redundancy cost		Job quality							
Dismissal due to redundancy allowed by law?	Third-party notification if 1 worker is dismissed?	Third-party approval if 1 worker is dismissed?	Third-party notification if 9 workers are dismissed?	Third-party approval if 9 workers are dismissed?	Retraining or reassignment?[e]	Priority rules for redundancies?	Priority rules for reemployment?	Notice period for redundancy dismissal (weeks of salary)[d]	Severance pay for redundancy dismissal (weeks of salary)[d]	Equal remuneration for work of equal value?	Gender non-discrimination in hiring?	Paid/unpaid maternity leave mandated by law?[f]	Minimum length of maternity leave (calendar days)[g]	Receive 100% of wages on maternity leave?	Availability of five fully paid days of sick leave?	Whether an unemployment protection scheme exists after one year of employment[i]	Minimum duration of contribution period (in months) for unemployment protection
Yes	Yes	No	Yes	No	Yes	No	No	11.6	7.2	Yes	Yes	Yes	238	No	No	No	24.0
Yes	No	No	No	No	No	Yes	No	5.3	5.3	Yes	Yes	Yes	105	Yes	Yes	Yes	9.0
Yes	Yes	No	Yes	No	No	No	No	4.3	10.7	No	No	Yes	84	No	Yes	No	n.a.
Yes	No	No	No	No	No	No	No	4.3	23.1	No	No	Yes	98	No	No	No	n.a.
Yes	Yes	No	Yes	No	Yes	No	No	4.0	5.3	Yes	No	Yes	120	No	Yes	Yes	0.0
Yes	Yes	Yes	Yes	Yes	No	No	No	4.3	21.7	No	No	Yes	56	Yes	Yes	No	n.a.
Yes	Yes	No	Yes	No	No	No	No	2.1	15.2	Yes	No	Yes	112	Yes	No	Yes	12.0
Yes	Yes	Yes	Yes	Yes	No	No	No	4.3	54.2	No	No	Yes	84	Yes	Yes	No	n.a.
Yes	No	No	No	No	No	No	Yes	8.7	0.0	No	No	Yes	91	No	No	No	n.a.
Yes	Yes	No	Yes	No	No	No	No	3.7	9.3	Yes	Yes	Yes	91	No	Yes	No	n.a.
Yes	No	No	Yes	No	No	No	Yes	4.0	10.0	No	No	Yes	91	No	Yes	No	n.a.
Yes	Yes	Yes	Yes	Yes	No	No	No	4.3	21.7	No	No	Yes	56	Yes	Yes	No	n.a.
Yes	Yes	Yes	Yes	Yes	No	No	No	0.0	8.8	No	No	No	n.a.	n.a.	No	No	n.a.
Yes	No	No	Yes	No	No	Yes	No	5.9	8.7	No	No	Yes	14	Yes	Yes	No	n.a.
Yes	No	No	Yes	No	Yes	Yes	Yes	14.4	0.0	Yes	Yes	Yes	480	No	No	Yes	6.0
Yes	No	No	No	No	No	No	No	10.1	0.0	Yes	Yes	Yes	98	No	Yes	Yes	12.0
Yes	Yes	Yes	Yes	Yes	No	No	No	8.7	0.0	No	No	Yes	120	Yes	No	No	n.a.
Yes	Yes	No	Yes	No	Yes	No	Yes	3.8	11.6	Yes	Yes	Yes	56	Yes	No	Yes	12.0
Yes	Yes	No	Yes	No	Yes	Yes	No	8.7	13.0	Yes	Yes	Yes	140	Yes	No	No	18.0
Yes	Yes	Yes	Yes	Yes	No	No	Yes	4.0	5.3	Yes	Yes	Yes	84	Yes	Yes	No	n.a.
Yes	No	No	No	No	No	No	No	4.3	31.7	No	No	Yes	90	Yes	Yes	Yes	6.0
Yes	Yes	No	Yes	No	No	No	No	3.6	0.0	No	No	Yes	84	Yes	Yes	No	n.a.
Yes	Yes	No	Yes	No	No	Yes	Yes	4.3	8.8	Yes	Yes	Yes	98	Yes	Yes	No	n.a.
No	No	No	No	No	No	No	No	n.a.	n.a.	No	No	No	n.a.	n.a.	No	No	n.a.
Yes	No	No	Yes	No	No	No	No	6.4	14.1	No	Yes	Yes	98	Yes	Yes	No	n.a.
Yes	Yes	Yes	Yes	Yes	Yes	Yes	Yes	4.3	17.2	No	No	Yes	30	No	Yes	No	n.a.
Yes	No	No	No	No	No	No	Yes	6.7	23.1	Yes	Yes	Yes	112	No	Yes	Yes	6.0
Yes	No	No	No	No	No	No	No	8.7	0.0	Yes	No	Yes	84	Yes	Yes	No	n.a.
Yes	No	No	No	No	Yes	Yes	Yes	8.7	4.3	No	Yes	Yes	126	Yes	Yes	Yes	6.0
Yes	No	No	Yes	No	No	No	No	4.3	0.0	No	No	Yes	45	Yes	Yes	No	n.a.
Yes	No	No	No	No	No	No	No	5.3	4.0	Yes	Yes	Yes	14	No	No	Yes	0.0

LABOR MARKET REGULATION DATA

Economy	Hiring					Working hours								
	Fixed-term contracts prohibited for permanent tasks?	Maximum length of fixed-term contracts (months)[a]	Minimum wage for a cashier, age 19, with one year of work experience (US$/month)[b]	Ratio of minimum wage to value added per worker	Maximum length of probationary period (months)[c]	Maximum number of working days per week	Premium for night work (% of hourly pay)	Premium for work on weekly rest day (% of hourly pay)	Premium for overtime work (% of hourly pay)	Restrictions on night work?	Whether non-pregnant and non-nursing women can work the same night hours as men	Restrictions on weekly holiday work?	Restrictions on overtime work?	Paid annual leave (working days)[d]
United States (Los Angeles)	No	No limit	1,762.1	0.2	n.a.	6.0	0.0	0.0	50.0	No	Yes	No	No	0.0
United States (New York City)	No	No limit	1,846.0	0.3	n.a.	6.0	0.0	0.0	50.0	No	Yes	No	No	0.0
Uruguay	No	No limit	628.1	0.3	n.a.	6.0	0.0	100.0	100.0	No	Yes	No	No	21.0
Uzbekistan	Yes	60.0	129.2	0.5	3.0	6.0	50.0	100.0	100.0	No	Yes	No	No	15.0
Vanuatu	No	No limit	271.5	0.7	6.0	6.0	0.0	50.0	25.0	No	No	No	No	17.0
Venezuela, RB[h]	Yes	24.0	1,217.0	6.0	1.0	5.0	30.0	50.0	50.0	Yes	Yes	Yes	No	19.3
Vietnam	No	72.0	168.4	0.7	1.0	6.0	30.0	0.0	50.0	No	Yes	No	No	13.0
West Bank and Gaza	No	24.0	371.3	0.8	6.0	6.0	0.0	150.0	50.0	Yes	No	Yes	No	12.0
Yemen, Rep.	No	No limit	75.7	0.5	6.0	6.0	15.0	100.0	50.0	No	No	No	No	30.0
Zambia	Yes	No limit	176.4	0.8	n.a.	6.0	4.3	100.0	50.0	No	Yes	No	No	24.0
Zimbabwe	No	No limit	304.5	2.2	3.0	6.0	0.0	0.0	50.0	No	Yes	No	No	22.0

a. Including renewals.
b. Economies for which 0.0 is shown have no minimum wage in the private sector.
c. Some answers are not applicable (n.a.) for economies in which there is no statutory provision for a probationary period.
d. Average for workers with 1, 5 and 10 years of tenure.
e. Whether the law requires the employer to reassign or retrain a worker before making the worker redundant.
f. If no maternity leave is mandated by law, parental leave is measured if applicable.
g. The minimum number of days that legally have to be paid by the government, the employer or both.
h. Some answers are not applicable (n.a.) for economies where dismissal due to redundancy is disallowed.
i. Some answers are not applicable (n.a.) for economies that do not have an unemployment protection scheme.

The following data were collected jointly with the World Bank Group's *Women, Business and the Law* team:
- Can non-pregnant and non-nursing women work the same night hours as men?
- Equal remuneration for work of equal value?
- Gender non-discrimination in hiring?
- Paid/unpaid maternity leave mandated by law?
- Minimum length of maternity leave (calendar days)?
- Receive 100% of wages on maternity leave?

	Redundancy rules							Redundancy cost		Job quality							
Dismissal due to redundancy allowed by law?	Third-party notification if 1 worker is dismissed?	Third-party approval if 1 worker is dismissed?	Third-party notification if 9 workers are dismissed?	Third-party approval if 9 workers are dismissed?	Retraining or reassignment?[e]	Priority rules for redundancies?	Priority rules for reemployment?	Notice period for redundancy dismissal (weeks of salary)[d]	Severance pay for redundancy dismissal (weeks of salary)[d]	Equal remuneration for work of equal value?	Gender non-discrimination in hiring?	Paid/unpaid maternity leave mandated by law?[f]	Minimum length of maternity leave (calendar days)[g]	Receive 100% of wages on maternity leave?	Availability of five fully paid days of sick leave?	Whether an unemployment protection scheme exists after one year of employment[h]	Minimum duration of contribution period (in months) for unemployment protection
Yes	No	No	No	No	No	No	No	0.0	0.0	No	Yes	Yes	0	n.a.	Yes	Yes	12.0
Yes	No	No	No	No	No	No	No	0.0	0.0	No	Yes	Yes	0	n.a.	Yes	Yes	6.0
Yes	No	No	No	No	No	No	No	0.0	20.8	No	Yes	Yes	98	Yes	No	Yes	6.0
Yes	No	No	Yes	No	Yes	Yes	No	8.7	8.7	No	No	Yes	126	Yes	Yes	Yes	0.0
Yes	No	No	No	No	No	No	No	9.3	23.1	No	No	Yes	84	No	Yes	No	n.a.
No	n.a.	n.a.	n.a.	n.a.	n.a.	n.a.	n.a.	n.a.	n.a.	No	Yes	Yes	182	Yes	Yes	Yes	12.0
Yes	No	No	Yes	Yes	Yes	No	No	0.0	24.6	Yes	Yes	Yes	180	Yes	Yes	Yes	12.0
Yes	Yes	No	Yes	No	No	No	No	4.3	23.1	No	No	Yes	84	Yes	Yes	No	n.a.
Yes	Yes	No	Yes	No	No	No	Yes	4.3	23.1	No	No	Yes	70	Yes	Yes	No	n.a.
Yes	Yes	No	Yes	No	No	No	No	4.3	46.2	Yes	Yes	Yes	84	Yes	Yes	No	n.a.
Yes	Yes	No	Yes	No	Yes	No	No	13.0	12.3	No	Yes	Yes	98	Yes	Yes	No	n.a.

Doing Business 2018

Acknowledgments

Data collection and analysis for *Doing Business 2018* were conducted by a team led by Santiago Croci (Acting Manager, *Doing Business*) under the general direction of Rita Ramalho (Acting Director, Global Indicators Group, Development Economics). Overall guidance for the preparation of the report was provided by Shantayanan Devarajan (Senior Director, Development Economics) and Paul Romer (Senior Vice President and Chief Economist of the World Bank). The project was managed with the support of Adrian Gonzalez, Valentina Saltane and Hulya Ulku. Other team members included Nadine Abi Chakra, Ahmad AlKhuzam, Jean Arlet, Yuriy Valentinovich Avramov, Erica Bosio, Édgar Chávez, Maria Magdalena Chiquier, Cyriane Marie Coste, Baria Nabil Daye, Christian De la Medina Soto, Marie Lily Delion, Laura Diniz, Faiza El Fezzazi El Maziani, Imane Fahli, Cécile Ferro, Dorina Georgieva, Pelayo Gonzalez-Escalada Mena, Maksym Iavorskyi, Nan Jiang, Herve Kaddoura, Klaus Adolfo Koch-Saldarriaga, Olena Koltko, Magdalini Konidari, Khrystyna Kushnir, Nicole Anouk Leger, Tiziana Londero, Silvia Carolina Lopez Rocha, Raman Maroz, Brendan Meighan, Margherita Mellone, Nuno Filipe Mendes Dos Santos, Frédéric Meunier, Joanna Nasr, Marie-Jeanne Ndiaye, Albert Nogués i Comas, Nadia Novik, Kennedy Oyugi Okoyo, Tigran Parvanyan, Esperanza Pastor Nuñez De Castro, Madwa-Nika Phanord-Cadet, Martin Andres Poveda Amarfil, María Antonia Quesada Gámez, Parvina Rakhimova, Morgann Courtney Reeves, Anna Reva, Margarida Rodrigues, Julie Ryan, Jayashree Srinivasan, Mihaela Stangu, Erick Tjong, Camille Henri Vaillon, María Adelaida Vélez Posada, Jerry Wu, Yelizaveta Yanovich, Marilyne Florence Mafoboue Youbi, Inés Zabalbeitia Múgica, Philip Christopher Zager, Yasmin Zand, Muqiao Zhang and Geyi Zheng. Rami Abdulaziz Al Shaibani, Nyanya Browne, Melissa Bueno, Daniel De la Hormaza, Joseph El-Cassabgui, Francesca Ermice, Ismael Eduardo Wilson Franco Gonzales, Xu Han, Marcy Jagdeo Adekoya, Edison Jakurti, Zain Jarrar, Sarp Yanki Kalfa, Valeriya Khoroshun, Chung Myung Kim, Jamie Lee-Brown, Yousef Majzoub, Ahmed Medhat M Garoub, Marie Parent, Izabela Prager, Victoria Ryan, Egiimaa Tsolmonbaatar, Gergana Tsvetanova, Yarmi Jose Vidal Horscheck, Hong Jing Wang, David Weinstein, Anthony Paul Winszman, Xinyu Wu, Rongpeng Yang and Mohamed W. Zakaria assisted in the months before publication. Thomas Moullier and Keiko Sakoda contributed to the writing of the chapter on dealing with construction permits.

The online service of the *Doing Business* database is managed by Varun Doiphode, Fengsheng Huang, Manoj Mathew, Arun Chakravarthi Nageswaran, Kunal Patel, Kamalesh Sengaonkar, Bishal Raj Thakuri, Vinod Thottikkatu, and Hashim Zia. The *Doing Business 2018* outreach strategy is managed by Indira Chand, under the general direction of Phillip Jeremy Hay with support from World Bank Group communications colleagues around the world.

The team is grateful for the valuable comments provided by colleagues, both within and outside the World Bank Group, and for the guidance provided by World Bank Group Executive Directors. The team would especially like to acknowledge the comments and guidance of Gabi George Afram, Miah Rahmat Ali, Ashani Chanuka Alles, Amjad Bashir, Karim Ouled Belayachi, Eugene Bempon, Lilia Burunciuc, Cesar Calderon, Mierta Capaul, Efrem Zephnath Chilima, Ted Haoquan Chu, Amila Indeewari Dahanayake, Fernando Dancausa, Annette Dixon, Simeon Djankov, Christian Eigen-Zucchi, Jorge Familiar Calderon, Manuela V. Ferro, Alvaro Gonzalez, Cemile Hacibeyoglu, Lucia Hanmer, Caroline Heider, Andras Horvai, Joyce Antoine Ibrahim, Jane Jamieson, Aphichoke Kotikula, Aart Kraay, Esperanza Lasagabaster, Yue Li, John Litwack, Gladys Lopez-Acevedo, William F. Maloney, Trimor Mici, Mamo Esmelealem Mihretu, Andrei Mikhnev, Ashish Narain, Claudia Nassif, Tatiana Nenova, Juri Oka, Sandie Okoro, Alice Ouedraogo, Madalina Papahagi, Samuel Pienkangura, Martin Rama, M. Masrur Reaz, Massimiliano Santini, Jaehyang So, Sylvia Solf, The Corporate Registers Forum, Moussa Traore, Yvonne M. Tsikata, Linda Van Gelder, Carlos Alberto Vegh Gramont, Julien Vilquin, John Wille, Ali Zafa and Albert G. Zeufack.

The paying taxes project was conducted in collaboration with PwC, led by Stef van Weeghel.

Bronwen Brown edited the manuscript. Corporate Visions, Inc. designed the report and the graphs.

Doing Business would not be possible without the expertise and generous input of a network of more than 13,000 local partners, including legal experts, business consultants, accountants, freight forwarders, government officials and other professionals routinely administering or advising on the relevant legal and regulatory requirements in the 190 economies covered. Contact details for local partners are available on the Doing Business website at http://www.doingbusiness.org.

The names of the local partners wishing to be acknowledged individually are listed below. The global and regional contributors listed are firms that have completed multiple questionnaires in their various offices around the world.

GLOBAL CONTRIBUTORS

ADVOCATES FOR INTERNATIONAL DEVELOPMENT

AMERICAN BAR ASSOCIATION, SECTION OF INTERNATIONAL LAW

BAKER & MCKENZIE

BDO

DELOITTE

DENTONS

DLA PIPER

EY

FIABCI, THE INTERNATIONAL REAL ESTATE FEDERATION

GRANT THORNTON

GRATA INTERNATIONAL

IUS LABORIS - ALLIANCE OF LABOR, EMPLOYMENT, BENEFITS AND PENSIONS LAW FIRMS

KPMG

LAW SOCIETY OF ENGLAND AND WALES

LEX MUNDI, ASSOCIATION OF INDEPENDENT LAW FIRMS

PWC[1]

REED SMITH LLP

RUSSELL BEDFORD INTERNATIONAL

WHITE & CASE

REGIONAL CONTRIBUTORS

A.P. MOLLER - MAERSK GROUP

AL TAMIMI & COMPANY

ARIAS LAW

ASHURST LLP

ASSOCIATION OF CONSUMER CREDIT INFORMATION SUPPLIERS (ACCIS)

BOGA & ASSOCIATES

CENTIL LAW

DFDL

ENSAFRICA

EVERSHEDS SUTHERLAND

GARCÍA & BODÁN

JOHN W. FFOOKS & CO.

LEXINCORP

MAYER BROWN

SCHOENHERR

SORAINEN

TALAL ABU-GHAZALEH LEGAL (TAG-LEGAL)

TRANSUNION INTERNATIONAL

VDA - VIEIRA DE ALMEIDA & ASSOCIADOS

AFGHANISTAN

Taqi Ahmad
A.F. FERGUSON & CO., CHARTERED ACCOUNTANTS, A MEMBER FIRM OF PWC NETWORK

Gloria Ahmadi
KAKAR ADVOCATS

Bari Alkozai
PRAELEGAL

Shaheryar Aziz
A.F. FERGUSON & CO., CHARTERED ACCOUNTANTS, A MEMBER FIRM OF PWC NETWORK

Mazhar Bangash
RIAA BARKER GILLETTE AFG

Haidar Barak
RGM INTERNATIONAL GROUP LLC

Nadia Bazidwal
THE ASIA FOUNDATION

Sultan Maqsood Fazel
QADERDAN ELECTRICITY COMPANY

Hasibullah Ghaforzai
PRAELEGAL

Chantal Grut
ROSENSTOCK LEGAL SERVICES

Naheed Habibi
DA AFGHANISTAN BANK

Khan Hadawal
DA AFGHANISTAN BANK

Mohammad Afzal Hassanzada
DA AFGHANISTAN BANK

Khalid Hatam
RIAA BARKER GILLETTE AFG

Saduddin Haziq
AFGHAN UNITED BANK

Hussain Ali Hekmat
IKMAL ENGINEERING CONSTRUCTION COMPANY

Rashid Ibrahim
A.F. FERGUSON & CO., CHARTERED ACCOUNTANTS, A MEMBER FIRM OF PWC NETWORK

Waheed Iqbal
LEGAL ORACLES

Sanzar Kakar
AFGHANISTAN HOLDING GROUP

M. Wissal Khan
LEGAL ORACLES

Thomas Kraemer
KAKAR ADVOCATS

Khalid Massoudi
MASNAD LEGAL CONSULTANCY

Ghulam Reza Mohammady
KAKAR ADVOCATS

Saqib Naseer
A.F. FERGUSON & CO., CHARTERED ACCOUNTANTS, A MEMBER FIRM OF PWC NETWORK

Abdul Nasser Nazari
RAINBOW CONSULTING SERVICES

Tariq Nazarwall
DEHSABZ CITY DEVELOPMENT AUTHORITY, INDEPENDENT BOARD OF KABUL NEW CITY DEVELOPMENT

Habibullah Pirzada
ACCL INTERNATIONAL

Habiburahman Qaderdan
QADERDAN ELECTRICITY COMPANY

Shakir Rahimi
PRAELEGAL

Tamsil Rashid
AFGHANISTAN INTERNATIONAL BANK

Irisglyn Rivero
RGM INTERNATIONAL GROUP LLC

Abdul Wahid Rizwanzai
RIAA BARKER GILLETTE AFG

Ali Saberi
IKMAL ENGINEERING CONSTRUCTION COMPANY

Abdul Sami Sabir
DA AFGHANISTAN BANK

Zahid Safi
RIAA BARKER GILLETTE AFG

Abdul Nasser Sahak
DA AFGHANISTAN BANK

Saeeq Shajjan
SHAJJAN & ASSOCIATES

Aali Shan Ahmed
ICON TRADING AND FORWARDING COMPANY

Haris Syed Raza
GERRY'S DNATA PVT. LTD.

Mohammad Taimur Taimur
DA AFGHANISTAN BANK

Roshan Kumar Thapa
RGM INTERNATIONAL GROUP LLC

Madan Upadhyay
RGM INTERNATIONAL GROUP LLC

Najibullah Wardak
MINISTRY OF FINANCE

Maseeh Ahmad Wassil
DA AFGHANISTAN BANK

Rohullah Zarif
ACCL INTERNATIONAL

ALBANIA

WOLF THEISS

Anjola Aliaj
OPTIMA LEGAL AND FINANCIAL

Artur Asllani
TONUCCI & PARTNERS

Artan Babaramo
GENERAL DIRECTORATE OF TAXATION

Sabina Baboci
KALO & ASSOCIATES

Eglantina Bakiu Lala
BITRI & BAKIU LAW FIRM

Ledia Beçi
HOXHA, MEMI & HOXHA

Renis Bega
HOXHA, MEMI & HOXHA

Boiken Bendo
BENDO LAW, ADVOCATES & LEGAL CONSULTANTS

Jona Bica
EY

Artan Bozo
BOZO & ASSOCIATES LAW FIRM

Njazuela Braholli
GJIKA & ASSOCIATES

Irma Cacaj
BOGA & ASSOCIATES

Doris Carcani
ALBANIAN ENERGY REGULATOR (ERE)

Megi Caushi
AVANNTIVE CONSULTING SH.P.K.

Rozana Çelmeta
GENERAL DIRECTORATE OF TAXATION

Ilir Daci
OPTIMA LEGAL AND FINANCIAL

Besnik Duraj
DRAKOPOULOS LAW FIRM

Ana Dylgjeri
BANK OF ALBANIA

Sokol Elmazaj
BOGA & ASSOCIATES

Dorina Fezollari
AVANNTIVE CONSULTING SH.P.K.

Lorena Gega
PRICEWATERHOUSECOOPERS AUDIT SH.P.K.

Enida Gerxholli
REGISTRY OF SECURITY PLEDGES

Gjergji Gjika
GJIKA & ASSOCIATES

Valbona Gjonçari
BOGA & ASSOCIATES

Shirli Gorenca
KALO & ASSOCIATES

Bojana Hajdini
DRAKOPOULOS LAW FIRM

Esa Hala
TONUCCI & PARTNERS

Ergys Hasani
GJIKA & ASSOCIATES

Shpati Hoxha
HOXHA, MEMI & HOXHA

Elira Hroni
KALO & ASSOCIATES

Evis Jani
GJIKA & ASSOCIATES

Brunilda Jegeni
REGISTRY OF SECURITY PLEDGES

Ilir Johollari
HOXHA, MEMI & HOXHA

Bledar Kabashi
MINISTRY OF JUSTICE

Neritan Kallfa
TONUCCI & PARTNERS

Miranda Kapllani
BENIMPEX & CO.

Olta Kaziaj
AVANNTIVE CONSULTING SH.P.K.

Migena Kolonja
BOGA & ASSOCIATES

Rudi Laze
BOZO & ASSOCIATES LAW FIRM

Gilda Lika
BENDO LAW, ADVOCATES & LEGAL CONSULTANTS

Petraq Lika
OSHEE (OPERATORI I SHPERNDARJES SE ENERGJISE ELEKTRIKE)

Arbër Lloshi
OPTIMA LEGAL AND FINANCIAL

Tetis Lubonja
MINISTRY OF JUSTICE

Rezarta Mataj
TIRANA DISTRICT COURT

Andi Memi
HOXHA, MEMI & HOXHA

Eglon Metalia
EY

Naim Mete
GENERAL DIRECTORATE OF TAXATION

Aigest Milo
KALO & ASSOCIATES

Orgita Milo
BOGA & ASSOCIATES

1. *"PwC" refers to the network of member firms of PricewaterhouseCoopers International Limited (PwCIL) or, as the context requires, individual member firms of the PwC network. Each member firm is a separate legal entity and does not act as agent of PwCIL or any other member firm. PwCIL does not provide any services to clients. PwCIL is not responsible or liable for the acts or omissions of any of its member firms nor can it control the exercise of their professional judgment or bind them in any way. No member firm is responsible or liable for the acts or omissions of any other member firm nor can it control the exercise of another member firm's professional judgment or bind another member firm or PwCIL in any way.*

Eno Muja
BOGA & ASSOCIATES

Kristo Myridinas
PRICEWATERHOUSECOOPERS
AUDIT SH.P.K.

Gjergji Nestor
GENERAL DIRECTORATE
OF TAXATION

Dorina Nika
LAWYER

Albulen Pano
PRICEWATERHOUSECOOPERS
AUDIT SH.P.K.

Loreta Peci
PRICEWATERHOUSECOOPERS
AUDIT SH.P.K.

Ardjana Shehi
KALO & ASSOCIATES

Enian Sina
GENERAL DIRECTORATE
OF TAXATION

Ketrin Topçiu
BOZO & ASSOCIATES
LAW FIRM

Anora Topi
GENERAL DIRECTORATE
OF TAXATION

Bruno Turabi
BOGA & ASSOCIATES

Alketa Uruçi
BOGA & ASSOCIATES

Gerhard Velaj
BOGA & ASSOCIATES

Flavia Xhafo
KALO & ASSOCIATES

Donald Xhelili
FIRST COURT OF TIRANA

Evis Zaja
OPTIMA LEGAL
AND FINANCIAL

Enida Zeneli
BOZO & ASSOCIATES
LAW FIRM

Lareda Zenunaj
GJIKA & ASSOCIATES

ALGERIA

CABINET MOHAMMED
TAHAR BENABID

TRANSIT SAIDJI

Amel Aiad
ACCOUNTANT

Mohamed Nadir Aissani
PWC ALGERIA

Salima Aloui
LAW FIRM GOUSSANEM
& ALOUI

Arab Aoudj
CABINET D'AUDIT ET DE
CONTRÔLE DES COMPTES

Djelloul Aouidette
UNION NATIONALE
DES TRANSITAIRES ET
COMMISSIONNAIRES
ALGÉRIENS (UNTCA)

Mohamed Atbi
ETUDE NOTARIALE
MOHAMED ATBI

Hind Belhachmi
LPA-CGR AVOCATS

Abdelouahab Benali
TRANSIT MOUHOUB KAMAL

Othmane Benali
ACCOUNTANT

Adnane Bouchaib
BOUCHAIB LAW FIRM

Hamid Boughenou
BECOME SCP

Rachida Boughenou
BECOME SCP

Hafida Bounefrat
ACCOUNTANT

Merouane Chabane
SOCIÉTÉ DE DISTRIBUTION
DE L'ELECTRICITÉ ET DU
GAZ D'ALGER (SDA)

Djamel Chorfi

Said Dib
BANQUE D'ALGÉRIE

Ahmed Djouadi
LAW FIRM HADJ-HAMOU
& DJOUADI - ASSOCIATE
OFFICE OF DENTONS

Mourad El Besseghi
CABINET EL BESSEGHI

Hamil Faidi
STUDIO A

Mohamed Lahbib Goubi
BANQUE D'ALGÉRIE

Khaled Goussanem
LAW FIRM GOUSSANEM
& ALOUI

Mohamed El-Amine Haddad
CABINET DE MAÎTRE
AMINE HADDAD

Samir Hamouda
CABINET D'AVOCATS
SAMIR HAMOUDA

Halim Karabadji
SOCIÉTÉ DE DISTRIBUTION
DE L'ELECTRICITÉ ET DU
GAZ D'ALGER (SDA)

Abdelmalek Kherbachene
BOUCHEMLA LANOUAR
& ASSOCIÉS

Farouk Lakli
LAKELEC

Mohamed Lanouar
BOUCHEMLA LANOUAR
& ASSOCIÉS

Walid Laouar
CABINET LAOUAR

Vincent Lunel
DS AVOCATS

Harous Madjid
PWC ALGERIA

Sid-Ahmed Mekerba
GHELLAL & MEKERBA

Mohamed Mokrane
MINISTÈRE DES FINANCES -
DIRECTION GÉNÉRALE DU
DOMAINE NATIONAL

Hamid Ould Hocine
STUDIO A

Malika Redouani
PWC ALGERIA

Lazhar Sahbani
PWC ALGERIA

Mourad Seghir
BENNANI & ASSOCIÉS LLP

Madiha Silini
LPA-CGR AVOCATS

Rabah Tafighoult
CABINET TAFIGHOULT

Redouane Tazerouti
MICHEL HUREL ALGERIE SARL

Hachemi Yanat
ACCOUNTANT

Hakim Zerbout
MICHEL HUREL ALGERIE SARL

ANGOLA

Luís Andrade
PWC ANGOLA

Sika Awoonor
GLOBAL CHOICE ANGOLA LDA

Jeanine Batalha Ferreira
PWC PORTUGAL

Pedro Bequengue
CÂMARA DOS DESPACHANTES
OFICIAIS DE ANGOLA

Edvaldo Cahombo
GUICHÉ ÚNICO DE EMPRESA

Guilherme Carreira
EDIFER ANGOLA

Luis Filipe Carvalho
ADCA LAW FIRM, MEMBER
OF DLA PIPER AFRICA GROUP

Jaime Carvalho Esteves
PWC PORTUGAL

Irineu Chingala
LOURDES CAPOSSO FERNANDES
& ASSOCIADOS (LCF)

Nelson Couto-Cabral
3C INTERNATIONAL

Inês Barbosa Cunha
PWC PORTUGAL

Alwin Leon Das
FAMS TRANSITÁRIOS LDA

Patricia Dias
AVM ADVOGADOS

Fernando F. Bastos
FBL ADVOGADOS

Lourdes Caposso Fernandes
LOURDES CAPOSSO
FERNANDES & ASSOCIADOS

João Fialho
VDA - VIEIRA DE ALMEIDA
& ASSOCIADOS

Marcelino Franco
GUICHÉ ÚNICO DE EMPRESA

Luís Fraústo Varona
ABREU ADVOGADOS

Marilia Frias
VDA - VIEIRA DE ALMEIDA
& ASSOCIADOS

Alberto Galhardo Simões
MIRANDA & ASSOCIADOS

Paulo Lobo
ABREU CARGA E TRÂNSITOS,
LDA - ANGOLA

Dilma Lopes
FBL ADVOGADOS

Chindalena Lourenço
FÁTIMA FREITAS ADVOGADOS

António Manuel da Silva
INSTITUTO REGULADOR DOS
SERVIÇOS DE ELECTRICIDADE
E ÁGUAS (IRSEA)

Arcelio Matias
ARCÉLIO INÁCIO DE
ALMEIDA MATIAS – ARDJA-
PRESTAÇÃO DE SERVIÇOS
E CONSULTORIA, LDA

Antonio Morgado
GUICHÉ ÚNICO DE EMPRESA

Marcos Neto
BANCO NACIONAL DE ANGOLA

Henrique Nogueira Nunes
ALBUQUERQUE & ASSOCIADOS

Janota Nzogi
ENERGY AND WATER MINISTRY

Joana Pacheco
ANGOLA COUNSEL

Júlio Pascoal
ENDE-EP

Antonio Pereira
EY

Joaquim Piedade
UNICARGAS

Djamila Pinto de Andrade
LEAD ADVOGADOS

André Miguel Pitéu
TRANSITEX ANGOLA

Laurinda Prazeres Cardoso
LEAD ADVOGADOS

José Quarta
INSTITUTO REGULADOR DOS
SERVIÇOS DE ELECTRICIDADE
E ÁGUAS (IRSEA)

Gonçalo Antunes Rita
BANCO NACIONAL DE ANGOLA

Sandra Saraiva
GABINETE LEGAL
ANGOLA – ADVOGADOS

Bruno Serejo
ELA – EXPERT LEGAL
ASSISTANCE

Dinamukueno Lukie Sérgio
OLICARGO ANGOLA SA

Tatiana Serrão
FBL ADVOGADOS

Gervasio Simao
GEPLI ANGOLA

Hugo Sipitali
ANGOLA COUNSEL

Beatriz Calcida Soares
Catumbela

Daniela Tavares Nunes
ABREU ADVOGADOS

Elsa Tchicanha
GABINETE LEGAL
ANGOLA – ADVOGADOS

Renata Valenti
GABINETE LEGAL
ANGOLA – ADVOGADOS

Ricardo Veloso
PWC ANGOLA

António Vicente Marques
AVM ADVOGADOS

Orlanda Vuite
ADCA LAW FIRM, MEMBER
OF DLA PIPER AFRICA GROUP

ANTIGUA AND BARBUDA

ANTIGUA & BARBUDA
INTELLECTUAL PROPERTY &
COMMERCE OFFICE (ABIPCO)

MINISTRY OF LABOR

Aisha Caleb
MINISTRY OF INFORMATION,
BROADCASTING,
TELECOMMUNICATIONS
AND INFORMATION
TECHNOLOGY - CUSTOMS
AND EXCISE DIVISION

Neil Coates
GRANT THORNTON

Nkosi Cochrane
DEVELOPMENT CONTROL
AUTHORITY

Gilbert Findlay
ANTIGUA PUBLIC UTILITIES
AUTHORITY (APUA)

Colin John Jenkins
ROBERTS CONSTRUCTION
& ENGINEERING CO. LTD.

Hugh C. Marshall
MARSHALL & CO.

Gloria Martin
FRANCIS TRADING
AGENCY LIMITED

David Matthias
ANTIGUA BARBUDA SOCIAL
SECURITY BOARD

Septimus A. Rhudd
RHUDD & ASSOCIATES

Stedroy Roache
ANTIGUA PUBLIC UTILITIES
AUTHORITY (APUA)

Andrea Roberts
ROBERTS & CO.

Safiya Roberts
ROBERTS & CO.

Megan Samuel-Fields
SAMUEL FIELDS CONSULTING
GROUP LTD.

Sharon Simmons
LAND REGISTRY

Owren Smith
DEVELOPMENT CONTROL
AUTHORITY

Eleanor R. Solomon
CLARKE & CLARKE

Frederick Southwell
DEVELOPMENT CONTROL
AUTHORITY

Arthur Thomas
THOMAS, JOHN & CO.

Marietta Warren
INTERFREIGHT LTD.

ARGENTINA

PETROBRAS

Lucas Abal
RIVERA & ASOCIADOS

Ignacio Acedo
GONZALEZ & FERRARO MILA

Cecilia Andrea Acosta
MBB BALADO BEVILACQUA
ABOGADOS

Pablo J. Alliani
ALLIANI & BRUZZON

Jose María Allonca
ALLONCA ABOGADOS LEGAL
& BUSINESS CONSULTING

Marina Altieri
DE DIOS & GOYENA
ABOGADOS CONSULTORES

Ignacio E. Aramburu
ESTUDIO MOLTEDO

Sebastian Ariel Uberti
CITY OF BUENOS AIRES

Ariadna Artopoulos
M. & M. BOMCHIL

María Fernanda Arturi
CENTRAL BANK OF ARGENTINA

Mercedes Balado Bevilacqua
MBB BALADO BEVILACQUA
ABOGADOS

Vanesa Balda
VITALE, MANOFF & FEILBOGEN

Gonzalo Carlos Ballester
J.P. O'FARRELL ABOGADOS

Maria Laura Barbosa
ZANG, BERGEL &
VIÑES ABOGADOS

Federico Martín Basile
M. & M. BOMCHIL

Néstor J. Belgrano
M. & M. BOMCHIL

Pilar Etcheverry Boneo
MARVAL, O'FARRELL & MAIRAL, MEMBER OF LEX MUNDI

Ignacio Fernández Borzese
LUNA REQUENA & FERNÁNDEZ BORZESE TAX LAW FIRM

Fernando L. Brunelli
ALLIANI & BRUZZON

Damián Burgio
SALAVERRI, DELLATORRE, BURGIO & WETZLER MALBRÁN

Eduardo Bustamante
ESTUDIO MOLTEDO

Adriana Paola Caballero
WIENER SOTO CAPARRÓS

Federico Carenzo
LEONHARDT & DIETL

Gabriela Carissimo
ALFARO ABOGADOS

Mariano E. Carricart
BADENI, CANTILO, LAPLACETTE & CARRICART

Luciano Cativa
LUNA REQUENA & FERNÁNDEZ BORZESE TAX LAW FIRM

Ma. Cecilia Herrero de Pratesi
REGISTRO DE LA PROPIEDAD INMUEBLE DE LA CAPITAL FEDERAL

Hector Osvaldo Chomer
JUZGADO DE PRIMERA INSTANCIA EN LO COMERCIAL

Agustín Comastri
G. BREUER

Roberto O. Condoleo
RCBM AUDITORES Y CONSULTORES TRIBUTARIOS

Julio Condomí Alcorta
ESCRIBANÍA CONDOMÍ

Roberto H. Crouzel
ESTUDIO BECCAR VARELA

Gabriel de Albadalejo
ECOVIS ARGENTINA RAMOGNINO, DE ALBALADEJO & ASOCIADOS SC

Oscar Alberto del Río
CENTRAL BANK OF ARGENTINA

Noelia Aldana Di Stéfano
J.P. O'FARRELL ABOGADOS

Analía Verónica Durán
MBB BALADO BEVILACQUA ABOGADOS

Dana Eizner
SEVERGNINI, ROBIOLA, GRINBERG & TOMBEUR

Daniel Fernandez de la Torre
CONSULTORES SRL

Sonia Ferrari
CONSULTORES SRL

Pablo Ferraro Mila
GONZALEZ & FERRARO MILA

Diego M. Fissore
G. BREUER

María Victoria Funes
M. & M. BOMCHIL

Ignacio Funes de Rioja
FUNES DE RIOJA & ASOCIADOS, MEMBER OF IUS LABORIS

Eduardo Galleazzi
ARCHITECT

Alfredo Garcia Samartino
SMART LOGISTICS

Martín Gastaldi
ESTUDIO BECCAR VARELA

Javier M. Gattó Bicain
CANDIOTI GATTO BICAIN & OCANTOS

Juan José Glusman
PWC ARGENTINA

Gonzalo María Gros
J.P. O'FARRELL ABOGADOS

Eduardo Guglielmini
MINISTRY OF ENERGY AND MINING

Sandra S. Guillan
DE DIOS & GOYENA ABOGADOS CONSULTORES

Federico Guillermo Absi
G. BREUER

Carlos Hernandez
CONSULTORES SRL

Gabriela Hidalgo

Fabián Hilal
CASELLA & HILAL ABOGADOS

Mailen Hilen Rico
ESTUDIO MOLTEDO

Daniel Intile
RUSSELL BEDFORD ARGENTINA - MEMBER OF RUSSELL BEDFORD INTERNATIONAL

Andrea Junquera
CANDIOTI GATTO BICAIN & OCANTOS

Federico Leonhardt
LEONHARDT, DIETL, GRAF & VON DER FECHT

Francisco Lobos
LLERENA & ASOCIADOS ABOGADOS

Pilar Lodewyckx Hardy
ESTUDIO BECCAR VARELA

Juan Manuel Magadan
PWC ARGENTINA

Tomas Martinez Casas
LLERENA & ASOCIADOS ABOGADOS

Andrés May
SECRETARÍA GENERAL DEL GOBIERNO DE LA CIUDAD DE BUENOS AIRES

Pedro Mazer
ALFARO ABOGADOS

Julián Melis
CANDIOTI GATTO BICAIN & OCANTOS

María Fernanda Mierez
ESTUDIO BECCAR VARELA

Diego Minerva
MITRANI CABALLERO OJAM & RUIZ MORENO

Jorge Miranda
CLIPPERS SA

Ino Mosse
CONSTRUIMOS

Miguel P. Murray
MURRAY, ANGUILLESI, GUYOT, ROSSI & SIRITO DE ZAVALÍA

Pedro Nicholson
ESTUDIO BECCAR VARELA

Luciano José Nístico
J.P. O'FARRELL ABOGADOS

Alfredo Miguel O'Farrell
MARVAL, O'FARRELL & MAIRAL, MEMBER OF LEX MUNDI

Matías Olcese
HOLT ABOGADOS

Laura Piedrahita Abella
RIVERA & ASOCIADOS

Segundo Pinto
LLERENA & ASOCIADOS ABOGADOS

Alejandro Poletto
ESTUDIO BECCAR VARELA

Gustavo M. Prestipino
INEC INGENIERIA ELECTRICA SA

María Clara Pujol
WIENER SOTO CAPARRÓS

Julio R. Martinez
MITRANI CABALLERO OJAM & RUIZ MORENO

Rafael Ramognino
ECOVIS ARGENTINA RAMOGNINO, DE ALBALADEJO & ASOCIADOS SC

Natalia Rauchberger
MITRANI CABALLERO OJAM & RUIZ MORENO

Federico José Reibestein
REIBESTEIN & ASOCIADOS

Juan Manuel Reyes Santa Cruz
PLANOSNET.COM CONSULTORIA MUNICIPAL

Julio Cesar Rivera
RIVERA & ASOCIADOS

Matías Rivera
SALAVERRI, DELLATORRE, BURGIO & WETZLER MALBRÁN

Sebastián Rodrigo
ALFARO ABOGADOS

Ignacio Rodriguez
PWC ARGENTINA

Juan Ignacio Ruiz
ALFARO ABOGADOS

Diego Salaverri
SALAVERRI, DELLATORRE, BURGIO & WETZLER MALBRÁN

Luz María Salomón
J.P. O'FARRELL ABOGADOS

Juan Martin Salvadores de Arzuaga
DE DIOS & GOYENA ABOGADOS CONSULTORES

Gonzalo J. Sanchez
SANCHEZ, LUPI & ASOCIADOS

Ramiro Santurio
LEONHARDT, DIETL, GRAF & VON DER FECHT

Mariela Alejandra Sas
M. & M. BOMCHIL

Enrique Schinelli
LEONHARDT, DIETL, GRAF & VON DER FECHT

Carolina Serra
ESTUDIO BECCAR VARELA

Maria Shakespear
ESTUDIO BECCAR VARELA

Osvaldo Solari Costa
INTERNATIONAL UNION OF NOTARIES

Federico Sosa
ESTUDIO BECCAR VARELA

Maria Florencia Sota Vazquez
ALFARO ABOGADOS

Pablo Staszewski
STASZEWSKI & ASSOCIATES

Ricardo Tavieres
PWC ARGENTINA

María Paula Terrel
HOLT ABOGADOS

Adolfo Tombolini
RUSSELL BEDFORD ARGENTINA - MEMBER OF RUSSELL BEDFORD INTERNATIONAL

Valentina Toquier
M. & M. BOMCHIL

María Paola Trigiani
ALFARO ABOGADOS

María Victoria Tuculet
M. & M. BOMCHIL

Gonzalo Ugarte
BARBOSA ABOGADOS

Emilio Beccar Varela
ESTUDIO BECCAR VARELA

Abraham Viera
PLANOSNET.COM CONSULTORIA MUNICIPAL

Eduardo J. Viñales
FUNES DE RIOJA & ASOCIADOS, MEMBER OF IUS LABORIS

Germán Wetzler Malbrán
SALAVERRI, DELLATORRE, BURGIO & WETZLER MALBRÁN

Roberto Wiman
GREEN INGENIERÍA

Joaquín Emilio Zappa
J.P. O'FARRELL ABOGADOS

ARMENIA

THE STATE COMMITTEE OF REAL PROPERTY CADASTRE OF THE GOVERNMENT OF THE REPUBLIC OF ARMENIA

Mher Aghabekyan
YEREVAN MUNICIPALITY

Sergey Aghinyan
PUBLIC SERVICES REGULATORY COMMISSION OF ARMENIA

Mike Ahern
PWC

Amalia Artemyan
PARADIGMA ARMENIA CJSC

Zaruhi Arzuamnyan
LEGELATA

Hayk Asatryan
YEREVAN MUNICIPALITY

Ella Atoyan
PWC ARMENIA

Gayane Babayan
AVENUE CONSULTING GROUP

Anushik Baghdasaryan
AVENUE CONSULTING GROUP

Artur Buduryan
LEGELATA

Hovhannes Chamsaryan
AVENUE CONSULTING GROUP

Aharon Chilingaryan
PARADIGMA ARMENIA CJSC

Arsen Chitchyan
THE COLLEGIUM OF BUSINESS-MANAGERS' BANKRUPTCY - SRO

Azat Dunamalyan
ARSHINBANK CJSC

Aikanush Edigaryan
TRANS-ALLIANCE

Shoghik Gharibyan
KPMG

Mihran Grigoryan
AVENUE CONSULTING GROUP

Tigran Grigoryan
AVENUE CONSULTING GROUP

Alla Hakhnazaryan
LEGELATA

Anahit Hakhumyan
MINISTRY OF URBAN DEVELOPMENT

Gevorg Hakobyan
ELAWPHANT LAW FIRM

Andranik Harutyunyan
ELECTRIC NETWORKS OF ARMENIA

Hasmik Harutyunyan
PWC ARMENIA

Artak Hovakimyan
BIG ENERGO LLC

Izabela Hovhannisyan

Mariam Hovsepyan
TER-TACHATYAN LEGAL AND BUSINESS CONSULTING

Angela Hovshannisyan
TER-TACHATYAN LEGAL AND BUSINESS CONSULTING

Vahe G. Kakoyan

Anna Karapetyan
MINISTRY OF JUSTICE

Andranik Kasaryan
YEREVAN MUNICIPALITY

David Khachatryan
AVENUE CONSULTING GROUP

Georgi Khachatryan
AVENUE CONSULTING GROUP

Rafik Khachatryan
KPMG

Vigen Khachatryan
AVENUE CONSULTING GROUP

Stanislav Kolesnikov
ELECTRIC NETWORKS OF ARMENIA

Hayk Mamajanyan
ARLEX INTERNATIONAL CJSC

Gor Margaryan
LEGELATA

Nshan Martirosyan
MINISTRY OF URBAN DEVELOPMENT

Lilit Matevosyan
PWC ARMENIA

Nshan Matevosyan
ARLEX INTERNATIONAL CJSC

Armen Melkumyan
FIDELITY CONSULTING CJSC

Rajiv Nagri
GLOBALINK LOGISTICS GROUP

Narine Nersisyan
PWC ARMENIA

Shavarsh Petakchyan
ILEX LAW FIRM

Naira Petrosyan
PARADIGMA ARMENIA CJSC

Sarhat Petrosyan
URBANLAB YEREVAN

Suren Petrosyan
SP CONSULTING LLC

Hayk Pogosyan
ARSARQTEX LLC

Nare Sahakyan
ARSHINBANK CJSC

Thomas Samuelian
ARLEX INTERNATIONAL CJSC

Gor Shahbazyan
PWC ARMENIA

Ruben Shakhmuradyan
COMFORT R&V

Aleksey Sukoyan
COURT OF FIRST INSTANCE

Hakob Tadevosyan
GRANT THORNTON LLP

Anoush Ter-Vardanyan
AVENUE CONSULTING GROUP

Liana Yordanyan
TER-TACHATYAN LEGAL AND BUSINESS CONSULTING

Aram Zakaryan
ACRA CREDIT BUREAU

AUSTRALIA

HILL SHIRE CITY COUNCIL

TREASURY OF AUSTRALIA

Paul Agnew
MCKAYS LAWYERS

Irene Argeres
WHITE & CASE AUSTRALIA

Mariam Azzo
CLAYTON UTZ, MEMBER OF LEX MUNDI

Harold Bolitho
KING & WOOD MALLESONS

Lynda Brumm
PWC AUSTRALIA

Andrea Castle
WHITE & CASE AUSTRALIA

Amanda Coneyworth
FERRIER HODGSON MH SDN BHD

Fiona Curl
WHITE & CASE AUSTRALIA

Mark Dalby
OFFICE OF STATE REVENUE, NSW TREASURY

Stephen Davis
NEXIA AUSTRALIA

Kristy Dixon
MARQUE LAWYERS

Paul Evans
MCKAYS LAWYERS

Philip Harvey
KING & WOOD MALLESONS

Stephen Jauncey
HENRY DAVIS YORK

Morgan Kelly
FERRIER HODGSON MH SDN BHD

Felicia Lal
MARQUE LAWYERS

Melanie Lam
CAMPHIN BOSTON - MEMBER OF RUSSELL BEDFORD INTERNATIONAL

John Martin
THOMSON GEER

Mitchell Mathas
NORTON ROSE FULBRIGHT

Nicholas Mavrakis
CLAYTON UTZ, MEMBER OF LEX MUNDI

Aaron McKenzie
MARQUE LAWYERS

Patricia Muscat
PWC AUSTRALIA

Mia Rafa
MCKAYS LAWYERS

Dean Schiller
FAYMAN INTERNATIONAL PTY. LTD.

Ruwan Senanayake

Jeremy Shelley
ATTORNEY-GENERAL'S DEPARTMENT

Amy Stiles
NSW OFFICE OF THE REGISTRAR GENERAL

Damian Sturzaker
MARQUE LAWYERS

Simon Truskett
CLAYTON UTZ, MEMBER OF LEX MUNDI

Cameron Watson
WHITE & CASE AUSTRALIA

Bruce Whittaker
ASHURST LLP

Kellie Woodward
MCKAYS LAWYERS

Amanda Wu
ASHURST LLP

AUSTRIA

MINISTRY FOR SCIENCE, RESEARCH AND ECONOMY

Thomas Bareder
OESTERREICHISCHE NATIONAL BANK

Henri Bellando
GRAF & PITKOWITZ RECHTSANWÄLTE GMBH

Markus Bitterl
GRAF & PITKOWITZ RECHTSANWÄLTE GMBH

Sonja Bydlinski
MINISTRY OF JUSTICE

Thomas Deutinger
FRESHFIELDS BRUCKHAUS DERINGER

Martin Ebner
SCHOENHERR

Tibor Fabian
BINDER GRÖSSWANG RECHTSANWÄLTE GMBH

Julian Feichtinger
CHSH CERHA HEMPEL SPIEGELFELD HLAWATI, MEMBER OF LEX MUNDI

Martin Foerster
GRAF & PITKOWITZ RECHTSANWÄLTE GMBH

Ferdinand Graf
GRAF & PITKOWITZ RECHTSANWÄLTE GMBH

Andreas Hable
BINDER GRÖSSWANG RECHTSANWÄLTE GMBH

Sebastian Haensse
GRAF & PITKOWITZ RECHTSANWÄLTE GMBH

Herbert Herzig
AUSTRIAN CHAMBER OF COMMERCE

Alexander Hofmann
LAWYER

Marianne Hrdlicka

Armin Immervoll
MINISTRY OF FINANCE

Alexander Isola
GRAF & PITKOWITZ RECHTSANWÄLTE GMBH

Rudolf Kaindl

Amith Gururaj Karanth
PPC INSULATORS AUSTRIA GMBH

Zsofia Kerkapoly
SCWP SCHINDHELM AUSTRIA

Birgit Kettlgruber
FRESHFIELDS BRUCKHAUS DERINGER

Alexander Klauser
BRAUNEIS KLAUSER PRÄNDL RECHTSANWÄLTE GMBH

Florian Klimscha
FRESHFIELDS BRUCKHAUS DERINGER

Christian Köttl
MINISTRY OF FINANCE

Rudolf Krickl
PWC AUSTRIA

Michaela Krist
CHSH CERHA HEMPEL SPIEGELFELD HLAWATI, MEMBER OF LEX MUNDI

Gerald Mitteregger
INTERNATIONAL LOGISTIC GATEWAY

Johannes Mrazek
AUSTRIAN REGULATORY AUTHORITY

Gerhard Muggenhuber
BEV - FEDERAL OFFICE OF METROLOGY & SURVEYING

Thomas Müller
FRESHFIELDS BRUCKHAUS DERINGER

Elke Napokoj
BPV HÜGEL RECHTSANWÄLTE OG

Nikolaus Neubauer
PWC AUSTRIA

Felix Neuwirther
FRESHFIELDS BRUCKHAUS DERINGER

Christopher Peitsch
CHSH CERHA HEMPEL SPIEGELFELD HLAWATI, MEMBER OF LEX MUNDI

Verena Pöchlinger
PWC AUSTRIA

Moritz Salzgeber
BINDER GRÖSSWANG RECHTSANWÄLTE GMBH

Johannes Samaan
FRESHFIELDS BRUCKHAUS DERINGER

Edwin Scharf
SCWP SCHINDHELM AUSTRIA

Georg Schima
KUNZ SCHIMA WALLENTIN RECHTSANWÄLTE OG, MEMBER OF IUS LABORIS

Stephan Schmalzl
GRAF & PITKOWITZ RECHTSANWÄLTE GMBH

Daniel Schmidt
BINDER GRÖSSWANG RECHTSANWÄLTE GMBH

Ernst Schmidt
HALPERN & PRINZ

Helmut Sprongl
AUSTRIAN REGULATORY AUTHORITY

Thomas Trettnak
CHSH CERHA HEMPEL SPIEGELFELD HLAWATI, MEMBER OF LEX MUNDI

Eugen Velicu
STRABAG SE

Birgit Vogt-Majarek
KUNZ SCHIMA WALLENTIN RECHTSANWÄLTE OG, MEMBER OF IUS LABORIS

Gerhard Wagner
KSV 1870

Lukas A. Weber
BRAUNEIS KLAUSER PRÄNDL RECHTSANWÄLTE GMBH

Elisabeth Zehetner-Piewald
AUSTRIAN CHAMBER OF COMMERCE

Anton Zeilinger
MINISTRY OF FINANCE

Kathrin Zeller
FRESHFIELDS BRUCKHAUS DERINGER

AZERBAIJAN

AZERSUN

Parviz Abdullayev
PWC AZERBAIJAN

Husniyye Abdullayeva
MINISTRY OF TAXES

Chingiz Agarzaev

Mike Ahern
PWC

Ilham Ahmedov
BAKU ADMINISTRATIVE-ECONOMICAL COURT NO. 1

Iftikhar Akhundov
MINISTRY OF TAXES

Nigar Alimova
MINISTRY OF TAXES

Jamil Alizada
BAKER & MCKENZIE - CIS, LIMITED

Aykhan Asadov
BM MORRISON PARTNERS LLC

Ismail Askerov
MGB LAW OFFICES

Zulfigar Babayev
BHM BAKU LAW CENTRE LLC

Jamal Baghirov
BM MORRISON PARTNERS LLC

Natavan Baghirova
BM MORRISON PARTNERS LLC

Aida Bagirova
UNIBANK

Farid Bakhshiyev
GRATA INTERNATIONAL

Khayyam Bayramov
MINISTRY OF JUSTICE

Orkhan Beydiyev
CASPIAN LEGAL CENTER

Eyyub Fataliyev
PWC AZERBAIJAN

Ikram Fikretoglu
BUSINESS SERVICE CENTRE

Jahangir Gafarov
BAKER & MCKENZIE - CIS, LIMITED

Rustam Gasimov
BAKER & MCKENZIE - CIS, LIMITED

Arif Guliyev
PWC AZERBAIJAN

Konul Guliyeva
PWC AZERBAIJAN

Shaban Gurbanov
BM MORRISON PARTNERS LLC

Ayten Gurbanova
EXPERT SM LTD.

Fatima Gurbanova
PWC AZERBAIJAN

Elchin Habibov
FINANCIAL MARKETS SUPERVISORY AUTHORITY

Arzu Hajiyeva
EY

Kamala Hajiyeva
EY

Shamkhal Hasanov
BAKER & MCKENZIE - CIS, LIMITED

Farid Huseynov
EKVITA

Ruhiyya Isayeva
DENTONS

Gadir Ismayilov
AZERISHIQ OJSC

Delara Israfilova
BM MORRISON PARTNERS LLC

Zaki Jabiyev

Aladdin A. Jafarov
BAKU CITY YASAMAL DISTRICT COURT

Ummi Jalilova
GRATA INTERNATIONAL

Anar Janmammadov
MGB LAW OFFICES

Gunduz Karimov
BAKER & MCKENZIE - CIS, LIMITED

Bahar Kavuzova
PWC AZERBAIJAN

Elnur Mammadov
PWC AZERBAIJAN

Sahib Mammadov
CITIZENS' LABOUR RIGHTS PROTECTION LEAGUE

Zaur Mammadov
EY

Aysel Mammadova
BHM BAKU LAW CENTRE LLC

Faiq S. Manafov
UNIBANK

Gumru Mehdiyeva
BHM BAKU LAW CENTRE LLC

Ilgar Mehti
EKVITA

Rauf Memmedov
AZERBAIJAN CUSTOMS COMMITTEE

Telman Memmedov
MINISTRY OF TAXES

Elkhan Mikayilov
SECTOR OF ASSISTANT SERVICE OF THE PRESIDENT OF AZERBAIJAN REPUBLIC ON ECONOMIC REFORMS

Farhad Mirzayev
BM MORRISON PARTNERS LLC

Ruslan Mirzayev
ADREM ATTORNEYS

Ruslan Mukhtarov
BM MORRISON PARTNERS LLC

Aynur Musayeva
EXPERT SM LTD.

Altay Mustafayev
BAKER & MCKENZIE - CIS, LIMITED

Turkan Mustafayeva
BHM BAKU LAW CENTRE LLC

Sabina Orujova
DENTONS

Ramiz Rustamov
SIN RRG MMC

Zenfira Rzayeva
MINISTRY OF EMERGENCY SITUATIONS, STATE AGENCY FOR CONTROL OVER CONSTRUCTION SAFETY

Shabnam Sadigova
GRATA INTERNATIONAL

Leyla Safarova
BM MORRISON PARTNERS LLC

Mustafa Salamov
BM MORRISON PARTNERS LLC

Nazim Shukurov
AUDIT AZERBAIJAN

Sona Taghiyeva
DENTONS

Anar A. Umudov
ALIBI PROFESSIONAL LEGAL
& CONSULTING SERVICES

Ilkin Veliyev
MINISTRY OF TAXES

Michael Wilson
MICHAEL WILSON &
PARTNERS LTD.

Javid Yusifov
CASPIAN LEGAL CENTER

Aygun Zeynalova
MGB LAW OFFICES

Ulvia Zeynalova-Bockin
DENTONS

BAHAMAS, THE

Jane Adams
KPMG

Kevin Basden
BAHAMAS ELECTRICITY
CORPORATION

Sonia Brown
GRAPHITE ENGINEERING LTD.

Dayrrl Butler
MOORE STEPHENS BUTLER
& TAYLOR CHARTERED
ACCOUNTANTS AND
BUSINESS ADVISORS

Kimberley Cleare
PWC BAHAMAS

Kandice Davis
UTILITIES REGULATION &
COMPETITION AUTHORITY

Surinder Deal
HIGGS & JOHNSON

Craig G. Delancy
MINISTRY OF WORKS
& TRANSPORT

Randol Dorsett
UTILITIES REGULATION &
COMPETITION AUTHORITY

Amos J. Ferguson Jr.
FERGUSON ASSOCIATES
& PLANNERS

Wendy Forsythe
IMPORT EXPORT BROKERS LTD.

Vann P. Gaitor
HIGGS & JOHNSON

Bryan A. Glinton

Pamela Hill
BAHAMAS POWER AND LIGHT

Amanda John
LENNOX PATON

Yolande Julien

Ja'Ann Major
HIGGS & JOHNSON

Simone Morgan-Gomez
CALLENDERS & CO.

Lester J. Mortimer Jr.
CALLENDERS & CO.

Michael Moss
MINISTRY OF FINANCE

Andrea Moultrie
HIGGS & JOHNSON

Portia Nicholson
HIGGS & JOHNSON

Andrew G.S. O'Brien II
GLINTON | SWEETING | O'BRIEN

Arthur K. Parris, Jr.
PARRISWHITTAKER

Courtney Pearce-Hanna
CALLENDERS & CO.

Prince Rahming
PWC BAHAMAS

Chad D. Roberts
CALLENDERS & CO.

Castino D. Sands
LENNOX PATON

Rochelle Sealy
PWC BAHAMAS

Merrit A. Storr
CHANCELLOR CHAMBERS

Burlington Strachan
BAHAMAS ELECTRICITY
CORPORATION

Roy Sweeting
GLINTON | SWEETING | O'BRIEN

Peter Whitehead
OSPREY CONSTRUCTION

Thomas Whitehead
OSPREY CONSTRUCTION

Dwayne Whylly
LENNOX PATON

BAHRAIN

Ahmed Abbas Abdulla
HASSAN RADHI & ASSOCIATES

Ahmed Abdulla
MINISTRY OF WORKS,
MUNICIPALITIES AND
URBAN PLANNING

Mohammed Al Ali
AL ALI & LEGAL
CONSULTANTS LAW OFFICE

Amel Al Aseeri
ZEENAT AL MANSOORI
& ASSOCIATES

Zeenat Al Mansoori
ZEENAT AL MANSOORI
& ASSOCIATES

Salem Al Quti
MINISTRY OF WORKS,
MUNICIPALITIES AND
URBAN PLANNING

Reem Al Rayes
ZEENAT AL MANSOORI
& ASSOCIATES

Waleed Al Sabbagh
BAHRAIN CUSTOMS

Noor Al Taraif
ZU'BI & PARTNERS ATTORNEYS
& LEGAL CONSULTANTS

Dana Alghareeb
HAYA RASHED AL KHALIFA

Shehbaz Ameen
AGILITY LOGISTICS

Nada Azmi
BAHRAIN ECONOMIC
DEVELOPMENT BOARD

Laverne Bacaser
EY

Piyush Bhandari
INTUIT MANAGEMENT
CONSULTANCY

Steven Brown
ASAR – AL RUWAYEH
& PARTNERS

Samir Can'an
GULF HOUSE ENGINEERING SPC

Laith Damer
TALAL ABU-GHAZALEH
LEGAL (TAG-LEGAL)

Qays H. Zu'bi
ZU'BI & PARTNERS ATTORNEYS
& LEGAL CONSULTANTS

Najma Hassan
MINISTRY OF WORKS,
MUNICIPALITIES AND
URBAN PLANNING

Hessa Hussain
THE BENEFIT COMPANY

Khaled Jamsheer
BAHRAIN ENGINEERING
BUREAU

Jawad Habib Jawad
BDO

Anil Kumar
KANOO SHIPPING - YUSUF
BIN AHMED KANOO WLL

Khalid Leila
MINISTRY OF INDUSTRY
& COMMERCE

Ali Makki
MINISTRY OF INDUSTRY
& COMMERCE

Omar Manassaki
ZU'BI & PARTNERS ATTORNEYS
& LEGAL CONSULTANTS

Ali Marhoon
MINISTRY OF INDUSTRY
& COMMERCE

Eman Omar
ZU'BI & PARTNERS ATTORNEYS
& LEGAL CONSULTANTS

Hassan Ali Radhi
HASSAN RADHI & ASSOCIATES

Noor Radhi
HASSAN RADHI & ASSOCIATES

Najib F. Saade
ASAR – AL RUWAYEH
& PARTNERS

Naji Sabt
SURVEY AND LAND
REGISTRATION BUREAU

Oleg Shmal
PWC BAHRAIN

Baiju Thomas
AGILITY LOGISTICS

Aseel Zimmo
SUPREME JUDICIAL COUNCIL

BANGLADESH

CHITTAGONG WATER SUPPLY
AND SEWERAGE AUTHORITY

DHAKA ELECTRICITY SUPPLY
COMPANY LTD. (DESCO)

Munir Uddin Ahamed
WAC LOGISTICS LIMITED

Suprim Ahammed
KPMG

Gias Ahmed
AUKO-TEX GROUP

Rajin Ahmed
DOULAH & DOULAH

Sayeed Abdullah Al Mamun
Khan
A.S. & ASSOCIATES

K.M. Tanjib-Ul Alam
TANJIB ALAM AND ASSOCIATES

Nafiu Alam
FM ASSOCIATES

Shajib Mahmood Alam
COUNSELS LAW PARTNERS

Mahdi Amin
COMFORT GROUP
OF INDUSTRIES

Mohammed Asaduzzaman
SYED ISHTIAQ AHMED
& ASSOCIATES

A.S.A. Bari
A.S. & ASSOCIATES

Kazi Bari
K.A. BARI & CO.

Avijit Barua
GEOSERVICES MARITIME
BD PVT. LTD.

Kapil Basu
PRICEWATERHOUSECOOPERS
PVT. LTD.

Sushmita Basu
PRICEWATERHOUSECOOPERS
PVT. LTD.

Md. Halim Bepari
HAFIZ AND HAQUE SOLICITORS

Mir Osman Bin Nasim
LAWYER

Paavan Chhabra
HEALY CONSULTANTS
GROUP PLC

Arif Moinuddin Chowdhury
MUNIM & ASSOCIATES

Junayed A. Chowdhury
VERTEX CHAMBERS

Md. Liaquat H. Chowdhury
M.L.H. CHOWDHURY & CO.

Mohammed Chowdhury
ANCHOR LOGISTICS

Swad Chowdhury
COUNSELS LAW PARTNERS

Md Khademul Islam Choyon
OBITER DICTUM

Nasirud Doulah
DOULAH & DOULAH

Shamsud Doulah
DOULAH & DOULAH

Dewan Faisal
A.S. & ASSOCIATES

Osman Goni
OGR LEGAL

Simon Guidecoq

Muhammad Tanvir Hashem
Munim
MUNIM & ASSOCIATES

Anam Hossain
FM ASSOCIATES

Farhana Hossain
FM ASSOCIATES

Faria Huq
A.S. & ASSOCIATES

Ashiq Imran
FIALKA

Arif Imtiaz

Aminur Islam
LEX JURIS

Md Aminul Islam
CITY APPAREL-TEX CO.

Shairee Islam
TANJIB ALAM AND ASSOCIATES

Abdul Jabbar
A.S. & ASSOCIATES

Mohammed Jabbar
DBL GROUP

Abdul Khaleque
FIALKA

Abdul Monem Khan
VERTEX CHAMBERS

Afsana Khan
LEE, KHAN & PARTNERS

Anwar A. Khan
GENESIS DENIM

Farhana Islam Khan
SYED ISHTIAQ AHMED
& ASSOCIATES

Mashfiqul Haque Khan
LEX JURIS

Md. Mydul H. Khan
LEX JURIS

Rukhsana Khan
LEX JURIS

Sarjean Rahman Lian
FM ASSOCIATES

Kazi Mahboob
A. WAHAB & CO.

Saqeb Mahbub
MAHBUB & COMPANY

Shyikh Mahdi
VERTEX CHAMBERS

Mohammad Moniruzzaman
THE LAW COUNSEL

Kamrun Nahar

Sifat Jahan Nikita
VERTEX CHAMBERS

Tanvir Quader
VERTEX CHAMBERS

Al Amin Rahman
FM ASSOCIATES

Habiba Rahman
SELF FASHION LIMITED

Md. Saidur Rahman
SELF FASHION LIMITED

Tameem Rahman
OGR LEGAL

Zarin Rahman
FM ASSOCIATES

Badhan Roy
RAHMAN'S CHAMBERS

Saroj Gopal Roy
RAHMAN'S CHAMBERS

Ridi Rubaiyat
TANJIB ALAM AND ASSOCIATES

Sadia Sarah
FM ASSOCIATES

Ammatul Uzma Sathi
A.S. & ASSOCIATES

Mohd. Shariful Islam Shaheen
BANGLADESH ENERGY
REGULATORY COMMISSION

Sohail Shakoor
PRONAYON

Karisma Sharif
HR SOLUTIONS

Imran Siddiq
THE LAW COUNSEL

Tasnia Siddiqui
FM ASSOCIATES

A.M. Mahbub Uddin
MAHBUB & COMPANY

Abdul Wahab
A. WAHAB & CO.

Nurul Wahab
A. WAHAB & CO.

Alicia Yen
HEALY CONSULTANTS
GROUP PLC

Sabrina Zarin
FM ASSOCIATES

BARBADOS

CLARKE GITTENS FARMER

Alicia Archer
ARTEMIS LAW

Kevin Boulard
*ROTHERLEY
CONSTRUCTION INC.*

Patricia Boyce
*EVERSON R. ELCOCK
& CO. LTD.*

Andrew F. Brathwaite
KPMG BARBADOS

Kevin Burke
*ROTHERLEY
CONSTRUCTION INC.*

Vincent Burnett
*MINISTRY OF LABOR AND
SOCIAL SECURITY AND HUMAN
RESOURCE DEVELOPMENT*

Trevor A. Carmichael
CHANCERY CHAMBERS

Adrian Carter
*THE BARBADOS LIGHT AND
POWER COMPANY LTD.*

Berkeley Clark
BJS CUSTOMS SERVICE INC.

Heather A. Clarke
*CORPORATE AFFAIRS
AND INTELLECTUAL
PROPERTY OFFICE*

Andrew Cox
*MINISTRY OF LABOR AND
SOCIAL SECURITY AND HUMAN
RESOURCE DEVELOPMENT*

Sherica J. Mohammed
Cumberbatch
CARRINGTON & SEALY

Adrian W. Cummins
CARRINGTON & SEALY

Gloria Eduardo
PWC BARBADOS

Adrian M. Elcock
*EVERSON R. ELCOCK
& CO. LTD.*

Antonio Elcock
*EVERSON R. ELCOCK
& CO. LTD.*

Andrew C. Ferreira
CHANCERY CHAMBERS

Mark Franklin

Sharalee M.J. Gittens
CHANCERY CHAMBERS

Anice C.N. Granville
LEX CARIBBEAN

Marianne Greenidge
KPMG BARBADOS

Liza A. Harridyal-Sodha
*HARRIDYAL-SODHA
& ASSOCIATES*

Jomo Crowther McGlinne
Hope
ARTEMIS LAW

Claudette Hope-Greenidge
*MINISTRY OF LABOR AND
SOCIAL SECURITY AND HUMAN
RESOURCE DEVELOPMENT*

Nicholas Hughes
BDO BARBADOS

Keisha N. Hyde Porchetta
*HARRIDYAL-SODHA
& ASSOCIATES*

Louisa Lewis-Ward
KPMG BARBADOS

Percy Murrell
*BIG P. CUSTOMS BROKERS
AND AIR SEA AND LAND
TRANSPORT INC.*

Laurel Odle
PWC BARBADOS

Rohan Pennegan
KPMG BARBADOS

Sheridan A. Reece
CARRINGTON & SEALY

Thayreesha Singh
LEX CARIBBEAN

Lynthia Skeete
*MOUNT GAY DISTILLERIES
LTD./REMY AMERICAS*

Heather Tull
*DAVID KING & CO.,
ATTORNEYS-AT-LAW*

Kaye A. Williams
PINEBRIDGE LAW

Stephen Worme
*THE BARBADOS LIGHT AND
POWER COMPANY LTD.*

BELARUS

RUP BELENERGOSETPROEKT

Anastasia Akulich
BOROVTSOV & SALEI

Aliaksandr Anisovich
PROMAUDIT

Anastasia Belenkevich
FBK BEL - PKF INTERNATIONAL

Vladimir G. Biruk
CAPITAL GROUP

Sergei Boiko
*MINSK CABLE (ELECTRICAL)
NETWORK*

Dmitry Bokhan
*VERKHOVODKO &
PARTNERS LLC*

Katsiaryna Buraya
*SYSOUEV, BONDAR,
KHRAPOUTSKI SBH LAW OFFICE*

Irina Butko
*EGOROV PUGINSKY AFANASIEV
AND PARTNERS (EPA&P)*

Alexander Buzo
*EGOROV PUGINSKY AFANASIEV
AND PARTNERS (EPA&P)*

Maksim Chernykh
*MINSK CABLE (ELECTRICAL)
NETWORK*

Eugenia Chetverikova
PWC BELARUS

Sergey Chistyakov
*STEPANOVSKI, PAPAKUL &
PARTNERS ATTORNEYS-AT-LAW*

Aliaksandr Danilevich
DANILEVICH & VOLOZHINETS

Tatsiana Fadzeyeva
BNT LEGAL & TAX

Aliaksei Fidzek
PWC BELARUS

Valentine Galich
VERDICT LAW OFFICE

Maria Golovko
*ARZINGER & PARTNERS
INTERNATIONAL LAW FIRM*

Nikolai Gorelik
*ARZINGER & PARTNERS
INTERNATIONAL LAW FIRM*

Elena Hmeleva
*VERKHOVODKO &
PARTNERS LLC*

Antonina Ivanova
*ANTONINA IVANOVA
LEGAL PRACTICE*

Ulyana Kavalionak
BNT LEGAL & TAX

Yurij Kazakevitch
RÖDL & PARTNER, BELARUS

Dmitry Khalimonchyk
SOFTCLUB LLC

Alexandre Khrapoutski
*SYSOUEV, BONDAR,
KHRAPOUTSKI SBH LAW OFFICE*

Sergey Khromov
*VERKHOVODKO &
PARTNERS LLC*

Siarhei Khvastovich
ALTHAUS LTD.

Alexander Kirienko
*AGENCY OF TURNAROUND
TECHNOLOGIES*

Nina Knyazeva
*VERKHOVODKO &
PARTNERS LLC*

Alexander Kononov
GRANT THORNTON

Nadezhda Koroleva
*SYSOUEV, BONDAR,
KHRAPOUTSKI SBH LAW OFFICE*

Alexander Korsak
*ARZINGER & PARTNERS
INTERNATIONAL LAW FIRM*

Mikhail Y. Kostyukov
ATTORNEY-AT-LAW

Dmitry Kovalchik
*STEPANOVSKI, PAPAKUL &
PARTNERS ATTORNEYS-AT-LAW*

Yuriy Kozikov
BOROVTSOV & SALEI

Yevgeniya Leonidovna
Kravchenko
AZ CONSULTANT

Inna Leus
MINISTRY OF JUSTICE

Yuliya Liashenko
VLASOVA MIKHEL & PARTNERS

Alexander Ließem
BNT LEGAL & TAX

Sergei Makarchuk
*CHSH CERHA HEMPEL
SPIEGELFELD HLAWATI BELARUS*

Natalya Makhanek
GRANT THORNTON

Maksim Maksimov
*VERKHOVODKO &
PARTNERS LLC*

Viktor Marinitch
RÖDL & PARTNER, BELARUS

Elena Mashonskaya
*ARZINGER & PARTNERS
INTERNATIONAL LAW FIRM*

Sergey Mashonsky
*ARZINGER & PARTNERS
INTERNATIONAL LAW FIRM*

Yuliya Matsiuk
*ARZINGER & PARTNERS
INTERNATIONAL LAW FIRM*

Irina Mazurina
VERDICT LAW OFFICE

Aleksei Mikhailov
*ARZINGER & PARTNERS
INTERNATIONAL LAW FIRM*

Anna Miritskaya
BNT LEGAL & TAX

Yulia Mironchik
*ARZINGER & PARTNERS
INTERNATIONAL LAW FIRM*

Aleksandr Mironichenko
MINISTRY OF ECONOMY

Dmitry Montik
LAWYER

Andrei Mucha
*MINSK CABLE (ELECTRICAL)
NETWORK*

Vitaliy Nasanovich
*VERKHOVODKO &
PARTNERS LLC*

Valentina Neizvestnaya
RSM BEL AUDIT

Elena Orda
*NATIONAL BANK OF THE
REPUBLIC OF BELARUS*

Veronika Pavlovskaya
*ARZINGER & PARTNERS
INTERNATIONAL LAW FIRM*

Dzina Pinchuk
PWC BELARUS

Sergey Pinchuk
LAWYER

Victor Pleonkin
*NATIONAL BANK OF THE
REPUBLIC OF BELARUS*

Vera Poklonskaya
*EGOROV PUGINSKY AFANASIEV
AND PARTNERS (EPA&P)*

Kirill Prihodko
*ARZINGER & PARTNERS
INTERNATIONAL LAW FIRM*

Anna Rusetskaya
*EGOROV PUGINSKY AFANASIEV
AND PARTNERS (EPA&P)*

Olga Rybakovskaya
MINISTRY OF ENERGY

Illia Salei
BOROVTSOV & SALEI

Vassili I. Salei
BOROVTSOV & SALEI

Elena Sapego
*STEPANOVSKI, PAPAKUL &
PARTNERS ATTORNEYS-AT-LAW*

Liubov Sergeevna Kulba
GOELLNER SPEDITION

Anna Shalimo
*VERKHOVODKO &
PARTNERS LLC*

Katsiaryna Shmatsina
*AMERICAN BAR
ASSOCIATION SECTION OF
INTERNATIONAL LAW*

Yuliya Shuba
BOROVTSOV & SALEI

Maksim Slepitch
*ARZINGER & PARTNERS
INTERNATIONAL LAW FIRM*

Vitaliy Sorokin
*NATIONAL BANK OF THE
REPUBLIC OF BELARUS*

Klim Stashevsky
*ARZINGER & PARTNERS
INTERNATIONAL LAW FIRM*

Alla Sundukova
*MINISTRY OF TAXES
AND DUTIES*

Dmitry Tihno
PWC BELARUS

Nikita Tolkanitsa
*CHSH CERHA HEMPEL
SPIEGELFELD HLAWATI BELARUS*

Elizaveta Trakhalina
*ARZINGER & PARTNERS
INTERNATIONAL LAW FIRM*

Nikita Nikolayevich Trosko
VLASOVA MIKHEL & PARTNERS

Dennis Turovets
*EGOROV PUGISNKY AFANASIEV
AND PARTNERS (EPA&P)*

Alena Usenia
*ARZINGER & PARTNERS
INTERNATIONAL LAW FIRM*

Pavel Velishkevich
GRANT THORNTON

Irina Veremeichuk
*VERKHOVODKO &
PARTNERS LLC*

Igor Verkhovodko
*VERKHOVODKO &
PARTNERS LLC*

Dmitry Viltovsky
*ARZINGER & PARTNERS
INTERNATIONAL LAW FIRM*

Ekaterina Zabello
VLASOVA MIKHEL & PARTNERS

Vadzim Zakreuski
MINISTRY OF ENERGY

Olga Zdobnova
VLASOVA MIKHEL & PARTNERS

Ekaterina Zheltonoga
VERDICT LAW OFFICE

Maksim Zhukov
*SYSOUEV, BONDAR,
KHRAPOUTSKI SBH LAW OFFICE*

Maxim Znak
JURZNAK LAW FIRM LLC

BELGIUM

Hubert André-Dumont
McGUIREWOODS LLP

Jan Bael
NOTARIAAT 14

Herlinde Baert
NOTARIAAT 14

Matthias Bastiaen
PWC BELGIUM

Michel Bonne
VAN BAEL & BELLIS

Patrick Boone
PWC BELGIUM

Hakim Boularbah
*LIEDEKERKE WOLTERS
WAELBROECK KIRKPATRICK,
MEMBER OF LEX MUNDI*

Stan Brijs
NAUTADUTILH

Sara Cappelle
MONARD LAW

Martijn De Meulemeester
PWC BELGIUM

Kris De Schutter
LOYENS & LOEFF

Didier De Vliegher
NAUTADUTILH

Eric Dirix
COUR DE CASSATION

Camille Dümm
NATIONAL BANK OF BELGIUM

David DuPont
ASHURST LLP

Danaïs Fol
LOYENS & LOEFF

Alex Franchimont
CROWELL & MORING

Alain François
EUBELIUS ATTORNEYS

Liesbet Fransen
*FEDERAL PUBLIC
SERVICE FINANCE*

Pierre-Yves Gillet
CABINET D'ARCHITECTE

Conny Grenson
EUBELIUS ATTORNEYS

Jean-Luc Hagon
NAUTADUTILH

Cedric Hauben
DLA PIPER UK LLP

Sophie Jacmain
NAUTADUTILH

An Jacobs
*LIEDEKERKE WOLTERS
WAELBROECK KIRKPATRICK,
MEMBER OF LEX MUNDI*

Evelien Jamaels
CROWELL & MORING

Stéphanie Kervyn de
Meerendré
DEMINOR SA

Marianne Laruelle

Stephan Legein
*FEDERAL PUBLIC
SERVICE FINANCE*

Nathalie Locht
MCGUIREWOODS LLP

Catherine Longeval
VAN BAEL & BELLIS

Axel Maeterlinck
SIMONT BRAUN

Allan Magerotte
EUBELIUS ATTORNEYS

Jan Moerkerke
*ROYAL FEDERATION OF
MORTGAGE KEEPERS
OF BELGIUM*

Pascale Moreau
PWC BELGIUM

Johan Mouraux
DLA PIPER UK LLP

Leo Peeters
PEETERS ADVOCATEN-AVOCATS

Emmanuel Plasschaert
CROWELL & MORING

Johan Poedts
SIBELGA

Aurélie Pollie
NAUTADUTILH

Eric Schmitz
PWC BELGIUM

Kristof Slootmans
DLA PIPER UK LLP

Frédéric Souchon
PWC BELGIUM

Timothy Speelman
MCGUIREWOODS LLP

Bernard Thuysbaert
DEMINOR SA

Bram Van Cauwenberge
NAUTADUTILH

Jan Van Celst
DLA PIPER UK LLP

Gill Van Damme
PWC BELGIUM

Yannick Van Ranst
*FEDERAL PUBLIC
SERVICE FINANCE*

Bart Van Rossum
B.T.V.

Robert Vermetten
*TRANSPORT & PROJECT
LOGISTICS*

Ivan Verougstraete
COUR DE CASSATION

Katrien Vorlat
MONARD LAW

Bram Vuylsteke
NOTARY BRAM VUYLSTEKE

Tom Wallyn
PWC BELGIUM

Luc Weyts

Dirk Wouters
*WOUTERS, VAN MERODE
& CO. BEDRIJFSREVISOREN
BVBA - MEMBER OF RUSSELL
BEDFORD INTERNATIONAL*

Nicola Zenoni
ASHURST LLP

BELIZE

Emil Arguelles
ARGUELLES & COMPANY LLC

Jenny Armstrong
*BELIZE COMPANIES AND
CORPORATE AFFAIRS REGISTRY*

Andrew Bennett
GLENN D. GODFREY & CO. LLP

Herbert Bradley
*HERBERT BRADLEY CUSTOM
HOUSE BROKERS*

Christopher Coye
COURTENAY COYE LLP

Ana Maria Espat
STRUKTURE ARCHITECTS

Russell Longsworth
*CARIBBEAN SHIPPING
AGENCIES LTD.*

Fred Lumor
FRED LUMOR & CO.

Tania Moody
BARROW & WILLIAMS

Estevan Perera
*ESTEVAN PERERA &
COMPANY LLP*

Vanessa Retreage
REYES RETREAGE LLP

Aldo Reyes
REYES RETREAGE LLP

Wilfred Rhaburn
W. RHABURN CONSULTING

Patricia Rodriguez
*BELIZE COMPANIES AND
CORPORATE AFFAIRS REGISTRY*

Giacomo Sanchez
GRANT THORNTON LLP

Llewelyn Usher
*INTERNATIONAL FINANCIAL
SERVICES COMMISSION*

Saidi Vaccaro
ARGUELLES & COMPANY LLC

Lisa Zayden
HORWATH BELIZE LLP

BENIN

BCEAO

*FIDUCIAIRE CONSEIL ET
ASSISTANCE (FCA)*

GUOCE

JOHN W. FFOOKS & CO.

Modeste Abiala
*BOLLORÉ TRANSPORT
& LOGISTICS*

Abdou Kabir Adoumbou
*CABINET MAÎTRE SAKARIYAOU
NOURO-GUIWA*

Rodolphe Kadoukpe Akoto

Rafikou Agnila Alabi
*CABINET MAÎTRE
RAFIKOU ALABI*

Françoise Amoussou
NOUVELLE VISION

Aum Rockas Amoussouvi
CABINET RAFIKOU A. ALABI

Charles Badou
*CABINET D'AVOCATS
CHARLES BADOU*

Ferdinand Bokossa Yaou
ENGINEER

Is-Dine Bouraima
*AGENCE DE PROMOTION DES
INVESTISSEMENTS ET DES
EXPORTATIONS (APIEX)*

Sètondji Pierre Codjia
*CABINET D'AVOCATS
CHARLES BADOU*

Bonaventure Dansou
*AFRICA HANDLING
AND LOGISTICS*

Michel Degbo
*SOCIÉTÉ BÉNINOISE
D'ENERGIE ELECTRIQUE*

Nadine Dossou Sakponou
CABINET ROBERT M. DOSSOU

Rodrigue Dossou-Togbe

Djakaridja Fofana
PWC CÔTE D'IVOIRE

Nadege Honvo

Narcisse Justin Soglo
*ORDRE NATIONAL DES
ARCHITECTES ET URBANISTES*

Noel Kelembho
SDV LOGISTICS

William Kodjoh-Kpakpassou
*TRIBUNAL DE PREMIÈRE
INSTANCE DE ABOMEY CALAVI*

Monique Kothofa Faihun
*ETUDE MAÎTRE
KOTHOFA FAIHUN*

Victorien D. Kougblenou
*AGENCE NATIONALE
DU DOMAINE ET DU
FONCIER (ANDF)*

Alain René Kpetehoto
CABINET ARTECH

Sakariyaou Nourou-Guiwa
*CABINET MAÎTRE SAKARIYAOU
NOURO-GUIWA*

Arouna Oloulade
*SOCIÉTÉ BÉNINOISE
D'ENERGIE ELECTRIQUE*

Claude Olympio
*MINISTERE DE LA JUSTICE
ET DE LA LEGISLATION*

Jules Pofagi

Alexandrine Falilatou
Saizonou-Bedie
*CABINET D'AVOCATS
ALEXANDRINE F.
SAIZONOU-BEDIE*

Olagnika Salam
*OFFICE NOTARIAL
OLAGNIKA SALAM*

Alidou Sare
*AGENCE NATIONALE
DU DOMAINE ET DU
FONCIER (ANDF)*

Hermann Senou
*ENTREPRISE GÉNÉRALE DE
CONSTRUCTION MACKHO*

Agbodjan Serge Prince
LAWYER

Yessoufou Tanda
*MINISTÈRE DU CADRE DE VIE ET
DU DÉVELOPPEMENT DURABLE*

Jean-Bosco Todjinou
ECOPLAN SARL

Gilles Togan
MAERSK BENIN SA

Augustin Fatondji Tonan
*PORT AUTONOME
DE COTONOU*

Bénoit Wandi
*AGENCE NATIONALE
DU DOMAINE ET DU
FONCIER (ANDF)*

Adjété Fabrice O. Wilson
*CABINET MAÎTRE
RAFIKOU ALABI*

BHUTAN

*BHUTAN POWER
CORPORATION LTD.*

Tika Ram Bhandari
*CONTINENTAL ACCOUNTS
& CONSULTANCY SERVICE*

Sonam Chophel
*CREDIT INFORMATION
BUREAU OF BHUTAN*

Samten Dhendup
THIMPHU THROMDE

Bhim Dhungel
ZORIG CONSULTANCY PVT. LTD.

Kencho Dorji
LEKO PACKERS

Kencho Dorji
MINISTRY OF FINANCE

Choki Gyeltshen
MINISTRY OF FINANCE

Goutam Mukherjee
KCR PRIVATE LIMITED

Tenzin Namgay
*NATIONAL LAND
COMMISSION SECRETARIAT*

Tashi Penjor
*MINISTRY OF
ECONOMIC AFFAIRS*

Dorji Phuntsho
*ROYAL SECURITIES EXCHANGE
OF BHUTAN LTD.*

Shrowan Pradhan
NICHE FINANCIAL SERVICES

Parishad Rai
*BHUTAN SILICON METAL
PRIVATE LIMITED*

Jamyang Sherab
GARUDA LEGAL SERVICES

Neelam Thapa
LEKO PACKERS

Karma Tshewang
VISIT ASIA

Prakash Veer Tyagi
GATEWAY RAIL FRIGHT LIMITED

Kinley Wangdi
*CREDIT INFORMATION
BUREAU OF BHUTAN*

Phuntsho Wangdi
MINISTRY OF FINANCE

Sonam Wangdi
*MINISTRY OF LABOUR AND
HUMAN RESOURCES*

Karma Yeshey
*MINISTRY OF
ECONOMIC AFFAIRS*

BOLIVIA

PWC BOLIVIA

Fernando Aguirre
BUFETE AGUIRRE SOC. CIV.

Ignacio Aguirre
BUFETE AGUIRRE SOC. CIV.

Carolina Aguirre Urioste
BUFETE AGUIRRE SOC. CIV.

René Alcázar
*AUTORIDAD DE SUPERVISIÓN
DEL SISTEMA FINANCIERO*

Richard César Alcócer Garnica
*AUTORIDAD DE FISCALIZACIÓN
Y CONTROL SOCIAL DE
ELECTRICIDAD (AE)*

Daniela Aragonés Cortez
*SANJINÉS &
ASOCIADOS - ABOGADOS*

Geovanni Armaza R.
A. R. LOGISTICS BOLIVIA

Johnny Arteaga Chavez
*DIRECCIÓN GENERAL DE
TIERRAS DE SANTA CRUZ*

Pedro Asturizaga
*AUTORIDAD DE SUPERVISIÓN
DEL SISTEMA FINANCIERO*

Sergio Avendaño
*RIGOBERTO PAREDES
& ASSOCIATES*

Rigoberto Paredes Ayllón
*RIGOBERTO PAREDES
& ASSOCIATES*

Leonardo Azurduy Saunero
*QUINTANILLA, SORIA &
NISHIZAWA SOC. CIV.*

Andrea Bollmann-Duarte
*SALAZAR SALAZAR
& ASOCIADOS*

Walter B. Calla Cardenas
*COLEGIO DEPARTAMENTAL
DE ARQUITECTOS DE LA PAZ*

Grisett Carrasco Guerra
*C.R. & F. ROJAS ABOGADOS,
MEMBER OF LEX MUNDI*

Asdrúval Columba Jofre
AC CONSULTORES LEGALES

Carla De la Barra
*RIGOBERTO PAREDES
& ASSOCIATES*

Sergio Delgadillo
BOLIVIAN BANK LAWYER

Jose Diaz
DM CONSULTORES LEGALES

Cynthia Diaz Quevedo
FERRERE ATTORNEYS

Jose Luis Diaz Romero
*SERVICIOS GENERALES
EN ELECTRICIDAD Y
CONSTRUCCIÓN (SGEC)*

Alejandra Guevara
GUEVARA & GUTIÉRREZ SC

Sergio Gutierrez
*GUTIERREZ CONSTRUCCION
Y MATERIALES*

Jorge Herrera
DM CONSULTORES LEGALES

Juan Carlos Ibañez Pereyra
*GLOBAL LINES - FREIGHT
AND CARGO SRL*

Jorge Luis Inchauste
GUEVARA & GUTIÉRREZ SC

Jaime M. Jiménez Alvarez
*COLEGIO DE INGENIEROS
ELECTRICISTAS Y
ELECTRÓNICOS LA PAZ*

Rodrigo Jiménez-Cusicanqui
*SALAZAR SALAZAR
& ASOCIADOS*

Paola Justiniano Arias
*SANJINÉS &
ASOCIADOS - ABOGADOS*

Fernando Krutzfeldt
Monasterio
*VON BORRIES BLANCO
ESTUDIO DE ABOGADOS*

Omar Martinez Velasquez
*AUTORIDAD DE FISCALIZACIÓN
Y CONTROL SOCIAL DE
ELECTRICIDAD (AE)*

Alejandra Bernal Mercado
*C.R. & F. ROJAS ABOGADOS,
MEMBER OF LEX MUNDI*

Rubí Mondaca
*AUTORIDAD DE SUPERVISIÓN
DEL SISTEMA FINANCIERO*

Ariel Morales Vasquez
*C.R. & F. ROJAS ABOGADOS,
MEMBER OF LEX MUNDI*

Ramiro Moreno
*MORENO BALDIVIESO
ESTUDIO DE ABOGADOS*

Ana Carola Muñoz Añez
INDACOCHEA & ASOCIADOS

Mirko Olmos
*C.R. & F. ROJAS ABOGADOS,
MEMBER OF LEX MUNDI*

David Pando
*AUTORIDAD DE SUPERVISIÓN
DEL SISTEMA FINANCIERO*

Carlos Pinto
FERRERE ATTORNEYS

Rocío Plata
*RIGOBERTO PAREDES
& ASSOCIATES*

Oscar Antonio Plaza Ponte
Sosa
*BURO DE INFORMACIÓN
INFOCENTER SA*

Guillermo Pou Munt
CEAS SRL

Ilda Raga Prado
*SOCIEDAD DE INGENIEROS
DE BOLIVIA*

Joaquín Rodríguez
*AUTORIDAD DE FISCALIZACIÓN
Y CONTROL SOCIAL DE
ELECTRICIDAD (AE)*

Patricio Rojas
*C.R. & F. ROJAS ABOGADOS,
MEMBER OF LEX MUNDI*

Mariela Rojas Mendieta
*BURO DE INFORMACIÓN
INFOCENTER SA*

Sergio Salazar-Arce
*SALAZAR SALAZAR
& ASOCIADOS*

Sergio Salazar-Machicado
*SALAZAR SALAZAR
& ASOCIADOS*

Sandra Salinas
*C.R. & F. ROJAS ABOGADOS,
MEMBER OF LEX MUNDI*

Raúl Sanjinés Elizagoyen
*SANJINÉS &
ASOCIADOS - ABOGADOS*

Carla Saracho
WBC ABOGADOS SRL

Jorge N. Serrate
*WÜRTH BEDOYA COSTA
DU RELS ABOGADOS*

Diego Tamayo
*WÜRTH BEDOYA COSTA
DU RELS ABOGADOS*

A. Mauricio Torrico Galindo
*QUINTANILLA, SORIA &
NISHIZAWA SOC. CIV.*

Ramiro Velasco
*COLEGIO DE INGENIEROS
ELECTRICISTAS Y
ELECTRÓNICOS LA PAZ*

BOSNIA AND
HERZEGOVINA

Jasmin Bešo
*FERK (REGULATORY
COMMISSION FOR ENERGY IN
THE FEDERATION OF BOSNIA
AND HERZEGOVINA)*

Dario Biščević
DB SCHENKER

Bojana Bošnjak-London
MARIĆ & CO. LAW FIRM

Mubera Brkovic
*PWC BOSNIA AND
HERZEGOVINA*

Zlatko Čengić
UNIONINVEST D.D.

Mia Delić
SPAHO LAW OFFICE

Slaven Dizdar
MARIĆ & CO. LAW FIRM

Višnja Dizdarević
MARIĆ & CO. LAW FIRM

Amina Dugum

Feđa Dupovac
*ADVOKATSKO DRUŠTVO
SPAHO D.O.O. SARAJEVO*

Dina Grebo
*CHAMBER OF COMMERCE
OF CANTON SARAJEVO*

Arijana Hadžiahmetović-Softić
MARIĆ & CO. LAW FIRM

Kemal Hadzimusic
*CHAMBER OF COMMERCE
OF CANTON SARAJEVO*

Vedran Hadžimustafić
WOLF THEISS D.O.O. SARAJEVO

Nermina Hadziosmanovich
*PWC BOSNIA AND
HERZEGOVINA*

Samra Hadžović
*LAW OFFICE HADZOVIC
IN ASSOCIATION WITH
WOLF THEISS*

Zijad Hasović
KOMORA REVIZORA FBIH

Amir Husić
*LAGERMAX AED BOSNA I
HERZEGOWINA D.O.O.*

Nusmir Huskić
HUSKIC LAW OFFICE

Emir Ibisevic
*DELOITTE ADVISORY
SERVICES D.O.O.*

Arela Jusufbasić-Goloman
*LAWYERS' OFFICE TKALCIC-
DULIC, PREBANIC, RIZVIC &
JUSUFBASIC-GOLOMAN*

Harun Kahvedžić
*PUBLIC EMPLOYMENT OFFICE
OF ZENICA-DOBOJ CANTON
AND UNIVERSITY IN ZENICA*

Nedžada Kapidžić
NOTARY

Salko Kruho
DB SCHENKER

Sejda Kruščica-Fejzić
*JP ELEKTROPRIVREDA
BIH PODRUŽNICA
ELEKTRODISTRIBUCIJA
SARAJEVO*

Emil Kučković
LRC CREDIT BUREAU

Muamer Mahmutovic
*CHAMBER OF COMMERCE
OF CANTON SARAJEVO*

Nebojsa Makaric
*ATTORNEY-AT-LAW
OFFICE LAWYERS
RUZICA TOPIC, NEBOJSA
MAKARIC, SASA TOPIC*

Branko Marić
MARIĆ & CO. LAW FIRM

Mejrima Memić-Drino
*PUBLIC EMPLOYMENT OFFICE
OF ZENICA-DOBOJ CANTON*

Emir Naimkadić
*JP ELEKTROPRIVREDA
BIH PODRUŽNICA
ELEKTRODISTRIBUCIJA
SARAJEVO*

Indir Osmic
*CMS REICH-ROHRWIG
HAINZ D.O.O.*

Aida Plivac
*PWC BOSNIA AND
HERZEGOVINA*

Lejla Popara

Olodar Prebanić
*LAWYERS' OFFICE TKALCIC-
DULIC, PREBANIC, RIZVIC &
JUSUFBASIC-GOLOMAN*

Đorđe Racković
*CENTRAL BANK OF BOSNIA
AND HERZEGOVINA*

Sanja Saf
UNIONINVEST D.D.

Hasib Salkić
JUMP LOGISTICS D.O.O.

Lana Sarajlic

Arjana Selimić
*JP ELEKTROPRIVREDA
BIH PODRUŽNICA
ELEKTRODISTRIBUCIJA
SARAJEVO*

Nihad Sijerčić
KN KARANOVIĆ & NIKOLIĆ

Emir Spaho
*ADVOKATSKO DRUŠTVO
SPAHO D.O.O. SARAJEVO*

Mehmed Spaho
*ADVOKATSKO DRUŠTVO
SPAHO D.O.O. SARAJEVO*

Selma Spaho
*ADVOKATSKO DRUŠTVO
SPAHO D.O.O. SARAJEVO*

Mile Srdanović
*FERK (REGULATORY
COMMISSION FOR ENERGY IN
THE FEDERATION OF BOSNIA
AND HERZEGOVINA)*

Bojana Tkalčić-Djulić
*LAWYERS' OFFICE TKALCIC-
DULIC, PREBANIC, RIZVIC &
JUSUFBASIC-GOLOMAN*

Sasa Topic
*ATTORNEY-AT-LAW
OFFICE LAWYERS
RUZICA TOPIC, NEBOJSA
MAKARIC, SASA TOPIC*

Ružica Topić
*ATTORNEY-AT-LAW
OFFICE LAWYERS
RUZICA TOPIC, NEBOJSA
MAKARIC, SASA TOPIC*

Edin Zametica
*DERK (STATE ELECTRICITY
REGULATORY COMMISSION)*

BOTSWANA

Jeffrey Bookbinder
BOOKBINDER BUSINESS LAW

Andrew Chifedi
*ANDREWS REMOVAL
& FREIGHT*

One Damane
MODIMO & ASSOCIATES

Nigel Dixon-Warren
KPMG

Candice Dubane
COLLINS NEWMAN & CO.

Lesego Gabasiane
COLLINS NEWMAN & CO.

Vasie Hager
PWC BOTSWANA

Julius Mwaniki Kanja
*CHIBANDA,
MAKGALEMELE & CO.*

We-Bathu Kwele
*CHIBANDA,
MAKGALEMELE & CO.*

Naledi Leepile
PWC BOTSWANA

Fidellis Lekhao
*BOTSWANA UNIFIED
REVENUE SERVICE (BURS)*

Queen Letshabo
RAHIM KHAN & COMPANY

City Mafa
*TECTURA INTERNATIONAL
BOTSWANA*

Mercia Bonzo Makgalemele
*CHIBANDA,
MAKGALEMELE & CO.*

Kgaotsang Matthews
MORIBAME MATTHEWS

Kusigani Mbambo
BOOKBINDER BUSINESS LAW

Finola McMahon
OSEI-OFEI SWABI & CO.

Ntandoyakhe Mhlanga
RAHIM KHAN & COMPANY

Gaselabotlhe Mmolawa
*BRANDBUCKET
INVESTMENT PTY. LTD.*

Peo Malaika Mmopi
BOOKBINDER BUSINESS LAW

Abel Walter Modimo
MODIMO & ASSOCIATES

Doreen Moeletsi
*BOTSWANA UNIFIED
REVENUE SERVICE (BURS)*

Tiroeaone Mojatale
*BRANDBUCKET
INVESTMENT PTY. LTD.*

Khumo Morupisi
*KUA MOSI ENTERPRISES
PTY. LTD.*

Johannes Mosanawe
*MINISTRY OF LABOUR
AND HOME AFFAIRS*

Petros Mosholombe
*BOTSWANA POWER
CORPORATION*

Bone Motau
COLLINS NEWMAN & CO.

Mmatshipi Motsepe
MANICA AFRICA PTY. LTD.

Robert Mpabanga
*TRANSUNION BOTSWANA
(PTY) LTD.*

Walter Mushi
COLLINS NEWMAN & CO.

Olebile Daphney Muzila
BOOKBINDER BUSINESS LAW

Gasepale Nametso
SLIGHT SHIFT PTY. LTD.

Rajesh Narasimhan
GRANT THORNTON LLP

Kwadwo Osei-Ofei
OSEI-OFEI SWABI & CO.

Onalenna Otlaadisa Diloro
BOOKBINDER BUSINESS LAW

Rory Peynado
GABORONE CITY COUNCIL

Fred Phiri
*DALGLIESH LINDSAY
GROUP ARCHITECTS*

Karen Phiri
ARMSTRONGS ATTORNEYS

Butler Phirie
PWC BOTSWANA

Joanne Robinson
OSEI-OFEI SWABI & CO.

Piyush Sharma
PIYUSH SHARMA ATTORNEYS

Moemedi J. Tafa
ARMSTRONGS ATTORNEYS

Girlie Tobedza
*CHIBANDA,
MAKGALEMELE & CO.*

Nilusha Weeraratne
PWC BOTSWANA

BRAZIL

Maysa Abrahao Tavares
Verzola
*SOUZA, CESCON, BARRIEU
& FLESCH ADVOGADOS*

Eduardo Abrantes
*SOUZA, CESCON, BARRIEU
& FLESCH ADVOGADOS*

Marina Agueda
*DE LUCA, DERENUSSON,
SCHUTTOFF E AZEVEDO
ADVOGADOS*

Antônio Aires
DEMAREST ADVOGADOS

Luiz Albieri
ALBIERI E ASSOCIADOS

Maria Lúcia Almeida
Prado e Silva
DEMAREST ADVOGADOS

Leila Alves
*DE LUCA, DERENUSSON,
SCHUTTOFF E AZEVEDO
ADVOGADOS*

Franklin Alves de Oliveira
Gomes Filho
*LOBO & DE RIZZO
ADVOGADOS*

Ivana Amorim de Coelho
Bomfim
*MACHADO, MEYER, SENDACZ
E OPICE ADVOGADOS*

Gabriel Araujo
*OLIVERIO DAL FABBRO
ADVOGADOS*

Gianvito Ardito
PINHEIRO NETO ADVOGADOS

Amanda Arêas
SOUZA, CESCON, BARRIEU & FLESCH ADVOGADOS

Luiza Arjona
SOUZA, CESCON, BARRIEU & FLESCH ADVOGADOS

Ticiana Ayala
CHEDIAK, LOPES DA COSTA, CRISTOFARO, MENEZES CÔRTES, RENNÓ E ARAGÃO ADVOGADOS

Matheus Azevedo Bastos de Oliveira
DEMAREST ADVOGADOS

Josef Azulay
BARBOSA, MÜSSNICH & ARAGÃO ADVOGADOS

Aldo Azullini
GRUPO BECHTRANS

Bruno Balduccini
PINHEIRO NETO ADVOGADOS

Rafael Baptista Baleroni
SOUZA, CESCON, BARRIEU & FLESCH ADVOGADOS

Rodrigo Baraldi dos Santos
BARALDI ADVOCACIA EMPRESARIAL

Sarah Barbassa
SOUZA, CESCON, BARRIEU & FLESCH ADVOGADOS

Priscyla Barbosa
VEIRANO ADVOGADOS

Matheus Barcelos
BARBOSA, MÜSSNICH & ARAGÃO ADVOGADOS

Sergio Basso
AES ELETROPAULO

Fernanda Bastos
SOUZA, CESCON, BARRIEU & FLESCH ADVOGADOS

Leonardo Bastos Carvalho
LETECH ENGENHARIA

Júlio Henrique Batista
GUERRA E BATISTA ADVOGADOS

Roberto Bekierman
FRAGA, BEKIERMAN E CRISTIANO ADVOGADOS

Gilberto Belleza
BELLEZA & BATALHA C. DO LAGO ARQUITETOS ASSOCIADOS

Marcello Bernardes
PINHEIRO NETO ADVOGADOS

Leonardo Bertolazzi
BRAGA NASCIMENTO E ZILIO LAW FIRM

Camila Biral Vieira da Cunha Martins
DEMAREST ADVOGADOS

Rodrigo Bittencourt
ULHÔA CANTO, REZENDE E GUERRA-ADVOGADOS

Alexander Blanco de Oliveira
WORLD LINE FREIGHT FORWARDER LTDA

Amir Bocayuva Cunha
BARBOSA, MÜSSNICH & ARAGÃO ADVOGADOS

Mellina Bortoli Caliman
PINHEIRO NETO ADVOGADOS

Carlos David Albuquerque Braga
SOUZA, CESCON, BARRIEU & FLESCH ADVOGADOS

Diana Braga Nascimento Toscani
BRAGA NASCIMENTO E ZILIO LAW FIRM

Leonardo Brandao
EY SERVIÇOS TRIBUTÁRIOS SS

Natalia Brasil Correa da Silva

Sergio Bronstein
VEIRANO ADVOGADOS

João Henrique Brum
DOMINGES E. PINHO CONTADORES

Marcus Brumano
DEMAREST ADVOGADOS

Cristina de Freitas Bueno
SOUZA, CESCON, BARRIEU & FLESCH ADVOGADOS

Fernanda Ferreira Bastos Buhatem
SOUZA, CESCON, BARRIEU & FLESCH ADVOGADOS

Frederico Buosi
VELLA PUGLIESE BUOSI GUIDONI

Luiz Guilherme Camargo
SOUZA, CESCON, BARRIEU & FLESCH ADVOGADOS

Paulo Campana
FELSBERG ADVOGADOS

Raíssa Campelo
PINHEIRO NETO ADVOGADOS

Renato Canizares
DEMAREST ADVOGADOS

Angela Carvalho
SOUZA, CESCON, BARRIEU & FLESCH ADVOGADOS

Angela Pedreira de Freitas Joaquim de Carvalho
SOUZA, CESCON, BARRIEU & FLESCH ADVOGADOS

David Carvalho
KRAFT ADVOGADOS ASSOCIADOS

Érika Carvalho
SOUZA, CESCON, BARRIEU & FLESCH ADVOGADOS

Thiago Carvalho Stob
NORONHA ADVOGADOS

Ramon Castilho
SOUZA, CESCON, BARRIEU & FLESCH ADVOGADOS

Roberto Castro
MACHADO, MEYER, SENDACZ E OPICE ADVOGADOS

Fernanda Cirne Montorfano Gibson
SOUZA, CESCON, BARRIEU & FLESCH ADVOGADOS

Ricardo E. Vieira Coelho
PINHEIRO NETO ADVOGADOS

Roberta Coelho de Souza Batalha
DEMAREST ADVOGADOS

Vivian Coelho dos Santos Breder
ULHÔA CANTO, REZENDE E GUERRA-ADVOGADOS

Caroline Cordeiro
COSTA E TAVARES PAES SOCIEDADE DE ADVOGADOS

Luiz Felipe Cordeiro
CHEDIAK, LOPES DA COSTA, CRISTOFARO, MENEZES CÔRTES, RENNÓ E ARAGÃO ADVOGADOS

Marcel Cordeiro
PWC BRAZIL

Pedro Costa
BARBOSA, MÜSSNICH & ARAGÃO ADVOGADOS

Bruno Henrique Coutinho de Aguiar
RAYES & FAGUNDES ADVOGADOS

Maria Cibele Crepaldi Affonso dos Santos
COSTA E TAVARES PAES SOCIEDADE DE ADVOGADOS

Marcelo Leonardo Cristiano
FRAGA, BEKIERMAN E CRISTIANO ADVOGADOS

Camilla Cunha
BARBOSA, MÜSSNICH & ARAGÃO ADVOGADOS

Gabriel da Câmara de Queiroz
DEMAREST ADVOGADOS

Carlos da Costa e Silva Filho
VIEIRA, REZENDE, BARBOSA E GUERREIRO ADVOGADOS

Pedro da Cunha e Silva de Carvalho
VELLA PUGLIESE BUOSI GUIDONI

Adriana Daiuto
DEMAREST ADVOGADOS

João Luis Ribeiro de Almeida
DEMAREST ADVOGADOS

Ana Beatriz de Almeida Lobo
VEIRANO ADVOGADOS

Fernando Amaral de Almeida Prado
SINERCONSULT

Fabíola Meira de Almeida Santos
BRAGA NASCIMENTO E ZILIO LAW FIRM

João Victor de Barros
VEIRANO ADVOGADOS

Rodrigo de Castro
VEIRANO ADVOGADOS

Rafael De Conti
DE CONTI LAW OFFICE

Otavio Augusto De Farias Carratu
GUERRA E BATISTA ADVOGADOS

João Claudio De Luca Junior
DE LUCA, DERENUSSON, SCHUTTOFF E AZEVEDO ADVOGADOS

Beatriz Gross Bueno de Moraes Gomes de Sá
DE VIVO, WHITAKER E CASTRO ADVOGADOS

Daniela de Pontes Andrade
LOBO & DE RIZZO ADVOGADOS

Gabriela Dell Agnolo de Carvalho
ZEIGLER E MENDONÇA DE BARROS SOCIEDADE DE ADVOGADOS (ZMB)

Nádia Demoliner Lacerda da Silva
MUNDIE E ADVOGADOS

Eduardo Depassier
LOESER E PORTELA ADVOGADOS

Claudia Derenusson Riedel
DE LUCA, DERENUSSON, SCHUTTOFF E AZEVEDO ADVOGADOS

Heloisa Bonciani Nader di Cunto
DUARTE GARCIA, CASELLI GUIMARÃES E TERRA ADVOGADOS

Cristiano Dias
COSTA E TAVARES PAES SOCIEDADE DE ADVOGADOS

Wagner Douglas Dockhorn
COPREVI ADVOCACIA PREVIDENCIÁRIA

José Ricardo dos Santos Luz Júnior
BRAGA NASCIMENTO E ZILIO LAW FIRM

Rodrigo Duarte
VEIRANO ADVOGADOS

Brigida Melo e Cruz Gama Filho
PINHEIRO NETO ADVOGADOS

Marcelo Elias
PINHEIRO GUIMARÃES ADVOGADOS

Bruna Esch
BARBOSA, MÜSSNICH & ARAGÃO ADVOGADOS

Renata Espinola Gomes
EY SERVIÇOS TRIBUTÁRIOS SS

João Paulo F.A. Fagundes
RAYES & FAGUNDES ADVOGADOS

Fabio Falkenburger
MACHADO, MEYER, SENDACZ E OPICE ADVOGADOS

Vanessa Felício
VEIRANO ADVOGADOS

Thomas Benes Felsberg
FELSBERG ADVOGADOS

Josney Ferraz
UNITS AUDITORES INDEPENDENTES

João Guilherme Ferreira
NORONHA ADVOGADOS

Marilia Ferreira de Miranda
TABELIÃ DE NOTAS E PROTESTO DE SANTA BRANCA/SP

Gabriella Ferreira do Nascimento

Renata Fialho
VEIRANO ADVOGADOS

Wesley Figueira
RUSSELL BEDFORD INTERNATIONAL

Guilherme Filardi
DE LUCA, DERENUSSON, SCHUTTOFF E AZEVEDO ADVOGADOS

Nadio Filho
SMX LOGISTICS

Rodolpho Finimundi
BRAGA NASCIMENTO E ZILIO LAW FIRM

Leandro Amorim C. Fonseca
COSTA E TAVARES PAES SOCIEDADE DE ADVOGADOS

Alessandra Fonseca de Morais
PINHEIRO NETO ADVOGADOS

Julian Fonseca Peña Chediak
CHEDIAK, LOPES DA COSTA, CRISTOFARO, MENEZES CÔRTES, RENNÓ E ARAGÃO ADVOGADOS

Luiz Carlos Fraga
FRAGA, BEKIERMAN E CRISTIANO ADVOGADOS

Jessica Frisch Rozes Kimelblat
SOUZA, CESCON, BARRIEU & FLESCH ADVOGADOS

Everton Gabriel Monezzi
BRAGA NASCIMENTO E ZILIO LAW FIRM

Rafael Gagliardi
DEMAREST ADVOGADOS

Rodrigo Garcia da Fonseca
FONSECA E SALLES LIMA ADVOGADOS ASSOCIADOS

Rafaella Gentil Gervaerd
CHEDIAK, LOPES DA COSTA, CRISTOFARO, MENEZES CÔRTES, RENNÓ E ARAGÃO ADVOGADOS

Luis Filipe Gentil Pedro
MACHADO, MEYER, SENDACZ E OPICE ADVOGADOS

Murilo Germiniani
MACHADO, MEYER, SENDACZ E OPICE ADVOGADOS

Daniel Giacomini
BRAGA NASCIMENTO E ZILIO LAW FIRM

Deborah Christina Giacomini
SOUZA, CESCON, BARRIEU & FLESCH ADVOGADOS

Luiz Marcelo Góis
BARBOSA, MÜSSNICH & ARAGÃO ADVOGADOS

Rodrigo Gomes Maia
NORONHA ADVOGADOS

Diógenes Gonçalves
PINHEIRO NETO ADVOGADOS

Renata Gonçalves
HALLIBURTON PRODUTOS LTDA

Jean Stnio Goncalves Feitosa
BRL GLOBAL LOGISTICS

Maria Eduarda Goston Tisi Ferraz
MACHADO, MEYER, SENDACZ E OPICE ADVOGADOS

Eduardo Ferraz Guerra
GUERRA E BATISTA ADVOGADOS

Marco Guerra
KÖNIG DO BRASIL CARGA INTERNACIONAL LTDA

Raphael Guerra
KÖNIG DO BRASIL CARGA INTERNACIONAL LTDA

António Carlos Guidoni Filho
VELLA PUGLIESE BUOSI GUIDONI

Bruno Habib Negreiros Barbosa
VEIRANO ADVOGADOS

Enrique Hadad
LOESER E PORTELA ADVOGADOS

Felipe Hanszmann
VIEIRA, REZENDE, BARBOSA E GUERREIRO ADVOGADOS

Luis Hiar
LEFOSSE ADVOGADOS

Alberto Jun II Shin
SOUZA, CESCON, BARRIEU & FLESCH ADVOGADOS

Carlos Augusto Leite Junqueira
SOUZA, CESCON, BARRIEU & FLESCH ADVOGADOS

Flavio Kelner
RAF ARQUITETURA E PLANEJAMENTO LTDA

Breno Kingma
*VIEIRA, REZENDE, BARBOSA
E GUERREIRO ADVOGADOS*

Dan Kraft
*KRAFT ADVOGADOS
ASSOCIADOS*

Gabriela Krieck
*SOUZA, CESCON, BARRIEU
& FLESCH ADVOGADOS*

Laila Kurati
SERASA SA

Sergio André Laclau
VEIRANO ADVOGADOS

José Paulo Lago Alves
Pequeno
NORONHA ADVOGADOS

Daniel Lago Rodrigues
*REGISTRO DE IMÓVEIS DE
TABOÃO DA SERRA*

Alessandro Lambiasi
DE CONTI LAW OFFICE

Thomás Lampster
PINHEIRO NETO ADVOGADOS

José Augusto Leal
*CASTRO, BARROS, SOBRAL,
GOMES ADVOGADOS*

André Leão
*COSTA E TAVARES PAES
SOCIEDADE DE ADVOGADOS*

Alexandre Leite Ribeiro do
Valle
*VM&L SOCIEDADE
DE ADVOGADOS*

Charles Lenzi
AES ELETROPAULO

Karina Lerner
*BARBOSA, MÜSSNICH &
ARAGÃO ADVOGADOS*

Rafael Lins e Silva Nascimento
*COSTA E TAVARES PAES
SOCIEDADE DE ADVOGADOS*

Guilherme Lippel
*SOUZA, CESCON, BARRIEU
& FLESCH ADVOGADOS*

Maury Lobo de Athayde
*CHAVES, GELMAN, MACHADO,
GILBERTO E BARBOZA*

Odilon Lopes
*UNITS AUDITORES
INDEPENDENTES*

Tiago Lopes
*SOUZA, CESCON, BARRIEU
& FLESCH ADVOGADOS*

Letícia Lucas
*BARALDI ADVOCACIA
EMPRESARIAL*

Zora Lyra
*VIEIRA, REZENDE, BARBOSA
E GUERREIRO ADVOGADOS*

Marina Maccabelli
DEMAREST ADVOGADOS

Thiago Machado
*SOUZA, CESCON, BARRIEU
& FLESCH ADVOGADOS*

Pedro Maciel
LEFOSSE ADVOGADOS

Lucilena Madaleno
EY SERVIÇOS TRIBUTÁRIOS SS

Renato G.R. Maggio
*MACHADO, MEYER, SENDACZ
E OPICE ADVOGADOS*

José Guilherme do
Nascimento Malheiro
*SOUZA, CESCON, BARRIEU
& FLESCH ADVOGADOS*

Estêvão Mallet
*MALLET E ADVOGADOS
ASSOCIADOS*

Glaucia Mara Coelho
*MACHADO, MEYER, SENDACZ
E OPICE ADVOGADOS*

Johnatan Maranhao
PINHEIRO NETO ADVOGADOS

Manuel Marinho
PWC BRAZIL

Deborah Marques
*SOUZA, CESCON, BARRIEU
& FLESCH ADVOGADOS*

Ana Marra
EY SERVIÇOS TRIBUTÁRIOS SS

Stefania Martignago
*DE LUCA, DERENUSSON,
SCHUTTOFF E AZEVEDO
ADVOGADOS*

Aldo Martinez
*SOUZA, CESCON, BARRIEU
& FLESCH ADVOGADOS*

Larissa Martins
NORONHA ADVOGADOS

Vinicius Martins
*SOUZA, CESCON, BARRIEU
& FLESCH ADVOGADOS*

Renata Martins de Oliveira
*MACHADO, MEYER, SENDACZ
E OPICE ADVOGADOS*

Roberta R. Matheus
LEFOSSE ADVOGADOS

Gisela Mation
*MACHADO, MEYER, SENDACZ
E OPICE ADVOGADOS*

Eduardo Augusto Mattar
*PINHEIRO GUIMARÃES
ADVOGADOS*

Gustavo Mattos
*VELLA PUGLIESE
BUOSI GUIDONI*

Marcelo Mattos
VEIRANO ADVOGADOS

Thiago Medaglia
FELSBERG ADVOGADOS

Davi Medina Vilela
*VIEIRA, REZENDE, BARBOSA
E GUERREIRO ADVOGADOS*

Aloysio Meirelles de Miranda
*ULHÔA CANTO, REZENDE
E GUERRA-ADVOGADOS*

Adlilon Melo
PWC BRAZIL

Adriano Mendes
ASSIS E MENDES ADVOGADOS

Camila Mendes
Vianna Cardoso
*KINCAID | MENDES
VIANNA ADVOGADOS*

Marianne Mendes Webber

Marina Meyer
*DE LUCA, DERENUSSON,
SCHUTTOFF E AZEVEDO
ADVOGADOS*

Mônica Missaka
NORONHA ADVOGADOS

Aline Moraes
NORONHA ADVOGADOS

Lycia Moreira
*FRAGA, BEKIERMAN E
CRISTIANO ADVOGADOS*

Gustavo Morel
VEIRANO ADVOGADOS

Vladimir Mucury Cardoso
*CHEDIAK, LOPES DA
COSTA, CRISTOFARO,
MENEZES CÔRTES, RENNÓ
E ARAGÃO ADVOGADOS*

Ian Muniz
VEIRANO ADVOGADOS

Ana Carolina Musa
*VIEIRA, REZENDE, BARBOSA
E GUERREIRO ADVOGADOS*

Cássio S. Namur
*SOUZA, CESCON, BARRIEU
& FLESCH ADVOGADOS*

Jorge Nemr
LEITE, TOSTO E BARROS

Flavio Nicoletti Siqueira
STTAS

Walter Nimir
*ZEIGLER E MENDONÇA DE
BARROS SOCIEDADE DE
ADVOGADOS (ZMB)*

Sergio Niskier

Vitor Novo
LEITE, TOSTO E BARROS

Flavio Nunes

Michael O'Connor
*GUERRA E BATISTA
ADVOGADOS*

Evany Oliveira
PWC BRAZIL

João Oliveira
VEIRANO ADVOGADOS

Lidia Amalia Oliveira Ferranti
*VM&L SOCIEDADE
DE ADVOGADOS*

Eduardo Ono Terashima
DEMAREST ADVOGADOS

Lucas Passos
*MACHADO, MEYER, SENDACZ
E OPICE ADVOGADOS*

Ivana Pedreira Coelho
*CASTRO, BARROS, SOBRAL,
GOMES ADVOGADOS*

Rogério Rabelo Peixoto
BANCO CENTRAL DO BRASIL

Gabrielle Pelegrini
*VIEIRA, REZENDE, BARBOSA
E GUERREIRO ADVOGADOS*

Rafaela Pepe
*SOUZA, CESCON, BARRIEU
& FLESCH ADVOGADOS*

Paula Pereira
*SOUZA, CESCON, BARRIEU
& FLESCH ADVOGADOS*

Nivio Perez dos Santos
NEW-LINK COM. EXT. LTDA

Maria Pia Bastos-Tigre
Buchheim
*BASTOS - TIGRE, COELHO DA
ROCHA E LOPES ADVOGADOS*

Claudio Pieruccetti
*VIEIRA, REZENDE, BARBOSA
E GUERREIRO ADVOGADOS*

Antonio Claudio Pinto
da Fonseca
CONSTRUTORA MG LTDA

Cássia Pizzotti
DEMAREST ADVOGADOS

Renato Poltronieri
DEMAREST ADVOGADOS

Durval Araulo Portela Filho
PWC BRAZIL

Marcos Prado
*SOUZA, CESCON, BARRIEU
& FLESCH ADVOGADOS*

Antonio Celso Pugliese
*VELLA PUGLIESE
BUOSI GUIDONI*

Marcelo Pupo
FELSBERG ADVOGADOS

Ricardo Quaresma
XYZ EXPORT

João Ramos
*SOUZA, CESCON, BARRIEU
& FLESCH ADVOGADOS*

Ronaldo Rayes
*RAYES & FAGUNDES
ADVOGADOS*

Gabriella Reao
*ULHÔA CANTO, REZENDE
E GUERRA-ADVOGADOS*

Anita Reis
*SOUZA, CESCON, BARRIEU
& FLESCH ADVOGADOS*

Elisa Rezende
VEIRANO ADVOGADOS

Andreza Ribeiro
*SOUZA, CESCON, BARRIEU
& FLESCH ADVOGADOS*

Erika Ribeiro
de Menezes Pascoal
DE CONTI LAW OFFICE

Laura Ribeiro Vissotto
*1º CARTÓRIO DE NOTAS DE
SÃO JOSÉ DOS CAMPOS*

Luis Fernando Riskalla
*LEITE, TOSTO E BARROS
ADVOGADOS*

Beatriz Roditi Lilenbaum
NORONHA ADVOGADOS

Viviane Rodrigues
*SOUZA, CESCON, BARRIEU
& FLESCH ADVOGADOS*

Marcelo Rolim
ROLINVEST

Fábio Rosas
*SOUZA, CESCON, BARRIEU
& FLESCH ADVOGADOS*

José Luiz Rossi
SERASA SA

Lia Roston
*RAYES & FAGUNDES
ADVOGADOS*

Jorge Roylei Kou
*VELLA PUGLIESE
BUOSI GUIDONI*

Victor Saldanha
*BRAGA NASCIMENTO
E ZILIO LAW FIRM*

Cristina Salvador
*BARALDI ADVOCACIA
EMPRESARIAL*

Rodrigo Sanchez
SERASA SA

Rafael Santos
*SOUZA, CESCON, BARRIEU
& FLESCH ADVOGADOS*

Priscilla Saraiva
*ULHÔA CANTO, REZENDE
E GUERRA-ADVOGADOS*

Carolina Guerra Sarti
*COSTA E TAVARES PAES
SOCIEDADE DE ADVOGADOS*

Julia Schulz Rotenberg
DEMAREST ADVOGADOS

Sabine Schuttoff
*DE LUCA, DERENUSSON,
SCHUTTOFF E AZEVEDO
ADVOGADOS*

Fernando Semerdjian
*LOBO & DE RIZZO
ADVOGADOS*

Erik Sernik
*VELLA PUGLIESE
BUOSI GUIDONI*

Donizetti Antonio Silva
DAS CONSULTORIA

Eduardo Simões Lanna
*SOUZA, CESCON, BARRIEU
& FLESCH ADVOGADOS*

Michel Siqueira Batista
*VIEIRA, REZENDE, BARBOSA
E GUERREIRO ADVOGADOS*

Livia Sousa Borges Leal
DEMAREST ADVOGADOS

Guilherme Spinacé
DEMAREST ADVOGADOS

Walter Stuber
*WALTER STUBER
CONSULTORIA JURÍDICA*

Marcos Tabatschnic
PWC BRAZIL

Rodrigo Takano
*MACHADO, MEYER, SENDACZ
E OPICE ADVOGADOS*

Bruno Tanus Job e Meira
*SOUZA, CESCON, BARRIEU
& FLESCH ADVOGADOS*

Celina Teixeira
18º OFICIO DE NOTAS

Rodrigo Teixeira
*LOBO & DE RIZZO
ADVOGADOS*

Maurício Teixeira Santos
*SOUZA, CESCON, BARRIEU
& FLESCH ADVOGADOS*

Milena Tesser
*RAYES & FAGUNDES
ADVOGADOS*

Carlos Augusto Texeira
da Silva

Gustavo Treistman
VEIRANO ADVOGADOS

Gisele Trindade
*VELLA PUGLIESE
BUOSI GUIDONI*

Bruno Valente
PWC BRAZIL

Luiz Fernando Valente
De Paiva
PINHEIRO NETO ADVOGADOS

Nickolas Valentin Risovas
*MACHADO, MEYER, SENDACZ
E OPICE ADVOGADOS*

Christiane Valese
*RAYES & FAGUNDES
ADVOGADOS*

Kamile Medeiros Valle
*SOUZA, CESCON, BARRIEU
& FLESCH ADVOGADOS*

Ronaldo C. Veirano
VEIRANO ADVOGADOS

Maria Tereza Vellano
AES ELETROPAULO

Anna Carolina Venturini
PINHEIRO NETO ADVOGADOS

Ademilson Viana
DEMAREST ADVOGADOS

Marcelo Viegas
MAR & MAR ENGENHARIA

Ana Cecilia Viegas Madasi
PINHEIRO NETO ADVOGADOS

Hugo Vieira
MUNDIE E ADVOGADOS

Victoria Villela Boacnin
PINHEIRO NETO ADVOGADOS

Eric Visini
FELSBERG ADVOGADOS

Rafael Vitelli Depieri
1º CARTÓRIO DE NOTAS DE SÃO JOSÉ DOS CAMPOS

José Carlos Wahle
VEIRANO ADVOGADOS

Eduardo Guimarães Wanderley
VEIRANO ADVOGADOS

Karin Yamauti Hatanaka
SOUZA, CESCON, BARRIEU & FLESCH ADVOGADOS

Natalia Yazbek
VEIRANO ADVOGADOS

Flavio Yoshida
RAYES & FAGUNDES ADVOGADOS

Andre Zanin de Oliveira
FEDERAÇÃO NACIONAL DAS AGÊNCIAS DE NAVEGAÇÃO MARÍTIMA FENAMAR

BRUNEI DARUSSALAM

ABDULLAH AHMAD ARCHITECTS

ARKITEK IBRAHIM

ECO BUMI ARKITEK

KHA ARKITEK

RIDZLAN LIM ADVOCATES & SOLICITORS

Zainon Abang
LANDS DEPARTMENT, MINISTRY OF DEVELOPMENT

Rena Azlina Abd Aziz
REGISTRY OF COMPANIES & BUSINESS NAMES

Amiruddin Abdul Aziz
ARKITEK AZIZ

HJH Siti Norishan HJ Abdul Ghafor
AUTORITI MONETARI BRUNEI DARUSSALAM

Nur Shahreena Abdullah
TABUNG AMANAH PEKERJA

Saharana Ahmad
LANDS DEPARTMENT, MINISTRY OF DEVELOPMENT

Hajah Norajimah Haji Aji
DEPARTMENT OF LABOR, MINISTRY OF HOME AFFAIRS

Erma Ali Rahman
REGISTRY OF COMPANIES & BUSINESS NAMES

Aishah Alkaff

Najibah Aziz
ROYAL CUSTOMS AND EXCISE DEPARTMENT

Mohammed Roaizan bin Haji Johari
AUTORITI MONETARI BRUNEI DARUSSALAM

Kasmat Bin Hj Kaling
NBT (BRUNEI)

Mahri Bin Hj Latif
GEMILANG LATIF ASSOCIATES

Mohamad Iskandar Zulkarnain Bin Omar Ali
ZULS PARTNERS LAW OFFICE

Penigran Nina Jasmine Binti
AUTORITI MONETARI BRUNEI DARUSSALAM

Siti Norzainah Binti Azharan
AUTORITI MONETARI BRUNEI DARUSSALAM

Robin Cheok
CHEOK ADVOCATES & SOLICITORS

Wong Chung Hong
CHUNG HONG SDN. BHD.

Zul'Amali DP H Idris
ARKITEK IDRIS

Kunal Fabiani

Simon Guidecoq

Mohammad Faizal Haji Ali
BRUNEI METHANOL COMPANY

Nina Jasmine Haji Bahrin
AUTORITI MONETARI BRUNEI DARUSSALAM

Norzanah Hambali
LANDS DEPARTMENT, MINISTRY OF DEVELOPMENT

Norizzah Hazirah Hj Awg Hussin
DEPARTMENT OF LABOR, MINISTRY OF HOME AFFAIRS

Farah Kong
AUTORITI MONETARI BRUNEI DARUSSALAM

Susan Law
D'SUNLIT SDN BHD

Simon Leong
KR KAMARULZAMAN & ASSOCIATES

Kathy Lim
C H WILLIAMS TALHAR & WONG SDN BHD

Muhammad Billy Lim Abdul Aziz
ARKITEK REKAJAYA

Harold Ng
CCW PARTNERSHIP

Ahmad Norhayati
SEPAKAT SETIA PERUNDING ENGINEERING CONSULTANT

Siti Norishan
AUTORITI MONETARI BRUNEI DARUSSALAM

Ghazalin Pengarah
LANDS DEPARTMENT, MINISTRY OF DEVELOPMENT

Awangku Aziz Fengiran Ali Hassan
ENERGY AND INDUSTRY DEPARTMENT

Dayang Hajah Rahayu Dato Paduka Haji Abdul Razak
DARUSSALAM ASSETS SDN BHD

Veronica K Rajakanu
ZULS PARTNERS LAW OFFICE

Yvonne Sim

Wario Tacbad
ARKITEK HAZA

C.K Tan
B.T. FORWARDING COMPANY

Bernard Tan Thiam Swee

Amanda Ting

Ting Tiu Pheng
ARKITEK TING

Cecilia Wong
TRICOR (B) SDN BHD

Kie Kong Yeong
B.T. FORWARDING COMPANY

Soon Teck Yu
PETAR PERUNDING SDN BHD

Mahmoud Syaheer Yusoff
TABUNG AMANAH PEKERJA

Zulina Zainal Abidin
ROYAL CUSTOMS AND EXCISE DEPARTMENT

BULGARIA

Svetlin Adrianov
PENKOV, MARKOV & PARTNERS

Stefan Angelov
V CONSULTING BULGARIA

Rusalena Angelova
DJINGOV, GOUGINSKI, KYUTCHUKOV & VELICHKOV

Elitsa Asenova
KINKIN & PARTNERS

Ina Bankovska
KINKIN & PARTNERS

Mileslava Bogdanova-Misheva
TSVETKOVA BEBOV KOMAREVSKI

Marina Borisova
KINKIN & PARTNERS

Plamen Borissov
BORISSOV & PARTNERS

Emil Cholakov
LM LEGAL SERVICES LTD.

Christopher Christov
PENEV LLP

Nikolay Cvetanov
PENKOV, MARKOV & PARTNERS

Ralitza Damyanova
DELCHEV & PARTNERS LAW FIRM

Maria Danailova
DANAILOVA, TODOROV AND PARTNERS LAW FIRM

Emil Delchev
DELCHEV & PARTNERS LAW FIRM

Daniel Borisov Delev
SOFIA MUNICIPALITY - TOWN HALL

Kostadinka Deleva
GUGUSHEV & PARTNERS

Valeria Dieva
KALAIDJIEV & GEORGIEV

George Dimitrov
DIMITROV, PETROV & CO.

Tzvetelina Dimitrova
GEORGIEV, TODOROV & CO.

Alexandra Doytchinova
SCHOENHERR

Simeon Draganov
GEODESY, CARTOGRAPHY AND CADASTER AGENCY

Silvia Dulevska
BULGARIAN NATIONAL BANK

Krasimir Gebrev
GEODESY, CARTOGRAPHY AND CADASTER AGENCY

Zornitsa Genova
CEZ DISTRIBUTION BULGARIA AD, MEMBER OF CEZ GROUP

Ani Petkova Georgieva
NATIONAL REVENUE AGENCY

Tatiana Gerganova
SOFIA MUNICIPALITY - TOWN HALL

Ralitsa Gougleva
DJINGOV, GOUGINSKI, KYUTCHUKOV & VELICHKOV

Kristina Gouneva
DOBREV & LYUTSKANOV

Katerina Gramatikova
DOBREV & LYUTSKANOV

Hristian Gueorguiev
DINOVA RUSEV & PARTNERS

Stefan Gugushev
GUGUSHEV & PARTNERS

Yassen Hristev
KINKIN & PARTNERS

Hristina Hristova
DHL EXPRESS BULGARIA

Velyana Hristova
PENKOV, MARKOV & PARTNERS

Krasimira Ignatova
PWC BULGARIA

Iliya Iliev
PRIMORSKA AUDIT COMPANY - MEMBER OF RUSSELL BEDFORD INTERNATIONAL

Ginka Iskrova
PWC BULGARIA

Rossen Ivanov
ARSOV, NACHEV, GANEVA

Vesela Kabatliyska
DINOVA RUSEV & PARTNERS

Angel Kalaidjiev
KALAIDJIEV & GEORGIEV

Vladi Kalinov
SOFIA MUNICIPALITY - TOWN HALL

Dessislava Karpulska
PWC BULGARIA

Hristina Kirilova
KAMBOUROV & PARTNERS

Violeta Kirova
BOYANOV & CO.

Nikolay Kolev
BOYANOV & CO.

Rada Koleva
PWC BULGARIA

Ilya Komarevski
TSVETKOVA BEBOV KOMAREVSKI

Yavor Kostov
ARSOV, NACHEV, GANEVA

Yordan Kostov

Stephan Kyutchukov
DJINGOV, GOUGINSKI, KYUTCHUKOV & VELICHKOV

Anita Laleva
NATIONAL REVENUE AGENCY

Nina Lazarova
REGISTRY AGENCY OF BULGARIA

Jordan Manahilov
BULGARIAN NATIONAL BANK

Todor Manev
DOBREV & LYUTSKANOV

Svetozar Manolov
SOFIA MUNICIPALITY - TOWN HALL

Hristina Manolova
DANAILOVA, TODOROV AND PARTNERS LAW FIRM

Ivan Marinov
DELCHEV & PARTNERS LAW FIRM

Elena Marinova
BULGARIAN NATIONAL BANK

Dimitrinka Metodieva
GUGUSHEV & PARTNERS

Slavi Mikinski
LEGALEX LAW OFFICE

Yordan Minkov
DINOVA RUSEV & PARTNERS

Lyubomira Miteva
KINKIN & PARTNERS

Yordanka Mravkova
REGISTRY AGENCY OF BULGARIA

Vladimir Natchev
ARSOV, NACHEV, GANEVA

Yordan Naydenov
BOYANOV & CO.

Hristo Nihrizov
DIMITROV, PETROV & CO.

Maria Pashalieva
PENKOV, MARKOV & PARTNERS

Viktor Pavlov
DIRECTORATE FOR STATE SUPERVISION CONTROL IN CONSTRUCTION

Ilian Petkov
ISPDD

Teodora Popova
PENEV LLP

Bozhko Poryazov
DELCHEV & PARTNERS LAW FIRM

Maria Pramatarova
SOFIA MUNICIPALITY - TOWN HALL

Nikolay Radev
KINKIN & PARTNERS

Silvia Ribanchova
SCHOENHERR

Milen Rusev
DINOVA RUSEV & PARTNERS

Aneta Sarafova
DANAILOVA, TODOROV AND PARTNERS LAW FIRM

Boiko Sekiranov
SOFIA MUNICIPALITY - TOWN HALL

Gergana Shinikova
KINKIN & PARTNERS

Julian Spassov
MCGREGOR & PARTNERS

Krum Stanchev
ELIA PLC

Petar Stefanov
RUTEX

Nina Stoeva
LEGALEX LAW OFFICE

Tsvetelina Stoilova
KINKIN & PARTNERS

Roman Stoyanov
PENKOV, MARKOV & PARTNERS

Donka Stoyanova
DIMITROV, PETROV & CO.

Vessela Tcherneva-Yankova
V CONSULTING BULGARIA

Yordan Terziev
ARSOV, NACHEV, GANEVA

Alexandrina Terziyska
GUGUSHEV & PARTNERS

Laura Thomas
LM LEGAL SERVICES LTD.

Kaloyan Todorov
DANAILOVA, TODOROV AND PARTNERS LAW FIRM

Svilen Todorov
*TODOROV & DOYKOVA
LAW FIRM*

Lyubomira Todorova
KINKIN & PARTNERS

Toma Tomov
DOBREV & LYUTSKANOV

Dilyana Tsoleva
KINKIN & PARTNERS

Georgi Tzvetkov
*DJINGOV, GOUGINSKI,
KYUTCHUKOV & VELICHKOV*

Dimitar Georgiev Valkanov
SOFIA WATER

Miroslav Varnaliev
UNIMASTERS LOGISTICS PLC

Siyana Veleva
KINKIN & PARTNERS

Dimitar Plamenov Velichkov
*GEODESY, CARTOGRAPHY
AND CADASTER AGENCY*

Mariana Velichkova
*TSVETKOVA BEBOV
KOMAREVSKI*

Nedyalka Vylcheva
*DELCHEV & PARTNERS
LAW FIRM*

Monika Yaneva
KALAIDJIEV & GEORGIEV

Sofia Yordanova
PENEV LLP

Iliyana Zhoteva
*REGISTRY AGENCY
OF BULGARIA*

BURKINA FASO

BCEAO

CREDITINFO VOLO

GIFA SARL

JOHN W. FFOOKS & CO.

NAVITRANS

Pierre Abadie
CABINET PIERRE ABADIE

Seydou Balama
*ETUDE MAÎTRE
BALAMA SEYDOU*

Victoire Bambara
*CABINET D'AVOCATS
MOUMOUNY KOPIHO*

Arsène Bazi
AB ENERGIE

Aimé Bonkoungou
SONABEL

Dieudonne Bonkoungou
SCPA THEMIS-B

Bobson Coulibaly
*CABINET D'AVOCATS
BARTHÉLEMY KERE*

Sansan Césaire Kambou
*CABINET D'ARCHITECTURE
AGORA BURKINA*

Aly Kanaté
EY

Vincent Armand Kobiané
ARDI – ARCHITECTES CONSEILS

Moumouny Kopiho
*CABINET D'AVOCATS
MOUMOUNY KOPIHO*

Armand Kpoda
SCPA THEMIS-B

Sawadogo Natou
*CABINET D'AVOCATS
MOUMOUNY KOPIHO*

Ali Neya
CABINET D'AVOCATS ALI NEYA

Sayouba Neya
CABINET D'AVOCATS ALI NEYA

Eric N'Guessan
EY

Lamoussa H. Ouattara
*CABINET D'AVOCATS
MOUMOUNY KOPIHO*

Anna T. Ouattara-Sory
*CABINET ME PAULIN
SALAMBÉRÉ*

André Ouedraogo
CABINET BONKOUNGOU

Madina Ouedraogo
*BUREAU D'ASSISTANCE À LA
CONSTRUCTION (BAC) SARL*

Martin Ouedraogo
*UNION INTERNATIONALE
DE NOTARIAT*

N. Henri Ouedraogo
*DIRECTION GÉNÉRALE
DES IMPÔTS*

Oumarou Ouedraogo
CABINET OUEDRAOGO

Ousmane Honore Ouedraogo
*MAISON DE L'ENTREPRISE
DU BURKINA FASO*

Roger Omer Ouédraogo
*ASSOCIATION
PROFESSIONNELLE
DES TRANSITAIRES &
COMMISSIONNAIRES EN
DOUANE AGRÉES*

Assana Pare
*CABINET D'AVOCATS
MOUMOUNY KOPIHO*

Jules Sadou
*CABINET D'AVOCATS
MOUMOUNY KOPIHO*

Kady Salia
*CABINET D'AVOCATS
MOUMOUNY KOPIHO*

Hermann Lambert Sanon
GROUPE HAGE

Moussa Ousmane Sawadogo
*DIRECTION GÉNÉRALE
DES IMPÔTS*

Abdoul Aziz Son
CABINET PIERRE ABADIE

Marc N. Souga
*CABINET D'AVOCATS
MOUMOUNY KOPIHO*

Alassane Tiemtore
*AUTORITÉ DE RÉGULATION
DU SOUS-SECTEUR DE
L'ÉLECTRICITÉ (ARSE)*

Franceline Toé-Bouda
*CABINET D'AVOCATS ME
FRANCELINE TOÉ-BOUDA*

Bouba Yaguibou
SCPA YAGUIBOU & ASSOCIÉS

Raïssa Yo
CABINET D'AVOCATS ALI NEYA

Albert Zoma
CABINET D'AVOCATS ALI NEYA

Ousmane Prosper Zoungrana
*TRIBUNAL DE GRANDE
INSTANCE DE OUAGADOUGOU*

BURUNDI

*AGENCE DE PROMOTION
DES INVESTISSEMENTS*

*BANQUE DE LA RÉPUBLIQUE
DU BURUNDI*

MINISTÈRE DES FINANCES

OBR

PSD

Gahama Alain
FINABANK SA

Jean Marie Barambona
UNIVERSITÉ DU BURUNDI

Cyprien Bigirimana
MINISTÈRE DE LA JUSTICE

Remy Bigirimana
GUICHET UNIQUE DE BURUNDI

Jean-Marie Bukware
*GUICHET UNIQUE DE
CRÉATION D'ENTREPRISE*

Joseph Gitonyotsi

Ange-Dorine Irakoze
RUBEYA & CO. ADVOCATES

René-Claude Madebari
LEGAL SOLUTION CHAMBERS

Stanislas Makoroka
UNIVERSITÉ DU BURUNDI

Anatole Miburo
CABINET ANATOLE MIBURO

Anatole Nahayo
UNIVERSITÉ DU BURUNDI

Horace Ncutiyumuheto
*NCUTI LAW FIRM &
CONSULTANCY*

Claude Ndayimirije
CGPR

Charles Nihangaza
*CONSULTANT CHARLES
NIHANGAZA*

Janvier Nsengiyumva
REGIDESO

Emmerence Ntahonkuriye
*DIRECTION GÉNÉRAL
DE L'URBANISME ET
L'HABITAT (DGUH)*

Happy-Hervé Ntwari
LEGAL SOLUTION CHAMBERS

Patrick-Didier Nukuri
BURUNDI LEGAL SPACE

Déogratias Nzemba
AVOCAT À LA COUR

Hubert Jacques Nzigamasabo
ABUTIP

Willy Rubeya
RUBEYA & CO. ADVOCATES

Benjamin Rufagari
*GPO PARTNERS BURUNDI,
A CORRESPONDENT
FIRM OF DELOITTE*

Fabien Segatwa
ETUDE ME SEGATWA

Gabriel Sinarinzi
CABINET ME GABRIEL SINARINZI

CABO VERDE

Tiago Albuquerque Dias
DELOITTE

David Almada
*D. HOPFFER ALMADA
& ASSOCIADOS*

Bruno Andrade Alves
PWC PORTUGAL

Luís Filipe Bernardo
DELOITTE

Jelson C. Vicente
*AGENCIA DESPACHO
ADUANEIRO JOSE MARIA LBV*

Susana Caetano
PWC PORTUGAL

Vasco Carvalho Oliveira Ramos
*ENGIC ENGENHEIROS
ASSOCIADOS LDA*

Ilídio Cruz
*ILIDIO CRUZ &
ASSOCIADOS - SOCIEDADE
DE ADVOGADOS RL*

Paulo David
*UBAGO GROUP -
FRESCOMAR, SA*

Manuel de Pina
*SAMP - SOCIEDADES
DE ADVOGADOS*

Daniel Delgado
*INLOGISTICS - AGÊNCIA
DE NAVEGAÇÃO E
TRANSITÁRIOS SA*

Dúnia Delgado
PWC PORTUGAL

Jorge Lima Delgado Lopes
*CONSULTOR GOVERNAÇÃO
ELETRÓNICA*

Amanda Fernandes
*ILIDIO CRUZ &
ASSOCIADOS - SOCIEDADE
DE ADVOGADOS RL*

Brites Fernandes
PMAR CABO VERDE

Tomás Garcia Vasconcelos
DELOITTE

Joana Gomes Rosa
ADVOCACIA - CONSULTORIA

Avdesh Kumar
JMD TRADING, LDA

Mirco Lima
*PISO - SOC. DE IMOBILIÁRIA
E CONTRUÇÕES, LDA*

José Maria Lima Barbosa
Vicente
*AGENCIA DESPACHO
ADUANEIRO JOSE MARIA LBV*

Teresa Livramento Monteiro
*DULCE LOPES, SOLANGE
LISBOA RAMOS, TERESA
LIVRAMENTO MONTEIRO-
SOCIEDADE DE ADVOGADOS*

Ana Cristina Lopes Semedo
BANCO DE CABO VERDE

João Medina
*NEVILLE DE ROUGEMONT
& ASSOCIADOS*

Fernando Aguiar Monteiro
ADVOGADOS ASSOCIADOS

Wanderleya Nascimento
*SAMP - SOCIEDADES
DE ADVOGADOS*

Alexandra Nunes
PWC PORTUGAL

João Nunes
*CSA – CABO VERDE
SHIPPING AGENCY, LDA*

João Pereira
FPS

Luis Quinta
MAERSK LINE CABO VERDE, SA

Clóvis Ramos
*ILIDIO CRUZ &
ASSOCIADOS - SOCIEDADE
DE ADVOGADOS RL*

Rafael Rocha Fernandes
MUNICIPALITY OF PRAIA

José Rui de Sena
*AGÊNCIA DE DESPACHO
ADUANEIRO FERREIRA
E SENA LDA*

Lidia Sancha
*ILIDIO CRUZ &
ASSOCIADOS - SOCIEDADE
DE ADVOGADOS RL*

Viviane Santos
*SAMP - SOCIEDADES
DE ADVOGADOS*

Tito Lívio Santos
Oliveira Ramos
*ENGIC ENGENHEIROS
ASSOCIADOS LDA*

Lanre Smith
BOM SPEC, LDA

Armindo Sousa
FPS

José Spinola
FPS

Salvador Varela
*ADVOCACIA CONSULTORIA
JURÍDICA*

Leendert Verschoor
PWC PORTUGAL

CAMBODIA

*CREDIT BUREAU
(CAMBODIA) CO. LTD.*

Chankoulika Bo
BNG LEGAL

Lam Bui
MAERSK LINE CAMBODIA

Seng Bun Huy
MAR ASSOCIATES

Buth Bunsayha
ACLEDA BANK PLC

Sreypeou Chaing
CSP & ASSOCIATES LAW FIRM

Vajiravann Chamnan
*DFDL MEKONG
(CAMBODIA) CO. LTD.*

Eaknguon Chea
HBS LAW

Phanin Cheam
*MUNICIPALITY OF PHNOM PENH
BUREAU OF URBAN AFFAIRS*

Heng Chhay
R&T SOK & HENG LAW OFFICE

Rina Chhun
HBS LAW

Ouk Chittra
*ELECTRICITÉ DU
CAMBODGE (EDC)*

Sopheak Virya Chroeng
*ARBITRATION COUNCIL
FOUNDATION*

Sou Doungchay
MAR ASSOCIATES

Monyrith Eng
*HML LAW GROUP &
CONSULTANTS*

Darwin Hem
BNG LEGAL

Pagnawat Heng
P&A ASIA LAW OFFICE

Charles Ngoc-Khoi Hoang
HBS LAW

Sovanvotey Hok
HBS LAW

Hans Hwang
SOK XING & HWANG

Xing Jiajia
SOK XING & HWANG

Sophorne Kheang
*DFDL MEKONG
(CAMBODIA) CO. LTD.*

Robert M. King
EY

Sereyrath Kiri
SCIARONI & ASSOCIATES

Kunthy Koy
KN LEGAL CONSULTING

Sylvain Larbi
BNG LEGAL

Alex Larkin
*DFDL MEKONG
(CAMBODIA) CO. LTD.*

Kang Leap
*HML LAW GROUP &
CONSULTANTS*

Souhuoth Leng
P&A ASIA LAW OFFICE

Chanmakara Ly
*DFDL MEKONG
(CAMBODIA) CO. LTD.*

Tayseng Ly
HBS LAW

Samvutheary Mao
*HML LAW GROUP &
CONSULTANTS*

Sadao Matsubara
HBS LAW

Nimmith Men
*ARBITRATION COUNCIL
FOUNDATION*

Samorn Mike
HBS LAW

Sophanny Mom
*ARBITRATION COUNCIL
FOUNDATION*

Kaing Monika
*THE GARMENT
MANUFACTURERS
ASSOCIATION IN CAMBODIA*

Koy Neam
KN LEGAL CONSULTING

Vandeth Nguon
PWC CAMBODIA

Nith Niteyana
SOK SIPHANA & ASSOCIATES

Daniel Noonan
SCIARONI & ASSOCIATES

Clint O'Connell
*DFDL MEKONG
(CAMBODIA) CO. LTD.*

Sophea Om
ACLEDA BANK PLC

Sokvirak Pheang
PWC CAMBODIA

Porchhay Phoung
SCIARONI & ASSOCIATES

Charkreymorkord Pok
BNG LEGAL

Sok Ren Polina
SOK SIPHANA & ASSOCIATES

Robert Porter
VDB LOI

Allen Prak
P&A ASIA LAW OFFICE

Borapyn Py
*DFDL MEKONG
(CAMBODIA) CO. LTD.*

Matthew Rendall
SOK SIPHANA & ASSOCIATES

Navinth Rethda
R&T SOK & HENG LAW OFFICE

Chris Robinson
*DFDL MEKONG
(CAMBODIA) CO. LTD.*

Somarith Sam
*ELECTRICITÉ DU
CAMBODGE (EDC)*

Vattanakvisal San
BNG LEGAL

Chhe Sao Elen
SOK SIPHANA & ASSOCIATES

Neak Seakirin
NEAK LAW OFFICE

Leung Seng
VDB LOI

Bopha Sin
BNG LEGAL

Sao Socheata
SOK SIPHANA & ASSOCIATES

Chanraksa Soeung
P&A ASIA LAW OFFICE

Lor Sok
SOK XING & HWANG

Neou Sonika
SOK SIPHANA & ASSOCIATES

Tiv Sophonnora
R&T SOK & HENG LAW OFFICE

Samnangvathana Sor
*DFDL MEKONG
(CAMBODIA) CO. LTD.*

Sou Sorphea
SOK XING & HWANG

Nget Sovannith
P&A ASIA LAW OFFICE

Kun Sovanrithy
SOK SIPHANA & ASSOCIATES

Kheng Taingpor
MAR ASSOCIATES

Heng Thy
PWC CAMBODIA

Thavsothaly Tok
BNG LEGAL

Reangsey Darith Touch
EY

Kong Vibol
*GENERAL DEPARTMENT
OF TAXATION*

Vannida Yen
*ARBITRATION COUNCIL
FOUNDATION*

Lyhout Yin
HBS LAW

Thearith You
SOK SIPHANA & ASSOCIATES

Potim Yun
VDB LOI

CAMEROON

ETUDE ME ETOKE

Armelle Silvana Abel
*MOJUFISC MONDE
JURIDIQUE ET FISCAL*

Armelle Silvana
Abel Piskopanis
*MOJUFISC MONDE
JURIDIQUE ET FISCAL*

Roland Abeng
THE ABENG LAW FIRM

Elisabeth Ajamen
BEAC SIÈGE

Oscar Alebga
THE ABENG LAW FIRM

Rosine Pauline Amboa
*MOJUFISC MONDE
JURIDIQUE ET FISCAL*

Cyrano Atoka
CABINET FRANCINE NYOBE

Lolita Bakala Mpessa
*CAMEROUN AUDIT
INTERNATIONAL (CAC
INTERNATIONAL)*

Thomas Didier Remy
Batoumbouck
CADIRE

Pierre Bertin Simbafo
BICEC

Isidore Biyiha
*GUICHET UNIQUE DES
OPERATIONS DU COMMERCE
EXTERIEUR-GIE*

Ahmadou Bouba Oumarou

Elvis Chenwi
CHENWI & ASSOCIES

Paul Marie Djamen
*MOBILE TELEPHONE NETWORKS
CAMEROON (MTN)*

Aurélien Djengue Kotte
CABINET EKOBO

Joseph Djeuga
SOTRAFIC

Laurent Dongmo
JING & PARTNERS

William Douandji
ARCHITECT AND PARTNERS

Narcisse Ekome Essake
EKOME ESSAKE & ASSOCIÉS

Ebot Elias Arrey
ARC CONSULTANTS LTD.

Philippe Claude Elimbi Elokan

Marie Marceline Enganalim
*ETUDE ME ENGANALIM
MARCELINE*

Cédric Enyime
VANTURE CONSULTING

Hyacinthe Clément Fansi
Ngamou
*NGASSAM, FANSI & MOUAFO
AVOCATS ASSOCIÉS*

Berlise Fimeni Djieya
ATANGA LAW OFFICE

Sorelle Fonssouo Mogo
JING & PARTNERS

Marie Cécile Fopoussi

Philippe Fouda Fouda
BEAC SIÈGE

Nicaise Ibohn
THE ABENG LAW FIRM

Paul T. Jing
JING & PARTNERS

Manguele Joseph
BOLLORÉ AFRICA LOGISTICS

Thérèse Joumessi
ATANGA LAW OFFICE

Christian Kamdoum
PWC CAMEROUN

Claude Koumba
CFAO CAMEROON

Jean-Aime Kounga
THE ABENG LAW FIRM

Gaelle Kuitche
*NGASSAM, FANSI & MOUAFO
AVOCATS ASSOCIÉS*

Serge Madola

Tchande Magloire
PWC CAMEROUN

Philippe Mbele

Michel-Antoine Mben
*NGASSAM, FANSI & MOUAFO
AVOCATS ASSOCIÉS*

Augustin Yves Mbock Keked
CADIRE

Jacques Mbongue Eboa
*CABINET D'AVOCATS
GÉRARD WOLBER*

Constantin Didier Medou
Medou
CABINET MEDOU

Ivan Mélachéo
VANTURE CONSULTING

Jules Minamo
KARVAN FINANCE

Mungu Mirabel
THE ABENG LAW FIRM

Danielle Moukouri
D. MOUKOURI & PARTNERS

Jean Jacques Mpanjo Lobe
MCA AUDIT & CONSEIL

Arielle Christiane Marthe
Mpeck
ATANGA LAW OFFICE

Marie Agathe Ndeme
CADIRE

Manfred Ndock Ekoume
GUINESS CAMEROON

Bernard Ngaibe
THE ABENG LAW FIRM

Ntah Charlote Ngara
ATANGA LAW OFFICE

Virgile Ngassam Njiké
*NGASSAM, FANSI & MOUAFO
AVOCATS ASSOCIÉS*

Dieu le Fit Nguiyan
UNIVERSITÉ DE DOUALA

Urbain Nini Teunda

George Njangtang
CONTEC SARL

Carine Obama Fossey
*MOJUFISC MONDE
JURIDIQUE ET FISCAL*

Jacob Oben
JING & PARTNERS

Jasmine Ouethy
*MUEKE A DOUALA
AU CAMEROUN*

Ernest Pilo

Ilias Poskipanis
*MOJUFISC MONDE
JURIDIQUE ET FISCAL*

Paul-Gérard Pougoue

Bolleri Pym
UNIVERSITÉ DE DOUALA

Claude Simo
CL AUDIT ET CONSEI

Linda Tatabod Amuteng

Aurelie Joelle Tatang Ngadjeu
ATANGA LAW OFFICE

Hélène Florette Tchidjip
Kapnang
ATANGA LAW OFFICE

Alain Tchiegang Dieukwa
ATANGA LAW OFFICE

Emmanuel Tchiffo
ATANGA LAW OFFICE

Pierre Morgant Tchuikwa
CADIRE

Marcelle Tello
*NGASSAM, FANSI & MOUAFO
AVOCATS ASSOCIÉS*

Floriand Tiemeni Djieya
ATANGA LAW OFFICE

Nadine Tinen Tchadgoum
*PRICEWATERHOUSECOOPERS
TAX & LEGAL SARL*

Chrétien Toudjui
*AFRIQUE AUDIT CONSEIL
BAKER TILLY*

Bergerele Reine
Tsafack Dongmo
*MOJUFISC MONDE
JURIDIQUE ET FISCAL*

Eliane Yomsi
KARVAN FINANCE

Philippe Zouna
PWC CAMEROUN

CANADA

TRANSUNION CANADA

David Bish
TORYS LLP

Paul Boshyk
MCMILLAN LLP

David Chapman
PWC CANADA

John Craig
*FASKEN MARTINEAU
DUMOULIN LLP*

Kim Deochand
CORPORATIONS CANADA

Audrey Diamant
PWC CANADA

Isabelle Foley
CORPORATIONS CANADA

Ross Francis
FOGLER RUBINOFF

Robert Frazer
*BLAKE, CASSELS & GRAYDON,
MEMBER OF LEX MUNDI*

Paul Gasparatto
ONTARIO ENERGY BOARD

Attila Gaspardy
PWC CANADA

Salma Gilani
*BLAKE, CASSELS & GRAYDON,
MEMBER OF LEX MUNDI*

Christopher Gillespsie
GILLESPIE-MUNRO INC.

Yoine Goldstein
MCMILLAN LLP

Talia Gordner
BLANEY MCMURTRY LLP

John Gotts
PWC CANADA

Mary Grozdanis
FOGLER RUBINOFF

John J. Humphries
TORONTO CITY HALL

A. Max Jarvie
MCMILLAN LLP

Andrew Kent
MCMILLAN LLP

Jordan Knowles
*BLAKE, CASSELS & GRAYDON,
MEMBER OF LEX MUNDI*

Joshua Kochath
COMAGE CONTAINER LINES

Eric Leinveer
*BLAKE, CASSELS & GRAYDON,
MEMBER OF LEX MUNDI*

Jon A. Levin
*FASKEN MARTINEAU
DUMOULIN LLP*

Alex Liszka
IBI GROUP INC.

Catherine MacInnis
IBI GROUP INC.

Mike Maodus
*BLAKE, CASSELS & GRAYDON,
MEMBER OF LEX MUNDI*

Matthew Merkley
*BLAKE, CASSELS & GRAYDON,
MEMBER OF LEX MUNDI*

William Northcote
SHIBLEY RIGHTON LLP

Meaghan Parry
*BLAKE, CASSELS & GRAYDON,
MEMBER OF LEX MUNDI*

Daniel Peterson
*DAVIES WARD PHILLIPS &
VINEBERG LLP (TORONTO)*

Martin Pinard
CORPORATIONS CANADA

Gautam Rishi
PWC CANADA

Gaynor Roger
SHIBLEY RIGHTON LLP

Harris M. Rosen
FOGLER RUBINOFF

Patrick Shaunessy
TORYS LLP

Daniel Styler
*BLAKE, CASSELS & GRAYDON,
MEMBER OF LEX MUNDI*

John Tobin
TORYS LLP

Shane Todd
*FASKEN MARTINEAU
DUMOULIN LLP*

Sharon Vogel
BORDEN LADNER GERVAIS LLP

George Waggott
MCMILLAN LLP

Andrea White
SHIBLEY RIGHTON LLP

CENTRAL AFRICAN REPUBLIC

*GUICHET UNIQUE
DE FORMALITÉS DES
ENTREPRISES (GUFE)*

Elisabeth Ajamen
BEAC SIÈGE

Jean Christophe Bakossa
*L'ORDRE CENTRAFRICAIN
DES ARCHITECTES*

Jean-Noël Bangue
*COUR DE CASSATION
DE BANGUI*

Blaise Banguitoumba
*ENERCA (ENERGIE
CENTRAFRICAINE)*

Thierry Chaou
SOFIA CREDIT

Maurice Dibert-Dollet
MINISTÈRE DE LA JUSTICE

Emile Doraz-Serefessenet
*CABINET NOTAIRE
DORAZ-SEREFESSENET*

Jacques Eboule
SDV LOGISTICS

Philippe Fouda Fouda
BEAC SIÈGE

Cyr Gregbanda
BAMELEC

Marious Guibaut Metongo
*BOLLORÉ AFRICA LOGISTICS EN
RÉPUBLIQUE CENTRAFRICAINE*

Laurent Hankoff
*ENERCA (ENERGIE
CENTRAFRICAINE)*

Ludovic Médard
Kolengue Kaye
AVOCATS SANS FRONTIÈRES

Jean Paul Maradas Nado
MINISTÈRE DE L'URBANISME

Serge Médard Missamou
*CLUB OHADA RÉPUBLIQUE
CENTRAFRICAINE*

Yves Namkomokoina
*TRIBUNAL DE COMMERCE
DE BANGUI*

Rigo-Beyah Parse
CABINET PARSE

Tahina Nathalie Rajaonarivelo
JOHN W. FFOOKS & CO.

Francky Rakotondrina
JOHN W. FFOOKS & CO.

Ghislain Samba Mokamanede
BAMELEC

CHAD

*3ACE COMMERCE
ENERGIE ET ÉTUDE*

Elisabeth Ajamen
BEAC SIÈGE

Oscar d'Estaing Deffosso

Thomas Dingamgoto
*CABINET THOMAS
DINGAMGOTO*

Mahamat Ousman Djidda
ARCHITECTURAL

Philippe Fouda Fouda
BEAC SIÈGE

Prosper Kemayou
TRANSIMEX TCHAD SA

Mahamat Kikigne

Jean Paul Nendigui
N CONSULTING

Guy Emmanuel Ngankam
*PRICEWATERHOUSECOOPERS
TAX & LEGAL SARL*

Issa Ngarmbassa
ETUDE ME ISSA NGAR MBASSA

Benga Nomen Christopher
EXPRESS CARGO

Joseph Pagop Noupoué
EY JURIDIQUE ET FISCAL TCHAD

Jean Bernard Padare
*SOCIÉTÉ CIVILE
PROFESSIONNELLE
PADARE & GONFOULI*

Nissaouabé Passang
ETUDE ME PASSANG

Anselme Patipéwé Njiakin
EY JURIDIQUE ET FISCAL TCHAD

Diane Sobmeka Pofinet
*SOCIÉTÉ CIVILE
PROFESSIONNELLE
PADARE & GONFOULI*

Tahina Nathalie Rajaonarivelo
JOHN W. FFOOKS & CO.

Claudia Randrianavory
JOHN W. FFOOKS & CO.

Nastasja Schnorfeil-Pauthe

Ahmat Senoussi
ARCHITECTURAL

Abakar Ousman Sougui
*DIRECTION DE LA
PROMOTION ECONOMIQUE
ET DU SECTEUR PRIVÉ*

Nadine Tinen Tchadgoum
*PRICEWATERHOUSECOOPERS
TAX & LEGAL SARL*

Masrangue Trahogra
CABINET D'AVOCATS ASSOCIÉS

Abdoulaye Yacouba
MAIRIE DE N'DJAMENA

Mahamat Tahir Youssouf
Nahar
*GUICHET UNIQUE DE
CREATIONS D'ENTREPRISES*

Sobdibé Zoua
CABINET SOBDIBÉ ZOUA

Patedjore Zoukalne
*MINISTÈRE DE L'URBANISME,
DE L'HABITAT, DES AFFAIRES
FONCIÈRES ET DES DOMAINES*

CHILE

*BOLETÍN DE INFORMACIONES
COMERCIALES*

Andrea Abdala
MORALES, BESA & CÍA LTDA

Leticia Acosta Aguirre
REDLINES GROUP

Rodrigo Albagli
*ALBAGLI ZALIASNIK
ABOGADOS*

Fernando Arab
MORALES, BESA & CÍA LTDA

Luis Avello
PWC CHILE

Angeles Barría
*PHILIPPI, PRIETOCARRIZOSA
FERRERO DU & URÍA*

María José Becker
MORALES, BESA & CÍA LTDA

Sandra Benedetto
PWC CHILE

Jorge Benitez Urrutia
URREJOLA Y CIA

María José Bernal
*PHILIPPI, PRIETOCARRIZOSA
FERRERO DU & URÍA*

Mario Bezanilla
ALCAÍNO ABOGADOS

Fernando Binder
PWC CHILE

Rodrigo Cabrera Ortiz
ENEL DISTRIBUCIÓN CHILE SA

Marcelo Caceres Jara
*CACERES STUDIO
ARQUITECTURA*

Raimundo Camus Varas
*YRARRÁZAVAL, RUIZ-TAGLE,
GOLDENBERG, LAGOS & SILVA*

Miguel Capo Valdes
BESALCO SA

Héctor Carrasco
*SUPERINTENDENCIA DE
BANCOS Y INSTITUCIONES
FINANCIERAS*

María Jesus Carrasco
*URENDA, RENCORET,
ORREGO Y DÖRR*

Isaac Cea
*ICEA PROYECTOS E
INSTALACIONES ELECTRICAS*

Andrés Chirgwin
CHIRGWIN LARRETA PEÑAFIEL

Nury Clavería
BESALCO SA

Gonzalo Cordero
MORALES, BESA & CÍA LTDA

M. Alejandra Corvalán A.
*YRARRÁZAVAL, RUIZ-TAGLE,
GOLDENBERG, LAGOS & SILVA*

Francisco De Sarratea
PWC CHILE

Gonzalo Errázuriz
*URENDA, RENCORET,
ORREGO Y DÖRR*

José Tomás Errázuriz
BARROS & ERRÁZURIZ

Peter Faille
*URENDA, RENCORET,
ORREGO Y DÖRR*

Sebastian Garcia
*URENDA, RENCORET,
ORREGO Y DÖRR*

Sebastian Garrido
ALESSANDRI ABOGADOS

Silvio Geroldi Iglesias
GEROARQ

Raúl Gómez Yáñez
*URENDA, RENCORET,
ORREGO Y DÖRR*

Carolina Gonzalez
PWC CHILE

Diego González
MORALES, BESA & CÍA LTDA

Sofía Haupt
ALESSANDRI ABOGADOS

Cristian Hermansen Rebolledo
ACTIC CONSULTORES

Daniela Hirsch
*ALBAGLI ZALIASNIK
ABOGADOS*

Javier Hurtado
*CÁMARA CHILENA DE
LA CONSTRUCCIÓN*

Fernando Jamarne Banduc
ALESSANDRI ABOGADOS

Daniel Labbé V.
*YRARRÁZAVAL, RUIZ-TAGLE,
GOLDENBERG, LAGOS & SILVA*

Tomás Landeta
*URENDA, RENCORET,
ORREGO Y DÖRR*

Ignacio Larraín
*PHILIPPI, PRIETOCARRIZOSA
FERRERO DU & URÍA*

Michel Laurie
PWC CHILE

Juan Ignacio León Lira
REYMOND & CÍA, ABOGADOS

Jose Luis Letelier
CARIOLA DIEZ PEREZ-COTAPOS

Jorge Lohse

Santiago Lopez
PWC CHILE

María Esther López Di Rubba
BANCO DE CHILE

Gianfranco Lotito
*CLARO & CÍA, MEMBER
OF LEX MUNDI*

Nicolás Maillard
MAILLARD & CELIS ABOGADOS

Dominque Manzur
*URENDA, RENCORET,
ORREGO Y DÖRR*

Juan Pablo Matus
CARIOLA DIEZ PEREZ-COTAPOS

Sebastian Melero
*PHILIPPI, PRIETOCARRIZOSA
FERRERO DU & URÍA*

Nicolás Miranda Larraguibel
ALESSANDRI ABOGADOS

Raúl Muñoz Prieto
*RUSSELL BEDFORD
CHILE - MEMBER OF RUSSELL
BEDFORD INTERNATIONAL*

Juan Pablo Navarrete
CAREY Y CÍA LTDA

Pablo Novoa
CARIOLA DIEZ PEREZ-COTAPOS

Nicolás Ocampo
CAREY Y CÍA LTDA

Alberto Oltra
DHL GLOBAL FORWARDING

Sergio Orrego
*URENDA, RENCORET,
ORREGO Y DÖRR*

Gerardo Ovalle Mahns
*YRARRÁZAVAL, RUIZ-TAGLE,
GOLDENBERG, LAGOS & SILVA*

Luis Parada Hoyl
BAZ|DLA PIPER

Miguel Pávez B.
*RUSSELL BEDFORD
CHILE - MEMBER OF RUSSELL
BEDFORD INTERNATIONAL*

Daniela Peña Fergadiott
BARROS & ERRÁZURIZ

Vicente Portales
*CLARO & CÍA, MEMBER
OF LEX MUNDI*

Alberto Pulido A.
*PHILIPPI, PRIETOCARRIZOSA
FERRERO DU & URÍA*

Nina Radovic Fanta
BESALCO SA

Gianfranco Raglianti
CAREY Y CÍA LTDA

Felipe Rencoret
*URENDA, RENCORET,
ORREGO Y DÖRR*

Alfonso Reymond Larrain
REYMOND & CÍA, ABOGADOS

Ignacio Riffo
CHIRGWIN LARRETA PEÑAFIEL

Cristian Riquelme
*ALBAGLI ZALIASNIK
ABOGADOS*

Edmundo Rojas García
*CONSERVADOR DE BIENES
RAÍCES Y COMERCIO
DE SANTIAGO*

Alvaro Rosenblut
*ALBAGLI ZALIASNIK
ABOGADOS*

Bernardita Saez
ALESSANDRI ABOGADOS

Hugo Sánchez Ramírez
*SUPERINTENDENCIA
DE INSOLVENCIA Y
REEMPRENDIMIENTO*

Andrés Sanfuentes
*PHILIPPI, PRIETOCARRIZOSA
FERRERO DU & URÍA*

Francisco Selamé
PWC CHILE

Ximena Silberman
CAREY Y CÍA LTDA

Andrés Siles
*URENDA, RENCORET,
ORREGO Y DÖRR*

Marcela Silva
*PHILIPPI, PRIETOCARRIZOSA
FERRERO DU & URÍA*

Luis Fernando Silva Ibañez
*YRARRÁZAVAL, RUIZ-TAGLE,
GOLDENBERG, LAGOS & SILVA*

Alan Smith
SMITH Y CÍA

Jorge Timmermann
BAZ|DLA PIPER

Ricardo Tisi
CARIOLA DIEZ PEREZ-COTAPOS

Carlos Torres
REDLINES GROUP

Víctor Hugo Valenzuela Millán

Felipe Valle
CARIOLA DIEZ PEREZ-COTAPOS

Nicolás Velasco Jenschke
SUPERINTENDENCIA
DE INSOLVENCIA Y
REEMPRENDIMIENTO

Sergio Yávar
GUERRERO OLIVOS

Arturo Yrarrázaval Covarrubias
YRARRÁZAVAL, RUIZ-TAGLE,
GOLDENBERG, LAGOS & SILVA

Jean Paul Zalaquett
ENEL DISTRIBUCIÓN CHILE SA

Matías Zegers
BAZ|DLA PIPER

Barbara Zlatar
CARIOLA DIEZ PEREZ-COTAPOS

CHINA

SHANGHAI JIALIANG
CPAS LIMITED

SHANGHAI XUNNIU
INVESTMENT MANAGEMENT
CO. LTD.

STEINBERG HKC

WHITE & CASE LLP

Jacob Blacklock
LEHMAN, LEE & XU

Russell Brown
LEHMANBROWN

Qiang Chai
CHINA INSTITUTE OF
REAL ESTATE APPRAISERS
AND AGENTS

Elliott Youchun Chen
JUNZEJUN LAW OFFICES

Jie Chen
JUN HE LAW OFFICE,
MEMBER OF LEX MUNDI

Jun Chen
SHANGHAI CITY
DEVELOPMENT LAW FIRM

Li Chen
JINAN SHANTONG
TAX CONSULTING

Mingqing Chen
JUN HE LAW OFFICE,
MEMBER OF LEX MUNDI

Tao Chen
JUN HE LAW OFFICE,
MEMBER OF LEX MUNDI

Xiaofeng Chen
BEIJING HUANZHONG
& PARTNERS

Xinping Chen
ZHONG LUN LAW FIRM

Diogo Colaço
OLICARGO INTERNATIONAL
FREIGHT FORWARDER
(SHANGHAI) CO. LTD.

Lei Cui
WEIHENG LAW FRIM

Fei Dang
MMLC GROUP

Michael Diaz Jr.
DIAZ, REUS & TARG, LLP

Zhitong Ding
CREDIT REFERENCE CENTER OF
PEOPLE'S BANK OF CHINA

Tina Dong
LEHMAN, LEE & XU

Zack Dong
REEDSMITH

Lijing Du
JUN HE LAW OFFICE,
MEMBER OF LEX MUNDI

Helen Feng
ANGELA WANG & CO.

Shuai Gao
AEROSPACE CONSTRUCTION
COMPANY OF CHINA

Grace Geng
ZHONG LUN LAW FIRM

Adam Gilbourne
EASY IMEX LTD.

Shuquan He
SHANGHAI UNIVESITY

Sherry Hu
HOGAN LOVELLS

Ziyan Huang
JUN HE LAW OFFICE,
MEMBER OF LEX MUNDI

Wilson Huo
ZHONG LUN LAW
FIRM - BEIJING

Shan Jin
KING & WOOD MALLESONS

Xin Jin
KING & WOOD MALLESONS

Catherine Jing
REEDSMITH

Jiang Junlu
KING & WOOD MALLESONS

Ioana Kraft
EUROPEAN UNION CHAMBER
OF COMMERCE IN CHINA

Jack Kai Lei
KUNLUN LAW FIRM

Audry Li
ZHONG LUN LAW FIRM

Juan Li
CHINA INSTITUTE OF
REAL ESTATE APPRAISERS
AND AGENTS

Qing Li
JUN HE LAW OFFICE,
MEMBER OF LEX MUNDI

Rachel Li
ZHONG LUN LAW
FIRM - BEIJING

Ellen Liu
MAYER BROWN JSM

Grace Liu
RUSSELL BEDFORD HUA-ANDER
CPAS - MEMBER OF RUSSELL
BEDFORD INTERNATIONAL

Ning Liu
JUN HE LAW OFFICE,
MEMBER OF LEX MUNDI

Sherry Liu
NORONHA ADVOGADOS

Yanyan Liu
KUNLUN LAW FIRM

Lucy Lu
KING & WOOD MALLESONS

Scarlett Lu
KING & WOOD MALLESONS

Xiaomin Luo
PENGYUAN CREDIT
SERVICES CO. LTD.

Hongli Ma
JUN HE LAW OFFICE,
MEMBER OF LEX MUNDI

Jonathan Mok
ANGELA WANG & CO.

Matthew Mui
PWC CHINA

Matthew Murphy
MMLC GROUP

Xiaochen Ni
EUROPEAN UNION CHAMBER
OF COMMERCE IN CHINA

Lei Niu
ZHONG LUN LAW FIRM

Peng Pan
KING & WOOD MALLESONS

Giovanni Pisacane
GWA GREATWAY ADVISORY

Han Shen
KING & WOOD MALLESONS

Tina Shi
MAYER BROWN JSM

Ruiqiu Song
KING & WOOD MALLESONS

Ice Sun
PWC CHINA

Yufan Sun
JUN HE LAW OFFICE,
MEMBER OF LEX MUNDI

Terence Tung
MAYER BROWN JSM

Angela Wang
ANGELA WANG & CO.

Eric Wang
MAYER BROWN JSM

Guoqi Wang
RUSSELL BEDFORD HUA-ANDER
CPAS - MEMBER OF RUSSELL
BEDFORD INTERNATIONAL

Jessica Wang
J & BACH INTERNATIONAL
LOGISTICS CO. LTD.

Jinghua Wang
JUN HE LAW OFFICE,
MEMBER OF LEX MUNDI

Lihua Wang
JUN HE LAW OFFICE,
MEMBER OF LEX MUNDI

Longxin Wang
YINGKE LAW FIRM

Thomas Wang
SHANGHAI BOSS & YOUNG

Wallace Wang
MAYER BROWN JSM

Xiaolei Wang
CREDIT REFERENCE CENTER OF
PEOPLE'S BANK OF CHINA

Xiaolu Wang
ENHESA

Xuehua Wang
BEIJING HUANZHONG
& PARTNERS

Anthea Wong
PWC CHINA

Kent Woo
GUANGDA LAW FIRM

Yuanbao Wu
XIONGZHI LAW FIRM

Xiaosong Xie
BEIJING HUANZHONG
& PARTNERS

Xiaohong Xiong
PENGYUAN CREDIT
SERVICES CO. LTD.

Benny Xu
J & BACH INTERNATIONAL
LOGISTICS CO. LTD.

Yuan Xu
SHANDONG STARMEN CO. LTD.

Qing Yang
KUNLUN LAW FIRM

Tianyao Yang
LEHMANBROWN

Yuan Yang
CREDIT REFERENCE CENTER OF
PEOPLE'S BANK OF CHINA

Andy Yeo
MAYER BROWN JSM

Hang Yu
SIEMENS CHINA

Natalie Yu
SHANGHAI LI YAN

Xia Yu
MMLC GROUP

Jianan Yuan
JUN HE LAW OFFICE,
MEMBER OF LEX MUNDI

Alan Zhang
KING & WOOD MALLESONS

Jessica Zhang
PWC CHINA

Lingjuan Zhang
YINGKE LAW FIRM

Xin Zhang
GLOBAL LAW OFFICE

Yi Zhang
KING & WOOD MALLESONS

Young Zhang
BEIJING XINHAI CUSTOMS
CLEARANCE CO. LTD.

George Zhao
KING & WOOD MALLESONS

Xingjian Zhao
DIAZ, REUS & TARG, LLP

Crys Zheng
LEHMAN, LEE & XU

Fei Zheng
JUN HE LAW OFFICE,
MEMBER OF LEX MUNDI

Jianying Zheng
JUN HE LAW OFFICE,
MEMBER OF LEX MUNDI

Christina Zhu
HOGAN LOVELLS

Viviane Zhu
DACHENG LAW OFFICES

Wei Zhu
SHANGHAI XINHAI CUSTOMS
BROKERS COMPANY

Weina Zhu
DENTONS

Delong Zou
JUN HE LAW OFFICE,
MEMBER OF LEX MUNDI

Roy Zou
HOGAN LOVELLS

COLOMBIA

EINCE LTDA

Enrique Álvarez
JOSÉ LLOREDA
CAMACHO & CO.

Méndez Andrea Daniela
PWC COLOMBIA

Santiago Arango
JOSÉ LLOREDA
CAMACHO & CO.

Alexandra Arbeláez Cardona
RUSSELL BEDFORD
COLOMBIA - MEMBER
OF RUSSELL BEDFORD
INTERNATIONAL

Laura Arboleda
PARRA RODRÍGUEZ
ABOGADOS SAS

Felipe Aristizábal
NIETO & CHALELA

Laura Ariza
REAL CARGA LTDA

Patricia Arrázola-Bustillo
GÓMEZ-PINZÓN ZULETA
ABOGADOS SA

Estefania Arteaga
TMF COLOMBIA LTDA

Cesar Barajas
PARRA RODRÍGUEZ
ABOGADOS SAS

Maria Cristina Barco Becerra
PRODESA Y CIA SA

Luis Alfredo Barragán
BRIGARD & URRUTIA,
MEMBER OF LEX MUNDI

Santiago Barrientos
PARRA RODRÍGUEZ
ABOGADOS SAS

Aurora Barroso
PARRA RODRÍGUEZ
ABOGADOS SAS

Claudia Benavides Galvis
BAKER & MCKENZIE

Fernando Bermúdez Durana
MUÑOZ TAMAYO
& ASOCIADOS

Andres Bernal
REAL CARGA LTDA

Joe Ignacio Bonilla Gálvez
MUÑOZ TAMAYO
& ASOCIADOS

Juan Pablo Bonilla Sabogal
POSSE HERRERA RUIZ

Martha Bonnet
CAVELIER ABOGADOS

Mario Camargo
HM & COMPANY LTDA

Claudia Marcela Camargo
Arias
PWC COLOMBIA

Samuel Cano
JOSÉ LLOREDA
CAMACHO & CO.

Darío Cárdenas
CÁRDENAS & CÁRDENAS

Natalia Caroprese
JOSÉ LLOREDA
CAMACHO & CO.

Carlos Carvajal
JOSÉ LLOREDA
CAMACHO & CO.

Luis Miguel Carvajal
CODENSA SA ESP

Fernando Castañeda
ORGANIZACIÓN CORONA

Elvin Chiviri
CAMACOL

Felipe Cuberos
PHILIPPI PRIETOCARRIZOSA
FERRERO DU & URÍA

Lyana De Luca
BRIGARD & URRUTIA,
MEMBER OF LEX MUNDI

Patrick Del Duca
ZUBER LAWLER & DEL DUCA

Jennifer Diaz
PRODESA Y CIA SA

Juan Carlos Diaz
GENELEC DE COLOMBIA SAS

Maria Fernanda Diaz Chacon
BAKER & MCKENZIE

Luis Aurelio Diaz Jiménez
GRUPO EMPRESARIAL OIKOS SAS

Carlos Fradique-Méndez
BRIGARD & URRUTIA, MEMBER OF LEX MUNDI

Luis Gallo Medina
GALLO MEDINA ABOGADOS ASOCIADOS

Wilman Garzón
CODENSA SA ESP

Julianna Giorgi
POSSE HERRERA RUIZ

Hugo Gonzalez
CAVELIER ABOGADOS

Sandra Liliana Gutiérrez
RUSSELL BEDFORD COLOMBIA - MEMBER OF RUSSELL BEDFORD INTERNATIONAL

Santiago Gutiérrez
JOSÉ LLOREDA CAMACHO & CO.

William Rene Gutierrez Oregon
INSTITUTO COLOMBIANO AGROPECUARIO

Edwar Hernandez
GENELEC DE COLOMBIA SAS

Thomas Holguin
BRIGARD & URRUTIA, MEMBER OF LEX MUNDI

Carlos Jair Gómez Guzmán
PARRA RODRÍGUEZ ABOGADOS SAS

Carlos Mario Lafaurie Escorce
PWC COLOMBIA

Nubia Lamprea
CODENSA SA ESP

Jorge Lara-Urbaneja
ARCINIEGAS LARA BRICEÑO PLANA

Margarita Llorente Carreño
AMARILO SA

William Marín
PRODUCTOS FAMILIA

Miguel Martinez
GENELEC DE COLOMBIA SAS

Camilo Martínez Beltrán
DLA PIPER MARTINEZ BELTRÁN

Néstor Humberto Martínez Neira
MARTINEZ NEIRA ABOGADOS

Alejandro Medina
PHILIPPI PRIETOCARRIZOSA FERRERO DU & URÍA

Juan Camilo Medina Contreras
PWC COLOMBIA

Christoph Möller
PARRA RODRÍGUEZ ABOGADOS SAS

Juan Felipe Morales Acosta
JOSÉ LLOREDA CAMACHO & CO.

Luis Gabriel Morcillo-Méndez
BRIGARD & URRUTIA, MEMBER OF LEX MUNDI

Francisco Javier Morón López
PARRA RODRÍGUEZ ABOGADOS SAS

Luis E. Nieto
NIETO & CHALELA

Caterine Noriega Cárdenas
GESTIÓN LEGAL COLOMBIA

Juan Sebastián Noriega Cárdenas
GESTIÓN LEGAL COLOMBIA

Adriana Carolina Ospina Jiménez
BRIGARD & URRUTIA, MEMBER OF LEX MUNDI

Juan Guillermo Otero Gonzalez
BAKER & MCKENZIE

Juan Andrés Palacios
LEWIN & WILLS ABOGADOS

Álvaro Parra
PARRA RODRÍGUEZ ABOGADOS SAS

Santiago Parra Salazar
PARRA RODRÍGUEZ ABOGADOS SAS

Naufal Pedraza
PRODUCTOS FAMILIA

Carolina Posada
POSSE HERRERA RUIZ

Daniel Posse
POSSE HERRERA RUIZ

Natalia Eugenia Quijano Uribe
CODENSA SA ESP

Luisa Rico Sierra
LEYVA ONTIER

Irma Isabel Rivera
BRIGARD & URRUTIA, MEMBER OF LEX MUNDI

Cristina Robayo Herrera
PARRA RODRÍGUEZ ABOGADOS SAS

Luis Carlos Robayo Higuera
RUSSELL BEDFORD COLOMBIA - MEMBER OF RUSSELL BEDFORD INTERNATIONAL

Laura Rodriguez
CAVELIER ABOGADOS

Adrián Rodríguez
LEWIN & WILLS ABOGADOS

Jaime Alberto Rodríguez Cuestas
NOTARÍA 13 DE BOGOTÁ

Bernardo Rodríguez Ossa
PARRA RODRÍGUEZ ABOGADOS SAS

Sonia Elizabeth Rojas Izaquita
GALLO MEDINA ABOGADOS ASOCIADOS

Leonardo Romero
PRODESA Y CIA SA

Katherine Romero Hinestrosa
PARRA RODRÍGUEZ ABOGADOS SAS

Cristina Rueda Londoño
PRIETO & CARRIZOSA SA

Ricardo Saldarriaga
JOSÉ LLOREDA CAMACHO & CO.

Nader Samih
PRODUCTOS FAMILIA

Paula Samper Salazar
GÓMEZ-PINZÓN ZULETA ABOGADOS SA

Ana Sanabria
TMF GROUP

Jorge Sarmiento
CAVELIER ABOGADOS

Raúl Alberto Suárez Arcila
SUÁREZ ARCILA & ABOGADOS ASOCIADOS

Diego Muñoz Tamayo
MUÑOZ TAMAYO & ASOCIADOS

Gustavo Tamayo Arango
JOSÉ LLOREDA CAMACHO & CO.

Olga Viviana Tapias
RUSSELL BEDFORD COLOMBIA - MEMBER OF RUSSELL BEDFORD INTERNATIONAL

Paola Tapiero
TRADE LEADER

Faunier David Toro Heredia
CODENSA SA ESP

Natalia Tovar Ibagos
EXPERIAN - DATACRÉDITO

Nataly Traslaviña
PARRA RODRÍGUEZ ABOGADOS SAS

Maria Camila Valdés
GALLO MEDINA ABOGADOS ASOCIADOS

Daniel Vargas Umaña
EXPERIAN - DATACRÉDITO

Frank Velandia
TECLOGIC LTDA

Patricia Vergara
GÓMEZ-PINZÓN ZULETA ABOGADOS SA

Lilalba Vinasco
INSTITUTO COLOMBIANO AGROPECUARIO

Alirio Virviescas
NOTARÍA 41 DE BOGOTÁ

Adriana Zapata
CAVELIER ABOGADOS

COMOROS

BANQUE CENTRALE DES COMORES

CABINET D'AVOCATS SAÏD IBRAHIM

Mohamed Abdou
PRÉFECTURE MORONI

Hilmy Aboudsaid
COMORES CARGO INTERNATIONAL

Zainoudine Ahamada
MINISTÈRE DE L'ÉCONOMIE ET DU COMMERCE

Aida Ahmed Yahaia
I2A SOCIETE IMMOBILIERE DES COMORES

Moissi Ali
ENERGIE COMOROS

Feissoili Ali Oubeidi
CABINET FEISSOILI

Omar Said Allaoui
ECDI

Salim Amir

Mouzaoui Amroine
MOUVEMENT DES ENTREPRENEURS COMORIENNES (MODEC)

Youssoub Ibn Ismael Aticki
BARREAU DE MORONI

Assoumani Hassani
MINISTÈRE DE L'ÉCONOMIE ET DU COMMERCE

Kabasse Ibrahima
MINISTÈRE DE L'ÉCONOMIE ET DU COMMERCE

Madiane Mohamed Issa
CABINET D'AVOCAT BAHASSANI

Faouzi Mohamed Lakj
TRIBUNAL DE COMMERCE COMOROS

Mohamed Maoulida
AUDIT CONSEIL-INTERNATIONAL

Farahati Moussa
MOUVEMENT DES ENTREPRENEURS COMORIENNES (MODEC)

Azad Mze
CABINET D'AVOCATS MZE

Ibrahim A. Mzimba
CABINET MZIMBA AVOCATS

Halidi Ali Omar
MINISTÈRE DE L'ÉCONOMIE ET DU COMMERCE

Marco Raymond

Abdillah Mohamed Soihiri
KILNIC SERVICES

CONGO, DEM. REP.

Albert-Blaise Akoka
DELOITTE RDC

Nathalie Banza
SDV LOGISTICS

Billy Batunzy
CABINET BATUNZY

Siku Beya
CABINET LUKOMBE & LES AVOCATS

Hugo Bolanshi
YAV & ASSOCIATES

Jonathan Bononge
ROCAT SARL

Guillaume Bononge Litobaka
ROCAT SARL

François Bota kilukidi
WILVAN ARCHITECTURE

Claude Cherubala
VARCONN

Nicaise Chikuru Munyiogwarha
CHIKURU & ASSOCIÉS

Kankenga Daniel
CONSORTIUM DE CONSTRUCTION D'ELECTRICITÉ ET MULTI SERVICE (COCEM)

Siegfried Dibong
PWC CONGO (DEMOCRATIC REPUBLIC OF)

Prosper Djuma Bilali
CABINET MASAMBA

Holly Embonga Tomboli
CHIKURU & ASSOCIÉS

Jose Engbanda Mananga
GUICHET UNIQUE DE CRÉATION D'ENTREPRISE

Irénée Falanka
CABINET IRÉNÉE FALANKA

Amisi Herady
GUICHET UNIQUE DE CRÉATION D'ENTREPRISE

Lydie Isengingo Luanzo
BARREAU DE KINSHASA/ MATETE

Cedrick Kala Konga
EGEC

Rene Kala Konga
EGEC

Nicky Kanyiki Katshindi
PROCREDIT BANK

Benoit Kapila
SDV LOGISTICS

Donatien Kasseyet Kalume
AXCESS-CONGO

Gracia Kavumvula
MINISTÈRE DES AFFAIRES FONCIÈRES

Dieu Donné Kfuma
CABINET KHUMA ET BEKOMBE

Arly Khuty
CABINET EMERY MUKENDI WAFWANA & ASSOCIÉS

Marc Kongomayi Mulumba
SOCIÉTÉ NATIONALE D'ELECTRICITÉ (SNEL)

Christ Kuty
CABINET EMERY MUKENDI WAFWANA & ASSOCIÉS

Emmanuel Le Bras
PWC

Jean-Marie Lepriya Molenge
CABINET NGALIEMA

Desiré Likolo
EGEC

Jean-Pierre Kevin Lofumbwa
DELOITTE RDC

Francis Lugunda Lubamba
CABINET LUKOMBE & LES AVOCATS

Carol Lutaladio
DIRECTION GÉNÉRALE DES DOUANES ET ACCISES

Brigitte Luyambuladio
EGEC

Aubin Mabanza
KLAM & PARTNERS AVOCATS

Béatrice Mabanza
KLAM & PARTNERS AVOCATS

Yves Madre
DELOITTE RDC

Robert Majambo
YAV & ASSOCIATES

Steve Manuana
CABINET EMERY MUKENDI WAFWANA & ASSOCIÉS

Aristide Mbayo Makyata
DIRECTION GÉNÉRALE DES DOUANES ET ACCISES

Patou Monkinda Molanga
PROCREDIT BANK

Louman Mpoy
MPOY LOUMAN & ASSOCIÉS

Christine Mpunga Tshim
BANQUE CENTRALE DU CONGO

Tarin Muhongo
PWC CONGO (DEMOCRATIC REPUBLIC OF)

Céléstine Mukalay Kionde
SOCIÉTÉ NATIONALE D'ELECTRICITÉ (SNEL)

Vaval Mukobo
CABINET NGALIEMA

Eliance Muloji Wa Mbuyi
CABINET NGALIEMA

Jean Pierre Muyaya Kasanzu
CABINET EMERY MUKENDI WAFWANA & ASSOCIÉS

Philippe Mvita Kabasele
BANQUE CENTRALE DU CONGO

Jean-Paul Mvuni Malanda
CABINET NGALIEMA

Gabriel Mwepu Numbi
DIRECTION GÉNÉRALE DES DOUANES ET ACCISES

Nicaise Navanga
SDV LOGISTICS

Joseph Ngalamulume Lukalu
CABINET YOKO ET ASSOCIÉS

Patrick Ngandu
CABINET NGALIEMA

Placide Nkala Basadilua
*GUICHET UNIQUE DE
CRÉATION D'ENTREPRISE*

Victorine Bibiche Nsimba
Kilembe
CABINET YOKO ET ASSOCIÉS

Marlyne Nzailu
*PWC CONGO (DEMOCRATIC
REPUBLIC OF)*

Léon Nzimbi
*PWC CONGO (DEMOCRATIC
REPUBLIC OF)*

Laurent Okitonembo
CABINET DJUNGA & RISASI

Pierre Risasi
CABINET DJUNGA & RISASI

Freddy Mulamba Senene
*MULAMBA & ASSOCIATES
LAW FIRM*

Moise Tangala
CABINET IRÉNÉE FALANKA

Antoine Tshibuabua Mbuyi
*SOCIÉTÉ NATIONALE
D'ELECTRICITÉ (SNEL)*

Seraphin Umba
YAV & ASSOCIATES

Willy Vangu Malanda
WILVAN ARCHITECTURE

Ngaliema Zephyrin
CABINET NGALIEMA

CONGO, REP.

Elisabeth Ajamen
BEAC SIÈGE

Patrice Bazolo
PWC

Prosper Bizitou
PWC

Claude Coelho
*CABINET D'AVOCATS
CLAUDE COELHO*

Alexis Debi
PWC

Lydie Diawara
*SNE (SOCIÉTÉ NATIONALE
D'ELECTRICITÉ)*

Georges Ebale
*TRIBUNAL DE COMMERCE
DE BRAZZAVILLE*

Zahour El Hiouli
*BUSINESS LAWYER
AND INTERPRETER*

Mathias Essereke
*CABINET D'AVOCATS
MATHIAS ESSEREKE*

Philippe Fouda Fouda
BEAC SIÈGE

Joe Pépin Foundoux
PWC

Gaston Gapo
*ATELIER D'ARCHITECTURE
ET D'URBANISME*

Moïse Kokolo
PWC

Sylvert Bérenger
Kymbassa Boussi
*ETUDE MAÎTRE BÉATRICE
DIANZOLO, HUISSIER
DE JUSTICE*

Salomon Louboula
ETUDE NOTARIALE LOUBOULA

Jay Makoundou
PWC

Benic Mbanwie Sarr
PWC

Françoise Mbongo
CABINET MBONGO

Gaspard Ngoma
*MINISTÈRE DE LA
CONSTRUCTION, DE
L'URBANISME, DE LA VILLE
ET DU CADRE DE VIE*

Paul Obambi
*CHAMBRE DE COMMERCE,
D'INDUSTRIE, D'AGRICULTURE
ET DES METIERS DE
BRAZZAVILLE*

Jean-Marc Ognango
DELOITTE

Regina Nicole Okandza Yoka
*DIRECTION GÉNÉRALE
DES IMPÔTS*

Claude Joël Paka
*ORDRE NATIONAL DES
AVOCATS DU CONGO
BARREAU DE BRAZZAVILLE*

Aimé Pambou
*BOLLORÉ TRANSPORTS
& LOGISTIQUES*

Andre François Quenum
*CABINET ANDRE
FRANCOIS QUENUM*

Francky Rakotondrina
JOHN W. FFOOKS & CO.

Jean Jacques Youlou

Volana Sandra Zakariasy
JOHN W. FFOOKS & CO.

Alpha Zinga Moko
PWC

COSTA RICA

BATALLA SALTO LUNA

TRANSUNION

Luis Acuna
*ASESORES LEGALES EN
PROPIEDAD INDUSTRIAL*

John Aguilar-Quesada
AGUILAR CASTILLO LOVE

Paula Amador
PWC COSTA RICA

Arnoldo André
LEXINCORP

Alejandro Antillón
PACHECO COTO

Arturo Apéstegui
PACHECO COTO

Carlos Araya
*CENTRAL LAW - QUIROS
ABOGADOS*

Carlos Arias
OLLER ABOGADOS

Luis Diego Barahona
PWC COSTA RICA

Alejandro Bettoni Traube
*DONINELLI &
DONINELLI - ASESORES
JURÍDICOS ASOCIADOS*

Arturo Bonilla Merino
SOLANO, ROJAS & BONILLA

Eduardo Calderón-Odio
BLP ABOGADOS

Natalia Callejas Aquino
AGUILAR CASTILLO LOVE

Giorginella Carranza
G LOGISTICS COSTA RICA SA

Adriana Castro
BLP ABOGADOS

Margot Chinchilla
SOCIACO

Andrey Dorado
ARIAS LAW

Roberto Esquivel
OLLER ABOGADOS

Dieter Gallop Fernández
G LOGISTICS COSTA RICA SA

Miguel Golcher Valverde
*COLEGIO DE INGENIEROS
ELECTRICISTAS, MECÁNICOS
E INDUSTRIALES*

Karla González-Bolaños
BLP ABOGADOS

Jorge Hernández
*COLEGIO DE INGENIEROS
ELECTRICISTAS, MECÁNICOS
E INDUSTRIALES*

Randall Zamora Hidalgo
COSTA RICA ABC

Stephanie Howard Peña
AGUILAR CASTILLO LOVE

Elvis Jiménez Gutiérrez
*SUPERINTENDENCIA GENERAL
DE ENTIDADES FINANCIERAS*

Vicente Lines
ARIAS LAW

José Pablo Masís

Andrés Mercado
OLLER ABOGADOS

Pamela Meza
OLLER ABOGADOS

Ignacio Monge Dobles
PACHECO COTO

Jorge Montenegro
*SCGMT ARQUITECTURA
Y DISEÑO*

Eduardo Montoya Solano
*SUPERINTENDENCIA GENERAL
DE ENTIDADES FINANCIERAS*

Ana Cristina Mora
EXPERTIS GHP ABOGADOS

Ricardo Murillo
SOCIACO

Cecilia Naranjo
LEX COUNSEL

Pedro Oller
OLLER ABOGADOS

Diana Pál-Hegedüs
*PÁL-HEGEDÜS &
ORTEGA ABOGADOS*

Marianne Pál-Hegedüs Ortega
*GÓMEZ & GALINDO
ABOGADOS*

Mauricio París
EXPERTIS GHP ABOGADOS

Natasha Perez
LEXINCORP COSTA RICA

Andrea Saenz
AGUILAR CASTILLO LOVE

Juliana Salamanca Valderrama
BDG BUILDING PROJECTS SA

Cristina Salas Trejos
LEXINCORP COSTA RICA

José Luis Salinas
*GRUPO INMOBILIARIO
DEL PARQUE*

Luis Sánchez
*FACIO & CAÑAS, MEMBER
OF LEX MUNDI*

Tracy Varela Calderón
ARIAS LAW

Alonso Vargas
LEXINCORP

Eugenio Vargas
LEXINCORP

Marianela Vargas
PWC

Abril Villegas
OLLER ABOGADOS

Jonathan Villegas Alvarado
SOCIACO

Guillermo Emilio Zúñiga
González
EXPERTIS GHP ABOGADOS

Jafet Zúñiga Salas
*SUPERINTENDENCIA GENERAL
DE ENTIDADES FINANCIERAS*

CÔTE D'IVOIRE

BCEAO

CABINET EXPERTISES

CREDITINFO VOLO

EOLIS

Claude Aman
BOLLORÉ AFRICA LOGISTICS

Nathalie Assou
ELISHA & ASSOCIÉS

Alexandre Bairo
KSK SOCIÉTÉ D'AVOCATS

Abou Berte
TIERI

Binde Binde
*AFRICA TRANS-LOGISTICS
INTERNATIONAL*

Amaury Boscio

Lassiney Kathann Camara
CLK AVOCATS

Thierry Court
TIERI

Arsène Dablé
*SCPA DOGUÉ-ABBÉ
YAO & ASSOCIÉS*

Zirignon Constant Delbe
*MINISTÈRE DE L'AGRICULTURE
ET DU DÉVELOPPEMENT RURAL*

Issa Diabaté
KOFFI & DIABATÉ

Lynn Diagou
*SCPA DOGUÉ-ABBÉ
YAO & ASSOCIÉS*

Aboubakar-Sidiki Diarrassouba
CLK AVOCATS

Cheick Diop
*CABINET DU DOCTEUR
CHEICK DIOP AVOCATS*

Aly Djiohou
IJF CONSEILS JURIDIQUES

Seydou Dongo
KOFFI & DIABATÉ

Yolande Doukoure Séhinabou
DSY ARCHITECTE

Dorothée K. Dreesen
ETUDE MAÎTRE DREESEN

Jean-Pierre Elisha
ELISHA & ASSOCIÉS

Esmel Emmanuel Essis
*GUICHET UNIQUE DE
L'INVESTISSEMENT EN
CÔTE D'IVOIRE - CEPICI*

Ramatou Fall
*GUICHET UNIQUE DE
L'INVESTISSEMENT EN
CÔTE D'IVOIRE - CEPICI*

Claude-Andrée Groga
*CABINET JEAN-FRANÇOIS
CHAUVEAU*

Annick Imboua-Niava
*IMBOUA-KOUAO-TELLA
(IKT) & ASSOCIÉS*

Nanette Kaba Ackah
BOLLORÉ AFRICA LOGISTICS

Barnabe Kabore

Kitifolo Kignaman-Soro
WEBB FONTAINE CÔTE D'IVOIRE

Kouamé Klemet
KSK SOCIÉTÉ D'AVOCATS

Angaman Koaudio
KSK SOCIÉTÉ D'AVOCATS

Guillaume Koffi
KOFFI & DIABATÉ

Noël Koffi
CABINET NOËL Y. KOFFI

Yocoli Grâce Konan
*SCPA DOGUÉ-ABBÉ
YAO & ASSOCIÉS*

Kiyobien Kone
KSK SOCIÉTÉ D'AVOCATS

Antoine Koné Yoha
ORAKYZEMA ARCHITECTOURA

Marc Arthur Kouacou
MAZARS CI

Guillaume Kouame
BOLLORÉ AFRICA LOGISTICS

Hermann Kouao
*IMBOUA-KOUAO-TELLA
(IKT) & ASSOCIÉS*

Marylene Kouassi
KSK SOCIÉTÉ D'AVOCATS

Blaise Kouassi Kouadio
SIELD

Marie Leonard
WEBB FONTAINE CÔTE D'IVOIRE

Charlotte-Yolande Mangoua
ETUDE DE MAÎTRE MANGOUA

Djimasna N'Doningar
*COUR COMMUNE DE
JUSTICE ET D'ARBITRAGE
(CCJA) DE L'OHADA*

Georges N'Goan
*CABINET N'GOAN,
ASMAN & ASSOCIÉS*

Eric N'Guessan
EY

Patricia N'Guessan
CABINET DE L'INDENIÉ

Isabelle Niamkey
CLK AVOCATS

Jacques Otro
*CONSEIL NATIONAL DE
L'ORDRE DES ARCHITECTES*

Madou Ouattara
TIERI

Athanase Raux
*CABINET RAUX, AMIEN
& ASSOCIÉS*

Zinda Sawadogo
KSK SOCIÉTÉ D'AVOCATS

Melissa Seri
*IMBOUA-KOUAO-TELLA
(IKT) & ASSOCIÉS*

Lanciné Sidibé
*GUICHET UNIQUE DU
PERMIS DE CONSTRUIRE*

Mamadou Sylla
*LABORATOIRE DU BATIMENT
ET DES TRAVAUX PUBLICS*

Osther Tella
*IMBOUA-KOUAO-TELLA
(IKT) & ASSOCIÉS*

Gwénaelle Teruin
*CABINET JEAN-FRANÇOIS
CHAUVEAU*

Euphrasie Tiacoh
ANYRAY & PARTNERS

Eloi Kouakou Yao
CLK AVOCATS

Didier Yao Koffi Kan
AITM

Volana Sandra Zakariasy
JOHN W. FFOOKS & CO.

Seydou Zerbo
*SCPA DOGUÉ-ABBÉ
YAO & ASSOCIÉS*

CROATIA

PWC CROATIA

ZAGREB STOCK EXCHANGE

Ivona Andelovic
*ODVJETNIČKO DRUŠTVO
GLINSKA & MIŠKOVIĆ D.O.O.*

Andrea August
*AGENCY FOR INVESTMENTS
AND COMPETITIVENESS*

Zoran Avramović
MINISTRY OF JUSTICE

Milan Bandić
*CENTRAL CITY
ADMINISTRATION OF ZAGREB*

Hrvoje Bardek
*BARDEK, LISAC, MUŠEC,
SKOKO D.O.O. IN
COOPERATION WITH CMS
REICHROHRWIG HAINZ
RECHTSANWÄLTE GMBH*

Maja Baričević
*CROATIAN BANK FOR
RECONSTRUCTION AND
DEVELOPMENT*

Marija Bartoluci
*LEKO I PARTNERI
ATTORNEYS-AT-LAW*

Nera Beroš
*LEKO I PARTNERI
ATTORNEYS-AT-LAW*

Zoran Bohaček
*CROATIAN BANKING
ASSOCIATION*

Martina Bosak
*LEKO I PARTNERI
ATTORNEYS-AT-LAW*

Željka Bregeš
COMMERCIAL COURT

Mijo Brković
HROK D.O.O.

Rajka Bunjevac
*CROATIAN CHAMBER
OF ARCHITECTS*

Belinda Čačić
ČAČIĆ & PARTNERS LAW FIRM

Iva Crnogorac
DIVJAK, TOPIĆ & BAHTIJAREVIĆ

Saša Divjak
DIVJAK, TOPIĆ & BAHTIJAREVIĆ

Renata Duka
MINISTRY OF JUSTICE

Mirta Dusparić
*CROATIAN BANK FOR
RECONSTRUCTION AND
DEVELOPMENT*

Bozidar Feldman
*MATIC, FELDMAN &
HERMAN LAW FIRM*

Mirela Fučkar
MINISTRY OF JUSTICE

Tomislava Furčić
LAW OFFICE FURCIC

Ivan Gjurgjan
*GJURGJAN & ŠRIBAR
RADIĆ LAW FIRM*

Marta Glasnovic
EY SAVJETOVANJE D.O.O.

Dino Gliha
ČAČIĆ & PARTNERS LAW FIRM

Krešimir Golubić
GOLMAX D.O.O.

Anja Grbeš
MAČEŠIĆ & PARTNERS LTD.

Iva Grgić
*BARDEK, LISAC, MUŠEC,
SKOKO D.O.O. IN
COOPERATION WITH CMS
REICHROHRWIG HAINZ
RECHTSANWÄLTE GMBH*

Sonja Herceg
*CROATIAN BANK FOR
RECONSTRUCTION AND
DEVELOPMENT*

Sandra Hutter
*CROATIAN ENERGY
REGULATORY AGENCY*

Branimir Iveković
IVEKOVIĆ LAW OFFICE

Tina Jakupak
COMMERCIAL COURT

Vinka Jelavić
*AGENCY FOR INVESTMENTS
AND COMPETITIVENESS*

Irina Jelčić
*HANŽEKOVIĆ & PARTNERS
LTD., MEMBER OF LEX MUNDI*

Tamara Jelić Kazić
*ODVJETNIČKO DRUŠTVO
BARDEK, LISAC, MUŠEC,
SKOKO D.O.O. IN
COOPERATION WITH CMS
REICH-ROHRWIG HAINZ*

Saša Jovičić
WOLF THEISS

Ana Junaković
*LAKTIC & PARTNERS
LAW FIRM LTD.*

Tena Jurišić
*ODVJETNIČKO DRUŠTVO
GLINSKA & MIŠKOVIĆ D.O.O.*

Ančica Kačić
*CENTRAL CITY
ADMINISTRATION OF ZAGREB*

Andrijana Kastelan
ŽURIĆ I PARTNERI D.O.O.

Mislav Kemec

Filip Kočiš
*AGENCY FOR INVESTMENTS
AND COMPETITIVENESS*

Bruno Kokot

Iva Kemec Kokot
ZAGREB CIVIL LAW NOTARY

Katarina Kokot

Vesna Kadić Komadina
*CUSTOMS DIRECTORATE
OF CROATIA*

Dean Kovač
*AGENCY FOR INVESTMENTS
AND COMPETITIVENESS*

Linda Križić
DIVJAK, TOPIĆ & BAHTIJAREVIĆ

Anita Krizmanić
MAČEŠIĆ & PARTNERS LTD.

Dinko Lauš
LAURA D.O.O.

Sandra Lauš
LAURA D.O.O.

Ivan Ljubic
*CROATIAN CHAMBER
OF ARCHITECTS*

Marko Lovrić
DIVJAK, TOPIĆ & BAHTIJAREVIĆ

Ana Lubura
GARK KONZALTING D.O.O.

Miran Mačešić
MAČEŠIĆ & PARTNERS LTD.

Josip Madirazza
MADIRAZZA & PARTNERS

Mihaela Malenica
VIDAN ATTORNEYS-AT-LAW

Ivan S. Maleš
*ODVJETNIČKO DRUŠTVO
GLINSKA & MIŠKOVIĆ D.O.O.*

Ivana Manovelo
MAČEŠIĆ & PARTNERS LTD.

Danko Markovinović
*STATE GEODETIC
ADMINISTRATION*

Josip Martinić
WOLF THEISS

Iva Masten
VIDAN ATTORNEYS-AT-LAW

Tin Matić
TIN MATIĆ LAW OFFICE

Danijel Meštrić
VARAŽDIN COUNTY

Damir Mikulić
THE CITY OF VARAŽDIN

Andrea Mršić
BOŽIĆ AND PARTNERS

Zeljana Muslim
*FINANCIAL AGENCY - HITRO.
HR CENTER*

Dominik Musulin
DIVJAK, TOPIĆ & BAHTIJAREVIĆ

Vladimir Nol
EY SAVJETOVANJE D.O.O.

Jelena Orlic
WOLF THEISS

Marina Pavić
PRALJAK & SVIĆ

Josip Peric
BOŽIĆ AND PARTNERS

Igor Periša
*HIGH COMMERCIAL COURT OF
THE REPUBLIC OF CROATIA*

Tatjana Pinhak
MINISTRY OF JUSTICE

Ivan Pižeta
ŠAVORIĆ & PARTNERS

Miroslav Plašćar
ŽURIĆ I PARTNERI D.O.O.

Lucija Popov
CROATIAN NOTARIES CHAMBER

Marko Praljak
PRALJAK & SVIĆ

Branimir Puskarić
KORPER & PARTNERI LAW FIRM

Hrvoje Radić
*GJURGJAN & ŠRIBAR
RADIĆ LAW FIRM*

Josipa Rebrina
EY SAVJETOVANJE D.O.O.

Tihana Ana Relijic
VIDAN ATTORNEYS-AT-LAW

Sanja Rodek
*LEKO I PARTNERI
ATTORNEYS-AT-LAW*

Boris Šavorić
ŠAVORIĆ & PARTNERS

Katarina Savuk
*ODVJETNIČKO DRUŠTVO
GLINSKA & MIŠKOVIĆ D.O.O.*

Slaven Šego
ŠEGO LAW OFFICE

Zvonimir Sever
*CROATIAN CHAMBER
OF CIVIL ENGINEERS*

Dino Simonoski Bukovski
ŽURIĆ I PARTNERI D.O.O.

Dušanka Šimunović
*CROATIAN CHAMBER
OF ARCHITECTS*

Ana-Marija Skoko
*BARDEK, LISAC, MUŠEC,
SKOKO D.O.O. IN
COOPERATION WITH CMS
REICHROHRWIG HAINZ
RECHTSANWÄLTE GMBH*

Valentina Šokec
KORPER & PARTNERI LAW FIRM

Alan Soric
*ALAN SORIC & ALEKSANDRA
TOMEKOVIC DUNDA
LAW OFFICE*

Morena Šoštarić
*GJURGJAN & ŠRIBAR
RADIĆ LAW FIRM*

Irena Šribar Radić
*GJURGJAN & ŠRIBAR
RADIĆ LAW FIRM*

Marko Stilinović
ČAČIĆ & PARTNERS LAW FIRM

Jana Štrangarević
ČAČIĆ & PARTNERS LAW FIRM

Vatroslav Subotic
*MINISTRY OF LABOUR
AND PENSION SYSTEM*

Ivana Sučević-Sorić
MELIN

Goranka Šumonja Laktić
*LAKTIC & PARTNERS
LAW FIRM LTD.*

Marin Svić
PRALJAK & SVIĆ

Tin Težak
MADIRAZZA & PARTNERS

Ana Udiljak
PRALJAK & SVIĆ

Luka Urbac
*ODVJETNIČKO DRUŠTVO
GLINSKA & MIŠKOVIĆ D.O.O.*

Hrvoje Vidan
VIDAN ATTORNEYS-AT-LAW

Igor Vidra
MINISTRY OF JUSTICE

Željko Vrban
*HEP DISTRIBUTION SYSTEM
OPERATOR LTD.*

Mario Vukelić
*HIGH COMMERCIAL COURT OF
THE REPUBLIC OF CROATIA*

Petar Živković
DIVJAK, TOPIĆ & BAHTIJAREVIĆ

Jelena Zjacic
MAČEŠIĆ & PARTNERS LTD.

Bosiljko Zlopaša
*CUSTOMS DIRECTORATE
OF CROATIA*

Andrej Žmikić
*DIVJAK, TOPIĆ &
BAHTIJAREVIĆ LAW FIRM*

Ivan Zornada
WOLF THEISS

Anamaria Zuvanic
*ODVJETNIČKO DRUŠTVO
GLINSKA & MIŠKOVIĆ D.O.O.*

CYPRUS

*DEPARTMENT OF
CUSTOMS & EXCISE*

Olga Adamidou
*ANTIS TRIANTAFYLLIDES
& SONS LLC*

Achilleas Amvrosiou
*ARTEMIS BANK INFORMATION
SYSTEMS LTD.*

Irene Anastasiou
MINISTRY OF INTERIOR

Irene Anastassiou
*DR. K. CHRYSOSTOMIDES
& CO. LLC*

Andreas Andreou
CYPRUS GLOBAL LOGISTICS

Marios Andreou
PWC CYPRUS

Chryso Antoniou
ALEXANDROS ECONOMOU LLC

Ioanna Apostolidou
*MINISTRY OF FINANCE,
TAX DEPARTMENT*

Katia Argyridou
PWC CYPRUS

Pavlos Aristodemou
HARNEYS

Anita Boyadjian
INFOCREDIT GROUP LTD.

Charalambos Charalambous
MINISTRY OF INTERIOR

Georgia P. Charalambous
DELOITTE

Harry S. Charalambous
KPMG

Hadjinicolaou Christina
*MINISTRY OF FINANCE,
TAX DEPARTMENT*

Antonis Christodoulides
PWC CYPRUS

Stavros Christofi
KPMG

Constantinos Christofides

Kypros Chrysostomides
*DR. K. CHRYSOSTOMIDES
& CO. LLC*

Chrysostomos Chrysostomou
*TOWN PLANNING AND
HOUSING DEPARTMENT*

Chryso Dekatris
*DR. K. CHRYSOSTOMIDES
& CO. LLC*

Achilleas Demetriades
*LELLOS P. DEMETRIADES
LAW OFFICE LLC*

Eleni Droussioti
*DR. K. CHRYSOSTOMIDES
& CO. LLC*

Alexandros Economou
ALEXANDROS ECONOMOU LLC

Lefteris S. Eleftheriou
*CYPRUS INVESTMENT
PROMOTION AGENCY*

Elikkos Elia
*DEPARTMENT OF LANDS
AND SURVEYS*

Elena Frixou
ARTEMIS BANK INFORMATION SYSTEMS LTD.

Demetris Georgiades
HARNEYS

Elvira Georgiou
ANTIS TRIANTAFYLLIDES & SONS LLC

Phedra Gregoriou
MINISTRY OF JUSTICE AND PUBLIC ORDER

Michael Grekas
KPMG

Marios Hadjigavriel
ANTIS TRIANTAFYLLIDES & SONS LLC

Costas Hadjimarcou
LEPTOS ESTATES

Andreas Ioannides
ELECTRICITY AUTHORITY OF CYPRUS

Elena Ioannides
DR. K. CHRYSOSTOMIDES & CO. LLC

Kypros Ioannides
HADJIANASTASSIOU, IOANNIDES LLC (DELOITTE LEGAL)

Elefhteria Ioannou
MINISTRY OF ENERGY, COMMERCE, INDUSTRY AND TOURISM

Georgios Karrotsakis
INSOLVENCY SERVICE, DEPARTMENT OF REGISTRAR OF COMPANIES AND OFFICIAL RECEIVER

Erodotos Kassapis
RUSSELL BEDFORD INTERNATIONAL

Christia-Lydia Kastellani
DR. K. CHRYSOSTOMIDES & CO. LLC

Maria Katsikidou
ALEXANDROS ECONOMOU LLC

Harris Kleanthous
DELOITTE

Christina Kotsapa
ANTIS TRIANTAFYLLIDES & SONS LLC

Kyriacos Kouros
MINISTRY OF INTERIOR - TECHNICAL SERVICES

Theodoros Kringou
FIRST CYPRUS CREDIT BUREAU

Nicholas Ktenas
ANDREAS NEOCLEOUS & CO. LEGAL CONSULTANTS

Andrie Kypridemou
INSOLVENCY SERVICE, DEPARTMENT OF REGISTRAR OF COMPANIES AND OFFICIAL RECEIVER

Olga Lambrou-Ioannou
MOUAIMIS & MOUAIMIS LLC

Andreas Lelekis
CHRYSSES DEMETRIADES & CO. LLC

Margarita Liasi
KPMG

Antonis Loizou
ANTONIS LOIZOU & ASSOCIATES

Michalis Marcou
ELECTRICITY AUTHORITY OF CYPRUS

George V. Markides
KPMG

Pieris M. Markou
DELOITTE

Zoe Mina
DELOITTE

Michalis Mouaimis
MOUAIMIS & MOUAIMIS LLC

Panayotis Mouaimis
MOUAIMIS & MOUAIMIS LLC

Demetris Nicolaou
HARNEYS

Varnavas Nicolaou
PWC CYPRUS

Andry Panteli
P.G. ECONOMIDES & CO LIMITED - MEMBER OF RUSSELL BEDFORD INTERNATIONAL

Christos Papamarkides
DELOITTE

Andriana Patsalosavvi
MINISTRY OF INTERIOR - TECHNICAL SERVICES

Chrysilios Pelekanos
PWC CYPRUS

Carolos Petrou
PETA CO. LTD.

George Petrou
PETA CO. LTD.

Ioanna Petrou
PWC CYPRUS

Maria Petsa
CYPRUS STOCK EXCHANGE

Haris Satsias
LELLOS P. DEMETRIADES LAW OFFICE LLC

Louiza Shiali
PWC CYPRUS

Ioanna Siammouti
ANTIS TRIANTAFYLLIDES & SONS LLC

Andreas Sokratous
MINISTRY OF INTERIOR

Eliza Stasopoulou
CYPRUS STOCK EXCHANGE

Athina Stephanou
MINISTRY OF FINANCE, TAX DEPARTMENT

Anna Stylianou
ARTEMIS BANK INFORMATION SYSTEMS LTD.

Electra Theodorou
ALEXANDROS ECONOMOU LLC

Georgia Theodorou
PWC CYPRUS

Stelios Triantafyllides
ANTIS TRIANTAFYLLIDES & SONS LLC

Vasiliki Triantafyllides
ANTIS TRIANTAFYLLIDES & SONS LLC

Tryfonas Tryfonos
DEPARTMENT OF REGISTRAR OF COMPANIES AND OFFICIAL RECEIVER

Andrie Tsima
MINISTRY OF FINANCE, TAX DEPARTMENT

Alexandros Tsirides
COSTAS TSIRIDES & CO. LLC

Ekaterina Varfolomeeva
PWC CYPRUS

Chrysilios Vassiliou
DELOITTE

Christiana Vassiliou Miliou
ANTIS TRIANTAFYLLIDES & SONS LLC

Olga-Maria Zenon
ANTIS TRIANTAFYLLIDES & SONS LLC

CZECH REPUBLIC

KPMG ČESKÁ REPUBLIKA, S.R.O.

Jan Andruško
WHITE & CASE

Denisa Assefová
SCHOENHERR

Lukáš Balada
MUNICIPALITY OF PRAGUE 1, TRADE LICENSING DEPARTMENT

Libor Basl
BAKER & MCKENZIE

Tomáš Běhounek
BNT ATTORNEYS-AT-LAW

Rudolf Bicek
SCHOENHERR

David Bujgl
SQUIRE PATTON BOGGS V.O.S. ADVOKÁTNÍ KANCELÁŘ

Jan Capek
EY

Ivan Chalupa
SQUIRE PATTON BOGGS V.O.S. ADVOKÁTNÍ KANCELÁŘ

Peter Chrenko
PWC CZECH REPUBLIC

Pavel Cirek
ENERGY REGULATOR OFFICE CZECH REPUBLIC

Vladimír Čížek
SCHOENHERR

Martin Dančišin
GLATZOVÁ & CO.

Kamila Daňková
WHITE & CASE

Pavel Dejl
KOCIÁN ŠOLC BALAŠTÍK, ADVOKÁTNÍ KANCELÁŘ, S.R.O.

Svatava Dokoupilova
CZECH OFFICE FOR SURVEYING, MAPPING AND CADASTRE

Kristýna Domokošová
WHITE & CASE

Dagmar Dubecka
KOCIÁN ŠOLC BALAŠTÍK, ADVOKÁTNÍ KANCELÁŘ, S.R.O.

Jiří Dvořák
TH ENERGO

Tereza Erényi
PRK PARTNERS S.R.O. ADVOKÁTNÍ KANCELÁŘ, MEMBER OF LEX MUNDI

Jindřich Fuka
GLATZOVÁ & CO.

Michal Hanko
BUBNIK, MYSLIL & PARTNERS

Marie Hasíková
SCHOENHERR

Tomas Hejny
WHITE & CASE

Vít Horáček
LEGALITÉ ADVOKÁTNÍ KANCELÁŘ S.R.O.

Ondřej Hromádko
MUNICIPALITY OF PRAGUE 1, TRADE LICENSING DEPARTMENT

David Ilczyszyn
WHITE & CASE

Anezka Janouskova
MINISTRY OF JUSTICE

Lucie Janouskova
CZECH ASSOCIATION OF ENERGY SECTOR EMPLOYERS

Lucie Kačerová
KOCIÁN ŠOLC BALAŠTÍK, ADVOKÁTNÍ KANCELÁŘ, S.R.O.

Jan Klas
CZECH ASSOCIATION OF ENERGY SECTOR EMPLOYERS

Martina Kneiflová
EY

Eva Koci
MINISTRY OF FINANCE

Filip Košťál
WOLF THEISS RECHTSANWÄLTE GMBH & CO.

Jan Krampera
DVOŘÁK HAGER & PARTNERS

Petr Kucera
CRIF - CZECH CREDIT BUREAU AS

Bohumil Kunc
NOTARIAL CHAMBER OF THE CZECH REPUBLIC - NOTÁŘSKÁ KOMORA ČESKÉ REPUBLIKY

Petr Kusy
MINISTRY OF FINANCE

Lukas Lejcek
BDP-WAKESTONE S.R.O.

Jakub Lichnovský
PRK PARTNERS S.R.O. ADVOKÁTNÍ KANCELÁŘ, MEMBER OF LEX MUNDI

Daniela Machova
NOTARIAL CHAMBER OF THE CZECH REPUBLIC - NOTÁŘSKÁ KOMORA ČESKÉ REPUBLIKY

Peter Maysenhölder
BNT ATTORNEYS-AT-LAW

Veronika Merjavá
WHITE & CASE

David Musil
PWC CZECH REPUBLIC

Barbora Nedvědová
WHITE & CASE

Jiří Nekovar
EURO-TREND, S.R.O. - MEMBER OF RUSSELL BEDFORD INTERNATIONAL

Radim Neubauer
NOTARIAL CHAMBER OF THE CZECH REPUBLIC - NOTÁŘSKÁ KOMORA ČESKÉ REPUBLIKY

Veronika Odrobinova
DVOŘÁK HAGER & PARTNERS

Tomáš Procházka
DVOŘÁK HAGER & PARTNERS

Štěpán Radkovský
CZECH NATIONAL BANK

Tomáš Richter
CLIFFORD CHANCE

Michal Rohacek
FINANCNI SPRAVA - GENERAL FINANCIAL DIRECTORATE

Jaroslav Schulz
INCZ CZ, S.R.O.

Mike Silin
DHL CZECH REPUBLIC

Dana Sládečková
CZECH NATIONAL BANK

Petr Smerkl
WHITE & CASE

Aleš Smetanka
KOCIÁN ŠOLC BALAŠTÍK, ADVOKÁTNÍ KANCELÁŘ, S.R.O.

Kristýna Solomonová
MUNICIPALITY OF PRAGUE 1, TRADE LICENSING DEPARTMENT

Pavel Srb
WOLF THEISS RECHTSANWÄLTE GMBH & CO.

Tomas Strelecek
MINISTRY OF JUSTICE

Petra Stupkova
PRK PARTNERS S.R.O. ADVOKÁTNÍ KANCELÁŘ, MEMBER OF LEX MUNDI

Marek Švehlík
ŠVEHLÍ & MIKULÁŠ ADVOKÁTI, S.R.O.

Sarka Tlaskova
NOTARIAL CHAMBER OF THE CZECH REPUBLIC - NOTÁŘSKÁ KOMORA ČESKÉ REPUBLIKY

Daniel Vejsada
PRK PARTNERS S.R.O. ADVOKÁTNÍ KANCELÁŘ, MEMBER OF LEX MUNDI

Aneta Vermachová
MINISTRY OF JUSTICE

Jiri Vlastnik
VEJMELKA & WÜNSCH, S.R.O.

Stanislav Votruba
PREDISTRIBUCE

Luděk Vrána
VRÁNA & PARTNERS

Andrea Vrbkova
VEJMELKA & WÜNSCH, S.R.O.

Jonathan Weinberg
WHITE & CASE

Tomas Zach
KOCIÁN ŠOLC BALAŠTÍK, ADVOKÁTNÍ KANCELÁŘ, S.R.O.

DENMARK

Elsebeth Aaes-Jørgensen
NORRBOM VINDING, MEMBER OF IUS LABORIS

Bo Andersen
REVISION KØBENHAVN I/S

Peter Bang
PLESNER

Thomas Bang
LETT LAW FIRM

Jacob Christensen
PLESNER

Frants Dalgaard-Knudsen
PLESNER

Agnes Cathrine Emdal Navntoft
KROMANN REUMERT, MEMBER OF LEX MUNDI

Anne Birgitte Gammeljord
ROVSING & GAMMELJORD

Thomas Hansen
PLESNER

Silan Harmankaya
PWC DENMARK

Anna Amalie Jensen
KROMANN REUMERT, MEMBER OF LEX MUNDI

Jens Steen Jensen
KROMANN REUMERT, MEMBER OF LEX MUNDI

Jacob C. Jørgensen
LAWYER

Trine Kahr
BRUUN & HJEJLE

Lars Kjaer
BECH-BRUUN LAW FIRM

Troels Kjersgaard
LETT LAW FIRM

Christian Kjølbye
PLESNER

Kamilla Krebs
*KROMANN REUMERT,
MEMBER OF LEX MUNDI*

Mikkel Stig Larsen
*KROMANN REUMERT,
MEMBER OF LEX MUNDI*

Susanne Schjølin Larsen
*KROMANN REUMERT,
MEMBER OF LEX MUNDI*

Lise Lauridsen
BECH-BRUUN LAW FIRM

Pelle Lykke Rørbæk
ROVSING & GAMMELJORD

Kasper Lykkegaard Sorensen
*SPEDMAN GLOBAL
LOGISTICS AB*

Nikolas Meyer-Karlsen
*KROMANN REUMERT,
MEMBER OF LEX MUNDI*

Robert Mikelsons
NJORD LAW FIRM

Morten Bang Mikkelsen
PWC DENMARK

Jesper Mortensen
PLESNER

Andreas Nielsen
BRUUN & HJEJLE

Michael Vilhelm Nielsen
PLESNER

Susanne Norgaard
PWC DENMARK

Jim Øksnebjerg
*ADVOKATPARTNERSELSKABET
HORTEN*

Carsten Pedersen
BECH-BRUUN LAW FIRM

Lars Lindencrone Petersen
BECH-BRUUN LAW FIRM

Marianne Philip
*KROMANN REUMERT,
MEMBER OF LEX MUNDI*

Sofie Precht Poulse
BECH-BRUUN LAW FIRM

Tessa Maria Rosenberg
BECH-BRUUN LAW FIRM

Kim Sejberg

Thomas Christian Thune
BECH-BRUUN LAW FIRM

DJIBOUTI

*BANQUE CENTRALE
DE DJIBOUTI*

*DIRECTION DE L'HABITAT
ET DE L'URBANISME*

Mohamed Abayazid Houmed
*CABINET AVOCATS ASSOCIÉS
DJIBOUTI ABAYAZID &
ABDOURAHMAN*

Mohamed Abdi Hassan
CABINET ARKIMED

Ahmed Abdourahman Cheik

Sadik Ali Imael
CABINET ZK

Idriss Assoweh
*CABINET ASSOWEH
& ASSOCIÉS*

Houssein Mahamoud Barreh
*SERVICE DES DOMAINES ET DE
LA CONSERVATION FONCIÈRE*

Thierno Barry

Loubna Bawazir
BANK OF AFRICA MER ROUGE

Idriss Bouha
MASSIDA SMART SOLUTIONS

Sofia Curradi

Ali Dini
AVOCAT À LA COUR

Hassan Mohamed Egue
*DIRECTION LEGISLATION
& CONTENTIEUX DE LA
DIRECTIONS DES IMPOTS*

Félix Emok N'Dolo
GROUPE CHD

Fahmi Fouad
SELECT

Djama Guelleh
ELECTRICITÉ DE DJIBOUTI

Mélanie Guerinot
MÉLANIE GUERINOT

Tolmone A. Haid
GOBAD ARCHITECTS

Ramiss Houmed
HLB DJIBOUTI

Moustafa Houssein Ali
ELECTRICITÉ DE DJIBOUTI

Zeinab Kamil Ali
CABINET ZK

Ismael Mahamoud
UNIVERSITÉ DE DJIBOUTI

Abdoulrazak Mohamed Ali
*CABINET AVOCATS ASSOCIÉS
DJIBOUTI ABAYAZID &
ABDOURAHMAN*

Ibrahim Mohamed Omar
CABINET CECA

Abdallah Mohammed Kamil
*ETUDE MAÎTRE
MOHAMMED KAMIL*

Idriss Omar
*BUREAU D'ETUDE TECHNIQUE
ET CONSEILS (BETC)*

Mahado Omar
*BUREAU D'ETUDE TECHNIQUE
ET CONSEILS (BETC)*

Mohamed Robleh Djama
CABINET D'AVOCAT ROBLEH

Ayman Said
AVOCAT

Aicha Youssouf Abdi
CABINET CECA

DOMINICA

Kertist Augustus
*WATERFRONT AND ALLIED
WORKERS UNION*

A.D. Jno Baptiste
*JNO. BAPTISTE SHIPPING
& CUSTOMS BROKERAGE
INTERNATIONAL*

Rose Anne Charles
*LAWRENCE ALICK
C. CHAMBERS*

Jo-Anne Commodore
SUPREME COURT REGISTRY

Yakima Cuffy
*DE FREITAS & DE FREITAS
AND JOHNSON*

Lisa de Freitas
*DE FREITAS & DE FREITAS
AND JOHNSON*

Evelina E-M. Baptiste
MAGISTRATE COURT

Marvlyn Estrado
*KPB CHARTERED
ACCOUNTANTS*

Rhoda Joseph
INVEST DOMINICA AUTHORITY

Glen Khan
*INDEPENDENT REGULATORY
COMMISSION*

Noelize Knight Didier
HARRIS & HARRIS

Michelle Matthew
*NATIONAL CO-OPERATIVE
CREDIT UNION LIMITED*

Bertilia McKenzie
*DOMINICA ELECTRICITY
SERVICES LIMITED (DOMLEC)*

Severin McKenzie
*MCKENZIE ARCHITECTURAL &
CONSTRUCTION SERVICES INC.*

Richard Peterkin
GRANT THORNTON

Eugene G. Royer
*EUGENE G. ROYER
CHARTERED ARCHITECT*

Dawn Yearwood
YEARWOOD CHAMBERS

DOMINICAN REPUBLIC

Rhadys Abreu de Polanco
*UNION INTERNACIONAL
DEL NOTARIADO LATINO*

María Teresa Acta
*HEADRICK RIZIK ALVAREZ
& FERNÁNDEZ*

Juan Alcalde
OMG

Melba Alcántara
*HEADRICK RIZIK ALVAREZ
& FERNÁNDEZ*

Merielin Almonte
*MERIELIN ALMONTE
ESTUDIO LEGAL*

Patricia Álvarez
MEDINA GARRIGÓ ABOGADOS

Ana Alvira Mera
AGENCIA DE ADUANAS MERA

Maria Amalia Lorenzo
DELOITTE RD, SRL

Tamara Aquino
JJ ROCA & ASOCIADOS

Flavia Baez de George
CASTILLO Y CASTILLO

Jennifer Beauchamps
JIMÉNEZ CRUZ PEÑA

Luis Eduardo Bernard
GONZÁLEZ TAPIA ABOGADOS

Gustavo Biaggi
BIAGGI & MESSINA

Laura Bobea
MEDINA GARRIGÓ ABOGADOS

Marvin Cardoza
*DIRECCIÓN GENERAL DE
IMPUESTOS INTERNOS*

Roberto Carvajal Polanco
*CARVAJAL POLANCO
& ASOCIADOS SRL*

Andre Ceara
*DMK LAWYERS
SANTO DOMINGO*

Milvio Coiscou Castro
COISCOU & ASOCIADOS

José Colón
EDESUR

Ludovino Colón
EY

Pamela Contreras
JJ ROCA & ASOCIADOS

Leandro Corral
GUZMÁN-ARIZA

Rachel Cortes
*HEADRICK RIZIK ALVAREZ
& FERNÁNDEZ*

José Cruz Campillo
JIMÉNEZ CRUZ PEÑA

Caleb de la Rosa
DYNATEC

Leonardo de la Rosa
DYNATEC

Sarah de León Perelló
*HEADRICK RIZIK ALVAREZ
& FERNÁNDEZ*

Rosa Díaz
JIMÉNEZ CRUZ PEÑA

Rafael Dickson Morales
*DICKSON MORALES -
ABOGADOS | CONSULTORES*

Ruben Edmead
MARÍTIMA DOMINICANA

Zenon Felipe
MARÍTIMA DOMINICANA

Ingrid Fermín-Terrero
*SEIBEL DARGAM
HENRÍQUEZ & HERRERA*

María Fernández A. de Pou
*RUSSIN, VECCHI &
HEREDIA BONETTI*

Alejandro Fernández de Castro
PWC DOMINICAN REPUBLIC

Mary Fernández Rodríguez
*HEADRICK RIZIK ALVAREZ
& FERNÁNDEZ*

Romina Figoli
*HEADRICK RIZIK ALVAREZ
& FERNÁNDEZ*

Milagros Figuereo
*JOB, BÁEZ, SOTO &
ASOCIADOS - MEMBER
OF RUSSELL BEDFORD
INTERNATIONAL*

Gloria Gasso
OMG

Sandra Goico
*SEIBEL DARGAM
HENRÍQUEZ & HERRERA*

Víctor Gómez
*HEADRICK RIZIK ALVAREZ
& FERNÁNDEZ*

Pablo González Tapia
GONZÁLEZ TAPIA ABOGADOS

María Hernández
EY

Paula Hernández Mera
GONZÁLEZ TAPIA ABOGADOS

David Infante
DELOITTE RD, SRL

Luis J. Jiménez
JIMÉNEZ CRUZ PEÑA

Alejandro Lama
*HEADRICK RIZIK ALVAREZ
& FERNÁNDEZ*

José M. López
LOPESA

Paola Mañón Taveras
*SEIBEL DARGAM
HENRÍQUEZ & HERRERA*

Fernando Marranzini
*HEADRICK RIZIK ALVAREZ
& FERNÁNDEZ*

Carlos Marte
*AGENCIA DE COMERCIO
EXTERIOR CM*

Jesús Geraldo Martínez
Alcántara
SUPERINTENDENCIA DE BANCOS

Vanessa Mateo
JJ ROCA & ASOCIADOS

Fabiola Medina
MEDINA GARRIGÓ ABOGADOS

Laura Medina
JIMÉNEZ CRUZ PEÑA

Ligia Melo
MEDINA GARRIGÓ ABOGADOS

Melissa Mercedes
JJ ROCA & ASOCIADOS

Rodolfo Mesa Chávez
MESA & MESA ABOGADOS

Apolinar Muñoz
SCHAD CONSULTING

Natia Núñez
*HEADRICK RIZIK ALVAREZ
& FERNÁNDEZ*

Indira Ogando
DELOITTE RD, SRL

Pamela Ogando
*DIRECCIÓN GENERAL DE
IMPUESTOS INTERNOS*

Ramón Ortega
PWC

Henry Pastrano Lluberes
JIMENEZ CRUZ PEÑA

Elisabetta Pedersini
AARON SUERO & PEDERSINI

Kaulynam Peralta
EDESUR

Yakaira Pérez
EY

Luisa Ericka Pérez Hernández
SUPERINTENDENCIA DE BANCOS

Edward Piña Fernández
BIAGGI & MESSINA

Julio Pinedo
PWC DOMINICAN REPUBLIC

Aimée Prieto
*PRIETO CABRERA &
ASOCIADOS*

Arturo Ramirez
AARON SUERO & PEDERSINI

Sayra J. Ramirez
*PRIETO CABRERA &
ASOCIADOS*

Alejandro Miguel Ramírez
Suzaña
*RAMIREZ SUZAÑA
& ASOCIADOS*

Eduardo Ramos E.
*COMISIÓN NACIONAL DE
DEFENSA DE LA COMPETENCIA
(PRO-COMPETENCIA)*

Reynaldo Ramos Morel
RAMOS MOREL & ASOCIADOS

Jaime Roca
JJ ROCA & ASOCIADOS

Naomi Rodríguez
*HEADRICK RIZIK ALVAREZ
& FERNÁNDEZ*

Mariel Romero
EDESUR

Katherine Rosa
JIMÉNEZ CRUZ PEÑA

Juan Rosario
EDESUR

Wendy Sánchez
TRANSUNION DOMINICAN
REPUBLIC

Felicia Santana
JJ ROCA & ASOCIADOS

Melissa Siiie
MEDINA GARRIGÓ ABOGADOS

Manuel Silverio
JIMÉNEZ CRUZ PEÑA

Llilda Solano
DMK LAWYERS
SANTO DOMINGO

Juan Tejeda
PWC DOMINICAN REPUBLIC

Laura Troncoso
OMG

Richard Troncoso
DELOITTE RD, SRL

Robert Valdez
SCHAD CONSULTING

Gisselle Valera Florencio
JIMÉNEZ CRUZ PEÑA

Vilma Veras Terrero
JIMÉNEZ CRUZ PEÑA

Jeannerette Vergez Soto
JOB, BÁEZ, SOTO &
ASOCIADOS - MEMBER
OF RUSSELL BEDFORD
INTERNATIONAL

Monica Villafaña
RUSSIN, VECCHI &
HEREDIA BONETTI

Dilcia Villanueva
EDESUR

Chery Zacarías
MEDINA GARRIGÓ ABOGADOS

ECUADOR

Claudio Mesias
Agama Chiluisa
EMPRESA ELECTRICA DE QUITO

Pablo Aguirre
PWC ECUADOR

María Isabel Aillón
PÉREZ, BUSTAMANTE Y PONCE,
MEMBER OF LEX MUNDI

Mario Armendáriz
DLL LAW OFFICE

Mariella Baquerizo
EQUIFAX ECUADOR BURÓ DE
INFORMACIÓN CREDITICIA C.A.

Esteban Baquero
FERRERE ABOGADOS

Diego Cabezas-Klaere
CABEZAS & CABEZAS-KLAERE

Luis Cabezas-Klaere
CABEZAS & CABEZAS-KLAERE

Juan José Campaña
del Castillo
P&P ABOGADOS

David Cornejo
PWC ECUADOR

Augusto Curillo
EMPRESA ELECTRICA DE QUITO

Juan Carlos Darquea
FERRERE ABOGADOS

Fernando Del Pozo Contreras
GALLEGOS, VALAREZO & NEIRA

Paola Gachet
FERRERE ABOGADOS

Martín Galarza Lanas
PUENTE SÁENZ & GALARZA
ATTORNEYS-AT-LAW, CIA LTDA

Leopoldo González R.
PAZ HOROWITZ ABOGADOS

Arturo Griffin Valdivieso
PÉREZ, BUSTAMANTE Y PONCE,
MEMBER OF LEX MUNDI

Pedro José Hajj Ferri
FERRERE ABOGADOS

Rubby Lucero
CABEZAS & CABEZAS-KLAERE

Marisol Naranjo Benites
SOUTH TRADE &
SOLUTIONS ECUADOR

Francisco Javier Naranjo
Grijalva
FEDLEX

Jessahe Navarrete
DLL LAW OFFICE

Luis Nolivos
NOLIVOS LAWYERS

Wolfgang Oberer
SCHRYVER

Letty Ordoñez
EMPRESA PÚBLICA DE
MOVILIDAD Y OBRAS PÚBLICAS

Andrea Pavón
VICSAN LOGISTICS SA

Ciro Pazmiño Yánez
P&P ABOGADOS

Ciro Pazmiño Zurita
P&P ABOGADOS

Rodrigo Martin Pesantes Sáenz
PÉREZ, BUSTAMANTE Y PONCE,
MEMBER OF LEX MUNDI

Ramiro Pinto
PINTO & GARCÉS ASOC. CÍA
LTDA - MEMBER OF RUSSELL
BEDFORD INTERNATIONAL

Patricia Ponce Arteta
BUSTAMANTE & BUSTAMANTE

Sandra Reed-Serrano
PÉREZ, BUSTAMANTE Y PONCE,
MEMBER OF LEX MUNDI

Santiago Reyes
DLL LAW OFFICE

Leonardo Sempértegui
SEMPÉRTEGUI ONTANEDA

Estefanía Sigcha Orrico
DLL LAW OFFICE

José Urizar
FERRERE ABOGADOS

Hernan Vela Albuja
ISEFE

David Villafuerte
TRADING SOLUTIONS
CONSULTORES SA

Manuel Zurita
MZ SISTEMAS ELECTRICOS
Y ELECTRONICOS

EGYPT, ARAB REP.

CAIRO GOVERNORATE
UTILITY DATA CENTER

EGYPTIAN HOLDING COMPANY
OF WATER AND WASTE WATER

ISLAND AGENCIES
AND SERVICES

Naguib Abadir
NACITA CORPORATION

Omar Abd el Salam
AL KAMEL LAW OFFICE

Alaa Abd E! Wahed
GENERAL ORGANIZATION OF
EXPORT & IMPORT CONTROL

Mohamed Abd El-Sadek
INTERNATIONAL CENTER FOR
LAW, INTELLECTUAL PROPERTY
AND ARBITRATION (ICLIPA)

Ayman Abdallah
AM LAW FIRM

Abdel Latif Abdel Moneam
3A INTERNATIONAL

Mostafa Abdel Rahim
HELMY, HAMZA & PARTNERS,
MEMBER FIRM OF BAKER &
MCKENZIE INTERNATIONAL

Mohamed Abdel-Aziz
SOUTH CAIRO ELECTRICITY
DISTRIBUTION COMPANY

Doha Abdelfattah
AM LAW FIRM

Hanan Abdelgamad Aly
ECG ENGINEERING
CONSULTANTS GROUP SA

Mostafa Abdel-Rahim
HELMY, HAMZA & PARTNERS,
MEMBER FIRM OF BAKER &
MCKENZIE INTERNATIONAL

Sherine Abdullah
EGYPTIAN ELECTRICITY UTILITY
AND CONSUMER PROTECTION

Amr Mohamed Abo El Fetouh
GENERAL AUTHORITY
FOR INVESTMENT GAFI

Ahmed Abou Ali
HASSOUNA & ABOU ALI

Gamal A. Abou Ali
HASSOUNA & ABOU ALI

Abeer Abu Zeid
YOUSSRY SALEH & PARTNERS

Nermine Abulata
MINISTRY OF INDUSTRY
AND FOREIGN TRADE

Mona Adel Hussein
TALAL ABU-GHAZALEH
LEGAL (TAG-LEGAL)

Hoda Adel Saleh
KARIM ADEL LAW OFFICE

Mohamed Reda Afifi
ENGINEERING
CONSULTANCIES OFFICE

Mohamed Aggag
MINISTRY OF JUSTICE

Karim Ahmed
ASMA MARINE GLOBAL
LOGISTICS AND FREIGHT
FORWARDER

Suzan Saad Ahmed
AL-SAAD FOR
ENGINEERING DESIGNS

Yulia V. Akinfieva
YOUSSRY SALEH & PARTNERS

Ashraf Al Wakeel
CENTRAL BANK OF EGYPT

Mahmoud AlFeki

Nadia Ali
CAIRO GOVERNORATE

Mamdouh Ali Ahmed

Ashraf Alkafrawy

Mohamed Allam
AM LAW FIRM

Serene Almaleh
SULTANS LAW

Abd El Wahab Aly Ibrahim
ABD EL WAHAB SONS

Mahmoud Alzayat
ALZAYAT LAW FIRM

Ahmed Amin
SCOPE

Sayed Ammar
AL KAMEL LAW OFFICE

Madonna Azmy
MAHER MILAD
ISKANDER & CO.

Tarek Badawy
SARWAT A. SHAHID LAW FIRM

Waleed Badr
EASTMED SHIPPING GROUP

Shaban Baker
CENTRAL BANK OF EGYPT

Khaled Balbaa
KPMG HAZEM HASSAN

Wagih Barakat
AAW CONSULTING ENGINEERS

Salma Basset
NOUR AND SELIM, IN
ASSOCIATION WITH AL
TAMIMI & COMPANY

Alah Bassyouni

Mansour Boriek
ALEXANDRIA PORT AUTHORITY,
MINISTRY OF TRANSPORTATION

Joseph Sami Boutros
AL ALAMEYA COMPANY

Helena Constantine
MAHER MILAD
ISKANDER & CO.

Mohamed Darwish
EL SAID DARWISH & PARTNERS

Menna El Abdeeny
MINISTRY OF INDUSTRY
AND FOREIGN TRADE

Abdallah El Adly
PWC EGYPT

Yehia H. El Bably
EL BABLY LAW FIRM

Assem El Hawy
NOUR AND SELIM, IN
ASSOCIATION WITH AL
TAMIMI & COMPANY

Mohamed Refaat El Houshi
THE EGYPTIAN CREDIT
BUREAU I-SCORE

Medhat El Kaddy
KADMAR

Hassan El Maraashly
AAW CONSULTING ENGINEERS

Mohamed El Rafie
ALLIANCE LAW FIRM

Ibrahim El Salamoni
HEGAZI LAW

Ramy El Sayed Fawzy
GENERAL AUTHORITY
FOR INVESTMENT GAFI

Yasmine El Shahed
SHALAKANY LAW OFFICE,
MEMBER OF LEX MUNDI

Aly El Shalakany
SHALAKANY LAW OFFICE,
MEMBER OF LEX MUNDI

Emad El Shalakany
SHALAKANY LAW OFFICE,
MEMBER OF LEX MUNDI

Khaled El Shalakany
SHALAKANY LAW OFFICE,
MEMBER OF LEX MUNDI

Sherry El Shalakany
SHALAKANY LAW OFFICE,
MEMBER OF LEX MUNDI

Khaled El Sharkawy
SARWAT A. SHAHID LAW FIRM

Mohamed El Sherbini
SARWAT A. SHAHID LAW FIRM

Passant El Tabei
PWC EGYPT

Hossam Elden Fida

Ashraf Elibrachy
IBRACHY LEGAL CONSULTANCY

Alaa Elkadry
PRIVATE PRACTITIONER

Mostafa Elshafei
IBRACHY LEGAL CONSULTANCY

Ehab Ahmed Elsharaby
KARIM ADEL LAW OFFICE

Essam Elshazly
HORUS AIR AND SEA
TRANSPORT

Karim Emam
PWC EGYPT

Mohsen Emam
CENTRAL BANK OF EGYPT

Shahdan Essam
TALAL ABU-GHAZALEH
LEGAL (TAG-LEGAL)

Haitham Essmat
JOUDY INTERNATIONAL
FOR IMPORT & EXPORT

Ahmed Ezzat
NOUR AND SELIM, IN
ASSOCIATION WITH AL
TAMIMI & COMPANY

Salma Ezzat
SHALAKANY LAW OFFICE,
MEMBER OF LEX MUNDI

Mariam Fahmy
SHALAKANY LAW OFFICE,
MEMBER OF LEX MUNDI

Hazem Fathi
HASSOUNA & ABOU ALI

Shereen Fouad
EGYPTIAN ELECTRICITY
HOLDING COMPANY

Mennatullah Hamdy
MINISTRY OF INDUSTRY
AND FOREIGN TRADE

Hany Hanna
MINISTRY OF JUSTICE

Mohamed Hashish
SOLIMAN, HASHISH
AND PARTNERS

Hassan Hassaan
DLA MATOUK BASSIOUNY
(PART OF DLA PIPER GROUP)

Dina Hassan
SHALAKANY LAW OFFICE,
MEMBER OF LEX MUNDI

Mohab Hassan
HELMY, HAMZA & PARTNERS,
MEMBER FIRM OF BAKER &
MCKENZIE INTERNATIONAL

Tarek Hassib
AL KAMEL LAW OFFICE

Mostafa Helmy
IBRACHY LEGAL CONSULTANCY

Omneia Helmy
FACULTY OF ECONOMICS
AND POLITICAL SCIENCE,
CAIRO UNIVERSITY

Taher Helmy
HELMY, HAMZA & PARTNERS,
MEMBER FIRM OF BAKER &
MCKENZIE INTERNATIONAL

Hossam Hilal
GRANT THORNTON LLP

Mohamed Hisham Hassan
MINISTRY OF INVESTMENT

Badawi Hozaien
HOZAIEN LAW OFFICE

Haytham Hussein
EGYPTIAN GLOBAL LOGISTICS

Nada Hussein
*SHALAKANY LAW OFFICE,
MEMBER OF LEX MUNDI*

Muhammad Hussein Sabaa
*FACHHOCHSCHULE
SÜDWESTFALEN*

Abdel Hamid Ibrahim
*EGYPTIAN FINANCIAL
SUPERVISORY AUTHORITY*

Badawy Ibrahim
MINISTRY OF FINANCE

Mona Ibrahim
UTI

Mehiar Joulji
SARWAT A. SHAHID LAW FIRM

Saif Allah Kadry
*SOLIMAN, HASHISH
AND PARTNERS*

Mohamed Kafafi
*THE EGYPTIAN CREDIT
BUREAU I-SCORE*

Omar Sherif Kamal El Din
*SHALAKANY LAW OFFICE,
MEMBER OF LEX MUNDI*

Khaled Sherif Kamal El Dine
*SHALAKANY LAW OFFICE,
MEMBER OF LEX MUNDI*

Mohamed Kamel
AL KAMEL LAW OFFICE

Mohamed Kandel
AL KAMEL LAW OFFICE

Ahmed Khairi
MINISTRY OF JUSTICE

Mohanad Khaled
BDO KHALED & CO.

Taha Khaled
BDO KHALED & CO.

Ahmed Khaleel

Mohamed Khodeir
*GENERAL AUTHORITY
FOR INVESTMENT GAFI*

Ashraf Maamoun Farag
BOSCH CENTER

Gomaa M. Madny
*MINISTRY OF TRADE
AND INDUSTRY*

Ibrahim Maher
*DLA MATOUK BASSIOUNY
(PART OF DLA PIPER GROUP)*

Ahmed Maher Badr Afifi
MINISTRY OF JUSTICE

Lamia Mahgoub
PWC EGYPT

Yaser Gamaluddin Mahmoud
Hamam
THE EGYPTIAN LAW FIRM

Magdy Makky
CUSTOMS ADMINISTRATION

Mustafa Makram
BDO KHALED & CO.

Abouelela Mohamed
ORIENTAL WEAVERS

Ahmed Mohamed
*MINISTRY OF INDUSTRY
AND FOREIGN TRADE*

Yasmin Mohamed Mahran
*TALAL ABU-GHAZALEH
LEGAL (TAG-LEGAL)*

Ola Mohammed Hassan
*TALAL ABU-GHAZALEH
LEGAL (TAG-LEGAL)*

Eman Mohey
HASSOUNA & ABOU ALI

Alia Monieb
IBRACHY LEGAL CONSULTANCY

Mohamed Ahmed Salah El Din
Mostafa El Sayed
MINISTRY OF JUSTICE

Marina Mouris
*IBRACHY & DERMARKAR
LAW FIRM*

Mostafa Nagi
*TANTA ECONOMIC
COURT OF APPEAL*

Mariam Negm
AM LAW FIRM

Shimaa Omar
*READYMADE GARMENTS
EXPORT COUNCIL*

Ryham Ragab
RAGAB LAW FIRM

Tamer Ragy
RAGY & PARTNERS LAW FIRM

Said Ramadan Arafa
*EGYPTIAN FINANCIAL
SUPERVISORY AUTHORITY*

Hoda Sabry
*ALEXANDRIA PORT AUTHORITY,
MINISTRY OF TRANSPORTATION*

Nouv Salama
AL KAMEL LAW OFFICE

Maaly Salim
*MINISTRY OF TRADE
AND INDUSTRY*

Zeinab Samir
AL KAMEL LAW OFFICE

Mohamed Serry
SERRY LAW OFFICE

Khalil Shaat
*MUNICIPALITY OF
GREATER CAIRO*

Doaa M. Shabaan
*INTERNATIONAL CENTER FOR
LAW, INTELLECTUAL PROPERTY
AND ARBITRATION (ICLIPA)*

Mohammad Shamroukh
MINISTRY OF JUSTICE

Sharif Shihata
*SHALAKANY LAW OFFICE,
MEMBER OF LEX MUNDI*

Mohamed Fakhry Shousha
*EGYPTIAN FINANCIAL
SUPERVISORY AUTHORITY*

Shaimaa Solaiman
CHALLENGE LAW FIRM

Frédéric Soliman
*SOLIMAN, HASHISH
AND PARTNERS*

Mamdouh Taha
*GENERAL ORGANIZATION OF
EXPORT & IMPORT CONTROL*

Randa Tharwat
NACITA CORPORATION

Nariman Wagdy
YOUSSRY SALEH & PARTNERS

Sara Wagdy
NACITA CORPORATION

Mona Wahba Aly El Din
*GENERAL AUTHORITY
FOR INVESTMENT GAFI*

Haidy Waheed
AM LAW FIRM

Amr Youssef
IBRACHY LEGAL CONSULTANCY

Mohamed Youssef
*INTERNATIONAL
COMPANY FOR YARN*

Darah Zakaria
*SHARKAWY & SARHAN
LAW FIRM*

Mona Zobaa
*GENERAL AUTHORITY
FOR INVESTMENT GAFI*

EL SALVADOR

LEÓN SOL ARQUITECTOS

Francisco Armando Arias
Rivera
ARIAS LAW

Mauricio Bernal
AES EL SALVADOR

Abraham Bichara
AES EL SALVADOR

Rafael Burgos
ARIAS LAW

Alexander Cader
PWC EL SALVADOR

Claudia Castellanos
*LA OFICINA DE PLANIFICACIÓN
DEL ÁREA METROPOLITANA DE
SAN SALVADOR (OPAMSS)*

Carlos Roberto Alfaro Castillo
AGUILAR CASTILLO LOVE

Christian Castro
AES EL SALVADOR

Armando Chacon
LEXINCORP

Walter Chávez
GOLD SERVICE

Eduardo Iván Colocho Catota
*INNOVATIONS & INTEGRATED
SOLUTIONS, SA DE CV*

Luis Alfredo Cornejo Martínez
*CORNEJO & UMAÑA, LTDA
DE CV - MEMBER OF RUSSELL
BEDFORD INTERNATIONAL*

Celina Cruz
*LA OFICINA DE PLANIFICACIÓN
DEL ÁREA METROPOLITANA DE
SAN SALVADOR (OPAMSS)*

Porfirio Díaz Fuentes
*DLM, ABOGADOS, NOTARIOS
& CONSULTORES*

David Ernesto Claros Flores
GARCÍA & BODÁN

Enrique Escobar
LEXINCORP

Guillermo Escobar
LEXINCORP

Roberta Gallardo de Cromeyer
ARIAS LAW

Edwin Gálvez
AES EL SALVADOR

Gabriela García
*SUPERINTENDENCIA DEL
SISTEMA FINANCIERO*

Raúl González
*CONSEJO NACIONAL
DE ENERGÍA (CNE)*

Yudy Guerrero
GOLD SERVICE

Gerardo Guidos
EXPERTIS

Guillermo Guidos
EXPERTIS

Antonio Guirola Moze
LEXINCORP

Luis Roberto Hernández Arita
HERNÁNDEZ ARITA INGENIEROS

Benjamín Valdez Iraheta

Hexiell Jarquin
*DLM, ABOGADOS, NOTARIOS
& CONSULTORES*

Ligia Maria Lazo Ventura
*LAZO ARQUITECTOS
ASOCIADOS*

Thelma Dinora Lizama de
Osorio
*SUPERINTENDENCIA DEL
SISTEMA FINANCIERO*

Mario Lozano
ARIAS LAW

Lorena Madrid
AGUILAR CASTILLO LOVE

Guillermo Massana
*ATCASAL ASOCIACIÓN
DE TRANSPORTISTAS DE
CARGA DE EL SALVADOR*

Astrud María Meléndez de
Chávez
*ASOCIACIÓN PROTECTORA
DE CRÉDITOS DE EL
SALVADOR (PROCREDITO)*

Antonio R. Méndez-Llort
*ROMERO PINEDA &
ASOCIADOS, MEMBER
OF LEX MUNDI*

Raúl Alberto García Mirón
BUFETE GARCÍA MIRÓN & CÍA

Miriam Eleana Mixco Reyna
GOLD SERVICE

Ricardo Molina
NOVITAS

Fernando Montano
ARIAS LAW

Jose Navas
ALL WORLD CARGO, SA DE CV

Moises Orlando Pacas M.
*ATCASAL ASOCIACIÓN
DE TRANSPORTISTAS DE
CARGA DE EL SALVADOR*

Geraldine Palma
AES EL SALVADOR

Carlos Pastrana
*RESTAURO ELETTRICITÀ
È COSTRUZIONI*

Sergio Perez
AES EL SALVADOR

Mónica Pineda Machuca
PACHECO COTO

Adriana Portillo
LEXINCORP

Ana Patricia Portillo Reyes
*LATAMLEX - GUANDIQUE
SEGOVIA QUINTANILLA*

Emilio Rivera
PWC EL SALVADOR

Carlos Roberto Rodríguez
*CONSORTIUM CENTRO
AMÉRICA ABOGADOS*

Rene Rodas
GEMMA LOGISTICS

Otto Rodríguez Salazar

Mario Enrique Sáenz
SÁENZ & ASOCIADOS

Jaime Salinas
GARCÍA & BODÁN

Oscar Samour
*CONSORTIUM CENTRO
AMÉRICA ABOGADOS*

Ernesto Sánchez
ARIAS LAW

Alonso V. Saravia
*ASOCIACIÓN SALVADOREÑA
DE INGENIEROS Y
ARQUITECTOS (ASIA)*

Luis Tevez
*BENJAMÍN VALDEZ
& ASOCIADOS*

Oscar Torres
GARCÍA & BODÁN

Laura Urrutia

Mauricio Antonio Urrutia
Urrutia
*SUPERINTENDENCIA DEL
SISTEMA FINANCIERO*

Julio C. Vargas Solano
GARCÍA & BODÁN

Karla Elizabeth Zelaya
Rodríguez
*SUPERINTENDENCIA DEL
SISTEMA FINANCIERO*

EQUATORIAL GUINEA

EY

*SEGESA (SOCIEDAD
DE ELECTRICIDAD DE
GUINEA ECUATORIAL)*

Elisabeth Ajamen
BEAC SIÈGE

Rui Andrade
*VDA - VIEIRA DE ALMEIDA
& ASSOCIADOS*

Maria Araujo
*VDA - VIEIRA DE ALMEIDA
& ASSOCIADOS*

Irene Balaguer Delgado
L&S ABOGADOS

Francisco Campos Braz
SOLEGE

Angel-Francisco Ela Ngomo
Nchama
*JUZGADO DE INSTRUCCION
DE BATA*

Philippe Fouda Fouda
BEAC SIÈGE

Soraia Lacerda
MIRANDA ALLIANCE

Marta López-Pena González
L&S ABOGADOS

João Mayer Moreira
*VDA - VIEIRA DE ALMEIDA
& ASSOCIADOS*

Jose Mbara
PWC EQUATORIAL GUINEA

Paulino Mbo Obama
OFICINA DE ESTUDIOS - ATEG

Ponciano Mbomio Nvo
*GABINETE JURIDICO DE
PONCIANO MBOMIO NVO*

Diosdado Nchama
*MINISTERIO DE MINAS,
INDUSTRIA Y ENERGIA*

Frida Ndong
K5 FREEPORT OIL CENTRE

José Emilio Ndong
ABUY ASESORES

Honorio Ndong Obama
ATTORNEY-AT-LAW

Nanda Nzambi
PWC EQUATORIAL GUINEA

Edna Oliveira
MIRANDA ALLIANCE

Antonio Ondo Obiang
Mangue
ARAB CONTRACTORS CO.

Zenika Sanogho
PWC EQUATORIAL GUINEA

Raquel Teresa Serón Calvo
L&S ABOGADOS

Sergio Abeso Tomo
GABINETE Y AGENCIA T&E

Boulbaba Zitouni Ben Yahia
GUINEA SERVICES PROVIDERS SL

ERITREA

Senai Andemariam
BERHANE GILA-MICHAEL LAW FIRM

Berhane Gila Michael
BERHANE GILA-MICHAEL LAW FIRM

ESTONIA

Juulika Aavik
ADVOKAADIBÜROO SORAINEN AS

Angela Agur
NJORD LAW FIRM

Oliver Ämarik
ADVOKAADIBÜROO SORAINEN AS

Aet Bergmann
BNT ATTORNEYS-AT-LAW ADVOKAADIBÜROO OÜ

Nikita Divissenko
VARUL MEMBER OF TARK GRUNTE SUTKIENE

Ülleke Eerik
ESTONIAN LAND BOARD

Kelli Eilart
ADVOKAADIBÜROO SORAINEN AS

Carri Ginter
ADVOKAADIBÜROO SORAINEN AS

Janek Hamidžanov
METAPRINT LTD.

Andres Juss
ESTONIAN LAND BOARD

Sander Kärson
VARUL MEMBER OF TARK GRUNTE SUTKIENE

Katre Kasepold
ESTONIAN LOGISTICS AND FREIGHT FORWARDING ASSOCIATION

Jevgeni Kazutkin
HOUGH, HUTT & PARTNERS OÜ

Kätlin Klaos
PWC ESTONIA

Edward Kostjuk
HOUGH, HUTT & PARTNERS OÜ

Villu Kõve
ESTONIAN SUPREME COURT

Tanja Kriisa
PWC ESTONIA

Paul Künnap
ADVOKAADIBÜROO SORAINEN AS

Tanel Küün
LAW OFFICE TARK

Gaily Kuusik
DELOITTE ADVISORY AS

Martti Lemendik
METAPRINT LTD.

Hannes Lentsius
PWC ESTONIA

Kerstin Linnart
ALIANCE OF INDEPENDENT LEGAL ADVISERS

Berit Loog
MINISTRY OF JUSTICE

Karin Madisson
ADVOKAADIBÜROO SORAINEN AS

Ants Mailend
ADVOKAADIBÜROO SORAINEN AS

Kaps Meelis
ELEKTRILEVI OÜ

Veiko Meos
CREDITINFO EESTI AS

Margus Mugu
COBALT LEGAL

Sandra-Kristin Noot
ELLEX RAIDLA ADVOKAADIBÜROO OÜ

Arne Ots
ELLEX RAIDLA ADVOKAADIBÜROO OÜ

Olavi Ottenson
DELOITTE ADVISORY AS

Kaitti Persidski
ESTONIAN CHAMBER OF NOTARIES

Martin-Johannes Raude
ELLEX RAIDLA ADVOKAADIBÜROO OÜ

Tõnu Roosve
ELEKTRILEVI OÜ

Einar Rosin
KPMG BALTICS OÜ

Kertu Ruus
ADVOKAADIBÜROO SORAINEN AS

Katrin Sarap
NJORD LAW FIRM

Häli Sokk
ADVOKAADIBÜROO SORAINEN AS

Lisette Suik
ADVOKAADIBÜROO SORAINEN AS

Aivar Taro
COBALT LEGAL

Triin Toom
ADVOKAADIBÜROO SORAINEN AS

Veikko Toomere
NJORD LAW FIRM

Neve Uudelt
ALIANCE OF INDEPENDENT LEGAL ADVISERS

Kai Vainola
ADVOKAADIBÜROO SORAINEN AS

Ingmar Vali
CENTRE OF REGISTERS & INFORMATION SYSTEMS

Paul Varul
VARUL MEMBER OF TARK GRUNTE SUTKIENE

Peeter Viirsalu
VARUL MEMBER OF TARK GRUNTE SUTKIENE

ETHIOPIA

Dagnachew Tesfaye Abetew
DAGNACHEW TESFAYE AND MAHLET MESGANAW LAW OFFICE

Million Alemu
LEGAL PRACTITIONER AND CONSULTANT

Girma Alemu Mengesha
ASSEFA & ASSOCIATES

Assefa Ali Beshir
ASSEFA & ASSOCIATES

Fikadu Asfaw
FIKADU ASFAW AND ASSOCIATES LAW OFFICE

Sisay Asres
FLK TRADING PLC

Henok Assefa
PRECISE CONSULT

Yodit Assefa
THE MOTOR & ENGINEERING COMPANY

Ato Awoke Asfaw
AWOKE ASFAW AUTHORIZED ACCOUNTING

Asrat Bekele
ASGB CONSULTING

Fekadu Bekele
ETHIOPIA REVENUES AND CUSTOMS AUTHORITY (ERCA)

Semere Wolde Bonger
NATIONAL BANK OF ETHIOPIA

Hailu Burayu
LAWYER

Kumlachew Dagne

Abinet Damtachew
CONSTRUCTION PROXY

Wondowosen Degefa
ETHIOPIA REVENUES AND CUSTOMS AUTHORITY (ERCA)

Teklay Gebrehiwot
ZENITH

Simon Getachew Kassaye
PWC

Berhane Ghebray
BERHANE GHEBRAY & ASSOCIATES

Solomon Gizaw
HST CONSULTING

Yodit Gurji
FIKADU ASFAW AND ASSOCIATES LAW OFFICE

Deborah Haddis Berhanu
MESFIN TAFESSE AND ASSOCIATES LAW OFFICE

Getu Jemaneh
DELOITTE CONSULTING PVT. LTD. CO.

Apollo Karumba
PWC

Belay Ketema
BELAY KETEMA LAW OFFICE

Tamrat Kidanemariam Domenico
TAMRAT KIDANEMARIAM DOMENICO LAW OFFICE

Tadesse Kiros
TADESSE KIROS LAW OFFICE

Mehrteab Leul
MEHRTEAB LEUL & ASSOCIATES

Yenehun Mamo
YENEHUN BIRLIE LAW OFFICE

Mahlet Mesganaw Getu
DAGNACHEW TESFAYE AND MAHLET MESGANAW LAW OFFICE

Mekdes Mezgebu
MESFIN TAFESSE AND ASSOCIATES LAW OFFICE

Nuredin Mohammed

Belayneh Molla Adgeh
MB CONSULTING PRIVATE LIMITED COMPANY

Titus Mukora
PWC KENYA

Mekonnen Muluneh Shiferaw
PWC

Habte Petros
YICHALAL TRANSIT SERVICE AND FREIGHT FORWARDING PLC

Nigussie Seid
ETHIOPIA REVENUES AND CUSTOMS AUTHORITY (ERCA)

Meklit Seifu
DELNESSAHOU TADESSE - COUNSELOR AND ATTORNEY-AT-LAW

Biruh Setargew
PWC

Kebede Shai
ETHIOPIA REVENUES AND CUSTOMS AUTHORITY (ERCA)

Kidist Sheferaw
MESFIN TAFESSE AND ASSOCIATES LAW OFFICE

Getu Shiferaw
MEHRTEAB LEUL & ASSOCIATES

Mekdes Shiferaw
GREEN INTERNATIONAL LOGISTIC SERVICES

Ameha Sime
AMEHA SIME B.C.

Delnessahou Tadesse
DELNESSAHOU TADESSE - COUNSELOR AND ATTORNEY-AT-LAW

Fasil Tadesse
FLK TRADING PLC

Mesfin Tafesse
MESFIN TAFESSE AND ASSOCIATES LAW OFFICE

Dereje Taffese

Solomon Demissie Tegegn
NET ENGINEERING CONSULTANCY

Michael Tekie
MEHRTEAB LEUL & ASSOCIATES

Gaim Yibrah Tesema
GAIM YIBRAH

Seyoum Yonhannes Tesfy
ADDIS ABABA UNIVERSITY

Gizeshwork Tessema
GIZE PLC

Wossenyeleh Tigu
MESFIN TAFESSE AND ASSOCIATES LAW OFFICE

Osborne Wanyoike
PWC

Getahun Worku
LAWYER

Haileyesus Worku
WOYN CHEMICALS PLC

Mekidem Yehiyes
MESFIN TAFESSE AND ASSOCIATES LAW OFFICE

Seyoum Yohannes Tesfay
ADDIS ABABA UNIVERSITY

Sintayehu Zeleke
FEDERAL HIGH COURT

FIJI

WAF NATIONAL OFFICE

Eddielin Almonte
PWC FIJI

Lisa Apted
KPMG

Nicholas Barnes
MUNRO LEYS

Jone Cavubati
FIJI EXPORT COUNCIL

Rhea Chand
MUNRO LEYS

Sangeeta Chand
MINISTRY OF JUSTICE

William Wylie Clarke
HOWARDS LAWYERS

Visvanath Das
FIJI REVENUE AND CUSTOMS AUTHORITY

Isireli Fa
THE FIJI LAW SOCIETY / FA & COMPANY BARRISTERS & SOLICITORS

Dilip Jamnadas
JAMNADAS AND ASSOCIATES

Jerome Kado
PWC FIJI

Viren Kapadia
SHERANI & CO.

Azam Khan
MINISTRY OF LOCAL GOVERNMENT

Mohammed Afzal Khan
KHAN & CO. BARRISTERS & SOLICITORS

Emily King
MUNRO LEYS

Peter Ian Knight
CROMPTONS SOLICITORS

Krishneel Krishna
FIJI REVENUE AND CUSTOMS AUTHORITY

Madhulesh Lakhan
WILLIAMS & GOSLING LTD.

Hemendra Nagin
SHERANI & CO.

Supreena Naidu
AP LEGAL

Jon Orton
ORTON ARCHITECTS

Armish Pal
AP LEGAL

Pradeep Patel
BDO

Mohnish Prasad
FIJI REVENUE AND CUSTOMS AUTHORITY

Varunendra Prasad
VP LAWYERS

Mele Rakai
SHERANI & CO.

Janet Raman
MUNRO LEYS

Shelvin Singh
SHELVIN SINGH LAWYERS

Narotam Solanki
PWC FIJI

Eparama Tawake
FIJI ELECTRICITY AUTHORITY

Ana Tuiketei
AP LEGAL

FINLAND

Manne Airaksinen
ROSCHIER ATTORNEYS LTD.

Timo Airisto
WHITE & CASE

Petri Avikainen
WHITE & CASE

Hillevi Ekstrom
OY NIKLASHIPPING LTD.

Marja Eskola
PWC FINLAND

Oona Fromholdt
*CASTRÉN & SNELLMAN
ATTORNEYS LTD.*

Esa Halmari
HEDMAN PARTNERS

Johanna Haltia-Tapio
*HANNES SNELLMAN
ATTORNEYS LTD.*

Joni Hatanmaa
HEDMAN PARTNERS

Seppo Havia
DITTMAR & INDRENIUS

Henrietta Hindström
ROSCHIER ATTORNEYS LTD.

Harri Hirvonen
PWC FINLAND

Lauri Jääskeläinen
*MINISTRY OF THE
ENVIRONMENT*

Pekka Jaatinen
*CASTRÉN & SNELLMAN
ATTORNEYS LTD.*

Johanna Jarvinen
PANALPINA AB

Sarianna Järviö
WHITE & CASE

Juuso Jokela
SUOMEN ASIAKASTIETO OY

Mika Karppinen
*HANNES SNELLMAN
ATTORNEYS LTD.*

Milla Kokko-Lehtinen
PWC FINLAND

Sini Laajala
HEDMAN PARTNERS

Kaisa Lamppu
PWC FINLAND

Anna-Ilona Lehtonen
ROSCHIER ATTORNEYS LTD.

Jan Lilius
*HANNES SNELLMAN
ATTORNEYS LTD.*

Johanna Lilja
ROSCHIER ATTORNEYS LTD.

Jaakko Maijala
*RUSSELL BEDFORD
INTERNATIONAL*

Olli Mäkelä
*HANNES SNELLMAN
ATTORNEYS LTD.*

Kimmo Mettälä
KROGERUS ATTORNEYS LTD.

Linda Miettinen
EVERSHEDS ATTORNEYS LTD.

Mia Mokkila
ROSCHIER ATTORNEYS LTD.

Marta Monteiro
*HANNES SNELLMAN
ATTORNEYS LTD.*

Eeva-Leena Niemelä
ROSCHIER ATTORNEYS LTD.

Janne Nurminen
ROSCHIER ATTORNEYS LTD.

Emma Nyyssölä
*ASIANAJOTOIMISTO
WHITE & CASE OY*

Jani Pitkänen
EVERSHEDS ATTORNEYS LTD.

Arttur Puoskari
WHITE & CASE

Mikko Rajala
BIRD & BIRD ATTORNEYS LTD.

Vuokko Rajamäki
ROSCHIER ATTORNEYS LTD.

Krista Rekola
WHITE & CASE

Ingrid Remmelgas
ROSCHIER ATTORNEYS LTD.

Peter Salovaara
EVERSHEDS ATTORNEYS LTD.

Petri Seppälä
PWC FINLAND

Nikolas Sjöberg
KROGERUS ATTORNEYS LTD.

Aatos Solhagen
*ASIANAJOTOIMISTO
WHITE & CASE OY*

Dina Stolt
ROSCHIER ATTORNEYS LTD.

Petri Taivalkoski
ROSCHIER ATTORNEYS LTD.

Jenni Teurokoski
HEDMAN PARTNERS

Tuuli Vapaavuori-Vartiainen
EVERSHEDS ATTORNEYS LTD.

Seija Vartiainen
PWC FINLAND

Marko Vuori
KROGERUS ATTORNEYS LTD.

Gunnar Westerlund
ROSCHIER ATTORNEYS LTD.

FRANCE

EAU DE PARIS

MAIRIE DE PARIS

Claire Adenis-Lamarre
MILLER ROSENFALCK LLP

Nadhia Ameziane
DENTONS

Yves Ardaillou
BERSAY ASSOCIES

Vincent Audoir
ALLEZ & ASSOCIÉS

Julien Bellapianta
ATS INTERNATIONAL

Hervé Beloeuvre
*FIDUCIAIRE BELOEUVRE
ET ASSOCIÉS*

Stéphane Bénézant
SCP GRANRUT AVOCATS

Florence Bequet-Abdou
PWC SOCIÉTÉ D'AVOCATS

Pierre Binon
BANQUE DE FRANCE

Andrew Booth
ANDREW BOOTH ARCHITECT

Isabelle-Victoria Carbuccia
IVCH PARIS

Frédéric Cauvin
PWC SOCIÉTÉ D'AVOCATS

Stéphanie Chatelon
*TAJ, MEMBER OF DELOITTE
TOUCHE TOHMATSU LIMITED*

Chloé Chiapusso-Ello
SCP GRANRUT AVOCATS

Jean-Pierre Clavel
SCP JEAN-PIERRE CLAVEL

Stephan de Groër
JEANTET AARPI

Jean-Paul Decorps
*ETUDE MAÎTRE JEAN-
PAUL DECORPS*

Antoine Delacarte
GUILLEMIN FLICHY AARPI

Djaffer Doulache
CABINET RCA

Segolene Dufetel
*MAYER BROWN
INTERNATIONAL LLP*

Jean-Marc Dufour
*FRANCE ECOMMERCE
INTERNATIONAL*

Odile Dupeyré
SOLVEIG AVOCATS

Philippe Durand
PWC SOCIÉTÉ D'AVOCATS

Thomas Ehrecke

Benoit Fauvelet
BANQUE DE FRANCE

Ingrid Fauvelière
JEANTET AARPI

Ivan Féron
PWC SOCIÉTÉ D'AVOCATS

Louis Feuillee
WHITE & CASE

Nataline Fleury
ASHURST LLP

Lionel Galliez
*CONSEIL SUPÉRIEUR DU
NOTARIAT (PARIS)*

Nassim Ghalimi
VEIL JOURDE

Régine Goury
*MAYER BROWN
INTERNATIONAL LLP*

François Grenier

Kevin Grossmann
CABINET GROSSMANN

Karl Hepp de Sevelinges
JEANTET AARPI

Marc Jobert
JOBERT & ASSOCIÉS

Ruben Koslar
JEANTET AARPI

Paul Lafuste
VEIL JOURDE

Daniel Arthur Laprès
*AVOCAT À LA COUR
D'APPEL DE PARIS*

Annie Le Berre
PWC SOCIÉTÉ D'AVOCATS

Alann Le Guillou
WHITE & CASE

Olivier Lopez
COHEN & GRESSER, AARPI

Elsa Lourdeau
*MAYER BROWN
INTERNATIONAL LLP*

Alexandre Majbruch
DENTONS

Wladimir Mangel
*MAYER BROWN
INTERNATIONAL LLP*

Frederic Mercier
*MATHEZ TRANSPORTS
INTERNATIONAUX SA*

Orane Mikolajayk

Nathalie Morel
*MAYER BROWN
INTERNATIONAL LLP*

Nathalie Nègre-Eveillard
WHITE & CASE

Michel Nisse
PWC SOCIÉTÉ D'AVOCATS

Catherine Ottaway
HOCHE SOCIÉTÉ D'AVOCATS

Sabine Paul
MILLER ROSENFALCK LLP

Arnaud Pédron
TAJ SOCIÉTÉ D'AVOCATS

Arnaud Pelpel
PELPEL AVOCATS

Thomas Philippe
*MAYER BROWN
INTERNATIONAL LLP*

Marie-Hélène Pinard-Fabro
PWC SOCIÉTÉ D'AVOCATS

Emmanuelle Ries
MILLER ROSENFALCK LLP

Jean-Francois Riffard
*UNIVERSITE CLERMONT
AUVERGNE, ECOLE DU DROIT*

Nicolas Rontchevsky
*AVOCAT ET PROFESSEUR
AGRÉGÉ DES FACULTÉS
DE DROIT*

Pierre-Yves Rossignol
SCP GRANRUT AVOCATS

Guillaume Rougier-Brierre
*GIDE LOYRETTE NOUEL,
MEMBER OF LEX MUNDI*

Philippe Roussel Galle
UNIVERSITÉ PARIS DESCARTES

Hugues Roux
BANQUE DE FRANCE

Abibatou Samb-Diouck
ETUDE SAMB-DIOUCK

Michael Samol
JEANTET AARPI

Maxime Samson

Pierre-Nicolas Sanzey
STEPHENSON HARWOOD

Emmanuel Schulte
BERSAY ASSOCIES

Maxime Simonnet
DENTONS

Johannes Singelnstein
RACINE AVOCATS

Isabelle Smith Monnerville
SMITH D'ORIA

Lionel Spizzichino
*WILLKIE FARR &
GALLAGHER LLP*

Jean Tarrade
*CONSEIL SUPÉRIEUR DU
NOTARIAT (PARIS)*

Steven Theallier
*MAYER BROWN
INTERNATIONAL LLP*

François Vergne
*GIDE LOYRETTE NOUEL,
MEMBER OF LEX MUNDI*

Nicolas Walker
REED SMITH

Ronène Zana
PWC SOCIÉTÉ D'AVOCATS

GABON

JOHN W. FFOOKS & CO.

MUNICIPALITÉ DE LIBREVILLE

Angéla Adibet
DELOITTE JURIDIQUE ET FISCAL

Elisabeth Ajamen
BEAC SIÈGE

Philippe Bergon
ACTION RAPIDE TRANSIT

Jean-Pierre Bozec
PROJECT LAWYERS

Nicolas Chevrinais
EY FFA JURIDIQUE ET FISCAL

Regine D'Almeida Mensah
OHADA LEGIS

Sylvain Diangatebe Malongo
*SOCIÉTÉ D'ENERGIE ET
D'EAU DU GABON (SEEG)*

Anaïs Edzang Pouzere
*PRICEWATERHOUSECOOPERS
TAX & LEGAL SA*

Gilbert Erangah
ETUDE MAÎTRE ERANGAH

Augustin Fang
CABINET AUGUSTIN FANG

Philippe Fouda Fouda
BEAC SIÈGE

Gagan Gupta
OLAM INTERNATIONAL

Désiré Lasseghe
CNSS

Kevin Lebreton
ACTION RAPIDE TRANSIT

Athanase Ndoye Loury
SYNDIC JUDICIAIRE

Eric Mbah
*CONSERVATION DE LA
PROPRIETÉ FONCIÈRE ET
DES HYPOTHÈQUES*

Louis Pascal Mbighi
MINISTÈRE DE L'ECONOMIE

Gaetan Mboza
3M-PARTNERS & CONSEILS

Davy Mendoume
MINISTÈRE DE L'ECONOMIE

Yannick Mokanda
MINISTÈRE DE L'ECONOMIE

Claude Mombo
MINISTÈRE DE L'ECONOMIE

Haymard Moutsinga
AVOCAT À LA COUR

Thierry Ngomo
ARCHI PRO INTERNATIONAL

Lubin Ntoutoume
*CABINET SCP NTOUTOUME
ET MEZHER*

Jean Serge Ogoula
CELLULE E-TAXES

Laurent Pommera
*PRICEWATERHOUSECOOPERS
TAX & LEGAL SA*

Christophe Adrien Relongoué
*PRICEWATERHOUSECOOPERS
TAX & LEGAL SA*

Anne Rodot
ACTION RAPIDE TRANSIT

Fabien Tannhof
*SOCIÉTÉ D'ENERGIE ET
D'EAU DU GABON (SEEG)*

H. Tchiffambeu
3M-PARTNERS & CONSEILS

Ines Vaz
*PRICEWATERHOUSECOOPERS
TAX & LEGAL SA*

Laetitia Yuinang
OLAM INTERNATIONAL

GAMBIA, THE

Malick Bah
*NATIONAL ENVIRONMENT
AGENCY*

Abdul Aziz Bensouda
AMIE BENSOUDA & CO.

Amie N.D. Bensouda
AMIE BENSOUDA & CO.

Odzangbateh Dake
PWC GHANA

Ida Denise Drameh
IDA D. DRAMEH & ASSOCIATES

Dzidzedze Fiadjoe
PWC GHANA

Sheriff Gaye
*BOLLORÉ TRANSPORT
& LOGISTICS*

Sarane Hydara
*MAHFOUS ENGINEERING
CONSULTANTS*

Lamin S. Jatta
ACCORD ASSOCIATES

Kebba Jobe
*DABANI ELECTRICAL
ENTERPRISE*

Sulayman Jobe
*DT ASSOCIATES, INDEPENDENT
CORRESPONDENCE FIRM
OF DELOITTE TOUCHE
TOHMATSU LIMITED*

Sulayman M. Joof
S.M. JOOF AGENCY

Mariam Kante
*BOLLORÉ TRANSPORT
& LOGISTICS*

Abdoullah Konateh
*MAHFOUS ENGINEERING
CONSULTANTS*

George Kwatia
PWC GHANA

Anna Njie
AMIE BENSOUDA & CO.

Clement Okey
PWC GHANA

Baboucarr Owl
*NATIONAL WATER AND
ELECTRICITY COMPANY LTD.*

Ibrahima Salla
TRUST BANK LTD.

Janet Ramatoulie Sallah-Njie
TORODO CHAMBERS

Mary Abdoulie
Samba-Christensen
LEGAL PRACTITIONER

Aji Penda B. Sankareh
*DT ASSOCIATES, INDEPENDENT
CORRESPONDENCE FIRM
OF DELOITTE TOUCHE
TOHMATSU LIMITED*

Bakary Sanneh
*DEPARTMENT OF PHYSICAL
PLANNING AND HOUSING*

Joseph E. Sarre
*GAMBIA ARCHITECTURAL AND
PLANNING CONSULTANTS*

Yassin Senghore
SENGHORE LAW PRACTICE

Hawa Sisay-Sabally
LAWYER

Salieu Taal
TEMPLE LEGAL PRACTITIONERS

GEORGIA

Marekh Amirashvili
*INTERNATIONAL
ADVOCATES LLC*

Davit Askurava
*NATIONAL BUREAU
OF ENFORCEMENT*

Nino Bakhia
*NATIONAL AGENCY OF
PUBLIC REGISTRY*

Sandro Bakhsoliani
INSTA LLC

Mikheil Baliashvili
ARCHITECTURAL BUREAU

David Bardavelidze
OCEANNET GEORGIA LTD.

Giorgi Begiashvili
*BEGIASHVILI & CO.
LIMITED LAW OFFICES*

Levan Berdzenishvili
*GEORGIAN TRANS
EXPEDITION LTD.*

Tatia Berekashvili
*MINISTRY OF ECONOMY AND
SUSTAINABLE DEVELOPMENT*

Nino Berianidze
*MINISTRY OF ECONOMY AND
SUSTAINABLE DEVELOPMENT*

Revaz Beridze
ERISTAVI & PARTNERS

Nino Bezhitashvili
*MINISTRY OF ECONOMY AND
SUSTAINABLE DEVELOPMENT*

Sandro Bibilashvili
BGI LEGAL

Temur Bolotashvili
*GEORGIAN INSTITUTE
OF BUILDING*

Arsen Bortsvadze
*AMPER CO. ENERGY
SOLUTIONS*

Giorgi Chichinadze
*MINISTRY OF ECONOMY AND
SUSTAINABLE DEVELOPMENT*

Zurab Chkheidze
*BEGIASHVILI & CO.
LIMITED LAW OFFICES*

Ekaterine Danelia
*NODIA, URUMASHVILI
& PARTNERS*

Giorgi Eliadze
FINE LIFE

Khatia Esebua
ALLIANCE GROUP HOLDING

Mariam Gabashvili
ERISTAVI & PARTNERS

Zviad Gabisonia
FINE LIFE

Nikoloz Gamkrelidze
CAUCASTRANSEXPRESS LTD.

Teymuraz Gamrekelashvili
TELASI

Teona Gaprindashvili
*NODIA, URUMASHVILI
& PARTNERS*

Ekaterina Gazadze
GEORGIAN STOCK EXCHANGE

Archil Giorgadze
DECHERT GEORGIA LLC

Givi Giorgadze
INVESTORS COUNCIL

Lasha Gogiberidze
BGI LEGAL

Lali Gogoberidze
*MINISTRY OF ECONOMY AND
SUSTAINABLE DEVELOPMENT*

Alexander Gomiashvili
JSC CREDIT INFO GEORGIA

Levan Gotua
*BEGIASHVILI & CO.
LIMITED LAW OFFICES*

Goga Gujejiani
*KAUKASUS TRANSPORT
LOGISTIK*

Nana Gurgenidze
*LEGAL PARTNERS
ASSOCIATED (LPA) LLC*

Jaba Gvelebiani
*LEGAL PARTNERS
ASSOCIATED (LPA) LLC*

Gia Jandieri
NEW ECONOMIC SCHOOL

David Javakhadze
*MINISTRY OF ECONOMY AND
SUSTAINABLE DEVELOPMENT*

George Jugeli
INVESTORS COUNCIL

David Kakabadze

Grigol Kakauridze
*MINISTRY OF ECONOMY AND
SUSTAINABLE DEVELOPMENT*

Nikoloz Kakauridze
AZIMUTI LTD.

David Kakhiani
MONTAGE GEORGIA

Irakli Kandashvili

Oguz Kaan Karaer
MAQRO CONSTRUCTION

Irma Kavtaradze
*MINISTRY OF ECONOMY AND
SUSTAINABLE DEVELOPMENT*

Mari Khardziani
*NATIONAL AGENCY OF
PUBLIC REGISTRY*

Dachi Kinkladze
GEORGIA REVENUE SERVICE

Sergi Kobakhidze
PWC GEORGIA

Aieti Kukava
ALLIANCE GROUP HOLDING

Sophio Kurtauli
*NATIONAL BUREAU
OF ENFORCEMENT*

Nino Kvinikadze
*NODIA, URUMASHVILI
& PARTNERS*

Natia Lapiashvili
DECHERT GEORGIA LLC

Danelia Lasha
AZIMUTI LTD.

Ela Lekishvili
F-CHAIN

Irakli Lekishvili
TOYOTA CAUCASUS LLC

Tea Loladze
*MINISTRY OF ECONOMY AND
SUSTAINABLE DEVELOPMENT*

Mirab-Dmitry Lomadze

Sofia Machaladze
ERISTAVI & PARTNERS

Irakli Mamaladze
TEGETA MOTORS

Jaba Mamulashvili
*BEGIASHVILI & CO.
LIMITED LAW OFFICES*

Nicola Mariani
DECHERT GEORGIA LLC

Elene Mebonia
*LEGAL PARTNERS
ASSOCIATED (LPA) LLC*

Salome Meladze
BGI LEGAL

Salome Meunargia
*LEGAL PARTNERS
ASSOCIATED (LPA) LLC*

Roin Migriauli
*LAW OFFICE MIGRIAULI
& PARTNERS*

Giorgi Mikautadze
TBILISI CITY COURT

Ia Mikhelidze
GEORGIA REVENUE SERVICE

Sophie Natroshvili
BGI LEGAL

Lasha Nodia
*NODIA, URUMASHVILI
& PARTNERS*

Tamta Nutsubidze
*BEGIASHVILI & CO.
LIMITED LAW OFFICES*

Papuna Papiashvili
*NATIONAL BUREAU
OF ENFORCEMENT*

George Paresishvili
GEORGIAN STOCK EXCHANGE

Simon Parsons
PWC GEORGIA

Tsisnami Sabadze
*MINISTRY OF ECONOMY AND
SUSTAINABLE DEVELOPMENT*

Natia Sakhokia
*NATIONAL BUREAU
OF ENFORCEMENT*

Levan Samanishvili
OCEANNET GEORGIA LTD.

Mikheil Sarjveladze
MINISTRY OF JUSTICE

Manzoor Shah
GLOBALINK LOGISTICS GROUP

Tea Sonishvili
*MINISTRY OF ECONOMY AND
SUSTAINABLE DEVELOPMENT*

Levan Targamadze
SABA CONSTRUCTION

Giorgi Tavartkiladze
DELOITTE

Tamara Tevdoradze
BGI LEGAL

Antonina Tselovalnikova
GIANTI LOGISTICS

Besik Tsimakuridze

Tamar Tvildiani
TOYOTA CAUCASUS LLC

Kote Ukleba
ELECTRICAL SERVICE GROUP

Samson Uridia
GEORGIA REVENUE SERVICE

Zviad Voshakidze
TELASI

Emre Yetiskin
MAQRO CONSTRUCTION

GERMANY

Helge Aulmann
REED SMITH LLP

Marc Bäumer
REED SMITH LLP

Anna-Lena Baur
GSK STOCKMANN + KOLLEGEN

Judith Becker
REED SMITH LLP

Mark Bekker
BEKKER LOGISTICA

Henning Berger
WHITE & CASE

Philipp Johannes Bergmann
REED SMITH LLP

Jennifer Bierly
GSK STOCKMANN + KOLLEGEN

Justus Binder
REED SMITH LLP

Heiko Büsing
*PRICEWATERHOUSECOOPERS
LEGAL AKTIENGESELLSCHAFT
RECHTSANWALTSGESELLSCHAFT*

Thomas Büssow
PWC GERMANY

Andreas Eckhardt
*PRICEWATERHOUSECOOPERS
LEGAL AKTIENGESELLSCHAFT
RECHTSANWALTSGESELLSCHAFT*

Sigrun Erber-Faller
*NOTARE ERBER-FALLER
UND VORAN*

Johann-Friedrich Fleisch
DLA PIPER UK LLP

Alexander Freiherr von Aretin
*GRAF VON WESTPHALEN
RECHTSANWÄLTE
PARTNERSCHAFT*

Simon Grieser
REED SMITH LLP

Andrea Gruss
MERGET + PARTNER

Klaus Günther
OPPENHOFF & PARTNER

Daniel Hacker
*PRICEWATERHOUSECOOPERS
LEGAL AKTIENGESELLSCHAFT
RECHTSANWALTSGESELLSCHAFT*

Marc Alexander Häger
OPPENHOFF & PARTNER

Sebastian Harder
*PRICEWATERHOUSECOOPERS
LEGAL AKTIENGESELLSCHAFT
RECHTSANWALTSGESELLSCHAFT*

Nadine Haubner
MAYER BROWN LLP

Tina Hoffmann
MAYER BROWN LLP

Götz-Sebastian Hök
*DR. HÖK STIEGLMEIER
& PARTNER*

Elke Holthausen-Dux
*MOCK PARTNERSCHAFT VON
RECHTSANWÄLTEN MBB*

Peter Holzhäuser
*PRICEWATERHOUSECOOPERS
LEGAL AKTIENGESELLSCHAFT
RECHTSANWALTSGESELLSCHAFT*

Markus Jakoby
JAKOBY RECHTSANWÄLTE

Helmuth Jordan
*JORDAN & WAGNER
RECHTSANWALTSGESELLSCHAFT
MBH*

Alexander Kollmorgen
K&L GATES LLP

Jörg Kraffel
WHITE & CASE

Ernst-Otto Kuchenbrandt
DEUTSCHE BUNDESBANK

Baerbel Kuhlmann
EY

Claudia Kuhn
REED SMITH LLP

Andreas Lange
MAYER BROWN LLP

Peter Limmer
*NOTARE DR. LIMMER
& DR. FRIEDERICH*

Steffen Lindemann
MAYER BROWN LLP

René Lochmann
REED SMITH LLP

Sabine Malik
SCHUFA HOLDING AG

Werner Meier
SIMMONS & SIMMONS

Frank Mizera
REED SMITH LLP

Marius Moeller
PWC GERMANY

Isaschar Nicolaysen
DLA PIPER UK LLP

Dirk Otto
DENK RECHTSANWAELTE

John Piotrowski
JAKOBY RECHTSANWÄLTE

Sebastian Prügel
WHITE & CASE

Angela Reimer
DIAZ REUS & TARG LLP

Anselm Reinertshofer
REED SMITH LLP

Sebastian Reinsch
JANKE & REINSCH

Alexander Reus
DIAZ REUS & TARG LLP

Malte Richter
MAYER BROWN LLP

Martina Rothe
ASHURST LLP

Jan Rudolph
LINKLATERS LLP

Philipp Ruehland
*PRICEWATERHOUSECOOPERS
LEGAL AKTIENGESELLSCHAFT
RECHTSANWALTSGESELLSCHAFT*

Diedrich Schröder
DLA PIPER UK LLP

Volker Schwarz
*HEUSSEN
RECHTSANWALTSGESELLSCHAFT
MBH*

Kirstin Schwedt
LINKLATERS LLP

Mike Silin
DHL CZECH REPUBLIC

Marce Spielberger
REED SMITH LLP

Kai Sebastian Staak
*PRICEWATERHOUSECOOPERS
LEGAL AKTIENGESELLSCHAFT
RECHTSANWALTSGESELLSCHAFT*

Dirk Stiller
PWC GERMANY

Karl-Thomas Stopp
*MOCK PARTNERSCHAFT VON
RECHTSANWÄLTEN MBB*

Tobias Taetzner
PWC GERMANY

Kévin Paul-Hervé Tanguy
*PRICEWATERHOUSECOOPERS
LEGAL AKTIENGESELLSCHAFT
RECHTSANWALTSGESELLSCHAFT*

Jonathan Tobler
DLA PIPER UK LLP

Matei Ujica
REED SMITH LLP

Arne Vogel
*M&P DR. MATZEN &
PARTNER MBB*

Oscar Weller
JANKE & REINSCH

Hartmut Wicke
*NOTARE DR. WICKE
UND HERRLER*

Marco Wilhelm
MAYER BROWN LLP

Thomas Winkler
*DOMUS AG - MEMBER
OF RUSSELL BEDFORD
INTERNATIONAL*

Gerlind Wisskirchen
CMS HASCHE SIGLE

Uwe Witt
*PRICEWATERHOUSECOOPERS
LEGAL AKTIENGESELLSCHAFT
RECHTSANWALTSGESELLSCHAFT*

GHANA

Solomon Ackom
GRIMALDI GHANA LTD.

George Kingsley Acquah
*STANDARD CHARTERED
BANK GHANA LIMITED*

John Acquah
GRIMALDI GHANA LTD.

Larry Adjetey
LAW TRUST COMPANY

Sena Agbekoh
AB & DAVID

Irene Agyenim-Boateng
AB & DAVID

George Ahiafor
XDSDATA GHANA LTD.

Kweku Ainuson
AB LEXMALL & ASSOCIATES

Cecilia Akyeampong
*TOWN AND COUNTRY
PLANNING DEPARTMENT*

Mellisa Amarteifio
SAM OKUDZETO & ASSOCIATES

Nene Amegatcher
SAM OKUDZETO & ASSOCIATES

Kennedy Paschal Anaba
LAWFIELDS CONSULTING

Kweku Brebu Andah
*BAKER TILLY ANDAH + ANDAH
CHARTERED ACCOUNTANTS*

Wilfred Kwabena
Anim-Odame
LANDS COMMISSION

Iris Annan
*BENTSI-ENCHILL, LETSA
& ANKOMAH, MEMBER
OF LEX MUNDI*

Daisy Joana Antwi
NTRAKWAH & CO.

Kwabena Asante Offei
*BENTSI-ENCHILL, LETSA
& ANKOMAH, MEMBER
OF LEX MUNDI*

Akousa Akoma Asiama
NTRAKWAH & CO.

Bridget Atta-Konadu
NTRAKWAH & CO.

Nana Akwasi Awuah
AB LEXMALL & ASSOCIATES

Joyce Bediako
NTRAKWAH & CO.

Ayesha Bedwei
PWC GHANA

Thomas Blankson
XDSDATA GHANA LTD.

Binditi Chitor
AB LEXMALL & ASSOCIATES

Diana Asonaba Dapaah
SAM OKUDZETO & ASSOCIATES

Ras Afful Davis
CLIMATE SHIPPING & TRADING

Jerry Dei
SAM OKUDZETO & ASSOCIATES

Judith Donkoh
NTRAKWAH & CO.

Kofi Edem Penty
RENAISSANCE LAW CHAMBERS

Christina Furler
FURLER ARCHITECTS LTD.

Abeku Gyan-Quansah
PWC GHANA

Rhoda Gyepi-Garbrah
NTRAKWAH & CO.

Roland Horsoo
BOUYGUES CONSTRUCTION

Daniel Imadi
*BENTSI-ENCHILL, LETSA
& ANKOMAH, MEMBER
OF LEX MUNDI*

Rosa Kudoadzi
*BENTSI-ENCHILL, LETSA
& ANKOMAH, MEMBER
OF LEX MUNDI*

Isaac Kunko
AB LEXMALL & ASSOCIATES

Mary Kwarteng
PWC GHANA

George Kwatia
PWC GHANA

Yaw Kyere
AB LEXMALL & ASSOCIATES

Eric Nii Yarboi Mensah
SAM OKUDZETO & ASSOCIATES

Godwin Ofosuhene Nkrumah
*BENTSI-ENCHILL, LETSA
& ANKOMAH, MEMBER
OF LEX MUNDI*

Kwadwo Ntrakwah
NTRAKWAH & CO.

Nana Yaw Ntrakwah
NTRAKWAH & CO.

Abena Ntrakwah-Mensah
NTRAKWAH & CO.

Wordsworth Odame Larbi
CONSULTANT

Sam Okudzeto
SAM OKUDZETO & ASSOCIATES

Rexford Assasie Oppong
KNUST

Prince Oppong Boakye
*BENTSI-ENCHILL, LETSA
& ANKOMAH, MEMBER
OF LEX MUNDI*

Patience Ose-Nyarko
*TOWN AND COUNTRY
PLANNING DEPARTMENT*

Vera Owusu Osei
AB & DAVID

Cynthia Jumu Quarcoo
CQ LEGAL & CONSULTING

Henry Layea Quartey
*BAKER TILLY ANDAH + ANDAH
CHARTERED ACCOUNTANTS*

Benjamin Quaye
*MINISTRY OF LAND AND
NATURAL RESOURCES OF
THE REPUBLIC OF GHANA*

Jacob Saah
SAAH & CO.

Shirley Somuah
NTRAKWAH & CO.

Ebenezer Teye Agawu
*CONSOLIDATED SHIPPING
AGENCIES LIMITED*

Joyce Franklyn Thompson
NTRAKWAH & CO.

M.C. Vasnani
*CONSOLIDATED SHIPPING
AGENCIES LIMITED*

Thecla Wricketts
*BENTSI-ENCHILL, LETSA
& ANKOMAH, MEMBER
OF LEX MUNDI*

GREECE

EYDAP SA

Sophia Ampoulidou
DRAKOPOULOS LAW FIRM

Evangelos Angelopoulos
E ANGELOPOULOS LAW OFFICE

Amalia Balla
POTAMITIS-VEKRIS

George Bersis
POTAMITIS-VEKRIS

Dimitris Bimpas
IME GSEVEE

Ira Charisiadou
CHARISIADOU LAW OFFICE

Viktoria Chatzara
IKRP ROKAS & PARTNERS

Theodora Christodoulou
KLC LAW FIRM

Alkistis Christofilou
IKRP ROKAS & PARTNERS

Evangelia Christopoulou
NOTARY

Vasiliki Christou
KLC LAW FIRM

Leda Condoyanni
*HELLENIC CORPORATE
GOUVERNANCE COUNCIL*

Eleni Dikonimaki
*TEIRESIAS SA - BANK
INFORMATION SYSTEMS*

Sotirios Douklias
KG LAW FIRM

Panagiotis Drakopoulos
DRAKOPOULOS LAW FIRM

Anastasia Dritsa
*KYRIAKIDES GEORGOPOULOS
LAW FIRM*

Elisabeth Eleftheriades
KG LAW FIRM

Stergios Frastanlis
*ZEPOS & YANNOPOULOS LAW
FIRM, MEMBER OF LEX MUNDI*

Dionyssia I. Gamvrakis
SARANTITIS LAW FIRM

Georgios Garoufis
PWC GREECE

Dionysios Gavounelis
KIP LAW FIRM

Gerasimos Georgopoulos
*GENIKO EMBORIKO
MITROO - GEMI*

Antonis Giannakodimos
*ZEPOS & YANNOPOULOS LAW
FIRM, MEMBER OF LEX MUNDI*

Antonios Gkiokas
PWC GREECE

Christos Goulas
*KREMALIS LAW FIRM,
MEMBER OF IUS LABORIS*

Aikaterini Grivaki
PWC GREECE

Dimitris V. Hatzihristidis
ELECTRICAL ENGINEER

Efthymios Kallitsis

Theodora D. Karagiorgou
KOUTALIDIS LAW FIRM

Artemis Karathanassi
PWC GREECE

Catherine Karatzas
KARATZAS & PARTNERS

Aristotelis Katranis
*KYRIAKIDES GEORGOPOULOS
LAW FIRM*

Rita Katsoula
POTAMITIS-VEKRIS

Dionysios Kazaglis
SARANTITIS LAW FIRM

Anna Kazantzidou
*VAINANIDIS ECONOMOU &
ASSOCIATES LAW FIRM*

Anastasia Kelveridou
*KYRIAKIDES GEORGOPOULOS
LAW FIRM*

Efthymios Kleftogiannis
PWC GREECE

Constantinos Klissouras
KIP LAW FIRM

Ioanna Kompou
PWC GREECE

Georgia Konstantinidou
DRAKOPOULOS LAW FIRM

Lena Kontogeorgou
NOTARY

Panos Koromantzos
*BAHAS, GRAMATIDIS
& PARTNERS*

Olga Koromilia
PWC GREECE

Liana Kosmatou
*C. PAPACOSTOPOULOS
& ASSOCIATES*

Zafiria Kosmidou
KARATZAS & PARTNERS

Dimitrios Kotsionis
*MICHAEL KYPRIANOU
& CO. LLC*

Vasiliki (Cecilia) Kousouri
*KYRIAKIDES GEORGOPOULOS
LAW FIRM*

Dimitrios Kremalis
*KREMALIS LAW FIRM,
MEMBER OF IUS LABORIS*

Irene C. Kyriakides
*KYRIAKIDES GEORGOPOULOS
LAW FIRM*

Panos Lolonis
*HELLENIC CADASTRE AND
MAPPING AGENCY*

Artemis Malliaropoulou
*INTERNATIONAL
CRIMINAL COURT*

Effrosyni-Maria Mantalia
*ELIAS PARASKEVAS
ATTORNEYS 1933*

Evangelos Margaritis
DRAKOPOULOS LAW FIRM

Emmanuel Mastromanolis
*ZEPOS & YANNOPOULOS LAW
FIRM, MEMBER OF LEX MUNDI*

Alexandros N. Metaxas
SARANTITIS LAW FIRM

Maria Moschopoulou
*ELIAS PARASKEVAS
ATTORNEYS 1933*

Marilisa Myrat
KARATZAS & PARTNERS

Anthony Narlis
CALBERSON SA

Anastasia Oikonomopoulou
KLC LAW FIRM

Athina Palli
*ZEPOS & YANNOPOULOS LAW
FIRM, MEMBER OF LEX MUNDI*

Christina Papachristopoulou
KIP LAW FIRM

Elena Papachristou
*ZEPOS & YANNOPOULOS LAW
FIRM, MEMBER OF LEX MUNDI*

Konstantinos Papadiamantis
POTAMITIS-VEKRIS

Lily Papakiriaki
KYRIAKIDES GEORGOPOULOS LAW FIRM

Dimitris Papamentzelopoulos
KLC LAW FIRM

Christina Papanikolopoulou
ZEPOS & YANNOPOULOS LAW FIRM, MEMBER OF LEX MUNDI

Stavros Papantonis
ACTION AUDITING SA - MEMBER OF RUSSELL BEDFORD INTERNATIONAL

Martha Papasotiriou
UNITYFOUR

Dimitris E. Paraskevas
ELIAS PARASKEVAS ATTORNEYS 1933

Marios Petropoulos
KREMALIS LAW FIRM, MEMBER OF IUS LABORIS

Spiros Pilios
GENESIS WORLD TRANS

Katerina Politi
KYRIAKIDES GEORGOPOULOS LAW FIRM

Panagiotis Polychronopoulos
KELEMENIS & CO.

Stathis Potamitis
POTAMITIS-VEKRIS

Vicky Psaltaki
SARANTITIS LAW FIRM

Mary Psylla
PWC GREECE

Eva Rodaki
PWC GREECE

Vasiliki Salaka
KARATZAS & PARTNERS

Ioannis Sarakinos
SARAKINOS LAW

Nikolaos Siakantaris
UNITYFOUR

Konstantinos Siakoulis
GENIKO EMBORIKO MITROO - GEMI

Ioannis Skandalis
PWC GREECE

Ioanna Stamou
KARATZAS & PARTNERS

Alexia Stratou
KREMALIS LAW FIRM, MEMBER OF IUS LABORIS

Georgios Thanopoulos
IME GSEVEE

Athanasios Thoedorou

John Tripidakis
JOHN TRIPIDAKIS & ASSOCIATES LAW FIRM

Kimon Tsakiris
KG LAW FIRM

Angeliki Tsatsi
KARATZAS & PARTNERS

Antonios Tsavdaridis
IKRP ROKAS & PARTNERS

Panagiota Tsinouli
KYRIAKIDES GEORGOPOULOS LAW FIRM

Panagiota D. Tsitsa
NOTARY PANAGIOTA TSITSA

Katerina Tzamalouka
KYRIAKIDES GEORGOPOULOS LAW FIRM

Alexia Tzouni
POTAMITIS-VEKRIS

Spyros Valvis
PWC GREECE

Penny Vithoulka
C. PAPACOSTOPOULOS & ASSOCIATES

Konstantinos Vlachakis
NOTARY

Kalliopi Vlachopoulou
KELEMENIS & CO.

Lydia Vradi
KARATZAS & PARTNERS

Sofia Xanthoulea
JOHN TRIPIDAKIS & ASSOCIATES LAW FIRM

Fredy Yatracou
PWC GREECE

Stergios Zygouras
KOUTALIDIS LAW FIRM

GRENADA

DANNY WILLIAMS & CO.

GRENADA ELECTRICITY SERVICES LTD.

W.R. Agostini
W.R. AGOSTINI & CO.

Raymond Anthony
RAYMOND ANTHONY & CO.

James Bristol
HENRY, HENRY & BRISTOL

Carlyle Felix
MINISTRY OF ECONOMIC DEVELOPMENT, PLANNING, TRADE, COOPERATIVES AND INTERNATIONAL BUSINESS

Melissa Garraway
SEON & ASSOCIATES

Kim George
KIM GEORGE & ASSOCIATES

Carlyle Glean Jr.
GLEAN'S CONSTRUCTION & ENGINEERING CO.

Cyrus Griffith
LABOUR DEPARTMENT

Annette Henry
MINISTRY OF LEGAL AFFAIRS

Keith Hosten
HOSTEN'S (ELECTRICAL SERVICES) LTD.

Ernie James
MINISTRY OF ECONOMIC DEVELOPMENT, PLANNING, TRADE, COOPERATIVES AND INTERNATIONAL BUSINESS

Nigel A. John
LATITUDES CONSULT

Garvey Louison
LOUISON CONSULTING

Debra Brenda Mason
GRENADA NUTMEG & COCOA PRODUCTS

Gail Ann Newton
GRENADA PORT AUTHORITY

Karen Samuel
SAMUEL PHILLIP & ASSOCIATES

Safiya Sawney
TRADSHIP INTERNATIONAL

Valentino Sawney
TRADSHIP INTERNATIONAL

David R. Sinclair
SINCLAIR ENTERPRISES LIMITED

Isabelle Slinger
INSTITUTE OF CHARTERED ACCOUNTANTS OF THE EASTERN CARIBBEAN

Sharon Tenny
GRENADA INDUSTRIAL DEVELOPMENT CORPORATION

Alana Twum-Barimah
SUPREME COURT REGISTRY

Shireen Wilkinson
WILKINSON, WILKINSON & WILKINSON

GUATEMALA

EMPRESA ELÉCTRICA DE GUATEMALA SA

PROTECTORA DE CRÉDITO COMERCIAL

Oty Aixa Farfán Álvarez
SUPERINTENDENCIA DE ADMINISTRACIÓN TRIBUTARIA

Erwin Ronaldo Alvarez Urbina
INSTAELECTRA XPRESS

Nancy Amaya
ATA SERVICIOS

Pedro Aragón
ARAGÓN & ARAGÓN

Mario René Archila Cruz
ARIAS LAW

Jorge Luis Arenales de la Roca
ARIAS LAW

José Alejandro Arévalo Alburez
SUPERINTENDENCIA DE BANCOS

Elías Arriaza Sáenz
CONSORTIUM - RACSA

Sandra Audicio
MARINE CARGO LINE, SA

María de los Angeles Barillas Buchhalter
SARAVIA & MUÑOZ

Nancy Barrera
PWC GUATEMALA

Jose Rodrigo Barrillas Garcia
NOVALES ABOGADOS

Jorge Rolando Barrios
BONILLA, MONTANO, TORIELLO & BARRIOS

Elmer Erasmo Beltetón Morales
REGISTRO GENERAL DE LA PROPIEDAD DE GUATEMALA (RGP)

Luis Gustavo Berganza
REGISTRO GENERAL DE LA PROPIEDAD DE GUATEMALA (RGP)

Axel Beteta

Eva Cacacho González
QIL+4 ABOGADOS SA

Emanuel Callejas
CARRILLO & ASOCIADOS

Natalia Callejas Aquino
AGUILAR CASTILLO LOVE

Rodrigo Callejas Aquino
CARRILLO & ASOCIADOS

Delia Cantoral
EY

Jorge Castañeda
SPEC

Raul Castañeda
SPEC

Juan Carlos Castillo Chacón
AGUILAR CASTILLO LOVE

Eduardo Castillo Cortes
CASTILLO ARQUITECTOS

Maria Mercedes Castro
GARCÍA & BODÁN

Juan Carlos Chavarría
EY

Jose Andres Fuxet Ciani
LEXINCORP

Julio Contreras
REGISTRO GENERAL DE LA PROPIEDAD DE GUATEMALA (RGP)

Juan Luis De la Roca
REGISTRO MERCANTIL

Eleonora de Palma
ATA SERVICIOS

Luis Pedro Del Valle
ARIAS LAW

Claudia Lavinia Figueroa
REGISTRO GENERAL DE LA PROPIEDAD DE GUATEMALA (RGP)

José María Flores Tintí

Abel Francisco Cruz Calderón
SUPERINTENDENCIA DE ADMINISTRACIÓN TRIBUTARIA

Joel Estuardo Gamarro Palomo

Giovanni Garcia
ATA SERVICIOS

Jose Gonzalez
PRECON

Omar Gonzalez
ARQUITECTURA Y DISENO

Liz Gordillo Anleu
ARIAS LAW

Diego Hernández
QIL+4 ABOGADOS SA

Carlos Guillermo Herrera
REGISTRO GENERAL DE LA PROPIEDAD DE GUATEMALA (RGP)

Pamela Jimenez
ARIAS LAW

Eva Maria Lima
MUNICIPALIDAD DE GUATEMALA

Ruy Llanera
COMERICAL AMERICANA DE CONSTRUCCIONES (CONAME)

María Isabel Luján Zilbermann
QIL+4 ABOGADOS SA

Juan Andrés Marroquín
CARRILLO & ASOCIADOS

César Enrique Marroquín Fernández
SUPERINTENDENCIA DE BANCOS

Marco Antonio Martinez
CPS LOGISTICS

Luis Amilcar Mazariegos Ramos

Abelardo Medina
MINISTRY OF ECONOMY

Magbis Mardoqueo Méndez López
REGISTRO GENERAL DE LA PROPIEDAD DE GUATEMALA (RGP)

Ricardo Mendez Tello
EEGSA

Edgar Mendoza
PWC GUATEMALA

Pedro Mendoza Montano
IURISCONSULTI ABOGADOS Y NOTARIOS

Edvin Montoya
LEXINCORP

Maria Eugenia Morales Aceña
CORTE SUPREMA DE JUSTICIA GUATEMALA

Anajoyce Oliva
MUNICIPALIDAD DE GUATEMALA

Julio César Ordóñez Montenegro
BANCO G&T CONTINENTAL

Carlos Ortega
MAYORA & MAYORA SC

Jorge A. Osoy
MUNICIPALIDAD DE GUATEMALA

Roberto Ozaeta
PWC GUATEMALA

Marco Antonio Palacios
PALACIOS & ASOCIADOS

Raul Antonio Palma Cruz
ATA SERVICIOS

Erick Palomo
REGISTRO GENERAL DE LA PROPIEDAD DE GUATEMALA (RGP)

Maria Jose Pepio Pensabene
CÁMARA GUATEMALTECA DE LA CONSTRUCCIÓN

Claudia Pereira
MAYORA & MAYORA SC

Hugo Arévalo Perez
ARÉVALO PEREZ, IRALDA Y ASOCIADOS SC

Mélida Pineda
CARRILLO & ASOCIADOS

Edi Orlando Pineda Ramírez
SUPERINTENDENCIA DE BANCOS

Gabriela Posadas
QIL+4 ABOGADOS SA

Manuel Ramírez
EY

Ada Celeste Rios Cruz De Sandoval
REGISTRO DE GARANTIAS MOBILIARIAS

Andres Rivera
ACEROS ARQUITECTÓNICOS

Francisco Rivera
SUPERINTENDENCIA DE ADMINISTRACIÓN TRIBUTARIA

Alfredo Rodríguez Mahuad
CONSORTIUM - RACSA

Ranulfo Rafael Rojas Cetina
CORTE SUPREMA DE JUSTICIA GUATEMALA

Federico Rolz
MR. BODEGUITAS

Jose Rosales
GARCÍA & BODÁN

Luis Alfonso Ruano
CGW

Maricela Sagastume
REGISTRO GENERAL DE LA PROPIEDAD DE GUATEMALA (RGP)

Glendy Salguero
PWC GUATEMALA

Salvador Augusto Saravia Castillo
SARAVIA & MUÑOZ

Alfredo Skinner-Klee
SKINNER-KLÉE & ASOCIADOS

Alejandro Solares
QIL+4 ABOGADOS SA

Claudia Solares
REGISTRO DE GARANTIAS MOBILIARIAS

Francisco Solórzano
SUPERINTENDENCIA DE ADMINISTRACIÓN TRIBUTARIA

José Augusto Toledo Cruz
ARIAS LAW

Arelis Yariza Torres de Alfaro
SUPERINTENDENCIA DE BANCOS

Rodrigo Valladares
REGISTRO MERCANTIL

Elmer Vargas
PACHECO COTO

Ivar Vega
RV INSTALACIONES

Roselyn Villatoro
NOVALES ABOGADOS

Marlon Virula
EY

GUINEA

Camara Abdoul Kabele
CABINET CAMARA ABDOUL

Yves Constant Amani
CABINET D'AVOCATS BAO & FILS

Toure Aïssata Aribot
PORT AUTONOME DE CONAKRY

Pierre Kodjo Avode
SYLLA & PARTNERS

Mohamed Aly Baldé
PWC GUINEA

Mody Sory Barry
DIRECTION NATIONALE DES IMPÔTS

Aguibou Bérété
MINISTÈRE DE L'INDUSTRIE, DES PME ET DE LA PROMOTION DU SECTEUR PRIVÉ

Renaud Bidault
DÉMÉNAGEMENTS INTERNATIONAUX ET GARDE-MEUBLES

Ismaila Camara
MAERSK LOGISTICS SA

Souleymane Camara

Francis Charles Haba
CABINET BABADY ET FRANCIS SCPA

Sally Oussouby Cissoko
DIRECTION NATIONALE DES IMPÔTS

Fatoumata Condé
APIP GUINÉE - AGENCE DE PROMOTION DES INVESTISSEMENTS PRIVÉS

Abdelaziz Derrahi
ELECTRICITÉ DE GUINÉE

Ahmadou Diallo
CHAMBRE DES NOTAIRES

Mamadou Aliou Diallo
GROUPE MAD

Youssouf Diallo
CHAMBRE DES NOTAIRES

Hann Dienaba Keita
APIP-GUINÉE

Barry Fatoumata
CABINET ARCHI PLUS

Naby Moussa Fofana
BANQUE CENTRALE DE GUINÉE (BCRG)

Soukeina Fofana
BANQUE CENTRALE DE GUINÉE (BCRG)

Guy Laurent Fondjo
AFRILAND FIRST BANK

Joachim Gbilimou

Yéké Goumou
MINISTÈRE DE L'INDUSTRIE, DES PME ET DE LA PROMOTION DU SECTEUR PRIVÉ

Madigbe Kaba
SYLLA & PARTNERS

Rene-Marie Kadouno
EY

Diawara Karamokoba
APIP-GUINÉE DIRECTION GÉNÉRALE DES DOUANES

Aribot Karim
DIRECTION NATIONALE DES IMPÔTS

Namory Keita
DIRECTION NATIONALE DES IMPÔTS

Mariama Ciré Keita Diallo
NIMBA CONSEIL SARL

Fatoumata Koulibaly
BANQUE CENTRALE DE GUINÉE (BCRG)

Maténin Kourouma
APIP GUINÉE - AGENCE DE PROMOTION DES INVESTISSEMENTS PRIVÉS

Nounké Kourouma
ADMINISTRATION DES GRANDS PROJETS ET DES MARCHÉS PUBLICS

Boua Kouyaté
SECRÉTARIAT DU DIALOGUE PERMANENT PUBLIC-PRIVÉ

Gbamon Kpoulomou
TRIBUNAL DE PREMIÈRE INSTANCE DE MAFANCO

Mohamed Lahlou
PWC GUINEA

Augustin Lovichi
ELECTRICITÉ DE GUINÉE

Jean Alfred Mathos
NOTAIRE MATHOS JEAN ALFRED

Kaba Moriba
CABINET D'AVOCAT KABA MORIBA

Badara Niang
EY

Lamah Pierre
COMMISSION NATIONALE OHADA DE GUINÉE

Rassi Raja
CABINET D'AVOCAT KOUMY

Mamadou Saliou Baldé
MINISTÈRE DE LA CONSTRUCTION, DE L'URBANISME ET HABITAT

David Sandouno
BUREAU DES TRAVAUX TOPOGRAPHIQUES

Camara Mamadou Sanoussy
NOTAIRE CAMARA MAMADOU SANOUSSY

Satouma Yari Sounah
ETUDE YANSANE

Mohamed Sidiki Sylla
SYLLA & PARTNERS

Paul Tchagna
PWC GUINEA

Abdourahamane Tounkara
GUINÉE CONSULTING

Aboubacar Salimatou Toure
BANQUE DE DÉVELOPPEMENT DE GUINÉE

Mohamed Lamine Touré
BANQUE CENTRALE DE GUINÉE (BCRG)

Mariama Cire Traore
EY

Barry Traoré
CABINET MAÎTRE FATOUMATA AMADOU BARRY

Diallo Youssouf
TRANSMAR SA

Kalivogui Zeze
CABINET D'AVOCAT DE ME KALIVOGUI ZEZE

Togba Nicolas Zomy
CABINET MAÎTRE ZOMY

GUINEA-BISSAU

BCEAO

CREDITINFO VOLO

ELECTRICIDADE E AGUAS DA GUINE-BISSAU

MINISTÉRIO DA ECONOMIA E INTEGRAÇÃO REGIONAL

MINISTÉRIO DA JUSTIÇA

Serge Agbomenou
BISSAU EQUIPAMENTOS

José Alves Té
MINISTÉRIO DA JUSTIÇA

Duarte Amaral da Cruz
MC&A - SOCIEDADE DE ADVOGADOS RL

Emílio Ano Mendes
GB LEGAL - MIRANDA ALLIANCE

Luís Antunes
LUFTEC – TÉCNICAS ELÉCTRICAS LDA

Jorcelene Badilé Nhaga
LUD TRÂNSITO - TRANSITÁRIOS BISSAU

Serafim Baptista
LUD TRÂNSITO - TRANSITÁRIOS BISSAU

Tiago Bastos
AICEP PORTUGAL GLOBAL

Humiliano Alves Cardoso
GABINETE ADVOCACIA

Malam Cassama
PRIVATE SECTOR REHABILITATION AND AGRO-INDUSTRIAL DEVELOPMENT PROJECT

Januario Pedro Correia
BANCO DA ÁFRICA OCCIDENTAL

Seco Dafe
BANCO DA ÁFRICA OCCIDENTAL

Adelaida Mesa D'Almeida
JURISCONTA SRL

Ibrahim Demba
MAERSK LOGISTICS

Mamadjan Djalo
MADJENS SARL

Jose Carlos Esteves
JCE CONSULTING

Juliano Augusto Fernandes
JULAFER & LOPESFINO ADVOGADOS ASSOCIADOS

Alcide Gomes
QUID JURIS SARL

Fernando Gomes
TSK LEGAL ADVOGADOS E JURISCONSULTOS

Vladimir Jorge Gomes
BANQUE ATLANTIQUE

Neil Gomes Pereira
CENTRO DE FORMALIZAÇÃO DE EMPRESAS

Liliane Gomis
MAERSK LINE

Numna Gorky Mendes de Medina
GENERAL DIRECTORATE OF CONTRIBUTIONS AND TAXES

Monica Indami
BISSAU FIRST INSTANCE COURT, COMMERCIAL DIVISION

Alceine Indjai
BUREAU PROSPECTIVA BISSAU

Carlos Leles
CÁMARA MUNICIPAL DE BISSAU

Suzette Maria Lopes da Costa Graça
CONSERVATÓRIA DO REGISTO PREDIAL, COMERCIAL E AUTOMÓVEL

Gregorio Malu
TRANSMAR SERVICES LDA

Miguel Mango
AUDI - CONTA LDA

Duarte Marques da Cruz
MC&A - SOCIEDADE DE ADVOGADOS RL

Vítor Marques da Cruz
MC&A - SOCIEDADE DE ADVOGADOS RL

Marciano Mendes
EQUITAS-ADVOCACIA & CONSULTORIA JURIDICA

Ismael Mendes de Medina
GB LEGAL - MIRANDA ALLIANCE

Ruth Monteiro
TSK LEGAL ADVOGADOS E JURISCONSULTOS

Halen Armando Napoco
EQUITAS-ADVOCACIA & CONSULTORIA JURIDICA

Eduardo Pimentel
CENTRO DE FORMALIZAÇÃO DE EMPRESAS

Carlos Pinto Pereira
PINTO PEREIRA & ASSOCIADOS

Tony Luis Pires

Armando Procel
REPÚBLICA DA GUINÉ-BISSAU

Fernando Resina da Silva
VDA - VIEIRA DE ALMEIDA & ASSOCIADOS

Marta Sampaio
MEDITERRANEAN SHIPPING COMPANY LISBON (MSC)

Frederico Sanca
MAERSK LINE

Suleimane Seide
MINISTRY OF FINANCE

José Semedo
TSK LEGAL ADVOGADOS E JURISCONSULTOS

Dickson Siedi
ARQUIDIS ESTUDOS E PROJECTOS

Alfredo Silva
CÁMARA MUNICIPAL DE BISSAU

A. Ussumane So
LOSSER LDA BUSINESS DEVELOPMENT CONSULTANTS

Jorge Sousa
CAMARA DE COMERCIO INDUSTRIA PORTUGAL GUINÉ BISSAU (CCIPGB)

Fernando Tavares
TRANSMAR SERVICES LDA

Fernando Teixeira
ORDEM NACIONAL DOS ARQUITECTOS

Gabriel Umabano
TSK LEGAL ADVOGADOS E JURISCONSULTOS

Carlos Vamain
GOMES & VAMAIN ASSOCIADOS

GUYANA

DIGICOM

RODRIGUES ARCHITECTS LTD.

Tracey Bancroft
CITY ENGINEERS OFFICE MAYOR & COUNCILLORS OF CITY OF GEORGETOWN

Wiston Beckles
CORREIA & CORREIA LTD.

Marcel Bobb
FRASER, HOUSTY & YEARWOOD ATTORNEYS-AT-LAW

Julius Campbell
CORREIA & CORREIA LTD.

Desmond Correia
CORREIA & CORREIA LTD.

Lucia Desir-John
D & J SHIPPING SERVICES

Rocky Hanoman
POLLONAIS, BLANC, DE LA BASTIDE & JACELON

Renford Homer
GUYANA POWER & LIGHT INC.

Kalam Azad Juman-Yassin
GUYANA OLYMPIC ASSOCIATION

Kashir Khan
ATTORNEY-AT-LAW

Rhonda La Fargue
GUYANA POWER & LIGHT INC.

Edward Luckhoo
LUCKHOO & LUCKHOO

Alexis Monize
GUYANA OFFICE FOR INVESTMENT

Harry Noel Narine
PKF INTERNATIONAL

Charles Ogle
MINISTRY OF LABOUR, HUMAN SERVICES AND SOCIAL SECURITY

Carolyn Paul
AMICE LEGAL CONSULTANTS INC.

Vishwamint Ramnarine
PFK BARCELLOS, NARINE & CO.

Reginald Roach
R&D ENGINEERING SERVICES

Ronald Roberts
INDEPENDENT CONTRACTOR

Ryan Ross
GUYANA POWER & LIGHT INC.

Shantel Scott
FRASER, HOUSTY & YEARWOOD ATTORNEYS-AT-LAW

Judy Semple-Joseph
CREDITINFO GUYANA

Leslie Sobers
ATTORNEY-AT-LAW

Allyson West
PRICEWATERHOUSECOOPERS LIMITED

Tonika Wilson-Gabriel
PRICEWATERHOUSECOOPERS LIMITED

Horace Woolford
GUYANA POWER & LIGHT INC.

Roger Yearwood
BRITTON, HAMILTON & ADAMS

HAITI

BANQUE DE LA RÉPUBLIQUE D'HAÏTI

MÉROVÉ-PIERRE - CABINET D'EXPERTS-COMPTABLES

Theodore Achille III
UNOPS

Marc Kinson Antoine
ADEKO ENTERPRISES

Jude Baptiste
CABINET JUDE BAPTISTE ET ASSOCIÉS

Larissa Bogat
CABINET LISSADE

Jean Baptiste Brown
BROWN LEGAL GROUP

Martin Camille Cangé
ÉLECTRICITÉ D'HAÏTI

Karl B. Couba

David Lafortune
BROWN LEGAL GROUP

Ronald Laraque
AAU

Patrick Laurent
CABINET PATRICK LAURENT & ASSOCIÉS

Camille Leblanc
CABINET LEBLANC & ASSOCIÉS

Garry Lhérisson
ATELIER D'ARCHITECTURE ET D'URBANISME

Dieuphète Maloir
SAM CONSTRUCTION

Joel Nexil
AIR COURRIER & SHIPPING

Jean Yves Noël
NOËL, CABINET D'EXPERTS-COMPTABLES

Joseph Paillant
BUCOFISC

Micosky Pompilus
CABINET D'AVOCATS CHALMERS

Margarette Antoine Sanon
CABINET MARGARETTE ANTOINE SANON

Michel Succar
CABINET LISSADE

Salim Succar
CABINET LISSADE

Jean Vandal
VANDAL & VANDAL

HONDURAS

CNBS - COMISIÓN NACIONAL DE BANCOS Y SEGUROS

COMISIÓN NACIONAL DE ENERGÍA

Mario Aguero
ARIAS LAW

Daniel Aguilera
TRANSCOMA

Edward Aguilera
TRANSCOMA

Olvin Aguilera
TRANSCOMA

Vanessa Aguilera
TRANSCOMA

Juan José Alcerro Milla
AGUILAR CASTILLO LOVE

Alberto Alvarez
AGUILAR CASTILLO LOVE

Valmir Araujo
OPERADORA PORTUARIA CENTROAMERICANA

Geovanni Ayestas
EMPRESA NACIONAL DE ENERGIA

José Simón Azcona
INMOBILIARIA ALIANZA SA

Freddy Castillo
GARCÍA & BODÁN

Helui Castillo
COHEP (CONSEJO HONDUREÑO DE LA EMPRESA PRIVADA)

Jaime Alberto Colindres Rosales
DYCELES S DE RL

Natalie Ann Cooper Umaña
INVERSIONES CELAQUE SA

Alejandra Cruz
CASCO-FORTIN, CRUZ & ASOCIADOS

Graciela Cruz
GARCÍA & BODÁN

Heidy Cruz
GARCÍA & BODÁN

Gilda Espinal Veliz
ASJ - ASOCIACIÓN PARA UNA SOCIEDAD MÁS JUSTA

Jose Luis Haya
ARQUITECNIC

Evangelina Lardizábal
ARIAS LAW

Erick Lezama
ARIAS LAW

Rafael Enrique Medina Elvir
CÁMARA DE COMERCIO E INDUSTRIA DE TEGUCIGALPA

Jesús Humberto Medina-Alva
CENTRAL LAW MEDINA, ROSENTHAL & ASOCIADOS

Juan Carlos Mejía Cotto
INSTITUTO DE LA PROPIEDAD

E. Mendoza
COHEP (CONSEJO HONDUREÑO DE LA EMPRESA PRIVADA)

Ramón E. Morales
PWC HONDURAS

Juan Diego Napky
GARCÍA & BODÁN

Vanessa Oquelí
GARCÍA & BODÁN

Gabriela Padilla
CASCO-FORTIN, CRUZ & ASOCIADOS

Dino Rietti
ARQUITECNIC

José Rafael Rivera Ferrari
CONSORTIUM LEGAL

Milton Gabriel Rivera Urquía
PWC HONDURAS

Conrado Rodriguez
ADVOCATUS LAW FIRM

Enrique Rodriguez Burchard
AGUILAR CASTILLO LOVE

Fanny Rodríguez del Cid
ARIAS LAW

Germany Salgado
ADVOCATUS LAW FIRM

René Serrano
ARIAS LAW

Juan Sinclair
EMPRESA NACIONAL DE ENERGÍA ELÉCTRICA

Gustavo Solorzano
COHEP (CONSEJO HONDUREÑO DE LA EMPRESA PRIVADA)

Cristian Stefan Handal
ADVOCATUS LAW FIRM

Valerya Theodoracopoulos
ARIAS LAW

Mariano Turnes
OPERADORA PORTUARIA CENTROAMERICANA

Daysi Gricelda Urquía Hernández
TRANSUNION

Armando Urtecho López
COHEP (CONSEJO HONDUREÑO DE LA EMPRESA PRIVADA)

Lizzeth Villatoro
CASCO-FORTIN, CRUZ & ASOCIADOS

Mauricio Villeda Jr.
GUTIERREZ FALLA & ASOCIADOS

Jose Emilio Zablah Ulloa
PWC HONDURAS

Mario Rubén Zelaya
ENERGÍA INTEGRAL S. DE RL DE CV

Benito Arturo Zelaya Cálix
LEXINCORP

HONG KONG SAR, CHINA

AECOM ASIA COMPANY LIMITED

ALLEN & OVERY

STEINBERG HKC

Albert P.C. Chan
THE HONG KONG POLYTECHNIC UNIVERSITY

Nick Chan
SQUIRE PATTON BOGGS

Vashi Chandiramani
EXCELLENCE INTERNATIONAL

Jacqueline Chiu
MAYER BROWN JSM

Nikki Chong
ASHURST HONG KONG

Lillian Chow
THE OFFICIAL RECEIVER'S OFFICE OF THE SPECIAL ADMINISTRATIVE REGION OF HONG KONG

Selraniy Chow
PWC HONG KONG

Robert Chu
FINANCIAL SERVICES AND THE TREASURY BUREAU OF THE GOVERNMENT OF THE HONG KONG SPECIAL ADMINISTRATIVE REGION

Tony Chu
VICTON REGISTRATIONS LTD.

Cynthia Chung
DEACONS, MEMBER OF LEX MUNDI

Jimmy Chung
RUSSELL BEDFORD HONG KONG - MEMBER OF RUSSELL BEDFORD INTERNATIONAL

Joanna Chung
FINANCIAL SERVICES AND THE TREASURY BUREAU OF THE GOVERNMENT OF THE HONG KONG SPECIAL ADMINISTRATIVE REGION

Victor Dawes
TEMPLE CHAMBERS

Jorge Forton
DUN & BRADSTREET (HK) LTD.

Wilson Fung
MAYER BROWN JSM

Keith Man Kei Ho
WILKINSON & GRIST

Samuel Ho
TRANSUNION LIMITED

Reynold Hung
PWC HONG KONG

Peter Kwon
ASHURST HONG KONG

Billy Lam
MAYER BROWN JSM

Christie Lam
HONG KONG FINANCIAL SECRETARY

Kai Chiu Lam
CLP POWER HONG KONG LIMITED

Eva Lau
THE LAND REGISTRY OF HONG KONG

Ka Shi Lau
BCT FINANCIAL LIMITED (BCTF) / BANK CONSORTIUM TRUST COMPANY LIMITED (BCTC)

Yolanda Lau
ADDLESHAW GODDARD

Gina Lee
TRANSUNION LIMITED

Camille Leung
SQUIRE PATTON BOGGS

Jenny Liu
ASHURST HONG KONG

Terry LK Kan
SHINEWING SPECIALIST ADVISORY SERVICES LIMITED

Albert Lo
TRANSUNION LIMITED

Kathy Lo
FINANCIAL SERVICES AND THE TREASURY BUREAU OF THE GOVERNMENT OF THE HONG KONG SPECIAL ADMINISTRATIVE REGION

Psyche S.F. Luk
FAIRBAIRN CATLEY LOW & KONG

Louise Ng
SQUIRE PATTON BOGGS

Mat Ng
JLA-ASIA

James Ngai
RUSSELL BEDFORD HONG KONG - MEMBER OF RUSSELL BEDFORD INTERNATIONAL

Kok Leong Ngan
CLP POWER HONG KONG LIMITED

Yeung Or
INLAND REVENUE DEPARTMENT, HKSAR

Martinal Quan
METOPRO ASSOCIATES LIMITED

Hin Han Shum
SQUIRE PATTON BOGGS

Holden Slutsky
PACIFIC CHAMBERS

Brett Stewien
ADDLESHAW GODDARD

Keith Tam
DUN & BRADSTREET (HK) LTD.

Tammie Tam
MAYER BROWN JSM

Yuk Ting Fiona Fok
JLA-ASIA

Anita Tsang
PWC HONG KONG

William Tsang
Y H TSANG & CO.

Lawrence Tsong
TRANSUNION LIMITED

Paul Tsui
HONG KONG ASSOCIATION OF FREIGHT FORWARDING & LOGISTICS LTD. (HAFFA)

King Wai Leonard Chan
JLA-ASIA

Christopher Whiteley
ASHURST HONG KONG

Fergus Wong
PWC HONG KONG

David Wu
CYTS-SPIRIT LOGISTICS LTD.

Erica Xiong
RUSSELL BEDFORD HONG KONG - MEMBER OF RUSSELL BEDFORD INTERNATIONAL

Yuan Xu
SHANDONG STARMEN CO. LTD.

Kwok Kuen Yu
COMPANIES REGISTRY

Sunny Yu
FINANCIAL SERVICES AND THE TREASURY BUREAU OF THE GOVERNMENT OF THE HONG KONG SPECIAL ADMINISTRATIVE REGION

HUNGARY

HELLMANN WORLDWIDE LOGISTICS KFT

Balázs Balog
RETI, ANTALL AND PARTNERS LAW FIRM

Dénes Balog
ELMŰ HÁLÓZATI KFT

Sándor Békési
PARTOS & NOBLET HOGAN LOVELLS

Sándor Benkei
ÓBUDA-ÚJLAK ZRT

Hédi Bozsonyik
SZECSKAY ATTORNEYS-AT-LAW

Beata Bujnoczki
*PRICEWATERHOUSECOOPERS
HUNGARY LTD.*

Szilágyi Csaba
ÓBUDA-ÚJLAK ZRT

Sárosi Csanád
OBUDA-UJLAK

Zsuzsanna Cseri
*CSERI & PARTNERS
LAW OFFICES*

Krisztián Devecz
*PARTOS & NOBLET
HOGAN LOVELLS*

Nóra Elmer-Szabó
*SÁNDOR SZEGEDI
SZENT-IVÁNY KOMÁROMI
EVERSHEDS SUTHERLAND*

Gyula Gábriel
BOGSCH & PARTNERS

Laszlo Gaspar
FBIS ARCHITECTS

Mihály Gerhát
*PRICEWATERHOUSECOOPERS
HUNGARY LTD.*

Ervin Gombos
GMBS KFT

Zoltán Gurszky
ELMŰ HÁLÓZATI KFT

Csaba Attila Hajdu
BNT ATTORNEYS-AT-LAW

Tamás Halmos
*PARTOS & NOBLET
HOGAN LOVELLS*

Attila Horváth
ÓBUDA-ÚJLAK ZRT

Dóra Horváth
*RETI, ANTALL AND
PARTNERS LAW FIRM*

József Horváth
ÓBUDA-ÚJLAK ZRT

Andrea Jádi Németh
*BPV / JÁDI NÉMETH
ATTORNEYS-AT-LAW*

Atilla Jambor
*DR. JÁMBOR ATTILA
LAW OFFICE*

Zoltán Janosi
*PARTOS & NOBLET
HOGAN LOVELLS*

Ferenc Kalla
GTF KFT

Veronika Kiss
*PARTOS & NOBLET
HOGAN LOVELLS*

Andrea Kladiva
*CSERI & PARTNERS
LAW OFFICES*

Andrea Kocziha
*PRICEWATERHOUSECOOPERS
HUNGARY LTD.*

Csaba Kovács
ELMŰ HÁLÓZATI KFT

Gergely Kovács
BOGSCH & PARTNERS

Miklós Machács
*MEASUREMENT AND
TECHNICAL SAFETY AUTHORITY
(BUDAPEST CAPITAL CITY
GOVERNMENT OFFICE)*

Csaba Máté
ÓBUDA-ÚJLAK ZRT

Dóra Máthé
*PRICEWATERHOUSECOOPERS
HUNGARY LTD.*

Kinga Mekler
*SÁNDOR SZEGEDI
SZENT-IVÁNY KOMÁROMI
EVERSHEDS SUTHERLAND*

Zsolt Miklóshalmi
ÓBUDA-ÚJLAK ZRT

Mariann Miskovics
*SÁNDOR SZEGEDI
SZENT-IVÁNY KOMÁROMI
EVERSHEDS SUTHERLAND*

László Mohai
MOHAI LAW OFFICE

Gyorgy Nadas
UNIVERSITY OF DEBRECEN

Viktor Nagy
*BISZ CENTRAL CREDIT
INFORMATION PLC*

Sándor Németh
SZECSKAY ATTORNEYS-AT-LAW

Christopher Noblet
*PARTOS & NOBLET
HOGAN LOVELLS*

Galbavi Pál
ÓBUDA-ÚJLAK ZRT

Örs Pénzes

Sipka Péter
UNIVERSITY OF DEBRECEN

Eszter Piller
*PRICEWATERHOUSECOOPERS
HUNGARY LTD.*

Henriett Rabb
UNIVERSITY OF DEBRECEN

Rita Rado
*CSERI & PARTNERS
LAW OFFICES*

Richard Safcsak
*BISZ CENTRAL CREDIT
INFORMATION PLC*

Zsófia Sallai
BNT ATTORNEYS-AT-LAW

István Sándor
*KELEMEN, MESZAROS,
SANDOR & PARTNERS*

Szilvia Szeleczky
*BUDAPEST 1ST DISTRICT
MUNICIPALITY*

Ágnes Szent-Ivány
*SÁNDOR SZEGEDI
SZENT-IVÁNY KOMÁROMI
EVERSHEDS SUTHERLAND*

Adám Tóth
*DR. TÓTH ÁDÁM
KÖZJEGYZŐI IRODA*

József Vizer
*RSM HUNGARY TAX AND
FINANCIAL ADVISORY
SERVICES PLC*

Marton Leo Zaccaria
UNIVERSITY OF DEBRECEN

ICELAND

*REYKJAVIK MUNICIPAL
BUILDING CONTROL OFFICER*

Ásta Sólveig Andrésdóttir
REGISTERS ICELAND

Benedikt Egill Árnason
*LOGOS, MEMBER
OF LEX MUNDI*

Ragnar Tomas Árnason
*LOGOS, MEMBER
OF LEX MUNDI*

Heiðar Ásberg Atlason
*LOGOS, MEMBER
OF LEX MUNDI*

Stefán Árni Auðólfsson
LMB LEGAL SERVICES

Margrét Berg Sverrisdóttir
*COURT OF ARBITRATION
OF THE ICELAND CHAMBER
OF COMMERCE*

Arnar Bjarnason
FRAKT.IS

Jakob Björgvin Jakobsson
ARCTIC LEGAL SERVICES

Karen Bragadóttir
*TOLLSTJÓRI - DIRECTORATE
OF CUSTOMS*

Margret Anna Einarsdottir
*JÓNATANSSON & CO.
LEGAL SERVICES*

Eymundur Einarsson
*ENDURSKOÐUN OG
RÁÐGJÖF EHF*

Ásta Margrét Eiríksdóttir
BBA LEGAL

Ólafur Eiríksson
*LOGOS, MEMBER
OF LEX MUNDI*

Sigríður Anna Ellerup
REGISTERS ICELAND

Björg Finnbogadóttir
REGISTERS ICELAND

Anna Björg Guðjónsdóttir
BBA LEGAL

Gudrun Gudmundsdottir
JÓNAR TRANSPORT

Marta Guðrún Blöndal
*COURT OF ARBITRATION
OF THE ICELAND CHAMBER
OF COMMERCE*

Andri Gunnarsson
NORDIK LEGAL SERVICES

Reynir Haraldsson
JÓNAR TRANSPORT

Hörður Davíð Harðarson
*TOLLSTJÓRI - DIRECTORATE
OF CUSTOMS*

Burkni Maack Helgason
CREDITINFO ICELAND

Jón Ingi Ingibergsson
PWC ICELAND

Aðalsteinn E. Jónasson
LEX LAW OFFICES

Hróbjartur Jónatansson
*JÓNATANSSON & CO.
LEGAL SERVICES*

Lára V. Júlíusdóttir
LÖGMENN LAUGAVEGI 3 EHF

Antoine Lochet
BBA LEGAL

Bjorn Mar Olafsson
PWC ICELAND

Helga Melkorka Óttarsdóttir
*LOGOS, MEMBER
OF LEX MUNDI*

Kristján Pálsson
JÓNAR TRANSPORT

Ásgeir Á. Ragnarsson
BBA LEGAL

Arna Sigurjónsdóttir
LMB LEGAL SERVICES

Gunnar Sturluson
*LOGOS, MEMBER
OF LEX MUNDI*

Rúnar Svavar Svavarsson
*VEITUR, DISTRIBUTION-
ELECTRICAL SYSTEM*

Jón Þórarinsson
CREDITINFO ICELAND

Helgi Þór Þorsteinsson
LEX LAW OFFICES

Steinþór Þorsteinsson
*TOLLSTJÓRI - DIRECTORATE
OF CUSTOMS*

Jon Vilhjalmsson
EFLA CONSULTING ENGINEERS

INDIA

ASHOK DHINGRA ASSOCIATES

*ASIATIC ELECTRICAL
SWITCHGEAR (P) LTD.*

AUM ARCHITECTS

CONSULTA JURIS

*FCA INDIA AUTOMOBILES
PVT. LTD.*

JAYNIX ENGINEERING PVT. LTD.

M.D. ARCHITECTS

*MAHARANI LAXMI AMMANNI
CENTRE FOR SOCIAL
SCIENCE RESEARCH*

Ajay Abad
SKP BUSINESS CONSULTING LLP

Jolly Abraham
DESAI & DIWANJI

Alfred Adebare
LEXCOUNSEL

Ca Surabhi Agarwal
SS KOTHARI MEHTA & CO.

Kritika Agarwal
MAJMUDAR & PARTNERS

Sanjay Kumar Agarwal

Vinay Agarwal
MIRC ELECTRONICS LIMITED

Mayank Aggarwal
*LUTHRA & LUTHRA
LAW OFFICES*

Neeharika Aggarwal
KNM & PARTNERS

Rahul Agrawal
ZOOM IN GROUP

Padmakar Agte
POWER SOLUTIONS

Jotinder Ahluwalia
*RELIANCE INFRASTRUCTURE
LTD.*

Aqil Ahmed
*SOUTH DELHI MUNICIPAL
CORPORATION*

Praveen Alok
KHAITAN AND COMPANY

Saurabh Babulkar
SETH DUA & ASSOCIATES

Surendrakumar Badge
BEST

Tarun Baidya
*VARDHAMAN CUSTOMS
CLEARING & FORWARDING
AGENCIES*

Shashi Bala
*MUNICIPAL CORPORATION
OF GREATER MUMBAI*

Shrenik N. Bamb
*SHRENIK N. BAMB
& ASSOCIATES*

Pallavi Banerjee
*J. SAGAR ASSOCIATES,
ADVOCATES & SOLICITORS*

Pritam Banerjee
DEUTSCHE POST DHL GROUP

Anupam Bansal
ABRD ARCHITECTS

Neeraj Bansal
*JAWAHARLAL NEHRU
PORT TRUST*

Raghav Bansal
*RSB LEAGUE CONSULTANTS,
ATTORNEYS & SOLICITORS*

Shashwat Bansal
*RSB LEAGUE CONSULTANTS,
ATTORNEYS & SOLICITORS*

Subhash Bansal
*RSB LEAGUE CONSULTANTS,
ATTORNEYS & SOLICITORS*

Sumitava Basu
JURIS CORP

Sumant Batra
KESAR DASS B & ASSOCIATES

Neeraj Bhagat
NEERAJ BHAGAT & CO.

M.L. Bhakta
KANGA & CO.

Pradeep Bhandari
*INTUIT MANAGEMENT
CONSULTANCY*

M.P. Bharucha
BHARUCHA & PARTNERS

Deepak Bhaskar
TRILEGAL

Moksha Bhat
TRILEGAL

Gurleen Bhatia
KNM & PARTNERS

Gurpriya Bhatia
I.L.A. PASRICH & COMPANY

Saurav Bhattacharya
PWC INDIA

Sukanya Bhattacharya
*LUTHRA & LUTHRA
LAW OFFICES*

Mona Bhide
DAVE & GIRISH & CO.

Hetal Bilaye
NISHITH DESAI ASSOCIATES

Nidhi Bothra
*VINOD KOTHARI & CO.
PRACTICING COMPANY
SECRETARIES*

Amit Brid
BRID ELECTRIC CORPORATION

J.K. Budhiraja
*INSOLVENCY PROFESSIONAL
AGENCY OF INSTITUTE OF COST
ACCOUNTANTS OF INDIA*

K.K. Chadha
ARCHITECT

Harshala Chandorkar
TRANSUNION CIBIL LIMITED

Sravani Channapragada
*J. SAGAR ASSOCIATES,
ADVOCATES & SOLICITORS*

Charu Lata
UNIVERSAL LEGAL

Anand Chatrath
B. M. CHATRATH & CO.

Jyoti Chaudhari
LEGASIS SERVICES PRIVATE

Sanjiv Kumar Chaudhary

Aseem Chawla
PHOENIX LEGAL

Chandni Chawla
PHOENIX LEGAL

Daizy Chawla
*SINGH & ASSOCIATES,
ADVOCATES AND SOLICITORS*

Manjula Chawla
PHOENIX LEGAL

Vinita Chhatwal
I.L.A. PASRICH & COMPANY

Vinod Chithore
MUNICIPAL CORPORATION
OF GREATER MUMBAI

Priyanka Choksi
DESAI & DIWANJI

Poorvi Chothani
LAWYER

Sachin Chugh
SINGHI CHUGH & KUMAR,
CHARTERED ACCOUNTANTS

Chirag Dabhi
C & D LOGISTICS

Manish Dadhania
PRECISION SINTERED PRODUCTS

Chetan Daga
SUDIT K. PAREKH AND CO.

Neelesh Datir
ALBIEA

Amin Dayani

Rhuta Deobagkar
TRILEGAL

Sunil Deole
DEOLE BROS

Nimish Desai
NHD FORWARDERS PVT. LTD.

Vishwang Desai
DESAI & DIWANJI

Pushkar Deshpande
KOCHHAR & CO.

Rishi Dev
RISHI DEV ARCHITECTS
AND ASSOCIATES

Farida Dholkawala
DESAI & DIWANJI

Rajiv Dogra
KODIAK CONTAINER
LINES PVT. LTD.

Rakesh Dogra

Anagha Dongre
SUDIT K. PAREKH AND CO.

Rajesh Dongre
ABRD ARCHITECTS

Jigar Doshi
SKP BUSINESS CONSULTING LLP

Jitendra R. Doshi
SHREEJI SERVICES

Maulik Doshi
SKP BUSINESS CONSULTING LLP

Atul Dua
SETH DUA & ASSOCIATES

Manojkumar Dubal
MANOJ DUBAL & ASSOCIATES

Harshit Dusad
JURIS CORP

Riya Dutta
ADVAYA LEGAL

Sunil G. Ambre
SUNIL AMBRE & ASSOCIATES

Ritika Ganju
PHOENIX LEGAL

Anuj Garg
INDIA LAW OFFICES

Pankaj Garg
NATIONAL COMPANY
LAW TRIBUNAL

Rahul Garg
PWC INDIA

Sarthak Garg
PHOENIX LEGAL

Abhinav Gaur
LAWYER

Rajeev Kumar Gera
GERA & ASSOCIATES

Tarun Ghia

Arup Ghosh
TATA POWER DELHI
DISTRIBUTION LTD.

Manoj Gidwani
SKP BUSINESS CONSULTING LLP

Prabhakar Giri
VARDHAMAN CUSTOMS
CLEARING & FORWARDING
AGENCIES

Mukund Godbole
GODBOLEMUKADAM
AND ASSOCIATES

Ankit Goel
GTECH INFRA ENGINEERS
PVT. LTD.

Gourav Goyal
NEERAJ BHAGAT & CO.

Amit Gupta
AAY AAR ELECTRICALS
CONTROL (P) LTD.

Ashish Gupta
ARMS & ASSOCIATES

Atul Gupta
TRILEGAL

G. D. Gupta
AAY AAR ELECTRICALS
CONTROL (P) LTD.

Gunjan Gupta
SINGHANIA & PARTNERS LLP

Naveen Gupta
DASS GUPTA AND ASSOCIATES

Pulkit Gupta
EY

Sameer Gupta
PHOENIX LEGAL

Shubham Gupta
LUTHRA & LUTHRA
LAW OFFICES

Sudhanshu Gupta
SINGHANIA & PARTNERS LLP

Prakash Hamirwasia
SKP BUSINESS CONSULTING LLP

Parma Nand Hans
MNC MANAGEMENT
SOLUTIONS & KAPSON LAW

Anil Harish
D.M. HARISH & CO.

Bhanu Harish
SINGHANIA & PARTNERS LLP

Akil Hirani
MAJMUDAR & PARTNERS

Michael D. Holland
FIABCI

Suresh L. Hulikal
ALLIANZ DE ARCHITECTURE

Jomy Jacob
OFFICE OF CHIEF
COMMISSIONER OF CUSTOMS

Jyoti N. Jadhav
SUPER FREIGHT

Pravin Jadhav
VASTU SHILP

Bhagwan Jagwani
KRUTI SYSTEMS

Sameena Jahangir
RGM LEGAL

Anshul Jain
LUTHRA & LUTHRA
LAW OFFICES

Dheeraj Jain
RHA PRAXIS INITIATIVE

Nikita Jain
SKP BUSINESS CONSULTING LLP

Rohit Jain
SINGHANIA & PARTNERS LLP

Sanjiv Kumar Jain
VARDHAMAN CUSTOMS
CLEARING & FORWARDING
AGENCIES

Sanyogita Jain
KNM & PARTNERS

Chinmay Jani
CHINMAY JANI ARCHITECT

Abhinava Jayaswal
LAWYER

Anand Kumar Jha
CENTRAL BOARD OF
EXCISE & CUSTOMS

Abhijit Joglekar
RELIANCE INFRASTRUCTURE
LTD.

Sanjay Joseph
INCOME TAX
DEPARTMENT (INDIA)

Piyush Joshi
CLARUS LAW ASSOCIATES

Yogesh Joshi
SPEEDWELL TECHNOLOGIES
PVT. LTD.

Kunal Juneja
MP LAW OFFICES

Kumalya Kale
SHELTER ASSOCIATES

Vikas Kallianpur
VASTU SHILP

Atul Kansal
INDUS ENVIRONMENTAL
SERVICES PVT. LTD.

Pranay Kapadia
NAVYATA LIFESPACE

Aditi Kapoor
TRILEGAL

Vishal Kapoor
MINISTRY OF POWER

Rajas Kasbekar
RAJAS KASBEKAR
PRIVATE PRACTICE

Shrinath Kasi
RELIANCE INFRASTRUCTURE
LTD.

Kripi Kathuria
PHOENIX LEGAL

Vandita Kaul
DEPARTMENT OF
FINANCIAL SERVICES,
MINISTRY OF FINANCE

Charandeep Kaur
TRILEGAL

Ramneet Kaur
ASP ASSOCIATES

Mitalee Kaushal
KNM & PARTNERS

Arun Kedia
VAV LIFE SCIENCES P. LTD.

Sanjay Kesari
EMPLOYEE'S PROVIDENT
FUND ORGANISATION

Giridhar Kesavan
VINZAS SOLUTIONS
INDIA PVT. LTD.

Gautam Khaitan
O.P. KHAITAN & CO.

Farrukh Khan
DIWAN ADVOCATES

Mohd. Wasiq Khan
DIWAN ADVOCATES

Dhiraj Khandelwal
KHANDELWAL DHIRAJ
& ASSOCIATES

Naveen Khanna
SUNRISE FREIGHT FORWARDERS

Tanya Khare
KHAITAN AND COMPANY

Rajeev Kharyal
TATA POWER DELHI
DISTRIBUTION LIMITED

Gautam Khurana
INDIA LAW OFFICES

Ankit Khushu
KACHWAHA & PARTNERS

Kamal Kishore
SUNRISE FREIGHT FORWARDERS

Shashank Kokil

Ravinder Komaragiri
THE TATA POWER
COMPANY LIMITED

Shinoj Koshy
LUTHRA & LUTHRA
LAW OFFICES

Saniya Kothari
LEXCOUNSEL

Vinod Kothari
VINOD KOTHARI & CO.
PRACTICING COMPANY
SECRETARIES

Gordhan Kukreja
LAWYER

Abhijeet Kulkarni
CAPEX EQUIPMENT
RENTAL SOLUTIONS

Anup Kulkarni
J. SAGAR ASSOCIATES,
ADVOCATES & SOLICITORS

Ajai Kumar

Jagmohan Kumar
AARKITEK COMBINE

Manoj Kumar
MANOJ & ASSOCIATES

Mrityunjay Kumar
DHINGRA &
SINGH - ATTORNEYS-AT-LAW

Mukesh Kumar
KNM & PARTNERS

Nitin Kumar
AARKITEK COMBINE

Raj Kumar
RAJ ENGINEERS

Vinay Kumar
MADHAV DESIGN GROUP

Arvind Kumar Bhatnagar
ARVIND KUMAR & ASSOCIATES

Parveen Kumar Sharma
CERSAI

Manoj Kumar Singh
SINGH & ASSOCIATES,
ADVOCATES AND SOLICITORS

Shreedhar T. Kunte
SHARP & TANNAN
GROUP - MEMBER OF RUSSELL
BEDFORD INTERNATIONAL

Samira Lalani
PHOENIX LEGAL

Minhaz Lokhandwala
DESAI & DIWANJI

Khushboo Luthra
SINGHANIA & PARTNERS LLP

Balkrishna M. Mandrekar
SUPER FREIGHT

Divya Malcolm
KOCHHAR & CO.

Yogesh Malhan
SINGH & ASSOCIATES,
ADVOCATES AND SOLICITORS

Pragati Malik
SPACES ARCHITECTURE STUDIO

Vipender Mann
KNM & PARTNERS

Rishabh G. Mastaram
RGM LEGAL

Manish Mathur
MATHUR ASSOCIATES
N ARCHITECTS

HL Meena
DEPARTMENT OF INDUSTRIES

Ajoy Mehta
MUNICIPAL CORPORATION
OF GREATER MUMBAI

Atul Mehta
MEHTA & MEHTA

Dara Mehta
LITTLE & CO.

Dipti Mehta
MEHTA & MEHTA

Pankaj Mehta
FORTUNE LEGAL ADVOCATES
& LEGAL CONSULTANTS

Preeti G. Mehta
KANGA & CO.

Anand Mohan Mishra
UNO ARCH

Gunjan Mishra
LUTHRA & LUTHRA
LAW OFFICES

Nikhil Mohan Mishra
UNO ARCH

Nilendu Mishra
MINISTRY OF CORPORATE
AFFAIRS - REGISTRAR

Saurabh Misra
SAURABH MISRA
& ASSOCIATES,
INTERNATIONAL LAWYERS

Amit B. Mistry
LAXMICHAND CHHEDA
CONSULTANCY

Ajay Mital
SOUTH DELHI MUNICIPAL
CORPORATION

Bhavin Modi
SPACE VISION - ARCHITECT
& PLANNER

Hemal Modi
SHARP & TANNAN
GROUP - MEMBER OF RUSSELL
BEDFORD INTERNATIONAL

Priyanka Mongia
PHOENIX LEGAL

Avikshit Moral
JURIS CORP

Jitendra Mukadam
GODBOLEMUKADAM
AND ASSOCIATES

Hardik Mungekar
DAISARIA ASSOCIATES

Tanvi Muraleedharan
JURIS CORP

Priyanka Naik
SUDIT K. PAREKH AND CO.

Vijay Nair
KNM & PARTNERS

Ratnakar Nama
ARCHITECT

Vijayan Nambiar
DELIGHT LOGISTICS PVT. LTD.

Vaibhav Nautiyal
*INDUS ENVIRONMENTAL
SERVICES PVT. LTD.*

Harendar Neel
*J. SAGAR ASSOCIATES,
ADVOCATES & SOLICITORS*

Sanjay Nirmal
*MUNICIPAL CORPORATION
OF GREATER MUMBAI*

Parag Pai
MITI

Divyanshu Pandey
*J. SAGAR ASSOCIATES,
ADVOCATES & SOLICITORS*

Janak Pandya
NISHITH DESAI ASSOCIATES

Niraj Pangam
G.L. PANGAM & ASSOCIATES

Ajay Pant
*INDUS ENVIRONMENTAL
SERVICES PVT. LTD.*

Amit Parab
SHELTER ASSOCIATES

Rajiv Paralkar
DEOLE BROS

Kunal Pareek
*TATA POWER DELHI
DISTRIBUTION LTD.*

Amir Z. Singh Pasrich
I.L.A. PASRICH & COMPANY

Sameer Patel
DESAI & DIWANJI

Sanjay Patil
BDH INDUSTRIES LIMITED

Vijay E. Patil
*MUNICIPAL CORPORATION
OF GREATER MUMBAI*

Soumya Patnaik
*J. SAGAR ASSOCIATES,
ADVOCATES & SOLICITORS*

Alok Patnia
ALOK RANJAN & ASSOCIATES

Ashish Patole

Ashok Poojary
MARS SHIPPING AGENCY

Joseph Pookkatt
APJ-SLG LAW OFFICES

Rashmi Pradeep
*CYRIL AMARCHAND
MANGALDAS*

Anush Raajan
BHARUCHA & PARTNERS

Ajay Raghavan
TRILEGAL

Ravishankar Raghavan
MAJMUDAR & PARTNERS

Hafeez Rahman
I.L.A. PASRICH & COMPANY

Vasanth Rajasekaran
SETH DUA & ASSOCIATES

N.V. Raman
MP LAW OFFICES

Sharanya G. Ranga
ADVAYA LEGAL

Dipak Rao
SINGHANIA & PARTNERS LLP

Meghna Rao
SINGHANIA & PARTNERS LLP

Yomesh Rao
YMS CONSULTANTS LTD.

Shruti Rathore
DIWAN ADVOCATES

Ankita Ray
*CYRIL AMARCHAND
MANGALDAS*

Purushottam Redekar
GM ARCH PVT. LTD.

Hiren Ruparel
BALAJI SHIPPING AGENCY

Dheeraj Ruri
*DEEP CONSULTANCY AND
BUSINESS SERVICES*

Rajneesh Sabharwal
*TATA POWER DELHI
DISTRIBUTION LTD.*

Suparna Sachar
O.P. KHAITAN & CO.

Shamik Saha
PHOENIX LEGAL

Priyanka Sahi
GRANT THORNTON INDIA LLP

M. S. Sahoo
*INSOLVENCY AND BANKRUPTCY
BOARD OF INDIA (IBBI)*

Keshav Saini
KNM & PARTNERS

Sirisha Sampat
KANGA & CO.

Hitesh Sanghvi
HITESH SANGHVI LAW OFFICES

Kanwar Sanjay
SWAIT ARCH.

Daya Saran
SUPER FREIGHT

Jaspal Sarowa
JASPAL SAROWA

Heemanshu Satija
P. J. ASSOCIATES

Vijay Satpute
POWER SOLUTIONS

Sunil Sawant
POWER SOLUTIONS

Sukrit Seth
SETH DUA & ASSOCIATES

Tarun Sethi
AARKITEK COMBINE

Aashit Shah
*J. SAGAR ASSOCIATES,
ADVOCATES & SOLICITORS*

Dilip S. Shah
*RELIANCE INFRASTRUCTURE
LTD.*

Gunjan Shah
DESAI & DIWANJI

Manish Shah
SUDIT K. PAREKH AND CO.

Paresh Shah
RPS LOGISTICS

Prasham Shah
JURIS CORP

Raj Shah
*NINA ELECTRICAL
CORPORATION*

Vijay Shah
ARCHITECT

Garima Shahi
SINGHANIA & PARTNERS LLP

A. Shaila
*MAHARASHTRA SALES
TAX DEPARTMENT*

Ashwani Sharma
R.S. ASSOCIATES

Himani Sharma
AXON PARTNERS LLP

L.N. Sharma
R.S. ASSOCIATES

Manoranjan Sharma
KNM & PARTNERS

Rupali Sharma
KOCHHAR & CO.

Saumya Sharma
LEXCOUNSEL

Saurabh Sharma
JURIS CORP

Shipra Sharma
MINISTRY OF SHIPPING

Sangita Shet
MITI

Sujoy Shet
MITI

Santosh Shetty
*INTERNATIONAL
CARGO TERMINALS
AND INFRASTRUCTURE
PRIVATE LIMITED*

Ashutosh Shingate
*EATON INDUSTRIAL SYSTEMS
PRIVATE LIMITED*

Arjun Shiv
TRILEGAL

Vishnu Shriram
PHOENIX LEGAL

Prabhat Shroff
SHROFF & COMPANY

Vikram Shroff
NISHITH DESAI ASSOCIATES

Akash Shukla
PWC INDIA

A.K. Singh
*VARDHAMAN CUSTOMS
CLEARING & FORWARDING
AGENCIES*

Aakarsh Singh
UNIVERSAL LEGAL

Akanksha Singh
DIWAN ADVOCATES

Bhisham Singh
*MNC MANAGEMENT
SOLUTIONS & KAPSON LAW*

Dileep Singh
*SAMSUNG INDIA
ELECTRONICS PVT. LTD.*

Dinesh Singh
SCL PVT. LIMITED

Ranvir Singh
R.S. ASSOCIATES

Sajai Singh
*J. SAGAR ASSOCIATES,
ADVOCATES & SOLICITORS*

Shailendra Singh

Sheetlesh Singh
MNRD & ASSOCIATES

Subodh Singh
*OFFICE OF CHIEF
COMMISSIONER OF CUSTOMS*

Vijiya Singh
APJ-SLG LAW OFFICES

Amardeep Singh Bhatia
*MINISTRY OF CORPORATE
AFFAIRS - REGISTRAR*

Shakti Singh Champawat
DESAI & DIWANJI

Mukesh Singhal
KNM & PARTNERS

Ravinder Singhania
SINGHANIA & PARTNERS LLP

Alok Sinha
ALOK SINHA & CO.

Neha Sinha
*LUTHRA & LUTHRA
LAW OFFICES*

Praveer Sinha
*TATA POWER DELHI
DISTRIBUTION LIMITED*

Sanjay Sinha
*MINISTRY OF LABOUR
& EMPLOYMENT*

Suharsh Sinha
AZB & PARTNERS

Vineet Sinha
KNM & PARTNERS

Veena Sivaramakrishnan
JURIS CORP

Preetha Soman
NISHITH DESAI ASSOCIATES

Shweta Soni
*FORTUNE LEGAL ADVOCATES
& LEGAL CONSULTANTS*

Akhil Srivastava
Y R ELECTRICALS

Rudra Srivastava
SINGHANIA & PARTNERS LLP

Aravind Srivatsan
PWC INDIA

Nitim Subhash
INDIMET PVT. LTD.

Surendra Suri
*DEEP CONSULTANCY AND
BUSINESS SERVICES*

Abhishek Swaroop
*LUTHRA & LUTHRA
LAW OFFICES*

Anuja Talukder
PWC INDIA

Medha Tamhanekar
UNIVERSAL LEGAL

Rajesh Tayal
KNM & PARTNERS

Stephanie Tellis
LEGASIS SERVICES PRIVATE

Chetan Thakkar
KANGA & CO.

Anand Thakur
KEI INDUSTRIES LTD.

Piyush Thareja
NEERAJ BHAGAT & CO.

Pooja Thomas
PHOENIX LEGAL

Amit Tiwari
VENTRANS INDIA

Suhas Tuljapurkar
LEGASIS SERVICES PRIVATE

Prakash Veer Tyagi
GATEWAY RAIL FRIGHT LIMITED

Ramesh K. Vaidyanathan
ADVAYA LEGAL

Uday Y. Vajandar
*THE BRIHAN MUMBAI
ELECTRIC SUPPLY &
TRANSPORT UNDERTAKING*

Chahat Varma
INDIA LAW OFFICES

Ashok Vashist
R.S. ASSOCIATES

Ajay Verma
JURIS CHAMBERS

Dipankar Vig
MP LAW OFFICES

Sameep Vijayvergiya
*DHINGRA &
SINGH - ATTORNEYS-AT-LAW*

Nilesh Vikamsey
KHIMJI KUNVERJI & CO.

Vinayak Vishwas Patil
*CREATIVE CONSULTANTS
& DESIGNERS*

Rajiv Wadhwa
*AAY AAR ELECTRICALS
CONTROL (P) LTD.*

Rajiv Wadhwa
*PLVK POWER ENGINEERS
& CONSULTANTS*

Girish Wadwekar
MOKSHA COMMUNICATIONS

Abhijeet Yadav
*THE TATA POWER
COMPANY LIMITED*

Akriti Yadav
KNM & PARTNERS

Manoj Yadav
NEERAJ BHAGAT & CO.

Neha Yadav
LEXCOUNSEL

Sanjay Yadav
*SOUTH DELHI MUNICIPAL
CORPORATION*

Sumiti Yadava
CLARUS LAW ASSOCIATES

INDONESIA

BPJS KETENAGAKERJAAN

*HERMAWAN JUNIARTO
LAW FIRM*

*INDONESIA NOTARY
ORGANIZATION*

MENTARI FREIGHT SERVICES

PT ANTAR BENUA CAHAYA

PT MULYA ABADI ASRO

Hizban Achmad
INDO KARYA SENIOR

Robertus Adinugraha
MELLI DARSA & CO.

Shamy Adrian
*LAND DATA AND
INFORMATION CENTER*

Nafis Adwani
*ALI BUDIARDJO, NUGROHO,
REKSODIPUTRO, MEMBER
OF LEX MUNDI*

Widiarahmi Afiandari
*NURJADIN SUMONO
MULYADI & PARTNERS*

Eko Agus Supiadi
*UPTSA (UNIT PELAYANAN
TERPADU SATU ATAP)
SURABAYA TIMUR
(ONE-STOP SHOP)*

Hilman Ahmad
*LAND DATA AND
INFORMATION CENTER*

Lia Alizia
MAKARIM & TAIRA S.

Fessy Alwi
NOTARY

Cindy Anjani
*ADNAN KELANA HARYANTO
& HERMANTO*

Karina Antonio
*NURJADIN SUMONO
MULYADI & PARTNERS*

Sasono Ardi Hersubeno
*PT PLN (PERSERO), EAST
JAVA DISTRIBUTION*

Hizkia Ardianto
EY

Cucu Asmawati
SIMBOLON & PARTNERS LAW FIRM

Ibrahim Assegaf
ASSEGAF, HAMZAH & PARTNERS

Nyoman Astawa
PT PLN (PERSERO) INDONESIA STATE ELECTRICITY CORPORATION

Hamud M. Balfas
LAW OFFICE OF HBP & PARTNERS

Reynalda Basya Ilyas
BUDIDJAJA & ASSOCIATES

Dimas Bimo
MELLI DARSA & CO.

Fabian Buddy Pascoal
HANAFIAH PONGGAWA & PARTNERS

Prianto Budi
PT PRATAMA INDOMITRA KONSULTAN - MEMBER OF RUSSELL BEDFORD INTERNATIONAL

Tony Budidjaja
BUDIDJAJA & ASSOCIATES

Didin Cahya Wahyudin
INDONESIAN PUBLIC TAX CONSULTANTS ASSOCIATION (AKP2I ASOSIASI KONSULTAN PAJAK PUBLIK INDONESIA)

Deded Chandra
BPJS KESEHATAN

Teresa Chiquita
MAKARIM & TAIRA S.

Roy Coastrio
LAWYER

Juni Dani
BUDIDJAJA & ASSOCIATES

Melli Darsa
MELLI DARSA & CO.

Reginald A. Dharma
ADNAN KELANA HARYANTO & HERMANTO

Nawangwulan Dilla Savitri
RIVAI TRIPRASETIO & PARTNERS

Natasha Djamin
OENTOENG SURIA & PARTNERS

Bama Djokonugroho
BUDIDJAJA & ASSOCIATES

Estu Dyah

Asma El Moufti
PT TERMINAL PETIKEMAS SURABAYA

Ahmad Fadli
BRIGITTA I. RAHAYOE & PARTNERS

Nurulita Fauzie
BRIGITTA I. RAHAYOE & PARTNERS

Edly Febrian Widjaja
BUDIDJAJA & ASSOCIATES

Fajar Febriandi
PT TOYOTA MOTOR MANUFACTURING

Ratna Febrina
SF CONSULTING

Lr. Fetnayeti
MINISTRY OF TRADE

Aprilda Fiona Butarbutar
APRILDA FIONA & PARTNERS LAW FIRM

Sinuhadji Frans Yoshua
OENTOENG SURIA & PARTNERS

Widigdya Gitaya
WSG & COMPANY

Michael Hadi
PT KREDIT BIRO INDONESIA JAYA (KBIJ)

Joei Hadi Nata Tan
TYCON CONTRACTOR

Mohammad Iqbal Hadromi
HADROMI & PARTNERS

Melanie Sri Handayani
BANK INDONESIA

Abdul Haris M. Rum
HIMPUNAN KONSULTAN HUKUM PASAR MODAL

Hariyanto S.H.
HARIYANTO & PARTNERS

Stefanus Haryanto
ADNAN KELANA HARYANTO & HERMANTO

Ibnu Hasan
TNB & PARTNERS

Yansah Hasstriansyah
BADAN PELAYANAN TERPADU SATU PINTU (BPTS)

Erwandi Hendarta
HADIPUTRANTO, HADINOTO & PARTNERS

Anang Hidayat
PT GPI LOGISTICS

Nurman Hidayat
INDONESIA INVESTMENT COORDINATING BOARD

Brigitta Imam Rahayoe
BRIGITTA I. RAHAYOE & PARTNERS

Adiwidya Imam Rahayu
BRIGITTA I. RAHAYOE & PARTNERS

Deshaputra Intanperdana
HADROMI & PARTNERS

Jamaslin James Purba
JAMES PURBA & PARTNERS

Pak Jatmiko
DISTRICT COURT OF SURABAYA

Edy Junaedi
BADAN PELAYANAN TERPADU SATU PINTU (BPTS)

Brinanda Lidwina Kaliska
MAKARIM & TAIRA S.

Mirza Karim
KARIMSYAH LAW FIRM

Othman Karim
KARIMSYAH LAW FIRM

Shakuntala Kartikasari
PTI ARCHITECTS

Anita Lucia Kendarto
NOTARIS & PEJABAT PEMBUAT AKTA TANAH

Johan Kurnia
HADIPUTRANTO, HADINOTO & PARTNERS

Ayu Katarina Kusnadi
OENTOENG SURIA & PARTNERS

Winita E. Kusnandar
KUSNANDAR & CO.

Diana Kusumasari
BUDIDJAJA & ASSOCIATES

Jatmiko Adi Kusumo
INTERIORS & CO.

Rosevelt Riedel Lontoh
ALI BUDIARDJO, NUGROHO, REKSODIPUTRO, MEMBER OF LEX MUNDI

Noorfina Luthfiany
BANK INDONESIA

Syamsul Ma'Arif
MAHKAMAH AGUNG REPUBLIK INDONESIA

Bobby R. Manalu
SIREGAR SETIAWAN MANALU

Yasser Mandela
BUDIDJAJA & ASSOCIATES

Manumpak Manurung

Benny Marbun
PT PLN (PERSERO) INDONESIA STATE ELECTRICITY CORPORATION

Ahmad Maulana
ASSEGAF, HAMZAH & PARTNERS

Mario Maurice Sinjal
NURJADIN SUMONO MULYADI & PARTNERS

Amalia Mayasari
SIMBOLON & PARTNERS LAW FIRM

Ella Melany
HANAFIAH PONGGAWA & PARTNERS

Any Miami
PWC INDONESIA

Kristo Molina
WITARA CAKRA ADVOCATES (IN ASSOCIATION WITH WHITE & CASE LLP)

Fifiek Mulyana SH
MULYANA ABRAR & ADVOCATES

Sri Mulyati
RIVAI TRIPRASETIO & PARTNERS

Alexander Nainggolan
HADROMI & PARTNERS

Safita Ratna Narthfilda
OENTOENG SURIA & PARTNERS

Imran Nating
INDONESIAN ASSOCIATION OF RECEIVERS AND ADMINISTRATORS (AKPI)

Ratih Nawangsari
OENTOENG SURIA & PARTNERS

Rizana Noor
PT KREDIT BIRO INDONESIA JAYA (KBIJ)

Monasisca Noviannei
INDONESIA INVESTMENT COORDINATING BOARD

Putra Nugraha
WITARA CAKRA ADVOCATES (IN ASSOCIATION WITH WHITE & CASE LLP)

Reza Nurtjahja
PT URBANE INDONESIA

Inta Oviyantari
PTI ARCHITECTS

Heru Pambudi
MINISTRY OF FINANCE

Agung Pangestu Wijaya
PT DANADIPA BERTU

Ay Tjhing Phan
PWC INDONESIA

Abraham Pierre
KPMG

Deni Prasetyo
LAND DATA AND INFORMATION CENTER

Norbertus Hengky Pratoko
INDONESIAN LOGISTICS AND FORWARDERS ASSOCIATION

Fredie Pratomo
PT BINATAMA AKRINDO

Ety Puspitasari
CKB LOGISTICS

Indra Raharja
APRILDA FIONA & PARTNERS LAW FIRM

Dewi Sri Rahayu
NOTARIS & PPAT

Tantia Rahmadhina
RIVAI TRIPRASETIO & PARTNERS

Dhamma Ratna
NOTARIS & PEJABAT PEMBUAT AKTA TANAH

Jean H. Reksodiputro
PT PEFINDO BIRO KREDIT

Sophia Rengganis
PWC INDONESIA

Rengganis Rennganis
HADROMI & PARTNERS

Reza Riztama
PT PRATAMA INDOMITRA KONSULTAN - MEMBER OF RUSSELL BEDFORD INTERNATIONAL

Mahesa Rumondor
ADNAN KELANA HARYANTO & HERMANTO

Valdano Ruru
MAKARIM & TAIRA S.

Ayudi Rusmanita
NURJADIN SUMONO MULYADI & PARTNERS

Indra Safitri
HIMPUNAN KONSULTAN HUKUM PASAR MODAL

Ayundha Sahar
OENTOENG SURIA & PARTNERS

Rika Salim
OENTOENG SURIA & PARTNERS

Darma Saputra
BANK INDONESIA

Widodo Saputro
PT ANDHIKA PRIMA PERKASA

Mahardika K. Sardjana
HADIPUTRANTO, HADINOTO & PARTNERS

Nur Asyura Anggini Sari
BANK INDONESIA

Haryo Sedewo
INDONESIA INVESTMENT COORDINATING BOARD

Harment Sembiring
INDONESIA NATIONAL SINGLE WINDOW

Ibrahim Senen
ARMAND YAPSUNTO MUHARAMSYAH & PARTNERS (AYMP)

Erwin Setiawan
EY

Indra Setiawan
ALI BUDIARDJO, NUGROHO, REKSODIPUTRO, MEMBER OF LEX MUNDI

Arief Setyadi
PKF ACCOUNTANTS & BUSINESS ADVISERS

Lardi SH
LARDI & PARTNERS

Taji M. Sianturi
TAJI & REKAN

Kevin Omar Sidharta
ALI BUDIARDJO, NUGROHO, REKSODIPUTRO, MEMBER OF LEX MUNDI

Obed Simamora
LAND OFFICE OF SURABAYA

Ricardo Simanjuntak
RICARDO SIMANJUNTAK & PARTNERS

Yudianta Medio N. Simbolon
SIMBOLON & PARTNERS LAW FIRM

Nien Rafles Siregar
SIREGAR SETIAWAN MANALU

Risbert Soelaiman

Ardi Haqi Solla
OTORITAS JASA KEUANGAN - INDONESIA FINANCIAL SERVICES AUTHORITY

Nadia Soraya
TNB & PARTNERS

Selvana Stella Oviona
BUDIDJAJA & ASSOCIATES

Tirtamarta Sudarman
PT PESAT JAYA UTAMA

Bambang Suprijanto
EY

Puspita W. Surono
MINISTRY OF FINANCE

Atik Susanto
OENTOENG SURIA & PARTNERS

Hantriono Susizo
MINISTRY OF FINANCE

Otje Sutedi
PTI ARCHITECTS

ST Suwandi
PT BINTANG TIMUR

Randy Suwenli
HANAFIAH PONGGAWA & PARTNERS

Aria Suyudi
CONSULTANT

Pieter Talaway
PIETER TALAWAY & ASSOCIATES

Kurniawan Tanzil
MAKARIM & TAIRA S.

Arief Tejo S.
INDONESIAN LOGISTICS AND FORWARDERS ASSOCIATION

Achmad Tri Cahyono
OTORITAS JASA KEUANGAN - INDONESIA FINANCIAL SERVICES AUTHORITY

Gatot Triprasetio
RIVAI TRIPRASETIO & PARTNERS

Runi Tusita
PWC INDONESIA

Trina Uli
SIMBOLON & PARTNERS LAW FIRM

Sony Panji Wicaksono
BANK INDONESIA

Haykel Widiasmoko
ABDUL HAKIM GARUDA NUSANTARA, HARMAN & PARTNER

Arojoto Wisanto
BAM DECORIAT INDONESIA

Garry Wood
PT KREDIT BIRO INDONESIA JAYA (KBIJ)

Pelopor Yanto
LAND DATA AND INFORMATION CENTER

Jono Yeo
BUDIDJAJA & ASSOCIATES

Akbar Zainuri
KARIMSYAH LAW FIRM

Mohammad Zamroni
ZAMRO LAW FIRM

Jacob Zwaan
KPMG

IRAN, ISLAMIC REP.

*TRADE PROMOTION
ORGANIZATION OF IRAN*

Sareh Abadtalab
*STATE ORGANIZATION
FOR REGISTRATION OF
DEEDS AND PROPERTIES*

Camellia Abdolsamad
*INTERNATIONAL LAW
OFFICE OF DR. BEHROOZ
AKHLAGHI & ASSOCIATES*

Morteza Adab
*COMPANY REGISTRATION
OFFICE*

Ali Ahmadi
*TEHRAN CHAMBER OF
COMMERCE, INDUSTRIES
AND MINES*

Mousa Ahmadi
ISLAMIC AZAD UNIVERSITY

Behrooz Akhlaghi
*INTERNATIONAL LAW
OFFICE OF DR. BEHROOZ
AKHLAGHI & ASSOCIATES*

Hamidreza Alipour Shirsavar
ISLAMIC AZAD UNIVERSITY

Ali Amani
*DAYA-RAHYAFT AUDITING &
MANAGEMENT SERVICES*

Gholam Ali Asghari
*GREAT TEHRAN
ELECTRICITY DISTRIBUTION
COMPANY (GTEDC)*

Zayer Ayat
*IRANIAN NATIONAL TAX
ADMINISTRATION (INTA)*

Toktam Aynehkar
PERSOL CORPORATION

Fatemeh Bagherzadeh
FARJAM LAW OFFICE

Rambod Barandoust
CONSULTANT

Hamid Berenjkar
OFFICE OF HAMID BERENJKAR

Somayeh Bodaghi
*CENTRAL BANK OF THE
ISLAMIC REPUBLIC OF IRAN*

Golsa Daghighi
*INTERNATIONAL LAW
OFFICE OF DR. BEHROOZ
AKHLAGHI & ASSOCIATES*

Gholam-Hossein Davani
*DAYA-RAHYAFT AUDITING &
MANAGEMENT SERVICES*

Morteza Dezfoulian

Sofie Djagharbekian
*TOROSSIAN, AVANESSIAN
& ASSOCIATES*

Sepideh Dowlatshahi
BARTAR ASSOCIATES LAW FIRM

Maryam Ebrahimi
DENTONS

Maryam Ebrahimi Ghaleaziz
*STATE ORGANIZATION
FOR REGISTRATION OF
DEEDS AND PROPERTIES*

Roza Einifar
*INTERNATIONAL LAW
OFFICE OF DR. BEHROOZ
AKHLAGHI & ASSOCIATES*

Shirin Ozra Entezari
*DR. SHIRIN O. ENTEZARI
& ASSOCIATES*

Seyyed Amir Hossein Etesami
*SECURITIES AND EXCHANGE
ORGANIZATION OF IRAN*

Shahin Fadakar
*INTERNATIONAL LAW
OFFICE OF DR. BEHROOZ
AKHLAGHI & ASSOCIATES*

Soroosh Falahati
*BAYAN EMROOZ
INTERNATIONAL LAW FIRM*

Allahyar Ghajar
*TEHRAN MUNICIPALITY -
FANAVARAN SHAHR CO.*

Nasim Gheidi
*GHEIDI & ASSOCIATES
LAW OFFICE*

S. Arash H. Mirmalek
PERSOL CORPORATION

Amir Hosseini
PERSOL CORPORATION

Nasim Jahanbani
*GREAT TEHRAN
ELECTRICITY DISTRIBUTION
COMPANY (GTEDC)*

Mohammad Jalili
IRAN CREDIT SCORING

Jafar Jamali
*SECURITIES AND EXCHANGE
ORGANIZATION OF IRAN*

Hossein Kakhki
IRAN CUSTOMS OFFICE

Farid Kani
ATIEH ASSOCIATES

Majid Mahallati
A.M. MAHALLATI & CO.

Gholam Reza Malekshoar
*CENTRAL BANK OF THE
ISLAMIC REPUBLIC OF IRAN*

Mahnaz Mehrinfar
*INTERNATIONAL LAW
OFFICE OF DR. BEHROOZ
AKHLAGHI & ASSOCIATES*

Fatemeh Sadat Mirsharifi
MINISTRY OF COMMERCE

Ali Mirzaie
*STATE ORGANIZATION
FOR REGISTRATION OF
DEEDS AND PROPERTIES*

Golazin Mokhtari
ATIEH ASSOCIATES

Hamidreza Mokhtarian
*MEHR INTERNATIONAL
LAW FIRM*

Mehdi Mousavi
PERSOL CORPORATION

Vahid Nasiri
*BAYAN EMROOZ
INTERNATIONAL LAW FIRM*

Fariba Norouzi
PARSIAN INSURANCE CO.

Rasoul Nowrouzi

Zohreh Papi
*CENTRAL BANK OF THE
ISLAMIC REPUBLIC OF IRAN*

Farmand Pourkarim
*TEHRAN MUNICIPALITY -
FANAVARAN SHAHR CO.*

Mohammad Rahmani
*BAYAN EMROOZ
INTERNATIONAL LAW FIRM*

Yahya Rayegani
PRAELEGAL IRAN

Atiyeh Rezaei
*DR. SHIRIN O. ENTEZARI
& ASSOCIATES*

Negin Saberi
*INTERNATIONAL LAW
OFFICE OF DR. BEHROOZ
AKHLAGHI & ASSOCIATES*

Emadaldin Sakhaei
*MINISTRY OF ECONOMIC
AND FINANCE AFFAIRS*

Encyeh Seyed Sadr
*INTERNATIONAL LAW
OFFICE OF DR. BEHROOZ
AKHLAGHI & ASSOCIATES*

Ahmad Shabanifard
*INTERNATIONAL CENTRE
OF HIGHER EDUCATION,
AUSTRALIA*

Sara Shabanifard
RS COMPONENT

Khatereh Shahbazi
*INTERNATIONAL LAW
OFFICE OF DR. BEHROOZ
AKHLAGHI & ASSOCIATES*

Farzan Shirvanbeigi
*TEHRAN MUNICIPALITY -
FANAVARAN SHAHR CO.*

Rajat Ratan Sinha
*RCS PVT. LTD. BUSINESS
ADVISORS GROUP*

Pedram Soltani
PERSOL CORPORATION

Sepideh Taheri
*STATE ORGANIZATION
FOR REGISTRATION OF
DEEDS AND PROPERTIES*

Mohammad Reza Talischi
PERSOL CORPORATION

Ebrahim Tavakoli
BARTAR ASSOCIATES LAW FIRM

Vrej Torossian
*TOROSSIAN, AVANESSIAN
& ASSOCIATES*

Gholam Hossein Vahidi
DR. VAHIDI & ASSOCIATES

Zohreh Yazdani Paraei
ENGINEER

Ahmad Yousefi
ATTORNEY-AT-LAW

Parham Zahedi
*GHEIDI & ASSOCIATES
LAW OFFICE*

Hamed Zamami
BARTAR ASSOCIATES LAW FIRM

Elham Zareie
*INTERNATIONAL LAW
OFFICE OF DR. BEHROOZ
AKHLAGHI & ASSOCIATES*

IRAQ

EY

*GEZAIRI TRANSPORT
IRAQI COMPANY LTD.*

Ahmed Abboud Al Janabi
*MENA ASSOCIATES,
MEMBER OF AMERELLER
RECHTSANWÄLTE*

Hadeel Salih Abboud Al-Janabi
*MENA ASSOCIATES,
MEMBER OF AMERELLER
RECHTSANWÄLTE*

Mohammad Abdul Hassan

Ammar Abdul Jabbar
PROGER SPA

Alkaznaji Abdulhassan
ALKAZNAJI ABDULHASSAN

Hazim Akram
ATTORNEY-AT-LAW

Qussay Jafar Al Alawi

Mohammed Al-Badri
*AMANAT BAGHDAD
(BAGHDAD MAYORALTY)*

Hussein Al-Fadhili
ATTORNEY-AT-LAW

Hussein Al-Hadeethi

Nafa Ali
MINISTRY OF ELECTRICITY

Qismah Ali
CENTRAL BANK OF IRAQ

Ihsan Jasim Al-Khalidi
MINISTRY OF PLANNING

Rashid Al-Khouri
RASHID AL-KHOURI

Zuhair Al-Maliki
*AL-MALIKI & ASSOCIATES
LAW FIRM*

Ghath Raad Al-Nidawi
MINISTRY OF PLANNING

Rukaya Sabaah Al-Oqabee
MINISTRY OF PLANNING

Sattar Al-Qassy
ACCOUNTANT

Azhar Al-Rubaie
MINISTRY OF PLANNING

Ali Al-Rubaii

Maysa Alshukr
MAYSA ALSHUKR

Florian Amereller
AMERELLER RECHTSANWÄLTE

Suhaib Asad
PWC JORDAN

Raad N. Athab
RAAD N. ATHAB

Munther B. Hamoudi
*AL-BURAQ ENGINEERING
CO. LTD.*

Malik Bair
*MENA ASSOCIATES,
MEMBER OF AMERELLER
RECHTSANWÄLTE*

Ahmed Dawood
BHC LAW FIRM LLC

Greg Englefield
CONFLUENT LAW GROUP

Rafeef Hadeed
CENTRAL BANK OF IRAQ

Safaa Hadi Ghani
CENTRAL BANK OF IRAQ

Nadhim Mansi Hafid

Daniel Heintel
*MENA ASSOCIATES,
MEMBER OF AMERELLER
RECHTSANWÄLTE*

Abdulaziz Jabbar Abdulaziz
*COMPANY REGISTRAR
DIRECTOR GENERAL*

Mohamad Rasool Jaber

Riyadh Hassan Japak

Shahad Jassem
BHC LAW FIRM LLC

Deepak John
*BRIDGEWAY SHIPPING &
CLEARING SERVICES*

Jwad Kadhim Kareem
AL-SHAMS SHOW

Mohamad Khalil

Ahmed Abbas Khareem

Mohamad Khareem

Zaid Mahdi
ADIB COMPANY

Modher Taha Majeed
*AL TAMIMI & COMPANY
ADVOCATES & LEGAL
CONSULTANTS*

Hassan Melih
HASSAN MELIH

Ali Mohammad Kanbar

Khalid Mozan
AL MOZAN COMPANIES GROUP

Rasha Nadeem
BHC LAW FIRM LLC

Adnan K. Nahidh
SIYAH GROUP

Ammar Naji
CONFLUENT LAW GROUP

Tom Nolda
CONFLUENT LAW GROUP

Ammar Ralobide
AMMAR RALOBIDE

Akram Saeed
ATTORNEY-AT-LAW

Dhirar Salim
KASB GENERAL CONTRACTING

Kareem Salim Kamash
*GENERAL COMMISSION
FOR TAXES*

Mohammed Mustafa Sami
PROGER SPA

Ahmed Sauode
AHMED SAUODE

Abdelrahman Sherif
*DLA MATOUK BASSIOUNY
(PART OF DLA PIPER GROUP)*

Stephan Stephan
PWC JORDAN

Khaled Yaseen
*AL-SAQER ADVISERS
& LEGAL SERVICES*

Dahlia Zamel
*MENA ASSOCIATES,
MEMBER OF AMERELLER
RECHTSANWÄLTE*

Haythem Zayed
PWC JORDAN

IRELAND

ESB INTERNATIONAL

Seán Barton
MCCANN FITZGERALD

John Comerford
*COONEY CAREY CONSULTING
LTD. - MEMBER OF RUSSELL
BEDFORD INTERNATIONAL*

Miranda Cox
PWC IRELAND

Emma Doherty
MATHESON

Gavin Doherty
EUGENE F. COLLINS SOLICITORS

Gillian Dully
*LK SHIELDS SOLICITORS,
MEMBER OF IUS LABORIS*

Kenneth Egan
*ARTHUR COX, MEMBER
OF LEX MUNDI*

Garret Farrelly
MATHESON

Laura Feely
EUGENE F. COLLINS SOLICITORS

Frank Flanagan
MASON HAYES & CURRAN

Orla Hegarty
UNIVERSITY COLLEGE DUBLIN

Thomas Johnson
IRISH BUILDING CONTROL INSTITUTE

William Johnston
ARTHUR COX, MEMBER OF LEX MUNDI

Liam Kennedy
A&L GOODBODY

Eamonn Madden
COONEY CAREY CONSULTING LTD. - MEMBER OF RUSSELL BEDFORD INTERNATIONAL

Bernadette McArdle
IRISH BUILDING CONTROL INSTITUTE

Gerry McCartney
IRISH CREDIT BUREAU

Brid McCoy
AMOSS SOLICITORS

Eddie Meaney
DHL EXPRESS

Kevin Meehan
COMPASS MARITIME LTD.

Heather Murphy
MATHESON

James O'Boyle
THE PROPERTY REGISTRATION AUTHORITY

Brian O'Malley
A&L GOODBODY

Laura O'Sullivan
MASON HAYES & CURRAN

Maurice Phelan
MASON HAYES & CURRAN

Kevin Quinn
PWC IRELAND

Brendan Ringrose
WHITNEY MOORE

Mark Traynor
A&L GOODBODY

Joe Tynan
PWC IRELAND

Marcus Walsh
A&L GOODBODY

Patrick Walshe
PHILIP LEE SOLICITORS

Emma Weld-Moore
DANIEL MURPHY SOLICITORS

Maura Young
IRISH CREDIT BUREAU

ISRAEL

Ben Baharav
S. HOROWITZ & CO., MEMBER OF LEX MUNDI

Moshe Balter
BALTER, GUTH, ALONI LLP

Yuval Bar-Gil
YIGAL ARNON & CO.

Jacob Ben-Chitrit
YIGAL ARNON & CO.

Jeremy Benjamin
GOLDFARB SELIGMAN & CO.

Marina Benvenisti
RUTH CARGO

Rona Bergman Naveh
GROSS, KLEINHENDLER, HODAK, HALEVY, GREENBERG & CO.

Roy Caner
ERDINAST BEN NATHAN & CO. ADVOCATES

Doron Cohen
RAVEH, RAVID & CO. CPAS - MEMBER OF RUSSELL BEDFORD INTERNATIONAL

Itay Deutsch
NASCHITZ, BRANDES, AMIR & CO.

Jonathan Finklestone
ERDINAST BEN NATHAN & CO. ADVOCATES

Eliran Furman
YIGAL ARNON & CO.

Viva Gayer
ERDINAST BEN NATHAN & CO. ADVOCATES

Tuvia Geffen
NASCHITZ, BRANDES, AMIR & CO.

Ido Gonen
GOLDFARB SELIGMAN & CO.

Amos Hacmun
HESKIA-HACMUN LAW FIRM

Liron HaCohen
YIGAL ARNON & CO.

Yael Hershkovitz
GROSS, KLEINHENDLER, HODAK, HALEVY, GREENBERG & CO.

Tali Hirsch Sherman
MINISTRY OF CONSTRUCTION AND HOUSING

Mirit Hoffman Reif
DAVE WOLF & CO. LAW FIRM

Yossi Katsav
RUTH CARGO

Zeev Katz
PWC ISRAEL

Vered Kirshner
PWC ISRAEL

Adam Klein
GOLDFARB SELIGMAN & CO.

Gideon Koren
GIDEON KOREN & CO. LAW OFFICES

Andrew Larah
STEINMETZ, HARING, GURMAN & CO.

Hadas Lavi
S. HOROWITZ & CO., MEMBER OF LEX MUNDI

Dana Leshem
ERDINAST BEN NATHAN & CO. ADVOCATES

Michelle Liberman
S. HOROWITZ & CO., MEMBER OF LEX MUNDI

Sharon Liberman
PWC ISRAEL

Amnon Lorch
YIGAL ARNON & CO.

Liron Mendelevitz
KRIEF ALBATROS LTD.

Michael Mograbi
PELTRANSPORT

Rotem Muntner
RUTH CARGO

Gil Oren
YIGAL ARNON & CO.

Daniel Justin Permut
STEINMETZ, HARING, GURMAN & CO.

Doron Sadan
PWC ISRAEL

Dan Sharon
DAN SHARON - CONSULTING ENGINEERS 2002 LTD.

Daniel Singerman
COFACEBDI

Yoav Tal
ERDINAST BEN NATHAN & CO. ADVOCATES

Eran B. Taussig
BALTER, GUTH, ALONI LLP

Eylam Weiss
WEISS-PORAT & CO.

Zeev Weiss
WEISS-PORAT & CO.

Ita Yarmish
DAVE WOLF & CO. LAW FIRM

Michal Zohar Neistein
NASCHITZ, BRANDES, AMIR & CO.

ITALY

WHITE & CASE LLP

Paolo Acciari
MINISTERO DELL'ECONOMIA E FINANZE

Fabrizio Acerbis
PWC ITALY

Giuseppe Alemani
ALEMANI E ASSOCIATI

Iacopo Aliverti Piuri
DENTONS

Federico Antich
STUDIO DELL'AVVOCATO ANTICH

Umberto Antonelli
STUDIO LEGALE ASSOCIATO AD ASHURST LLP

Gea Arcella
CIVIL LAW NOTARY, LAWYER

Claudia Adele Aresu
PWC - TAX AND LEGAL SERVICES

Roberto Argeri
CLEARY GOTTLIEB STEEN & HAMILTON LLP

Gaetano Arnò
PWC - TAX AND LEGAL SERVICES

Clemente Arricale
PRIVATE ENGINEER - CLEMENTE ARRICALE

Gianluigi Baroni
PWC - TAX AND LEGAL SERVICES

Alvise Becker
PWC - TAX AND LEGAL SERVICES

Vlad Beffa
STUDIO SAVOIA

Susanna Beltramo
STUDIO LEGALE BELTRAMO

Claudia Beranzoli
COURT OF APPEAL OF ROME

Carlo Berarducci
CARLO BERARDUCCI ARCHITECTURE

Paola Bernardo
PWC - TAX AND LEGAL SERVICES

Marta Bianchi
PWC - TAX AND LEGAL SERVICES

Edoardo Augusto Bononi
STUDIO LEGALE ASSOCIATO AD ASHURST LLP

Gianluca Borraccia
PWC - TAX AND LEGAL SERVICES

Giampaolo Botta
SPEDIPORTO - ASSOCIAZIONE SPEDIZIONIERI CORRIERI E TRASPORTATORI DI GENOVA

Giuseppe Broccoli
BDA STUDIO LEGALE

Marco Buffarini
MINISTERO DELL'ECONOMIA E FINANZE

Claudio Burello
PWC - TAX AND LEGAL SERVICES

Sergio Calderara
CLEGAL

Federico Calloni
STUDIO CORNO - MEMBER OF RUSSELL BEDFORD INTERNATIONAL

Claudia Caluori
STUDIO DELL'AVVOCATO ANTICH

Gianluca Cambareri
TONUCCI & PARTNERS

Antonio Campagnoli
IL PUNTO REAL ESTATE ADVISOR

Paolo Canal
ORSINGHER ORTU – AVVOCATI ASSOCIATI

Stefano Cancarini
PWC - TAX AND LEGAL SERVICES

Gianni Carfì Pavia
PWC - TAX AND LEGAL SERVICES

Cecilia Carrara
LEGANCE AVVOCATI ASSOCIATI

Sandro Cecili
ARIETI S.P.A. ACEA GROUP

Nicla Cimmino
PWC ITALY

Ludovica Citarella
BDA STUDIO LEGALE

Ottavia Civardi
A. HARTRODT ITALIANA SRL

Domenico Colella
ORSINGHER ORTU – AVVOCATI ASSOCIATI

Stefano Colla
PWC - TAX AND LEGAL SERVICES

Fabrizio Colonna
STELÉ PERELLI

Mattia Colonnelli de Gasperis
COLONNELLI DE GASPERIS STUDIO LEGALE

Barbara Corsetti
PORTOLANO CAVALLO STUDIO LEGALE

Filippo Corsini
CHIOMENTI STUDIO LEGALE

Barbara Cortesi
STUDIO LEGALE GUASTI

Marco Cosa
NCTM STUDIO LEGALE

Antonio Cutini
PWC ITALY

Salvatore Cuzzocrea
PWC - TAX AND LEGAL SERVICES

Mariano Davoli
PIROLA PENNUTO ZEI & ASSOCIATI

Daniele De Giorgi
CLEARY GOTTLIEB STEEN & HAMILTON LLP

Antonio De Martinis
SPASARO DE MARTINIS LAW FIRM

Francesca De Paolis
STUDIO LEGALE SALVATORE DE PAOLIS

Rosa Del Sindaco
ABBATESCIANNI STUDIO LEGALE E TRIBUTARIO

Claudio Di Falco
CLEARY GOTTLIEB STEEN & HAMILTON LLP

Claudio Di Mario
ADL CONSULTING

Silvia Digregorio
COURT OF APPEAL OF ROME

Francesco Falsetti
SALINI IMPREGILO

Maddalena Ferrari
STUDIO NOTARILE FERRARI

Giuseppe Ferrelli
STUDIO LEGALE SINATRA

Barbara Mirta Ferri
PWC - TAX AND LEGAL SERVICES

Gianclaudio Fischetti
PWC - TAX AND LEGAL SERVICES

Paolo Franceschetti
AGENZIA DELLE ENTRATE

Emanuele Franchi
PWC ITALY

Pier Andrea Fré Torelli Massini
CARABBA & PARTNERS

Filippo Frigerio
PORTOLANO CAVALLO STUDIO LEGALE

Marialaura Frittella
COCUZZA E ASSOCIATI

Bruno Frugis
ITALIAN REVENUE AGENCY

Paolo Gallarati
NCTM STUDIO LEGALE

Andrea Gangemi
PORTOLANO CAVALLO STUDIO LEGALE

Daniele Geronzi
LEGANCE AVVOCATI ASSOCIATI

Vincenzo Fabrizio Giglio
GIGLIO & SCOFFERI STUDIO LEGALE DEL LAVORO

Antonio Grieco
GRIECO E ASSOCIATI

Valentino Guarini
PWC - TAX AND LEGAL SERVICES

Federico Guasti
STUDIO LEGALE GUASTI

Francesca Inchingolo
COURT OF APPEAL OF ROME

Francesco Iodice
CLEARY GOTTLIEB STEEN & HAMILTON LLP

Alberto Irace
ARIETI S.P.A. ACEA GROUP

Giovanni Izzo
ABBATESCIANNI STUDIO LEGALE E TRIBUTARIO

Ignazio La Candia
*PIROLA PENNUTO ZEI
& ASSOCIATI*

Pietro La Fortezza
DLA PIPER

Cecilia Laporta
BDA STUDIO LEGALE

Francesco Laureti
NCTM STUDIO LEGALE

Stefano Liotta
ARIETI S.P.A. ACEA GROUP

Alessandra Livreri
A. HARTRODT ITALIANA SRL

Enrico Lodi
CRIF S.P.A.

Ottavia Lombardo
DLA PIPER

Claudio Lumaca
AGENZIA DELLE ENTRATE

Stefano Macchi di Cellere
*MACCHI DI CELLERE
GANGEMI LLP*

Federico Magi
*PWC - TAX AND
LEGAL SERVICES*

Carlo Majer
LEXELLENT

Roberta Marconi
ITALIAN REVENUE AGENCY

Anna Chiara Margottini
*ORSINGHER ORTU –
AVVOCATI ASSOCIATI*

Laura Marretta
ROMOLOTTI MARRETTA

Donatella Martinelli
*STUDIO LEGALE ASSOCIATO
TOMMASINI E MARTINELLI*

Federico Mattei
*PWC - TAX AND
LEGAL SERVICES*

Carloandrea Meacci
*STUDIO LEGALE ASSOCIATO
AD ASHURST LLP*

Gianluca Medina
*STUDIO LEGALE ASSOCIATO
AD ASHURST LLP*

Gilberto Melchiorri
*UNITED NATIONS ECONOMIC
COMMISSION FOR EUROPE*

Michele Melchiorri
*UNITED NATIONS ECONOMIC
COMMISSION FOR EUROPE*

Laura Mellone
BANK OF ITALY

Priscilla Merlino
NUNZIANTE MAGRONE

Marco Monaco Sorge
TONUCCI & PARTNERS

Maria Teresa Monteduro
*MINISTERO DELL'ECONOMIA
E FINANZE*

Micael Montinari
*PORTOLANO CAVALLO
STUDIO LEGALE*

Davide Moretti
BANK OF ITALY

Valeria Morosini
*TOFFOLETTO E SOCI LAW FIRM,
MEMBER OF IUS LABORIS*

Monica Negrini
BDA STUDIO LEGALE

Gianmatteo Nunziante
NUNZIANTE MAGRONE

Luca Occhetta
*PIROLA PENNUTO ZEI
& ASSOCIATI*

Fabiana Padroni
RISTUCCIA & TUFARELLI

Luciano Panzani
COURT OF APPEAL OF ROME

Ignazio Pasquetti
STUDIO PASQUETTI S.I.P. 2C

Giovanni Patti
*ABBATESCIANNI STUDIO
LEGALE E TRIBUTARIO*

Gino Pazienza
ENER-PRICE

Federica Periale
*STUDIO LEGALE ASSOCIATO
AD ASHURST LLP*

Federica Pianta
COCUZZA E ASSOCIATI

Annamaria Pinzuti
*STUDIO LEGALE ASSOCIATO
AD ASHURST LLP*

Maria Progida
*PWC - TAX AND
LEGAL SERVICES*

Daniele Raynaud
RAYNAUD STUDIO LEGALE

Valentina Ricci
STELÉ PERELLI

Marianna Ristuccia
RISTUCCIA & TUFARELLI

Filippo Maria Riva
*PWC - TAX AND
LEGAL SERVICES*

Cinzia Romano
*STUDIO LEGALE
SALVATORE DE PAOLIS*

Tommaso Edoardo Romolotti
ROMOLOTTI MARRETTA

Michele Salemo
STUDIOCREDIT

Francesca Salerno
LEGANCE AVVOCATI ASSOCIATI

Mike Salerno
KRCOM

Giuseppe Santarelli
TONUCCI & PARTNERS

Vera Santomartino
*MINISTERO DELL'ECONOMIA
E FINANZE*

Arturo Santoro
*PIROLA PENNUTO ZEI
& ASSOCIATI*

Guido Savelli
*SPASARO DE MARTINIS
LAW FIRM*

Paolo Savini
AGENZIA DELLE ENTRATE

Filippo Savoia
STUDIO SAVOIA

Felice Schipani
AGENZIA DELLE ENTRATE

Alice Scotti
STUDIO LEGALE GUASTI

Lidia Maria Sella
*STUDIO CORNO - MEMBER
OF RUSSELL BEDFORD
INTERNATIONAL*

Andrea Semmola
*STUDIO LEGALE ASSOCIATO
AD ASHURST LLP*

Susanna Servi
CARABBA & PARTNERS

Chiara Sestagalli
*STUDIO LEGALE ASSOCIATO
AD ASHURST LLP*

Ginevra Sforza
*PORTOLANO CAVALLO
STUDIO LEGALE*

Massimiliano Silvetti
LEGÁLIA

Carlo Sinatra
STUDIO LEGALE SINATRA

Manlio Carlo Soldani

Lorenzo Sozio
*SPASARO DE MARTINIS
LAW FIRM*

Elisa Sulcis
STUDIO LEGALE SINATRA

Maria Antonietta Tanico
STUDIO LEGALE TANICO

Andrea Tedioli
STUDIO LEGALE TEDIOLI

Giuseppe Telesca
AGENZIA DELLE ENTRATE

Roberto Tirone
COCUZZA E ASSOCIATI

Francesca Tironi
*PWC - TAX AND
LEGAL SERVICES*

Davide Tollardo
*SPASARO DE MARTINIS
LAW FIRM*

Giacinto Tommasini
*STUDIO LEGALE ASSOCIATO
TOMMASINI E MARTINELLI*

Stefano Tresca
ISEED

Luca Tufarelli
RISTUCCIA & TUFARELLI

Valentina Turco
*PORTOLANO CAVALLO
STUDIO LEGALE*

Rachele Vacca de Dominicis
GRIECO E ASSOCIATI

Mario Valentini
*PIROLA PENNUTO ZEI
& ASSOCIATI*

Elisabetta Ventrella
BDA STUDIO LEGALE

Fabio Zanchi
BDA STUDIO LEGALE

Emilio Zendri
ARIETI S.P.A. ACEA GROUP

Domenico Zuccaro
*CLEARY GOTTLIEB STEEN
& HAMILTON LLP*

Filippo Zucchinelli
*PWC - TAX AND
LEGAL SERVICES*

JAMAICA

CARL CHEN & ASSOCIATES

FREIGHT HANDLERS LIMITED

INTERPLAN

*MARITIME AND
TRANSPORT LIMITED*

*RIVI GARDENER &
ASSOCIATE LTD.*

*THE SHIPPING ASSOCIATION
OF JAMAICA*

Rollin Alveranga
*MINISTRY OF WATER,
LAND, ENVIRONMENT
AND CLIMATE CHANGE*

Althea Anderson
LEX CARIBBEAN

Danielle Archer
*THE LAW PRACTICE OF
DANIELLE S. ARCHER
& ASSOCIATES*

Gregory Bennett
*NATIONAL ENVIRONMENT
& PLANNING AGENCY*

Rachel Bond
PATTERSON MAIR HAMILTON

Christopher Bovell
DUNNCOX

Errington Case
*JAMAICA PUBLIC SERVICE
COMPANY LIMITED*

Terrence Cooper
*CRIF NM CREDIT
ASSURE LIMITED*

Jemelia Davis
*THE SUPREME COURT
OF JAMAICA*

Brian Denning
PWC JAMAICA

Damion Dodd
PWC JAMAICA

Joan Ferreira-Dallas
ABTAX LIMITED

Nicole Foga
FOGA DALEY

Thalia Francis
KPMG

Lecia Gaye Taylor
HYLTON & HYLTON

Kay-Ann Graham
*NUNES, SCHOLEFIELD
DELEON & CO.*

Narda Graham
DUNNCOX

Gabrielle Grant
*MYERS, FLETCHER & GORDON,
MEMBER OF LEX MUNDI*

Howard Harris
FOGA DALEY

Marsha Henry-Martin
*MINISTRY OF LOCAL
GOVERNMENT & COMMUNITY
DEVELOPMENT*

Matthew A. Hogarth
WILMOT HOGARTH & CO.

Donovan Jackson
*NUNES, SCHOLEFIELD
DELEON & CO.*

Topaz Johnson
DUNNCOX

Grace Lindo
*NUNES, SCHOLEFIELD
DELEON & CO.*

Melinda Lloyd
*JAMAICA PUBLIC SERVICE
COMPANY LIMITED*

Rachael Lodge
FOGA DALEY

Marlon Lowe
*JAMAICA CUSTOMS
DEPARTMENT*

Zaila McCalla
*THE SUPREME COURT
OF JAMAICA*

Karen McHugh
PWC JAMAICA

Karlene McKenzie
*CABINET OFFICE OF THE
GOVERNMENT OF JAMAICA*

Jaime Mendoza
*UNITED NATIONS CONFERENCE
ON TRADE & DEVELOPMENT
(UNCTAD), GENEVA*

Alton Morgan
*LEGIS-ALTON E. MORGAN &
CO. ATTORNEYS-AT-LAW*

Sharon Neil Smith
PATTERSON MAIR HAMILTON

Camara Nelson
*WEST INDIES HOME
CONTRACTORS*

Sandralyn Nembhard
ABTAX LIMITED

Shyvonne Osborne
FOGA DALEY

Gina Phillipps Black
*MYERS, FLETCHER & GORDON,
MEMBER OF LEX MUNDI*

Shalise Porteous
NATIONAL LAND AGENCY

Norman Rainford
KPMG

Judith Ramlogan
COMPANIES OFFICE

Paul Randall
CREDITINFO JAMAICA LIMITED

Hilary Reid
*MYERS, FLETCHER & GORDON,
MEMBER OF LEX MUNDI*

Norman Shand
*KINGSTON AND ST.
ANDREW CORPORATION*

Jacqueline Simmonds
*JAMAICA PUBLIC SERVICE
COMPANY LIMITED*

Chantal Simpson
*MYERS, FLETCHER & GORDON,
MEMBER OF LEX MUNDI*

Tana'ania Small Davis
*LIVINGSTON, ALEXANDER &
LEVY ATTORNEYS-AT-LAW*

Hakon Stefansson
CREDITINFO JAMAICA LIMITED

Craig Stephen
CREDITINFO JAMAICA LIMITED

Danielle Stiebel
*MYERS, FLETCHER & GORDON,
MEMBER OF LEX MUNDI*

Humprey Taylor
TAYLOR CONSTRUCTION LTD.

Sherica Taylor
LEX CARIBBEAN

Marvalyn Taylor-Wright
TAYLOR-WRIGHT & COMPANY

Lorraine Thomas-Harris
*LTN LOGISTICS
INTERNATIONAL CO. LTD.*

Lori-Ann Thompson
NATIONAL LAND AGENCY

John Vassell
DUNNCOX

Cheriese Walcott
NATIONAL LAND AGENCY

Dominic Williams
*JAMAICA PUBLIC SERVICE
COMPANY LIMITED*

Lisa Williams
*LIVINGSTON, ALEXANDER &
LEVY ATTORNEYS-AT-LAW*

Anwar Wright
TAYLOR-WRIGHT & COMPANY

Scott Wright
TAYLOR-WRIGHT & COMPANY

Angelean Young-Daley
*JAMAICA PUBLIC SERVICE
COMPANY LIMITED*

JAPAN

KANSAI ELECTRIC POWER

Daiki Akanane
LAW OFFICES OF AKAHANE, ISEKI & HONDA (AIH LAW)

Fumika Cho
WHITE & CASE

Jeffrey Dressler
WHITE & CASE

Takuya Eguchi
MORI HAMADA & MATSUMOTO - OSAKA

Toyoki Emoto
ATSUMI & SAKAI

Shuntaro Fujii
ANDERSON MORI & TOMOTSUNE

Kiyoshi Fujita
ADACHI, HENDERSON, MIYATAKE & FUJITA

Miho Fujita
ADACHI, HENDERSON, MIYATAKE & FUJITA

Tatsuya Fukui
ATSUMI & SAKAI

Shinnosuke Fukuoka
NISHIMURA & ASAHI

David Gilmore
HERBERT SMITH FREEHILLS

Tomoko Goto
NISHIMURA & ASAHI

Taichi Haraguchi
ERNST & YOUNG TAX CO.

Yuichi Hasegawa
ADACHI, HENDERSON, MIYATAKE & FUJITA

Shunsuke Honda
ANDERSON MORI & TOMOTSUNE

Kai Hoshino
EY

Keisuke Imon
WHITE & CASE

Hiroshi Inagaki
HANKYU HANSHIN EXPRESS CO. LTD.

Ryuji Ino
ERNST & YOUNG TAX CO.

Akiko Isoyama
PWC TAX JAPAN

Jun Ito
KINTETSU WORLD EXPRESS, INC.

Saki Kamiya
ANDERSON MORI & TOMOTSUNE

Kazuo Kasai
WHITE & CASE

Hiroshi Kasuya
BAKER & MCKENZIE

Yuijro Katayama
NISHIMURA & ASAHI

Kenji Kawakami
FUTABA CORPORATION

Toriuchi Kazuki
ALPS LOGISTICS CO. LTD.

Takumi Kiriyama
NISHIMURA & ASAHI

Akemi Kito
PWC TAX JAPAN

Akiko Kobayashi
CREDIT INFORMATION CENTER CORP.

Masayoshi Kobayashi
BAKER & MCKENZIE

Hiroyuki Konishi
KONISHI TAX AND ACCOUNTING

Yasuyuki Kuribayashi
CITY-YUWA PARTNERS

Takafumi Masukata
NIPPON EXPRESS CO., LTD.

Hiroaki Matsui
NISHIMURA & ASAHI

Naoki Matsuo
CITY-YUWA PARTNERS

Nakano Michiaki
SOUTH TORANOMON LAW OFFICES

Kazuya Miyakawa
PWC TAX JAPAN

Toshio Miyatake
ADACHI, HENDERSON, MIYATAKE & FUJITA

Teppei Mogi
OH-EBASHI LPC & PARTNERS

Michihiro Mori
NISHIMURA & ASAHI

Tatsuaki Murakami
NISHIMURA & ASAHi

Hirosato Nabika
CITY-YUWA PARTNERS

Hideto Nakai
KINDEN CORP.

Ken Nakatsuka
NAKATSUKA KEN TAX ACCOUNTING OFFICE

Keisuke Nishimura
WHITE & CASE

Miho Niunoya
ATSUMI & SAKAI

Fumiya Obinata
NISHIMURA & ASAHI

Takeshi Ogura
OGURA ACCOUNTING OFFICE

Kotaro Okamoto
EY

Daisuke Omote
ATSUMI & SAKAI

Takashi Saito
CITY-YUWA PARTNERS

Hitomi Sakai
KOJIMA LAW OFFICES

Yuka Sakai
CITY-YUWA PARTNERS

Sara Sandford
GARVEY SCHUBERT BARER LAW FIRM

Kei Sasaki
ANDERSON MORI & TOMOTSUNE

Tetsuro Sato
BAKER & MCKENZIE

Yuri Sugano
NISHIMURA & ASAHI

Sachiko Sugawara
ATSUMI & SAKAI

Tomoyuki Susukida
WHITE & CASE

Junya Suzuki
BAKER & MCKENZIE

Yasuyuki Suzuki
STANDARD CHARTERED BANK

Yoshimasa Takagi
EY

Hiroaki Takahashi
ANDERSON MORI & TOMOTSUNE

Hiroto Takahashi
ATSUMI & SAKAI

Y. Takahashi
SANKYU INC.

Junichi Tobimatsu
TOBIMATSU LAW

Yamamoto Tomohide
KINDEN CORP.

Takaharu Totsuka
ANDERSON MORI & TOMOTSUNE

Naohiro Toyoda
AEON FINANCIAL SERVICE CO. LTD.

Yoshito Tsuji
OBAYASHI CORPORATION

Takeo Tsukamoto
NISHIMURA & ASAHI

Ichiro Tsumiomri
EY

Shougo Tsuruta
PWC TAX JAPAN

Yoshihiro Tsutaya
ANDERSON MORI & TOMOTSUNE

Yuichi Urata
OH-EBASHI LPC & PARTNERS

Jun Usami
WHITE & CASE

Kenji Utsumi
NAGASHIMA OHNO & TSUNEMATSU

Tatsuya Yagishita
DAITO KOUN CO. LTD.

Mizuho Yamada
WHITE & CASE

Michi Yamagami
ANDERSON MORI & TOMOTSUNE

Shunichi Yamamoto

JORDAN

DEPARTMENT OF LANDS & SURVEY

EY

Hayja'a Abu Al Hayja'a
TALAL ABU GHAZALEH LEGAL SERVICES CO.

Nayef Abu Alim
PREMIER LAW FIRM LLP

Hanin Abughazaleh
AL TAMIMI & COMPANY ADVOCATES & LEGAL CONSULTANTS

Fatina Abweini
MINISTRY OF JUSTICE

Waleed Adi
EMRC ENERGY AND MINERALS REGULATORY COMMISSION

Malak Al Hasoun
MINISTRY OF JUSTICE

Haifa Al Kiali
MAGISTRATES COURT

Zeina Al Nabih
AL TAMIMI & COMPANY ADVOCATES & LEGAL CONSULTANTS

Abd El Rahman M. Al Qatawenh
ATTORNEY

Wijdan Al Rabadi
EMRC ENERGY AND MINERALS REGULATORY COMMISSION

Ziad Al Shufiyyen
EMRC ENERGY AND MINERALS REGULATORY COMMISSION

Maha Al-Abdallat
CENTRAL BANK OF JORDAN

Mohammad Al-Akhras
PWC JORDAN

Rawan Alameddin
HAMMOURI & PARTNERS LAW FIRM

Eman M. Al-Dabbas
INTERNATIONAL BUSINESS LEGAL ASSOCIATES

Ashraf Alja'fari

Zeinab Aljaafreh
CENTRAL BANK OF JORDAN

Omar Aljazy
ALJAZY & CO. ADVOCATES & LEGAL CONSULTANTS

Sabri S. Al-Khassib
AMMAN CHAMBER OF COMMERCE

Liana Al-Mufleh
HAMMOURI & PARTNERS LAW FIRM

Naser Al-Mughrabi
PWC JORDAN

Moath Alsbin
EMRC ENERGY AND MINERALS REGULATORY COMMISSION

Ghada Al-Sha'arawi
BEIRUTI ATTORNEYS & COUNSELORS AT LAW

Zaid Al-Sha'rawi
CENTRAL BANK OF JORDAN

Hussien Alsorakhi
ISTD

Eid M. Alwrikat
JUSTICE PALACE

Essa Amawi
AMAWI & CO. ADVOCATES & LEGAL CONSULTANTS

Mohammed Amawi
AMAWI & CO. ADVOCATES & LEGAL CONSULTANTS

Ahmad Amoudi
CRIF JORDAN

Faisal Asfour
KHALIFEH & PARTNERS LAWYERS

Raaed Asfour
ISTD

Murad Awamleh
GREATER AMMAN MUNICIPALITY

Hatem Barakat

Jafar Barham
JORDAN CUSTOMS

Aya Bassoumi
HAMMOURI & PARTNERS LAW FIRM

Ayham Batarseh
ZALLOUM & LASWI LAW FIRM

Raeda Bawadi
MAGISTRATES COURT

Mohammad Beiruti
BEIRUTI ATTORNEYS & COUNSELORS AT LAW

Yotta Bulmer
HAMMOURI & PARTNERS LAW FIRM

Anwar Ellaian
THE JORDANIAN ELECTRIC POWER CO. LTD. (JEPCO)

Vincent Flamant
AQABA CONTAINER TERMINAL

Fadiz A. Freij
BEIRUTI ATTORNEYS & COUNSELORS AT LAW

Talah Ghosheh
AMAWI & CO. ADVOCATES & LEGAL CONSULTANTS

Rami Hadidi
HADIDI & CO. ATTORNEYS

Tariq Hammouri
HAMMOURI & PARTNERS LAW FIRM

George Hazboun
INTERNATIONAL CONSOLIDATED FOR LEGAL CONSULTATIONS

Reem Hazboun
INTERNATIONAL CONSOLIDATED FOR LEGAL CONSULTATIONS

Jenan Hijjawi
COMPANIES CONTROL DEPARTMENT

Mohammad Hussein
AL REFA'I INTERNATIONAL TRANSPORT & CLEARING EST.

Tayseer Ismail Ibrahim
NOUR ALSHARQ TRADE COMPANY ENGINEERING & COMPANY SERVICES

Abdullah Jaradat
ABDULLAH & PARTNERS

Farah Jaradat
HAMMOURI & PARTNERS LAW FIRM

Emad Karkar
PWC JORDAN

Rakan Kawar
ALI SHARIF ZU'BI, ADVOCATES & LEGAL CONSULTANTS, MEMBER OF LEX MUNDI

Samer Kawar
SAMER KAWAR & ASSOCIATES, CONSULTANTS AND LEGAL ADVISORS

Ahmed Khalifeh
HAMMOURI & PARTNERS LAW FIRM

Nadeen Khraset
ABDULLAH & PARTNERS

Nadeen Khresab
ABDULLAH LAW FIRM

Hussein Kofahy
CENTRAL BANK OF JORDAN

Ammar Krayim
KRAYIM CONSTRUCTION

Lama Krayim
KRAYIM CONSTRUCTION

Rasha Laswi
ZALLOUM & LASWI LAW FIRM

Firas Malhas
INTERNATIONAL BUSINESS LEGAL ASSOCIATES

Ola Khalil Mohammad
CENTRAL BANK OF JORDAN

Nour Nayef Momani
CENTRAL BANK OF JORDAN

Hala Mujalli
GREATER AMMAN MUNICIPALITY

Khaldoun Nazer
KHALIFEH & PARTNERS LAWYERS

Majd Nemeh
*INTERNATIONAL CONSOLIDATED
FOR LEGAL CONSULTATIONS*

Hamza Obidat
*INTERNATIONAL CONSOLIDATED
FOR LEGAL CONSULTATIONS*

Mohammad Ouglat
ISTD

Mhanna Qattan
*GREATER AMMAN
MUNICIPALITY*

Naji Qutieshat
*INTERNATIONAL BUSINESS
LEGAL ASSOCIATES*

Osama Y. Sabbagh
*THE JORDANIAN ELECTRIC
POWER CO. LTD. (JEPCO)*

Tareq Sahouri
SAHOURI & PARTNERS LLC

Siwar Saket
*KHALIFEH & PARTNERS
LAWYERS*

Majdi Salaita
*ALI SHARIF ZU'BI, ADVOCATES
& LEGAL CONSULTANTS,
MEMBER OF LEX MUNDI*

Lana Salameh
JC LAW

Omar Salhea
ISTD

Omar Sawadha
*HAMMOURI & PARTNERS
LAW FIRM*

Manhal Sayigh
*THE JORDANIAN ELECTRIC
POWER CO. LTD. (JEPCO)*

Adele Shaban
JC LAW

Mohammed Y. Shaban
AMIN KAWAR & SONS CO.

Nadia Shahin
AMIN KAWAR & SONS CO.

Areen Shraideh
*INTERNATIONAL BUSINESS
LEGAL ASSOCIATES*

Stephan Stephan
PWC JORDAN

Mohammed-Hanif Tarajia
ABDULLAH & PARTNERS

Moawyah Tarawneh
*KHALIFEH & PARTNERS
LAWYERS*

Khaled Tuffaha
*KPMG KAWASMY &
PARTNERS CO.*

Azzam Zalloum
ZALLOUM & LASWI LAW FIRM

Mahmoud Ziuod
*THE JORDANIAN ELECTRIC
POWER CO. LTD. (JEPCO)*

Deema Abu Zulaikha
*TALAL ABU GHAZALEH
LEGAL SERVICES CO.*

Kareem Zureikat

KAZAKHSTAN

Dinara Abdirova
OLYMPEX ADVISERS

Emil Halilyevich Abdrashitov
*NOTARY ASSOCIATION
OF THE ALMATY CITY*

Sardar Inarovich Abdysadykov
*NOTARY ASSOCIATION
OF THE ALMATY CITY*

Kuben Abzhanov
BAKER & MCKENZIE

Kuben Abzhanov
GRATA INTERNATIONAL

Saule Akhmetova
GRATA INTERNATIONAL

Altynbek Akpanov
*ECONOMIC RESEARCH
INSTITUTE KAZAKHSTAN*

Akmaral Akylbayeva
ARNA PARTNERS

Gaukhar Alibekova
*MINISTRY OF NATIONAL
ECONOMY*

Assel Aralbayeva
*SUPREME COURT OF THE
REPUBLIC OF KAZAKHSTAN*

Andrey Artyushenko
ARTYUSHENKO & PARTNERS

Samat Aryshev
ALMATY ENERGO ZBYT

Yermek Aubakirov
*MICHAEL WILSON &
PARTNERS LTD.*

Zarina Baikenzhina
WHITE & CASE

Rakhat Baisuanov
ARNA PARTNERS

Aigul Baizhanova
MINISTRY OF JUSTICE

Elmira Battal
SYNERGY PARTNERS LAW FIRM

Aidos Bekov
JSC STATE CREDIT BUREAU

Arman Berdalin
SAYAT ZHOLSHY & PARTNERS

Aidyn Bikebayev
SAYAT ZHOLSHY & PARTNERS

Timur Bizhanov
*MINISTRY OF REGIONAL
DEVELOPMENT*

Aizhan Bozaeva
MINISTRY OF FINANCE

Aziza Bozhakanova
MINISTRY OF JUSTICE

Victoria Chagay
ARTYUSHENKO & PARTNERS

Alexander Chumachenko
AEQUITAS LAW FIRM

Yuliya Chumachenko
AEQUITAS LAW FIRM

Dmitriy Chumakov
SAYAT ZHOLSHY & PARTNERS

Saltanat Dauletova
KPMG KAZAKHSTAN

Ruslan Degtyarenko
DENTONS KAZAKHSTAN LLP

Inara Elemanova
CENTIL LAW FIRM

Sungat Essimkhanov
*NUCLEAR AND ENERGY
SUPERVISION AND CONTROL
COMMITTEE OF THE
MINISTRY OF ENERGY*

Alexander Giros
*PARADIGM PROJECTS
KAZAKHSTAN*

Ardak Idayatova
AEQUITAS LAW FIRM

Majra Iskakova
ALMATY ENERGO ZBYT

Kamil Jambakiyev
NORTON ROSE FULBRIGHT

Galiya Joldybayeva
*MINISTRY OF NATIONAL
ECONOMY*

Mariyash Kabikenova
REHABILITATION MANAGER

Elena Kaeva
PWC KAZAKHSTAN

Aybek Kambaliyev
GRATA INTERNATIONAL

Saltanat Kamenova
*ECONOMIC RESEARCH
INSTITUTE KAZAKHSTAN*

Maksud Karaketov
CENTIL LAW FIRM

Alimzhan Karkinbaev
*MINISTRY OF REGIONAL
DEVELOPMENT*

Anel Kassabulatova
SIGNUM LAW FIRM

Aigerim Kauldasheva
*SUPREME COURT OF THE
REPUBLIC OF KAZAKHSTAN*

Madina Kazhimova
*MINISTRY OF NATIONAL
ECONOMY*

Saltanat Kemalova
SIGNUM LAW FIRM

Lyazzat Kereitbayeva
*MINISTRY OF NATIONAL
ECONOMY*

Yekaterina Khamidullina
AEQUITAS LAW FIRM

Olga Kim
CENTIL LAW FIRM

Askar Konysbayev
GRATA INTERNATIONAL

Alexander Korobeinikov
BAKER & MCKENZIE

Nurlan Kubenov
KPMG KAZAKHSTAN

Gaukhar Kudaibergenova
SIGNUM LAW FIRM

Tair Kulteleev
AEQUITAS LAW FIRM

Gulmira Lamacharipova
MINISTRY OF JUSTICE

Elena Lee
*MICHAEL WILSON &
PARTNERS LTD.*

Madina Makanova

Yerzhan Manasov
LINKAGE & MIND LLP

Marzhan Mardenova
PWC KAZAKHSTAN

Yessen Massalin
OLYMPEX ADVISERS

Nurkhan Mermankulov
*SUPREME COURT OF THE
REPUBLIC OF KAZAKHSTAN*

Bolat Miyatov
GRATA INTERNATIONAL

Victor Mokrousov
DECHERT KAZAKHSTAN LLP

Elena Motovilova
MINISTRY OF FINANCE

Andrei Mukazhanov
ALMATY ENERGO ZBYT

Daniyar Mussakhan
NORTON ROSE FULBRIGHT

Abylkhair Nakipov
SIGNUM LAW FIRM

Yevgeniya Nossova
DECHERT KAZAKHSTAN LLP

Kulbatyrov Nurlan
*ECONOMIC RESEARCH
INSTITUTE KAZAKHSTAN*

Islambek Nurzhanov
SYNERGY PARTNERS LAW FIRM

Ruslan Omarov
FIRST CREDIT BUREAU

Sergazy Omash
*SUPREME COURT OF THE
REPUBLIC OF KAZAKHSTAN*

Kazieva Orynkul
STATE REVENUE COMMITTEE

Yuliya V. Petrenko
BMF PARTNERS LAW FIRM LLP

Andrey Yuriyevich
Ponomarenko
*ALMATY BRANCH OF THE RSE
RESEARCH AND PRODUCTION
CENTER OF LAND CADASTRE*

Aigerim Raikhanova
CENTIL LAW FIRM

Taizhanova Roza
OLYMPEX ADVISERS

Darya Ryapissova
GRATA INTERNATIONAL

Gaukhar Sapina
*MINISTRY OF NATIONAL
ECONOMY*

Talgat Sariev
SIGNUM LAW FIRM

Nazym Seidakhmetova
SIGNUM LAW FIRM

Yerlan Serikbayev
*MICHAEL WILSON &
PARTNERS LTD.*

Aida Shadirova
DECHERT KAZAKHSTAN LLP

Abai Shaikenov
DENTONS KAZAKHSTAN LLP

Elmira Shamayeva
WHITE & CASE

Sofia Shaykhrazieva
CENTIL LAW FIRM

Meruert Sisembaeva
MINISTRY OF FINANCE

Alzhan Stamkulov
SYNERGY PARTNERS LAW FIRM

Nurzhan Stamkulov
SYNERGY PARTNERS LAW FIRM

Ulan Stybayev
SIGNUM LAW FIRM

Zhaslan Alimgazinovich
Sultanbekov
FIRMA PARITET LTD.

Zarina Syzdykova
GRATA INTERNATIONAL

Dana Tokmurzina
PWC KAZAKHSTAN

Mirat Tokombayev
*NUCLEAR AND ENERGY
SUPERVISION AND CONTROL
COMMITTEE OF THE
MINISTRY OF ENERGY*

Yerzhan Toktarov
SAYAT ZHOLSHY & PARTNERS

Botanova Totynur
STATE REVENUE COMMITTEE

Shynggys Turez
*ECONOMIC RESEARCH
INSTITUTE KAZAKHSTAN*

Maria Turganbaeva
MINISTRY OF JUSTICE

Nurken Turmakhambetov
*MINISTRY OF REGIONAL
DEVELOPMENT*

Alexandr Tyo
CENTIL LAW FIRM

Aigerim Tyurebayeva
KPMG KAZAKHSTAN

Anara Urakova
BMF PARTNERS LAW FIRM LLP

Azim Usmanov
CENTIL LAW FIRM

Aliya Utegaliyeva
PWC KAZAKHSTAN

Nikita Sergeevich Vasilchuk
*ENERGOPROMSTROIPROEKT
LLC*

Sergei Vataev
DECHERT KAZAKHSTAN LLP

Larissa Yemelyanova
AEQUITAS LAW FIRM

Aigerim Yermahanova
*MINISTRY OF NATIONAL
ECONOMY*

Olga Olegovna Yershova
*NOTARY ASSOCIATION
OF THE ALMATY CITY*

Yerzhan Yessimkhanov
GRATA INTERNATIONAL

Bakytgul Zhabaginova
*ECONOMIC RESEARCH
INSTITUTE KAZAKHSTAN*

Saken Zhailauov
SAEN ENGINEERING GROUP

Zhanar Zhandossova
BMF PARTNERS LAW FIRM LLP

Bulat Zhulamanov
*SUPREME COURT OF THE
REPUBLIC OF KAZAKHSTAN*

Liza Zhumakhmetova
SIGNUM LAW FIRM

Balykov Daulen Zhumalovich
*INTER-DISTRICT ECONOMIC
COURT OF ALMATY*

Sofiya Zhylkaidarova
SIGNUM LAW FIRM

KENYA

PYRAMID BUILDERS

Philip Aluku
SDV TRANSAMI

Barack Barkwang
COULSON HARNEY LLP

Mohammed A. Bhatti
BHATTI ELECTRICAL LIMITED

Hillary Biwott
CAPITAL MARKETS AUTHORITY

Dennis Chiruba
*ANJARWALLA & KHANNA
ADVOCATES*

Philip Coulson
COULSON HARNEY LLP

Oliver Fowler
KAPLAN & STRATTON

Peter Gachuhi
KAPLAN & STRATTON

Francis Gichuhi Kamau
A4 ARCHITECT

Ben Githinji
APT DESIGN SOLUTIONS

William Ikutha Maema
*ISEME, KAMAU &
MAEMA ADVOCATES*

Milly Jalega
*ISEME, KAMAU &
MAEMA ADVOCATES*

Abdilatif Jarso
*B.M. MUSAU & CO.
ADVOCATES*

Kenneth Kamaitha
KAPLAN & STRATTON

Martha Kamanu-Mutugi
KENYA POWER

Cathrine Kamau
DELUXE INKS LIMITED

Reuben Njoroge Kamau Kabbau
DREAMS ARCHITECTS

Samuel Kamunyu
CAPITAL MARKETS AUTHORITY

Apollo Karumba
PWC KENYA

Ronald Khavagali
B.M. MUSAU & CO. ADVOCATES

Hassan Kibet
ISEME, KAMAU & MAEMA ADVOCATES

Alan Kigen
KAMOTHO MAIYO & MBATIA ADVOCATES

William M. Kilonzo
ASSOCIATED SERVICES

Timothy Kiman
SIGINON FREIGHT LTD.

Meshack T. Kipturgo
SIGINON FREIGHT LTD.

Owen Koimburi
MAZARS KENYA

Emmanuel Kubo
SISULE MUNYI KILONZO & ASSOCIATES

Evelyn Kyania
B.M. MUSAU & CO. ADVOCATES

David Lekerai
ISEME, KAMAU & MAEMA ADVOCATES

Eric Lukoye
KENYA TRADE NETWORK AGENCY (KENTRADE)

Dominic Makau
CENTRAL ELECTRICALS INTERNATIONAL LTD.

Jacob Malelu
B.M. MUSAU & CO. ADVOCATES

Nicholas Malonza
SISULE MUNYI KILONZO & ASSOCIATES

Esther Manthi
CAPITAL MARKETS AUTHORITY

James Mburu Kamau
ISEME, KAMAU & MAEMA ADVOCATES

Ken Melly
ISEME KAMAU & MAEMA ADVOCATES (DLA PIPER)

Emma Miloyo
DESIGN SOURCE

Mansoor A. Mohamed
RUMAN SHIPCONTRACTORS LIMITED

Peter Momanyi
MAZARS KENYA

Titus Mukora
PWC KENYA

Teresia Munywoki
B.M. MUSAU & CO. ADVOCATES

John Muoria
WARUHIU K'OWADE & NG'ANG'A ADVOCATES

Benjamin Musau
B.M. MUSAU & CO. ADVOCATES

Peter Musyimi
KENYA LAW REFORM COMMISSION

Susan Mutinda
B.M. MUSAU & CO. ADVOCATES

Arnold Mutisya
COULSON HARNEY LLP

Joshua Mutua
KENYA POWER

Jane Mutulili
LA FEMME ENGINEERING SERVICES LTD.

Jacob W. Mwangi
THE ARCHITECTURAL ASSOCIATION OF KENYA

Peter Mwaura
ANJARWALLA & KHANNA ADVOCATES

James Ndegwa
KENYA POWER

Christina Nduba-Banja
COULSON HARNEY LLP

Mbage Ng'ang'a
WARUHIU K'OWADE & NG'ANG'A ADVOCATES

Christine Njau
ISEME, KAMAU & MAEMA ADVOCATES

Victor Njenga
KAPLAN & STRATTON

Chege Njoroge
LESINKO NJOROGE & GATHOGO

Jacqueline Njoroge
B.M. MUSAU & CO. ADVOCATES

Alex Nyagah
ARCHBUILD LIMITED

Rose Nyongesa
ISEME, KAMAU & MAEMA ADVOCATES

Conrad Nyukuri
AXIS KENYA

Robert Oimeke
ENERGY REGULATORY COMMISSION (ERC)

John Ojwang
NAIROBI CITY COUNTY GOVERNMENT

Sam Omukoko
METROPOL CORPORATION LTD.

Esther Omulele
MMC AFRICA LAW

Andrew Ondieki
PWC KENYA

Phillip Onyango
KAPLAN & STRATTON

Tom Odhiambo Onyango
TRIPLEOKLAW ADVOCATES

Cephas Osoro
HORWATH ERASTUS & CO. MEMBER, CROWE HORWARTH INTERNATIONAL

Charles Osundwa
KAPLAN & STRATTON

Andrew Ragui
PWC KENYA

Sonal Sejpal
ANJARWALLA & KHANNA ADVOCATES

Joseph Taracha
CENTRAL BANK OF KENYA

Maureen W. Makutano
AXIS KENYA

Angela Waki
COULSON HARNEY LLP

Evelyn Wamae
KENYA TRADE NETWORK AGENCY (KENTRADE)

Arphaxade Wanjala

Angela Waweru
KAPLAN & STRATTON

John Wekesa
KENYA POWER

Edmond Wesonga
B.M. MUSAU & CO. ADVOCATES

KIRIBATI

MINISTRY OF PUBLIC WORKS AND UTILITIES

Kenneth Barden
ATTORNEY-AT-LAW

Susan Barrie
TOBARAOI TRAVEL

Raweita Beniata
OLP KIRIBATI

Ierevita Biriti
KIRIBATI CHAMBER OF COMMERCE AND INDUSTRY

Tomitiana Eritama
MINISTRY OF LABOUR & HUMAN RESOURCES DEVELOPMENT

Mantaia Kaongotao
MK LAW & CO.

Tieri Kautuntamoa
BUSINESS & COMPANIES REGULATORY DIVISION, BUSINESS REGULATORY CENTRE, MINISTRY OF COMMERCE, INDUSTRY & COOPERATIVES

Motiti Moriati Koae
DEVELOPMENT BANK OF KIRIBATI

Laokiri Koreaua
KIRIBATI TAX OFFICE

Tion Neemia
SHIPPING AGENCY OF KIRIBATI

Tiiroa Roneti
MINISTRY OF COMMERCE, INDUSTRY AND TOURISM

Mautaake Tannang
KIRIBATI ELECTRICAL CONSULTING & CONTRACTING SERVICES

Naata Tekeaa
DEVELOPMENT BANK OF KIRIBATI

Tauniu Teraoi Moy
TOBARAOI TRAVEL

Reei Tioti
MINISTRY OF ENVIRONMENT, LANDS & AGRICULTURE DEVELOPMENT (MELAD)

KOREA, REP.

Arnold Yoohum Baek
KIM & CHANG

Jennifer Min-Sook Chae
KOREA CREDIT BUREAU

Kyoung Soo Chang
SHIN & KIM

Seung Hee Grace Chang
SHINHAN CUSTOMS SERVICE INC.

Paavan Chhabra
HEALY CONSULTANTS GROUP PLC

Junghoon Cho
KOREAN ELECTRICAL CONTRACTORS ASSOCIATION

Min Kyong Cho
WHITE & CASE LLP FOREIGN LEGAL CONSULTANT OFFICE

Sung-Min Cho
JOYANG LOGISTICS

Young-Dae Cho
KIM & CHANG

Jinhyuk Choi
BARUN LAW LLC

Kyung-Joon Choi
KIM, CHANGE & LEE

Paul Jihoon Choi
BARUN LAW LLC

Sung-Soo Choi
KIM & CHANG

Isabel Cleaver
HEALY CONSULTANTS GROUP PLC

Robert Flemer
KIM & CHANG

Mark Goodrich
WHITE & CASE LLP FOREIGN LEGAL CONSULTANT OFFICE

Jason Ha
BARUN LAW LLC

Sang-Goo Han
YOON & YANG LLC

Sang-Hoon Han
SHIN & KIM

Young Huh
HEALY CONSULTANTS GROUP PLC

Ji-Sang Hur
KOREA CUSTOMS SERVICE

C.W. Hyun
KIM & CHANG

James I.S. Jeon
SOJONG PARTNERS

Jae-Wook Jeong
SHIN & KIM

Changho Jo
SAMIL PRICEWATERHOUSECOOPERS

Bo Moon Jung
KIM & CHANG

Haeng Chang Jung
HANARO TNS

Hyukjun Jung
BARUN LAW LLC

Jinku Kang
LEE & KO

Kyung-won Kang
SAMIL PRICEWATERHOUSECOOPERS

Young-Seok Ki
SHIN & KIM

Byung-Tae Kim
SHIN & KIM

Chul Man Kim
YULCHON LLC

Jennifer Min Sun Kim
SOJONG PARTNERS

Jong-Hyun Kim
SHIN & KIM

Ki Young Kim
YULCHON LLC

Rieu Kim
BARUN LAW LLC

Sang-jin Kim
KEPCO

Seong Won (David) Kim
HANARO TNS

Sun Kyoung Kim
YULCHON LLC

Wonhyung Kim
YOON & YANG LLC

Yoon Young Kim
HWANG MOK PARK PC

Youn Jong Kim
SHINHAN CUSTOMS SERVICE INC.

Seong-Cheon Ko
SAMIL PRICEWATERHOUSECOOPERS

Joonghoon Kwak
LEE & KO

Alex Joong-Hyun Lee
SAMIL PRICEWATERHOUSECOOPERS

Dong Hun Lee
KOREA CUSTOMS SERVICE

Eugene Lee
BARUN LAW LLC

Hongyou Lee
PANALPINA KOREA LTD.

Jae-Hahn Lee
KIM, CHANGE & LEE

Kyu Wha Lee
LEE & KO

Kyung Yoon Lee
KIM & CHANG

Moonsub Lee
SOJONG PARTNERS

Sangmin Lee
KIM & CHANG

Seung Yoon Lee
KIM & CHANG

Su Yeon Lee
YULCHON LLC

Young Jin Lee
SUPREME COURT OF KOREA

Yong-Hee Lim
SAMIL PRICEWATERHOUSECOOPERS

Yunseok Lim
SUPREME COURT OF KOREA

Young Min Kim
YOON & YANG LLC

Jae Wook Oh
BARUN LAW LLC

Yon Kyun Oh
KIM & CHANG

Danbi Park
KIM & CHANG

Grace Park
KIM & CHANG

Jihye Park
LEE & KO

Sang Il Park
HWANG MOK PARK PC

Yong Seok Park
SHIN & KIM

Sang-ug Ryu
SUPREME COURT OF KOREA

Jeong Seo
KIM & CHANG

Minah Seo
HWANG MOK PARK PC

Ji Seon Kim
HWANG MOK PARK PC

Changho Seong
*SEOUL CENTRAL
DISTRICT COURT*

Mi-Jin Shin
KIM & CHANG

Philippe Shin
SHIN & KIM

Moon-Bae Sohn
KOREA CREDIT BUREAU

Ahn Sooyoung
HWANG MOK PARK PC

Kiwon Suh
*CHEONJI ACCOUNTING
CORPORATION*

Catherine J. Yeo
KIM & CHANG

Elizabeth Shinwon Yoon
*SHINHAN CUSTOMS
SERVICE INC.*

Jae-Yoon Yoon
KOREA CUSTOMS SERVICE

Huiwon Yun
*HUIWON YUN PRIVATE
PRACTITIONER*

KOSOVO

KPMG ALBANIA SHPK

*MINISTRY OF ECONOMIC
DEVELOPMENT (MED)*

*MINISTRY OF TRADE
AND INDUSTRY*

*USAID PARTNERSHIPS FOR
DEVELOPMENT PROJECT*

Leonora Beka
KALO & ASSOCIATES

Gani Bucaj
ENERGY REGULATORY OFFICE

Destan Bujupaj
*DESTAN BUJUPAJ
ENFORCEMENT AGENT*

Shyqiri Bytyqi
VALA CONSULTING

Ali Curri
KESCO

Naim Devetaku
VALA CONSULTING

Sokol Elmazaj
BOGA & ASSOCIATES

Mirjeta Emini
BOGA & ASSOCIATES

Yllka Emini
*TAX ADMINISTRATION
OF KOSOVO*

Haxhi Gashi
*UNIVERSITY OF PRISHTINA,
LAW FACULTY*

Adea Geci
AB OLIVIER & ASSOCIATES LLC

Lorena Gega
*PRICEWATERHOUSECOOPERS
AUDIT SH.P.K.*

Jashar Goga
KOSOVO CUSTOMS

Valon Hasani
LAWYER

Bujar Haxhidauti
KOSOVO CUSTOMS

Rudina Heroi-Puka
KESCO

Naim Huruglica
KOSOVO CUSTOMS

Rifat Hyseni
*TAX ADMINISTRATION
OF KOSOVO*

Albert Islami
ALBERT ISLAMI & PARTNERS

Liresa Kadriu
VALA CONSULTING

Arben Kelmendi
KELMENDI & PARTNERS LLC

Leonik Mehmeti
DELOITTE

Fitore Mekaj
BOGA & ASSOCIATES

Delvina Nallbani
BOGA & ASSOCIATES

Driton Nikaj
*RAIFFEISEN LEASING
KOSOVA SH.P.K.*

Besim Osmani
AB OLIVIER & ASSOCIATES LLC

Besim Osmani
INTERLEX ASSOCIATES LLC

Valdet Osmani
*ARCHITECT ASSOCIATION
OF KOSOVO*

Loreta Peci
*PRICEWATERHOUSECOOPERS
AUDIT SH.P.K.*

Naser Prapashtica
CRIMSON CAPITAL

Blerim Prestreshi
SCLR PARTNERS

Ilaz Ramajli
RAMAJLI & PARTNERS CO.

Vigan Rogova
ETHEM ROGOVA LAW FIRM

Ariana Rozhaja
VALA CONSULTING

Shendrit Sadiku
*PRICEWATERHOUSECOOPERS
KOSOVO*

Sami Salihu
*TAX ADMINISTRATION
OF KOSOVO*

Arbena Shehu
*NOTARY CHAMBER OF THE
REPUBLIC OF KOSOVO*

Teki Shehu

Ardi Shita

Fatmir Stublla

Arbresha Tuhina
BAKER TILLY KOSOVO

Gëzim Xharavina
*ARCHITECTURAL, DESIGN
AND ENGINEERING*

Arta Xhema
BAKER TILLY KOSOVO

Lulzim Zeka
BAKER TILLY KOSOVO

Petrit Zeka
BAKER TILLY KOSOVO

Shpend Zeka
*PRICEWATERHOUSECOOPERS
KOSOVO*

Ruzhdi Zenelaj
DELOITTE

Ruzhdi Zeqiri
CRIMSON CAPITAL

Shaha Zylfiu
*CENTRAL BANK OF THE
REPUBLIC OF KOSOVO*

KUWAIT

*TALAL ABU-GHAZALEH
LEGAL (TAG-LEGAL)*

Maged Abd Al Hady
*HORWATH AL-MUHANNA
& CO.*

Mohammad Abdal
ZAIN GROUP

Nader Abdelaziz
*ASAR – AL RUWAYEH
& PARTNERS*

Sherif Shawki Abdel-Fattah
*PRICEWATERHOUSECOOPERS
AL-SHATTI & CO.*

Farid Abdin
MAERSK KUWAIT CO. W.L.L.

Ahmed Abdou
*ASAR – AL RUWAYEH
& PARTNERS*

Abdulrazzaq Abdullah
*ABDULRAZZAQ ABDULLAH
& PARTNERS LAW FIRM*

Hossam Abdullah
AL-HOSSAM LEGAL

Hani Abu Daqa
*CREDIT INFORMATION
NETWORK*

Mohammad Abulwafa
*ASAR – AL RUWAYEH
& PARTNERS*

Lina A.K. Adlouni
*ADLOUNI & PARTNERS
LEGAL CONSULTANTS &
ATTORNEYS LAW FIRM*

Hossam Afify
*PRICEWATERHOUSECOOPERS
AL-SHATTI & CO.*

Basma Akbar
*CAPITAL MARKET
AUTHORITY OF KUWAIT*

Khaldah Al Ali
MINISTRY OF FINANCE

Hanan Al Gharabally
*CAPITAL MARKET
AUTHORITY OF KUWAIT*

Jasim Mohammad Al Habib
KUWAIT MUNICIPALITY

Hamad M. Al Mashaan
*AL-AHLIA CONTRACTING
GROUP*

Heyam Al Mehri
MINISTRY OF JUSTICE

Meshari Al Nusf
KUWAIT INSURANCE COMPANY

Hashem Al Qallaf
*KUWAIT CITY FIRST
INSTANCE COURT*

Rezq Al Sammak
KUWAIT INSURANCE COMPANY

Nouf Al Sanea
*CAPITAL MARKET
AUTHORITY OF KUWAIT*

Ahmed Abdul Aziz Al
Thuwaikh
*KUWAIT CITY FIRST
INSTANCE COURT*

Fahad Al Zumai
KUWAIT UNIVERSITY

Ayyad Al-Adwani
AL-ADWANI LAW FIRM

Aiman Alaraj
*KEO INTERNATIONAL
CONSULTANTS*

Waleed Al-Awadhi
CENTRAL BANK OF KUWAIT

Abdullah Al-Ayoub
*ABDULLAH KH. AL-AYOUB
& ASSOCIATES, MEMBER
OF LEX MUNDI*

Abrar Alazemi
MINISTRY OF FINANCE

Anwar Al-Bisher
ALBISHER LEGAL GROUP

Ahmed Aldhoayan
ALRAAI LAW FIRM

Areej Aldulaimi
MINISTRY OF JUSTICE

Omar Hamad Yousuf Al-Essa
*THE LAW OFFICE OF
AL-ESSA & PARTNERS*

Lulwha Alfahad
MINISTRY OF FINANCE

Nada F.A. Al-Fahad
*GEC DAR GULF ENGINEERS
CONSULTANTS*

Adaweyah Alfailakawi
*MINISTRY OF COMMERCE
AND INDUSTRY*

Rawan M. Al-Ghazali
*THE LAW OFFICES OF MISHARI
AL-GHAZALI AND RAWAN
MISHARI AL-GHAZALI*

Nora Al-Haroun
*CAPITAL MARKET
AUTHORITY OF KUWAIT*

Shaikhah Alhelali

Hanan Almudhahkah
MINISTRY OF FINANCE

Rasha Al-Naibari
*CAPITAL MARKET
AUTHORITY OF KUWAIT*

Jasem Al-Oun
AREF INVESTMENT GROUP

Waleed Alowaiyesh
*CAPITAL MARKET
AUTHORITY OF KUWAIT*

Yousef Alroumi
*CAPITAL MARKET
AUTHORITY OF KUWAIT*

Jasem Alsharekh
ALRAAI LAW FIRM

Adnan Alsharrah
*CREDIT INFORMATION
NETWORK*

Tariq Hamad Alshatti
AL-DOSTOUR LAW FIRM

Fahed Al-Subaih
*CAPITAL MARKET
AUTHORITY OF KUWAIT*

Haya Alzayed
MINISTRY OF JUSTICE

Najed Abdul Aziz
*ABDULRAHMAN MOHAMAD
AL-BAHAR AND SONS WLL*

Akusa Batwala
*ASAR – AL RUWAYEH
& PARTNERS*

Lutfi Ben Fatma
AL-TWAIJRI & PARTNERS

Waleed BenHassan
*CREDIT INFORMATION
NETWORK*

Piyush Bhandari
*INTUIT MANAGEMENT
CONSULTANCY*

Priyanka Bhandari
*INTUIT MANAGEMENT
CONSULTANCY*

Nada Bourahmah
*THE LAW OFFICES OF MISHARI
AL-GHAZALI AND RAWAN
MISHARI AL-GHAZALI*

Najmah Brown
AL-ADWANI LAW FIRM

Maysaa Mousa Bushihri
KUWAIT MUNICIPALITY

Twinkle Anie Chacko
*ABDULRAZZAQ ABDULLAH
& PARTNERS LAW FIRM*

Alok Chugh
EY

Bader Ali Dashti
*CUSTOMS - GENERAL
ADMINISTRATION*

Fouad Douglas
*PRICEWATERHOUSECOOPERS
AL-SHATTI & CO.*

Talal Edan
*CUSTOMS - GENERAL
ADMINISTRATION*

Haya Essa Al Zayed
MINISTRY OF JUSTICE

Mahmoud Ezzat
*CAPITAL MARKET
AUTHORITY OF KUWAIT*

Jomon George
*HORWATH AL-MUHANNA
& CO.*

Michel Ghanem
MEYSAN PARTNERS

Marc-Aurele Grassin
MEYSAN PARTNERS

Sam Habbas
*ASAR – AL RUWAYEH
& PARTNERS*

Mohammed Haneefa
MAERSK KUWAIT CO. W.L.L.

Hussein M. Hassan
*ABDULLAH KH. AL-AYOUB
& ASSOCIATES, MEMBER
OF LEX MUNDI*

Samir Ibrahim
ALRAAI LAW FIRM

Jad Jabre
*ASAR – AL RUWAYEH
& PARTNERS*

Wael S. Khalifa
*GLOBAL CLEARINGHOUSE
SYSTEMS*

Mazen A. Khoursheed
*PACKAGING & PLASTIC
INDUSTRIES CO. KSCC*

Dany Labaky
*THE LAW OFFICE OF
AL-ESSA & PARTNERS*

Ahmed Labib
*ASAR – AL RUWAYEH
& PARTNERS*

Anju Menon
*ABDULLAH KH. AL-AYOUB
& ASSOCIATES, MEMBER
OF LEX MUNDI*

Abdulrahman Mohamad
*CAPITAL MARKET
AUTHORITY OF KUWAIT*

Ayman Nada
AL MARKAZ LAW FIRM

Seth Ochieng
*HEALY CONSULTANTS
GROUP PLC*

Rabea Saad Al-Muhanna
*HORWATH AL-MUHANNA
& CO.*

Mohammed Radwan
ALRAAI LAW FIRM

Johnson Rajan
INTUIT MANAGEMENT
CONSULTANCY

Ganesh Ramanath
PRICEWATERHOUSECOOPERS
AL-SHATTI & CO.

Abdulwahab Abdullatif Sadeq
MEYSAN PARTNERS

Aya Salih
AL-ADWANI LAW FIRM

Ibrahim Sattout
ASAR – AL RUWAYEH
& PARTNERS

Afrah Shabeeb
THE LAW OFFICES OF MISHARI
AL-GHAZALI AND RAWAN
MISHARI AL-GHAZALI

Chetan Sharma
ABDULLAH KH. AL-AYOUB
& ASSOCIATES, MEMBER
OF LEX MUNDI

Emad Tawfiq

David Walker
ASAR – AL RUWAYEH
& PARTNERS

Abdullah Y. Al Khurafi
MIRAS LEGAL

Ahmed Zakaria
BOUBYAN CAPITAL
INVESTMENT

KYRGYZ REPUBLIC

Almaz Abdiev
DEPARTMENT OF CADASTRE
AND REGISTRATION OF RIGHTS
ON IMMOVABLE PROPERTY

Yulia Abdumanapova
BAKER TILLY BISHKEK LLC

Gulnara Akhmatova
LAWYER

Atabek Akhmedov
GRATA INTERNATIONAL

Sanzhar Aldashev
GRATA INTERNATIONAL

Bayansulu Bassepova
PWC KAZAKHSTAN

Kerim Begaliev
CENTIL LAW FIRM

Elena Bit-Avragim
VERITAS LAW AGENCY

Samara Dumanaeva
KOAN LORENZ

Nurlan Dzhusumaliev
MINISTRY OF ECONOMY

Bakytbek Dzhusupbekov
DEPARTMENT OF CADASTRE
AND REGISTRATION OF RIGHTS
ON IMMOVABLE PROPERTY

Victor Efremov
VERITAS LAW AGENCY

Akjoltoi Elebesova
CREDIT INFORMATION
BUREAU ISHENIM

Chynara Esengeldieva
KOAN LORENZ

Kymbat Ibakova
KOAN LORENZ

Indira Ibraimova
MEGA STROY LLC

Aidaraliev Erkin Isagalievich
ALTERNATIVA GARANT
LAW FIRM

Saara Kabaeva
KOAN LORENZ

Merim Kachkynbaeva
KALIKOVA & ASSOCIATES
LAW FIRM

Elena Kaeva
PWC KAZAKHSTAN

Amanbek Kebekov
DEPARTMENT OF CADASTRE
AND REGISTRATION OF RIGHTS
ON IMMOVABLE PROPERTY

Sultan Khalilov
KALIKOVA & ASSOCIATES
LAW FIRM

Evgeny Kim
KOAN LORENZ

Nurdin Kumushbekov
USAID BEI BUSINESS
ENVIRONMENT IMPROVEMENT
PROJECT (BY PRAGMA
CORPORATION)

Kuttubai Marzabaev
ORION CONSTRUCTION
COMPANY

Chinara Moldobaeva

Umtul Muratkyzy
KOAN LORENZ

Mariya Nazarova
PWC KAZAKHSTAN

Karlygash Ospankulova
IGROUP, PUBLIC ASSOCIATION

Elena Petrova
JSC BISHKEKKYRYLUSH

Nargiz Sabyrova
VERITAS LAW AGENCY

Aisanat Safarbek Kyzy
GRATA INTERNATIONAL

Emil Saryazhiev
CREDIT INFORMATION
BUREAU ISHENIM

Erkin Saryazhiev
KOMPANION BANK CJSC

Kanat Seidaliev
GRATA INTERNATIONAL

Saodat Shakirova
ARTE LAW FIRM

Tatyana Shapovalova

Aidin Omuralievich Sharsheev
CENTRAL COLLATERAL
REGISTRATION OFFICE UNDER
MINISTRY OF JUSTICE

Anvar Suleimanov
PWC KAZAKHSTAN

Guljan Tashimova
ORION CONSTRUCTION
COMPANY

Nurlan Sadykovich Temiraliev
MINISTRY OF JUSTICE

Jibek Tenizbaeva
KOAN LORENZ

Idaiat Toktash
LAW FIRM LEX

Asel Tursuniiazova
KUMAREL NURAMIR LLC

Gulnara Uskenbaeva
AUDIT PLUS

Gulnara Uskenbaeva
SUPPLIER ASSOCIATION -
COMMITTEE MEMBER OF CCI

Mansur Usmanov
MEGA STROY LLC

LAO PDR

Chonchanok Akarakitkasem
LS HORIZON LIMITED (LAO)

Anthony Assassa
VDB LOI

Phetmany Boualivong
ELECTRICITE DU LAOS

Thatsnachone Bounthanh
XANGLAO ENGINEERING
CONSULTANTS

Siri Boutdakham
LAO LAW &
CONSULTANCY GROUP

Khammuan Bouxatry
ZICOLAW (LAOS)
SOLE CO. LTD.

Xaynari Chanthala
LS HORIZON LIMITED (LAO)

Chatchai Chanyuttasart
HUNG HUANG (LAO)
LOGISTICS CO. LTD.

Nawika Charoenkitchatorn
LAO PREMIER INTERNATIONAL
LAW OFFICE

Sirikarn Chattrastrai
LAO PREMIER INTERNATIONAL
LAW OFFICE

Rawat Chomsri
LAO PREMIER INTERNATIONAL
LAW OFFICE

Agnès Couriol
DFDL

Bounyong Dalasone
LAO PREMIER INTERNATIONAL
LAW OFFICE

Bounyasith Daopasith
LAO PREMIER INTERNATIONAL
LAW OFFICE

Aristotle David
ZICOLAW (LAOS)
SOLE CO. LTD.

Simeuang Douangbouddy
XANGLAO ENGINEERING
CONSULTANTS

Somlith Duangchanpasert
VDB LOI

Daodeuane Duangdara
VDB LOI

Steve Goddard
ARION LEGAL

Petlumpanh Inthajuck
ELECTRICITE DU LAOS

Bounlay Kangmanivanh
VDB LOI

Valyna Keochomsi
LS HORIZON LIMITED (LAO)

Dokkeo Keovongsa
BANK OF LAO PDR

Phetlamphone Khanophet
BANK OF LAO PDR

Sisomephieng Khanthalivanh
BANK OF LAO PDR

Kan Khuprasert
LAO PREMIER INTERNATIONAL
LAW OFFICE

Ganesan Kolandevelu
KPMG LAO CO. LTD.

Natchar Leedae
LAO PREMIER INTERNATIONAL
LAW OFFICE

Anna Linden
SCIARONI & ASSOCIATES

Ha Manh Nguyen
EY

Christian Metzger

Vongsa Nanthavong
ELECTRICITE DU LAOS

Tuan Nhu Nguyen
EY

Souvanno S. Phabmixay
SV LEGAL ADVOCATE
(LAO) CO. LTD.

Viengsavanh Phanthaly
ZICOLAW (LAOS)
SOLE CO. LTD.

Nampanya Phayboun
ZICOLAW (LAOS)
SOLE CO. LTD.

Komonchanh Phet-asa
ELECTRICITE DU LAOS

Vassana Phetlamphanh
ELECTRICITE DU LAOS

Sengny Phimmany
SCIARONI & ASSOCIATES

Khamphaeng Phochanthilath
ZICOLAW (LAOS)
SOLE CO. LTD.

Ketsana Phommachanh
MINISTRY OF JUSTICE

Chansamone Phommachanto
T.E.C. LOGISTICS

Viengsamone Phommavongsa
BANK OF LAO PDR

Phonexay Southiphong
DESIGN GROUP CO. LTD.

Latsamy Sysamouth
MINISTRY OF JUSTICE

Danyel Thomson
DFDL

Arpon Tunjumras
LAO PREMIER INTERNATIONAL
LAW OFFICE

Huong Vu
EY

Patthana Xaykosy
LAO PREMIER INTERNATIONAL
LAW OFFICE

Monmany Yaganagi
LAO INTERCONSULT CO. LTD.

LATVIA

COLLIERS INTERNATIONAL

Raivis Bušmanis
STATE LABOUR INSPECTORATE

Andis Čonka
LATVIJAS BANKA

Ainis Dabols
LATVIAN ASSOCIATION
OF TAX ADVISERS

Andris Dimants
COBALT LEGAL

Anete Dimitrovska
ELLEX KLAVINS, MEMBER
OF LEX MUNDI

Valters Diure
ELLEX KLAVINS, MEMBER
OF LEX MUNDI

Edvīns Draba
LAW FIRM SORAINEN
& PARTNERS

Jānis Dreimanis
COURT ADMINISTRATION

Zlata Elksniņa-Zaščirinska
PWC LATVIA

Kalvis Engīzers
COBALT LEGAL

Kaspars Freimanis
PRIMUS ATTORNEYS-AT-LAW

Kristīne Gailīte
COBALT LEGAL

Janis Gavars
ELLEX KLAVINS, MEMBER
OF LEX MUNDI

Andris Ignatenko
ESTMA LTD.

Viesturs Kadiķis
PUBLIC UTILITIES COMMISSION

Valters Kalme
PUBLIC UTILITIES COMMISSION

Snezhina Kazakova
DHL EXPRESS LATVIA

Irina Kostina
ELLEX KLAVINS, MEMBER
OF LEX MUNDI

Dainis Leons
SADALES TIKLS AS

Indriķis Liepa
COBALT LEGAL

Dainis Locs
COURT ADMINISTRATION

Rolands Lūsveris
SADALES TIKLS AS

Zane Markvarte
MARKVARTE LEXCHANGE
LAW OFFICE

Ivo Maskalans
COBALT LEGAL

Baiba Orbidane
ELLEX KLAVINS, MEMBER
OF LEX MUNDI

Guna Paidere
REGISTER OF ENTERPRISES

Ilze Rauza
PWC LATVIA

Lelde Rozentale
STATE LAND SERVICE OF
THE REPUBLIC OF LATVIA

Elina Rozulapa
ER3

Andris Škutāns
AB WAYS

Sandra Stipniece
CHAMBER OF SWORN
NOTARIES OF LATVIA

Darja Tagajeva
PWC LATVIA

Ruta Teresko
AZ SERVICE LTD.

Jānis Timermanis
AS KREDĪTINFORMĀCIJAS
BIROJS

Edgars Timpa
STATE LABOUR INSPECTORATE

Ingus Užulis
PUBLIC UTILITIES COMMISSION

Maris Vainovskis
EVERSHEDS BITĀNS

Elina Vilde
EVERSHEDS BITĀNS

Sabine Vilka
COBALT LEGAL

Armands Viskers
BALTIC LEGAL

Krista Zariņa
ELLEX KLAVINS, MEMBER
OF LEX MUNDI

Agate Ziverte
PWC LATVIA

Daiga Zivtina
ELLEX KLAVINS, MEMBER
OF LEX MUNDI

Vadims Zvicevics
COBALT LEGAL

LEBANON

Nadim Abboud
*LAW OFFICE OF A.
ABBOUD & ASSOCIATES*

Nina Abdallah
KHATTAR ASSOCIATES

Nada Abdelsater-Abusamra
*ABDELSATER ABUSAMRA &
ASSOCIATES - ASAS LAW*

Marie Abi Antoun
*ABDELSATER ABUSAMRA &
ASSOCIATES - ASAS LAW*

Nancy Abou Ghaida
MENA CITY LAWYERS

Riham Al Ali
SMAYRA LAW OFFICE

Zeina Azzi
OBEID & MEDAWAR LAW FIRM

Corinne Baaklini
MENA CITY LAWYERS

Jean Baroudi
BAROUDI & ASSOCIATES

Boutros Bou Lattouf
EBL BUREAU IN BEIRUT

Tony Boutros
*RUSSELL BEDFORD
INTERNATIONAL*

Najib Choucair
CENTRAL BANK OF LEBANON

Alice Choueiri
MENA CITY LAWYERS

Hadi Diab
SMAYRA LAW OFFICE

Mario El Cheikh
AGC SAL

Richard El Mouallem
PWC LEBANON

Nada Elsayed
PWC LEBANON

Hadi Fathallah
ESCO FATHALLAH & CO.

Izzat Fathallah
ESCO FATHALLAH & CO.

Wafic Fathallah
ESCO FATHALLAH & CO.

Ribal Fattal
*LAW OFFICE OF A.
ABBOUD & ASSOCIATES*

Elie Feghali
*BADRI AND SALIM EL
MEOUCHI LAW FIRM,
MEMBER OF INTERLEGES*

Lea Ferzli
BAROUDI & ASSOCIATES

Serena Ghanimeh
*ABDELSATER ABUSAMRA &
ASSOCIATES - ASAS LAW*

Ghassan Haddad
*BADRI AND SALIM EL
MEOUCHI LAW FIRM,
MEMBER OF INTERLEGES*

Rawad Halawi

Rayan Hdayfe
EMEA LEGAL COUNSELS

Walid Honein
*BADRI AND SALIM EL
MEOUCHI LAW FIRM,
MEMBER OF INTERLEGES*

Chawkat Houalla
ADIB & HOUALLA LAW OFFICE

Fady Jamaleddine
MENA CITY LAWYERS

Mohammad Joumaa
PWC LEBANON

Georges Jureidini
*COSERV SARL -
PANALPINA AGENTS*

Elie Kachouh
ELC TRANSPORT SERVICES SAL

Georges Kadige
KADIGE & KADIGE LAW FIRM

Michel Kadige
KADIGE & KADIGE LAW FIRM

Raydan Kakoun
*BADRI AND SALIM EL
MEOUCHI LAW FIRM,
MEMBER OF INTERLEGES*

Tatiana Kehdy
BAROUDI & ASSOCIATES

Najib Khattar
KHATTAR ASSOCIATES

Abdo Maatouk
SMAYRA LAW OFFICE

Georges Mallat
HYAM G. MALLAT LAW FIRM

Nabil Mallat
HYAM G. MALLAT LAW FIRM

Aline Matta
*TALAL ABU-GHAZALEH
LEGAL (TAG-LEGAL)*

Rachad Medawar
OBEID & MEDAWAR LAW FIRM

Mirvat Moustapha
MENA CITY LAWYERS

Andre Nader
NADER LAW OFFICE

Rana Nader
NADER LAW OFFICE

Toufic Nehme
*LAW OFFICES OF
TOUFIC NEHME*

Rana Osman
MENA CITY LAWYERS

Nehman Rhayem
ELECTRICITÉ DU LIBAN

Mireille Richa
TYAN & ZGHEIB LAW FIRM

Jihan Rizk
KHATTAR ASSOCIATES

Jihad Rizkallah
*BADRI AND SALIM EL
MEOUCHI LAW FIRM,
MEMBER OF INTERLEGES*

Yara Romanos
*BADRI AND SALIM EL
MEOUCHI LAW FIRM,
MEMBER OF INTERLEGES*

Mustafa Saadeh
TYAN & ZGHEIB LAW FIRM

Christelle Sakr
TYAN & ZGHEIB LAW FIRM

Nisrine Mary Salhab
HYAM G. MALLAT LAW FIRM

Rached Sarkis
CONSULTANT

Mona Sfeir
HYAM G. MALLAT LAW FIRM

Rami Smayra
SMAYRA LAW OFFICE

Nady Tyan
TYAN & ZGHEIB LAW FIRM

Alaa Zeineddine
EMEA LEGAL COUNSELS

LESOTHO

ARCHIPLAN STUDIO

BIDVEST PANALPINA LOGISTICS

*KHATLELI TOMANE MOTEANE
(KTM) ARCHITECTS*

MASERU MUNICIPAL COUNCIL

Emile du Toit
EY

Motselisi Khiba
HARLEY & MORRIS

Mannete Khotle
COMPUSCAN LESOTHO

Makali Lepholisa
LESOTHO REVENUE AUTHORITY

Qhalehang Letsika
MEI & MEI ATTORNEYS INC.

Mateboho Litlhakanyane
QUANTUM CONSULTANTS

Monica Louro
WEBBER NEWDIGATE

Veronica Matiea
HIGH COURT

John Mclean
COMPUSCAN LESOTHO

Renate Mholo
EY

Denis Molyneaux
WEBBER NEWDIGATE

Tseliso Monaphathi
HIGH COURT

Ntlatlapa Mosae
SELLO-MAFATLE ATTORNEYS

Molupe Mothepu
LESOTHO REVENUE AUTHORITY

Daan Roberts
WEBBER NEWDIGATE

Duduzile Seamatha
PWC

Tiisetso Sello-Mafatle
SELLO-MAFATLE ATTORNEYS

Lindiwe Sephomolo
*ASSOCIATION OF LESOTHO
EMPLOYERS AND BUSINESS*

Starford Sharite
HIGH COURT

Hennie Smit
PWC SOUTH AFRICA

Mooresi Tau Thabane

Marorisang Thekiso
PWC

Phoka Thene
LETŠENG DIAMONDS

Mark Frederick Webber
HARLEY & MORRIS

Dieter Winkler
COMPUSCAN LESOTHO

LIBERIA

Arthur Abdulai
EXPRESS HANDLING SERVICES

Kofi Abedu-Bentsi
BAKER TILLY LIBERIA

Adebayo M. Adeyemi
*TSC ENGINEERING
AND CONSTRUCTION
CONSULTANTS, INC.*

Rajesh Angepat
BOLLORÉ AFRICA LOGISTICS

Patrick Bono
FRONTIER LOGISTICS INC

Henry N. Brunson
FEDEX

William Buku
LIBERIA REVENUE AUTHORITY

F. Augustus Caesar Jr.
CAESAR ARCHITECTS, INC.

Eva-Mae Campbell
CAESAR ARCHITECTS, INC.

Preston Chea Doe
THELMA LAW & ASSOCIATES

Clarence Cooper
FRONTIER LOGISTICS INC

Henry Reed Cooper
*COOPER & TOGBAH
LAW OFFICE*

John Davis
*LIBERIA BANK FOR
DEVELOPMENT AND
INVESTMENT*

Morris Davis
KEMP & ASSOCIATES

Frank Musah Dean
DEAN & ASSOCIATES

Samuel Dennis Jr.
SEB ELECTRICAL TEAM

Moses Dolo
*LIBERIA ELECTRICITY
CORPORATION*

Fonsia Donzo
CENTRAL BANK OF LIBERIA

Folbay Edwin
FRONTIER LOGISTICS INC

Emmanuel Enders
SEB ELECTRICAL TEAM

Francis Folleh
*BRO'S ELECTRIC
AND CONSTRUCTION
ASSOCIATES (BECCA)*

George Fonderson
BAKER TILLY LIBERIA

Christine Sonpon Freeman
*COOPER & TOGBAH
LAW OFFICE*

Arthur W.B. Fumbah
BAKER TILLY LIBERIA

Lucia Gbala
*HERITAGE PARTNER &
ASSOCIATES, INC.*

Deweh Gray
*FEMALE LAWYERS
ASSOCIATION OF LIBERIA*

Ernest Hughes
*LIBERIA ELECTRICITY
CORPORATION*

Ruth Jappah
*JSGB & ASSOCIATES
LEGAL CONSULTANTS*

Cyril Jones
JONES & JONES

Abu Kamara
LIBERIA BUSINESS REGISTRY

Momolu G. Kanda Kai
*CONGLOE AND
ASSOCIATES INC.*

Sophie Kayemba Mutebi
PWC

Boakai Kollie
*ALLIANCE CONSULTING
ENGINEERS, PLANNERS
& SURVEYORS INC.*

Jonah Soe Kotee
*ASSOCIATION OF LIBERIAN
HUMAN RESOURCE
PROFESSIONALS (ALHRP)*

Kwaiwo Kotee
*ASSOCIATION OF LIBERIAN
HUMAN RESOURCE
PROFESSIONALS (ALHRP)*

Cooper Kruah
HENRIES LAW FIRM

Bob Weetol Livingstone
*UNITED METHODIST
UNIVERSITY*

Jura Lynch
ATTORNEY-AT-LAW

Nim'ne E. Mombo
PKF INTERNATIONAL

Brenda Brewer Moore
*ASSOCIATION OF LIBERIAN
HUMAN RESOURCE
PROFESSIONALS (ALHRP)*

Klade Neufville
*ASSOCIATION OF LIBERIAN
HUMAN RESOURCE
PROFESSIONALS (ALHRP)*

Ndubuisi Nwabudike
SANNOH & PARTNERS

James Nyenpan
LEGAL WATCH

Bill Nyumah
*BRO'S ELECTRIC
AND CONSTRUCTION
ASSOCIATES (BECCA)*

Manzuer A. Raji
AFSAT CORPORATION

Arabella Reed
PWC

Sylvester Rennie
LEGAL WATCH

Boye A. Robertson
*MONROVIA CITY
CORPORATIONS (MCC)*

Philomena Bloh Sayeh
*CENTER FOR NATIONAL
DOCUMENTS & RECORDS
(NATIONAL ARCHIVES)*

Ocelia Scott
CENTRAL BANK OF LIBERIA

Yancy Seeboe
*NATIONAL CUSTOM BROKERS
ASSOCIATION OF LIBERIA*

Steven D. Seimavula
PKF INTERNATIONAL

Roland D. Siaka
*WEST CONSTRUCTION
LIBERIA, INC.*

Albert S. Sims
SHERMAN & SHERMAN

Robert Smallwood
PWC

Victor B. Smith
*ALLIANCE CONSULTING
ENGINEERS, PLANNERS
& SURVEYORS INC.*

Christoper C. Swen
*BEST BRAINS TECHNOLOGY
LIBERIA LTD. (BBTELL)*

Darlington Y. Talery
LIBERIA REVENUE AUTHORITY

Ambrose Taplah
KEMP & ASSOCIATES

Justin Tengbeh
*NATIONAL CUSTOM BROKERS
ASSOCIATION OF LIBERIA*

Benjamin M. Togbah
*COOPER & TOGBAH
LAW OFFICE*

Nyenati Tuan
TUAN WREH LAW FIRM

J. Awia Vankan
*HERITAGE PARTNER &
ASSOCIATES, INC.*

T. Negbalee Warner
*HERITAGE PARTNER &
ASSOCIATES, INC.*

LIBYA

ALTERAZ ENGINEERING
CONSULTANTS

GOLDEN PLANNER
ARCHITECTURE AND
ENGINEERING

ZAHAF & PARTNERS LAW FIRM

Ahmed Abdulaziz
MUKHTAR, KELBASH
& ELGHARABLI

Abdallah B. Al Hasse
CONSULTANCY HOUSE

Abdudayem Elgharabli
MUKHTAR, KELBASH
& ELGHARABLI

Abdul Salam El-Marghani
PWC

Husam Elnaili
PWC

Mahmoud ELSheikh
UNIVERSITY OF TRIPOLI

Ahmed Ghattour
AHMED GHATTOUR & CO.

Paolo Greco
P&A LEGAL

Jalal Hamad
CONSULTANCY HOUSE

Hassan Hassaan
DLA MATOUK BASSIOUNY
(PART OF DLA PIPER GROUP)

Bahloul Kelbash
MUKHTAR, KELBASH
& ELGHARABLI

Belkasem Magid Obadi
GENERAL ELECTRICITY
COMPANY OF LIBYA (GECOL)

Ibrahim Maher
DLA MATOUK BASSIOUNY
(PART OF DLA PIPER GROUP)

Mahmud Mukhtar
MUKHTAR, KELBASH
& ELGHARABLI

Ali Naser
LIBYAN CREDIT
INFORMATION CENTER

Abuejila Saif Annaser
SAIF ANNASER LAW OFFICE

Muftah Saif Annaser
SAIF ANNASER LAW OFFICE

Abdulkarim Tayeb
LiBYAN CREDIT
INFORMATION CENTER

Mazen Tumi
TUMI LAW FIRM

LITHUANIA

Loreta Andziulyte
ECOVIS PROVENTUSLAW
LAW FIRM

Artūras Asakavičius
LAW FIRM SORAINEN
& PARTNERS

Andrea August
AGENCY FOR INVESTMENTS
AND COMPETITIVENESS

Pavel Balbatunov

Lina Balbatunova

Rimgailė Baliūnaitė
NATIONAL COMMISSION FOR
ENERGY CONTROL AND PRICES

Petras Baltusevičius
DSV TRANSPORT UAB

Jomilė Baranauskaitė
VALIUNAS ELLEX

Donatas Baranauskas
VILNIAUS MIESTO 14 - ASIS
NOTARU BIURAS

Kornelija Basijokiene
GLIMSTEDT

Vilius Bernatonis
TARK GRUNTE SUTKIENE

Andrius Bogdanovičius
JSC CREDITINFO LIETUVA

Ausra Brazauskiene
LAW FIRM ELLEX VALIUNAS
IR PARTNERIAI, MEMBER
OF LEX MUNDI

Alina Burlakova
LAW FIRM ELLEX VALIUNAS
IR PARTNERIAI, MEMBER
OF LEX MUNDI

Daiva Čekanavičienė
GLIMSTEDT

Robertas Čiočys
LAW FIRM ELLEX VALIUNAS
IR PARTNERIAI, MEMBER
OF LEX MUNDI

Justas Ciomanas
LITHUANIAN CHAMBER
OF NOTARIES

Giedre Dailidenaite
PRIMUS ATTORNEYS-AT-LAW

Ignas Dargužas
LAW FIRM SORAINEN
& PARTNERS

Aurelija Daubaraitė
LAW FIRM SORAINEN
& PARTNERS

Asta Daudaitė
MINISTRY OF ECONOMY

Gintaras Daugela
BANK OF LITHUANIA

Giedre Domkute
AAA LAW

Artur Drapeko
LAW FIRM SORAINEN
& PARTNERS

Dalia Foigt
COBALT LEGAL

Reda Gabrilavičiūtė
MINISTRY OF JUSTICE

Aida Ganusauskaitė
LAW FIRM ELLEX VALIUNAS
IR PARTNERIAI, MEMBER
OF LEX MUNDI

Karolina Gasparke
BNT ATTORNEYS-AT-LAW

Yvonne Goldammer
BNT ATTORNEYS-AT-LAW

Živilė Golubevė
NATIONAL COMMISSION FOR
ENERGY CONTROL AND PRICES

Joana Gramakovaitė
PWC LITHUANIA

Dovile Greblikiene
VALIUNAS ELLEX

Kostas Grigaitis
AAA LAW

Skomantas Grigas
D. ZABIELA, M. RINDINAS AND
S. GRIGAS LAW FIRM ZRG

Arturas Gutauskas
PRIMUS ATTORNEYS-AT-LAW

Frank Heemann
BNT ATTORNEYS-AT-LAW

Rokas Jankus
MOTIEKA & AUDZEVIČIUS

Ieva Kairytė
PWC LITHUANIA

Inga Karulaityte-Kvainauskiene
ECOVIS PROVENTUSLAW
LAW FIRM

Romualdas Kasperavičius
STATE ENTERPRISE
CENTRE OF REGISTERS

Milda Kaupelienė
MINISTRY OF ECONOMY

Jonas Kiauleikis
LAW FIRM SORAINEN
& PARTNERS

Laura Kirilevičiūtė
MINISTRY OF ECONOMY

Agnė Kisieliauskaitė
VALIUNAS ELLEX

Augustas Klezys
LAW FIRM SORAINEN
& PARTNERS

Tomas Kontautas
LAW FIRM SORAINEN
& PARTNERS

Dalius Kontrimavičius
NATIONAL COMMISSION FOR
ENERGY CONTROL AND PRICES

Ieva Krivickaitė
LAW FIRM SORAINEN
& PARTNERS

Gediminas Kuncevicius
INTERMODAL
CONTAINER SERVICE

Egidijus Kundelis
PWC LITHUANIA

Lauras Lukosius
BALTIC FREIGHT SERVICES

Odeta Maksvytytė
PRIMUS ATTORNEYS-AT-LAW

Linas Margevicius
LEGAL BUREAU OF
LINAS MARGEVICIUS

Vilius Martišius
METIDA LAW FIRM
ZABOLIENE AND PARTNERS

Laura Matukaityte
LAW FIRM SORAINEN
& PARTNERS

Jolita Meškelytė
MINISTRY OF JUSTICE

Tautginas Mickevicius
MINISTRY OF JUSTICE

Bronislovas Mikūta
STATE ENTERPRISE
CENTRE OF REGISTERS

Donata Montvydaitė
LAW FIRM ELLEX VALIUNAS
IR PARTNERIAI, MEMBER
OF LEX MUNDI

Nerijus Nedzinskas
PWC LITHUANIA

Michail Parchimovič
MOTIEKA & AUDZEVIČIUS

Algirdas Pekšys
LAW FIRM SORAINEN
& PARTNERS

Šarūnė Prankonytė
PRIMUS ATTORNEYS-AT-LAW

Justina Rakauskaitė
GLIMSTEDT

Marius Rindinas
D. ZABIELA, M. RINDINAS AND
S. GRIGAS LAW FIRM ZRG

Greta Roguckytė
TARK GRUNTE SUTKIENE

Vytautas Sabalys
LAW FIRM SORAINEN
& PARTNERS

Svajone Saltauskiene
VILNIUS CITY 29TH
NOTARY'S OFFICE

Simona Šarkauskaitė
D. ZABIELA, M. RINDINAS AND
S. GRIGAS LAW FIRM ZRG

Arvydas Sedekerskis
LITHUANIAN ELECTRIC
ENERGY ASSOCIATION

Aušra Sičiūnienė
VILNIUS CITY MUNICIPALITY

Donatas Šliora
TARK GRUNTE SUTKIENE

Agneska Stanulevic
PWC LITHUANIA

Gintarė Stonienė
GINTARE

Marius Stračkaitis
LITHUANIAN CHAMBER
OF NOTARIES

Ieva Tarailiene
STATE ENTERPRISE
CENTRE OF REGISTERS

Monika Tukačiauskaitė
LAW FIRM SORAINEN
& PARTNERS

Daiva Ušinskaitė-Filonovienė
TARK GRUNTE SUTKIENE

Vygantas Vaitkus
NATIONAL COMMISSION FOR
ENERGY CONTROL AND PRICES

Vilija Vaitkutė Pavan
VALIUNAS ELLEX

Adrijus Vegys
BANK OF LITHUANIA

Agnietė Venckiene
LAW FIRM SORAINEN
& PARTNERS

Darius Zabiela
D. ZABIELA, M. RINDINAS AND
S. GRIGAS LAW FIRM ZRG

Ernesta Žiogienė
PRIMUS ATTORNEYS-AT-LAW

Povilas Žukauskas
LAW FIRM ELLEX VALIUNAS
IR PARTNERIAI, MEMBER
OF LEX MUNDI

Audrius Žvybas
GLIMSTEDT

LUXEMBOURG

Tom Baumert
CHAMBER OF COMMERCE
OF THE GRAND-DUCHY
OF LUXEMBOURG

Louis Berns
ARENDT & MEDERNACH SA

Sébastien Binard
ARENDT & MEDERNACH SA

Eleonora Broman
LOYENS & LOEFF
LUXEMBOURG SARL

Christel Dumont
DENTONS

Catherine Dupont
PWC LUXEMBOURG

Gérard Eischen
CHAMBER OF COMMERCE
OF THE GRAND-DUCHY
OF LUXEMBOURG

Thomas Feider
ADMINISTRATION DE
L'ENREGISTREMENT ET
DES DOMAINES

Margherita Gentili
DENTONS

Peggy Goossens
PIERRE THIELEN AVOCATS

Andreas Heinzmann
GSK STOCKMANN + KOLLEGEN

Véronique Hoffeld
LOYENS & LOEFF
LUXEMBOURG SARL

Chantal Keereman
BONN & SCHMITT

François Kremer
ARENDT & MEDERNACH SA

Paul Lanois
LAWYER

Florence Lhyvernay
OPF PARTNERS

Tom Loesch
LAW FIRM LOESCH

Evelyne Lordong
ARENDT & MEDERNACH SA

Laurent Lucius
CHAMBER OF COMMERCE
OF THE GRAND-DUCHY
OF LUXEMBOURG

Hawa Mahamoud
GSK STOCKMANN + KOLLEGEN

Jeannot Medinger
CREOS LUXEMBOURG SA

Philipp Metzschke
ARENDT & MEDERNACH SA

Marco Peters
CREOS LUXEMBOURG SA

Wim Piot
PWC LUXEMBOURG

Elisa Ragazzoni
PAUL WURTH GEPROLUX SA

Judith Raijmakers
LOYENS & LOEFF
LUXEMBOURG SARL

Jean-Luc Schaus
DECKER BRAUN AVOCATS

Roger Schintgen
PAUL WURTH GEPROLUX SA

Phillipe Schmit
ARENDT & MEDERNACH SA

Alex Schmitt
BONN & SCHMITT

Valerio Scollo
GSK STOCKMANN + KOLLEGEN

Marielle Stevenot
MNKS LAW FIRM

Massimo Trifilio
PWC LUXEMBOURG

Davide Visin
PWC LUXEMBOURG

Candice Wiser
BONN & SCHMITT

MACEDONIA, FYR

Igor Aleksandrovski
APOSTOLSKA &
ALEKSANDROVSKI

Ljubinka Andonovska
CENTRAL REGISTRY OF THE
REPUBLIC OF MACEDONIA

Natasha Andreeva
NATIONAL BANK OF THE
REPUBLIC OF MACEDONIA

Zlatko Antevski
LAWYERS ANTEVSKI

Dina Apostolova
EMIL MIFTARI LAW OFFICE

Dina Apostolovska
EMIL MIFTARI LAW OFFICE

Maja Atanasova
GEORGI DIMITROV ATTORNEYS

Dragan Blažev
TIMELPROJECT ENGINEERING

Vladimir Bocevski
CAKMAKOVA ADVOCATES

Jela Boskovic Ognjanoska
LAWELL ATTORNEYS

Ljupco Cvetkovski
DDK ATTORNEYS-AT-LAW

Dragan Dameski
DDK ATTORNEYS-AT-LAW

Irene Dimitrievikj
CAKMAKOVA ADVOCATES

Elena Dimova
CAKMAKOVA ADVOCATES

Ana Georgievska
DIMA FORWARDERS

Dimche Georgievski
DIMA FORWARDERS

Bojan Gerovski
IKRP ROKAS & PARTNERS

Katarina Ginoska
GEORGI DIMITROV ATTORNEYS

Marijana Gjoreska
*CENTRAL REGISTRY OF THE
REPUBLIC OF MACEDONIA*

Angelina Gogusevska
TITANIJA DOOEL – SKOPJE

Verica Hadzi
Vasileva-Markovska
*AAG - ANALYSIS AND
ADVISORY GROUP*

Ana Hadzieva-Angelovska
DDK ATTORNEYS-AT-LAW

Aleksandar Ickovski

Maja Jakimovska
*THE LAW OFFICE OF
MAJA JAKIMOVSKA*

Aneta Jovanoska Trajanovska
LAWYERS ANTEVSKI

Emilija Kelesoska Sholjakovska
DDK ATTORNEYS-AT-LAW

Risto Kitev
MEPOS OPERATIVA LTD.

Zlatko T. Kolevski
KOLEVSKI LAW OFFICE

Stanko Korunoski
*CENTRAL REGISTRY OF THE
REPUBLIC OF MACEDONIA*

Vladimir Kostoski
*APOSTOLSKA &
ALEKSANDROVSKI*

Andrea Lazarevska
GEORGI DIMITROV ATTORNEYS

Ivana Lekic
PWC MACEDONIA

Georgi Markov
PWC MACEDONIA

Emil Miftari
EMIL MIFTARI LAW OFFICE

Vlatko Mihailov
EMIL MIFTARI LAW OFFICE

Petra Mihajlovska
CAKMAKOVA ADVOCATES

Oliver Mirchevski
EVN MACEDONIA

Irena Mitkovska
LAWYERS ANTEVSKI

Biljana Mladenovska Dimitrova
LAWYERS ANTEVSKI

Martin Monevski
MONEVSKI LAW FIRM

Vojdan Monevski
MONEVSKI LAW FIRM

Svetlana Neceva
LAW OFFICE PEPELJUGOSKI

Ilija Nedelkoski
CAKMAKOVA ADVOCATES

Elena Nikodinovska
EMIL MIFTARI LAW OFFICE

Marina Nikoloska
CAKMAKOVA ADVOCATES

Martin Odzaklieski
*MINISTRY OF TRANSPORT
AND COMMUNICATIONS*

Bojana Paneva
LAW FIRM TRPENOSKI

Aleksandar Penovski
LAW FIRM TRPENOSKI

Ana Pepeljugoska
LAW OFFICE PEPELJUGOSKI

Valentin Pepeljugoski
LAW OFFICE PEPELJUGOSKI

Iva Petrovska
CAKMAKOVA ADVOCATES

Andrea Popovski
*CENTRAL REGISTRY OF THE
REPUBLIC OF MACEDONIA*

Sonja Risteska
ANALYTICA MK

Ljubica Ruben
MENS LEGIS LAW FIRM

Sasho Saltirovski
EVN MACEDONIA

Radovan Sanclic
LAW FIRM TRPENOSKI

Lidija Sarafimova-Danevska
*NATIONAL BANK OF THE
REPUBLIC OF MACEDONIA*

Simonida
Shosholceva-Giannitsakis
IKRP ROKAS & PARTNERS

Djino Skrijelj
VICTORIA SPED D.O.O. SKOPJE

Sonja Stojcevska
CAKMAKOVA ADVOCATES

Blagoj Stojevski
EVN MACEDONIA

Ana Stojilovska
ANALYTICA MK

Dragica Tasevska
*NATIONAL BANK OF THE
REPUBLIC OF MACEDONIA*

Paul Tobin
PWC BULGARIA

Elena Todorovska
LAWELL ATTORNEYS

Toni Trajanov
*MACEDONIAN CREDIT
BUREAU AD SKOPJE*

Dragan Trajkovski
ELTEK

Svetlana Trendova
*APOSTOLSKA &
ALEKSANDROVSKI*

Stefan Trost
EVN MACEDONIA

Natasha Trpenoska
Trenchevska
LAW FIRM TRPENOSKI

Slavce Trpeski
*AGENCY FOR REAL
ESTATE CADASTRE*

Vladimir Vasilevski
BETASPED D.O.O.

Ivana Velkovska
PWC MACEDONIA

Tome Velkovski
*AAG - ANALYSIS AND
ADVISORY GROUP*

Sladjana Zafirova
*TIVA-AS D.O.O.E.L. -
VALANDOVO*

Dragisa Zlatkovski
SISKON LTD.

MADAGASCAR

JOHN W. FFOOKS & CO.

Natacha Adrianjakamanarivo
CABINET MAZARS FIVOARANA

Liva Harisoa Andriamahady
MADAGASCAR LAW OFFICES

Laura Andriamanjato
SMR & HR ASSOCIATES SA

Eric Robson Andriamihaja
*ECONOMIC DEVELOPMENT
BOARD OF MADAGASCAR*

Tsiry Andriamisamanana

Aimée Andrianasolo
*OFFICE DE REGULATION
ÉLECTRICITÉ (ORE)*

Lalaina Andrianina Rakotonaivo
LEXEL JURIDIQUE & FISCAL

Andry Andriantsilavo
*OFFICE DE REGULATION
ÉLECTRICITÉ (ORE)*

Cedric Catheline
BUREAU DE LIAISON SGS

Frédéric Christophe Ranjatoely
LEXEL JURIDIQUE & FISCAL

Eric Diore De Perigny
S.E.A.L.

Yves Duchateau
*BOLLORÉ AFRICA LOGISTICS
MADAGASCAR*

Raphaël Jakoba
*MADAGASCAR CONSEIL
INTERNATIONAL*

Hanna Keyserlingk
CABINET HK JURIFISC

Jody Pruvot
CABINET HK JURIFISC

Pascaline R. Rabearisoa
DELTA AUDIT DELOITTE

Mirado Ambininjara
Rabearintsoa
MADAGASCAR LAW OFFICES

Rija Rabeharisoa
CABINET MAZARS FIVOARANA

Ketakandriana Rabemananjara
*OFFICE DE REGULATION
ÉLECTRICITÉ (ORE)*

Sahondra Rabenarivo
MADAGASCAR LAW OFFICES

Jeannot Julien Padoue
Rafanomezana
*ETUDE DE ME JEANNOT
RAFANOMEZANA*

Tahina Rajaona
MADAGASCAR LAW OFFICES

Pierrette Rajaonarisoa
*BOLLORÉ AFRICA LOGISTICS
MADAGASCAR*

Jean Sylvio Rajaonson
ETUDE ME. RAJAONSON

Fetrahanta Sylviane
Rakotomanana
*PRICEWATERHOUSECOOPERS
TAX & LEGAL MADAGASCAR -
PWC MADAGASCAR*

Corinne Holy Rakotoniaina
*PRICEWATERHOUSECOOPERS
TAX & LEGAL MADAGASCAR -
PWC MADAGASCAR*

Hery Rakotonindrainy
*OFFICE DE REGULATION
ÉLECTRICITÉ (ORE)*

Fidèle Armand Rakotonirina
CABINET MAZARS FIVOARANA

Harotsilavo Rakotoson
SMR & HR ASSOCIATES SA

Lanto Tiana Ralison
*PRICEWATERHOUSECOOPERS
TAX & LEGAL MADAGASCAR -
PWC MADAGASCAR*

Handry Orlando Ramananarivo
ARTCHIC MADAGASCAR

Andriamahafaly Ramanantsoa
*MINISTÈRE DE L'EQUIPEMENT,
DES PROJETS PRÉSIDENTIELS
ET DE L'AMÉNAGEMENT
DU TERRITOIRE*

Aviva Ramanitra
LEXEL JURIDIQUE & FISCAL

Roland Ramarijaona
DELTA AUDIT DELOITTE

Laingo Ramarimbahoaka
*MADAGASCAR CONSEIL
INTERNATIONAL*

Tsiry Ramiadanarivelo

William Randrianarivelo
*PRICEWATERHOUSECOOPERS
TAX & LEGAL MADAGASCAR -
PWC MADAGASCAR*

Felanasoa Randrianjafy
MINISTÈRE DE LA JUSTICE

Oméga Rasetanarimalala
*MINISTÈRE DE L'EQUIPEMENT,
DES PROJETS PRÉSIDENTIELS
ET DE L'AMÉNAGEMENT
DU TERRITOIRE*

Sylvia Rasoarilala
*BANKY FOIBEN'I
MADAGASIKARA / BANQUE
CENTRALE DE MADAGASCAR*

Sahondra Rasoarisoa
DELTA AUDIT DELOITTE

Henintsoa Ratiarison
MADAGASCAR LAW OFFICES

Michael Ratrimo
*MADAGASCAR INTERNATIONAL
CONTAINER TERMINAL
SERVICES LTD.*

Mahery Ratsimandresy
PRIME LEX

Rotsy Ratsimbarison
*MADAGASCAR CONSEIL
INTERNATIONAL*

Théodore Raveloarison
*JARY - BUREAU D'ÉTUDES
ARCHITECTURE INGÉNIERIE*

Princy Raveloharison
*PRICEWATERHOUSECOOPERS
TAX & LEGAL MADAGASCAR -
PWC MADAGASCAR*

Andriamisa Ravelomanana
*PRICEWATERHOUSECOOPERS
TAX & LEGAL MADAGASCAR -
PWC MADAGASCAR*

Landy Raveloson
CABINET HK JURIFISC

Jean Marcel Razafimahenina
DELTA AUDIT DELOITTE

Chantal Razafinarivo
CABINET RAZAFINARIVO

Parson Harivel Razafindrainibe
*ETUDE RAZAFINDRAINIBE
/ RAVOAJANAHARY*

Lisiniaina Razafindrakoto
BUREAU DE LIAISON SGS

Olivier Ribot
LEXEL JURIDIQUE & FISCAL

Louis Sagot
*CABINET D'AVOCAT
LOUIS SAGOT*

MALAWI

Everson Bandawe
*ALLIANCE FREIGHT
SERVICES LIMITED*

Andrew Chimpololo
*UNIVERSITY OF MALAWI
(POLYTECHNIC COLLEGE)*

Runcain Chimwala
*CONTINENTAL FREIGHT
AGENCY LIMITED*

Richard Chinawa
OCEAN AIR FREIGHT SERVICES

Ricky Chingota
SAVJANI & CO.

Maryann Chitseko
EY

Gautoni D. Kainja
KAINJA & DZONZI

Innocent Kalua
D&A ATTORNEYS

Griffin Kamanga
SPINE CARGO CO.

Cyprian Kambili

Dannie J. Kamwaza
*KAMWAZA DESIGN
PARTNERSHIP*

Frank Edgar Kapanda
SUPREME COURT OF APPEAL

Alfred Kaponda
ESCOM

Mavbuto Kasote
*KAMWAZA DESIGN
PARTNERSHIP*

Alfred Majamanda
*MBENDERA & NKHONO
ASSOCIATES*

James Masumbu
TEMBENU, MASUMBU & CO.

Noel Misanjo
SAVJANI & CO.

Vyamala Aggriel Moyo
PWC MALAWI

Misheck Msiska
EY

Arthur Alick Msowoya
WILSON & MORGAN

Charles Mvula
*DUMA ELECTRICS LTD. -
CONTROL SYSTEMS AND
ENERGY MANAGEMENT*

Matthews Mwadzangati
BLANTYRE CITY COUNCIL

Mtchuka Mwale
NICHOLLS & BROOKES

Patricia Mwase
*CREDIT DATA CREDIT
REFERENCE BUREAU LTD.*

Yusuf Nthenda
*CHIDOTHE, CHIDOTHE
& COMPANY*

Grant Nyirongo
ELEMECH DESIGNS

Reena Purshtam

Donns Shawa
RD CONSULTANTS

MALAYSIA

BANK NEGARA MALAYSIA

BURSA MALAYSIA

INLAND REVENUE BOARD
OF MALAYSIA

PLATINUM TAX
CONSULTANTS SDN BHD

WORLDGATE EXPRESS
SERVICES SDN BHD

Aniza Abd Manaf
CREDIT BUREAU
MALAYSIA SDN BHD

Azura Abd Rahman
LAND & MINES OFFICE

Nor Azimah Abdul Aziz
COMPANIES COMMISSION

Idayu Abdul Rahim
COMPANIES COMMISSION

Sonia Abraham
AZMAN, DAVIDSON & CO.

Wilfred Abraham
ZUL RAFIQUE & PARTNERS,
ADVOCATE & SOLICITORS

Wan Nur Ain Nabilah
AZMI & ASSOCIATES

Muhammad Arif Harinder
TITIMAS LOGISTICS SDN BHD

Nur Sajati Binti Asan
Monamed
AZMI & ASSOCIATES

Wan Amir Azlan
AZMI & ASSOCIATES

Shamsuddin Bardan
MALAYSIAN EMPLOYERS
FEDERATION

Mohd Nawawi bin Hj Said
Abdullah
TENAGA NASIONAL BERHAD

Ahmad Fuad bin Md Kasim
TENAGA NASIONAL BERHAD

Che Adnan Bin Mohamad
NADI CONSULT ERA SDN BHD

Tahir bin Mohd Deni
TENAGA NASIONAL BERHAD

YM Tengku Rohana Binti
Tengku Nawawi
LAND & MINES OFFICE

KC Chan
FREIGHT TRANSPORT
NETWORK SDN BHD

Hong Yun Chang
TAY & PARTNERS

Lee Cheng Keat
PERUNDING MEKTRIK SDN BHD

Chow Keng Chin
INDRA GANDHI & CO.

Eric Chin
CTOS DATA SYSTEMS SDN BHD

Jacky Choi
JEFF LEONG, POON & WONG

Jack Chor
CHRISTOPHER LEE & CO.

Melinda Marie D'Angelus
AZMI & ASSOCIATES

Ruzaida Daud
ENERGY COMMISSION

Indra Gandhi
INDRA GANDHI & CO.

Puan Morhaniza Hamir
MALAYSIA PRODUCTIVITY
CORPORATION

Khalid Hashim
AZMI & ASSOCIATES

Noor Hassan
MALAYSIA PRODUCTIVITY
CORPORATION

Andrew Heng
FERRIER HODGSON
MH SDN BHD

Abdul Hafiz Bin Hidzir
TENAGA NASIONAL BERHAD

Wong Hin Loong
AZMAN, DAVIDSON & CO.

Ang Seng Hing
USHAMAS FORWARDING
(M) SDN BHD

Wei En Hoong
TAY & PARTNERS

Mohamad Ali Abdul Husain
NORTH PORT (MALAYSIA) BHD

Dato' Dr. Sallehudin Ishak
LAND & MINES OFFICE

Kumarakuru Jai
FERRIER HODGSON
MH SDN BHD

Abdul Azis Japri
TENAGA NASIONAL BERHAD

Norhaiza Jemon
COMPANIES COMMISSION

Manfred Tee Jeok Renn
SHEARN DELAMORE & CO.

Jamielyn Jimmy
JEFF LEONG, POON & WONG

Dato' Dr. Ir. Andy K. H. Seo

Komathi P. Karuppanan
AZMI & ASSOCIATES

Amos Kok
JEFF LEONG, POON & WONG

LOH Kok Leong
RUSSELL BEDFORD LC
& COMPANY - MEMBER
OF RUSSELL BEDFORD
INTERNATIONAL

Christopher Lee
CHRISTOPHER LEE & CO.

Cing-Cing Lee
AZMI & ASSOCIATES

Richard Lee
JEFF LEONG, POON & WONG

Seen Yin Lee
JEFF LEONG, POON & WONG

Jeff Leong
JEFF LEONG, POON & WONG

Alex Lian
JEFF LEONG, POON & WONG

Koon Huan Lim
SKRINE, MEMBER
OF LEX MUNDI

San Peen Lim
PWC MALAYSIA

Lim Litt
FERRIER HODGSON
MH SDN BHD

Kin Sin Low
JEFF LEONG, POON & WONG

Ahmad Lutfi Abdull Mutalip
AZMI & ASSOCIATES

Ir. Bashir Ahamed Maideen
NADI CONSULT ERA SDN BHD

John Matthew
CHRISTOPHER LEE & CO.

Khairon Niza Md Akhir
COMPANIES COMMISSION

Arvind Menon
RANHILL BERSEKUTU SDN BHD

Hasliana Mohamad
TENAGA NASIONAL BERHAD

Hanani Hayati Mohd Adhan
AZMI & ASSOCIATES

Azmi Mohd Ali
AZMI & ASSOCIATES

Nik Mohd Fadhil Bin Salleh
FIRE AND RESCUE DEPARTMENT
OF KUALA LUMPUR

Muzzamir Mohd Mydin
AZMI & ASSOCIATES

Zuhaidi Mohd Shahari
AZMI & ASSOCIATES

Rohaizad Mohd Yusof
NORTH PORT (MALAYSIA) BHD

Mohd Yusoff Mokhzani Aris
MALAYSIA PRODUCTIVITY
CORPORATION

Marina Nathan
COMPANIES COMMISSION

Swee Kee Ng
SHEARN DELAMORE & CO.

Noor Wahida Noordin
MINISTRY OF INTERNATIONAL
TRADE AND INDUSTRY

Allison Ong
AZMAN, DAVIDSON & CO.

Hock An Ong
BDO

Tamilmaran A/L Palaniappan
NORTH PORT (MALAYSIA) BHD

Kim Yong Pang
FERRIER HODGSON
MH SDN BHD

Tan Kar Peng
KAMARUDDIN WEE & CO.
ADVOCATES & SOLICITORS

Aurobindo Ponniah
PWC MALAYSIA

Aminah Bt Abd Rahman
MINISTRY OF URBAN
WELLBEING, HOUSING AND
LOCAL GOVERNMENT

Ahmad Ridha Abdul Razak
ABRAZ ARKITECTS

Muzawipah Bt Md. Salim
TENAGA NASIONAL BERHAD

Sugumar Saminathan
MALAYSIA PRODUCTIVITY
CORPORATION

Victor Saw Seng Kee
PRICEWATERHOUSECOOPERS
ADVISORY SERVICES SDN BHD

Zamzuri Selamat
SYARIKAT BEKALAN AIR
SELANGOR SDN BHD (SYABAS)

Fiona Sequerah
CHRISTOPHER LEE & CO.

Jagdev Singh
PWC MALAYSIA

Adeline Thor Sue Lyn
RUSSELL BEDFORD LC
& COMPANY - MEMBER
OF RUSSELL BEDFORD
INTERNATIONAL

Muhendaran Suppiah
MUHENDARAN SRI

Esther Tan
ZUL RAFIQUE & PARTNERS,
ADVOCATE & SOLICITORS

Shu Shuen Tan
ZUL RAFIQUE & PARTNERS,
ADVOCATE & SOLICITORS

Raphael Tay
CHOOI & COMPANY

Hemant Thakore
RANHILL BERSEKUTU SDN BHD

Kenneth Tiong
THE ASSOCIATED CHINESE
CHAMBERS OF COMMERCE
AND INDUSTRY OF
MALAYSIA (ACCCIM)

Vijayakumar Varutharaju
TENAGA NASIONAL BERHAD

Siti Wahida Binti Sheikh
Hussien
CREDIT BUREAU
MALAYSIA SDN BHD

Anne Wai Yee Wong
JEFF LEONG, POON & WONG

Wan Rosmawati Wan Ibrahim
MALAYAN BANKING BERHAD

Chee Lin Wong
SKRINE, MEMBER
OF LEX MUNDI

Keat Ching Wong
ZUL RAFIQUE & PARTNERS,
ADVOCATE & SOLICITORS

Yeoh Keng Yao
TITIMAS LOGISTICS SDN BHD

Khairani M. Yusof
MALAYSIA PRODUCTIVITY
CORPORATION

MALDIVES

AVANT-GARDE LAWYERS

BANK OF MALDIVES PLC

Samih Adam
MALDIVES MONETARY
AUTHORITY

Junaina Ahmed
SHAH, HUSSAIN & CO.
BARRISTERS & ATTORNEYS

Mohamed Ahsan
ARCHENG STUDIO

Mohamed Shahdy Anwar
SUOOD ANWAR & CO. -
ATTORNEYS-AT-LAW

Jatindra Bhattray
PWC MALDIVES

Asma Chan-Rahim
SHAH, HUSSAIN & CO.
BARRISTERS & ATTORNEYS

Fazleena Fakir
MALDIVES MONETARY
AUTHORITY

Aishath Haifa
SHAH, HUSSAIN & CO.
BARRISTERS & ATTORNEYS

Mohamed Hameed
ANTRAC HOLDING PVT. LTD.

Ameelia Hussain
MALDIVES MONETARY
AUTHORITY

Abdul Rasheed Ibrahim
CUSTOMS SERVICE

Ishan Ibrahim
ASIA FORWARDING PVT. LTD.

Yameen Ibrahim
SUOOD ANWAR & CO. -
ATTORNEYS-AT-LAW

Savithri Karunaratne
EY

Prasanta Misra
PWC MALDIVES

Mohamed Munavvar
MUNAVVAR & ASSOCIATES
LAW FIRM

Ahmed Murad
MAZLAN & MURAD
LAW ASSOCIATES

Ismail Nashid
MALDIVES CUSTOMS SERVICE

Hassan Raaif Mohamed
MALDIVES MONETARY
AUTHORITY

Sulakshan Ramanan
EY

Sumeera Rodrigo
EY

Ahmed Saif
STELCO

Shuaib M. Shah
SHAH, HUSSAIN & CO.
BARRISTERS & ATTORNEYS

Mizna Shareef
SHAH, HUSSAIN & CO.
BARRISTERS & ATTORNEYS

Manal Shihab
SUOOD ANWAR & CO. -
ATTORNEYS-AT-LAW

Fathimath Sodhaf
MALDIVES CUSTOMS SERVICE

Sumudu Wijesundara
EY

Lubna Zahir Hussain
THE LAW COMMISSION
OF THE MALDIVES

MALI

BCEAO

CREDITINFO VOLO

Assadeck Allasane
DIRECTION GÉNÉRALE
DES DOUANES

Oumar Bane
JURIFIS CONSULT

Mariam Bocoum
MATRANS

Mahamane I. Cisse
CABINET LEXIS CONSEILS

Boubacar Coulibaly
MATRANS

Sekou Dembele
ETUDE MAÎTRE
SEKOU DEMBELE

Fatoumata D. Diarra
AFRICAN LEGAL & TAX
MALI (ALT-MALI)

Mamadou Diarra
CABINET JURI-PARTNER

Mariama Doumbia
MATRANS

Abdoulaye Fofana
MATRANS

Baba Haidara
ETUDE GAOUSSOU HAIDARA

Gaoussou Haïdara
ETUDE GAOUSSOU HAIDARA

Mamadou Ismaïla Konate
JURIFIS CONSULT

Abdoul Karim Samba Timbo
Konaté
AGENCE D'ARCHITECTURE
CADET

Gaoussou A.G. Konaté
AGENCE D'ARCHITECTURE
CADET

Mohamadi Magassa
ICON SARL

Celestin Maiga
SYTRAM

Bérenger Y. Meuke
JURIFIS CONSULT

Claudia Randrianavory
JOHN W. FFOOKS & CO.

Bourema Sagara
JURIFIS CONSULT

Alassane T. Sangaré
NOTARY

Oumar Sanogo
*DIRECTION DE L'INSPECTION
DU TRAVAIL*

Djibril Semega
CABINET SEAG CONSEIL

Mamadou Moustapha Sow
CABINET SOW & ASSOCIÉS

Boubacar Thiam
*ASSOCIATION
PROFESSIONNELLE DES
BANQUES ET ÉTABLISSEMENT
FINANCIERS DU MALI*

Abdoulaye Toure
*CELLULE TECHNIQUE
DES RÉFORMES ET DU
CLIMAT DES AFFAIRES*

Moctar Toure
*COMMISSION DE RÉGULATION
DE L'ÉLECTRICITE ET DE L'EAU*

Imirane A. Touré
*DIRECTION NATIONALE DE
L'URBANISME ET DE L'HABITAT*

Lasseni Touré
ETUDE GAOUSSOU HAIDARA

Alassane Traoré
ICON SARL

MALTA

CENTRAL BANK OF MALTA

Shawn Agius
INLAND REVENUE DEPARTMENT

Matthew Attard
GANADO ADVOCATES

Nicole Attard
GVZH ADVOCATES

Mark Attard Montalto
MINISTRY OF JUSTICE

Anthony Azzopardi
*DEPARTMENT OF INDUSTRIAL
AND EMPLOYMENT RELATIONS*

Kevan Azzopardi
*MALTA FINANCIAL SERVICES
AUTHORITY (MFSA)*

Leonard Bonello
GANADO ADVOCATES

Amanda Bonnci
GVZH ADVOCATES

Christopher Borg
ENEMALTA PLC

Kris Borg
*DR. KRIS BORG &
ASSOCIATES - ADVOCATES*

Mario Raymond Borg
INLAND REVENUE DEPARTMENT

Martina Borg Steven
GVZH ADVOCATES

Karl Briffa
GVZH ADVOCATES

Josianne Brimmer
FENECH & FENECH ADVOCATES

Joseph Buhagiar
MALTA ENTERPRISE

Jeanelle Cachia
GVZH ADVOCATES

Katia Cachia
GVZH ADVOCATES

Simon Camilleri
CREDITINFO

Joseph Caruana
*MALTA FINANCIAL SERVICES
AUTHORITY (MFSA)*

Laragh Cassar
*CAMILLERI CASSAR
ADVOCATES*

Kyle DeBattista
CAMILLERI PREZIOSI

David Felice
ARCHITECTURE PROJECT

Neville Gatt
PWC MALTA

Steve Gingell
PWC MALTA

Sandro Grech
*SG MALTA LIMITED -
CORRESPONDENT OF RUSSELL
BEDFORD INTERNATIONAL*

Karl Grech Orr
GANADO ADVOCATES

Roberta Gulic Hammett
PWC MALTA

Kurt Hyzler
GVZH ADVOCATES

Consuelo Marzi
GANADO ADVOCATES

Michael Mifsud
IDENTITY MALTA AGENCY

Henri Mizzi
CAMILLERI PREZIOSI

John Paris
CREDITINFO

Jonathan Scerri
ENEMALTA PLC

Jude Schembri
PWC MALTA

Ian Stafrace
IAN STAFRACE LEGAL

Pierre Theuma
MALTA ENTERPRISE

Dimitris Tsoukalas
W.J. PARNIS ENGLAND

Andrei Vella
CAMILLERI PREZIOSI

Luca Vella
GVZH ADVOCATES

Simone Vella Lenicker
ARCHITECTURE PROJECT

Quentin Zahra
EUROFREIGHT

Andrew J. Zammit
GVZH ADVOCATES

MARSHALL ISLANDS

BANK OF MARSHALL ISLANDS

MARSHALLS ENERGY
COMPANY

Helkena Anni
MARSHALL ISLANDS REGISTRY

Kenneth Barden
ATTORNEY-AT-LAW

Tune Carlos
PACIFIC INTERNATIONAL, INC.

Raquel De Leon
*MARSHALL ISLANDS SOCIAL
SECURITY ADMINISTRATION*

Kenneth Gideon
PII SHIPPING

Avelino R. Gimao Jr.
*MARSHALL ISLANDS SOCIAL
SECURITY ADMINISTRATION*

Richard W. Hamlin
OKNEY & HAMLIN

Don Hess
*COLLEGE OF THE
MARSHALL ISLANDS*

Jerry Kramer
PACIFIC INTERNATIONAL, INC.

Lani Milne
*ENVIRONMENTAL PROTECTION
AGENCY - MARSHALL ISLANDS*

Philip A. Okney
*LAW OFFICE OF
PHILIP A. OKNEY*

Steve Philip
CHAMBER OF COMMERCE

Dennis James Reeder
REEDER & SIMPSON

Michael Slinger
CHAMBER OF COMMERCE

David M. Strauss
ATTORNEY-AT-LAW

MAURITANIA

Mohamed Abdallahi Bellil

Wane Abdelaziz
*CHAMBRE DE COMMERCE,
D'INDUSTRIE ET D'AGRICULTURE
DE MAURITANIE*

Sid'Ahmed Abeidna
SOGECO MAURITANIA

Jemal Abde Nasser Ahmed
*DIRECTION GÉNÉRALE
DES DOUANES*

Kane Aly
GUICHET UNIQUE MAURITANIA

Mohamed Lemine Ould Babiye
*BANQUE CENTRALE
DE MAURITANIE*

Dieng Adama Boubou
*BANQUE CENTRALE
DE MAURITANIE*

Mohamed Marouf Bousbe

Moulaye Ahmed Boussabou
*BANQUE CENTRALE
DE MAURITANIE*

Mohamed Cheikh Abdallah
*AFACOR - AUDIT FINANCE
ASSISTANCE COMPTABLE
ORGANISATION SARL*

Brahim Ebety

Moulaye El Hassen Kamara
*SOCERE LAMBERT SOMEC
MAURITANIE (SLSM)*

Fadel Elaoune
*MINISTÈRE DES AFFAIRES
ÉCONOMIQUES ET DU
DÉVELOPPEMENT*

Boumiya Hamoud

Cheikhany Jules
CHEIKHANY JULES LAW OFFICE

Oumar Sada Kelly
ASSURIM CONSULTING

Mohamed Koum Maloum
*BETEM INGENIERIES DE
L'ENERGIE ET DE L'EAU*

Mohamed Lemine O/Bah

Mohamed Lemine Selmane
*MINISTÈRE DES AFFAIRES
ÉCONOMIQUES ET DU
DÉVELOPPEMENT*

Mohamed Salem Mah
*TRIBUNAL DE COMMERCE
DE NOUAKCHOTT*

Moustapha Maouloud
GUICHET UNIQUE MAURITANIA

Bah Elbar M'beirik
*CHAMBRE COMMERCIALE
AUPRÈS DE LA COUR
D'APPEL DE NOUAKCHOTT*

Abdou M'Bodj

Ould Med Yahya
*DIRECTION GÉNÉRALE
DES DOMAINES ET DU
PATRIMOINE DE L'ÉTAT*

Mazar Mohamed Mahmoud
Hmettou
*SOCIÉTÉ MAURITANIENNE
D'ELECTRICITÉ (SOMELEC)*

Ahmed Salem Mohamed Vall
*DIRECTION GÉNÉRALE
DES IMPÔTS*

Layti Ndiaye
SOGECO MAURITANIA

Mine Ould Abdoullah
*CABINET D'AVOCAT
OULD ABDOULLAH*

Ishagh Ould Ahmed Miské
CABINET ISHAGH MISKE

Moustapha Ould Bilal
*TRIBUNAL DE COMMERCE
DE NOUAKCHOTT*

M'Hamed Ould Bouboutt
*MINISTÈRE DES AFFAIRES
ECONOMIQUES ET DU
DÉVELOPPEMENT*

Abdellahi Ould Charrouck
*ATELIER ARCHITECTURE
ET DESIGN*

Hassena Ould Ely
*PORT AUTONOME DE
NOUAKCHOTT*

Ahmed Ould Radhi
*BANQUE CENTRALE
DE MAURITANIE*

Haimoud Ould Ramdan
MINISTÈRE DE LA JUSTICE

Mohamed Elmokhtar Roueiha
BUREAU CAUPID

Aliou Sall
*ETUDE ME ALIOU
SALL & ASSOCIÉS*

Sophie Teffahi
*PORT AUTONOME DE
NOUAKCHOTT*

Mohamed Yarguett
*MINISTÈRE DU PÉTROLE, DE
L'ENERGIE ET DES MINES*

MAURITIUS

SUPREME COURT

Daygarasen Amoomoogum
*MAURITIUS CHAMBER OF
COMMERCE AND INDUSTRY*

Wasoudeo Balloo
KPMG

Keshav Beeharry
MCB GROUP LIMITED

Khoushwant Bheem Singh
NOTARY

Valerie Bisasur
BLC CHAMBERS

Urmila Boolell
*BANYMANDHUB
BOOLELL CHAMBERS*

Satyajit Bundhoo
*BANYMANDHUB
BOOLELL CHAMBERS*

Adele Catherine
ENSAFRICA (MAURITIUS)

Bernard Chan Sing
*MAURITIUS NETWORK
SERVICES LTD.*

D.P. Chinien
*REGISTRAR OF COMPANIES
AND BUSINESSES,
CORPORATE AND BUSINESS
REGISTRATION DEPARTMENT*

Stephanie Chong Mei Lin
Ah Tow
MCB GROUP LIMITED

Jenifer Chung
PWC MAURITIUS

Jessen Coolen
MCB GROUP LIMITED

Asmaa Coowar
PWC MAURITIUS

Amritraj Dassyne
*CHAMBERS OF NOTARIES
OF MAURITIUS*

Veda Dawoonauth
*EVERSHEDS SUTHERLAND
(MAURITIUS)*

Martine de Fleuriot de la
Colinière
ENSAFRICA (MAURITIUS)

A. Delbar
*CUSTOMS HOUSE
BROKERS ASSOCIATION*

Carolyn Desvaux de Marigny
ENSAFRICA (MAURITIUS)

Shalinee Dreepaul-Halkhoree
JURISTCONSULT CHAMBERS

Amil Emandin
*ASSOCIATION
PROFESSIONNELLE DES
TRANSITAIRES*

Yannick Fok
*EVERSHEDS SUTHERLAND
(MAURITIUS)*

J. Gilbert Gnany
MCB GROUP LIMITED

Tilotma Gobin Jhurry
BANK OF MAURITIUS

Chavi Gonpot
BLC CHAMBERS

Yandraduth Googoolye
BANK OF MAURITIUS

Moorari Gujadhur
*MADUN GUJADHUR
CHAMBERS*

Gopaul Gupta
VELOGIC LTD.

Arvin Halkhoree
JURISTCONSULT CHAMBERS

Arzeenah Hassunally
PWC MAURITIUS

Rubishwur Hemoo
*MINISTRY OF LOCAL
GOVERNMENT AND
OUTER ISLANDS*

Nooreena Hosany
*MINISTRY OF LOCAL
GOVERNMENT AND
OUTER ISLANDS*

Deoyani Hurrynag
REGISTRAR GENERAL

Navin Jowaheer
*WASTEWATER MANAGEMENT
AUTHORITY*

Nishi Kichenin
JURISTAX

Thierry Koenig
ENSAFRICA (MAURITIUS)

Anthony Leung Shing
PWC MAURITIUS

Jayram Luximon
CENTRAL ELECTRICITY BOARD

Malcolm Moller
APPLEBY

Bala Moonsamy
CMT INTERNATIONAL LTD.

Ramdas Mootanah
ARCHITECTURE & DESIGN LTD.

Manisha Mootoocurpen
BANYMANDHUB
BOOLELL CHAMBERS

Ashwin Mudhoo
JURISTCONSULT CHAMBERS

Loganayagan Munian
ARTISCO INTERNATIONAL

Khemila Narraidoo
JURISTCONSULT CHAMBERS

Nicholas Ng
EVERSHEDS SUTHERLAND
(MAURITIUS)

Daniel Ng Cheong Hin
MAURITIUS CARGO
COMMUNITY SERVICES LTD.

Stéphanie Odayen
JURISTCONSULT CHAMBERS

Nawsheen Oozeer
BOARD OF INVESTMENT
(MAURITIUS)

Cristelle Parsooramen
BANYMANDHUB
BOOLELL CHAMBERS

Elsie Rasolohery Pascal
ENSAFRICA (MAURITIUS)

Hasanali Pirbhai
MADUN GUJADHUR
CHAMBERS

Varuna Punchoo
NOTARY

Iqbal Rajahbalee
BLC CHAMBERS

Li'owtee Rajmun
MAURITIUS EXPORT
ASSOCIATION

Vivekanand Ramburun
CUSTOMS AND EXCISE
DEPARTMENT

Dhanraj Ramdin
MAURITIUS REVENUE
AUTHORITY

Jayshen Rammah
MERITS CONSULTING
ENGINEERS LTD.

Annabelle Ribet
JURISTCONSULT CHAMBERS

Nicolas Richard
JURISTCONSULT CHAMBERS

André Robert
BLC ROBERT & ASSOCIATES

Purmessur Sarwansingh
MINISTRY OF LOCAL
GOVERNMENT AND
OUTER ISLANDS

Hurrydeo Seebchurrun
CENTRAL ELECTRICITY BOARD

Geetanjali Seewoosurrun
CENTRAL ELECTRICITY BOARD

Gilbert Seeyave
BDO FINANCIAL SERVICES LTD.

Steven Sarangavany Sengayen
STEVEN & ASSOCIATES
LAW FIRM

Bhavish Sewraz
JURISTCONSULT CHAMBERS

Deviantee Sobarun
REGISTRAR GENERAL

Menzie Sunglee
CENTRAL ELECTRICITY BOARD

Dhanesswurnath Vikash
Thakoor
BANK OF MAURITIUS

Muhammad R.C. Uteem
UTEEM CHAMBERS

Amy Vaulbert de Chantilly
JURISTCONSULT CHAMBERS

Nashenta Vuddamalay Zindel
ENSAFRICA (MAURITIUS)

Bobby Yerkiah
KPMG

MEXICO

COMISIÓN REGULADORA
DE ENERGÍA

INSTITUTO REGISTRAL Y
CATASTRAL DEL ESTADO
DE NUEVO LEÓN

NOTARÍA PÚBLICA 62

SECRETARIAT OF LABOUR
AND SOCIAL WELFARE

Andrea Melissa Alanís Ochoa
PENA MOURET ABOGADOS SC

Jaime Alejandro Gutiérrez Vidal
INSTITUTO FEDERAL
DE ESPECIALISTAS DE
CONCURSOS MERCANTILES

Federico Alvarez Gonzalez
WHITE & CASE SC

Miguel Andrade Gómez
ASOCIACIÓN MEXICANA
DE AGENTES

Lesly Arellano
RIVADENEYRA, TREVINO
& DE CAMPO SC

Francisco Samuel Arias
González
NOTARY PUBLIC 28

Francisco Javier Arias Vazque
MINISTRY OF FINANCE

José Alejandro Astorga Hilbert
INSTITUTO FEDERAL
DE ESPECIALISTAS DE
CONCURSOS MERCANTILES

Rodrigo Avendano
WHITE & CASE SC

Maria Paulina
Avendaño Verduzco
GOODRICH, RIQUELME
Y ASOCIADOS

Alberto Avila
FEDERATION OF
INTERAMERICAN
CONSTRUCTION
INDUSTRY (FIIC)

Elsa Regina Ayala Gómez
SECRETARÍA DE ECONOMÍA,
DIRECCIÓN GENERAL
DE NORMATIVIDAD
MERCANTIL (RUG)

Alfonso Azcona Anaya
ZITYMERKA SA DE CV

Vanessa Barajas
HUB LOGISTICS MEXICO

Jorge Barrero Stahl
SANTAMARINA Y STETA SC

Rodrigo Barros
MINISTRY OF FINANCE

Hernando Becerra de Cima
GONZALEZ CALVILLO SC

Luis Horacio Bortoni Vazquez
SECRETARIA DE DESARROLLO
URBANO (SEDUE) -
SECRETARIAT FOR URBAN
DEVELOPMENT AND ECOLOGY

Andrea Burgos Harfush
CREEL, GARCÍA-CUÉLLAR,
AIZA Y ENRIQUEZ SC

Gilberto Calderon
GALAZ, YAMAZAKI, RUIZ
URQUIZA SC, MEMBER
OF DELOITTE TOUCHE
TOHMATSU LIMITED

Adrian Martin Camacho
Fernandez
COMISIÓN FEDERAL
DE ELECTRICIDAD

Enrique Camarena Dominguez
MAQUEO, DE GARAY
Y AGUILAR SC

Samuel Campos Leal
GONZALEZ CALVILLO SC

Carlos Cano
PWC MEXICO

Jaime Cantú
MULTITRASLADOS

Tomás Cantú González
CANTU ESTRADA Y MARTINEZ
(CEM ABOGADOS)

Carlos Carbajal
J.A. TREVIÑO ABOGADOS
SA DE CV

Fernando Antonio Cardenas
Gonzalez
NOTARY PUBLIC #44

Lisa Carral F.
SANTAMARINA Y STETA SC

Pedro Carreon
PWC MEXICO

María Casas López
BAKER & MCKENZIE

Kathalina Chapa Peña
CAF-SIAC CONTADORES

Carlos Chávez
GALICIA ABOGADOS SC

Ernesto Chávez
INTERCONTINENTAL
NETWORK SERVICES

Carlos A. Chávez Pereda
J.A. TREVIÑO ABOGADOS
SA DE CV

Rodrigo Conesa
RITCH MUELLER, HEATHER
Y NICOLAU, SC

Bruno Cordova
PWC MEXICO

Samanta Cornu Sandoval
SECRETARIA DE DESARROLLO
URBANO (SEDUE) -
SECRETARIAT FOR URBAN
DEVELOPMENT AND ECOLOGY

Nancy Mireya Coronado Perez
DIRECCION DE
PROTECCION CIVIL (CIVIL
PROTECTION AGENCY)

Jose Covarrubias-Azuela
SOLÓRZANO, CARVAJAL,
GONZÁLEZ Y PÉREZ-CORREA SC

Juan Paulo Cruz de la Curz
PODER JUDICIAL DEL
ESTADO DE NUEVO LEÓN

David Cuellar
PWC MEXICO

Carlos De la Garza
MARTINEZ, ALGABA, DE HARO,
CURIEL Y GALVAN-DUQUE SC

Jorge de Presno
BASHAM, RINGE Y CORREA,
MEMBER OF IUS LABORIS

Franco Alberto Del Valle Prado
DEL VALLE, PRADO Y
FERNANDEZ, SC

Tracy Delgadillo Miranda
J.A. TREVIÑO ABOGADOS
SA DE CV

Julia Díaz
MULTITRASLADOS

Carlos Diez Garcia
GONZALEZ CALVILLO SC

Felipe Dominguez
MOORE STEPHENS
OROZCO MEDINA SC

Dolores Enriquez
PWC MEXICO

David Escalante
KPMG CARDENAS DOSAL SC

Isaura Escobar
DELEGACIÓN DE
AZCAPOTZALCO

Miguel Espitia
BUFETE INTERNACIONAL

Miguel Espitia
GLOBAL BUSINESS UNIVERSITY

Alfredo Falconer Orbe
COMISION NACIONAL
BANCARIA Y DE VALORES

Lucía Fernández
GONZALEZ CALVILLO SC

Victor Fernandez Sanchez
COMISIÓN FEDERAL
DE ELECTRICIDAD

Pedro Flores
MOORE STEPHENS
OROZCO MEDINA SC

Julio Flores Luna
GOODRICH, RIQUELME
Y ASOCIADOS

Valente Fuentes Tello
MAQUEO, DE GARAY
Y AGUILAR SC

Manuel Galicia
GALICIA ABOGADOS SC

Maria Antonieta Galvan
Carriles
TRIBUNAL SUPERIOR
DE JUSTICIA DEL LA
CIUDAD DE MÉXICO

Mauricio Gamboa
TRANSUNION DE
MEXICO SA SIC

Brenda Garcia
PWC MEXICO

Eduardo Garcia Fraschetto
SÁNCHEZ DEVANNY
ESEVERRI SC

Paulo Gabriel Garza González
PODER JUDICIAL DEL
ESTADO DE NUEVO LEÓN

Arturo Garza-Mátar
SÁNCHEZ DEVANNY
ESEVERRI SC

Jose Alberto Gonzalez
KPMG CARDENAS DOSAL SC

Pamela Gonzalez
GONZALEZ CALVILLO SC

Ricardo Gonzalez Orta
GALAZ, YAMAZAKI, RUIZ
URQUIZA SC, MEMBER
OF DELOITTE TOUCHE
TOHMATSU LIMITED

Antonio Gonzalez Rodriguez
GALAZ, YAMAZAKI, RUIZ
URQUIZA SC, MEMBER
OF DELOITTE TOUCHE
TOHMATSU LIMITED

Jose Gonzalez-Elizondo
BAKER & MCKENZIE

Alvaro Gonzalez-Schiaffino
BASHAM, RINGE Y CORREA,
MEMBER OF IUS LABORIS

James Graham
3CT

Sergio Granados
PWC MEXICO

Adrian Guarneros
SERVICIO DE ADMINISTRACIÓN
TRIBUTARIA

Antonio Guerra Gomez
GUERRA GOMEZ, ABOGADOS

Mario Alberto Gutiérrez
PWC MEXICO

Yves Hayaux-du-Tilly
NADER, HAYAUX & GOEBEL

F. Abimael Hernández
SOLÓRZANO, CARVAJAL,
GONZÁLEZ Y PÉREZ-CORREA SC

Roberto Hernandez Garcia
COMAD SC

David Hoyos de la Garza
SÁNCHEZ DEVANNY
ESEVERRI SC

Ricardo Ibarra
SERVICIO DE ADMINISTRACIÓN
TRIBUTARIA

Ivan Imperial
KPMG CARDENAS DOSAL SC

María Concepción Isoard
Viesca
RITCH MUELLER, HEATHER
Y NICOLAU, SC

Jorge Jiménez
RUSSELL BEDFORD MÉXICO
- MEMBER OF RUSSELL
BEDFORD INTERNATIONAL

Diana Juárez Martínez
BAKER & MCKENZIE

Adrian Kohlmann
KOVA INNOVACIÓN

Alfredo Kupfer Dominguez
SÁNCHEZ DEVANNY
ESEVERRI SC

Ricardo León-Santacruz
SÁNCHEZ DEVANNY
ESEVERRI SC

Luis Leyva Martinez
COMISION NACIONAL
BANCARIA Y DE VALORES

Carlos López Juárez
GOODRICH, RIQUELME
Y ASOCIADOS

Alfonso López Lajud
SÁNCHEZ DEVANNY
ESEVERRI SC

Rogelio Lopez-Velarde
LOPEZ VELARDE,
HEFTYE Y SORIA SC

Jose Antonio Lozada Capetillo
TRIBUNAL SUPERIOR
DE JUSTICIA DEL LA
CIUDAD DE MÉXICO

Arturo Lozano Guerrero
*CANTU ESTRADA Y MARTINEZ
(CEM ABOGADOS)*

Gerardo Maltos
GRUPO SYS

Gabriel Manrique
*RUSSELL BEDFORD MÉXICO -
MEMBER OF RUSSELL
BEDFORD INTERNATIONAL*

Esteban Maqueo Barnetche
*MAQUEO, DE GARAY
Y AGUILAR SC*

José Antonio Marquez
González
NOTARY PUBLIC #2

Renato Martínes Quezada
EC LEGAL

Carlos Manuel Martinez
PWC MEXICO

Gerardo Martínez
*RIVADENEYRA, TREVINO
& DE CAMPO SC*

Victor Hugo Núñez Martínez
*MEXICAN TAX
ADMINISTRATION
SERVICE (SAT)*

Juan Sergio Alfonso Martínez
González
*COMISIÓN FEDERAL
DE ELECTRICIDAD*

Ana Lilia Martínez Valdés
*SECRETARÍA DE ECONOMÍA -
MINISTRY OF ECONOMY*

Mariana Maxinez
*GALAZ, YAMAZAKI, RUIZ
URQUIZA SC, MEMBER
OF DELOITTE TOUCHE
TOHMATSU LIMITED*

Jose Alberto Miguel Perez
*SECRETARÍA DE ECONOMÍA,
DIRECCIÓN GENERAL
DE NORMATIVIDAD
MERCANTIL (RUG)*

Angel Humberto Montiel
Trujano
*TRIBUNAL SUPERIOR
DE JUSTICIA DEL LA
CIUDAD DE MÉXICO*

Ignacio R. Morales Lechuga
NOTARÍA 116

Daniel Moran
GONZALEZ CALVILLO SC

Guillermo Moran
*GALAZ, YAMAZAKI, RUIZ
URQUIZA SC, MEMBER
OF DELOITTE TOUCHE
TOHMATSU LIMITED*

Emilio Rodriguez Muniz
*MEXICAN TAX
ADMINISTRATION
SERVICE (SAT)*

Eloy F. Muñoz M.
*IMEYEL SOLUCIONES
INTEGRALES SA DE CV*

Juan Nájera
NDA NAJERA DANIELI & ASOCS

Jorge Narváez Hasfura
BAKER & MCKENZIE

Javier Luis Navarro Velasco
BAKER & MCKENZIE

Mario Neave
*GALAZ, YAMAZAKI, RUIZ
URQUIZA SC, MEMBER
OF DELOITTE TOUCHE
TOHMATSU LIMITED*

Pablo Nosti Herrera
MIRANDA & ESTAVILLO SC

María José Ortiz Haro
GALICIA ABOGADOS SC

Gilberto Osio
*SOLÓRZANO, CARVAJAL,
GONZÁLEZ Y PÉREZ-CORREA SC*

Cynthia Irene Osio Sanchez
COMAD SC

Raúl Paniahua
NADER, HAYAUX & GOEBEL

Sonia Paredes Sepúlveda
PENA MOURET ABOGADOS SC

Victor Paz
CAF-SIAC CONTADORES

Gabriel Peña Mouret
PENA MOURET ABOGADOS SC

Sergio Peña Zazueta
*TRANSUNION DE
MEXICO SA SIC*

Arturo Perdomo
GALICIA ABOGADOS SC

Eduardo Perez Armienta
*MOORE STEPHENS
OROZCO MEDINA SC*

Luis Uriel Pérez Delgado
*GOODRICH, RIQUELME
Y ASOCIADOS*

José Jacinto Pérez Silva
OPERADORA TERRA REGIA SA

Pablo Perezalonso Eguía
*RITCH MUELLER, HEATHER
Y NICOLAU, SC*

Fernando Pérez-Correa
*SOLÓRZANO, CARVAJAL,
GONZÁLEZ Y PÉREZ-CORREA SC*

Guillermo Piecarchic
PMC LAW SC

José Piecarchic Cohen
PMC LAW SC

Federico Pineda
HUB LOGISTICS MEXICO

Ricardo Platt
*FEDERATION OF
INTERAMERICAN
CONSTRUCTION
INDUSTRY (FIIC)*

Gizeh Polo
*CREEL, GARCÍA-CUÉLLAR,
AIZA Y ENRIQUEZ SC*

Víctor Manuel Ponce Rosendo
*JUNTA LOCAL DE
CONCILIACIÓN Y ARBITRAJE
DE NUEVO LEON*

David Eugenio Puente-Tostado
*SÁNCHEZ DEVANNY
ESEVERRI SC*

Eric Quiles Gutierrez
WHITE & CASE SC

Olga Cristina Ramirez Acosta
*SECRETARIA DE DESARROLLO
URBANO (SEDUE) -
SECRETARIAT FOR URBAN
DEVELOPMENT AND ECOLOGY*

Jorge Francisco Ramirez
Mazlum
*MEXICAN TAX
ADMINISTRATION
SERVICE (SAT)*

Manuel Ramos
*BUFETE DE OBRAS, SERVICIOS
Y SUMINISTROS SA DE CV*

Carolina Ramos Ballesteros
MIRANDA & ESTAVILLO SC

Brindisi Reyes Delgado
*RITCH MUELLER, HEATHER
Y NICOLAU, SC*

Eduardo Reyes Díaz-Leal
BUFETE INTERNACIONAL

Héctor Reyes Freaner
BAKER & MCKENZIE

Hector Francisco Reyes Lopez
*SECRETARIA DE DESARROLLO
URBANO (SEDUE) -
SECRETARIAT FOR URBAN
DEVELOPMENT AND ECOLOGY*

Claudia Ríos
PWC MEXICO

Fernando Rivadeneyra
*RIVADENEYRA, TREVINO
& DE CAMPO SC*

Jose Ignacio Rivero
GONZALEZ CALVILLO SC

Beatriz Robles
CAF-SIAC CONTADORES

Alba Rodriguez Chamorro
*COMISION NACIONAL
BANCARIA Y DE VALORES*

Irazu Rodríguez Garza
*COMISIÓN FEDERAL
DE ELECTRICIDAD*

Cecilia Rojas
GALICIA ABOGADOS SC

Maria Eugenia Romero Torres
MINISTRY OF FINANCE

Raúl Sahagun
BUFETE INTERNACIONAL

Juan Pablo Sainz
NADER, HAYAUX & GOEBEL

José Roberto Salinas
*SALINAS PADILLA, ROMAN
ÁVILA & ASSOCIATES,
LEGAL FIRM SC*

Jorge Sanchez
*GALAZ, YAMAZAKI, RUIZ
URQUIZA SC, MEMBER
OF DELOITTE TOUCHE
TOHMATSU LIMITED*

Lucero Sánchez de la Concha
BAKER & MCKENZIE

Luis Sanchez Galguera
*GALAZ, YAMAZAKI, RUIZ
URQUIZA SC, MEMBER
OF DELOITTE TOUCHE
TOHMATSU LIMITED*

Rodrigo Sanchez Mejorada
*SÁNCHEZ-MEJORADA,
VELASCO Y RIBÉ*

Karla Sanchez Reyes
*SECRETARÍA DE ECONOMÍA,
DIRECCIÓN GENERAL
DE NORMATIVIDAD
MERCANTIL (RUG)*

Alberto Sanchez Rodriguez
*DIRECCION DE
PROTECCION CIVIL (CIVIL
PROTECTION AGENCY)*

Cristina Sanchez Vebber
*SÁNCHEZ DEVANNY
ESEVERRI SC*

Carlos Sánchez-Mejorada y
Velasco
*SÁNCHEZ-MEJORADA
Y ASOCIADOS*

Cristina Sánchez-Urtiz
MIRANDA & ESTAVILLO SC

Quetzalcoatl Sandoval Mata
VELEZ Y SANDOVAL SC

Ricardo Sandoval Ortega
*COMISIÓN FEDERAL
DE ELECTRICIDAD*

María Esther Sandoval Salgado
*INSTITUTO FEDERAL
DE ESPECIALISTAS DE
CONCURSOS MERCANTILES*

José Santiago
GRUPO IMEV, SA DE CV

Monica Schiaffino Pérez
LITTLER MEXICO

Arturo Suárez
KPMG CARDENAS DOSAL SC

Juan Francisco Torres Landa
Ruffo
HOGAN LOVELLS

Jaime A. Tovar Villegas
NOTARÍA 116

Jaime A. Treviño
J.A. TREVIÑO ABOGADOS

Roberto Treviño Ramos
*PODER JUDICIAL DEL
ESTADO DE NUEVO LEÓN*

Alfonso Vargas
*RITCH MUELLER, HEATHER
Y NICOLAU, SC*

Layla Vargas Muga
*GOODRICH, RIQUELME
Y ASOCIADOS*

Camilo Vazquez Lopez
SANTAMARINA Y STETA SC

Denise Carla Vazquez Wallach
*SECRETARÍA DE ECONOMÍA,
DIRECCIÓN GENERAL
DE NORMATIVIDAD
MERCANTIL (RUG)*

José Luis Vega Garrido
*GOODRICH, RIQUELME
Y ASOCIADOS*

Rodrigo Vejar Félix
*MAQUEO, DE GARAY
Y AGUILAR SC*

Luis Miguel Velasco Lizárraga
*SÁNCHEZ DEVANNY
ESEVERRI SC*

Enrique Lavin Velez
*MEXICAN TAX
ADMINISTRATION
SERVICE (SAT)*

Adrian Roberto Villagomez
Aleman
COMAD SC

Claudio Villavicencio
*GALAZ, YAMAZAKI, RUIZ
URQUIZA SC, MEMBER
OF DELOITTE TOUCHE
TOHMATSU LIMITED*

Paula Villavicencio
GONZALEZ CALVILLO SC

Juan Pablo Villela Vizcaya
*CREEL, GARCÍA-CUÉLLAR,
AIZA Y ENRIQUEZ SC*

Antonio Zuazua
KPMG CARDENAS DOSAL SC

MICRONESIA, FED. STS.

Marcelino Actouka
*POHNPEI UTILITIES
CORPORATION*

Nixon Anson
*POHNPEI UTILITIES
CORPORATION*

Rusty Carlos
*POHNPEI STATE
ENVIRONMENTAL
PROTECTION AGENCY*

Lam Dang
CONGRESS OF THE FSM

Erick Divinagracia
RAMP & MIDA LAW FIRM

Mark Heath
*MICRONESIA REGISTRATION
ADVISORS, INC.*

Jerry Kramer
PACIFIC INTERNATIONAL, INC.

Simon Lihpai
*DIVISION OF FORESTRY &
MARINE CONSERVATION*

Ronald Pangelinan
A&P ENTERPRISES INC.

Salomon Saimon
*MICRONESIAN LEGAL
SERVICES CORPORATION*

Nora Sigrah
FSM DEVELOPMENT BANK

Joseph Vitt
*POHNPEI TRANSFER &
STORAGE, INC.*

MOLDOVA

*NATIONAL COMMISSION
FOR FINANCIAL MARKETS*

UNION FENOSA

Alexei Bosneaga
*MINISTRY OF REGIONAL
DEVELOPMENT AND
CONSTRUCTION*

Andrei Caciurenco
ACI PARTNERS LAW OFFICE

Olga Ceban
*NATIONAL UNION OF
JUDICIAL OFFICERS*

Roman Ceban
*MOLDOVA BUSINESS
PEOPLE ASSOCIATION*

Valeriu Cernei
GLADEI & PARTNERS

Valentina Chiper
MINISTRY OF ECONOMY

Ludmila Ciubaciuc
PWC MOLDOVA

Daniel Cobzac
COBZAC & PARTNERS

Andrei Crigan
*MOLDOVA BUSINESS
PEOPLE ASSOCIATION*

Anastasia Dereveanchina
PWC MOLDOVA

Silviu Foca
BIROUL DE CREDIT - MOLDOVA

Iulia Furtuna
TURCAN CAZAC

Ana Galus
TURCAN CAZAC

Vasile Gherasim
POPA & ASSOCIATES

Roger Gladei
GLADEI & PARTNERS

Victoria Goncearuc
COBZAC & PARTNERS

Silvia Grosu
PWC MOLDOVA

Andrian Guzun
SCHOENHERR

Patricia Handraman
GLADEI & PARTNERS

Ana Iovu
COBZAC & PARTNERS

Vladimir Iurkovski
SCHOENHERR

Roman Ivanov
VERNON DAVID & ASSOCIATES

Cristina Martin
ACI PARTNERS LAW OFFICE

Angela Matcov
AGENCY OF LAND RELATIONS AND CADASTRE STATE ENTERPRISE "CADASTRU"

Mihaela Mitroi
PWC ROMANIA

Alexandru Munteanu
PWC MOLDOVA

Serghei Munteanu
MINISTRY OF REGIONAL DEVELOPMENT AND CONSTRUCTION

Oxana Novicov
NATIONAL UNION OF JUDICIAL OFFICERS

Igor Odobescu
ACI PARTNERS LAW OFFICE

Aelita Orhei
GLADEI & PARTNERS

Vladimir Palamarciuc
TURCAN CAZAC

Bodiu Pantelimon
SRL RECONSCIVIL

Carolina Parcalab
ACI PARTNERS LAW OFFICE

Iulian Pașatii
GLADEI & PARTNERS

Maya Pircalab
ACI PARTNERS LAW OFFICE

Vladimir Plehov

Dumitru Popescu
PWC MOLDOVA

Irina Popușoi
COBZAC & PARTNERS

Irina Rotari
MINISTRY OF ECONOMY

Elena Sadovici
CUSTOMS SERVICE OF THE REPUBLIC OF MOLDOVA

Alexandru Savva

Adrian Sorocean
ACI PARTNERS LAW OFFICE

Tatiana Stavinschi
PWC MOLDOVA

Liviu Surdu
GLORINAL SRL

Lilia Tapu
PWC MOLDOVA

Cristina Tiscul-Diaconu
ACI PARTNERS LAW OFFICE

Alexander Tuceac
TURCAN CAZAC

Alexander Turcan
TURCAN CAZAC

MONGOLIA

Amarmurun Amartuvshin
LEHMAN, LEE & XU

Odgerel Amgalan
MONLOGISTICS WORLDWIDE LLC

Dunnaran Baasankhuu
MINTER ELLISON

Munkhjargal Baashuu
GTS ADVOCATES LLP

Telenged Baast
MONLOGISTICS WORLDWIDE LLC

Minjae Baek
ANDERSON AND ANDERSON LLP

Molor Bakhdal
TSETS LLP

Nandinchimeg Banzragch
TSOGT & NANDIN

Delgermaa Bataa
NEW LOGISTICS LLC

Uranzaya Batdorj
TSETS LLP

Dashzeveg Bat-Erdene
DELOITTE

Azzaya Batsuuri
ELECTROSETIPROJECT, LLC

Solongo Battulga
GTS ADVOCATES LLP

Altanduulga Bazarragchaa
UBEDN

Jacob Blacklock
LEHMAN, LEE & XU

Bayar Budragchaa
ELC LLP ADVOCATES

David C. Buxbaum
ANDERSON AND ANDERSON LLP

Tsendmaa Choijamts
PWC MONGOLIA

Khatanbat Dashdarjaa
ARLEX CONSULTING SERVICES

Zoljargal Dashnyam
GTS ADVOCATES LLP

Otgontuya Davaanyam
ANDERSON AND ANDERSON LLP

Tseveensuren Davkharbayar
MONGOL ADVOCATES

Onchinsuren Dendevsambuu
DELOITTE

Elisabeth Ellis
MINTER ELLISON

Gerel Enebish
LEHMAN, LEE & XU

Sanjkhand Erdenebaatar
PWC MONGOLIA

Alimaa Erdenebat
HOGAN LOVELLS

Oyunbold Ganchimeg
THE BANK OF MONGOLIA

Dulguun Gantumur
MINTER ELLISON

Simon Guidecoq

Dermot Kane
KANE TUNELLING LLC

Undram Lhagvasuren
ANAND ADVOCATES LAW FIRM

Azzaya Lkhachin
PWC MONGOLIA

Amarjargal Lkhagvaa
LEHMAN, LEE & XU

Ganzorig Luvsan
UBEDN

Bayarmanla Manljav
MONGOLYN ALT (MAK) CORPORATION

Christopher Melville
HOGAN LOVELLS

Ulziimaa Naidandorj
MONGOLIAN COMPANY FORMATION LLC

Mend-Amar Narantsetseg
GTS ADVOCATES LLP

Tsogt Natsagdorj
TSOGT & NANDIN

Enkhtsetseg Nergui
ANAND ADVOCATES LAW FIRM

Bayarsaikhan Nyamragchaa
TSAST CONSTRUCTION LLC

Sebastian Rosholt
MINTER ELLISON

Scott Schlink
MINTER ELLISON

Bayarjargal Sodbaatar
ANAND ADVOCATES LAW FIRM

Tumurkhuu Sukgbaatar
UBEDN

Ganbayar Surmaajav
THE BANK OF MONGOLIA

Ganbagana Togtokhbayar
DELOITTE

Enkhtuvshin Tsetsegmaa
ANDERSON AND ANDERSON LLP

Ganzaya Tsogtgerel
ANDERSON AND ANDERSON LLP

Dudgen Turbat
THE BANK OF MONGOLIA

Munkh-Orgil Tuvaandorj
ANAND ADVOCATES LAW FIRM

Alicia Yen
HEALY CONSULTANTS GROUP PLC

Khosbayar Zorig
ARLEX CONSULTING SERVICES

MONTENEGRO

CEDIS

MINISTRY OF ECONOMY

Anja Abramovic
PRELEVIĆ LAW FIRM

Jelena Bogetić
BDK ADVOKATI

Bojana Bošković
MINISTRY OF FINANCE

Bojan Božović
HARRISONS SOLICITORS

Dragoljub Cibulić
BDK ADVOKATI

Milan Dakic
BDK ADVOKATI

Vladimir Dašić
BDK ADVOKATI

Savo Djurović
ADRIATIC MARINAS D.O.O.

Dragan Draca
PRICEWATERHOUSECOOPERS CONSULTING D.O.O.

Veselin Dragićević
CHAMBER OF ECONOMY OF MONTENEGRO, SECTOR FOR ASSOCIATIONS AND ECONOMIC DEVELOPMENT

Sladana Dragović
NORMAL COMPANY

Dragana Filipovic
MINISTRY OF SUSTAINABLE DEVELOPMENT AND TOURISM

Mile Gujić
NORMAL COMPANY

Danilo Gvozdenović
MINISTRY OF SUSTAINABLE DEVELOPMENT AND TOURISM

Fata Hodžić
LAW OFFICE VUJAČIĆ

Ana Jankov
BDK ADVOKATI

Nada Jovanovic
CENTRAL BANK OF MONTENEGRO

Milica Jovicevic
MONTENOMAX

Radoš-Lolo Kastratović
ADVOKATSKA KANCELARIJA

Milica Komar
VUKMIROVIC MISIC LAW FIRM

Ana Krsmanović
MINISTRY OF FINANCE

Nikola Martinović
ADVOKATSKA KANCELARIJA

Milica Milanovic
PRICEWATERHOUSECOOPERS CONSULTING D.O.O.

Ivan Nikolic
TOTAL SPED

Novica Pesic
PESIC & BAJCETA

Zorica Pesic Bajceta
PESIC & BAJCETA

Luka Popović
BDK ADVOKATI

Dragana Radević
CEED

Radovan Radulovic
MONTENOMAX

Ivan Radulović
MINISTRY OF FINANCE

Dražen Raičković
FINANCEPLUS

Branka Rajicic
PRICEWATERHOUSECOOPERS CONSULTING D.O.O.

Sead Salkovic
FINANCEPLUS

Slaven Šćepanović
SCEPANOVIC LAW OFFICE

Marko Tintor
CENTRAL BANK OF MONTENEGRO

Vera Vucelic
HARRISONS SOLICITORS

Saša Vujačić
LAW OFFICE VUJAČIĆ

Jelena Vujisić
LAW OFFICE VUJAČIĆ

Tatjana Vujosevic
MINISTRY OF SUSTAINABLE DEVELOPMENT AND TOURISM

Lana Vukmirovic Misic
VUKMIROVIC MISIC LAW FIRM

Sandra Zdravkovic
MONTECCO INC D.O.O.

Djordje Zejak
BDK ADVOKATI

Jelena Zivkovic
EUROFAST GLOBAL

MOROCCO

PORTNET SA

Idriss Abou Mouslim
BHIRAT

Sidimohamed Abouchikhi
CREDITINFO MAROC

Abdelkrim Karim Adyel
CABINET ADYEL

Samir Agoumi
DAR ALKHIBRA

Ali Alamri
MOROCCAN CARGO PARTNER

Aishah Alkaff

Amina Ammor
CREDITINFO MAROC

Maïlis Andrieu
CHASSANY WATRELOT & ASSOCIÉS

Redouane Assakhen
CENTRE RÉGIONAL D'INVESTISSEMENT

Adnane Bahija
DAR ALKHIBRA

Fassi-Fihri Bassamat
CABINET BASSAMAT & ASSOCIÉE

Toufiq Benali
MINISTÈRE DE L'URBANISME ET DE L'AMÉNAGEMENT DU TERRITOIRE

Meriem Benis
HAJJI & ASSOCIÉS

Badria Benjelloun
MINISTÈRE DE L'URBANISME ET DE L'AMÉNAGEMENT DU TERRITOIRE

Karim Benkirane
ESPACE TRANSIT

Mohamed Benkirane
ESPACE TRANSIT

Meriem Benzakour
CABINET D'AVOCATS MORSAD

Oussama Boualam
LYDEC

Ali Bougrine
UGGC LAW FIRM

Bouchaib Chahi
AGENCE NATIONALE DE LA CONSERVATION FONCIÈRE DU CADASTRE ET DE LA CARTOGRAPHIE (ANCFCC)

Abdallah Chater
CENTRE RÉGIONAL D'INVESTISSEMENT

Anas Chorfi
AGENCE MAROCAINE POUR LE DEVELOPPEMENT DE L'ENTREPRISE (AMDE)

Mahat Chraibi
PWC ADVISORY MAROC

Marie-Amélia da Silva Marques
CHASSANY WATRELOT & ASSOCIÉS

Driss Debbagh
KETTANI LAW FIRM

Merieme Diouri
ETUDE DE NOTARIAT MODERNE

Mohssin El Makoudi
DAR ALKHIBRA

Hamid Errida
ACCOUNTHINK MAROC SARLAU

Kunal Fabiani

Safia Fassi-Fihri
BFR ASSOCIÉS

Simon Guidecoq

Houda Habachi
BAKOUCHI & HABACHI - HB LAW FIRM LLP

Kamal Habachi
BAKOUCHI & HABACHI - HB LAW FIRM LLP

Amin Hajji
HAJJI & ASSOCIÉS

Zohra Hasnaoui
CABINET H-AVOCATS

Ahmad Hussein
CABINET H-AVOCATS

Bahya Ibn Khaldoun
UNIVERSITÉ M.V. SOUISSI RABAT, MAROC

Younes Jalal
TRANSIT JALAL

Nadia Kettani
KETTANI LAW FIRM

Rita Kettani
KETTANI LAW FIRM

Yassir Khalil
YASSIR KHALIL STUDIO

Abdelatif Laamrani
LAAMRANI LAW OFFICE

Hakim Lahlou
LAHLOU-ZIOUI & ASSOCIÉS

Mhammed Lahlou
ETUDE DE NOTARIAT MODERNE

Zineb Laraqui
CABINET ZINEB LARAQUI

Mohamed Amine Mahboub
ETUDE DE ME MAHBOUB

Amine Mahfoud
AMINE MAHFOUD NOTAIRE

Noureddine Marzouk
PWC ADVISORY MAROC

Adil Morsad
CABINET D'AVOCATS MORSAD

Ahmed Morsad
CABINET D'AVOCATS MORSAD

Tayeb Mohamed Omar
*AVOCAT AU BARREAU
DE CASABLANCA*

Hicham Oughza
DAR ALKHIBRA

Mohamed Oulkhouir
*CHASSANY WATRELOT
& ASSOCIÉS*

Abderrahim Outass
FONCTION LIBÉRALE

Mohamed Rifi
PWC ADVISORY MAROC

Morgane Saint-Jalmes

Mehdi Salmouni-Zerhouni
*SALMOUNI-ZERHOUNI
LAW FIRM*

Ghalia Sebti
AIT MANOS

Farhat Smail
*ADMINISTRATION DES
DOUANES ET IMPOTS INDIRECTS*

Rachid Tahri
*ASSOCIATION DES FREIGHT
FORWARDERS DU MAROC*

Rim Tazi
LPA-CGR AVOCATS

Kenza Yamani
*CHASSANY WATRELOT
& ASSOCIÉS*

Amine Zniber
ETUDE DE NOTAIRE ZNIBER

Meryem Zoubir
*CHASSANY WATRELOT
& ASSOCIÉS*

MOZAMBIQUE

HPF ADVOGADOS

Amina Abdala
*TTA – SOCIEDADE DE
ADVOGADOS*

Duarte Amaral da Cruz
*MC&A - SOCIEDADE
DE ADVOGADOS RL*

Luís Antunes
*LUFTEC – TÉCNICAS
ELÉCTRICAS LDA*

Henrique Castro Amaro
*AMARO ARQUITECTOS
E ASSOCIADOS LDA*

Carolina Balate
PWC MOZAMBIQUE

Goncalo Barros Cardoso
*GUILHERME DANIEL
& ASSOCIADOS*

Ebrahim Bhikhá
PWC MOZAMBIQUE

Abubacar Calú
ELECTROVISAO LDA

Eduardo Calú
*SAL & CALDEIRA,
ADVOGADOS, LDA*

Alexandra Carvalho
Monjardino
ATTORNEY-AT-LAW

Natércio Chambule
*MAPUTO CITY COURT
(COMMERCIAL CHAMBER)*

Pedro Chilengue
*MOTT MACDONALD PDNA
MOÇAMBIQUE, LDA*

Pedro Couto
*CGA - COUTO, GRAÇA E
ASSOCIADOS, SOCIEDADE
DE ADVOGADOS*

Avelar da Silva
INTERTEK INTERNATIONAL LTD.

Thera Dai
*CGA - COUTO, GRAÇA E
ASSOCIADOS, SOCIEDADE
DE ADVOGADOS*

Guilherme Daniel
*GUILHERME DANIEL
& ASSOCIADOS*

Fabrícia de Almeida Henriques
*HENRIQUES, ROCHA &
ASSOCIADOS (MOZAMBIQUE
LEGAL CIRCLE ADVOGADOS)*

Arlinda de Lurdes Nhaquila
*CONSERVATÓRIA DO REGISTO
DAS ENTIDADES LEGAIS*

Alferio Dgedge
*FL&A - FERNANDA LOPES &
ASSOCIADOS ADVOGADOS*

Fulgêncio Dimande
*MANICA FREIGHT
SERVICES SARL*

Teresa Empis Falcão
*VDA - VIEIRA DE ALMEIDA
& ASSOCIADOS*

Ahmad Essak
PWC MOZAMBIQUE

Vanessa Fernandes
*CGA - COUTO, GRAÇA E
ASSOCIADOS, SOCIEDADE
DE ADVOGADOS*

Telmo Ferreira
*CGA - COUTO, GRAÇA E
ASSOCIADOS, SOCIEDADE
DE ADVOGADOS*

Arsénio Ricardo
ELECTROCUAMBA

Maria Fatima Fonseca
*MAPUTO CITY COURT
(COMMERCIAL CHAMBER)*

Pinto Fulane
BANCO DE MOÇAMBIQUE

Nipul K. Govan
*HENRIQUES, ROCHA &
ASSOCIADOS (MOZAMBIQUE
LEGAL CIRCLE ADVOGADOS)*

Jorge Graça
*CGA - COUTO, GRAÇA E
ASSOCIADOS, SOCIEDADE
DE ADVOGADOS*

Abdul Satar Hamid
BDO MOZAMBIQUE

Zara Jamal
JLA

Adriano João
PWC MOZAMBIQUE

Katia Jussub
*CM&A - CARLOS MARTINES
& ASSOCIADOS*

Gimina Langa
*SAL & CALDEIRA,
ADVOGADOS, LDA*

Rui Loforte
*CGA - COUTO, GRAÇA E
ASSOCIADOS, SOCIEDADE
DE ADVOGADOS*

B. Longamane
*FL&A - FERNANDA LOPES &
ASSOCIADOS ADVOGADOS*

Fernanda Lopes
*FL&A - FERNANDA LOPES &
ASSOCIADOS ADVOGADOS*

Mara Lopes
*HENRIQUES, ROCHA &
ASSOCIADOS (MOZAMBIQUE
LEGAL CIRCLE ADVOGADOS)*

Eugénio Luis
BANCO DE MOÇAMBIQUE

Duarte Marques da Cruz
*MC&A - SOCIEDADE
DE ADVOGADOS RL*

Vítor Marques da Cruz
*MC&A - SOCIEDADE
DE ADVOGADOS RL*

Stayleir Marroquim
*MARROQUIM, NKUTUMULA,
MACIA & ASSOCIADOS*

Carlos Martins
*CM&A - CARLOS MARTINES
& ASSOCIADOS*

João Martins
PWC MOZAMBIQUE

Tiago Martins
*TRANSITEX GLOBAL LOGISTICS
OPERATIONS PTY. LTD.*

João Mayer Moreira
*VDA - VIEIRA DE ALMEIDA
& ASSOCIADOS*

Ana Berta Mazuze
*HENRIQUES, ROCHA &
ASSOCIADOS (MOZAMBIQUE
LEGAL CIRCLE ADVOGADOS)*

Jean-Louis Neves Mandelli
SHEARMAN & STERLING LLP

Ilidio Nhamahango
BDO MOZAMBIQUE

Kekobad Patel
*CONFEDERAÇÃO DAS
ASSOCIAÇÕES ECONÓMICAS
DE MOÇAMBIQUE (CTA)*

Diana Ramalho
*SAL & CALDEIRA,
ADVOGADOS, LDA*

Arsénio Ricardo
ELECTROCUAMBA

Christopher Tanner
FAO REPRESENTATION

Acacio Tembe
*MOTT MACDONALD PDNA
MOÇAMBIQUE, LDA*

Constancio Tevete
*FL&A - FERNANDA LOPES &
ASSOCIADOS ADVOGADOS*

Liana Utxavo
*MANICA FREIGHT
SERVICES SARL*

Cesar Vamos Ver
*SAL & CALDEIRA,
ADVOGADOS, LDA*

Ricardo Veloso
PWC ANGOLA

Joaquim Vilanculos
*FL&A - FERNANDA LOPES &
ASSOCIADOS ADVOGADOS*

MYANMAR

*AGX LOGISTICS
MYANMAR CO. LTD.*

*DUANE MORRIS & SELVAM
LLP MYANMAR*

*PRICEWATERHOUSECOOPERS
MYANMAR CO. LTD.*

RAJAH & TANN LLP

Quamruddin Ahmed
BAY LINE SHIPPING PTE. LTD.

Mar Mar Aung
DFDL

Sam Britton
ZICOLAW MYANMAR LTD.

Sher Hann Chua
*TILLEKE & GIBBINS
MYANMAR LTD.*

William Greenlee
DFDL

Yu Lin Khoo
ZICOLAW MYANMAR LTD.

Nay Myo Myat Ko
CARE FREIGHT SERVICES LTD.

U Moe Kyaw Aye
MYANMAR CUSTOMS

Yan Lin
*YANGON CITY ELECTRICITY
SUPPLY BOARDS*

Jean Loi
VDB LOI

Ah Lonn Maung
DFDL

Myo Min
*DIRECTORATE OF
INVESTMENT AND COMPANY
ADMINISTRATION (DICA)*

Yee Mon Mon
*YANGON CITY ELECTRICITY
SUPPLY BOARDS*

Nila Mu
DICA

Mya Myint Zu
DFDL

Win Naing
WIN & CHO LAW FIRM

Nwe Oo
*TILLEKE & GIBBINS
MYANMAR LTD.*

Su Wai Phyo
ZICOLAW MYANMAR LTD.

Key Pwint Phoo Wai
CARE FREIGHT SERVICES LTD.

U San Lwin
JLPW LEGAL SERVICES

Kyaw Soe Min
MYANMA APEX BANK

Cheah Swee Gim
KELVIN CHIA YANGON LTD.

Yuwadee Theanngarm
*TILLEKE & GIBBINS
MYANMAR LTD.*

U Myint Thein
MYINT THEIN & SON

Danyel Thomson
DFDL

Su Su Tin
WIN THIN & ASSOCIATES

Hnin Thet Wai
ZICOLAW MYANMAR LTD.

Lucy Wayne
*LUCY WAYNE &
ASSOCIATES LIMITED*

Htut Khaung Win
*YANGON CITY DEVELOPMENT
COMMITTEE*

Khin Phyu Win
MYANMAR GLOBAL LAW FIRM

Myo Win
VDB LOI

Zaw Win
*YANGON CITY DEVELOPMENT
COMMITTEE*

Cho Cho Wynn
*THILAWA SPECIAL ECONOMIC
ZONE MANAGEMENT
COMMITTEE*

Kyaw Ye Tun
MINISTRY OF FINANCE

NAMIBIA

Gino Absai
*KPMG ADVISORY SERVICES
(NAMIBIA) PTY. LTD.*

Joos Agenbach
KOEP & PARTNERS

Tiaan Bazuin
NAMIBIAN STOCK EXCHANGE

Adeline Beukes
*STANDARD BANK
NAMIBIA LIMITED*

Daneale C. Beukes
*ENGLING, STRITTER
& PARTNERS*

Clifford Bezuidenhout
*ENGLING, STRITTER
& PARTNERS*

Benita Blume
H.D. BOSSAU & CO.

Hanno D. Bossau
H.D. BOSSAU & CO.

Stephanie Busch
ENSAFRICA | NAMIBIA

Andy Chase
*STAUCH+PARTNERS
ARCHITECTS*

Esi Chase
ADVOCATE

Dirk Hendrik Conradie
CONRADIE & DAMASEB

Myra Craven
ENS

André Davids
MAERSK NAMIBIA PTY. LTD.

Britt du Plessis
STANDARD BANK NAMIBIA

Marcha Erni
TRANSUNION

Johann Espag
CLARKE ARCHITECTS

Ulrich Etzold
ETZOLD-DUVENHAGE FIRM

Stefan Hugo
PWC NAMIBIA

Frank Köpplinger
KÖPPLINGER BOLTMAN

Norbert Liebich
*TRANSWORLD CARGO
PTY. LTD.*

Anneri Lück
PWC NAMIBIA

Prisca Mandimika
*MINISTRY OF LANDS
AND RESETTLEMENT*

John Mandy
MMM CONSULTANCY

Marie Mandy
MMM CONSULTANCY

Tiago Martins
*TRANSITEX GLOBAL LOGISTICS
OPERATIONS PTY. LTD.*

Memory Mbai
*KPMG ADVISORY SERVICES
(NAMIBIA) PTY. LTD.*

Johan Nel
PWC NAMIBIA

Tim Parkhouse
*NAMIBIAN EMPLOYER'S
FEDERATION*

Frank Sauerbach
*DEUTSCHE GESELLSCHAFT
FÜR INTERNATIONALE
ZUSAMMENARBEIT (GIZ)*

Johny M. Smith
WALVIS BAY CORRIDOR GROUP

Helmut Stolze
CONRADIE & DAMASEB

Axel Stritter
*ENGLING, STRITTER
& PARTNERS*

Erentia Tromp
*INSTITUTE OF CHARTERED
ACCOUNTANTS OF NAMIBIA*

Willem van Greunen
KÖPPLINGER BOLTMAN

Stefan van Zijl
KOEP & PARTNERS

NEPAL

Lalit Aryal
*LA & ASSOCIATES CHARTERED
ACCOUNTANTS*

Narayan Bajaj
NARAYAN BAJAJ & ASSOCIATES

Jaya Raj Bhandari
NEPAL ELECTRICITY AUTHORITY

Ankit Dhakal
*DHAKAL & GHIMIRE LAW
OFFICES, PVT. LTD.*

Sarita Duwal
JKK AND ASSOCIATES

Suraj Guragain
*LA & ASSOCIATES CHARTERED
ACCOUNTANTS*

Janak Raj Joshi
*MINISTRY OF LAND REFORM
AND MANAGEMENT*

Rabin K.C.
CORPORATE LAW ASSOCIATES

Shreedhar Kapali
SHANGRI-LA FREIGHT PVT. LTD.

Jha Kaushlendra
JKK AND ASSOCIATES

Gourish K. Kharel
KTO INC.

Amir Maharjan
*SAFE CONSULTING ARCHITECTS
& ENGINEERS PVT. LTD.*

Ashok Man Kapali
SHANGRI-LA FREIGHT PVT. LTD.

Bijaya Mishra
*PRADHAN, GHIMIRE
& ASSOCIATES*

Anjan Neupane
NEUPANE LAW ASSOCIATES

Usha Pandey
*PRADHAN, GHIMIRE
& ASSOCIATES*

Dev Raj Paudyal
*UNIVERSITY OF SOUTHERN
QUEENSLAND*

Devendra Pradhan
*PRADHAN, GHIMIRE
& ASSOCIATES*

Rajan Sharma
*NEPAL FREIGHT FORWARDERS
ASSOCIATION*

P. L. Shrestha
*EVERGREEN CARGO
SERVICES PVT. LTD.*

Rajeshwor Shrestha
SINHA VERMA LAW CONCERN

Ramji Shrestha
*PRADHAN, GHIMIRE
& ASSOCIATES*

Suman Lal Shrestha
H.R. LOGISTIC PVT. LTD.

Mahesh Kumar Thapa
SINHA VERMA LAW CONCERN

NETHERLANDS

MINISTRY OF FINANCE

Joost Achterberg
KENNEDY VAN DER LAAN

Maarten Appels
VAN DOORNE NV

Ruud Berndsen
LIANDER

Gert Jan Boeve
VAN BENTHEM & KEULEN NV

Reint Bolhuis
*AKD LAWYERS & CIVIL
LAW NOTARIES*

Matthijs Bolkenstein
EVERSHEDS SUTHERLAND BV

Roland Brandsma
PWC NETHERLANDS

Ate Bremmer
KENNEDY VAN DER LAAN

Martin Brink
VAN BENTHEM & KEULEN NV

Margriet de Boer
*JUST LITIGATION
ADVOCATUUR BV*

Wyneke de Gelder
PWC NETHERLANDS

Taco de Lange
*AKD LAWYERS & CIVIL
LAW NOTARIES*

Rolef de Weijs
HOUTHOFF BURUMA

Marc Diepstraten
PWC NETHERLANDS

Menno Duin
*VERENIGING VAN
ROTTERDAMSE CARGADOORS*

Sharon Edoo
EVERSHEDS SUTHERLAND BV

Noël Ellens
*FRUYTIER LAWYERS
IN BUSINESS*

Arjan Enneman
EXPATAX BV

Jan Hockx
LEXENCE

Mick Hurks
HÖCKER ADVOCATEN

Niels Huurdeman
HOUTHOFF BURUMA

Marcel Kettenis
PWC NETHERLANDS

Edwin M.A.J. Kleefstra
*STOLP+KAB ADVISEURS
EN ACCOUNTANTS BV*

Christian Koedam
PWC NETHERLANDS

Gerard Koster
*BAKER & MCKENZIE
AMSTERDAM NV*

Thomas Kraan
*STICHTING BUREAU
KREDIET REGISTRATIE*

Andrej Kwitowski
AKADIS BV

Martijn Lentz
CHAMBER OF COMMERCE

Lucas Lustermans
EVERSHEDS SUTHERLAND BV

Danique Meijer
HVK STEVENS LEGAL BV

Sharon Neven
PWC NETHERLANDS

Matthias Noorlander
*AUTHORITY FOR CONSUMERS
AND MARKETS*

Peter Plug
*OFFICE OF ENERGY
REGULATION*

Hugo Reumkens
VAN DOORNE NV

Jan Willem Schenk
HVK STEVENS LEGAL BV

Rutger Schimmelpenninck
HOUTHOFF BURUMA

Jack Schrijver
*BAKER & MCKENZIE
AMSTERDAM NV*

Maaike Sips
PWC NETHERLANDS

Fedor Tanke
*BAKER & MCKENZIE
AMSTERDAM NV*

Manon Ultee
PWC NETHERLANDS

Kor Van Dijk
*BAKER & MCKENZIE
AMSTERDAM NV*

Gert-Jan van Gijs
*VAT LOGISTICS (OCEAN
FREIGHT) BV*

Wies van Kesteren
*DE BRAUW BLACKSTONE
WESTBROEK*

IJsbrand Van Straten
STIBBE

Frédéric Verhoeven
HOUTHOFF BURUMA

Janine Verweij
*OFFICE OF ENERGY
REGULATION*

Reinout Vriesendorp
*DE BRAUW BLACKSTONE
WESTBROEK*

Floris-Jan Werners
VAN DOORNE NV

Stephan Westera
LEXENCE

Marcel Willems
FIELDFISHER NV

Bianco Witjes
LIANDER

Bob Zonderwijk
VAN DOORNE NV

NEW ZEALAND

*RSM NEW ZEALAND
(AUCKLAND)*

Mo Al Obaidi
HESKETH HENRY LAWYERS

Michael Brosnahan
*MINISTRY OF BUSINESS,
INNOVATION & EMPLOYMENT*

Daniel Brunt
*NEW ZEALAND
CUSTOMS SERVICE*

Paul Chambers
*ANDERSON CREAGH
LAI LIMITED*

Philip Coombe
*PANALPINA WORLD
TRANSPORT LLP*

Robyn Cox
*MINISTRY OF BUSINESS,
INNOVATION & EMPLOYMENT*

George Culver
PWC NEW ZEALAND

John Cuthbertson
PWC NEW ZEALAND

Matthew Davie
BELL GULLY

Corey Dixon
PWC NEW ZEALAND

Laura Drake
*SIMPSON GRIERSON,
MEMBER OF LEX MUNDI*

Igor Drinkovic
MINTER ELLISON RUDD WATTS

Ashton Dunn
ASTECH ELECTRICAL LTD.

Jonathan Embling
MINTER ELLISON RUDD WATTS

Alexandra Flaus
WEBB HENDERSON

Michael Gartshore
WEBB HENDERSON

Ian Gault
BELL GULLY

Tony Gault
PWC NEW ZEALAND

Syvaie Ghamry
MINTER ELLISON RUDD WATTS

Lucy Harris
*SIMPSON GRIERSON,
MEMBER OF LEX MUNDI*

James Hawes
*SIMPSON GRIERSON,
MEMBER OF LEX MUNDI*

Matthew Kersey
RUSSELL MCVEAGH

Jeffrey Lai
*ANDERSON CREAGH
LAI LIMITED*

Kate Lane
MINTER ELLISON RUDD WATTS

Michael Langdon
MINTER ELLISON RUDD WATTS

Alex MacDuff
RUSSELL MCVEAGH

Annaliese McIntyre
WEBB HENDERSON

Andrew Minturn
*QUALTECH
INTERNATIONAL LTD.*

Phillipa Muir
*SIMPSON GRIERSON,
MEMBER OF LEX MUNDI*

Robert Muir
*LAND INFORMATION
NEW ZEALAND*

Ian Page
BRANZ

Mihai Pascariu
MINTER ELLISON RUDD WATTS

Jose Paul
AUCKLAND CITY COUNCIL

Marcus Playle
RUSSELL MCVEAGH

Silvana Schenone
MINTER ELLISON RUDD WATTS

Kelvin Sue
*SIMPSON GRIERSON,
MEMBER OF LEX MUNDI*

Andrew Tetzlaff
*SIMPSON GRIERSON,
MEMBER OF LEX MUNDI*

Jennifer Tunna
LOWNDES

Ben Upton
*SIMPSON GRIERSON,
MEMBER OF LEX MUNDI*

Simon Vannini

Mike Whale
LOWNDES

NICARAGUA

Guillermo Abella
INTERMODAL | CMA CGM

Samantha Aguilar
LATAMLEX NICARAGUA

Yara Valesia Alemán Sequeira
ARIAS LAW

Bernardo Arauz
BAUTRANS & LOGISTICS

Humberto Argüello
CETREX

Alfredo Artiles
KPMG

Maria Alejandra Aubert
Carcamo
GARCÍA & BODÁN

Juan Ramon Aviles Molina
LAWYER

Soledad Balladares
SUPERINTENDENCIA DE BANCOS

Henrik Bang
EXPORTADORA ATLANTIC SA

Ana Carolina Baquero Urroz
LATIN ALLIANCE

Minerva Adriana Bellorín
Rodríguez
PACHECO COTO

Flavio Andrés Berríos Zepeda
MULTICONSULT & CIA LTDA

Blanca Buitrago
GARCÍA & BODÁN

Edmundo Castillo
EXPERTIS CASTILLO Y FIALLOS

Francisco Castro
PWC NICARAGUA

Brenda Darce
CETREX

Maricarmen Espinosa de
Molina
*MOLINA & ASOCIADOS
CENTRAL LAW*

Ana Gabriel Espinoza
ARIAS LAW

Maria Antonieta Fiallos
EXPERTIS CASTILLO Y FIALLOS

Diana Fonseca
ARIAS LAW

Terencio Garcia Montenegro
GARCÍA & BODÁN

Maryeling Suyen Guevara
Sequeira
ARIAS LAW

Federico Gurdian
GARCÍA & BODÁN

Eduardo Gutierrez
PACHECO COTO

Denisse Gutiérrez Rayo
GARCÍA & BODÁN

Gerardo Hernandez
CONSORTIUM LEGAL

Rodrigo Ibarra Rodney
ARIAS LAW

Eduardo Lacayo
TRANSUNION

Brenda Ninoska Martínez
Aragón
CONSORTIUM LEGAL

Jose Ivan Mejia Miranda
GARCÍA & BODÁN

Xiomara Mena
CETREX

Fernando Midence Mantilla
*ALVARADO Y ASOCIADOS,
MEMBER OF LEX MUNDI*

Soraya Montoya Herrera

Jeanethe Morales Núñez
SUPERINTENDENCIA DE BANCOS

Tania Muñoz
KPMG

Luis Murillo
REX CARGO NICARAGUA SA

Ramón Ortega
PwC

Jose René Orúe Cruz
*CENTRO DE MEDIACION
Y ARBITRAJE CMA*

Silvio Guillermo Otero Quiroz
GLOBALTRANS INTERNACIONAL

Ivania Paguaga
ARIAS LAW

Antonio Palomares
DISNORTE-DISSUR

Andrea Paniagua
PwC DOMINICAN REPUBLIC

Wilder Pérez
AIMAR GROUP

Rigoberto Pineda
PINEDA GARCÍA & ASOCIADOS

Alonso Porras
PACHECO COTO

Olga Renee Torres
LATIN ALLIANCE

Yader Oswaldo Reyes
Membreno
GRUPO VESTA

Erwin Rodriguez
PwC NICARAGUA

Carlos Taboada Rodríguez
CONSORTIUM LEGAL

Patricia Rodríguez
MULTICONSULT & CIA LTDA

Alfonso José Sandino Granera
CONSORTIUM LEGAL

Rodrigo Taboada
CONSORTIUM LEGAL

Carlos Téllez
GARCÍA & BODÁN

Joe Henry Thompson
ESTUDIO JURÍDICO ADUANERO

Diógenes Velásquez V.
PACHECO COTO

Gustavo Viales
*ASOCIACIÓN NICARAGÜENSE
DE AGENTES NAVIERAS*

Diana Zelaya
GARCÍA & BODÁN

Mario Zelaya
DGUERRERO INGS. SA

NIGER

BCEAO

CREDITINFO VOLO

*MINISTÈRE DE L'ENERGIE
ET DU PETROLE*

*PROJET SÉCURITÉ DES
INSTALLATIONS ÉLECTRIQUES
INTÉRIEURES AU NIGER (SIEIN)*

VILLE DE NIAMEY

Abdallah Abdoulati
*BANQUE CENTRALE DES ETATS
DE L'AFRIQUE DE L'OUEST*

Cyprien Abdoulaye
*DIRECTION GÉNÉRALE
DES IMPÔTS*

Daouda Adamou
OFFICE NOTARIAL AHD

Issoufou Adamou
NIGELEC

Mohamadou Amadou
FIDUCIAIRE CONSEILS ET AUDIT

Issouf Baco
*SOCIÉTÉ NIGÉRIENNE
DE TRANSIT (NITRA)*

Ibrahim Boubacar Arbi
*CABINET D'INGÉNIERIE
CONSEIL (CIC-NIGER SARL)*

Amadou Boukar
*CELLULE DE PARTENARIAT
PUBLIC PRIVÉ*

Mohamed Amadou Boukar
*ETUDE DE MAÎTRE MOHAMED
AMADOU BOUKAR*

Moustapha Boukari
CABINET BOUKARI

Moussa Coulibaly
*CABINET D'AVOCATS
SOUNA-COULIBALY*

Moussa Dantia
*MAISON DE
L'ENTREPRISE NIGER*

Aïssatou Djibo
*ETUDE DE MAÎTRE
DJIBO AÏSSATOU*

Ali Djimba
CAT LOGISTICS

Mai Moussa Ellhadji Basshir
*TRIBUNAL DE GRANDE
INSTANCE HORS CLASSE
DE NIAMEY*

Boureïma Fodi
*CABINET D'AVOCATS
SOUNA-COULIBALY*

Abder Rhamane Halidou
Abdoulaye
*CHAMBRE NATIONALE DES
NOTAIRES DU NIGER*

Souley Hammi Illiassou
CABINET KOUAOVI

Ali Idrissa Sounna
TOUTELEC NIGER SA

Seybou Issifi
URBAMED CONSULT

Habibou Kane Kadoure
AGENCE PROJEDIS AFRIQUE

Bernar-Oliver Kouaovi
CABINET KOUAOVI

Fati Kountche-Adji
CABINET FATI KOUNTCHE

Zeinabou Labo Maiga
MINISTÈRE DE LA JUSTICE

Lambert Lainé
*ETUDE DE MAÎTRE
ACHIMI RILIWANOU*

Aly Mamadou Ousmane
*MINISTÈRE DU COMMERCE
ET DE LA PROMOTION
DU SECTEUR PRIVÉ*

Sabiou Mamane Naissa
*TRIBUNAL DE COMMERCE
DE NIAMEY*

Mamane Sani Manane
*BUREAU D'ETUDES
BALA & HIMO*

Ali Moctar
*CHAMBRE DES
NOTAIRES DU NIGER*

Sadou Mounkaila
HASKÉ SOLAIRE

Yayé Mounkaïla
*CABINET D'AVOCATS
MOUNKAILA-NIANDOU*

Ibrahim Mounouni
*BUREAU D'ETUDES
BALA & HIMO*

Ali Hamidou Nafissatou
*CELLULE DE PARTENARIAT
PUBLIC PRIVÉ*

Linda Rakotonavalona
JOHN W. FFOOKS & CO.

Achimi M. Riliwanou
*ETUDE DE MAÎTRE
ACHIMI RILIWANOU*

Idrissa Tchernaka
SCPA LBTI & PARTNERS

Hamadou Yacouba
*ETUDE DE MAÎTRE DODO
DAN GADO HAOUA*

Wouro Yahia
*ETUDE D'AVOCATS MARC LE
BIHAN & COLLABORATEURS*

Ali Yeya
*DIRECTION GÉNÉRALE
DES IMPÔTS*

Tinni Younoussa
BATE INTERNATIONAL

NIGERIA

ASO VILLA DEMO DAY

*CREDIT REGISTRY SERVICES
(CREDIT BUREAU) PLC*

*FEDERAL INLAND
REVENUE SERVICE*

LAGOS STATE GOVERNMENT

*NIGERIAN MARITIME
ADMINISTRATION &
SAFETY AGENCY*

Ijeoma Abalogu
GBENGA BIOBAKU & CO.

Ismail Abdulaziz
POINTBLANK ATTORNEYS

Stella Abdulkadir
JACOBS & BIGAELS

Bala Abdullahi
BANK OF AGRICULTURE

Fariha Abdullahi
*DIKKO AND MAHMOUD
SOLICITORS AND ADVOCATES*

Mohammed K. Abdulsalam
GITRAS LTD.

Innocent Abidoye
NNENNA EJEKAM ASSOCIATES

Lemea Abina
STERLING PARTNERSHIP

Oluseyi Abiodun Akinwunmi
*AKINWUNMI & BUSARI
LEGAL PRACTITIONERS*

Zainab Abolarin
CRC CREDIT BUREAU LIMITED

Akinbiyi Abudu
EY

Peter Adaji
*CORPORATE AFFAIRS
COMMISSION*

Bashir H. Adamu
DESIGN PLUS

Alawale Adebambo
PERCHSTONE & GREAYS

Olufunmilayo Adebanjo
FIRST BANK OF NIGERIA PLC

Olaleye Adebiyi
WTS ADEBIYI & ASSOCIATES

Olasupo Musa Adedokun
*NATIONAL COLLATERAL
REGISTRY*

Joseph Adegbite
NIGERIAN PORTS AUTHORITY

Kunle Adegbite
CANAAN SOLICITORS

Bode Adegoke
BLOOMFIELD LAW PRACTICE

Steve Adehi
STEVE ADEHI AND CO.

Olufunke Adekoya
*AELEX, LEGAL PRACTITIONERS
& ARBITRATORS*

Ademola Adesalu
CRC CREDIT BUREAU LIMITED

Adebayo Adewale
BAWAG CHAMBERS

Agbolade Adeyemi
UDO UDOMA & BELO-OSAGIE

Tunji Adeyemi
BANWO & IGHODALO

Olamilekan Adeyemo
PwC NIGERIA

Mary Adeyi
*DIKKO AND MAHMOUD
SOLICITORS AND ADVOCATES*

Albert Adu
ALLIANCE LAW FIRM

Dayo Adu
BLOOMFIELD LAW PRACTICE

Daniel Agbor
UDO UDOMA & BELO-OSAGIE

Akram Ahmed
*BHAGAVAN CLEARING
AGENCY NIGERIA LTD.*

Balarabe Ahmed
MAERSK LINE NIGERIA

Fatima Aigbomian
STERLING PARTNERSHIP

Michael Ajaegbo
ALLIANCE LAW FIRM

Kunle Ajagbe
PERCHSTONE & GREAYS

Babatunde Ajibade
SPA AJIBADE & CO.

Odein Ajumogobia
AJUMOGOBIA & OKEKE

Blessing Ajunwo
ALLIANCE LAW FIRM

Ahmed Akanbi
*AKANBI & WIGWE LEGAL
PRACTITIONERS*

Azeez Akande
JACKSON, ETTI & EDU

Manuel Akinshola
JACOBS & BIGAELS

Iwilade Akintayo
KUSAMOTU & KUSAMOTU

Bukola Akinwonmi
OLANIWUN AJAYI LP

Jesuloba Akinyele
OLANIWUN AJAYI LP

Dafe Akpeneye
PwC NIGERIA

Folake Alabi
OLANIWUN AJAYI LP

Temidayo Alade
OLANIWUN AJAYI LP

Ezinne Alajemba
*AKANBI & WIGWE LEGAL
PRACTITIONERS*

Toyosi Alasi
BANWO & IGHODALO

Joke Aliu
ALUKO & OYEBODE

Al-Amin Aliyu
*CORPORATE AFFAIRS
COMMISSION*

Maimunat Aliyu
*CORPORATE AFFAIRS
COMMISSION*

Usman Aliyu Mahmud
*NIGERIAN COMMUNICATIONS
COMMISSION*

Jonathan Aluju
OLANIWUN AJAYI LP

Chioma Amadi
*AKANBI & WIGWE LEGAL
PRACTITIONERS*

Kayode Amodu
J.B. MAJIYAGBE & CO.

Sola Arifayan
IKEYI & ARIFAYAN

Oluseye Arowolo
DELOITTE

Jude Ashiedu
EDUJETAGE

Oluwapelumi Asiwaju
*G. ELIAS & CO. SOLICITORS
AND ADVOCATES*

Zion Athora
EY

Ebunoluwa Awosika
AJUMOGOBIA & OKEKE

Anthony Ayalogu
NIGERIAN CUSTOMS

Israel Aye
STERLING PARTNERSHIP

Seth Azubuike
PERCHSTONE & GREAYS

Tomilehin Babafemi
*G. ELIAS & CO. SOLICITORS
AND ADVOCATES*

Zainab Babalola
*AKINWUNMI & BUSARI
LEGAL PRACTITIONERS*

Bisola Babington
PERCHSTONE & GREAYS

Jerry Bakut
*NIGERIAN EXPORT PROCESSING
ZONE AUTHORITY*

Mohammed Bawa
CENTRAL BANK OF NIGERIA

Risikat Bukola Bello
MINISTRY OF PHYSICAL
PLANNING AND URBAN
DEVELOPMENT

Gilbert Benson-Oladeinbo
G. ELIAS & CO. SOLICITORS
AND ADVOCATES

Ibifubara Berenibara
AELEX, LEGAL PRACTITIONERS
& ARBITRATORS

Betty Biayeibo
PUNUKA ATTORNEYS
& SOLICITORS

Taofeek Bola Shittu
IKEYI & ARIFAYAN

Cephas Caleb
ALUKO & OYEBODE

Afolabi Caxton-Martins
ADCAX NOMINEES LTD.

Mercy Chibuike-Iheama
CENTRE FOR MANAGEMENT
DEVELOPMENT (CMD)

Ukata Christian
AFRIGLOBE SHIPPING LINES LTD.

Kyzito Dakyen
CENTRAL BANK OF NIGERIA

Bisola Dere
STERLING PARTNERSHIP

Obinna Dike
ALLIANCE LAW FIRM

Damilola Durosimi-Etti
OLANIWUN AJAYI LP

Colin Egemonye
GOLDSMITHS SOLICITORS

Osaro Eghobamien S.A.N.
PERCHSTONE & GRAEYS

Emmanuel Egwuagu
OBLA & CO.

Nnenna Ejekam
NNENNA EJEKAM ASSOCIATES

Tunde Ekundayo
GIANT VIEWS PLUS

David Elesinmogun
ELESINMOGUN & EGWUATU

Theophilus I. Emuwa
AELEX

Kenneth Erikume
PWC NIGERIA

Idongesit Essien
NIGERIAN EXPORT PROMOTION
COUNCIL (NEPC)

Samuel Etuk
1ST ATTORNEYS

Samuel Etukakpan
ENABLING BUSINESS
ENVIRONMENT SECRETARIAT

Ekiomado Ewere-Isaiah
JACKSON, ETTI & EDU

William Ezeagu
NIGERIAN EXPORT PROMOTION
COUNCIL (NEPC)

Ncsike Ezebo
IKEYI & ARIFAYAN

Anse Agu Ezetah
CHIEF LAW AGU EZETAH & CO.

Kenechi Ezezika
IKEYI & ARIFAYAN

Babatunde Fagbohunlu
ALUKO & OYEBODE

Omowumi Fajemiroye
OLANIWUN AJAYI LP

Oluwabamise Fatoke
PERCHSTONE & GRAEYS

Yetunde Filani
WTS ADEBIYI & ASSOCIATES

Augustine Fischer
APM TERMINALS

Fatai Folarin
DELOITTE

Tajudeen Funsho
TAJUDEEN AO FUNSHO
AND ASSOCIATE

Bolaji Gabari
SPA AJIBADE & CO.

Peter Gai
CORPORATE AFFAIRS
COMMISSION

Hassana Gambo
UNIVERSAL ARCHITECTS AND
ENGINEERING CONSULTS

Lionel Garrick
FORTELEGAL PARTNERS

Remi Gbajumo
MAGISTRATE COURT (LAGOS)

Akalonu Gertrude Uzochikwa
CORPORATE AFFAIRS
COMMISSION

Sagir Gezawa
S. S. GEZAWA & CO.

Temitope Giwa
OLANIWUN AJAYI LP

Osayaba Giwa-Osagie
GIWA-OSAGIE & CO

Lateefat Hakeem-Bakare
AJUMOGOBIA & OKEKE

Ibrahim Hashim
ELECTROMECH PRIME
UTILITY RESOURCES LTD.

Tokunbo Ibrahim
PWC NIGERIA

Joseph Idiong
ASSOCIATION OF
NIGERIAN EXPORTERS

Maymunah Idris
FEDERAL MINISTRY OF JUSTICE

Anjola Ige
OLANIWUN AJAYI LP

Chimezie Ihekweazu
CHIKWEM CHAMBERS

Chidinma Ihemedu
ALLIANCE LAW FIRM

Oluwabukola Iji
SPA AJIBADE & CO.

Emmanuel Ikeakonwu
DELOITTE

Nduka Ikeyi
IKEYI & ARIFAYAN

Meshach Ikpe
ABUBAKAR D. SANI & CO.

Funmi Ilamah
ENABLING BUSINESS
ENVIRONMENT SECRETARIAT

Ifedolapo Ilesanmi
KUSAMOTU & KUSAMOTU

Oyeniyi Immanuel
STREAMSOWERS & KÖHN

Ifedayo Iroche
PERCHSTONE & GRAEYS

Paul Kalejaiye
KUSAMOTU & KUSAMOTU

Okorie Kalu
PUNUKA ATTORNEYS
& SOLICITORS

Evarist Kameja
MKONO & CO. ADVOCATES

Jelilat Kareem
CRC CREDIT BUREAU LIMITED

Olatunde King
BANWO & IGHODALO

Dolapo Kokuyi
DETAIL COMMERCIAL
SOLICITORS

Ayodele Kusamotu
KUSAMOTU & KUSAMOTU

Folabi Kuti
PERCHSTONE & GRAEYS

Alhassan L. Alhassan
HOPE ATTORNEYS

Mobolaji Ladapo
OLANIWUN AJAYI LP

Abubakar Ladi Dahiru
CORPORATE AFFAIRS
COMMISSION

Ishaya Livinus Etsu
NIGERIAN ELECTRICITY
REGULATORY
COMMISSION (NERC)

Tahav Iorse-Sheriffs
ASSOCIATED ATTORNEY

Obinna Maduako
OLANIWUN AJAYI LP

Abubakar Mahmoud
DIKKO AND MAHMOUD
SOLICITORS AND ADVOCATES

Muhammad Mainassara
CENTRAL BANK OF NIGERIA

Abdu Maiwada Abubakar
KANO MAGISTRATE COURT

Oghogho Makinde
ALUKO & OYEBODE

Brenda Masangwa
MKONO & CO. ADVOCATES

Kolawole Mayomi
SPA AJIBADE & CO.

Felicia Mosuro
ADCAX NOMINEES LTD.

Bashir Mudi
KANO URBAN PLANNING
AND DEVELOPMENT
AUTHORITY (KNUPDA)

Oluwatoyin Nathaniel
G. ELIAS & CO. SOLICITORS
AND ADVOCATES

Ugochi Ndebbio
KPMG

Juliet Ndoh
IMO STATE UNIVERSITY

Justine Nidiya
CORPORATE AFFAIRS
COMMISSION

Ifunanya Nwajagu
FEDERAL MINISTRY OF JUSTICE

Obinna Nwankwo
NATIONAL COLLATERAL
REGISTRY

Ugochukwu Obi
PERCHSTONE & GRAEYS

V. Uche Obi
ALLIANCE LAW FIRM

Nnamdi Obinwa
KPMG

Chijioke Odo
DELOITTE

Onyinye Odogwu
PUNUKA ATTORNEYS
& SOLICITORS

Abutu Odu
OLAJIDE OYEWOLE LLP

E.A. Offiong
NATIONAL COLLATERAL
REGISTRY

Ugonna Ogbuagu
IKEYI & ARIFAYAN

Nelson Ogbuanya
NOCS CONSULTS

Godson Ogheneochuko
UDO UDOMA & BELO-OSAGIE

Ozofu Ogiemudia
UDO UDOMA & BELO-OSAGIE

Abimbola Ogunbanjo
CHRIS OGUNBANJO & CO.

Makinde Ogunleye
CORPORATE CASTLES LTD.

Yvonne Ogunoiki
IKEYI & ARIFAYAN

Adebola Ogunsanya
OLANIWUN AJAYI LP

Gloria Ogwu
PUNUKA ATTORNEYS
& SOLICITORS

Oladimeji Ojo
ALUKO & OYEBODE

Cindy Ojogbo
OLANIWUN AJAYI LP

Mercy Ojukwu
CENTRAL BANK OF NIGERIA

Chinyere Okafor
G. ELIAS & CO. SOLICITORS
AND ADVOCATES

Ikenna Okafor
PERCHSTONE & GRAEYS

Ngo-Martins Okonmah
ALUKO & OYEBODE

Chukwuma Okoroafor
SOLOLA & AKPANA

Chidubem Okoye
OLANIWUN AJAYI LP

Oluwatosin Okunrinboye
AJUMOGOBIA & OKEKE

Stephen Ola Jagun
JAGUN ASSOCIATES

Eniola Oladunjoye
BANWO & IGHODALO

Moshood Olajide
PWC NIGERIA

Kola B. Olatunbosun
ARCHITEXT ASSOCIATES

Funmilayo Olofintuyi
KUSAMOTU & KUSAMOTU

Adebayo Ologe
PERCHSTONE & GRAEYS

Olumide Ologe
CORPORATE AFFAIRS
COMMISSION

Ajibola Olomola
KPMG

Afolasade Olowe
JACKSON, ETTI & EDU

Temi Olowu
UDO UDOMA & BELO-OSAGIE

Uma Olugo
1ST ATTORNEYS

Olufunke Olutoye
ALUKO & OYEBODE

Peter Oluwafemi
JUDE & PARTNERS

Tolulope Omidiji
PWC NIGERIA

Emmanuel Omoju
WTS ADEBIYI & ASSOCIATES

Bayo Omole
MATRIX SOLICITORS

David Omoleye
KANO DISTRIBUTION
ELECTRICITY COMPANY

Seun Omothosho
CRC CREDIT BUREAU LIMITED

Oluwatunmise Omotoyinbo
OLANIWUN AJAYI LP

Funke Onakoya
AKINWUNMI & BUSARI
LEGAL PRACTITIONERS

Adetola Onayemi
OFFICE OF THE VICE PRESIDENT

Gabriel Onojason
ALLIANCE LAW FIRM

Fred Onuobia
G. ELIAS & CO. SOLICITORS
AND ADVOCATES

Aaron Onyebuchi
STRACHAN PARTNERS

Amede Oputa
DE SPLENDOR SOLICITORS

Nnamdi Oragwu
PUNUKA ATTORNEYS
& SOLICITORS

Benedict Oregbemhe
SPA AJIBADE & CO.

Gbenga Oregun
GMT LIMITED

Ola Orewale
AELEX, LEGAL PRACTITIONERS
& ARBITRATORS

Tunde Osasona
WHITESTONE WORLDWIDE LTD.

Olufunmilayo Osifuye
LAGOS STATE PHYSICAL
PLANNING & DEVELOPMENT
AUTHORITY

Olufemi Ososanya
HLB Z.O. OSOSANYA & CO.

Ignatius Nwosu Owelle
HOMELUX CONSTRUCTION
& EQUIPMENT CO. LTD.

Abraham Oyakhilome
FIRST & FIRST INTERNATIONAL
AGENCIES

Olajumoke Oyebode
PWC NIGERIA

Oluwatomiwa Oyedara
AKINWUNMI & BUSARI
LEGAL PRACTITIONERS

Taiwo Oyedele
PWC NIGERIA

Abiodun Oyeledun
DETAIL COMMERCIAL
SOLICITORS

Bukola Oyeneyin
AKANBI & WIGWE LEGAL
PRACTITIONERS

Olubukola Oyerinde
PWC NIGERIA

Ademola Oyewuni
TIGER SHIPPING

Samuel Oyeyipo
NIGERIAN EXPORT PROMOTION
COUNCIL (NEPC)

Patrick Oyong
FEDERAL MINISTRY OF JUSTICE

Samuel Pamah
BENSON AND BROTHERS
COMPANY

Mahendra Pandey
EKO ELECTRICITY
DISTRIBUTION PLC

Tunde Popoola
CRC CREDIT BUREAU LIMITED

Sulayman Bolanle Raheem
*MINISTRY OF PHYSICAL
PLANNING AND URBAN
DEVELOPMENT*

Nura Sagir Umar
*HIGH COURT OF
JUSTICE - KANO*

Kofo Salam-Alada
CENTRAL BANK OF NIGERIA

Sheriff Salami
CRC CREDIT BUREAU LIMITED

Simisola Salu
PWC NIGERIA

Temitope Samagbeyi
EY

Abubakar Sani
ABUBAKAR D. SANI & CO.

Yewande Senbore
OLANIWUN AJAYI LP

Eric Sesu
PWC NIGERIA

Taofeek 'Bola Shittu
IKEYI & ARIFAYAN

Christine Sijuwade
UDO UDOMA & BELO-OSAGIE

Olusina Sipasi
*AELEX, LEGAL PRACTITIONERS
& ARBITRATORS*

Olugbenga Sodipo
IKEYI & ARIFAYAN

Similoluwa Somuyiwa
OLANIWUN AJAYI LP

Adeola Sunmola
UDO UDOMA & BELO-OSAGIE

Femi Sunmonu
*FEMI SUNMONU &
ASSOCIATES-QAIS CONRAD
LAUREATE SOLICITORS
& NOTARY PUBLIC*

Rafiu Sunmonu
*DELMORE ENGINEERING
AND CONSTRUCTION
COMPANY LIMITED*

Kolade T. Olawuni
BABALAKIN & CO.

Ijeoma Uche
KPMG

Kelechi Ugbeva
BLACKWOOD AND STONE LP

Chinyerugo Ugoji
AELEX

Ovie E. Ukiri
AJUMOGOBIA & OKEKE

Aniekan Ukpanah
UDO UDOMA & BELO-OSAGIE

Adamu M. Usman
F.O. AKINRELE & CO.

Ebere Uzum
UDO UDOMA & BELO-OSAGIE

Uzoamaka Wemambu
STANBIC IBTC BANK LTD.

Uchechukwu Wigwe
*AKANBI & WIGWE LEGAL
PRACTITIONERS*

Kamaluddeen Yahaya
KAMALUDDEEN YAHAYA & CO.

Samuel Yisa
KPMG

Naomi Zayumba
MKONO & CO. ADVOCATES

NORWAY

*NORWEGIAN BUILDING
AUTHORITY*

Nanette Arvesen
*ADVOKATFIRMAET
THOMMESSEN AS*

Jan L. Backer
WIKBORG, REIN & CO.

Eli Beck Nilsen
PWC NORWAY

Stig Berge
*ADVOKATFIRMAET
THOMMESSEN AS*

Elin Bergman
MENON ECONOMICS

John Ole Bjørnerud
HAFSLUND

Ingrid Fladberg Brucker
*ADVOKATFIRMA
SIMONSEN VOGT WIIG*

Camilla Bull
*HOMBLE OLSBY
ADVOKATFIRMA AS*

Per Arne Dæhli
ADVOKATFIRMAET SELMER DA

Tron Dalheim
*ARNTZEN DE BESCHE
ADVOKATFIRMA AS*

Lars Davidsen
HAFSLUND

Lill Egeland
*ADVOKATFIRMA
SIMONSEN VOGT WIIG*

Knut Ekern
PWC NORWAY

Turid Ellingsen
STATENS KARTVERK

Marius Moursund Gisvold
WIKBORG, REIN & CO.

Gjermund Grimsby
MENON ECONOMICS

Leo A. Grünfeld
MENON ECONOMICS

Jarand Gule
YARA INTERNATIONAL ASA

Erlend Haaskjold
*ARNTZEN DE BESCHE
ADVOKATFIRMA AS*

Johan Astrup Heber
WIKBORG, REIN & CO.

Hilde Høksnes
ADVOKATFIRMAET SELMER DA

Heidi Holmelin
ADVOKATFIRMAET SELMER DA

Odd Hylland
PWC NORWAY

Anette Istre
*ADVOKATFIRMA
SIMONSEN VOGT WIIG*

Andreas Jarbø
ADVOKATFIRMAET SELMER DA

Kyrre Width Kielland
ADVOKATFIRMA RÆDER DA

Jarle Kjelingtveit
UNIL AS

Eirin Kogstad
*ARNTZEN DE BESCHE
ADVOKATFIRMA AS*

Bente Langsrud
*ARNTZEN DE BESCHE
ADVOKATFIRMA AS*

Per Einar Lunde
PWC NORWAY

Leif Petter Madsen
WIKBORG, REIN & CO.

William Peter Nordan
*ADVOKATFIRMA
SIMONSEN VOGT WIIG*

Christina Norland
ADVOKATFIRMAET SELMER DA

Ole Kristian Olsby
*HOMBLE OLSBY
ADVOKATFIRMA AS*

Einar Riddervold
PWC NORWAY

Ståle Skutle Arneson
*ADVOKATFIRMA
SIMONSEN VOGT WIIG*

Fredrik Sparre-Enger
ADVOKATFIRMAET SELMER DA

Iselin Stolpestad
*THE BRONNOYSUND
REGISTER CENTER*

Svein Sulland
ADVOKATFIRMAET SELMER DA

Liss Sunde
ADVOKATFIRMA RÆDER DA

Kaare Christian Tapper
WIKBORG, REIN & CO.

Ragnar Ulsund
HAFSLUND

Kai Sølve Urke
WIKBORG, REIN & CO.

Oyvind Vagan
*THE BRONNOYSUND
REGISTER CENTER*

OMAN

*MUSCAT ELECTRICITY
DISTRIBUTION COMPANY*

MUSCAT MUNICIPALITY

Hussein Al Balushi
*MAZOON ELECTRICITY
COMPANY*

Dali Al Habboub
SNR DENTON & CO.

Hamed Amur Al Hajri
*OMAN CABLES
INDUSTRY (SAOG)*

Mohammed Al Khalili
*AL BUSAIDY MANSOOR
JAMAL & CO.*

Al Waleed Al Kiyumi
SNR DENTON & CO.

Abdulredha Al Lawati
SNR DENTON & CO.

Habib Murad Ali Al Raisi
*CENTRAL BANK OF
OMAN (CBO)*

Hamood Al Rawahi
*SAHAR ASKALAN
LEGAL ADVOCACY &
CONSULTANCY (SALEGAL)*

Ahmed Al Salmi
*SAHAR ASKALAN
LEGAL ADVOCACY &
CONSULTANCY (SALEGAL)*

Eman Al Shahry
*SASLO - SAID AL
SHAHRY & PARTNERS*

Said bin Saad Al Shahry
*SASLO - SAID AL
SHAHRY & PARTNERS*

Thamer Al Shahry
*SASLO - SAID AL
SHAHRY & PARTNERS*

Wafa Al Shuaibi
*SASLO - SAID AL
SHAHRY & PARTNERS*

Zuhaira Al Sulaimani
*CURTIS MALLET - PREVOST,
COLT & MOSLE LLP*

Haitham Omar Albalulah
*MOHAMMED IBRAHIM
LAW FIRM*

Najat Al-Ismaily
SNR DENTON & CO.

Ahmed Aljahweri
M.O. HOUSING

Adil Alsobhi
ALSOBHI CONSTRUCTION

Umaima Al-Wahaibi
SNR DENTON & CO.

Ahmed Amor Al Esry
EY

Sahar Askalan
*SAHAR ASKALAN
LEGAL ADVOCACY &
CONSULTANCY (SALEGAL)*

Russell Aycock
PWC OMAN

Azhar Azmi
*SAHAR ASKALAN
LEGAL ADVOCACY &
CONSULTANCY (SALEGAL)*

Piyush Bhandari
*INTUIT MANAGEMENT
CONSULTANCY*

Priyanka Bhandari
*INTUIT MANAGEMENT
CONSULTANCY*

Sadaf Buchanan
SNR DENTON & CO.

Francis D'Souza

Jamie Gibson
TROWERS & HAMLINS

Justine Harding
SNR DENTON & CO.

Davis Kallukaran
HORWATH MAK GHAZALI LLC

Faiz Khan
*AL BUSAIDY MANSOOR
JAMAL & CO.*

Pushpa Malani
PWC OMAN

Mansoor Jamal Malik
*AL BUSAIDY MANSOOR
JAMAL & CO.*

Fathia Mbarak
TROWERS & HAMLINS

Yashpal Mehta

Unmi Muraleedharan
*MUAMIR DESIGN & ENGG
CONSULTANCY LLC*

Ahmed Naveed Farooqui
*OMAN CABLES
INDUSTRY (SAOG)*

Raghavendra Pangala
SEMAC & PARTNERS LLC

Dhanalakshmi Pillai Perumal
SNR DENTON & CO.

Johnson Rajan
*INTUIT MANAGEMENT
CONSULTANCY*

Mohammed Raza
EY

Khalid Rhamtalah Al-Badwi
*RAJAB AL KATHIRI &
ASSOCIATES LEGAL
CONSULTANTS*

Nick Simpson
SNR DENTON & CO.

Ahmed Subai
*SASLO - SAID AL
SHAHRY & PARTNERS*

Roy Thomas
*OMAN CABLES
INDUSTRY (SAOG)*

Rajesh Vaidyanathan
KHIMJI RAMDAS

Simon Ward
*CURTIS MALLET - PREVOST,
COLT & MOSLE LLP*

PAKISTAN

CARGO CORPORATION

FEDERAL BOARD OF REVENUE

MAERSK LINE

*NATIONAL ELECTRIC POWER
REGULATORY AUTHORITY*

Tahir Abbas
MCC PORT QASIM

Zaheer Abbas Chughtai
*QAISER & ABBAS ATTORNEYS
& CORPORATE COUNSELLORS*

Mahmood Abdul Ghani
*MAHMOOD ABDUL
GHANI & CO.*

Umer Abdullah
ABDULLAH & HUSSAIN

Farid Ud Din Ahmad
KPMG

Khalil Ahmad
KARIM CHAMBER

Nadeem Ahmad
*ORR, DIGNAM & CO.
ADVOCATES*

Rana Ahmad
RANA IJAZ & PARTNERS

Jawad Ahmed
*MUHAMMAD FAROOQ & CO.
CHARTERED ACCOUNTANTS*

Shabbir Ahmed
MCC PORT QASIM

Shahid Ahmed
*PROCON ENGINEERING PVT.
LTD., PART OF MASTER MOTOR
CORPORATION PVT. LTD.*

Waheed Ahmed
*LEGIS INN ATTORNEYS &
CORPORATE CONSULTANTS*

Jamil Ahmed Khan
*ERECTION ENGINEERS
AND CONTRACTORS*

Majid Ahmed Khan
*ERECTION ENGINEERS
AND CONTRACTORS*

Muhammed Anas Ajmal
NAVEENA EXPORTERS

Mehmood Alam
TMT LAW SERVICES

Abbas Ali
EY

Akhtar Ali
AKHTAR ALI ASSOCIATES

Syed Ahmed Ali
SURRIDGE & BEECHENO

Tabassum Ali
TMT LAW SERVICES

Syed Ali Zafar
MANDVIWALLA & ZAFAR

A.R. Asad
*DACO INTERNATIONAL
TRANSPORT PVT. LTD.*

Jam Asif Mehmood
AHMED & QAZI

Bushra Aslam
SECURITIES AND EXCHANGE
COMMISSION

Muhammad Awais
EY

Jahanzeb Awan
KHALID ANWER & CO.

Anum Azhar
SAAD RASOOL LAW
ASSOCIATES

Shaezer Azmat
EY

Fawad Baluch
KHALID ANWER & CO.

Hasan Hameed Bhatti
LAHORE WASTE
MANAGEMENT COMPANY

Akeel Bilgrami
NAJMI BILGRAMI
COLLABORATIVE PVT. LTD.

Huzaima Bukhari
HUZAIMA & IKRAM

Aitzaz Aslam Chaudhary
SAAD RASOOL LAW
ASSOCIATES

Waheed Chaudhary
LEGIS INN ATTORNEYS &
CORPORATE CONSULTANTS

Salman Chima
CHIMA & IBRAHIM

Khurram Shehzad Chughtai
JUS & REM

Faisal Daudpota
KHALID DAUDPOTA & CO.

Junaid Daudpota
KHALID DAUDPOTA & CO.

Diana Dsouza
DATACHECK PVT. LTD.

Huma Ejaz Zaman
MANDVIWALLA & ZAFAR

Ikram Fayaz
QAMAR ABBAS & CO.

Kausar Fecto
KAUSAR FECTO & CO.
CHARTERED ACCOUNTANTS

Aman Ghanchi
UNILEVER PAKISTAN LIMITED

Asma Ghayoor
SINDH BUILDING
CONTROL AUTHORITY

Irfan Mir Halepota
LAW FIRM IRFAN M. HALEPOTA

Asma Hameed Khan
SURRIDGE & BEECHENO

Ikramul Haq
HUZAIMA & IKRAM

Salman Haq
EY

Khalil Hashmi
SYNTHETIC PRODUCTS
ENTERPRISES LIMITED

Saim Hashmi
AHMED & QAZI

Faiz-ul Hassan
LAND ADMINISTRATION &
REVENUE MANAGEMENT
INFORMATION SYSTEM
(LARMIS)

Mohammad Hassan Bakshi
ASSOCIATION OF BUILDERS
AND DEVELOPERS OF
PAKISTAN (ABAD)

Khizer Hayat
DANYAL AGENCIES

Dilawar Hussain
DS ENGINEERING SERVICES

Shaukat Hussain

Syed Intisar Hussain
AL HAJ FAW MOTORS
(PVT.) LIMITED

Azhar Iqbal
QURESHI LAW ASSOCIATES

Hasan Irfan Khan
IRFAN & IRFAN

Fiza Islam
LEGIS INN ATTORNEYS &
CORPORATE CONSULTANTS

Muzaffar Islam
LEGIS INN ATTORNEYS &
CORPORATE CONSULTANTS

Ilyas Jabbar
STATE BANK OF PAKISTAN

Tariq Nasim Jan
DATACHECK PVT. LTD.

Zafarullah Jan
KARACHI INTERNATIONAL
CONTAINER TERMINAL

Ismail Javed
JAVED UMAR ENTERPRISES

Rubina Javed
TEXPERTS INTERNATIONAL

M. Javed Hassan
TEXPERTS INTERNATIONAL

Babur Kabir
MCC PORT QASIM

Minam Karim
LMA EBRAHIM HOSAIN,
BARRISTERS, ADVOCATES
& CORPORATE LEGAL
CONSULTANTS

Habib Kazi
KHALID ANWER & CO.

Mayhar Kazi
RIAA BARKER GILLETTE
KARACHI

Aftab Ahmed Khan
SURRIDGE & BEECHENO

Ahmad Shahzad Khan
MARIUM ASSOCIATES

Ameer Khan
INDUS MOTORS CO. LTD.

Arif Khan
QAMAR ABBAS & CO.

Bilal Khan
AL HAJ FAW MOTORS
(PVT.) LIMITED

Hilal Khan
AL HAJ FAW MOTORS
(PVT.) LIMITED

Jahan Khan
SHAHEEN LOGISTICS PVT. LTD.

Shahzeb N. Khan
RIAA BARKER GILLETTE

Shair Khan
MCC PORT QASIM

Faiz Ullah Khan Niazi
SAAD RASOOL LAW
ASSOCIATES

Misbah Kokab
TMT LAW SERVICES

Muhammad Saleem Kundi
KUNDI SERVICES LTD.

Ali Abbas Lali
SAAD RASOOL LAW
ASSOCIATES

Irfan Majeed
NAVEENA EXPORTERS

Mohsin Malik
BUILDERS ASSOCIATES
PVT. LTD.

Nadeem Malik
PROCON ENGINEERING PVT.
LTD., PART OF MASTER MOTOR
CORPORATION PVT. LTD.

Muhammad Mansoor
UF LOGISTICS

Basharat Mehmood
QURESHI LAW ASSOCIATES

Aitzaz Manzoor Memon
RIAA BARKER GILLETTE
KARACHI

Muhammad Mudassir
ADVOCATE HIGH COURT

Syed Muhammad Ijaz
HUZAIMA & IKRAM

Kashif Mukhtar
NATIONAL INDUSTRIES

Anwar Kashif Mumtaz
SAIDUDDUN & CO.

Faiza Muzaffar
LEGIS INN ATTORNEYS &
CORPORATE CONSULTANTS

Mohammad Nadeem
PROCON ENGINEERING PVT.
LTD., PART OF MASTER MOTOR
CORPORATION PVT. LTD.

Muhammad Gohar Nawaz
LAHORE WASTE
MANAGEMENT COMPANY

Faryal Nazir
LMA EBRAHIM HOSAIN,
BARRISTERS, ADVOCATES
& CORPORATE LEGAL
CONSULTANTS

Omaimah Nazir

Owais Patel
DATACHECK PVT. LTD.

Ahmad Pervez Mirza
ARCHITECTS AFFILIATION

Faisal Perwaiz Umer
PERWAIZ UMAR ENTERPRISES

Shahbakht Pirzada
RIAA BARKER GILLETTE
KARACHI

Khushbakht Qaiser
QAISER & ABBAS ATTORNEYS
& CORPORATE COUNSELLORS

Zarfishan Qaiser
QAISER & ABBAS ATTORNEYS
& CORPORATE COUNSELLORS

Naveed Qamar
PROCON ENGINEERING PVT.
LTD., PART OF MASTER MOTOR
CORPORATION PVT. LTD.

Adnan Qureshi
QURESHI LAW ASSOCIATES

Junaid Qureshi
PAKISTAN INTERNATIONAL
CONTAINER TERMINAL

Abdul Rahman
QAMAR ABBAS & CO.

Nageen Rahman
KPMG

Zaki Rahman
LMA EBRAHIM HOSAIN,
BARRISTERS, ADVOCATES
& CORPORATE LEGAL
CONSULTANTS

Arslan Rana
MCC PORT QASIM

Kashif Rasheed
PAK SUZUKI MOTOR CO. LTD.

Ghulam Rasool
HAIDER SHAMSI & CO.,
CHARTERED ACCOUNTANTS

Saad Rasool
SAAD RASOOL LAW
ASSOCIATES

Tayyab Raza
TMT LAW SERVICES

Abdur Razzaq
QAMAR ABBAS & CO.

Khalid A. Rehman
SURRIDGE & BEECHENO

Saad Saboor
EY

Ahmed Saeed
SAAD RASOOL LAW
ASSOCIATES

Rana Sajjad
RANA IJAZ & PARTNERS

Aftab Salahuddin
EY

Jawad A. Sarwana
ABRAHAM & SARWANA

Shakil Sarwar
GHANDHARA NISSAN LTD.

Mohammad Ali Seena
SURRIDGE & BEECHENO

Zulfiqar Shah
LAND ADMINISTRATION &
REVENUE MANAGEMENT
INFORMATION SYSTEM
(LARMIS)

Muhammad Shahid
SYNTHETIC PRODUCTS
ENTERPRISES LIMITED

Shabir Sharif
MASTRADE21

Arshad Shehzad
TAXPERTS

Adnan Sheikh
AKRAM SHEIKH LAW
ASSOCIATES

Barrister Sherjeel
AKRAM SHEIKH LAW
ASSOCIATES

Muneeb Ahmed Shiekh
MANDVIWALLA & ZAFAR

Muhammad Siddique
SECURITIES AND EXCHANGE
COMMISSION

Masood Siddiqui
ASHAKOOR & BROS

Ameena Suhail
QURESHI LAW ASSOCIATES

Haris Syed Raza
GERRY'S DNATA PVT. LTD.

Muhammad Tahir
STATE BANK OF PAKISTAN

Waqas Ahmed Tamimi
DELOITTE YOUSUF ADIL,
CHARTERED ACCOUNTANTS

Ali Thaheem
SURRIDGE & BEECHENO

Saud ul-Hassan
EY

Farhan Ullah
ATTORNEY

Fiza Usama
LEGIS INN ATTORNEYS &
CORPORATE CONSULTANTS

Chaudhary Usman
LMA EBRAHIM HOSAIN,
BARRISTERS, ADVOCATES
& CORPORATE LEGAL
CONSULTANTS

Hana Yahyal
SAIDUDDUN & CO.

Muhammad Yousuf
HAIDER SHAMSI & CO.,
CHARTERED ACCOUNTANTS

Syed Zeeshan Ali
EY

PALAU

Jun Aclan
CTSI LOGISTICS

Kenneth Barden
ATTORNEY-AT-LAW

Tito Cabunagan
PALAU PUBLIC UTILITY
CORPORATION

Maria Cristina Castro
WESTERN CAROLINE
TRADING CO.

Anthony Frazier

Sterlina Gabriel
BUREAU OF LAND
AND SURVEYS

Wilbert Kamerang
PALAU SHIPPING
COMPANY, INC.

Mouias Kangichi
KOROR STATE GOVERNMENT

Carlos Mariano
CARLOS MARIANO LAW FIRM

Ramsey Ngiraibai
KOROR PLANNING AND
ZONING OFFICE

Techur Rengulbai
BUREAU OF PUBLIC WORKS

William L. Ridpath
WILLIAM L. RIDPATH,
ATTORNEY-AT-LAW (AMCIT)

V. Tikei Sbal
FINANCIAL INSTITUTIONS
COMMISSION

Rhinehart Silas
BUREAU OF REVENUE,
CUSTOMS AND TAXATION

Ken Sugiyama
PALAU PUBLIC UTILITY
CORPORATION

Sylcerius Tewalei
BUREAU OF LABOUR

PANAMA

Alvaro Aguilar
LOMBARDI AGUILAR GROUP

Gabriel Aguilar
LOMBARDI AGUILAR GROUP

Aristides Anguizola
MORGAN & MORGAN

Mercedes Araúz de Grimaldo
MORGAN & MORGAN

Khatiya Asvat
PATTON, MORENO & ASVAT

Fernando Aued
PATTON, MORENO & ASVAT

Francisco A. Barrios G.
PWC PANAMA

Gustavo Adolfo Bernal
ETESA

Klaus Bieberach Schriebl
TAX@PANAMA

Giovanna Cardellicchio
APC BURÓ SA

Johanna Castillo
ARIAS-LAW

Luis Chalhoub
ICAZA, GONZALEZ-RUIZ & ALEMAN

Julio César Contreras III
AROSEMENA NORIEGA & CONTRERAS

Gonzalo Córdoba
APC BURÓ SA

Juan Carlos Croston
MANZANILLO INTERNATIONAL TERMINAL OPERATOR MIT

Eduardo De Alba
ARIAS, FÁBREGA & FÁBREGA

Claudio De Castro
ARIAS, FÁBREGA & FÁBREGA

Jorge G. Lombardi Dutari
LOMBARDI AGUILAR GROUP

Marisol Ellis
ICAZA, GONZALEZ-RUIZ & ALEMAN

Felipe Escalona
GALINDO, ARIAS & LÓPEZ

Ricardo Eskildsen Morales
ESKILDSEN & ESKILDSEN

María Cristina Fábrega
ARIAS LAW

Juan Pablo Fabrega Polleri
FABREGA, MOLINO & MULINO

L. Fernandes
THE PANAMA MARITIME CHAMBER

Michael Fernandez
CÁMARA PANAMEÑA DE LA CONSTRUCCIÓN (CAPAC)

Enna Ferrer
ALFARO, FERRER & RAMÍREZ

Angie Guzmán
MORGAN & MORGAN

Edgar Herrera
GALINDO, ARIAS & LÓPEZ

Jorge L. Lara T.
INGENIERÍA LARA SA

Cristina Lewis de la Guardia
GALINDO, ARIAS & LÓPEZ

Esteban Lopez Moreno
KATZ Y LOPEZ

Ivette Elisa Martínez Saenz
PATTON, MORENO & ASVAT

Olmedo Miranda Boyd
AROSEMENA NORIEGA & CONTRERAS

David M. Mizrachi Fidanque
MIZRACHI, DAVARRO & URIOLA

Erick Rogelio Muñoz
SUCRE, ARIAS & REYES

Mayrolis Parnther
ARIAS LAW

Hassim Patel
PWC PANAMA

Sebastián Perez
UNION FENOSA - EDEMET - EDECHI

Nayda Price
PATTON, MORENO & ASVAT

Linda Quintero
PINZON LOZANO & ASOCIADOS ARQUITECTOS

Anel Roach
ALEMAN, CORDERO, GALINDO & LEE

Mario Rognoni
AROSEMENA NORIEGA & CONTRERAS

Nelson E. Sales
ALFARO, FERRER & RAMÍREZ

Daniel Sessa
GALINDO, ARIAS & LÓPEZ

Yinnis Solís de Amaya
UNION FENOSA - EDEMET - EDECHI

Hermes Tello
ELECTROMECHANICAL CONSULTING GROUP

Ramón Varela
MORGAN & MORGAN

Gabriela Vasquez
GALINDO, ARIAS & LÓPEZ

Mario Vlieg
ALEMAN, CORDERO, GALINDO & LEE

PAPUA NEW GUINEA

CREDIT & DATA BUREAU LIMITED

PWC PAPUA NEW GUINEA

Rob Addis
PENTAGON FREIGHT SERVICES (PNG) LTD.

Ian Clarke
DENTONS

Paul Cullen
DENTONS

Rebecca Cullen
DENTONS

Gibson Geroro
GERORO LAWYERS

Simon Guidecoq
DENTONS

Lea Henao
STEAMSHIPS TRADING COMPANY LTD.

Clarence Hoot
INVESTMENT PROMOTION AUTHORITY

Lauari Ikavape
INVESTMENT PROMOTION AUTHORITY

Timothy Koris
PNG POWER LTD.

Sarah Kuman
ALLENS

Peter Lowing
LEAHY LEWIN NUTLEY SULLIVAN

Doug Mageo
PNG POWER LTD.

Stephen Massa
DENTONS

Steve Patrick
GADENS LAWYERS

Ray Paul
PNG CUSTOMS SERVICE

Daroa Peter
INVESTMENT PROMOTION AUTHORITY

Lou Pipi
NCDC MUNICIPALITY

Nancy Pogla
ALLENS LINKLATERS

Desmond Pokajam
INVESTMENT PROMOTION AUTHORITY

Herjit Saini
DENTONS

Renee Siaguru
ALLENS

Sinton Spence Mbe
SINTON SPENCE CHARTERED ACCOUNTANTS

Lilian Sukot
PNG POWER LTD.

Alex Tongayu
INVESTMENT PROMOTION AUTHORITY

Sally Weatherstone
DENTONS

Stuart Wilson
LCS ELECTRICAL & MECHANICAL CONTRACTORS

Alicia Yen
HEALY CONSULTANTS GROUP PLC

PARAGUAY

Perla Alderete
VOUGA ABOGADOS

Bruno Angulo
PWC PARAGUAY

Sandybelle Avalos
RUSSELL BEDFORD INTERNATIONAL

Enrique Benitez
BDO AUDITORES CONSULTORES

Maximo Gustavo Benitez Gimenez
SUPERINTENDENCIA DE BANCOS - BCP

Alex Berkemeyer
BERKEMEYER, ATTORNEYS & COUNSELORS

Hugo T. Berkemeyer
BERKEMEYER, ATTORNEYS & COUNSELORS

Juan Ramírez Biedermann
ESTUDIO JURÍDICO LIVIERES GUGGIARI

Carlos Cañete
BDO AUDITORES CONSULTORES

Pedro Cuevas
ADMINISTRACIÓN NACIONAL DE ELECTRICIDAD

Sergio Dejesus
KEMPER – DEJESUS & PANGRAZIO ABOGADOS Y CONSULTORES

Natalia Enciso Benitez
NOTARY PUBLIC

Maria Ines Galeano
OLMEDO ABOGADOS

Néstor Gamarra
SERVIMEX SACI

Liliana Maria Giménez de Castillo
DIRECCIÓN GENERAL DE LOS REGISTROS PÚBLICOS

Lourdes Gonzalez
DIRECCIÓN GENERAL DE LOS REGISTROS PÚBLICOS

Nadia Gorostiaga
PWC PARAGUAY

Sigfrido Gross Brown
ESTUDIO JURIDICO GROSS BROWN

Marcelo Gul Pavoni
TMF GROUP

Carl Gwynn
GWYNN & GWYNN - LEGAL COUNSELLORS

Norman Gwynn
SUPREME COURT OF JUSTICE

Manfred Heyn
FERRERE ABOGADOS

Christian Kemper
KEMPER – DEJESUS & PANGRAZIO ABOGADOS Y CONSULTORES

Gabriel Lamas
ONIX SACI CONSULTING + ENGINEERING

Pablo Livieres Guggiari
ESTUDIO JURÍDICO LIVIERES GUGGIARI

Nestor Loizaga
FERRERE ABOGADOS

Augusto Mengual
MIATERRA

Oscar A. Mersan Galli
MERSÁN ABOGADOS

María Esmeralda Moreno Rodríguez Alcalá
MORENO RUFFINELLI & ASOCIADOS

Monica Núñez
BERKEMEYER, ATTORNEYS & COUNSELORS

Anibal Pangrazio
KEMPER – DEJESUS & PANGRAZIO ABOGADOS Y CONSULTORES

Rocío Penayo
MORENO RUFFINELLI & ASOCIADOS

Yolanda Pereira
BERKEMEYER, ATTORNEYS & COUNSELORS

María Antonia Ramírez de Gwynn
GWYNN & GWYNN - LEGAL COUNSELLORS

Veronica Recalde
KEMPER – DEJESUS & PANGRAZIO ABOGADOS Y CONSULTORES

Mauricio Salgueiro
VOUGA ABOGADOS

Rafael Salomoni
SALOMONI & ASOCIADOS

Cecilia Sánchez
VOUGA ABOGADOS

Angela Schaerer de Sosa
ESCRIBANA PÚBLICA

Carlos Torres
GRUPO IBD

Maria Gloria Triguis Gonzalez
BERKEMEYER, ATTORNEYS & COUNSELORS

Emmanuel Trulls
FERRERE ABOGADOS

Andres Vera
VOUGA ABOGADOS

David Vera
VOUGA ABOGADOS

Walter Vera
VOUGA ABOGADOS

Carlos Vouga
VOUGA ABOGADOS

Rodolfo Vouga Muller
VOUGA ABOGADOS

PERU

AGUIRRE ABOGADOS & ASESORES

WHITE & CASE SC

Guillermo Acuña Roeder
RUBIO LEGUÍA NORMAND

Marco Antonio Alarcón Piana
ESTUDIO LUIS ECHECOPAR GARCÍA SRL

Cesar Angulo
MUÑIZ, RAMÍREZ, PERÉZ-TAIMAN & OLAYA ABOGADOS

Evelin Aragon Grados
ADEX

Jimy Atunga Rios
M.A.V. LOGISTICA Y TRANSPORTE SA

Guilhermo Auler
AULER Y PINTO ABOGADOS

Brian Avalos
PAYET, REY, CAUVI, PÉREZ ABOGADOS

Arelis Avila Tagle
CONUDFI

Jose Luis Ayllon Carreño
CÁMARA PERUANA DE LA CONSTRUCCIÓN

Guillermo Bracamonte
MIRANDA & AMADO

Stephany Giovanna Bravo de Rueda Arce
RANSA COMERCIAL SA

Wilfredo Caceres
ESTUDIO MUÑIZ, RAMIREZ, PEREZ-TAIMAN & OLAYA

Renzo Camaiora
GALLO BARRIOS PICKMANN

Fernando Castro
MUÑIZ, RAMÍREZ, PERÉZ-TAIMAN & OLAYA ABOGADOS

Alvaro Chuquipiondo
BARRIOS & FUENTES ABOGADOS

Sandra Copacondori
BARRIOS & FUENTES ABOGADOS

Tomas Cosco
RUSSELL BEDFORD PERÚ - MEMBER OF RUSSELL BEDFORD INTERNATIONAL

Ricardo de la Piedra
ESTUDIO OLAECHEA, MEMBER OF LEX MUNDI

Jose Dedios
PAYET, REY, CAUVI, PÉREZ ABOGADOS

Carlos Roberto Drago Llanos
SUNAT

Alex Espinoza
PWC PERU

Hugo Espinoza Rivera
SUNARP

María del Pilar Falcón Castro
ESTUDIO LLONA & BUSTAMANTE ABOGADOS

Napoleón Fernández
SUNARP

Fiama Fernandez Saldamando
CONUDFI

Luis Enrique Narro Forno
SUNAT

Luis Fuentes
BARRIOS & FUENTES ABOGADOS

Julio Gallo
GALLO BARRIOS PICKMANN

Lorena Galvez
GALLO BARRIOS PICKMANN

Alejandra Giufra Chavez
ESTUDIO LLONA & BUSTAMANTE ABOGADOS

Diego Gomez
BARRIOS & FUENTES ABOGADOS

Rafael Gonzales
*BARRIOS & FUENTES
ABOGADOS*

Gerardo Guzman
DELMAR UGARTE ABOGADOS

Carlos Hernández Ladera
RANSA COMERCIAL SA

Jose Antonio Honda
*ESTUDIO OLAECHEA,
MEMBER OF LEX MUNDI*

Diego Huertas del Pino
*BARRIOS & FUENTES
ABOGADOS*

Felipe Eduardo Iannacone Silva
SUNAT

César Ballón Izquierdo
RANSA COMERCIAL SA

Sacha Larrea
SCOTIABANK PERU

Alexandra Lemke
*BARRIOS & FUENTES
ABOGADOS*

Gonzalo Leo
*BARRIOS & FUENTES
ABOGADOS*

Juan Carlos Leon Siles
ADEX

German Lora
*PAYET, REY, CAUVI,
PÉREZ ABOGADOS*

Rafael Lulli Meyer
*REBAZA, ALCÁZAR & DE
LAS CASAS ABOGADOS
FINANCIEROS*

Cesar Luna Victoria
RUBIO LEGUÍA NORMAND

Milagros Maravi Sumar
RUBIO LEGUÍA NORMAND

Orlando Marchesi
PWC PERU

Carlos Martínez Ebell
RUBIO LEGUÍA NORMAND

Jesús Matos
*ESTUDIO OLAECHEA,
MEMBER OF LEX MUNDI*

Gino Menchola
PWC PERU

Jorge Miranda
RUBIO LEGUÍA NORMAND

Diego Muñiz
*ESTUDIO OLAECHEA,
MEMBER OF LEX MUNDI*

Juan Carlos Novoa
*SOCIEDAD NACIONAL DE
MINERÍA, PETRÓLEO Y ENERGÍA*

Lilian Oliver
SUNARP

Alexandra Orbezo
*REBAZA, ALCÁZAR & DE
LAS CASAS ABOGADOS
FINANCIEROS*

Luis Orrego
DELMAR UGARTE ABOGADOS

Ariel Orrego-Villacorta
*BARRIOS & FUENTES
ABOGADOS*

Cristina Oviedo
*PAYET, REY, CAUVI,
PÉREZ ABOGADOS*

David Pacheco
*ESTUDIO OLAECHEA,
MEMBER OF LEX MUNDI*

Nélida Palacios
SUNARP

Roxana Antonieta Pantigozo
Delgado
SUNAT

Edmundo Paredes
*SUPERINTENDENCY OF
BANKING, INSURANCE
AND PRIVATE PENSION
FUND ADMINISTRATOR*

Lucianna Polar
*ESTUDIO OLAECHEA,
MEMBER OF LEX MUNDI*

Angélica Portillo Flores
SUNARP

Juan Manuel Prado
Bustamante
*ESTUDIO LLONA &
BUSTAMANTE ABOGADOS*

Maribel Príncipe Hidalgo
RUBIO LEGUÍA NORMAND

María José Puertas
GALLO BARRIOS PICKMANN

Cesar Puntriano
PWC PERU

Manuel Quindimil
*CÁMARA DE COMERCIO
AMERICANA DEL PERÚ*

Bruno Marchese Quintana
RUBIO LEGUÍA NORMAND

Fernando M. Ramos
*BARRIOS & FUENTES
ABOGADOS*

Alonso Rey Bustamante
*PAYET, REY, CAUVI,
PÉREZ ABOGADOS*

José Miguel Reyes
*BARRIOS & FUENTES
ABOGADOS*

Andrea Rieckhof
GALLO BARRIOS PICKMANN

Andres Rieckhof
*REBAZA, ALCÁZAR & DE
LAS CASAS ABOGADOS
FINANCIEROS*

Anggie Rivera
*BARRIOS & FUENTES
ABOGADOS*

Juan Manuel Robles
RUBIO LEGUÍA NORMAND

Erick Rojas
*CÁMARA PERUANA DE
LA CONSTRUCCIÓN*

Martin Ruggiero
*PAYET, REY, CAUVI,
PÉREZ ABOGADOS*

Felix Arturo Ruiz Sanchez
RUBIO LEGUÍA NORMAND

Carolina Sáenz
RUBIO LEGUÍA NORMAND

Carolina Salcedo
*ESTUDIO MUÑIZ, RAMIREZ,
PEREZ-TAIMAN & OLAYA*

Raúl Sanchez
*BARRIOS & FUENTES
ABOGADOS*

Raul Sanchez Sabogal
ADEX

Pablo Santos
CONUDFI

Pablo Santos Curo
ADEX

Victor Scarsi
LUZ DEL SUR

Martin Serkovic
*ESTUDIO OLAECHEA,
MEMBER OF LEX MUNDI*

Hugo Silva
*RODRIGO, ELÍAS,
MEDRANO ABOGADOS*

Ricardo P. Silva
*ESTUDIO MUÑIZ, RAMIREZ,
PEREZ-TAIMAN & OLAYA*

Carla Sinchi
*PAYET, REY, CAUVI,
PÉREZ ABOGADOS*

Enrique Sebastián Soto Ruiz
CONGRESO DE LA REPUBLICA

Jose Steck
NPG ABOGADOS

Edmundo Taboada
*BARRIOS & FUENTES
ABOGADOS*

Carlos Tapia
NPG ABOGADOS

Claudia Tejada
*BARRIOS & FUENTES
ABOGADOS*

Xenia Tello
*ESTUDIO OLAECHEA,
MEMBER OF LEX MUNDI*

Ricardo Arturo Toma Oyama
SUNAT

Arturo Tuesta
PWC PERU

Manuel A. Ugarte
DELMAR UGARTE ABOGADOS

Jean A. Unda Valverde
*SOCIEDAD NACIONAL DE
MINERÍA, PETRÓLEO Y ENERGÍA*

Jack Vainstein
VAINSTEIN & INGENIEROS SA

Erick Valderrama
*RUSSELL BEDFORD PERÚ
- MEMBER OF RUSSELL
BEDFORD INTERNATIONAL*

Yelitza Valdivia
MIRANDA & AMADO

Mitchell Alex Valdiviezo Del
Carpio
RUBIO LEGUÍA NORMAND

Manuel Villa-García
*ESTUDIO OLAECHEA,
MEMBER OF LEX MUNDI*

Rafael Villaran
*ESTUDIO LUIS ECHECOPAR
GARCÍA SRL*

Agustín Yrigoyen
GARCÍA SAYÁN ABOGADOS

Sabino Zaconeta Torres
*ASOCIACIÓN PERUANA DE
AGENTES MARÍTIMOS*

PHILIPPINES

*CREDIT INFORMATION
CORPORATION*

DEPARTMENT OF ENERGY

Go Abigail
*SIGUION REYNA MONTECILLO
& ONGSIAKO*

Juan Paolo Agbayani
*MARTINEZ VERGARA
GONZALEZ & SERRANO*

Ma. Carmen Agcaoili-Orena
AGCAOILI & ASSOCIATES

Shirley Alinea
*MARTINEZ VERGARA
GONZALEZ & SERRANO*

Charina Amanda B. Javier
SKALA ARCHITECTS

Henry D. Antonio
KPMG R.G. MANABAT & CO.

Rosario Carmela Asutria
SEC

Francis Avellana
BAP CREDIT BUREAU, INC.

Alex B. Runes
MERALCO

Manuel Batallones
BAP CREDIT BUREAU, INC.

Merope Bautista
*TRADECON TRADING
& CONSTRUCTION*

Vera Marie Bautista
*SYCIP SALAZAR HERNANDEZ
& GATMAITAN*

Rosario Cherry Bernaldo
*SHAREHOLDERS
ASSOCIATION OF THE
PHILIPPINES (SHAREPHIL)*

Ronald Bernas
*QUISUMBING TORRES,
MEMBER FIRM OF BAKER &
MCKENZIE INTERNATIONAL*

Irene Joy Besido Garcia
*KAPUNAN GARCIA &
CASTILLO LAW OFFICES*

Kristine Bongcaron
*MARTINEZ VERGARA
GONZALEZ & SERRANO*

Pearl Grace Cabali
*PUYAT JACINTO SANTOS
LAW OFFICE*

Juan Arturo Iluminado
Cagampang de Castro
*DE CASTRO & CAGAMPANG-
DE CASTRO LAW FIRM*

Justina Callangan
SEC

Renato Calma
*ORTEGA, BACORRO, ODULIO,
CALMA & CARBONELL*

Roselle Caraig
ISLA LIPANA & CO.

Mia Carmela Imperial
*QUISUMBING TORRES,
MEMBER FIRM OF BAKER &
MCKENZIE INTERNATIONAL*

Domingo Castillo
*SYCIP SALAZAR HERNANDEZ
& GATMAITAN*

Jon Edmarc R. Castillo
*SYCIP SALAZAR HERNANDEZ
& GATMAITAN*

Luis M. Catibayan
BUREAU OF IMPORT SERVICES

Ria Danielle Ching
KPMG R.G. MANABAT & CO.

Kenneth L. Chua
*QUISUMBING TORRES,
MEMBER FIRM OF BAKER &
MCKENZIE INTERNATIONAL*

Juan Paolo E. Colet

Toni Angeli Coo

Karl Raymond Cruz
*SYCIP SALAZAR HERNANDEZ
& GATMAITAN*

Robert Dalaodao
IN-LINE FORWARDER

Thomas John Thaddeus de
Castro
AGCAOILI & ASSOCIATES

Emerico O. de Guzman
*ANGARA ABELLO CONCEPCION
REGALA & CRUZ LAW
OFFICES (ACCRALAW)*

Hector De Leon, Jr.
*SYCIP SALAZAR HERNANDEZ
& GATMAITAN*

Ann Sherrol De los Santos
*SHAREHOLDERS
ASSOCIATION OF THE
PHILIPPINES (SHAREPHIL)*

Anthony Dee
*SYCIP SALAZAR HERNANDEZ
& GATMAITAN*

Corazon Del Castillo
*SIGUION REYNA MONTECILLO
& ONGSIAKO*

Evelyn Dela Cerna
FAST LINK

Aimee Rose dela Cruz
ISLA LIPANA & CO.

Jenny Jean Domino
*SYCIP SALAZAR HERNANDEZ
& GATMAITAN*

Rolando Ducut
IN-LINE FORWARDER

Alexander Dy
*VILLANUEVA GABIONZA
& DY LAW OFFICES*

Karla Eunice
*PAREDES GARCIA AND
GOLEZ LAW OFFICE*

Colonel Jesus Fernandez
*LOCAL GOVERNMENT
OF QUEZON CITY*

Florida Fomaneg
ISLA LIPANA & CO.

Catherine Franco
*QUISUMBING TORRES,
MEMBER FIRM OF BAKER &
MCKENZIE INTERNATIONAL*

Arnelito Garcia
*AB GARCIA
CONSTRUCTION INC.*

Geraldine S. Garcia
*FOLLOSCO MORALLOS
& HERCE*

Vicente Gerochi IV
*SYCIP SALAZAR HERNANDEZ
& GATMAITAN*

Ma. Cecilia Gironella
GIRONELLA LAW OFFICE

Carlo Miguel Romeo S. Go
*SYCIP SALAZAR HERNANDEZ
& GATMAITAN*

Manuel Z. Gonzalez
*MARTINEZ VERGARA
GONZALEZ & SERRANO*

George Matthew Habacon
*SYCIP SALAZAR HERNANDEZ
& GATMAITAN*

Judy Hao
*ANGARA ABELLO CONCEPCION
REGALA & CRUZ LAW
OFFICES (ACCRALAW)*

Jose Emmanuel Hernandez
*DE GUZMAN SAN DIEGO
MEJIA & HERNANDEZ*

Tadeo F. Hilado
*ANGARA ABELLO CONCEPCION
REGALA & CRUZ LAW
OFFICES (ACCRALAW)*

Benito Jose L. de los Santos
ABS LAW FIRM

Charmane Kanahashi
*PAREDES GARCIA AND
GOLEZ LAW OFFICE*

Justin Vincent La Chica
*ROMULO, MABANTA,
BUENAVENTURA, SAYOC
& DE LOS ANGELES,
MEMBER OF LEX MUNDI*

Carina Laforteza
*SYCIP SALAZAR HERNANDEZ
& GATMAITAN*

Frederic Landicho
NAVARRO AMPER & CO.

Hiyasmin Lapitan
*SYCIP SALAZAR HERNANDEZ
& GATMAITAN*

Everlene Lee
*ANGARA ABELLO CONCEPCION
REGALA & CRUZ LAW
OFFICES (ACCRALAW)*

Jennifer Lee
*QUASHA ANCHETA
PENA & NOLASCO*

Jeva Lee
*AB GARCIA
CONSTRUCTION INC.*

Ana Liezl Pelayo
IN-LINE FORWARDER

Joyce Liza Chan
*QUISUMBING TORRES,
MEMBER FIRM OF BAKER &
MCKENZIE INTERNATIONAL*

Roane Alfredo Lopez
*ORTEGA, BACORRO, ODULIO,
CALMA & CARBONELL*

Herbert M. Bautista
*LOCAL GOVERNMENT
OF QUEZON CITY*

Mel A. Macaraig
*CASTILLO LAMAN TAN
PANTALEON & SAN JOSE*

Sam Angelo Maducdoc
KPMG R.G. MANABAT & CO.

Marlon G. Mariano
*LOCAL GOVERNMENT
OF QUEZON CITY*

Hector A. Martinez
*PLATON, MARTINEZ FLORES
SAN PEDRO & LEAÑO*

Michael Mejia
*DE GUZMAN SAN DIEGO
MEJIA & HERNANDEZ*

Enriquito J. Mendoza
*ROMULO, MABANTA,
BUENAVENTURA, SAYOC
& DE LOS ANGELES,
MEMBER OF LEX MUNDI*

Maria Teresa Mercado-Ferrer
*SYCIP SALAZAR HERNANDEZ
& GATMAITAN*

Marianne Miguel
*SYCIP SALAZAR HERNANDEZ
& GATMAITAN*

Jesusito G. Morallos
*FOLLOSCO MORALLOS
& HERCE*

Gregorio S. Navarro
NAVARRO AMPER & CO.

Perpetua Calliope Ngo
*MARTINEZ VERGARA
GONZALEZ & SERRANO*

Krisanto Karlo Nicolas
*NICOLAS & DE VEGA
LAW OFFICES*

Harold Ocampo
ISLA LIPANA & CO.

Jude Ocampo
*OCAMPO & SURALVO
LAW OFFICES*

Karen Ocampo
*OCAMPO & SURALVO
LAW OFFICES*

Gwyneth Ong
*MARTINEZ VERGARA
GONZALEZ & SERRANO*

Mariah-Rose Rafaela Ong
KPMG R.G. MANABAT & CO.

Maria Christina Ortua
*SYCIP SALAZAR HERNANDEZ
& GATMAITAN*

Ma. Milagros Padernal
UY SINGSON ABELLA & CO.

Sheila Mae Panares
SEC

Benedicto Panigbatan
*SYCIP SALAZAR HERNANDEZ
& GATMAITAN*

Gil Christopher Paredes
KPMG R.G. MANABAT & CO.

Hilario Paredes
*PAREDES GARCIA &
GOLEZ LAW OFFICE*

Ma. Patricia Paz
*SYCIP SALAZAR HERNANDEZ
& GATMAITAN*

Maria Pilar Pilares-Gutierrez
*CASTILLO LAMAN TAN
PANTALEON & SAN JOSE*

Maybellyn Pinpin-Malayo
ISLA LIPANA & CO.

Hailin Quintos
*SYCIP SALAZAR HERNANDEZ
& GATMAITAN*

Revelino Rabaja
ISLA LIPANA & CO.

Janice Kae Ramirez
*QUASHA ANCHETA
PENA & NOLASCO*

Frederika Rentoy
*LOCAL GOVERNMENT
OF QUEZON CITY*

Elaine Patricia S.
Reyes-Rodolfo
*ANGARA ABELLO CONCEPCION
REGALA & CRUZ LAW
OFFICES (ACCRALAW)*

Leandro Ben Robediso
KPMG R.G. MANABAT & CO.

Pedro P. Rodriguez
*LOCAL GOVERNMENT
OF QUEZON CITY*

Ricardo J. Romulo
*ROMULO, MABANTA,
BUENAVENTURA, SAYOC
& DE LOS ANGELES,
MEMBER OF LEX MUNDI*

Renz Jeffrey A. Ruiz
*SYCIP SALAZAR HERNANDEZ
& GATMAITAN*

Patrick Henry D. Salazar
*QUISUMBING TORRES,
MEMBER FIRM OF BAKER &
MCKENZIE INTERNATIONAL*

Neptali Salvanera
*ANGARA ABELLO CONCEPCION
REGALA & CRUZ LAW
OFFICES (ACCRALAW)*

Rodolfo San Diego
*DE GUZMAN SAN DIEGO
MEJIA & HERNANDEZ*

Jennilyn Sio
*SHAREHOLDERS
ASSOCIATION OF THE
PHILIPPINES (SHAREPHIL)*

Neil Sison
SISON CORILLO PARONE & CO.

Felice Suzanne Soria
*ANGARA ABELLO CONCEPCION
REGALA & CRUZ LAW
OFFICES (ACCRALAW)*

Manilyn Rose Sotelo
ISLA LIPANA & CO.

Erdan Suero

Cristina Suralvo
*OCAMPO & SURALVO
LAW OFFICES*

Shennan Sy
*KALAW SY VIDA
SELVA & CAMPOS*

Fidel T. Valeros
*PUYAT JACINTO SANTOS
LAW OFFICE*

Gloria Victoria Y. Taruc
*ENERGY REGULATORY
COMMISSION*

Carlos Martin Tayag
*ROMULO, MABANTA,
BUENAVENTURA, SAYOC
& DE LOS ANGELES,
MEMBER OF LEX MUNDI*

Amando Tetangco Jr.
BANGKO SENTRAL NG PILIPINAS

Jolina Pauline Tuazon
*PUYAT JACINTO SANTOS
LAW OFFICE*

Roland Glenn Tuazon
*ROMULO, MABANTA,
BUENAVENTURA, SAYOC
& DE LOS ANGELES,
MEMBER OF LEX MUNDI*

Martin Victorino Cusi
*VILLANUEVA GABIONZA
& DY LAW OFFICES*

Virginia B. Viray
*PUYAT JACINTO SANTOS
LAW OFFICE*

Gil Roberto Zerrudo
*QUISUMBING TORRES,
MEMBER FIRM OF BAKER &
MCKENZIE INTERNATIONAL*

POLAND

ENERGY REGULATORY OFFICE

*NAPRAWA KABLI
ENERGETYCZNYCH
ANDRZEJ ROGOWSKI*

Wojciech Andrzejewski
*KANCELARIA PRAWNA PISZCZ,
NOREK I WSPÓLNICY SP.K.*

Marcin Bącal
*CHAJEC, DON-SIEMION &
ZYTO LEGAL ADVISORS*

Tomasz Baranczyk
PWC POLAND

Michał Barłowski
WARDYŃSKI & PARTNERS

Justyna Bartnik
*MORAWSKI & PARTNERS
LAW FIRM*

Wojciech Bieganski
DLA PIPER WIATER SP.K.

Paulina Blukacz
MINISTRY OF FINANCE

Joanna Bugajska
JAMP

Rafał Burda
DLA PIPER WIATER SP.K.

Kinga Cekiera
*BREVELLS CEKIERA
OLEKSIEWICZ SP.K.*

Olga Chodorowska
*KAMIŃSKI & PARTNERS
KANCELARIA PRAWNICZA SP.K.*

Małgorzata Chruściak
CMS CAMERON MCKENNA

Łukasz Chruściel
*RACZKOWSKI PARUCH LAW
FIRM IUS LABORIS POLAND
GLOBAL HR LAWYERS*

Karolina Czapska
*RACZKOWSKI PARUCH LAW
FIRM IUS LABORIS POLAND
GLOBAL HR LAWYERS*

Katarzyna Czwartosz
*WHITE & CASE M. STUDNIAREK
I WSPÓLNICY - KANCELARIA
PRAWNA SP.K.*

Michał Dąbrowski
MINISTRY OF JUSTICE

Aleksandra Danielewicz
DLA PIPER WIATER SP.K.

Andrzej Dmowski
*RUSSELL BEDFORD POLAND SP.
Z O.O. - MEMBER OF RUSSELL
BEDFORD INTERNATIONAL*

Ewa Don-Siemion
*CHAJEC, DON-SIEMION &
ZYTO LEGAL ADVISORS*

Bartosz Draniewicz
*KANCELARIA PRAWA
GOSPODARCZEGO I
EKOLOGICZNEGO DR
BARTOSZ DRANIEWICZ*

Edyta Dubikowska
SQUIRE PATTON BOGGS

Patryk Filipiak
*FILIPIAKBABICZ LEGAL,
ZIMMERMAN FILIPIAK
RESTRUKTURYZACJA SA*

Maciej Geromin
ALLERHAND INSTITUTE

Michał Gliński
WARDYŃSKI & PARTNERS

Magdalena Gmur
DLA PIPER WIATER SP.K.

Rafał Godlewski
WARDYŃSKI & PARTNERS

Bartosz Groele
ALLERHAND INSTITUTE

Andrzej Grześkiewicz
GRIDNET

Marcin Hołówka
*KANCELARIA ADWOKATA
MARCINA HOŁÓWKI*

Łukasz Iwański
ENERGOMIX

Michal Jadwisiak
*WHITE & CASE M. STUDNIAREK
I WSPÓLNICY - KANCELARIA
PRAWNA SP.K.*

Jakub Jędrzejak
*WKB WIERCIŃSKI,
KWIECIŃSKI, BAEHR SP.K.*

Magdalena Kalińska
*WKB WIERCIŃSKI,
KWIECIŃSKI, BAEHR SP.K.*

Mateusz Kaliński
*KANCELARIA PRAWA
RESTRUKTURYZACYJNEGO I
UPADLOSCIOWEGO TATARA
I WSPOLPRACOWNICY*

Karolina Kalucka
DLA PIPER WIATER SP.K.

Aleksandra Kaminska
DENTONS

Tomasz Kański
*SOŁTYSIŃSKI KAWECKI
& SZLĘZAK*

Iwona Karasek-Wojciechowicz
JAGIELLONIAN UNIVERSITY

Zbigniew Korba
*DELOITTE DORADZTWO
PODATKOWE SP. Z O.O.*

Jacek Korzeniewski
BAKER & MCKENZIE

Aleksandra Kozlowska
DLA PIPER WIATER SP.K.

Adam Królik
*KANCELARIA PRAWA
RESTRUKTURYZACYJNEGO I
UPADLOSCIOWEGO TATARA
I WSPOLPRACOWNICY*

Iga Kwasny
*MOORE STEPHENS CENTRAL
AUDIT SP. Z O.O.*

Ewa Łachowska-Brol
*WIERZBOWSKI EVERSHEDS
SUTHERLAND SP.K., MEMBER
OF EVERSHEDS SUTHERLAND
(EUROPE) LIMITED*

Wojciech Langowski
MILLER CANFIELD

Katarzyna Lawinska
BAKER & MCKENZIE

Agnieszka Lehwark
DLA PIPER WIATER SP.K.

Monika Leszko
DLA PIPER WIATER SP.K.

Konrad Piotr Lewandowski
*MAURICE WARD &
CO. SP. Z.O.O.*

Agnieszka Lisiecka
WARDYŃSKI & PARTNERS

Tomasz Listwan
*MOORE STEPHENS CENTRAL
AUDIT SP. Z O.O.*

Paweł Ludwiniak
ELTECH

Konrad Marciniuk
MILLER CANFIELD

Adam Marszałek
DLA PIPER WIATER SP.K.

Pawel Meus
*GIDE LOYRETTE NOUEL
POLAND WARSAW*

Tomasz Michalik
*MDDP MICHALIK DŁUSKA
DZIEDZIC I PARTNERZY*

Anna Miernik
CLIFFORD CHANCE

Tomasz Milewski
MILLER CANFIELD

Joanna Młot
CMS CAMERON MCKENNA

Adam Morawski
*MORAWSKI & PARTNERS
LAW FIRM*

Grzegorz Namiotkiewicz
CLIFFORD CHANCE

Michal Niemirowicz-Szczytt
*LEX IUVAT KANCELARIA
RADCY PRAWNEGO MICHAL
NIEMIROWICZ-SZCZYTT*

Dominika Nowak
DLA PIPER WIATER SP.K.

Marta Osowska
*WHITE & CASE M. STUDNIAREK
I WSPÓLNICY - KANCELARIA
PRAWNA SP.K.*

Tomasz Ostrowski
*WHITE & CASE M. STUDNIAREK
I WSPÓLNICY - KANCELARIA
PRAWNA SP.K.*

Sławomir Paruch
*RACZKOWSKI PARUCH LAW
FIRM IUS LABORIS POLAND
GLOBAL HR LAWYERS*

Krzysztof Pawlak
*SOŁTYSIŃSKI KAWECKI
& SZLĘZAK*

Agata Pawlak-Jaszczak
KANCELARIA PRAWNA PISZCZ, NOREK I WSPÓLNICY SP.K.

Małgorzata Pietrzak-Paciorek
BAKER & MCKENZIE

Mariusz Purgał
TOMASIK, PAKOSIEWICZ, GROELE ADWOKACI I RADCOWIE PRAWNI SP.P.

Anna Ratajczyk-Sałamacha
GIDE LOYRETTE NOUEL POLAND WARSAW

Radosław Rudnik
CHAJEC, DON-SIEMION & ZYTO LEGAL ADVISORS

Szymon Sakowski
DLA PIPER WIATER SP.K.

Marek Sawicki
DLA PIPER WIATER SP.K.

Gabriela Siegmund
SOŁTYSIŃSKI KAWECKI & SZLĘZAK

Karol Skibniewski
SOŁTYSIŃSKI KAWECKI & SZLĘZAK

Michal Snitko-Pleszko
BLACKSTONES

Marek Sosnowski
GIDE LOYRETTE NOUEL POLAND WARSAW

Maciej Stepien
PWC POLAND

Małgorzata Studniarek
DLA PIPER WIATER SP.K.

Michał Subocz
WHITE & CASE M. STUDNIAREK I WSPÓLNICY - KANCELARIA PRAWNA SP.K.

Michal Suska
ENERGOMIX

Filip Świtała
MINISTRY OF FINANCE

Jadwiga Szabat
ECOVIS SYSTEM REWIDENT SP. Z O.O.

Leonart Szanajca-Kossakowski
DLA PIPER WIATER SP.K.

Emil Szczepanik
MINISTRY OF JUSTICE

Łukasz Szegda
WARDYŃSKI & PARTNERS

Marcelina Szwed
DLA PIPER WIATER SP.K.

Maciej Szwedowski
SQUIRE PATTON BOGGS

Karol Tatara
KANCELARIA PRAWA RESTRUKTURYZACYJNEGO I UPADLOSCIOWEGO TATARA I WSPOLPRACOWNICY

Dariusz Tokarczuk
GIDE LOYRETTE NOUEL POLAND WARSAW

Mateusz Tusznio
WARDYŃSKI & PARTNERS

Dominika Wagrodzka
BNT NEUPERT ZAMORSKA & ZAMORSKA PARTNERZY SP.J.

Emilia Waszkiewicz
BAKER & MCKENZIE

Cezary Wernic
MINISTRY OF FINANCE

Sebastian Wieczorek
DENTONS

Anna Wietrzyńska-Ciołkowska
DLA PIPER WIATER SP.K.

Anna Wojciechowska
WKB WIERCIŃSKI, KWIECIŃSKI, BAEHR SP.K.

Jakub Woliński
BNT NEUPERT ZAMORSKA & ZAMORSKA PARTNERZY SP.J.

Steven Wood
BLACKSTONES

Anna Wyrzykowska
WKB WIERCIŃSKI, KWIECIŃSKI, BAEHR SP.K.

Edyta Zalewska
GIDE LOYRETTE NOUEL POLAND WARSAW

Maciej Zalewski
WHITE & CASE M. STUDNIAREK I WSPÓLNICY - KANCELARIA PRAWNA SP.K.

Anna Ziemian
DLA PIPER WIATER SP.K.

Darius Zimnicki
CHAJEC, DON-SIEMION & ZYTO LEGAL ADVISORS

Agnieszka Ziółek
CMS CAMERON MCKENNA

Katarzyna Zukowska
WARDYŃSKI & PARTNERS

Krzysztof Żyto
CHAJEC, DON-SIEMION & ZYTO LEGAL ADVISORS

PORTUGAL

Victor Abrantes
INTERNATIONAL SALES AGENT

Anabela Aguilar Salvado
PEDRO RAPOSO & ASSOCIADOS

Bruno Andrade Alves
PWC PORTUGAL

Igor Amarii
MBS ADVOGADOS

Joana Andrade Correia
RAPOSO BERNARDO & ASSOCIADOS

Luís Antunes
LUFTEC – TÉCNICAS ELÉCTRICAS LDA

Filipa Arantes Pedroso
MORAIS LEITÃO, GALVÃO TELES, SOARES DA SILVA & ASSOCIADOS, MEMBER OF LEX MUNDI

Miguel Azevedo
GARRIGUES PORTUGAL SLP - SUCURSAL

João Banza
PWC PORTUGAL

Manuel P. Barrocas
BARROCAS ADVOGADOS

Jeanine Batalha Ferreira
PWC PORTUGAL

Mark Bekker
BEKKER LOGISTICA

Antonio Belmar da Costa
ASSOCIAÇÃO DOS AGENTES DE NAVEGAÇÃO DE PORTUGAL (AGEPOR)

Andreia Bento Simões
MORAIS LEITÃO, GALVÃO TELES, SOARES DA SILVA & ASSOCIADOS, MEMBER OF LEX MUNDI

João Bettencourt da Camara
CREDINFORMAÇÕES - EQUIFAX

João Cadete de Matos
BANCO DE PORTUGAL

Susana Caetano
PWC PORTUGAL

Vicente Caldeira Pires
PEDRO RAPOSO & ASSOCIADOS

Inês Calor
CICS.NOVA, UNIVERSIDADE NOVA DE LISBOA

Francisco Campilho
EDP DISTRIBUIÇÃO - ENERGIA, SA

Vitor Campos
NATIONAL LABORATORY FOR CIVIL ENGINEERING - LNEC

Rui Capote
PLEN - SOCIEDADE DE ADVOGADOS, RL

Fernando Cardoso da Cunha
GALI MACEDO & ASSOCIADOS

João Carneiro
MIRANDA & ASSOCIADOS

Petra Carreira
GARRIGUES PORTUGAL SLP - SUCURSAL

Isa Carvalho
MBS ADVOGADOS

Jaime Carvalho Esteves
PWC PORTUGAL

Filipa Castanheira de Almeida
MORAIS LEITÃO, GALVÃO TELES, SOARES DA SILVA & ASSOCIADOS, MEMBER OF LEX MUNDI

Tiago Castanheira Marques
ABREU ADVOGADOS

João Duarte de Sousa
GARRIGUES PORTUGAL SLP - SUCURSAL

Sara Ferraz Mendonça
MORAIS LEITÃO, GALVÃO TELES, SOARES DA SILVA & ASSOCIADOS, MEMBER OF LEX MUNDI

Ana Luisa Ferreira
ABREU ADVOGADOS

Rita Ferreira Lopes
MORAIS LEITÃO, GALVÃO TELES, SOARES DA SILVA & ASSOCIADOS, MEMBER OF LEX MUNDI

Eduardo Fonseca
PWC PORTUGAL

Rui Gloria
TOCHA, CHAVES & ASSOCIADOS, SROC - MEMBER OF RUSSELL BEDFORD INTERNATIONAL

Nuno Gundar da Cruz
MORAIS LEITÃO, GALVÃO TELES, SOARES DA SILVA & ASSOCIADOS, MEMBER OF LEX MUNDI

Tiago Lemos
PLEN - SOCIEDADE DE ADVOGADOS, RL

Bruno Lobato
MOUTEIRA GUERREIRO, ROSA AMARAL & ASSOCIADOS - SOCIEDADE DE ADVOGADOS RL

Helga Lopes Ribeiro
MOUTEIRA GUERREIRO, ROSA AMARAL & ASSOCIADOS - SOCIEDADE DE ADVOGADOS RL

Tiago Gali Macedo
GALI MACEDO & ASSOCIADOS

Ana Margarida Maia
MIRANDA & ASSOCIADOS

Carlos Pedro Marques
EDP DISTRIBUIÇÃO - ENERGIA, SA

Catarina Medeiros
PWC PORTUGAL

Patricia Melo Gomes
MORAIS LEITÃO, GALVÃO TELES, SOARES DA SILVA & ASSOCIADOS, MEMBER OF LEX MUNDI

Joaquim Luís Mendes
GRANT THORNTON CONSULTORES LDA.

Andreia Morins
PWC PORTUGAL

António Mouteira Guerreiro
MOUTEIRA GUERREIRO, ROSA AMARAL & ASSOCIADOS - SOCIEDADE DE ADVOGADOS RL

Rita Nogueira Neto
GARRIGUES PORTUGAL SLP - SUCURSAL

Eduardo Paulino
MORAIS LEITÃO, GALVÃO TELES, SOARES DA SILVA & ASSOCIADOS, MEMBER OF LEX MUNDI

João Branco Pedro
NATIONAL LABORATORY FOR CIVIL ENGINEERING - LNEC

Inga Petkelyte-Kilikeviciene
KPL LEGAL

Pedro Catão Pinheiro
GALI MACEDO & ASSOCIADOS

Acácio Pita Negrão
PLEN - SOCIEDADE DE ADVOGADOS, RL

Margarida Ramalho
ASSOCIAÇÃO DE EMPRESAS DE CONSTRUÇÃO, OBRAS PÚBLICAS E SERVIÇOS

Sara Reis
MIRANDA & ASSOCIADOS

Maria João Ricou
CUATRECASAS, GONÇALVES PEREIRA, RL (PORTUGAL)

Ana Robin de Andrade
MORAIS LEITÃO, GALVÃO TELES, SOARES DA SILVA & ASSOCIADOS, MEMBER OF LEX MUNDI

Telmo Rodrigues
ABREU ADVOGADOS

Filomena Rosa
INSTITUTO DOS REGISTOS E DO NOTARIADO

Pedro Rosa
GARRIGUES PORTUGAL SLP - SUCURSAL

Francisco Salgueiro
NEVILLE DE ROUGEMONT & ASSOCIADOS

Maria do Ceu Santiago
MBS ADVOGADOS

Filipe Santos Barata
GÓMEZ-ACEBO & POMBO ABOGADOS, SLP SUCURSAL EM PORTUGAL

Cláudia Santos Malaquias
MIRANDA & ASSOCIADOS

Cristina Serrazina
PEDRO RAPOSO & ASSOCIADOS

Ana Sofia Silva
CUATRECASAS, GONÇALVES PEREIRA, RL (PORTUGAL)

Rui Silva
PWC PORTUGAL

João Silva Pereira
BARROCAS ADVOGADOS

Inês Sousa Godinho
GÓMEZ-ACEBO & POMBO ABOGADOS, SLP SUCURSAL EM PORTUGAL

Francisco Sousa Guedes
SGOC SOUSA GUEDES, OLIVEIRA COUTO & ASSOCIADOS, SOC. ADVOGADOS RL

Carmo Sousa Machado
ABREU ADVOGADOS

Rui Souto
RAPOSO SÁ MIRANDA & ASSOCIADOS

Ricardo Veloso
PWC ANGOLA

Diogo Vitorino Martins
MOUTEIRA GUERREIRO, ROSA AMARAL & ASSOCIADOS - SOCIEDADE DE ADVOGADOS RL

PUERTO RICO (U.S.)

AUTORIDAD DE ENERGÍA ELÉCTRICA

Martha L. Acevedo-Peñuela
O'NEILL & BORGES LLC

Olga Angueira
COLEGIO DE ARQUITECTOS Y ARQUITECTOS PAISAJISTAS DE PUERTO RICO

Antonio A. Arias-Larcada
MCCONNELL VALDÉS LLC

Hermann Bauer
O'NEILL & BORGES LLC

Jorge Capó Matos
O'NEILL & BORGES LLC

Odemaris Chacon
ESTRELLA, LLC

Manuel De Lemos
MANUEL DE LEMOS AIA ARQUITECTOS

Carla Diaz
PWC PUERTO RICO

Antonio Escudero Viera
MCCONNELL VALDÉS LLC

Ubaldo Fernandez
O'NEILL & BORGES LLC

Alfonso Fernández
IVY GROUP

Nelson William González
COLEGIO DE NOTARIOS DE PUERTO RICO

Pedro Janer
CMA ARCHITECTS & ENGINEERS LLP

Rubén M. Medina-Lugo
CANCIO, NADAL, RIVERA & DÍAZ

Oscar O. Meléndez-Sauri
MALLEY TAMARGO & MELÉNDEZ-SAURI LLC

Juan Carlos Méndez
REICHARD & ESCALERA

Antonio Molina
PIETRANTONI MÉNDEZ & ALVAREZ LLC

Luis Mongil-Casasnovas
*CANCIO, NADAL,
RIVERA & DÍAZ*

Jose Armando Morales
Rodriguez
JAM CARGO SALES INC.

Jhansel Núñez
ATTORNEY

Virmarily Pacheco
*COLEGIO DE NOTARIOS
DE PUERTO RICO*

Diego R. Puello Álvarez
MCCONNELL VALDÉS LLC

Marta Ramirez
O'NEILL & BORGES LLC

Roberto E. Reyes Perez
*REYES PEREZ &
ASSOCIATES LLC*

Jesus Rivera
*BANCO POPULAR DE
PUERTO RICO*

Kenneth Rivera-Robles
*FPV & GALÍNDEZ CPAS,
PSC - MEMBER OF RUSSELL
BEDFORD INTERNATIONAL*

Victor Rodriguez
*MULTITRANSPORT
& MARINE CO.*

Victor Rodriguez
PWC PUERTO RICO

Edgardo Rosa
*FPV & GALÍNDEZ CPAS,
PSC - MEMBER OF RUSSELL
BEDFORD INTERNATIONAL*

Jorge M. Ruiz Montilla
MCCONNELL VALDÉS LLC

Jaime Santos
*PIETRANTONI MÉNDEZ
& ALVAREZ LLC*

Tania Vazquez Maldonado
*BANCO POPULAR DE
PUERTO RICO*

Raúl Vidal y Sepúlveda
*OMNIA ECONOMIC
SOLUTIONS LLC*

QATAR

Hani Al Naddaf
*AL TAMIMI & COMPANY
ADVOCATES & LEGAL
CONSULTANTS*

Abdulla Mohamed Al Naimi
QATAR CREDIT BUREAU

Grace Alam
*BADRI AND SALIM EL
MEOUCHI LAW FIRM,
MEMBER OF INTERLEGES*

Rashed Albuflasa
NOBLE GLOBAL LOGISTICS

Mohammad Alkhalifa
MINISTRY OF JUSTICE

Maitha Al-Naemi
MINISTRY OF JUSTICE

Maryam Al-Thani
QATAR CREDIT BUREAU

Zied Alzobi
MINISTRY OF JUSTICE

Amira Awad
MINISTRY OF JUSTICE

Imran Ayub
KPMG QATAR

Piyush Bhandari
*INTUIT MANAGEMENT
CONSULTANCY*

Priyanka Bhandari
*INTUIT MANAGEMENT
CONSULTANCY*

Alexis Coleman
PINSENT MASONS LLP

Michael Earley
*SULTAN AL-ABDULLA
& PARTNERS*

Fouad El Haddad
LALIVE LLC

Ahmed Eljaale
*AL TAMIMI & COMPANY
ADVOCATES & LEGAL
CONSULTANTS*

Dalal K. Farhat Harb
FD CONSULT

Mohammed Fouad
*SULTAN AL-ABDULLA
& PARTNERS*

Walid Honein
*BADRI AND SALIM EL
MEOUCHI LAW FIRM,
MEMBER OF INTERLEGES*

Rafiq Jaffer
*AL TAMIMI & COMPANY
ADVOCATES & LEGAL
CONSULTANTS*

Tamsyn Jones
KPMG QATAR

Dani Kabbani
EVERSHEDS

Upuli Kasthuriarachchi
PWC QATAR

Pradeep Kumar
DIAMOND SHIPPING SERVICES

Frank Lucente
*AL TAMIMI & COMPANY
ADVOCATES & LEGAL
CONSULTANTS*

Seem Maleh
*AL TAMIMI & COMPANY
ADVOCATES & LEGAL
CONSULTANTS*

Julie Menhem
EVERSHEDS

Muhammad Mitha
*AL TAMIMI & COMPANY
ADVOCATES & LEGAL
CONSULTANTS*

Peter Motti
DENTONS

Sujani Nisansala
PWC QATAR

Neil O'Brien
PWC QATAR

Ferdinand Ray Ona II
NOBLE GLOBAL LOGISTICS

Michael Palmer
*SQUIRE PATTON
BOGGS (MEA) LLP*

Sony Pereira
*NATIONAL SHIPPING
AND MARINE SERVICES
COMPANY WLL*

Johnson Rajan
*INTUIT MANAGEMENT
CONSULTANCY*

Sohaib Rubbani
PWC QATAR

Lilia Sabbagh
*BADRI AND SALIM EL
MEOUCHI LAW FIRM,
MEMBER OF INTERLEGES*

Mohamed Samy
MINISTRY OF JUSTICE

Murad Sawalha
*AL TAMIMI & COMPANY
ADVOCATES & LEGAL
CONSULTANTS*

Zain Al Abdin Sharar
*QATAR INTERNATIONAL
COURT AND DISPUTE
RESOLUTION CENTRE*

Ali Sophie
*TALAL ABU-GHAZALEH
LEGAL (TAG-LEGAL)*

Abdul Aziz Mohammed
Sorour
MINISTRY OF JUSTICE

Tabara Sy
LALIVE LLC

ROMANIA

ARHIPAR SRL

Elena Abdulgani
MCGREGOR & PARTNERS SCA

Daniel Alexie

Cosmin Anghel
CLIFFORD CHANCE BADEA SCA

Mihai Anghel
ȚUCA ZBÂRCEA & ASOCIAȚII

Gabriela Anton
ȚUCA ZBÂRCEA & ASOCIAȚII

Francesco Atanasio
ENEL

Ioana Avram
EVERSHEDS LINA & GUIA SCA

Andreea Badea
DLA PIPER DINU SCA

Andrei Badiu
*3B EXPERT AUDIT - MEMBER
OF RUSSELL BEDFORD
INTERNATIONAL*

Georgiana Balan
D&B DAVID ȘI BAIAS LAW FIRM

Florina Balanescu
ENEL

Irina Elena Bănică
*POP & PARTNERS SCA
ATTORNEYS-AT-LAW*

Paula Boteanu
DLA PIPER DINU SCA

Mihai Bucuiuman

Sandra Cahu
DLA PIPER DINU SCA

Maria Cambien
PWC ROMANIA

Victor Cândea
*STATE INSPECTORATE
FOR CONSTRUCTIONS*

Ioana Cercel
D&B DAVID ȘI BAIAS LAW FIRM

Marius Chelaru
*STOICA & ASOCIAȚII -
SOCIETATE CIVILĂ DE AVOCAȚI*

Teodor Chirvase

Veronica Cocârlea
JINGA & ASOCIAȚII

Raluca Coman
CLIFFORD CHANCE BADEA SCA

Razvan Constantinescu
*DENTONS EUROPE - TODOR
SI ASOCIATII SPARL*

Paula Corban
DLA PIPER DINU SCA

Anamaria Corbescu
*DENTONS EUROPE - TODOR
SI ASOCIATII SPARL*

Oana Cornescu
ȚUCA ZBÂRCEA & ASOCIAȚII

Sergiu Cretu
ȚUCA ZBÂRCEA & ASOCIAȚII

Alexandru Cristea
ȚUCA ZBÂRCEA & ASOCIAȚII

Tiberiu Csaki
*DENTONS EUROPE - TODOR
SI ASOCIATII SPARL*

Radu Damaschin
*NESTOR NESTOR DICULESCU
KINGSTON PETERSEN*

Anca Danilescu
*ZAMFIRESCU RACOȚI &
PARTNERS ATTORNEYS-AT-LAW*

Dan Dascalu
D&B DAVID ȘI BAIAS LAW FIRM

Adrian Deaconu
TAXHOUSE SRL

Luminița Dima
*NESTOR NESTOR DICULESCU
KINGSTON PETERSEN*

Rodica Dobre
PWC ROMANIA

Monia Dobrescu
MUȘAT & ASOCIAȚII

Constantin Dragos-Mircea
OFFICE OF ARCHITECTURE

Laura Adina Duca
*NESTOR NESTOR DICULESCU
KINGSTON PETERSEN*

Alina Dumitrascu
*CABINET CONSULTANTA
ECONOMICA MERCESCU*

Geanina Dumitru
*ENEL (FORMER ELECTRICA
MUNTENIA SUD)*

Nastasia Dumitru
DLA PIPER DINU SCA

Lidia Dutu
DLA PIPER DINU SCA

Serban Epure
BIROUL DE CREDIT

Iulia Ferăstrău-Grigore
MARAVELA & ASOCIAȚII

Raluca Gabor
ȚUCA ZBÂRCEA & ASOCIAȚII

Adriana Gaspar
*NESTOR NESTOR DICULESCU
KINGSTON PETERSEN*

Monica Georgiadis
DLA PIPER DINU SCA

Ștefan Ghenciulescu
*ORDINUL ARHITECȚILOR
DIN ROMANIA*

George Ghitu
MUȘAT & ASOCIAȚII

Fanizzi Giuseppe
ENEL

Magda Grigore
MARAVELA & ASOCIAȚII

Adina Grosu
*DENTONS EUROPE - TODOR
SI ASOCIATII SPARL*

Ana-Maria Hrituc
*PROTOPOPESCU,
PUSCAS SI ASOCIAȚII*

Florentina Hurdubei
ȚUCA ZBÂRCEA & ASOCIAȚII

Romina Iancu
DLA PIPER DINU SCA

Camelia Iantuc
CLIFFORD CHANCE BADEA SCA

Alexandra Ichim

Alina Ignat
*REGIONAL INSPECTORATE FOR
CONSTRUCTIONS BUCHAREST*

Mariana Ionescu
*ORDINUL ARHITECȚILOR
DIN ROMANIA*

Cătălina Iordache
BUCHAREST CITY HALL

Diana Emanuela Ispas
*NESTOR NESTOR DICULESCU
KINGSTON PETERSEN*

Horia Ispas
ȚUCA ZBÂRCEA & ASOCIAȚII

Cristian Lina
EVERSHEDS LINA & GUIA SCA

Edita Lovin
*RETIRED JUDGE OF ROMANIAN
SUPREME COURT OF JUSTICE*

Ileana Lucian
MUȘAT & ASOCIAȚII

Madalina Mailat
CLIFFORD CHANCE BADEA SCA

Smaranda Mandrescu
*POP & PARTNERS SCA
ATTORNEYS-AT-LAW*

Gelu Titus Maravela
MARAVELA & ASOCIAȚII

Alexandra-Mikaela Măruțoiu
*NESTOR NESTOR DICULESCU
KINGSTON PETERSEN*

Neil McGregor
MCGREGOR & PARTNERS SCA

Mariana Mercescu
*CABINET CONSULTANTA
ECONOMICA MERCESCU*

Mirela Metea
MARAVELA & ASOCIAȚII

Maria Cristina Metelet
*POP & PARTNERS SCA
ATTORNEYS-AT-LAW*

Cătălina Mihăilescu
ȚUCA ZBÂRCEA & ASOCIAȚII

Stefan Mihartescu
D&B DAVID ȘI BAIAS LAW FIRM

Mihaela Mitroi
PWC ROMANIA

Marian Mustareata
NATIONAL BANK OF ROMANIA

Adriana Neagoe
NATIONAL BANK OF ROMANIA

Larisa-Georgiana Negoias
DLA PIPER DINU SCA

Manuela Marina Nestor
*NESTOR NESTOR DICULESCU
KINGSTON PETERSEN*

Andreea Nica
DLA PIPER DINU SCA

Theodor Catalin Nicolescu
*NICOLESCU & PERIANU
LAW FIRM*

Raluca Onufreiciuc
SĂVESCU & ASOCIAȚII

Gabriela Oprea
CLIFFORD CHANCE BADEA SCA

Andrei Ormenean
MUȘAT & ASOCIAȚII

Bogdan Papandopol
*DENTONS EUROPE - TODOR
SI ASOCIATII SPARL*

Mircea Parvu
SCPA PARVU SI ASOCIATII

Gheorghe Pătrașcu
BUCHAREST CITY HALL

Laurentiu Petre
SĂVESCU & ASOCIAȚII

Sergiu Petrea
SC TECTO ARHITECTURA SRL

Ana Maria Placintescu
MUȘAT & ASOCIAȚII

Carolina Pletniuc
EVERSHEDS LINA & GUIA SCA

Claudiu Pop
POP & PARTNERS SCA
ATTORNEYS-AT-LAW

Mihai Popa
MUȘAT & ASOCIAȚII

Alina Elena Popescu
MARAVELA & ASOCIAȚII

Iulian Popescu
MUȘAT & ASOCIAȚII

Mariana Popescu
NATIONAL BANK OF ROMANIA

Tiberiu Potyesz
BITRANS LTD.

Olga Preda
POP & PARTNERS SCA
ATTORNEYS-AT-LAW

Elena Monica Preotescu
DLA PIPER DINU SCA

Sebastian Radocea
ȚUCA ZBÂRCEA & ASOCIAȚII

Laura Radu
STOICA & ASOCIAȚII -
SOCIETATE CIVILĂ DE AVOCAȚI

Magdalena Raducanu
DENTONS EUROPE - TODOR
SI ASOCIATII SPARL

Alexandra Radulescu
DLA PIPER DINU SCA

Dana Rădulescu

Argentina Rafail
DENTONS EUROPE - TODOR
SI ASOCIATII SPARL

Corina Ricman
CLIFFORD CHANCE BADEA SCA

Bogdan Riti
MUȘAT & ASOCIAȚII

Ioan Roman
MARAVELA & ASOCIAȚII

Angela Rosca
TAXHOUSE SRL

Florica Salaytah
STATE INSPECTORATE
FOR CONSTRUCTIONS

Cristina Sandu
TAXHOUSE SRL

Raluca Sanucean
ȚUCA ZBÂRCEA & ASOCIAȚII

Andrei Săvescu
SĂVESCU & ASOCIAȚII

Corina Simion
PWC ROMANIA

Alina Solschi
MUȘAT & ASOCIAȚII

Oana Soviani
DENTONS EUROPE - TODOR
SI ASOCIATII SPARL

Diana Stan
ORDINUL ARHITECȚILOR
DIN ROMANIA

Georgiana Stan
DLA PIPER DINU SCA

Ionut Stancu
NESTOR NESTOR DICULESCU
KINGSTON PETERSEN

Marie-Jeanna Stefanescu
RATEN-CITON

Tania Stefanita
TAXHOUSE SRL

Sorin Corneliu Stratula
STRATULA MOCANU
& ASOCIATII

Cătălina Sucaciu
MARAVELA & ASOCIAȚII

Alina Tacea
MUȘAT & ASOCIAȚII

Felix Tapai

Diana Tătulescu
NESTOR NESTOR DICULESCU
KINGSTON PETERSEN

Amelia Teis
D&B DAVID ȘI BAIAS LAW FIRM

Iulian Țepure
ORDINUL ARHITECȚILOR
DIN ROMANIA

Ciprian Timofte
ȚUCA ZBÂRCEA & ASOCIAȚII

Anda Todor
DENTONS EUROPE - TODOR
SI ASOCIATII SPARL

Adela Topescu
PWC ROMANIA

Andra Trantea
DLA PIPER DINU SCA

Madalina Trifan
DENTONS EUROPE - TODOR
SI ASOCIATII SPARL

Ada Țucă
JINGA & ASOCIAȚII

Cristina Tutuianu
PWC ROMANIA

Andrei Vartires
DENTONS EUROPE - TODOR
SI ASOCIATII SPARL

Cosmin Vasilescu
DENTONS EUROPE - TODOR
SI ASOCIATII SPARL

Cristina Gabriela Vedel
POP & PARTNERS SCA
ATTORNEYS-AT-LAW

Luigi Vendrami
DHL INTERNATIONAL ROMANIA

Daniel Nicolae Vinerean

Maria Vlad
JINGA & ASOCIAȚII

Andrei Zaharescu
BUCHAREST CITY HALL

Stefan Zamfirescu
ZAMFIRESCU RACOȚI &
PARTNERS ATTORNEYS-AT-LAW

RUSSIAN FEDERATION

FEDERAL CUSTOMS SERVICE

FEDERAL SERVICE FOR STATE
REGISTRATION, CADASTER AND
CARTOGRAPHY IN MOSCOW

FEDERAL SERVICE FOR STATE
REGISTRATION, CADASTER
AND CARTOGRAPHY
IN ST. PETERSBURG

HYUNDAI MOTOR
MANUFACTURING RUS, LLC

INTRANS

MOSENERGOSBYT

SAINT PETERSBURG
SUPPLY COMPANY

WHITE & CASE LLP RUSSIA

Andrei Afanasiev
BAKER & MCKENZIE - CIS,
LIMITED

Teymur Akhundov
ALRUD LAW FIRM

Vera Akimkina

Andrei Andreev
UNIFEEDER

Anatoly E. Andriash
NORTON ROSE FULBRIGHT
(CENTRAL EUROPE) LLP

Aleksei Anisimov
KHAZOV, KASHKIN
& PARTNERS

Vitaly Anisimov
GRATA INTERNATIONAL

Irina Anyukhina
ALRUD LAW FIRM

Suren Avakov
AVAKOV TARASOV
& PARTNERS

Vladimir S. Averyanov
LAW OFFICE OF
AVERYANOV & OLENEV

Anna Babich
MANNHEIMER SWARTLING

Vladimir Barbolin
CLIFFORD CHANCE

Marc Bartholomy
CLIFFORD CHANCE

Gleb Bazurin
LINIYA PRAVA LAW FIRM

Edward Bekeschenko
BAKER & MCKENZIE - CIS,
LIMITED

Evgenia Belokon
NORTON ROSE FULBRIGHT
(CENTRAL EUROPE) LLP

Victoria Belykh
OKB - UNITED CREDIT BUREAU

Artem Berlin
KACHKIN & PARTNERS

Mikhail Beshtoyev

Dmitry Bessolitsyn
PRICEWATERHOUSECOOPERS
LEGAL

Roman Bevzenko
PEPELIAEV GROUP

Ekaterina Boeva
ALRUD LAW FIRM

Sergey Bogatyev
BEITEN BURKHARDT
RECHTSANWÄLTE
(ATTORNEYS-AT-LAW)

Andrey Bondarchuk
COMMITTEE ON URBAN
DEVELOPMENT AND
ARCHITECTURE OF
ST PETERSBURG

Natalia Borisevich
UNITED CONSULTING GROUP

Julia Borozdna
PEPELIAEV GROUP

Thomas Brand
BRAND & PARTNER

Olga Chirkova
HANNES SNELLMAN
ATTORNEYS LTD.

Alexander Chizhov
EY

Dmitry Churin
CAPITAL LEGAL SERVICES

Marat Davletbaev
NEKTOROV, SAVELIEV
& PARTNERS

Darya Degtyareva
ALRUD LAW FIRM

Svetlana Demicheva
DENTONS

German Derbushev
PRICEWATERHOUSECOOPERS
LEGAL

Yana Dianova
GRATA INTERNATIONAL

Daniel Dmitriev
ENERGIA LLC

Olga Duchenko
KACHKIN & PARTNERS

Elizaveta Dvoinishnikova
CAPITAL LEGAL SERVICES

Arslan Dyakiev
PRICEWATERHOUSECOOPERS
LEGAL

Natalia Dybina
KHAZOV, KASHKIN
& PARTNERS

Sergey Fedorov
BORENIUS ATTORNEYS
RUSSIA LTD.

Victoria Feleshtin
LEVINE BRIDGE

Ilya Fomin
GOLSBLAT BLP

Dzhaniko Gagua
N-LOGISTICS

Marsel Galiautdinov
JSC LUKOIL

Magomed Gasanov
ALRUD LAW FIRM

Vladimir Vladimirovich
Golobokov
CENTER FOR INNOVATION
AND INFORMATION
TECHNOLOGY FOUNDATION

Lidia Gorshkova
PEPELIAEV GROUP

Anton Grebennikov
FWD FREIGHT AND
FORWARDING

Vladimir Grigoriyev
COMMITTEE ON URBAN
DEVELOPMENT AND
ARCHITECTURE OF
ST PETERSBURG

Anna Grishchenkova
KORELSKIY ISCHUK
ASTAFIEV (KIAP)

Igor Guschev
DUVERNOIX LEGAL

Teymur Guseynov
EGOROV PUGINSKY
AFANASIEV & PARTNERS

George Gutiev
GOLSBLAT BLP

Roman Ibriyev
MOESK

Anton Isakov
GOLSBLAT BLP

Roman Ishmukhametov
BAKER & MCKENZIE

Polina Kachkina
KACHKIN & PARTNERS

Nikita Kalinichenko
NEKTOROV, SAVELIEV
& PARTNERS

Maxim Kalinin
BAKER & MCKENZIE

Lilia Kalinina
PENNVILLE HOLDINGS LIMITED

Nadezhda Karavanova
DEPARTMENT OF URBAN
PLANNING POLICY
OF MOSCOW

Kamil Karibov
BEITEN BURKHARDT
RECHTSANWÄLTE
(ATTORNEYS-AT-LAW)

Pavel Karpunin
CAPITAL LEGAL SERVICES

Ekaterina Karunets
BAKER & MCKENZIE - CIS,
LIMITED

Roman Kashkin
KHAZOV, KASHKIN
& PARTNERS

Ivan Khaydurov
HOUGH TROFIMOV
& PARTNERS

Evgeny Khazanov
ROLL STANDARD

Snezhana Kitaeva
LENENERGO

Ksenia Kochneva
DLA PIPER

Vadim Kolomnikov
DEBEVOISE & PLIMPTON LLP

Oleg Kolotilov
KULKOV, KOLOTILOV &
PARTNERS (KK&P)

Aleksey Konevsky
PEPELIAEV GROUP

Anastasia Konovalova
NORTON ROSE FULBRIGHT
(CENTRAL EUROPE) LLP

Vadim Konyushkevich
LINIYA PRAVA LAW FIRM

Alexander Korkin
PEPELIAEV GROUP

Evgenia Korotkova
DECHERT LLP

Evgeniy Koshkarov
ARIVIST

Igor Kostennikov
YUST LAW FIRM

Vadim Kovalyov
CAPITAL LEGAL SERVICES

Dmitriy Kozlov
UNITED CONSULTING GROUP

Alyona Kozyreva
NORTON ROSE FULBRIGHT
(CENTRAL EUROPE) LLP

Leonid Kropotov
DLA PIPER

Ekaterina Krylova
AGENCY FOR STRATEGIC
INITIATIVES

Elena Kukushkina
BAKER & MCKENZIE - CIS,
LIMITED

Leonid Kulakov
COMMITTEE ON URBAN
DEVELOPMENT AND
ARCHITECTURE OF
ST PETERSBURG

Dmitry Kunitsa
MORGAN LEWIS

Roman Kuzmin
LINIYA PRAVA LAW FIRM

Sergei L. Lazarev
RUSSIN & VECCHI

Ekaterina Lazorina
PWC RUSSIA

Bogdan Lebed
BUDMAKS CONSTRUCTION

Sergei Lee
*CASTRÉN & SNELLMAN
INTERNATIONAL LTD.*

Evgeny Lidzhiev
LIDINGS LAW FIRM

Sergey Likhachev
GOLSBLAT BLP

Anastasiya Likhanova
GEOMETRIYA

Gregory Linkov
*CENTER FOR INNOVATION
AND INFORMATION
TECHNOLOGY FOUNDATION*

Yulia Litovtseva
PEPELIAEV GROUP

Dmitry Lobachev
KHRENOV & PARTNERS

Maxim Losik
*CASTRÉN & SNELLMAN
INTERNATIONAL LTD.*

Stepan Lubavsky
FINEC

Yulia Ludinova
*COMMITTEE ON URBAN
DEVELOPMENT AND
ARCHITECTURE OF
ST PETERSBURG*

Sergey Lyadov
TRANS BUSINESS

Ilya Lyubchenko
UNITED CONSULTING GROUP

Aleksandr Lyuboserdov
PROFESSIONAL LEGAL CENTER

Alexei Yurievich Makarovsky
MOESK

Bagel Maksim Anatolyevich
GARANT ENERGO

Sofya Mamonova
*NORTON ROSE FULBRIGHT
(CENTRAL EUROPE) LLP*

Alisa Manaka
MOESK

Vilena Mandrika
RUSSIN & VECCHI

Igor Marmalidi
PEPELIAEV GROUP

Igor Matveyev
*BORENIUS ATTORNEYS
RUSSIA LTD.*

Ekaterina Mayorova
ALRUD LAW FIRM

Vladimir Meleshin
EXPRESS REGISTRATOR

Anastasia Mergasova
CAPITAL LEGAL SERVICES

Maria Mikhailova
MORGAN LEWIS

Stanislav Mikhaylov
HOLDING RBI

Nadezhda Minina
*NEKTOROV, SAVELIEV
& PARTNERS*

Dmitry Mishin
*PRICEWATERHOUSECOOPERS
LEGAL*

Michael Morozov
KPMG RUSSIA

Natalya Morozova
VINSON & ELKINS

Ivan Nasonov
N-LOGISTICS

Elena Nazarova
SCHNEIDER GROUP

Kliment Nechaev
CAPITAL LEGAL SERVICES

Tatiana Nikolayevna Nekrasova
MOESK

Dmitry Nekrestyanov
KACHKIN & PARTNERS

Tatyana Neveeva
*EGOROV PUGINSKY
AFANASIEV & PARTNERS*

Petr Nikitenko
LIDINGS LAW FIRM

Alexey Nikitin
*BORENIUS ATTORNEYS
RUSSIA LTD.*

Pavel Novikov
*BAKER & MCKENZIE - CIS,
LIMITED*

Anton Novoseltsev
LIDINGS LAW FIRM

Gennady Odarich
*PRICEWATERHOUSECOOPERS
LEGAL*

Elena Ogawa
LEVINE BRIDGE

Irina Onikienko
CAPITAL LEGAL SERVICES

Julia Oprenko
*NORTON ROSE FULBRIGHT
(CENTRAL EUROPE) LLP*

Ekaterina Orlova
ATTORNEY

Olga Pankova
BAKER & MCKENZIE

Sergey Petrachkov
ALRUD LAW FIRM

Maya Petrova
*BORENIUS ATTORNEYS
RUSSIA LTD.*

Sergei Pikin
ENERGY DEVELOPMENT FUND

Ivan Podbereznyak
DEBEVOISE & PLIMPTON LLP

Anna Ponomareva
GOLSBLAT BLP

Sergei Vladimirovich Popov
OOO SKIV

Ilya Povetkin
LENENERGO

Natalia Prisekina
RUSSIN & VECCHI

Svetlana Prokofieva
LENENERGO

Alexandr Pyatigor
MOESK

Daniil Rivin
BAKER & MCKENZIE

Anton Romanov
DMSTR CONSTRUCTION

Alexander Rostovsky
*CASTRÉN & SNELLMAN
INTERNATIONAL LTD.*

Kirill Rubashevskiy
LINIYA PRAVA LAW FIRM

Ekaterina Rudova
CAPITAL LEGAL SERVICES

Alexander Rudyakov
YUST LAW FIRM

Anna Rybalko
DELOITTE & TOUCHE CIS

Marianna Rybynok
KHRENOV & PARTNERS

Gudisa Sakania
MOESK

Artem Samoylov
LINIYA PRAVA LAW FIRM

Kirill Saskov
KACHKIN & PARTNERS

Ulf Schneider
SCHNEIDER GROUP

Maxim Semenyako
IUSLAND LAW OFFICES

Vladimir Shabanov
YIT SAINT-PETERSBURG JSC

Alexei Shcherbakov
TSDS GROUP OF COMPANIES

Alexander Shevchuk
*ASSOCIATION OF
INSTITUTIONAL INVESTORS*

Yulia Aleksandrovna Shirokova
MOESK

Vladimir Skrynnik
JUST PRIVATUM LAW FIRM

Yury Smolin
*DE BERTI JACCHIA FRANCHINI
FORLANI STUDIO LEGALE*

Mihail Sergeevich Smolko
GSP GROUP

Nikolay Solodovnikov
PEPELIAEV GROUP

Julia Solomkina
LEVINE BRIDGE

Ksenia Soloschenko
*CASTRÉN & SNELLMAN
INTERNATIONAL LTD.*

Elena Solovyeva
*AGENCY FOR STRATEGIC
INITIATIVES*

Sergey Sosnovsky
PEPELIAEV GROUP

Ksenia Stepanischeva
LIDINGS LAW FIRM

Elena Subocheva
RUSSIN & VECCHI

Ilya Sukharnikov
*EY VALUATION AND
ADVISORY SERVICES LLC*

Andrey Sukhov
*DEPARTMENT OF URBAN
PLANNING POLICY
OF MOSCOW*

Fredrik Svensson
MANNHEIMER SWARTLING

Dagadina Svetlana
CLIFF LEGAL SERVICES

Dmitry Tarasov
*AVAKOV TARASOV
& PARTNERS*

Julia Tarasova
LEVINE BRIDGE

Ilya Tarbaev
ABZ-DORSTROY

Vladlena Terekhina
*PRICEWATERHOUSECOOPERS
LEGAL*

Tatiana Tereshchenko
*PRIME ADVICE ST.
PETERSBURG LAW OFFICE*

Evgeny Timofeev
GOLSBLAT BLP

Evgeniy Tregubenko
T&T SERVICES, LLC

Sergey A. Treshchev
*SQUIRE PATTON BOGGS
MOSCOW LLC*

Alexander Tsakoev
*NORTON ROSE FULBRIGHT
(CENTRAL EUROPE) LLP*

Alexandra Ulezko
KACHKIN & PARTNERS

Olga Varlamova
PENNVILLE HOLDINGS LIMITED

Anastasia Vasilieva
*BEITEN BURKHARDT
RECHTSANWÄLTE
(ATTORNEYS-AT-LAW)*

Sergey Vasilliev
DLA PIPER

Artem Vasyutin
DELOITTE & TOUCHE CIS

Inna Vavilova
*PRIME ADVICE ST.
PETERSBURG LAW OFFICE*

Stanislav Veselov
ALRUD LAW FIRM

Denis E. Voevodin
DENTONS

Aleksei Volkov
*NATIONAL BUREAU OF
CREDIT HISTORIES*

Yuriy Vorobyev
PEPELIAEV GROUP

Viktoria Aleksandrovna
Vostrosablina
MOESK

Andrey Yakushin
CENTRAL BANK OF RUSSIA

Vadim Yudenkov
OOO GEOTECHNIC

Sergey Yurov
*MONASTYRSKY, ZYUBA,
STEPANOV & PARTNERS*

Vladislav Zabrodin
CAPITAL LEGAL SERVICES

Roman Zaitsev
DENTONS

Marina Zaykova
*CLOSED STOCK COMPANY
STS ENERGY*

Andrey Zelenin
LIDINGS LAW FIRM

Andrey Zharskiy
ALRUD LAW FIRM

Roman Zhavner
*EGOROV PUGINSKY
AFANASIEV & PARTNERS*

Artem Zhavoronkov
DENTONS

Evgeny Zhilin
YUST LAW FIRM

Ekaterina Znamenskaya
*NEKTOROV, SAVELIEV
& PARTNERS*

RWANDA

BOLLORÉ AFRICA LOGISTICS

*GM CORPORATE CONSULT
LIMITED (GMCC)*

Emmanuel Abijuru
*CAPITAL PERFORMANCE
ADVOCATES*

Angel Phionah Ampurire
TRUST LAW CHAMBERS

Ray Amusengeri
PWC

Richard Balenzi
TRUST LAW CHAMBERS

Alberto Basomingera
CABINET ZÉNITH LAW FIRM

Natacha Bugondo

Flavia Busingye
*EAST AFRICAN COMMUNITY
SECRETARIAT*

Louis de Gonzague
Mukerangabo
*VISION TECHNOLOGIES
COMPANY*

Paul Frobisher Mugambwa
PWC

Claver Gakwavu
RWANDA ENERGY GROUP

Patrick Gashagaza
GPO PARTNERS RWANDA

Jean Havugimana
ECODESEP LTD.

Francois Xavier Kalinda
UNIVERSITY OF RWANDA

Désiré Kamanzi
ENSAFRICA RWANDA

Wilson Karegyeya
*RWANDA UTILITIES AND
REGULATORY AUTHORITY*

Tushabe Karim
*RWANDA DEVELOPMENT
BOARD*

Didas Kayihura
FOUNTAIN ADVOCATES

Eudes Kayumba
LANDMARK STUDIO

Théophile Kazeneza
*CABINET D'AVOCATS
KAZENEZA*

Valence Kimeny
NATIONAL BANK OF RWANDA

Patrice Manirakiza
REPRO LTD.

Isaïe Mhayimana
ZENITH LAW FIRM

Alvin Mihigo
R & PARTNERS LAW FIRM

Calvin Mitali
EQUITY JURIS CHAMBERS

Merard Mpabwanamaguru
*CITY OF KIGALI - ONE STOP
CENTER FOR CONSTRUCTION*

Alex Mugire
RWANDA CUSTOMS

Richard Mugisha
TRUST LAW CHAMBERS

Elonie Mukandoli
NATIONAL BANK OF RWANDA

Léopold Munderere
CABINET D'AVOCATS-CONSEILS

Jacques Munyandamutsa
*RWANDA ENERGY UTILITY
CORPORATION LIMITED*

Pascal Mutesa
*RWANDA ENERGY UTILITY
CORPORATION LIMITED*

Patrick Mutimura
BMP CONSULTING

Pothin Muvara
*RWANDA NATURAL RESOURCES
AUTHORITY, OFFICE OF THE
REGISTRAR OF LAND TITLES*

Grace Nishimwe
*RWANDA NATURAL RESOURCES
AUTHORITY, OFFICE OF THE
REGISTRAR OF LAND TITLES*

Aimable Nkuranga
TRANSUNION RWANDA

Martin Nkurunziza
GPO PARTNERS RWANDA

Pius Ntazinda
TRUST LAW CHAMBERS

Fred Nuwagaba
EAST AFRICAN COMMUNITY SECRETARIAT

Christy Nyarwaya
PWC

Emile Nzabamwita
CASE CONSULTANTS

Dieudonne Nzafashwanayo
ENSAFRICA RWANDA

Aaron Nzeyimana
CMA-CGM RWANDA

Seth Ochieng
HEALY CONSULTANTS GROUP PLC

Nelson Ogara
PWC

Josue Penaloza Quispe
BRALIRWA LTD.

Fred Rwihunda
RFM ENGINEERING LTD.

Yves Sangano
RWANDA DEVELOPMENT BOARD, OFFICE OF THE REGISTRAR GENERAL OF RWANDA

Pierre Valery Singizumukiza
SINGIZUMUKIZA PIERRE VALERY - NOTARY PUBLIC

Asante Twagira
ENSAFRICA RWANDA

Nelly Umugwaneza

M. Aimee Uwanyiligira
RWANDA ENERGY UTILITY CORPORATION LIMITED

Maureen Wamahiu
TRANSUNION RWANDA

Stephen Zawadi
MILLENNIUM LAW CHAMBERS

SAMOA

BETHAM BROTHERS ENTERPRISES LTD.

LESA MA PENN

Ferila Brown
PLANNING AND URBAN MANAGEMENT AGENCY

Lawrie Burich
QUANTUM CONTRAX LTD.

Shelley Burich
QUANTUM CONTRAX LTD.

Henry Tamotu Ah Ching

Fiona Ey
CLARKE EY LAWYERS

Patrick Fepulea'I
FEPULEA'I & SHUSTER

Taulapapa Brenda Heather-Latu
LATU LAWYERS

Komisi Koria
CLARKE EY LAWYERS

Herman Kruse
KRUSE, ENARI & BARLOW

Matafeo George Latu
LATU LAWYERS

Tima Leavai
LEAVAI LAW

Peato Sam Ling
SAMOA SHIPPING SERVICES LTD.

Sala Theodore Sialau Toalepai
SAMOA SHIPPING SERVICES LTD.

Keilani Soloi
SOLOI SURVEY SERVICES

Leiataua Tom Tinai
INSTITUTION OF PROFESSIONAL ENGINEERS SAMOA (IPES)

Leilani Va'a-Tamat
VAAI HOGLUND & TAMATI LAW FIRM

Shane Wulf
MWK LAWYERS

SAN MARINO

Renzo Balsimelli
UFFICIO URBANISTICA

Dennis Beccari
AVV. ERIKA MARANI

Gian Luca Belluzzi
STUDIO COMMERCIALE BELLUZZI

Gianna Burgagni
STUDIO LEGALE E NOTARILE

Cecilia Cardogna
STUDIO LEGALE E NOTARILE

Vincent Cecchetti
CECCHETTI, ALBANI & ASSOCIATI

Debora Cenni

Alberto Chezzi
STUDIO CHEZZI

Marco Ciacci
BANCA AGRICOLA

Sara Cupioli
UFFICIO TRIBUTARIO DELLA REPUBBLICA DI SAN MARINO

Alessandro de Mattia
AZIENDA AUTONOMA DI STATO PER I SERVIZI PUBBLICI

Laura Ferretti
SEGRETERIA DI STATO INDUSTRIA ARTIGIANATO E COMMERCIO TRASPORTI E RICERCA - DIPARTIMENTO ECONOMIA

Marcello Forcellini
STUDIO CHEZZI

Davide Gasperoni
UFFICIO TRIBUTARIO DELLA REPUBBLICA DI SAN MARINO

Simone Gatti
WORLD LINE

Cinzia Guerretti
WORLD LINE

Anna Maria Lonfernini
STUDIO LEGALE E NOTARILE LONFERNINI

Erika Marani
AVV. ERIKA MARANI

Lucia Mazza
UFFICIO TECNICO DEL CATASTO

Daniela Mina

Gianluca Minguzzi
ANTAO PROGETTI S.P.A.

Emanuela Montanari

Lorenzo Moretti
STUDIO LEGALE E NOTARILE

Alfredo Nicolini
LAWYER

Sara Pelliccioni
STUDIO LEGALE E NOTARILE AVV. MATTEO MULARONI - IN ASSOCIAZIONE CON BUSSOLETTI NUZZO & ASSOCIATI

Giuseppe Ragini
STUDIO LEGALE E NOTARILE GIUSEPPE RAGINI

Daniela Reffi
UFFICIO TECNICO DEL CATASTO

Marco Giancarlo Rossini
STUDIO LEGALE E NOTARILE

SÃO TOMÉ AND PRÍNCIPE

AGER - AUTORIDADE GERAL DE REGULACAO

CÂMARA DOS DESPACHANTES OFICIAIS - SÃO TOMÉ E PRÍNCIPE

António de Barros A. Aguiar
SOCOGESTA

Eudes Aguiar
AGUIAR & PEDRONHO STUDIO

Adelino Amado Pereira
AMADO PEREIRA & ASSOCIADOS, SOCIEDADE DE ADVOGADOS

André Aureliano Aragão
JURISCONSULTA & ADVOGADO

Nuno Barata
MIRANDA & ASSOCIADOS

Jeanine Batalha Ferreira
PWC PORTUGAL

Lara Beirao
CENTRAL BANK OF SÃO TOMÉ E PRÍNCIPE

Angelo De Jesus Bonfim
AMADO PEREIRA & ASSOCIADOS, SOCIEDADE DE ADVOGADOS

Miris Botelho Bernardo
TRIBUNAL DE 1A INSTANCIA DE SAO TOMÉ (JUIZO CIVEL)

Sukayna Braganca
BANCO INTERNACIONAL DE SÃO TOMÉ E PRÍNCIPE

Paula Caldeira Dutschmann
MIRANDA & ASSOCIADOS

Jaime Carvalho Esteves
PWC PORTUGAL

Tânia Cascais
MIRANDA & ASSOCIADOS

Mirian Castelo David Pontífice
BANCO INTERNACIONAL DE SÃO TOMÉ E PRÍNCIPE

Francisco Chibeles
ECOMOVEL

Olinto Costa
DIRECTORATE OF TAXES

Inês Barbosa Cunha
PWC PORTUGAL

Jaime de Oliveira
ODL & ASSOCIADOS

Celiza Deus Lima
ODL & ASSOCIADOS

Cláudia do Carmo Santos
MIRANDA & ASSOCIADOS

Stela dos Santoa Soares
POSSER DA COSTA ADVOGADOS ASSOCIADOS

Agostinho Fernandes
BANCO INTERNACIONAL DE SÃO TOMÉ E PRÍNCIPE

Edmar Ferriera Carvalho
LAWYER

Maria Figueiredo
MIRANDA & ASSOCIADOS

Salvador Fonseca
DIRECTORATE OF TAXES

Abdulay Godinho
DIRECÇÃO DOS REGISTOS E NOTARIADO DE SÃO TOMÉ

Ronísima Gomes Santana
BANCO INTERNACIONAL DE SÃO TOMÉ E PRÍNCIPE

Fernando Lima da Trindade
MINISTRY OF PUBLIC WORKS, GEOGRAPHICAL-CADASTRE, NATURAL RESOURCES, AND ENVIRONMENT

Pascoal Lima Dos Santos Daio
LAWYER

João Mayer Moreira
VDA - VIEIRA DE ALMEIDA & ASSOCIADOS

Herlander Rossi Medeiros
DIRECÇÃO GERAL DOS REGISTROS E DO NOTARIADO

Silvino Mendes
DIRECÇÃO DE OBRAS PÚBLICAS E URBANISMO

Manuel Morais
EQUADOR - VIAGENS E TURISMO LDA (AGENTE BELLETRANS)

Raul Mota Cerveira
VDA - VIEIRA DE ALMEIDA & ASSOCIADOS

Victor Nascimento
DESPACHANTE VICTOR NASCIMENTO

Virna Neves
STP COUNSEL, MEMBER OF THE MIRANDA ALLIANCE

Zerna Nezef
STP COUNSEL, MEMBER OF THE MIRANDA ALLIANCE

Anastácio Oliveira

Ana Posser
POSSER DA COSTA ADVOGADOS ASSOCIADOS

Guilherme Posser da Costa
POSSER DA COSTA ADVOGADOS ASSOCIADOS

Cosme Bonfim Afonso Rita
CÂMARA DE COMÉRCIO, AGRICULTURA E SERVIÇOS

Ilma Salvaterra
GUICHÉ ÚNICO PARA EMPRESAS

Vitor Santos
EBIC – EMPRESA DE CONSTRUÇÃO CIVIL

Edinha Soares Lima
SOLIMA & ASSOCIADOS

Manikson Trigueiros
POSSER DA COSTA ADVOGADOS ASSOCIADOS

Afonso Varela
PRIVATE PRACTITIONER

Idalécio Viana

SAUDI ARABIA

DELOITTE & TOUCHE

EY

THE LAW FIRM OF HATEM ABBAS GHAZZAWI & CO.

Khalid Abdulaziz
PWC SAUDI ARABIA

Rupert Agius-Pease
KPMG

Naif Bader Al-Harbi
UNIFIED REGISTRY - MINISTRY OF COMMERCE & INDUSTRY

Omar Al Ansari
LEGAL ADVISORS, ABDULAZIZ I. AL-AJLAN & PARTNERS IN ASSOCIATION WITH BAKER & MCKENZIE LIMITED

Fayez Al Debs
PWC SAUDI ARABIA

Abdulrahman Saleh Alzeraigi Al Sohaibani
ABDULNASIR AL SOHAIBANI

Abdullah Al Tamimi
AL TAMIMI & COMPANY ADVOCATES & LEGAL CONSULTANTS

Sulaiman Al Tuwaijri
SAUDI ARABIAN GENERAL INVESTMENT AUTHORITY

Khalid Al-Abdulkareem
CLIFFORD CHANCE

Luay Alamr
ALAMR GROUP COMPANY FOR ENGINEERING CONSULTANCY

Nizar Al-Awwad
SAUDI CREDIT BUREAU - SIMAH

Fahad AlDehais
EVERSHEDS LAW FIRM

Eisa Aleisa
SAUDI ARABIA CUSTOMS

Nasser Alfaraj
LEGAL ADVISORS, ABDULAZIZ I. AL-AJLAN & PARTNERS IN ASSOCIATION WITH BAKER & MCKENZIE LIMITED

Afnan K. Al-Haboudal
AL-GHAZZAWI PROFESSIONAL ASSOCIATION

Fatima Alhasan
LEGAL ADVISORS, ABDULAZIZ I. AL-AJLAN & PARTNERS IN ASSOCIATION WITH BAKER & MCKENZIE LIMITED

Nicholas Diacos Al-Hejailan
THE LAW FIRM OF SALAH AL-HEJAILAN

Omar AlHoshan
ALHOSHAN CPAS & CONSULTANTS - MEMBER OF RUSSELL BEDFORD INTERNATIONAL

Abdulaziz Alhussan
OSOOL LAW FIRM

Naif Aljbaly
NAIF ALJBALY LAW FIRM

Sultan Almasoud
SHERMAN & STERLING IN ASSOCIATION WITH DR. SULTAN ALMASOUD & PARTNERS

Saud Almelhem
DEPARTMENT OF ZAKAT & INCOME TAX

Aiman Meqham Almeqham
AL-MEQHAM CERTIFIED PUBLIC ACCOUNTANTS

Nabil Abdullah Al-Mubarak

Naif I. Alnammi
SAUDI ARABIA CUSTOMS

Sultan Alqudiry
SAUDI CREDIT BUREAU - SIMAH

Waleed Khaled AlRudaian
SAUDI ARABIAN GENERAL INVESTMENT AUTHORITY

Ahmad Alsadhan
CLIFFORD CHANCE

Abdulmohsen Alshenify
SAUDI ARABIA CUSTOMS

Wisam AlSindi
ALSINDI LAW FIRM

Abdullah Alsowayan
*SAUDI ARABIAN
MONETARY AGENCY*

Hussain Alsudairy
*MINISTRY OF MUNICIPAL
AND RURAL AFFAIRS*

Faisal Alzamil
EVERSHEDS LAW FIRM

Haroon Ansary
PWC SAUDI ARABIA

Lamisse Bajunaid
ALSINDI LAW FIRM

John Balouziyeh
DENTONS

Nada Bashammakh
ALSINDI LAW FIRM

Piyush Bhandari
*INTUIT MANAGEMENT
CONSULTANCY*

Priyanka Bhandari
*INTUIT MANAGEMENT
CONSULTANCY*

Kamal El-Batnigi
KPMG

Emad El-Hout
ALFANAR PRECAST

Majed Mohammed Garoub
*LAW FIRM OF MAJED
M. GAROUB*

Fehem Hashmi
CLIFFORD CHANCE

Amgad Husein
DENTONS

Christopher H. Johnson
*JOHNSON & PUMP IN
ASSOCIATION WITH
AL-SHARIF LAW FIRM*

Zaid Mahayni
SEDCO HOLDING

Mohammed Majed AlQahtani
*UNIFIED REGISTRY - MINISTRY
OF COMMERCE & INDUSTRY*

Justin McGettigan
KPMG

Rukn Eldeen Mohammed
OMRANIA & ASSOCIATES

Humaid Mudhaffr
*SAUDI CREDIT
BUREAU - SIMAH*

Grahame Nelson
*AL TAMIMI & COMPANY
ADVOCATES & LEGAL
CONSULTANTS*

Johnson Rajan
*INTUIT MANAGEMENT
CONSULTANCY*

Faisal Saad Al-Bedah
SAUDI ARABIA CUSTOMS

Emad Salameh
*AL TAMIMI & COMPANY
ADVOCATES & LEGAL
CONSULTANTS*

Muhammad Anum Saleem
EVERSHEDS LAW FIRM

Subahi Mohammed Subahi
*AL-GHAZZAWI PROFESSIONAL
ASSOCIATION*

Mohammed Yaghmour
PWC SAUDI ARABIA

Soudki Zawaydeh
PWC SAUDI ARABIA

SENEGAL

BCEAO

CREDITINFO VOLO

Baba Aly Barro
*PRICEWATERHOUSECOOPERS
TAX & LEGAL SA*

Mamadou Berthe
ATELIER D'ARCHITECTURE

Ibrahima Diagne
GAINDE 2000

Amadou Dioulé Diallo
*MINISTÈRE DE L'URBANISME
ET DE L'ASSAINISSEMENT*

Abdoul Aziz Dieng
*CENTRE DE GESTION
AGRÉE DE DAKAR*

Malick Dieng
CAFIJEX

Alioune Badara Diop
ONAS

Amadou Diop
GAINDE 2000

Angelique Pouye Diop
*APIX AGENCE CHARGÉE
DE LA PROMOTION DE
L'INVESTISSEMENT ET DES
GRANDS TRAVAUX*

Fodé Diop
ART INGÉNIERIE SUARL

Medieumbe Diouf
ONAS

Abdoulaye Drame
CABINET ABDOULAYE DRAME

Fama de Sagama Fall Gueye
ONAS

Ibrahim Faye
SCI LA PROMOBILIERE

Moustapha Faye
*SOCIÉTÉ CIVILE
PROFESSIONNELLE D'AVOCATS
FRANÇOIS SARR & ASSOCIÉS*

Catherine Faye Diop
*ORDRE DES ARCHITECTES
DU SÉNÉGAL*

Balla Gningue
*SCP MAME ADAMA
GUEYE & ASSOCIÉS*

Antoine Gomis
*SCP SENGHOR & SARR,
NOTAIRES ASSOCIÉS*

Matthias Hubert
*PRICEWATERHOUSECOOPERS
TAX & LEGAL SA*

Abdou Kader Konaté
ARCHITECTE DPLG

Malick Kandji
*APIX AGENCE CHARGÉE
DE LA PROMOTION DE
L'INVESTISSEMENT ET DES
GRANDS TRAVAUX*

Abdou Dialy Kane
*CABINET MAÎTRE
ABDOU DIALY KANE*

Mahi Kane
*PRICEWATERHOUSECOOPERS
TAX & LEGAL SA*

Sidy Kanoute
AVOCAT À LA COUR

Mouhamed Kebe
GENI & KEBE

Mamadou Lamine Ba
APIX

Doudou Charles Lo
FINKONE TRANSIT SA

Cheikh Loum Pouye
FINKONE TRANSIT SA

Mamadou Mbaye
*SCP MAME ADAMA
GUEYE & ASSOCIÉS*

Ngouda Mbaye
HECTO ENERGY

Saliou Mbaye
HECTO ENERGY

Birame Mbaye Seck
*DIRECTION DU
DEVELOPPEMENT URBAIN*

Elodie Dagneaux Ndiaye
*APIX AGENCE CHARGÉE
DE LA PROMOTION DE
L'INVESTISSEMENT ET DES
GRANDS TRAVAUX*

Sadel Ndiaye
SCP NDIAYE & MBODJ

Absatou Ndiaye Samaké
GENI & KEBE

Moustapha Ndoye
*CABINET MAITRE
MOUSTAPHA NDOYE*

Macoumba Niang
*REGISTRE DU COMMERCE
ET DU CREDIT MOBILIER*

Herinjiva Tahirisoa
Rakotonirina

Abibatou Samb-Diouck
ETUDE SAMB-DIOUCK

François Sarr
*SOCIÉTÉ CIVILE
PROFESSIONNELLE D'AVOCATS
FRANÇOIS SARR & ASSOCIÉS*

Daniel-Sédar Senghor
*SCP SENGHOR & SARR,
NOTAIRES ASSOCIÉS*

Codou Sow-Seck
GENI & KEBE

Ndatté Sy
SENELEC

Ibra Thiombane
*CABINET JURAFRIK CONSEIL
EN AFFAIRES (JCA)*

Ndèye Khoudia Tounkara
*ETUDE ME MAYACINE
TOUNKARA ET ASSOCIÉS*

SERBIA

HARRISONS

Milos Anđelković
WOLF THEISS

Senka Anđelković
*NATIONAL ALLIANCE
FOR LOCAL ECONOMIC
DEVELOPMENT*

Aleksandar Andrejic
PRICA & PARTNERS LAW OFFICE

Aleksandar Arsic
*PRICEWATERHOUSECOOPERS
CONSULTING D.O.O.*

Vlado Babic
AIR SPEED

Jovan Beara
UVRA

Slavko Bingulac
*IMMORENT SINGIDUNUM
D.O.O.*

Jelena Bojovic
*NATIONAL ALLIANCE
FOR LOCAL ECONOMIC
DEVELOPMENT*

Bojana Bregovic
WOLF THEISS

Milan Brkovic
*ASSOCIATION OF
SERBIAN BANKS*

Marina Bulatovic
WOLF THEISS

Marija Čabarkapa
AVS LEGAL

Ana Čalić Turudija
PRICA & PARTNERS LAW OFFICE

Dragoljub Cibulić
BDK ADVOKATI

Vladimir Dabić
*THE INTERNATIONAL
CENTER FOR FINANCIAL
MARKET DEVELOPMENT*

Marina Dacijar
*BELGRADE COMMERCIAL
COURT*

Milan Dakic
BDK ADVOKATI

Jovica Damnjanovic
*DEVELOPMENT
CONSULTING GROUP*

Vladimir Dašić
BDK ADVOKATI

Gili Dekel
DIRECT CAPITAL S D.O.O.

Lidija Djeric
*LAW OFFICES POPOVIC,
POPOVIC & PARTNERS*

Uroš Djordjević
*ŽIVKOVIĆ & SAMARDŽIĆ
LAW OFFICE*

Zeljko Djuric
CONTINENTAL WIND

Jelena Kuveljic Dmitric

Dragan Draca
*PRICEWATERHOUSECOOPERS
CONSULTING D.O.O.*

Ilija Drazic
*DRAŽIĆ, BEATOVIĆ &
PARTNERS LAW OFFICE*

Dragan Gajin
NEWTON LAW GROUP

Jovana Gavrilovic
PRICA & PARTNERS LAW OFFICE

Jelena Gazivoda
*LAW OFFICES JANKOVIĆ,
POPOVIĆ & MITIĆ*

Danica Gligorijevic
PRICA & PARTNERS LAW OFFICE

Miloš Ilić
*ŽIVKOVIĆ & SAMARDŽIĆ
LAW OFFICE*

Marko Janicijevic
*TOMIC SINDJELIC
GROZA LAW OFFICE*

Ana Jankov
BDK ADVOKATI

Mihajlo Jovanović
*ADVOKATSKA KANCELARIJA
OLJACIC & TODOROVIC*

Nemanja Kačavenda
A.D. INTEREUROPA, BELGRADE

Irena Kalmić
BDK ADVOKATI

Dušan Karalić
DMK TAX & FINANCE

Marija Karalić
DMK TAX & FINANCE

Milica Košutić
*LAW OFFICES JANKOVIĆ,
POPOVIĆ & MITIĆ*

Vidak Kovacevic
WOLF THEISS

Ivan Krsikapa
NINKOVIĆ LAW OFFICE

Zach Kuvizic
KUVIZIC & TADIC LAW OFFICE

Kosta D. Lazic
LAW OFFICE KOSTA D. LAZIC

Milan Lazić
KN KARANOVIĆ & NIKOLIĆ

Ružica Mačukat
*SERBIAN BUSINESS REGISTERS
AGENCY (SBRA)*

Miladin Maglov
*SERBIAN BUSINESS REGISTERS
AGENCY (SBRA)*

Aleksandar Mančev
PRICA & PARTNERS LAW OFFICE

Djordje Mijatov
LAW OFFICE ILIĆ

Predrag Milenković
*DRAŽIĆ, BEATOVIĆ &
PARTNERS LAW OFFICE*

Milena Mitić
KN KARANOVIĆ & NIKOLIĆ

Aleksandar Mladenović
*MLADENOVIC & STANKOVIC
IN COOPERATION WITH ROKAS
INTERNATIONAL LAW FIRM*

Veljko Nešić
PRICA & PARTNERS LAW OFFICE

Dimitrije Nikolić
GEBRUDER WEISS D.O.O.

Djurdje Ninković
NINKOVIĆ LAW OFFICE

Bojana Noskov
WOLF THEISS

Zvonko Obradović
*SERBIAN BUSINESS REGISTERS
AGENCY (SBRA)*

Igor Oljačić
*ADVOKATSKA KANCELARIJA
OLJACIC & TODOROVIC*

Stefan Pavlovic
*MLADENOVIC & STANKOVIC
IN COOPERATION WITH ROKAS
INTERNATIONAL LAW FIRM*

Časlav Petrović
ZAVIŠIN SEMIZ & PARTNERS

Jasmina Petrović
*CITY OF BELGRADE,
URBANISM DEPARTMENT*

Mihajlo Prica
PRICA & PARTNERS LAW OFFICE

Branka Rajicic
*PRICEWATERHOUSECOOPERS
CONSULTING D.O.O.*

Branimir Rajsic
*KARANOVIC & NIKOLIC
LAW FIRM*

Marko Repić
*ADVOKATSKA KANCELARIJA
OLJACIC & TODOROVIC*

Sonja Sehovac
*ŽIVKOVIĆ & SAMARDŽIĆ
LAW OFFICE*

Stojan Semiz
ZAVIŠIN SEMIZ & PARTNERS

Neda Spajić
*ŽIVKOVIĆ & SAMARDŽIĆ
LAW OFFICE*

Marko Srdanovic
MUNICIPALITY OF SURCIN

Mirjana Stankovic
*DEVELOPMENT
CONSULTING GROUP*

Dragana Stanojević
USAID BUSINESS ENABLING PROJECT - BY CARDNO EMERGING MARKETS USA LTD.

Milica Stojanović
LAW OFFICES JANKOVIĆ, POPOVIĆ & MITIĆ

Petar Stojanović
JOKSOVIC, STOJANOVIĆ AND PARTNERS

Nikola Sugaris
ZAVIŠIN SEMIZ & PARTNERS

Robert Sundberg
DEVELOPMENT CONSULTING GROUP

Marko Tesanovic
WOLF THEISS

Ana Tomic
JOKSOVIC, STOJANOVIĆ AND PARTNERS

Jovana Tomić
ŽIVKOVIĆ & SAMARDŽIĆ LAW OFFICE

Snežana Tosić
SERBIAN BUSINESS REGISTERS AGENCY (SBRA)

Goran Vucic
JOKSOVIC, STOJANOVIĆ AND PARTNERS

Srećko Vujaković
MORAVCEVIC, VOJNOVIC & PARTNERS IN COOPERATION WITH SCHOENHERR

Tanja Vukotić Marinković
SERBIAN BUSINESS REGISTERS AGENCY (SBRA)

Milena Vuković Buha
AJILON SOLUTIONS

Miloš Vulić
PRICA & PARTNERS LAW OFFICE

Djordje Zejak
BDK ADVOKATI

Miloš Živković
ŽIVKOVIĆ & SAMARDŽIĆ LAW OFFICE

Igor Živkovski
ŽIVKOVIĆ & SAMARDŽIĆ LAW OFFICE

SEYCHELLES

PUBLIC UTILITIES CORPORATION

Fanette Albert
SEYCHELLES PLANNING AUTHORITY

Clifford Andre
LAW CHAMBER OF CLIFFORD ANDRE

Justin Bacharie
ELECTRICAL CONSULTANT SEYCHELLES

Karishma Beegoo
APPLEBY

Terry Biscornet
SEYCHELLES PLANNING AUTHORITY

Cyril Bonnelame
OCEANA FISHERIES

Juliette Butler
APPLEBY

Petar Chakarov
HEALY CONSULTANTS GROUP PLC

Francis Chang-Sam
LAW CHAMBERS OF FRANCIS CHANG-SAM

Alex Ellenberger
ADD LOCUS ARCHITECTS LTD.

Joseph Francois
SEYCHELLES PLANNING AUTHORITY

Bernard Georges
GEORGES & GEORGES

Fred Hoareau
COMPANY AND LAND REGISTRY

Brian Julie
BRYAN JULIE LAW CHAMBERS

Conrad Lablache
PARDIWALLA TWOMEY LABLACHE

Alison Lister
SEYCHELLES REVENUE COMMISSION

Carlos Loizeau
CENTRAL BANK OF SEYCHELLES

Malcolm Moller
APPLEBY

Marcus Naiken
HUNT, DELTEL & CO. LTD.

Margaret Nourice
STAMP DUTY COMMISSION

Brian Orr
MEJ ELECTRICAL

Zara Pardiwalla
PARDIWALLA TWOMEY LABLACHE

Wendy Pierre
COMPANY AND LAND REGISTRY

Victor Pool
OFFICE OF THE ATTORNEY GENERAL

Lisa Rouillon
ATTORNEY-AT-LAW

Serge Rouillon
ATTORNEY-AT-LAW

Divino Sabino
PARDIWALLA TWOMEY LABLACHE

Veerghese Samuel
OFFICE OF THE ATTORNEY GENERAL

Anthony Savy de St. Maurice
AQUARIUS SHIPPING AGENCY LTD.

Kieran B. Shah
BARRISTER & ATTORNEY-AT-LAW

Brohnsonn Winslow
WINSLOW NAYA CONSULTING

SIERRA LEONE

Amos Odame Adjei
PWC GHANA

Alfred Akibo-Betts
NATIONAL REVENUE AUTHORITY

Padrina Ardua Annan
PWC GHANA

Awoonor Renner
BCAR - BEACARD CHAMBERS AWOONOR RENNER

Gideon Ayi-Owoo
PWC GHANA

Isiaka Balogun
KPMG

Abdul Akim Bangura
ASSOCIATION OF CLEARING AND FORWARDING AGENCIES SIERRA LEONE

Mallay F. Bangura
ELECTRICITY DISTRIBUTION AND SUPPLY AUTHORITY

Philip Bangura
BANK OF SIERRA LEONE

Ayesha Bedwei
PWC GHANA

Adiatu Iyamide Betts
KPMG

Anthony Y. Brewah
BREWAH & CO.

Nicholas Colin Browne-Marke
COURT OF APPEALS

Siman Mans Conteh
INCOME TAX BOARD OF APPELLATE COMMISSIONERS

Kwesi Amo Dadson
PWC GHANA

Samiria Decker
CLAS CONSULT LTD.

Momoh Dumbuya
ELECTRICITY DISTRIBUTION AND SUPPLY AUTHORITY

Manilius Garber
JARRETT-YASKEY, GARBER & ASSOCIATES: ARCHITECTS (JYGA)

Francis Kwame Gerber
HALLOWAY & PARTNERS SOLICITORS

Cyril Jalloh
NATIONAL SOCIAL SECURITY AND INSURANCE TRUST

Mohamed Jalloh
AKIM AND SATU C&F AGENCY

Ahmed Yassin Jallo-Jamboria

Ransford Johnson
LAMBERT & PARTNERS, PREMIERE CHAMBERS

Jerrie Kamara
KPMG

Alieyah Keita

Patrick Syl Kongo
NATIONAL REVENUE AUTHORITY

Lansana Kotor-Kamara
FAST TRACK COMMERCIAL COURT

George Kwatia
PWC GHANA

Millicent Lewis-Ojumu
CLAS CONSULT LTD.

Michala Mackay
CORPORATE AFFAIRS COMMISSION OF SIERRA LEONE

Ibrahim Mansaray
FAST TRACK COMMERCIAL COURT

Clifford Marcus-Roberts
KPMG

Tamba P. Ngegba
MINISTRY OF WORKS HOUSING AND INFRASTRUCTURE (MWH&I)

Francis Nyama
ELECTRICITY DISTRIBUTION AND SUPPLY AUTHORITY

Afolabi Oluwole
CUSTOMERWORTH

Eduard Parkinson
ELECTRICITY DISTRIBUTION AND SUPPLY AUTHORITY

Alusine Sesay
JUDICIARY OF SIERRA LEONE

Sahid Mohammed Sesay
SERRY KAMAL & CO

Mohamed Sherrington Samura
ELECTRICITY GENERATION AND TRANSMISSION COMPANY (EGTC)

Vivian Solomon
SUPREME COURT OF SIERRA LEONE

Millicent Stronge
DELUXE CHAMBER

Donald Samuel Williams
NATIONAL REVENUE AUTHORITY (NRA), LARGE TAXPAYERS OFFICE (LTO), DOMESTIC TAX DEPARTMENT (DTD)

Oluyemisi Williams
CLAS CONSULT LTD.

Prince Williams
CORPORATE AFFAIRS COMMISSION OF SIERRA LEONE

SINGAPORE

MINISTRY OF TRADE & INDUSTRY

STATE COURTS

Lim Ah Kuan
SP POWERGRID LTD.

Yvonne Ang
PUBLIC UTILITIES BOARD

Caroline Berube
HJM ASIA LAW & CO LLC

Piyush Bhandari
INTUIT MANAGEMENT CONSULTANCY

Priyanka Bhandari
INTUIT MANAGEMENT CONSULTANCY

Andrew Chan
ALLEN & GLEDHILL LLP

Ewe Jin Chan
ECAS CONSULTANT PTE. LTD.

Jason Chan
ALLEN & GLEDHILL LLP

Tan Chau Yee
HARRY ELIAS PARTNERSHIP

YC Chee
RSM CHIO LIM LLP

Hooi Yen Chin
POLARIS LAW CORPORATION

Ng Chin Lock
SP POWERGRID LTD.

Chee Beow Chng
CHIP ENG SENG CORPORATION LTD.

Eng Christopher
INSOLVENCY AND PUBLIC TRUSTEE'S OFFICE

Kit Min Chye
TAN PENG CHIN LLC

Kamil Dada
TETRAFLOW PTE LTD.

Charmaine Deng
BUILDING & CONSTRUCTION AUTHORITY

Miah Fok
CREDIT BUREAU SINGAPORE PTE. LTD.

Joseph Foo
THE NATIONAL ENVIRONMENT AGENCY

Sandy Foo
DREW NAPIER

Kohe Hasan
REED SMITH

Kaiwei Ho
MINISTRY OF MANPOWER

Jay Jay
JUST R. TRANSPORT ENTERPRISE PTE. LTD.

Chong Kah Kheng
RAJAH & TANN SINGAPORE LLP

Poh Chee Kai
BUILDING & CONSTRUCTION AUTHORITY

Soo How Koh
PWC SINGAPORE

Wong Kum Hoong
ENERGY MARKET AUTHORITY

Huen Poh Lai
RSP ARCHITECTS PLANNERS & ENGINEERS (PTE) LTD.

K. Latha
ACCOUNTING & CORPORATE REGULATORY AUTHORITY, ACRA

Dave Lau
ACCOUNTING & CORPORATE REGULATORY AUTHORITY, ACRA

Yvonne Lay
INLAND REVENUE AUTHORITY OF SINGAPORE

Lee Lay See
RAJAH & TANN SINGAPORE LLP

Eng Beng Lee
RAJAH & TANN SINGAPORE LLP

Yuan Lee
WONG TAN & MOLLY LIM LLC

Edwin Leow
NEXIA TS TAX SERVICES PTE. LTD.

Yik Wee Liew
WONG PARTNERSHIP LLP

Joshua Lim
ACCOUNTING & CORPORATE REGULATORY AUTHORITY, ACRA

Kenneth Lim
ALLEN & GLEDHILL LLP

Meng May Lim
BUILDING & CONSTRUCTION AUTHORITY

Peng Hong Lim
PH CONSULTING PTE. LTD.

William Lim
CREDIT BUREAU SINGAPORE PTE. LTD.

Wai Hui Ling
BUILDING & CONSTRUCTION AUTHORITY

Joseph Liow
STRAITS LAW

Eugene Luah
DREW NAPIER

Chang Bek Mei
BUILDING & CONSTRUCTION AUTHORITY

Loh Meiling
NEXIA TS TAX SERVICES PTE. LTD.

Nikisha Mirpuri
REED SMITH

Girish Naik
PWC SINGAPORE

Daryl Ng
DNKH LOGISTICS

Beng Hong Ong
WONG TAN & MOLLY LIM LLC

Teo Han Ping
MINISTRY OF MANPOWER

Mark Quek
ALLEN & GLEDHILL LLP

Teck Beng Quek
LAND TRANSPORT AUTHORITY

Johnson Rajan
INTUIT MANAGEMENT CONSULTANCY

Lim Bok Hwa Sandy
JUST R. TRANSPORT ENTERPRISE PTE. LTD.

Jimmy Soh
YUSEN LOGISTICS SINGAPORE PTE LTD.

Hak Khoon Tan
ENERGY MARKET AUTHORITY

Henry Tan
NEXIA TS TAX SERVICES PTE. LTD.

Kristy Tan
ALLEN & GLEDHILL LLP

Martin Tan
URBAN REDEVELOPMENT AUTHORITY

Tay Lek Tan
PWC SINGAPORE

Yong Seng Tay
ALLEN & GLEDHILL LLP

Joo Heng Teh
TEH JOO HENG ARCHITECTS

Siu Ing Teng
SINGAPORE LAND AUTHORITY

Edwin Tong
ALLEN & GLEDHILL LLP

Keam Tong Wong
WOH HUP PRIVATE LIMITED

Kok Siong Wong
STEVEN TAN RUSSELL BEDFORD PAC - MEMBER OF RUSSELL BEDFORD INTERNATIONAL

Siew Kwong Wong
ENERGY MARKET AUTHORITY

Isaac Yong
FIRE SAFETY & SHELTER DEPARTMENT

Lin Zhan
REED SMITH

Yin Zili
BUILDING & CONSTRUCTION AUTHORITY

SLOVAK REPUBLIC

ZÁRECKÝ ZEMAN

Beáta Babačová
ČECHOVÁ & PARTNERS S.R.O.

Ján Budinský
CRIF - SLOVAK CREDIT BUREAU, S.R.O.

Peter Čavojský
CLS ČAVOJSKÝ & PARTNERS, S.R.O

Katarína Čechová
ČECHOVÁ & PARTNERS S.R.O.

Tomas Cermak
WEINHOLD LEGAL

Tomáš Cibuľa
WHITE & CASE S.R.O.

Peter Drenka
HAMALA KLUCH VÍGLASKÝ S.R.O.

Jan Dvorecky
SCM LOGISTICS S.R.O.

Matúš Fojtl
GEODESY, CARTOGRAPHY AND CADASTRE AUTHORITY

Marek Follrich
SQUIRE PATTON BOGGS

Roman Hamala
HAMALA KLUCH VÍGLASKÝ S.R.O.

Tatiana Hlušková
MINISTRY OF ECONOMY

Peter Hodál
WHITE & CASE S.R.O.

Veronika Hrušovská
PRK PARTNERS S.R.O.

Lucia Huntatová
JNC LEGAL S.R.O.

Miroslav Jalec
ZÁPADOSLOVENSKÁ DISTRIBUČNÁ AS

Mária Juraševská
PWC SLOVAKIA

Michaela Jurková
ČECHOVÁ & PARTNERS S.R.O.

Tomáš Kamenec
ZUKALOVÁ - ADVOKÁTSKA KANCELÁRIA S.R.O.

Marián Kapec
ZÁPADOSLOVENSKÁ DISTRIBUČNÁ AS

Kristina Klenova
WHITE & CASE S.R.O.

Martin Kluch
HAMALA KLUCH VÍGLASKÝ S.R.O.

Ivan Kolenič
ČECHOVÁ & PARTNERS S.R.O.

Roman Konrad
PROFINAM, S.R.O.

Miroslav Kopac
NATIONAL BANK OF SLOVAKIA

Jakub Kováčik
CLS ČAVOJSKÝ & PARTNERS, S.R.O

Karol Kovács
NOTARSKA KOMORA SLOVENSKEJ REPUBLIKY

Gabriela Kubicová
PWC SLOVAKIA

Soňa Lehocká
ALIANCIAADVOKÁTOV AK, S.R.O.

Alex Medek
WHITE & CASE S.R.O.

Nina Molcanova
PWC SLOVAKIA

Petra Murínová
DEDÁK & PARTNERS

Miloš Nagy
ZÁPADOSLOVENSKÁ DISTRIBUČNÁ AS

Jaroslav Niznansky
JNC LEGAL S.R.O.

Andrea Olšovská
PRK PARTNERS S.R.O.

Simona Rapavá
WHITE & CASE S.R.O.

Gerta Sámelová-Flassiková
ALIANCIAADVOKÁTOV AK, S.R.O.

Zuzana Satkova
PWC SLOVAKIA

Nikoleta Scasna
PWC SLOVAKIA

Christiana Serugova
PWC SLOVAKIA

Michal Simunic
ČECHOVÁ & PARTNERS S.R.O.

Jaroslav Škubal
PRK PARTNERS S.R.O.

Jakub Vojtko
JNC LEGAL S.R.O.

Otakar Weis
PWC SLOVAKIA

Katarina Zaprazna
PWC SLOVAKIA

Michal Záthurecký
WHITE & CASE S.R.O.

Miroslav Zaťko
ČECHOVÁ & PARTNERS S.R.O.

Dagmar Zukalová
ZUKALOVÁ - ADVOKÁTSKA KANCELÁRIA S.R.O.

SLOVENIA

Nika Bosnič
ODVETNIKI ŠELIH & PARTNERJI

Maša Drkušič
ODI LAW FIRM

Andrej Ekart
LOCAL COURT MARIBOR

Mojca Fakin
FABIANI, PETROVIČ, JERAJ, REJC ATTORNEYS-AT-LAW LTD.

Aleksander Ferk
PWC SVETOVANJE D.O.O.

Ana Filipov
FILIPOV O.P.D.O.O.

Pavle Flere

Alenka Gorenčič
DELOITTE

Mia Gostinčar
LAW FIRM MIRO SENICA AND ATTORNEYS LTD.

Eva Gostisa
JADEK & PENSA D.O.O. - O.P.

Hermina Govekar Vičič
BANK OF SLOVENIA

Damijan Gregorc
LAW FIRM MIRO SENICA AND ATTORNEYS LTD.

Barbara Hočevar
PWC SVETOVANJE D.O.O.

Branko Ilič
ODI LAW FIRM

Andraž Jadek

Matjaž Jan
ODI LAW FIRM

Andrej Jarkovič
LAW FIRM JANEŽIČ & JARKOVIČ LTD.

Jernej Jeraj
FABIANI, PETROVIČ, JERAJ, REJC ATTORNEYS-AT-LAW LTD.

Boris Kastelic
FINANCIAL INSTITUTION OF THE REPUBLIC OF SLOVENIA

Lovro Kleindienst
TRANSOCEAN SHIPPING

Sašo Koderman
ODVETNIK SEDMAK

Miro Košak
NOTARY OFFICE KOŠAK

Gregor Kovačič
JADEK & PENSA D.O.O. - O.P.

Neža Kranjc
ODVETNIKI ŠELIH & PARTNERJI

Nina Kristarič
JADEK & PENSA D.O.O. - O.P.

Uroš Križanec
SKM LAW FIRM

Sabina Lamut
LAMUTS D.O.O

Borut Leskovec
JADEK & PENSA D.O.O. - O.P.

Vesna Ložak
ODVETNISKA DRUZBA NEFFAT

Jera Majzelj
ODVETNIKI ŠELIH & PARTNERJI

Miroslav Marchev
PWC SVETOVANJE D.O.O.

Nastja Merlak
JADEK & PENSA D.O.O. - O.P.

Matjaž Miklavčič
SODO D.O.O.

Bojan Mlaj
ENERGY AGENCY OF THE REPUBLIC OF SLOVENIA

Eva Možina
SCHOENHERR

Domen Neffat
ODVETNISKA DRUZBA NEFFAT

Mateja Odar
ODVETNIKI ŠELIH & PARTNERJI

Neli Okretič
JADEK & PENSA D.O.O. - O.P.

Ela Omersa
FABIANI, PETROVIČ, JERAJ, REJC ATTORNEYS-AT-LAW LTD.

Sonja Omerza
DELOITTE

Aljaz Perme

Nataša Pipan-Nahtigal
ODVETNIKI ŠELIH & PARTNERJI

Petra Plevnik
LAW FIRM MIRO SENICA AND ATTORNEYS LTD.

Bojan Podgoršek
NOTARIAT

Anja Primožič
DELOITTE

Špela Remec
ODVETNIKI ŠELIH & PARTNERJI

Jasmina Rešidović
NOTARY OFFICE KOŠAK

Patricija Rot
JADEK & PENSA D.O.O. - O.P.

Sanja Savič
DELOITTE

Bostjan Sedmak
ODVETNIK SEDMAK

Branka Sedmak
JADEK & PENSA D.O.O. - O.P.

Andreja Škofič Klanjšček
DELOITTE

Nives Slemenjak
SCHOENHERR

Rok Starc
NOTARY OFFICE KOŠAK

Gregor Strojin
SUPREME COURT OF THE REPUBLIC OF SLOVENIA

Tilen Terlep
ODVETNIKI ŠELIH & PARTNERJI

Katarina Vodopivec
SUPREME COURT OF THE REPUBLIC OF SLOVENIA

Irena Vodopivec Jean
BANK OF SLOVENIA

Ana Vran
FABIANI, PETROVIČ, JERAJ, REJC ATTORNEYS-AT-LAW LTD.

Katja Wostner
BDO SVETOVANJE D.O.O.

Petra Zapušek
JADEK & PENSA D.O.O. - O.P.

Nina Žefran
DELOITTE

Tina Žvanut Mioč
JADEK & PENSA D.O.O. - O.P.

SOLOMON ISLANDS

CREDIT & DATA BUREAU LIMITED

Agnes Atkin
MINISTRY OF LAND, HOUSING AND SURVEY

Don Boykin
PACIFIC ARCHITECTS LTD.

Anthony Frazier

Julie Haro
PREMIERE GROUP OF COMPANIES LTD.

John Katahanas
SOL - LAW

Sebastian Keso
TRADCO SHIPPING

Judy Kirchner
BJS AGENCIES LTD.

Silverio Lepe
SOL - LAW

Wayne Morris
MORRIS & SOJNOCKI CHARTERED ACCOUNTANTS

Maurice Nonipitu
KRAMER AUSENCO

Andrew Radclyffe

Gregory Joseph Sojnocki
MORRIS & SOJNOCKI CHARTERED ACCOUNTANTS

John Sullivan
SOL - LAW

Makario Tagini
GLOBAL LAWYERS, BARRISTERS & SOLICITOR

Whitlam K. Togamae
WHITLAM K TOGAMAE LAWYERS

Yolande Yates
GOH & PARTNERS

SOMALIA

Abdul Rahmad Haji Abdalla Abdalla
BANADIR REGIONAL ADMINISTRATION - MUNICIPALITY OF MOGADISHU

Ismail Abdullahi
MINISTRY OF LABOUR AND SOCIAL AFFAIRS

Abdikarin Mohamed Ahmed
HORN LEGAL CONSULTING SERVICES

Tahlil H. Ahmed
HORN LEGAL CONSULTING SERVICES

Maryan Ahmed Harun
HORN LEGAL CONSULTING SERVICES

Mohamed Ali
SIMATECH INTERNATIONAL - SIMA MARINE LTD.

Daud Ali Abdulle
HOLAC CONSTRUCTION
COMPANY

Abdulkadir Ali Adow
MAYOR'S OFFICE AT THE
MUNICIPALITY OF MOGADISHU

Bile Dhoore
EAST AFRICA MODERN
ENGINEERING COMPANY
(EAMECO)

Abdi Abshir Dorre
SOMALI CHAMBER OF
COMMERCE & INDUSTRY

Mohamed Dubad
EAST AFRICA MODERN
ENGINEERING COMPANY
(EAMECO)

Hassan Mohammed Farah
HOLAC CONSTRUCTION
COMPANY

Omar Mohamed Farah
HOLAC CONSTRUCTION
COMPANY

Abdiwahid Osman Haji
MOGADISHU LAW OFFICE

Mahad Hassan
HORN LEGAL CONSULTING
SERVICES

Mahdi Hassan
DARYEEL SHIPPING
AND FORWARDING

Sadia Hassan

Abdirahman Hassan Wardere
MOGADISHU UNIVERSITY

Hassan Abukar Hirabe
HOLAC CONSTRUCTION
COMPANY

Said Mohamed Hussein
MINISTRY OF COMMERCE
& INDUSTRY

Ahmed Jama Kheire
ADAMI GENERAL SERVICE

Godfrey Maina Macharia

Ahmed Mahmoud

Abdiwahid Mohamed
SOMALI CHAMBER OF
COMMERCE & INDUSTRY

Mariam Mohamed

Bashir Mohamed Sheikh
MOGADISHU UNIVERSITY

Ali Mohamud Mahadalle
HIJAZ CLEARANCE AND
FORWARDING SERVICE

Samia Saciid
EAST AFRICA MODERN
ENGINEERING COMPANY
(EAMECO)

Hassan Yussuf
INTERNATIONAL BANK
OF SOMALIA

SOUTH AFRICA

BIDVEST PANALPINA LOGISTICS

PINSENT MASONS AFRICA LLP

Douglas Ainslie
BOWMANS

Nicolaos Akritidis
PARADIGM ARCHITECTS

Okyerebea Ampofo-Anti
WEBBER WENTZEL

Kobus Blignaut
ATTORNEY

Zamadeyi Cebisa
WEBBER WENTZEL

Brendon Christian
BUSINESS LAW BC

Haydn Davies
WEBBER WENTZEL

Gretchen de Smit
ENS

Heather Dodd
SAVAGE + DODD ARCHITECTS

Anine Greef
TRANSUNION

Daneille Halters
TRANSUNION

Nastascha Harduth
WERKSMANS INC.

Julian Jones
CLIFFE DEKKER HOFMEYR INC.

Tobie Jordaan
CLIFFE DEKKER HOFMEYR INC.

J. Michael Judin
JUDIN COMBRINCK
INC. ATTORNEYS

Lisa Koenig
TRANSUNION

Jeffrey Kron
NORTON ROSE FULBRIGHT
SOUTH AFRICA

David Kruyer
CONCARGO PTY. LTD.

Johnathan Leibbrandt
WEBBER WENTZEL

Eric Levenstein
WERKSMANS INC.

Shoayb Loonat
ENUMERATE CONSULTING

Kyle Mandy
PWC SOUTH AFRICA

Venashrie Mannar
ADAMS & ADAMS

Tiago Martins
TRANSITEX GLOBAL LOGISTICS
OPERATIONS PTY. LTD.

Patt Mazibuko
CITY OF JOHANNESBURG -
BUILDING DEVELOPMENT
MANAGEMENT

Terrick McCallum
BAKER & MCKENZIE

Katlego Mmuoe

Azwindini Molaudzi
CITY OF JOHANNESBURG -
BUILDING DEVELOPMENT
MANAGEMENT

Laban Naidoo
CITY OF JOHANNESBURG -
BUILDING DEVELOPMENT
MANAGEMENT

Graeme Palmer
GARLICKE & BOUSFIELD INC.

Shannon Quinn
JUDIN COMBRINCK
INC. ATTORNEYS

Kwanele Radebe
THE STANDARD BANK OF
SOUTH AFRICA LIMITED

Malope Ramagaga
CITYPOWER

Lucinde Rhoodie
CLIFFE DEKKER HOFMEYR INC.

Wesley Rosslyn-Smith
UNIVERSITY OF PRETORIA

Richard Shein
BOWMANS

David Short
FAIRBRIDGES ATTORNEYS

Rajat Ratan Sinha
RCS PVT. LTD. BUSINESS
ADVISORS GROUP

Richard Steinbach
NORTON ROSE FULBRIGHT
SOUTH AFRICA

Danie Strachan
ADAMS & ADAMS

Zaidah Swart
WOLFSOHN AND ASSOCIATES

Anton Theron
TONKIN CLACEY PRETORIA

Paul Vermeulen
CITYPOWER

Jean Visagie
PWC SOUTH AFRICA

Rory Voller
COMPANIES AND INTELLECTUAL
PROPERTY COMMISSION (CIPC)

Anthony Whittaker
CITYPOWER

St. Elmo Wilken
ENS

Gareth Williams-Wynn
KARTER MARGUB
& ASSOCIATES

Colin Wolfsohn
WOLFSOHN AND ASSOCIATES

SOUTH SUDAN

Mufti Othaneil Akum
MINISTRY OF JUSTICE

Roda Allison Dokolo
LOMORO & CO. ADVOCATES

Monyluak Alor Kuol
LIBERTY ADVOCATES LLP

Jimmy Araba Parata
ENGINEERING COUNCIL
OF SOUTH SUDAN

Gabriel Isaac Awow
MINISTRY OF JUSTICE

Premal Bataviya
INFOTECH GROUP

Leo Bouma
NEWTON LAW GROUP

Soro Edward Eli
IMPORT FORUM
INTERNATIONAL LIMITED

Halim Gebeili
NEWTON LAW GROUP

Ajo Noel Julius Kenyi
AJO & CO. ADVOCATES

Benson Karuiru
EY

Jimmy Kato
JIREH SERVICES
COMPANY LIMITED

Nawaz Khan
SOUTH SUDAN ENGINEERING
SOLUTIONS

Hellen Achiro Lotara
NATIONAL MINISTRY OF
LABOUR, PUBLIC SERVICE
& HUMAN RESOURCES
DEVELOPMENT

Monywiir Marial
AJO & CO. ADVOCATES

Ramadhan A.M. Mogga
RAMADHAN & LAW
ASSOCIATES

Issa Muzamil
JUBA ASSOCIATED ADVOCATES

Peter Atem Ngor
RHINO STARS

Peter Pitya
MINISTRY OF HOUSING

Lomoro Robert Bullen
LOMORO & CO. ADVOCATES

Jeremaih Sauka
MINISTRY OF JUSTICE

James Tadiwe
NATIONAL CONSULTANTS
ASSOCIATION

Mut Turuk
TURUK & CO.ADVOCATES

Daniel Wani
ENGINEERING COUNCIL
OF SOUTH SUDAN

Simon Patrick Wani
AJO & CO. ADVOCATES

SPAIN

EQUIFAX IBERICA

MINISTERIO DE ECONOMÍA,
INDUSTRIA Y COMPETITIVIDAD

Basilio Aguirre
REGISTRO DE LA
PROPIEDAD DE ESPAÑA

Iñigo Alejandre
ASHURST LLP

Maria Alonso
DLA PIPER SPAIN

Angel Alonso Hernández
URÍA & MENÉNDEZ,
MEMBER OF LEX MUNDI

Alfonso Alvarado Planas
DIRECCIÓN GENERAL DE
INDUSTRIA, ENERGÍA Y MINAS

Javier Álvarez
J&A GARRIGUES SLP

Jacobo Archilla Martín-Sanz
ASOCIACION/
COLEGIO NACIONAL DE
INGENIEROS DEL ICAI

Irene Arévalo
WHITE & CASE

Serena Argente Escartín
RAPOSO BERNARDO
& ASSOCIADOS

Nuria Armas
BANCO DE ESPAÑA

Ana Armijo
ASHURST LLP

Denise Bejarano
PÉREZ - LLORCA

Monika Beltram
MONEREO MEYER
MARINEL-LO ABOGADOS

Vicente Bootello
J&A GARRIGUES SLP

Agustín Bou
JAUSAS

Héctor Bouzo Cortejosa
SOLCAISUR S.L.

Antonio Bravo
EVERSHEDS NICEA

Laura Camarero
BAKER & MCKENZIE

Rosalia Cambronero
DIRECCIÓN GENERAL
DEL ESPACIO PÚBLICO,
AYUNTAMIENTO DE MADRID

Lola Cano
BANCO DE ESPAÑA

Ignacio Castrillón Jorge
IBERDROLA DISTRIBUCIÓN
ELÉCTRICA SAU

Miguel Cruz Amorós
PWC SPAIN

Pelayo de Salvador Morell
DESALVADOR REAL
ESTATE LAWYERS

Iván Delgado González
PÉREZ - LLORCA

Rossanna D'Onza
BAKER & MCKENZIE

Iván Escribano
J&A GARRIGUES SLP

Julia Fernández Esteban
EVERSHEDS NICEA

Adriadna Galimany
GÓMEZ-ACEBO &
POMBO ABOGADOS

Patricia Garcia
BAKER & MCKENZIE

Valentín García González
CUATRECASAS,
GONÇALVES PEREIRA

Ignacio García Silvestre
BAKER & MCKENZIE

Borja García-Alamán
J&A GARRIGUES SLP

Cristino Gomez
ARKITANDEM SL

Manuel Gomez
J&A GARRIGUES SLP

Juan Ignacio Gomeza Villa
NOTARIO DE BILBAO

Flaminia González-Barba Bolza
WHITE & CASE

Alvaro González-Escalada
LOGESTA

David Grasa Graell
AGG

Carlos Hernández
METROPOLITANA DE
ADUANAS Y TRANSPORTES
& ICONTAINERS.COM

Juan Miguel Hernandez
Herrera
URÍA & MENÉNDEZ,
MEMBER OF LEX MUNDI

Gabriele Hofmann
FOURLAW ABOGADOS

Pablo Hontoria
PÉREZ - LLORCA

Alejandro Huertas León
J&A GARRIGUES SLP

Guillermo Lillo Jaramillo
J&A GARRIGUES SLP

María Lourdes López Rivera
PWC SPAIN

Esperanza Lopez Rodriguez
URÍA & MENÉNDEZ,
MEMBER OF LEX MUNDI

Marina Lorente
J&A GARRIGUES SLP

Alberto Lorenzo
BANCO DE ESPAÑA

Julio Isidro Lozano
LVA LUIS VIDAL + ARCHITECTS

Joaquin Macias
ASHURST LLP

Alberto Manzanares
ASHURST LLP

Gregorio Marañon Medina
MARAÑON LONGORIA SL

Daniel Marín
GÓMEZ-ACEBO &
POMBO ABOGADOS

Ignacio Martín Martín
Fernández
CAZORLA ABOGADOS, SLP

Marina Martinez
BAKER & MCKENZIE

Jorge Martín-Fernández
CLIFFORD CHANCE

Alberto Mata
THE SPAIN AMERICAN
BAR ASSOCIATION

José Manuel Mateo
J&A GARRIGUES SLP

María Jesús Mazo Venero
CONSEJO GENERAL
DEL NOTARIADO

José María Menéndez Sánchez
ASOCIACION/
COLEGIO NACIONAL DE
INGENIEROS DEL ICAI

Valentín Merino López
VALENTÍN MERINO
ARQUITECTOS SL

Alberto Monreal Lasheras
PWC SPAIN

Pedro Manuel Moreira Dos
Santos
SCA LEGAL SLP

Enrique Moreno Serrano
URÍA & MENÉNDEZ,
MEMBER OF LEX MUNDI

Pedro Neira
CAZORLA ABOGADOS, SLP

Àlex Nistal Vázquez
MONEREO, MEYER &
MARINEL-LO ABOGADOS SLP

Nicolás Nogueroles Peiró
COLEGIO DE REGISTRADORES
DE LA PROPIEDAD Y
MERCANTILES DE ESPAÑA

Rafael Núñez-Lagos de Miguel
URÍA & MENÉNDEZ,
MEMBER OF LEX MUNDI

Álvaro Felipe Ochoa Pinzón
J&A GARRIGUES SLP

Juan Oñate
LINKLATERS

Francisco Pablo
DHL EXPRESS

Isabel Palacios
CLIFFORD CHANCE

Daniel Parejo Ballesteros
J&A GARRIGUES SLP

Julio Peralta de Arriba
WHITE & CASE

Patricia Pila
DLA PIPER SPAIN

María José Plaza
ASOCIACION/
COLEGIO NACIONAL DE
INGENIEROS DEL ICAI

Carlos Pol
JAUSAS

Carolina Posse
GÓMEZ-ACEBO &
POMBO ABOGADOS

Ignacio Quintana Elena
PWC SPAIN

Nelson Raposo Bernardo
RAPOSO BERNARDO
& ASSOCIADOS

Álvaro Rifá
URÍA MENÉNDEZ

Javier Rodríguez
GÓMEZ-ACEBO &
POMBO ABOGADOS

Eduardo Rodríguez-Rovira
URÍA & MENÉNDEZ,
MEMBER OF LEX MUNDI

Álvaro Rojo
J&A GARRIGUES SLP

Javier Romeu
TIBA INTERNACIONAL SA

Mireia Sabate
BAKER & MCKENZIE

Jaime Salvador
RUSSELL BEDFORD ESPAÑA
AUDITORES Y CONSULTORES
SL - MEMBER OF RUSSELL
BEDFORD INTERNATIONAL

Eduardo Santamaría Moral
J&A GARRIGUES SLP

Pablo Santos Fita
DELOITTE ABOGADOS

Marcos Soberón
LINKLATERS

Raimon Tagliavini
URÍA MENÉNDEZ

Francisco Téllez de Gregorio
FOURLAW ABOGADOS

Adrián Thery
J&A GARRIGUES SLP

Ivan Tintore Subirana
METROPOLITANA DE
ADUANAS Y TRANSPORTES
& ICONTAINERS.COM

Alejandro Valls
BAKER & MCKENZIE

Adrián Vázquez
URÍA & MENÉNDEZ,
MEMBER OF LEX MUNDI

Juan Verdugo
J&A GARRIGUES SLP

Fernando Vives Ruiz
J&A GARRIGUES SLP

SRI LANKA

Asanka Abeysekera
TIRUCHELVAM ASSOCIATES

Anushika Abeywickrama
F.J. & G. DE SARAM

Nihal Sri Ameresekere
CONSULTANTS 21 LTD.

Nandi Anthony
CREDIT INFORMATION
BUREAU OF SRI LANKA

Surangi Arawwawala
PWC SRI LANKA

Peshala Attygalle
NITHYA PARTNERS

Harsha Cabral
CHAMBERS OF
HARSHA CABRAL

Dilmini Cooray
D.L. & F. DE SARAM

Savantha De Saram
D.L. & F. DE SARAM

Chamari de Silva
F.J. & G. DE SARAM

Suvendrini Dimbulana
D.L. & F. DE SARAM

Nilmini Ediriweera
JULIUS & CREASY

Manjula Ellepola
F.J. & G. DE SARAM

Amila Fernando
JULIUS & CREASY

Anjali Fernando
F.J. & G. DE SARAM

Ayomi Fernando
EMPLOYERS' FEDERATION
OF CEYLON

P.N.R. Fernando
COLOMBO MUNICIPAL
COUNCIL

Thuwaraka Ganeshan
TIRUCHELVAM ASSOCIATES

Thambippillai Gobalasingam
DELOITTE

Jivan Goonetilleke
D.L. & F. DE SARAM

Naomal Goonewardena
NITHYA PARTNERS

Shehara Gunasekera
F.J. & G. DE SARAM

M. Basheer Ismail
DELOITTE

David Jacob
FITS EXPRESS PVT. LTD.

Sonali Jayasuriya-Rajapakse
D.L. & F. DE SARAM

Niral Kadawatharatchie
FREIGHT LINKS
INTERNATIONAL (PTE.) LTD.

Rajah Kadirgama
FAST TRANSIT LOGISTICS
PVT. LTD.

Charana Kanankegamage
F.J. & G. DE SARAM

H.E.I. Karunarathna
COLOMBO MUNICIPAL
COUNCIL

Chamila Karunarathne
F.J. & G. DE SARAM

Sankha Karunaratne
F.J. & G. DE SARAM

Janaka Lakmal
CREDIT INFORMATION
BUREAU OF SRI LANKA

Ishara Madarasinghe
F.J. & G. DE SARAM

Sujeewa Mudalige
PWC SRI LANKA

Kandiah Neelakandan
NEELAKANDAN &
NEELAKANDAN

Abirami Nithiananthan
TIRUCHELVAM ASSOCIATES

Nirosha Peiris
TIRUCHELVAM ASSOCIATES

Priyantha Peiris
COLOMBO MUNICIPAL
COUNCIL

Dayaratne Perera
COLOMBO MUNICIPAL
COUNCIL

Nissanka Perera
PWC SRI LANKA

W.A. Chulananda Perera
DEPARTMENT OF CUSTOMS

Sunil Premarathna
DEPARTMENT OF CUSTOMS

Nishan Premathiratne
CHAMBERS OF
HARSHA CABRAL

Sabaratnam Rajendran
DEPARTMENT OF CUSTOMS

Rasheedha Ramjani
TIRUCHELVAM ASSOCIATES

Hiranthi Ratnayake
PWC SRI LANKA

Sanjeewanie Ratnayake
CREDIT INFORMATION
BUREAU OF SRI LANKA

Mohamed Rizni
SPEED INTERNATIONAL
FREIGHT SYSTEMS LTD.

Heshika Rupasinghe
TIRUCHELVAM ASSOCIATES

Shane Silva
JULIUS & CREASY

Priya Sivagananathan
JULIUS & CREASY

A.H. Sumathipala
NEELAKANDAN &
NEELAKANDAN

Harshana Suriyapperuma
SECURITIES & EXCHANGE
COMMISSION

J.M. Swaminathan
JULIUS & CREASY

Shehara Varia
F.J. & G. DE SARAM

G.G. Weerakkody
COLOMBO MUNICIPAL
COUNCIL

Charmalie Weerasekera
LAWYER

Oshani Wijewardena
D.L. & F. DE SARAM

John Wilson
JOHN WILSON PARTNERS

ST. KITTS AND NEVIS

Michella Adrien
THE LAW OFFICES OF
MICHELLA ADRIEN

Charlene Berry
SCOTIABANK

Neil Coates
GRANT THORNTON

Rayana Dowden
WEBSTER LAW FIRM

Bernie Greaux
TROPICAL SHIPPING

Dahlia Joseph Rowe
JOSEPH ROWE
ATTORNEYS-AT-LAW

Adeola Moore
INLAND REVENUE AUTHORITY

Shaunette Pemberton
GRANT THORNTON

Steadroy Pemberton
FIVE DIAMOND SERVICES
COMPANY LTD

Tony Scatliffe II
R & T DESIGN-BUILD
CONSULTANTS GROUP LTD.

Heidi Lynn Sutton
LAW OFFICES OF T.A.C.T.
LIBURD & H.D. SUTTON

Sanshe N.N. Thompson
ST. KITTS ELECTRICITY
DEPARTMENT

Deborah Tyrell
HALIX CORPORATION

Larry Vaughan
CUSTOMS AND EXCISE
DEPARTMENT

Leonora Walwyn
WALWYNLAW

Lennox Warner
LENNOX WARNER
AND PARTNER

Charles Wilkin QC
KELSICK, WILKIN & FERDINAND

Collin Williams
ROYAL LOGISTICS

ST. LUCIA

Clive Antoine
MINISTRY OF SUSTAINABLE
DEVELOPMENT, ENERGY,
SCIENCE AND TECHNOLOGY

Natalie Augustin
GLITZENHIRN AUGUSTIN & CO.

Oswald Augustin
JOSEPH SHIPPING

Judge Francis Belle
EASTERN CARIBBEAN
SUPREME COURT

Sardia Cenac-Prospere
FLOISSAC FLEMING
& ASSOCIATES

Geoffrey Duboulay
FLOISSAC FLEMING
& ASSOCIATES

Michael Duboulay
FLOISSAC FLEMING
& ASSOCIATES

Lydia Faisal
RICHARD FREDERICK AND
LYDIA FAISALS' CHAMBERS

Sylma Finisterre
FINISTERRE ATTORNEYS

Brenda Floissac-Fleming
FLOISSAC FLEMING
& ASSOCIATES

Peter I. Foster
PETER I. FOSTER & ASSOCIATES

Carol J. Gedeon
CHANCERY CHAMBERS

Garth George
ST. LUCIA ELECTRICITY
SERVICES LTD.

Cheryl Goddard-Dorville
FLOISSAC FLEMING
& ASSOCIATES

Claire Greene-Malaykhan
PETER I. FOSTER & ASSOCIATES

Natasha James
EASTERN CARIBBEAN
SUPREME COURT

John Larcher
J.H. LARCHER'S ELECTRICS LTD.

Kareem Larcher
J.H. LARCHER'S ELECTRICS LTD.

Bradley Paul
BRADLEY PAUL ASSOCIATES

Richard Peterkin
GRANT THORNTON

Candace Polius
POLIUS & ASSOCIATES

Martin S. Renee
RENEE'S CONSTRUCTION
COMPANY

Matthew T. Sargusingh
TRI-FINITY ENGINEERING

Catherine Sealys
PROCUREMENT SERVICES
INTERNATIONAL

Chala Smith
REGISTRY OF COMPANIES AND
INTELLECTUAL PROPERTY

Finelle Smith
GRANT THORNTON

Avery Trim
MINISTRY OF PHYSICAL
DEVELOPMENT, HOUSING,
AND URBAN RENEWAL

Leandra Gabrielle Verneuil
CHAMBERS OF JENNIFER
REMY & ASSOCIATES

ST. VINCENT AND THE GRENADINES

CENTRAL WATER AND SEWERAGE AUTHORITY

ST. VINCENT ELECTRICITY SERVICES LTD.

Kay R.A. Bacchus-Browne
KAY BACCHUS-BROWNE CHAMBERS

Stanley DeFreitas
DEFREITAS & ASSOCIATES

Vilma Diaz de Gonsalves
CORPORATE SERVICES INC.

Theona R. Elizee-Stapleton
COMMERCE & INTELLECTUAL PROPERTY OFFICE (CIPO)

Zhinga Horne Edwards
LAW CHAMBERS OF ZHINGA HORNE EDWARDS

Stanley John
ELIZABETH LAW CHAMBERS

Moulton Mayers
MOULTON MAYERS ARCHITECTS

Martin Sheen
COMMERCE & INTELLECTUAL PROPERTY OFFICE (CIPO)

Shelford Stowe
MINISTRY OF HOUSING, INFORMAL HUMAN SETTLEMENTS, LANDS AND SURVEYS

Trevor Thompson
TVA CONSULTANT

SUDAN

Omer Abdel Ati
OMER ABDELATI LAW FIRM

Ali Abdelrahman Khalil
SHAMI, KHALIL & SIDDIG ADVOCATES

Mohammed Abdullah Mohammed
SDV LOGISTICS

Wala Hassan Aboalela
EL KARIB & MEDANI ADVOCATES

Abdalla Abuzeid
ABDALLA A. ABUZEID & ASSOCIATES

Mohamed Ibrahim Adam
DR. ADAM & ASSOCIATES

Hatim Al Hag

Abdalla Bashir Ibrahim Alataya
MAHMOUD ELSHEIKH OMER & ASSOCIATES ADVOCATES

Imtinan Ali
CIASA

Omer El Sharif Abdulla
EMIRATES ISLAMIC BANK

Ahmed Eldirdiri
SUDANESE COMMERCIAL LAW OFFICE (SCLO)

Mohamed Elebodi
CIASA

Ahmed M. Elhillali
AMERICAN SUDANESE CONSULTING INC.

Mustafa Elshiekh
CIASA

Hatim Elshoush
EL BARKAL ENGINEERING COMPANY

Eyhab Fadl
MAHMOUD ELSHEIKH OMER & ASSOCIATES ADVOCATES

Huzeifa Fareed Ahmed Osman
MAHMOUD ELSHEIKH OMER & ASSOCIATES ADVOCATES

Nazar Hamad
AL SHAIEA COMPANY

Amr Hamad Omar
EMIRATES ISLAMIC BANK

Ahmed Hamoda Elnour
SUDAN ELECTRIC DISTRIBUTION COMPANY

Elwaleed Hussein
CIASA

Mohamed Ibrahim
SOMARAIN ORIENTAL CO.

Alaa Jalal Eldin Mohamed Ibrahim
MAHMOUD ELSHEIKH OMER & ASSOCIATES ADVOCATES

Ahmed Mahdi
MAHMOUD ELSHEIKH OMER & ASSOCIATES ADVOCATES

Ghada Mahmoud Eljeedawi
SOMARAIN ORIENTAL CO.

Tarig Mahmoud Elsheikh Omer
MAHMOUD ELSHEIKH OMER & ASSOCIATES ADVOCATES

Amin Mekki Medani
EL KARIB & MEDANI ADVOCATES

Lamis Mohamed Abdalgadir Osman
MAHMOUD ELSHEIKH OMER & ASSOCIATES ADVOCATES

Sayab Mohamed Osman Ibrahim Swar
MAHMOUD ELSHEIKH OMER & ASSOCIATES ADVOCATES

Tarig Monim
TM ADVISORY

Tariq Mubarak
EL KARIB & MEDANI ADVOCATES

Abdulhakim Omar
SDV LOGISTICS

Rayan Omer
OMER ABDELATI LAW FIRM

Enas Salih
SHAMI, KHALIL & SIDDIG ADVOCATES

Abdelkhalig Shaib
ASAR – AL RUWAYEH & PARTNERS

Wafa Shami
SHAMI, KHALIL & SIDDIG ADVOCATES

Husameldin Taha
SUDANESE COMMERCIAL LAW OFFICE (SCLO)

Marwa Taha
SHAMI, KHALIL & SIDDIG ADVOCATES

Abdel Gadir Warsama Ghalib
DR. ABDEL GADIR WARSAMA GHALIB & ASSOCIATES LEGAL FIRM

Mohamed Zain
KAYAN CONSULTANCY

SURINAME

NOTARIAAT BLOM

Robert Bottse
HBN LAW

Sieglien Burleson

Dennis Chandansingh
DCA ACCOUNTANTS & CONSULTANTS

Anneke Chin-A-Lin

Joanne Danoesemito
VSH SHIPPING

Anoeschka Debipersad
A.E. DEBIPERSAD & ASSOCIATES

Norman Doorson
MANAGEMENT INSTITUTE GLIS

Marcel K. Eyndhoven
N.V. ENERGIEBEDRIJVEN SURINAME

Kenneth Foe A. Man

Dirk Heave

Rachelle Jong-Along-Asan
HAKRINBANK NV

Antoon Karg
LIM A. PO LAW FIRM

Johan Kastelein
KASTELEIN DESIGN

Satish Mahes
HAKRINBANK NV

Henk Naarendorp
CHAMBER OF COMMERCE & INDUSTRY

Joanne Pancham
CHAMBER OF COMMERCE & INDUSTRY

Edwards Redjosentone
N.V. ENERGIEBEDRIJVEN SURINAME

Adiel Sakoer
NV EKLIPZE LOGISTICS

Tjanderwatie Sieglien Sewdien
COSTER ADVOCATEN

Prija Soechitram
CHAMBER OF COMMERCE & INDUSTRY

Albert D. Soedamah
LAWFIRM SOEDAMAH & ASSOCIATES

Jane Peggy Tjon
COSTER ADVOCATEN

Silvano Tjong-Ahin
MANAGEMENT INSTITUTE GLIS

Carol-Ann Tjon-Pian-Gi
LAWYER AND SWORN TRANSLATOR

Milton van Brussel
BDO

Jennifer van Dijk-Silos
LAW FIRM VAN DIJK-SILOS

Kenneth van Gom
GOM FOOD INDUSTRIES NV

Baboelal Widjindra
CHAMBER OF COMMERCE & INDUSTRY

Andy Wong
N.V. ENERGIEBEDRIJVEN SURINAME

Anthony Wong
GENERAL CONTRACTORS ASSOCIATION OF SURINAME

SWAZILAND

FEDERATION OF SWAZILAND EMPLOYERS AND CHAMBER OF COMMERCE

KPMG

Lucas Bhembe
EZULWINI MUNICIPALITY

Ray Dlamini
BICON CONSULTING ENGINEERS

Veli Dlamini
INTERFREIGHT PTY. LTD.

Chris Forte
SWAZI SURVEYS

Earl John Henwood
HENWOOD & COMPANY

Andrew Linsey
PWC SWAZILAND

Mangaliso Magagula
MAGAGULA & HLOPHE

Nhlanhla Maphanga
LANG MITCHELL ASSOCIATES

Gabsile Maseko
ROBINSON BERTRAM

Tshidi Masisi-Hlanze
MASISI-HLANZE ATTORNEYS

Sabelo Masuku
HOWE MASUKU NSIBANDE ATTORNEYS

Thandiwe Mkandla
HENWOOD & COMPANY

Kenneth J. Motsa
ROBINSON BERTRAM

George Mzungu
M&E CONSULTING ENGINEERS

Knox Nxumalo
ROBINSON BERTRAM

Kobla Quashie
KOBLA QUASHIE AND ASSOCIATES

José Rodrigues
RODRIGUES & ASSOCIATES

Bongani Simelane
MUNICIPAL COUNCIL OF MBABANE

Pieter Smoor
INTEGRATED DEVELOPMENT CONSULTANTS (IDC)

John Thomson
MORMOND ELECTRICAL CONTRACTORS

Manene Thwala
THWALA ATTORNEYS

Bradford Mark Walker
BRAD WALKER ARCHITECTS

Patricia Zwane
TRANSUNION ITC SWAZILAND PTY. LTD.

SWEDEN

STOCKHOLM CITY HALL

Charles Andersson
ASHURST ADVOKATBYRÅ AB

Therese Andersson
ÖHRLINGS PRICEWATERHOUSECOOPERS AB

Mats Berter
MAQS LAW FIRM

Alexander Broch
ÖRESUNDS REDOVISNING AB

Laura Carlson
STOCKHOLM UNIVERSITY, DEPARTMENT OF LAW

Åke Dahlqvist
UC

Mia Edlund
BAKER & MCKENZIE

Lars Hartzell
ELMZELL ADVOKATBYRÅ AB, MEMBER OF IUS LABORIS

Elisabeth Heide
ASHURST ADVOKATBYRÅ AB

Erik Hygrell
WISTRAND ADVOKATBYRÅ

Rickard Jansson
PANALPINA AB

Kim Jokinen
ÖHRLINGS PRICEWATERHOUSECOOPERS AB

Elena Kadelburger
MILLER ROSENFALCK LLP

Almira Kashani
MILLER ROSENFALCK LLP

Jarle Kjelingtveit
UNIL AS

Rikard Lindahl
ADVOKATFIRMAN VINGE KB, MEMBER OF LEX MUNDI

Dennis Linden
LANTMÄTERIET

Inger Lindhe
LANTMÄTERIET

Heléne Lindqvist
BOLAGSVERKET - SWEDISH COMPANIES REGISTRATION OFFICE (SCRO)

Christoffer Monell
MANNHEIMER SWARTLING ADVOKATBYRÅ

Karl-Arne Olsson
WESSLAU SODERQVIST ADVOKATBYRA

Jesper Schönbeck
ADVOKATFIRMAN VINGE KB, MEMBER OF LEX MUNDI

Mikael Söderman
ADVOKATFIRMAN BASTLING & PARTNERS

Astrid Trolle Adams
MILLER ROSENFALCK LLP

Petter Vaeren
FLOOD HERSLOW HOME

Albert Wållgren
ADVOKATFIRMAN VINGE KB, MEMBER OF LEX MUNDI

Carl Johan Wallnerström
SWEDISH ENERGY MARKETS INSPECTORATE (ENERGIMARKNADSINSPEKTIONEN)

Magnus Wennerhorn
WHITE & CASE

Anna Werner
ELMZELL ADVOKATBYRÅ AB, MEMBER OF IUS LABORIS

SWITZERLAND

Rashid Bahar
BÄR & KARRER AG

Marc Bernheim
STAIGER ATTORNEYS-AT-LAW LTD.

Myriam Büchi-Bänteli
PWC SWITZERLAND

Lukas Bühlmann
PWC SWITZERLAND

Martin Burkhardt
LENZ & STAEHELIN

Massimo Calderan
ALTENBURGER LTD. LEGAL + TAX

Ivo Cathry
FRORIEP LEGAL AG

Boudry Charles
LALIVE

Flavio Delli Colli
LENZ & STAEHELIN

Stefan Eberhard
OBERSON ABELS SA

Suzanne Eckert
WENGER PLATTNER

Jana Essebier
VISCHER AG

Robert Furter
PESTALOZZI, MEMBER
OF LEX MUNDI

Gaudenz Geiger
STAIGER ATTORNEYS-
AT-LAW LTD.

Riccardo Geiser
ALTENBURGER LTD.
LEGAL + TAX

Matthias Giger
CEVA LOGISTICS

Olivier Hari
SCHELLENBERG WITTMER LTD.

Thomas H. Henle
IL INDUSTRIE-LEASING LTD.

Anouk Hirt
BÄR & KARRER AG

Ani Homberger
LALIVE

David Jenny
VISCHER AG

L. Mattias Johnson
FRORIEP LEGAL AG

Cyrill Kaeser
LENZ & STAEHELIN

Michael Kramer
PESTALOZZI, MEMBER
OF LEX MUNDI

Cédric Lenoir
LALIVE

Beat Luescher
AZ ELEKTRO AG

Valerie Meyer Bahar
NIEDERER KRAFT & FREY AG

Kaisa Miller
EY

Andrea Molino
MAG LEGIS SA

Konrad Moor
BÜRGI NÄGELI LAWYERS

Marco Mühlemann
EY

Angela Oppliger
VISCHER AG

Daniela Reinhardt
PWC SWITZERLAND

Alexander Reus
DIAZ REUS & TARG LLP

Roman Rinderknecht
EY

Ueli Schindler
AECOM/URS

Daniel Schmitz
PWC SWITZERLAND

Corinne Studer
HANDELSREGISTERAMT
DES KANTONS

Jean-Paul Vulliéty
LALIVE

Patrick Weber
EKZ ELEKTRIZITÄTSWERKE
DES KANTONS ZÜRICH

Stefan Zangger
BELGLOBE INTERNATIONAL LLC

Marc Zimmermann
LENZ & STAEHELIN

SYRIAN ARAB REPUBLIC

EY

Alaa Ahmad
SYRIAN STRATEGIC THINK
TANK RESEARCH CENTER

Sadi Alkhouri
KPMG SYRIA

Serene Almaleh
SULTANS LAW

Layla Alsamman
DELOITTE SYRIA

Jamil Ammar
RUTGERS LAW SCHOOL

Ghada Armali
SARKIS & ASSOCIATES

Reem Awad
COMMERCE & ENGINEERING
CONSULTANTS

Mohammad Khaled
Darwicheh
TALAL ABU-GHAZALEH
LEGAL (TAG-LEGAL)

Richard El Mouallem
PWC LEBANON

Nada Elsayed
PWC LEBANON

Anas Ghazi
MEETHAK - LAWYERS
& CONSULTANTS

Gordon Gray
NATIONAL U.S.-ARAB
CHAMBER OF COMMERCE

Fadi Kardous
KARDOUS LAW OFFICE

Mamon Katbeh
CENTRAL BANK OF SYRIA

Hussein Khaddour
SYRIAN LEGAL BUREAU

Alaa Nizam
ALAA NIZAM LAW OFFICE

Gabriel Oussi
OUSSI LAW FIRM

Fadi Sarkis
SARKIS & ASSOCIATES

Arem Taweel
EBRAHEEM TAWEEL
LAW OFFICE

Ebraheem Taweel
EBRAHEEM TAWEEL
LAW OFFICE

TAIWAN, CHINA

Jack Chang
YANGMING PARTNERS

Kuo-Ming Chang
JOINT CREDIT
INFORMATION CENTER

Sur-Form Chang
ACER INCORPORATED

Victor Chang
LCS & PARTNERS

Christine Chen
WINKLER PARTNERS

Daniel Chen
WINKLER PARTNERS

Edgar Y. Chen
TSAR & TSAI LAW FIRM,
MEMBER OF LEX MUNDI

Emily Chen
LCS & PARTNERS

Nicholas V. Chen
PAMIR LAW GROUP

Romy Chen
NATIONAL DEVELOPMENT
COUNCIL

Ying-Hua Chen
TAIWAN STOCK EXCHANGE

Yo-Yi Chen
FORMOSA TRANSNATIONAL

Chun-Yih Cheng
FORMOSA TRANSNATIONAL

Cathy Chin
TAIWAN INTERNATIONAL
LOGISTICS & SUPPLY
CHAIN ASSOCIATION

May Chou
APL

Philip T. C. Fei
FEI & CHENG ASSOCIATES

Mark Harty
LCS & PARTNERS

Sophia Hsieh
TSAR & TSAI LAW FIRM,
MEMBER OF LEX MUNDI

Chin-Yun Hsu
SECURITIES AND FUTURES
BUREAU, FINANCIAL
SUPERVISORY COMMISSION

Robert Hsu
BOLLORÉ LOGISTICS
TAIWAN LTD.

Jamie Huang
HUANG & PARTNERS

Margaret Huang
LCS & PARTNERS

T.C. Huang
HUANG & PARTNERS

Charles Hwang
YANGMING PARTNERS

Gloria Juan
YANGMING PARTNERS

Jung-Chang Lai
TAIPEI CITY GOVERNMENT

Wei-Ping Lai
YU-DING LAW FIRM

En-Fong Lan
PRIMORDIAL LAW FIRM

Jenny Lee
PAMIR LAW GROUP

Max Lee
TSAR & TSAI LAW FIRM,
MEMBER OF LEX MUNDI

Vivian Lee
HUANG & PARTNERS

John Li
LCS & PARTNERS

Justin Liang
BAKER & MCKENZIE

Angela Lin
LEXCEL PARTNERS

Frank Lin
REXMED INDUSTRIES CO. LTD.

Jeffrey Lin
JOINT CREDIT
INFORMATION CENTER

Kien Lin
JOINT CREDIT
INFORMATION CENTER

Lilian Lin
FINANCIAL SUPERVISORY
COMMISSION,
BANKING BUREAU

Ming-Yen Lin
DEEP & FAR,
ATTORNEYS-AT-LAW

Nelson J. Lin
HUANG & PARTNERS

Rich Lin
LCS & PARTNERS

Sheau Chyng Lin
PRIMORDIAL LAW FIRM

Tien-Tsai Lin
NATIONAL CUSTOMS BROKERS
ASSOCIATION OF ROC

Veronica Lin
EIGER

You-Jing Lin
CHI-SHENG LAW FIRM

Julia Liu
BOLLORÉ LOGISTICS
TAIWAN LTD.

Kang-Shen Liu
LEXCEL PARTNERS

Shu-Ying Liu
MINISTRY OF
ECONOMIC AFFAIRS

Wanyi Liu
FINANCIAL SUPERVISORY
COMMISSION,
BANKING BUREAU

Stacy Lo
LEXCEL PARTNERS

Alice Lu
LCS & PARTNERS

Judy Lu
LEE AND LI,
ATTORNEYS-AT-LAW

Wan-Chu Lu
MINISTRY OF INTERIOR

Joseph Ni
GOOD EARTH CPA

Patrick Pai-Chiang Chu
LEE AND LI,
ATTORNEYS-AT-LAW

Shiaw-Der Pan
MOTC

Lloyd Roberts
EIGER

Ching-Ping Shao
NATIONAL TAIWAN UNIVERSITY

Scarlett Tang
TSAR & TSAI LAW FIRM,
MEMBER OF LEX MUNDI

Tanya Y. Teng
HUANG & PARTNERS

Bee Leay Teo
BAKER & MCKENZIE

David Tien
LEE AND LI,
ATTORNEYS-AT-LAW

C.F. Tsai
DEEP & FAR,
ATTORNEYS-AT-LAW

Chiun-Yi Tsai
MINISTRY OF
ECONOMIC AFFAIRS

David Tsai
LEXCEL PARTNERS

Rita Tsai
APL

Yu-ti Tsai
WINKLER PARTNERS

Huan-Kai Tseng
PWC TAIWAN

Vivian W. Chen
PWC TAIWAN

Antoine Wang
TBBC LTD.

Felix Yifan Wang
YANGMING PARTNERS

Richard Watanabe
PWC TAIWAN

Huang William
GIBSIN ELECTRICAL
CONSULTANCY

Chun-Feng Wu
TAIWAN INTERNATIONAL
PORTS CORP. LTD.

Ja-Lin Wu
NATIONAL DEVELOPMENT
COUNCIL

Pei-Yu Wu
BAKER & MCKENZIE

Yen-yi Wu
WINKLER PARTNERS

Alex Yeh
LCS & PARTNERS

TAJIKISTAN

AITEN CONSULTING GROUP

ASSOCIATION OF BANKS
OF TAJIKISTAN

BAKER TILLY TAJIKISTAN

Bakhtiyor Abdulloev
ABM TRANS SERVICE LLC

Manuchehr Abdusamadzoda
CIBT - CREDIT INFORMATION
BUREAU IN TAJIKISTAN

Zarrina Adham
CJSC MDO HUMO

Zulfiya Akchurina
GRATA INTERNATIONAL

Ilhom Amirhonov
ABM TRANS SERVICE LLC

Dzhamshed Asrorov
CJSC MDO HUMO

Gulanor Atobek
DELOITTE & TOUCHE LLC

Amirbek Azizov
MINISTRY OF LABOR,
MIGRATION AND EMPLOYMENT
OF POPULATION

Denis Bagrov
CENTIL LAW FIRM

Abdulbori Baybabaev
LAW FIRM LEX

Petar Chakarov
HEALY CONSULTANTS
GROUP PLC

Akhror Edgarov
CJSC MDO HUMO

Manvel Harutyunyan
GRANT THORNTON LLP

Elena Kaeva
PWC KAZAKHSTAN

Assel Khamzina
PWC KAZAKHSTAN

Alisher Khoshimov
CENTIL LAW FIRM

Khurshed Mirziyoev
TAX COMMITTEE UNDER
GOVERNMENT OF THE
REPUBLIC OF TAJIKISTAN

Kamoliddin Mukhamedov
GRATA INTERNATIONAL

Rustam Nazrisho
NAZRISHO & MIRZOEV
LAW FIRM LLC

Temirlan Nildibayev
PWC KAZAKHSTAN

Ganchina Nuralieva
CENTIL LAW FIRM

Bahodur Nurov
GRATA INTERNATIONAL

Anjelika Pazdnyakova
GRANT THORNTON LLP

Faizali Rajabov
ASSOCIATION OF
CONSTRUCTORS OF TAJIKISTAN

Firdavs S. Mirzoev
NAZRISHO & MIRZOEV LAW FIRM LLC

Aisanat Safarbek Kyzy
GRATA INTERNATIONAL

Nadir Saidovich
SAID LTD.

Emin Sanginzoda
MINISTRY OF LABOR, MIGRATION AND EMPLOYMENT OF POPULATION

Kanat Seidaliev
GRATA INTERNATIONAL

Marina Shamilova
LEGAL CONSULTING GROUP

Takdir Sharifov
TAKDIR SHARIFOV PRIVATE PRACTITIONER

Sherzod Sodatkadamov
NAZRISHO & MIRZOEV LAW FIRM LLC

Farzona Tilavova
KAMOLOT 1 CONSULTING GROUP

Aliya Utegaliyeva
PWC KAZAKHSTAN

Abdurakhmon Yuldoshev
MINISTRY OF LABOR, MIGRATION AND EMPLOYMENT OF POPULATION

TANZANIA

ILALA MUNICIPAL COUNCIL

KINONDONI MUNICIPAL COUNCIL

Said Athuman
TANZANIA REVENUE AUTHORITY

Lydia Dominic

Lucas Elingaya
EAST AFRICAN LAW CHAMBERS

Esther April Erners
CRB AFRICA LEGAL

Asma Hilal
CRB AFRICA LEGAL

Anitha Ishengoma
TANESCO LTD.

Protase R.G. Ishengoma
ISHENGOMA, KARUME, MASHA & MAGAI ADVOCATES

Sujata Jaffer
NEXIA SJ TANZANIA

Faustin Joseph Kahatano
ASSOCIATION ARCHITECTS OF TANZANIA

Alex Kalanje
ZIMBABWE ELECTRICITY TRANSMISSION & DISTRIBUTION COMPANY

Njerii Kanyama
ENSAFRICA TANZANIA ATTORNEYS

Charles Kisoka
EAST AFRICAN LAW CHAMBERS

Stanley Mabiti
ABENRY & COMPANY ADVOCATES

Nkanwa Magina
BANK OF TANZANIA

Mandisa Maketa
BOLLORÉ AFRICA LOGISTICS

Sunil Maru
SUMAR VARMA ASSOCIATES

Salome Masenga
I & M BANK TANZANIA

Umaiya Masoli
BANK OF TANZANIA

Abdul Masunga
ZIMBABWE ELECTRICITY TRANSMISSION & DISTRIBUTION COMPANY

Verediana Mkabahati
BOLLORÉ AFRICA LOGISTICS

Deogratius Mmasy
PWC TANZANIA

Freddy Moshy
TANZANIA REVENUE AUTHORITY

Mirumbe Mseti
PWC TANZANIA

Ayoub Mtafya
NEXLAW ADVOCATES

Angel Mwesiga
ABENRY & COMPANY ADVOCATES

Deogratias Myamani
BANK OF TANZANIA

Athanasius Nangali
ZIMBABWE ELECTRICITY TRANSMISSION & DISTRIBUTION COMPANY

Gerald Nangi
AKO LAW IN ASSOCIATION WITH CLYDE & CO.

Stella Ndikimi
EAST AFRICAN LAW CHAMBERS

Janet Ndyetabura
VELMA LAW

Raymond Ngatuni
ENSAFRICA TANZANIA ATTORNEYS

Burure Ngocho
ISHENGOMA, KARUME, MASHA & MAGAI ADVOCATES

Alex Thomas Nguluma
ENSAFRICA TANZANIA ATTORNEYS

Hope Paul
ENSAFRICA TANZANIA ATTORNEYS

Charles R.B. Rwechungura
CRB AFRICA LEGAL

Eve Hawa Sinare
REX CONSULTING LIMITED

Ambassador Mwanaidi Sinare Maajar
ENSAFRICA TANZANIA ATTORNEYS

Henry Sondo
ABENRY & COMPANY ADVOCATES

Miriam Sudi
PWC TANZANIA

David Tarimo
PWC TANZANIA

Vulfrida Teye
VELMA LAW

Regis Tissier
BOLLORÉ AFRICA LOGISTICS

Camilla Yusuf
CRB AFRICA LEGAL

THAILAND

ADVANCE ADJUSTING ASSOCIATES CO. LTD. (AAA)

C.K. & P. ELECTRIC CO. LTD.

INSPECTRUM ENGINEERING SERVICES

LS HORIZON LIMITED

MESI ENGINEERING CO. LTD.

METROPOLITAN ELECTRICITY AUTHORITY

MINISTRY OF FINANCE

NEOEX ENTERPRISE CO. LTD.

PEL ENGINEERING CO. LTD.

Panida Agkavikai
BANGKOK GLOBAL LAW OFFICES LIMITED

Chavapol Akkaravoranun
BAKER & MCKENZIE

Narupat Amornkosit
ENERGY REGULATORY COMMISSION (ERC)

Somsak Anakkasela
PWC THAILAND

Salinthip Anpattanakul
SILK LEGAL COMPANY LTD.

Puangrat Anusanti
EY

Janist Aphornratana
TMF THAILAND LIMITED

Jedsada Ariyachatkul
THAI CUSTOMS DEPARTMENT

Amara Bhuwanawat
SIAM PREMIER INTERNATIONAL LAW OFFICE LIMITED

Nuttapon Boonchokchuay
PORT AUTHORITY OF THAILAND

Janpen Boonmool
TVL GLOBAL LOGISTICS

Anawat Buraphachon
DEPARTMENT OF PUBLIC WORKS AND TOWN & COUNTRY PLANNING

Thanakorn Busarasopitkul
PWC THAILAND

Guillaume Busschaert
COMIN THAI ENGINEERING SOLUTIONS CO. LTD.

Brendan Carroll
BAKER & MCKENZIE

Nopadol Chaipunya
BANGKOK METROPOLITAN ADMINISTRATION

Panotporn Chalodhorn
OFFICE OF THE JUDICIARY

Aye Chananan
PANU & PARTNERS

Albert T. Chandler
CHANDLER MHM LIMITED

Isorn Chandrawong
BANGKOK JURIST LTD.

Udomphan Chantana
DEPARTMENT OF LANDS

Phadet Charoensivakon
NATIONAL CREDIT BUREAU CO. LTD.

Damrong Charoenying
BANGKOK METROPOLITAN ADMINISTRATION

Chonlada Chayjaroensuksakul
TVL GLOBAL LOGISTICS

Cheewin Chiangkan
BAKER & MCKENZIE

Chinnavat Chinsangaram
WEERAWONG, CHINNAVAT & PEANGPANOR LTD.

Weerawong Chittmittrapap
WEERAWONG, CHINNAVAT & PEANGPANOR LTD.

Suphakorn Chueabunchai
CHANDLER MHM LIMITED

Pakwan Chuensunwankul
DEPARTMENT OF BUSINESS DEVELOPMENT, MINISTRY OF COMMERCE

Suwanna Chuerboonchai
SECURITIES AND EXCHANGE COMMISSION

Nuttita Chungsawat
ANTARES ADVISORY LTD.

Paul Connelly
INTERNATIONAL LEGAL COUNSELLORS THAILAND LIMITED (ILCT)

Samruay Daengduang
DEPARTMENT OF BUSINESS DEVELOPMENT, MINISTRY OF COMMERCE

Monnira Danwiwat
BANGKOK GLOBAL LAW OFFICES LIMITED

Thanathat Ghonkaew
COMIN THAI ENGINEERING SOLUTIONS CO. LTD.

Thirapa Glinsukon
PWC THAILAND

Manita Hengriprasopchoke
THANATHIP & PARTNERS COUNSELLORS LIMITED

Kullakarn Indrasawat
THAI CUSTOMS DEPARTMENT

Chalermpol Intarasing
TILLEKE & GIBBINS

Monthcai Itisurasing
LEED AP

Kanok Jullamon
THE SUPREME COURT OF THAILAND

Suthatip Jullamon
THE SUPREME COURT OF THAILAND

Wallaya Kaewrungruang
SIAM COMMERCIAL BANK PCL

Nuttinee Kaewsa-ard
NATIONAL CREDIT BUREAU CO. LTD.

Prasert Kongkauroptham
THAI CONTRACTORS ASSOCIATION UNDER HM THE KING'S PATRONAGE

Amnart Kongsakda
BANGKOK GLOBAL LAW OFFICES LIMITED

Alan Laichareonsup
TILLEKE & GIBBINS

Phannarat La-Ongmanee
TMF THAILAND LIMITED

Chanida Leelanuntakul
BAKER & MCKENZIE

William Lehane
SIAM PREMIER INTERNATIONAL LAW OFFICE LIMITED

Woraphong Leksakulchai
HUGHES KRUPICA CONSULTING CO. LTD.

Atthapong Limchaikit
INTER CONNECTIONS LOGISTICS

Sakchai Limsiripothong
WEERAWONG, CHINNAVAT & PEANGPANOR LTD.

Wassana Limwattanakul
TVL GLOBAL LOGISTICS

Weerasak Loysaior
THAI CUSTOMS DEPARTMENT

Prateep Lumrungruang
DFDL

Arunee Mahathorn
THANATHIP & PARTNERS COUNSELLORS LIMITED

Florian Maier
ANTARES ADVISORY LTD.

Thanissorn Masuchand
BAKER & MCKENZIE

Rudeewan Mikhanorn
EY

Pongphan Narasin
MAZARS THAILAND LTD.

Anuwat Ngamprasertkul
PWC THAILAND

Bowornsith Nitiyavanich
HUGHES KRUPICA CONSULTING CO. LTD.

Nicha Nutchayangkul
LAWPLUS LTD.

Surapol Opasatien
NATIONAL CREDIT BUREAU CO. LTD.

Wynn Pakdeejit
BAKER & MCKENZIE

Rangsima Pakkoh
ENERGY REGULATORY COMMISSION (ERC)

Pakinee Pipatpoka
NATIONAL CREDIT BUREAU CO. LTD.

Viroj Piyawattanametha
BAKER & MCKENZIE

Harit Na Pombejra
SILK LEGAL COMPANY LTD.

Panitt Pongpakdee
ONESTOP EXPORT SERVICE

Ratana Poonsombudlert
CHANDLER MHM LIMITED

Ruengrit Pooprasert
BLUMENTHAL RICHTER & SUMET

Predee Pravichpaibul
WEERAWONG, CHINNAVAT & PEANGPANOR LTD.

Kanya Pujjusamai
THAI CONTRACTORS ASSOCIATION UNDER HM THE KING'S PATRONAGE

Rangsima Rattana
LEGAL EXECUTION DEPARTMENT

Warantorn Rattanasombat
SIAM PREMIER INTERNATIONAL LAW OFFICE LIMITED

Vunnipa Ruamrangsri
PWC THAILAND

Ruthai Rugrachagarn
THAI CONTRACTORS ASSOCIATION UNDER HM THE KING'S PATRONAGE

Chaiwat Rungsipanodorn
BANGKOK METROPOLITAN ADMINISTRATION

Watchara Sanghattawattana
THAI CONTRACTORS ASSOCIATION UNDER HM THE KING'S PATRONAGE

Peangnate Sathiensopon
CHANDLER MHM LIMITED

Ubolmas Sathiensopon
CHANDLER MHM LIMITED

Peangnate Sawatdipong
CHANDLER MHM LIMITED

Alexander James Seeley
INTERNATIONAL LEGAL COUNSELLORS THAILAND LIMITED (ILCT)

Pradujduan Sirion
*BANGKOK GLOBAL LAW
OFFICES LIMITED*

Panya Sittisakonsin
BAKER & MCKENZIE

Kulit Sombatsiri
THAI CUSTOMS DEPARTMENT

Ratanavadee Somboon
*LEGAL EXECUTION
DEPARTMENT*

Kowit Somwaiya
LAWPLUS LTD.

Audray Souche
DFDL

Korapat Sukhummek
PWC THAILAND

Atchara Suknaibaiboon
TMF THAILAND LIMITED

Picharn Sukparangsee
*BANGKOK GLOBAL LAW
OFFICES LIMITED*

Malee Sumanotayan
THAI CUSTOMS DEPARTMENT

Nuchapa Sungkakorn
THAI CUSTOMS DEPARTMENT

Apinan Suntharanan
SIAM COMMERCIAL BANK PCL

Pattamakan Suparp
TMF THAILAND LIMITED

Tanatis Suraborworn
*BANGKOK METROPOLITAN
ADMINISTRATION*

Nattapon Suraratrangsi
ZICOLAW

Ruenvadee Suwanmongkol
*LEGAL EXECUTION
DEPARTMENT*

Naddaporn Suwanvajukkasikij
LAWPLUS LTD.

Hunt Talmage
CHANDLER MHM LIMITED

Jedsadaporn Tamnanjit
MTOUCHE CO. LTD. THAILAND

Jeffery Tan
*TRICHAROEN ENGINEERING
CO., LTD.*

Sasivimol Tanasarnti
*LEGAL EXECUTION
DEPARTMENT*

Kornjan Tangkrisanakajorn
*THANATHIP & PARTNERS
COUNSELLORS LIMITED*

Thitima Tangprasert
EY

Ornanong Tesabamroong
*S.J. INTERNATIONAL
LEGAL CONSULTING AND
ADVISORY CO., LTD.*

Noppramart
Thammateeradaycho
*SIAM PREMIER INTERNATIONAL
LAW OFFICE LIMITED*

Norarat Theeranukoon
*BANGKOK GLOBAL LAW
OFFICES LIMITED*

Atitaya Thongboon
*LEGAL EXECUTION
DEPARTMENT*

Waraporn Tungwatcharobol
RAJAH & TANN

Kitipong Urapeepatanapong
BAKER & MCKENZIE

Supawadee Vajasit
RAJAH & TANN

Surasak Vajasit
RAJAH & TANN

Chinachart Vatanasuchart
TILLEKE & GIBBINS

Kanokkorn Viriyasutum
CHANDLER MHM LIMITED

Anthony Visate Loh
DELOITTE

Somboon Weerawutiwong
PWC THAILAND

Auradee P. Wongsaroj
CHANDLER MHM LIMITED

Somchai Yungkarn
CHANDLER MHM LIMITED

Yada Yuwataepakorn
BAKER & MCKENZIE

TIMOR-LESTE

Jose Abilio
*CUSTOMS, MINISTRY
OF FINANCE*

Nur Aini Djafar Alkatiri
*BANCO CENTRAL DE
TIMOR-LESTE*

Rui Amendoeira
*VDA - VIEIRA DE ALMEIDA
& ASSOCIADOS*

José Borges Guerra
MIRANDA & ASSOCIADOS

Paula Caldeira Dutschmann
MIRANDA & ASSOCIADOS

Miguel Carreira Martins
WONG ALLIANCE

João Cortez Vaz
*VDA - VIEIRA DE ALMEIDA
& ASSOCIADOS*

Joana Custóias
MIRANDA & ASSOCIADOS

Octaviana Da S. A. Maxanches
*BANCO CENTRAL DE
TIMOR-LESTE*

Pascoela M. R. da Silva
*BANCO CENTRAL DE
TIMOR-LESTE*

Francisco de Deus Maia
*BANCO CENTRAL DE
TIMOR-LESTE*

Luis de Oliveira Sampaio
*JSMP - JUDICIAL SYSTEMS
MONITORING PROGRAMME*

Casimiro dos Santos
*JSMP - JUDICIAL SYSTEMS
MONITORING PROGRAMME*

Tony Duarte

Anthony Frazier

João Galamba de Oliveira
ABREU AND C&C ADVOGADOS

Tereza Garcia André
MIRANDA & ASSOCIADOS

Adi Ghanie
PWC INDONESIA

Eusebio Guterres
*UNIDO BUSINESS
REGULATORY CONSULTANT*

João Leite
MIRANDA & ASSOCIADOS

Carolina Letra
*CAIXA GERAL DE
DEPOSITOS (CGD)*

Andre Lopez
ANL TIMOR, UNIPESSOAL LDA

Elisa Pereira
ABREU AND C&C ADVOGADOS

Vega Ramadhan
PWC INDONESIA

Gaurav Sareen
DELOITTE

Ricardo Silva
MIRANDA & ASSOCIADOS

Erik Stokes
*RMS ENGINEERING AND
CONSTRUCTION*

Fernando Torrão Alves
*CAIXA GERAL DE
DEPOSITOS (CGD)*

Tim Robert Watson
PWC INDONESIA

TOGO

BCEAO

CREDITINFO VOLO

A. M. Abbi Toyi
*DIRECTION DES AFFAIRES
DOMANIALES ET CADASTRALES*

Abbas Aboulaye
*AUTORITÉ DE
RÉGLEMENTATION DU SECTEUR
DE L'ELECTRICITÉ (ARSE)*

Claude Adama
*AQUEREBURU AND PARTNERS,
SOCIÉTÉ D'AVOCATS
JURIDIQUE ET FISCAL*

Djifa Emefa Adjale Suku
SCP DOGBEAVOU & ASSOCIES

Mensah Adje
*AQUEREBURU AND PARTNERS,
SOCIÉTÉ D'AVOCATS
JURIDIQUE ET FISCAL*

Kossi Mawuse Adjedomole
MARTIAL AKAKPO ET ASSOCIÉS

Komi Adjivon Kowuvi
SOCIÉTÉ TOGOLAISE DES EAUX

Koudzo Mawuéna Agbemaple
*AUTORITÉ DE
RÉGLEMENTATION DU SECTEUR
DE L'ELECTRICITÉ (ARSE)*

Martial Akakpo
MARTIAL AKAKPO ET ASSOCIÉS

Nicolas Kossi Akidjetan
*ORDRE NATIONAL
DES ARCHITECTES DU
TOGO (ONAT)*

Yves Yaovi Akoue
ETINSEL

Kossi Adotê Akpagana
SCP DOGBEAVOU & ASSOCIES

Eklu Patrick Amendah
*ORDRE NATIONAL
DES ARCHITECTES DU
TOGO (ONAT)*

Coffi Alexis Aquereburu
*AQUEREBURU AND PARTNERS,
SOCIÉTÉ D'AVOCATS
JURIDIQUE ET FISCAL*

Cécile Assogbavi
ETUDE NOTARIALE ASSOGBAVI

Kossi Ayate
TRIBUNAL DE LOME

Antoine Ayivi
LIGUE DES GENIES

Sandrine Badjili
MARTIAL AKAKPO ET ASSOCIÉS

Ibrahima Beye
*PRÉSIDENCE DE LA
RÉPUBLIQUE DU TOGO*

Assiom Kossi Bokodjin
*CABINET D'AVOCATS
ME TOBLE GAGNON*

Cedric Chalvon
SEGUCE TOGO

Essenouwa Degla
*COMPAGNIE ENERGIE
ELECTRIQUE DU TOGO (CEET)*

Kokou Djegnon
*MINISTÈRE DE L'URBANISME
ET DE L'HABITAT*

Sédjro Koffi Dogbeavou
SCP DOGBEAVOU & ASSOCIES

Essiame Koko Dzoka
LAWYER

Aklesso Louis-Edson Edeou
VERSUS ARCHITECTURE

Bassimsouwé Edjam-Etchaki
*DIRECTION DES SERVICES
TECHNIQUE DE LA MAIRIE*

Mathias A. Edorh-Komahe
LAWYER

Koffi Mawunyo Equagoo
*CABINET D'AVOCATS
MAÎTRE MENSAH-ATTOH,
KOFFI SYLVAIN*

Bérenger Ette
PWC CÔTE D'IVOIRE

N'dane Felibigou-Edjeou
*OTR – COMMISSARIAT
DES DOUANES*

Akossiwa Fonouvi
*CABINET DE MAÎTRE
GALOLO SOEDJEDE*

Ayélé Annie Gbadoe Deckon
*AQUEREBURU AND PARTNERS,
SOCIÉTÉ D'AVOCATS
JURIDIQUE ET FISCAL*

Mèmèssilé Dominque Gnazo
CABINET DE NOTAIRE GNAZO

Tchakoura Gnon
*OTR – COMMISSARIAT
DES DOUANES*

Tino Hoffer
*AQUEREBURU AND PARTNERS,
SOCIÉTÉ D'AVOCATS
JURIDIQUE ET FISCAL*

Atchroe Leonard Johnson
SCP AQUEREBURU & PARTNERS

Sandra Ablamba Johnson
*PRÉSIDENCE DE LA
RÉPUBLIQUE DU TOGO*

Gilbert Josias
*CHAMBRE DE COMMERCE ET
D'INDUSTRIE DU TOGO (CCIT)*

Molgah Kadjaka-Abougnima
*CABINET DE NOTAIRE
KADJAKA-ABOUGNIMA*

Amatékóé Kangni
MARTIAL AKAKPO ET ASSOCIÉS

Komivi Kassegne
*COMPAGNIE ENERGIE
ELECTRIQUE DU TOGO (CEET)*

Kodko Cephas Keoula
*CHAMBRE DE COMMERCE ET
D'INDUSTRIE DU TOGO (CCIT)*

Agbéwonou Koudasse
*CABINET DE MAÎTRE
GALOLO SOEDJEDE*

Kokou Kpeglo
*OTR – COMMISSARIAT
DES DOUANES*

Hokaméto Kpenou
*AUTORITÉ DE
RÉGLEMENTATION DU SECTEUR
DE L'ELECTRICITÉ (ARSE)*

Emmanuel Mamlan
MARTIAL AKAKPO ET ASSOCIÉS

Koffi Sylvain Mensah Attoh
*CABINET MAÎTRE
MENSAH-ATTOH*

Colette Migan
*CABINET MAÎTRE
MENSAH-ATTOH*

Laname Nayante
CALAFI

Kwami Obossou
*OTR – COMMISSARIAT
DES DOUANES*

Dissadama Ouro-Bodi
*OFFICE TOGOLAIS
DES RECETTES*

Francky Rakotondrina
JOHN W. FFOOKS & CO.

Tihana Ana Relijic
VIDAN ATTORNEYS-AT-LAW

Samuel Sanwogou
*CHAMBRE DE COMMERCE ET
D'INDUSTRIE DU TOGO (CCIT)*

Adjémida Douato Soededjede
SAFECO

Galolo Soedjede
*CABINET DE MAÎTRE
GALOLO SOEDJEDE*

Lazare Sossoukpe
SCP DOGBEAVOU & ASSOCIES

Mouhamed Tchassona Traore
*ETUDE ME MOUHAMED
TCHASSONA TRAORE*

Gagnon Yawo Toble
*CABINET D'AVOCATS
ME TOBLE GAGNON*

Fafavi Tossah Adom
SCP DOGBEAVOU & ASSOCIES

Senyo Komla Wozufia
COMELEC ÉLECTRICITÉ

Apotevi Zekpa
*COMPAGNIE ENERGIE
ELECTRIQUE DU TOGO (CEET)*

Komla Edem Zotchi
MARTIAL AKAKPO ET ASSOCIÉS

TONGA

Delores Elliott

Pipiena Faupula
*MINISTRY OF REVENUE
AND CUSTOMS*

Lopeti Heimuli
MINISTRY OF INFRASTRUCTURE

Taaniela Kula
*MINISTRY OF LANDS, SURVEY,
NATURAL RESOURCES
& ENVIRONMENT*

Loupua Kuli
*LEGISLATIVE ASSEMBLY
OF TONGA*

Mosese Lavemai
PORTS AUTHORITY TONGA

Samisoni Masila
TONGA DEVELOPMENT BANK

Seini Movete
TONGA DEVELOPMENT BANK

Sione Tomasi Naite Fakahua
*FAKAHUA-FA'OTUSIA
& ASSOCIATES*

Laki M. Niu
LAKI NIU OFFICES

Sipiloni Raass
*JAIMI ASSOCIATES
- ARCHITECTS*

Tuipulotu Taufoou
DATELINE TRANS-AM SHIPPING

Vaimoana Taukolo
MINISTRY OF COMMERCE,
TOURISM AND LABOUR

Fine Tohi
DATELINE TRANS-AM SHIPPING

Lesina Tonga
LESINA TONGA LAW FIRM

Pesalili Tuiano
MINISTRY OF INFRASTRUCTURE

Distquaine P. Tu'ihalamaka
MINISTRY OF COMMERCE,
TOURISM AND LABOUR

Paula Tupou
ALPA ELECTRIC
COMPANY LIMITED

Christine M. 'Uta'atu
UTA'ATU & ASSOCIATES

Tahifisi Vehikite
KTEC CONSULTANTS.
KINGDOM OF TONGA
ENGINEERING CONSULTANTS

Fotu Veikune
MINISTRY OF INFRASTRUCTURE

Dianne Warner
SKIP'S CUSTOM JOINERY LTD.

TRINIDAD AND TOBAGO

REGULATED INDUSTRIES
COMMISSION

Ashmead Ali
ASHMEAD ALI & CO.

Linda M. Besson
CARIBBEAN EMPLOYERS
CONFEDERATION

Luis Dini
HSMDT LTD.

Rosanne Dopson
J.D. SELLIER & CO.

Thomas Escalante
TRANSUNION

Dennis Fakoory
FAKOORY & COMPANY LTD.

Hadyn-John Gadsby
J.D. SELLIER & CO.

Glenn Hamel-Smith
M. HAMEL-SMITH & CO.,
MEMBER OF LEX MUNDI

Melissa Inglefield
M. HAMEL-SMITH & CO.,
MEMBER OF LEX MUNDI

Randall Karim
MINISTRY OF TRADE,
INDUSTRY AND INVESTMENT

Sunil Lalloo
GA FARRELL AND ASSOCIATES

Mariella Lange
HSMDT LTD.

Orrisha Maharajh
JOHNSON, CAMACHO & SINGH

Kevin Maraj
PRICEWATERHOUSECOOPERS
LIMITED

Christian Marquez
MINISTRY OF TRADE,
INDUSTRY AND INVESTMENT

Imtiaz Mohammed
DELTA ELECTRICAL
CONTRACTORS, LTD.

Nassim Mohammed
EY

David Montgomery
HLB MONTGOMERY & CO.

Evelyn Murphy
TROPICAL SHIPPING
AGENCY UNLIMITED

Sheldon Mycoo
SYNOVATIONS LIMITED

Kevin Nurse
JOHNSON, CAMACHO & SINGH

Kerry Pariag
TOWN AND COUNTRY
PLANNING DIVISION

Yolander Persaud
ASHMEAD ALI & CO.

Sonji Pierre Chase
JOHNSON, CAMACHO & SINGH

Catherine Ramnarine
M. HAMEL-SMITH & CO.,
MEMBER OF LEX MUNDI

Krystal Richardson
M. HAMEL-SMITH & CO.,
MEMBER OF LEX MUNDI

Clyde Roach
ROTECH SERVICES LTD.

Keith Robinson
PRICEWATERHOUSECOOPERS
LIMITED

Andre Rudder
J.D. SELLIER & CO.

Alana T.G. Russell
ASHMEAD ALI & CO.

Arun Seenath
DELOITTE

Neshan Singh
MINISTRY OF TRADE,
INDUSTRY AND INVESTMENT

Stephen A. Singh
JOHNSON, CAMACHO & SINGH

Tammy Timal-Toonday
GRANT THORNTON ORBIT
SOLUTIONS LIMITED

Jonathan Walker
M. HAMEL-SMITH & CO.,
MEMBER OF LEX MUNDI

Turkessa Warwick
BROKERAGE SOLUTION

Tonika Wilson-Gabriel
PRICEWATERHOUSECOOPERS
LIMITED

TUNISIA

Mourad Abdelmoula
AFINCO, A MEMBER OF
NEXIA INTERNATIONAL

Ilhem Abderrahim
SOCIÉTÉ TUNISIENNE DE
L'ELECTRICITÉ ET DU GAZ (STEG)

Adly Bellagha
ADLY BELLAGHA & ASSOCIATES

Zied Ben Ali
SOCIÉTÉ TUNISIENNE
D'INDUSTRIE ELECTRIQUE
ET DE LUMIÈRE (STIEL)

Thouraya Ben Ghenia
TRIBUNAL IMMOBILIER - TUNISIE

Wassim Ben Mahmoud
BUREAU WASSEM
BEN MAHMOUD

Amel Ben Rahal
BANQUE CENTRALE DE TUNISIE

Anis Ben Said
GLOBAL AUDITING & ADVISING

Abdelfetah Benahji
FERCHIOU & ASSOCIÉS

Slah-Eddine Bensaid
SCET-TUNISIE

Abdessattar Berraies
CABINET ZAANOUNI
& ASSOCIÉS

Peter Bismuth
TUNISIE ELECTRO TECHNIQUE

Omar Boukhdir
BOLLORÉ AFRICA LOGISTICS

Mongi Bousbia
SOCIÉTÉ TUNISIENNE DE
L'ELECTRICITÉ ET DU GAZ (STEG)

Salaheddine Caid Essebsi
CAID ESSEBSI & BEN
SALEM ASSOCIÉS

Elyes Chafter
CHAFTER RAOUADI LAW FIRM

Zine el Abidine Chafter
CHAFTER RAOUADI LAW FIRM

Ali Chaouali
SOCIÉTÉ TUNISIENNE DE
L'ELECTRICITÉ ET DU GAZ (STEG)

Faouzi Cheikh
BANQUE CENTRALE DE TUNISIE

Mona Cherif
GIDE LOYRETTE NOUEL,
MEMBER OF LEX MUNDI

Abdelmalek Dahmani
DAHMANI TRANSIT
INTERNATIONAL

Mohamed Derbel
BDO

Mohamed Lotfi El Ajeri
EL AJERI LAWYERS EAL

Sarra Elloumi
CABINET ZAANOUNI
& ASSOCIÉS

Abderrahmen Fendri
CAF MEMBRE DU RÉSEAU
INTERNATIONAL PWC

Noureddine Ferchiou
FERCHIOU & ASSOCIÉS

Rym Ferchiou
FERCHIOU & ASSOCIÉS

Amina Fradi
CAF MEMBRE DU RÉSEAU
INTERNATIONAL PWC

Imen Guettat
CAF MEMBRE DU RÉSEAU
INTERNATIONAL PWC

Anis Jabnoun
GIDE LOYRETTE NOUEL,
MEMBER OF LEX MUNDI

Badis Jedidi
MEZIOU KNANI & ASSOCIÉS

Sami Kallel
KALLEL & ASSOCIATES

Mabrouk Maalaoui
CAF MEMBRE DU RÉSEAU
INTERNATIONAL PWC

Slim Malouche
MALOUCHE
AVOCATS-CONSEILS

Samia Mayara
ACCELEA ENGINEERING

Sarah Mebazaa
ARCHITECT

Mohamed Mgazzen
SOCIÉTÉ TUNISIENNE DE
L'ELECTRICITÉ ET DU GAZ (STEG)

Amel Mrabet
EL AJERI LAWYERS EAL

Mohamed Taieb Mrabet
BANQUE CENTRALE DE TUNISIE

Hichem M'rabet
SOCIÉTÉ TUNISIENNE DE
L'ELECTRICITÉ ET DU GAZ (STEG)

Imen Nouira
CONSERVATION
FONCIÈRE TUNISIA

Sofian Obbaia
CENTRAL BANK OF TUNISIA

Olfa Othmane
BANQUE CENTRALE DE TUNISIE

Habiba Raouadi
CHAFTER RAOUADI LAW FIRM

Nizar Sdiri
NIZAR SDIRI LAW FIRM

Ferid Smida
OFFICE DE LA TOPOGRAPHIE
ET DU CADASTRE - TUNISIE

Hafedeh Trabelsi
CABINET D'ARCHITECTURE
HAFEDEH TRABELSI

Wassim Turki
AWT AUDIT & CONSEIL

Anis Wahabi
AWT AUDIT & CONSEIL

Mohamed Zaanouni
CABINET ZAANOUNI
& ASSOCIÉS

TURKEY

BOĞAZIÇI ELEKTIK
DAĞITIM AŞ (BEDAŞ)

GUNDUZ SIMSEK GAGO
AVUKATLIK ORTAKLIGI

Metin Abut
MOROĞLU ARSEVEN

Hakan Ağu
PENETRA YMM LTD.

Zeynep Ahmetoğlu
MOROĞLU ARSEVEN

Deniz Akbaş
SERAP ZUVIN LAW OFFICES

Fatih Akbulut
CAYA GROUP

Efe Can Akıncı
ADMD - MAVIOGLU &
ALKAN LAW OFFICE

Seda Akipek
CERRAHOĞLU LAW FIRM

Mey Akkayan
HERGUNER BILGEN OZEKE

Müjdem Aksoy Çevik
CERRAHOĞLU LAW FIRM

Sinan Akyüz
MINISTRY OF CUSTOMS
AND TRADE

Simge Akyüz-Haybat
DEVRES LAW OFFICE

Duygu Alkan
ADMD - MAVIOGLU &
ALKAN LAW OFFICE

Ekin Altıntaş
PWC TURKEY

Selin Barlin Aral
PAKSOY LAW FIRM

Ergun Benan Arseven
MOROĞLU ARSEVEN

Mehmet Mücahit Arvas
MINISTRY OF CUSTOMS
AND TRADE

Aysun Atıl
MINISTRY OF CUSTOMS
AND TRADE

Serdar Ay
MINISTRY OF CUSTOMS
AND TRADE

Aykut Aydın
BEZEN & PARTNERS

Murat Ayyıldız
ERYÜREKLI LAW OFFICE

Elvan Aziz
PAKSOY LAW FIRM

Burak Babacan
KPMG

Derya Baksı
TARLAN – BAKSI LAW FIRM

Aslihan Balci
SOMAY HUKUK BÜROSU

Naz Bandik Hatipoglu
ÇAKMAK AVUKATLIK ORTAKLIĞI

Ayça Bayburan
ADMD - MAVIOGLU &
ALKAN LAW OFFICE

Harun Bayramoglu
ITKIB ISTANBUL TEXTILE
AND APPAREL EXPORTERS'
ASSOCIATION

Imge Besenk
PEKIN & PEKIN

Serdar Bezen
BEZEN & PARTNERS

Yeşim Bezen
BEZEN & PARTNERS

Ayşe Eda Biçer
ÇAKMAK AVUKATLIK ORTAKLIĞI

Cansin Bilal
PWC TURKEY

Aysegul Bogrun
ERSOY BILGEHAN LAWYERS
AND CONSULTANTS

Seyma Boydak
SERAP ZUVIN LAW OFFICES

Başak Bumin
PERA CONSTRUCTION

Esin Çamlıbel
TURUNÇ LAW OFFICE

Ümit Can
SARIIBRAHIMOĞLU LAW OFFICE

Nabi Can Acar
MOROĞLU ARSEVEN

Zeynep Cantimur
CAPITAL MARKETS
BOARD OF TURKEY

Maria Lianides Çelebi
BENER LAW OFFICE,
MEMBER OF IUS LABORIS

Ersay Cete
MINISTRY OF CUSTOMS
AND TRADE

Huseyin Batuhan Çolak
HERGUNER BILGEN OZEKE

Sertaç Coşgun
PWC TURKEY

Yavuz Dayıoğlu
PWC TURKEY

Gizem Demirci
SARIIBRAHIMOĞLU LAW OFFICE

Ebru Demirhan
TABOGLU & DEMIRHAN

Rüçhan Derici
3E DANIŞMANLIK LTD. ŞTI.

Emine Devres
DEVRES LAW OFFICE

Şule Dilek Çelik
CERRAHOĞLU LAW FIRM

Deniz Dinçer Öner
PWC TURKEY

Derya Doğan
MOROĞLU ARSEVEN

Orkun Dokener
3E DANIŞMANLIK LTD. ŞTI.

Safa Mustafa Durakoğlu
ÇAKMAK AVUKATLIK
ORTAKLIĞI

Hakan Durusel
PEKIN & PEKIN

Elsen Ece Otlu
PWC TURKEY

Gülşen Engin
ÇAKMAK AVUKATLIK ORTAKLIĞI

Gökben Erdem Dirican
PEKIN & PEKIN

Goktug Ersoy
PAKSOY LAW FIRM

Naz Esen
TURUNÇ LAW OFFICE

Özgür Can Geçim
EY

Tuba Gedik
PWC TURKEY

Oya Gençay
CENTRAL BANK OF THE REPUBLIC OF TURKEY

Mehmet Emir Göka
ÇAKMAK AVUKATLIK ORTAKLIĞI

Göksu Gökay
PEKIN & PEKIN

Hafize Gökçe
ADMD - MAVIOGLU & ALKAN LAW OFFICE

Alev Güçlüer
MOROĞLU ARSEVEN

Serkan Gul
HERGUNER BILGEN OZEKE

Kenan Güler
GÜLER DINAMIK GÜMRÜK MÜŞAVIRLIĞI AŞ

Onur Gülsaran
CERRAHOĞLU LAW FIRM

Omer Gumusel
PEKIN & BAYAR LAW FIRM

Arzum Gunalcin
GÜNALÇIN HUKUK BÜROSU

Nurettin Gündoğmuş
AKTIF INVESTMENT BANK AS

Zeki Gündüz
PWC TURKEY

Burcu Güray
MOROĞLU ARSEVEN

Can Gürlek
MINISTRY OF ECONOMY

Ayşegül Gürsoy
CERRAHOĞLU LAW FIRM

Tuna Gürsu
MINISTRY OF CUSTOMS AND TRADE

Göktuğ Halaç
BEZEN & PARTNERS

Gülin Halebak Kuşakoğlu
TUYID - TURKISH IR SOCIETY

Timur Hülagü
CENTRAL BANK OF THE REPUBLIC OF TURKEY

Tolga İpek
HERGUNER BILGEN OZEKE

Mustafa Isik
MINISTRY OF CUSTOMS AND TRADE

Sevi Islamagec
MOROĞLU ARSEVEN

M. Yağız Kacar
TURUNÇ LAW OFFICE

Ali Can Kahya
MINISTRY OF ECONOMY

Zeynep Kalaycı
PAKSOY LAW FIRM

Ilker Karabulut
3E DANIŞMANLIK LTD. ŞTI.

Özgür Karacaoğlu
MINISTRY OF CUSTOMS AND TRADE

Başak Karakoç
MOROĞLU ARSEVEN

Elçin Karatay
PEKIN & PEKIN

Özge Kavasoğlu
THE BANKS ASSOCIATION OF TURKEY

Betül Kencebay
TUYID - TURKISH IR SOCIETY

Burak Kepkep
PAKSOY LAW FIRM

Süleyman Kisaç
TURK TELEKOM

Serhat Kisakurek
BENER LAW OFFICE, MEMBER OF IUS LABORIS

Özlem Kızıl Voyvoda
ÇAKMAK AVUKATLIK ORTAKLIĞI

Selman Koç
CERRAHOĞLU LAW FIRM

Serhan Koçaklı
KOLCUOĞLU DEMIRKAN KOÇAKLI ATTORNEYS-AT-LAW

Korhan Kocali
CERRAHOĞLU LAW FIRM

Galya Kohen
TABOGLU & DEMIRHAN

Umut Korkmaz
PEKIN & PEKIN

Vedia Nihal Koyuncu
TARLAN – BAKSI LAW FIRM

Nazım Olcay Kurt
HERGUNER BILGEN OZEKE

Aybala Kurtuldu
SERAP ZUVIN LAW OFFICES

Dilara Leventoğlu
TABOGLU & DEMIRHAN

Orhan Yavuz Mavioğlu
ADMD - MAVIOGLU & ALKAN LAW OFFICE

Maral Minasyan
KOLCUOĞLU DEMIRKAN KOÇAKLI ATTORNEYS-AT-LAW

Gokhan Mirahmetoglu
UNION OF CHAMBERS AND COMMODITY EXCHANGES OF TURKEY

Busra Nur
ODAMAN & TASKIN LAW FIRM

Zumbul Odaman Taskin
ODAMAN & TASKIN LAW FIRM

Pelin Oguzer
MOROĞLU ARSEVEN

Mert Oner
KPMG

Yavus Oner
KPMG

Volkan Oray
GÜLER DINAMIK GÜMRÜK MÜŞAVIRLIĞI AŞ

Mine Orer
ÇAKMAK AVUKATLIK ORTAKLIĞI

Kerem Utku Örer
TARLAN – BAKSI LAW FIRM

Burcu Osmanoglu
OSMANOGLU HUKUK | OSMANOGLU LAW FIRM

Nursen Osmanoglu
OSMANOGLU HUKUK | OSMANOGLU LAW FIRM

Mert Özden
SARIIBRAHIMOĞLU LAW OFFICE

Yusuf Mansur Özer
ERSOY BILGEHAN LAWYERS AND CONSULTANTS

Duygu Ozmen
PEKIN & BAYAR LAW FIRM

Özlem Özyiğit
YASED - INTERNATIONAL INVESTORS ASSOCIATION

Ahmed Pekin
PEKIN & PEKIN

Ferhat Pekin
PEKIN & BAYAR LAW FIRM

İlknur Peksen
ERSOY BILGEHAN LAWYERS AND CONSULTANTS

Ecem Pirler
ÇAKMAK AVUKATLIK ORTAKLIĞI

Erenalp Rençber
PEKIN & PEKIN

Dilara Saatçioğlu
PWC TURKEY

Gülbin Şahinbeyoğlu
CENTRAL BANK OF THE REPUBLIC OF TURKEY

Batuhan Şahmay
BENER LAW OFFICE, MEMBER OF IUS LABORIS

Bulent Sarac
MINISTRY OF CUSTOMS AND TRADE

Selim Sarıibrahimoğlu
SARIIBRAHIMOĞLU LAW OFFICE

Gülce Saydam Pehlivan
PAKSOY LAW FIRM

Uğur Sebzeci
BEZEN & PARTNERS

Şimal Şeker
PWC TURKEY

Selen Şenocak
KOLCUOĞLU DEMIRKAN KOÇAKLI ATTORNEYS-AT-LAW

Ömer Kayhan Seyhun
CENTRAL BANK OF THE REPUBLIC OF TURKEY

Irmak Seymen
ADMD - MAVIOGLU & ALKAN LAW OFFICE

Sinan Şığva
GENERAL DIRECTORATE OF LAND REGISTRY AND CADASTRE

Sezil Simsek
PWC TURKEY

Murat Soylu
BEZEN & PARTNERS

Çağıl Sünbül
PWC TURKEY

Esin Taboğlu
TABOGLU & DEMIRHAN

Aysenaz Tahmaz
ÇAKMAK AVUKATLIK ORTAKLIĞI

Dilara Tamtürk
ADMD - MAVIOGLU & ALKAN LAW OFFICE

Elif Tan
MOROĞLU ARSEVEN

Eda Tanriverdi
TURUNÇ LAW OFFICE

Bekir Tarik Yigit
GENERAL DIRECTORATE OF LAND REGISTRY AND CADASTRE

Aylin Tarlan Tüzemen
TARLAN – BAKSI LAW FIRM

Eser Taşcı
TUYID - TURKISH IR SOCIETY

Mehmet Ali Taskin
ODAMAN & TASKIN LAW FIRM

Selen Terzi Özsoylu
PAKSOY LAW FIRM

Deniz Torun
ADMD - MAVIOGLU & ALKAN LAW OFFICE

Oguz Tumis
3E DANIŞMANLIK LTD. ŞTI.

Mehmet Selcuk Turkoglu
CAPITAL MARKETS BOARD OF TURKEY

Ibrahim Tutar
PENETRA YMM LTD.

Burcu Tuzcu Ersin
MOROĞLU ARSEVEN

Kayra Üçer
HERGUNER BILGEN OZEKE

Sait Uğur
ADMD - MAVIOGLU & ALKAN LAW OFFICE

Leyla Ulucan
ERSOY BILGEHAN LAWYERS AND CONSULTANTS

Özlem Üntez
MINISTRY OF ECONOMY

Burcu Urganci
HERGUNER BILGEN OZEKE

Ü. Barış Urhan
TÜSIAD

Doğa Usluel
ÇAKMAK AVUKATLIK ORTAKLIĞI

Anil Uysal
TALAL ABU-GHAZALEH LEGAL (TAG-LEGAL)

Ufuk Yalçın
HERGUNER BILGEN OZEKE

Ayşegül Yalçınmani
CERRAHOĞLU LAW FIRM

Hasan Yaşar
PEKIN & PEKIN

Cüneyt Yetgin
GÜLER DINAMIK GÜMRÜK MÜŞAVIRLIĞI AŞ

Muhammet Yiğit
BENER LAW OFFICE, MEMBER OF IUS LABORIS

Beste Yıldızili
TURUNÇ LAW OFFICE

Can Yilmaz
SERAP ZUVIN LAW OFFICES

Senay Yılmaz
TOBB - THE UNION OF CHAMBERS AND COMMODITY EXCHANGES OF TURKEY

Melis Yüksel
SARIIBRAHIMOĞLU LAW OFFICE

Murat Yülek
PGLOBAL GLOBAL ADVISORY AND TRAINING SERVICES LTD.

Izzet Zakuto
SOMAY HUKUK BÜROSU

Serap Zuvin
SERAP ZUVIN LAW OFFICES

UGANDA

MMAKS ADVOCATES

MaryRose Akii
FBW GROUP

Daniel Angualia
ANGUALIA, BUSIKU & CO. ADVOCATES

Robert Apenya
ENGORU, MUTEBI ADVOCATES

Leria Arinaitwe
SEBALU & LULE ADVOCATES

Justine Bagyenda
BANK OF UGANDA

Edward Balaba
EY

Robert Bbosa
KYEYUNE ROBERT

Alice Namuli Blazevic
KATENDE, SSEMPEBWA & CO. ADVOCATES

Joseph Buwembo
BUWEMBO & CO. ADVOCATES

Mark Bwambale
KAMPALA CAPITAL CITY AUTHORITY (KCCA)

Mulindwa Muwonge Desire
BUWEMBO & CO. ADVOCATES

Matovu Emmy
MARMA TECHNICAL SERVICES

Nasali Joan
BUWEMBO & CO. ADVOCATES

Lwanga John Bosco
MARMA TECHNICAL SERVICES

Nicholas Kabonge
PWC UGANDA

Marion Kakembo
KSK ASSOCIATES

Francis Kamulegeya
PWC UGANDA

Ali Kankaka
KYAZZE, KANKAKA & CO. ADVOCATES

Doreen Kansiime
SEBALU & LULE ADVOCATES

Stephen Kasenge
KSK ASSOCIATES

Allan Katangaza
BOWMANS (AF MPANGA, ADVOCATES)

Arthur Katende
KATENDE, SSEMPEBWA & CO. ADVOCATES

Baati Katende
KATENDE, SSEMPEBWA & CO. ADVOCATES

David Katende
ENVIROKAD

Sim K. Katende
KATENDE, SSEMPEBWA & CO. ADVOCATES

Collins Dicksons Kateshumbwa
UGANDA REVENUE AUTHORITY

Vincent Katutsi
KATEERA & KAGUMIRE ADVOCATES

Assumpta Kemigisha
NANGWALA, REZIDA & CO. ADVOCATES

Lucy Kemigisha
EY

Sebaggala M. Kigozi
UGANDA MANUFACTURERS ASSOCIATION

Kenneth Kihembo
KSK ASSOCIATES

Mubaraka Nkuutu Kirunda
*UGANDA MANUFACTURERS
ASSOCIATION*

Lillian Helen Kuteesa
*NANGWALA, REZIDA
& CO. ADVOCATES*

Mercy
Kyomugasho-Kainobwisho
*UGANDA REGISTRATION
SERVICES BUREAU*

Musuuza Lawrence
BUWEMBO & CO. ADVOCATES

Arnold Lule
ENGORU, MUTEBI ADVOCATES

Michael Malan
COMPUSCAN CRB LTD.

Richard Marshall
PWC UGANDA

Alex Mbonye Manzi
UGANDA SHIPPERS COUNCIL

Paul Moores
FBW GROUP

Robert Mugabe
*UGANDA REGISTRATION
SERVICES BUREAU*

Patrick Mugalula
*KATENDE, SSEMPEBWA
& CO. ADVOCATES*

Albert Mukasa
BKA ADVOCATES

Cornelius Mukiibi
*C. MUKIIBI SENTAMU
& CO. ADVOCATES*

Priscilla Mutebi
ENGORU, MUTEBI ADVOCATES

Miriam Nabatanzi
*UGANDA REGISTRATION
SERVICES BUREAU*

Harriet Nakaddu
PWC UGANDA

Victoria Nakaddu
SEBALU & LULE ADVOCATES

Eva Nalwanga Gitta
*KASIRYE BYARUHANGA
AND CO.*

Matthias Nalyanya
*LEX UGANDA ADVOCATES
& SOLICITORS*

Priscilla Namusikwe
SHONUBI, MUSOKE & CO.

Jane Nankabirwa
FBW GROUP

Diana Nannono
*KATENDE, SSEMPEBWA
& CO. ADVOCATES*

Nusula Kizito Nassuna
CAPITAL MARKETS AUTHORITY

Martin Ngugi
*BROSBAN CONSULTANTS
ARCHITECTURE AND PLANNING*

Charles Odere
*LEX UGANDA ADVOCATES
& SOLICITORS*

Mercy Odu
*BOWMANS (AF MPANGA,
ADVOCATES)*

William Okello

Joseph Oteng Otogo
*ELECTRICITY REGULATORY
AUTHORITY*

Alex Rezida
*NANGWALA, REZIDA
& CO. ADVOCATES*

Moses Segawa
SEBALU & LULE ADVOCATES

Paul Semanda
FBW GROUP

Alan Shonubi
SHONUBI, MUSOKE & CO.

Charles Lwanga Ssemanda
BESTIN LIMITED

Ambrose Turyahabwe
*DHL GLOBAL
FORWARDING (U) LTD.*

Bemanya Twebaze
*UGANDA REGISTRATION
SERVICES BUREAU*

UKRAINE

Yaroslav Abramov
INTEGRITES

Denys Absalyamov
JSC UKRENERGOCHERMET

Igor Agarkov
ROKADA GROUP

Mykola Agarkov
*EGOROV PUGINSKY
AFANASIEV & PARTNERS*

Mykola Aleksandrov
*EGOROV PUGINSKY
AFANASIEV & PARTNERS*

Rotov Alexander
*CONFEDERATION OF
BUILDERS OF UKRAINE*

Anna Babych
AEQUO

Anastasia Belkina
PWC

Gleb Bialyi
*EGOROV PUGINSKY
AFANASIEV & PARTNERS*

Aleksandr Biryukov
LCF LAW GROUP

Oleg Boichuk
*EGOROV PUGINSKY
AFANASIEV & PARTNERS*

Bohdan Bon
DENTONS

Yulia Bondar
HLB UKRAINE

Timur Bondaryev
ARZINGER

Alexander Borodkin
VASIL KISIL & PARTNERS

Pavlo Byelousov
AEQUO

Kateryna Chechulina
*CMS CAMERON
MCKENNA LLC*

Iaroslav Cheker
KPMG

Sergey Chulkov
KIEVENERGO

Graham Conlon
*CMS CAMERON
MCKENNA LLC*

Ivan Demtso
KPMG

Aleksandr Deputat
ELIT GROUP

Dmytro Donenko
*ENGARDE
ATTORNEYS-AT-LAW*

Mariana Dudnyk
PWC

Igor Dykunskyy
DLF ATTORNEYS-AT-LAW

Anna Folvarochna
ASTERS

Oleksandr Fomenko
KIEVENERGO

Andriy Fortunenko
AVELLUM

Oleksandr Frolov
*CMS CAMERON
MCKENNA LLC*

Ivan Nikolaevich Gelyukh
KIEVENERGO

Leonid Gilevich
ILYASHEV & PARTNERS

Vitalii Grusevych
*CONFEDERATION OF
BUILDERS OF UKRAINE*

Yaroslav Guseynov
PWC

Ilhar Hakhramanov
AVELLUM

Vitalii Hamalii
PWC

Mykola Heletiy
*CMS CAMERON
MCKENNA LLC*

Dmytro Honcharenko
ETERNA LAW

Oksana Ilchenko
*EGOROV PUGINSKY
AFANASIEV & PARTNERS*

Olga Ivanova
ARZINGER

Tetyana Ivanovich
SPENSER & KAUFFMANN

Jon Johannesson
IBCH

Oleg Kachmar
VASIL KISIL & PARTNERS

Oleg Kanikovskyi
PROXEN & PARTNERS

Kostiantyn Karaianov
DLA PIPER UKRAINE LLC

Yuriy Katser
KPMG

Pavlo Khodakovsky
ARZINGER

Halyna Khomenko
EY

Vadym A. Kizlenko
ILYASHEV & PARTNERS

Uliana Kolodii
ZAMMLER 3PL

Maryana Kolyada
PWC

Nataliia Kondrashyna
ASTERS

Stanislav Koptilin
ILYASHEV & PARTNERS

Andrey Kosharny
ELIT GROUP

Andrii Koshman
KPMG

Vladimir Kotenko
EY

Alla Kozachenko
DLA PIPER UKRAINE LLC

Alona Kravchenko
INYURPOLIS LAW FIRM

Alina Kuksenko
ASTERS

Vitaliy Kulinich
*EGOROV PUGINSKY
AFANASIEV & PARTNERS*

Tatyana Kuzmenko
AIG LAW FIRM

Oles Kvyat
ASTERS

Yulia Kyrpa
AEQUO

Oleksii Latsko
*EGOROV PUGINSKY
AFANASIEV & PARTNERS*

Yevgen Levitskyi
AEQUO

Nikolay Alexandrovich Lezin
KIEVGORSTROY

Maksym Libanov
*NATIONAL SECURITIES AND
STOCK MARKET COMMISSION*

Nickolas Likhachov
SPENSER & KAUFFMANN

Artem Lukyanov
DENTONS

Anastasiya Lytvynenko
ALKIRIS LAW FIRM

Dmytro Makarenko
*STATE SERVICE FOR GEODESY,
CARTOGRAPHY AND CADASTER*

Oleh Malskyy
ETERNA LAW

Victor Marchan
DENTONS

Olexander Martinenko
*CMS CAMERON
MCKENNA LLC*

Olena Martsynovska
DLA PIPER UKRAINE LLC

Larysa Melnychuk
ZAMMLER 3PL

Arsenyy Milyutin
*EGOROV PUGINSKY
AFANASIEV & PARTNERS*

Ivan Mustanien
EY

Adam Mycyk
DENTONS

Mariya Natsyna
AIG LAW FIRM

Artem Naumov
INYURPOLIS LAW FIRM

Yuriy Nechayev
AVELLUM

Mykola Negrych
*GEOS DEVELOPMENT
AND CONSTRUCTION*

Anna Ogrenchuk
LCF LAW GROUP

Olena Ohonovska
*EGOROV PUGINSKY
AFANASIEV & PARTNERS*

Kateryna Oliynyk
*EGOROV PUGINSKY
AFANASIEV & PARTNERS*

Maryna Opirska
DLA PIPER UKRAINE LLC

Liliya Palko
KPMG

Olena Papazova
KPMG

Alesya Pavlynska
ARZINGER

Yuriy Petrenko
SPENSER & KAUFFMANN

Konstantin Pilkov
CAI & LENARD

Serhiy Piontkovsky
BAKER & MCKENZIE

Sergiy Popov
KPMG

Viktor Poternak
AIG LAW FIRM

Viktoriia Prokharenko
AURORA PJSC

Vadym Samoilenko
ASTERS

Olga Samusieva
HLB UKRAINE

Iuliia Savchenko
ASTERS

Maryana Sayenko
ASTERS

Natalia Selyakova
DENTONS

Viktor Semenyuta
KIEVENERGO

Olga Serbul
LAW FIRM IP & C CONSULT LLC

Anna Shabinskaya
*PRIVATE NOTARY -
SHABINSKAYA ANNA
VIKTOROVNA*

Stepan Shef
HLB UKRAINE

Victor Shekera
KPMG

Naida Shykhkerimova
KPMG

Dmytro Simashko
DLA PIPER

Anton Sintsov
*EGOROV PUGINSKY
AFANASIEV & PARTNERS*

Anastasia Sotir
AEQUO

Yulia Spolitak
ETERNA LAW

Natalia Spyrydonova
*EGOROV PUGINSKY
AFANASIEV & PARTNERS*

Andriy Stelmashchuk
VASIL KISIL & PARTNERS

Roman Stepanenko
*EGOROV PUGINSKY
AFANASIEV & PARTNERS*

Andriy Stetsenko
*CMS CAMERON
MCKENNA LLC*

Mykola Stetsenko
AVELLUM

Artem Stoyanov
LCF LAW GROUP

Dmitriy Sykaluk
DLF ATTORNEYS-AT-LAW

Dmytro Symanov
CAI & LENARD

Marharyta Tatarova
ETERNA LAW

Anna Tkachenko
DENTONS

Dmytro Tkachenko
DLA PIPER UKRAINE LLC

Dmytro Tkachenko
RIQUEZA CAPITAL GROUP, LLC

Ivan Trofimenko
*DEPT. OF STATE REGISTRATION
AND NOTARIAT AT THE
MINISTRY OF JUSTICE
OF UKRAINE*

Oleg Tsvyah
STATE GEOKADASTRE

Andriy Tsvyetkov
*ATTORNEYS' ASSOCIATION
GESTORS*

Serhii Uvarov
AVELLUM

Camiel van der Meij
PWC

Andriy Valentinovich Vavrish
CHIEF DEPARTMENT OF TOWN-PLANNING, ARCHITECTURE AND URBAN ENVIRONMENT DESIGN OF THE KIEV CITY STATE ADMINISTRATION

Slava Vlasov
PWC

Yuliia Volkova
AEQUO

Elena Volyanskaya
LCF LAW GROUP

Olexiy Yanov
LAW FIRM IP & C CONSULT LLC

Yulia Yashenkova
AIG LAW FIRM

Aleksandra Yevstafyeva
EGOROV PUGINSKY AFANASIEV & PARTNERS

Vasyl Yurmanovych
INTEGRITES

Anton Zaderygolova
DLA PIPER UKRAINE LLC

Galyna Zagorodniuk
DLA PIPER UKRAINE LLC

Anna Zorya
ARZINGER

UNITED ARAB EMIRATES

AL HAMD ELECTROMECHANICAL WORKS LLC

PEARL HOMES TECHNICAL SERVICES LLC DUBAI UAE

REED SMITH

Qurashi Abdulghani
DUBAI MUNICIPALITY

Nadia Abdulrazagh
NADIA ABDULRAZAGH ADVOCACY & LEGAL CONSULTATIONS

Saleh Abdurahman
ARAA GROUP ADVOCATES & LEGAL CONSULTANTS

Laith Abu Qauod
TALAL ABU-GHAZALEH LEGAL (TAG-LEGAL)

Hesam Aghaloui
OHM ELECTROMECHANIC

Laila Al Asbahi
TAMLEEK REAL ESTATE REGISTRATION TRUSTEE

Mahmood Al Bastaki
DUBAI TRADE

Obaid Saif Atiq Al Falasi
DUBAI ELECTRICITY AND WATER AUTHORITY

Yousuf Mohd Al Khazraji
DUBAI ELECTRICITY AND WATER AUTHORITY

Abdullah Al Nasser
ARAA GROUP ADVOCATES & LEGAL CONSULTANTS

Marwan Sultan Al Sabbagh
DUBAI ELECTRICITY AND WATER AUTHORITY

Buti Al Subosi
TAMLEEK REAL ESTATE REGISTRATION TRUSTEE

Faizan Asif Ali
BLUE ZONE ELECTROMECHANICAL LLC

Hussain Almatrood
AL TAMIMI & COMPANY ADVOCATES & LEGAL CONSULTANTS

Layali AlMulla
DUBAI MUNICIPALITY

Mohammed Alsuboosi
DUBAI COURTS

Yousaf Al-Suwaidi
DUBAI COURTS

Piyush Bhandari
INTUIT MANAGEMENT CONSULTANCY

Priyanka Bhandari
INTUIT MANAGEMENT CONSULTANCY

Maryam Bin Lahej Al-Falasi
DUBAI COURTS

Mazen Boustany
BAKER & MCKENZIE

Omar Bushahab
BUSINESS REGISTRATION IN DEPARTMENT OF ECONOMIC DEVELOPMENT

Diego Carmona
AL TAMIMI & COMPANY ADVOCATES & LEGAL CONSULTANTS

R. Chandran
TRANSWORLD SHIPPING

Maggie Chang
PWC UNITED ARAB EMIRATES

Pooja Dabir
PWC UNITED ARAB EMIRATES

Niaz Ebrahim
BRIGHT ELECTRICAL WORKS LLC

Ghassan El Asmar
DUBAI ELECTRICITY AND WATER AUTHORITY

Amany El Bagoury
AL SAFAR & PARTNERS ADVOCATES AND LEGAL CONSULTANTS

Syed Ali Hussnain Gilani
AL MEHER CONTRACTING CO. LLC

Nasim Hashim
AFRIDI & ANGELL, MEMBER OF LEX MUNDI

Talal Mohammed Hassan Al-Tamimi
AL TAMIMI & COMPANY ADVOCATES & LEGAL CONSULTANTS

Ahmed Hegazy
TAMLEEK REAL ESTATE REGISTRATION TRUSTEE

Bedarul Hoque
POWER ELECTROMECHANICAL WORKS LLC

Rita Jaballah
AL TAMIMI & COMPANY ADVOCATES & LEGAL CONSULTANTS

Tara Jamieson
AFRIDI & ANGELL, MEMBER OF LEX MUNDI

Edger Larose Joseph
AMPTEC ELECTROMECHANICAL LLC

Sony Joseph
INTERTECHS ELECTROMECHANICAL CONTRACTORS LLC

Gul Kalam
OHM ELECTROMECHANIC

Jonia Kashalaba
PWC UNITED ARAB EMIRATES

Khaled Kilani
ARAMEX EMIRATES LLC

Saurbh Kothari
AFRIDI & ANGELL, MEMBER OF LEX MUNDI

Vipul Kothari
KOTHARI AUDITORS & ACCOUNTANTS

Ravi Kumar
DUBAI TRADE

Charles S. Laubach
AFRIDI & ANGELL, MEMBER OF LEX MUNDI

Daniele Lavalle
AL ETIHAD CREDIT BUREAU

Rana Madi
DUBAI MUNICIPALITY

Christine Maksoud
BAROUDI & ASSOCIATES

Arslan Malik
OHM ELECTROMECHANIC

Junaid Malik
AL ETIHAD CREDIT BUREAU

Srikrishnan Mannapara
SONY MEA

Shammas Manthadathil
AL MURJAN ELECTRICAL INSTALLATION LLC

Lorance Mathew
SAFE PLUS TECHNICAL SERVICES LLC

Mohamed Mihlar
INTERGULF LTD. (AN IFFCO GROUP CO.)

Abdulla Mohamed
ARAA GROUP ADVOCATES & LEGAL CONSULTANTS

Badih Moukarzel
HUQOOQ LEGAL PRACTICE

Udayan Mukherjee
DENTONS

Mohammed Murshed Alam
AL MURJAN ELECTRICAL INSTALLATION LLC

Sarathe Natarajan
NAFFCO

Himadri Pathak
INTUIT MANAGEMENT CONSULTANCY

Vijendra Vikram Singh Paul
TALAL ABU-GHAZALEH LEGAL (TAG-LEGAL)

Iqbal Pedhiwala
SHABMANS TRADING EST

Sinoj Philip

Silvia Pretorius
AFRIDI & ANGELL, MEMBER OF LEX MUNDI

Motaz Qaoud
AL KHAWAJA ENGINEERING CONSULTANCY

Samer Qudah
AL TAMIMI & COMPANY ADVOCATES & LEGAL CONSULTANTS

Mohamed Younus Rafeeq
BINLAHEJ ELECTROMECHANICAL LLC

Yusuf Rafiudeen
DUBAI ELECTRICITY AND WATER AUTHORITY

Ashraf M. Rahman
ADAM GLOBAL

Azizur Rahman
CHANCE ELECTROMECHANICAL WORKS LLC

Mohammed Sanaur Rahman
AL BADHA ELECTRICAL & SANITARY INS. LLC

Nooshin Rahmanijade
ARAA GROUP ADVOCATES & LEGAL CONSULTANTS

Johnson Rajan
INTUIT MANAGEMENT CONSULTANCY

Mehul Rajyaguru
AL HILI STAR ELECTROMECHANICAL WORKS LLC

Chatura Randeniya
AFRIDI & ANGELL, MEMBER OF LEX MUNDI

Jochem Rossel
PWC UNITED ARAB EMIRATES

Mohammad Safwan
AL HASHEMI PLANNERS, ARCHITECTS, ENGINEERS

Said Said
DUBAI TRADE

Mohammed Ahmed Saleh
DUBAI MUNICIPALITY

Osama Shabaan
TALAL ABU-GHAZALEH LEGAL (TAG-LEGAL)

Hassan Shakrouf
GLOBAL TEAM UAE

Advaita Sharma
ADAM GLOBAL

Clinton Slogrove
AL TAMIMI & COMPANY ADVOCATES & LEGAL CONSULTANTS

Izabella Szadkowska
AL TAMIMI & COMPANY ADVOCATES & LEGAL CONSULTANTS

Walid Takrouri
AL ETIHAD CREDIT BUREAU

Hamad Thani Mutar
DUBAI COURTS

Nitin Tirath
DUBAI TRADE

Mohsen Tomh
OPTIONS ENGINEERING CONSULTANCIES

Arun Udayabhanu
BRIGHT ELECTRICAL WORKS LLC

Hannan Uddin
CHANCE ELECTROMECHANICAL WORKS LLC

Sriram Viswanathan
DYNATRADE AUTOMOTIVE GROUP

Gary Watts
AL TAMIMI & COMPANY ADVOCATES & LEGAL CONSULTANTS

Jody Waugh
AL TAMIMI & COMPANY ADVOCATES & LEGAL CONSULTANTS

Anna White
AFRIDI & ANGELL, MEMBER OF LEX MUNDI

Alan Wood
PWC UNITED ARAB EMIRATES

Victoria Yates
AFRIDI & ANGELL, MEMBER OF LEX MUNDI

Baher Yousef
ENGINEERING CONSULTANTS GROUP (ECG)

Mohammed Zeen
NAFFCO

UNITED KINGDOM

EXPERIAN LTD.

THE INSOLVENCY SERVICE

WHITE & CASE LLP LONDON

Alexandra Adams
CLYDE & CO.

Philip Allenby
DLA PIPER UK LLP

Clare Barras
CMS CAMERON MCKENNA LLP

Corina Barsa
CLYDE & CO.

Ravi Basra
LUBBOCK FINE - MEMBER OF RUSSELL BEDFORD INTERNATIONAL

Marie Batchelor
BIRKETTS LLP

Andrew Booth
ANDREW BOOTH ARCHITECT

Moshe Bordon
MILBANK, TWEED, HADLEY & MCCLOY LLP

Marlies Braun
WEDLAKE BELL LLP

Rob Briggs
CMS CAMERON MCKENNA LLP

Howard Bushell
HER MAJESTY'S LAND REGISTRY

Jonathan Caldwell
DLA PIPER UK LLP

Brendon Christian
BUSINESS LAW BC

Karen Clarke
CMS CAMERON MCKENNA LLP

Colin Cochrane
REED SMITH LLP

Simon Cohen
SHEARMAN & STERLING LLP

Michael Collard
5 PUMP COURT CHAMBERS

James Collinson
DLA PIPER UK LLP

James Cross
REED SMITH LLP

Ashley Damiral
CMS CAMERON MCKENNA LLP

John Dewar
MILBANK, TWEED, HADLEY & MCCLOY LLP

Shannon Diggory
REED SMITH LLP

Zaki Ejaz
RIGHT LEGAL ADVICE

Thomas Fancett
CMS CAMERON MCKENNA LLP

Paul Fleming
DECHERT LLP

Claire Fourel
ASHURST LLP

Nick Francis
PWC UNITED KINGDOM

Robert Franklin
CLYDE & CO.

Jack Gardener
CLYDE & CO.

Donald Gray
DARWIN GRAY LLP

Louise Gullifer
OXFORD UNIVERSITY,
COMMERCIAL LAW CENTER

Marc Harvey
DLA PIPER UK LLP

Andrew Haywood
PENNINGTONS MANCHES LLP

Nicky Heathcote
HER MAJESTY'S
LAND REGISTRY

Robert Hillhouse
CLYDE & CO.

Jess Hogan
DLA PIPER UK LLP

Chris Horrocks
DECHERT LLP

Daden Hunt
BIRKETTS LLP

Karl Hurley
OFGEM

Michael Josypenko
INSTITUTE OF EXPORT

Katherine Keenan
WEDLAKE BELL LLP

Pascal Lalande
HER MAJESTY'S
LAND REGISTRY

Keavy Larkin
OFGEM

Mickael Laurans
THE LAW SOCIETY OF
ENGLAND & WALES

Bob Ledsome
DEPARTMENT FOR
COMMUNITIES AND
LOCAL GOVERNMENT

Sarah Leslie
SHEPHERD & WEDDERBURN

Monika Lorenzo-Perez
REED SMITH LLP

Suzy Lovell
CMS CAMERON MCKENNA LLP

Ryan Lynch
MEMERY CRYSTAL LLP

Joanna Macintosh
LATHAM & WATKINS LLP

Neil Maclean
SHEPHERD & WEDDERBURN

Neil Magrath
UK POWER NETWORKS

Christopher Mallon
SKADDEN, ARPS, SLATE,
MEAGHER & FLOM LLP

Peter Manning
SIMMONS & SIMMONS LLP

Jane Marsden
MEMERY CRYSTAL LLP

Charles Mayo
SIMMONS & SIMMONS LLP

Antoinette McManus
PWC UNITED KINGDOM

Monika Mecevic
DECHERT LLP

Paul Miller
REED SMITH LLP

Charlotte Moller
REED SMITH LLP

Agnes Molnar
REED SMITH

Becca Naylor
REED SMITH LLP

Tom Neilson
MILBANK, TWEED, HADLEY
& MCCLOY LLP

Peter Newman
MILBANK, TWEED, HADLEY
& MCCLOY LLP

Kevin Nicholson
PWC UNITED KINGDOM

Phil Norton
CLYDE & CO.

Felicia Hanson Ofori-Quaah
MILBANK, TWEED, HADLEY
& MCCLOY LLP

Elizabeth Ormesher
CMS CAMERON MCKENNA LLP

Ivan Orsolini
REED SMITH LLP

Karolina Pechanova
DIAZ REUS & TARG LLP

Ross Pooley
LATHAM & WATKINS LLP

Helena Potts
LATHAM & WATKINS LLP

Alexander Reus
DIAZ REUS & TARG LLP

Lizzette Robleto de Howarth
THE LAW SOCIETY OF
ENGLAND & WALES

Alex Rogan
SKADDEN, ARPS, SLATE,
MEAGHER & FLOM LLP

David Rough
FREEDOM INFRASTRUCTURE
SERVICES

Philippa Scott
SHEARMAN & STERLING LLP

Angela Shaw
HER MAJESTY'S
LAND REGISTRY

Sandra Simoni
DEPARTMENT FOR
COMMUNITIES AND
LOCAL GOVERNMENT

Stuart Swift
MILBANK, TWEED, HADLEY
& MCCLOY LLP

Alex Turner
DEPARTMENT FOR
COMMUNITIES AND
LOCAL GOVERNMENT

Julia Vaynzof
CLYDE & CO.

Amelia Villiers-Stuart
WEDLAKE BELL LLP

Alistair White
DLA PIPER UK LLP

Geoff Wilkinson
WILKINSON CONSTRUCTION
CONSULTANTS

Nicholas Williams
REED SMITH

Alexandra Wood
CLYDE & CO.

David Ziyambi
LATHAM & WATKINS LLP

UNITED STATES

LOS ANGELES DEPARTMENT
OF WATER AND POWER

Sam J. Alberts
DENTONS

Benjamin Alexander
GREENBERG GLUSKER FIELDS
CLAMAN & MACHTINGER LLP

Manish Antani
EISNER JAFFE PC

Pamy J. S. Arora
CORNELL GROUP, INC.

Eve Brackmann
STUART KANE

Steven Clark
CLARK FIRM PLLC

Federico Cruz

María Amalia Cruz

Vilas Dhar
DHAR LAW, LLP

Joshua L. Ditelberg
SEYFARTH SHAW LLP

Motsa Dubois
FIABCI

Michael Dyll
TEXAS INTERNATIONAL FREIGHT

David Elden
PARKER, MILLIKEN, CLARK,
O'HARA & SAMUELIAN

Julia Fetherston
BOSTON CONSULTING GROUP

Irma Foley
ORRICK, HERRINGTON
& SUTCLIFFE LLP

Robert Goethe
CORNELL GROUP, INC.

William Gould
TROYGOULD PC

Javier Gutierrez
STUART KANE

Tony Hadley
EXPERIAN

Thomas Halket
HALKET WEITZ LLP

Timi Anyon Hallem
MANATT, PHELPS &
PHILLIPS, LLP

Donald Hamman
STUART KANE

Dennis Harber
MIAMI LEGAL, TITLE
& REMEDIATION

Sanford Hillsberg
TROYGOULD PC

Neil Jacobs
NI JACOBS & ASSOCIATES

Christopher Kelleher
SEYFARTH SHAW LLP

Joshua Kochath
COMAGE CONTAINER LINES

John LaBar
HENRY, MCCORD,
BEAN, MILLER, GABRIEL
& LABAR PLLC

Jen Leary
CLIFTONLARSONALLEN LLP

Wen-Ching Lin
LAW OFFICES OF
WEN-CHING LIN

Bradford L. Livingston
SEYFARTH SHAW LLP

Jeffrey Makin
ARENT FOX LLP

Dietrick Miller
TROYGOULD PC

Stephanie Moura
RUSSELL BEDFORD
INTERNATIONAL

Kelly J. Murray
PWC UNITED STATES

David Newberg
COLLIER, HALPERN,
NEWBERG, NOLLETTI, LLP

Samuel Nolen
RICHARDS, LAYTON & FINGER,
P.A., MEMBER OF LEX MUNDI

Christopher O'Connell
PARKER, MILLIKEN, CLARK,
O'HARA & SAMUELIAN

Richard O'Neill
CONSOLIDATED EDISON
CO. OF NY, INC.

Eric Pezold
SNELL & WILMER

Darrell Pierce
DYKEMA

Shanen Prout
LAW OFFICE OF
SHANEN R. PROUT

Kenneth Rosen
UNIVERSITY OF ALABAMA
SCHOOL OF LAW

Richard Rosen
NYC DEPARTMENT
OF BUILDINGS

Daren M. Schlecter
LAW OFFICE OF DAREN
M. SCHLECTER

William Shawn
SHAWNCOULSON LLP

Joseph Tannous
JT CONSTRUCTION

Michael Temin
FOX ROTHSCHILD LLP

Magda Theodate
GLOBAL EXECUTIVE
TRADE CONSULTING

Julie Travis
KAMINE CONSTRUCTION LAW

Frederick Turner
TURNER & TURNER

James J. Varellas III
VARELLAS & VARELLAS

Javier Villa
RUSSELL BEDFORD
INTERNATIONAL

Robert Wallace
STUART KANE

Ann Marie Zaletel
SEYFARTH SHAW LLP

Olga Zalomiy
LAW OFFICES OF OLGA
ZALOMIY, PC

Isaac B. Zaur
CLARICK GUERON
REISBAUM LLP

Malka Zeefe
DENTONS

URUGUAY

EQUIFAX - CLEARING
DE INFORMES

GRAETZ NUÑEZ

JIMÉNEZ DE ARÉCHAGA,
VIANA & BRAUSE

Marta Alvarez
ADMINISTRACIÓN NACIONAL
DE USINAS Y TRANSMISIÓN
ELÉCTRICA (UTE)

Bernardo Amorín
AMORIN ABOGADOS

Alfredo Arocena
FERRERE ABOGADOS

Gaston Atchugarry
GASTON ATCHUGARRY
ARQUITECTURA-URUGUAY

Leticia Barrios

Juan Bonet
GUYER & REGULES,
MEMBER OF LEX MUNDI

Sofia Borba
ARCHITECT

Luis Burastero Servetto
LUIS BURASTERO & ASOC.

Valeria Cabrejos
AMORIN ABOGADOS

Lucia Carbajal
POSADAS, POSADAS & VECINO

Federico Caresani
GALANTE & MARTINS

Augusto Cibils
PWC URUGUAY

Maria Noel Corchs
TMF GROUP

Victoria Costa
HUGHES & HUGHES

Leonardo Couto
JOSE MARIA FACAL & CO.

Hernán de la Fuente
ESCRIBANÍA DE LA FUENTE

Fernando De Posadas
POSADAS, POSADAS & VECINO

Rosana Díaz
SUPERINTENDENCIA DE
SERVICIOS FINANCIEROS
- BANCO CENTRAL
DEL URUGUAY

Carolina Diaz De Armas
GUYER & REGULES,
MEMBER OF LEX MUNDI

Analía Fernández Gonzalez
BERGSTEIN ABOGADOS

Javier Fernández Zerbino
BADO, KUSTER, ZERBINO
& RACHETTI

Hector Ferreira
HUGHES & HUGHES

Fabiana Ferreyra
TMF GROUP

Juan Federico Fischer
FISCHER & SCHICKENDANTZ

Federico Florin
GUYER & REGULES,
MEMBER OF LEX MUNDI

Sergio Franco
PWC URUGUAY

Andrés Fuentes
ARCIA STORACE FUENTES
MEDINA ABOGADOS

Diego Galante
GALANTE & MARTINS

Margarita Garcia
ESTUDIO LOZANO LTDA.

Alejandra García
FERRERE ABOGADOS

Daniel García
PWC URUGUAY

Enrique Garcia Pini
ADMINISTRACIÓN NACIONAL
DE USINAS Y TRANSMISIÓN
ELÉCTRICA (UTE)

Rodrigo Goncalvez
GUYER & REGULES,
MEMBER OF LEX MUNDI

Daniel Gonzalez
POSADAS, POSADAS & VECINO

Nelson Alfredo Gonzalez
SDV URUGUAY

Pablo Gonzalez
TMF GROUP

Renato Guerrieri
*GUYER & REGULES,
MEMBER OF LEX MUNDI*

Tomas Gurmendez
POSADAS, POSADAS & VECINO

Andrés Hessdörfer
OLIVERA ABOGADOS

Marcela Hughes
HUGHES & HUGHES

Alfredo Inciarte Blanco
ESTUDIO INCIARTE

Jimena Lanzani
*GUYER & REGULES,
MEMBER OF LEX MUNDI*

Santiago Madalena
*GUYER & REGULES,
MEMBER OF LEX MUNDI*

Leandro Marques
PWC URUGUAY

Ana Claudia Marrero
BERGSTEIN ABOGADOS

Enrique Martínez
Schickendantz
*ASOCIACIÓN DE
DESPACHANTES DE
ADUANA DEL URUGUAY*

Leonardo Melos

Ricardo Mezzera
MEZZERA ABOGADOS

Alejandro Miller Artola
*GUYER & REGULES,
MEMBER OF LEX MUNDI*

Daniel Ignacio Mosco Gómez
*GUYER & REGULES,
MEMBER OF LEX MUNDI*

Pablo Mosto
*ADMINISTRACIÓN NACIONAL
DE USINAS Y TRANSMISIÓN
ELÉCTRICA (UTE)*

Mateo Noseda
*GUYER & REGULES,
MEMBER OF LEX MUNDI*

María Concepción Olivera
OLIVERA ABOGADOS

Juan Martín Olivera Amato
OLIVERA ABOGADOS

Lucía Patrón
FERRERE ABOGADOS

Mariana Pisón
BERGSTEIN ABOGADOS

Walter Planells
FERRERE ABOGADOS

Maria Clara Porro
FERRERE ABOGADOS

María Posada
*SUPERINTENDENCIA DE
SERVICIOS FINANCIEROS -
BANCO CENTRAL
DEL URUGUAY*

María Carolina Queraltó
*ARCIA STORACE FUENTES
MEDINA ABOGADOS*

María Macarena Rachetti
PWC URUGUAY

Agustín Rachetti Pérez
*BADO, KUSTER, ZERBINO
& RACHETTI*

Cecilia Ricciardi
FISCHER & SCHICKENDANTZ

Carolina Sarroca
*ARCIA STORACE FUENTES
MEDINA ABOGADOS*

Eliana Sartori
PWC URUGUAY

Leonardo Slinger
*GUYER & REGULES,
MEMBER OF LEX MUNDI*

Fabiana Steinberg
HUGHES & HUGHES

Dolores Storace
*ARCIA STORACE FUENTES
MEDINA ABOGADOS*

Carolina Techera
PWC URUGUAY

Lucia Techera
*GUYER & REGULES,
MEMBER OF LEX MUNDI*

Juan Ignacio Troccoli
FISCHER & SCHICKENDANTZ

Gerardo Viñoles
VIÑOLES ARQUITECT STUDIO

Mario Vogel
TMF GROUP

María Eugenia Yavarone
FERRERE ABOGADOS

UZBEKISTAN

UZBEKENERGO

Ulugbek Abdullaev
DENTONS

Jahongir Abdurasulov
*CHARGES REGISTRY OF THE
CENTRAL BANK OF UZBEKISTAN*

Ravshan Adilov
CENTIL LAW FIRM

Azizbek Akhmadjonov
KOSTA LEGAL

Rustam Akramov
GRATA INTERNATIONAL

Bobir Artukmetov

Elvina Asanova
GRATA INTERNATIONAL

Bokhodir Atakhanov
*CENTER FOR COORDINATION
AND DEVELOPMENT OF
SECURITIES MARKET*

Jakhongir Azimov
DIPLOMAT LAW FIRM

Alisher Chaykhov
*CHAMBER OF COMMERCE
AND INDUSTRY OF
UZBEKISTAN (CCIU)*

Maxim Dogonkin
KOSTA LEGAL

Nail Hassanov
KOSTA LEGAL

Nadira Hassanova
AZALIA IMPREX

Kamilla Khamraeva
CENTIL LAW FIRM

Sergey Mayorov
SIMAY KOM

Muzaffar Salomov
*CREDIT BUREAU CREDIT
INFORMATIONAL-
ANALYTICAL CENTRE LLC*

Nizomiddin Shakhabutdinov
LEGES ADVOKAT LAW FIRM

Alisher Shaykhov
*CHAMBER OF COMMERCE
AND INDUSTRY UZBEKISTAN*

Sofia Shaykhrazieva
CENTIL LAW FIRM

Otabek Suleimanov
CENTIL LAW FIRM

Nargiza Turgunova
GRATA INTERNATIONAL

VANUATU

*UTILITIES REGULATORY
AUTHORITY OF VANUATU*

Barry Amoss
*SOUTH SEA SHIPPING
(VANUATU) LTD.*

Loïc Bernier
CAILLARD & KADDOUR

Alan Brown
FLETCHER CONSTRUCTION

Shirley Bule
BARRETT & PARTNERS

Laurence Cameron
*PACIFIC CUSTOMS &
FREIGHT AGENCIES*

Frederic Derousseau
UNELCO

Delores Elliott

David Hudson
HUDSON & SUGDEN

Bill Jimmy
VANUATU'S OWN LOGISTICS

Chris Kernot
FR8 LOGISTICS LTD.

Sandy Mwetu
MUNICIPALITY OF PORT VILA

Mark Pardoe
*SOUTH SEA SHIPPING
(VANUATU) LTD.*

Nisha Rambay
BARRETT & PARTNERS

Mark Stafford
BARRETT & PARTNERS

Martin St-Hilaire
*CABINET AJC, AN INDEPENDENT
CORRESPONDENT MEMBER
OF DFK INTERNATIONAL*

VENEZUELA, RB

Claudia Abreu
BAKER & MCKENZIE

Tamara Adrian
ADRIAN & ADRIAN

Yanet Aguiar
*DESPACHO DE ABOGADOS
MIEMBROS DE NORTON
ROSE FULBRIGHT SC*

Juan Enrique Aigster
*HOET PELAEZ CASTILLO
& DUQUE*

Servio T. Altuve Jr.
*SERVIO T. ALTUVE R.
& ASOCIADOS*

Leidys Amengual
CONAPRI

Aixa Añez
*D'EMPAIRE REYNA
& ASOCIADOS*

Carlos Bachrich Nagy
*DE SOLA PATE & BROWN,
ABOGADOS - CONSULTORES*

Marian Basciani
*DE SOLA PATE & BROWN,
ABOGADOS - CONSULTORES*

Francesco Castiglione
BAKER & MCKENZIE

Geraldine d'Empaire
*D'EMPAIRE REYNA
& ASOCIADOS*

Arturo De Sola Lander
*DE SOLA PATE & BROWN,
ABOGADOS - CONSULTORES*

Carlos Domínguez Hernández
*HOET PELAEZ CASTILLO
& DUQUE*

Omar Fernandez Russo
CEPACEX

Jose Javier Garcia
PWC VENEZUELA

Maria Geige
*DESPACHO DE ABOGADOS
MIEMBROS DE NORTON
ROSE FULBRIGHT SC*

Luis Ignacio Gil Palacios
*PALACIOS, ORTEGA
Y ASOCIADOS*

Adriana Goncalves
BAKER & MCKENZIE

Andres Gonzalez Crespo
*CASAS RINCON GONZALEZ
RUBIO & ASOCIADOS*

Diego Gonzalez Crespo
*CASAS RINCON GONZALEZ
RUBIO & ASOCIADOS*

Enrique Gonzalez Crespo
*CASAS RINCON GONZALEZ
RUBIO & ASOCIADOS*

Alfredo Hurtado
*HURTADO ESTEBAN Y
ASOCIADOS - MEMBER
OF RUSSELL BEDFORD
INTERNATIONAL*

Carla Hurtado

Enrique Itriago
RODRIGUEZ & MENDOZA

Daniela Jaimes
*DESPACHO DE ABOGADOS
MIEMBROS DE NORTON
ROSE FULBRIGHT SC*

Gabriela Longo
*PALACIOS, ORTEGA
Y ASOCIADOS*

Sarai Lopez
*TRANSPORTE INTERNACIONAL
LÓGICA OCEÁNICA, CA*

Greta Marazzi
ADRIAN & ADRIAN

Rafael Alberto Medina Ulacio
EMPRESAS MEDINA

Pedro Mendoza
MENDOZA DAVILA TOLEDO

Maritza Meszaros
BAKER & MCKENZIE

Lorena Mingarelli Lozzi
*DE SOLA PATE & BROWN,
ABOGADOS - CONSULTORES*

José Manuel Ortega
*PALACIOS, ORTEGA
Y ASOCIADOS*

Pedro Pacheco
PWC VENEZUELA

Bruno Paredes
LOGISTIKA TSM

Ruth Paz
PWC VENEZUELA

Bernardo Pisani
RODRIGUEZ & MENDOZA

Eduardo Porcarelli
CONAPRI

Juan Carlos Pró-Rísquez
*DESPACHO DE ABOGADOS
MIEMBROS DE NORTON
ROSE FULBRIGHT SC*

Carlos Rivero
*CÁMARA DE CONSTRUCCION
DE VENEZUELA*

Andreína Rondón
CONAPRI

Pedro Saghy
*DESPACHO DE ABOGADOS
MIEMBROS DE NORTON
ROSE FULBRIGHT SC*

Eva Marina Santos
*HOET PELAEZ CASTILLO
& DUQUE*

Laura Silva Aparicio
*HOET PELAEZ CASTILLO
& DUQUE*

Lenhy Saraid Torrealba Flores
EMPRESAS MEDINA

Oscar Ignacio Torres
*TRAVIESO EVANS ARRIA
RENGEL & PAZ*

Arnoldo Troconis
*D'EMPAIRE REYNA
& ASOCIADOS*

Jose Valecillos
*D'EMPAIRE REYNA
& ASOCIADOS*

Delfin Zambrano

VIETNAM

GRANT THORNTON LLP

*HO CHI MINH CITY POWER
CORPORATION (EVN HCMC)*

Viet Anh Hoang
DIMAC LAW FIRM

Frederick Burke
*BAKER & MCKENZIE
(VIETNAM) LTD.*

Tran Cong Quoc
BIZCONSULT LAW FIRM

Giles Thomas Cooper
DUANE MORRIS LLC

Thi Bich Tram Dao
INDOCHINE COUNSEL

Thuy Linh Do
*RUSSELL BEDFORD KTC
ASSURANCE & BUSINESS
ADVISORS - MEMBER
OF RUSSELL BEDFORD
INTERNATIONAL*

Linh Doan
LVN & ASSOCIATES

Dang The Duc
INDOCHINE COUNSEL

Thanh Duong
DIMAC LAW FIRM

Thanh Long Duong
ALIAT LEGAL

Lien Duong Hong
PWC VIETNAM

Le Hong Phong
BIZCONSULT LAW FIRM

Dai Thang Huynh
DFDL

Milton Lawson
*FRESHFIELDS BRUCKHAUS
DERINGER*

Anh Tuan Le
*THE NATIONAL CREDIT
INFORMATION CENTRE - THE
STATE BANK OF VIETNAM*

Nhan Le
DUANE MORRIS LLC

Phuong Uyen Le Hoang
RUSSIN & VECCHI

Loc Le Thi
YKVN

Logan Leung
RAJAH & TANN LCT LAWYERS

Tien Ngoc Luu
VISION & ASSOCIATES

Christopher Marjoram
PWC VIETNAM

Hoang Minh Duc
DUANE MORRIS LLC

Duy Minh Ngo
VB LAW

Anh Thi Tu Nguyen
INDOCHINE COUNSEL

Ha Nguyen
DIMAC LAW FIRM

Huong Nguyen
MAYER BROWN LLP

Khanh Ly Nguyen
*RUSSELL BEDFORD KTC
ASSURANCE & BUSINESS
ADVISORS - MEMBER
OF RUSSELL BEDFORD
INTERNATIONAL*

Minh Tuan Nguyen
VIET PREMIER LAW LTD.

Oanh Nguyen
*BAKER & MCKENZIE
(VIETNAM) LTD.*

Quoc Phong Nguyen
ALIAT LEGAL

Thi Minh Ngoc Nguyen
*THE NATIONAL CREDIT
INFORMATION CENTRE - THE
STATE BANK OF VIETNAM*

Thi Phuong Lan Nguyen
*VIETNAM CREDIT
INFORMATION JSC (PCB)*

Thi Phuong Thao Nguyen
*VIETNAM CREDIT
INFORMATION JSC (PCB)*

Tien Hoa Nguyen
S&B LAW

Tieu My Nguyen
*HONOR PARTNERSHIP LAW
COMPANY LIMITED (HPLAW)*

Tram Nguyen
LVN & ASSOCIATES

Tram Nguyen
YKVN

Trang Nguyen
*THE NATIONAL CREDIT
INFORMATION CENTRE - THE
STATE BANK OF VIETNAM*

Dong Huong Nguyen Thi
RAJAH & TANN LCT LAWYERS

Hung Duy Pham
*RUSSELL BEDFORD KTC
ASSURANCE & BUSINESS
ADVISORS - MEMBER
OF RUSSELL BEDFORD
INTERNATIONAL*

Huong Pham
YKVN

Thanh Huong Pham
*THE NATIONAL CREDIT
INFORMATION CENTRE - THE
STATE BANK OF VIETNAM*

Anh Vu Phan
INDOCHINE COUNSEL

Phan Nguyen Minh Phuong
VN COUNSEL

Dang Anh Quan
RUSSIN & VECCHI

Nguyen Que Tam
CSP LEGAL LLC

Van Anh Thai
*RUSSELL BEDFORD KTC -
MEMBER OF RUSSELL
BEDFORD INTERNATIONAL*

Nguyen Thi Hong Thang
VN COUNSEL

Dinh The Phuc
*ELECTRICITY REGULATORY
AUTHORITY OF VIETNAM*

Tan Heng Thye
CSP LEGAL LLC

Chi Anh Tran
*BAKER & MCKENZIE
(VIETNAM) LTD.*

Son Tran Duc
RAJAH & TANN LCT LAWYERS

Nam Hoai Truong
INDOCHINE COUNSEL

Tran Yen Uyen
CSP LEGAL LLC

Dzung Vu
LVN & ASSOCIATES

Hong Hanh Vu
MAYER BROWN LLP

Phuong Vu
LVN & ASSOCIATES

Thu Hang Vu
*HONOR PARTNERSHIP LAW
COMPANY LIMITED*

Que Vu Thi
RAJAH & TANN LCT LAWYERS

Son Ha Vuong
VISION & ASSOCIATES

WEST BANK AND GAZA

*PALESTINE TRADE
CENTER - PALTRADE*

Khaldon Abu Alsoud
ARAB BANK

Nidal Abu Lawi
*PALESTINE REAL ESTATE
INVESTMENT CO.*

Tareq Al Masri
*MINISTRY OF NATIONAL
ECONOMY*

Shadi Al-Haj
PWC

Sharhabeel Al-Zaeem
AL-ZAEEM & ASSOCIATES

Haytham L. Al-Zubi
AL-ZUBI LAW OFFICE

Moayad Amouri
PWC

Thaer Amro
*AMRO & ASSOCIATES
LAW OFFICE*

Muhanad Assaf
ITTQAN CONSULTING SERVICES

Firas Attereh
*HUSSAM ATTEREH GROUP
FOR LEGAL SERVICES*

Duaa Aweida
ITTQAN CONSULTING SERVICES

Anan Boshnaq
E-FREIGHT INTERNATIONAL CO.

Imad Dayyah
*TRAINING & MANAGEMENT
INSTITUTE (TAMI)*

Ashraf Far
ITTQAN CONSULTING SERVICES

Ali Faroun
*PALESTINIAN MONETARY
AUTHORITY*

Philip Farrage
BAKER TILLY INTERNATIONAL

Victor Ghattas
ARCO

Lina Ghbeish
*PALESTINE CAPITAL
MARKETS AUTHORITY*

Hussein Habbab
PALESTINE IJARA COMPANY

Nadeen Haddad
*THE PALESTINIAN COMPANY
FOR OPERATIONAL AND
CAPITAL LEASE (PALLEASE)*

Mohannad Hajali
EY

Ali Hamoudeh
*JERUSALEM DISTRICT
ELECTRICITY COMPANY
(JDECo)*

George Handal
BETHLEHEM FREIGHT

Omar Hannoun
*PALESTINE REAL ESTATE
INVESTMENT CO.*

Samir Hulileh
PADICO HOLDINGS

Hiba I. Husseini
HUSSEINI & HUSSEINI

Ayman Jbail
EY

Bilal Kamal
KAMAL LAW FIRM

Rasem Kamal
*KAMAL & ASSOCIATES -
ATTORNEYS AND
COUNSELLORS-AT-LAW*

Mohamed Khader
*LAUSANNE TRADING
CONSULTANTS*

Deena Khalaf
*AL KAMAL SHIPPING AND
CLEARING CO. (LTD.)*

Raja Khwialed
COMPANIES CONTROL

Mahmoud Kittana
KAMAL LAW FIRM

Sireen Lubbadeh
*MINISTRY OF NATIONAL
ECONOMY*

Dima Saad Mashaqi
RAMALLAH MUNICIPALITY

Wroud Meliji
*THE PALESTINIAN COMPANY
FOR OPERATIONAL AND
CAPITAL LEASE (PALLEASE)*

Emir Mushahwar
*LAW OFFICES OF NABIL
A. MUSHAHWAR*

Manal Nassar
*JERUSALEM DISTRICT
ELECTRICITY COMPANY
(JDECo)*

Tony H. Nassar
*A.F. & R. SHEHADEH
LAW OFFICE*

Mark-George Nesnas
ITTQAN CONSULTING SERVICES

Raed Rajab

Wael Saadi
PWC

Hazem Salah
ARAB BANK

Maysa Sarhan
*PALESTINIAN MONETARY
AUTHORITY*

Suhaib Sharief
*THE PALESTINIAN COMPANY
FOR OPERATIONAL AND
CAPITAL LEASE (PALLEASE)*

Kareem Fuad Shehadeh
*A.F. & R. SHEHADEH
LAW OFFICE*

Mazin Theeb
*SHAHD ELECTRICAL
ENGINEERING CONSULTANTS*

Tareq Z. Touqan
EQUITY LEGAL GROUP

Yazeed Zakarneh
*PALESTINIAN SHIPPERS'
COUNCIL*

Kosty Ziadeh
ZIADEH LAW OFFICE

YEMEN, REP.

Khalid Abdullah
*SHEIKH MOHAMMED
ABDULLAH SONS (EST. 1927)*

Tariq Abdullah
*LAW OFFICES OF SHEIKH
TARIQ ABDULLAH*

Shafiq Adat
*LAW OFFICES OF SHEIKH
TARIQ ABDULLAH*

Jamal Adimi
JAMAL ADIMI LAW OFFICE

Ghazi Shaif Al Aghbari
*AL AGHBARI &
PARTNERS LAW FIRM*

Maher Al Kladi
*LAW OFFICES OF SHEIKH
TARIQ ABDULLAH*

Khaled Al Wazir
KHALED AL WAZIR LAW FIRM

Noura Yahya H. Al-Adhhi
CENTRAL BANK OF YEMEN

Yaser Al-Adimi
*ABDUL GABAR A. AL-ADIMI
FOR CONSTRUCTION & TRADE*

Ramzi Al-Ariqi
GRANT THORNTON YEMEN

Khaled Al-Buraihi
*KHALED AL-BURAIHI FOR
ADVOCACY & LEGAL SERVICES*

Ahmed Al-Gharasi
AL-GHASARI TRADING

Mohamed Taha Hamood
Al-Hashimi
*MOHAMED TAHA
HAMOOD & CO.*

Omar Al-Qatani
CENTRAL BANK OF YEMEN

Qais Alsanabani
Q&A LAW OFFICE

Mahmood Abdulaziz
Al-sharmani
LAWYER

Abdulla Farouk Luqman
*LUQMAN LEGAL ADVOCATES
& LEGAL CONSULTANTS*

Amani Hail
CENTRAL BANK OF YEMEN

Ejlal Mofadal
CENTRAL BANK OF YEMEN

Laila A. Mohammed
*AL AGHBARI &
PARTNERS LAW FIRM*

Zuhair Abdul Rasheed
*LAW OFFICES OF SHEIKH
TARIQ ABDULLAH*

Khaled Mohammed Salem Ali
*LUQMAN LEGAL ADVOCATES
& LEGAL CONSULTANTS*

Nigel Truscott
DAMAC GROUP

ZAMBIA

*ENERGY MANAGEMENT
SERVICES*

Sudhir Balsure
*SWIFT FREIGHT
INTERNATIONAL LTD.*

Agatha Ntutuma Banda
*MINISTRY OF LANDS AND
NATURAL RESOURCES*

Salome Banda
KPMG

Wilson Banda
*PATENTS AND COMPANIES
REGISTRATION
AGENCY (PACRA)*

Lewis K. Bwalya
ZESCO LTD.

Anthony Bwembya
*PATENTS AND COMPANIES
REGISTRATION
AGENCY (PACRA)*

Lilian Chibale
KPMG

Bonaventure Chibamba
Mutale
ELLIS & CO.

Mwelwa Chibesakunda
*CHIBESAKUNDA & COMPANY,
MEMBER OF DLA PIPER GROUP*

Sydney Chipoyae
*JOHN KAITE LEGAL
PRACTITIONERS*

Alick Chirwa
SINOK LOGISTICS LTD.

Sydney Chisenga
CORPUS LEGAL PRACTITIONERS

Bradley Choonga
PWC ZAMBIA

Namuyombe Gondwe
*SWIFT FREIGHT
INTERNATIONAL LTD.*

Prasad Hettiarachchi
*ELECTRICAL MAINTENANCE
LUSAKA LTD.*

Jackie Jhala
CORPUS LEGAL PRACTITIONERS

Malcolm G.G. Jhala
DELOITTE

Bruce Kaemba
*ZAMBIA CUSTOMS AND
FORWARDING AGENTS
ASSOCIATION*

Charles Kafunda
HIGH COURT

John K. Kaite
*JOHN KAITE LEGAL
PRACTITIONERS*

Kelly Kalumba
GREEN COLD ARCHITECTS

Arnold Kasalwe
EY ZAMBIA

Johan Lombaard
MANICA AFRICA PTY. LTD.

Fumanikile Lungani
CORPUS LEGAL PRACTITIONERS

Christopher Mapani
*PATENTS AND COMPANIES
REGISTRATION
AGENCY (PACRA)*

Ernest Mate
CORPUS LEGAL PRACTITIONERS

Bonaventure Mbewe
BONAVENTURE MBEWE

Harriet Mdala
MUSA DUDHIA & COMPANY

Jyoti Mistry
PWC ZAMBIA

Mukuka Mubanga
ZESCO LTD.

Monde Mukela
ENTRY POINT AFRICA

Chintu Y. Mulendema
CYMA

Muchinda Muma
CORPUS LEGAL PRACTITIONERS

Charles Musonda
SIMSURVEY MAPPING & CONSULTANTS

Lloyd Musonda
PATENTS AND COMPANIES REGISTRATION AGENCY (PACRA)

Chanda Musonda-Chiluba
AFRICA LEGAL NETWORK (ALN)

Arthi Muthusamy
PWC ZAMBIA

Inonge Elizabeth Muuba
MUSA DUDHIA & COMPANY

Kafula Mwiche
MADISON FINANCIAL SERVICES PLC

Hope Ndao
MUSA DUDHIA & COMPANY

Peter Ngoma
SIMSURVEY MAPPING & CONSULTANTS

Miriam Sabi
ZRA - TAXPAYER SERVICES

Namakuzu Shandavu
CORPUS LEGAL PRACTITIONERS

Lindiwe Shawa
PWC ZAMBIA

Clavel M. Sianondo
MALAMBO AND COMPANY

Chitembo Simwanza
ZESCO LTD.

Mutengo Sindano
MINISTRY OF LANDS AND NATURAL RESOURCES

Mildred Stephenson
CREDIT REFERENCE BUREAU AFRICA LIMITED T/A TRANSUNION

Jimmy Zulu
DELOITTE

Lungisani Zulu
BANK OF ZAMBIA

ZIMBABWE

FINANCIAL CLEARING BUREAU

Richard Beattie
THE STONE/BEATTIE STUDIO

Tim Boulton
MANICA AFRICA

Peter Cawood
PWC ZIMBABWE

Shaxious Cheza
ZIMBABWE INVESTMENT AUTHORITY

Simplicius Julius Chihambakwe
CHIHAMBAKWE, MUTIZWA & PARTNERS

Clayton Z. Chikara
DHLAKAMA B. ATTORNEYS

Nonhlanhla Chiromo
RESERVE BANK OF ZIMBABWE

Ruzayi Chiviri
RESERVE BANK OF ZIMBABWE

Beloved Dhlakama
DHLAKAMA B. ATTORNEYS

Farayi Dyirakumunda
EXPERT DECISION SYSTEMS ZIMBABWE

Paul Fraser
LOFTY & FRASER

Takunda Gumbo
CHINAWA LAW CHAMBERS

Takura Gumbo
ATHERSTONE & COOK

Obert Chaurura Gutu
GUTU & CHIKOWERO

Charles Jaure
ZIMBABWE INVESTMENT AUTHORITY

Shamiso Khupe
GUTU & CHIKOWERO

Charity Machiridza
BDO TAX & ADVISORY SERVICES PVT. LTD.

Rita Makarau
HIGH COURT ZIMBABWE

Zanudeen Makorie
COGHLAN, WELSH & GUEST

Chatapiwa Malaba
KANTOR AND IMMERMAN

Oleen Maponga nee Singizi
EXPERT DECISION SYSTEMS ZIMBABWE

Gertrude Maredza
GUTU & CHIKOWERO

R. R. Mariwa
ZIMBABWE ELECTRICITY TRANSMISSION & DISTRIBUTION COMPANY

Tsungirirai Marufu-Maune
GUTU & CHIKOWERO

David Masaya
PWC ZIMBABWE

Collen Masunda
RESERVE BANK OF ZIMBABWE

Norman Mataruka
RESERVE BANK OF ZIMBABWE

Thembiwe Mazingi
COGHLAN, WELSH & GUEST

Jim McComish
PEARCE MCCOMISH ARCHITECTS

Nyasha Mhunduru
EXPERT DECISION SYSTEMS ZIMBABWE

H.P. Mkushi
SAWYER & MKUSHI

Kundai Msemburi
SECURITIES & EXCHANGE COMMISSION

Sithembinkosi Msipa
JUDICIAL SERVICES COMMISSION

Benjamin Mukandi
FREIGHT WORLD PVT. LTD.

Haruperi Mumbengegwi
MANOKORE ATTORNEYS

Tiri Muringani
SPEARTEC

Eldard Mutasa
HIGH COURT ZIMBABWE

Ostern Mutero
SAWYER & MKUSHI

Alec Tafadzwa Muza
MAWERE & SIBANDA LEGAL PRACTITIONERS

Christina Muzerengi
GRANT THORNTON ZIMBABWE

Christopher Muzhingi
PWC ZIMBABWE

Sympathy Muzondiwa
SAWYER & MKUSHI

Duduzile Ndawana
GILL, GODLONTON & GERRANS

Itayi Ndudzo
MUTAMANGIRA AND ASSOCIATES

Maxwell Ngorima
BDO TAX & ADVISORY SERVICES PVT. LTD.

Edwell Ngwenya
FREIGHT WORLD PVT. LTD.

Tatenda Nhemachena
MAWERE & SIBANDA LEGAL PRACTITIONERS

Farai Nyabereka
MANOKORE ATTORNEYS

Michael Nyamazana
AFRICA CORPORATE ADVISORS

Dorothy Pasipanodya
GILL, GODLONTON & GERRANS

Phillipa M. Phillips
PHILLIPS LAW

Nobert Musa Phiri
MUVINGI & MUGADZA LEGAL PRACTITIONERS

John Ridgewell
BCHOD AND PARTNERS

Edward Rigby
CASLING, RIGBY, MCMAHON

Unity Sakhe
KANTOR & IMMERMAN

Bellina Sigauke
RESERVE BANK OF ZIMBABWE

Sichoni Takoleza
ZIMBABWE INVESTMENT AUTHORITY

Ruby Tapera
ZIMBABWE INVESTMENT AUTHORITY

Murambiwa Tarabuku
PEARCE MCCOMISH ARCHITECTS

Takunda Timbe
MUVINGI & MUGADZA LEGAL PRACTITIONERS

Sonja Vas
SCANLEN & HOLDERNESS

Adam Bongani Wenyimo
GUTU & CHIKOWERO

Ruvimbo Zakeo
GILL, GODLONTON & GERRANS

www.ingramcontent.com/pod-product-compliance
Lightning Source LLC
Chambersburg PA
CBHW050835220326
41598CB00006B/370